30ᵀᴴ EDITION
SCHOOL LAW

New York State School Boards Association • New York State Bar Association

Information about the New York State Education Law, Regulations and Decisions of the Commissioner of Education, and Other Laws and Legal Opinions Relating to Education for the Guidance of School Boards and School Administrators in New York State

NYSBA

This publication is intended to provide information about general questions pertaining to various statutory enactments and administrative decisions affecting public schools. It is not intended to provide the answers to specific questions. The answers to the questions are brief and are intended to call attention to the applicable law rather than provide a definitive review. Laws are changed by each session of the New York State Legislature and United States Congress, and interpretive court decisions are handed down continually. To obtain answers to specific legal questions, seek legal advice from your school board's attorney.

Printed in the United States of America

Softcover:
    ISBN   0-8205-8782-6   Product Number 3070311   (Pub. 30703)
Hardcover:
    ISBN   0-8205-8784-2   Product Number 3070811   (Pub. 30703)

15M-Lexis/Nexis-9/04

Distributed by LexisNexis™

New for the 30ᵗʰ Edition – School Law PLUS!

An expanded online research site exclusively for purchasers of **School Law**

How to activate your account:

1) Go to the following website:

   http://schoollaw30.lexisnexis.com/registration.aspx

2) In the box labeled "Account Number" please enter the following unique account number:

NAP87162SL

3) In the box labeled "Product ID" please enter **30703** and hit "Continue"

4) Follow the registration instructions on your screen to start using the website!

If you have questions or need assistance accessing the website, please send an email to *llp.clp@lexisnexis.com* with "School Law" in the subject line. Please include your customer account number (from your invoice) in the email.

---

*Access **School Law 30ᵗʰ Edition** online, and research a wide range of primary legal materials anywhere and any time with **School Law Plus!***

Enter your account information here for your records:

User ID: _____

Password: _____

Login / Homepage: **http://schoollaw30.lexisnexis.com**

ABOUT THE CD

HOW TO USE IT

If you experience any problems during the installation procedure, please call Technical Support at **1-800-223-5297** for assistance.

1. Insert the CD into the CD-ROM drive; the installation should begin automatically.

   (If the installation fails to launch, select *Run* from the Start menu. Type *d:\setup* and click on OK. (If the CD reader drive is not *D:*, substitute the correct letter.)

2. In the Welcome screen, click **Next**. Read and *accept* the Master Agreement. You must accept the Master Agreement to complete the installation process. (Declining will cancel installation.)

3. Your 20-digit Codeword should be hard-coded in your installation. If it is not, locate it on your packing slip, and enter it in the corresponding fields. Click **Next**.

4. Click Close in the Products & Publications screen. Select a directory and/or drive to receive the software; click **Next**.

5. Complete the installation by following the prompts.

FEATURES

Hypertext Links. Instantly move from the integrated table of contents to your desired section, from section to section, and then back to your original location. All in the blink of an eye.

Search Engine. Now with faster searches! Folio Views® software allows the user to search by note, by section, by words and phrases, and even allows wild card searches! Scroll through your "hit list" in seconds to find the information you need.

Customize Electronically. Use a bookmark to mark your favorite spots; a highlighter to mark a key word in long sections; and a notepad to jot down important notes. Save them all for future use.

Print And Save. Print and save blocked text, a whole section, or a series of selected records. Download the information into Word, WordPerfect, text files, and/or many other word processing formats.

Support. With on-line help, full-time technical support, an easy-to-use on-line user manual, and point and click Windows access, you can do research with the security that LexisNexis's expert staff will back you up.

Expanded Content. Contains all of the material included in the book, plus full-text versions of all federal and state cases and selective administrative decisions.

SYSTEM REQUIREMENTS

- Intel® Pentium®-based 133-Mhz or faster PC
- 32 MB RAM for Win 95/98/98SE; 64 MB RAM for Win ME/NT4/2000/XP
- 35 MB free hard disk space
- 8x or faster CD-ROM drive
- Microsoft Windows 95® or higher

SUPPORT

For support call **1-800-223-5297.**

Press **3** for questions regarding installation.

Press **2** for questions related to use of the product (searching, printing, etc.)

30TH EDITION

SCHOOL LAW

New York State School Boards Association • New York State Bar Association

CONTENTS

PREFACE

What you hold in your hands is the 30th edition of *School Law*. Since its inception in 1945, *School Law* has evolved with the times to provide school board members, administrators, and others who use it with accurate, up-to-date, clearly written information on common legal problems most school districts face.

This marks the second time the New York State School Boards Association has worked with LexisNexis as our publishing partner on this book. LexisNexis is one of the premier legal publishing houses in the country and brings its considerable publishing and marketing expertise to the project. *School Law* again includes a companion searchable CD-ROM for readers to quickly find information. This edition also includes *School Law Plus*, an online version of this book.

This edition of *School Law* has been revised and expanded — by more than 100 pages — to reflect the latest additions in relevant law and cases. The material has been thoroughly checked by staff members of the New York State School Boards Association.

For the sixth time we welcome the New York State Bar Association as co-publisher of *School Law*. We appreciate their review of the book and thank them for all their help. The State Bar Association's sound reputation as a legal publisher continues to enhance the scope and content of this handbook.

School Law, 30th Edition, will help school board members develop a more comprehensive understanding of their roles as policy makers, and offer school administrators with a ready and complete source for making informed operational decisions. It will also provide the public with a greater understanding of the vast legal details involved in operating a school district.

Sources for the information contained in this handbook include New York State law, the Rules of the Board of Regents, decisions and regulations of the commissioner of education, opinions of the state comptroller, federal laws and regulations, and court decisions from all levels of the judicial system. In short, it is a highly customized collection of materials from a vast array of resources.

We are proud of the fact that over the years, you have come to rely on *School Law's* practical advice on complicated legal issues pertaining to the operation of school districts. We are confident that the changes we've made to the 30th edition will further enhance its usefulness to members of the education community.

Timothy G. Kremer
Executive Director

ACKNOWLEDGMENT

This handbook was originated in 1945 as an outgrowth of the doctoral thesis of the late William J. Hageny, Distinguished Service Professor Emeritus, State University of New York, College at New Paltz, New Paltz, New York. We have appreciated Dr. Hageny's work on the handbook from its inception through 1988 and his contributions to creating a ready school law reference for school board members, administrators, and attorneys alike. This handbook is an effort to make school law accessible and understandable to all.

Dr. Hageny's past contributions to education include chairman of the Department of Educational Administration and professor of education, State University of New York, College at New Paltz; executive secretary of the Mid-Hudson School Study Council; and member of the Board of Trustees, Ulster County Community College. He served as president of the New York Collegiate Association for the Development of Educational Administration, New York State Association of Secondary School Principals and Council of Administrative Leadership. He also served for many years as the chief school administrator of Haldane Central School, Cold Spring, New York. Dr. Hageny graduated from Hobart College and Syracuse University and received his doctorate from Columbia University.

SCHOOL LAW

General Information

This 30th edition of *School Law* is a compendium of information about New York State school law arranged according to 26 topics, represented by the chapter headings, in a question-and-answer format. The questions are numbered according to the chapters in which they appear and their order in those chapters. When question numbers are referred to, they are set in boldface type (**14:5**).

There are two considerations to remember when using *School Law*. First, all legal references throughout the handbook are to the New York State Education Law unless noted otherwise in unnumbered footnotes at the beginning of chapters or sections. Second, when a specific number of days is referred to in a statute or elsewhere in the law, Saturdays, Sundays, and holidays are included when calculating such days unless otherwise stated in specific provisions of the law, or the period of time is two days or less (Gen. Constr. Law § 20) or the period of time specified ends on a Saturday, Sunday, or a public holiday. In such cases, the specified time will occur on the next succeeding business day (Gen. Constr. Law § 25-a).

Abbreviations

The following abbreviations represent sources

Case Law Citations

United States Supreme Court

U.S.	United States Reports
S.Ct.	Supreme Court Reporter
U.S.L.W.	United States Law Week

Federal Courts of Appeals

F., F.2d, F.3d	Federal Reporter

Federal District Courts

F.Supp., F.Supp.2d	Federal Supplement

New York State Court of Appeals

N.Y.2d, N.Y.3d	New York Reports

New York State Supreme Court, Appellate Division

A.D.2d, A.D.3d	Appellate Division Reports

New York State Lower Courts

Misc.2d, Misc. 3d	New York Miscellaneous Reports

Other Reports

Educ. Dep't Rep.	(State) Education Department Reports
Fair Empl. Prac. Case	(BNA) Fair Employment Practice Cases
IDELR	Individuals with Disabilities Education Law Reporter
Opn. Att'y Gen.	New York State Attorney General's Opinions
Opn. St. Comp.	State Comptroller's Opinions
PERB	Public Employment Relations Board's Rules of Procedure
SRO	State Review Officer Decisions
St. Dep't Rep.	State Department Report
LEXIS	LexisNexis Total Research System

Statutory Citations

Federal

USC	United States Code
Pub. Law	Public Law
CFR	United States Code of Federal Regulations

State

NYCRR	New York Code of Rules and Regulations
8 NYCRR	Regulations of the Commissioner of Education

New York State Law

Arts & Cult. Aff. Law	Arts and Cultural Affairs Law
C.P.L.R.	Civil Practice Law and Rules
Civ. Rights Law	Civil Rights Law
Civ. Serv. Law	Civil Service Law
Educ. Law	Education Law
Elec. Law	Election Law
Envtl. Conserv. Law	Environmental Conservation Law
Exec. Law	Executive Law
Gen. Constr. Law	General Construction Law
Gen. Mun. Law.	General Municipal Law
High. Law	Highway Law
Jud. Law	Judiciary Law
Lab. Law	Labor Law
Local Fin. Law	Local Finance Law
Mil. Law	Military Law
NYS Const.	New York State Constitution
Pub. Auth. Law	Public Authorities Law

Pub. Health Law	Public Health Law
Pub. Off. Law	Public Officers Law
Real. Prop. Law	Real Property Law
Real Prop. Tax Law	Real Property Tax Law
Retire. and Soc. Sec. Law	Retirement and Social Security Law
State Fin. Law	State Finance Law
Tax Law	Tax Law
Unconsol. Laws	Unconsolidated Laws
Veh. and Traf. Law	Vehicle and Traffic Law
Work. Comp. Law	Workers' Compensation Law

INTRODUCTION

A number of legal changes have taken place since *School Law* was last published in 2002. While most of the changes have been incorporated into the main body of this book, some also have been included in the introduction because of their significance.

This introduction is organized into three main sections: new statutory and regulatory law, recent statutory changes approved by the state Legislature but awaiting action by the governor at press time, and new case law. For the latest update on specific statutes, contact the New York State School Boards Association at 800-342-3360.

The information in this introduction is current through August 9, 2004.

New Statutory and Regulatory Law

Not every statute and regulation that has been enacted since the publication of *School Law, 29th Edition* can be summarized in this section. Only the most significant ones are included here.

Contrary to expectations, the federal government did not reauthorize the Individuals with Disabilities Education Act (IDEA). For its part, the State of New York failed to enact reforms necessary to comply with the New York Court of Appeals decision in *Campaign for Fiscal Equity, Inc. v. State*, 100 N.Y.2d 893 (2003), which declared that the current state-aid system for funding public education fails to provide students in New York City a "sound basic education."

State Statutes

Compulsory Education Age

Chapter 183 of the Laws of 2004 amended the compulsory education law to extend to all school boards the authority to require minors ages 16 through 17 who are not employed to attend school until the last day of the school year in which they become 17 years of age, effective July 1, 2005.

Conditional Hiring

Chapter 100 of the Laws of 2003 extended until July 1, 2005 the ability of school districts, BOCES, and charter schools to make conditional and emergency conditional appointments of prospective employees pending clearance for employment by the commissioner of education under certain conditions.

Farm Product Purchases

Assembly bill 6024-A (signed by the governor in 2004 but still un-chaptered when this publication went to press) amended the state's General Municipal Law to require that school districts buying food items directly from farmers make such purchases only from New York farmers. In addition, districts may ask the commissioner of education for permission to make such purchases from an association of producers and growers of more than 10 owners, when no other producers or growers have offered to sell to the district.

Hazardous Materials

Chapter 270 of the Laws of 2004 prohibits school districts from using paradichlorobenzene as a urinal or toilet deodorizer in any school building or other facility under the control of the district. Chapter 145 of the Laws of 2004 bans use of elemental (free-flowing) mercury in school science labs.

Homeless Students

Chapter 101 of the Laws of 2003 conformed the definition of homeless child in section 3209 (1)(a) of the Education Law to the definition of homeless children and youths in the McKinney-Vento Homeless Education Assistance Improvements Act amended in Title X of the No Child Left Behind Act (NCLB). Consistent with NCLB requirements, this law also requires that local educational agencies designate a liaison for homeless children and comply with applicable provisions relating to immediate enrollment of homeless children, records of homeless children, dispute resolution procedures, comparable services, and coordination of services for homeless children.

Immunizations

Chapter 207 of the Laws of 2004 amended the state's Public Health Law to require students born after January 1, 2005 also be immunized against pertussis and tetanus before starting school, in addition to poliomyelitis, mumps, measles, diphtheria, rubella, varicella, Haemophilus influenzae type b (Hib), and hepatitis B.

Special Education

Chapter 194 of the Laws of 2004 expanded the definition of who can serve as the additional parent member in a committee on special education (CSE) to include the parent of a declassified student no longer eligible for special education or of a disabled student who has graduated for up to five years beyond the student's declassification or graduation.

Reserve Funds

Chapter 260 of the Laws of 2004 amended the state's General Municipal Law to allow municipal corporations including school districts other than city school districts with a population of more than 125,000 and boards of cooperative educational services (BOCES) to establish a retirement contribution reserve fund for the purpose of financing retirement contributions. The chief fiscal officer of a district or BOCES must account for such a fund separate and apart from all other funds, and give the board a detailed report of the operation and condition of this fund.

Retirees

Chapter 25 of the Laws of 2004 extended until May 15, 2005, the prohibition against reductions in health insurance benefits for retirees and their dependents, or a school district's contributions for such health insurance coverage unless there is a corresponding reduction of benefits or contributions for the corresponding group of active employees for such retirees.

Sex Offenders

Chapter 106 of the Laws of 2004 defines what elements constitute the crime of disseminating a false registered sex offender notice. A person is guilty of such a crime when, knowing the information to be false or baseless, he or she disseminates a purportedly official notice that an individual is a registered sex offender.

Student Disciplinary Records

Chapter 101 of the Laws of 2003 added a new subdivision 7 to section 3214 of the Education Law to require that school districts establish procedures to facilitate the transfer of student disciplinary records relating to the suspension or expulsion of a student to any public or nonpublic school in which the student enrolls or seeks, intends or is instructed to enroll on a full-time or part-time basis.

Transportation

Chapter 97 of the Laws of 2003 extended until June 30, 2005, the authority of school boards to establish child safety zones and provide transportation to students who face hazardous conditions in parts of a district where transportation otherwise is not provided because of transportation limits.

State Statutory Changes Awaiting Action by the Governor

Campaign Expenditure Statements

Assembly bill 8558-A would add a new requirement that, in addition to campaign expenditure statements, school board candidates file statements on contributions to their campaigns in excess of $500 or a statement that the candidates did not receive contributions exceeding that amount. It would also require school board candidates to file expenditure and contribution statements on three separate specific occasions. Two of those would precede the election, and one would follow the election. The contribution statement would have to specify the dollar amount or the fair market value of the contribution received, the name and address of the donor, including political committees and the political unit represented by such a committee, and the date of receipt.

Nutrition Advisory Committees

Assembly bill 10454-A would authorize school boards to establish a child nutrition advisory committee to study all facets of their respective district's nutritional policies and to report on practices designed to educate teachers, parents, and children about healthy nutrition and raise awareness of the dangers of obesity. The committee would further report to the board on the implementation of district programs to improve student nutritional awareness and healthy diet.

Power and Energy Purchases

Assembly bill 10556-E would add school districts to the list of New York Power Authority's mandated customers. It would allow the Authority to make available to school districts energy efficiency services, clean energy technologies, and, if supplies of power and energy are available from the competitive market for this purpose, power and energy.

Special Act School Districts

Assembly bill 11670 would require that the school board of a special act school district also include two public members who are neither employed by nor are members of the board of trustees of the child care institution where the children are placed. The commissioner of education would appoint the two public members from a list of potential candidates who submit a letter of intent to the State Education Department.

The Board of Regents and State Regulations

Athletic Trainers

The Board of Regents approved changes to the commissioner's regulations requiring that athletic trainers employed by a school district be certified by the State of New York. The practice of the profession of athletic training involves the management of athletic injuries and instruction to coaches, athletes, parents, medical personnel, and communities in the areas of care and prevention of athletic injuries.

Diploma Requirements

The Board of Regents approved changes to the commissioner's regulations to allow students who first enter grade 9 in the 2001–02 school year and those entering grade 9 prior to the 2005–06 school year to receive either a Regents or a local high school diploma if they earn at least 22 units of credit. Students first entering grade 9 in 2005–06 and thereafter will only have the option to receive a Regents diploma.

School districts may consider a passing score of 55–64 on the required Regents exams as an option to meet local diploma requirements for students who entered grade 9 in the school years 2000–01, 2001–02, 2002–03, 2003–04 and for those who will enter grade 9 in the 2004–05 school year.

The safety net for students with disabilities was extended to include students who enter grade 9 prior to the 2010–11 school year. Under the safety net, students with disabilities who fail to pass a required Regents exam may meet local diploma requirements by taking and passing the corresponding Regents Competency Test.

No Child Left Behind Act

The Board of Regents approved several changes to the commissioner's regulations to implement various requirements of the federal No Child Left Behind Act of 2001 (NCLB). First, the definition of a homeless child and various responsibilities of a school district liaison for homeless children now conform with the McKinney-Vento Homeless Education Assistance Improvements Act as amended by Title IX of the NCLB and state law as amended by Chapter 101 of the Laws of 2003, discussed above.

Second, the definition of students with limited English proficiency (LEP) was changed to include those who score below a state-designated level of proficiency in the Language Assessment Battery-Revised (LAB-R) or the New York State English as a Second Language Achievement Test (NYSESLAT). Initial identification as a LEP student is based on LAB-R results. The NYSESLAT results determine a student's continued status as a LEP student. In addition, districts must submit to the commissioner a report by building of "the number" of students initially identified as limited English proficient and those served during the preceding school year, as well as "a report by building of the number of pupils annually evaluated as being limited English proficient in the preceding school year" and the "qualifications" of teachers and support personnel providing services to such students.

Third, amendments to previously adopted public school choice regulations clarified that students in schools identified as in need of improvement, corrective action, or restructuring may not transfer to a school that has been designated as persistently dangerous. These students may transfer to a magnet school or special focus school with entrance requirements based on academic or other skills only if they meet those requirements. In addition, districts must offer a choice of more than one school if there is more than one school that children would be able to transfer to, and take into account parental preferences among the choices offered.

Fourth, amendments to previously adopted supplemental educational services (SES) regulations clarified that when notifying parents of the identity of approved SES providers within the district, a school district must also include any approved providers of technology-based or distance learning supplemental educational services. Districts must ensure students with disabilities eligible to receive supplemental educational services receive appropriate services and accommodations in the provision of those services, and that eligible limited English proficient students receive appropriate supplemental educational services and language assistance in the provision of those services. In addition, when monitoring SES providers, districts must ensure that funds are not used for religious worship or instruction.

Fifth, the changes conform the commissioner's schools under registration review regulations (SURR) with NCLB requirements. Consistent with the state's NCLB accountability plan, the SURR regulations now provide a single system of accountability for identifying schools and school districts as requiring academic progress and, if they receive NCLB Title I funds, as in need of improvement, corrective action, or restructuring. The regulations also establish performance criteria and additional indicators applicable to the identification of such schools, as well as the basis for identifying schools as SURR schools.

Sixth, the changes require that each school district submit to the commissioner of education electronic records for each student enrolled in a public school in the district or placed out of the district for educational services by the committee on special education or a district official. The records must include the information specified in the regulations.

Seventh, the changes establish a new format for the State School Report Card and procedures for the distribution of the report card to parents and the community at both the district and school level.

School Bus Drivers, Attendants and Monitors

The Board of Regents approved several changes to the commissioner's regulations relating to the qualifications and standards for school bus drivers, monitors, and attendants. First, school bus monitors and attendants must be at least 19 years of age, complete a physical performance test, receive pre-service and annual refresher training, and complete a basic course of instruction if hired after July 1, 2003.

Second, school bus drivers, monitors, and attendants share responsibility for ensuring the safety of students, including making sure no student is left unattended in a bus or left behind in a bus at the end of a route.

Third, school bus attendants serving students with a disabling condition obtain training and certification in cardiopulmonary resuscitation (CPR) if such skills are required as part of the individualized education plan prepared for a student. Those hired after January 1, 2004 must satisfy this requirement prior to assuming their duties as a school bus attendant. Those hired before then had until July 1, 2004.

Fourth, both school bus attendants and school bus monitors serving students with a disabling condition must receive instruction relating to special needs transportation, including, but not limited to, the proper techniques for assisting disabled students in entering and exiting a school bus. Those hired after January 1, 2004 must have received such training prior to assuming their duties. Those hired before then had until July 1, 2004.

Students with Disabilities

The Board of Regents approved several changes to commissioner's regulations related to the education of students with disabilities. First, school boards must adopt a written policy that establishes administrative practices and procedures that ensure staff responsible for implementing a student's individualized education plan (IEP) receive a copy of, or access to, the IEP prior to implementation, as required by law and regulation. Each staff member with responsibility relating to the implementation of the IEP must be informed of his or her respective responsibility and the specific accommodations, modifications, and supports that must be provided under the IEP.

Second, the approved changes repealed prior requirements that a school board initiate a due process hearing when a parent did not provide consent for the *initial* provision of special education services.

Third, school district space requirement plans must include an appraisal of and provide for sufficient instructional space to meet the current and future special education program and service needs of students with disabilities, and to serve them in settings with non-disabled students. Such plans must be consistent with regional needs and the special education space requirements plan developed by the local board of cooperative educational services (BOCES). The commissioner of education must approve all plans and specifications for the creation of new instructional space and leases for space to be used for special education programs and services. In addition, BOCES superintendents must annually report to the commissioner on the actual number and projected numbers and percentages of students with disabilities in settings with non-disabled peers in the regions, any expected significant changes to the space requirements plan, and procedures that ensure the stability and continuity of program placements for students with disabilities.

Fourth, changes intended to streamline due process hearing procedures require that an impartial hearing officer (IHO) may not accept appointment if he or she is unavailable to start a hearing within the first 14 days after being *appointed* as opposed to the first 14 days of being contacted by a district. IHOs may schedule a pre-hearing conference to discuss various matters necessary to complete a hearing in a timely manner, require a stipulation of facts and introduction of joint exhibits, whenever practicable, accept testimony by telephone or affidavit, and exclude evidence and limit the number of witnesses whose testimony he or she deems irrelevant, immaterial, unreliable, or unduly repetitious. In addition, each party has up to one day to present its case, unless the IHO determines that additional time is necessary for a full, fair disclosure of the facts to arrive at a decision. Extensions may not be granted based solely on agreement of the parties. The IHO must consider the impact of a delay, student's educational interest or well-being, and other factors. Moreover, an IHO may grant only one extension of no more than 30 days duration for settlement discussions. If a settlement is not reached, the hearing continues.

Fifth, other changes related to appeals to the State Review Officer (SRO) from an IHO's decision establish new deadlines for submitting a petition for review, and new rules regarding the content and format for pleadings and memorandum of law, and require that the original exhibits accepted into evidence at the hearing, instead of copies thereof, be forwarded to the SRO along with the decision of the impartial hearing officer and a written and electronic transcript of the hearing. The school board must certify that the record submitted is the complete hearing record. Staff at the Office of State Review may schedule and direct the attorneys for the parties to participate in a preview telephone conference. Absent good cause, the SRO will dismiss the petition of any party whose attorney fails to attend and participate in such a conference. The SRO's decision will be mailed to the district's attorney and the superintendent of schools, and the superintendent must forward a copy of the decision to the building principal and the chairperson of the committee on special education involved in developing the most recent individualized education program that was in contention in the appeal.

Sixth, appeals from an SRO's decision in state court must now proceed through Article 4 of the Civil Practice Law and Rules, instead of Article 78. This change allows a court to hear additional evidence at the request of a party. The court must base its decision on the preponderance of the evidence rather than the substantial evidence standard applied in Article 78 proceedings.

Teacher Mentoring Program

The Board of Regents approved amendments to the commissioner's regulations requiring that school districts and boards of cooperative educational services (BOCES) include in a professional development plan (PDP) in effect after February 2, 2004, a mentoring program for teachers certified under new rules that went into effect on that date. The new certification rules require that candidates for a "professional" certificate must successfully complete three years of teaching experience or its equivalent. If they fulfill the teaching experience requirements by teaching in New York public schools, they also must participate in a mentored program in their first year of employment (unless they have successfully completed two years of teaching prior to such service).

The PDP mentoring program must describe the procedure for selecting mentors, the role of mentors, the preparation of mentors, types of mentoring activities, and time allotted for mentoring. Aspects of the mentoring program such as pay for mentor training, time allocated for mentoring activities, and for activities occurring beyond the hours of a regular teacher workday are subject to collective bargaining.

The PDP mentoring program requirement is separate and distinct from the New York State Mentor Teacher-Internship Program (MTIP) that some district may have had in place under separate provisions of the Education Law and commissioner's regulations.

New Case Law

Employee Constitutional Rights

The U.S. Court of Appeals for the Second Circuit ruled that school officials had the right to search the classroom of a teacher suspended during the pendency of disciplinary charges alleging improper dealings with a student both for non-investigatory work-related purposes such as preparing the classroom for a substitute teacher, and for evidence relevant to its investigation into work-related misconduct. The court recognized that "public employees can have a 'substantial' expectation of privacy in private possessions kept in their workplace, but their expectation can be diminished by workplace realities such as work-related visits by fellow employees and others." In this case, the teacher had surrendered his classroom keys and had been given an opportunity to gather his personal belongings, which were scattered throughout the classroom and intermingled with school property (*Shaul v. Cherry Valley-Springfield CSD*, 363 F.3d 177 (2d Cir. 2004)).

Employee Discipline

The Appellate Division, Third Department ruled that a school district properly terminated a school bus driver who made death threats against a co-worker even though the employee had worked for the district for 13 years without prior incident. The court noted that the termination was based on the employee's "poor judgment and lack of remorse the disturbing nature of her comments, various safety issues and the District's strict policy concerns regarding threats of violence." Even if a lesser penalty may have been more appropriate, the circumstances in the case did not make the penalty of termination so shocking to a sense of fairness as to warrant the court set it aside (*Bottari v. Saratoga Springs City School Dist.*, 3 A.D.3d 832 (3d Dep't 2004)).

Interscholastic Sports

The U.S. Court of Appeals for the Second Circuit ruled that school districts violated Title IX of the Education Amendments of 1972 and its governing regulations by scheduling girls' high school soccer in the spring while scheduling boys' high school soccer in the fall (*McCormick v. The School Dist. of Mamaroneck and The School Dist. of Pelham*, 370 F.3d 275 (2d Cir. 2004)). The schedule deprived the girls of the opportunity to compete in the regional and state championships held in the fall. In addition, girls' soccer was the only sport scheduled outside the State championship game season. According to the court, the opportunity to play for a championship title is so "fundamental" to the athletic experience that it "is inconsistent with Title IX's mandate of equal opportunity for both sexes" to deprive the girls' soccer team of this opportunity.

Parent Visitation Rights

The Appellate Division, Third Department, ruled that a school district did not violate the due process or free speech rights of a parent who was banned by the principal from school until further notice after she brought a weapon to school and refused to secure it either in her car or off-campus (*Cina v. Waters*, 779 N.Y.S.2d 289 (3d Dep't 2004)). The parent worked as a parole officer and was licensed to carry a weapon. However, schools have the right to prevent visitors to school grounds from carrying firearms or weapons, even if they may lawfully possess such weapons. In addition, the parent had prior notice of the district's policy against bringing firearms or weapons to school without prior written permission, and was given the opportunity to appeal the principal's decision to the school board. The court also determined that the school did not violate the parent's fundamental interest in the upbringing and education of her children because she was able to communicate with the school by phone and through the mail. Moreover, according to the court, parents do not have a right to be physically present on school grounds.

Pledge of Allegiance

The U.S. Supreme Court dismissed on procedural grounds the lawsuit of a non-custodial parent who objected to his daughter having to listen to the daily recitation of the Pledge of Allegiance by her classmates based on the words "under God" included in the pledge (*Elk Grove Unified School Dist. v. Newdow*, 124 S.Ct. 2301 (2004)). His daughter's classmates recited the pledge daily as required by California state law. In dismissing the case on the basis that, as a non-custodial parent, the student's father did not have "standing" to maintain the lawsuit under California's domestic relations law, the Court failed to answer whether recitation of the pledge is unconstitutional.

Preferred Eligibility Rights

The Appellate Division, Third Department, decided several cases regarding preferred eligibility rights. In one case, it ruled that an administrator whose position was eliminated and thereafter formally retired severed her rights to be placed on a preferred eligibility list (PEL). In so ruling, the court explained that "recall rights . . . will survive . . . acceptance of other employment, but . . . not . . . an individual's formal retirement . . . unless it can be demonstrated that the decision to retire was involuntary or made under duress." According to the court, "economic reasons alone will not constitute compelling circumstances sufficient to undermine the "finality [that] must be given to resignations and retirements from service" (*Donato v. Mills*, 6 A.D.3d 966 (3d Dep't 2004)).

In another case, the Third Department ruled that a teacher who was fired by a board of cooperative educational services (BOCES) for unsatisfactory performance after a BOCES "takeover" of a component district's program, but who had performed satisfactorily for the component district before the

BOCES takeover, retained PEL rights for reemployment by the component district (*Bojarczuk v. Mills*, 6 A.D.3d 774 (3d Dep't 2004)).

School Principal

The commissioner of education ruled that a school principal must possess the requisite certification at the time of appointment. In addition, a superintendent of schools may not serve simultaneously as principal without a waiver from the commissioner because each building must employ a full-time principal (*Appeal of Giardina*, 43 Educ. Dep't Rep. ___, dec. no. 14,959 (2003)).

Students with Disabilities

The U.S. Court of Appeals for the Second Circuit ruled that a school district did not violate the Individuals with Disabilities Education Act (IDEA) or section 504 of the Rehabilitation Act when it denied a learning disabled student the use of an advanced calculator. The student did not need that particular model to pass his class, and its use actually would have interfered with the student's ability to develop certain skills. According to the court, it would have been a violation of the IDEA to provide the student with an unneeded assistive device and award him passing grades based on the use of the device (*Sherman v. Mamaroneck UFSD*, 340 F.3d 87 (2d Cir. 2003)).

Student Discipline

The commissioner of education decided several appeals concerning the conditions that a district may impose in a behavior contract used in cases involving long-term student suspensions. Generally, in exchange for staying such a suspension, a district may ask that the student involved promise to abide by the rules of the school. A student's failure to maintain that promise would result in the reinstatement of the suspension. However, in one case, the commissioner clarified that a district may not condition the return of a student to school upon the student's agreement to execute such a behavior contract (*Appeal of R.M. and L.M.*, 43 Educ. Dep't Rep. ___, dec. no. 14,951 (2003)). In another case, the commissioner explained that a long-term suspension behavior contract may not require a student to participate in anger management counseling (*Appeal of M.F. and P.F.*, 43 Educ. Dep't Rep. ___, dec. no. 14,960 (2003)). In that same case, the commissioner further stated that a school principal does not need parental consent to conduct an investigation and obtain a statement from a student that can be used as evidence for disciplinary purposes. There is no constitutional or statutory requirement that a parent be present when a school official questions a student.

In another case, the commissioner ruled that a school district is responsible for enforcing its code of conduct on a school bus, even when the district hires an independent contractor to transport students (*Appeal of M.H.*, 43 Educ. Dep't Rep. ___, dec. no. 14,973 (2003)).

A number of commissioner's decisions involving student discipline concerned compliance with the procedures applicable to the suspension of students from school for five or fewer days. Generally, parents must receive written notice of the suspension and the right to an informal conference with the principal regarding the suspension. The notice must be provided by means calculated to ensure the parents receive it within 24 hours of the decision to propose suspension. Failure to comply with these requirements will result in an order annulling and expunging the suspension. In one case, the commissioner ruled that notice by regular mail was not sufficient (*Appeal of C.D.*, 44 Educ. Dep't Rep. ___, dec. no. 15,041 (2004)). In another, he ruled that notification by phone followed the same day by written notice sent via regular mail was insufficient, as well (*Appeal of R.F.*, 43 Educ. Dep't Rep. ___, dec. no. 14,972 (2003)). In both cases, the commissioner stressed that the informal conference must occur before the short-term suspension takes place, unless the student's continuing presence at the school poses an ongoing danger or threat of disruption that justifies an immediate suspension. In yet another case, the commissioner ruled that written notice sent via regular mail return receipt requested did not satisfy the notice requirements. In addition, a meeting with someone other than the school principal, in this case the hall principal, also violates the rules applicable to short-term suspensions (*Appeal of V.R. and C.R.*, 43 Educ. Dep't Rep. ___, No. 14,934 (2003)).

Regarding permanent suspensions, the commissioner ruled that such a penalty is educationally unsound except in extraordinary circumstances such as when a student demonstrates "alarming disregard for the safety of others" (*Appeal of Y.M.*, 43 Educ. Dep't Rep. ___, dec. no. 14,968 (2003)). In that same case, the commissioner further ruled that 80 prior disciplinary incidents could not serve as a basis for a permanent suspension when viewed with the current incident because not one of the prior incidents carried a suspension exceeding five days.

Student Records

The Family Policy Compliance Office (FPCO) at the U.S. Department of Education, responsible for enforcing the Family Educational Rights and Privacy Act (FERPA), determined that an impartial hearing officer improperly ordered a school district to provide the parents of a student with disabilities involved in a hearing with a "complete and accurate copy" of his disciplinary records. Those records included the names and other personally identifiable information of other students who had signed allegations charging the disabled student with serious or criminal behavior. In reaching this determination, FPCO clarified that a disabled student's due process rights under the Individuals with Disabilities Education Act (IDEA) do not override FERPA's prohibition against the release of such information without prior written parental consent. The IDEA does not provide a greater right of access than FERPA. Furthermore, where joint records cannot be easily redacted, or the information segregated out, a district can satisfy a request for access by informing the parent about the contents of the record (*Letter to Attorney from School Dist.*, Family Policy Compliance Officer, 40 IDELR 99 (10/31/03)).

Student Residency

The New York Court of Appeals ruled that when a child is placed in foster care, the cost of the child's education in the public schools remains the responsibility of the district where the child resided at the time social services takes over the child's maintenance and support (*Longwood CSD v. Springs UFSD*, 1 N.Y.3d 385 (2004)).

The commissioner of education ruled that children who lived with their mother in an apartment subsidized by a federal program were not homeless because under the program their residence was not temporary or transitional. Therefore, the children were required to attend school in the district where the apartment was located, rather than the district in which they lived when their mother entered the rental assistance program (*Appeal of D.R.*, 43 Educ. Dep't Rep. ___, dec. no. 14,994 (2003)).

The commissioner also ruled that the children of divorced parents were entitled to attend school without the payment of tuition at the district designated by a family court after the children's parents asked the court to make that decision because they could not agree on the district the children should attend (*Appeal of T.K.*, 43 Educ. Dep't Rep. ___, dec. no. 14,935 (2003)).

Substitute Teaching Assistants

The commissioner of education ruled that absent statutory or contractual provisions requiring otherwise, a school district lacks authority to pay a certified teacher substituting for a teaching assistant at a higher rate of pay than the teacher assistant rate (*Appeal of Barkley*, 43 Educ. Dep't Rep. ___, dec. no. 14,912 (2003)).

Tenure and Seniority

The Appellate Division, Third Department, ruled that teaching assistants enjoy layoff rights based on seniority, the same as teachers. In addition, all teaching assistants serve within the same single tenure area. Therefore, a board of cooperative educational services had no authority to establish different tenure areas for teaching assistants and determine who to layoff based on seniority within the applicable separate tenure areas (*Matter of Madison-Oneida BOCES v. Mills*, 2 A.D.3d 1240 (3d Dep't 2004)). This decision was on appeal to the New York Court of Appeals at the time this publication went to press.

Vouchers

The U.S. Supreme Court upheld a Washington state law that specifically prohibits the use of state scholarship funds to pay college tuition for students who wish to pursue a degree in theology (*Locke v. Davey*, 124 S.Ct. 1307 (2004)). According to the Court, Washington State could have funded scholarships for such individuals but was not required to do so. The prohibition did not disfavor religion in violation of the federal constitution. The state of Washington merely chose not to fund a distinct category of instruction. It is permissible for a state to draw a more stringent line. However, the Court chose not to answer the question as to whether a state constitutional prohibition against funding any institution under the direct control of a religious denomination is inconsistent with the federal constitution.

1. The Structure of the New York State School System

Legal Framework

1:1. What is the University of the State of New York?

The University of the State of New York consists of all public and private elementary and secondary schools in the state; all privately and publicly controlled institutions of higher education, including the schools in the State University of New York (SUNY) system; and all libraries, museums, and other educational and cultural institutions admitted to or incorporated by the University (§ 214). It is vested with broad regulatory powers and is governed by the Board of Regents. Its primary purpose is to encourage and promote education (§§ 201, 202; see also *Moore v. Board of Regents*, 44 N.Y.2d 593 (1978)).

The University of the State of New York should not be confused with the State University of New York (SUNY), which was established in 1948 (§ 352). SUNY consists of 34 state-operated and statutory campuses and 30 community colleges. It is governed by a 16-member board of trustees: 15 are appointed by the governor with the advice and consent of the state Senate and one member is president of the Student Assembly of the State University (SASU), ex officio (§ 353(1)). The board of trustees appoints a chancellor who heads SUNY (§ 353(3)).

1:2. What is the general framework of New York State's public education system?

The general framework of New York State's public education system consists of several levels of authority and resembles a pyramid. The base, which carries the most authority, is the federal government. Its authority resides in the United States Constitution, federal laws and regulations, and federal court decisions. The next level, the state, relies on the New York State Constitution, state laws and regulations, including the rules of the state Board of Regents, regulations and decisions of the commissioner of education, and state court decisions.

Legal authority for and jurisdiction of school boards are at the top of the pyramid. As local entities, school boards have the narrowest band of authority and may set policy only in areas in which their jurisdiction is not superseded by federal or state authority.

1:3. What is the role of the federal government regarding the operation of school districts in New York State?

The Tenth Amendment to the United States Constitution leaves the function of education to the individual states by providing that "[t]he powers not delegated to the United States by the Constitution, nor prohibited by it to the States, are reserved to the States respectively, or to the people."

Although not as common as state laws, federal statutes place certain responsibilities on local school districts. For example, under the federal Individuals with Disabilities Education Act (IDEA), districts have certain duties with regard to providing education to students with disabilities (20 USC §§ 1400–1487). The No Child Left Behind Act (NCLB), which constitutes the 2001 Reauthorization of the Elementary and Secondary Education Act, (20 USC §§ 6301–7941) establishes certain national standards and testing requirements. Federal regulations established by federal agencies also stand as the law of the land unless challenged and overturned by federal courts, or changed or overruled by the particular agency.

1:4. What is the role of the state government regarding the operation of school districts in New York State?

The basis for free public education in New York State is contained in article 11, section 1, of the state constitution, which declares that the Legislature "shall provide for the maintenance and support of a system of free common schools, wherein all the children of this state may be educated." Article 11 provides the legal authority given to the Board of Regents and to the Legislature to provide for the maintenance and support of public schools.

Both the governor and the Legislature propose and enact numerous statutes that affect education at the state level. The following statutes in the Education Law specify the authority of the state's school boards:

- Section 1604, for trustees of common school districts.
- Section 1709, for union free school board members.
- Section 1804, for central school district boards.
- Section 1950 for boards of cooperative educational services (BOCES).
- Articles 51, 52, and 52a for city school district boards.

In addition, the state delegates powers to school districts as it does to municipalities. School districts are considered political subdivisions of the state government (*Burlaka v. Greece CSD*, 167 Misc.2d 281 (1996); *Koch v. Webster CSD*, 112 Misc.2d 10 (1981)).

Through the enactment of Article 56 of the Education Law, the state also provides for charter schools that operate as autonomous public schools independent of existing school districts. For further discussion on charter schools, see **chapter 25**.

1:5. What is the role of the New York State Board of Regents and the State Education Department regarding the operation of school districts?

The New York State Board of Regents and the State Education Department (SED) exercise the powers and functions delegated to them through the Education Law. They also establish policy by adopting rules and regulations within the limitations of state law (see **1:6–1:10**). These regulations have the authority of law unless they are overruled by decisions of the state's courts or the Legislature, or until they are superseded by the promulgating agency (§§ 101, 101(a), 207. Also see *Board of Educ. of Northport-East Northport UFSD v. Ambach*, 90 A.D.2d 227, 458 N.Y.S.2d 680, *aff'd*, 60 N.Y.2d 748 (1982), *cert. denied*, 465 U.S. 1101 (1984); and *Van Allen v. McCleary*, 27 Misc.2d 81, 211 N.Y.S.2d 501 (1961)).

In addition, all public elementary, middle, and secondary schools, other than charter schools, must be registered by the Board of Regents, and all are deemed to be admitted to the University of the State of New York (8 NYCRR § 3.32)

The New York State Board of Regents

1:6. What is the New York State Board of Regents?

The New York State Board of Regents is the governing body of the University of the State of New York. It was established by the state Legislature in 1784 and is the oldest continuous state educational agency in the United States.

The Regents exercise legislative functions over the state educational system, determine its educational policies, and, except as related to the judicial functions of the commissioner of education, establish rules for carrying out the state's laws and policies relating to education and the functions, powers, duties, and trusts granted to or authorized by the University of the State of New York and the State Education Department (§ 207).

The Regents also sponsor a Regents College Examinations (RCE) program. Through this nationwide, nontraditional program, adults earn credit toward college degrees in such areas as nursing, liberal arts, business, and technology.

1:7. What is the composition of the Board of Regents?

There are 16 members of the Board of Regents. Each is elected to a five-year term by a concurrent resolution of both houses of the state Legislature. One Regent is selected from each of the state's 12 judicial districts, and four Regents are chosen from the state at large (§ 202). There are no ex officio Regents; that is, members of the Regents do not serve simply by virtue of their holding an elected or appointed position (§ 202).

A Regent's term of office expires April 1. The Legislature's concurrent resolution electing a Regent must be adopted on or before the first Tuesday of the preceding March. Absent adoption of a concurrent resolution, both houses of the state Legislature must meet in a joint session on the second Tuesday in March to select a Regent by joint ballot (§ 202).

1:8. What are the Regents' powers and duties?

The Regents have broad authority over all the state's educational institutions *(Moore v. Board of Regents,* 44 N.Y.2d 593 (1978)). For example, they appoint the commissioner of education, who becomes the president of the University of the State of New York (§ 302; 8 NYCRR § 3.5). They establish and enforce educational and professional standards in the interests of the people of the state.

In the performance of these functions, the Regents are empowered to charter, register, visit, examine into and inspect any school or institution under the educational supervision of the state (§§ 215, 216, 2851(3)(c), 2853(1)(c), 2853(2), (2853(2-a)), to license practitioners in 38 major professions (§ 6504), and to certify teachers and librarians (§§ 3004, 3006).

The Regents meet monthly (except in August), usually in Albany. They serve without compensation, but are reimbursed for travel and other expenses. They elect their own chancellor and vice chancellor (§ 203).

The New York State Education Department

1:9. What is the New York State Education Department?

The New York State Education Department (SED), under the direction of the commissioner of education, is the administrative arm of the University of the State of New York. It is charged with carrying out legislative mandates and the Regents' policies (§§ 101, 207, 305). The principal functions of SED are carried out within six major areas: Office of Management Services; Office of Cultural Education; Office of Elementary, Middle, Secondary and Continuing Education; Office of Higher and Professional Education; Office of the Professions; and Office of Vocational and Educational Services for Individuals with Disabilities. The Office of Elementary, Middle, Secondary and Continuing Education (EMCS) and the

Office of Vocational and Educational Services for Individuals with Disabilities (VESID) directly pertain to elementary and secondary education.

For more information about SED and its offices, contact SED at 518-474-3852, or via its general Web site at http://www.nysed.gov or the individual office Web sites, including, for example, http://www.emsc.nysed.gov (EMSC) and http://web.nysed.gov/vesid (VESID).

1:10. What is the function of the State Education Department?

The State Education Department (SED) is charged with the general management and supervision of all public schools and all the education work of the state (§ 101), from prekindergarten to graduate school, and is responsible for setting educational policy, standards, and rules. SED also supervises the state's nonpublic schools (§ 807; 8 NYCRR Parts 100, 125), oversees the 38 licensed professions (§§ 6500, 6501, 6504), provides vocational and educational services to people with disabilities (§ 4400; 8 NYCRR § 15.2), guides local government records programs (§§ 229, 230, 231), and operates the State Archives, Library, and Museum (§ 232; 8 NYCRR § 10.1).

The Commissioner of Education

1:11. Who is the commissioner of education?

The commissioner of education is the chief executive officer of the State Education Department and the Board of Regents (§§ 101, 301, 305(1); 8 NYCRR § 3.7; see **1:6, 1:8–10**).

1:12. What are the commissioner of education's powers and duties?

The commissioner of education's powers and duties are contained primarily in section 305 of the Education Law. They include, for example, enforcement of laws relating to the educational system, execution of all educational policies determined by the Board of Regents, issuance of regulations, general supervision of all schools and institutions subject to the provisions of the Education Law, grant and annulment of teaching certificates, approval of school transportation and cafeteria contracts, review of appeals and petitions pursuant to section 310, removal of school officers and withholding of state aid pursuant to section 306, and execution of such other powers and duties as determined by the Board of Regents.

For more specific information and examples of the commissioner's powers and duties, see **7:2** (school administrators), **8:14–57** (teachers), **12:11–14** (students), **14:4, 14:6–7** (school day/hours), **14:23–27, 14:29, 14:33, 14:36, 14:39, 14:42, 14:45–51, 14:53–54** (curriculum), **14:116** (library), **15:8** (school district reorganization), **17:1, 17:16–30, 17:49, 17:51, 17:56** (school building safety), **22:89–92** (transportation).

1:13. What are the commissioner's regulations?

The commissioner's regulations are rules that govern how the schools, institutions, and other entities under the commissioner's jurisdiction are to be operated. They have the effect of law on the schools of the state unless the courts overturn them. They are officially compiled and published by the New York Department of State and are found in Title VIII of the Official Compilation of Codes, Rules and Regulations of the State of New York (8 NYCRR). They include, among other things, certification requirements for teachers, curriculum requirements, mandates on the building of schools, and standards for the various professions.

1:14. Can a school district apply for a waiver from regulation?

Yes. A school district can apply for a waiver from any regulatory mandate issued by the commissioner of education or other state agencies, provided the intent of the mandate can be achieved in a more cost-effective manner. State agencies have broad power to exempt a school district from regulatory mandates that would not compromise environmental quality, health, or safety concerns, or reduce any employee rights or benefits or violate a collective bargaining agreement (N.Y. Adm. Pro. § 204-a).

1:15. How is an appeal brought to the commissioner of education?

Any person believing himself or herself to be aggrieved by an official act of any officer or school authority, or by any action taken at a meeting concerning any matter under the Education Law or pertaining to the schools of the state, may appeal to the commissioner of education (§ 310). For example, that person must be aggrieved in the sense that he or she has suffered personal damage or injury to his or her rights (*Appeal of Goldin*, 43 Educ. Dep't Rep.___, dec. no. 15,009 (2004); *Appeal of M.H.*, 43 Educ. Dep't Rep.___, dec. no. 14,973 (2003); *Appeal of Simms*, 42 Educ. Rep. 50 (2002)).

All appeals to the commissioner must be brought within 30 days after the decision or act complained of, or from the time knowledge of the cause of the complaint came to the person appealing the decision. However, the commissioner, in his sole discretion, may excuse a failure to commence an appeal in a timely manner for good cause (8 NYCRR § 275.16). The party against whom an appeal is filed and served must answer the appeal within 20 days of service (8 NYCRR § 275.13).

The procedures regarding appeals to the commissioner of education are detailed in *Handbook 1—Regulations of the Commissioner of Education Relating to Appeals and Other Proceedings Before the Commissioner and the State Review Officer* (State Education Department, rev. Sept. 1999). It is available from SED's Office of Counsel at 518-474-8927 or by visiting their Web site at http://www.counsel.nysed.gov.

1:16. Are there any limitations on the commissioner's ability to review an appeal?

The commissioner will not determine moot or advisory questions but will determine only actual matters in controversy (*Appeal of D'Orazio and Carey*, 41 Educ. Dep't Rep. 292 (2002); *Appeal of D.M. and M.M.*, 41 Educ. Dep't Rep. 302 (2002); *Appeal of N.C.*, 40 Educ. Dep't Rep. 542 (2000); *Appeal of Eckert*, 40 Educ. Dep't Rep. 433 (2000); *Appeal of Doro*, 40 Educ. Dep't Rep. 281 (2000)).

The commissioner will not decide the constitutionality of a statute (*Appeal of St. Cyr*, 27 Educ. Dep't Rep. 351 (1988); *Matter of Van Druff*, 21 Educ. Dep't Rep. 635 (1982)) or violations of the Open Meetings Law, Freedom of Information Law, and the Family Education Rights and Privacy Act (*Appeal of Barnett*, 40 Educ. Dep't Rep. 403 (2000); *Appeal of Instone-Noonan*, 39 Educ. Dep't Rep. 413 (1999); *Appeal of Razzano*, 39 Educ. Dep't Rep. 303 (1999); *Appeal of Tsu, Iannacone and Dunne*, 39 Educ. Dep't Rep. 84 (1999)).

In addition, the commissioner will not resolve "novel questions of constitutional law" in an administrative appeal (*Appeal of Almedina*, 33 Educ. Dep't Rep. 383 (1993); *Ware v. Valley Stream High*, 75 N.Y.2d 114 (1989)).

Furthermore, the commissioner will not substitute his or her judgment for that of a board or school official in any decision absent a showing that the decision is arbitrary, capricious, or contrary to law or the dictates of sound educational policy (*Appeal of Chan and Grogan*, 41 Educ. Dep't Rep. 178 (2001)).

Once an appeal has been decided, it will not be reopened by the commissioner unless it is established that there is new and material evidence that was not available at the time of the original proceedings or that the original decision was rendered under a misunderstanding of the facts (8 NYCRR § 276.8; *Application to Reopen the Appeal of D.H.*, 41 Educ. Dep't Rep. 283 (2002); *Appeal of Wroblewski*, 36 Educ. Dep't Rep. 294 (1997); *Appeal of Bach*, 34 Educ. Dep't Rep. 18 (1994); *Appeal of Strada*, 33 Educ. Dep't Rep. 666 (1994)).

1:17. Are the commissioner of education's decisions reviewable by the courts?

Yes. The actions of the commissioner of education are subject to court review, the same as those of other state officials. The commissioner's decisions are subject to review in the courts by means of a proceeding under Article 78 of the Civil Practice Law and Rules. The commissioner's decisions are published in Education Department Reports (Educ. Dep't Rep.). Ordinarily they can be found in any county courthouse law library, or they can be obtained by writing directly to the State Education Department's Publication Sales, Education Building, Room 309, 89 Washington Avenue, Albany, NY 12234, 518-474-3806. Currently, only some are available through the Web site of SED's Office of Counsel at http://www.counsel.nysed.gov.

Local School Districts

Editor's Note: For additional information about school districts, see A Guide to the Reorganization of School Districts in New York State *(Albany, N.Y.: State Education Department, 1998).*

1:18. What is a common school district?

A *common school district* is a school district first created by legislative action in 1812 to operate elementary schools (kindergarten through eighth grade). Even though they lack legal authority to operate a high school, common school districts remain responsible for ensuring a secondary education for their resident children.

A common school district is administered by either a sole trustee or a school board of three trustees (§ 1602(1)). The number of members of the board of trustees of a common school district may be increased or decreased as set forth in law (§ 1602; see **2:6**).

1:19. What is a union free school district?

A *union free school district* is a school district generally formed from one or more common school districts to operate a high school program, which common school districts cannot do. First authorized by legislation in 1853, union free school districts are administered by a school board of between three and nine members. The number of board members of a union free school district may be increased or decreased as set forth in law (§§ 1702, 1703; see **2:6**).

Currently, not all union free school districts operate a secondary school program, and some have been established solely as special act school districts to serve children who reside in specified childcare institutions (see **1:23**).

1:20. What is a central school district?

A *central school district* is a school district formed by combining any number of common, union free, and central school districts. First established in 1914, the central school district is the most common form of district organization in the state. Like union free districts, central school districts may operate a high school. Their school boards may consist of five, seven, or nine members (§ 1804(1)). The number of board members may be increased or decreased as set forth in law (§ 1804(3); see **2:6**).

1:21. What is a central high school district?

A *central high school district* is a school district that provides only secondary education to children from two or more common or union free school districts. Only three such districts exist in the state, and the Legislature has prohibited the formation of additional such districts, except in Suffolk County.

A central high school district's governing board is composed of representatives from each of its participating districts. The number of members of such board shall be not less than five. A central high school district is part of a supervisory district (§§ 1912–1914; see **6:2**).

1:22. What is a city school district?

A *city school district* is a school district whose school boundary lines are identical with that of a city. There are two types of city school districts: those with a population under 125,000 and those with a population of 125,000 or more (§§ 2501, 2550). The enlargement of a city school district by the addition of one or more union free, common, or central school districts contiguous to the city school district results in an enlarged city school district (§ 1526).

Article 51 of the Education Law applies to city school districts with less than 125,000 inhabitants. Their governing boards may consist of five, seven, or nine members (§ 2502(2)).

Article 52 of the Education Law applies to cities with populations of 125,000 or more. There are five in New York State, commonly referred to as the Big 5 school districts: Buffalo, New York City, Rochester, Syracuse, and Yonkers. Rochester and Syracuse have seven-member boards, chosen by the voters at either a general or municipal election (§§ 2552, 2553(2)). Yonkers has a nine-member school board, each member appointed by the mayor (§§ 2552, 2553(3)). Buffalo has a nine-member school board: one member elected by the qualified voters in each of the city's six school subdistricts, and three members elected in a citywide, at-large election by the qualified voters (§ 2553(10)(c)).

In New York City, the citywide Panel for Educational Policy has 13 members (§ 2590-b(1)(a)). Five of them are appointed by the city's borough presidents, and eight are appointed by the city's mayor, including the chancellor, who serves as a member of the board and as its chairperson at the pleasure of the mayor (§ 2590-h).

In addition, New York City has 32 community district education councils, each composed of 11 voting members and one non-voting member (§ 2590-c(1)). Nine of the voting members are parents of children attending a public school within the district who are selected by the presidents and officers of the parents' association or parent-teacher association. They serve for a term of two years (§ 2590-c(1)(a)). Two of the 11 voting members are appointed by the borough presidents corresponding to such district. They must be residents of, or own or operate a business within the district and have extensive business, trade, or education experience and knowledge. Such members serve for two years and may be reappointed but only for one additional two-year term (§ 2590-c(1)(6)). The non-voting member is a high school senior appointed by the superintendent forum among the elected student leadership (§ 2590-c(1)(c)). The community district education councils are responsible for prekindergarten, nursery, kindergarten, elementary, intermediate, junior high schools, and related community district programs within the community district (§ 2590-e).

1:23. What is a special act school district?

Special act school districts are those that are created by a special act of the Legislature rather than through a procedure provided in the Education Law. In general, these districts have been established on the grounds of charitable institutions caring for children and youth.

They are designated by the state Legislature as public school districts authorized to receive state financial aid. For example, Abbott House in Westchester County is known legally as Union Free School District No. 13, and Mother Cabrini School in Ulster County is known legally as West Park Union Free School District. Section 3602 of the Education Law outlines the details on apportionment of state aid for such districts.

1:24. What is a board of cooperative educational services (BOCES)?

A board of cooperative educational services (BOCES) is a voluntary, cooperative association of school districts in a geographic area that have banded together to provide educational or business services more economically than each district could offer by itself. Each BOCES is governed by a board of between five and 15 members elected by the component school boards (see **chapter 5** for more detailed information).

1:25. What is the relationship of a school district to local and county governments?

The relationship between a school district and local or county government is a multifaceted one that is based on the necessity for close communication and cooperation regarding the development and administration of programs and services to be provided by the governmental bodies to the schools of the district.

In addition to their concern regarding the education of the students of their districts, school boards must perform a variety of functions related to the security, safety, health and well being of their students. Thus, boards must work with numerous agencies of local governments, such as the police and fire departments as well as health, fiscal, taxation and civil defense authorities.

Many school districts also find they work closely with county government bodies, such as planning and zoning commissions, in the selection and acquisition of school sites, and in the construction of school buildings and related structures or additions.

1:26. Who determines the official name of a school district?

The Education Law provides that school districts, other than city school districts, adopt simplified legal names subject to the approval of the commissioner of education (§ 315).

The commissioner's centralization order designates the name of a centralized school district (§ 1801(2); 8 NYCRR Part 240). However, the name of a central school district established or reorganized by such an order may be changed by the district's school board if a written request is filed with the commissioner at least 14 days before the establishment or reorganization of the district (§ 315; see **15:2** on centralization).

The State Education Department (SED) shall issue, on request, certificates certifying the name of a school district and the names of the towns and counties in which the territory of the district is located, or in the case of school districts other than city school districts, which are wholly or partly located within a city, the names of the city, as well as the towns and counties in which the territory of the district is located (§ 315).

The Parent-Teacher Association

1:27. What is the parent-teacher association's relationship to the public schools?

The New York State Congress of Parents and Teachers, otherwise known as the parent-teacher association (PTA), is a voluntary group of citizens that acts in an advisory capacity to school boards, superintendents, and principals. School boards are responsible for the administration of the schools and the development of the policies that govern their operation.

Section 2590-d(2)(a) of the Education Law states that a New York City community education council must provide for either a parent association or a parent-teacher association in each school under its jurisdiction and maintain regular communications with each association. In addition, community education counsels must meet quarterly with elected officers of the parent and parent-teacher association and provide them with information on student achievement, including but not limited to the following: annual reading scores, comparison of the achievement of students in comparable grades and schools, as well as the record of achievement of the same children as they progress through the school. The information may not be disclosed in a manner that would identify individual pupils (§ 2590-d(2)(b)).

1:28. May PTA members serve on school boards?

Yes. Service as an officer or member of a PTA does not bar individuals from membership on a school board. However, a member of the PTA who is a teacher within the same district may not serve, as teachers may not serve on the school board of the district in which they are employed (§ 2103(4); see **2:27**).

1:29. Where can information about the PTA and its publications be obtained?

Information about the PTA can be obtained from the New York State Congress of Parents and Teachers, Inc., One Wembley Square, Albany, N.Y. 12205; telephone 518-452-8808 or via its Web site at http://www.nypta.com.

2. School Boards

2:1. What is a school board?

A school board is a corporate body that oversees and manages a public school district's affairs, personnel, and properties (§§ 1601, 1603, 1701, 2502(1), 2551)). Its members are elected by the residents of the school district that the board oversees (see **2:3**).

The term *corporate body* indicates that a school board is treated as a corporation, a legal entity that has an existence distinct and apart from its members and has the capacity for continuous existence without regard to changes in its membership. As such, the legalities of a school board's contracts, as well as the validity of a board's policies and resolutions, do not depend on its individual members.

Board members do not assume any personal liability for the school district even though they may be personally liable for certain conduct (see **18:1–2, 18:25**). Generally, school board members take official action only by majority vote at an official meeting (see **2:15**).

2:2. What is the composition of a school board?

A school board is composed of its elected members. One member is elected by the board at its annual reorganizational meeting to serve as president (see **3:1–3**). At its discretion, the board also may elect a vice president, who exercises the duties of the president in case of that officer's absence or disability. If the office of president becomes vacant, the vice president acts as president until a new president is elected (§ 1701).

2:3. What is the difference between a trustee and a school board member?

The term *trustee* generally refers to a member of a school board of a common school district, whereas the term *school board member* generally refers to a member of the school board of any other type of school district. These terms are sometimes used interchangeably, but the more contemporary and commonly used term is board member.

Board member is also the term used throughout this book, unless a distinction is necessary for accuracy or clarity.

2:4. May a student be a member of a school board?

Yes, but only as a non-voting member. The Education Law expressly allows union free, central, and small city school districts to have a high school student serve as an ex officio non-voting member of the school board if district voters approve having a student serve in that capacity. A district may offer voters this option once every two years (§§ 1702(3), (3-a), 1804(12), (12-a), 2502(10), (10-a)).

Generally, the student board member is the elected student president of the high school, with a rotating system in the case of multiple high schools. If there is no high school student president, the student government selects the student board member. Where there is neither a high school student president nor a student government, the high school principal selects a student who will serve on the school board. The student selected must be at least 18 years old, a senior at the high school, and have attended the high school for at least two years prior to the selection (§§ 1702 (3)(c), (d), (e); 1804(12)(c), (d), (e); 2502(10)(c), (d), (e)). Although the student board member is not entitled to vote, he or she can sit with the board at all public meetings and participate in all board hearings and meetings, except executive sessions (§§ 1702(3); 1804(12); 2502(10)).

In New York City, community district education councils must have a high school senior serve as a non-voting council member. The superintendent appoints a student from among the elected student leadership (§ 2590-c(1)(c)).

2:5. How many school board members serve on a school board?

It depends on the type of school district. As the voters of the district determine, a common school district may have from one to three trustees (§§ 1602(1), 2101(1)). A union free school district may have from three to nine board members (§§ 1702(1), 2101(2)). A central school district may have a board consisting of five, seven, or nine members (§ 1804(1)). The board of a central high school district is comprised of a minimum of five members, at least one from each common school district and at least two from each union free school district within the central high school district (§§ 1901, 1914). A small city school district with a population under 125,000 may have a board consisting of five, seven, or nine members (§ 2502(2)). Union free, central, and small city districts may also have an ex-officio student member (see 2:3).

Except in New York City, a large city school district's board may have between three and nine members (§ 2552). For example:

- In Yonkers, nine school board members are appointed by the mayor from the city at large (§§ 2552(d), 2553(3)).
- In both Rochester and Syracuse, seven board members are elected by the voters at large, at either a general or municipal election or both (§§ 2552(b), (c), 2553(2)).
- In Buffalo, a total of nine school board members are elected by the voters from a combination of specific districts and at-large seats. Six of these board members are elected from six subdistricts of

equal population created by the Buffalo Common Council. Three members are elected from the city at large (§§ 2552(a), 2553(10)).

In New York City, eight of the 13-member Panel for Educational Policy (i.e., the central board) are appointed by the mayor, including the chancellor who serves as a member of the board and as its chairperson. The remaining five members are appointed by each of the five borough presidents (§ 2590-b(1)(a)). The seven members appointed by the mayor must reside in the city, whereas each of the five borough president appointees must reside in his or her respective borough. Each of the 32 community district education councils is composed of 11 voting members and one non-voting member (§ 2590-c(1)). Nine of the voting members are parents of children attending a public school within the district and are selected by the presidents and officers of the parents' association or parent-teacher association. They serve for a term of two years (§ 2590-c(1)(a)). Two are appointed by the borough presidents corresponding to such district and must be residents of, or own or operate a business within the district and have extensive business, trade, or education experience and knowledge. They serve for two years and may be reappointed only for one additional two-year term (§ 2590-c(1)(6)). The non-voting member is a high school senior appointed by the superintendent from among the elected student leadership (§ 2590-c(1)(c)). The community district education councils are responsible for prekindergarten, nursery, kindergarten, elementary, intermediate, junior high schools, and related community district programs within the community district (§ 2590-e).

A board of cooperative educational services (BOCES) has between five and 15 members elected by the members of the school boards of the BOCES' component school districts (§ 1950(1),(2)). A more detailed discussion of BOCES members' terms, as well as other issues related to BOCES, is provided in **chapter 5**.

2:6. May the number of members on a school board be changed?

Yes. In common school districts that have only one trustee, two-thirds of the legal voters present and voting at any annual meeting may vote to increase the size of the board to three trustees (§ 1602(3); see also *Matter of Gillison*, 70 State Dep't Rep. 60 (1949)). In common school districts that already have three trustees, a simple majority of the voters present and voting may decrease the size of the board to one trustee (§ 1602(2)). When the voters determine to decrease the number of trustees to one, the trustees in office continue in office until their terms expire, and thereafter only one trustee will be elected (§ 1602(2)).

In union free and central school districts, the number of members of a board can be increased or decreased by a majority vote of the qualified voters present and voting at the annual meeting. A proposition to increase or decrease the size of the board of education must be put before the voters upon petition of 25 voters or 5 percent of the number of people who voted in the previous annual election, whichever is greater (§§ 1703(2), 1804(3); *Matter of Degioia,* 17 Educ. Dep't Rep. 451 (1978). See also *Matter of Swanson,* 29 Educ. Dep't Rep. 503 (1990)).

In small city school districts, the board may, on its own motion, and must, on a written petition signed by 500 qualified voters of the district, submit a proposition at the annual election to increase or decrease the number of members of the board (§ 2502(4)(a)).

Petitions to change the number of members on a school board must be submitted enough in advance, according to the procedures prescribed by the board, to allow a statement giving notice of the proposition to be included in the notice of the annual meeting (§§ 1703(2), 2035(2), 2502(4)(b); see also *Matter of Presutti,* 17 Educ. Dep't Rep. 445 (1978)).

For information on the boards of cooperative educational services (BOCES), see **5:5.**

2:7. When do changes to the number of members on a school board take effect?

When the voters determine to increase the number of board members, the additional members are elected at a special meeting to be held for that purpose, between 30 and 60 days from the annual meeting approving the increase (§§ 1703(3), 1804(3); *Matter of the Appeal of Beck,* 74 St. Dep't Rep. 78 (1953); *Matter of Gillison,* 70 State Dep't Rep. 60 (1949), except in small city school districts where the additional members are elected at the next annual meeting §§ 1602(3), 2502(4)(c)). The terms of the new members must be established to ensure that as nearly as possible an equal number of terms expire each year (§§ 1602(3), 1804(3), 2105(9), 2502(3), (4)(c)(3)).

If the voters approve a decrease in the number of board members, no election may be held until the number of members on the board is equal to or less than the number to which the board has been decreased. At subsequent elections in union free, central, and small city school districts, board members are to be elected for terms of no more than five years, again with the aim that an equal number of terms are to expire each year (§§ 1602(2), 1804(3), 2105(10), 2502(4)(c)).

2:8. What is the term of office for board members?

It depends on the type of school district. In common school districts that have just one trustee, the trustee serves only a one-year term (§§ 1602(1), 2105(1)). However, in common school districts with three trustees, the trustees are elected for three-year terms (§§ 1602(1), 2105(2)). In union free and central school districts, board members are elected for terms of three, four, or five years (§§ 1702(1), 1804(1), 2105(3)).

Members of a central high school board must be members of the school board of a component district while they are members of the central high school board. However, the term of office on the central high school board can be shorter than the term on the school board of the component district (*Appeal of Carbonaro*, 35 Educ. Dep't Rep. 257 (1996); see also §§ 1901, 1914).

The term of office for city board members varies among the various city school districts. In most city school districts with less than 125,000 inhabitants, the term of office of a school board member is three or five years, as determined by the district (§ 2502(2)). In the Albany City School District, a board member's term is four years (§ 2502(3)). In the Rensselaer City School District, the term is five years (§ 2502(9-a)(n)).

In city school districts with 125,000 or more inhabitants (the Big 5), the term of office of school board members is as follows:

- In Buffalo, board members elected from the city school subdistricts each are elected for three-year terms, while the term of office for members of the school board elected at large is five years (§ 2553(10)(n)).

- In New York City, members of the Panel for Educational Policy (i.e., the central board) serve at the pleasure of the appointing authority. Community education council members hold two-year terms, except for terms that began on July 1, 2004, which were limited to one year (§ 2590-c; see **2:5**).

- In both Rochester and Syracuse, board members are elected to four-year terms (§ 2553(4)).

- In Yonkers, board members are appointed to five-year terms (§ 2553(4)).

BOCES board members generally serve three-year terms (§ 1950(2)). A more detailed discussion of BOCES members' terms, as well as other issues related to BOCES, is provided in **chapter 5**.

2:9. May the term of office for a board member be changed?

Yes. In central and union free school districts, board members serve either a three-, four- or five-year term. Education Law section 2105(3) specifically authorizes the voters of such districts to decrease the full term of a board member to three or four years or increase the full term of a member to four or five years. Such changes can be accomplished by adopting a proposition at any annual meeting or election to do so (§ 2105(3); *Appeal of Atkins*, 35 Educ. Dep't Rep. 375 (1996)).

Board members in city school districts with less than 125,000 inhabitants serve either a three- or five-year term. Education Law section 2502(3) specifically authorizes such districts to decrease the full term of a board to three years or increase it to five by adopting a proposition at any regular meeting or election to do so (§ 2502(3)).

The current term of office of incumbent board members may not be increased or decreased by any such proposition. In addition, propositions to increase or decrease the term of office must specify that vacancies during each of the three years next succeeding the adoption of such proposition will be filled for terms that ensure, as nearly as possible, that equal numbers of board members will be elected each year (§§ 2105(3); 2502(3); *Appeal of Atkins*).

2:10. Are school board members local officials or state officials?

School board members are local officials.

Section 2 of the Public Officers Law defines *state officers* as those who are elected by all of the state's voters (such as the governor, lieutenant governor, comptroller, and attorney general); members of the state Legislature; justices of the state Supreme Court; Regents of the University of the State of New York; and every officer, appointed by one or more state officers, or by the Legislature, and authorized to exercise his or her official functions throughout the state or without limitation to any political subdivision of the state. All others are considered to be local officers, including school board members. However, their authority and duties are defined by the state and federal constitutions and laws, as well as by rules and regulations promulgated by the Board of Regents and commissioner of education.

2:11. Are members of a school board required to take a constitutional oath of office?

Yes. School board members are not able to exercise the duties of office until they take the following oath: "I do solemnly swear (or affirm) that I will support the constitution of the United States and the constitution of the State of New York, and that I will faithfully discharge the duties of the office of . . . , according to the best of my ability" (State Constitution Art. 13 § 1). This oath must be filed with the district clerk. In the case of a board of cooperative educational services (BOCES), each board member files an oath in the office of the clerk of the county in which that member resides (Pub. Off. Law § 10).

The refusal or neglect of a school board member to file an oath of office within 30 days after the commencement of the term of office to which the person is elected, or if appointed, within 30 days after notice of appointment, causes the office to become vacant (Pub. Off. Law § 30(1)(h); *Appeal of Rausch*, 41 Educ. Dep't Rep. 351 (2002)).

Usually the president of the board or the district clerk administers the oath to newly elected school board members at the board's annual reorganizational meeting. The fact that the oath has been administered should be noted in the board's minutes. An individual who has not properly taken and filed an oath of office has no authority to administer oaths to others (*Application of Karpen*, 39 Educ. Dep't Rep. 98 (1999)).

Members who are reelected to the school board also must take the oath at the beginning of their new term of office, just as at the beginning of the first term they held. Board officers, such as the president, vice president, clerk and treasurer, must be administered the oath each year at the time of their appointment or reappointment.

2:12. Must school board members file statements disclosing their personal financial status?

No. The Ethics in Government Act, which requires individuals holding or running for office to make financial disclosure statements, applies to municipalities with populations of 50,000 or more, but not to school districts (Gen. Mun. Law §§ 810(1), 811). Candidates for school boards, however, are required to file campaign expenditure statements under the Education Law (§§ 1528–1531; see **4:68** for more information).

Powers and Duties

2:13. What are the powers and duties of a school board?

"A board of education has no inherent powers and possesses only those powers expressly delegated by statute or necessarily and reasonably implied therefrom" (*Appeal of McKenna*, 42 Educ. Dep't Rep. 54 (2002); *Appeal of Rosenkranz,* 37 Educ. Dep't Rep. 330 (1998); *Appeal of Bode*, 33 Educ. Dep't Rep. 260 (1993)).

The general powers and duties of school boards are outlined in the Education Law, which assigns different powers and duties to different types of school districts, some of which are common to various types of districts, others of which are specific to a single type of district. Figure 1 below lists the different types of school districts and the Education Law sections that govern their respective responsibilities.

Fig. 1

School Board Responsibilities

Type of school district	Education Law section
common school districts	1604
union free school districts	1709
central school districts	1804
central high school districts	1903
small city school districts	2503
large city school districts	2554
New York City Panel for Educational Policy (formerly, the central board)	2590-g
New York City community district educational councils	2590-c, 2590-d

Additional powers and duties may be found in other state laws such as the General Municipal Law, the Local Finance Law, the Real Property Tax Law and the Public Officers Law, as well as in federal law and regulations, and the state education commissioner's regulations.

However, all school boards are similar in that they are responsible for the education of the children residing in their respective districts.

Generally, school boards are responsible for the admission, instruction, discipline, grading, and, as appropriate, classification of students attending the public schools in its district; for the employment and management of necessary professional and support staff; and for purchasing, leasing, maintaining, and insuring school buildings, properties, equipment, and supplies (see generally § 1709). With the exception of large city school districts, they also must present a detailed statement of estimated expenditures (i.e., the proposed budget) for the ensuing school year, which must be submitted to the district voters annually for approval (§§ 1608, 1716, 2022, 2601-a; see also **4:1–2; 4:14–29**).

In addition, school boards are one of the charter entities authorized to receive and approve applications for charter schools proposed to be operated within their respective school district's geographic boundaries, and the only charter entity authorized to receive and approve an application for the conversion of one of their existing public schools into a charter school (§ 2851(a), (c)). For more information on charter schools, see **chapter 25**.

Consistent with law, school boards also have the authority and duty to adopt whatever policies, rules, and bylaws they deem will best meet their statutory responsibilities and secure the best educational results for the students in their charge (see, e.g., §§ 1709(1), (2), 2503(2); 2590-g(1); 2590-d(2); see also **2:93–97**).

2:14. What is devolution, and how does it affect the powers and duties of school boards?

Devolution is the process by which the powers and duties assigned to specific school districts at the top of the list in Figure 2 below devolve and become applicable to other types of school districts through specific provisions of the Education Law (§§ 1710, 1804(1), 1805, 1903, 2503(1), 2554(1)). As shown in this figure, districts lower on the list are granted many of the powers of districts higher on the list by reference to the powers possessed by those districts. As these powers and duties devolve down to other types of districts, they are joined by additional powers and duties that then devolve to school districts located lower on the list. The additional powers, however, do not apply to school districts located higher on the table. Powers and duties devolve down but not up.

Fig. 2

Devolution

Type of District	Ed. Law Article	Ed. Law Section(s)
Common School District	33	—
Union Free School District	35	1710
Central School District	37	1804(1), 1805
Central High School District	39	1903
Small City School District	51	2503(1)
Large City School District	52	2554(1)

Unless the powers that devolve are inconsistent with other specific provisions of the Education Law applicable to a particular type of school district, such a district has all of the powers and duties assigned specifically to it, as well as all of the powers and duties assigned to the other types of school districts located above it on the list (see *Matter of Felicio*, 19 Educ. Dep't Rep. 414 (1980)). The figure above indicates the order of the devolution of powers and duties of school districts. The figure also refers to the article of the Education Law that governs each type of school district, as well as the section of the Education Law that provides for such devolution.

In this handbook, a general reference or citation to powers and duties of school districts refers to those of union free school districts, as set forth in section 1709, which usually apply, through devolution, to all other school districts, with the exception of common school districts.

2:15. Do individual members of a school board have the right to take official action on the board's behalf?

Generally, no. A school board acting in its corporate capacity is required to transact its business in the same manner as the governing body of any corporation; that is, its acts are required to be authorized by resolutions or motions duly adopted or passed by a majority of the whole board (Gen. Constr. Law § 41; *Matter of Coughlan v. Cowan*, 21 Misc.2d 667 (1959); *Appeal of Instone-Noonan*, 39 Educ. Dep't Rep 413 (1999); *Matter of Ascher*, 12 Educ. Dep't Rep. 97 (1972)). Unless the board has taken official action to designate an individual member as the representative of the board for a particular purpose, an individual board member has no more authority than any other qualified voter of the district (see Gen. Constr. Law § 41; *Coughlan v. Cowan*; *Appeal of Silano*, 33 Educ. Dep't Rep. 20 (1993); *Matter of Bruno*, 4 Educ. Dep't Rep. 14 (1964)).

However, occasionally the board may delegate authority to a board officer, such as an auditor (§§ 1709(20-a), 2554(2-a)). It may also delegate the power to perform ministerial acts to other district officers or employees, such as authorizing the business manager to make purchases with appropriated funds of certain items that do not require competitive bidding (8 NYCRR § 170.2(b)).

2:16. What happens if a school board fails to take official action?

A transaction has no legal effect and is not considered an official action unless made at a properly constituted meeting of the board (Gen. Constr. Law § 41). For example, a state appellate court ruled that litigation commenced on a district's behalf by the school attorney with the knowledge and tacit approval of the board was invalid and without effect because the board failed to formally vote in a public meeting to authorize such litigation. As a result, the district lost its victory before the lower court (*Gersen v. Mills,* 290 A.D.2d 839 (3d Dep't 2002)).

2:17. Do individual school board members have the right to visit schools?

Yes. Every board member has the same right as parents or school district residents to visit the schools in accordance with whatever district procedures apply to the public in general. However, individual board members may visit schools for official purposes, such as for building inspection, interviewing staff, or inspection of personnel records, only with the authorization of the board (*Appeal of Silano*, 33 Educ. Dep't Rep. 20 (1993); *Matter of Bruno*, 4 Educ. Dep't Rep. 14 (1964)).

2:18. May a school board hire a superintendent of schools?

Yes. A school board has the authority to hire a superintendent of schools and enter into employment contracts of varying duration with its superintendent as permitted by law (§§ 1604(8), 1711, 2503(5), 2554(2); see **7:23–27**). A board may also agree to extend the superintendent's contract, so long as the entire term of the contract plus any extensions does not exceed the maximum term authorized by statute (*Appeal of Boyle*, 35 Educ. Dep't Rep. 162 (1995); see also **7:25**).

2:19. May a school board remove its superintendent?

Generally, yes. The board, however, must comply with any applicable provisions set forth in law or in the superintendent's contract (see also **7:33–34**).

2:20. May a school board evaluate staff?

Yes. Although school superintendents may perform this function, neither the Education Law nor commissioner's regulations reserve this authority exclusively to the school superintendent. However, a board may not unilaterally reprimand tenured employees (*Appeal of Fusco*, 39 Educ. Dep't Rep. 836 (2000)). For more information on reprimands and other forms of disciplinary action, see **7:16, 8:125–128, 178–180, 191, 198–200; 9:31–43**.

2:21. May an outgoing school board extend a superintendent's contract and thus bind successor boards?

Yes. The commissioner of education has ruled that even last-minute extensions of a superintendent's contract by an outgoing board, while not democratic, are legal and bind a successor board, because there is specific statutory authority permitting multi-year contracts with a superintendent (*Appeal of Dillon*, 33 Educ. Dep't Rep. 544 (1994); *Appeal of Knapp*, 34 Educ. Dep't Rep. 207 (1994); see **7:25–26**). However, an outgoing board may not extend an already existing agreement that is scheduled to expire during the successor's board term. Such an action would constitute impermissible "tacking" by creating two simultaneous contracts that circumvent the statutory time limits on superintendent's contracts (*Appeal of Boyle*, 35 Educ. Dep't Rep. 162 (1995); see **7:24–26**).

2:22. May an outgoing school board bind a successor board to a contract with a school attorney?

No. It is improper for an outgoing board of education to bind its successor to a contract with a school district attorney (*Harrison CSD v. Nyquist*, 59 A.D.2d 434 (3d Dep't 1977). Outgoing boards may not enter into employment contracts for professional services that bind a successor board absent express statutory authority to do so (see *Karedes v. Colella,* 292 A.D.2d 138 (2002); as in the case of a superintendent's contract, see **2:21**).

2:23. May a school board enter into a "pouring rights" contract?

Yes, a school may enter into a contract that grants a vendor the exclusive right to supply beverages such as soft drinks and fruit juices in school buildings, vending areas, concessions, or other school property, subject to nutrition laws and regulations applicable to schools. In exchange, the vendor pays commissions or fees to the district. However, districts may not permit the use of school premises or staff to facilitate the sale of a vendor's products to fund-raising groups. Nor may a board allow a member to distribute beverages to students free of charge (*Appeal of American Quality Beverages LLC,* 42 Educ. Dep't Rep. 153 (2002); *Appeal of American Quality Beverages LLC,* 42 Educ. Dep't Rep. 144 (2002); *Appeal of Citizens for Responsible Fiscal and Educational Policy,* 40 Educ. Dep't Rep. 315 (2000)).

Such contracts are not subject to competitive bidding unless the products purchased under the contract value at least $10,000. Neither are they contracts for services by private food service companies otherwise subject to prior approval by the commissioner (*Appeal of American Quality Beverages LLC*). However, districts should not accept any advance payment that they are required to pay back in the event of early termination, so as not to bind successor boards (*Id.*).

In addition, the sale of presweetened beverages does not violate a district's obligation to provide physical and health education in an environment conducive to healthful living. Nonetheless, districts should consider whether the installation of vending machines in school is in the best interest of students' health, particularly at the elementary level. Although lighted vending machine panels do not violate state constitutional or regulatory provisions, districts should further consider whether promotional statements on such panels are appropriate for school environments (*Id.*).

2:24. May a school board authorize credit unions to open and maintain student branches within elementary and secondary schools?

Yes. However, use of such branches is restricted to students and excludes faculty, staff, or students' families. Approval from the board of education is a prerequisite to a branch opening, and student membership expires 30 days after secondary school graduation or immediately upon transfer to another school or termination of enrollment (Banking Law § 450-b). This authority facilitates and fosters the skills necessary to fulfill learning standards requirements for mathematics and career development outlined in commissioner's regulations at 8 NYCRR § 100.1(t). According to the law's sponsor's memo, it helps students "obtain the skills, knowledge and experience necessary to manage their personal finances and obtain general financial literacy," which helps prepare them for the workforce and financial independence.

2:25. May a school board establish a school camp?

Yes. An individual school district, or two or more school districts jointly, may establish and operate a school camp on school land or land acquired for that purpose. A city school district also may establish and operate a school camp on land provided for that purpose in state parks adjacent to the district. The camp may be used to furnish education in subjects deemed proper by the board, as well as to provide physical training, recreation, and maintenance for all children of school age whether they attend public or private school. Districts may charge a reasonable fee to cover costs of food and instructional materials, although the law requires that provision be made for children who cannot afford these fees (§§ 4501–4502).

2:26. What are the school board's responsibilities with respect to a school census?

In the cities of New York, Buffalo, and Rochester, the board of education must take a school census for the purpose of enforcing the provisions of the compulsory education law (§ 3240). In small city school districts, each board of education also serves as a permanent census board that has a duty to maintain a continuous census of all children residing in the district from birth to 18 years of age, and of children with disabilities to the age of 21. The census board is required to provide information to the commissioner of education (§ 3241(1)).

All other school districts are simply authorized, rather than required, to take a census of all children residing in the district from birth to 18 years of age (§ 3242).

However, all school districts have an obligation to locate and identify students with disabilities residing in their district and establish a register of such students entitled to attend school or receive preschool services (§ 4402(1)(a); 8 NYCRR § 200.2(a); see also **13:12**).

Membership

2:27. What are the qualifications for membership on a school board?

To qualify for membership on a school board in a common, union free, central, central high school, or small city school district, an individual:

- Must be able to read and write (§ 2102).
- Must be a qualified voter of the district; that is, a citizen of the United States, at least 18 years of age or older, and not adjudged to be an incompetent (§§ 2102, 2012, 2502(7); Elec. Law § 5-106(6)).

  (Note: a convicted felon is barred from running for a seat on a board of education if his or her maximum prison sentence has not expired or if he or she has not been pardoned or discharged from parole (Elec. Law § 5-106(2)).

- Must be and have been a resident (but need not be a taxpayer) of the district for a continuous and uninterrupted period of at least one year (30 days in the city of Rensselaer (§ 2502(9-a)(d)) immediately before the election (§§ 2102, 2502(7), (9)(d); see also *Appeal of Baleno*, 30 Educ. Dep't Rep. 358 (1991)).
- May not have been removed from any school district office within the preceding year (§ 2103(2)).
- May not reside with another member of the same school board as a member of the same family (§ 2103(3); *Rosenstock v. Scaringe*, 40 N.Y.2d 563 (1976)).
- May not be a current employee of the school board (§§ 2103(4); see **2:29, 2:59**).
- May not simultaneously hold another incompatible public office (*Matter of Schoch and Betheil*, 21 Educ. Dep't Rep. 300 (1981); see also **2:54–58**).

In large city school districts, different rules of law and/or exceptions to the above rules may govern membership on the school board (see §§ 2553(1), 2590-b(1)(a), (4)(e), 2590-c(1), (5)). For example, in New York City, community district education council members may not serve on more than one such council or on both a community council and the citywide Panel for Educational Policy or the citywide council on special education (§§ 2590-b(4)(e); 2590-c(4)).

2:28. May a school district impose additional requirements for school board membership?

No. A school district may not require candidates for a school board position to meet eligibility requirements in addition to those imposed by statute (*Matter of Guilderland CSD*, 23 Educ. Dep't Rep. 262 (1984)).

In one case, the commissioner of education invalidated a "gentlemen's agreement" observed by a school district for more than 60 years, under which seats of elected school board members were allocated among the communities comprising the district (*Appeal of Gravink*, 37 Educ. Dep't Rep. 393 (1998)).

2:29. May a former employee of the school district serve on the school board?

Yes. Even where the school board could address a matter directly pertaining to the former employee's personal interests, such as continuing retiree health insurance benefits because contracts with a teachers' union, which is a "voluntary nonprofit association," are exempt from the provisions of the conflict of interest law (*Application of Casazza*, 32 Educ. Dep't Rep. 462 (1993); Gen. Mun. Law § 802(1)(f); see **2:47–53**, for more information on conflicts of interest).

2:30. May an individual be a school board member if that person's spouse is employed by the district?

Yes. There is no prohibition against the employment of spouses, children, or other relatives of board members to positions in the district.

Furthermore, due to a specific statutory exception, a "contract of employment" between the district and a relative does not create a prohibited conflicting interest for the board member (Gen. Mun. Law § 800(3)(a); *Appeal of Behuniak and Lattimore*, 30 Educ. Dep't Rep. 236 (1991); see **2:47, 2:52**).

The Education Law, however, requires a two-thirds vote by the board to employ a teacher who is related to a board member by blood or by marriage (§ 3016). The two-thirds vote requirement does not apply and has no effect on the continued employment of a tenured teacher who is initially hired before his or her relative is elected or appointed to the school board (*Appeal of Heizman*, 31 Educ. Dep't Rep. 387 (1992)).

In one decision, the commissioner ruled that a person who sought employment as a social worker in the district where her spouse was a member of the board of education, was a teacher for the purposes of this section of law and therefore needed approval from two-thirds of the board in order to be appointed (*Appeal of McNamara*, 30 Educ. Dep't Rep. 272 (1991)).

2:31. May a member of the clergy seek office as a member of a school board?

Yes. The United States Supreme Court declared unconstitutional any ban on the eligibility of members of the clergy to run for public office, provided they meet all the statutory qualifications (*McDaniel v. Paty*, 435 U.S. 618 (1978)).

2:32. May a school board member resign from office?

Yes. Under the Education Law, a board member or other school district officer who wishes to resign may do so at a district meeting (i.e., annual meeting, special meeting) or by filing a written resignation with the district (BOCES) superintendent of his or her district, which becomes effective only upon the approval of the district superintendent and filing with the school district clerk (§ 2111; see also Opn. Att'y Gen. 97-1).

Alternatively, a board member may resign under the Public Officers Law by delivering to or filing a written resignation with the district clerk (Pub. Off. Law § 31(1)(h), (3); *Matter of Verity*, 28 Educ. Dep't Rep. 171 (1988); see also Opn. Att'y Gen. 97-1). The clerk must then notify the school board and the state board of elections (Pub. Off. Law § 31(5)).

A resignation becomes effective on the date specified in the resignation or if no effective date is specified, then immediately upon delivery to or filing with the district clerk. In no event shall the effective date be more than 30 days after its proper filing (Pub. Off. Law § 31(2)).

A successor may not be appointed or elected until after the resignation becomes effective (*Roberts v. Allen*, 54 Misc.2d 746 (1962)).

2:33. Once a school board member has submitted his or her resignation, may it be withdrawn?

Yes, but only with the consent of the person to whom the resignation was delivered, such as the district clerk if the resignation was submitted under the Public Officers Law or the district (BOCES) superintendent if submitted under the Education Law (see **2:30**). The school board has no authority to consent to a request to withdraw a resignation (Pub. Off. Law § 31(4); *Matter of Verity*, 28 Educ. Dep't Rep. 171 (1988)).

2:34. May a school board member be removed from office?

Yes. A board member may be removed by the commissioner of education for the willful violation or neglect of duty or the willful disobedience of a law or a decision, order, or regulation of the commissioner of education or Board of Regents (§§ 306, 1706, 2559; see also 8 NYCRR Part 277). New York City community district education council members are subject to removal by the city schools chancellor (§ 2590-l). To be considered willful, a school board member's actions must have been "intentional and with a wrongful purpose" to disregard a lawful duty or violate a legal requirement (*Application of Student with a Disability*, 43 Educ. Dep't Rep. __ dec. no. 14,979 (2003); *Application of Santicola*, 42 Educ. Dep't Rep. 356 (2003);

Application of Lilker, 40 Educ. Dep't Rep. 704 (2001); *Appeal of Gaul*, 40 Educ. Dep't Rep. 105 (2000)).

Generally, a board member who acts in good faith on the advice of counsel will not be found to have acted with the requisite willfulness to warrant removal from office (*Application of Fix*, 39 Educ. Dep't Rep. 728 (2000); *Appeal of McCall*, 34 Educ. Dep't Rep. 29 (1994); see also *Application of Goldin*, 36 Educ. Dep't Rep. 319 (1997)). However, if the advice of counsel directly contradicts established law, reliance on such advice will "not necessarily shield a board member from removal under section 306" (*Appeal of Scarrone*, 35 Educ. Dep't Rep. 443 (1996); see also *Matter of BOCES*, 32 Educ. Dep't Rep. 519 (1993)).

The commissioner has removed a board member, for instance, for behavior that interfered with the board's ability to function in a case where that board member threatened and initiated a physical altercation with another board member during a board meeting. Such conduct breached the board member's "duty to engage in constructive discussion" on matters affecting the governance of the district (*Appeal of Kozak*, 34 Educ. Dep't Rep. 501 (1995)).

2:35. May a school board remove one of its members from office?

Yes. A school board may remove any of its members for "official misconduct"; that is, misconduct clearly relating to a board member's official duties. This is so when a board member engages in an unauthorized exercise of power or intentionally fails to exercise power to the detriment of the district (§ 1709(18); *Appeal of Taber*, 42 Educ. Dep't Rep 251 (2003); *Appeals of Gill and Burnett*, 42 Educ. Dep't Rep. 89 (2002); *Application of Balen*, 40 Educ. Dep't Rep. 479 (2001); *Matter of Cox*, 27 Educ. Dep't Rep. 353 (1988)).

In one case, the commissioner upheld a board's removal of a fellow board member after a hearing before the board. The board member was charged and found guilty of settling employee grievance and contacting staff without board authorization, using threatening and profane language, and demanding that an acting supervisor not schedule a particular maintenance employee for overtime work. He also sent unauthorized written directives to an acting supervisor, supposedly on behalf of the board's plant committee. The board appointed special counsel who investigated and then presented the charges of official misconduct to the board at the hearing (*Application of Balen*).

A school board's authority to remove one of its members from office is separate and distinct from the commissioner of education's authority to remove a board member. However, a board's decision to remove a school board member from office may be reviewed by the commissioner on appeal (*Appeal of Taber*; see **2:34**).

2:36. What is the process for removing a school board member?

The removal may take place only after a hearing on the charges either before the commissioner, at which the board member has a right to be represented by counsel (§ 306(1)), or before the board itself (§§ 1709(18), 2559; see **2:46, 2:53**). A written copy of the charges must be served at least 10 days before the hearing. The board member must be afforded a "full and fair opportunity to refute the charges before the removal" (*Appeal of Taber*, 42 Educ. Dep't Rep. 251 (2002)).

2:37. May a school board member be removed as president of the board without being removed as a school board member?

Yes. Although it is unlikely that the same circumstances that would support the removal of a school board president would not also give cause for the removal of that individual from the board, both offices are separate and distinct from one another (*Matter of Motoyama*, 12 Educ. Dep't Rep. 244 (1973)). Therefore, it is possible to remove someone as president of the school board without removing that person from the board.

However, because under section 2105(6) the board president serves in that capacity for a statutory period of one year, he or she does not serve at the pleasure of the board. As such, a board member may be removed from the office of board president only for cause. In addition, the sole decision on this matter indicates that only the commissioner may remove an individual from office as president when that individual is not being removed from the board as well (*Matter of Motoyama*).

2:38. May a school board member be censured or reprimanded?

No. Nothing in the Education Law authorizes either a board of education or the commissioner of education to censure or reprimand a school board member (*Appeal of Philips*, 41 Educ. Dep't Rep. 10 (2001); *Appeal of Kozak*, 39 Educ. Dep't Rep. 278 (1999); *Appeal of Silano*, 33 Educ. Dep't Rep. 20 (1993)). However, a school board may criticize the actions of a board member for exhibiting poor judgment (*Appeal of Silano*).

There is no legal basis either for ordering a school board member to apologize (*Appeal of Lloyd*, 39 Educ. Dep't Rep. 537 (2000)).

2:39. Can school board members be paid for their service as board members?

Generally, no. Opinions of the state comptroller have consistently held that school board members may not receive compensation for their services unless expressly authorized by an act of the state Legislature (Opn. St. Comp. 72-342, 71-985; see also §§ 2590-(b)(1), 2590-c(1)).

However, school board members may be reimbursed for expenses actually and necessarily incurred in the performance of their official duties (§§ 2118; 2590-b(1)(a)). Board members also may receive reimbursement to cover the costs of conferences, such as those sponsored by the New York State School Boards Association, if they are believed to be of benefit to the district and if they are authorized by a resolution approved by a majority of the board, or approved by a duly authorized designee of the board, prior to attendance at such a conference (Gen. Mun. Law § 77-b; see **19:16–17**).

Board Vacancies

2:40. How do vacancies occur on a school board?

In addition to the timely expiration of a board member's term of office, vacancies on a school board may occur due to death, incapacity, resignation, removal from office, or refusal to serve (§ 2112; *Matter of Turchiarelli*, 31 Educ. Dep't Rep. 402 (1992); see also **2:41**).

A position also may become vacant if an incumbent board member moves to a residence outside the district (Pub. Off. Law § 30(1)(d); see also *Matter of Willard*, 23 Educ. Dep't Rep. 448 (1984)). However, "an individual's residence is not lost until a new residence is established through both intent and action" (*Appeal of Lavelle*, 28 Educ. Dep't Rep 189 (1988)).

A vacancy also will occur if a board member is convicted of a felony or crime involving his or her oath of office, is declared incompetent, or refuses or fails to file an oath of office (see Pub. Off. Law § 30(1); *Appeal of Rausch*, 41 Educ. Dep't Rep. 351 (2002); Opn. Att'y Gen. F 97-7, I 99-3; see also **2:11**). In an informal opinion, the New York State Attorney General indicated that a school board member who pled guilty to a misdemeanor petit larceny charge after being charged with a felony for illegally collecting unemployment insurance violated her oath of office and vacated her position as a school board member by operation of law. The crime involved "willful deceit" and a "calculated disregard for honesty" (Opn. Att'y Gen. I 99-3, see also F 97-7).

2:41. May a vacancy on a school board be declared if a member is absent from three successive meetings?

Yes. A vacancy may be declared if the record clearly shows that a board member has failed to attend three successive meetings and has no sufficient excuse for the absence (§§ 2109, 2502(8), 2553(8), 2590-b (4)(f), 2590-c(6)(a); see *Matter of Cox*, 28 Educ. Dep't Rep. 156 (1988)). If the board member has sufficient excuse to warrant absence from the meetings, a vacancy cannot be declared (*Appeal of Rowe*, 31 Educ. Dep't Rep. 280 (1992); *Application of Shader*, 31 Educ. Dep't Rep. 252 (1992)).

2:42. Are school districts obligated to fill a vacancy when one arises?

The applicable laws impose upon union free and central school districts the power and duty to fill a vacancy (§§ 1709(17), 1804(1)) and require common school districts to immediately call a special meeting to fill the vacancy when it occurs (§ 1607(2)).

According to the commissioner of education, small city school boards are not obligated to fill a vacancy because the statutory language governing vacancies in small city schools makes filling a vacancy optional (§ 2502(6); *Appeal of Keyrouze*, 34 Educ. Dep't Rep. 468 (1995)). However, the Albany and Rensselaer city school districts are governed by special provisions of law not examined in the commissioner's decision above. The law applicable to those districts provides that whenever a vacancy occurs other than because of the expiration of a board member's term of office or because of an increase in the size of the board, the board "shall" appoint a qualified person to fill the vacancy (§§ 2502(9)(n), 2502(9-a)(n)). In large city school districts, different rules of law and/or exceptions apply (see §§ 2553(6), (7), (9)(e), (10)(n), 2590-b(1)(a); 2590-c(6)(b), (c)).

2:43. What is the procedure to fill a vacancy on a school board?

Any school board may call a special election to fill such a vacancy within 90 days after it occurs. If that does not happen, the district (BOCES) superintendent may fill it by appointment in school districts under his or her jurisdiction (§ 2113(1)). Common school districts must call a special district meeting immediately to fill a vacancy (§ 1607(2)). Alternatively, the commissioner of education may order a special election to fill a vacancy in a union free school district (§ 2113(2)). If a vacancy is filled by a special district election, the elected board member serves for the remainder of the unexpired term (§ 2113(3)).

In union free, central, and small city school districts, the school board may choose instead to appoint a qualified person to fill a vacancy (§§ 1709(17), 1804(1), 2502(6)). Consistent with the limitation on the board's authority to act as a corporate body, a vote of the majority of the whole board ordinarily is required to fill a vacancy by appointment (see 2:14). But in small city school districts, due to a unique provision of law, only a "majority of the remaining members of the board" is needed to appoint a qualified person to fill a board vacancy (§§ 2502(6), (9)(n), (9-a)(n)). If the vacancy is filled by appointment, the new board member serves only until the next regular school district election (NYS Const. Art. XIII, § 3; §§ 1709(17), 2113(3), 2502(6)).

Special rules of law govern the appointment of board members in the Albany and Rensselaer city school districts (§§ 2502(9)(n), 2502(9-a)(n)), and in large city school districts (§§ 2553(6),(7), (9)(e), (10)(n), 2590-b(1)(a), 2590-c(6)(b), (c)).

A person elected or appointed to fill a vacancy takes office immediately upon filing the oath of office (§§ 1709(17), 2502(6), see also NYS Const. Art. XIII, § 3; 2:11).

Ethics and Conflicts of Interest

2:44. Must a school board adopt a code of ethics and operate according to its tenets?

Yes. The General Municipal Law requires all school boards to adopt a code of ethics for the guidance of its officers and employees that sets forth the standards of conduct reasonably expected of them (Gen. Mun. Law § 806).

The law requires school district codes of ethics to "provide standards for officers and employees with respect to disclosure of interest in legislation before the local governing body, holding of investments in conflict with official duties, private employment in conflict with official duties, future employment and such other standards relating to the conduct of officers and employees as may be deemed advisable" (Gen. Mun. Law § 806(1)(a); see also Opn. St. Comp. 82-189).

However, the board's code may not violate state law (*Appeal of Grinnell*, 37 Educ. Dep't Rep. 504 (1998)). For example, the commissioner of education has held improper a board's attempt to apply a provision of its code of ethics as an additional qualification for membership on the board, eligibility for which is governed specifically by the Education Law (*Matter of Guilderland CSD*, 23 Educ. Dep't Rep. 262 (1984)). In another case, the commissioner declared null and void a portion of a board's code of ethics that prohibited board members from voting on the employment contracts of their relatives (*Appeal of Behuniak and Lattimore*, 30 Educ. Dep't Rep. 236 (1991)). Likewise, a board's code of ethics may not preclude a board member from voting on a contract involving a collective bargaining unit if the board member is or was a member of a similar bargaining unit while employed in another district, or regardless of current employment (*Appeal of Grinnell*).

For more information on codes of ethics, contact the New York State Department of State, Office of Counsel, 41 State Street, 8th Floor, Albany, N.Y. 12231; telephone: 518-474-6740.

2:45. Must the school district's code of ethics be distributed or filed?

Both. The superintendent of schools, as chief executive officer of the district, must distribute a copy of the code of ethics to every district officer and employee, who must enforce and comply with the code, even if they do not actually receive a copy (Gen. Mun. Law § 806(2)). The district clerk must file a copy of the code, and any amendments to it, with the office of the state comptroller (Gen. Mun. Law § 806(3)(a)).

In addition, the superintendent must ensure that the district posts a copy of the provisions of the General Municipal Law regarding conflicts of interest, in each public building in a place conspicuous to its officers and employees. However, failure to post the provisions will have no effect on the duty to comply with the law or with its enforcement (Gen. Mun. Law § 807).

2:46. Are there certain actions by school board members, district officers, and employees that are specifically prohibited by law?

Yes. Public officers and employees — including school board members, district officers and employees — are specifically prohibited from:

- Soliciting or accepting any gift worth more than $75 under circumstances where it reasonably could be inferred that the gift was intended to influence or reward official action. School districts, through their own codes of ethics, can set the figure lower than $75, though not higher (Gen. Mun. Law § 805-a(1)(a); Opn. Att'y Gen. I 99-16; see also Penal Law §§ 200.00, 200.10).
- Disclosing confidential information acquired during the course of their official duties or using such information to further their personal interests (Gen. Mun. Law § 805-a(1)(b)). Allegations that a board member has disclosed confidential information must be supported by competent evidence (see *Application of Balen*, 40 Educ. Dep't Rep. 250 (2000); *Application of Bd. of Educ. of Middle Country CSD*, 33 Educ. Dep't Rep. 511 (1994)).
- Representing clients for compensation before the board or district (Gen. Mun. Law § 805-a(1)(c)).

Entering into contingency arrangements with clients for compensation in any matter before the school board or district (Gen. Mun. Law § 805-a(1)(d)).

- With certain limited exceptions, having an interest in any contract, lease, purchase, or sale over which they have any responsibility to negotiate, prepare, authorize, approve, or audit (Gen. Mun. Law §§ 800-805).

In addition to any penalty contained in any other provision of law, any person who knowingly and intentionally violates these rules of law may be fined, suspended, or removed from office or employment (Gen. Mun. Law § 805-a(2)).

2:47. What is a conflict of interest?

The term *conflict of interest* describes a situation in which a school board member, district officer, or employee is in a position to benefit financially from a decision he or she may make on behalf of the district through the exercise of official authority or disposing of public funds. Financial interests that are prohibited by law include:

- Interest in a contract with the school district where a school board member, district officer, or employee has the power or may appoint someone who has the power to negotiate, authorize, approve, prepare, make payment, or audit bills or claims under the contract unless otherwise exempted under law (Gen. Mun. Law §§ 801(1), 802).
- Interest by a chief fiscal officer, treasurer, or his or her deputy or employee in a bank or other financial institution that is used by the school district he or she serves (Gen. Mun. Law § 801(2)).

Interest is defined as a direct or indirect pecuniary benefit that runs to the officer, or employee as a result of a contract with the school district (Gen. Mun. Law § 800(3)). The General Municipal Law expressly makes the provisions regarding conflicts of interest applicable to school districts (Gen. Mun. Law § 800).

Contract is defined to include any claim, account, or demand against, or agreement, express or implied, as well as the designation of a depository of public funds or a newspaper for use by the school district (Gen. Mun. Law § 800(2)).

2:48. In what instances would a board member, district officer, or employee have an interest that could result in a prohibited conflict of interest?

A school board member, district officer, or employee is deemed to have an interest in a firm, partnership, or association of which he or she is a member or employee; a corporation of which he or she is an officer, director, or employee; or a corporation in which he or she owns or directly or indirectly controls any stock.

A board member, district officer or employee also is deemed to have an interest in a contract between the district and his or her spouse, minor child, or dependents, except a contract of employment as the law specifically allows a school district officer's or employee's spouse, minor child, or dependent to enter into an employment contract with the district (Gen. Mun. Law § 800(3); see also *Application of Kravitsky*, 41 Educ. Dep't Rep. 231 (2001)). Board members are required to disclose any interest they may have or acquire in any actual or proposed contract involving the district, even though it is not a prohibited interest (Gen. Mun. Law § 803; *Matter of Ackerberg*, 25 Educ. Dep't Rep. 232 (1985)).

In addition, interests that are not prohibited but which nonetheless may create an appearance of impropriety may be properly restricted by the district's code of ethics, as long as the restriction is not inconsistent with other provisions of law (Opn. St. Comp. 88-77; *Appeal of Behuniak and Lattimore*, 30 Educ. Dep't Rep. 236 (1991)).

2:49. How can a school board determine whether one of its members has a prohibited conflict of interest?

To decide whether one of its members has a prohibited conflict of interest, a board must determine:

- Whether there is a contract with the school district.
- Whether the board member in question has an interest in that contract.
- Whether the board member is authorized to exercise any of his or her powers or duties with respect to the agreement (see Gen. Mun. Law § 801(1); see **2:47**).
- Whether any exception to the conflict of interest law is applicable (Gen. Mun. Law § 802; see also Opn. St. Comp. 89-39; see **2:51–52**).

2:50. What are some examples of conflicts of interest for school board members?

A school board member had a conflict of interest, for instance, when the district purchased heating oil from the company of which the board member was president and in which he owned more than 5 percent of the stock (*Appeal of Golden*, 32 Educ. Dep't Rep. 202 (1992)). By contrast, where a vice president of a corporation that both installed and continued to maintain a school telephone system was elected to a board of education, there was no prohibited conflict of interest in the contracts entered into with his corporation prior to his election. However, there was the potential for a conflict of interest after he became a board member, depending upon his responsibilities as an officer of the company (if any), in connection with the contracts at issue (Opn. St. Comp. 86-58).

2:51. What are some examples of situations which do not involve a conflict of interest?

Section 802 of the General Municipal Law lists several specific exceptions. For example:

- A contract entered into by the district with a person who later is elected or appointed to the school board remains valid, except that the contract may not be renewed (Gen. Mun. Law § 802(1)(h)).
- A board member may enter into a contract or multiple contracts with the school district if the total consideration paid under the contract is, or contracts are, less than $750 (Gen. Mun. Law § 802(2)(e)).
- A school board member who is a bank officer at the bank's main office has no conflict of interest, where the school district has designated a branch of that bank as a depository for district funds and the bank employee would never have occasion to become involved in any school district transactions occurring at that bank branch (Gen. Mun. Law § 802(1)(a); Opn. St. Comp. 77-504).
- The conflict of interest provisions do not apply to employment of a school board member as school physician upon authorization by a two-thirds vote of the board (Gen. Mun. Law § 802(1)(i)).

Additionally, there is no conflict of interest where a board member lives in the same house and splits expenses with a district employee (*Appeal of Santicola*, 42 Educ. Dep't Rep. 356 (2002)).

Board members voting on the collective bargaining agreements of their relatives do not have a prohibited conflict of interest (Gen. Mun. Law § 800(3), Educ. Law § 3016(2); *Appeal of Behuniak and Lattimore*, 30 Educ. Dep't Rep. 236 (1991); see also **2:30, 2:44, 2:47**).

2:52. Does an interest arising from a collective bargaining agreement constitute a prohibited conflict of interest?

No. Collective bargaining agreements fall within a statutory exception to the general rule regarding contracts with membership corporations or other voluntary, nonprofit corporations or associations. Therefore, a personal interest arising from such a contract is not a prohibited interest under the law (Gen. Mun. Law § 802(1)(f); *Stettine v. County of Suffolk*, 66 N.Y.2d 354 (1985); see also Opn. St. Comp. 89-24)).

The commissioner of education, citing the *Stettine* case, has rejected petitions attacking the election of board members who are retired district employees with continuing health insurance benefits under the district's collective bargaining agreement (see *Application of Casazza*, 32 Educ. Dep't Rep. 462 (1993); *Appeal of Samuels*, 25 Educ. Dep't Rep. 228 (1985); see **2:29**). This, of course, does not affect the prohibition against current employees serving as board members (see **2:27**).

2:53. What are the consequences of violating the conflict of interest law?

Any contract willfully entered into by or with a school district in which there is a prohibited interest is void and unenforceable (Gen. Mun. Law § 804). Furthermore, a school board member who knowingly and willfully violates the law in this regard or fails to disclose an interest in a contract may be guilty of a misdemeanor (Gen. Mun. Law § 805) and/or subject to removal from office by the commissioner of education (see *Appeal of Golden*, 32 Educ. Dep't Rep. 202 (1992); see also **2:34**).

Incompatibility of Office

2:54. May a school board member run for or hold an additional public office?

There is no general prohibition against holding two or more public offices at the same time (Opn. Att'y Gen. I 82-1 (1982)). However, two issues must be addressed: first, whether there is an express prohibition against the board member holding or running for the office in question; and second, whether the duties of the two offices may be legally incompatible (see **2:55–57**).

2:55. What makes two public offices or positions of employment incompatible with one another?

One person cannot simultaneously hold two public offices or positions of employment if one office is subordinate to the other, such that the person would essentially be his or her own boss, or if the functions of the two positions are inherently inconsistent with each other, such as serving simultaneously as the district's finance officer and as the auditor responsible for the integrity of the district's finances (see *O'Malley v. Macejka*, 44 N.Y.2d 530 (1978); Opn. Att'y Gen. I 92-13).

There must be a great likelihood of a division of loyalties or a conflict of duties between the offices, not merely a possibility that such complications may arise on occasion.

The doctrine of compatibility of office does not prohibit an individual from being a candidate for election to a second office where that office is incompatible with the first, if he or she intends to resign from the first office if elected to the second. However, if there is a specific provision of law that makes two offices or positions incompatible, such a provision of law may expressly disqualify a person from even being a candidate for a second incompatible office or position (Opn. Att'y Gen. I 89-62; see, for example, **2:56**). Once elected and upon accepting the second office, an individual vacates the first office automatically (Opn. Att'y Gen. I 89-62; *People ex rel. Ryan v. Green*, 58 N.Y. 295 (1874)).

Even where two public offices or positions of employment are compatible, a situation may arise in which holding both offices creates a conflict of interest. If this occurs, the conflict can be avoided by declining to participate in the conflicted matter (Opn. Att'y Gen. I 92-13).

2:56. Are there any positions a school board member is specifically prohibited by statute from holding?

Yes. The Education Law specifically prohibits a board member from also holding the positions of district superintendent, supervisor, clerk, tax collector, treasurer, or librarian simultaneously (§ 2103(1)), or from being an employee of his or her school board (§ 2103(4)). In union free and central school districts, however, a board member may be appointed clerk of the board and of the district (§§ 2130(1), 1804(1); *Matter of Hurtgam*, 22 Educ. Dep't Rep. 219 (1982)). A board member of a board of cooperative educational services (BOCES) may not be employed by any of that BOCES' component districts (§ 1950(9); *Appeal of Reynolds*, 42 Educ. Dep't Rep. 278 (2003)).

In small city school districts, the Education Law provides that school board members may not hold any city office other than that of police officer or firefighter (§ 2502(7); Opn. Att'y Gen. I 90-80, I 87-6). Decisions determining whether an employee holds an office within the meaning of this provision turn on the presence of traditional indicia of office, such as the taking of an oath of office, the filing of an undertaking or bond, designation as an office holder in a city charter, significant policy-making authority and other job characteristics including duties and supervisory relationships (*Application of Washock*, 41 Educ. Dep't Rep. 280 (2002); Opn. Att'y Gen. I 90-80, I 87-6). Thus, in a case where the titles of Water Department Director and Director of Parks and Recreation involved limited supervisory and administrative duties, were classified as civil service positions, and did not have a reporting relationship to the mayor or city council, the individuals holding these positions were not precluded from serving as school board members. Although both positions required the taking of an oath of office, all city employees were required to do so (*Application of Washock*).

In New York City no one individual may simultaneously serve on the citywide Panel on Educational Policy and the citywide council on special education or a community district education council (§§ 2590-b (4)(e); 2590-c(4)).

Additionally, a town supervisor may not be a trustee of a school district (Town Law § 23(1)). But there is no prohibition against a deputy town supervisor serving as a member of a board of education (see **2:57**).

2:57. Are there any offices that have been found to be incompatible with the office of school board member?

Yes. For example, counsel to the state attorney general has expressed the opinion that a public school board member may not serve simultaneously as a member of the board of education of a private school within the district (Opn. Att'y Gen. I 87-58), a director of weights and measures in small city school districts (Opn. Att'y Gen. I 90-80), a county elections commissioner in any city school district (Opn. Att'y Gen. I 87-50; see also Elec. Law § 3-200(4)), or as a district attorney with jurisdiction over the school district (Opn. Att'y Gen. I 2000-13), or on a city's common council in small city school districts (Opn. Att'y Gen. I 84-61).

The state Advisory Committee on Judicial Ethics has indicated that a part-time judge may not seek election to a local board of education because the Rules of the Chief Administrator of the Courts prohibit judges from campaigning for elective office (Joint Opn. of Advisory Committee on Judicial Ethics 89-157/90-7; 22 NYCRR § 100.7).

The Advisory Committee has also stated that a judge who already has been elected to a school board should resign because the "position on the school board [is] one that may involve dealing with quasi-political and highly controversial issues" that are incompatible with holding judicial office (*Id.*, see also 22 NYCRR § 100.5(h)). But a part-time justice may accept "appointment" to the board of trustees of a publicly-funded school district for children with disabilities, because by virtue of the "appointment," the justice would not be required to compete in a public, political election in order to obtain a seat on the school board, and because in that particular type of school district there is no public referendum on the school district's budget (Joint Opn. of Advisory Committee on Judicial Ethics 94-59; 22 NYCRR § 100.5(b) (h)).

2:58. Are there any offices that are compatible with the office of school board member?

Yes. A school board member may serve simultaneously in the following offices:

- trustee of a public library (*Matter of Schoch*, 21 Educ. Dep't Rep. 300 (1981); see also Opn. Att'y Gen. I 81-110);
- town assessor (Opn. St. Comp. 2000-14 and 73-1174);
- employee of a BOCES (*Appeal of Reynolds*, 42 Educ. Dep't Rep. 278 (2003); *Matter of Todd*, 19 Educ. Dep't Rep. 277 (1979);
- village mayor (Opn. Att'y Gen. I 91-59; see also Village Law § 3-300);
- member of a town zoning board of appeals (Opn. Att'y Gen. I 84-68);

- member of a city school board and county director of real property tax services (Opn. Att'y Gen. I 93-9);
- volunteer in an athletic department of the school, depending upon the significance of the volunteer's responsibilities (Opn. Att'y Gen. I 92-13); and
- deputy town supervisor (Opn. Att'y Gen. I 96-29).

This is only a partial list of opinions on compatibility of office. For more information, contact the state Attorney General's Office.

2:59. May a school board member apply for and be appointed to a position of employment with the district in which he or she serves as a school board member?

Only if expressly authorized by law, as in the case of district clerk (see **3:12**). Otherwise, a board may not appoint one of its members to a position of employment with the district (*Wood v. Whitehall*, 120 Misc. 124, *aff'd*, 206 A.D. 786 (3d Dep't 1923); Opn. Att'y Gen. I 87-4 (1987); *Appeal of Boeddener*, 28 Educ. Dep't Rep. 578 (1989)). Furthermore, an appointment following resignation from the board may or may not be proper depending upon the facts and circumstances. For example, it would not be proper for a board to decide to appoint one of its members to an employment position with the district at a future date, prior to the board member's resignation when the board member still sat on the board (Opn. Att'y Gen. I 87-4; *Appeal of Boeddener*).

Board Meetings

Editor's Note: For more information on the requirements of the Open Meetings Law, see The Sunshine Laws, 2nd Edition, *a handbook published by the New York State School Boards Association (2001). Additional information is also available from the Committee on Open Government at New York Department of State, Committee on Open Government, 41 State Street, Albany, N.Y. 12231; telephone: 518-474-2518; or Web site at http://www.dos.state.ny.us/coog/coogwww.html.*

2:60. What types of meetings are conducted by school boards?

School board meetings fall into the following categories:
- The annual *organizational* or *reorganizational* meeting is when the school board elects and appoints its officers and committees for the coming year, and board members take or renew their oaths of office. In most school districts, this meeting must be held each year in July. For specific dates and times (where applicable) that school districts must hold their annual organizational meeting, see **3:2**.

- *Regular* board meetings, which are the regularly scheduled business meetings held throughout the year (see **2:62**).
- *Special* board meetings, which are not regularly scheduled and may be called by any member of the board to address a particular item or items (see **2:63**).

"Board" meetings are distinct from school "district" meetings, such as the annual district meeting, at which a school board presents its annual budget to voters in the district and at which school board elections are held, or special district meetings, called for either by the voters or by the school board for district residents to vote on specific issues and propositions. See **chapter 4** for more information on school district meetings.

2:61. Must school board meetings be held within the school district limits?

No. However, meeting in a location intended to avoid the public and news media may be deemed a violation of the Open Meetings Law, which may result in the annulment of any action taken at the meeting (see Pub. Off. Law §§ 103, 107(1)).

2:62. Are school boards required to hold a certain number of regular meetings?

Yes. The Education Law requires school boards to meet at least once each quarter of the year (§ 1708(1)). Most boards, however, meet at least once a month. In city school districts, monthly meetings are required (§§ 2504(2), 2563(2), 2590-b(1)(b); 2590-e(14)), except that in New York City, community district educational councils also must meet at least quarterly with the community superintendent, each building principal and all parent and parent-teacher associations (§ 2590-d (2)(b)).

2:63. Who may call a special meeting of the school board?

Any school board member has the authority to call a special meeting of the board (see *Matter of Felicio*, 19 Educ. Dep't Rep. 414 (1980)), as long as notice of the meeting is given to the other board members at least 24 hours in advance (§ 1606(3); see also *Application of Bean*, 42 Educ. Dep't Rep. 171 (2002)). The notice provided normally states the purpose of the meeting, although there is no specific requirement that it do so.

A majority of the board cannot decide to hold a meeting and dispense with providing notice to the remaining members. The law requires good faith efforts to give actual notice of a special or emergency meeting to each board member. Failure to do so may invalidate any action taken at the meeting (see *Matter of Colasuonno*, 22 Educ. Dep't Rep. 215 (1982)).

However, if it is determined that one board member did not receive notice, the action taken may be sustained if the member signs an affidavit waiving notice (*Matter of Bd. of Educ. of UFSD No. 1 of the Town of Hume*, 29 St. Dep't Rep. 624 (1923)). It is advisable, therefore, in situations where notice cannot be given within 24 hours, that each board member sign a waiver of notice to be entered in the minutes.

Although special meetings are ordinarily held to consider a single item of business, other items of business may be included on the agenda for that meeting by consent of the board members present. There is no requirement that the notice of a special board meeting contain any notice of a proposed agenda (*Matter of Neversink*, 10 Educ. Dep't Rep. 203 (1971)).

Care should be taken, however, to see that the special board meeting does not usurp the place of regularly scheduled board meetings for the consideration of regular school district business.

2:64. What are the requirements for holding a school board meeting?

There must be a quorum of the board and public notice of the time and place of the meeting (see **2:65–68**).

2:65. What constitutes a quorum of a school board?

A *quorum* is a simple majority (more than half) of the total number of board members (Gen. Constr. Law § 41). A quorum is required for the board to conduct any business. A majority of the entire board, not simply of those present, is required for the board to take any official action (Opn. of Counsel #70, 1 Educ. Dep't Rep. 770 (1952); see also *Appeal of Greenwald*, 31 Educ. Dep't Rep. 12 (1991); Gen. Constr. Law § 41). For example, if a board has five members and three are present at a meeting, all three would have to vote in favor of a resolution for it to pass; a two-to-one vote would not be sufficient.

Generally, a school board may not adopt a policy requiring affirmative votes by more than a majority of the whole number of the board to take official action, because neither the Education Law nor the General Construction Law authorizes a board to adopt requirements in excess of those already provided by statute (*Matter of Miller*, 17 Educ. Dep't Rep. 275 (1978); but see *Appeal of Volpe*, 25 Educ. Dep't Rep. 398 (1986)).

2:66. Can school board members vote by telephone or videoconference?

According to the Director of the Committee on Open Government, a series of communications between individual members or telephone calls among members that result in a collective decision, a meeting held by means of a telephone conference, or a vote taken by phone or mail would be inconsistent with the Open Meetings Law. Under the law, a person's physical presence is required for a vote (NYS Department of State, Committee on Open Government, OML-AO-#3025, May 12, 1999; see also OML-AO-#2779, July 28, 1997; OML-AO-#2480, Mar. 27, 1995).

In an unreported opinion, the New York State Supreme Court, Broome County, reached a similar conclusion regarding telephone conference discussions of tax assessment reductions by members of a town board (*Cheevers v. Town of Union* (Sept. 3, 1998) cited in OML-AO-#3025, May 12, 1999).

In comparison, any public body, including a school board, may meet via videoconferencing. Thus, a school board may properly conduct a meeting and vote on public matters through the use of videoconferencing. In such an instance, the public notice of the meeting must indicate that videoconferencing will be used, specify the location(s) for the meeting, and state that the public may attend at any of the locations (see Chapter 289 of the Laws of 2000; Gen. Const. Law § 41; Pub. Off. Law §§ 102, 103, and 104).

2:67. What type of notice of meetings of the school board is required?

The Education Law does not require notice of board meetings to be published (*Matter of Thomas et al.*, 10 Educ. Dep't Rep. 108 (1971)). However, under the Open Meetings Law, with which school boards must comply, public notice stating the time and place of any board meeting must be given to the news media and conspicuously posted in one or more designated public locations at least 72 hours before the meeting, if it has been scheduled at least one week before it occurs (Pub. Off. Law § 104(1)). Although school boards are required to provide notice of when and where its meetings will take place, such notice does not have to include the matters to be discussed (*Appeal of Allen and Wong*, 40 Educ. Dep't Rep. 372 (2000); *Matter of the CSD No. 1 of the Towns of Neversink, Fallsburgh and Liberty et al.*, 10 Educ. Dep't Rep. 203 (1971)).

If the meeting is scheduled less than a week in advance, public notice of the time and place must be given to the news media "to the extent practicable" and posted conspicuously a reasonable time before the meeting (Pub. Off. Law § 104(2); *Previdi v. Hirsch*, 138 Misc.2d 436 (Sup. Ct. Westchester County 1988)).

In addition, school board members must receive at least 24 hours notice of any board meeting (Educ. Law § 1606(3); see also *Application of Bean*, 42 Educ. Dep't Rep. 171 (2000)). A board majority may not dispense with notice of a board meeting to other board members, but individual board members may waive this 24-hour notice requirement in case of an emergency (*Matter of Colasuonno*, 22 Educ. Dep't Rep. 215 (1982); *Matter of Carlson*, 11 Educ. Dep't Rep. 284 (1972)).

2:68. Is an agenda necessary for a board meeting?

Although good business practice may indicate that an agenda of the regular session is in order, an agenda is not specifically required for either regular meetings or executive sessions. Moreover, the procedure to be followed at school board meetings is left to the policies adopted by the board (*Matter of Kramer*, 72 St. Dep't Rep. 114 (1951); but see § 2590-c(4)).

2:69. Are school board meetings open to the public?

Yes. Because school boards are public bodies, the Open Meetings Law (Pub. Off. Law § 103) requires school board meetings that discuss school district business to be open to the public (see also Educ. Law § 1708(3)). The public may be excluded only from properly convened executive sessions of the board and other meetings exempted under the law (Pub. Off. Law §§ 105(2), 108; Educ. Law § 1708(3); see **2:70; 2:73-2:74**).

Public business includes not only binding votes of the board, but also any activity that is preliminary to such a vote or involves consideration of a matter that could be the subject of board action (Pub. Off. Law § 102; *Goodson Todman Enters., Ltd. v. Kingston Common Council*, 153 A.D.2d 103 (3d Dep't 1990); but see *Hill v. Planning Bd. of Amherst*, 140 A.D.2d 967 (4th Dep't 1988)).

A school board's authority to adopt rules and regulations for the maintenance of public order on school property does not give a board the right to automatically exclude members of the public from attending a board meeting (*Matter of John Goetschius et al. v. Board of Educ. of Greenburg 11 UFSD*, 244 A.D.2d 552 (2d Dep't 1997)). But a school board's use of a metal detector as a security measure at the entrance to public meetings does not necessarily constitute a violation of the Open Meetings Law (*Goetschius v. Board of Educ. of Greenburg 11 UFSD*, 281 A.D.2d 416 (2d Dep't 2001)).

2:70. Are there any types of meeting not covered by the Open Meeting Law?

Yes. The Open Meeting Law exempts the following types of meetings:
1. "judicial or quasi-judicial proceeding" and
2. "any matter made confidential by federal or state law" (Pub. Off. Law § 108(3)).

An example of an exempt meeting regarding a matter made confidential by a federal law is a meeting to discuss student records. A federal law known as the Family Educational Rights and Privacy Act (FERPA) prohibits school officials from divulging, without parental consent, education records that are specifically identifiable to a particular student or students (20 USC § 1232(g); see **2:88**). A meeting where a school board reviews the transcript and evidence presented at a student disciplinary meeting when parents appeal their child's suspension would be considered a quasi-judicial proceeding. However, a school board vote to uphold or modify the suspension must take place in open session at a meeting conducted under the Open Meeting Law (see *Cheevers v. Town of Union, unreported, Broome Co.* (Sup. Ct. Sept. 3, 1998)).

An example of an exempt meeting regarding a matter made confidential by state law is a meeting between a board of education and the board's attorney that is protected by attorney-client privilege pursuant to the New York's Civil Practice Law and Rules (CPLR § 4503; for a review of the nature and scope of the privilege itself, see *Appeal of Goldin*, 40 Educ. Dep't Rep. 628 (2001)).

2:71. Are work sessions and planning meetings of the school board open to the public?

Yes. Any meeting of at least a quorum of a public body in which public business is to be conducted, even if only for the purpose of informal discussions, must be open to the public unless it is a properly convened executive session or otherwise exempted under the law (Pub. Off. Law §§ 102(1), 103(1)108; *Goodson Todman Enters., Ltd., v. Kingston Common Council*, 153 A.D.2d 103 (3d Dep't 1990); see also **2:72**).

2:72. Are board committee meetings open to the public?

Meetings of a committee or subcommittee consisting solely of board members that discusses or conducts public business are subject to the Open Meetings Law (Pub. Off. Law § 102; OML-AO-2588 (Mar. 28, 1996); OML-AO-2472 (Feb. 23, 1995); see *Syracuse United Neighbors v. City of Syracuse*, 80 A.D.2d 984 (1981); compare OML-AO-2481 (Dec. 12, 1994)).

However, meetings of board advisory committees, which do not consist exclusively of board members, are created solely to advise and make recommendations to the board. They have no power to take final action and are not subject to the requirements of the Open Meetings Laws (see *Goodson-Todman Enters., Ltd v. Town Board of Milan*, 151 A.D.2d 642 (2d Dep't 1989); *Poughkeepsie Newspapers v. Mayor's Intergovernmental Task Force*, 145 A.D.2d 65 (2d Dep't 1989)).

According to the Committee on Open Government, districtwide shared-decision-making committees are subject to the Open Meetings Law because they perform a governmental function to the extent that school boards may not adopt a shared-decision-making plan without their collaboration and participation (NYS Department of State, Committee on Open Government,

OML-AO-2456, Jan. 31, 1995). School-based shared-decision-making committees are subject to the Open Meetings Law if a district's shared-decision-making plan provides them with decision-making authority (NYS Department of State, Committee on Open Government, OML-AO-3265, Jan. 17, 2001).

2:73. What is an executive session?

An executive session is a portion of the school board meeting that is not open to the public. It can take place only upon a majority vote of the total membership of the board taken at an open meeting (Pub. Off. Law. § 105(1)). The motion should specify the subject or subjects to be discussed (*Gordon v. Village of Monticello*, 207 A.D.2d 55 (3d Dep't 1994)), *rev'd on other grounds*, 87 N.Y.2d 124 (1995)).

Executive sessions are permitted only for a limited number of specific purposes. A board may call an executive session only on the following subjects:

- Matters that will imperil the public safety if disclosed.
- Any matter that may disclose the identity of a law enforcement agent or informer.
- Information relating to current or future investigation or prosecution of a criminal offense that would imperil effective law enforcement if disclosed.
- Discussions involving proposed, pending, or current litigation.
- Collective negotiations pursuant to article 14 of the Civil Service Law.
- The medical, financial, credit, or employment history of a particular person or corporation, or matters leading to the appointment, employment, promotion, demotion, discipline, suspension, dismissal, or removal of a particular person or corporation.
- The preparation, grading, or administration of exams.
- The proposed acquisition, sale, or lease of real property or the proposed acquisition, sale, or exchange of securities, but only when publicity would substantially affect the value of these things (Pub. Off. Law § 105(a-h)).

With certain limited exceptions, no official action can be taken on issues discussed in executive session without first returning to open session (see § 1708; *Matter of Crapster*, 22 Educ. Dep't Rep. 29 (1982)). An exception includes voting on charges against a tenured teacher (Educ. Law §§ 1708(3), 3020-a(2); *Sanna v. Lindenhurst Bd. of Educ.*, 85 A.D.2d 157 (2d Dep't 1987), *aff'd*, 58 N.Y.2d 626 (1987); *United Teachers of Northport v. Northport UFSD*, 50 A.D.2d 897 (2d Dep't 1975); *Matter of Cappa*, 14 Educ. Dep't Rep 80 (1974); Formal Opn. of Counsel No. 239, 16 Educ. Dep't Rep.

457 (1976)). No public body, including a school board, may vote to appropriate money during an executive session (Pub. Off. Law § 105(1)).

2:74. Who is entitled to attend executive sessions?

All members of the board of education (other than a student board member) and "any other persons authorized by" the board may attend executive sessions (Pub. Off. Law § 105(2); see also Educ. Law § 1708(3); see **2:4**). Thus, only those people who are invited by the board may attend. It should be noted in this context, however, that in both large and small city school districts, the superintendent possesses the power "to have a seat on the board of education and the right to speak on all matters before the board, but not to vote" (§§ 2508(1); 2566(1)).

It is important that a school board exercise discretion in deciding whom to invite into executive session because of important confidentiality issues. In one case, the commissioner of education ruled that the attendance at an executive session of a former school board member, who was awaiting the results of an appeal of the election he lost, was in conflict with statutory and regulatory provisions providing for the confidentiality of personnel and student records (*Appeal of Whalen*, 34 Educ. Dep't Rep. 282 (1994)). Moreover, board members themselves also must be careful to maintain confidential information acquired in executive session (see Gen. Mun. Law § 805-a(1)(b); see also Opn. Att'y Gen. I 2000-2; Family Educational Rights and Privacy Act (20 USC § 1232g)).

2:75. Does the public have a right to speak at school board meetings?

Although school board meetings must be open to the public (Educ. Law § 1708(3); Pub. Off. Law § 103; see also **2:69**), there is no requirement that school boards allow members of the public to speak at school board meetings except in New York City, where community district educational councils must hold monthly meetings at which the public must be allowed to speak (§ 2590-e(14)). Elsewhere, the commissioner of education encourages school boards, whenever possible, to allow citizens to speak on matters under consideration (*Appeal of Wittneben*, 31 Educ. Dep't Rep. 375 (1992)). Boards can limit the time for a person to speak (see *Matter of Kramer*, 72 St. Dep't Rep. 114 (1951)).

The commissioner has ruled that a school board need not permit nonresidents to speak at public board meetings, even where the board has a policy of permitting residents to speak (*Matter of Martin*, 32 Educ. Dep't Rep. 381 (1992)). However, the state Committee on Open Government has indicated that such a practice would violate the Open Meetings Law. The committee concurs with the commissioner that school boards are not required to allow members of the public to speak at board meetings in the first place, but cautions that if a school board permits public participation, it may not discriminate between residents and nonresidents (NYS Department of State, Committee on Open Government, OML-AO-#2696, Jan. 8, 1997 and OML-AO-#2717, Feb. 27, 1997).

2:76. Do people attending a public school board meeting have the right to audiotape the meeting?

As a general rule, yes. There is no justifiable basis for prohibiting the use of unobtrusive, hand-held tape-recording devices at public board meetings (*Mitchell v. Board of Educ. of Garden City UFSD*, 113 A.D.2d 924 (2d Dep't 1985)). In one case, a judge found that a school board's bylaw prohibiting the use of recording devices at board meetings violated public policy (*People v. Ystueta*, 99 Misc.2d 1105 (District Court Suffolk Co. 1979); see also NYS Department of State Committee on Open Government OML-AO-3037, June 18, 1999). However, the use of a tape recorder by members of the public attending a board meeting may not cause public inconvenience, annoyance or alarm, or disturb the meeting (see *Feldman v. Town of Bethel*, 106 A.D.2d 695 (3d Dep't 1984)).

2:77. Do people attending a public school board meeting have the right to videotape a meeting?

Yes. According to one state appellate court, a school board cannot outright prohibit videotaping of its meetings. However, a board may regulate the use of cameras to ensure it does not interfere with the meeting. (*Csorny v. Shoreham Wading River CSD*, 305 A.D.2d 83 (2d Dep't 2003); see also *Matter of Peloquin v. Arsenault*, 162 Misc. 2d 306 (Sup. Ct. Franklin Co. 1994); NYS Department of State Committee on Open Government OML-AO-1317). The interference must be genuine. Board member objections to appearing on television or fears of publicly airing comments at a public meeting are not sufficient to prohibit the use of a videotape camera (*Csorny; Matter of Peloquin*).

2:78. What penalties may be assessed against a school board that violates the Open Meeting Law?

Courts have the power to declare void any action taken in violation of the Open Meetings Law (Pub. Off. Law § 107(1); *Gernatt Asphalt Prods. v. Town of Sardinia*, 87 N.Y.2d 668 (1996); *Matter of MCI Telecomm. Corp. v. Public Serv. Comm'n of the State of New York*, 231 A.D.2d 284 (3d Dep't 1997)). However, in order to invalidate action that already has been taken by a school board, the courts have held that a complaint alleging a violation of the Open Meeting Law must demonstrate the complainant was prejudiced by the board's failure to comply with the law (*Smithtown v.*

Illion Housing Auth., 130 A.D.2d 965 (4th Dep't 1988), *aff'd,* 72 N.Y.2d 1034 (1988); *Matter of Inner-City Press/Community on the Move v. New York State Banking Bd.*, 170 Misc. 2d 684 (1996)). In one case, a court invalidated a school board's appeal from an adverse decision by the commissioner of education, because the board failed to take a formal vote at a public meeting to approve the litigation (*Gersen v. Mills*, 290 A.D.2d 839 (3d Dep't 2002)).

Moreover, courts may award reasonable attorneys' fees to a party who sues a school district for a violation of the Open Meetings Law and prevails (Pub. Off. Law § 107(2); see also *Matter of Gordon v. Village of Monticello*, 87 N.Y.2d 124 (1995); *Matter of Orange County Pubs. Div. of Ottawa Newspapers Inc. v. County of Orange*, 120 A.D.2d 596 (2d Dep't 1986)).

2:79. Is the president or presiding officer of the school board entitled to vote at board meetings?

Yes. A school board member does not lose a vote while serving as presiding officer. His or her vote is expected on every matter and should not be reserved only for tie votes (Opn. of Counsel No. 70, 1 Educ. Dep't Rep. 770 (1952)).

2:80. May a school board rescind action previously taken at a board meeting?

Generally, the courts have held that a school board may rescind an action it has taken at any time before such action becomes final. For example, the New York State Court of Appeals has held that a board may not be barred from reconsidering a prior decision not to dismiss a probationary employee. Such a dismissal need not be for cause, and it would be illogical not to allow a board to reconsider its decision not to terminate a probationary employee based, for example, on changing needs and requirements of the district (*Venes v. Community Sch. Bd.*, 43 N.Y.2d 520 (1978)).

According to section 34 of *Robert's Rules of Order*, a board may not rescind a previous action which, as a result of the vote on the main motion, may not be undone. For example, a board may not undo a contract it has already agreed to by motion, and the other party of that contract has been notified of the original vote.

2:81. May school board members prevent action on a matter by refusing to vote on a motion?

If a majority of the school board votes in favor of a motion, it is approved, whether the remaining members of the board vote against it, abstain, or otherwise refuse to vote (see **2:65**).

When a motion is voted on, board members are expected to be counted and must be reported in the minutes either as voting for or against each motion, or as having abstained from voting (Pub. Off. Law § 87(3)(a)).

In one case, the commissioner of education ruled that school board members may not abstain from voting on whether to grant tenure to a school employee based upon philosophical objections to the state's tenure system. Board members who abstain from voting on tenure recommendations on that basis face possible removal from office for dereliction of duty (*Appeal of Craft and Dworkin*, 36 Educ. Dep't Rep. 314 (1997); see **8:128**.

2:82. Must minutes be taken at school board meetings?

Yes. Formal minutes of all actions must be taken at open meetings. Minutes must consist of a record or summary of all motions, proposals, resolutions, and other matters formally voted upon, including the result of any vote (Pub. Off. Law § 106(1)). Records of votes must include the final vote of each board member on every matter voted on (Pub. Off. Law § 87(3)(a)). Secret ballots are not allowed for any purpose (*Smithtown v. Illion Housing Auth.*, 130 A.D.2d 965 (4th Dep't 1988), *aff'd*, 72 N.Y.2d 1034 (1988)).

There is no requirement that the minutes be comprehensive in nature, although the board may impose additional requirements by adopting a policy on minutes.

Generally, school boards are not authorized to take action in executive sessions. Where boards have such authority (see **2:72**), minutes of an executive session must be taken. However, they need only contain a record of any final determinations, the date, and the vote. They need not contain any matter that is not available to the public under the Freedom of Information Law (see Pub. Off. Law § 106(2); *Plattsburgh Pub. Co., Div. of Ottoway Newspapers, Inc. v. City of Plattsburgh*, 185 A.D.2d 518 (3d Dep't 1992)).

2:83. Is the public entitled to access the minutes of school board meetings?

Yes. According to the provisions of the Open Meetings Law, minutes of school board meetings must be available to the public within two weeks from the date of the meeting. Minutes taken at a properly convened executive session are not available to the public under the Open Meetings Law unless action is taken by a formal vote in the executive session as authorized by law (*Kline and Sons, Inc. v. County of Hamilton*, 235 A.D.2d 44 (3d Dep't 1997); see **2:73, 2:82**). Minutes taken at executive sessions recording actions taken by formal vote of the board must be available to the public within one week (Pub. Off. Law § 106).

Minutes must be made available to the public even if they have not been approved by the board (NYS Department of State, Committee on Open Government FOIL-AO-#8543, Nov. 17, 1994). The law also requires that the district maintain a record of the final votes of each member of the board (Pub. Off. Law §§ 87(3)(a), 106(1)). These records may not be destroyed (see **2:93**).

Minutes may be amended in order to clarify what actually occurred at a meeting, but not to reflect a change of mind, which occurred after the meeting. If there is a change of mind, according to accepted rules of order, there should follow a motion to rescind or amend the motion previously adopted, and the recision or amendment should be included in the minutes of the meeting where this occurred (see *Robert's Rules of Order*, 10th Ed., §§ 35, 48).

School District Records

Editor's Note: For more information on this subject and the Freedom of Information Law, see The Sunshine Laws, *2nd Edition, a handbook published by the New York State School Boards Association (2001). Additional information is available from the Committee on Open Government at New York State, Department of State, Committee on Open Government, 41 State Street, Albany, N.Y. 12231; telephone: 518-474-2518 or Web site at http://www.dos.state.ny.us/coog/coogwww.html.*

2:84. Are school district records subject to public access and inspection?

Yes. Each school board is required by the Education Law and the Public Officers Law to have school district records available for inspection and copying at all reasonable times (§ 2116; Pub. Off. Law § 87). The Freedom of Information Law, which is part of the Public Officers Law and is also commonly referred to as FOIL, requires government bodies and agencies, including school districts, to allow the public access to official documents and records (Pub. Off. Law Art. 6, §§ 84–90). Any member of the public has the right to examine and/or copy these records or documents according to procedures adopted by the district in accordance with the law (see Pub. Off. Law § 87(1)(b)). A fee may be charged for copies (see **2:91**). (For a definition of school district records subject to public access, see **2:86–88**).

FOIL also allows districts to withhold access to certain categories of documents, including those that are required by law to be kept confidential (see Pub. Off. Law §§ 87(2), 89(7); **2:83**).

2:85. Are there any restrictions on who may access school district records?

Although there are restrictions on the types of district records accessible under FOIL (see **2:84, 2:87**), there is no restriction as to who may access district records. While section 2116 of the Education Law provides that district records are to be available for inspection to any qualified voter, FOIL has been held to broaden the category of such persons to include individuals living outside the school district as well (*Duncan v. Savino*, 90 Misc.2d 282 (1977)).

Parents and eligible students have the right to see educational records pertaining to the student under the Family Educational Rights and Privacy Act (FERPA), also known as the Buckley Amendment (20 USC § 1232g; see also **2:88**).

2:86. What types of school district records are subject to public access and inspection?

The Education Law provides that the records, books, and papers of the office of any officer of a school district are the property of the district and open for inspection and copying (§ 2116).

However, according to the commissioner of education, the same exceptions from disclosure that are available under the Freedom of Information Law (FOIL) also apply to records requested pursuant to section 2116 of the Education Law. In other words, a school district can refuse to disclose records requested under this section, to the same extent that it could deny a FOIL request pursuant to one of the exceptions from disclosure available under FOIL. There is no broader scope of disclosure under section 2116 of the Education Law than under FOIL (*Appeal of Martinez*, 37 Educ. Dep't Rep. 435 (1998)).

FOIL defines a record as "any information kept, held, filed, produced or reproduced by, with or for" the school district, "in any form, including but not limited to, reports, statements, examinations, memoranda, opinions, folders, files, books, manuals, pamphlets, forms, papers, designs, drawings, maps, photos, letters, microfilm, computer tapes or disks, rules, regulations or codes" (Pub. Off. Law § 86(4)). Examples of recorded information that may be inspected by interested citizens are school contracts, statements of expenditures, and minutes of board meetings.

Only existing records are subject to disclosure. An agency does not need to prepare a record that does not already exist solely for the purpose of responding to a request for information (Pub. Off. Law § 89(3); *Curro v. Capasso*, 209 A.D.2d 346 (1st Dep't 1994)). However, according to one state supreme court, the creation of a computer program to redact confidential information from electronic files does not constitute the creation of a new record (*New York Pub. Interest Research Group, Inc. v. Cohen*, 188 Misc.2d 658 (New York County, 2001)).

2:87. May any district records be withheld from public access and inspection?

Yes. While the Freedom of Information Law (FOIL) generally requires access to be given to all public records, it also specifically exempts the following records from mandatory disclosure:

- Those specifically exempted by a state or federal statute (see, e.g., **2:88**).
- Certain law enforcement documents and records.
- Records that, if disclosed, would constitute an "unwarranted invasion of personal privacy" (see Pub. Off. Law § 89(2)).
- Records that, if disclosed, would impair current or imminent contract awards or collective bargaining negotiations.
- Interagency and intra-agency materials that are not statistical or factual tabulations or data; instructions to staff that affect the public; final agency policy or determinations; or external audits.
- Information that, if disclosed, would endanger the life or safety of any person.
- Questions or answers to an exam that has not yet been administered.
- Computer access codes (see Pub. Off. Law § 87(2)).
- The name or home address of an applicant for appointment to public employment (Pub. Off. Law § 89(7); but see *Mothers on the Move, Inc. v. Messer*, 236 A.D.2d 408 (2d Dep't 1997); *Daily News, L.P. v. New York City Office of Payroll Administration*, N.Y.L.J. (4/17/03)).

Exceptions are treated very narrowly. For example, a budget examiner's worksheets have been determined to be subject to inspection as "statistical or factual tabulations," not exempt as internal documents (Pub. Off. Law § 87(2)(g)(i); see *Dunlea v. Goldmark*, 54 A.D.2d 446 (1976), *aff'd*, 43 N.Y.2d 754 (1977)).

Government agencies may not immunize documents from disclosure under FOIL by designating them as confidential, either unilaterally or by agreement with a private party. FOIL does not permit exempting from public disclosure government records that do not otherwise qualify for exception pursuant to a specific provision of the Freedom of Information Law. (*In re City of Newark v. Law Department of the City of New York*, 305 A.D.2d 28 (1st Dep't 2003).

2:88. Are students' records accessible under FOIL?

No. FOIL exempts from disclosure records that are specifically exempted by federal or state statute (Pub. Off. Law § 87(2)(a)). Under the federal Family Educational Rights and Privacy Act (FERPA), also known as the

"Buckley Amendment," only parents or eligible students (meaning any student who has reached 18 years of age or is attending an institution of post-secondary education) have the right to see educational records pertaining to the student. Disclosure to anyone else without the prior written consent of the parent or eligible student is limited except as provided by law (see 20 USC § 1232g *et seq.*; see also 34 CFR Part 99; *Owasso Independent School Dist. No. I-0111 v. Falvo,* 534 U.S. 426 (2002); *Taylor v. Vermont Dep't of Education,* 313 F.3d 768 (2d Cir. 2003).

However, there are certain exceptions to the prior consent requirement. For example, districts may disclose student records without parental consent to other school officials who have "legitimate educational interests" and certain other state and federal officials (20 USC § 1232g(b)). Moreover, all school records are subject to inspection by court order or pursuant to any lawfully issued subpoena, provided that parents and students are notified by the school district in advance of compliance with the court order or the subpoena (20 USC § 1232g(b)(2)(B)).

In addition, districts may disclose "directory information" about students, such as their names and addresses, if they notify parents of the categories of information so designated, and give parents or eligible students a reasonable period of time to inform the district that such information should not be released without their consent (20 USC § 1232g(a)(5)(A), (B)).

But even if a district does not otherwise release directory information, if it receives federal funds under the No Child Left Behind Act of 2001, it must provide to post-secondary schools and the military, upon request, the names, addresses, and telephone numbers of high school students. It also must provide military recruiters the same access to students that it generally provides to post-secondary schools or prospective employees, unless parents refuse consent (20 USC § 7908).

State law prohibits the use of student social security numbers for public listing of grades, class rosters, or other lists provided to teachers, identification cards, student directories, or similar listings, except as otherwise specifically authorized or required by law (§ 2-b).

2:89. Are 3020-a settlement agreements available to the public under FOIL?

Yes. Generally, agreements settling disciplinary charges are subject to disclosure under the Freedom of Information Law (FOIL). However, certain portions of such agreements should be reviewed and edited before disclosure to the public in order to protect privacy, including charges that were denied and charges mentioning the names of other employees or students (*LaRocca v. Board of Educ. of Jericho UFSD,* 220 A.D.2d 424 (2d Dep't 1995); see also *Anonymous v. Board of Educ. for the Mexico CSD,*

162 Misc.2d 300 (Sup. Ct. Oswego County 1994); *Buffalo Evening News, Inc. v. Board of Educ. of the Hamburg CSD* (unreported, Sup. Ct. Erie County 1987)).

2:90. Do school board members have access to school employees' personnel records?

Yes, under certain circumstances. The commissioner's regulations provide that any board member may request that personnel records be examined by the board in executive session, but only for inspection and use in the deliberation of specific matters before the board and if certain procedures are followed (see 8 NYCRR Part 84). A school board that permitted a nonboard member in attendance at an executive session to have access to personnel records violated the regulation (*Appeal of Whalen*, 34 Educ. Dep't Rep. 282 (1994)).

According to these regulations, information obtained from employees' personnel records by school board members may be used only to help make decisions on personnel matters, such as appointments, assignments, promotions, demotions, pay, discipline, or dismissal; to aid in the development and implementation of personnel policies; and to enable the board to carry out its legal responsibilities (8 NYCRR § 84.3; *Matter of Krasinski*, 29 Educ. Dep't Rep. 375 (1990)). For example, a board may review personnel files to determine whether the district's legal obligation are being met by the superintendent and /or other administrative staff, such as whether or not employee evaluations are being performed (*Application of Bean*, 42 Educ. Dep't Rep. 171 (2002)).

Any board member may request that the superintendent bring the personnel records of a designated employee or group of employees to the public board meeting. The board must then decide to meet in executive session to examine the records. Even if a majority of the board does not wish to view the records, a single member or minority of the board may insist that a majority of the board meet in executive session so that the interested members may do so (*Gustin v. Joiner*, 95 Misc.2d 277, *aff'd*, 68 A.D.2d 880 (2d Dep't 1979)). Records are brought by the superintendent to the executive session and returned to the superintendent at the end of the session (8 NYCRR § 84.2).

Under other circumstances, an individual board member has no greater right of access to district records than any other member of the public (*Matter of Bruno*, 4 Educ. Dep't Rep. 14 (1964)). Therefore, that individual board member would be able to access only that which is available under FOIL (see *Buffalo Teachers Fed'n, Inc. v. Buffalo Bd. of Educ.*, 156 A.D.2d 1027 (4th Dep't 1989), *appeal denied*, 75 N.Y.2d 708 (1990)).

2:91. What are the procedures to gain access to school district records?

School districts are required under the Freedom of Information Law (FOIL) to adopt procedures by which interested citizens may review district records. These procedures must specify the times when and places where records are available, the names or titles of persons responsible for providing records, and any fees for copying records. Districts must accept FOIL requests and permit inspection of records during all hours they are regularly open for business (Pub. Off. Law § 87(1)(b)(i); 21 NYCRR § 1401.4). Copying fees may be the actual cost of reproduction, excluding fixed overhead costs, up to 25 cents per 9-inch-by-14-inch page, or any fee specified by law (Pub. Off. Law § 87(1)(b)).

Interested persons must make their request for records in writing to the school district and must identify the desired records in sufficient detail for the request to be honored. Requests should be directed to the records access officer, the individual whom school districts must designate by law to be responsible for ensuring compliance with FOIL (Pub. Off. Law § 87(1)(b)).

The school district must respond within five business days of the receipt of a written request by making the record available, by issuing a written denial, or by acknowledging the request and stating approximately when the request will be granted or denied (Pub. Off. Law § 89(3)).

School districts also must maintain a procedure for people to appeal the denial of records. The procedure must allow a person to appeal a denial within 30 days to the individual designated by the school board to receive and decide such appeals. Within 10 business days of receipt of the appeal, that person must either provide the record requested or a written explanation of the reason for the further denial (Pub. Off. Law § 89(4)(a)).

The district must provide a "particularized and specific justification for denying access" or a "factual basis" for claiming an exemption (*Rushford v. Oneida-Herkimer Solid Waste Auth.*, 217 A.D.2d 966 (4th Dep't 1995)). The district must also file each appeal and its outcome with the Committee on Open Government (Pub. Off. Law § 89(4)(a); 21 NYCRR § 1401.7(g)) at the following address: New York State Department of State, Committee on Open Government, 41 State Street, Albany, N.Y. 12231.

Anyone who is dissatisfied with the district's final decision on a request for access to records may appeal the decision to the supreme court of the appropriate county (Pub. Off. Law § 89(4)(b)). The commissioner of education does not hear appeals regarding alleged violations of the FOIL, FERPA, or the Open Meetings Law (*Appeal of Rowe*, 41 Educ. Dep't Rep 189 (2001); *Appeal of a Student Suspected of Having a Disability*, 40 Educ. Dep't Rep. 75 (2000)).

2:92. What penalties may be imposed against a school district for denying access to district records?

If records of clearly significant public interest are withheld without a reasonable basis under FOIL, the school district may be assessed reasonable attorneys' fees and other costs of litigation incurred by a person who has sued for disclosure (Pub. Off. Law § 89(4)(c); see also *Gordon v. Village of Monticello*, 87 N.Y.2d 124 (1995)).

The willful concealment or destruction of public records with the intent to prevent public inspection of such records is also a violation of section 240.65 of the Penal Law and section 89(8) of the Public Officers Law, punishable by a fine of up to $250 and/or a jail term of up to 15 days (Penal Law §§ 70.15(4), 80.05(4)).

2:93. Are there any restrictions on the destruction of school district records?

Yes. Public records must be maintained and preserved in accordance with the "Local Government Records Law," which is contained in article 57-A of the New York's Arts and Cultural Affairs Law. Pursuant to this law, the commissioner of education has created a document called the "Records Retention and Disposition Schedule ED-1" with which school districts must comply (Arts & Cult. Aff. Law §§ 57.17(1), 57.23, 57.25; 8 NYCRR § 185.12; 8 NYCRR Appendix I; see also Pub. Off. Law § 80; Educ. Law § 2121(7)). The document can be accessed at http://www.nysarchives.org/a/nysaservices/ns_mgr_pub_ed1.shtml#Top.

Records may be destroyed only after being retained for a period specified in the Schedule ED-1 (Arts & Cult. Aff. Law § 57.25(2)). Moreover, before any records listed on the Schedule ED-1 may be disposed of, the board of education must formally adopt the Schedule ED-1 by passing a resolution (8 NYCRR Appendix I, p. vii; see p. xi for a sample resolution).

Documents that are not listed in the schedule may be destroyed only with the permission of the commissioner (8 NYCRR § 185.6(a)). Records of employee disciplinary matters, investigations, and evaluations may be disposed of according to the terms of a collective bargaining agreement (8 NYCRR § 185.6(d)).

Records may be preserved on microfilm and the originals disposed of, unless they date from before 1910 or have "enduring statewide significance," according to the commissioner's criteria (8 NYCRR §§ 185.6(c), 185.7), in which case they may be destroyed only with the commissioner's approval. Film reproductions are treated legally as original documents (Arts & Cult. Aff. Law § 57.29).

The destruction of canceled bonds and notes and similar obligations is governed by regulations of the state comptroller (Loc. Fin. Law § 63.10; Opn. St. Comp. 80-351).

School Board Policies

2:94. What is a policy?

A *policy* is a statement that establishes standards and/or objectives to be attained by the district. A school board policy should clearly state the board's view of what it considers to be the mission of the district, the objectives to be reached and the standards to be maintained; the manner in which the district is to perform these tasks, including the allocation of responsibilities and delegation of duties to specific staff members; and the methods to be used, the procedures to be followed and the reasoning to be applied in conducting the district's business, whether by the administration, instructional staff, other employees, students, parents, or the public.

2:95. What is the function of school board policies?

Policies are the means by which a school board leads and governs its school district. Policies form the bylaws and rules for the governance of the district and serve as the standards to which the board, administration, and students are held accountable (see § 1709). A board's policies ensure that the school district performs its established mission and operates in an effective, uniform manner. They are legally binding and serve as the local law of the school district that may be enforced by the district. Moreover, if a school district violates its own policies, the commissioner of education may enforce the policy against the district (see *Appeal of Fusco,* 39 Educ. Dep't Rep. 836 (2000); *Appeal of Marek,* 35 Educ. Dep't Rep. 314 (1996); *Appeal of Joannides,* 32 Educ. Dep't Rep. 278 (1992)).

2:96. Must school boards maintain policy manuals?

No. Districts may be required to adopt policies on certain issues, but they are not required to maintain or organize them in any particular manner. However, it is a common practice to organize and number policies in a single manual for ease of reference and access for the board, district staff, and the public. Such policies may also be maintained for easy board, administrator and public access by storing them in an online, fully searchable format, such as the one offered through the New York State School Boards Association and its Policy Plus service.

2:97. What is the difference between a policy and a regulation?

Policies are statements by the board of education establishing standards and/or objectives to be attained by the district. Policies can only be adopted or amended by the vote of a majority of the board members at an open meeting. Regulations are generally more detailed directives developed by the administration to implement the board's policies. Policies give direction and goals for the district, while regulations give specific orders and procedures to be followed to move in that direction and to attain those goals. Unless otherwise specified by the bylaws of the board of education, it is the power and duty of the superintendent to enforce all provisions of law, rules, and regulations relating to the management of the schools and other educational, social, and recreational activities under the direction of the board of education (§§ 1711(2)(b), 2508(2)).

It is important that board policies be both broad enough to allow administrators to exercise discretion in dealing with day-to-day problems, yet specific enough to provide clear guidance. It is equally important that regulations be written to implement, but not modify, the board's policies.

2:98. What services do the New York State School Boards Association provide to assist local school boards in developing and maintaining up-to-date policies?

The New York State School Boards Association (NYSSBA) offers a variety of free and fee-based services to assist local school boards in developing and maintaining policy manuals for more effective decision making and administration. Services include:

- Customized services specifically tailored to meet a district's policy needs, including customized policy manuals and maintenance/update services that keep custom policy manuals current.
- School Policy Alert subscription that provides school boards with annotated information on all the latest policy requirements.
- Online School Policy Encyclopedia that highlights sample policies.
- Policy workshops tailored to address issues related to a district's policy needs.

For more information, visit NYSSBA's Web site at http://www.nyssba.org and click onto the Policy Services page or contact the Legal/Policy Services Department directly.

3. School Board Organization

3:1. What is the annual school board reorganizational meeting?

The annual school board reorganizational or organizational meeting is the school board's meeting after the annual election of school board members. Here, the organization of the board is established, school board officers are elected, and other district officers are appointed for the upcoming year. In addition, at this meeting, boards often appoint other personnel, such as the internal auditor, school attorney, records access officer, and records management officer, and designate depositories for district funds and newspapers for required notices (§§ 1701, 2502(9)(o)).

In city school districts with a population less than 125,000 inhabitants, the school board must also set the dates and times for its regular school board meetings, which are required to occur at least monthly (§ 2504(2)).

The school board's annual reorganizational meeting is different and apart from the annual district meeting, at which district voters vote on the district's annual budget and elect school board members (see **4:1**).

3:2. Is there a specific time set by law for the annual school board reorganizational meeting?

Yes. In union free and central school districts, the reorganizational meeting must be held on the first Tuesday in July. If that day is a legal holiday, then the meeting must be held on the first Wednesday in July (§ 1707(1)). Alternatively, a board of education in these districts may, by resolution, decide to hold the annual reorganizational meeting at any time during the first 15 days in July (§ 1707(2)).

The annual reorganizational meeting of central high school districts in Nassau County must be held on the second Tuesday in July (§ 1904).

In city school districts with less than 125,000 inhabitants, the reorganizational meeting must be held during the first week in July, unless otherwise specified by law (§§ 2504(1), 2502(9)(o), 2502(9-a)(o)).

In large city school districts, the reorganizational meeting occurs on the second Tuesday in May, except as otherwise specified by law (§§ 2563(1), 2553(9)(f), 2553(10)(o)).

3:3. Which school board officers are chosen at the annual reorganizational meeting?

A school board is required by law to elect a president and may, at its discretion, elect a vice president (§§ 1701, 2504(1)).

The board may exercise fairly broad discretion in determining its internal organization, officers, and staff. It may appoint staff assistants and a school attorney, designate board and/or advisory committees to assist in a wide variety of functions, and employ consultants as desired for the efficient management of its work.

3:4. May a school board vest in a vice president all the powers of the president of the board in the event of the president's absence, or disability?

Yes. Section 1701 of the Education Law authorizes a school board to elect one of its members as vice president with the power to exercise the duties of the president in case of his or her absence or disability.

3:5. What happens when there is a vacancy in the office of president?

When there is a vacancy in the office of president, the vice president shall act as president until a new president is elected (§ 1701).

3:6. May a school board govern through the appointment of standing committees?

No. While there is no state law that either prohibits or requires standing committees, board committees that constitute less than a quorum of the entire board cannot take official action for the board (Gen. Constr. Law § 41; see *Appeal of Greenwald*, 31 Educ. Dep't Rep. 12 (1991); see also **2:14**).

However, a school board may appoint advisory committees to assist in addressing specific problems or issues. Those asked to serve on these committees should understand that their role is advisory and that the final decision on all issues considered rests ultimately with the board.

Certain advisory committees are required by law or commissioner's regulations, and their composition and duties are prescribed therein. For example, the Education Law requires visitation committees to visit every school under the board's jurisdiction at least once annually (§ 1708(2)). The commissioner's regulations require each school board to establish an acquired immune deficiency syndrome (AIDS) advisory council to advise the board concerning the content, implementation, and evaluation of an AIDS instruction program (8 NYCRR §§ 135.3(b)(2), (c)(2)(i)).

The School District's Officers

3:7. Who are the school district's officers?

The school district's officers are individuals who are elected or appointed to administer the district's affairs. In addition to school board members and trustees, school district officers include a district superintendent, superintendent of schools, supervisor of attendance or attendance officer, school district clerk, treasurer, and tax collector employed by the school district (§§ 2(13), 2101(1), 2506; Town Law § 38).

3:8. Is the school board's legal counsel or school attorney a school district officer?

No. The school attorney and those in similar positions are not school district officers (*Matter of McGinley*, 23 Educ. Dep't Rep. 350 (1984), citing *Matter of Harrison CSD v. Nyquist*, 59 A.D.2d 434 (3d Dep't 1977), *appeal denied*, 44 N.Y.2d 645 (1978)). They are either an employee or an independent contractor (*Matter of Burke*, 11 Educ. Dep't Rep. 275 (1972)).

3:9. Which school district officers are appointed by the school board?

School district officers appointed by the school board generally include a clerk, treasurer, tax collector, and auditor (§§ 2130, 1709(20-a), 2503(15), 2526).

A critical appointment made by the board is that of a superintendent of schools who, as chief executive officer of the district, is responsible for the day-to-day administration of the school district (§§ 1604(8), 1711, 2507, 2508, 2554(2)). The superintendent is not necessarily appointed at the board's reorganizational meeting, because he or she is usually appointed for a certain number of years (see **7:23–26**).

3:10. What are the qualifications of school district officers?

The general rule is that a school district officer must be able to read and write and must be a qualified voter of the district (§ 2102; for further information on the qualifications for school board members, see **2:27**).

Residency in the school district is not a statutory requirement for the district superintendent, superintendent of schools, district clerk, treasurer, or tax collector (§ 2102). Therefore, these school district officers are not required to be qualified voters of the district.

3:11. Are a school district's officers required to take a constitutional oath of office?

Yes. A school district's officers, such as board members and trustees, the clerk and the treasurer, are required to take and file an oath of office with the district clerk (Pub. Off. Law § 10). Usually the oath is administered at the board's annual reorganizational meeting by either the board president or the district clerk. Whoever administers the oath must have properly taken and filed an oath of office before administering oaths to others (*Application of Karpen*, 39 Educ. Dep't Rep. 98 (1999); for further information on the oath of office for school board members, see **2:11**). The fact that the oath has been administered should be noted in the board's minutes.

A district superintendent also must take an oath upon the discharge of the duties of his or her office. This must be done no later than five days after the date on which his or her term of office begins (§ 2206; Pub. Off. Law § 10).

3:12. May a school board member be appointed district clerk?

Yes. The school board has the power to appoint either one of its members or another individual as clerk (§ 2130(1); *Matter of Hurtgam*, 22 Educ. Dep't Rep. 219 (1982)).

3:13. May the school board appoint someone to fulfill the district clerk's duties if the current clerk is unavailable?

Although the Education Law does not specifically provide for the appointment of a deputy or acting clerk, certain duties of the district clerk must be carried out, notwithstanding the clerk's temporary incapacitation. For example, the notice of an annual meeting must be given whether or not the clerk is available to carry out this function (§ 2004(1)).

Therefore, by practical necessity, a board may designate an individual to carry out the district clerk's duties when he or she is incapacitated or otherwise unavailable.

3:14. May the offices of school tax collector and school district treasurer be held by the same person?

No. Separate individuals must hold each of the offices of school tax collector, school district treasurer, school district clerk, and school district auditor, if one is appointed (§ 2130; 8 NYCRR § 170.2(a)).

3:15. May the school board appoint a deputy treasurer?

Yes. The board may appoint a deputy treasurer to sign checks in lieu of the treasurer or other officer required to sign such checks, in case of his or her absence or inability. The deputy treasurer must also execute and file an "official undertaking" (a bond) in the same manner and amount as required of the treasurer (§ 1720(2); see also **3:21**).

3:16. May the school board appoint a bank to act as the district's treasurer?

No. The school district's treasurer must be an individual. However, a school board, by resolution, may enter into a contract to provide for the deposit of the school district's periodic payroll in a bank or trust company for district disbursal in accordance with provisions of section 96-b of the Banking Law (§§ 1719, 1720).

3:17. Must the school board designate a bank or trust company as an official school district depository?

Yes. The school board must designate one or more banks or trust companies as depository(ies) for district funds in accordance with section 10 of the General Municipal Law. The board resolution designating a depository must specify the maximum amount that may be kept on deposit at any time in each designated bank or trust company. These designations and monetary amounts may be changed at any time by further resolution (Gen. Mun. Law § 10(2)).

3:18. May the board designate a bank or trust company to fulfill its financial needs if an officer of that bank or trust company has been appointed as the school district's treasurer?

The general rule is that a school board may not designate a bank or trust company as a depository, paying agent, registration agent, or its agent for investment of its funds if the school district's treasurer or his or her deputy or employee has an interest in that bank or trust company. This would constitute a prohibited conflict of interest (Gen. Mun. Law § 801(2), see § 802(1)(a) for exception; see **3:23**).

3:19. May the school board appoint one of its members to sign checks?

Yes. The school board may, by resolution, appoint a member to sign checks in lieu of the treasurer in case of his or her absence or inability, or in addition to the treasurer, if the board decides to require another district officer to countersign all checks. This board member must also execute and file a bond in the same manner and amount as is required of the treasurer (§ 1720(2); Opn. St. Comp. § 73-1122; see **3:21**).

3:20. Must a school board appoint an internal auditor?

No. The position of the school district's internal auditor is a discretionary appointment of the school board. The Education Law stipulates, however, that the following may *not* be appointed as the district's internal auditor: a member of the school board, the district clerk, the district treasurer, the official responsible for the district's business management, the district's designated purchasing agent, or a clerk directly involved in the accounting function (§§ 1709(20-a), 2509(4), 2526; 8 NYCRR § 170.2(a); Opn. St. Comp. § 67-290).

3:21. Must certain school district officers file a bond?

Yes. The school board must establish the limits of a bond (known in the law as an "official undertaking") and require the treasurer, tax collector, and auditor to file one. As an alternative, the board may include these officers in a blanket bond (§§ 2130(5), 2527; Pub. Off. Law § 11(2); 8 NYCRR § 170.2(d); see **3:15, 3:19**).

3:22. Who determines the amount of compensation received by a school district officer appointed by the school board?

The school board determines the amount of compensation for the district treasurer, tax collector, superintendent of schools, and auditor. The board may also determine the amount of compensation to be provided to the district clerk if it was not decided at the annual meeting (§§ 2123, 2130(3), 2506; *Appeal of Palillo*, 6 Educ. Dep't Rep. 117 (1967)).

3:23. May a school district officer do business with the school by which he or she is employed?

No, unless allowed by the conflict of interest law, which is applicable to school district officers and employees as well as school board members (Gen. Mun. Law § 800 *et seq.*; see **2:47–53**).

3:24. Can the school board remove school district officers from their positions?

Both the school district treasurer and collector serve at the pleasure of the school board, which means the board has the right to dismiss them at any time without cause (§§ 2130(4), 2503(15), 2506(1); *Matter of Probeck*, 58 St. Dep't Rep. 470 (1937)). District clerks and other board officers, however, may only be removed for cause except that in small city school districts, the district clerk also serves at the pleasure of the board (§ 2503(15); see *Matter of Motoyama*, 12 Educ. Dep't Rep. 244 (1973); see also **2:34, 2:37** for details on the removal of board members, and **6:8, 7:33–34** on the removal of district superintendents and superintendents of schools).

3:25. What is the procedure for removing a district clerk who may be removed only for cause?

The commissioner of education may remove a clerk or other school officer from office after a hearing at which the officer has a right to be represented by counsel. Removal of the clerk can be for any willful violation, neglect of duty under the Education Law, or any other act pertaining to common schools or other educational institutions participating in state funds, or for willful disobedience of any decision, order, rule, or regulation of the Board of Regents or the commissioner of education (§ 306; see *Matter of Motoyama*, 12 Educ. Dep't Rep. 244 (1973)).

Shared Decision Making

3:26. What is shared decision making?

The terms *shared decision making* and *school-based management* refer to a model for decision making in the schools that emphasizes both the involvement and meaningful participation of administrators, teachers, and parents in the process (8 NYCRR § 100.11).

Every board of education and board of cooperative educational services (BOCES) must have in place a district plan for the participation by teachers, parents, and administrators in school-based planning and shared decision making (8 NYCRR § 100.11(b)). The adopted plan must be made available to the public and must be filed with the district superintendent and the commissioner of education within 30 days of adoption (8 NYCRR § 100.11(d)(1)).

3:27. How is a district's shared-decision-making plan developed?

The commissioner's regulations provide that a school board must consult certain individuals when developing and amending the district's plan for school-based management and shared decision making. The plan the board develops with input from the districtwide committee (also referred to as the central planning committee) must outline both the creation of the school-based shared-decision-making teams and detail those educational issues on which the teams are to provide input. However, nothing in the regulations requires that a board obtain the approval of a school-based planning team before implementing a decision (*Appeal of Gillespie*, 34 Educ. Dep't Rep. 240 (1994)).

3:28. What must be addressed in a school district's shared-decision-making plan?

The district plan must address the following:
- The educational issues that are subject to cooperative planning and shared decision making at the building level.
- The manner and the extent of involvement of each of the parties.
- The means and standards to be used in evaluating the improvement in student achievement.
- The method of holding each party accountable for the decisions they helped make.
- The process for resolving disputes on educational issues at the local level.

- The manner in which all state and federal requirements for the involvement of parents in planning and decision making will be coordinated and met by the overall district plan (8 NYCRR § 100.11(c)).

3:29. Are there any limitations on which educational issues a shared-decision-making committee may address?

The commissioner's regulations do not define which educational issues the school-based committees must consider. A school board is expected to work together with its districtwide planning committee to define what issues the school-based shared-decision-making committee will examine.

School-based committees might consider a range of issues, such as mission statements, school schedules, grouping for instruction, the allocation of discretionary resources, and links with community organizations.

In working with shared-decision-making committees, board members should be aware that while some education issues may be appropriate for input, they may not be appropriate for delegation. For example, a school board is required to formulate the school district budget, and that obligation cannot be delegated to a shared-decision-making team (§§ 1716, 1804(1), 1906(3), 2601-a(3); *Appeal of Kastberg*, 35 Educ. Dep't Rep. 208 (1995)). Similarly, while student performance is an appropriate issue for discussion, it is the school board that must set the course of study by which students are graded and classified (§ 1709(3); *Appeal of Orris and Kelly*, 35 Educ. Dep't Rep. 184 (1995)). Final decisions regarding what instructional programs will be offered in a district's schools are also the school board's responsibility (*Appeal of Zaleski and Gimmi*, 36 Educ. Dep't Rep. 284 (1997)), as are decisions regarding reorganization of a district's schools (*Appeal of Woodward*, 36 Educ. Dep't Rep. 445 (1997)).

The commissioner has found that nothing in the shared-decision-making regulation mandates that a school board obtain the approval of a school-based planning team before implementing a decision. In one case, the commissioner determined that a board may establish a day care center at one of its school facilities, despite opposition from the building's shared-decision-making committee (*Appeal of Gillespie*, 34 Educ. Dep't Rep. 240 (1994)).

And while there is no specific case that addresses this particular issue with regard to shared decision making, board members should also be aware that a school board cannot delegate its responsibility to grant or deny tenure to an employee (*Cohoes City Sch. Dist. v. Cohoes Teachers Ass'n*, 40 N.Y.2d 774 (1976)).

3:30. How often must the shared-decision-making plan be reviewed?

The plan must be reviewed biennially and amended or recertified without change, as appropriate, following the same procedures as for the original plan. The amended or recertified plan must be filed with the district superintendent and submitted to the commissioner for approval, together with a statement of the plan's success in meeting its objectives, no later than February 1 of the year in which the review occurs. The next biennial review must be completed by February 1, 2006 (8 NYCRR § 100.11(f)).

3:31. Who must be involved in the biennial review of a district's school-based planning and shared-decision-making plan?

The school board must conduct the biennial review of its district's plan in collaboration with a districtwide committee composed of the superintendent of schools, administrators selected by the administrative bargaining organization(s), teachers selected by the teachers' bargaining organization(s) and parents selected by the school-related parent organization(s) (8 NYCRR § 100.11(b), (f); *Application of Newburg Teachers Ass'n*, 36 Educ. Dep't Rep. 264 (1996); see *Appeal of Chester*, 35 Educ. Dep't Rep. 512 (1996)).

Parents who are employed by the district or employed by a collective bargaining organization representing teachers and/or administrators in the district may not serve on the committee. In those districts in which teachers or administrators are not represented by a collective bargaining organization, or where there are no school-related parent organizations, teachers, administrators and/or parents are to be selected by their peers in a manner prescribed by the school board or board of cooperative educational services (BOCES) (8 NYCRR § 100.11(b); *Appeal of Greenburg Eleven Fed'n of Teachers*, 34 Educ. Dep't Rep. 606 (1995)).

While the board must seek the districtwide committee's endorsement of any amendments to the plan, the board of education has the final say over the district plan (8 NYCRR § 100.11(d), see *Appeal of Meyer*, 34 Educ. Dep't Rep. 329 (1995); *Appeal of Newburg Teacher's Ass'n*, 34 Educ. Dep't Rep. 621 (1995)). It is not required that all committee members agree on all elements of the plan (*Appeal of Leet*, 42 Educ. Dep't Rep. 253 (2003); see *Appeal of Victor*, 33 Educ. Dep't Rep. 679 (1994)). In addition, school boards may revisit modifications suggested in earlier years (*Appeal of Leet*).

3:32. Can a board member be a member of the districtwide committee?

No. The commissioner of education has held that the intent of the regulation is not for board members to serve on the committee itself, but to work in collaboration with the districtwide committee in developing and amending the shared-decision-making plan (*Appeal of Trombley*, 39 Educ. Dep't Rep. 115 (1999); *Appeal of Chester*, 35 Educ. Dep't Rep. 512 (1996)).

3:33. Who may be a member of the school-based shared-decision-making team?

According to the commissioner's regulations, school-based committees engaged in shared decision making at the building level are to be composed of administrators, teachers, parents, and others at the discretion of the board of education or board of cooperative educational services (BOCES) (for example, students, support staff, or community members) (8 NYCRR § 100.11(c)(1)).

3:34. What is the process for challenging a shared-decision-making plan?

According to the commissioner's regulations, anyone who feels the school board failed to properly adopt, amend, or recertify the plan may appeal to the commissioner no later than 30 days after the plan was adopted, amended, or recertified (8 NYCRR § 100.11(e)(1); *Appeal of Lawrence Teachers' Ass'n,* 39 Educ. Dep't Rep. 119 (1999)). Anyone who participated in the plan's development and claims that the plan is deficient or fails to provide for meaningful participation in the decision-making process may also file an appeal with the commissioner (8 NYCRR § 100.11(e)(2)). The grounds for such an appeal include noncompliance with any of the six enumerated requirements of the plan (8 NYCRR § 100.11(e)(2); see **3:28**).

3:35. Must school districts negotiate with their unions over shared decision making?

It depends on the circumstance. The Public Employment Relations Board (PERB) has held that a school district did not violate its bargaining obligation by refusing to negotiate over teachers' participation on a shared-decision-making committee or over the alleged impact of an increased workload. PERB held that the teachers were not acting in their capacity as employees of the district but rather as volunteers, and that the terms of their participation on the committee were not a mandatory subject of bargaining (*Deer Park Teachers Ass'n v. Deer Park UFSD,* 26 PERB ¶ 4642 (1993)).

However, where a school district has developed or implemented a plan for the participation of teachers and/or administrators in school-based shared decision making as a result of a collective bargaining agreement, any such negotiated provisions must be incorporated into the district's shared-decision-making plan (8 NYCRR § 100.11(h)).

3:36. Is the shared-decision-making process subject to the Open Meetings Law?

Although there are no court decisions that address this issue, whenever a districtwide planning committee is required to have a quorum to conduct business and is actively involved in the process of formulating recommendations at any level, the meetings of that committee are subject to the Open Meetings Law, according to the state Committee on Open Government (Department of State, Committee on Open Government, OML-AO-2204 (Apr. 1, 1993)). Therefore, advance notice of meetings must be provided (*MFY Legal Servs. Inc. v. Toia*, 93 Misc.2d 147 (1977); Department of State, Committee on Open Government, FOIL-AO-9989 (Mar. 26, 1997), OML-AO-2305 (Jan. 19, 1994)).

School-based shared-decision-making committees would be subject to the Open Meetings Law if the district's shared-decision-making plan gives them decision-making authority or requires that the board seek their input and recommendations prior to taking action, even if the board rejects their recommendations (Department of State, Committee on Open Government OML-AO-3265 (Jan. 17, 2001) and OML-AO-2305 (Jan. 19, 1994)).

In addition, if the meeting is required to be open to the public, it must be accessible to people with disabilities (Pub. Off. Law § 103(b); 42 USC § 12102 *et seq.*; see also **2:69**).

4. Annual and Special School District Meetings

The Annual Meeting and Election

4:1. What is the annual meeting and election?

Historically, the annual school district meeting was an actual meeting of the residents of a school district, which occurred immediately prior to or simultaneously with the vote on the proposed school district budget for the upcoming school year. However, school districts now must present the proposed budget for the ensuing school year to the voters at a public hearing held seven to 14 days prior to the date of the annual meeting and election. The public hearing replaces the annual meeting as the forum for presentation of the proposed budget to the voters (see **4:27–29**).

Therefore, the only remaining significance of the term "annual meeting" is that the date set by law for holding the annual meeting is the date that the budget vote and school board elections must occur.

4:2. Must a school district hold an annual meeting and election?

Yes, except large city school districts (the Big 5) and special act school districts. The purpose of the annual meeting and election is to allow qualified voters residing in the school district to vote on the school district's budget for the upcoming school year and to elect candidates to fill any vacancies on the board of education (Article 41).

For information on the annual meeting of a board of cooperative educational services (BOCES), see **5:35–37**.

4:3. When is the annual meeting and election held?

Each school district must hold its annual meeting and election on the third Tuesday in May, which constitutes the statewide day for conducting school district budget votes. If, at the request of a local school board, the commissioner of education certifies no later than March 1 that the election would conflict with religious observances, the election may be held on the second Tuesday in May (§§ 1804(4), 1906(1), 2002(1), 2022(1), 2601-a(2)). Voting on school budgets and board member elections on separate days and/or on a date other than the one set by law is not permitted.

The Albany City School District holds its annual budget vote on the third Tuesday in May, just like other school districts to which the law applies. However, by specific provision of law, members of the Albany Board of Education are elected at a general election the first Tuesday in November conducted by the Albany County Board of Elections (§§ 2502(9)(b), (p),

2602(1)). School board elections in the Big 5 take place at different dates and times as specified by law (§ 2553).

4:4. Is there a specific time of day that the annual meeting and election must be held?

Yes. Most school districts must hold their annual meeting and election during at least six consecutive hours after 6:00 a.m., two hours of which must be after 6:00 p.m., as determined by resolution of the trustees or board of education (§ 2002(1)).

Small city school districts must hold their annual meeting and election during at least nine consecutive hours, beginning not earlier than 7:00 a.m., two hours of which must be after 6:00 p.m., as established by board resolution (§ 2602(3)).

School districts that are not divided into election districts and conduct their election or vote by a show of hands or voice vote must hold their annual meeting and election at 7:30 p.m., unless the time is changed by a vote at a previous district meeting (§ 2002(1)). In such districts, once the proposed budget has been presented, the meeting may not be adjourned or concluded until the budget has been voted on (*Appeal of Mazzurco*, 6 Educ. Dep't Rep. 101 (1967); see also *Appeal of Kerr*, 76 St. Dep't Rep. 121 (1955)).

4:5. What happens if a district fails to hold its annual meeting and election on the required date?

If this happens, the school board or the district clerk must call a special district meeting to transact the business of the annual meeting within 10 days after the time for holding the annual meeting has passed. If the school board or district clerk fails to call such a special meeting, the district superintendent or the commissioner of education may order a special district meeting to conduct the business of the annual meeting.

The officers elected at such a special meeting hold their offices only until the next annual meeting, and until their elected successors have been qualified (§ 2005; see **3:10** for qualification of officers).

4:6. What happens if a school district holds its annual meeting and election on a day or time not allowed by law?

The commissioner of education may annul the results of the meeting and order a special district meeting (see *Appeal of Glier*, 1 Educ. Dep't Rep. 695 (1961)).

4:7. May the annual meeting and election be postponed pending settlement of collective bargaining negotiations?

No. The date for holding the annual meeting and election is fixed by law and may not be altered to await the outcome of contract negotiations (§§ 2002(1), 1804(4), 1906(1), 2022(1), 2601-a(2); see Opn. of Counsel No. 228, 8 Educ. Dep't Rep. 227 (1969)).

In cases where a budget must be presented and voted on before the settlement of contract negotiations, a school board may estimate the amount it will need to meet salary and other obligations under the contract. Once the contract is settled, if insufficient funds are provided for in the budget or if the budget is defeated, the board may appropriate an additional amount to meet these obligations (see *Matter of New Paltz CSD*, 30 Educ. Dep't Rep. 300 (1991), citing *Matter of Fagan*, 15 Educ. Dep't Rep. 296 (1976)). The board also may issue a budget note during the last nine months of the school year, in an amount not to exceed 5 percent (more with voter approval) of the district's annual budget (Local Fin. Law § 29(3)).

However, if the budget is defeated, the total contingency budget, including the additional amount appropriated by the board, is subject to certain caps on contingency budget expenditures (§ 2023; see also **19:47–48**).

4:8. Where is the annual meeting and election held?

The annual meeting and election is held at the school(s) designated by the board of education for this purpose. If the district has no school or if the school is not accessible or adequate, then the annual meeting and election may be held in any place suitable for the occasion (§ 2002(1)).

4:9. Who calls the annual meeting and election to order?

In common school districts, the annual meeting and election is called to order by the sole trustee, the chairperson of the board of trustees, or a person chosen by the trustee or trustees. Once the meeting is called to order, the qualified district voters present at the meeting nominate and elect a qualified voter in attendance to serve as permanent chairperson (§§ 2021(1), 2025(1)). As qualified voters, members of the school board are eligible to serve as chairperson (*Appeal of Uciechowski*, 32 Educ. Dep't Rep. 511 (1993)).

In union free, central, and small city school districts, a qualified voter appointed by the school board as permanent chairperson declares the polls open and closed at the appropriate time (§§ 2025(2), 2601-a(2)).

4:10. What notice must be given to the public regarding the annual meeting and election?

The district clerk must publish notice of the date, time, and place of the annual meeting and election four times during the seven weeks preceding the date of the annual meeting and election, in two newspapers having general circulation, or one newspaper of general circulation, if there is only one, with the first publication occurring at least 45 days before the date of the annual meeting and election (§§ 2003(1), 2004(1), 2121(4), 2601-a(2)).

A newspaper of general circulation is, with narrow exceptions, one that is published at least weekly; that contains news, editorials, features, advertising or other matter regarded as of current interest; that is of paid circulation; and that is sent by at least second class mail (Gen. Constr. Law § 60).

The fees that newspapers may charge for publishing the notice of annual meeting are set forth in section 8007 of the Civil Practice Law and Rules. A school district may not pay a claim for publication of a notice in a newspaper that does not meet the legal definition of a newspaper of general circulation (Opn. St. Comp. 93-33).

If no newspaper of general circulation is available, or if both newspapers having general circulation in the district refuse to publish the notice at the rates prescribed by law, the notice must be posted in at least 20 of the most public places 45 days before the meeting (§§ 2003(1), 2004(1), 2601-a(2)).

4:11. What must be included in the notice of the annual meeting and election?

The notice must state the date, time, and place of the annual district meeting and election (§§ 2003(1), 2004(1), 2601-a(2)). It also must include the following:

- The date, time, and place of the public hearing on the budget (§§ 1608(2), 1716(2), 2601-a(2)).
- A statement that district residents may obtain a copy of the proposed budget at any district schoolhouse, during designated hours, on each day other than a Saturday, Sunday, or holiday during the 14 days preceding the date of the annual meeting and election (§§ 1608(2), 1716(2), 2004(6)(d)).
- Notice of any proposed tax, together with a statement specifying both the purpose and the amount of spending for which the tax will be levied, where such tax is proposed to finance: (1) an addition to or change of site or purchase of a new site; (2) purchase of any new site or structure; (3) grading or improving a school site; (4) purchase of an addition to the site of any schoolhouse; (5) purchase of lands and

buildings for agricultural, athletic, playground or social center purposes; (6) construction of any new schoolhouse or the erection of an addition to any schoolhouse already built; and (7) payment or refund of any outstanding bonded indebtedness (§ 416(3)).

- Where required by statute, the substance of each specific proposition to be voted on, for example, a proposition:

  1. To levy a tax by installments as a condition prerequisite to the adoption of a bond resolution or capital note resolution where such bonds or capital notes will be issued to finance a specific object or purpose. The notice of the meeting at which such a proposition shall be voted upon must state the estimated maximum cost of each item of such specific object or purpose and the estimated total cost of all the items (§§ 416(2), 2009; see also Local Fin. Law § 41.10). "There is no legal requirement that the notice of the election specify the term of the bonds" (*Appeal of Brousseau*, 39 Educ. Dep't Rep. 397 (1999)).

  2. To rescind a district vote to raise money or to reduce the amount thereof (§ 416(5)).

  3. To establish certain reserve funds and/or to make expenditures therefrom (§ 3651(1)(b), (3)).

  4. To increase or decrease the number of members of the board of education (§§ 1703(2), 2502(4)(b); see also *Appeal of Rosenberg*, 31 Educ. Dep't Rep. 398 (1992); *Appeal of Como*, 30 Educ. Dep't Rep. 214 (1990); *Appeal of Swanson*, 29 Educ. Dep't Rep. 503 (1990); *Appeal of Presutti*, 17 Educ. Dep't Rep. 445 (1978)).

  5. To increase or decrease the term of office (i.e., the number of years served) of board members in small city school districts (§ 2502(4)(b)).

- A statement that qualified voters may apply for absentee ballots at the district clerk's office and that a list of persons to whom absentee ballots have been issued will be available for inspection in the district clerk's office during each of the five days prior to the day of the election, except Sundays (§ 2004(7)).

- The time and place that the board of registration will meet to prepare the register of the school district, together with notice that any person who is not already registered, upon proving that he or she is entitled to vote in the district, may have his or her name placed upon the register. In addition, the notice shall state that the register containing the names of qualified voters will be available for inspection in the clerk's office during the hours determined by the district on each of the five days prior to the day of the election, except Sundays (§ 2004(5), (6)).

In addition, the notice also must state that petitions for nominating candidates for office of school board member must be filed in the district clerk's office between 9:00 a.m. and 5:00 p.m. no later than 30 days (20 days in small city districts) before the election (§§ 2003(2), 2004(2), 2601-a(2), 2608(1)). Note that if the deadline for filing petitions falls on "a Saturday, Sunday or public holiday," the filing may be performed on the "next succeeding business day" (Gen. Constr. Law § 25-a(1); see also *Appeal of Williams*, 36 Educ. Dep't Rep. 270 (1996)). Therefore, when this situation occurs, districts may want to inform voters in the notice of annual meeting and election that nominating petitions may be filed with the district clerk, during the hours specified by law, on the Monday following the 30th day before the election (specify date).

4:12. What happens if the notice of the annual meeting and election does not comply with the law?

If a district fails to comply with the legal requirements for providing adequate public notice, the results of the budget vote and/or board member elections, in all likelihood, will be upheld and will not be found illegal, unless it appears that the failure to give proper notice was willful or fraudulent (§ 2010; see also *Appeals of Campbell and Coleman*, 41 Educ. Dep't Rep. 207 (2001)). "Where the notice given is reasonably calculated to and effectively does give notice to the public of the election, a technical failure to give proper notice is not a basis for invalidating the result" (*Appeal of Winograd*, 42 Educ. Dep't Rep. 180 (2002)).

For example, in one case, a district provided correct information for publication in the local newspaper, indicating that it would hold its budget hearing on May 6 of that year. However, the newspaper incorrectly advertised the date of the hearing as May 5. Observing that all the other information the district provided to community residents listed the correct date, the commissioner of education found nothing willful or fraudulent about the error in the notice of the budget hearing and refused to overturn the results of the election (*Appeal of Leman*, 39 Educ. Dep't Rep. 35 (1999)).

In another case, the commissioner refused to overturn the election results where the district had published notice in only one newspaper, not realizing until just five days before the election that the law generally requires publication in two newspapers, at which point in time it was too late to correct the error. The commissioner found that the error was not willful or fraudulent, especially since, upon discovering the error, the district mailed and hand-delivered a flyer regarding the election to district households (*Appeal of Hebel*, 34 Educ. Dep't Rep. 319 (1994); see also *Appeal of Winograd*, 42 Educ. Dep't Rep. 180 (2002)); *Appeal of Bartosik*, 37 Educ. Dep't Rep. 531 (1998); and *Application of Martin*, 32 Educ. Dep't Rep. 208 (1992)).

4:13. Are school boards required to provide a financial report for the prior school year at the annual meeting?

Only in common school districts. In such districts, the trustees must provide a financial statement at the annual meeting that accounts for all moneys received for the use of the district, or raised or collected by taxes, in the preceding year, and which indicates how they were spent (§ 1610). The trustees' willful neglect or refusal to do so will result in members forfeiting their offices (§ 1611). Other types of school districts are required by law to publish an annual financial statement instead of presenting it at the annual meeting (see **19:5**).

The School District Budget

4:14. Is there a deadline by which a school board must complete the budget that it plans to submit to the voters for approval?

Yes. The school board must complete the proposed budget document at least seven days before the public hearing at which the board will present the budget to the voters. Since the budget hearing must be held seven to 14 days before the annual meeting and election, the school board must complete the budget 14 to 21 days prior to the date of the annual meeting and election, depending upon the hearing date selected by the board (§§ 1608(2), 1716(2), 2601-a(2)). This provision also applies to a budget re-vote (see **4:84**).

In addition, boards have to share certain budget estimates with the State Education Department (SED) prior to the budget vote (§§ 1608(7), 1716(7), 2601-a(3)). These estimates must be included in the district's "Property Tax Report Card" (see **4:24**) and transmitted to the SED immediately following approval by the board of education, but in no event later than 24 days prior to the statewide uniform voting day, which is the third Tuesday in May (§§ 1608(7), 1716(7), 2601-a(3)). Therefore, as a practical matter, since the estimates provided in the Property Tax Report Card depend upon the district's budget projections, school boards may find it necessary to complete their budgets in time to make the calculations that must be stated in this Report Card for timely transmittal to the SED.

4:15. Can a school board make adjustments to a completed proposed budget?

Once a school board settles upon the final dollar amount of the district budget and the corresponding tax levy, it still may be possible for the board to adjust various projected budgetary expenditures within the total dollar amount without changing the total budget amount and estimated tax levy submitted to the State Education Department. Where a district proposes a budget that will increase spending in the upcoming fiscal year, it would be able to report its total spending and total estimated tax levy as well as the percentage increase in total spending and in the levy. But it also might be able to make line item adjustments in the budget without affecting either total spending or the estimated tax levy, depending on a variety of factors, such as state aid. For example, if a district chose to delete a $300,000 spending item and simply replace it with another $300,000 spending item, its total spending would not be altered, but its estimated tax levy might be, depending on the aidability of the alternate spending items.

4:16. Must the school board make a copy of the proposed school district budget available to the public before the district meeting at which it is presented?

Yes. Copies of the budget, together with the attachments required by law (see **4:21-24**), must be made available upon request to district residents during the 14 days immediately preceding the date of the annual meeting and election or special district meeting at which a budget vote will occur. The school board also must indicate in the notice of the annual meeting and election or special district meeting at which a budget vote will occur that residents may obtain a copy of the budget at any schoolhouse in the district, during designated hours, on each day other than a Saturday, Sunday, or holiday, during the 14 days immediately preceding the date of the annual meeting and election. Furthermore, at least once during the school year, the board must include in a district wide mailing notice of the availability of copies of the budget (§§ 1608, 1716, 2004(6)(d), 2601-a(3)). There is no legal requirement that the actual text of the budget be published in a newspaper. Similarly, there is no legal requirement that a school district mail copies of a proposed district budget to anyone (*Appeal of Chernish and DeRidder*, 39 Educ. Dep't Rep. 204 (1999); see also *Appeal of Herloski*, 43 Educ. Dep't Rep.___, dec. no. 15,014 (2004)).

A school board also has to make available a true and correct copy of any budget being resubmitted to the voters to "provide up-to-date, accurate information to the electorate" prior to the revote (*Appeal of Walker*, 41 Educ. Dep't Rep. 365 (2002)).

4:17. What kind of information must be included in the proposed school district budget?

School districts must present a detailed written statement of the amount of money that will be required for the coming school year for school purposes, specifying the various purposes of proposed funding and the amount of each. This statement must show the total amount necessary to pay boards of cooperative educational services (BOCES) in full, with no deduction of estimated state aid. It must also include the amount of state aid to be provided and its percentage relationship to the total expenditures. This statement must be completed at least seven days before the budget hearing at which it is to be presented (§§ 1608(1), 1716(1), 2601-a(3); see **4:14, 4:27**).

The proposed budget must be written in plain language; in other words, easy to read and understand. It must include a complete, accurate, and detailed written statement of estimated revenues, including payments in lieu of taxes, and property tax refunds from certiorari proceedings, proposed expenditures, transfers to other funds, and the amount of fund balance to be used in support of budgetary appropriations, as well as a comparison with the prior year's data (§§ 305(26), 1608(3), 1716(3), 2601-a(3); 8 NYCRR § 170.9; see also, *Appeal of Herloski*, 43 Educ. Dep't Rep. ___, dec. no. 15,014 (2004)).

Districts must present their proposed budgets in three component parts: (1) a program component; (2) a capital component; and (3) an administrative component (§§ 1608(4), 1716(4), 2601-a(3), see also 8 NYCRR § 170.8).

Districts must also append a number of attachments to the budget document, including a statement on administrative salaries, a school district report card, and a property tax report card (see **4:21–24**).

4:18. What must be included in the program component of the proposed budget?

The program component must include, but need not be limited to, all program expenditures of the school district, including the salaries and benefits of teachers and any school administrators and supervisors who spend the majority of their time performing teaching duties, and all transportation operating expenses (§§ 1608(4), 1716(4), 2601-a(3); see also 8 NYCRR § 170.8).

4:19. What must be included in the capital component of the proposed budget?

The capital component must include, but need not be limited to, all transportation capital, debt service and lease expenditures and costs resulting from judgments in tax certiorari proceedings or the payment of awards from court judgments, administrative orders or settled or compromised claims. It must also include all facilities costs of the school district, including facilities lease expenditures, the annual debt service and total debt service for all facilities financed by bonds and notes of the school district, and the costs of construction, acquisition, reconstruction, rehabilitation, or improvement of school buildings. This part of the budget must include a rental, operations, and maintenance section that includes base rental costs, total rent costs, operation and maintenance charges, costs per square foot for each facility leased by the school district, and any and all expenditures associated with custodial salaries and benefits, service contracts, supplies, utilities, and maintenance and repair of school facilities (§§ 1608(4), 1716(4), 2601-a(3); see also 8 NYCRR § 170.8).

4:20. What must be included in the administrative component of the proposed budget?

The administrative component must include at least, office and central administrative expenses; traveling expenses and salaries and benefits of all certified school administrators and supervisors who spend a majority of their time performing administrative or supervisory duties; any and all expenditures associated with the operation of the board of education, the office of the superintendent of schools, general administration, the school business office; consulting costs not directly related to student services and programs, planning, and all other administrative activities (§§ 1608(4), 1716(4), 2601-a(3); see also 8 NYCRR § 170.8).

4:21. What attachments must be appended to the proposed budget?

A school board must append to its proposed budget (1) an administrative salaries statement; (2) the New York State school report card; and (3) a property tax report card (see **4:22–24**).

4:22. What must be included in the administrative salaries statement that must be attached to the proposed budget?

The administrative salaries statement must detail the total compensation, including salary, benefits and any in-kind or other form of remuneration, to be paid to the superintendent of schools, and assistant or associate superintendents, together with a list of any administrator(s) who will earn a salary of $101,000 or more in the upcoming year with their position title and salary. This dollar amount increases annually. For updated information, go to: http://www.emsc.nysed.gov/mgtserv/cdlead.htm.

This statement must also be submitted to the commissioner of education within five days of its preparation on a form prescribed by the commissioner. The commissioner then compiles such data into a single statewide compilation and makes it available to the governor, the Legislature, and other interested parties upon request (§§ 1608(5), 1716(5), 2601-a(3)).

4:23. What must be included in the New York State school report card that must be attached to the proposed budget?

Each school board must append to copies of its proposed budget its New York State school report card. This report card consists of the following reports prepared by the State Education Department, based on data submitted by each district:

- An overview of School Performance and Analysis of Student Subgroup Performance;
- the Comprehensive Information Report;
- the School Accountability Report; and
- the Fiscal Supplement (8 NYCRR § 100.2(m); see also **14:86–87**).

In addition to attaching this report card to the proposed budget, school districts also must make it available for distribution at the annual meeting, transmit it to local newspapers of general circulation, and make it available to parents (8 NYCRR § 100.2(m)(3)).

Note: The commissioner's regulations at 8 NYCRR § 100.2(bb), pertaining to what previously was known as the "School District Report Card" were amended in 2003 to conform with various requirements under the federal No Child Left Behind Act (NCLB). Regulatory amendments to section 100.2(m) then renamed the "School District Report Card" the "New York State School Report Card" and altered the contents of the report as well. However, as before, the purpose of this report card is to provide data about the academic performance of each district in a comparable format. Notably, the underlying statutory provisions that authorize the commissioner of education to promulgate regulations setting forth the contents of the report card still refer to it as the "School District Report Card" (see §§ 1608(6); 1716(6); 2554(24); 2590-e(23); 2601-a(7)).

4:24. What must be included in the property tax report card that must be attached to the proposed budget?

The property tax report card must contain the following information:

- The amount of total spending and the total estimated school tax levy that would result from the adoption of the proposed budget.
- The percentage increase or decrease in total spending and in the total school tax levy as compared with the school district budget and tax levy for the preceding school year.
- The projected enrollment growth for the school year for which the budget is prepared, and the percentage change in enrollment from the previous year. The commissioner's regulations require use of the definition of "enrollment" as set forth in Education Law section 3602(1)(n)(2) (see 8 NYCRR § 170.11(a)(6), (7)).

- The percentage increase in the consumer price index (CPI) averaged during the 12 months preceding January 1 of the prior school year as compared with the average CPI for the 12-month period immediately preceding January 1 of the current school year (§§ 1608(7)(c), 1716(7)(c); 8 NYCRR § 170.11(a)(8).

In addition to attaching it to the proposed budget, districts must make this tax report card available for distribution on the day of the budget vote and transmit it to local newspapers of general circulation.

4:25. Must a school board submit a copy of the property tax report card to the State Education Department?

Yes. A copy of the tax report card must be submitted to the State Education Department (SED) by the end of the business day immediately following its approval by the board of education, but no later than 24 days prior to the statewide uniform voting day — the third Tuesday in May (§§ 1608(7), 1716(7), 2601-a(3); 8 NYCRR § 170.11(e)). SED then must compile such data from all school districts whose budgets are subject to a vote of the qualified voters and shall make such compilation available electronically at least 10 days prior to the statewide uniform voting day (§§ 1608(7), 1716(7), 2601-a(3)).

4:26. Must the proposed budget include an estimate of the tax "rate" needed to generate the estimated tax levy?

No. However, while not required to do so, school districts may provide the voters with an estimate of the tax rate that would result from voter approval of the proposed budget. Any school district supplying such information to the voters should consider including an appropriate disclaimer about the accuracy and reliability of the information (*Appeal of Russo*, 41 Educ. Dep't Rep. 182 (2001)).

4:27. Are school districts required to hold a public hearing on the proposed budget prior to the budget vote?

Yes. Each school district must hold a public hearing on the budget at least seven days but not more than 14 days prior to the annual meeting and election or special district meeting at which a school budget vote will occur (§§ 1608(1), 1716(1), 2022(2)). At the public hearing, the board of education presents the proposed budget for the upcoming school year to the voters.

Notice of the date, time and place of the public hearing must be included in the notice of annual meeting and election or special district meeting (§§ 1608(2), 1716(2); see **4:11**).

4:28. Are large city school districts required to hold a public hearing on the proposed budget?

No. In large city school districts (the Big 5), school boards do not adopt a budget. Instead, they prepare an itemized estimate of the sum needed for necessary and other authorized expenses. The estimate is then filed with and acted upon by designated city officials (§§ 2576, 2590-q).

In Buffalo, it is filed with the city official authorized to receive department estimates and acted upon by such officer and the city council (§ 2576(4)).

In New York City, community district education councils submit their budget estimates to the chancellor. The chancellor then submits the estimates adopted by the city board to the mayor in the manner prescribed by the city charter (§ 2590-q). In addition, each community superintendent must prepare semi-annual and year-end reports, which include, but are not limited to, an accounting of all funds received and spent by the subject community district education council from all sources. Copies of these reports are given to the chancellor and the community district education council and must be available to the public. For specific information, see section 2590-q(17) of the Education Law.

In Rochester, Syracuse, and Yonkers, the estimate is filed with the mayor or city manager and then evaluated and dealt with in a manner similar to estimates from other city departments (§ 2576(2)).

4:29. What budget information must districts provide to residents after the public hearing on the budget?

Each school district must mail a school "Budget Notice" to all qualified voters in the district, at a point in time after the date of the public hearing on the budget, but no later than six days prior to the annual meeting and election or special district meeting at which a school budget vote will occur. The budget notice must compare the percentage increase or decrease in total spending under the proposed budget with total spending under the district budget adopted for the current school year. In addition, the budget notice must compare the percentage increase or decrease in total spending under the proposed budget with the percentage increase or decrease in the consumer price index (CPI) from January 1 of the prior school year to January 1 of the current school year.

The budget notice must also contain a description of how total spending and the tax levy resulting from the proposed budget would compare with a projected contingency budget, if a contingency budget were adopted on the same day as the vote on the proposed budget. This comparison must be in total, and also broken down by budget components (i.e., program, administrative, and capital). It must include a statement explaining the assumptions made in estimating the projected contingency budget (§ 2022(2-a)(a)).

In addition, the budget notice must include, in a format and in a manner prescribed by the commissioner, a comparison of the basic School Tax Relief (STAR) exemption and the increase or decrease in school taxes from the prior year. It must also include the resulting net taxpayer savings, based on a hypothetical home in the district with a full value of $100,000 under the existing district budget, and with such savings under the proposed budget (§ 2022(2-a)(b)).

Finally, the budget notice must state the date, time, and place of the budget vote, in the same manner as in the notice of annual meeting (§ 2022(2-a)).

4:30. Is a minimum percentage of eligible voters required in order to approve a district's budget?

No. There is no such requirement in law (*Appeal of Sherrill*, 43 Educ. Dep't Rep. ___, dec. no. 15,004 (2003)).

4:31. What happens if the voters reject the proposed school district budget?

A school board may do one of the following:

- Prepare and adopt a contingency (or austerity) budget without going back to the voters, subject to the cap on contingency budgets. In this case, the board has the authority to levy a tax sufficient to pay for teachers' salaries and items that constitute ordinary contingent expenses (§§ 2022(4), (5), 2023, 2601-a(4), (5); see **19:45–55**).
- Present the original budget for a second vote, or a revised budget, at a special district meeting, within the limitations set by law (§§ 2022(4), 2601-a(4); see also **4:83–85**).
- Adopt a contingency budget, and then present one or more propositions to the voters, giving them the opportunity to vote to fund services that cannot be provided without voter approval. A separate proposition may be presented for each such service, or several services may be included in one proposition (*Appeal of Aarseth*, 32 Educ. Dep't Rep. 506 (1993)). Nothing in the law prohibits school districts from combining several unrelated objects and purposes in a single proposition (*Appeal of Friedman*, 36 Educ. Dep't Rep. 431 (1997)).

A school board is under no obligation to submit a budget to the voters more than once prior to the adoption of a contingency budget, and the voters cannot compel it to do so (§ 2022(4), (5); see also *Appeal of Osten*, 35 Educ. Dep't Rep. 160 (1995); *Appeal of Brosseau*, 31 Educ. Dep't Rep. 155 (1991)).

For information on contingency budgets, see **19:45–55**.

4:32. How many times can a school board submit a budget or any proposition involving the expenditure of money for a vote at a district meeting?

Two times. If the voters fail to approve a proposed budget after the second submission, or if the board elects not to put the proposed budget to a public vote a second time, the board must adopt a contingency (austerity) budget (§§ 2022 (4), 2601-a(4)).

In addition, school districts cannot submit to the voters more than twice during any 12-month period a proposition for the construction of a new schoolhouse or an addition to an existing schoolhouse at the same site. Moreover, districts cannot submit the second proposition to the voters within 90 days of the first vote. However, neither of these limitations applies where the voters approve a building project, but the bids that subsequently are received on the project exceed the amount approved by the voters (§ 416(6)).

4:33. May the commissioner of education impose a budget on school districts?

No. The commissioner does not have the authority to do this. However, questions as to what may be included in a contingency budget may be referred to the commissioner for a final decision (§§ 2024, 2601-a(5)(g), (6)).

4:34. Can a school board submit supplemental budget propositions to the voters?

Yes. A school board has the power to submit additional items of expenditure to the voters separate and apart from those specified in the proposed budget, either on the board's own initiative or pursuant to a petition of voters (§§ 2022(2), 2035(2); see **4:36–43**). However, this authority is subject to the two-vote limit on budget propositions (see **4:32**).

4:35. Should a school board place propositions on the ballot concerning matters that do not require voter approval?

No. Although technically not illegal, the commissioner consistently has advised against this practice because advisory votes may infer voter determination of the issue submitted for consideration (see *Appeal of D'Orazio and Carey*, 41 Educ. Dep't Rep. 292 (2002); *Appeal of Moonan and Richards*, 28 Educ. Dep't Rep. 390 (1989); *Matter of Feldheim*, 8 Educ. Dep't Rep. 136 (1969)).

In addition, although such a vote is not legally binding on a board of education, "it can easily lead to the inference that the board is seeking to avoid its responsibility to make decisions within its legal powers, and is therefore . . . an undesirable practice and should be discouraged" (*Matter of Feldheim*; see also *Appeal of Rosenberg*, 31 Educ. Dep't Rep. 398 (1992)).

A nonbinding referendum is "particularly ill-advised" when the matter can only be remedied by a change in the law, and the board of education fails to inform the voters of the advisory nature of the vote" (see *Appeal of Marshall and Troge*, 41 Educ. Dep't Rep. 219 (2001); see also *Appeal of Moonan and Richards*).

Voter Propositions

4:36. Can voters petition their local board of education to have propositions placed on the ballot?

Yes, subject to the two-vote limit on budget propositions (see **4:32**). However, the school board may refuse such a proposition if its purpose is not within the power of the voters, or if it requires an expenditure of money but fails to specify the amount for which voter approval is sought (§§ 2021, 2035; *Appeal of Leman*, 32 Educ. Dep't Rep. 579 (1993); *Matter of Sampson*, 14 Educ. Dep't Rep. 162 (1974)).

A school board also may refuse to place a proposition on the ballot if the petition submitted to the board is ambiguous, unfeasible, would cause difficulty interpreting voting results (see **4:39**), or if it fails to contain the requisite number of petition signatures set by board policy (**4:41**).

4:37. Who determines whether a particular proposition is within the power of the voters?

The school board makes this determination, subject to review by the commissioner of education. This authority must be exercised with care because the commissioner has warned that it does not give school districts unfettered discretion to refuse propositions (*Appeal of Como*, 30 Educ. Dep't Rep. 214 (1990)).

In one case, for example, the commissioner sustained a school board's refusal to place a proposition on the ballot that amounted to an attack on the board and other district officials. The proposition asked the voters to set aside $200,000 to fund a lawsuit against school officials. The commissioner ruled that the proposition was not within the power of the voters (*Appeal of Cox*, 37 Educ. Dep't Rep. 404 (1998)).

In another case, the commissioner sustained a school board's decision to reject a proposition which would have required the board to submit a budget to the voters more than once before adopting a contingency budget. School boards, not the voters, have the authority to determine whether to place a budget before the voters a second time, or adopt a contingency budget (*Appeal of Osten*, 35 Educ. Dep't Rep. 160 (1995)).

Similarly, a school board may reject a voter proposition that would require the board to schedule a vote on an alternative budget proposed by a citizens' group before adopting a contingency budget. The authority to develop a budget rests with the school board, not the voters (*Appeal of Sperl*, 33 Educ. Dep't Rep. 388 (1994)).

4:38. Can a school board reject a voter petition on an issue previously submitted to the voters?

Yes. Once any issue has been placed before the voters in a particular year, a school board may refuse to place the issue before the voters again in the same year (*Appeal of Brush*, 34 Educ. Dep't Rep. 273 (1994)).

4:39. Can a school board reject a voter petition to add a ballot proposition that is ambiguous, unfeasible, or would cause difficulty interpreting voting results?

Yes. According to the commissioner of education, "A board of education may not be compelled to place before the voters at an annual meeting all propositions submitted in conformity with section 2035 and its bylaws, regardless of ambiguity, feasibility, or difficulty in interpreting election results when conflicting matters are voted on simultaneously. A board must exercise its independent judgment within the law to be certain that the will of the voters can be ascertained" (*Appeal of Krause*, 27 Educ. Dep't Rep. 57 (1987); see also *Appeal of Huber,* 41 Educ. Dep't Rep. 240 (2001)).

For example, two conflicting propositions, one for construction, and the other for renovation, should not be placed on the same ballot (*Appeal of McDougal & Murphy*, 37 Educ. Dep't Rep. 611 (1998); see also *Appeal of Martin*, 32 Educ. Dep't Rep. 567 (1993); and *Appeal of Huber*; but compare with *Appeal of Kohilakis*, 33 Educ. Dep't Rep. 513 (1994)).

4:40. Can a school board alter the language of an ambiguous proposition submitted by the voters?

Yes. A school board has the power to alter the language of a proposition submitted by the voters to bring the proposition into conformity with the law. However, it is not required to do so (*Appeal of Como*, 30 Educ. Dep't Rep. 214 (1990); *Appeal of Krause*, 27 Educ. Dep't Rep. 57 (1987); *Appeal of Welch*, 16 Educ. Dep't Rep. 397 (1977)).

In addition, where it is possible for the school board to make minor modifications to two otherwise mutually inconsistent propositions, such that the voters are presented with a clear choice between alternatives, there is nothing improper about the board submitting both propositions to the voters

(*Appeals of the Board of Trustees of the George F. Johnson Mem. Library,*
40 Educ. Dep't Rep. 331 (2000)). For example, according to the
commissioner, it was perfectly acceptable for a board of education to
submit one proposition to the voters to eliminate the annual tax levy for a
particular library, while placing a second proposition on the ballot at the
same election, proposing that the tax levy for the very same library be
increased in the event that the voters did not adopt the first proposition
eliminating library funding (*Appeal of the Board of Trustees of the George
F. Johnson Mem. Library*).

4:41. Is there a minimum number of signatures that a voter petition must have to place a proposition on the ballot at the annual meeting and election?

It depends upon the policy of the particular school board. The law
requires each school board to adopt a rule for submitting voter-initiated
propositions that specifies the minimum number of signatures required for
such petitions (*Appeal of Huber,* 41 Educ. Dep't Rep. 240 14,676 (2001)).
School boards must comply with any such rules and regulations after they
have been established (*Matter of Fetta,* 8 Educ. Dep't Rep. 201 (1969)).
However, a board may, in its discretion, amend such rules (§ 2035).

4:42. Must a voter petition include the addresses of those signing the petition?

No. The law does not require voters to list their addresses on a petition to
add a proposition to the ballot, nor does it require that such a petition
contain a sworn statement (*Appeal of Atkins,* 35 Educ. Dep't Rep. 375
(1996)).

4:43. Is there a deadline for filing a voter petition to place a proposition on the ballot at the annual meeting and election?

Such a voter petition must be filed with the school board at least 30 days
before the election date, unless the proposition is required by law to be
included in the published or posted notice of the annual or special district
meeting (§ 2035).

In addition, a board may establish rules that require the proposition be
submitted a reasonable period of time before the first publication or posting
of notice (see *Appeal of Rosenberg,* 31 Educ. Dep't Rep. 398 (1992); see
also *Appeal of Como,* 30 Educ. Dep't Rep. 214 (1990); *Appeal of Presutti,*
17 Educ. Dep't Rep. 445 (1978)). The commissioner of education has
sustained as reasonable board policies requiring the submission of
propositions to the board 90 and 60 days in advance of the annual meeting,
where such propositions are of the type that must be included in the notice

of annual meeting (see, *Appeal of Reynolds*, 42 Educ. Dep't Rep. 231 (2003); see also, *Presutti* at 446).

Improper Advocacy

4:44. May a school district urge voters to vote in favor of a proposed school district budget or other ballot proposition?

No. School districts must take care to avoid spending public money to encourage voters to vote in favor of the school budget or any proposition. District funds may not be used to express "favoritism, partisanship, partiality, approval or disapproval . . . of any issue, worthy as it may be" (*Phillips v. Maurer*, 67 N.Y.2d 672 (1986); see also *Appeal of Hubbard*, 39 Educ. Dep't Rep. 363 (1999)).

This prohibition is not limited to advocating a "yes" vote. Even subtle promotional activities are prohibited (*Appeal of Meyer*, 38 Educ. Dep't Rep. 285 (1998)).

However, "it is not impermissible *per se* to state that rejection of the budget may result in the elimination of programs" (*Appeal of Julian*, 42 Educ. Dep't Rep. 300 (2003)). In addition, there is nothing wrong with stating, as fact, in a district newsletter, that a particular proposition has the "unanimous support of the board of education" if indeed that is the case (*Appeal of Brown*, 43 Educ. Dep't Rep. ___, dec. no. 14,980 (2003)).

4:45. May school board members acting in their personal capacity urge voters to vote in favor of a proposed school district budget or other ballot proposition?

Yes. School board members and other school officials, acting in their personal capacity, have the same right as any other member of the community to express their views on public issues. They may actively support a proposed budget and other ballot propositions, as long as they do so at their own expense and on their own behalf. In other words, they cannot use district funds, facilities, or channels of communication, or claim to be speaking on behalf of the board (*Appeal of Goldin*, 40 Educ. Dep't Rep. 628 (2001); see also *Appeal of Eisenkraft*, 38 Educ. Dep't Rep. 553 (1999); *Appeal of Dinan*, 36 Educ. Dep't Rep. 370 (1997); *Appeal of Carroll*, 33 Educ. Dep't Rep. 219 (1993); *Appeal of Weaver*, 28 Educ. Dep't Rep. 183 (1988); *Matter of Wolff*, 17 Educ. Dep't Rep. 297 (1978)).

In one case, for example, the commissioner found that while it would be improper for a board member to use the district's postage permit to mail partisan materials, there would be nothing improper about the same board member using his own private bulk mail permit to distribute campaign literature in support of candidates running for the board of education (*Appeal of Allen*, 39 Educ. Dep't Rep. 528 (2000)).

In another case, the commissioner dismissed an appeal filed against a school board where a board candidate inadvertently included a school district telephone number on a campaign flyer but did not actually use the district's telephone for campaign purposes (*Appeal of Grant*, 42 Educ. Dep't Rep. 184 (2002)).

4:46. May school districts provide factual materials to the voters about the school budget and other ballot propositions?

Yes. Districts may provide purely factual materials on the school budget or other ballot propositions through means aimed at reaching the electorate as a whole in order to help them make an informed decision (*Appeal of Prentice*, 38 Educ. Dep't Rep. 736 (1999); see also *Appeal of Loriz*, 27 Educ. Dep't Rep. 376 (1988)). In fact, school boards and school superintendents have a "statutory obligation to present and publicize school budgets so as to 'promote public comprehension'" (*Gersen v. Mills*, Sup. Ct., Albany Co., Special Term, Sheridan, J., Apr. 21, 2000, unreported, *rev'd on other grounds*, 290 A.D.2d 839 (3d Dep't 2002)). Such activities promote "the general public policy of this State to foster public awareness and understanding of governmental actions and to encourage participation therein" (*Gersen*, citing Pub. Off. Law § 84).

4:47. May a school board use a videotape to communicate budget information to the voters?

It depends. In one case, the commissioner of education admonished a district for using a promotional video to characterize as minimal the tax increase that would result from voter approval of the proposed budget. In the video, the superintendent stated, "The budget will result in a tax increase of *only* 1.9 percent." According to the commissioner, characterizing the percentage increase as "only" a given percentage sought "to persuade residents to vote in favor of the budget and propositions" (*Appeal of Hubbard*, 39 Educ. Dep't Rep. 363 (1999)).

In another case, however, the commissioner upheld a district's decision to allow various factions within the community to videotape the condition of school facilities in connection with a proposed bond proposition asking district voters to approve a major renovation project. The "sufficiency and condition" of the facilities were "obviously relevant" for voters to decide whether to approve the proposition and the district did not restrict access to videotaping of its facilities to anyone (*Appeal of Huber*, 41 Educ. Dep't Rep. 240 (2001), but compare *Appeal of Karpoff*, 40 Educ. Dep't Rep. 459

(2000), 192 Misc.2d 487 (2001), *aff'd*, 296 A.D.2d 691 (3d Dep't 2002), *appeal denied*, 99 N.Y.2d 501 (2002)).

4:48. What are some examples of improper budget advocacy by a school district?

Determining precisely what type of language constitutes improper advocacy can be difficult. For example, in one case, a district pamphlet included a statement indicating that a favorable vote on a bond referendum for school construction and renovation would "bring families back" to the community. The commissioner of education ruled that while the district's use of the statement "presents a close question . . . on balance . . . the statement is intended to persuade the public by promoting the positive consequences of a "yes" vote. It does not set forth objective facts designed to educate or inform the public. Thus, this statement constitutes improper advocacy." The commissioner then admonished the district "to refrain from speculating about the effect future proposals might have on bringing families back to the city in an attempt to persuade the public to take a particular position on such propositions" (*Appeal of D'Oronzio*, 41 Educ. Dep't Rep. 457 (2002)).

In yet another case, the commissioner of education admonished a district based on a letter from the superintendent that included the sentence: "*Unfortunately*, with a school budget defeat and the adoption of an austerity budget, we are not able to make these purchases or provide the services as stated above without voter authorization [emphasis added]." According to the commissioner, "[t]he use of '*unfortunately*,' in the context of the letter, could be construed as improper advocacy on behalf of the propositions and the use of such term or similar language should be avoided" (*Appeal of Schadtle*, 38 Educ. Dep't Rep. 599 (1999); see also *Appeal of Eckert*, 40 Educ. Dep't Rep. 433 (2000); and *Appeal of Miller*, 39 Educ. Dep't Rep. 348 (1999)).

In contrast, a court overturned a commissioner's decision, which held that a school district's use of the word "need" in informational materials describing the proposed school budget constituted improper advocacy (*Gersen v. Mills*, Sup. Ct., Albany Co., Special Term, Sheridan, J., Apr. 21, 2000, unreported, *rev'd on other grounds*, 290 A.D.2d 839 (3d Dep't 2002)). According to the court, the district was simply "explaining the reasons for various provisions in the budget, [and] such relatively neutral language neither advocates a position nor 'patently exhorts' the voters to cast their ballots in favor of the proposed budget." More recently, the commissioner ruled that a district report stating that "we educate children in hallways and converted closets. The overburdened cafeterias force them to have lunch at 10:40 in the morning or, at the high school, to go off campus to eat. There is not enough gym space . . ." constituted factual information and did not amount to improperly exhorting the electorate (*Appeal of Meyer & Mittlestaedt, Jr.*, 40 Educ. Dep't Rep. 34 (2000); see also *Appeal of Boni*, 41 Educ. Dep't Rep. 214 (2001)).

4:49. May school officials treat as "fact" statements about property values diminishing if the school budget is defeated at the polls?

No. Although there is a common perception in many communities that property values correspond directly with the quality of the public schools, the commissioner has directed school officials to "refrain from speculating about the effect future proposals might have on property values in an attempt to persuade the public to take a particular position" on a ballot proposition (*Appeal of Karpoff*, 40 Educ. Dep't Rep. 459 (2000), 192 Misc.2d 487 (2001), *aff'd*, 296 A.D.2d 691 (3d Dep't 2002), *appeal denied*, 99 N.Y.2d 501 (2002); see also *Appeal of Eckert*, 40 Educ. Dep't Rep. 433 (2000)).

4:50. What are some examples of communications by a school district that do not constitute improper budget advocacy?

General statements that a district's "extra-curricular activities in music, art, and sports have, again, been superlative" have been deemed "mere platitudes" that do "not exhort the electorate to vote in any particular way or otherwise convey favoritism, partisanship, partiality, approval or disapproval for the budget proposal or any particular candidates" (*Appeal of Carroll*, 42 Educ. Dep't Rep. 326 (2003)).

Similarly, the commissioner found nothing wrong with the following factual statement included in a description of the district's long-term facilities plan: ". . . we educate children in hallways and converted closets. The overburdened cafeterias force them to have lunch at 10:40 in the morning or, at the high school to go off campus to eat. There is not enough gym space. . ." (*Appeal of Meyer & Middlestadt, Jr.*, 40 Educ. Dep't Rep. 34 (2000)).

4:51. What happens if a district advocates on behalf of the proposed budget or other proposition?

If the commissioner of education finds that such advocacy affected the outcome of the vote, he or she may annul the results of the vote and order a new election (*Appeal of Leman*, 38 Educ. Dep't Rep. 683 (1999); see also 4:115). The commissioner also may remove from office school officials who engage in a willful violation of *Phillips v. Maurer* (67 N.Y.2d 672 (1986); see 2:34–35) or neglect their duty to adhere to the court's ruling in that case (see § 306(1)). In addition, the commissioner can withhold state funding from any district that willfully advocates on behalf of the proposed budget or other proposition (see § 306(2)).

4:52. Should districts avoid creating an "appearance of impropriety" when engaging in activities that technically do not constitute partisan advocacy?

Yes. According to the commissioner of education, districts should avoid engaging in activities that create an "appearance of impropriety," even if the activity itself technically does not violate the prohibition against partisan advocacy.

For example, in one case, the commissioner found that the use of district phones by students and administrators to call potential voters to encourage them to vote creates the appearance of improper partisan activity, where selective phone lists are used (*Appeal of Boni*, 40 Educ. Dep't Rep. 292 (2000); *Appeal of Schadtle*, 38 Educ. Dep't Rep. 599 (1999); see also *Appeal of Tortorello*, 29 Educ. Dep't Rep. 306 (1990)). However, in the absence of partisan phone lists, the use of district phones to remind residents to vote is not improper (*Appeal of Gang*, 32 Educ. Dep't Rep. 337 (1992); *Appeal of Boni;* see **4:119**).

4:53. Can school officials permit private individuals and organizations to use district facilities or channels of communication to encourage the electorate to vote in a particular way?

No. The commissioner of education has ruled that districts cannot do indirectly that which they cannot do directly. In general, this means that school officials can neither actively encourage nor tacitly permit anyone else to use district facilities or channels of communication to engage in promotional activities. School boards are "ultimately accountable for how district facilities and resources are used and must avoid even the appearance of impermissible partisan activity" (*Appeal of Maliha*, 41 Educ. Dep't Rep. 367 (2002); see also, *Appeal of McBride*, 39 Educ. Dep't Rep. 702 (2000); *Appeal of Karpoff*, 40 Educ. Dep't Rep. 459 (2000), 192 Misc.2d 487 (2001), *aff'd*, 296 A.D.2d 691 (3d Dep't 2002), *appeal denied*, 99 N.Y.2d 501 (2002)).

For example, the commissioner has ruled that a board of education should not make sets of mailing labels available to outside organizations in the absence of safeguards to ensure that such district resources will not be used to exhort the electorate to vote in a particular way (*Appeal of Allen*, 39 Educ. Dep't Rep. 528 (2000); see also *Appeal of Lawson*, 38 Educ. Dep't Rep. 713 (1999)).

However, a district may allow outside organizations to videotape facilities that are the subject of an upcoming vote on a capital project proposition, if the district does not single out specific organizations and provides such access to everyone (Appeal of Huber, 41 Educ. Dep't Rep. 240 (2001); *Appeal of Karpoff*).

In addition, the "mere presence" of a link on a district's Web site to another Web site where partisan views are advocated does not constitute an improper use of district communication channels; however, it is recommended that the district include a disclaimer on its Web site "to clarify that the district is not responsible for facts or opinions contained on any linked sites" (Appeal of Hager and Scheuerman, 43 Educ. Dep't Rep.___, dec. no. 15,019 (2004)).

4:54. Can school officials permit employee unions, staff, or students to use district facilities or channels of communication to encourage a particular vote?

No. Where a local teachers' union used school mailboxes to distribute flyers to union members urging them to vote for certain preferred board candidates, despite the fact that the superintendent told union leaders to desist and directed building principals to retrieve the flyers from the mailboxes upon learning of the distribution, the commissioner admonished the district to take steps to prevent other groups from taking similar action in the future (*Appeal of Van Allen*, 38 Educ. Dep't Rep. 701 (1999); see also *Appeal of Hoefer*, 41 Educ. Dep't Rep. 203 (2001); but compare with *Appeal of Huber*, 41 Educ. Dep't Rep. 240 (2001)).

Districts also must take affirmative steps to ensure that teachers and staff do not espouse partisan positions to students on school time on matters pending before the voters (*Appeal of Lawson*, 36 Educ. Dep't Rep. 450 (1997); compare with *Appeal of Roxbury Taxpayers Alliance*, 34 Educ. Dep't Rep. 576 (1995)), in which the commissioner ruled that there was nothing improper about a teacher explaining the meaning of a "contingency budget" to students in class because the teacher only provided factual information to the students).

However, according to the commissioner, school officials may permit student editors of a district-funded newspaper to editorialize in support of particular school board candidates or the proposed school budget, provided that the district does not act to influence the content of such editorials. Moreover, students may distribute literature on school grounds expressing their opinions about school budget votes and elections, subject to the imposition of reasonable restrictions by the district on the time, place, and manner of distribution; provided, however, that the district does not use district personnel or funds to support such activities (*Appeal of Doro*, 40 Educ. Dep't Rep. 281 (2000)).

4:55. May school officials allow the PTA and other organizations and individuals to use district facilities or channels of communication to disseminate nonpartisan information about board candidates and/or budget propositions?

Yes. The commissioner of education has stated that while districts may not allow PTAs to use district facilities or established channels of communication for partisan purposes, they may do so for informational and nonpartisan purposes (*Appeal of McBride*, 39 Educ. Dep't Rep. 702 (2000)).

In one case, the commissioner ruled that it was permissible for a school district to allow the PTA to distribute to students on school grounds a flyer consisting of copies of the biographies of each of the candidates running for the board of education, as well as their verbatim responses to a survey containing five questions that the commissioner found objective and nonpartisan. Specifically, the commissioner found that the "questions were broad and open-ended, and each candidate's response was distributed without editing, censoring or alteration." Under the circumstances, the commissioner concluded, "[T]he questions served to educate and inform the public about the candidate's positions and qualifications, and [did] not advocate a particular position." (*Appeal of Boni*, 41 Educ. Dep't Rep. 214 (2001)).

4:56. May a school district prohibit the distribution of anonymous literature on the school budget?

No. The United States Supreme Court ruled that a state statute that prohibited the distribution of anonymous literature violated the First Amendment. The literature at issue expressed opposition to a proposed school tax levy and did not identify the author, but rather purported to express the views of "concerned parents and taxpayers." The individual who distributed the literature was fined $100 after a school official filed a complaint against her with the Elections Commission for violating the state law that prohibited the distribution of campaign literature that did not contain the name and address of the person or campaign official issuing the literature (*McIntyre v. Ohio Elections Comm'n*, 514 U.S. 334 (1995)).

Election of School Board Members

4:57. How are school board candidates nominated for election?

Nominating petitions must be signed by at least 25 qualified district voters or 2 percent of the number of voters who voted in the previous annual election of the members of the board of education, whichever is greater (§ 2018(a)). In small city school districts, nominating petitions must be signed by at least 100 qualified voters (§ 2608(1)).

Ordinarily, nominating petitions are for specific seats on the school board (§ 2018(a)). However, district voters may choose to make all seats "at large," which means that each nominee is eligible for every vacancy, rather than only for a specific seat (§ 2018(b)) and nominating petitions do not state a specific seat (see *Appeal of Martin*, 32 Educ. Dep't Rep. 567 (1993)). A duly adopted "at large" proposition becomes effective at the next election and remains valid until repealed by the voters (§ 2018(b)).

Board members in small city school districts run "at large." The nominating petition must name the specific seat for which the board member is running only if the voters have adopted a proposition requiring candidates to run for specific seats (§ 2608(1)).

In districts where candidates run for specific seats, not only must the petition include the candidate's name and residence and the residences of the people who signed the petition, it must also identify the specific seat for which the candidate is running, including the name of the incumbent, and the length of the term of office to be filled (§§ 2018(a), 2608(1)). Candidates may be nominated for only one vacancy (§ 2018(a)).

For information about write-in candidates, please see **4:64–65**.

4:58. Must the nominating petition of an incumbent board member running for reelection identify the incumbent as the candidate in the petition?

Yes. In one case the commissioner of education ruled that an incumbent board member who sought reelection to his own seat and wrote his name in the space on the nominating petition identifying himself as the incumbent, technically violated the Education Law because he failed to list his name in the space identifying himself as the "candidate." However, the record established that as each person was asked to sign the nominating petition, the person gathering the signatures explained who was running and described the seat for which the candidate was running. Moreover, there was no proof that any voter was confused about who was seeking the nomination. Therefore the commissioner dismissed the challenge to the election (*Appeal of Grant*, 42 Educ. Dep't Rep. 184 (2002)).

4:59. Can a person who is not a registered voter sign a nominating petition for school board candidates?

Yes. While only qualified voters may sign a board candidate's nominating petition, a person need not be a registered voter to satisfy the legal definition of a "qualified voter." (*Appeal of Dreyer*, 18 Educ. Dep't Rep. 235 (1978); see also *Appeal of Crowley*, 39 Educ. Dep't Rep. 665

(2000)). If a person is a citizen of the United States, at least 18 years old, and a "resident" of the school district for at least 30 days immediately prior to the election at which he or she seeks to vote, then that person satisfies the legal definition of "qualified voter" and may sign nominating petitions, even if that person is not a registered voter and therefore would be unable to vote in a district that requires voter registration.

4:60. Can a person sign a nominating petition for more than one candidate for the same board seat?

Generally, yes. There is no limit on the number of nominating petitions a district resident may sign.

4:61. Do nominating petitions have to be verified?

Generally, no. In school districts that conduct their school board elections pursuant to the provisions of the Education Law, it is impermissible to require that nominating petitions be verified (*Appeal of Loughlin*, 35 Educ. Dep't Rep. 432 (1996)). However, in city school districts that may conduct certain aspects of their school board elections pursuant to provisions of the Election Law, different rules sometimes apply.

4:62. What is the deadline for the submission of nominating petitions?

Nominating petitions must be filed in the office of the district clerk no later than 30 days (20 days in small city school districts) before the annual or special district meeting at which the school board election will occur, between 9:00 a.m. and 5:00 p.m. (§§ 2018(a), 2608(1)). Notice of the deadline for filing nominating petitions must be published in the notice of the annual or special district meeting (§§ 2003(2), 2004(2), 2007(1), 2601-a(2), 2602(2); see also **4:11**). Under certain specified circumstances, the nominating deadline may be extended (see **4:66**).

Nothing in the Education Law specifies the earliest date that candidates may begin collecting signatures on nominating petitions. In one case, the commissioner ruled that it was not unreasonable for a district to accept nominating petitions that contained signatures collected prior to the posting of the notice of the annual meeting, absent evidence that this practice gave some candidates an unfair advantage over others (*Appeal of Leman*, 32 Educ. Dep't Rep. 579 (1993)).

If the deadline for filing nominating petitions falls on "a Saturday, Sunday or public holiday, the filing may be performed on the next succeeding business day" (Gen. Constr. Law § 25-a(1); see also *Appeal of Williams*, 36 Educ. Dep't Rep. 270 (1996)).

4:63. May the school board reject a nominating petition?

Yes. A nominating petition may be rejected if the nominating petition has been incorrectly filed, or if the candidate is ineligible for office or has declared an unwillingness to serve (§ 2035(2)). Although nominating petitions are presented to the district clerk, the board of education is authorized to determine whether a board candidate is eligible to serve and to reject a nominating petition from an ineligible candidate (*Appeal of Martin*, 31 Educ. Dep't Rep. 441 (1992)).

A failure to include the candidate's name and address or the specific seat or term of office on each page of a multi-sheet petition does not provide sufficient grounds to reject a nominating petition absent proof that persons signing the petition did not know what they were signing (*Appeal of Taubenfeld*, 18 Educ. Dep't Rep. 10 (1978)).

4:64. Must a person have filed a nominating petition in order to be elected?

No. A person need not file a nominating petition in order to be elected to serve on a board of education. All ballots must have one blank space for each vacancy on the board of education, in which voters may write in the name of any candidate who is not listed on the ballot (§§ 2032(2)(e), 2608(2)). If the ballot does not have an open space for write-in votes, and the outcome of the election is affected as a result of the omission, the election may be nullified by the commissioner of education (*Appeal of Bd. of Trustees of Syosset Pub. Library*, 32 Educ. Dep't Rep. 460 (1993)).

There is no requirement in the Education Law that a voter place a check mark or an "x" or any other kind of mark next to the name of the write-in candidate (*Appeal of Titus*, 36 Educ. Dep't Rep. 407 (1997); *Appeal of Gresty*, 31 Educ. Dep't Rep. 90 (1991)). If the name of a qualified person is written on a write-in ballot, it must be counted.

Write-in ballots with minor misspellings of a candidate's name should be credited to that candidate in the absence of a showing that there is another district resident with the same or a similar name (*Appeal of Cook*, 20 Educ. Dep't Rep. 1 (1980)).

Where voting machines are used, it is improper to require voters to cast write-in ballots in a separate ballot box (*Matter of Yost*, 21 Educ. Dep't Rep. 140 (1981)).

4:65. What happens if there are no candidates or not enough candidates properly nominated for each vacancy?

If this happens, the election must still be held, and the vacancies will be filled by the individuals with the most write-in votes (§§ 2032(2)(e), 2034(7)(a)). If there are not enough write-in candidates to fill vacancies, any remaining vacancy may be filled pursuant to the provisions of sections 1709(17), 2502(6), or 2113 of the Education Law (see **2:42–43**).

4:66. What happens if a candidate who has properly filed a nominating petition withdraws, dies, or becomes ineligible for office before the election?

If a board candidate, for whom a nominating petition has been duly filed, withdraws the petition, dies, or otherwise becomes ineligible to hold the office of board member at a point in time later than 15 days before the last day for the filing of nominating petitions, the district is required to extend the nominating deadline by as much as 15 days; provided, however, that in no event may nominating petitions be filed later than 5:00 p.m. on the seventh day before the date of the election (§§ 2018(d), 2608(1)).

4:67. May a candidate who withdraws from an election resubmit his or her candidacy?

Yes, but that person must file a new petition within the same time limitations applicable to other candidates (§ 2018(a)).

4:68. Are school board candidates required to file campaign expenditure statements?

Yes. If a school board candidate's campaign expenditures exceed $500, the candidate must file a sworn statement with both the district clerk and the commissioner of education itemizing their expenditures (§§ 1528–1531). This statement must list the amounts of all money or other valuable things paid, given, expended or promised by the candidate, or incurred for or on the candidate's behalf with his or her approval (§ 1528).

A candidate who spends $500 or less is only required to file a sworn statement with the district clerk indicating this to be the case (§ 1528). No other campaign expenditure statement is required (see **2:12**).

A preliminary statement must be filed at least 10 days before the election, and a final statement must be filed within 20 days after the election (§ 1529(1)). The statement must cover the period up to and including the day next preceding the day specified for the filing of the statement (§ 1529(2)).

4:69. What happens if a board candidate fails to file a campaign expenditure statement?

In the event that the appropriate statement is not filed with the district clerk, the law provides that the candidate must promptly file a copy of such statement upon notice from the school district and/or the commissioner that the statement was not received. If a candidate still fails to file the statement, then the only way the law can be enforced is for any other "candidate voted for at the election" or "any five qualified voters" to commence legal action in state Supreme Court requesting the court to order the candidate to file the required statements (§ 1530).

In other words, school officials can and should remind candidates to file the appropriate expenditure statements, but only the state Supreme Court has the authority to order candidates to file these statements (see *Appeal of Muench*, 38 Educ. Dep't Rep. 649 (1999); see also *Appeal of Donnelly*, 33 Educ. Dep't Rep. 362 (1993)).

A candidate's failure to file a complete statement of election expenditures is an insufficient basis for setting aside the results of a school board election (See *Appeal of Muench*, 38 Educ. Dep't Rep. 649 (1999); see also *Appeal of Guttman*, 32 Educ. Dep't Rep. 228 (1992); *Matter of Pendergast*, 20 Educ. Dep't Rep. 127 (1980)).

4:70. How are school board members elected?

School board members are elected by a plurality of the votes cast for each vacancy (§§ 2034(7)(a)), 2502(9)(n), (9-a)(n), 2610(4)). In districts with "at-large" seats, if there are vacant positions of different lengths, positions are filled in decreasing order of the number of votes and length of office (§§ 2034(7)(c), 2502(9)(n), (9-a)(n), 2610(4)). Thus, the candidate with the highest number of votes is entitled to the position of the longest length.

Moreover, the law provides that where the term of office for a school board seat expires at the end of the school year, and the seat is vacant, or becomes vacant on the date of the annual meeting and election, "the person elected to fill the full term vacancy is deemed elected to fill the remainder of the term preceding the commencement of the full term"(§ 2105(14)). In other words, if the seat is vacant as of the date of the annual meeting and election, the winning candidate does not wait until the term of office expires on June 30 to begin serving in that seat. He or she takes the oath of office and immediately begins serving in that seat. This provision of law has added significance in districts where board candidates run "at-large," because the term of office for a board seat that is or becomes vacant as of the day of the election, when added to the full term of office, will be the seat with the longest term of office, and as such, must be awarded to the candidate with the highest number of votes.

In city school districts with 125,000 or more inhabitants, school board elections are conducted in accordance with section 2553 of the Education Law.

4:71. Must candidates' names appear on the ballot in any particular order?

Yes. Candidates' names must be grouped together in order, as determined by the drawing of lots, either under the specific vacancy for which they have been nominated, or all together for at-large seats. The district clerk conducts the drawing "the day after the last possible date for candidates to file a petition. In the event that any candidate is not present in person or by a person designated in a written proxy to accomplish the drawing, the district clerk shall be authorized to act as proxy" (§§ 2032(2)(b), 2608(2); see *Koppell v. New York State Bd. of Elections*, 108 F.Supp.2d 355 (S.D.N.Y. 2000)).

However, the commissioner of education has ruled that the failure of the district clerk to draw lots for placement on the ballot by the statutory deadline was a technical error that did not affect the outcome of the election (*Appeal of Reese*, 34 Educ. Dep't Rep. 187 (1994); see also *Appeal of Olivia*, 16 Educ. Dep't Rep. 355 (1977)). He also has dismissed an appeal from a losing candidate who failed to prove that she lost the election because a district's printer mistakenly printed the candidates' names on the ballot in the wrong order (*Appeal of Apgar*, 43 Educ. Dep't Rep.___, dec. no. 15,015 (2004)).

4:72. Are there special ballot requirements in elections where board members run for "specific seats?"

Yes. The Education Law requires that "at the top of each group" of candidates running for separate specific seats on a school board there must be a description that includes, at a minimum, "the length of the term of office and the name of the last incumbent, if any, and in addition, a direction that only one vote may be cast in each separate group" (§ 2032(2(b); see also *Appeal of Mead*, 42 Educ. Dep't Rep. 359 (2003); *Appeal of Kuschner and Pinto*, 39 Educ. Dep't Rep. 770 (2000)).

4:73. Who gives official notice of school board election results?

The chairperson of the meeting at which the election takes place declares the result of each ballot, as announced by the election inspectors (§ 2034(7)(a)). If the district has been divided into election districts and voting machines are used, the election inspectors must report the results to the chief election inspector of each district, who then reports the results to the district clerk within 24 hours. The school board must then tabulate and declare the result of the ballot within 24 hours of receiving the results (§ 2034(7)(b)).

The school district clerk, in turn, must notify in writing every person elected as a school board member (§§ 2108(1), 2121(5), 2610(5)). However, the presence of a person elected to the board at the district meeting at which he or she is elected is considered sufficient legal notice to the candidate of his or her election (§ 2108(2)).

The district clerk also must report the names and post office addresses of elected board members to the town clerk of the town where the district is situated. There is a $5 penalty for failing to do so (§ 2121(5)).

4:74. What happens if an election vote is tied?

If there is a tie vote for a board seat, the district must have a run-off election within 45 days. The only candidates in a run-off election are those who tied. No new nominating petitions are required (§§ 2034(10), 2610(6)).

4:75. Must newly elected school board members officially accept their election to office?

No. Newly elected school board members are considered to have accepted the office unless they file a written refusal with the school district clerk within five days after receiving notice of their election. However, they must take and file an oath of office prior to commencing service on the board (see **4:76**).

4:76. When does a newly-elected board member take office?

A new board member takes office when the incumbent's term of office expires, or if the seat is vacant at the time of the election, immediately after the election (§ 2105(14)).

However, the new board member must file an oath of office (NYS Const. Art. 13, § 1; Pub. Off. Law § 10; see **2:11**). If a new member has not filed an oath of office or is otherwise not qualified to take office when the term begins, the incumbent "holds over" in office until the new member becomes "qualified," that is, takes all the steps necessary to take office (Pub. Off. Law § 5; see *Appeal of Foshee*, 38 Educ. Dep't Rep. 346 (1998); see also *Matter of Waxman*, 19 Educ. Dep't Rep. 157 (1979)).

The failure or neglect of a board member to file an oath of office within 30 days after the commencement of his or her term causes the office to become vacant (Pub. Off. Law § 30(1)(h); see, for example, *Appeal of Rausch*, 41 Educ. Dep't Rep. 351 (2002); see also *Appeal of Karpen*, 39 Educ. Dep't Rep. 99 (1999)).

4:77. What happens if there is a dispute over the results of a school board election?

All disputes over any district meeting or election must be referred to the commissioner of education (§ 2037). "Once the results of an election are declared, there is no authority in the elections officials or the voters to recanvass the results" (*Appeal of LaValley*, 12 Educ. Dep't Rep. 33 (1972)).

The commissioner may, at his discretion, order a recount of the ballots or a new election (§§ 2034(6)(a), 2037; *Appeal of Murtagh*, 19 Educ. Dep't

Rep. 179 (1979)). Only the commissioner has the authority to order a recount of a vote on a school board election (*Appeal of Doro*, 41 Educ. Dep't Rep. 13 (2001); see also *Matter of Senecal*, 22 Educ. Dep't Rep. 367 (1983); but see *Appeal of Ell*, 34 Educ. Dep't Rep. 394 (1995); see also **4:115**).

4:78. What impact does a successful challenge to the results of a school board election have on the actions taken by the board pending appeal?

In such cases, the commissioner of education has determined that the person initially declared the winner is a *de facto* board member during the period of time that an appeal of the election results is pending. Therefore, the actions taken by the board during the pendency of the appeal are valid (*Appeal of Titus*, 36 Educ. Dep't Rep. 407 (1997); see also *Appeal of Loughlin*, 35 Educ. Dep't Rep. 432 (1996); and *Appeal of Heller*, 34 Educ. Dep't Rep. 220 (1994)).

Special School District Meetings

4:79. What is a special school district meeting?

A *special school district meeting* is a meeting of the qualified voters of the district called for a specific purpose or purposes, such as resubmitting the district budget for a re-vote or conducting an election to fill a vacancy on the board of education (§§ 2006–2008).

4:80. Must special school district meetings be held at a specific time?

Unlike the annual meeting and election, there is no date designated by law for holding special school district meetings. Moreover, the meeting generally need not continue for any specific period of time, so long as enough time is allowed for all voters present at the meeting to vote on the matters before them (see *Appeal of Faulkner*, 16 Educ. Dep't Rep. 93 (1976)).

However, in small city school districts, a special district meeting must be held at least nine consecutive hours beginning not earlier than 7:00 a.m., at least two hours of which must be after 6:00 p.m. (§ 2602(3)).

In addition, in union free and central school districts, a special district meeting for the purpose of electing school board members must be held for at least six consecutive hours between 7:00 a.m. (as opposed to 6:00 a.m. for annual elections) and 9:00 p.m., at least two hours of which must be after 6:00 p.m. Such an election may go longer than the statutory six hours so long as proper notice is given (§ 2007(4)). In one case, the commissioner of education upheld the results of a special district meeting held until after 10:00 p.m. (*Appeal of Demos*, 34 Educ. Dep't Rep. 54 (1994)).

4:81. How are special school district meetings called?

Generally, special district meetings are called by the school board when the board deems it necessary and proper (§§ 2006(1), 2007(1), 2602(2)), or when petitioned by 25 voters or 5 percent of those voting in the previous annual election, whichever is greater (§ 2008(2)).

The commissioner of education and district superintendent also have authority to call special meetings under certain circumstances as set forth in law (§§ 2005, 2008(1), 2113(2)).

4:82. May a school board refuse a voter's petition to call a special school district meeting?

Yes. A school board may refuse to call a special school district meeting if its purpose is to address matters not within the power of the voters (see § 2021); if its purpose is illegal; if the petition for such a meeting was not filed within 20 days of publication of the passage of a bond or note resolution, pursuant to Local Finance Law section 81.00 (see, for example, *Appeal of Johnson*, 41 Educ. Dep't Rep. 407 (2002); or if the district asserts another valid reason for refusing to call the requested meeting, subject to review by the commissioner (§ 2008(2)(a-d)).

However, school boards must either accept or reject petitions for a special school district meeting within 20 days of their submission (§ 2008(2); see *Appeal of French*, 32 Educ. Dep't Rep. 100 (1992)). If a petition is accepted, notice of the meeting must be given within 20 days of the petition's receipt (§ 2008(2)).

4:83. What notice must be given to the public regarding a special school district meeting?

In common school districts, notice of a special district meeting must be given to each resident by the district clerk (by hand delivery to their residence) at least six days before the meeting, unless district residents have voted at a district meeting to use another method. In the alternative, notice can be published in two newspapers (or one if there is only one) having general circulation once each week during the four weeks prior to the meeting, with the first publication at least 22 days before the meeting. If no newspaper is available, notice must be posted in at least 20 public places between 22 and 28 days before the meeting (§ 2006(1), (2)).

All other school districts must include the same items of information in the notice of a special district meeting as are required in the notice of annual meeting, which are applicable to the purpose or purposes for which the special district meeting was called (§§ 2006, 2007, 2004; see **4:11**).

4:84. When must notice be given to the public regarding a special school district meeting?

In general, notice of a special school district meeting must be published or posted in the same manner and following the same timeline required for the notice of the annual meeting: 45 days ahead of the meeting, with publication once each week for four weeks in two newspapers of general circulation (§ 2007(1); see also **4:11**).

However, there are two circumstances when a full 45-day notice of a special district meeting is not required:

- when a special meeting is called to "re-vote" on the same budget, a modified budget, or certain propositions after a defeated budget; or
- when the board of education rejects all bids for a contract or contracts for public work, transportation, or purchase, and the board deems it necessary and proper to call a special district meeting to take appropriate action.

Under either of these two circumstances, notice of the special district meeting is required only two weeks in advance, by publishing notice once each week during the two weeks before the vote, with the first publication being 14 days before the vote (§ 2007(3)(a)).

Districts should be mindful, however, that the law requires them to hold a public hearing seven to 14 days prior to any special district meeting at which a budget vote will occur (§§ 1608(1), 1716(1) 2022(1); see **4:27–28**). In addition, the law requires districts to mail a budget notice to all qualified voters in the district after the date of the public hearing, but no later than six days prior to a special district meeting at which a school budget vote will occur (§ 2022(2-a); see **4:29**). Therefore, as a practical matter, when preparing to hold a special district meeting for a budget re-vote, districts must allow time for a public hearing, mailing of the required budget notice, and newspaper publication of the notice of the special district meeting.

4:85. How is a special school district meeting conducted?

A special school district meeting is conducted in the same way as the annual meeting and election: the chairperson of a special school district meeting is appointed in the same manner and calls the meeting to order (see **4:9**). Written records of the proceedings must be kept, and the district clerk serves as the clerk of the meeting (§ 2025).

Qualifications of Voters

4:86. Who is a qualified voter?

A *qualified voter* is a person who is a citizen of the United States, at least 18 years old, a resident of the school district for at least 30 days prior to the meeting at which he or she offers to vote, and who is not otherwise prohibited from voting under the provisions of section 5-106 of the Election Law (for example, a person who has been adjudged to be mentally incompetent). Only qualified voters of the school district may vote on a question brought before an annual meeting and election or special school district meeting (§§ 2012, 2603).

A person need not be a registered voter to satisfy the legal definition of a "qualified voter" (*Appeal of Dreyer*, 18 Educ. Dep't Rep. 235 (1978); see also *Appeal of Crowley*, 39 Educ. Dep't Rep. 665 (2000); see **4:59**). Owning a home in a school district does not necessarily make the owner a district resident for purposes of being considered a qualified voter eligible to participate in school district annual or special school district meeting or election. "A person may have only one legal residence or domicile, and that is the place where such person intends to have his or her permanent residence or home. The residency of dual home owners is dependent on the intent and conduct of the owner" (*Appeal of Taylor*, 39 Educ. Dep't Rep. 712 (2000)).

School districts may not require voters to pay taxes or have children attending the public schools to be eligible to vote *(Kramer v. Union Free Sch. Dist. No. 15*, 395 U.S. 621 (1969)). Military personnel residing on a military base may also be qualified voters in the school district where that base is located (*Appeal of Kuleszo*, 30 Educ. Dep't Rep. 465 (1991)).

4:87. Is a convicted felon eligible to vote at a school district meeting and election?

It depends. A convicted felon has a right to vote, provided that he or she has been pardoned, his or her maximum prison sentence has expired, or he or she has been discharged from parole (Elec. Law § 5-106(2)).

4:88. What happens if an unqualified person votes or lies about his or her qualifications to vote?

The district may sue unqualified voters for a fine of $10 to be used for the benefit of the district (§ 2020(3)). In addition, a person who willfully makes a false statement about his or her qualifications to vote is guilty of a misdemeanor (§ 2020(1), (2)), and may be subject to a fine of up to $1,000 and/or imprisonment for up to one year (Penal Law §§ 55.10(2)(b), 70.15(1), 80.05(1)).

If it appears that the election results were affected by votes cast by unqualified persons, the commissioner may invalidate the vote and require a special meeting or election (*Appeal of Cobb*, 32 Educ. Dep't Rep. 139 (1992); see **4:115**).

Voter Registration

4:89. Must qualified voters be registered to vote in a school district meeting or election?

Yes. However, in districts that use personal registration, qualified voters can be registered with the school district's board of registration or with the county board of elections in order to vote (see also **4:90, 4:121**).

4:90. Must school districts have a system of personal registration?

No. But school boards in union free, central, and small city school districts may decide to provide for personal registration of voters in their districts (§§ 2014, 2606). Boards that adopt a resolution providing for personal registration must notify the appropriate board of elections within five days of the adoption (Elec. Law § 5-612(4)). They also must notify the board of elections at least 45 days before the date of the annual district meeting and election, and at least 14 days before the date of any special district meeting (Elec. Law § 5-612(5)).

4:91. In districts with personal registration, must voters be registered with the school district in order to vote?

Not necessarily. Although school districts may have a system of personal voter registration (§§ 2014, 2606), individuals registered to vote with the county board of elections are eligible to vote at school district meetings without further registration (Elec. Law § 5-612(2); see also *Appeal of Muench*, 38 Educ. Dep't Rep. 649 (1999); and *Appeal of Shortell*, 27 Educ. Dep't Rep. 190 (1987)).

The county board of elections is required to provide a list of voters to the school district at least 30 days prior to any regularly scheduled election, and a supplemental list at least 10 days before any regular or special election (Elec. Law § 5-612(3)).

4:92. When and where does personal registration take place?

The time and location of voter registration is set by school board resolution. However, the last day of registration must not be more than 14 days nor less than five days before the annual district meeting and election. Such registration must be open for at least four consecutive hours between 7:00 a.m. and 8:00 p.m. (§ 2014(2)).

The board of registration also must conduct registration at the annual meeting and election for the purpose of registering voters to vote in *future* school district elections (§ 2014(2)). However, it is improper for a school district to allow any person who registers with the district on election day to vote in the election occurring on that day (*Appeal of Collins*, 39 Educ. Dep't Rep. 226 (1999)).

Registration of voters prior to a special district meeting must occur not more than seven days nor less than two days before the date of the meeting (§ 2007(3)(b)) (for information about voter registration in small city school districts, see Educ. Law § 2606).

Subject to approval of the district voters, districts also may authorize registration during the same hours children may be enrolled for a school term or during specified hours of the school day at the office of the district clerk or assistant clerk or at the district's business office (§ 2014(2)).

4:93. May teachers register eligible students to vote in district elections?

Yes. In one case, the commissioner dismissed a complaint alleging that it was improper for a teacher to participate in registering high school seniors to vote in school district elections. According to the commissioner: "There is nothing inherently wrong with registering a student to vote provided the student is not directed to vote a certain way" (*Appeal of Hoefer*, 41 Educ. Dep't Rep. 203 (2001)).

4:94. What information is included in the voter registration list?

The registration list used for each district meeting must include the name of everyone who has registered to vote at the meeting, and may include anyone who has registered and voted in prior school district meetings in the preceding four calendar years. However, the name of anyone who has died or moved out of the school district, or become otherwise ineligible to vote, must be removed (§ 2014(2)). The registration list must include the name and street address of each voter on the list, arranged alphabetically by last name. If there is no street address, some description must be included that accurately locates the place of residence. It also must have a column or columns in which to indicate whether each person listed has voted previously in any school district election or elections or at any meetings (§ 2014(2)).

The registration list is not the same thing as a poll list (see **4:111**).

4:95. Who prepares the voter registration list?

This is prepared by the school district's board of registration (§ 2014(2)). This board consists of four qualified voters of the district appointed annually by the school board, not later than 30 days after the district's annual meeting or election, who serve until 30 days after the annual meeting or election the following year. The board of registration is entitled to compensation at a rate fixed by the school board for each day actually and necessarily spent on the duties of the office (§ 2014(1)).

4:96. Must school districts make voter registration lists available for public inspection?

Yes. Voter registration lists must be filed in the office of the district clerk at least five days before any school district meeting or election and must be open to public inspection by any qualified voter at all reasonable times and days of the week, except Sunday, up to and including the day of the election (§ 2015(1)).

4:97. May a school district discontinue its system of personal registration?

Yes. The board may discontinue personal registration by a board resolution passed at least two months before the next school district meeting or election. However, personal registration may not then be re-instituted without voter approval (§ 2014(3)).

The Voting Process

4:98. Do the provisions of the New York State Election Law apply to school districts?

The Election Law applies to school districts only as specifically provided by law (Elect. Law § 1-102; see also Educ. Law § 2609; *Appeal of Brown,* 43 Educ. Dep't Rep. ___, dec. no. 14,980 (2003)). In general, the Education Law governs school district meetings and elections, not the Election Law (Article 41).

4:99. Must voting booths be used at school board elections and budget votes?

Yes, in districts other than common school districts (§§ 2030(2), 2609(3)).

4:100. Must ballots be used in school board elections and budget votes?

Generally, yes. However, in school districts that prior to 1998 conducted their vote at the annual meeting, votes may be taken by recording the ayes and nays of the qualified voters attending and voting at the district meeting (§§ 2022(3), 2608, 2031, 2032).

4:101. May voting machines be used at the annual meeting and election or special school district meetings?

Yes. Although the use of voting machines is optional, it is considered to be in compliance with any provision of law requiring the vote to be by ballot (§§ 2035(1), 2611; *Hurd v. Nyquist*, 72 Misc.2d 213 (1972); *Matter of Nicoletti*, 21 Educ. Dep't Rep. 38 (1981)).

If voting machines are used, they must be examined by election inspectors before each use to ensure all the counters are set at zero, that the ballot labels are properly placed, and that each machine is in all respects in proper condition for use (§ 2035(1); see also *Appeal of Breud*, 38 Educ. Dep't Rep. 748 (1999)).

4:102. Who provides the ballots or voting machines used at school district meetings?

Ballots are provided by the school district. When used for school board elections, ballots must contain the names of candidates who have been nominated, listed in the order determined by drawing lots (§§ 2032(2)(e), 2608(2); see also **4:71**). If paper ballots are used, a choice is indicated by an "x" or a "√" by pencil or pen in a square before the name of the candidate. Regardless of whether paper ballots or voting machines are used, one blank space, must be provided under the name of the last candidate for each specific office for write-in candidates (§ 2032(2)(e); see also **4:64**).

A voting machine or machines may be purchased by the school district or, with the consent of the county board of elections, the school district may use voting machines belonging to the county or the town in which any part of the school district is located. Rental and other terms or conditions are set by resolutions of the board of elections (§ 2035(1); Elec. Law § 3-224).

4:103. May school districts be divided into election districts?

Yes. Union free and central school districts with personal registration of voters may be divided into election districts by action of the board or by a majority vote of the qualified voters present and voting at a district meeting (§ 2017(1); see also *Matter of Clarke*, 13 Educ. Dep't Rep. 256 (1974)). Each election district must have at least 300 qualified voters, and if possible, have a school building (§ 2017(1), (2)).

Once the decision is made, the school board must immediately adopt a resolution dividing the district into the number of election districts as it may determine. The election districts so formed continue in existence until modified by board resolution (§ 2017(2)). However, any such resolution must be adopted at least 30 days before the annual or special meeting or election. Voters then vote within their respective election districts.

Boards of education in small city school districts may pass a resolution modifying election districts already in existence. As with union free and central school districts, election districts in small city school districts should contain a public schoolhouse where possible, in which voting shall take place. A city school district with less than 10,000 inhabitants may designate the entire school district as a single election district (§ 2604).

4:104. May proxy votes be cast at school district meetings?

No. There is no statutory authority permitting the use of proxy votes at school district meetings (*Matter of Kirchhof*, 70 St. Dep't Rep. 33 (1949); *Matter of Dist. No. 1 of the Town of Pittstown*, 58 St. Dep't Rep. 423 (1937)).

4:105. May school districts conduct exit polls at the polling place?

There is nothing improper about conducting an "exit poll" at a polling place so long as voter access to the polls is not hampered (*Appeal of Tudor*, 38 Educ. Dep't Rep. 591 (1999)).

4:106. Must there be election inspectors at school district meetings?

Yes. There must be at least two election inspectors for each ballot box or voting machine in use (§ 2025(3)). It is their responsibility to count the ballots and tally and count the votes cast (*Appeal of Murtaugh*, 19 Educ. Dep't Rep. 179 (1979); see also § 2034; **4:113–114**).

In common school districts, election inspectors are elected by the voters. The election inspectors choose a chief election inspector (§ 2025(3)(a)).

In union free and central school districts, the board of education appoints the election inspectors, and also appoints assistant election inspectors, as needed, in connection with the conduct of a district meeting and election. The board also designates a chief election inspector. Where the district is divided into election districts, the board must appoint a chief election inspector for each election district (§ 2025(3)(b)).

In small city school districts, the board of education is required to appoint three qualified voters to serve as election inspectors for each election district, and may appoint additional election inspectors if necessary. The inspectors themselves elect one of their number as chairperson. The chairperson may appoint one of the inspectors as assistant poll clerk (§ 2607).

The failure to appoint the required number of election inspectors can invalidate a school district election only if the error affects the outcome of the election (*Appeal of Uciechowski*, 32 Educ. Dep't Rep. 511 (1993)).

Nothing in the Education Law prohibits district employees, school board members, relatives of board members or candidates from serving as election inspectors (*Appeal of Goldman*, 35 Educ. Dep't Rep. 126 (1995); *Appeal of*

Bleier, 32 Educ. Dep't Rep. 63 (1992); see also *Appeal of Crowley*, 39 Educ. Dep't Rep. 665 (2000)).

4:107. Are election inspectors entitled to compensation?

Election inspectors in union free and central school districts are compensated at a rate set by the board of education (§ 2025(5)). Election inspectors in small city school districts are compensated at a rate set by the board of education, not to exceed the basic compensation paid to election inspectors at the preceding general election, as fixed by the governing body of the city in which the school district is located (§ 2607).

4:108. May a school board candidate appoint poll watchers?

Yes, but only in school districts that have adopted a system of personal registration (§ 2019-a(2)(c), (d)). There is no authority for a candidate to appoint poll watchers in districts without personal registration (*Appeal of Chaplin, Jr.*, 30 Educ. Dep't Rep. 420 (1991)).

4:109. What happens if people are still in line waiting to vote at the time for closing the polls?

All qualified voters who are present at the polling place must be allowed to vote (§§ 2033, 2609(4); see also *Appeal of Fugle*, 32 Educ. Dep't Rep. 480 (1993)).

4:110. Must a written record be kept of the proceedings at an annual or special school district meeting or election?

Yes. The clerk and assistant clerk(s) of district meetings must keep a true and accurate written record of all of the proceedings of the district meeting or election and file a written record with the district clerk within 24 hours after the meeting (§§ 2025(4), 2121(1)).

Generally, the district clerk serves as the clerk of all district meetings and elections (§ 2025(3)). In common school districts, the voters elect assistant clerks as necessary. In union free and central school districts, the school board may appoint an acting clerk in the absence or disability of the district clerk, and also may appoint assistant clerks as is necessary in connection with the conduct of a district meeting and election. Such clerks may be compensated at a rate set by the board (§ 2025(3), (5)).

4:111. Must a poll list be made of those voting at school district meetings?

Yes. The district clerk or assistant clerk(s) maintain a poll list that contains the names and addresses of the people who actually vote in a district meeting or election. The clerk or assistant clerk(s) must record the name and legal residences of all voters as they deposit their ballots (§§ 2029, 2609(4); see *Appeal of Gang*, 32 Educ. Dep't Rep. 337 (1992)).

However, a school district's technical failure to maintain a complete and accurate poll list is no basis to invalidate an election, absent proof that this irregularity affected the outcome of the election (*Appeal of Crowley*, 39 Educ. Dep't Rep. 665 (2000); *Appeal of Diamond*, 39 Educ. Dep't Rep. 541 (2000)).

Moreover, discrepancies between the machine count and the sign-in sheets at the conclusion of an election do not necessarily require that the commissioner invalidate an election absent evidence "that the outcome of the election was affected by the apparent failure of some voters to sign the poll list." (*Appeals of Campbell & Coleman*, 41 Educ. Dep't Rep. 207 (2001)).

4:112. Are poll lists subject to public inspection?

Yes. Poll lists are public documents that must be made available for inspection and copying, including on the day of the election. However, on the day of the election, districts must take special care to provide access to the poll list(s) in an evenhanded manner and with minimal disruption to the electoral process (*Appeal of Walsh*, 34 Educ. Dep't Rep. 544 (1995); *Appeal of Schneider*, 29 Educ. Dep't Rep. 151 (1989); see also *Appeal of Crowley*, 39 Educ. Dep't Rep. 665 (2000)).

4:113. How are votes counted?

The election inspectors count the ballots and tally the votes (*Appeal of Murtagh*, 19 Educ. Dep't Rep. 179 (1979); see also § 2034). The inspectors first must count the ballots to determine if they agree with the number of names recorded on the voter list. If they exceed that number, enough ballots must be withdrawn at random by the chief election inspector to reduce the number of ballots to the number of voters. The inspectors then conduct the final ballot count and inform the chairperson of the results of the meeting (§ 2034; see § 2610 as to the procedure for canvassing the vote in small city school districts).

In one case, the school attorney read the voting machine counters, instead of the district's election inspectors. However, this was done in view of the election inspectors, and the tallies were then written onto the tabulation sheet by the chief election inspector, who declared the result and gave the tabulation sheet to the chairperson. Under the circumstances, the commissioner of education found that the deviation from the law was "*de minimis*" and refused to invalidate the vote absent proof that the any irregularity resulted "in an inaccurate vote tally or otherwise affected the outcome of the election" (*Appeal of Grant*, 42 Educ. Dep't Rep. 184 (2002)).

4:114. Who announces the results of the vote count?

The chairperson of the meeting at which the election takes place declares the result of each ballot, as announced by the election inspectors (§ 2034(7)(a)).

If a district has been divided into election districts, and voting machines are used, the election inspectors must make a written report of the results, signed by all the inspectors, to the chief election inspector of each district, who then reports the results to the district clerk within 24 hours. The school board then tabulates and declares the result of the ballot within 24 hours of receiving the results (§ 2034(7)(b)).

4:115. What happens if a school district election is found to have been improperly held?

The commissioner of education may set aside the election results and/or may order the district to conduct a new election (§ 2037). However, there is a presumption of regularity in the conduct of school district elections. The burden of proof rests on the person who challenges the results to establish all the facts based upon which he or she seeks to have the commissioner overturn the election results.

First, the challenger must first prove that the district engaged in improper conduct, such as a violation of the Education Law or commissioner's regulations. "Mere speculation as to the possible existence of irregularities provides an insufficient basis on which to annul election results" (*Appeal of DeBerardinis*, 39 Educ. Dep't Rep. 145 (1999)).

Second, the challenger must prove that the improper activity engaged in by the district actually affected the outcome of the election. If the improper activity occurred but did not affect the outcome of the election, the commissioner may admonish the district, but usually will decline to overturn the results of the election.

Although this standard has been upheld in court (*Appeal of Karpoff*, 40 Educ. Dep't Rep. 459 (2000), 192 Misc.2d 487 (2001), *aff'd*, 296 A.D.2d 691 (3d Dep't 2002)), *appeal denied*, 99 N.Y.2d 501 (2002)), on rare occasions, the commissioner has departed from it. In one case where the commissioner invalidated certain absentee ballots and the vote on a library voting proposition ended in a tie, he ordered a new vote even through there was no proof that the invalidated absentee ballots actually cast a vote on the library proposition. The commissioner found "the probability that the will of the voters was not expressed, because of illegally cast absentee votes, to be too high to allow the election results to stand" (*Appeal of the Weller Library Comm'n*, 42 Educ. Dep't Rep. 338 (2003); see also *Appeal of Cobb*, 32 Educ. Dep't Rep. 139 (1992)).

Alternatively, a challenger may be able to overturn the results of an election if the challenger can prove irregularities occurred that were "so pervasive that they vitiated the electoral process" or can "demonstrate a clear and convincing picture of informality to the point of laxity in adherence to the Education Law." The commissioner has made it clear, however, that "it is a rare case where errors in the conduct of the election become so pervasive that they vitiate the fundamental fairness of the election" (*Appeal of Huber*, 41 Educ. Dep't Rep. 240 (2001); *Appeal of D'Oronzio*, 41 Educ. Dep't Rep. 457 (2002); *Appeal of De Berardinis*).

4:116. How long must school boards keep district meeting and elections records?

The "Records Retention and Disposition Schedule ED-1" (8 NYCRR § 185.12 "Appendix I"; see **2:93**), which all school districts and boards of cooperative educational services (BOCES) must follow, sets forth specific periods of time that various types of school elections records must be maintained. For example, "final election results, including election inspectors' return and statement of canvass (where information is not duplicated in report of final election results) and election results report" must be *permanently* maintained. "Intermediate records used to compile final election results, including tally sheets and voting machine tabulations" must be maintained for one year after the election, or, if the election is contested, until any investigation and/or litigation is complete.

Schedule ED-1 is available on the following Web site: http://www.nysarchives.org/a/nysaservices/ns_mgr_pub_ed1.shtml#Top. Or contact the State Archives and Records Administration (SARA) at Local Government Records Services, SARA, 10A63 Cultural Education Center, Albany, N.Y. 12230; Telephone: 518-474-6926; Fax: 518-486-4923.

In addition, in districts that use paper ballots and ballot boxes, the Education Law further requires that after the election is over and the results have been announced, the election inspectors must lock and seal the ballot boxes, and the chief election inspector must deliver them to the district clerk. Thereafter, the ballot boxes cannot be opened, except: (1) upon order of the commissioner; or (2) after the elapse of a period of six months without challenge to the election, the board passes a resolution ordering the opening of the ballot boxes and the destruction of the ballots therein (§ 2034(6)).

Electioneering

4:117. Is electioneering permitted during school board elections or when voting on the school budget or propositions?

No. The Education Law prohibits electioneering on the day of the election within a 100-foot zone measured from the entrance to the polling place (§§ 2031-a, 2609(4-a)). District elections inspectors are required to post distance markers delineating the 100-foot zone (§§ 2031-a(1), 2609(4-a)(a); *Cullen v. Fliegner*, 18 F.3d 96 (2nd Cir. 1994)).

4:118. What constitutes electioneeering?

Electioneering includes, but is not limited to, such activity as distributing or displaying a candidate's campaign materials or materials in support of or in opposition to any proposition. It should be noted, however, that the law specifically allows a board of education to display within any polling place a copy or copies of any budget or proposition to be voted upon (§§ 2031-a(2), 2609(4-a)(b)). In addition, the commissioner of education has ruled that districts do not engage in electioneering when they distribute purely factual materials at polling places (see *Appeal of VanAllen*, 38 Educ. Dep't Rep. 701 (1999); see also *Appeal of Leman*, 38 Educ. Dep't Rep. 683 (1999); *Appeal of Hart*, 34 Educ. Dep't Rep. 299 (1994); *Appeal of Tomkins*, 34 Educ. Dep't Rep. 174 (1994)).

4:119. What are some examples of activities that do not constitute electioneering?

The meeting of a partisan group in a schoolhouse during the hours of an election in and of itself does not constitute electioneering (*Appeal of Giuliano*, 37 Educ. Dep't Rep. 572 (1998)). Similarly, the mere presence of partisan officials at a polling place in and of itself does not constitute electioneering (*Appeal of Loriz*, 35 Educ. Dep't Rep. 231 (1995)).

In addition, calling potential voters to encourage them to exercise their right to vote does not necessarily constitute electioneering (*Appeal of Gang*, 32 Educ. Dep't Rep. 337 (1992); see also *Appeal of Boni*, 40 Educ. Dep't Rep. 292 (2000)). However, it is improper for district personnel to make such calls using a selective list of voters, such as a list of district residents with children enrolled in public school (who arguably are more likely to support the district budget and/or other propositions) (*Appeal of Schadtle*, 38 Educ. Dep't Rep. 599 (1999); see also *Appeal of Eckert*, 40 Educ. Dep't Rep. 433 (2000)).

Holding a "[b]arbecue fund raiser at the same time as the election, even if the grill is within 100 feet of the voting booth, does not constitute electioneering in and of itself" (*Appeal of Santicola*, 36 Educ. Dep't Rep. 416

(1997); see also *Appeal of McBride*, 39 Educ. Dep't Rep. 702 (2000)). Neither does holding a school concert on the night of the budget vote, provided that the district gives notice of the concert to all district residents in the same manner and not just to those district residents whom the board believes will be supportive of the propositions on the ballot (*Appeal of Rampello*, 37 Educ. Dep't Rep. 153 (1997); *Appeal of Sowinski*, 34 Educ. Dep't Rep. 184 (1994)).

4:120. What is the penalty for violating the prohibition against electioneering?

Any person who willfully violates the prohibition on electioneering may be found guilty of a misdemeanor (§§ 2031-a(3), 2609(4-a)(c)). However, absent proof that electioneering affected the outcome of an election, proof that electioneering occurred is no basis to overturn the results of the election (*Appeal of Lawson*, 38 Educ. Dep't Rep. 713 (1999); see also *Appeal of Ponella*, 38 Educ. Dep't Rep. 610 (1999); and *Appeal of Karliner*, 36 Educ. Dep't Rep. 30 (1996)).

Challenges to Voter Qualifications

4:121. In a district with personal registration, how can a person's qualifications to vote be challenged?

Any qualified voter has the right, although not the duty to challenge, either prior to or at the district meeting, the qualifications of any other voter (§§ 2015(3), (4), 2019, 2609(5); *Matter of Thompson*, 76 St. Dep't Rep. 162 (1956)).

If a qualified voter challenges a person whose name is on the voter registration list, the chairperson presiding at the meeting or election shall require the person offering to vote to make the following declaration: "I do declare and affirm that I am, and have been, for 30 days last past, an actual resident of this school district and that I am qualified to vote at this meeting." If the person challenged makes this declaration, then he or she shall be permitted to vote, but if the person refuses, his or her vote must be rejected (§§ 2015(3), (4), 2019, 2609(5)).

If, however, a person's name cannot be found on the list of registered voters or in the registration poll ledger, then district elections officials shall not permit that person to vote, unless: (1) the person presents a court order requiring that he or she be permitted to vote in the manner otherwise prescribed for voters whose names are on the list of registered voters or in the registration poll ledger; or (2) the person submits an affidavit attesting to his or her qualifications to vote.

If the person is permitted to vote by affidavit, he or she must print on the outside of an envelope a sworn statement indicating (1) that he or she has duly registered to vote; (2) the address at which he or she is registered; (3) that he or she remains a duly qualified voter in the election district where he or she resides; (4) that his or her poll record appears to be lost or misplaced or that his or her name has been incorrectly omitted from the list of registered voters; and (5) that he or she understands that any false statement made therein is perjury punishable according to law.

A person who is permitted to vote by affidavit must vote by paper ballot, which is placed inside the envelope upon which the affidavit was written and then sealed therein until the close of the election and the canvassing of ballots (§ 2019-a(1); see also *Appeal of Brown*, 38 Educ. Dep't Rep. 816 (1999)). "If it is determined that a voter who cast an affidavit ballot was not registered, the ballot may not be counted" (*Appeal of Crowley*, 39 Educ. Dep't Rep. 665 (2000); *Appeal of Vaughan*, 33 Educ. Dep't Rep. 189 (1993)).

4:122. In a district without personal registration, how can a person's qualifications to vote be challenged?

Any qualified voter may challenge the qualifications of any other voter. If a qualified voter challenges the qualifications of another voter, then the chairman presiding at the meeting or election shall require the person offering to vote to make the following declaration: "I do declare and affirm that I am, and have been, for 30 days last past, an actual resident of this school district and that I am qualified to vote at this meeting." If the person challenged makes this declaration, then the person shall be permitted to vote, but if the person refuses, his or her vote must be rejected (§§ 2019, 2609(5)).

4:123. Is there a deadline for challenging a person's qualifications to vote?

Yes. All challenges to the qualifications of a voter must be raised no later than the time the voter goes to the polls to vote (*Appeal of Grant*, 42 Educ. Dep't Rep. 184 (2002); see also *Appeal of Pappas*, 38 Educ. Dep't Rep. 582 (1999); see also *Appeal of Carlson*, 37 Educ. Dep't Rep. 351 (1998); *Appeal of Fraser-McBride*, 36 Educ. Dep't Rep. 488 (1997)).

Moreover, anyone qualified to challenge a voter (see **4:59, 4:86, 4:121– 122**) who does not exercise such right is not allowed to object to such voter's participation (*Appeal of Crowley*, 39 Educ. Dep't Rep. 665 (2000); see also *Appeal of Horton*, 35 Educ. Dep't Rep. 168 (1995)).

"[I]f a person . . . has the opportunity to challenge, but does not do so . . . then he cannot be heard to complain, only after the event and only when the outcome is not according to such person's liking. . ." (*Matter of Kavanaugh*, 5 Educ. Dep't Rep. 19 (1965); see also *Appeal of Crowley*, 39

Educ. Dep't Rep. 665 (2000); and *Matter of Katz*, 18 Educ. Dep't Rep. 276 (1978)).

4:124. May school districts ask for proof of residency before allowing individuals to cast their vote?

Yes. In districts without personal registration, the Education Law authorizes (but does not require) district election officials to require voters at any school district meeting or election to provide one form of proof of residency, determined by the school district, such as a driver's license, non-driver I.D. card, utility bill or voter registration card. In addition, district election officials also may require such persons offering to vote to provide their signature, printed name, and address (§ 2018-c; see also *Appeal of Pugliese*, 40 Educ. Dep't Rep. 499 (2001)).

In addition, in districts with personal registration, the commissioner has recognized the right of school officials to request proof of residency from a voter prior to the election, as a condition of maintaining the voter's name on the voter registration list (*Appeal of Taylor*, 39 Educ. Dep't Rep. 712 (2000)). For example, a district may require a voter to supply a "redacted" copy of the voter's income tax return. This means that the voter can blacken out the tax information but must allow school officials to see what address the voter has declared as his or her residence for tax purposes (*Appeal of Taylor*).

Absentee Ballots

4:125. Must absentee ballots be made available to qualified voters?

Yes. All school districts are required by law to make absentee ballots available to qualified voters for the election of school board members, school district public library trustees, the adoption of the annual budget, and school district public library budgets and referenda (§§ 2018-a, 2018-b, 2613).

In general, absentee ballots must be provided to any qualified voter who will be unable to vote in person due to illness or physical disability, hospitalization, incarceration (unless incarcerated for conviction of a felony), travel outside the voter's county or city of residence for employment or business reasons, studies, or vacation on the day of the election (§§ 2018-a(2), 2018-b(2)).

4:126. What is the process for voting by absentee ballot?

The board of registration (in districts with personal registration) or district clerk or other designee of the school board (in districts without personal registration) must automatically mail an absentee ballot to each voter whose registration record on file with the county board of elections is marked "permanently disabled" (§§ 2018-a(2)(g), 2018-b(2)(g)).

All other voters (except as noted below, see also **4:127, 4:130**) must submit an application prior to obtaining an absentee ballot (§§ 2018-a(2)(a), 2018-b(2)(a)). The information that must be included in the application is set by statute (§§ 2018-a(2)(a), 2018-b(2)(a)). The application must be received by the district clerk or designee at least seven days before the election, if the ballot is to be mailed to the voter, or the day before the election, if the ballot is to be issued to the voter in person (§§ 2018-a(2)(a), 2018-b(2)(a)).

Upon receipt of an application, either the board of registration (in districts with personal registration) or district clerk or other designee of the board of education (in districts without personal registration) must review the application to determine if the applicant is a qualified voter and is otherwise entitled to vote by absentee ballot (§ 2018-a(3), 2018-b(3)).

If the application is proper in all respects, the board of registration or district clerk or other designee of the board, then mails or personally issues an absentee ballot to the voter. The board of registration or district clerk must then record the name of the voter to whom the absentee ballot was issued on the district's personal registration list or poll list (§§ 2018-a(3), 2018-b(3)).

4:127. Is absentee voting conducted differently in nursing homes and other adult care facilities?

Yes, under certain, limited circumstances. Chapter 195 of the Laws of 2001 added a new section 1501-c to the Education Law, which makes Election Law section 8-407 applicable to "all elections conducted . . . by a school district" pursuant to Title II of the Education Law, notwithstanding any inconsistent provision in Title II. Election Law section 8-407 provides that when a county or city board of elections receives 25 or more absentee ballot applications from a nursing home (or other qualifying adult care facility), that board of elections must send elections inspectors to the nursing home between one and 13 days before the election to supervise the completion of absentee ballots by the residents of that facility.

4:128. When must a school district make absentee ballots available to voters?

The law is generally silent on when districts must begin making absentee ballot applications available to voters. With the exception of absentee ballots issued upon receipt of a request by letter (see **4:130**), nothing in the law specifies how far in advance of the election school districts must begin making applications for absentee ballots available (see *Appeal of Roxbury Taxpayers Alliance*, 34 Educ. Dep't Rep. 576 (1995)).

However, since the notice of the district meeting must include a statement that qualified voters may apply for absentee ballots at the clerk's office (§ 2004(7)), as a practical matter, ballot applications should be made available at the time of the first publication of the notice of the district meeting and must be made available far enough in advance of the meeting date to permit voters to apply for and return completed ballots as required by law.

4:129. Can a person request more than one absentee ballot application?

Yes. There is no authority under the Education Law for a school district to demand a list of the voters who will use the applications from an individual seeking multiple copies of absentee ballot applications (*Appeal of the Roxbury Taxpayers Alliance*, 34 Educ. Dep't Rep. 576 (1995)).

4:130. May a district issue an absentee ballot to a voter who has not submitted an application?

Yes, but only under two limited circumstances. First, a district must automatically issue an absentee ballot to any voter whose registration record is marked "permanently disabled" (see **4:126**).

The only other time a district may issue a ballot prior to receiving a properly completed application is upon receipt of a request for an absentee ballot by letter signed by the voter. Moreover, this exception only applies in districts that do not use personal registration. In such districts, any qualified voter may request a ballot by signed letter, rather than by application. The letter must be received by the district clerk or designee no earlier than 30 days before the election and no later than seven days before the election. Upon receipt of the letter request, the clerk must send both an application and a ballot to the voter at the same time. The voter then completes both the application and the ballot and returns them together in the same envelope. In fact, the law specifically provides that the ballot will not be counted unless the completed application is returned with it (§ 2018-b(4)).

A word of caution is in order: this same procedure is not statutorily authorized in districts that use personal registration. In one case involving a district that used a system of personal registration, the commissioner invalidated the absentee ballots of two voters who returned their absentee ballot applications inside the same envelopes as their ballots. According to the commissioner, "the inclusion of the applications in the sealed ballot envelopes with the ballots was an act extrinsic to the ballot in violation of section 2034(3)(a), which voids the whole ballot" (*Appeal of McGrath*, 38 Educ. Dep't Rep. 707 (1999)).

4:131. What is the deadline for the submission of absentee ballots?

No absentee voter's ballot will be counted unless it is received in the office of the district clerk (clerk or designee of the school board in districts without personal registration) by 5:00 p.m. on the day of the election (§§ 2018-a(8), 2018-b(9)).

4:132. Must a school district maintain a list of individuals who have been issued absentee ballots?

Yes. The board of registration (in districts with personal registration) must make a list of all persons to whom absentee ballots have been issued, and file the list in the office of the district clerk, where it must be available for public inspection during regular office hours until the day of the election.

Similarly, the district clerk or other designee of the board of education (in districts without personal registration) must make a list of all persons to whom absentee ballots have been issued and make it available for public inspection during regular office hours until the day of the election (§§ 2018-a(6), 2018-b(7); see also, *Appeal of Laurie*, 42 Educ. Dep't Rep. 313 (2003); but see § 2004(7)).

4:133. Can an absentee ballot be challenged?

Yes. Any qualified voter may, prior to the election, file a written challenge to the qualifications of any person whose name appears on the list of absentee voters prepared for transmittal to the election inspectors on the day of the election, stating the reason for such challenge (§§ 2018-a(6), 2018-b(7)). The written challenge must be transmitted by the clerk or designee to the election inspectors on the day of the election (§§ 2018-a(6), 2018-b(7)).

The commissioner of education has ruled it improper under section 2018-a(10) to open and/or count absentee ballots before the polls close, and that pursuant to section 2018-a(11), any qualified voter present at the polling place has the right to object to the voting of an absentee ballot at that time (§ 2018-a(10), (11); *Appeal of Pappas*, 38 Educ. Dep't Rep. 582 (1999)). Therefore, in districts governed by section 2018-a, at least, any qualified voter may challenge an absentee ballot during the public canvassing of such ballots after the polls close.

Preventing a qualified voter from exercising his or her right to object to a submitted absentee ballot may be grounds for invalidating the election results (*Appeal of Heller*, 34 Educ. Dep't Rep. 220 (1994)).

4:134. Can a person wait until after the election to challenge an absentee ballot?

Not generally. The law does not permit a person to wait until after the election to challenge another person's right to vote by absentee ballot (see *Appeal of Karliner*, 36 Educ. Dep't Rep. 30 (1996)). However, in one case, the commissioner excused a petitioner's untimely challenge, finding that the board's failure to make available a list of all persons to whom absentee ballots were issued "prevented petitioner from having a reasonable opportunity to challenge the disputed absentee ballots at the time of the election" (*Matter of Levine*, 24 Educ. Dep't Rep. 172 (1984), *aff'd sub nom. Copobianco v. Ambach*, 112 A.D.2d 640 (3d Dep't 1985)). In another case, the commissioner excused an untimely challenge to absentee ballots cast in a district library vote, where it was alleged that a school board member fraudulently induced several voters to file false applications, and such fraud "was undetected at the time because the board member was somehow able to circumvent the statutory requirements for the handling of absentee ballots" (see *Appeal of the Weller Library Comm'n*, 42 Educ. Dep't Rep. 338 14,875 (2003)).

5. Boards of Cooperative Educational Services (BOCES)

Editor's Note: For additional information concerning BOCES, contact the State Education Department's Office of School District Organization and BOCES Services at 518-474-3936, or online at http://www.emsc.nysed.gov/ mgtserv/BOCES.

5:1. What is a board of cooperative educational services?

A board of cooperative educational services (BOCES) is a voluntary, cooperative association of school districts in a geographic area that share planning, services, and programs to provide educational and support activities more economically, efficiently, and equitably than could be provided by an individual district. The geographic area covered by a BOCES is known as a supervisory district (see **6:2**).

BOCES are organized under section 1950 of the Education Law. BOCES services are focused on education for students with disabilities, career education, academic and alternative programs, summer schools, staff development, computer services (managerial and instructional), educational communication, and burgeoning cooperative purchasing.

A BOCES board is considered a corporate body. All BOCES property is held by the BOCES board as a corporation (§ 1950(6)). BOCES boards are also considered municipal corporations, permitting them to contract with other municipalities on a cooperative basis under sections 119-n(a) and 119-o of the General Municipal Law.

For the sake of clarity, the governing body of the BOCES will be referred to as the BOCES board throughout this chapter.

5:2. How many BOCES are there?

There are 38 BOCES in New York State.

5:3. Do all school districts belong to a BOCES?

No. According to the State Education Department, of the 704 BOCES-eligible school districts, all but nine school districts belong to a BOCES as of January 2004. BOCES membership is not available to the Big 5 school districts (Buffalo, New York City, Rochester, Syracuse, and Yonkers). However, under certain circumstances, non-component districts, including the Big 5, may participate in BOCES instructional support services (see **5:33**).

5:4. Can a school district terminate its membership in a BOCES?

No. There is no authority or process by which a school district can terminate its status as a BOCES component.

BOCES Board Membership

5:5. How many members are on a BOCES board?

A BOCES board may consist of between five and 15 members. The number of BOCES board members may be increased or decreased within that range by the commissioner of education (§ 1950(1), (2-b)).

5:6. Can two residents of the same component district sit on a BOCES board at the same time?

The law prohibits the election of more than one candidate residing in a particular component school district, unless the number of seats on the BOCES board exceeds the number of component school districts or an unrepresented district declines to make a nomination, provided that a person nominated by a special act school district, a central high school district or any component thereof shall be deemed a resident of the district that nominated him or her (§ 1950 (2-a)(c)). This restriction applies, no matter which district initially nominated the person.

5:7. How long is the term of office of a BOCES board member?

BOCES board members are elected to three-year terms. BOCES board members' terms commence on the first day of July following their election (§ 1950(2-b); see also **5:12** and **5:16**).

5:8. What are the qualifications for serving as a BOCES board member?

A BOCES board candidate must reside within the boundaries of a component school district (§ 1950(9-a)). Any candidate nominated by a special act school district, a central high school district, or any component thereof, shall be considered a resident of the district that nominated that person (§ 1950(2-a)(b)).

A candidate need not be a member of a component district school board. However, no employee of a component district is eligible for BOCES board membership (§ 1950(9)), and a BOCES board member cannot accept employment in a component district. On the other hand, a BOCES employee may serve on a component school board (*Appeal of Reynolds*, 42 Educ. Dep't Rep. 278 (2003); *Application of a BOCES*, 38 Educ. Dep't

Rep. 224 (1998); *Matter of Todd*, 19 Educ. Dep't Rep. 277 (1979)). The commissioner of education encourages BOCES employees serving on component boards to recuse themselves from voting on issues that present a conflict (*Appeal of Reynolds*). Also, in an informal opinion, the Attorney General has held that the position of district attorney is incompatible with membership on a BOCES board (Opn. Att'y Gen. (Inf.) 2000-13).

Lastly, no more than one candidate per component district may be elected to serve, unless the number of BOCES seats exceeds the number of component districts or an unrepresented district declines to make a nomination (§ 1950(2-a)(c); see **5:6**).

5:9. How are BOCES board members nominated for office?

Members of a BOCES board are nominated by resolution of one or more of the school boards of its component districts. The resolution must be provided to the clerk of the BOCES board at least 30 days prior to the date of the election, as designated by the BOCES president (§ 1950(2-a)(b)).

5:10. Are there any restrictions on BOCES board nominations?

Yes. The clerk of the BOCES board must reject any nomination from a component school district that has another resident serving on the BOCES board unless that member's term will expire at the end of the current year, or the number of BOCES board seats exceeds the number of component school districts, or an unrepresented district declines to make a nomination (§ 1950(2-a)(b)). The clerk must also reject a nominee who is not a resident of any component school district of the BOCES (§ 1950(9-a)), or a nominee employed by a component district within the supervisory district (§ 1950(9); *Application of a BOCES*, 38 Educ. Dep't Rep. 224 (1998); see also *Appeal of Reynolds*, 42 Educ. Dep't Rep. 278 (2003)).

Any person or board member nominated by a special act school district, a central high school district, or any component thereof, will be deemed a resident only of the district that nominated that person (§ 1950(2-a)(b); see also *Appeal of Stris*, 40 Educ. Dep't Rep. 495 (2001)).

There are no limitations on the number of nominations an individual component district may make (see "Questions and Answers on the BOCES Reform Act," State Education Department, October 1993).

5:11. Does the BOCES have a responsibility to encourage nominations?

Yes, it is the duty of the BOCES to encourage the nomination of persons residing in districts not currently represented on the BOCES board (§ 1950(2-a)(b)).

5:12. How are the members of a BOCES board elected?

BOCES board members are elected by their component member boards. By February 1 of each year, the BOCES board president must set the date of election in each component district. It is the same day designated for the vote on the tentative administrative budget, between April 16th and 30th. All component school boards meet on that same date, except for central high school boards, which must hold their meetings the next business day (§ 1950(2-a)(b), (4)(b)(5)).

The BOCES clerk then must mail an election ballot to each component district at least 14 days prior to the election. On the date designated for the election, each component board is entitled to cast one vote per vacancy, but no more than one vote per candidate. BOCES board members are elected by resolution of the component boards on the ballot prepared by the BOCES clerk (§ 1950(2-a)(c)).

Each component district must mail or deliver its completed ballot to the BOCES clerk no later than one business day after the election (§ 1950(2-a)(c)). There must be a quorum of board members voting in each component district to have a valid ballot (see "Questions and Answers on the BOCES Reform Act," State Education Department, October 1993).

The candidates receiving the plurality of votes cast are elected with the candidate receiving the highest vote total elected to the position with the longest term, and the candidate with the second highest vote total elected to the position with the next longest term, and so on. If the length of term of all positions to be filled is equal, candidates are elected in order of the greatest number of votes received until all vacancies are filled (§ 1950(2-a)(c)).

5:13. What happens in the event of a tie vote?

In the event of a tie vote, the BOCES board president must call a run-off election within 20 days of the initial vote, with only the candidates who received an equal number of votes deemed nominated. If the run-off election results in a tie vote, the winning candidate is determined by drawing lots (§ 1950(2-a)(d)).

5:14. What happens if the school board of a component district is unable to obtain a quorum on the day designated for the election or fails to adopt a board resolution voting on the candidates?

If a component district fails to obtain a quorum on that date, the district's ballot is void. The candidates receiving a plurality of the votes actually cast on the day of election are elected (see "Questions and Answers on the BOCES Reform Act," State Education Department, October 1993).

5:15. What happens if all of the component school districts fail to vote, so that no candidate receives a plurality?

The BOCES board position(s) will remain open until there is an election that fills the vacancy. However, each component board has a duty to elect BOCES board members, and a willful neglect of this duty may constitute grounds for removal of the school board (see "Questions and Answers on the BOCES Reform Act," State Education Department, October 1993).

5:16. What is the procedure to fill a vacancy on the BOCES board?

If the vacancy occurs before January 1 or between the last five days before the nomination deadline (see **5:9, 5:13**) and the last day of the school year, a special election must be held on a date designated by the BOCES board president no later than 45 days after the date the vacancy occurred (§ 1950(2-a)(f)). If the vacancy occurs on or after January 1 and before the fifth day preceding the date for submitting nominations, the BOCES may appoint someone to fill the position until the next annual election (§ 1950(2-a)(f)).

When two or more BOCES have been merged or reorganized, elections may not be held to fill vacancies on the new board until a sufficient number of board member terms have expired so that the board has between five and 15 members (§ 1950(7)).

Duties and Powers of a BOCES Board

5:17. What are some of a BOCES board's duties?

The following are the chief duties of a BOCES board, as listed in section 1950(4) of the Education Law:

- Appoint a district superintendent of schools and, at its discretion, provide for the payment of a supplementary salary to the district (BOCES) superintendent of schools by the BOCES (§ 1950(4)(a)(1)).
- Prepare separate tentative budgets of expenditures for program, capital and administrative costs for the BOCES in accordance with the commissioner's regulations (§ 1950(4)(b)(1)).
- Adopt the final program, capital and administrative budgets no later than May 15. After applicable state aid has been deducted, component school districts are to be charged for their proportionate shares of the budget (§ 1950 (4)(b)(7)).

5:18. What responsibility does a BOCES have in determining the cooperative educational needs within its supervisory district?

Each BOCES has the duty to survey the need for cooperative educational services in its supervisory district and present the findings of its surveys to local school authorities. Each BOCES must prepare long-range plans to meet the projected need for such services in the supervisory district for the next five years "as may be specified by the commissioner." The plans and annual revisions are to be submitted to the commissioner before December 1 each year. Plans for special and career education programs are to be submitted every two years, no later than the date specified by the commissioner and in a form specified by the commissioner. These plans are also to be revised annually (§ 1950(4)(c)).

5:19. What powers does a BOCES board have?

A BOCES board may do, for example, the following:
- Employ administrative assistants, teachers, supervisors, clerical help, and other personnel recommended by the district superintendent as may be necessary to carry out its program (§ 1950(4)(e)).
- Rent, improve, alter, equip and furnish suitable land, classrooms, offices or buildings, with the commissioner of education's approval, in order to carry out its educational and administrative services (§ 1950(4)(p)(a); see **5:24–25**).
- Provide transportation for students to and from BOCES classes (§ 1950(4)(q)).
- Furnish any of the educational services provided for in the Education Law to school districts outside of the supervisory district, with the approval of the district superintendent of schools and the commissioner, on terms agreed to pursuant to contracts executed by the BOCES and the trustees or school boards of such districts (§ 1950(4)(r)).
- Contract with the federal government, the state government, community colleges, agricultural and technical colleges or other public agencies for the provision of career education programs (§ 1950(4)(h)(5)).
- Enter into contracts with not-for-profit corporations to participate in federal programs related to career training and experience (§ 1950(4)(h)(6)).
- Lease unneeded facilities to public or private agencies, individuals, partnerships or corporations (§ 1950(4)(p)(b); see **5:23**).
- Contract with the state government, community colleges, agricultural and technical colleges, or other public agencies for the purpose of

providing electronic data-processing services to such agencies (§ 1950(4)(h)(7)).

5:20. May a BOCES own a building?

Yes. A BOCES may own and construct buildings and obtain funds necessary for their acquisition. Purchase or acquisition of buildings, building sites, or additions by a BOCES, however, depends on authorization of the "qualified voters of the board"; that is, the qualified voters of the BOCES district (§ 1950(4)(t); *Board of Educ. of East Syracuse-Minoa CSD v. Commissioner of Educ.*, 145 A.D.2d 13 (3d Dep't 1989), *appeal denied*, 74 N.Y.2d 890 (1989)). A qualified voter of the BOCES is a person who is a citizen of the United States, at least 18 years of age, and a resident within the BOCES for a period of 30 days prior to the meeting at which he or she will vote (§ 1951(2)(c)). In purchasing a building site, a BOCES may not issue bonds to acquire real property.

5:21. May a BOCES contract with the New York State Dormitory Authority to construct facilities to house BOCES services?

Yes. A BOCES and its component school districts may enter into an agreement to acquire from the New York State Dormitory Authority facilities designed to house services to be provided by the BOCES and to share the cost of the acquisition (§ 1950(13)). No such agreement may be for longer than is required to retire the obligations or to pay the Dormitory Authority in full (§ 1950(11)).

The Dormitory Authority is authorized to construct facilities where the BOCES may operate its program, to finance their cost, lease them to the BOCES, and to transfer the facilities back to the BOCES when the costs and liabilities incurred by the authority have been paid (Pub. Auth. Law §§ 1676(2)(d), 1678(15), 1689).

5:22. Do renovations of BOCES buildings require a referendum?

No. Only the acquisition or construction of additional space requires voter approval (see *Board of Educ. of East Syracuse-Minoa CSD v. Commissioner of Educ.*, 145 A.D.2d 13 (3d Dep't 1989), *appeal denied*, 74 N.Y.2d 890 (1989); § 1950(4)(t)).

5:23. May a BOCES lease its unused facilities?

Yes. A BOCES may lease its unused facilities to public or private agencies and others, with the approval of the commissioner of education, for a term of not more than five years, which is renewable with the commissioner's approval (§ 1950(4)(p)(b); 8 NYCRR § 155.14).

5:24. May a BOCES rent real property?

Yes. A BOCES's authority to rent real property, however, is limited to a maximum period of 10 years, except for certain specified conditions or uses that are identified in section 1950(4)(p)(a) of the Education Law.

Before executing a lease, the BOCES board must adopt a resolution that explains why this action is in the best financial interests of the supervisory district, and that the rental payment is no more than fair market value as determined by the board. No such lease is enforceable against the BOCES unless and until it has been approved in writing by the commissioner of education (§ 1950(4)(p)(a); 8 NYCRR § 155.15).

5:25. May a BOCES lease personal property?

Yes. A BOCES may lease personal property such as relocatable classrooms constructed on land owned by the BOCES or leased from a third party. Before executing the agreement, the BOCES board must adopt a resolution to determine that the agreement is "in the best financial interests" of the BOCES, and the resolution must state the basis for that determination. In addition, such agreements are subject to the bidding requirements of the General Municipal Law (§ 1950(4)(y); 8 NYCRR § 155.15).

5:26. Are there any policy requirements that are unique to a BOCES?

Yes. A BOCES board is also required to develop and adopt a formal policy on the acquisition, sale, and disposal of personal property to be approved by the commissioner of education. The policy must include procedures for the acquisition of personal property by purchase of or gift, and the periodic inventory of personal property. It also must include procedures for the sale of valuable personal property to the highest bidder, except that a BOCES may give vehicles received at no cost for use in an authorized welfare-to-work program to eligible program participants. (§ 1950(18)).

BOCES Services

5:27. What educational services are available through a BOCES?

Any of the following services are available through a BOCES on a cooperative basis: school nurse-teacher; attendance supervisor; supervisor of teachers; psychologist; dental hygienist; teachers of art, music, physical education, and career education; guidance counselors; operation of classes for students with disabilities; student and financial accounting services; academic and other programs and services, including summer programs and services; advanced academic courses; interactive television and other technologies; and maintenance and operation of cafeteria or restaurant service for the use of students and teachers while at school and to furnish meals to senior citizens (§ 1950(4)(d), (4)(bb), (4)(bb)(3)). These services must be requested by component districts and approved by the commissioner of education (§ 1950(4)(d)).

In addition, a BOCES may provide activities and services pertaining to the arts, training adults for employment, and activities and services regarding environmental education (§ 1950(4)(dd), (gg), (hh)). Examples of other services not specifically mentioned in the law that have been approved by the commissioner in specific situations include adult education coordinator; supervisor of education for students with disabilities; shared school business manager; coordinator of language arts; coordinator of education for gifted children; cooperative purchasing; transportation service; printing services, psychiatric consultant service; coordinator of career education; clinical programs for reading and speech correction; school health coordinator; in-service workshops; and educational communications center.

5:28. How does a component school district secure educational services through a BOCES?

The annual procedure for securing such BOCES services is as follows:

- By February 1, component districts must file their requests for services with their BOCES (§ 1950(4)(d)(3)).
- By February 15, BOCES must submit proposed operating plans to the State Education Department (§ 1950(4)(d)(3)).
- By March 10, BOCES must notify their component school districts of the services that the commissioner of education has approved for the coming school year. This notice must include the local uniform cost for each service established in accordance with the Education Law and commissioner's regulations (§ 1950(4)(d)(3)).
- By May 1, component school districts must notify BOCES of their intent to participate in shared services and identify those services (§ 1950(4)(d)(4)).
- By June 1, BOCES must submit to the commissioner an operating plan and budget based upon component districts' requests. This must include the budgeted unit cost of programs and services calculated pursuant to the Education Law. If a BOCES receives requests for unanticipated shared services subsequent to the adoption of the budget, then it must submit an amended operating plan to the commissioner and include a statement concerning the availability of district funds to pay for the district's share of the additional services

from each superintendent who has requested the services (§ 1950(4)(d)(5)).

- By August 1, BOCES must file with the commissioner a copy of each contract for services executed with component districts (§ 1950 (4)(d)(4)).
- By September 1, BOCES must submit an annual program report and evaluation to the commissioner (§ 1950(4)(d)(5)).

It is up to a component's school board to decide whether to contract for particular BOCES programs (*Appeal of Williams III*, 42 Educ. Dep't Rep. 260 (2003); *Appeal of a Student with a Disability*, 42 Educ. Dep't Rep. 163 (2003)). When a school board determines to provide a program through BOCES, this has the same effect, legally, as providing that program in its own school. In such an instance, the BOCES is considered part of the component district (*Appeal of Kendrick and Sillato*, 32 Educ. Dep't Rep. 464 (1993)).

5:29. May a local school board limit student enrollment in particular BOCES programs?

A school board may establish prerequisites for admission to a BOCES program and deny admission to a student found to be unqualified for a particular course. In addition, a school board may limit enrollment in a BOCES career education program to 11th- and 12th-grade students (*Appeal of a Student with a Disability*, 42 Educ. Dep't Rep. 163 (2003); *Matter of Tripi*, 21 Educ. Dep't Rep. 349 (1981); see also § 4602(1)). Furthermore, a school district that makes available career education courses within its own curriculum does not have to contract with a BOCES for such program, even if its own offerings are different from those provided by the BOCES (*Appeal of a Student with a Disability*).

5:30. What is the maximum amount of time an itinerant teacher or worker may spend in a single component school district in order for the service to be approved as a shared BOCES service?

According to the State Education Department, a person whose services are to be shared may not spend any more than 60 percent or three days per week of his or her time in any one school district. A district may not expect to use most of such a person's time when engaged in a token sharing with one or two other districts.

5:31. What state aid is paid to districts to reimburse them for services purchased from BOCES?

Component districts are eligible to receive BOCES operating aid for approved services costs and administrative charges, BOCES facilities aid, and BOCES rental aid. BOCES operating aid is based on prior-year approved expenditures, while aid for facilities and rental are based on current-year expenditures. Approved expenditures include salaries of BOCES employees only up to $30,000.

BOCES aid is wealth-equalized so that districts poor in property taxes receive proportionately more than districts that are wealthy in property taxes. However, the total of the three types of aids is subject to a save-harmless provision; that is, no district will receive less BOCES aid than it received in the 1967-68 school year.

5:32. May transportation of students to BOCES be provided?

Yes. Transportation to and from classes operated by a BOCES may be provided at the request of one or more school districts. School districts and BOCES are authorized to enter into contracts with other districts, private contractors, BOCES, and any municipal corporations or authorities to provide the transportation (§ 1950(4)(q)).

5:33. May a non-component district receive BOCES instructional support services?

Yes. Any non-component school district, including members of the Big 5, can, upon consent of the BOCES and with the approval of the commissioner of education, participate as a component district of the BOCES serving its geographic area or an adjoining BOCES for the sole purpose of purchasing instructional support services. The district must pay its share of the expenses of the program, including a charge for administration costs (§ 1950 (8-c)).

5:34. Are there any services the BOCES are specifically prohibited from providing as aidable shared services?

Yes. Cooperative maintenance services or municipal services, including but not limited to lawn mowing services and heating, ventilation or air conditioning repair or maintenance or trash collection, or any other municipal service as defined by the commissioner of education, will not be authorized as an aidable BOCES shared service (§ 1950(4)(d)(2); see *Vestal Employees Ass'n v. PERB*, 94 N.Y.2d 409 (2000)).

BOCES Annual Meeting

5:35. When is the BOCES annual meeting held?

The BOCES annual meeting must be held between April 1 and April 15 on a date and at a place and hour designated by the BOCES board president (§1950(4)(o)).

5:36. What is the purpose of the BOCES annual meeting?

The purpose of the BOCES annual meeting is to present the tentative administrative, capital, and program budgets of the BOCES to school board members of component school districts prior to the vote on the tentative administrative budget, and to conduct other BOCES-wide business (§ 1950(4)(o); see "Questions and Answers on the BOCES Reform Act," State Education Department, October 1993).

5:37. What notice must be given of the BOCES annual meeting?

Notice of the time, date, and place of the annual meeting must be given to each of the members of the board and the clerk of each of the component districts by mail at least 14 days prior to the meeting (§ 1950(4)(o)). The BOCES must also publish the notice at least once each week within the two weeks preceding the annual meeting, the first publication to be at least 14 days before the meeting in newspapers having general circulation within the BOCES (§ 1950(4)(b)(4)).

In addition to the date, time, and place of the meeting, the notice also must contain the following:

- A statement that the tentative BOCES budgets will be presented to the component school board members at the meeting (§ 1950 (4)(b)(4)).
- A summary of the tentative BOCES capital and program budgets in a form prescribed by the commissioner (§ 1950 (4)(b)(4)).
- A summary of the tentative BOCES administrative budget in a form prescribed by the commissioner that includes the salary and benefits payable to supervisory and administrative staff of the BOCES and the total compensation payable to the district (BOCES) superintendent of schools (§ 1950(4)(b)(4)).
- When and where the tentative budgets will be available to the public for inspection ((§ 1950(4)(b)(4)).

Adoption of the BOCES Budget

5:38. How is the BOCES budget funded?

A BOCES budget is comprised of separate budgets for administrative, program, and capital costs. After state aid and federal aid are subtracted from the cost of operating a BOCES, all component districts must share in its administrative and capital costs. Each component district's share of these costs is determined either by resident weighted average daily attendance (RWADA), real property valuation, or resident public school district enrollment as defined in the Education Law. Only one method can be applied in any year, unless otherwise provided by law (§ 1950(4)(b)(7)).

In addition, each component district pays tuition or a service fee for programs in which its students participate. Generally, districts not participating in BOCES services are not required to pay for costs associated with those services, such as salaries for employees, equipment, supplies or student transportation. However, the BOCES board may allocate the cost of such services to component school districts in accordance with terms agreed upon between the BOCES board and three-quarters of the component school districts participating in the service (§§ 1950(4)(d)(4), 1951(1)).

A component district's contribution to BOCES expenditures is derived from state aid and its local tax levy.

5:39. Must a BOCES make available copies of its tentative administrative, program, and capital budgets?

Yes. The BOCES must provide copies of the tentative administrative, capital, and program budgets and attachments to the school boards of each component school district at least 10 days prior to the annual meeting. In addition, the BOCES must comply with any reasonable request for additional information made prior to the annual meeting.

Each component school board must make these budgets available to the residents of their respective school district, upon request (§ 1950(4)(b)(2) and (3); see also **5:40–41**).

5:40. What is included in the BOCES program and capital budgets?

As a general rule, the program budget includes costs for those BOCES shared services that have been requested by and contracted for by the component districts (§§ 1950(4)(b), 1951(1)). These costs must be based on local and statewide uniform unit costs calculated as set forth in the Education Law.

The capital budget includes, for instance, facility acquisition and construction costs; debt expenditures associated with repayment of indebtedness incurred for the acquisition of facilities and capital projects; and operation and maintenance costs such as rent, custodial salaries and benefits, and supplies and utilities. It also includes expenditures associated with the payment of court judgments and orders from administrative bodies and officers, and certain costs relating to employee retirement (§ 1950(4)(b)).

5:41. What is included in the administrative budget?

By law, the administrative budget must at least include office and central administrative expenses, traveling expenses, salaries and benefits of supervisors and administrative personnel necessary to carry out the central administrative duties of the supervisory district, any and all expenditures associated with the BOCES board, the office of the district superintendent, general administration, central support services, planning, and all other administrative activities.

The BOCES board also must attach to the administrative budget a detailed statement of the total compensation to be paid to the district (BOCES) superintendent of schools, delineating the salary, annualized cost of benefits, and any in-kind or other form of remuneration to be paid, plus a list of items of expense eligible for reimbursement on expense accounts in the ensuing school year and a statement of the amount of expenses paid to the district superintendent in the prior year for purposes of carrying out his or her official duties. The commissioner's regulations further specify the content of each of the tentative budgets and the circumstances under which salaries and benefits of BOCES administrators will be budgeted under program or administration (§ 1950(4)(b)(1); 8 NYCRR § 170.3).

In addition, each BOCES must prepare and append to the proposed administrative budget a report card that includes measures of academic performance of the BOCES educational services, fiscal performance of the supervisory district, and other measures that support the achievement of the Regents standards, as prescribed by the commissioner of education. The measures for each BOCES will be compared to the statewide averages for all BOCES. The BOCES report card must be distributed publicly as required by law (§ 1950(4)(kk); 8 NYCRR § 100.2(cc)). Beginning with the 2002–03 school year, the BOCES report card must include a summary of the BOCES annual violent or disruptive incident report in a format containing such information as the commissioner shall prescribe (8 NYCRR § 100.2 (cc)(4), (gg)).

5:42. Is there a deadline by which a BOCES board must adopt its final budget?

Yes. The BOCES board must adopt its final program, capital, and administrative budgets no later than May 15 (§ 1950(4)(b)(7)).

5:43. What is the process for adopting the BOCES program and capital budgets?

The BOCES tentative program, capital, and administrative budgets must be provided to the component districts 10 days prior to the annual meeting (§ 1950(4)(b)(2); see **5:39–40**). Component districts review the tentative program, capital, and administrative budgets at the annual meeting held between April 1 and April 15, on a date, place, and time designated by the BOCES president (§ 1950(4)(o); see **5:35–36**).

The component districts do not vote on the program and capital budgets. They only vote on the administrative budget (see **5:44–45**).

The BOCES board adopts the final BOCES program and capital budgets, along with the administrative budget approved by the component districts, no later than May 15 (§ 1950(4)(b)(7)). Once adopted by the BOCES board, the administrative and capital budgets became a charge against all the component school districts within the BOCES supervisory district (§ 1950(4)(b)(7)).

5:44. What is the process for adopting the BOCES administrative budget?

A tentative administrative budget must be provided to the component districts 10 days prior to the annual meeting (§ 1950(4)(b)(2); see **5:39, 5:41**). Component districts review the administrative budget at the annual meeting held between April 1 and April 15 (§ 1950(4)(o); see **5:35–36**). Thereafter, on the same day, between April 16 and 30, designated by the BOCES president for the election of the BOCES board, each component school board must conduct a public meeting, which may be a regular or special board meeting, to adopt a resolution to either approve or disapprove the BOCES tentative administrative budget (§ 1950(2-a)(b)). The BOCES board president must designate this date no later than February 1 of each year (§ 1950(2-a)(b), (4)(b), (5); see also **5:12**). In the case of a central high school district, this vote will take place on the day following the designated date (§ 1950(4)(b)(5)). This resolution approving or disapproving the administrative budget must be transmitted to the BOCES no later than one business day following the vote (§ 1950(4)(b)(7)).

Approval of the tentative administrative budget requires the approval of a majority of the component school boards actually voting (§ 1950(4)(b)(5)).

5:45. What happens if the tentative administrative budget is not approved by the component districts?

If the majority of the total number of component school districts actually voting do not approve the tentative administrative budget, or if there is a tie vote (half the districts approve, half disapprove), the BOCES must prepare and adopt a contingency administrative budget (§ 1950(4)(b)(5)).

5:46. Are there any limitations on a BOCES contingency administrative budget?

Yes. In a contingency budget for BOCES the amount of the administrative budget may not exceed the amount in the prior year's budget, except for expenditures incurred in the supplemental retirement allowances, including health insurance benefits for retirees (§ 1950(4)(b)(5)).

5:47. Are BOCES subject to financial audits?

Yes. There are two types of audits that are to be conducted in BOCES districts:

- *State audits.* The commissioner of education shall conduct periodic fiscal audits of the BOCES and, to the extent sufficient resources are provided to SED, shall assure that each BOCES is audited at least once every three years (§ 305 (25)). In addition, the state comptroller has the authority to examine the financial affairs of a BOCES (Gen. Mun. Law §§ 30, 33–34).
- *Independent audits.* The commissioner's regulations require that BOCES obtain an annual audit, in a form prescribed by the commissioner of education, of all funds by a certified public accountant or public accountant. The auditor's final report must be adopted by resolution of the BOCES board and a copy must be filed with the commissioner of education by October 1 of each year (NYCRR § 170.3(a)).

6. The District Superintendent

6:1. What is a district superintendent and how does this position differ from that of superintendent of schools?

A district superintendent is the chief executive officer of a board of cooperative educational services (BOCES) and the general supervising officer of the supervisory district that comprises the BOCES. This person is responsible for both the BOCES and its component districts, and also performs duties assigned by the commissioner of education, serving as the State Education Department's field representative in the supervisory district (§§ 1950(2), 2213, 2215). In comparison, a superintendent of schools is the chief executive officer of a single local school district (§ 1711). (See **chapter 5** for more information on BOCES and **7:20–34** for more information on superintendents of schools.)

6:2. What constitutes the supervisory district overseen by the district superintendent?

A supervisory district is made up of the total geographic area under the supervision of a district superintendent, as established under section 2201 of the Education Law.

6:3. What are the qualifications for the position of district superintendent of schools?

A district superintendent must be at least 21 years of age, a citizen of the United States, and a resident of New York State (§ 2205). That person must be a graduate of a college or university from a regionally accredited institution of higher education or from an institution approved by or registered with the State Education Department and must have completed 60 semester hours in graduate courses and an approved administrative/supervisory internship under the supervision of a practicing school administrator and of a representative of the sponsoring institution of higher education (§ 3003(1)(a)(b); 8 NYCRR § 80-2.4)). One year of satisfactory full-time experience in a school administrative or supervisory position may be substituted for the internship. The individual must also have a master's degree (8 NYCRR § 80-2.4(a)(1)).

At the time of his or her appointment, the district superintendent must have completed three years of teaching and/or supervision in public or nonpublic schools (§ 3003(1)(b); 8 NYCRR § 80-2.4(a)(2)). Any person applying for a superintendent's certificate on or after January 1, 1991 also must have completed two hours of course work or training on how to identify and report child abuse and maltreatment (§ 3003(4)). In addition, any person applying for a superintendent's certificate must have completed two hours of course work or training in school violence prevention and intervention (§ 3004(3); see 8 NYCRR § 80-2.4(a)).

For exceptionally qualified persons, the commissioner may waive the stated educational requirements (§ 3003(3); 8 NYCRR § 80-2.4(a)(3)).

6:4. Is a district superintendent subject to the fingerprinting requirements of the Education Law and commissioner's regulation?

It depends. Any district superintendent candidate who applies for an administrative certificate on or after July 1, 2001, who was not provisionally certified prior to that date, is subject to the fingerprinting requirements as a condition of obtaining certification (§ 3004-b; 8 NYCRR § 87.3; see also **7:2, 8:66**).

In addition, a district superintendent appointed on or after July 1, 2001, to a board of cooperative educational services (BOCES) in which he or she was not continuously employed prior to that date, also would be subject to the fingerprinting requirement to the extent that in his or her capacity as district superintendent, he or she would have direct, in-person, face-to-face contact with students under age 21 for more than five days during the school year (§ 1950(4)(a)(1); 8 NYCRR §§ 87.2, 87.4; see also **7:2, 8:66**).

6:5. How is a district superintendent appointed?

A district superintendent is appointed by the BOCES board of a supervisory district. When a vacancy occurs and the commissioner of education has not redistricted the county to provide a smaller number of supervisory districts, the commissioner will direct the board to meet to appoint a district superintendent. This appointment is subject to the commissioner's approval (§ 2204(1), (2)). If the vacancy is not filled at this meeting, the commissioner may appoint an interim district superintendent until the BOCES fills the vacancy (§ 2204(1); see **6:10**).

6:6. Is there a maximum length for the duration of a district superintendent's employment contract?

Yes. The duration of any employment contract between a BOCES and a district superintendent entered after July 1, 1993 may not exceed three years. Copies of the agreement and any amendments thereto must be filed within five days of the contract's execution with the commissioner (§ 1950(4)(a)(1)).

Regardless of any employment contract, however, a district superintendent can be removed from office at any time by a majority vote of the BOCES board or by the commissioner of education under section 306 of the Education Law (§ 2212; see **6:8**).

6:7. Must a district superintendent take an oath of office?

Yes. The district superintendent must take a constitutional oath of office before assuming his or her duties and not later than five days after the date on which the term of office is to start. The oath may be taken before a county clerk, a justice of the peace, or a notary public, and must be filed in the office of the secretary of state (§ 2206).

6:8. May a district superintendent be removed from office?

Yes. A district superintendent may be removed from office at any time by majority vote of the BOCES board or by the commissioner of education under section 306 of the Education Law (§ 2212). A district superintendent who is removed from office is ineligible for appointment as a district superintendent in any supervisory district for five years (§ 2205(3)).

6:9. Under what circumstances does a vacancy in the office of a district superintendent occur?

Under section 2208 of the Education Law, a district superintendent's office becomes vacant when the current incumbent dies; files a written resignation with the commissioner of education and the clerk of the BOCES; accepts the office of supervisor, town clerk, or trustee of a school district; or fails to take and file the oath of office. A vacancy will also occur if the district superintendent is removed from office by the BOCES board or the commissioner of education (§ 2208; 2212; see **6:8**).

6:10. How is a vacancy in the office of district superintendent filled?

When such a vacancy occurs, the commissioner of education shall direct the BOCES board to meet to appoint a new district superintendent, unless the commissioner has provided for a smaller number of supervisory districts. Each board member has one vote and the person receiving the majority of all votes cast shall be appointed, subject to the approval of the commissioner. A copy of the proceedings and the appointment certified by the BOCES board president and the BOCES board clerk must be filed in the county clerk's office and with the commissioner of education by the BOCES board clerk within five days of the appointment (§ 2204(1), (2), (3); see **6:5**).

If the vacancy is not filled at this meeting, the meeting may be adjourned to a subsequent date, and the commissioner may appoint a district superintendent who serves until the board fills the vacancy. A district superintendent from one supervisory district who is appointed to be a temporary or acting superintendent in another supervisory district does not receive any compensation for duties associated with the temporary or acting position (§ 2204(1), (4)).

6:11. How is a district superintendent's salary paid?

Each district superintendent receives an annual salary of $43,499 from the state, payable by the commissioner (§ 2209(1)). In addition, the BOCES may decide to pay the district superintendent a supplementary salary (§ 1950(4)(a)(1)). If the board decides to do so, this supplemental amount along with other supplementary benefits (see **6:12**) must be listed in the BOCES administrative budget that is provided to the trustees or board members of each component district (§ 1950(4)(b)(1)).

Additionally, the town supervisors in any supervisory district may vote to further increase the district superintendent's salary. This additional amount is paid by a tax levied on the towns comprising the supervisory district (§ 2209(2)).

6:12. Is there a limit or cap on a district superintendent's salary?

Yes. Starting with the 2003-04 school year, the total salary paid to district superintendents, including the amount paid by the state under section 2209 and the supplementary salary paid by the supervisory district, may not exceed the lesser of 6 percent of the salary cap of the preceding school year, or 98 percent of the commissioner's 2003-04 salary (§ 1950(4)(a)(2)). That 98 percent amounts to $166,572.

6:13. What items must be included in the total salary cap?

In addition to the amount paid by the state under section 2209 and the supplementary salary paid by the supervisory district, the following items must also be included in the total salary cap:

- payments for life insurance having a cash value;
- payments for the employee contribution, co-pay, or uncovered medical expenses under a health insurance plan;
- payments for transportation or travel expenses in excess of actual documented expenses incurred in the performance of BOCES and state functions; and
- any other lump sum payments that are not specifically excluded from total salary by Education Law (§ 1950(4)(a)(2)).

Any variation of these limitations may subject a district superintendent to penalties, including termination (§ 2212-b).

A statement describing the district superintendent's compensation must be included in the BOCES budget prior to the BOCES annual meeting (§ 1950(4)(b)(1)).

6:14. Are there limits on other benefits provided to a district superintendent?

Yes. Under the BOCES Reform Act, a district superintendent is an employee of the state (see also Opn. Att'y Gen. F 97-10). His or her maximum vacation time and sick leave and accrued or unused vacation or sick leave may not exceed the maximum permitted for management/confidential employees of New York State — 200 sick days and vacation without limit, except that as of January 1 each year, the amount of vacation cannot exceed 40 vacation days (4 NYCRR §§ 28-1.2, 28-1.3). This 40-day limitation on the accrual of vacation may be exceeded in a few special circumstances (see 4 NYCRR § 1.2(e).

A district superintendent may be granted up to 13 days of vacation leave during his or her first year of employment and one additional vacation day on each subsequent annual anniversary date, for a total of up to 20 vacation days per year (more if the district superintendent has 20 years of continuous state service) (4 NYCRR § 1.2(b), (c)).

A district superintendent who was in state service on December 31, 1985 may be provided up to 13 sick days per year (4 NYCRR § 28-1.3(b)). All other district superintendents to whom the BOCES Reform Act applies are limited to a maximum of eight days sick leave per year (4 NYCRR § 28-2.1(c)).

Further, at the time of separation from service, a district superintendent may not be compensated for accrued and unused vacation credits or sick leave, or use accrued and unused sick leave for retirement service credit or to pay health insurance premiums after retirement at a rate in excess of that allowed for other management/confidential employees (§ 1950(4)(a)(2)).

Specifically, a district superintendent may not be compensated for more than 30 accrued, unused vacation days upon separation of service (4 NYCRR § 30.1).

Upon separation from service, a district superintendent may be permitted to use up to 200 days of accumulated, unused sick leave to pay for health insurance in retirement (4 NYCRR §§ 28-1.3(b)–2.1(c)).

6:15. May the supervisory district give pay raises to the district superintendent based upon increases in other collective bargaining agreements within the supervisory district?

No. The terms of a district superintendent's contract may not be tied to any increases paid pursuant to any collective bargaining agreements made with other employees in the supervisory district (§ 1950(4)(a)(2)).

6:16. May the commissioner of education withhold payment of the district superintendent's salary?

Yes. If the commissioner determines that a district superintendent has persistently neglected to perform an official duty, he or she may withhold part or all the district superintendent's salary as it becomes due. However, the commissioner may also later decide to pay the withheld portion to the district superintendent at a later date (§ 2211).

Pursuant to section 2212-b of the Education Law, the commissioner must withhold from a district superintendent's state salary an amount of money equal to twice the value of any violation of the applicable salary and benefit caps (see **6:14–15**), unless the commissioner determines that the violation was inadvertent. In this case, the commissioner shall withhold the monetary value of the violation (§§ 2212-b(2), 1950(4)(a)(2)).

6:17. May a district superintendent hold another job during his or her term of office?

No. A district superintendent must devote his or her full time to the office and may not "engage in any other occupation or profession" (§ 2213). Additionally, a district superintendent, once appointed, must vacate any prior position with the BOCES upon appointment as district superintendent. The contract for employment as district superintendent must be the only contract the district superintendent holds with the BOCES (§1950(4)(a)(3)).

6:18. Are there any specific business activities in which district superintendents are prohibited from participating?

Yes. District superintendents are expressly prohibited from:
- having a direct or indirect interest, other than as an author, in the sale, publication, or manufacture of school books, maps, charts, or school apparatus, or in the sale or manufacture of school furniture or any other school supplies or library supplies;
- having a direct or indirect interest, in any contract made by the trustees of a school district;
- having a direct or indirect interest in any agency or bureau maintained to obtain or help obtain positions for teachers or superintendents;
- directly or indirectly receiving any emolument, gift, pay reward or promise of pay or reward for recommending or procuring the sale, use or adoption, or assisting in the sale, use or adoption of any book, map, chart, school apparatus or furniture or other supplies for any school or library or for recommending a teacher or helping a teacher obtain a teaching position (§ 2214).

6:19. What are the district superintendent's responsibilities in the organization and operation of a board of cooperative educational services (BOCES)?

The district superintendent is the chief executive officer of the BOCES board. Where a BOCES is composed of two or more supervisory districts, the district superintendents, together with the president of the BOCES board, serve as an executive committee (§ 1950(2)).

6:20. What are the general powers and duties of the district superintendent?

Section 2215 of the Education Law states that a district superintendent's general powers and duties are to:

- Ascertain and maintain records in regard to school district boundaries. In addition, district superintendents are authorized to determine where district boundary lines are located (*Board of Educ. of Shenendehowa CSD v. Commissioner of Educ.*, 182 A.D.2d 944 (3d Dep't 1992); but see **6:23**).
- Hold teacher conferences and counsel teachers in relation to discipline, school management and other schoolwork, and matters promoting the general good of all schools of the district.
- Counsel trustees and board members and other school officers in relation to their powers and duties.
- Direct trustees and board members to "abate any nuisance" in or on school grounds, at the direction of the commissioner of education.
- Approve the amount, or the sureties on bonds, of treasurers and tax collectors of school districts.
- Condemn a schoolhouse, at the direction of the commissioner of education (§ 412).
- Examine and license teachers pursuant to the provisions of the Education Law and conduct other examinations as directed by the commissioner of education.
- Examine any charges affecting the moral character of any teacher residing or employed within the supervisory district and to revoke that teacher's certificate pursuant to section 3018 of the Education Law.
- Take affidavits and administer oaths in all matters pertaining to the public school system, free of charge.
- Take and report testimony in cases under appeal to the commissioner of education, as the commissioner directs. In such a case or in any matter to be heard or determined by the district superintendent, he or she may issue a subpoena to compel the attendance of a witness.
- Exercise at his or her discretion any of the powers and perform any of the duties of another district superintendent at the written request of

that superintendent. A district superintendent also must perform such duties when directed to do so by the commissioner.

- Make an annual report to the commissioner by August 1 of each year, and submit any other reports he or she may request.
- Participate in the permanent computerized statewide school district address match and income verification system as provided by section 171 of the Tax Law and as directed by the commissioner.
- Report to the commissioner on cost-effective practices in school districts within his or her supervisory district.
- Fill, under certain circumstances, a vacancy on a school board (§ 2113).

In addition, the district superintendent or his or her designee shall represent the educational system on the interagency children's services team responsible for coordinating services for children with emotional and behavioral disorders within their county or local consortium of counties, along with appropriate local school district representatives determined by the district superintendent (Exec. Law §§ 448(3)(a)(ii),(b)(ii)).

6:21. What are the district superintendent's responsibilities in appointing teachers for probation and tenure in local districts and boards of cooperative educational services (BOCES)?

A district superintendent plays no role in appointing teachers for probation and tenure in local districts. These recommendations are made by the local superintendent of schools to the local school board (§§ 2509(1), (2), 2573, 3012(1),(3)).

However, the district superintendent does have the power to recommend BOCES staff members to the BOCES board, including teachers, administrative assistants, and supervisors, for a probationary period of up to three years (§ 3014(1)). The district superintendent is also charged with making tenure recommendations to the BOCES board for those employees (§ 3014(2)).

6:22. May the district superintendent revoke a teacher's certificate?

Yes, although this authority is seldom invoked. The district superintendent is empowered to examine any charge affecting the moral character of any teacher residing in or employed within his or her supervisory district and to revoke such teacher's certificate (§ 2215(10)). The teacher is given reasonable notice of the charge and an opportunity to defend himself or herself. If the charge is sustained, the teacher's certificate is annulled and the individual declared unfit to teach. The district superintendent must then notify the commissioner of education immediately of such annulment and declaration (§ 3018).

6:23. What are the powers and duties of the district superintendent in relation to the formation, alteration, and dissolution of school districts?

A district superintendent may organize a new common or union free school district out of the territory of one or more districts that are wholly within the geographic area served by his or her BOCES "whenever the educational interests of the community require it" (§ 1504(1)). The district superintendents of two or more adjoining supervisory districts may form a joint school district out of the adjoining portions of their respective districts "when public interests require it" (§ 1504(2)). A district superintendent may also order the partitioning of territory from an existing union free, central high school, or enlarged city school district; the dissolution and reformation of the existing district; and the formation of a new union free or city school district out of such territory (§ 2218).

In addition, any district superintendent may dissolve one or more school districts by order and may form a new district from this territory. He or she also may unite the territory or a portion thereof, by order, to an adjoining school district, except for a city school district (§ 1505(1)) and/or a central school district. The formation and changes of central school districts are completed by order of the commissioner of education (§§ 1801, 1802).

Section 1507 of the Education Law also authorizes a district superintendent to alter district boundaries with the written consent of all the districts to be affected (*Matter of Zeltmann*, 15 Educ. Dep't Rep. 47 (1975)).

A district superintendent, however, has no authority to change school district boundaries, except upon consent of all the affected districts (§§ 1507, 1508, 1509; *Appeal of Roberta*, 38 Educ. Dep't Rep. 690 (1999); *Appeal of Elacqua*, 32 Educ. Dep't Rep. 658 (1993)).

6:24. Is a district superintendent entitled to the protections of Public Officers Law section 17, which governs defense and indemnification of state employees?

Yes. A district superintendent of schools is a state employee entitled to the protections of Public Officers Law section 17 in connection with lawsuits that arise out of the performance of the district superintendent's state functions (Opn. Att'y Gen. F 97-10 (1997)). For further information on the issue of defense and indemnification, see **chapter 18**.

7. School Administrators

7:1. What are the typical school administrative positions in New York State?

Every school district in New York State may appoint a superintendent of schools (§§ 1604(8), 1711(1); 2503(5), 2554(2), 2590-g(2), 2590-h(17), (41); see **7:22**). School districts must appoint a full-time building principal for every school, unless the commissioner of education approves an alternative mode of building administration after reviewing evidence submitted by the district (8 NYCRR 100.2(a); *Appeal of Branch and McElfresh*, 41 Educ. Dep't Rep. 334 (2002); see **7:32**). Other common administrative positions in New York State, appointed at the option of the school board, are associate and assistant superintendents, supervisors, department chairpersons, and assistant principals.

7:2. What are the certification and fingerprinting requirements for school administrators in New York State?

For *certification requirements*, the commissioner's regulations set out three classes of certificates for school administrators (8 NYCRR § 80-2.4). These include:

- *School District Administrator (SDA)*. The SDA class includes district superintendents, superintendents of schools, deputy, associate and assistant superintendents, and any other persons having responsibilities involving general districtwide administration (8 NYCRR § 80-2.4(a)).

The certificate requirements are a baccalaureate and a master's degree, including at least 60 semester hours of graduate study. Of the 60 hours, 24 must be in school administration and supervision. An approved administrative/supervisory internship also must be completed or one year of satisfactory full-time experience may be substituted for it (8 NYCRR § 80-2.4(a)(1)).

In addition, any person applying for a superintendent's certificate must have completed two hours of course work on or training in the identification and reporting of child abuse and maltreatment (§ 3003(4); 8 NYCRR § 80-1.4).

Furthermore, any person applying for a certification or license valid for service as school administrator, supervisor, or superintendent must complete two hours of training in school violence prevention and intervention (§ 3004(3); 8 NYCRR § 80-1.4).

Three years of teaching and/or administrative and/or supervisory and/or pupil personnel service experience in nursery school through 12th grade are also required (8 NYCRR § 80-2.4(a)(2)).

- *School Administrator and Supervisor (SAS).* The SAS certificate is required for principals, housemasters, assistant principals, supervisors, department chairpersons, coordinators, unit heads, and any other persons serving more than 25 percent of his or her assignment (10 periods per week) in any administrative and/or supervisory position (8 NYCRR § 80-2.4(b); *Matter of Connor*, 22 Educ. Dep't Rep. 313 (1982)).

The requirements for a provisional SAS certificate are a baccalaureate degree; 30 semester hours of graduate study, 18 hours of which must have been taken in school administration and supervision; and an internship or one year of satisfactory full-time experience in a school administrative or supervisory position (8 NYCRR § 80-2.4(b)(1)(i)).

Three years of teaching and/or administrative and/or supervisory and/or pupil personnel service experience in nursery school through 12th grade are also required (8 NYCRR § 80-2.4(b)(1)(ii)).

In addition to requirements for provisional certification, permanent certification requires that an SAS candidate have completed two years of school experience in an administrative/supervisory position. Within the total program of preparation, the candidate must have been awarded a master's degree (8 NYCRR § 80-2.4(b)(2)).

- *School Business Administrator (SBA).* The SBA certificate is required for deputy superintendents of schools for business, associate and assistant superintendents of schools for business and any other person having professional responsibility for the business operation of the school district, such as a school business official or administrator (8 NYCRR § 80-2.4(c)).

The certificate requirements are identical to those of the SDA, except that one year of satisfactory full-time experience as the chief business official, rather than one year of full-time experience in a school administrative or supervisory position of a school district, may be substituted for the internship requirement (8 NYCRR § 80-2.4(c)(1)).

The holder of any certificate that would otherwise expire while that individual is on military active duty will be extended automatically for the period of active duty and for 12 months after release from active duty (Military Law §§ 308-a, 308-b).

For *fingerprinting requirements,* all "prospective" school district or BOCES employees, including administrators, must be fingerprinted. In general, commissioner's regulations define a "prospective employee" to mean any paid employee or contract service provider "who will reasonably be expected by [the district] to provide services which involve direct contract, meaning face-to-face communication or interaction, with students under the age of 21," more than five days during the school year (see **8:13**). This also includes individuals who are employed by or associated with providers of supplemental educational services required by the federal No Child Left Behind Act (20 USC § 6301 *et seq.*) if such individuals will have direct contact with children eligible for such services (§ 305 (33)(b)).

A prospective employee who refuses to be fingerprinted may not be hired. The district or BOCES is responsible for obtaining two sets of fingerprints from the prospective employee and forwarding them to the commissioner of education.

The commissioner then submits the fingerprints to the state Division of Criminal Justice Services (DCJS) for processing by DCJS and the Federal Bureau of Investigation. Upon receipt of a criminal history report, the commissioner will notify the school district or BOCES whether the prospective employee is cleared for employment (§§ 305(30), 1604(39), (40), 1709(39), (40), 1804(9), (10), 1950(4)(11)(mm), 2503(18), (19), 2554(25), (26), 2590-h (20), 3004-b, 3035; 8 NYCRR Part 87). Until July 1, 2005, the law provides for the conditional appointment of employees (including administrators) awaiting completion of the fingerprinting process (§ 3035(3)(b)).

For a more detailed explanation of the requirements of the fingerprinting law, see **8:66–79**.

7:3. May the requirements for certification as a school district administrator (SDA) be waived?

Yes. At the request of a school board or board of cooperative educational services (BOCES), the commissioner of education may waive the requirements for the school district administrator certificate for a person who is exceptionally qualified but does not meet all of the graduate course or teaching requirements, and whose training and experience are the substantial equivalent of such requirements (§ 3003(3); 8 NYCRR § 80-2.4(a)(3)).

In its formal request to the State Education Department, the board must note its approval of the request; the job description; its rationale for requesting such certification of the individual; a statement identifying the exceptional qualifications of the candidate; and the individual's completed application for certification, vitae and official transcripts of collegiate study. Such a certification, if issued, is valid only for service in the district requesting the waiver (8 NYCRR § 80-2.4(a)(3)).

In addition, a certification that would otherwise expire while the holder is on military active duty is automatically extended for 12 months after that individual's release from active duty (Military Law §§ 308-a, 308-b).

7:4. Is there a legal procedure for decertifying a school administrator?

No, but there is a procedure, specified in Part 83 of the commissioner's regulations, to make a determination of good moral character. This could lead to the revocation, annulment, or suspension of an administrator's certificate, or the imposition of another penalty prescribed by the commissioner's regulations (§ 305(7); 8 NYCRR §§ 83.5(c), 83.6; see *Matter of Kelly*, 20 Educ. Dep't Rep. 503 (1981)). For a complete discussion of the range of penalties available, see **8:51**.

7:5. How are school administrators appointed?

Principals, administrators, and all other members of the supervisory staff of school districts and BOCES must be appointed by the school board to a three-year probationary term (§ 3012(1)(b)). The appointment requires the recommendation of the superintendent of schools in a school district, or the district superintendent in a BOCES. This rule does not apply to superintendents of schools, associate and assistant superintendents in small city school districts, and executive directors, associate, assistant, district, and community superintendents and examiners in Buffalo, New York City, Rochester, Syracuse, and Yonkers (§§ 2509(1)(b), 2573(1)(b), 3012(1)(b), 3014(1)). Special rules apply to the appointment of individuals in these districts depending on the position and district involved (see §§ 2509 (3), (4), (9); 2573(3), (4)).

Unlike teachers, administrators who have received tenure in another school district in the state are not entitled to a shortened two-year probationary period, and must serve a three-year probationary period, according to the State Education Department (Opn. of Counsel, No. 235, 15 Educ. Dep't Rep. 538 (1975); see **8:96, 8:114**).

In New York City, principals and other supervisory personnel are employed in the manner prescribed by chanceller's regulations (see §§ 2590-f(1)(d),(e), 2590-h).

7:6. What tenure areas are applicable to school administrators?

There are no clearly defined guidelines for determining administrative and supervisory tenure areas (*Bell v. Board of Educ. of Vestal CSD*, 61 N.Y.2d 149 (1984)). Part 30 of the commissioner's regulations, which establishes teacher tenure areas, is not applicable to administrative and supervisory personnel (*Matter of Moore*, 15 Educ. Dep't Rep. 475 (1976); see 8 NYCRR Part 30). Instead, a board of education may maintain a single districtwide "administrator" tenure area or establish more defined administrative tenure areas (see *Bell*).

The tenure area of an administrator is the area in which the original probationary appointment was made (*Schlick v. Board of Educ. of Mamaroneck UFSD*, 227 A.D.2d 407 (2d Dep't 1996)).

7:7. How do school districts with more than one administrative tenure area determine what positions belong in a particular tenure area?

Where a school board has established more than one administrative tenure area, case law has identified factors that should be considered to determine whether certain administrative and supervisory positions must be considered to lie within the same tenure area. Among the factors to be considered are "the notice given to the individuals involved as to their tenure status, the duties of various positions, the adverse practical impact of non-recognition of a particular area and membership in collective bargaining units" (see *Matter of Plesent*, 16 Educ. Dep't Rep. 348 (1977)).

Documentation such as an appointment letter or a board resolution that refers to an administrator's tenure area and comparisons of duties and responsibilities are important factors in determining the tenure area of administrators (see, for example, *Matter of Roloff*, 16 Educ. Dep't Rep. 274 (1977); *Matter of Parsons*, 16 Educ. Dep't Rep. 134 (1976)). Under the principle commonly known as the "50 percent rule," positions will generally be deemed to lie within the same administrative tenure area if a majority of the job duties are similar (*Coates v. Ambach*, 52 A.D.2d 261, *aff'd*, 42 N.Y.2d 846 (1977)). Consequently, the mere fact that two positions, such as director and chairperson, are supervisory in nature does not compel the conclusion that they are within the same tenure area (see *Matter of Plesent*).

However, the 50 percent rule should not be rigidly applied. Emphasis should be on the type, quality, and breadth of responsibilities associated with the positions being compared (*Cowan v. Board of Educ. of the Brentwood UFSD*, 99 A.D.2d 831 (2d Dep't 1984), *appeal discontinued*, 63 N.Y.2d 708 (1984); *Matter of Plesent*; see *Appeal of Elmendorf*, 36 Educ. Dep't Rep. 308 (1997); *Matter of Abeles*, 18 Educ. Dep't Rep. 521 (1979); *Matter of Falanga*, 17 Educ. Dep't Rep. 267 (1978)).

The 50 percent rule has also been applied in determining whether a particular employee serves in an administrative or teacher tenure area. An employee will be deemed to serve in a administrative rather than teacher tenure area if the employee spends **over** 50 percent of his or her time on administrative duties (*Appeal of Klein*, 43 Educ. Dep't Rep. ___, dec. no. 15,003 (2003); see also *Maine-Endwell Teachers Ass'n v. Maine-Endwell CSD*, 92 A.D.2d 1052 (3d Dep't 1983); *Matter of Funnell*, 19 Educ. Dep't Rep. 448 (1980)).

7:8. Does service as a substitute administrator count toward an administrative probationary period?

No. Administrative employees do not receive so-called "Jarema credit" for time spent as substitutes for administrators who are temporarily unable to perform their duties (*McManus v. Board of Educ. of the Hempstead UFSD*, 87 N.Y.2d 183 (1995); see *Roberts v. Community Sch. Bd. of Community Dist. No. 6*, 66 N.Y.2d 652 (1985)). While teachers may apply Jarema credit for time spent as a substitute teacher towards the probationary period required before tenure (§§ 2509(1)(a), 2573(1)(a), 3012(1)(a); see **8:114–116**), administrators are not given similar rights (see §§ 2509(1)(b), 2573(1)(b), 3012(1)(b)).

7:9. Does service as an "acting" administrator in a vacant position count toward an administrative probationary period?

Yes. A board must count as service toward a probationary period time spent by an employee assigned to a vacant position in an "acting" capacity when that employee is subsequently appointed to a probationary term in that position. The employee will be deemed to have commenced the probationary term for that particular position when appointed to fill the vacant position (*McManus v. Board of Educ. of the Hempstead UFSD*, 87 N.Y.2d 183 (1995)).

7:10. Does service rendered outside an administrative tenure area pending the outcome of criminal charges count toward an administrative probationary period?

No. In *Feldman v. Community Sch. Dist.* 32, 231 A.D.2d 632 (2d Dep't 1996), *appeal denied*, 89 N.Y.2d 811(1997), an assistant principal who was reassigned to the central district office during his probationary period pending the outcome of criminal charges did not receive credit for the time spent in the central district office assignment because he did not perform the duties of assistant principal during that time.

7:11. Does part-time service as an administrator count toward an administrative probationary period?

An individual must spend over 50 percent of his or her time performing administrative duties for such part-time service to constitute service within an administrative tenure area. As such, a lesser amount of time spent on administrative duties may not count toward an administrative probationary period (see *Appeal of* Klein, 43 Educ. Dep't Rep. ___, dec. no. 15,003 (2003); *Matter of Funnell*, 19 Educ. Dep't Rep. 448 (1980)).

7:12. May administrators be transferred?

Yes. An administrator may be transferred to another position or assigned to perform other duties and functions encompassed within his or her tenure area (*Matter of Monaco*, 24 Educ. Dep't Rep. 48 (1984)). However, administrators may not be transferred outside their tenure area without their consent (*Appeal of Caruana*, 41 Educ. Dep't Rep. 227 (2001); *Matter of Zamek*, 19 Educ. Dep't Rep. 77 (1979); *Cowan v. Board of Educ.*, 99 A.D.2d 831 (2d Dep't 1984)).

Nor may a tenured administrator be transferred involuntarily as a means of discipline in lieu of affording the administrator his or her due process rights pursuant to Education Law section 3020-a (*Appeal of Irving*, 39 Educ. Dep't Rep. 761 (2002); see **7:16**). In *Appeal of Irving*, a district transferred a principal to the position of assistant principal at another school based on the superintendent's conclusion that the principal was "confrontational" and mistreated parents and students. According to the commissioner of education, the sole reason for the transfer was the principal's alleged misconduct, which violated her rights as a tenured administrator under section 3020-a, including the right to contest the charges.

A school board may transfer principals without the recommendation of the superintendent of schools (*Appeal of Lander*, 42 Educ. Dep't Rep. 201 (2002)).

7:13. May districts share administrators?

Yes. Under Education Law article 40-A, school districts may arrange to share the services of a superintendent, associate superintendent, assistant superintendent or any other employee with districtwide administrative or supervisory responsibilities, with one or more other school districts (§ 1981(1)).

A shared administrator who is not in a tenure-track position is considered an employee by all districts sharing his or her services. All decisions regarding the appointment or compensation of that administrator must be made with the consent of a majority of each participating school district's board. The compensation and benefits of a shared administrator are provided by each participating school district, based on an agreed-upon formula (§ 1981(2)(a)).

For a shared administrator who may be granted tenure, the participating districts must designate one of their own as the principal employing district. That administrator is considered to be employed by the principal employing district, but decisions on the probationary appointment and compensation package must be made with the consent of a majority of each of the school boards of each participating district.

The principal employing district makes decisions regarding the termination, discipline, or tenure of that administrator in consultation with all other participating districts. The services rendered by the shared administrator in any participating district is deemed to have been rendered in the principal employing district for all purposes, including tenure credit, seniority, and discipline (§ 1981(2)(b)).

All agreements to share personnel, such as administrators, between districts must be approved by the district superintendent (see **7:19**), or by the commissioner of education or his or her designee if there is no local district superintendent (§ 1981(4)).

7:14. May a school district collectively negotiate with its administrative employees, or contract with its superintendent, a cash payment for unused accumulated sick leave at retirement?

Yes. Sick leave is a term and condition of employment that must be negotiated with unionized employees under the Taylor Law (*City of Albany v. Helsby*, 48 A.D.2d 998 (3d Dep't), *aff'd*, 38 N.Y.2d 778 (1975)). Because there is no express statutory prohibition against providing a cash payment for unused accumulated sick leave at retirement, the district and the union may agree to such an arrangement (*Perrenod v. Liberty Bd. of Educ.*, 223 A.D.2d 870 (3d Dep't 1996); see **chapter 10** for more information on the Taylor Law and collective bargaining).

Employment contracts for superintendents may also contain such a provision because the Education Law specifically authorizes contracts to contain "such other terms as shall be mutually acceptable to the parties, including but not limited to, fringe benefits" (§ 1711(3); *Perrenod*; see §§ 2507(1), 2565(1)).

However, such payments may be found to violate the constitutional ban on gifts of public funds if there is no legal obligation to provide such payment under contract, collective bargaining agreement or policy prior to the accumulation of leave (*Rampello v. East Irondequoit CSD*, 236 A.D.2d 797 (4th Dep't 1997)).

7:15. Is a school board bound by an employment contract with an administrative employee?

Yes, if one exists. The courts have ruled that a school board that has appointed a probationary administrative employee is bound by a written employment contract between that employee and the board, including those provisions concerning dismissal during the probationary period (*Averback v. Board of Educ. of New Paltz CSD*, 147 A.D.2d 152 (3d Dep't 1989), *appeal denied*, 74 N.Y.2d 611 (1989); see also *Appeal of Charland*, 32 Educ. Dep't Rep. 291 (1992)).

In addition, the commissioner of education has held that an employment contract between a small city school district and a deputy superintendent of schools is statutorily authorized under the Education Law (*Appeal of Reilly*, 37 Educ. Dep't Rep. 688 (1998); see § 2509(3)).

7:16. Are there specific procedures for disciplining and/or terminating the employment of administrators or supervisors?

Yes. The probationary appointment of an administrative employee may be terminated at any time on the recommendation of the superintendent and by majority vote of the school board (§§ 2509(1)(b), 2573(1)(b), 3012(1)(b), 3014(1)), provided the employee is not terminated for an illegal or unconstitutional reason, and the notice requirements of section 3019-a of the Education Law are met (*Appeal of Wint*, 33 Educ. Dep't Rep. 9 (1993); see **8:126**).

Education Law section 3031 applies to the dismissal of probationary administrators and supervisors who are not recommended for tenure (*Appeal of Gold*, 34 Educ. Dep't Rep. 372 (1995); see § 3012(2)). The procedure is similar to that applicable to teachers (see **8:126–127, 8:129**).

Under certain circumstances an administrator who is terminated during his or her probationary period may be entitled to a name-clearing hearing. For example, the U.S. Court of Appeals for the Second Circuit found that an administrator who received negative evaluations and reasons for termination, which damaged the administrator's professional reputation to such a degree as to virtually preclude her from getting another job as an administrator in the future, was entitled to a name-clearing hearing (*Donato v. Plainview-Old Bethpage CSD*, 96 F.3d 623 (2nd Cir. 1996), *cert. denied*, 519 U.S. 1150 (1997), *remanded*, 985 F.Supp. 316 (E.D.N.Y. 1997)).

Tenured administrative employees, like tenured teachers, are subject to the protections of section 3020-a of the Education Law, except that in New York City, discipline and/or termination of principals and other supervisory personnel may be conducted exclusively pursuant to the provisions of certain collective bargaining agreements (§§ 3020(3), 3012(2); see **8:178–201**). Accordingly, a school district improperly transferred a tenured principal to the position of assistant principal at another school based solely on a superintendent's conclusion that the principal had engaged in misconduct (*Appeal of Irving*, 39 Educ. Dep't Rep. 761 (2000)). Collective bargaining agreements may place further restrictions on the dismissal of administrative employees.

However, a school district may not agree to withhold from law enforcement authorities the fact that an allegation of child abuse in an educational setting (see **12:82**) has been made against an administrator in exchange for the administrator's resignation or voluntary suspension. Any such agreement constitutes a class E felony and is also punishable by a civil penalty of up to $20,000 (§ 1133).

Like teachers, administrators enjoy freedom of expression rights and generally may not be disciplined for speaking out on matters of public concern. For example, a federal district court refused to dismiss a lawsuit brought by a high school principal who claimed that a school superintendent retaliated against him for expressing his opinion that the school superintendent behaved inappropriately by drinking in public and driving while intoxicated. The court denied the district's motion to dismiss the case, because the principal's comments were on a matter of public concern, the district did not claim that the comments caused disruption, and a jury could find that the comments were a substantial or motivating factor in an adverse employment action by the district (*DePace v. Flaherty*, 183 F.Supp.2d 633 (S.D.N.Y. 2002)).

On the other hand, a separate federal district court dismissed, on remand from the U.S. Court of Appeals for the Second Circuit, a lawsuit challenging the termination of an assistant superintendent who publicly criticized fellow administrators for failing to provide leadership and poor performance. The court dismissed the plaintiff's case, finding that his criticisms were at odds with the administration's goals and likely to cause disruption, because his remarks "ran counter to his job description and undermined the ability of the administration as a whole to carry out its responsibilities" (*McCullough v. Wyandanch UFSD*, 187 F.3d 272 (2d Cir. 1999), *dismissed on remand*, 132 F.Supp.2d 87 (E.D.N.Y. 2001))

7:17. Is a wrongfully terminated probationary administrator entitled to back pay?

No. Only "tenured employees . . . are entitled to back pay during periods of . . . improper termination" because their tenured status affords them a property interest in their salary (*Okebiyi v. Crew*, 303 A.D.2d 684 (2d Dep't 2003)).

7:18. May a school board abolish an administrative position?

Yes, if the position is no longer necessary to the school system. School boards have broad latitude to abolish, reorganize, or consolidate administrative and teaching positions (*Matter of Riendeau*, 23 Educ. Dep't Rep. 487 (1984); see *Girard v. Board of Educ. of City Sch. Dist. of City of Buffalo*, 168 A.D.2d 183 (4th Dep't 1991); *Ryan v. Ambach*, 71 A.D.2d 719 (3d Dep't 1979); see also **8:145–46**). However, a position may not be abolished as a pretext to circumvent an employee's tenure rights (*Matter of Riendeau*).

Whenever a board abolishes an administrative position, the administrator with the least amount of seniority in the tenure area is the first to be dismissed (§§ 2510(2), 2585(3), 2588(3)(b), 3013(2); for more information on administrative tenure areas, see **7:6–7**).

7:19. Is an administrator whose position is abolished entitled to another position in the school district?

Yes, under certain circumstances, an administrator may be reinstated to another position in the district for which appointments on tenure may be made under the Education Law (*Matter of Merz*, 21 Educ. Dep't Rep. 449 (1982); see *Appeal of Heath*, 37 Educ. Dep't Rep. 544 (1998)).

First, if a school board abolishes an office or position and creates another one with similar duties, the administrator whose position is to be abolished may be entitled to be appointed to the newly created position without reduction in salary or increment (§§ 2510(1), 2585(2), 2588(2), 3013(1); see § 1981(2)(b)(ii)). To claim such entitlement, the administrator must show that:

- The newly created position is in the same tenure area as the abolished position (*Appeal of Heath; Appeal of Elmendorf*, 36 Educ. Dep't Rep. 308 (1997)).
- The newly created and abolished positions have more than 50 percent of duties in common, provided that, in comparing the duties of two positions, the degree of comparable skill, experience, trainin,g and certification required to carry out the duties and responsibilities of each position also must be considered (*Appeal of Heath; Appeal of Elmendorf*). For example, the commissioner of education has held that the positions of building principal and assistant superintendent are not similar because of the districtwide responsibilities and the additional skill, training, and certification requirements of the position of assistant superintendent (*Appeal of Elmendorf*).

The administrator may have the right to a pre-termination hearing before the school board where there is a possibility that the duties of the position being abolished and the duties of a newly created position are similar (*Appeal of Elmendorf*; see also *Davis v. Mills*, 98 N.Y. 2d 120 (2002)).

Second, an administrator whose position is abolished has the right to be placed on a preferred eligible list (PEL) of candidates for appointment to a similar position within his or her tenure area. The administrator may be "called back" from the PEL for reinstatement for up to seven years after the position is abolished (§§ 2510(3)(a), 2585(4), 3013(3)(a); for more information on administrative tenure areas, see **7:6–7**).

Superintendent of Schools

7:20. What is a superintendent of schools?

A *superintendent of schools* is the chief executive officer of a school district (§§ 1711(2)(a), 2508(1), 2566(1)). Any reference to the terms district principal, supervising principal, or principal of the district generally refer to the superintendent of schools (Gen. Constr. Law § 47-a).

A *district superintendent*, on the other hand, is the chief executive officer of a board of cooperative educational services (BOCES) and is the general supervising officer of the supervisory district. The district superintendent has responsibilities for both the BOCES and the component districts that comprise the BOCES (see **chapter 6** for more information on the district superintendent).

7:21. Is a superintendent a member of the school board?

No, except in city school districts. However, in all school districts, the superintendent has the right to speak on all matters before the board, but he or she does not have the right to vote on matters before the board (§§ 1711(2)(a), 2508(1), 2566(1)).

7:22. Is a superintendent required to take an oath of office?

Although statutory law does not specifically require superintendents to take an oath of office (see §§ 2206 (district superintendents), 3002 (teachers); Pub. Off. Law §§ 2, 10 (board members, district clerk, treasurer)), the commissioner of education has held that superintendents must take an oath of office as a matter of public policy. According to the commissioner, "it is sound public policy to treat school superintendents as public officers with respect to oaths of office" (*Application of Karpen*, 39 Educ. Dep't Rep. 98 (1999)). The oath must be administered by someone who has properly taken or filed an oath of office (*Application of Karpen*; see Pub. Off. Law § 10).

7:23. How do superintendents of schools acquire their positions in New York State?

A school board may appoint a superintendent of schools (§§ 1604(8), 1711(1), 2503(5), 2554(2)). These superintendents serve at the pleasure of the board, unless they and their boards have entered into employment contracts. Such contracts, however, may include procedures for terminating the superintendent's services prior to the end of the term (§ 1711(3); see **7:24** for more information on superintendents' contracts).

7:24. Is a contract necessary to employ a superintendent?

No. However, many school boards enter into such contracts with their superintendents. This type of contract may include terms and conditions of employment such as duties, compensation, and termination of the contract (§ 1711(3); see §§ 2507(1), 2565(1); *Matter of Balen*, 20 Educ. Dep't Rep. 304 (1980)). In the absence of a contract, resolutions concerning term appointments embodied in minutes of board meetings may be used to identify the terms and conditions of employment.

A school board may not enter into a contract with a superintendent that contains any provisions relating to an increase in salary, compensation, or other benefits which are based on or tied to the terms of any contract or collective bargaining agreement with the district's teachers or other district employees (§§ 1711(3), 2507(1), 2565(1)).

7:25. How long may a superintendent's contract last?

School districts may enter into contracts with their superintendents for terms of from three to five years (§ 1711(3)).

City school districts, however, are prohibited from entering into a superintendent's contract that fixes the term or tenure of the super-intendent's services. Instead, superintendents serve at the pleasure of their board unless they are appointed to a term (§§ 2507(1), 2565(1),(3); *Matter of Brewster*, 15 Educ. Dep't Rep. 526 (1976); see *Appeal of Pratella*, 37 Educ. Dep't Rep. 693 (1998)). If appointed to a term, the term may not exceed five years in city school districts with a population of less than 250,000 and four years in Rochester and city school districts with a population of over 250,000 (§§ 2507(1), 2565(1), (3)). However, these school boards may have contracts that fix the other terms of employment, such as duties and salaries, with their superintendents (§§ 2507(1), 2565(1); *Matter of Venezia*, 19 Educ. Dep't Rep. 273 (1979); see *Matter of Balen*, 20 Educ. Dep't Rep. 304 (1980)), provided that terms and provisions relating to an increase in salary, compensation, or other benefits may not be based on or tied to the terms of any district contract or collective bargaining agreement entered into with teachers or other district employees (§§ 2507(1), 2565(1)).

School boards may not circumvent the statutory limitations on the length of employment contracts for superintendents by entering into multiple contracts that, when read together, create an obligation longer than that authorized by law (*Appeal of Boyle*, 35 Educ. Dep't Rep. 162 (1995)). For example, a five-year contract that was tacked onto an existing contract with three years remaining was invalid because these two contracts were in effect simultaneously and extended the service of the superintendent for three years beyond the statutory limit (*Appeal of Boyle*). However, school boards may extend an existing contract or supplant a prior contract with a new one, provided that the duration of the initial contract or the extension or subsequent contract does not exceed the statutory limitation (*Appeal of Knapp*, 34 Educ. Dep't Rep. 207 (1994); *Appeal of Stephens*, 28 Educ. Dep't Rep. 269, *aff'd sub nom. Lewiston-Porter CSD v. Sobol*, 154 A.D.2d 777 (3d Dep't 1989), *appeal dismissed*, 75 N.Y.2d 978 (1990); see *Appeal of Boyle*).

In New York City, the chancellor, who also sits on the city board and acts as its chairperson, serves at the pleasure of the mayor (§ 2590-h).

7:26. May an outgoing board extend a superintendent's contract?

Yes. The commissioner of education has ruled that, although it may be undemocratic, it is not illegal for a "lame-duck" board to extend the superintendent's contract and even award him or her a salary increase prior to the installation of the new board (*Appeal of Knapp*, 34 Educ. Dep't Rep. 207 (1994); *Appeal of Dillon*, 33 Educ. Dep't Rep. 544 (1994)). Because such an action taken by an outgoing board is procedurally correct, a new board may not nullify it (*Appeal of Dillon*).

7:27. Must the school board of a newly-consolidated school district honor the contract of a former superintendent of one of the merged districts?

Yes. The commissioner of education has determined that a consolidated district, which is a combination of common, central or union free school districts merged to form a new district (see **chapter 15**), as the successor in interest of the districts that have merged, is obligated to honor the contract entered into by the former superintendent and the former board (§ 1804(5)(b); *Matter of Foster*, 28 Educ. Dep't Rep. 29 (1988)).

However, the consolidated district need not employ the former superintendent. Instead, it may discharge its obligation by paying the former superintendent the salary that he or she would have earned pursuant to the contract, less any income the former superintendent earns from employment elsewhere during the term of the contract (*Matter of Foster*).

7:28. Is a school board required to evaluate its superintendent?

Yes. The commissioner's regulations require school boards to annually review the performance of their superintendents according to procedures developed by the school board in consultation with the superintendent. The evaluation procedures must be filed in the district office and available for public review no later than September 10 of each year (8 NYCRR § 100.2(o)(2)(v)).

7:29. What are the statutory powers and duties of a superintendent of schools?

Education Law section 1711(2) states that superintendents of schools have the following powers and duties, unless otherwise specified by the bylaws of the board of education:

- "To be the chief executive officer of the school district and the educational system, and to have the right to speak on all matters before the board, but not to vote.
- "To enforce all provisions of law and all rules and regulations relating to the management of the schools and other educational, social and recreational activities under the direction of the board of education.
- "To prepare the content of each course of study authorized by the board of education. The content of each such course shall be submitted to the board of education for its approval and, when thus approved, the superintendent shall cause such courses of study to be used in the grades, classes and schools for which they are authorized.
- "To recommend suitable lists of textbooks to be used in the schools.
- "To have supervision and direction of associate, assistant and other superintendents, directors, supervisors, principals, teachers, lecturers, medical inspectors, nurses, auditors, attendance officers, janitors and other persons employed in the management of the schools or the other educational activities of the district authorized by [the Education Law] and under the direction and management of the board of education; to transfer teachers from one school to another, or from one grade of the course of study to another grade in such course, and to report immediately such transfers to such board for its consideration and actions; to report to such board violations of regulations and cases of insubordination, and to suspend an associate, assistant or other superintendent, director, supervisor, expert, principal, teacher or other employee until the next regular meeting of such board, when all facts relating to the case shall be submitted to such board for its consideration and action.
- "To have supervision and direction over the enforcement and observance of the courses of study, the examination and promotion of pupils, and over all other matters pertaining to playgrounds, medical inspection, recreation and social center work, libraries, lectures, and all other education activities under the management, direction and control of the board of education." (For city school districts, see §§ 2508 and 2566.)

With regard to the transfer of teachers, the Education Law specifically provides that a collective bargaining agreement may modify the superintendent's authority (§§ 1711(4), 2508(7), 2566(9); *Board of Educ. of the*

Arlington CSD v. Arlington Teachers Ass'n, 78 N.Y.2d 33 (1991)). A superintendent may not transfer a tenured administrator to another position as a disciplinary measure (*Appeal of Irving*, 39 Educ. Dep't Rep. 761 (2000)).

In New York City, the chancellor also sits on the citywide Panel for Educational Policy and serves as its chairperson. He or she also has the power to appoint and set salaries for employees in nonrepresented managerial titles (§§ 2590-g(2), 2590-h(17), (41)).

7:30. May a superintendent of schools grant an employee leave to serve as a emergency service volunteer?

Yes. A superintendent of schools has the authority to grant emergency service volunteer leave to district employees certified by the American Red Cross to participate in specialized disaster relief operations upon written request by the American Red Cross. Such leave from work shall be with pay and not exceed 20 days in any calendar year. The employee must be paid while on leave at the regular rate of pay for those regular work hours he or she is absent from work while participating in authorized specialized disaster relief operations. There may be no loss of seniority, sick, or vacation leave or compensation to which the employer is otherwise entitled (Gen. Mun. Law § 92-c).

7:31. Does a superintendent of schools need school board approval to initiate legal proceedings on behalf of the school district?

Yes. A superintendent of schools has no authority to commence legal proceedings on behalf of a school district absent school board approval, including an appeal from a commissioner of education decision. In addition, any school board vote authorizing such action must take place within the applicable period of limitations for commencing the particular legal proceeding (*Gersen v. Mills*, 290 A.D.2d 839 (3d Dep't 2002).

7:32. Does the school board have the authority to change the superintendent's duties during his or her employment contract?

Generally, yes. The board retains the authority to change the superintendent's powers and duties unless the board has given up that authority in the superintendent's employment contract (§ 1711(2)). Except where that authority has been removed, a board has broad latitude in establishing work requirements (*Matter of Hagen*, 17 Educ. Dep't Rep. 400 (1978); *Appeal of Fusco*, 39 Educ. Dep't Rep. (2000)).

7:33. Under what circumstances may a school board terminate a superintendent's contract?

A superintendent's contract may be terminated through non-renewal. In this context, attention must be paid to any automatic extension, "roll-over" or "evergreen" provisions contained in the contract. Procedures for providing notice of non-renewal must be carefully observed (*Appeal of Hernandez*, 29 Educ. Dep't Rep. 508 (1990); *Matter of Northrup*, 24 Educ. Dep't Rep. 262 (1985)).

Prior to its expiration date, a superintendent's contract may be terminated for cause in accordance with the provisions of the contract and in compliance with applicable due process requirements. The services of a superintendent appointed for a specified period of time in city school districts may also be terminated for cause as long as applicable due process requirements are observed (*Matter of Brewster*, 15 Educ. Dep't Rep. 526 (1976); see **7:34**).

A superintendent's contract may also be terminated prior to its expiration date through mutual agreement between the board and the superintendent. The courts and the commissioner of education have held that "buy-out" agreements do not violate the constitutional prohibition against the gift of public funds (see *Ingram v. Boone*, 91 A.D.2d 1063 (2d Dep't 1983); *Matter of Berke*, 12 Educ. Dep't Rep. 93 (1972); *Matter of Loiacono*, 11 Educ. Dep't Rep. 270 (1972)). Any documents confirming a "buy-out" or similar agreement are subject to disclosure under the Freedom of Information Law (see **2:89**).

7:34. What legal restrictions apply to dismissal proceedings against school superintendents?

Dismissal of a superintendent during the term of his or her contract or appointment requires cause and adherence to the provisions of the contract and to applicable due process procedures. Due process procedures must be followed because this kind of contract gives rise to a legally founded expectation of continued employment and is a property right within the meaning of case law (see, for example, *Appeal of Pinckney*, 35 Educ. Dep't Rep. 461 (1996); *Matter of Driscoll*, 14 Educ. Dep't Rep. 148 (1974)).

Due process under such circumstances involves, at minimum, the right to: receive written charges and to respond in writing to such charges; be represented by counsel; a formal hearing, with the right to produce evidence and cross-examine witnesses who testify in support of the charges; obtain a transcript of such hearing; formal written findings sustaining or dismissing the charges (*Matter of DeFreitas*, 14 Educ. Dep't Rep. 329 (1975)); and continued pay until due process requirements are met (*Appeal of Pinckney*). The contract may modify or supplement these requirements.

It should be noted that the Education Law specifically authorizes the inclusion of procedures for termination of employment as a term of the contract between the board and the superintendent (§ 1711(3)).

Principals

7:35. Must there be a principal in each school?

Yes. The commissioner's regulations require that a full-time principal be employed and assigned to each school. The principal must hold appropriate certification (8 NYCRR § 100.2(a)). Thus, a teacher who does not have proper certification to serve as principal may not be appointed as "teacher in charge" upon the resignation of a building principal until a successor can be appointed (*Appeal of Giardina*, 43 Educ. Dep't Rep.___, dec. no. 14,959 (2003)).

If there are circumstances that do not justify the assignment of a principal to a particular school, or if another mode of building administration would be more effective, the commissioner of education may approve an alternative mode upon request for such a variance (8 NYCRR § 100.2(a); *Appeal of Henderson*, 43 Educ. Dep't Rep. ___, dec. no. 14,909 (2003); Appeal *of Branch and McElfresh*, 41 Educ. Dep't Rep. 334 (2002), *aff'd, Olean City School Dist. v. NYS Educ. Dep't*, 2 A.D.3d 1111 (3d Dep't 2003)). The commissioner has determined that a district may assign one principal to a school comprised of more than one building on the same site where the buildings are in close proximity to each other (*Matter of Middle Island Principals' Ass'n*, 19 Educ. Dep't Rep. 507 (1980)). Two buildings that house different grades and are located miles apart do not constitute one unit (see *Matter of Henderson*).

7:36. May a superintendent of schools serve simultaneously as a school principal?

A superintendent of schools may serve simultaneously as a building principal only with the approval of the commissioner of education. That is so even when the school board's appointment of the superintendent to serve as principal is temporary until a full-time principal can be appointed (*Appeal of Giardina*, 43 Educ. Dep't Rep. ___, dec. no. 14,959 (2003)).

7:37. May a school board transfer a principal without the recommendation of the superintendent of schools?

Yes. School boards have "the superintendence, management and control of the educational affairs of the school district" and "all the powers reasonably necessary to... discharge duties imposed expressly or by implication" by law. They also have an obligation to employ a full-time principal at each school. In contrast, nothing in the Education Law or commissioner of education regulations requires the recommendation of a superintendent of schools to effectuate a transfer (*Appeal of Lander*, 42 Educ. Dep't Rep. 201 (2002)).

7:38. Are school districts required to have assistant principals in school buildings?

No. There is no requirement that a school district employ assistant principals (*Matter of Ryan*, 17 Educ. Dep't Rep. 338 (1978), *aff'd*, 71 A.D.2d 719 (3d Dep't 1979)).

7:39. Who establishes a salary schedule for the school principal?

There is no statutory or regulatory requirement that a school board adopt a salary schedule for school principals. If a school district's principals are represented by a recognized or certified union, the district must negotiate with the union over salaries, hours, and other terms and conditions of employment (Civ. Serv. Law § 204(2), (3); see **10:43–44**), and the salary schedules that result from negotiations would be embodied in a collective bargaining agreement. Otherwise, salary schedules for principals may be found in school board resolutions.

7:40. Can a school board legally reduce a principal's salary?

A school board must adhere to all the terms and conditions of employment, including salary, embodied in a collectively negotiated agreement or a principal's contract (Civ. Serv. Law § 209-a(1)(d),(e); see **7:15**).

Whether or not a contract exists, a board cannot reduce a tenured principal's salary so much that it amounts to disciplinary action, because section 3020-a of the Education Law provides the exclusive procedure for disciplinary action against tenured school district employees (*Matter of Trono*, 18 Educ. Dep't Rep. 344 (1978)).

7:41. Can a school board, acting on its own, designate its school principals as "managerial" employees and thereby exclude them from membership in a negotiating unit?

No. This type of designation may be obtained only upon application to the Public Employment Relations Board (PERB) (4 NYCRR § 201.10).

Principals of schools or other administrative personnel who do not formulate districtwide policy, or who may not be reasonably required to assist directly in the preparation for and conduct of collective bargaining or who do not have a major role in contract or personnel administration, may not be so designated (Civ. Serv. Law § 201(7)(a); see **10:39–41** for further information about designating managerial personnel). While principals are not generally designated as "managerial" (see *Warsaw CSD*, 27 PERB ¶ 4022 (1994)), principals in small school districts might be because they are more likely to have a significant role in formulating policy and personnel administration (see *McGraw CSD*, 21 PERB ¶ 3001 (1988)).

8. Teachers

Editor's Note: The No Child Left Behind Act (NCLB) of 2001 has far-reaching effects on the employment of teachers and teaching assistants in New York State. This chapter incorporates a brief discussion on major issues. For more information see Leaving No Child Behind In New York, 2nd Edition, *a handbook published by the New York State School Boards Association and distributed by LexisNexis. Also visit the New York State Education Department Web site at http://www.highered.nysed.gov and http://www.emsc.nysed.gov/ deputy/ nclb/nclbhome.htm/.*

Teachers' Qualifications

8:1. What is the legal definition of a teacher?

No uniform definition of the term *teacher* exists. *Teacher* is most commonly understood to be any full-time member of the teaching staff of a school district. However, administrative and supervisory staff members are included within the definition in some provisions of the Education Law (see § 3101). Because the term *teacher* is defined differently within the Education Law, reference to the particular law under consideration is recommended.

8:2. What are the qualifications for teachers?

An individual is qualified to teach in a New York State public school if he or she is a citizen of the United States, is at least 18 years of age and possesses a New York State teacher's certificate (§ 3001; see **8:5, 8:14–65**). A teacher also must subscribe to an oath to support the federal and state constitutions (§ 3002).

In addition, as of July 1, 2001, applicants for certification and prospective employees of a school district or a board of cooperative educational services (BOCES), including teachers, must be fingerprinted. For more information on fingerprinting, see **8:66–79**.

Under the federal No Child Left Behind Act of 2001 (NCLB), all public school teachers of core academic subjects must meet the act's highly qualified teacher requirements by the end of the 2005–06 school year. Those hired to teach a core academic subject in a program supported with Title I funds on or after the first day of the 2002–03 school year must meet those requirements as of the moment of employment (20 USC § 6319 (a)(1), (2); 34 CFR § 200.55 (a)(1), (b)). Core academic subjects include English, reading, language arts, math, the sciences, foreign languages (other than English), cinema and government, economics, the arts (including dance, music, theater, public speaking, and drama) (20 USC 7801 (11); 34 CFR § 200.55; "Updated Guidance on Implementing the NCLB's Requirements for Teachers," NY State Education Department, November 2003).

What makes a teacher highly qualified under the NCLB depends on the teacher's specific teaching assignment and whether the teacher is new to the profession. Thus, different requirements apply to elementary and middle and secondary school teachers and to teachers who are in the first year of their first-ever certification. In general, however, all teachers of core academic subjects have to be certified for their teaching assignment and show subject matter competency in all the core subjects they teach. In turn, how teachers can demonstrate subject matter competency depends on the grade level they teach and their newness to the profession. For example, a high school teacher may show subject matter competency to teach physics, in part, by passing a state content specialty test in that subject, or having an undergraduate major or equivalent coursework in the subject, or having a graduate degree in the subject. Physics teachers not new to the profession could also show subject matter competency through the high objective uniform standard of evaluation (HOUSSE), which assesses teachers in a number of areas including their educational and work experience ("Updated Guidance on Implementing the NCLB's Requirements for Teachers," NY State Education Department, November 2003; "Updated Guidance on Implementing the NCLB's High Objective Uniform State Standard of Evaluation in New York State," NY State Education Department, August 2003; see also NYSSBA's *Leaving No Child Behind in New York, 2nd Edition*).

8:3. May a school district employ a teacher who is not legally qualified?

Generally, no. A district may not employ an unqualified teacher, nor may it pay the salary of an unqualified teacher (§§ 3001(2), 3009(1), 3010; see *Winter v. Board of Educ. for Rhinebeck CSD*, 79 N.Y.2d 1 (1992), *reconsideration denied*, 79 N.Y.2d 978 (1992); *Smith v. Board of Educ.*, 65 N.Y.2d 797 (1985); *Meliti v. Nyquist*, 41 N.Y.2d 183 (1976)); *Sullivan v. Windham-Ashland-Jewett CSD*, 212 A.D.2d 63 (3d Dep't 1995), *appeal denied*, 89 N.Y.2d 814 (1997). However, the commissioner of education may, in his discretion, "excuse the default" of a school board that employed and paid an unqualified teacher, and may legalize the past employment and authorize the payment of that teacher's salary (§ 3604(6)).

A district may employ an uncertified teacher only when no certified and qualified teacher is available after extensive and documented recruitment, and the commissioner grants a *modified temporary license* for classroom teaching (§ 3006; 8 NYCRR § 80-5.10; see **8:16**).

A certified teacher may, however, instruct five classroom hours of teaching per week in an area for which that teacher is uncertified, pursuant to the commissioner's regulations on "incidental teaching," provided that, despite extensive recruitment efforts, there are no certified or qualified individuals available for the position (see 8 NYCRR § 80-5.3; see **8:39**). However, incidental teachers providing instruction in core academic subjects must comply with the highly qualified teacher requirements of the federal No Child Left Behind Act of 2001 ("Updated Fact Sheet With Highlights of the NCLB's Requirements for Teachers and Title I Para-professionals in New York State," NY State Education Department, March 2004; "Updated Guidance on Implementing the NCLB's Requirements for Teachers," NY State Education Department, November 2003; see **8:39**).

Any board member "who applies, or directs or consents to the application of, any district money to the payment of an unqualified teacher's salary" commits a misdemeanor (§ 3010).

8:4. Must districts notify parents of the qualifications of their child's teacher?

Yes. At the beginning of each school year, school districts receiving federal Title I, Part A funds must notify the parents of each student attending any school receiving such funds that the parents may request, and the district will provide in a timely manner, information regarding the professional qualifications of the student's classroom teachers. This information must include, at a minimum, the following:

- whether the teacher has state certification for the classes in which the teacher provides instruction;
- the teacher's bachelor's degree major and any other certifications or degrees held by the teacher by field or discipline;
- whether the child is provided services by paraprofessionals and, if so, their qualifications (20 USC § 6311 (h)(2)(6)(A); 34 CFR § 200.61(a)).

In addition, a school that receives Title I, Part A funds must provide to parents timely notice that their child has been assigned or has been taught for four or more consecutive weeks by a teacher of a core academic subject who is not highly qualified under the federal No Child Left Behind Act of 2001 (20 USC § 6311 (h)(2)(6)(A),(B); 34 CFR § 200.61(a),(b); see **8:2** for more information on highly qualified teachers).

8:5. Under what circumstances may a non-United States citizen teach in the public schools?

A person who is not a United States citizen is qualified to teach, provided he or she is at least 18 years of age, possesses a New York State teacher's certificate, has petitioned to become a U.S. citizen and will become a citizen of this country within the time prescribed by law (§ 3001(3)).

The United States Supreme Court has found the citizenship requirement in the Education Law to be constitutional because of the important civic function of public school teachers in our democratic government (*Ambach v. Norwick*, 441 U.S. 68 (1979)).

However, through November 26, 2007, the citizenship requirements do not apply to an alien teacher employed on or after November 26, 2002 whose immigration status is that of a lawful, permanent resident of the United States, and who otherwise would be eligible to serve as a teacher or to apply for or receive permanent certification as a teacher, but for these requirements (§ 3001 (3); 8 NYCRR § 80-1.3(a)(2)).

In addition, a candidate for a teaching certificate who is not a United States citizen, has not declared an intent to become a United States citizen, and is not a permanent resident of the United States may be issued a modified temporary license, provisional, initial or transitional certificate, or other time-limited license authorized by the commissioner. This is provided that he or she has the appropriate educational qualifications set forth in the commissioner's regulations, and either 1) possesses skills and competencies not readily available among teachers who are United States citizens; or 2) demonstrates other good cause such as the need to facilitate his or her ability to meet certification requirements of another jurisdiction (8 NYCRR § 80-1.3(a)(3)).

An expired provisional, initial, or transitional certificate may be extended no more than two years upon application by a non-United States citizen whose application for citizenship has not been acted upon by the United States Immigration and Naturalization Service (8 NYCRR § 80-1.6(a)(5)).

Similarly, a person who is not a citizen of the United States may qualify to teach in the public schools pursuant to specific provisions in the Education Law such as section 3005, which permits teachers from foreign countries to teach in New York State for up to two years as part of a teacher exchange program with the approval of the commissioner of education (8 NYCRR § 80-1.3(b); see also § 3001-a; see **8:47**).

8:6. May a relative of a school board member be employed as a teacher by that board?

Yes. A person related by blood or marriage to a school board member may be employed as a teacher by the district on the consent of a two-thirds majority of the board. In common school districts, the employment of relatives of trustees as teachers must be approved by two-thirds of the voters of the district who are present and voting on the issue at an annual or special district meeting (§ 3016(1)). The board member related to the applicant may participate in the vote (§ 3016(2); see also Opn St. Comp. 80-34).

A two-thirds vote also may be required to grant tenure to that same teacher (Opn St. Comp. 80-34; see also *Application of Gmelch*, 32 Educ. Dep't Rep. 167 (1992)), but not where a preferred eligible list (see **8:148– 157**) mandates reappointment of a teacher related to a board member (*Gmelch*).

In New York City, city board members and other officers and employees under the jurisdiction of the citywide Panel for Educational Policy and chancellor must notify the chancellor in writing every year about the employment of "related" persons, as described in law, by the city board or any community district education council (§ 2590-h(39)).

There are no restrictions on the employment of relatives in nonteaching positions. For information concerning any potential conflict of interest resulting from the employment of board member relatives, see **2:30** and General Municipal Law Sections 801 and 800(3)(a).

8:7. May teacher "applicants" be required to submit to a medical examination?

No. Such a requirement would constitute a violation of the Americans with Disabilities Act (42 USC § 12112(d)(2)) and Section 504 of the Rehabilitation Act of 1976 (29 USC § 794 *et seq.*). However, a district may condition an "offer of employment" on a physical and/or psychological examination to ensure that a candidate has the physical and mental capacity to perform the duties of that position. This examination, if required, must be applied equally to all entering employees (42 USC § 12112(d)(3); 28 CFR §§ 35.140, 41.55, 42.513; 29 CFR §§ 1630.13, 1630.14; 34 CFR § 104.14).

8:8. May a district require a teacher to submit to a medical examination after the teacher has begun working for the district?

Yes, under certain circumstances. To safeguard the health of children attending the public schools, the school board, the BOCES board or, in New York City community school districts the superintendent, can require any employee to submit to a medical examination, including a psychiatric examination, to determine that person's physical or mental capacity to perform his or her duties (§§ 913, 2568; 42 USC § 12112(d)(4)(A); see also *Matter of Gordon v. City Sch. Dist. of the City of New York*, 26 A.D.2d 545 (2d Dep't 1966); *Brodsky v. Board of Educ. of Brentwood UFSD*, 64

A.D.2d 611 (2d Dep't (1978); and *Matter of Dobosen v. Board of Educ. of the City Sch. Dist. of the City of New York*, 192 A.D.2d 399 (1st Dep't 1993)).

The board may require a teacher to submit to additional examinations if necessary to permit a doctor to render a final determination regarding that individual's fitness to teach (*Matter of Almeter*, 30 Educ. Dep't Rep. 230 (1991)). The board may direct the examination to be conducted by its own physician or by a physician chosen by the teacher (*Matter of Hirsch*, 20 Educ. Dep't Rep. 211 (1980), *application to reopen denied*, 20 Educ. Dep't Rep. 389 (1981), see related case *In re Claim of Hirsch*, 126 A.D.2d 782 (3d Dep't 1987); *Matter of Gargiul*, 15 Educ. Dep't Rep. 360 (1976), *application to reopen denied*, 15 Educ. Dep't Rep. 520 (1976), *aff'd*, 54 A.D.2d 1085 (4th Dep't 1976), *appeal denied*, 41 N.Y.2d 802 (1977), *aff'd*, 69 A.D.2d 986 (4th Dep't 1979), *appeal denied*, 48 N.Y.2d 606 (1979); see also 525 F.Supp. 795 (1981)). The teacher is entitled to be accompanied by a physician or other person of his or her choice, including a union representative. Accordingly, the teacher must be given sufficient notice to arrange for the presence of his or her physician (§§ 913, 2568; *Schiffer v. Board of Educ.*, 112 A.D.2d 372 (2d Dep't 1985), *appeal dismissed*, 66 N.Y.2d 915 (1985)).

The findings of the examination must be reported to the school board, the BOCES board (§ 913) or, in New York City community school districts, to the superintendent of schools (§ 2568) and may be used for the performance evaluation of the employee or for disability retirement.

8:9. What happens if a teacher refuses to submit to a school-ordered examination?

A teacher's refusal to comply with an examination ordered by the school board may constitute insubordination, and if the teacher is tenured, may warrant the filing of formal disciplinary charges pursuant to section 3020-a (*McNamara v. Commissioner of Educ.*, 80 A.D.2d 660 (3d Dep't 1981), *appeal dismissed*, 64 N.Y.2d 1110 (1985)).

Moreover, "a board may suspend a teacher's pay if the teacher fails to comply with the school board's reasonable directive that he or she be examined" (*Appeal of El-Araby*, 28 Educ. Dep't Rep. 524 (1989); see also *Appeal of Grossberg*, 33 Educ. Dep't Rep. 64 (1993); *Appeal of McCall*, 33 Educ. Dep't Rep. 148 (1993), and connected cases at 34 Educ. Dep't Rep. 29, 484; 35 Educ. Dep't Rep. 38, 81). Such a teacher is not deemed suspended from employment but rather, precluded from teaching based upon his or her "own failure to comply with the board's reasonable directives" (*Kurzius v. Board of Educ.*, 81 A.D.2d 829 (2d Dep't 1981), *appeal withdrawn*, 54 N.Y.2d 1027 (1981); *Grassel v. Board of Educ. of the City of New York*, 301 A.D.2d 498 (2d Dep't 2003)).

Similarly, a school board's refusal to permit a teacher to return to work after an extended absence until the teacher provides medical records and submits to an examination by the board's appointed physician does not violate a tenured teacher's due process rights. The refusal to allow the teacher to return to work under such circumstances is not considered a suspension or termination (*Strong v. Board of Educ. of Uniondale UFSD*, 902 F.2d 208 (2d Cir. 1990)).

However, where a school board actually terminated its school superintendent based on its conclusion that the superintendent abandoned her position by remaining on medical leave without providing adequate medical documentation, the commissioner of education ruled that the board violated the superintendent's employment contract by failing to provide her with a due process hearing and establishing just cause for her termination (*Appeal of Cannie*, 43 Educ. Dep't Rep. ___ , dec. no. 15,056 (2004)).

8:10. Can a teacher's age be used as a qualification for employment and/or licensing?

No, except to the extent that teachers in the public schools of New York State must be at least 18 years of age (§ 3001; see **8:2**). Otherwise, state law bars age-based employment and licensing qualifications for persons 18 years old or older (Exec. Law §§ 291, 296). Moreover, age-related discrimination in hiring, promotion, and other conditions of employment for employees over age 40 is prohibited by the federal Age Discrimination in Employment Act (ADEA) (29 USC § 621 *et seq.*, § 623; see also *Renz v. Grey Advertising, Inc.*, 135 F.3d 217 (2d Cir. 1997); *Byrnie v. Town of Cromwell Bd. of Educ.*, 243 F.3d 93 (2d Cir. 2001); *cf. Golove v. Monroe Community College*, 29 Fed. Appx. 695, 2002 U.S. App. LEXIS 2649 (2d Cir. 2002)). Thus, districts may not specify an age requirement as a qualification for any teaching position.

Equally prohibited is mandatory retirement because of age, except where age is a "bona fide occupational qualification" (Exec. Law § 296(3-a), (d); Retire. & Soc. Sec. Law § 530). However, districts may offer an early retirement incentive, provided that the incentive meets certain criteria. In order for a retirement incentive to be lawful, it must be voluntary, available for a reasonable period of time, and may not arbitrarily discriminate on the basis of age (*Auerbach v. Board of Educ. of the Harborfields CSD*, 136 F.3d 104 (2d Cir. 1998); *O'Brien v. Board of Educ. of the Deer Park UFSD*, 127 F.Supp.2d 342 (E.D.N.Y. 2001); see **11:2**). In *O'Brien*, a provision of the teachers' contract diminished compensation paid to retiring teachers for accumulated sick leave for each school year that they continued to work past the date they first became eligible to retire. According to the court, such reductions in the amount of the retirement benefits based on the age of the retiree is impermissible.

In addition, collective bargaining agreement provisions that limit health benefits for subsequent retirees to current "older" workers does not violate the ADEA (*General Dynamics Laws Sys., Inc. v. Cline*, 124 S.Ct. 1236, ___ U.S.___ (2004)).

8:11. May a school district refuse to employ a qualified teacher on the basis of religion, race, sex, or other protected attributes?

No. State and federal laws prohibit discrimination against applicants or current employees on the basis of race, color, national origin, sex, sexual orientation, religion, creed or marital status. Thus, school districts may not disqualify a candidate for a teaching position based on any of these criteria (42 USC § 2000e *et seq.* (Title VII of the Civil Rights Act of 1964); 20 USC § 1681 *et seq.* (Title IX of the Education Amendments of 1972); Exec. Law § 290 *et seq.* (Human Rights Law); Civ. Rights Law § 40 *et seq.*; see **8:10, 8:12–13** regarding age and disability discrimination; see also **18:27– 49** for further discussion on employment discrimination).

Title VII prohibits unlawful employment practices such as failing or refusing to hire, discharge or otherwise discriminating against an individual with respect to employment because of his or her race, color, religion, sex or national origin (42 USC § 2000e-2). In addition, Title VII prohibits discrimination in employment on the basis of pregnancy and protects the right to reinstatement of women on leave for reasons related to pregnancy (42 USC § 2000e(k)).

Title IX bans sexual discrimination in education programs by providing for the termination of federal aid to institutions that support such discrimination (20 USC § 1681). The Civil Rights Restoration Act of 1987 broadened the scope of Title IX (Pub. Law 100-259) to permit the withholding not only of funding for specific discriminatory programs or activities within the institution, but funding from entire educational departments, organizations or institutions that support discriminatory programs or activities (20 USC § 1687).

State law also provides for equal protection of law for all persons within the state (Civ. Rights Law § 40-c(1)). School districts expressly are prohibited from making inquiries regarding the religion or religious affiliation of a candidate for employment (Civ. Rights Law § 40-a). Examples of other illegal inquiries are described in "Recommendations on Employment Inquiries," available from the New York State Division of Human Rights, 1 Fordham Plaza, Bronx, N.Y., 10458; 718-741-8400; http://www.nysdhr.com/employment.html.

8:12. May a school district refuse to employ an otherwise qualified teacher who has a disability?

No. State and federal laws prohibit discrimination against applicants or current employees on the basis of a disability (29 USC § 794 *et seq.* (Section 504 of the Rehabilitation Act of 1973); 42 USC § 12101 *et seq.* (Americans with Disabilities Act); Exec. Law § 290 *et seq.* (Human Rights Law); Civ. Rights Law § 40 *et seq.*; see **18:32–41**).

Section 504 of the Rehabilitation Act of 1973 prohibits discrimination based on an individual's disability by all recipients of federal financial assistance. The Americans with Disabilities Act of 1990 (ADA) is designed to eliminate both intended and unintended discrimination against individuals with disabilities in both private and governmental employment, public services, public accommodations and telecommunications. The employment provisions of the ADA cover employers with 15 or more employees. See **18:32–40** for further discussion under the ADA.

The United States Supreme Court has ruled that the ADA applies to people infected with the human immunodeficiency virus (HIV) (*Bragdon v. Abbott*, 524 U.S. 624 (1998); see **18:33** for a discussion of what constitutes a disability under the ADA). However, it is noteworthy that the ADA specifically excludes from its coverage any employee or job applicant who currently uses illegal drugs (42 USC §§ 12111(6), 12114). Furthermore, the ADA does not preclude an employer from refusing to hire an individual whose performance on the job would endanger his own health or safety (*Chevron USA Inc. v. Echazabal*, 536 U.S. 76 (2002)).

Under New York State law, a teacher may not be disqualified for a teaching position solely because of a disability, provided the disability does not interfere with that person's ability to teach (§ 3004; Civ. Rights Law § 40-c(2); Exec. Law § 296; see also *Peters v. Baldwin UFSD*, 320 F.3d 164 (2d Cir. 2003); *Antonsen v. Ward*, 77 N.Y.2d 506 (1991); *In re State Div. of Human Rights*, 70 N.Y.2d 100 (1987)).

8:13. Must a school district provide a reasonable accommodation to an employee with a disability?

Yes, under certain circumstances. A school district must make reasonable accommodation to the known physical or mental limitations of an otherwise qualified disabled applicant unless the school district can demonstrate that the accommodation would impose an undue hardship on the operation of its program (29 USC § 794; 42 USC § 12112(b)(5)(A); 34 CFR § 104.12(a); 45 CFR § 84.12(a); *Borkowski v. Valley CSD*, 63 F.3d 131 (2d Cir. 1995); see also *Mitchell v. Washingtonville CSD*, 190 F.3d 1 (2d Cir. 1999)).

Reasonable accommodations may include making facilities readily accessible to and usable by disabled persons, job restructuring, part-time or modified work schedules, acquisition or modification of equipment or devices, the provision of readers or interpreters, and other similar actions (42 USC § 12111(9); 34 CFR § 104.12(b); 45 CFR § 84.12(b); see also **18:36**).

Some of the factors to be considered in determining whether a particular accommodation would cause an undue hardship are the overall size of the district's program with respect to the number of employees, the number and type of facilities, the size of the district's budget, and the nature and cost of the accommodation needed (42 USC § 12111(10); 34 CFR § 104.12(c); 45 CFR § 84.12(c)).

Additional information on the rights and responsibilities of employers and individuals with disabilities is available from the U.S. Equal Employment Opportunity Commission (EEOC) and its Enforcement Guidance: Reasonable Accommodation and Undue Hardship Under the Americans with Disabilities Act, obtainable through the EEOC's Publication Center, 800-669-3362; http://www.eeoc.gov/policy/guidance.html.

Teacher Certification

8:14. What is a teacher's certificate?

A *teacher's certificate* is a license issued by the commissioner of education, which certifies that the holder meets all the necessary qualifications to teach in the public schools (§§ 3004, 3004-b; 8 NYCRR § 80-1.2(b)).

8:15. Is state certification required for all public school teachers in New York State?

Yes. With one limited exception for teachers in Buffalo, the law prohibits school districts from employing a person who does not have a valid teacher's certificate (§§ 2569, 3001). In Buffalo, members of the teaching and supervisory staff appointed prior to September 1, 2001 must meet local requirements for licenses issued by that city in lieu of state certification, but these local requirements must meet or exceed the minimums set by the state (see §§ 2569, 3008; 8 NYCRR § 80-2.2(d)). Members of the teaching and supervisory staff appointed on or after September 1, 2001 are required to hold a state teaching certificate, but not a local license (§ 2573).

Although teachers employed in New York City prior to 1991 held local certificates, teachers employed since that date must now hold teaching certificates issued from the State Education Department, as well as a local license (§ 2569; 8 NYCRR § 80-2.2(d)).

8:16. May a district employ an uncertified teacher?

Only upon approval by the commissioner of education and, only under limited circumstances (§§ 3006, 3009(1); 8 NYCRR § 80-5.10; see **8:3**). For example:

Employment of an Uncertified Teacher Under a Modified Temporary License. The commissioner of education may issue a modified temporary license for certificate titles in the classroom teaching service with a demonstrated shortage of certified teachers for use during the 2004-05 school year, and for a maximum of one year.

The commissioner will issue a modified temporary license only if no certified or qualified teacher are available after extensive and documented recruitment, and the superintendent of schools, or in the case of the city school district of the city of New York, the chancellor, submits an approved application for a modified temporary license together with the required fee (see **8:35**). The application must include:

- The justification for employment of an uncertified person.
- Evidence that the candidate has achieved a satisfactory level of performance on the NYS Teacher Certification Examination (NYSTCE) liberal arts and sciences test, has the minimum degree required for the corresponding initial certificate; and has completed at least 27 semester hours of coursework required in content core and/or pedagogical core for the initial certificate in the title for which the modified temporary license is sought.
- Official transcripts of all collegiate study completed to date by the applicant.

In addition, the superintendent of schools, or in the case of the New York City by the chancellor, must certify that:

- No certified teacher is available after extensive and documented recruitment.
- A candidate currently or previously employed by the district as a teacher has a record of satisfactory service.
- A candidate not currently or previously employed by the district as a teacher has been subjected to a rigorous interview and screening process.
- The candidate will not be assigned or otherwise permitted to teach in a building that is a "school under registration review" (see **14:89, 14:107**) or a "school in need of improvement" (see **14:89, 14:91, 14:98, 26:10**) or corrective action status (see **14:89, 14:99, 26:10**), unless the candidate

currently is employed in such building as a teacher and has rendered satisfactory service there as a teacher.

- The candidate will not be assigned to a position supported by Title I funds in violation of the federal No Child Left Behind Act of 2001 and its implementing regulations (8 NYCRR § 80-5.10).

Employment of a Teacher Whose Certificate Expired While Serving on Active Military Duty. Under state law, if the license, certification or registration of any professional expires while that person is serving on active military duty, it is automatically extended until 12 months after the date that person is released from active duty (Mil. Law § 308-b; see also **8:32**). Moreover, expired certificates held by individuals on active duty with the Armed Forces may be extended by the commissioner, upon application of the certificate holder, for the time of the active service (8 NYCRR § 80-1.6(b)).

8:17. What types of teaching certificates are currently issued by the State Education Department?

The State Education Department (SED) issues three types of certificates to all teachers applying for certification on or after February 2, 2004: *initial certificates, transitional certificates,* and *professional certificates.* Initial and transitional certificates allow an individual to teach in public schools, generally for three years, until he or she meets the requirements for a professional certificate. A professional certificate is valid for the life of the teacher, unless revoked for cause, and so long as continuing professional development requirements are met (see **8:158–172**). Each certificate is specific to the title or subject area for which it is issued (8 NYCRR §§ 80-1.1(b)(22), (26), (41), (42), (43), 80-3.1, see **8:25, 8:27**). For detailed information about the requirements a person must meet to obtain initial, transitional or professional certificates, contact the New York State Education Department, Office of Teaching, Albany, N.Y. 12234, or visit its Web site at http://www.highered.nysed.gov/tcert/.

8:18. What are the requirements for an initial certificate?

Candidates for an *initial certificate* must complete a required course of study in one of two ways. They may complete a registered teacher education program for the specific certificate title sought and earn a bachelor's (baccalaureate) or higher degree from a regionally accredited institution of higher education or from an institution authorized by the Board of Regents to confer degrees whose programs are registered by the State Education Department (SED).

In the alternative, they may complete "equivalent study" as determined by "individual evaluation" in accordance with the commissioner's regulations (8 NYCRR §§ 80-3.3(a)(3), 80-3.3(b)1), 80-3.7).

A bachelor's degree is not required for initial certificates in career and technical subjects within the field of agriculture, business and marketing, family and consumer sciences, health, a technical area, or a trade (grades 7–12) (8 NYCRR § 80-3.3c)(1),(2)). Teachers of those subjects with an associate (or higher) degree must have at least two years of work experience in the subject for which the certificate is sought (8 NYCRR § 80-3.3(c)(1)(iii)). Moreover, such teachers must achieve a satisfactory score on the NYS Teacher Certification Examination (NYSTCE) communication and quantitative skills test, written assessment of teaching skills (ATS-W) and content specialty test(s) (CSTs) in the area of the certificate (8 NYCRR § 80-3.3(c)(1)(ii)(a)). Individuals without such a degree must complete a registered program of instruction leading to the initial certificate, or its equivalent, and have four years of work experience in the subject for which the initial certificate is sought (8 NYCRR § 80-3.3(c)(2)(i)(a),(ii)). Such teachers must achieve a satisfactory score on the NYSTCE written assessment of teaching skills (ATS-W) and content specialty test(s) (CSTs) in the area of the certificate (8 NYCRR § 80-3.3(c)(2)(ii)(a)). Certain restrictions apply to specified family and consumer science, business and marketing and technical subjects (8 NYCRR § 80.3-3(c)(2)).

All candidates (except candidates for certification in specific career and technical subjects within the filed of agriculture, business and marketing, family and consumer sciences, health, a technical area or trade (grades 7 through 12)) must achieve satisfactory scores on the NYSTCE liberal arts and sciences test (LAST), written assessment of teaching skills (ATS-W), and content specialty test(s) (CSTs) in the area of the certificate.

Special rules apply to teachers seeking an initial certificate in the title of speech and language disabilities (all grades) (8 NYCRR §§ 80-3.3(b); 80-3.9), to teach a specific career and technical subject requiring federal or state licensure and/or registration to legally perform that service, and a certificate to teach practical nursing (8 NYCRR § 80-303(a)(4)).

An initial certificate generally is valid for three years from its effective date (8 NYCRR §§ 80-1.1(22), 80-3.3(b)(2)), but may be extended under certain circumstances (see **8:23**). Students enrolled in teacher preparation programs are recommended for an initial certificate by their educational institution upon completion of their program, and their certificates will be issued at that time (8 NYCRR § 80-3.3(a); see 8 NYCRR § 80-1.8). Applicants for an initial certificate qualifying through the individual evaluation process apply directly to SED. More information on these requirements is available from the NY State Education Department's Office of Teaching and their Web site at http://www.highered.nysed.gov.tcert/certificate/notice12122003.htm.

8:19. May teachers who have completed programs of study outside of New York State obtain an initial certificate?

Yes, provided they meet the education requirement by successfully completing a program of preparation for a teacher's certificate in the certificate title or its equivalent at an institution of higher education approved pursuant to the Interstate Agreement on the Qualifications of Educational Personnel (§ 3030; 8 NYCRR § 80-3.3(b)(1)(ii)).

In addition, the commissioner of education may issue a *conditional initial certificate* even if a candidate has not met examination requirements when the candidate holds a valid regular teacher's certificate in the same or an equivalent title sought that was issued by a state sharing reciprocity with New York pursuant to the Interstate Agreement on the Qualifications of Educational Personnel, and the candidate's out-of-state certificate evidences knowledge, skills and abilities comparable to those required for New York State certification (§ 3030). Under such circumstances, the commissioner may deem all other requirements for an initial certificate to have been met. Thereafter, to obtain a full initial certificate, the candidate must submit to the commissioner, at least 60 days prior to the expiration of the conditional certificate, proof of satisfying the examination requirement (8 NYCRR § 80-5.17).

8:20. Is there an alternate route for obtaining an initial certificate?

Yes. An individual with a bachelor's or higher degree who holds a certificate issued by the National Board for Professional Teaching Standards, may be deemed to have met the requirements for an initial certificate, if the State Education Department determines the title held is equivalent to the initial certificate sought (8 NYCRR § 80-3.3(a)(2)).

8:21. What is a transitional certificate?

A *transitional certificate* is a certificate issued for several types of teachers: those holding a graduate or professional degree who are teaching while enrolled in intensive programs; those enrolled in an alternative teacher certification program; those teaching specific agriculture, health or trade subjects; and those teaching specific occupational subjects. They generally are valid for three years (8 NYCRR §§ 52.21(b)(1)(xv), (xvi), (xvii); 80-1.1(41); 80-3.5, 80-5.13, 80-5.14, 5.16; see also **8:22**).

Holders of a transitional A certificate (for teachers of specified career and technical subjects within the filed of agriculture, health, or a trade) do not need to be matriculated in good standing in a teacher education program leading to a professional certificate (8 NYCRR § 80-3.5(a)(2)).

8:22. What requirements apply to candidates seeking a transitional certificate while enrolled in an alternative teacher certification program?

An alternative teacher certification program allows individuals who have a bachelor's degree but lack courses in teacher's education to be issued a special transitional B certificate. A candidate must complete a 200-hour pre-service program, pass two certification tests, and, work as a teacher, with mentoring support, while continuing to take additional college courses in the field of teaching.

Candidates for an alternative teacher certificate must have a bachelor's degree with a major of at least 30 semester hours in the area of the subject they wish to teach, 12 hours of which may be in related subjects. They must also have a 3.0 grade point average or a positive recommendation from the college that they have the knowledge and skills necessary to be successful in the program.

The 200-hour pre-service program to be completed by the candidate must include, among other required coursework, information on how children learn and develop, effective teaching strategies that work, an outline of the state learning standards, how to teach children with special needs, and the basics of school organization and classroom management. The program must also include at least 40 hours in an actual classroom with students.

Candidates in an alternative teacher certification program must pass two New York State certification tests: the liberal arts and sciences test (LAST) and the content specialty test (CST). After completing the 200-hour pre-service program and passing the two certification tests, candidates will be awarded a transitional certificate and placed in a teaching position in a school district (8 NYCRR §§ 52.21(b)(3)(xviii), 80-1.1(42), 80-5.13).

Upon completion of all necessary requirements, candidates who apply and qualify for a transitional certificate after February 4, 2004 will be entitled to be issued an initial certificate. Those who applied and qualified for a transitional certificate on or before February 4, 2004 will be entitled to a provisional certificate (8 NYCRR § 80-5.13(b)(2)). This allows holders of a transitional B certificate who were already on track for obtaining a provisional certificate under prior certification requirements to obtain that certificate ("Regulatory Impact Statement," NYS Register, April 14, 2004).

For more information about alternative teacher certification programs, visit the State Education Department's Office of Teaching's Web site at http://www.highered.nysed.gov/tcert/.

8:23. Can an expired initial or transitional certificate be extended?

Yes. Upon application of the certificate holder, an expired initial or transitional certificate may be extended for not more than two years, for the following reasons:

- leave taken for childbearing, childrearing, serious illness or extended illness;
- Peace Corps or other volunteer organization service;
- abolition of his or her teaching position in the employing school district;
- inaction by the U.S. Immigration and Naturalization Service on his or her application for citizenship.

An initial certificate may be extended for no more than one additional year to complete a master's or higher degree program for the education requirement for a professional certificate. The applicant must have completed at least 24 semester hours of such study by the end of the three-year period of the initial certificate and must demonstrate progress in the graduate program and the compelling need for additional time The certificate will not be extended again for this same purpose (8 NYCRR § 80-3.3(a)).

For holders of expired initial certificates who can satisfactorily document their inability to secure employment as a teacher, an initial certificate may be reissued one time only for a period of three years.

8:24. What are the requirements for a professional certificate?

A *professional certificate* is the final certificate issued to public school teachers applying for teacher certification on or after February 2, 2004 (8 NYCRR § 80-1.1(26)). Once issued, it is continuously valid, unless revoked for cause, so long as the professional certificate holder meets the professional development requirements (8 NYCRR § 80-3.4(a); see **8:158– 172)**).

In general, a teacher seeking a professional certificate must have either an initial or a transitional certificate for the title sought, a master's or higher degree in the content core of the title sought, and three years of teaching experience. The teaching experience must include participating in a mentored program in the first year of employment, unless the candidate has successfully completed two years of teaching prior to teaching in public schools (8 NYCRR § 80-3.4(a), (b)(1), (2)).

If a teacher possesses a master's degree in a field other than the content core of the title, he or she must have at least 12 semester hours of graduate study in the content core of the initial certificate (8 NYCRR § 80-3.4). In addition, teachers eligible for a transitional certificate because they already hold a graduate or professional degree must achieve a satisfactory score on the NYSTCE written assessment of teaching (ATS-W) before they are eligible for a professional certificate (8 NYCRR § 80-3.4(b)(3)(i)). Special rules apply for a professional certificate in speech and language disabilities (8 NYCRR § 80-3.4(b)(3)(ii)).

A master's degree is not required for a professional certificate in specific career and technical subjects within the field of agriculture, business and marketing, family and consumer sciences, health, a technical area, or a trade (grades 7–12), but those teachers must complete a registered teacher's education program leading to the certification sought, or through "equivalent study" as determined by "individual evaluation" in accordance with the commissioner regulations (8 NYCRR §§ 80-3.3(a)(3), 80-3.7)).

8:25. What types of teaching certificates were issued by the State Education Department to teachers who applied for certification before February 2, 2004?

For teachers who applied for certification before February 1, 2004, the State Education Department (SED) issued three types of teaching certificates: provisional certificates, permanent certificates, and internship certificates (8 NYCRR § 80-2.1(a)). Most of these teachers hold either provisional or permanent certificates. Individuals applying for certification after February 1, 2004 are issued different types of certificates (see **8:17**).

An *internship certificate* was issued to a student who was enrolled in a registered or approved graduate program of teacher education and who had completed at least one-half of the semester hour requirements of the program. The internship certificate was restricted to use within a particular school district, was valid for no more than two years, and was not renewable (8 NYCRR §§ 80-1.1(23), 80-5.9).

The requirement for a *provisional certificate* that allows an individual to teach in a public school for five years varied depending upon the area of teaching and the time the application was made (see 8 NYCRR § 80-2). Under certain circumstances, a provisional certificate could be extended by no more than two years or renewed for two periods of two years each (8 NYCRR §§ 80-1.6, 80-1.7, 80-1.8, 80-2). However, the commissioner will not accept any application for renewal of a provisional certificate that is submitted after February 1, 2004 (8 NYCRR § 80-1.7(b)).

In addition, prior to September 2, 1998, graduates of teachers' education programs and other qualified persons could receive a *certificate of qualification* indicating their eligibility for a provisional certificate. The certificate of qualification provided a teacher with additional time to complete the requirements for obtaining permanent certification while unemployed and made its holder is eligible for employment as a substitute teacher. The commissioner no longer issues certificates of qualification. They were valid for five years from the date of issuance and had to be surrendered upon beginning regular employment with any public school district to the chief school officer (usually the superintendent of schools), who forwarded the certificate to the commissioner in exchange for a provisional certificate (8 NYCRR §§ 80-1.1(b)(9), 80-5.11)).

A *permanent certificate* replaced a provisional certificate upon completion of the requirements for a permanent certificate, provided those requirements are met before the provisional certificate expires. The requirements for a permanent certificate vary depending on the time the provisional or renewable provisional certificate was issued (8 NYCRR § 80-1.7(a)(2)). As the name implies, a permanent certificate is valid for the life of a teacher unless revoked for cause (8 NYCRR § 80-1.1(b)(25), 80-2).

8:26. Are there any teachers still eligible for a permanent certificate?

Yes, those with an unexpired provisional certificate as of February 2, 2004. To obtain permanent certification, teachers must complete one year of a supervised internship or two years of teaching experience in a public or nonpublic school and obtain a master's degree that is functionally relevant to the area in which they seek permanent certification. They also must pass two competency examinations: a content specialty test and a performance assessment (see **8:34**; 8 NYCRR Part 80).

8:27. In what titles are teacher certificates currently issued?

Teachers who apply for certification on or after February 2, 2004, are issued teaching certificates with new certificate titles that are more closely aligned with academic subjects and grade levels than the certificate titles issued in the past. The new certificate titles are as follows:

Early Childhood Education (Birth–Grade 2)
Childhood Education (Grades 1–6)
Generalist in Middle Childhood Education (Grades 5–9)

Specified Academic Subjects (Grades 5–9)
- English Language Arts
- Language other than English (specified)
- Mathematics
- Biology
- Chemistry
- Earth Science
- Physics
- Social Studies

Students with Disabilities (Birth–Grade 2)
Students with Disabilities (Grades 1–6)
Students with Disabilities (Grades 5–9)
Students with Disabilities (Grades 7–12)
Deaf and Hard of Hearing (All Grades)
Blind and Visually Impaired (All Grades)
Speech and Language Disabilities (All Grades)

All Grades:
- Dance
- Health Education
- Music
- Physical Education
- Theatre
- Visual Arts
- Agriculture
- Family and Consumer Sciences
- Business and Marketing
- Technology Education
- English to Speakers of other Languages
- Library Media Specialist
- Educational Technology Specialist

Specified Subjects (Grades 7–12)
- English Language Arts
- Language other than English (specified)
- Mathematics
- Biology
- Chemistry
- Earth Science
- Physics
- Social Studies
- Specific agricultural subject titles
- Specific family and consumer science titles
- Specific technical subject titles
- Specific trade subject titles
- Specific health occupations subject titles
- Specific business & marketing subject titles

Literacy (Birth–Grade 6)
Literacy (Grades 5–12) (8 NYCRR § 80-3.2(e)).

Notwithstanding amendments to the commissioner's regulations creating a new certification title of theatre (all grades), any person employed as a teacher of theatre in New York State in a public school or other school for which theatre certification is required, for at least three of the five years preceding February 2, 2004, may be issued a statement of continued eligibility by SED which will enable them to continue to teach theatre in the classroom teaching service without the certificate prescribed by the commissioner's regulations, provided that the teacher holds a permanent certificate in the classroom teaching service (8 NYCRR § 80-3.8).

The certificate titles issued for pupil personnel, administrative and supervisory service remain the same (8 NYCRR § 80-3.2(e)(2)).

The certificate, license or credential titles for supplemental school personnel, teaching in nonregistered evening schools, regional credential, and internship certificate are prescribed in Subpart 80-5 (8 NYCRR § 80-3.2(e)(3); §§ 80-5.6 through 5.9).

Certification areas are narrowly construed in accordance with the commissioner's regulations (*Appeal of Dankleman*, 37 Educ. Dep't Rep. 415 (1998)).

8:28. What teaching certificate titles were issued to applicants who applied for certification before February 2, 2004?

Teachers who applied to the State Education Department (SED) for certification on or before February 1, 2004 were issued teaching certificates in the following classifications: lower and upper elementary grades pre-K–6 and 7–12 in academic subjects (8 NYCRR §§ 80-2.12, 80-2.13) which are valid for the life of the teacher, unless revoked for cause, and so long as continuing professional development requirements are met (see **8:158–172**).

SED also granted teachers who applied for certification on or before February 1, 2004, certificates in a number of special certification areas, including career occupational subjects (8 NYCRR § 80-2.5); special education, the deaf and hearing impaired, the blind and partially sighted, and students with speech and hearing disabilities (8 NYCRR § 80-2.6); reading teacher (8 NYCRR § 80-2.7); school media specialist (8 NYCRR § 80-2.8); bilingual education (8 NYCRR § 80-2.9); English as a second language (8 NYCRR § 80-2.10); teachers of adult, community and continuing education (8 NYCRR § 80-2.11); and certification to teach in nonregistered evening schools (8 NYCRR § 80-5.7).

8:29. What are the certification requirements for middle school teachers?

Certification regulations have posed problems for educators in middle schools because teachers' certificates traditionally had been issued either up to the sixth grade (elementary) or for grades 7–12 (secondary). Thus, grade-level organizational patterns that combine students from both traditional elementary and secondary grade levels have created. However, SED now issues specific teaching certification extensions, including, for example, certification extension titles in Middle Childhood Education for Grades (5–6) or (7-9), or in specific academic subjects, such as General Science (5-9) in addition to General Science (7-12); (8 NYCRR Subpart 80-4).

Prior to February 2, 2004, the commissioner's regulations provided for an extension of certificate validity to meet the needs of experimentation in grade-level organization (8 NYCRR § 80-5.12). Specifically, there was an extension of the pre-K–6 certificate to teach academic subjects in grades 7–9, and an extension of the 7–12 certificate to teach academic subjects in grades 5–6 (8 NYCRR §§ 80-2.12(d), 80-2.13(d), 80-4.1(a)). In order to obtain these extensions to teachers' certificates, districts were required to apply for approval of an experiment in school organization The commissioner then granted approval for districts to employ certified teachers in any teaching assignment within the scope of the experiment, for a five-year period. Such an experimental program could be renewed for a five-year period with the commissioner's permission (8 NYCRR § 80-5.12(a)(2)). However, as of February 2, 2004, the commissioner no longer accepts applications for approval or renewal of teaching assignments in connection with organizational change experiments, inasmuch as the new certificate titles have alleviated the need for this process (8 NYCRR § 80-5.12(b)).

8:30. Are there available extensions or annotations to teachers' certification titles that would enable teachers to expand the scope of their teaching?

Yes. In addition to the certification extension titles for middle school teachers (see **8:29**), certificate extensions also are available in bilingual education; language other than English (Birth-2) and (1-6); American Sign Language; gifted education; and coordinator of work-based learning programs (career awareness) and (career development) (8 NYCRR Subpart 80-4). The specific requirements for obtaining such extensions are set forth in the commissioner's regulations (8 NYCRR § 80-4.3).

SED also grants a provisional and permanent annotation to indicate special preparation for teachers of students with severe or multiple disabilities (8 NYCRR §§ 80-4.2(b), 80-2.12(e)). The specific requirements for obtaining such annotation are set forth in the commissioner's regulations (8 NYCRR § 80-4.4).

8:31. Can a teacher certified in one certification title becomes certified in another, different certification title?

Yes. An individual with a provisional, permanent, initial or professional certificate may be eligible for an initial certificate in another subject if his or her program of study is deemed equivalent by SED to that required for the new certificate sought, and the other criteria for an initial certificate are met (8 NYCRR § 80-3.3(b)(1)(i)).

Such an individual may meet the examination requirement for an initial certificate in another title by passing any New York State Certification Examination (NYSTCE) content specialty test(s) required for the certification title sought (8 NYCRR §§ 80-3.3(b)(2)(ii), 80-3.3(c)(1)(ii)(b), 80-3.3(c)(2)(ii)(b)).

8:32. What happens to candidates for provisional or permanent certification whose progress towards completing the certification requirements was delayed because of a call to active military service after September 11, 2001?

Candidates who were matriculated in a registered program leading to certification in the classroom teaching service, whose participation in that program was interrupted by mobilization in active military service between September 11, 2001 and February 1, 2004, are entitled to an extension of time to complete the requirements for provisional or permanent certification equal to the amount of time the candidate was in active military duty.

Candidates must provide documentation to SED both of their matriculation in a registered program as well as of their military service. The clock on the extension of time for completing the certification requirements begins to run September 1 immediately following the candidate's last date of active military service (8 NYCRR § 80-2.1(a)(3)).

8:33. Is training in school violence prevention and intervention child abuse identification and reporting a precondition for certification?

Yes. All candidates for a certificate or license valid for administrative or supervisory service, classroom teaching service or school service must have completed two clock hours of coursework or training regarding the identification and reporting of suspected child abuse or maltreatment. In addition, all such candidates who apply for a certificate or license on or after February 2, 2001, must have completed at least two clock hours of coursework or training in school violence prevention and intervention provided by a registered program or another approved provider (§§ 3004,

(2), (3); 8 NYCRR § 80-1.4). Individuals who are certified in other states and applying for certification in New York must also meet these requirements for a permanent or professional certificate (§ 3030; 8 NYCRR §§ 80-1.4, 80-2.2(e)).

8:34. Must candidates pass a competency examination to become certified to teach in New York State?

Yes. All candidates for a teaching certificate must pass designated examinations as part of the New York State Teacher Certification Examination (NYSTCE) program (8 NYCRR § 80-1.5(a)). The NYSTCE includes the Liberal Arts and Science Test (LAST), the Written Assessment of Teaching Skills (ATS-W), the Content Specialty Tests (CSTs), and the Performance Assessment of Teaching Skills (ATS-P). A satisfactory score on these competency examinations satisfies the subject matter competency requirement for highly qualified teachers under the federal No Child Left Behind Act of 2001 for the corresponding grade level/subject matter teaching assignment (20 USC § 7801 (23)(B); 34 CFR § 200.56(a), (b); ("Updated Fact Sheet with Highlights of the NCLB's Requirements for Teachers and Title I Paraprofessionals in New York State," NY State Education Department, March 2004; "Updated Guidance on Implementing the NCLB's Requirements for Teachers," NY State Education Department, November 2003).

8:35. Is there an application fee for a teacher's certificate?

Yes. The fee for a teacher's certificate based on completion of a New York State teachers' education program is $50, and the fee for a certificate based on education or experience completed in other than a New York State teaching program is $100 (§ 3006).

However, the law requires the commissioner of education to waive fees paid by applicants for the renewal of a temporary teaching certificate or license that lapsed while the applicant was deployed by the United States armed forces and any of its reserve components in a combat theater or combat zone of operations at any time on or after August 2, 1990 (§ 3004(1-a)).

8:36. Do state certification requirements apply to teachers in nonpublic and independent schools of New York State?

No. They apply only to teachers in public schools (§ 3001).

8:37. What rules apply to student teachers?

Student teachers practice the skills being learned in the teacher education program in which they are enrolled, and gradually assume increased responsibility for instruction, classroom management, and other related duties in the area in which they are seeking certification.

A student teacher generally practices these skills under the direct supervision of the certified teacher who has official responsibility for the class. However, a student teacher may teach a class without the presence of a certified teacher in the classroom, provided that the classroom teacher is available at all times and retains supervision of the student teacher.

The number of certified teachers employed in the district must not be reduced because of the presence of student teachers (§ 3001; 8 NYCRR § 80-1.1(36)).

8:38. May a school district employ supplementary school personnel for which no certification title exists?

Upon application of the superintendent of schools, the commissioner may grant a permit to a school district authorizing the district to employ a qualified person for which no certification title exists. The application must describe in detail the nature of the position to be filled, the qualifications deemed necessary for the position, and a list of the eligible candidates who possess the desired qualifications for appointment to the position.

The permit is valid for a period of up to two years for employment in the district for which it was granted, unless extended by the commissioner for intervals of up to five years (8 NYCRR § 80-5.6(d)).

8:39. May a certified teacher employed by a public school teach outside his or her certification area in that school?

Ordinarily, no. However, a superintendent of schools, with the approval of the commissioner of education, may assign a teacher to instruct a subject outside his or her certification area for no more than five classroom hours a week, when no certified or qualified teacher is available for the position, despite extensive recruitment efforts (8 NYCRR § 80-5.3). This commonly is referred to as *incidental teaching*. Incidental teachers providing instruction in core academic subjects must meet the highly qualified teacher requirements of the federal No Child Left Behind Act of 2001 ("Updated Fact Sheet with Highlights of the NCLB's Requirements for Teachers and Title I Paraprofessionals in New York State," NY State Education Department, March 2004; "Updated Guidance on Implementing the NCLB's Requirements for Teachers," NY State Education Department, November 2003).

Within 20 days of making an incidental teaching assignment, the superintendent of schools must file an application with the commissioner, in accordance with the commissioner's regulations, for approval of the assignment (8 NYCRR § 80-5.3(a)). The commissioner then has 20 days in which to approve or disapprove the assignment (8 NYCRR § 80-5.3(c)). If the commissioner approves the assignment, the approval takes effect retroactively as of the date the incidental teaching assignment began and continues in effect until the end of that school year. However, if the commissioner disapproves the assignment, the superintendent must terminate the assignment within seven business days of receipt of the notice of disapproval (8 NYCRR § 80-5.3(d)).

To renew an incidental teaching assignment for a subsequent school year, the superintendent must again submit an application for the commissioner's approval. In addition to including the same types of information that are required upon application for approval of an incidental teaching assignment in the first instance, a renewal application must provide assurances that the teacher given the incidental assignment has taken or will take at least three semester hours of instruction or the equivalent towards obtaining certification in the subject area in which the incidental assignment was made (8 NYCRR § 80-5.3(e)).

8:40. Must substitute teachers have a New York State teaching certificate?

Not always. Uncertified individuals may serve either on an intermittent or long-term basis. Which capacity depends on whether they are working, toward certification (see **8:41**).

In addition, the highly qualified teacher requirements of the federal No Child Left Behind Act of 2001 do not apply to substitute teachers and districts do not have to replace substitute teachers who are not highly qualified ("Updated Fact Sheet with Highlights of the NCLB's Requirements for Teachers and Title I Paraprofessionals in New York State," NY State Education Department, March 2004; "Updated Guidance on Implementing the NCLB's Requirements for Teachers," NY State Education Department, November 2003). However, schools receiving Title I funds must notify parents whenever their children are assigned to or thought for four or more consecutive weeks by a substitute teacher who is not highly qualified (20 USC § 6311 (h)(b)(B); 34 CFR § 200.61 (b); ("Updated Fact Sheet with Highlights of the NCLB's Requirements for Teachers and Title I Paraprofessionals in New York State," NY State Education Department, March 2004; "Updated Guidance on Implementing the NCLB's Requirements for Teachers," NY State Education Department, November 2003).

8:41. On what basis may districts employ substitute teachers?

There are three types of substitute teachers: those with certification or certificates of qualification (see **8:25**); those without certification who are completing college study toward certification at the rate of at least six semester hours annually; and those without certification who are not working toward certification (8 NYCRR § 80-5.4(c)).

Substitutes may be employed on an *itinerant* basis on the occasional days when the regularly appointed teacher calls in sick, or on a long-term basis when the regularly appointed teacher is absent for an extended period of time but is expected to return at the end of a planned leave (8 NYCRR § 80-5.4). A substitute teacher hired on an itinerant basis may be employed by a school district for up to 40 days during a school year (8 NYCRR § 80-5.4(a)(3)). A substitute teacher hired on a long-term basis may be employed by a school district for more than 40 days during a school year (8 NYCRR § 80-5.4(a)(2)).

Uncertified individuals who are not working toward certification may be employed legally on an itinerant basis only; in other words, not more than 40 days by a school district in any one school year. This same uncertified person likewise could be employed for 40 days the following year (8 NYCRR § 80-5.4(c)(3)).

An uncertified individual who is attending college to become eligible for certification may be employed on either an itinerant or a long-term basis. No limitations are placed on the number of days a district can employ this person. However, if the teacher serves on more than an itinerant basis, he or she must be employed in an area where he or she is seeking certification (8 NYCRR § 80-5.4(c)(2)).

A certified teacher or a person with a certificate of qualification may serve as a substitute in any capacity. Thus, a district may use a teacher who is certified in one area to serve as an itinerant substitute teacher in another. For example, a teacher certified in high school business education could teach as an itinerant substitute in the elementary grades. However, if employed on more than an itinerant basis, the teacher must be employed in an area in which he or she is certified (8 NYCRR § 80-5.4(c)(1)).

8:42. Must a teaching assistant be certified?

Yes. A teaching assistant must be certified, and depending on when he or she has been certified, may have one of six different types of certification. Different education and testing requirements apply for each type of certification.

In addition, teaching assistants providing instructional support services (see **8:44**) who work in a program supported with Title I Part A funds made available by the federal No Child Left Behind Act of 2001 also must demonstrate their knowledge of and ability to assist in instructing reading/language arts, writing or mathematics or readiness therein (20 USC § 6319 (c)(1), (2); 34 CFR §§ 200.58(a)(2)(i)(c), 200.59(b)); "Updated Fact

Sheet with Highlights of the NCLB's Requirements for Teachers and Title I Paraprofessionals in New York State," March 2004; "Update on the NCLB Requirements for Title I Paraprofessionals," NY State Education Department, June 2003). Teaching assistants applying for certification on or after February 1, 2004 automatically meet NCLB qualification requirements, as well as those certified prior to that date who have tenure, other than tenure acquired by estoppel. "Updated Fact Sheet with Highlights of the NCLB's Requirements for Teachers and Title I Paraprofessionals in New York State," NY State Education Department, March 2004. Others may meet those requirements by passing the New York State Assessment of Teaching Assistant Skills (NYSATAS) or a commercial or locally developed assessment that measures their knowledge and ability to assist in instruction (*Id.*).

8:43. What are the requirements for obtaining a teaching assistant certificate?

Those requirement vary according to the specific type of certification sought. For example:

Applications submitted prior to February 1, 2004: A candidate who submitted an application endorsed by the employing school district to the State Education Department (SED) on or before February 1, 2004 for credentials to work as a teaching assistant, and whose application is subsequently granted, must possess either a temporary license or a continuing certificate (8 NYCRR § 80-5.6(b)(2)(i)).

A candidate who has completed a four-year high school program or its equivalent and who has training and experience appropriate for the position is eligible for a *temporary license*. The temporary license is valid for one year and may be renewed once (8 NYCRR § 80-5.6(b)(2)(i)(a)).

An applicant for a *continuing certificate* must have completed six college credits in the field of education and one year of experience as a licensed teaching assistant or as a certified teacher in order to be eligible. A continuing certificate remains valid continuously, except when the person does not remain continuously employed as a teaching assistant in a New York State public school for a period of five consecutive years, the certificate lapses (8 NYCRR § 80-5.6(b)(2)(i)(b)).

Applications submitted after February 1, 2004: For teaching assistant candidates who apply for certification on or after February 2, 2004, there are four types of certification:

- A *Level I teaching assistant certificate* requires a high school diploma or its equivalent, and passing the New York State Assessment of Teaching Assistant Skills (NYSATAS). It is valid for one year and is not renewable, unless the certificate holder submits adequate evidence of the need to renew the certificate for one additional year to meet the experience requirement for the level II teaching assistant certificate (8 NYCRR § 80-5.6(b)(2)(ii)(a)(ii).

- A *Level II teaching assistant certificate* requires a high school diploma or its equivalent and at least six semester hours of college credit towards a bachelor's degree, passing the NYSATAS, and employment as a teaching assistant for one school year under a level I teaching assistant certificate or under a temporary license authorizing employment as a teaching assistant. It is valid for two years and is not renewable (8 NYCRR § 80-5.6(b)(2)(ii)(b)(ii)).

- *A Level III teaching assistant certificate* requires a high school diploma or its equivalent, at least 18 semester hours of college credit towards a bachelor's degree, passing the NYSATAS, and satisfactory employment as a teaching assistant for one school year under a level I or level II teaching assistant certificate or under a temporary license authorizing employment as a teaching assistant. It is continuously valid, provided that the professional development requirement is met (8 NYCRR § 80-5.6(b)(2)(ii)(c)(ii); see **8:158–172**)).

- A *pre-professional teaching assistant certificate* requires a high school diploma or its equivalent, at least 18 credits of college credit towards a bachelor's degree, and matriculation in a registered teacher certification program, or its equivalent, or in a program with an articulation agreement with such a program. Applicants must pass the NYSATAS and have satisfactory employment as a teaching assistant for one school year under a level I, level II or level III teaching assistant certificate, or under a temporary license or continuing certificate authorizing employment as a teaching assistant. It is valid for five years from its effective date, at which time it must be renewed. In order to be renewed, the holder of the certificate must show he or she is matriculated in a registered teacher certification program, or its equivalent, or in a program with an articulation agreement with such a program, and completion (during the five year period in which the certificate is held) of 30 semester hours of coursework in such a program (8 NYCRR § 80-5.6(b)(2)(ii),(d)(ii)).

8:44. Are certified teaching assistants qualified to teach without supervision?

No. Pursuant to commissioner's regulations, a teaching assistant serves under the *general* supervision of a licensed or certified teacher and provides direct instructional service to students (8 NYCRR § 80-5.6(b)(1)(i)), including the following functions:

- Work with individual students or groups of students on special instructional projects (8 NYCRR § 80-5.6(b)(1)(ii)(a)(1)).
- Provide the teacher with general information about students to aid the teacher in the development of appropriate learning experience (8 NYCRR § 80-5.6(b)(1)(ii)(a)(2)).
- Assist students in the use of instructional resources and assist in the development of instructional materials (8 NYCRR § 80-5.6 (b)(1)(ii)(a)(3)).
- Utilize his or her own special skills and abilities by assisting with instructional programs in such areas as foreign language, arts, crafts, music and similar subjects (8 NYCRR § 80-5.6 (b)(1)(ii)(a)(4)).
- Assist in related instructional work as required (§ 3009(2)(b); (8 NYCRR § 80-5.6(b)(1)(ii)(a)(5)). (See also *Appeal of Banschback*, 38 Educ. Dep't Rep. 493 (1998); *Appeal of Rees and Chachakis*, 34 Educ. Dep't Rep. 616 (1995)); *Appeal of Latorre*, 27 Educ. Dep't Rep. 367 (1988)).

However, pursuant to the federal No Child Left Behind Act of 2001 (NCLB), teaching assistants working in a program supported with Title I Part A funds available under the act must work under the *direct* supervision of, and in close and frequent proximity to the teacher they support. This means the teacher plans the instructional activities the teaching assistant carries out, and evaluates the achievement of the students with whom the teaching assistant works. In addition, the teacher must be in the same building and readily available to the teaching assistant when the teaching assistant is working with students (34 CFR § 200.59(c).

Furthermore, NCLB regulations expressly prohibit programs staffed entirely by Title I paraprofessionals (34 CFR § 200.59(c)) which in New York refers to teaching assistants working a program supported with NCLB Title I Part A funds ("Updated Fact Sheet with Highlights of the NCLB's Requirements for Teachers and Title I Paraprofessionals in New York State," NY State Education Department, March 2004; "Updated on the NCLB Requirements for Title I Paraprofessionals," NY State Education Department, June 2003). In addition, the NCLB limits the type of duties that maybe assigned to teaching assistants working in a program supported with Title I Part A funds. Additional guidance on the duties that may appropriately be assigned to teaching assistants, see "Guidelines on the Employment of Teacher Aides and Teaching Assistants" prepared by the Office of Teaching at the State Education Department, available at: http://www.highered.nysed.gov/tcert/resteachers/guidelinesforta.htm.

8:45. Must teacher aides be certified?

No. Individuals appointed to teacher aide positions are governed by civil service rules and regulations. They are classified in the noncompetitive class of the civil service (*Appeal of Latorre*, 27 Educ. Dep't Rep. 366 (1988)).

A teacher aide assists in noninstructional duties such as managing records, materials and equipment; attending to the physical needs of students; supervising students and performing nonteaching duties otherwise performed by the regular teacher or teachers under the supervision of a teacher (8 NYCRR § 80-5.6(a); see also § 3009(2)).

For additional guidance on the duties that may appropriately be assigned to teacher aides, see "Guidelines on the Employment of Teacher Aides and Teaching Assistants" by the Office of Teaching at the State Education Department, which is available at: http://www.highered.nysed.gov/tcert/resteachers/guidelinesforta.htm.

8:46. Must school counselors, school psychologists and school librarians be certified?

Yes. The commissioner of education issues certificates for those in pupil personnel service, such as school psychologists and school counselors (8 NYCRR § 80-2.3); and for school media specialists, such as school librarians (8 NYCRR § 80-2.8; see also **8:27,** which describes additional certificate titles, for example, Educational Technology Specialist (all grades)). Only fully certified persons can be employed in these areas.

8:47. Is a teacher who is certified in New York State also certified to teach in other states?

Not automatically. However, New York State has entered into a joint agreement with six other northeast certifying jurisdictions which establishes a Northeast Regional Credential that allows a teacher certified in any of the participating jurisdictions to teach in the area of certification in another of these states (§ 3030; 8 NYCRR § 80-5.8). Regional credentials are valid for two years (8 NYCRR § 80-5.8(d)), except in Maine, where they are good for one year, and the teacher must take all necessary steps to qualify for certification in the new state within that time. Besides New York, northeast regional credentials are valid in Connecticut, Maine, Massachusetts, New Hampshire, Rhode Island, and Vermont.

In addition, teachers from New York State may qualify for a license in certain states that participate with New York in the Interstate Agreement on Qualification of Educational Personnel (§ 3030; 8 NYCRR § 80-2.2(e)). For more information, write to the New York State Education Department,

Office of Teaching, Albany, N.Y. 12334, or check the Office of Teaching's Web site: http://www.nysed.gov/tcert/homepage.htm.

8:48. How are exchange teachers certified in New York State?

An exchange teacher from a foreign country whose qualifications are approved by the commissioner of education will be issued a two-year exchange permit, at no cost, that will qualify that person to teach (§ 3005). Approval of the exchange teacher's qualifications will be based on that teacher's application for certification, which identifies the position to be filled and the education completed by that teacher. The citizenship of the foreign teacher does not bar him or her from certification for this purpose (see **8:5**). However exchange teachers of core academic subjects must satisfy the highly qualified teacher requirements of the federal No Child Left Behind Act of 2001. Those requirements apply whether teachers are recruited and hired from within the United States or another country (Policy Letter to Chief State School Officers from U.S. Secretary of Education Rod Paige, March 24, 2003).

8:49. May a school district employ a visiting lecturer?

Yes. Upon application by the superintendent of schools, the commissioner of education may issue a license to a visiting lecturer who possesses unusual qualifications in a specific subject in order to authorize this person to supplement the regular program of instruction.

The application for such a license must indicate the specific subject for which the license will be issued, the program to be supplemented, the educational credentials and relevant experience of the visiting lecturer, and the extent of services that he or she will render.

A license issued to a visiting lecturer is valid for one year (8 NYCRR § 80-5.6(c)).

A visiting lecturer who will reasonably be expected by a covered school to provide services for it on more than five days per school year is subject to fingerprinting and criminal history record check requirements (8 NYCRR § 87.2(k)(3)(iii), see **8:66**).

8:50. Who enforces the teacher certification law?

It is the State Education Department's (SED) responsibility to enforce the law and regulations concerning teacher certification. SED's Office of Teaching, with assistance from superintendents and district superintendents, oversees compliance with these rules.

When matters arise that cast doubt on an applicant's or a teacher's moral character, and may warrant suspension or revocation of his or her certification, hearings are held under Part 83 (see **8:51–56**). This type of hearing to determine fitness for certification is different from a disciplinary hearing conducted by an employing district under section 3020-a of the Education Law (see **8:180–191**).

8:51. May a teacher's certificate be revoked or suspended?

Yes. The commissioner of education is authorized to revoke, or where appropriate, suspend a teacher's certification after a hearing where it has been determined that the teacher lacks good moral character (§ 305(7); 8 NYCRR §§ 83.4, 83.5(c)).

For individuals served with notice that a substantial question exists as to their moral character after November 1, 2000, a hearing officer or panel may recommend, and the commissioner may impose one of the following alternative penalties:

- revocation of a certificate;
- suspension of a certificate for a fixed period of time;
- suspension of a certificate until completion of retraining in the area to which the suspension applies;
- suspension of a certificate until completion of therapy or other such treatment;
- limitation of the scope of a certificate by revoking an extension to teach additional subjects or grades;
- a fine not to exceed five thousand dollars ($5,000);
- a requirement that the certificate holder pursue continuing education or training (§ 305(7); 8 NYCRR § 83.6).

8:52. What are some potential grounds for revoking a teacher's certification?

In addition to the lack of good moral character (see **8:51**), a teacher's failure to complete a contract of employment for a school year without good reason may be sufficient grounds for the revocation of his or her certificate (§ 3019). In addition, a teacher must give written notice to the school district of his or her intention to resign at least 30 days prior to the termination date (§ 3019-a).

8:53. Does a teacher's conviction of a crime constitute grounds for automatic revocation of his or her certification?

No. Proof of conviction of a crime, although admissible into evidence against the teacher, does not by itself create a conclusive presumption that the teacher lacks good moral character (8 NYCRR § 83.4(d)). Moreover, evidence of conviction of a crime is given different weight depending on the type of crime committed, and depending also on whether the criminal conviction occurred before or after the point in time when the teacher acquired certification (8 NYCRR § 83.4(d), (e)).

When a teacher who already is certified is subsequently convicted of certain specified drug-related crimes, crimes involving the physical or sexual abuse of minors or students, or any crimes committed while on school property or while in the performance of teaching duties, proof of the conviction creates a "rebuttable presumption" that the teacher lacks the necessary good moral character to retain a teaching certificate (8 NYCRR § 83.4(d)). In other words, after the state has introduced evidence of a teacher's conviction of one of these crimes at a hearing, the teacher must demonstrate that he or she continues to have a good moral character in order to keep his or her license to teach (8 NYCRR § 83.4(d)).

However, the hearing officer or panel must apply the standards for denial of a license or application set forth in Correction Law section 752, taking into consideration the factors set forth in Correction Law section 753 (8 NYCRR § 83.4(e); see also *Matter of Arrocha v. Board of Educ. of the City of New York*, 93 N.Y.2d 361 (1999)). For example, an application for a license may be denied based on a finding of lack of good moral character as a result of a criminal conviction if there is a direct relationship between the criminal offense and the specific license sought, or if the issuance of a license involves an unreasonable risk to property or to the safety or welfare of specific individuals or the general public (Correct. Law § 752; see *Matter of Arrocha*).

8:54. What role does a school district play in the process for revoking or suspending a teacher's certification?

Part 83 of the commissioner's regulations requires school superintendents to report to the professional conduct officer of the State Education Department (SED) "any information indicating that a person holding a teaching certificate has been convicted of a crime, or has committed an act which raises a reasonable question as to the individual's moral character" (8 NYCRR § 83.1(a)). A superintendent's failure to do so may result in a part 83 investigation into the moral character of the superintendent himself or herself (see *Skiptunas v. Mills*, 2000 U.S. Dist. LEXIS 65 (N.D.N.Y Jan. 5, 2000)).

Once information is referred to SED, the professional conduct officer then conducts an investigation and reports the findings from the investigation and recommendations for action to the Professional Standards and Practices Board for Teaching or a subcommittee of that body (8 NYCRR § 83.2). The board or subcommittee reviews the case to determine whether a substantial question about the moral character of the certified teacher exists and notifies the teacher of its decision (8 NYCRR §§ 3.14, 83.3).

If the board or subcommittee finds that a substantial question does exist, the teacher is entitled to request a hearing before either a hearing officer or a three member panel selected from the section 3020-a list maintained by the commissioner (8 NYCRR § 83.4(a), (b)).

The certified teacher is entitled to representation at the hearing by counsel, and the burden of proving the teacher's lack of good moral character rests with the Education Department (8 NYCRR § 83.4(c)).

8:55. Who else may refer a teacher for investigation?

Any individual may refer information of a criminal conviction or other act that raises a reasonable question as to the moral character of an individual holding a teaching certificate, or of an applicant for a teaching certificate, to the State Education Department professional conduct officer, or to the executive coordinator for the teaching professions, respectively (8 NYCRR § 83.1(c)). Once the information is referred, the same process followed for revoking a teachers certificate applies (see **8:56**).

Furthermore, information from the Division of Criminal Justice Services regarding an arrest and/or conviction of a certified teacher or an applicant for certification received by SED while conducting a criminal history record check, must also be forwarded to the Office of Teaching for a determination of that individual's good moral character (8 NYCRR § 87.6 (b); see **8:74, 8:77**).

In addition, the state also must review the findings and recommendations of 3020-a hearing officers or panels to consider whether or not teachers subject to such local disciplinary charges should retain their teaching certificates (8 NYCRR § 83.1(d)).

8:56. What are the procedures at hearings to revoke or suspend a teacher's certification or to deny an application for certification based on lack of good moral character?

The procedures generally followed are in part 83 of the commissioner's regulations (§§ 305(7), 2215(10), 3018, 8 NYCRR § 83).

The Office of Teaching must prove at a hearing that the teacher or applicant lacks good moral character. The teacher or applicant is entitled to be represented by an attorney at the hearing and may call witnesses and introduce other evidence of his or her good moral character. The hearing officer may issue subpoenas at the request of a party. At the end of the hearing, the hearing officer or hearing panel issues a decision on whether the teacher's certification should be revoked or suspended or whether an applicant's request for certification should be denied. The hearing officer must notify the commissioner and the teacher or applicant (8 NYCRR § 83.4(f)), who may appeal the decision to the commissioner within 30 days (8 NYCRR § 83.5(a)). The commissioner is authorized to appeal only in cases involving a teacher convicted of drug-related crimes, crimes involving the physical or sexual abuse of minors or students, or crimes committed while on school property or while in the performance of teaching duties (8 NYCRR § 83.5(b)).

8:57. Where can additional information about teacher certification be obtained?

Additional information about teacher certification is available from the State Education Department, Office of Teaching, Albany, N.Y. 12234; telephone 518-474-3901, or at: http://www.nysed.gov/tcert/.

Coaching and Athletic Trainer Certification Requirements

8:58. Must a teacher who coaches interscholastic sports be certified as a physical education teacher?

No. A certified physical education teacher may coach any sport in any school. However, a teacher certified in an area other than physical education also may coach any sport in any school, provided he or she has been trained in first aid, completes an education program for coaches within three years of appointment, completes an approved child abuse identification and reporting workshop within one year, and completes an approved course in philosophy, principles and organization of athletics within two years after initial appointment (§§ 3004(2), 3001-b; 8 NYCRR § 135.(c)(7)).

Where two or more certified teachers with coaching qualifications and experience apply for one available position, a district may appoint any one of the qualified applicants to the position (*Appeal of Chichester*, 39 Educ. Dep't Rep. 470 (1999). However, a district may have an obligation, based on the teachers' collective bargaining agreement or past practice, to offer available coaching positions to certified teachers who are members of the bargaining unit in that district before making such positions available to other certified teachers. Notably, the Public Employment Relations Board (PERB) has ruled that a single documented instance of offering the right of first refusal for available coaching positions to teachers in a district's collective bargaining unit does not establish a past practice that the district is obligated to follow in the future (*Canastota CSD*, 32 PERB ¶ 3003 (1999)).

8:59. May nonteachers coach interscholastic sports?

Yes, if they hold a *professional coaching certificate*. To qualify for such a certificate, the nonteacher must have:

- completed first aid and CPR requirements;
- completed, or demonstrate satisfactory progress towards completion of, the course requirements established for coaching by the State Education Department, and
- a minimum of three years coaching experience in a specific sport in a New York State interscholastic athletic program (§§ 3004, 3001-b, 8 NYCRR §§ 135.4 (c)(7)(i)(c)(4), 135.5). Each certificate is sport specific (i.e., football, field hockey, soccer, basketball, softball, track, etc.) (8 NYCRR § 135.4 (c)(7)(i)(c)(4)(i)).

A professional coaching certificate is valid for a three-year period, and may be renewed for an additional three-year period upon application to the commissioner (8 NYCRR § 135.4 (c)(7)(i)(c)(4)(ii)).

The commissioner's regulations place an applicant for a coaching position who possesses a professional coaching certificate on "equal footing" with certified teachers seeking appointment to the same position (*Appeal of Parisi*, 42 Educ. Dep't Rep. 271 (2003)).

Although fingerprinting and a criminal history record check are not a prerequisite for a professional coaching certificate, all prospective employees of a covered school must satisfy SED's fingerprinting requirements (8 NYCRR §§ 80-1.11, 87.2(k), 87.3(a); see **8:66**).

8:60. Must a school district evaluate the performance of a nonteacher coach?

Yes. A school district that employs an individual as a coach pursuant to a professional coaching certificate must ensure that the principal or athletic director responsible for supervision of that individual conducts an evaluation during each year in which the nonteacher coach is employed (8 NYCRR § 135.4 (c)(7)(i)(c)(4)(iii)). While not specifically required by statute or the commissioner's regulations, SED recommends that this review take place at the end of the season for that particular sport.

8:61. May a school district employ an uncertified person as a temporary coach?

Yes. A school district may employ an uncertified person as a temporary coach but only if there are no certified teachers with coaching qualifications and experience or a certified professional coach available (8 NYCRR § 135.4 (c)(7)(i)(c)(3)), *Appeal of Folsom*, 37 Educ. Dep't Rep. 343 (1998)); see also *Appeal of Cracchiolo*, 36 Educ. Dep't Rep. 230 (1996); 8 NYCRR § 135.4(c)(7)(i)(c)(4)). Similarly, school districts may not hire uncertified coaches in lieu of certified applicants based on subjective determinations that the certified applicant was "not qualified" (*Appeal of Folsom*; see also *Appeal of Feiss*, 37 Educ. Dep't Rep. 339 (1998); compare *Appeal of Brown*, 39 Educ. Dep't Rep. 343 (1999), where a district passed over a certified coach because during the previous year he had been ejected from two basketball games for unsportsmanlike conduct). Where no certified candidate applies for a particular coaching position for a particular season by the announced application deadline, and the district appoints an uncertified person with temporary coaching license and coaching qualifications and experience to the position, a certified teacher who comes forward for the first time after the application deadline has no claim to that coaching position for that season (*Appeal of Folsom*, 37 Educ. Dep't Rep. 343 (1998)).

A district seeking to employ a nonteacher coach who has not fulfilled the requirement for a professional coaching certificate (see **8:59**) must apply to the district superintendent of the local board of cooperative educational services (BOCES) for a temporary coaching license (see **8:63**).

8:62. Are there any requirements that an uncertified person must meet to serve as a temporary coach?

Yes. An uncertified person must obtain a temporary coaching license from the commissioner of education, must be trained in first aid, and have coaching qualifications and experience which satisfy the school board (8 NYCRR § 135.4(c)(7)(i)(c)(3)). Although not specifically required by statute or regulation, the State Education Department also requires uncertified individuals who apply for a temporary coaching license to complete a workshop in the identification and reporting of suspected child abuse and maltreatment. An uncertified person appointed to a coaching position by a school district may not undertake coaching responsibilities until he or she actually has received a temporary license (*Appeal of Kimball*, 36 Educ. Dep't Rep. 508 (1997)).

8:63. What is the process for obtaining a temporary coaching license?

The superintendent of schools must apply for a temporary coaching license and satisfactorily demonstrate the district's inability to obtain a certified teacher with coaching qualifications and experience or a certified professional coach (8 NYCRR § 135.4 (c)(7)(i)(c)(3)(i); see 8 NYCRR § 135.4(c)(7)(i)(c)(4)).

Applications for temporary coaching licenses must be filed with the district superintendent for the board of cooperative educational services (BOCES) district within which the school district is located. The district superintendent collects application fees and issues temporary coaching licenses on behalf of the commissioner (Memorandum of James A. Kadamus, Deputy Commissioner for Elementary, Middle, Secondary and Continuing Education, February 1999).

Applications in the city school districts of Buffalo, Yonkers, Syracuse and Rochester should be submitted to the respective district superintendents for those regions. For those school districts that are not members of a BOCES, applicants for temporary coaching licenses must submit their applications to the nearest district superintendent.

The temporary license is valid for one year but may be renewed once upon the enrollment in or completion of an approved course in philosophy, principles and organization of athletics, and may be renewed subsequently upon completion of an education program for coaches (8 NYCRR § 135.4(c)(7)(i)(c)(3)).

8:64. Are there any special certification requirements applicable to all coaches?

Yes. All coaches must hold valid certification in first aid or meet equivalent requirements of the commissioner of education. This must include instruction in the administration of adult cardiopulmonary resuscitation (CPR). In addition, prior to the beginning of each sports season, coaches must provide valid evidence to the superintendent that their first aid and adult CPR knowledge and skills are current under the requirements established by the American Red Cross or equivalent requirements certified by the commissioner of education (§§ 3001-b, 3001-c; 8 NYCRR § 135.5).

8:65. What are the licensing requirements applicable to school district athletic trainers?

Revised commissioner's regulations that became effective July 10, 2003, require athletic trainers employed by school districts to possess a valid license as a "Certified Athletic Trainer" pursuant to the professional licensing standards contained in Article 162 of the Education Law.

Athletic trainers who hold a valid certificate from the National Athletic Trainers' Association, or have completed a comparable course of study for certification by that Association, are eligible to apply for licensure under the revised regulations, provided they also have completed training pursuant to Public Health Law section 3000-b(3)(a) in the operation and use of an automatic external defibrillator (AED).

The revised regulations also clarify and expand the scope of duties and responsibilities of athletic trainers employed by school districts in alignment with Article 162, as well as with criteria established by the National Athletic Trainers' Association (8 NYCRR § 135.4(c)(7)(i)(d)).

Fingerprinting Requirements

8:66. What are the fingerprinting requirements for teachers?

The Education Law and commissioner's regulations generally require fingerprinting and a criminal history background check for applicants for certification, as well as prospective employees of school districts, charter schools, BOCES (hereinafter referred to as "covered schools"), and providers of supplemental educational services authorized by the No Child Left Behind Act of 2001.

Current Employees: Employees appointed prior to July 1, 2001, are exempt so long as they remain at the same place of employment. If such individuals seek new employment at another covered school, they then become subject to fingerprinting and criminal history background check requirements (8 NYCRR §§ 87.2(k), 87.4(b)).

Applicants for Certification: All individuals who apply on or after July 1, 2001 for certification as a superintendent of schools, teacher, administrator or supervisor, teaching assistant, or in any other title for which a teaching or administrative license or certificate is required pursuant to Part 80 of the commissioner's regulations, must submit their fingerprints to the State Education Department (SED) for a criminal history record check (§ 3004-b). However, applicants for permanent certification who hold a valid provisional certificate applied for prior to July 1, 2001, in the same title for which permanent certification is sought, are not subject to the fingerprinting requirements (8 NYCRR §§ 80, 80-1.11, 87.3). Nor are teachers applying for a modified temporary license pursuant to section 80-5.10 for employment by the New York City School District, if that district has cleared them for employment after fingerprinting and a criminal history record check (§§ 2590-h(20), 3004-b; 8 NYCRR §§ 80-1.11, 87.3).

Prospective Employees: The fingerprinting requirements also apply to prospective school employees appointed by the school board on or after July 1, 2001, who are reasonably expected by a covered school to provide services involving direct, in person, face-to-face communication or interaction with students under the age of 21 for more than five days per school year. This applies to individuals seeking a compensated position with a covered school, employees placed in the school by a contractual service provider, and employees placed directly or through contract in a covered school under a public assistance employment program (Social Services Law, Art. V, Title 9-B; 8 NYCRR § 87.2(k)) An employee who worked for a covered school in the previous year is not considered a prospective employee (8 NYCRR § 87.2(k)(3)(ii)).

An individual who the covered school expects provide services for it for no more than five days per school year does not have to be fingerprinted if the covered school provides in-person supervision while that individual is providing services. Such individuals may include, for example, visiting artists, guest lecturers and speakers, and sports officials (8 NYCRR § 87.2(k)(3)(iii)).

For more information about the fingerprinting and criminal history record check requirements, contact the NY State Education Department's Office of School Personnel Review and Accountability (OSPRA) by phone at 518-473-2998, or e-mail at OSPRA@mail.nysed.gov., or visit the OSPRA Web site at http://www.highered.nysed.gov/tcert/ospra/.

8:67. What is the procedure to have a prospective employee fingerprinted and a criminal history record check conducted by the State Education Department?

If a prospective employee is not already in the State Education Department's (SED) criminal history record file, then he or she must allow SED to make a request for his or her criminal history record and be fingerprinted by a designated fingerprinting entity (§ 3035). A "designated fingerprinting entity" is designated by SED and may include school districts, BOCES, charter schools, state and local criminal justice agencies, and colleges and universities (8 NYCRR §§ 87.2(i), 87.4). Either the covered school or the prospective employee must direct the designated fingerprinting entity to send two sets of the fingerprints to SED along with the consent form and required fees (see **8:76**; 8 NYCRR § 87.4 (a)(2), (b)(ii)). The commissioner must promptly transmit the fees and fingerprints to the state Division of Criminal Justice Services (DCJS) and to the Federal Bureau of Investigation (FBI). Both the DCJS and the FBI are required to provide a record of all convictions of crimes and any pending criminal charges to the commissioner. All criminal history records processed by the DCJS and the FBI and sent to the commissioner are confidential. These records may not be published or in any way disclosed to persons other than the commissioner, unless otherwise authorized by law (§ 3035(1); 8 NYCRR §§ 87.4, 87.5(a)).

If the prospective employee is already in the SED criminal history file, then he or she must notify the covered school of this fact, and the covered school must request a clearance for employment from SED. There is no department fee for this request (8 NYCRR § 87.4 (b)).

If the criminal history record check by SED reveals that a prospective employee has no criminal convictions or pending criminal charges, SED will issue a clearance for employment to the school and notify the prospective employee (§ 3035(3); 8 NYCRR § 87.5(a)(1)).

8:68. What is the procedure to have No Child Left Behind Act (NCLB) providers of supplemental educational services fingerprinted and a criminal history record check conducted by the State Education Department?

Any individual employed by or associated with a supplemental educational services provider approved by the commissioner, other than a school district, board of cooperative educational services (BOCES), or charter school, who will provide supplemental educational services through direct contact with eligible children, is deemed to be a prospective employee of each school district in which such provider is authorized to provide services. Therefore, they are fingerprinted according to the same procedures applicable to other prospective employees regardless of the location in which the services are delivered (§ 305(33)(b)).

8:69. Must a teacher previously fingerprinted and cleared for employment again undergo a criminal history record check when seeking employment in the New York City School District?

Not if the teacher authorizes the city school district to request from the State Education Department (SED) that the contents of his or her criminal history record be forwarded to officials of the city school district. In such instances SED also will send summary information to the city school district concerning any subsequent criminal history notifications that the Department receives from the Division of Criminal Justice Services concerning that person. When that employee separates from service with the city school district, the district must notify SED (8 NYCRR § 87.9).

8:70. Must a teacher previously fingerprinted and cleared for certification or employment by the New York City School District again undergo a criminal history record check by the State Education Department?

Not if the applicant is also in the criminal history file maintained by the State Education Department (SED) (see **8:67**), or the applicant who was previously cleared by the New York City School District:

- requests and authorizes the city school district to forward to SED a copy of his or her criminal history record and any subsequent criminal history received from Division of Criminal Justice Services (DCJS);
- was fingerprinted by the city school district on or after July 1, 1990, and those fingerprints are still on file with DCJS.

In addition, SED must be satisfied that the criminal history record received from the city school district is complete and sufficient for determining clearance, and the city school district must agree to provide

SED any subsequent criminal history notifications that it receives from DCJS concerning that person.

If these conditions are met, SED's review will consist of examining the criminal history transmitted by the city school district (§§ 3004-b(1); 3035(3-a); 8 NYCRR § 87.9).

8:71. Can a district hire a covered prospective employee who has not been cleared by the State Education Department?

Until July 1, 2005, a school board may, upon the recommendation of the superintendent of schools, conditionally appoint a covered prospective employee before he or she has final clearance from SED but only if SED grants that person conditional clearance for employment (see 8:72).

Under certain specified circumstances, a board also may make an emergency conditional appointment for 20 days or less (see 8:73). Otherwise, and after July 1, 2005, a covered school cannot employ or utilize a prospective school employee without clearance for employment from SED (§§ 1604(39), 1709(39), 1804(9),1950(4)(*ll*), 2503(18), 2554(25), 2854(3), 3035(3); 8 NYCRR § 87.4(a)).

A sample conditional appointment and emergency conditional appointment policy is available from NYSSBA.

8:72. What are the requirements for a conditional clearance appointment?

Conditional clearance for employment requires a determination by the State Education Department based upon its review of a prospective school employee's criminal history record obtained from the Division of Criminal Justice Services (DCJS), that such individual may be temporarily employed by the covered school, provided all other requirements for employment are met (8 NYCRR § 87.2(d)). The process involves a number of steps.

A district must obtain from the prospective employee a signed statement that, to the best of his or her knowledge, he or she has no pending criminal charges or convictions in any jurisdiction outside of New York State (§§ 1604(39)(b), 1709(39)(b), 1804(9), 1950(4)(*ll*), 2503(18), 2554(25), 2854(3); 8 NYCRR § 87.4(a)(3), (4), (b)(2), (3)). Either the district or the prospective employee may then request conditional clearance from SED. In either case, the prospective employee must sign and complete a request form (8 NYCRR § 87.4(a)(3), (4), (b)(2), (3)).

Within 15 business days after the commissioner receives the prospective employee's fingerprints, the commissioner must grant or deny conditional clearance or provide the employee and school with a good faith estimate of how much additional time is necessary to make a determination (3035(3)(b); 8 NYCRR § 87.5(a)(2), (3)).

A conditional appointment cannot commence until notification by the commissioner that the prospective employee has been conditionally cleared for appointment and must terminate when the prospective employer is notified of a determination by the commissioner to grant or deny clearance. If clearance is granted, the appointment continues and the conditional status is removed (§§ 1609(39)(b), 1709(39)(b), 1804(9)(b), 1950(4)(*ll*)(b), 2503(18)(b), 2554(25)(b), 2854(3)(a-2)(ii)).

A board cannot conditionally appoint employees unless it has developed a policy for the safety of the children who have contact with an employee holding conditional appointment or emergency conditional appointment §§ 1604(39)(d), 1709(39)(d), 1804(9)(d), 1950(4)(*ll*)(d), 2503(18)(d), 2554(25)(d), 2854(3)(a-2)(iv); 8 NYCRR § 87.2(c)). At the time of publication, the Education Law did not permit conditional appointments after July 1, 2005 (*Id.*). A sample conditional appointment policy is available from NYSSBA.

8:73. What are the requirements for an emergency conditional appointment?

A school board may make an emergency conditional appointment only when an unforeseen emergency vacancy has occurred. An *unforeseen emergency vacancy* must meet the following criteria:

- it occurs less than 10 business days before the start of or during any school session, including summer school, without sufficient notice to allow for clearance; or when the board determines that the covered school has been unable to fill the vacancy with sufficient time for clearance or conditional clearance despite good faith efforts to do so; and

- there is no other qualified person to fill the vacancy, and it is necessary to maintain services the covered school is legally required to provide or necessary to protect the health, education, or safety of students or staff (§§ 1604(39), 1709(39), 1804(9), 1950(4)(*ll*), 2503(18), 2554(25), 2854(3); 8 NYCRR § 87.2(j)).

The school board must obtain from the prospective employee a signed statement indicating whether, to the best of his or her knowledge, he or she has a pending criminal charge or conviction in any jurisdiction.

It also must initiate the process for conditional appointment discussed at **8:72** (§§ 1604(39)(c), 1709(39)(c), 1804(9)(c), 1950(4)(*ll*)(c), 2503(18)(c), 2554(25)(c), 2854(3)(a-2)(iii); 8 NYCRR § 87.2(j)).

An emergency conditional appointment may commence prior to notification from the commissioner on conditional clearance, but must terminate 20 business days from the date it starts, or upon notification by the commissioner regarding conditional clearance, whichever occurs first. If conditional clearance is granted, the appointment continues as a conditional appointment (*Id.*).

A board cannot make an emergency conditional appointment unless it has developed a policy for the safety of the children who have contact with an employee holding conditional appointment or emergency conditional appointment (§§ 1604(39)(d), 1709(39)(d), 1804(9)(d), 1950(4)(*ll*)(d), 2503(18)(d), 2554(25)(d), 2854(3)(a-2)(iii); 8 NYCRR § 87.2(c)).

8:74. If a criminal history record check reveals that a prospective employee has a record of convictions and/or pending charges, does that mean that he or she will be automatically denied clearance?

No. If the prospective employee has a record of criminal conviction(s) or pending criminal charge(s), SED must conduct a review in accordance with standards set forth in New York's Correction Law and Executive Law (see **8:53**). SED must assess factors such as whether there is a direct relationship between the criminal offense(s) and the employment sought, and whether employment of such individual will present an unreasonable risk to the safety, welfare or property of the public or specific individuals (Educ. Law § 3035(3); Corr. Law §§ 752, 753; Exec. Law § 296 (15), (16); 8 NYCRR § 87.5 (a)(4)(i), (iii)).

If SED determines that there is a basis to deny clearance for employment, it must notify the prospective employee of a possible denial of clearance and state the basis for this determination, including but not limited to a description of the criminal charge(s) or conviction(s) involved. The notification must state that a clearance for employment will be denied unless the prospective employee submits a response demonstrating to SED's satisfaction that clearance should be granted. The prospective employee must respond within 25 calendar days (or, if conditional clearance for employment has been requested or already granted, within 10 calendar days) from the date the notification was mailed (§ 3035(3); 8 NYCRR § 87.5 (a)(4)(v)).

The prospective employee's response may include any affidavits or other relevant written information which he or she wishes SED to consider, including, where applicable, information in regard to his or her good conduct and rehabilitation. SED must review the response and determine (subject to the criteria set forth in the Correction and Executive Laws) whether the information submitted by the prospective employee warrants granting clearance for employment (8 NYCRR § 87.5 (a)(4)(vi)).

If the prospective employee does not submit a response within the timeframe prescribed, or if after reviewing his or her response, SED determines that clearance must be denied, SED must cancel any conditional clearance previously granted and notify the prospective employee of such denial, along with the basis for its determination and instructions for an appeal. SED must also notify the covered school (8 NYCRR § 87.5 (a)(4)(vii), (viii)).

If clearance for employment is denied by SED prior to its receipt of information from the FBI which forms an additional basis to deny clearance for employment, and the prospective school employee has already appealed the department's determination, then SED must notify the prospective school employee of this additional information. The prospective school employee has 25 calendar days after the mailing of the notification to respond. After a review of the information provided by the FBI and the response of the prospective school employee, if any, SED must either notify the prospective employee that no change in the original denial of clearance determination will be made, or issue modified determinations denying clearance for employment including the FBI information. The modified determinations will not affect the validity of the original determinations (8 NYCRR § 87.5 (a)(4)(ix)).

8:75. What are the responsibilities of a school that hires a fingerprinted employee when the employee commences employment or separates from service?

Covered schools must notify SED of the name and other identifying information of the covered school employee, along with the date employment or service began, and the position held or service provided by that individual. Covered schools must also notify SED of any employee who was fingerprinted pursuant to the Education Law and has been separated from employment or ceased providing services and the date the employee left the employment of the school (8 NYCRR § 87.4(a)(5), (6)).

8:76. Who pays the fee for the State Education Department's criminal history record check?

Applicants for certification or licensure are responsible for the fee for clearance for certification (§ 3004-b(2); 8 NYCRR § 87.8 (b)). Prospective school employees must pay the fee for SED's clearance for employment, unless the covered school agrees to pay the fee. However, prospective school employees participating in a public assistance employment program under the provisions of the Social Services Law, or receiving employment services through the Federal Temporary Assistance for Needy Families Block Grant, are exempt from paying the fee. In such cases, the Social Services District pays the fee (Soc. Serv. Law, Art. V, Title 9-B; Educ. Law § 3035(4); 8 NYCRR § 87.8 (d)(1)).

A prospective school employee may submit a request to the school board that the fees be waived and paid by the board instead. The board may grant such a request and pay the fee if it determines that payment of such a fee would impose an unreasonable financial hardship on the prospective employee or his or her family. (§ 3035(4); 8 NYCRR § 87.8 (d)(2)).

Payment of such fees may be a negotiated item in a collective bargaining agreement (§ 3035(6); see **10:52–53; 10:55**). However, reimbursement of fingerprinting costs for new hires is not a mandatory subject of bargaining (see *Matter of Newark Valley Cardinal Bus Serv.*, 35 PERB ¶ 3006 (2002), *aff'd*, 36 PERB 7005, *aff'd*, *Newark Valley Cardinal Bus Driver, Local 4360, NYSUT, AFT, AFL-CIO*, 303 A.D.2d 888 (3d Dep't 2003), *appeal denied*, 100 N.Y.2d 504 (2003)).

8:77. What if there is a change in a teacher's criminal history record file after he or she has been employed by a covered school?

The State Education Department (SED) must notify a covered school if SED receives subsequent information regarding a covered employee's criminal history record and SED records show the individual is employed by the covered school. Upon receipt of such information from the Division of Criminal Justice Services, SED must notify the covered school of the date of any subsequent arrest of the covered employee and the court of jurisdiction (8 NYCRR § 87.6 (a)). For applicants for, or holders of, certification as a superintendent of schools, teacher, administrator or supervisor, teaching assistant, or any other title for which a teaching or administrative license or certificate is required pursuant to part 80 of the commissioner's regulations, SED will also forward the arrest information to its Office of Teaching for a determination of good moral character under part 83 of the commissioner's regulations (8 NYCRR § 87.6 (b); see **8:51–56**).

8:78. Can an applicant for certification or a prospective employee appeal the State Education Department's determination to deny clearance?

Yes. If the State Education Department (SED) denies clearance to an applicant or prospective employee (hereinafter "appellant"), he or she may appeal that determination to SED's Office of Teaching within 25 calendar days of the date clearance denial was mailed. The appeal will be heard by the Office of Teaching's executive coordinator or a designated state review officer who did not participate in SED's determination (8 NYCRR § 87.5 (a)(5)).

The appellant may submit any affidavits or other relevant written information that he or she wants considered, including, where applicable, information regarding his or her good conduct and rehabilitation. If timely requested, oral argument will be heard before the executive coordinator, or his designee, at which time the appellant may present additional affidavits, arguments or other relevant written information. While no testimony will be taken and no transcript will be made of the oral argument, the appellant may make an audio tape recording of the proceeding (8 NYCRR § 87.5(a)(5)(iv)).

The Office of Teaching, or the designated state review officer, must make a determination on the appeal based on a review of the appellant's criminal history record, the written information and arguments timely submitted by him or her, and the oral argument (if any). The hearing officer must apply the standards for granting or denying a license or employment application set forth in the Correction Law and Executive Law. If the appeal is denied, the decision must include the findings of fact and conclusions of law upon which the determination is based. A copy of the decision must be sent to the appellant, and the covered school must be notified of the denial or grant of clearance (Corr. Law §§ 752, 753; Exec. Law § 296 (16); 8 NYCRR § 87.5(a)(5)(v)).

8:79. Once an employee leaves the employment of a covered school, what becomes of their fingerprints on file at the Division of Criminal Justice Services (DCJS) and their criminal history file at the State Education Department?

The State Education Department (SED) will notify the DCJS to destroy the fingerprints of any individual separated from employment at a covered school who has not become employed at the same or another covered school within 12 months of separation. Any such individual may request that his or her fingerprints be destroyed prior to the expiration of this 12-month period. Individuals whose fingerprints are destroyed will be removed from SED's criminal history file (8 NYCRR § 87.7).

Teachers' Rights and Responsibilities

8:80. Is there a law that establishes a maximum length for a teacher's workday?

There are no laws that limit the hours of work a school board may establish for its teachers. However, the length of a teacher's workday is a mandatory subject of bargaining that must be negotiated with a collective bargaining unit, such as a teachers' union (Civ. Serv. Law §§ 201(4), 204(3); *Troy City Sch. Dist.*, 11 PERB ¶ 3056 (1978); see also **10:52–53**).

8:81. Do any standards exist for a teacher's daily teaching load?

Yes. The commissioner's regulations state the number of daily classroom periods of instruction for a teacher should not exceed five periods. A school district that requires teachers to instruct for more than six teaching periods a day or imposes a daily teaching load of more than 150 pupils must justify its deviation from this policy (8 NYCRR § 100.2(i); but see *Appeal of Romano*, 43 Educ. Dep't Rep. ___, dec. no. 15,052 (2004)).

The commissioner has ruled that deviation from the regulatory standards will be permitted only in unique and compelling circumstances (*Appeal of Baker*, 33 Educ. Dep't Rep. 395 (1994); *Appeal of LaForty*, 33 Educ. Dep't Rep. 161 (1993)). Districts that cannot comply with the regulation may be required to make annual reports to the commissioner on the progress made toward eventual compliance (see *Matter of Simon*, 1 Educ. Dep't Rep. 562 (1960); see also *Appeal of Lowell*, 26 Educ. Dep't Rep. 333 (1987)).

Limitations on teachers' workloads are frequently included as a provision in collective bargaining agreements.

8:82. Must teachers be given a free period for lunch?

All school districts, except New York City, must allow each teacher who is employed for more than five hours a day at least a 30-minute period free from assigned duties and scheduled, so far as practical, during the hours normally allotted for student lunch periods. Additionally, districts must schedule teaching assignments so that no full-time teacher will be assigned to continuous duty for more than five hours (§ 3029).

A collective bargaining agreement may contain a provision extending but not reducing this duty-free period (*Matter of Gordon*, 18 Educ. Dep't Rep. 518 (1979)).

8:83. May a school district unilaterally require its teachers to supervise or participate in extracurricular activities outside of regular school hours?

No. Hours of work and extra pay for extra work are mandatory subjects of collective bargaining under the Taylor Law. Thus, districts must negotiate with their teachers concerning assignment of and payment for after-school duties (*Beacon CSD*, 14 PERB ¶ 3084 (1981); see also **10:52–53**). Most school boards pay extra compensation for extracurricular supervision or participation, such as coaching athletics.

8:84. Do teachers have the right to participate in shared decision making and school-based planning?

Yes. The commissioner of education has adopted regulations, which require an increased level of shared decision making among teachers, administrators, parents and other members of the school community (8 NYCRR § 100.11; see **3:26–36**). The regulations require school districts to adopt a plan and to establish shared-decision-making committees at both the districtwide and building level. They also require that teachers be members of any such committee (8 NYCRR § 100.11(b)).

Teachers serving on the districtwide committee must be selected by the teachers' collective bargaining organization. However, the commissioner's regulations are silent regarding the method of selecting teacher representatives to building-level shared-decision-making committees (*Appeal of Roby*, 34 Educ. Dep't Rep. 654 (1995)). In this context, PERB dismissed an improper practice charge against a school district that refused to recognize teachers appointed by the union as building level members because the union purported to make their appointments subject to rescission by the union president if the teachers failed to represent the interests of the union. PERB rejected the union's claim that it had the legal right to appoint teachers of its choosing to building-level shared-decision-making committees subject to any conditions it chose to attach to such appointments (*West Genesee CSD*, 31 PERB ¶ 3005 (1998)).

8:85. What rights and obligations do teachers have over the curriculum being taught?

A school board has the power and obligation to establish curriculum within its schools (§ 1709(3)). In upholding a school district's change of its grading policy without having previously submitted the issue to a shared-decision-making committee, the commissioner explained that a school board is empowered to set the course of study by which students are graded and classified (see *Appeal of Orris*, 35 Educ. Dep't Rep. 184 (1995); see also *Appeal of Zaleski*, 36 Educ. Dep't Rep. 284 (1997)).

Teachers' claims of academic freedom to control the content of instruction must be balanced against the board's legitimate interest in establishing instructional programs. As such, a school board may prohibit a teacher from making references to religion in the delivery of the teacher's instructional program, except where the religious reference is a required element of the course and its use has been pre-approved by the teacher's supervisor (*Marchi v. BOCES*, 173 F.3d 469 (2d Cir. 1999), *cert. denied*, 528 U.S. 869 (1999)).

Similarly, a school district may direct a teacher to refrain from making sexual references in the classroom that are deemed inappropriate given the age and maturity of students (*Bernstein v. Norwich City Sch. Dist.*, 282 A.D.2d 70 (3d Dep't 2001), *appeal denied*, 96 N.Y.2d 937 (2001)).

However, a teacher's claim of academic freedom must be protected where the instructional material has educational value, is relevant to the curriculum, and is suitable to the age and maturity of the students (*Malverne UFSD v. Sobol*, 181 A.D.2d 371 (3d Dep't 1992), *appeal withdrawn*, 80 N.Y.2d 972 (1992); *Kingsville Indep. Sch. Dist. v. Cooper*, 611 F.2d 1109 (5th Cir. 1980)).

A district's policy on academic freedom must contain specific direction regarding the use of new or different teaching methods before it becomes a basis for imposing discipline against a teacher (*Malverne UFSD*). However, the placement of a critical letter in a teacher's personnel file regarding that teacher's use of material in the classroom deemed objectionable by a school board does not rise to the level of discipline such that any right to academic freedom retained by the teacher would be chilled (*O'Connor v. Sobol*, 173 A.D.2d 74 (3d Dep't 1991), *appeal dismissed*, 80 N.Y.2d 897 (1992)).

8:86. Do teachers enjoy freedom of expression rights?

Yes. However, public employers, including school districts, may discipline and dismiss employees for speech that is not on a matter of public concern or for speech that the district reasonably believes is disruptive. A district is entitled to make such a determination based on the facts surrounding the speech as the district reasonably believes them to be (*Waters v. Churchill*, 511 U.S. 661 (1994); *Connick v. Myers*, 461 U.S. 138 (1983)). A district is not required to demonstrate that an employee's speech actually caused disruption to the district's operation; rather, the district's burden is to show that the speech threatened to interfere with the district's operations (*Jeffries v. Harleston*, 52 F.3d 9 (2d Cir.), *cert. denied*, 516 U.S 862 (1995); see also *Marchi v. BOCES*, 173 F.3d 469 (2d Cir. 1999), *cert. denied*, 528 U.S. 869 (1999)).

In one case, the United States Supreme Court ruled that the discharge of a teacher for publicly criticizing, in a local newspaper, the school's allocation of financial resources between the school's educational and athletic programs violated the teacher's First Amendment rights, because the teacher was addressing a matter of public concern (*Pickering v. Board of Educ. of Township High Sch. Dist. 205*, 391 U.S. 563 (1968)).

In another case, the U.S. Court of Appeals for the Second Circuit, which has jurisdiction over New York State, ruled that a school board did not violate a teacher's First Amendment rights when it terminated him based on his active participation in the North American Man Boy Love Association (NAMBLA), an organization that advocates legalizing sexual relationships between men and underage boys (*Melzer v. Board of Educ. of the City Sch. Dist. of City of New York*, 336 F.3d 185 (2d Cir. 2003), *cert. denied*, 124 S.Ct. 1424 (2004)). The court found the dismissal justified because the teacher's much publicized active participation in NAMBLA would cause disruption if he were allowed to continue teaching. Concerns of the student body, a psychologist's testimony that students would experience anxiety by being exposed to a teacher who encouraged disavowal of the law and their families' moral codes, together with the teacher's own testimony that it would be difficult for him to objectively assess and report any sexual encounters he learned of between a man and underage boy, persuaded the court that the potential disruptiveness of returning the teacher to the classroom outweighed his First Amendment rights.

Applying a standard similar to the one used by the Second Circuit in *Melzer,* the commissioner of education ruled that a faculty advisor to an extracurricular student newspaper could not be disciplined for allowing the publication of a cartoon depicting board members and an administrator unfavorably. The teacher was entitled to the same constitutional protection safeguarding student expression, which can only be suppressed to avoid "substantial disruption or material interference with school activities or to maintain order and discipline in the operation of its schools" (*Appeal of Bd. of Educ. of Wappingers CSD*, 34 Educ. Dep't Rep. 323 (1994)). In another case, the commissioner ruled it was not improper for a school district to allow school employees to wear campaign buttons in support of school board candidates, under circumstances where there was a "minimal likelihood of disruption," because elections are a matter of public concern (*Appeal of Moessinger*, 33 Educ. Dep't Rep. 487 (1994)).

By comparison, the United States Court of Appeals for the Second Circuit, which has jurisdiction over New York, has ruled that policy-making employees do not have the same free speech rights as other employees and may suffer adverse action by their employer, even when they "speak out" on issues of public concern (see *McEvoy v. Spencer*, 124 F.3d 92 (2d Cir. N.Y. 1997), *on remand*, 49 F.Supp.2d 224 (S.D.N.Y. 1999)). Moreover, policy-making employees who "refuse to speak out" in support of and thereby actively promote their employer's policies also may face adverse action by their employer (*Lewis v. Cowen*, 165 F.3d 154 (2d Cir. Conn. 1999), *cert. denied*, 528 U.S. 823 (1999); see **7:16**).

8:87. Are there any restrictions on a school district's ability to impose a dress code on its faculty?

Yes. A school district may not unilaterally impose a dress code on its faculty. The imposition of a specific dress code for faculty is a mandatory subject of collective bargaining (*Catskill CSD*, 18 PERB ¶ 4612 (1985); see *also State of New York (Dep't of Taxation and Finance)* 30 PERB ¶ 3028 (1997); **10:52–53**). However, a PERB administrative law judge held a school district may require its staff to wear photo identification cards without first negotiating the issue with the union, where the identification system relates to the employer's mission to promote safety and accountability (*Middle Country CSD*, 30 PERB ¶ 4556 (1997)).

In addition, the United States Court of Appeals for the Second Circuit, which has jurisdiction over New York State, has held that a dress code that requires a teacher to wear a necktie does not infringe on First Amendment rights to free expression or the right to privacy (*East Hartford Educ. Ass'n v. Board of Educ.*, 562 F.2d 838 (2d Cir. 1977)). However, in a noteworthy case arising outside the school context, a New York appellate court ordered reinstatement and back pay where a Native American corrections officer was dismissed for refusing to cut his hair, as required by regulation, because of his religious beliefs. According to the court, there was no legitimate state interest shown which outweighed the employee's right to the free exercise of his religion (*Rourke v. NYS Dep't of Correctional Servs.*, 201 A.D.2d 179 (3d Dep't 1994); see connected cases at 224 A.D.2d 815 (3d Dep't 1996); and 245 A.D.2d 870 (3d Dep't 1997)).

8:88. Must a teacher comply with any code of ethics or other guidelines for his or her conduct?

Yes. The General Municipal Law prohibits certain conduct by school district employees that creates a conflict of interest (Gen. Mun. Law §§ 800, 801, 802, 805-a). For example, an employee must not accept a gift worth more than $75 under circumstances in which it reasonably could be inferred that the gift was intended to or could in fact influence the employee in the performance of the employee's official duties, or was intended as a reward for any official action by the employee (§ 805-a(1)(a); see Opn. Att'y Gen. 95-10). The school board can set the limit at less than $75, but not above $75 (Opn. Att'y Gen. 99-16).

It also is impermissible for school employees to disclose confidential information acquired in the course of their official duties or use such information for personal gain (§ 805-a(1)(b)), or to have an interest in certain types of contracts with the district (§ 805-a(1)(c), (d)).

In addition, each school district must adopt a code of ethics that provides guidance to its officers and employees regarding the standard of conduct reasonably expected of them (Gen. Mun. Law § 806; see also Opn. Att'y Gen. 99-16). This code of ethics must provide standards as may be deemed advisable, including limitations on outside employment and holding of investments in conflict with official duties. Thus, it may proscribe certain conduct in addition to that specifically prohibited by law (Gen. Mun. Law § 806(1)(a)).

Employees of the New York City Board of Education and community district education councils may be required by chancellor's regulations and bylaws to submit financial disclosure statements and are required by state law to disclose certain other information (§ 2590-h(39), (40)). The New York State Court of Appeals has held that disclosures for background investigations beyond what is required by law are a mandatory subject of bargaining (*Board of Educ. of the City of New York v. New York State PERB*, 75 N.Y.2d 660 (1990); see **10:52–53**).

8:89. Do teachers have the right to strike?

No. Teachers are subject to the provisions of the Taylor Law, which prohibits strikes by police officers, fire fighters, and other public employees (Civ. Serv. Law § 210). The law gives all public employees the right to form, join, and participate in labor organizations, and also grants public employees the right to be represented by labor organizations in collective bargaining of their terms and conditions of employment and in the administration of grievances (see **10:15**).

The Taylor Law defines a strike or illegal job action as "any strike or other concerted stoppage of work or slowdown by public employees" (Civ. Serv. Law § 201(9)). A refusal or even a threatened refusal by teachers to perform services in the usual and customary manner, including work not specified in the contract, is an illegal job action (*Haverling CSD*, 22 PERB ¶ 4554 (1989); *Horseheads Teacher Ass'n and New York State United Teachers*, 15 PERB ¶ 3110 (1982); *Penn Yan CSD*, 13 PERB ¶ 3046 (1980); *Webutuck Teachers Ass'n*, 13 PERB ¶ 3041 (1980); *Plainedge Fed'n of Teachers*, 11 PERB ¶ 3060 (1978); *Pearl River UFSD*, 11 PERB ¶ 3085, *aff'g* 11 PERB ¶ 4530 (1978)). Thus, boycotts of assignments, such as evening activities, extracurricular assignments, extra help, field trips and faculty meetings, are illegal strikes (see also **10:74**).

In addition, the threat of refusal or the actual refusal to perform volunteer duties during collective bargaining in order to gain an advantage, known as work-to-rule, is a strike or threat of a strike that is prohibited by the Taylor Law (*Haverling CSD*).

A school district may deduct twice a teacher's daily salary for each day he or she participates in a strike (Civ. Serv. Law § 210(2)(f)). The penalty for a strike of extracurricular duties is limited to a deduction of compensation for the extracurricular work (*Bd. of Educ. of Seaford UFSD*, 22 PERB ¶ 7533 (Sup. Ct. Nassau Co. 1989); see **10:75–76**).

In addition, if the Public Employment Relations Board (PERB) determines that the teachers' union has violated the strike ban, it will order forfeiture of the union's membership dues deduction and agency shop fee deduction privileges (Civ. Serv. Law § 210(3)(f); see, for example, *Yonkers Federation of Teachers*, 32 PERB ¶ 3075 (1999)).

8:90. May a teacher remove a student from his or her classroom for disruptive behavior?

Yes. A teacher has the authority to remove a "disruptive pupil" from the classroom. The removal must be consistent with the code of conduct adopted by the school board pursuant to section 2801 (§ 3214 (3-a), 8 NYCRR § 100.2(l)(2))(ii)(c)). A "disruptive pupil" is an elementary or secondary school student under age 21 who substantially disrupts the educational process or substantially interferes with the teacher's authority in the classroom (§ 3214 (2-a)(b)). The district must have established policies and procedures to provide for the continued education of students removed from the classroom (§ 3214(3-a)).

8:91. What is the procedure for a teacher's removal of a disruptive student from the teacher's classroom?

If the teacher finds that the student does not pose a continuing danger to person or property, nor an ongoing threat of disruption to the academic process, the teacher must, prior to removing the student, provide the student with a basis for the removal, and allow the student to informally present his or her version of relevant events. In all other cases, the teacher must provide the student with an explanation of the basis for removal and an informal opportunity to be heard within 24 hours of the student's removal. The teacher also must inform the principal of the reason for the removal. Until July 1, 2005, if the 24-hour period does not end on a school day, the time period is extended until the next school day. After July 1, 2005, the teacher must comply with the 24-hour time period, regardless of whether it ends on a school day (§ 3214(3-a)(a)).

Within 24 hours of the removal, the principal must inform a person in parental relation to the student of the removal and the basis for it. Until July 1, 2005, if this 24-hour period does not end on a school day, it is extended until the next school day. After July 1, 2005, however, the principal must comply with the 24-hour time period, regardless of whether it ends on a school day (§ 3214(3-a)(b)).

The student and his or her parents must be given an opportunity for an informal conference with the principal to discuss the reasons for the removal. If the student denies the charges, the principal must provide an explanation of the basis for removal and allow the student and/or his or her parents an opportunity to present the student's version of events. The informal hearing must be held within 48 hours of the student's removal. Until July 1, 2005, if any such time periods do not end on a school day, the time period is extended until the next school day (§ 3214(3-a)(b)). After July 5, 2005, however, the informal hearing must be held with 48 hours of the student's removal, even if the 48-hour period does not expire on a school day (§ 3214(3-a)(b)).

The principal cannot set aside the discipline imposed by the teacher unless the principal finds that the charges against the student are not supported by substantial evidence or the student's removal is otherwise in violation of law, or that the conduct warrants suspending the student from school, and such suspension is imposed. Any such determination by the principal must be made by the end of the school day after the 48-hour period for an informal hearing. Until July 1, 2005, if the time period for the principal's determination does not end on school day, the time period is extended until the next school day (§ 3214 (3-a)(c)). The pupil will not be returned to the classroom until the principal makes a final determination or the period of removal expires, whichever is less (§ 3214(3-a)).

A principal may, in his or her discretion, designate another school district administrator to carry out the principal's functions in this process (§ 3214(3-a)(d)).

8:92. May a teacher in New York State administer corporal punishment to a student?

No. Corporal punishment is forbidden in public schools in New York State, although the use of physical force is permitted where alternatives cannot be employed reasonably (8 NYCRR §§ 19.5(a), (c), 100.2(l)(3); for more information, see **12:117–118**).

8:93. Is a school district obligated to assist a teacher facing legal action as a result of his or her conduct in the discharge of his or her official duties?

Yes (see **18:53–55**). School districts must provide an attorney and pay legal fees in a case where civil or criminal action is brought against a teacher who, in the discharge of his or her duties, takes disciplinary action against a student (§ 3028; see, for example, *Inglis v. Dundee CSD Bd. of Educ.*, 180 Misc.2d 156 (Sup. Ct., Yates Co. 1999)). A district's obligation extends only to charges arising out of disciplinary action by a teacher as determined by the actual facts underlying the incident giving rise to the allegations of teacher misconduct, not just the allegations (*Lamb v. Westmoreland CSD*, 143 A.D.2d 535 (4th Dep't 1988), *appeal denied*, 73 N.Y.2d 704 (1989); *Cutler v. Poughkeepsie City Sch. Dist.*, 73 A.D.2d 967 (2d Dep't 1980)).

In addition, school districts must provide legal assistance to employees facing claims of alleged negligence or acts resulting in accidental bodily injury to any person within or outside of a school building, provided the employee at the time of the accident or injury was acting within the scope of his or her employment and/or under the direction of the school board (§ 3023). The teacher must deliver copies of the legal papers in the criminal or civil proceedings to the board of education within 10 days of being served to be eligible for district assistance (§§ 3023, 3028).

Education Law section 3811 provides that all costs and damages which are assessed against a teacher due to non-criminal conduct arising out of the good-faith exercise of his or her duties shall be a district charge, provided that the teacher gives the school district notice of the lawsuit within five days of its commencement.

However, unless the teacher notifies the district in writing within five days of being served with the legal papers, the district is exempt from paying for the costs and reasonable expenses of defending the action, as well as all costs and damages adjudged against the teacher (§ 3811). These requirements do not apply to an action or proceeding brought against an employee by the school district or a criminal prosecution.

School districts also should be aware that section 18 of the Public Officers Law permits a school board to adopt a resolution to supplant or supplement the protection provided by the Education Law (see *Matter of Percy*, 31 Educ. Dep't Rep. 199 (1991); **18:55**).

Tenure and Tenure Areas

8:94. What is tenure?

Tenure is an employment status a teacher may earn by successfully completing a period of probationary employment and then, upon the superintendent's recommendation, being granted this status by the school board (§§ 2509, 2573, 3012, 3014). A teacher who has received tenure has earned the right to keep his or her job; in other words, to be free from discipline or dismissal, except for just cause to be proven by school officials in a due process hearing under section 3020-a of the Education Law.

A teacher's tenure status will not be affected by accepting a part-time position with the district (*Tadken v. Board of Educ.*, 65 A.D.2d 820 (2d Dep't 1978), *appeal denied*, 46 N.Y.2d 711 (1979). However, upon submission of a resignation, a teacher relinquishes any tenure or seniority rights, even if the teacher subsequently accepts a part-time position (*Matter of Middleton*, 16 Educ. Dep't Rep. 50 (1976), *application to reopen denied*, 16 Educ. Dep't Rep. 366 (1977); *connected case at* 16 Educ. Dep't Rep. 368 (1977)).

8:95. Are teachers employed by a board of cooperative educational services (BOCES) eligible for tenure?

Yes. Probationary appointments and tenure at a BOCES are provided for by section 3014 of the Education Law.

8:96. May a teacher transfer his or her tenure when accepting a position in a different school district or BOCES?

No. Tenure is not transferable from one school district to another. Each school district is independent, and a teacher must serve a new probationary period whenever he or she moves to a different school district. However, a teacher who has acquired tenure in one district or board of cooperative educational services (BOCES) in New York State and moves to another district or BOCES, or changes tenure areas within the same school district (see **8:102, 8:104**), serves a probationary period of two years rather than the usual three (§§ 2509(1)(a), 3012(1)(a), 3014(1)).

Teachers who are transferred to a different school within the same district do not lose any tenure rights within that district.

Teachers who are transferred as a result of a BOCES takeover of services or a district takeover of BOCES services are entitled to full recognition of the tenure rights they previously held (§§ 3014-a, 3014-b; *Appeal of Adler*, 37 Educ. Dep't Rep. 95 (1997); *Appeal of Valentine*, 38 Educ. Dep't Rep. 39 (1998)). A comparable provision applies when teachers are transferred because a school district takes back students who were previously tuitioned out or takes in students tuitioned out from another district (§§ 3014-c, 3014-d). In *Adler* and *Valentine*, the commissioner held that a district that took over a BOCES program must credit former BOCES teachers now employed by the district with the BOCES service as well as any prior service and prior accumulated sick time credited by the BOCES.

8:97. What is the difference between tenure and tenure areas?

Tenure is a classification of employment granted to teachers who have completed a probationary period of satisfactory service with a school district (see **8:94**). Tenure areas are subject areas of teaching positions that are established by the Board of Regents (see **8:98**). Teachers are granted tenure in specific tenure areas established by the Board of Regents.

8:98. What is the legal definition of a tenure area?

A *tenure area* is defined as "the administrative subdivision within the organizational structure of a school district in which a professional educator is deemed to serve" (8 NYCRR § 30.1(h)). When a school board appoints a teacher to a probationary teaching position (see **8:107–132**), the teacher is appointed to a position in one or more of the tenure areas, or subject areas, established by law (8 NYCRR §§ 30.2, 30.3, 30.4; see **8:99**).

Part 30 of the Rules of the Board of Regents establishes the various "vertical" or subject tenure areas that must be used for teachers hired after August 1, 1975. The tenure areas under part 30 include, for example, elementary education, mathematics, English, science and art.

Teachers who were hired before August 1, 1975 are governed by the old tenure areas that were established by each district before the enactment of part 30 (*Baer v. Nyquist*, 34 N.Y.2d 291 (1974); *Matter of Waiters v. Board of Educ.*, 46 N.Y.2d 885 (1979); *Matter of Parcells*, 23 Educ. Dep't Rep. 61 (1983)). Tenure areas often were established by grade level and not by subject area under this "horizontal" system, where, for example, an English teacher and a science teacher teaching at the secondary grade level may be in the same tenure area.

As a result of this, a dual system of tenure areas will exist for many years, with one set of tenure area rules applying to persons appointed before August 1, 1975 and another set of rules governing those appointed after that date (*Rippe v. Board of Educ.*, 64 N.Y.2d 281 (1985); *Matter of Platania*, 20 Educ. Dep't Rep. 670 (1981); *Freeman v. Board of Educ.*, 205 A.D.2d 38 (2d Dep't 1994)).

8:99. What tenure areas are recognized by part 30 of the Rules of the Board of Regents?

The tenure areas for teachers hired after August 1, 1975 include elementary, middle grades, academic and special subject areas (8 NYCRR §§ 30.5, 30.6, 30.7, 30.8). The *elementary tenure area* encompasses prekindergarten through sixth grade (8 NYCRR §§ 30.4, 30.5). The *middle grades tenure area* applies when the instruction of seventh and eighth grades is not departmentalized by academic area (8 NYCRR §§ 30.4, 30.6).

Teachers at or above the seventh-grade level, where instruction in the core academic subjects is departmentalized, are placed into the *academic tenure areas* of English, social studies, mathematics, science and foreign languages (8 NYCRR §§ 30.4, 30.7).

In addition, there are 31 *special subject tenure areas,* encompassing 15 academic areas, six vocational education subject areas, nine ancillary or supportive educational services, and one teaching assistant area (8 NYCRR § 30.8; see **8:100**).

These tenure areas apply to all school districts except those in the cities of New York and Buffalo or to those employing fewer than eight teachers. They are not retroactive and apply only to teachers appointed to probationary teaching positions on or after August 1, 1975 (8 NYCRR § 30.2).

The commissioner of education has ruled that districts may only appoint teachers to those tenure areas designated in part 30 and may not create new tenure areas for teaching positions, such as a gifted and talented teacher, that do not easily fit within those areas (*Appeal of Bales*, 32 Educ. Dep't Rep. 559 (1993)). If a district should appoint a teacher to an unauthorized tenure area, the teacher will be deemed to actually serve within the authorized tenure area which encompasses the teacher's actual duties (*Kaufman v. Fallsburg CSD*

Bd. of Educ., 91 N.Y.2d 57 (1997); *Abrantes v. Board of Educ. of the Norwood-Norfolk CSD*, 233 A.D.2d 718, *appeal denied*, 89 N.Y.2d 812 (1997); *Herbert-Glover v. Board of Educ. of Wantagh UFSD*, 213 A.D.2d 404 (2d Dep't 1995); *Appeal of Lessing*, 34 Educ. Dep't Rep. 451 (1995)).

The position of "adult education teacher" is not a tenure-bearing position. According to the commissioner, all of the tenure areas set forth in Part 30 are for teachers of students who are under age 21 and eligible to receive a public education (*Appeal of Thomas*, 34 Educ. Dep't Rep. 181 (1994)).

8:100. What are special subject tenure areas under Part 30 of the Rules of the Board of Regents?

Special subject tenure areas are specific topical areas the Regents have designated as being tenure areas. There are four general types of special-subject tenure areas: academic areas, career education subject areas, supportive educational services, and a teaching assistant area (8 NYCRR § 30.8).

The *academic areas* include such subjects as art, music, driver education, business education, health, home economics (general), industrial arts (general), physical education, remedial reading, remedial speech, English as a second language, and four branches of education for the disabled (8 NYCRR § 30.8(a)).

Vocational education subject areas in which the tenure area is coextensive with the certification possessed by the teacher, such as, for example, agriculture, health occupations, home economics (occupational), technical subjects and trade subjects, are also special subject tenure areas (8 NYCRR § 30.8(c)).

Positions in *supportive educational services* include guidance counselor, school media specialist, school library media specialist, school educational communications media specialist, school psychologist, school social worker, school nurse teacher, school dental hygienist and school attendance teacher (8 NYCRR § 30.8(b)).

The commissioner's regulations designate the position of "teaching assistant" as a special subject tenure area (8 NYCRR § 30.8(d)). They do not allow districts to classify teaching assistant tenure areas by specific subject assignment, for example, "teaching assistant — science," or "teaching assistant — heavy equipment" (*Appeal of Krason*, 41 Educ. Dep't Rep. 305 (2002), *aff'd, Madison-Oneida Bd. of Co-op. Educational Servs.*, 2 A.D.3d 1240 (3d Dep't 2003), *appeal granted*, ___ N.Y.3d ___, 2004 N.Y. LEXIS 655 (2004)).

8:101. What tenure areas are recognized under the horizontal tenure practices?

Teachers hired before August 1, 1975 are subject to the old horizontal tenure areas plus several special subject areas (*Baer v. Nyquist*, 34 N.Y.2d 291 (1974)). Those teachers who serve at a given horizontal level, such as elementary, middle school, junior high or high school, frequently serve in a single grade-level tenure area, regardless of the subject they teach (such as English, mathematics, social studies, science and foreign languages). The courts and the commissioner of education also have recognized certain permissible special subject tenure areas for teachers hired before August 1, 1975 such as guidance counselor (*Steele v. Board of Educ.*, 40 N.Y.2d 456 (1976); *Matter of Glowacki*, 14 Educ. Dep't Rep. 122 (1974)) and music and physical education (*Baer v. Nyquist*).

Part 30 of the Rules of the Board of Regents may be used as a guideline in determining whether a subject may be considered a traditional special subject tenure area under horizontal tenure practices (*Steele v. Board of Educ.; Mitchell v. Board of Educ.*, 40 N.Y.2d 904 (1976)). In a case where it is unclear whether a teacher has served in a separate tenure area, resolution of the dispute depends on whether the district has treated the subject as being separate (*Hicksville Congress of Teachers v. Hicksville UFSD*, 118 A.D.2d 623 (2d Dep't 1986)). Separate tenure areas may have been created by school policy, board resolution or regulation (*Matter of Muzante*, 16 Educ. Dep't Rep. 149 (1976)), as well as by tenure appointment resolutions, schedules of appointment or employment records (*Matter of Zappulla*, 25 Educ. Dep't Rep. 54 (1985); *Matter of Platania*, 20 Educ. Dep't Rep. 670 (1981)).

Teachers and administrators must be notified that they are serving in a separate tenure area (*Waiters v. Board of Educ.*, 46 N.Y.2d 885 (1979); *Mitchell v. Board of Educ.*). When a district creates a separate tenure area, it cannot affect a teacher's seniority rights by eliminating that tenure area from the tenure structure (*Baer v. Nyquist*).

8:102. May a teacher serve in more than one tenure area at the same time?

Yes. Under part 30 of the commissioner's regulations, teachers are deemed to serve in any tenure area in which they spend at least 40 percent of their time. Teachers serving in more than one tenure area at the same time gain seniority credit under both tenure areas (8 NYCRR § 30.1(f), (g)), and also may acquire tenure in both tenure areas (8 NYCRR § 30.9(c)).

A teacher assigned to spend 40 percent or more of his or her time in a second tenure area may acquire tenure by estoppel (see **8:124**) in that area despite a district's failure to give him or her a formal probationary appointment (*Freeman v. Board of Educ.*, 205 A.D.2d 38 (2d Dep't 1994) see *Kaufman v. Fallsburg CSD Bd. of Educ.*, 91 N.Y. 2d 57 (1997)).

8:103. In what tenure areas do teachers who also perform administrative functions serve?

In determining whether particular employees serve in an administrative tenure area or a teacher tenure area, the courts and the commissioner of education have applied what is commonly known as the 50 percent rule: if *more than* 50 percent of an employee's duties are administrative in nature, he or she will be deemed to serve in an administrative tenure area (*Appeal of Klein*, 43 Educ. Dep't Rep.___, dec. no. 15,003 (2003); *Coates v. Ambach*, 52 A.D.2d 261, *aff'd*, 42 N.Y.2d 846 (1977); see also *Cowan v. Board of Educ. of Brentwood UFSD*, 99 A.D.2d 831 (2d Dep't 1984), *appeal withdrawn*, 63 N.Y.2d 702 (1984); see **7:7**).

Prior to the enactment of part 30, an individual who served in an administrative rather than a teacher tenure area under the 50 percent rule was not eligible for seniority credit in the teacher tenure area. Subsequent to the enactment of part 30, however, teachers are deemed to serve in any tenure area in which they serve at least 40 percent of their time (see **8:102**; *Sapphire v. Board of Educ.*, 96 A.D.2d 1033 (2d Dep't 1983), *appeal dismissed*, 60 N.Y.2d 1015 (1983)). Neither the commissioner nor the courts have decided yet whether an educator who spends more than 50 percent of the time on administrative duties who also serves at least 40 percent of his or her time in a part 30 tenure area would be eligible to receive seniority credit in both the administrative and part 30 teacher tenure areas under the 40 percent rule (see **8:102–103, 8:136**).

8:104. May a teacher who has tenure or who has probationary status be transferred to a position in a different tenure area?

A teacher who has tenure or who has probationary status may not be assigned without his or her consent to devote a substantial portion of his or her time outside his or her existing tenure area (8 NYCRR § 30.9(b); *Matter of Zamek*, 19 Educ. Dep't Rep. 77 (1979)). If transferred to a new tenure area with the teacher's consent, the teacher begins a new probationary period in a new tenure area (8 NYCRR § 30.9(d)). However, the teacher does not lose any previously earned tenure or seniority in the former area.

The general rule is that if a teacher is transferred to service in another tenure area without his or her consent, all service in that other area is deemed, as a matter of law, to constitute service for purposes of seniority in the teacher's prior tenure area (*Matter of Boron v. Sobol*, 205 A.D.2d 28 (3d Dep't 1994), *appeal denied*, 86 N.Y.2d 711 (1995); *Maine-Endwell Teachers Ass'n v.*

Maine-Endwell CSD, 92 A.D.2d 1052 (3d Dep't 1983); *Appeal of Lawrence,* 32 Educ. Dep't Rep. 398 (1992)).

However, the New York State Court of Appeals has ruled that a teacher who is transferred to another tenure area without his or her consent may knowingly and voluntarily waive his or her right to have his or her service in the later tenure area credited for purposes of seniority in the teacher's prior tenure area. Under such circumstances, a district may grant seniority credit for such service to the teacher in the second tenure area (*Kaufman v. Fallsburg CSD Bd. of Educ.*, 91 N.Y. 2d 57 (1997)).

A teacher who is certified in several subjects may be assigned to serve in another tenure area for less than 40 percent of the time without being deemed to work in a different tenure area (8 NYCRR §§ 30.1(g), 30.9(a); see **8:102; 8:112**).

An assignment from a teacher's current tenure area to a position in a tenure area in which the teacher previously acquired tenure is an assignment outside of the teacher's current area, and may only be effected with the teacher's consent (*Appeal of Pendl*, 28 Educ. Dep't Rep. 511 (1989); *Appeal of Singer,* 19 Educ. Dep't Rep. 297 (1979); *Matter of Adler*, 8 Educ. Dep't Rep. 6 (1968); see also *Appeal of Shayo*, 12 Educ. Dep't Rep. 143 (1973).

8:105. May a district transfer teachers in the elementary tenure area from one specific grade to another?

Yes. Staff assignments are within the discretion of the school authorities as long as the assignments are within the proper tenure area (*Mishkoff v. Nyquist*, 57 A.D.2d 649 (3d Dep't 1977), *appeal denied*, 43 N.Y.2d 641 (1977); *Matter of Gould*, 17 Educ. Dep't Rep. 283 (1978)).

8:106. What is the difference between tenure rights and seniority rights?

Tenure rights are those rights and privileges enjoyed by tenured teachers, the most important of which is the limitation pertaining to employment disciplinary proceedings (see **8:178–201**).

Seniority rights are those rights to job security based on appointment to a tenure area. Seniority rights apply to both tenured and probationary teachers, while tenure rights apply only to tenured teachers. (For more information on seniority see **8:133–157**.)

Probationary Teachers and the Granting of Tenure

8:107. What is a probationary teacher?

A *probationary teacher* is a teacher employed by a school district during a period of probation, which usually lasts three years. The probationary appointment allows districts to evaluate the competency of a teacher prior to making an appointment to tenure (see **8:114**).

8:108. What type of teaching position requires a probationary appointment?

A probationary appointment must be made when filling any vacant, unencumbered, full-time teaching position. There is no legal authority for a temporary appointment to evade the provisions of the tenure laws (*Board of Educ. of Oneida CSD v. Nyquist*, 59 A.D.2d 76 (3d Dep't 1977), *rev'd*, 45 N.Y.2d 975 (1978)).

When a teacher is granted a leave of absence, the position is encumbered by that leave and is not considered vacant (*Brewer v. Board of Educ.*, 51 N.Y.2d 855 (1980)). However, where an employee on extended leave tenders a resignation during the leave, the position should be considered vacant and unencumbered even if the resignation is dated prospectively (*Matter of Dionisio v. Board of Educ.*, 96 A.D.2d 1041 (2d Dep't 1983), *aff'd*, 63 N.Y.2d 862 (1984)).

A school district may not assign substitute teachers to temporarily fill vacant positions, even during the pendency of negotiations over the possible transfer of the duties of the vacant positions (*DiPiazza v. Board of Educ.*, 214 A.D.2d 729 (2d Dep't 1995)).

8:109. Do part-time teachers receive probationary appointments?

Normally, part-time teachers do not receive probationary appointments or credit toward tenure (*Ceparano v. Ambach*, 53 N.Y.2d 873 (1981); *Lilley v. Mills*, 274 A.D.2d 644 (3d Dep't 2000)). A school board may, however, extend credit to a part-time teacher either by a board resolution (*Moritz v. Board of Educ.*, 60 A.D.2d 161 (4th Dep't 1977)) or by a provision in a collective bargaining agreement (*Schlosser v. Board of Educ.*, 62 A.D.2d 207, *aff'd*, 47 N.Y.2d 811 (1979)).

The one exception to the general rule is kindergarten teaching, where the commissioner of education has construed the tenure statutes as encompassing both full-time (two sessions) and part-time (one session) positions (*Ablondi v. Commissioner of Educ.*, 54 A.D.2d 507 (3d Dep't 1976), *appeal denied*, 42 N.Y.2d 801 (1977); *Matter of Clark*, 17 Educ. Dep't Rep. 311 (1978)). Consequently, even where a district uses a combination of full-time and part-time teachers to meet its kindergarten needs, part-time kindergarten teachers still receive credit toward tenure.

If a school district does not grant a teacher a tenure-track probationary appointment because the district considers the teacher a part-time employee, but it is later determined that the teacher is in fact a full-time employee, then the teacher may be entitled to tenure by estoppel (see **8:124**), provided that he or she has served the requisite probationary period (*Walters v. Amityville UFSD*, 251 A.D.2d 590 (2d Dep't 1998)).

8:110. Are contracts with individual teachers used to employ probationary teachers?

Because probationary teachers are appointed by the school board, a contract of employment technically is not required. However, most districts enter into collective bargaining agreements with teachers unions (which include probationary teachers as members) that describe the terms and conditions of employment (see **10:1–5**).

8:111. May a prospective teacher waive his or her right to a probationary appointment in a tenure-bearing position?

Yes, under certain circumstances. The New York State Court of Appeals has held that a teacher's right to receive a probationary appointment and consideration for tenure may be waived through an agreement in certain cases. A teacher can be held to the terms of such waiver only as long as he or she freely, knowingly and voluntarily accepts them (*Feinerman v. BOCES*, 48 N.Y.2d 491 (1979); see also *Yastion v. Mills*, 229 A.D.2d 775 (3d Dep't 1996); *Kelland v. Commissioner of Educ.*, 96 A.D.2d 979 (3d Dep't 1983); *Matter of Anderson*, 22 Educ. Dep't Rep. 59 (1982); *Appeal of Thomas*, 34 Educ. Dep't Rep. 181 (1994)).

However, some courts have ruled that a district may not require all prospective teachers in a district to sign a waiver of their tenure rights as a condition to being hired by the district (*Costello v. Board of Educ. of East Islip*, 250 A.D.2d 846 (2d Dep't 1998); *Lambert v. Middle Country CSD*, 174 Misc.2d 487 (Sup. Ct. Nassau Co. 1997)).

8:112. How are teachers appointed to probation?

Teachers are appointed to full-time teaching positions for a probationary period by majority vote of the school board upon recommendation of the superintendent of schools (§§ 2509(1)(a), 2573(1)(a), 3012(1)(a), or in the case of a board of cooperative educational services (BOCES), by majority vote of the BOCES board upon recommendation of the district superintendent (§ 3014(1)).

For each probationary appointment, the board must indicate in its resolution the name of the appointee, the tenure area of the teaching position, the certification status of the teacher, and the beginning and end dates of the probationary appointment (8 NYCRR § 30.3).

Each tenure area that makes up 40 percent or more of a teacher's total instructional course load requires a separate probationary appointment (8 NYCRR § 30.9(c)). Thus, a teacher hired to divide his or her time equally between mathematics and science would need two separate probationary appointments. Likewise, a tenured teacher whose duties are reassigned to include instruction in a new tenure area for more than 40 percent of his or her work load is also entitled to a probationary appointment in the new tenure area (8 NYCRR § 30.9(d)).

Even in the absence of a probationary appointment, if a teacher is serving 40 percent or more of his or her time in multiple separate tenure areas, the teacher is deemed as having received a probationary appointment in each such area, notwithstanding the absence of a formal probationary appointment (*Freeman v. Board of Educ.*, 205 A.D.2d 38 (2d Dep't 1994)).

8:113. How is a teacher informed of a probationary appointment?

Usually the district sends a letter or a notice to the teacher, which indicates the appointment, the duration of the probationary period, and the salary that is sufficient to inform a teacher of a probationary appointment. The teacher should acknowledge the receipt of the notice and accept or reject the appointment.

Both the courts and the commissioner of education have emphasized the importance of clear and explicit notice to both probationary and tenured employees of the tenure area to which they have been appointed. Teachers must be alerted sufficiently when they are entering a different tenure area by board action (*Mitchell v. Board of Educ.*, 40 N.Y.2d 904 (1976); *Matter of Keeney*, 17 Educ. Dep't Rep. 314 (1978)).

8:114. What is the length of the probationary period?

The probationary period is three years for most teachers (§§ 2509 (1)(a), 2573(1)(a), 3012(1)(a), 3014(1)). However, there are two exceptions to the general rule.

First, a teacher who has received tenure in another school district or board of cooperative educational services (BOCES), or in another tenure area within the same district or BOCES, is entitled to a shortened two-year probationary period (§§ 2509(1)(a), 2573(1)(a), 3012(1)(a), 3014(1); see **8:96**).

Second, a teacher who serves as a regular substitute for at least a semester immediately preceding an appointment to a probationary position in the same tenure area is entitled to have up to two years of the prior substitute service applied toward completion of the probationary period (§§ 2509(1)(a), 2573(1)(a), 3012(1)(a); *Robins v. Blaney*, 59 N.Y.2d 393 (1983); *Appeal of Negri*, 19 Educ. Dep't Rep. 35 (1979), *aff'd, Negri v. Ambach* (Supreme Court, Albany Co., Hughes, J., unreported, 1980). This exception is sometimes referred to as *Jarema* credit. (See **8:115–116**; for information on *Jarema* credit for probationary administrators, see **7:8**.) The regular substitute service must immediately precede a probationary appointment for a teacher to be eligible for

Jarema credit. A teacher's acceptance of a part-time teaching position during the school year immediately preceding his probationary appointment creates a "gap" in earlier service as a full-time substitute teacher, which disqualifies a teacher from claiming entitlement to *Jarema* credit (*Appeal of McDonald*, 40 Educ. Dep't Rep. 560 (2001)).

8:115. How long must the regular substitute service last for purposes of determining *Jarema* credit?

A school district is only required to grant *Jarema* credit to an individual who is employed as a regular substitute for a full semester or more. Where the period of service as a regular substitute is for less than a full semester, as for example where the substitute teacher does not commence service at the beginning of the semester or does not finish the entire semester, that individual is not entitled to any credit toward his or her probationary period (*Lifson v. Board of Educ. of the Nanuet Public Schs.*, 109 A.D.2d 743 (2d Dep't 1985), aff'd, 66 N.Y.2d 896 (1985); *Appeal of Czajkowski*, 34 Educ. Dep't Rep. 589 (1995)). However, depending on the circumstances, a teacher's occasional absences during an otherwise full semester of regular, full-time substitute service will not defeat the teacher's entitlement to *Jarema* credit (*Appeal of Goldman*, 43 Educ. Dep't Rep.___, dec. no. 15,011 (2004)). In addition, summer months are included in calculating *Jarema* credit, such that a teacher who serves as a regular substitute for a school year is entitled to 12 months of *Jarema* credit (*Appeal of Creswell*, 41 Educ. Dep't Rep 235 (2001)).

The two exceptions cannot be combined to allow a teacher who previously held tenure and two years of substitute service to earn tenure without completing an additional probationary period (*Carpenter v. Board of Educ.*, 71 N.Y.2d 832 (1988); see *also Appeal of Balandis*, 27 Educ. Dep't Rep. 359 (1988)).

Part-time service does not count as part of the probationary period toward tenure (*Ceprano v. Ambach*, 53 N.Y.2d 873 (1981); *Lilley v. Mills*, 274 A.D.2d 644 (3d Dep't 2000); *Appeal of Mau*, 35 Educ. Dep't Rep. 275 (1996)). However, if it is later determined that even though the district considered the teacher a part-time employee, the teacher was in fact serving as a full-time employee, such service would count toward tenure (*Walters v. Amityville UFSD*, 251 A.D.2d 590 (2d Dep't 1998)).

8:116. What is the definition of "regular substitute" for purposes of determining *Jarema* credit?

There is no definition provided within the law. However, the New York State Court of Appeals has ruled that the term is defined by the actual nature and continuity of the substitute service, not by the anticipated duration of the replaced teacher's absence (*Speichler v. BOCES, Second*

Supervisory Dist., 90 N.Y.2d 110 (1997)); see also *Matter of Ducey*, 65 State Dep't Rep. 65 (1943)). In *Speichler*, a teacher who served as a "per diem substitute" in place of another teacher on leave for an indefinite time, and who taught continuously every school day for at least one full semester before her formal appointment to a probationary term, was entitled to *Jarema* credit for that time period.

In another case, a teacher who served as a "permanent" substitute, but served all of the functions of a "regular" substitute, was entitled to *Jarema* credit (*Hudson v. Board of Educ. of the Hempstead Pub. Sch. Dist.* (Sup. Ct. Nassau Co. 1997)).

However, according to one court, "*Jarema* credit cannot be given to a regular substitute who does not possess a valid teacher's certificate." Thus, a substitute teacher who only possessed a temporary license during her five years of employment was not entitled to it (*Pierce v. Monroe 2—Orleans BOCES*, 195 Misc.2d 178 (Sup. Ct. Monroe Co. 2003)).

8:117. May a district and a teacher agree to extend a probationary appointment for an additional year?

Yes. A district and a teacher may enter into an agreement to extend a probationary appointment for an additional year when the teacher will not be recommended for tenure (*Juul v. Board of Educ. of Hempstead UFSD*, 76 A.D.2d 837 (2d Dep't 1980), *aff'd*, 55 N.Y.2d 648 (1981)). Under such an agreement, called a *Juul* agreement, the district waives its right to dismiss the teacher at the end of the probationary period, and the teacher waives any claim of tenure by estoppel (see also **8:124**). The teacher is given a second chance to prove his or her worth and the district is free to grant or withhold tenure at the end of the fourth year (see *Appeal of Fink*, 33 Educ. Dep't Rep. 340 (1993)). *Juul* agreements are valid as long as they are entered into freely, with full knowledge of their consequences.

In addition, a district can enter into a collective bargaining agreement that permits an arbitrator to review procedural aspects of the tenure determination, but not a substantive review of the board's decision (*Vestal CSD v. Vestal Teachers Ass'n*, 60 A.D.2d 720 (3d Dep't 1977), *aff'd*, 46 N.Y.2d 746 (1978); *Board of Educ. v. Elwood Teachers Alliance*, 94 A.D.2d 692 (2d Dep't 1983)).

8:118. What is the procedure for granting a teacher tenure at the end of his or her probationary period?

Except for instances in which a teacher acquires tenure by estoppel (see **8:124**), tenure may only be bestowed upon a teacher with the superintendent's affirmative recommendation to grant tenure and the school board's acceptance of that recommendation (§§ 2573(5), 3012(2), 2509(2)).

Before the end of a teacher's probationary period, the superintendent recommends those teachers for tenure who are found competent, efficient, and satisfactory. This recommendation is made in writing to the school board. The board may then appoint to tenure, by majority vote, any or all of the teachers recommended (§§ 2509 (2), 2573(5), 3012(2), 3014(2)).

A tenure appointment must be considered separately for each tenure area that requires more than 40 percent of a teacher's instructional time (8 NYCRR § 30.9(c); see **8:102–103, 8:112, 8:136**). Thus, a teacher with two probationary appointments in separate tenure areas may be granted tenure in one, both, or neither.

8:119. Who has the final authority to appoint a teacher to tenure?

A school board has no power to make a tenure appointment without the recommendation of the superintendent (*Anderson v. Board of Educ.*, 46 A.D.2d 360 (2d Dep't 1974), *aff'd*, 38 N.Y.2d 897 (1976); *Matter of Burke*, 11 Educ. Dep't Rep. 231 (1972)). However, the school board by majority vote may appoint to tenure any or all of the persons recommended by the superintendent (§§ 2509(2), 3012(2); *Appeal of Spadone*, 39 Educ. Dep't Rep. 640 (2000)). Additionally, school boards, other than those in New York City and Buffalo, can reject any recommendation in favor of tenure from the superintendent and deny tenure despite that recommendation (§§ 2573(5), (6), 3031); see *Caraballo v. Community Sch. Bd.*, 49 N.Y.2d 488 (1980)).

On the other hand, when a superintendent recommends that the school board grant tenure to a particular probationary employee, the school board may vote to deny tenure despite the superintendent's affirmative recommendation to grant tenure. Such a vote is considered advisory in nature, and the school board must reconsider the issue at a second meeting. At least 30 days before final consideration of the recommendation, the board must notify the teacher of its intention to deny tenure and the date of the board meeting when it will take final action.

The power to grant or deny tenure may not be impaired by a collective bargaining agreement because the Education Law vests authority to make tenure decisions in the board of education (*Cohoes City Sch. Dist. v. Cohoes Teachers Ass'n*, 40 N.Y.2d 774 (1976); see **10:53** regarding prohibited subjects of bargaining). However, an arbitrator may direct a school district to extend the probationary period of a teacher and to re-evaluate the teacher at the end of the extended probationary period (*Cohoes City Sch. Dist.*). The Public Employment Relations Board (PERB) has imposed similar orders (see *Sag Harbor UFSD*, 8 PERB ¶ 4524, *aff'd*, 54 A.D.2d 391 (3d Dep't 1976)).

8:120. Can a teacher be granted tenure prior to the expiration of the probationary period?

Yes. However, it is not clear exactly how long before the expiration of the probationary period it is permissible to grant tenure. In *Weinbrown v. Board of Educ.*, 28 N.Y.2d 474 (1971), the New York State Court of Appeals ruled a school district could offer tenure to a teacher in the spring immediately preceding the expiration of the probationary period. In that case, the court found that since school districts must make tenure decisions at least 60 days prior to the expiration of the probationary period, there was "no purpose in requiring the district to withhold its favorable determinations until the last day" (see also *Remus v. Board of Educ. for Tonawanda City Sch. Dist. and Shaffer v. Schenectady Sch. Dist.,* 96 N.Y.2d 271 (2001); **8:121, 8:123**).

The commissioner of education has ruled that a school board can confer early tenure in a case where the employee had only served two out of three years in the probationary period at the time tenure was granted (*Appeal of Sullivan*, 33 Educ. Dep't Rep. 566 (1994); see also *Appeal of Allen and Wong*, 40 Educ. Dep't Rep. 372 (2000)). However, these decisions contradict an earlier opinion of the Westchester County Supreme Court, which had found that public policy, as embodied in section 3012 of the Education Law, precluded a school district from conferring tenure after two years (*Matter of Altamura*, Sup. Ct. Westchester County, Pirro, J.S.C. (Dec. 30, 1992)).

8:121. When does a board resolution granting tenure become effective?

According to New York's highest court, the Court of Appeals, tenure does not become effective, and a teacher granted tenure is not entitled to the benefits of tenure, until the effective date specified in the resolution (*Remus v. Board of Educ. for Tonawanda City Sch. Dist. and Shaffer v. Schenectady Sch. Dist.* 96 N.Y.2d 271(2001); see **8:123**).

8:122. Does a teacher awarded tenure still acquire tenure if he or she resigns before the effective date of the tenure?

Yes, according to one state appellate court. In *Marcus v. Bd. of Educ. of the Cohoes City Sch. Dist.*, 64 A.D.2d 475 (3d Dep't 1978), a teacher granted tenure resigned three weeks before his tenure became effective. A few years later, he received a probationary appointment in another district and claimed tenure by estoppel on the grounds that his receipt of tenure in the prior district reduced his probationary period to two years (see **8:96, 8:114, 8:124**).

A court rejected the argument that since the teacher's tenure at the prior district did not become effective until after he resigned, he was not tenured when he resigned. According to the court, to deny the teacher the tenure previously granted because he resigned before the effective date would defeat the "purpose and underlying logic" of the provision of law that provides that "two years is a sufficient probationary period for a teacher who has previously been appointed on tenure. . . ."

It remains to be seen whether the *Marcus* decision is still good law after the Court of Appeals' decision in *Remus v. Board of Educ. for Tonawanda City Sch. Dist. and Shaffer v. Schenectady Sch. Dist.*, 96 N.Y.2d 271 (2001), discussed at **8:123.**

8:123. Can a board rescind a prior grant of tenure?

The New York Court of Appeals addressed this question in two consolidated cases (*Remus v. Board of Educ. for Tonawanda City Sch. Dist. and Shaffer v. Schenectady City Sch. Dist.*, 96 N.Y.2d 271 (2001)).

In the first case, the name of a teacher whom the superintendent did not intend to recommend for tenure mistakenly appeared on a list of persons recommended to the school board for tenure due to clerical error. Unaware of the clerical error, the board passed a resolution granting tenure to every teacher on the list. Shortly thereafter, and still well before the effective date specified in the board resolution granting tenure, the board learned of its mistake and passed a subsequent resolution rescinding the prior grant of tenure. The Court of Appeals held that the teacher did not have the protection of tenure because the school district was entitled to rescind its erroneous grant of tenure prior to its effective date (*Shaffer*).

In the other case, the school board passed a resolution in June conferring tenure effective in September. Shortly thereafter, but still well before the September effective date, the district learned that the teacher, while acting as a school chaperone, had consumed alcoholic beverages with students. The teacher declined the district's offer to extend her probationary period one year, and the board rescinded its grant of tenure. The Court of Appeals ruled that a school board is not prohibited from making a deferred award of tenure, and the teacher did not have the benefits of tenure before the effective date previously stated by the board (*Id.*).

Where a school board rescinds a prospective grant of tenure prior to the date that tenure vests, the teacher reverts to the status of a non-tenured teacher approaching the end of the probationary period. As such, that teacher is entitled to the same termination notices as any other probationary teacher who is being denied tenure (see **8:129** for a description of the required notices) (*Appeal of Mahoney*, 43 Educ. Dep't Rep. ___, dec. no. 15,060 (2004)).

8:124. May a teacher acquire tenure by estoppel if a school board fails to take official action granting tenure?

Yes, in limited circumstances. Courts have granted tenure to teachers when school boards have not acted to grant tenure but have continued the teachers' employment after expiration of the probationary period (*Matter of Gould v. Board of Educ.*, 81 N.Y.2d 446 (1993); *Lindsey v. Board of Educ.*, 72 A.D.2d 185 (4th Dep't 1980)). This is known as *tenure by estoppel* or tenure by acquiescence.

Tenure by estoppel or acquiescence occurs only when a district "with full knowledge and consent" allows a teacher to continue to teach after the probationary period has expired (*Lindsey*). In essence, tenure is imposed on the district because it acquiesced or consented to the employment of the teacher under conditions that implied the granting of tenure.

In one case, the New York State Court of Appeals ruled a school district must permit a tenured teacher to rescind her resignation when she resigned under the mistaken belief that she had not yet acquired tenure and was going to be denied tenure (*Gould v. Board of Educ.*). The teacher had obtained tenure by estoppel because her probationary period was two rather than three years and she was employed as a "probationary teacher" for three years because neither she nor the district had noticed that she was entitled to a shortened probationary period (see **8:96, 8:114**).

8:125. Can a school district dismiss a teacher during his or her probationary period?

Yes. A teacher's probationary appointment may be terminated at any time on the recommendation of the superintendent, provided the dismissal is approved by a majority vote of the school board (§§ 2509(1)(a), 2573(1)(a), 3012(1); see also *Matter of Amnawah v. Board of Educ. of the City of New York*, 266 A.D.2d 455 (2d Dep't 1999)), or in the case of a board of cooperative educational services (BOCES), upon the recommendation of the district superintendent by majority vote of the BOCES board (§ 3014(1)).

However, a teacher cannot be terminated for an illegal or unconstitutional reason. The burden rests with the teacher to prove that he or she was terminated for an impermissible reason (*Amnawah*). In one case, the Unites States Supreme Court ruled that the discharge of a teacher for publicly criticizing, in a local newspaper, the school's allocation of financial resources between the school's educational and athletic programs violated the teacher's First Amendment rights. The teacher was addressing a matter of public concern and districts may not discipline or dismiss employees for engaging in such speech (*Pickering v. Board of Educ. of Township High Sch. Dist. 205*, 391 U.S. 563 (1968); see **8:86**).

Although the law does not require a hearing to effect a termination, the district must meet certain notice requirements in order to fire a teacher during his or her probationary period (§§ 2509(1)(a), 2573(1)(a), 3019-a; see also **8:126**).

Some collective bargaining agreements place further restrictions on the discharge of probationary teachers. Therefore, school officials should refer to those agreements before taking action against a probationary teacher.

8:126. What notice must be given to a probationary teacher who is dismissed during his or her probationary period?

The superintendent of schools must give the probationary teacher notice that he or she will recommend to the board that the teacher be dismissed at least 30 days prior to the board meeting at which such recommendation will be considered (§ 3031).

In all districts except New York City, if requested by the teacher no later than 21 days before the board meeting at which the recommendation will be considered, the superintendent of schools must provide the reason(s) for the proposed dismissal recommendation within seven days after the request. The teacher may file a written response with the clerk of the board seven days before the board meets to consider the recommendation for dismissal (§ 3031(b)).

The law does not require that the teacher be given an opportunity to speak or present evidence at the board meeting (*Strax v. Rockland County BOCES,* 257 A.D.2d 578 (2d Dep't 1999)). Failure to provide the requisite notice under section 3031 does not entitle the teacher to automatic reinstatement or back pay. The remedy is for the board to reconsider the termination recommendation with proper notice to the teacher and an opportunity for him or her to respond (*Appeal of Gold,* 34 Educ. Dep't Rep. 372 (1995)).

If a majority of the board accepts the recommendation and votes to dismiss, the teacher must then be given a 30-day written notice of termination (§ 3019-a). Failure to provide the termination notice required by section 3019-a entitles a dismissed teacher to back pay but not reinstatement (*Appeal of Madden-Lynch,* 31 Educ. Dep't Rep. 411 (1992); see also *Matter of Mutschler v. Board of Educ. of the William Floyd UFSD,* 177 A.D.2d 629 (2d Dep't 1991)). Back pay was not available, however, to a probationary teacher who was dismissed for lack of certification without proper notice because the Education Law precludes school districts from paying a teacher who is uncertified at the time of initial hiring (*Sullivan v. Windham-Ashland-Jewett CSD,* 212 A.D.2d 63 (3d Dep't 1995), *appeal denied,* 89 N.Y.2d 814 (1997)).

The two notification periods do not run concurrently (*Appeal of Madden-Lynch*; see also *Appeal of Slater*, 12 Educ. Dep't Rep. 275 (1973)).

8:127. Is a school district required to provide a terminated teacher with a name-clearing hearing?

A terminated teacher is not entitled to a name-clearing hearing unless the district's reasons for the termination have a stigmatizing effect upon the teacher and the district disseminates those reasons (*Appeal of Federico*, 35 Educ. Dep't Rep. 269 (1996)).

The United States Court of Appeals for the Second Circuit has ruled that a name-clearing hearing is required when the reasons for termination "denigrate the employee's competence as a professional and impugn the employee's professional reputation in such a fashion as to effectively put a significant roadblock in that employee's continued ability to practice his or her profession."

According to the court, the right to a name-clearing hearing was triggered when the reasons for termination were placed in the discharged employee's personnel file and were likely to be disclosed to prospective employers (*Donato v. Plainview-Old Bethpage CSD*, 96 F.3d 623 (2d Cir.), *cert. denied*, 519 U.S. 1150 (1997), *remanded*, 985 F.Supp. 316 (E.D.N.Y. 1997); see also *Patterson v. City of Utica*, 307 F.3d 322 (2d Cir. 2004); *Swinton v. Safir*, 93 N.Y.2d 758 (1999); but see *Aquilone v. City of New York*, 262 A.D.2d 13 (1st Dep't 1999), *appeal denied*, 93 N.Y.2d 819 (1999)).

On remand, the district court ruled that the school district was not required to prove the truth of the charges that formed the basis for terminating the employee. Rather, in a proceeding to clear her name, the burden of proof rested with the terminated employee to disprove the charges. The court also ruled that "to be meaningful, the name clearing proceeding must be run by the same actor who diminished the [employee's] reputation" (*Donato v. Plainview-Old Bethpage CSD*, 985 F.Supp. 316 (E.D.N.Y. 1997); see also *Patterson*).

If a name-clearing hearing is unlikely to remedy any ill effects caused by the employer's stigmatizing actions, a terminated employee may be able to recover monetary damages (*Patterson*).

8:128. For what reasons may a probationary teacher be denied tenure?

Although a school district generally has the "unfettered right" to terminate probationary teachers and deny tenure, the denial of tenure is invalid if the reason for the termination is unconstitutional or in violation of the law (*James v. Board of Educ.*, 37 N.Y.2d 891 (1975)). Therefore, unless a teacher demonstrates that the reasons given for the denial of tenure lack a rational basis, the courts will not find the district acted in bad faith in denying tenure (*Matter of Altamura* (Sup. Ct. Westchester County, Pirro, J.S.C., Dec. 30, 1992); *Strax v. Rockland County BOCES*, 257 A.D.2d 578 (2d Dep't 1999)).

In one case, the commissioner of education found a school district could deny tenure to a teacher who had been excessively absent, even though the absences did not exceed the number of sick days under the teachers' collective bargaining agreement (*Appeal of Toma*, 31 Educ. Dep't Rep. 477 (1992)).

A school district may not deny a teacher tenure based upon the school board's philosophical objection to the tenure system (*Conetta v. Board of Educ.*, 165 Misc.2d 329 (1995)). In addition, a school board member may not abstain from voting on whether to grant tenure to an employee based upon a philosophical objection to the state's tenure system (*Appeal of Craft & Dworkin*, 36 Educ. Dep't Rep. 314 (1997)).

8:129. What notice must be given to a probationary teacher who is being denied tenure?

The superintendent of schools must notify the teacher in writing at least 60 days prior to the expiration of the probationary period that an affirmative recommendation for appointment on tenure will not be made (§§ 2509(1)(a), 2573(1)(a), 3012(2); see also *Matter of Meehan*, 11 Educ. Dep't Rep. 34 (1971)). Notice must also be given that the board of education will review the failure to recommend for appointment on tenure at a board meeting to be held at least 30 days after the notice is given. Both notices may be contained within the same written statement, or they may be transmitted separately (§ 3031).

In all districts except New York City, if requested by the teacher no later than 21 days before the board meeting at which the recommendation will be considered, the school superintendent must provide the reason(s) for the recommendation to deny tenure in writing seven days after the request (§ 3031). The teacher may file a written response with the clerk seven days before the board meets to consider the recommendation for dismissal (§ 3031). The law does not require that the teacher be given an opportunity to speak or to present evidence at the board meeting.

The statement of reasons for the nonrecommendation of tenure cannot be vague. It must be sufficiently specific to enable the teacher to respond. However, a teacher's right to such a statement is a "procedural" right, not a "substantive" one. Therefore, the remedy afforded to a teacher who does not initially receive a sufficiently specific statement is to provide one (see *Farrell v. Board of Educ.*, 64 A.D.2d 703 (2d Dep't 1978); *Rathbone v. Board of Educ.*, 47 A.D.2d 172 (3d Dep't 1975)).

A district need not provide such notices to part-time employees who are not eligible for tenure in the district (*Appeal of Longshore*, 32 Educ. Dep't Rep. 311 (1992)). The notice procedures also are not applicable in the case of probationary teachers who resign voluntarily to prevent any reference of the discharge in their personnel file (*Biegel v. Board of Educ.*, 211 A.D.2d 969 (3d Dep't 1995)).

8:130. What happens if a school district fails to give the required denial of tenure notice?

If a district fails to provide the required notice for denial of tenure, the teacher is not entitled to automatic reinstatement or salary beyond the last day he or she rendered service. The remedy is for the board to reconsider the recommendation against tenure with notice to the teacher and an opportunity for him or her to respond (*Appeal of Gold*, 34 Educ. Dep't Rep. 372 (1995); *Appeal of Spadone,* 39 Educ. Dep't Rep. 638 (2000)).

In a case in which a district learned of inappropriate conduct by a probationary teacher 22 days before the end of the probationary period, the New York State Court of Appeals ruled the district could deny tenure to the teacher even though it was impossible for the district to comply with the notice requirements of section 2573(1) (*Tucker v. Community Sch. Dist. No. 10*, 82 N.Y.2d 274 (1993); see also *Appeal of Thier,* 36 Educ. Dep't Rep. 222 (1996)). However, the court did require the district to pay back wages to the teacher to ensure she had the required notice prior to termination (*Tucker*).

8:131. When is a decision to deny tenure final?

The Education Law provides that a superintendent's recommendation to deny tenure must be reviewed by the board of education (§ 3031; see **8:129**). However, according to the commissioner of education, when the superintendent fails to recommend tenure, "the probationary period expires as a matter of law upon the last day of the probationary period" (*Matter of Leviness*, 18 Educ. Dep't Rep. 213 (1978)). Moreover, "the refusal of the superintendent to make an affirmative recommendation that tenure be granted is not merely a recommendation, but rather a final act" (*Appeal of Clancy*, 29 Educ. Dep't Rep. 28 (1989)). Therefore, while it is not improper for a school board to vote in concurrence with a superintendent's recommendation to deny tenure, it is unnecessary (*Matter of Egan*, 15 Educ. Dep't Rep. 196 (1975)). However, at least one state appellate court disagrees with the commissioner (*Dembovich v. Liberty CSD Bd. of Educ.*, 296 A.D.2d 794 (3d Dep't 2002)).

When a school board votes to deny a teacher tenure despite a superintendent's recommendation that tenure be granted, such a vote is considered advisory in nature, and the board must meet again to reconsider the issue and take final action. The teacher is entitled to notice of the board's intention to deny tenure and the date of the meeting at which it will take final action at least 30 days prior to that meeting. No later than 21 days before the board meeting, the teacher may request a written statement giving the board's reasons for denial, which must be provided by the district within seven days of the request (§ 3031(b)). The teacher may file a written response with the district clerk seven days before the board meeting at which final consideration will take place (§ 3031(b)).

The statement provided by the board in support of its decision to deny tenure notwithstanding the superintendent's recommendation to grant tenure must be sufficiently specific to permit the teacher to make an "intelligent and meaningful" response (*Appeal of Dituri and Blake*, 42 Educ. Dep't Rep. 363 (2003)). The commissioner has found, for example, that a board's statement that probationary employees "failed to function effectively" was insufficient to enable them to prepare meaningful responses (*Appeal of Dituri and Blake*).

8:132. Does a teacher who resigns rather than be denied tenure have any rights?

A teacher who resigns rather than be denied tenure may be eligible for unemployment insurance benefits. A state Appellate Court held that the teacher's "resignation" under such circumstances is not voluntary and therefore, he or she is eligible for unemployment benefits (*In re the Claim of Harp*, 202 A.D.2d 876 (3d Dep't 1994)).

In addition, a teacher who resigns under a mistaken belief that he or she does not have and is going to be denied tenure has a right to rescind the resignation (*Gould v. Board of Educ.*, 81 N.Y.2d 446 (1993); see **8:124**)).

Seniority Rights

8:133. What are seniority rights?

Seniority rights are those rights to job security and priority within a school district based on length of actual paid service in a specific tenure area (*Volk v. Board of Educ. of City Sch. Dist. of Rochester*, 83 N.Y.2d 930 (1994)). Seniority rights are different from tenure rights because they apply to both tenured and probationary teachers.

The Education Law does not provide a definition of the term seniority, but it does require that seniority be used in determining the order in which teachers are dismissed in the event that teaching positions are abolished (§§ 2510(2), 2585(3), 3013(2); see *Appeal of Krason*, 41 Educ. Dep't Rep. 305 (2002)), *aff'd, Madison-Oneida BOCES*, 2 A.D.3d 1240 (3d Dep't

2003), *appeal granted*, ___ N.Y.3d ___, 2004 N.Y. LEXIS 655 (2004) (section 3013 applies to teaching assistants)).

Seniority is the sole criterion districts may use to decide which teacher will be excessed — tenured status may not be a consideration (*Matter of Fallick*, 18 Educ. Dep't Rep. 586 (1979), *aff'd*, Sup. Ct. Albany County, Hughes, J.S.C. (Feb. 11, 1980)). Likewise, certification may not be used as a factor in determining seniority (*Lynch v. Nyquist*, 41 A.D.2d 363, *aff'd*, 34 N.Y.2d 588 (1974); *Silver v. Board of Educ.*, 46 A.D.2d 427 (4th Dep't 1975)).

8:134. How do tenure areas affect seniority rights?

Seniority within a specific tenure area is the determining factor in establishing seniority credit prior to excessing a teacher following a school board's decision to abolish a position (*Lynch v. Nyquist*, 41 A.D.2d 363, *aff'd*, 34 N.Y.2d 588 (1974); *Matter of Daly*, 23 Educ. Dep't Rep. 147 (1983)). Thus, a teacher's seniority rights are tied directly to tenure areas.

A teacher who has several probationary or tenure appointments in separate tenure areas accrues seniority separately in each area, depending on the actual service performed. For example, if a teacher serves as a mathematics teacher and a science teacher for five years and then teaches only mathematics for two years, then that teacher has seven years of seniority credit in mathematics and five years of seniority credit in science.

Once a teacher is excessed and placed on a preferred eligible list for possible call back, however, seniority is determined by length of service within the district rather than service in a tenure area (*Mahony v. Board of Educ.*, 140 A.D.2d 33 (2d Dep't 1988), *appeal denied*, 73 N.Y.2d 703 (1988)). Thus, the same teacher described above would have seven years of seniority for purposes of reappointment to either a mathematics or science position. (For more information on the abolition of positions and the excessing of teachers see **8:145–157**.)

8:135. Can seniority rights be waived or altered by a written agreement?

Seniority rights may be waived but cannot be extended by a written agreement. In a case upheld by the Albany County Supreme Court, the commissioner of education ruled that a business education teacher was not entitled to continue to accrue seniority in a teaching tenure area while placed on special assignment in the district's business office, even though the district, the teachers' union, and the teacher signed a written agreement that the teacher would continue to accrue such seniority (*Appeal of Tropia*, 32 Educ. Dep't Rep. 606 (1993), *aff'd*, *Matter of Camden CSD*, Sup. Ct. Albany County, Keegan, J.S.C. (Jan. 11, 1994)).

Even though a school district cannot enter into an agreement to extend seniority rights, it can enter into an agreement whereby a teacher waives his or her seniority rights (*Matter of Cesaratto*, 17 Educ. Dep't Rep. 23 (1977)). A waiver is effective only if it is clearly evidenced and given with knowledge and consent (*Feinerman v. Board of Coop. Educ. Services*, 48 N.Y.2d 491 (1979); *Ambramovich v. Board of Educ.*, 46 N.Y.2d 450 (1979), *reconsideration denied*, 46 N.Y.2d 1076 (1979), *cert. denied*, 444 U.S. 845 (1979)).

8:136. How is seniority calculated?

The courts and the commissioner of education have defined seniority in terms of length of actual paid service within a tenure area to a school district (*Dreyfuss v. Board of Educ.*, 76 Misc.2d 479 (1973), *aff'd*, 45 A.D.2d 988 (2d Dep't 1974); *Matter of Halayko*, 23 Educ. Dep't Rep. 384 (1984)).

The first criterion for determining seniority is the actual full-time service rendered within the tenure area. If such full-time service is equal, the teachers' respective appointment dates are to be used for determining seniority (*Matter of Ferguson*, 14 Educ. Dep't Rep. 102 (1974); see also *Matter of Schoenfeld v. BOCES of Nassau County*, 98 A.D.2d 723 (2d Dep't 1983); *Appeal of Kulick*, 34 Educ. Dep't Rep. 613 (1995)). When two teachers have equal seniority and the same appointment date, the more senior teacher is the one whose appointment occurred first (*Matter of Ducey*, 65 State Dep't Rep. 65 (1943)). But if both were appointed in the same resolution, a school district may use any reasonable method to establish seniority, including factors such as the dates on which an employment agreement was signed or returned, and also may consider the salaries of the employees (*Schoenfeld; Matter of Sommers*, 19 Educ. Dep't Rep. 99 (1979); *Appeal of Kiernan*, 32 Educ. Dep't Rep. 618 (1993); *Matter of Cesaratto*, 17 Educ. Dep't Rep. 23(1977); *Matter of Nicolette*, 17 Educ. Dep't Rep. 381(1978)).

School districts are required to comply with the requirements of section 30.1 (which is applicable to all probationary appointments made after August 1, 1975). This section mandates that seniority "need not have been consecutive but shall, during each term for which seniority credit is sought, have constituted a substantial portion of the time of the professional educator" (i.e., equaling 40 percent or more of the total time spent by the professional educator in the performance of his or her duties) (8 NYCRR § 30.1(f), (g)). Thus, the commissioner has held that years of regular full-time substitute teaching service, which was interrupted by periods of part-time substitute service and ultimately led to a probationary appointment, should count for purposes of seniority by virtue of section 30.1(f) (*Appeal of Carey*, 31 Educ. Dep't Rep. 394 (1992)).

Days spent on unpaid leave of absence may not be included in determining seniority (*Matter of Halayko*). A district is not obliged to grant credit for interrupted service when the teacher has not obtained a leave of absence. However, a district may choose to grant credit for interrupted service pursuant to a collective bargaining agreement with its teachers (*Board of Educ. v. Lakeland Fed'n of Teachers*, 51 A.D.2d 1033 (2d Dep't 1976)).

8:137. Do teachers lose accrued seniority when they "voluntarily" sever service with the district?

Yes. Teachers lose their accrued seniority when they voluntarily sever service with the district that employs them, as for example, through resignation or retirement (*Kransdorf v. Bd. of Educ. of Northport-East Northport UFSD*, 81 N.Y.2d 871 (1993); *Appeal of Carey*, 31 Educ. Dep't Rep. 394 (1992); *Matter of Ducey*, 65 St. Dep't Rep. 65 (1943); *Appeal of Morehouse*, 37 Educ. Dep't Rep. 428 (1998), *aff'd,* 268 A.D.2d 767 (3d Dep't 2000), *appeal denied*, 95 N.Y.2d 751 (2000)).

However when a teacher's service with a district is "involuntarily" severed because the teacher's position is eliminated and the teacher is excessed, the teacher retains any accrued seniority upon returning to service with that district in the future; the seniority clock is not reset when a teacher returns to service after being excessed (*Appeal of Lamb*, 42 Educ. Dep't Rep. 406 (2003)).

8:138. Does service as a regular substitute teacher count towards "seniority" for purposes of calculating the length of service in the district generally, or in a particular tenure area?

Yes. A teacher must be given seniority credit for regular substitute service rendered any time prior to a probationary appointment, even if the substitute service is longer than two years (*Kransdorf v. Board of Educ. of Northport-East Northport UFSD*, 81 N.Y.2d 871 (1993); *Appeal of Carey*, 31 Educ. Dep't Rep. 394 (1992); *Appeal of Kahn and Cruz*, 35 Educ. Dep't Rep. 129 (1995)). Similarly, prior regular substitute service counts toward seniority even if it is for less than the full semester required for *Jarema* credit (*Kaufman v. Fallsburg CSN*, 91 N.Y.2d 57 (1997)).

Moreover, the New York State Court of Appeals and the commissioner of education have ruled that if a teacher has been continuously employed by a district, the regular substitute service need not immediately precede the probationary appointment to count as seniority credit (*Kransdorf; Carey*).

8:139. Do part-time teachers receive seniority credit for part-time service?

Generally, part-time service does not qualify a teacher for any seniority rights except in the case of part-time kindergarten teachers (see **8:109**). However, part-time service rendered after a full-time probationary appointment is included in calculation of seniority if the district requests the change in position (*Matter of Oursler*, 15 Educ. Dep't Rep. 258 (1975); *Matter of Blanchard*, 14 Educ. Dep't Rep. 260 (1975)), but not if the reduction to part-time status is at the request of the teacher. Seniority is "frozen" at this point (*Matter of Walsh*, 17 Educ. Dep't Rep. 434 (1978)). A collective bargaining agreement or board policy may oblige a school district to give seniority credit for part-time service (*Garcia v. Board of Educ.*, 100 A.D.2d 967 (2d Dep't 1984); *Schlosser v. Board of Educ.*, 62 A.D.2d 207, *aff'd*, 47 N.Y.2d 811 (1979)).

A teacher who has served full time does not lose existing seniority upon accepting or requesting a part-time position with a school district ((*Avila v. Board of Educ. of the North Babylon UFSD*, 240 A.D.2d 661 (2d Dep't 1997), *appeal denied*, 91 N.Y.2d 801 (1997); *Matter of Bellarosa*, 20 Educ. Dep't Rep. 252 (1980); *Matter of Walsh; Matter of Blanchard*).

8:140. What are the seniority rights of teachers, teaching assistants, and teacher aides when a board of cooperative educational services (BOCES) takes over a program under which they were employed?

When a teacher, teaching assistant, or teacher aide will be excessed because a district program is contracted out to a BOCES, the BOCES taking over the district program must continue the employment of the district's teachers, teaching assistants, and teacher aides who worked in the program (§ 3014-a(1)). If it cannot employ all, it must hire those teachers, teaching assistants, and teacher aides with the greatest seniority to fill the teaching positions for the program (§ 3014-a(2)). However, the law cannot be used by teachers who are not excessed by the change to obtain a superior placement with the new provider (see *Buenzow v. Lewiston-Porter CSD*, 101 A.D.2d 30 (4th Dep't 1984), *aff'd*, 64 N.Y.2d 676 (1984)).

The district must place all excessed teachers, teaching assistants, and teacher aides who cannot be employed on its preferred eligible list for similar positions (§§ 3014-a(2), 3014-b(2); *Acinapuro BOCES*, 89 A.D. 2d 329 (2d Dep't 1982)).

The teacher, teaching assistant, or teacher aide maintains the same tenure and seniority status he or she enjoyed before the takeover. The teacher, teaching assistant, or teacher aide may also be entitled to retain the salary step and sick days credited to him or her prior to the takeover (§§ 3014-a(3), 3014-b(3); *Appeal of Adler*, 37 Educ. Dep't Rep. 95 (1997), *rev'd on other grounds, Board of Educ. of the N. Tonawanda City Sch. Dist. v. Mills,* 263 A.D.2d 574 (3d Dep't 1999), *appeal denied,* 94 N.Y.2d 751 (1999)).

Even if a teacher accepts an offer of full-time employment with the BOCES, the excessed teacher still retains any preferred eligibility rights that he or she has acquired pursuant to sections 2510(3) and 3013(3) of the Education Law with the component district from which he or she was excessed (*Bojarczuk v. Mills,* 98 N.Y.2d 663 (2002); see also **8:142**).

8:141. Do teachers dismissed by a board of cooperative educational services (BOCES) after a BOCES takeover retain any preferred eligibility (PEL) rights with the component district?

Yes. A teacher fired by a BOCES following a BOCES takeover does not necessarily lose his or her PEL rights with the component district. Under the law, however, a teacher only retains preferred eligibility rights with the component district if the teacher's record with that district demonstrates "faithful, competent service in the office or position" that he or she filled (§§ 2510(3)(a), 3013). It is the teacher's record of service with the component that determines whether the teacher has preferred eligibility rights to a position of employment with that component, not the teacher's record of service with the BOCES. (*Borarczuk v. Mills,* ___A.D.3d ___, 2004 N.Y. App. Div. LEXIS 3681 (3d Dep't 2004)).

8:142. What are the seniority rights of teachers, teaching assistants and teacher aides when a school district takes back from a board of cooperative educational services (BOCES) a program under which they were employed?

When a teacher, teaching assistant or teacher aide is excessed from a BOCES because of a takeback by a component district, the former BOCES employee has a vested right to employment with the component district, and in fact, becomes an employee of the component district by operation of law, subject to availability of positions based on seniority (§ 3014-b(1); see **8:143**). In such cases, no vote of the component school board is necessary to hire the excessed BOCES teacher (*Appeal of Valentine,* 38 Educ. Dep't Rep. 39 (1998)).

Such employees maintain the same tenure and seniority status they enjoyed before the takeback and may also be entitled to retain the salary step and sick days credited to them prior to the takeback (§§ 3014-a(3), 3014-b(3); *Appeal of Adler,* 37 Educ. Dep't Rep. 95 (1997), *rev'd on other grounds, Board of Educ. of the N. Tonawanda City Sch. Dist. v. Mills,* 263 A.D.2d 574 (3d Dep't 1999), *appeal denied,* 94 N.Y.2d 751 (1999)).

A similar law provides the same rights to teachers whose positions are excessed as a result of tuitioning out students to another district (§ 3014-d) or taking back tuitioned-out students (§ 3014-c). However, the two provisions may not be combined to require a component district to employ BOCES teachers excessed when a district takes back students from a BOCES program and tuitions the students out to another component district (*Herrman v. Board of Educ.*, 194 A.D.2d 673 (2d Dep't 1993)). School counselors and social workers who lose their BOCES jobs due to a takeback of services by a component district are not entitled to these job protections (*Bd. of Educ. of the N. Tonawanda City Sch. Dist. v. Mills*).

8:143. What happens if a component district taking back a program from a board of cooperative educational services (BOCES) does not have enough positions for everyone employed by the BOCES in the program?

If a district cannot employ all of the teachers, teaching assistants and teacher aides in the program it takes back, it must hire those teachers, teaching assistants and teacher aides with the greatest seniority to fill the teaching positions for the program (§ 3014-b(2); *Buenzow v. Lewiston-Porter CSD*, 101 A.D.2d 30 (4th Dep't 1984), *aff'd*, 64 N.Y.2d 676 (1984); *Acinapuro v. BOCES*, 89 A.D.2d 329 (2d Dep't 1982); *Gill v. Dutchess County BOCES*, 99 A.D.2d 836 (2d Dep't 1984). However, the law cannot be used by teachers who are not excessed by the change to obtain a superior placement with the new provider (*Buenzow*). The district must place all excessed teachers, teaching assistants and teacher aides who cannot be employed on its preferred eligible list for similar positions (§ 3014-b(2); *Acinapuro*).

8:144. Do teachers excessed by a BOCES who accept employment with a component district retain preferred eligibility (PEL) rights with the BOCES?

Probably. An employees who is excessed by a BOCES and is offered and accepts employment with a component district may retain PEL rights with the BOCES consistent with a state appellate court's ruling in *Bojarczuk v. Mills*, ___ A.D.3d ___, 2004 N.Y. App. Div. LEXIS 3681 (3d Dep't 2004), (see **8:140**), which implicitly reversed a contrary ruling by the commissioner of education in *Appeal of Chernoff*, 37 Educ. Dep't Rep. 709 (1998), *aff'd*, (Albany Co. Supreme Ct., unpublished, 1999)).

Abolition of Positions and Excessing

8:145. May a school board abolish a teaching position?

Yes, if the position is no longer necessary to the school system. Traditionally, both the courts and the commissioner of education have given school boards broad latitude to abolish, reorganize, or consolidate positions (*Zurlo v. Ambach*, 53 N.Y.2d 1035 (1981); *Cohen v. Crown Point CSD*, 306 A.D.2d 732 (3d Dep't 2003); *Young v. Board of Educ.*, 35 N.Y.2d 31 (1974); *Currier v. Tompkins-Seneca-Tioga BOCES*, 80 A.D.2d 979 (3d Dep't 1981)). However, there should be a bona fide reason for abolition or reorganization.

Before a teaching position is abolished, school districts must consider adjusting teaching schedules in order to continue the services of a teacher within his or her certification (*Steele v. Board of Educ.*, 53 A.D.2d 674 (2d Dep't 1976), *aff'd*, 42 N.Y.2d 840 (1977); *Amos v. Board of Educ.*, 54 A.D.2d 297 (4th Dep't 1976), *aff'd*, 43 N.Y.2d 706 (1977)).

When teachers challenge the abolition of positions in cases where schedule shuffling has taken place, districts must demonstrate the impossibility of retaining the teachers through adjustment of schedules. A board can meet this burden by demonstrating that the educational and financial impact of the teaching assignment will be detrimental (*Chambers v. Board of Educ.*, 47 N.Y.2d 279 (1979)). A school district has no obligation to shuffle the schedules of teachers outside the tenure area of the particular teacher whose position is being abolished (*Appeal of Chaney*, 33 Educ. Dep't Rep. 12 (1993); see also *Appeal of Soukey*, 38 Educ. Dep't Rep. 626 (1999); but see *Matter of Taber v. Sherburne-Earlville CSD*, 244 A.D.2d 634 (3d Dep't 1997)).

A school board must adopt a formal resolution abolishing a particular position and provide notice to the teacher that his or her position is being abolished. The board's resolution must identify the tenure area in which a position is to be abolished (*Appeal of Lessing*, 34 Educ. Dep't Rep. 451 (1995)). In addition, the applicable collective bargaining agreement should be reviewed to determine if it requires a particular method or manner of giving notice to teachers whose positions are being abolished.

Where a school board appointed a teacher to a nonexistent tenure area, the court ruled the board could not abolish the position and terminate the teacher without first reclassifying the teacher's tenure area. The board was ordered to determine the teacher's proper tenure area based upon the work she actually performed (*Abrantes v. Board of Educ. of the Norwood-Norfolk CSD*, 233 A.D.2d 718 (3d Dep't 1996), *appeal denied*, 89 N.Y.2d 812 (1997)). School districts may only appoint teachers to the tenure areas designated in part 30 of the commissioner's regulations and may not create their own tenure areas for teaching positions (8 NYCRR Part 30).

8:146. May a district abolish a position rather than fire a teacher?

No. Abolishing a position may not be used as a way to fire a teacher or an administrator (*Young v. Board of Educ.*, 35 N.Y.2d 31 (1974); *Weimer v. Board of Educ.*, 76 A.D.2d 1046 (2d Dep't 1980); *Board of Educ. v.*

Niagara-Wheatfield Teachers' Ass'n, 54 A.D.2d 281 (4th Dep't 1976), *appeal denied*, 41 N.Y.2d 801 (1977); *Appeal of Stratton*, 33 Educ. Dep't Rep. 373 (1993)).

However, the commissioner of education has held that in a 3020-a proceeding involving a "schedule shuffling" question, a hearing panel cannot require a district to show why it abolished positions in one subject rather than another (*Rappold v. Board of Educ.*, 20 Educ. Dep't Rep. 664 (1981), *aff'd*, 95 A.D.2d 890 (3d Dep't 1983)).

8:147. Does a teacher whose position is being abolished have the right to take the job of a less senior teacher?

Yes. If a position is abolished, the teacher with the least seniority within the tenure area of that position in that school district must be the person dismissed (§§ 2510(2), 2585(3), 3013(2)). Although this is sometimes incorrectly referred to as "bumping" the junior teacher, the more senior teacher need not take over the assignment of the excessed teacher. The district retains the authority to make all teaching assignments.

True bumping rights are available only to teachers appointed under part 30 of the Rules of the Board of Regents. An excessed teacher cannot bump back into a pre-part 30 tenure area (*Rippe v. Board of Educ.*, 64 N.Y.2d 281 (1985)). These rights allow a teacher whose position is eliminated in one area and who accrued seniority based on prior service in a different tenure area to claim the position of another teacher serving in that previous tenure area, provided the first teacher has more seniority in the tenure area than other teachers (8 NYCRR § 30.13).

In addition, if a district creates a new position at the same time that it abolishes an existing position, the teacher who would be excessed must be hired at his or her existing salary for the new position if the duties performed under both positions are similar and the record of the person has been one of faithful, competent service in the prior position (§§ 2510(1), 2585(2), 3013(1)). The two positions are considered similar if more than 50 percent of the functions to be performed in the new position are the same as those performed under the old position (*Appeal of Klein*, 43 Educ. Dep't Rep.___, dec. no. 15,003 (2003); *Coates v. Ambach*, 52 A.D.2d 261 (3d Dep't 1976), *aff'd*, 42 N.Y.2d 846 (1977); see **8:149**). The 50 percent rule should not be applied rigidly, and the emphasis should be on the type of duties the employee could have been expected to perform in the old position (*Matter of Cowan v. Board of Educ. of Brentwood UFSD*, 99 A.D.2d 831 (2d Dep't 1984), *appeal withdrawn*, 63 N.Y.2d 702 (1984); *Appeal of Elmendorf*, 36 Educ. Dep't Rep. 308 (1997), see also *Elmendorf v. Howell*, 962 F.Supp. 326 (N.D.N.Y. 1997)).

An employee who claims entitlement to a similar position is entitled to a pre-termination hearing to offer proof of the similarity of positions (*DeSimone v. Board of Educ.*, 604 F.Supp. 1180 (E.D.N.Y. 1985), and 612 F.Supp.1568 (E.D.N.Y. 1985); *Fairbairn v. Board of Educ.*, 876 F.Supp. 432 (E.D.N.Y. 1995); *Appeal of Elmendorf*, 36 Educ. Dep't Rep. 308 (1997)) see also *Elmendorf v. Howell*, 962 F.Supp. 326 (N.D.N.Y. 1997)).

8:148. What rights of reappointment do excessed teachers have?

A teacher who is excessed because a teaching position has been abolished must be placed on a preferred eligible list of candidates for appointment to a similar position for seven years after the position is abolished (§§ 2510(3)(a), 3013(3)(a); *Brewer v. Board of Educ.*, 51 N.Y.2d 855 (1980); *Jester v. Board of Educ.*, 109 A.D.2d 1004 (3d Dep't 1985); *Greenspan v. Dutchess Co. BOCES*, 96 A.D.2d 1028 (2d Dep't 1983); *Appeal of Tucholski*, 28 Educ. Dep't Rep. 112 (1988), and in large city school districts, until his or her name is reached on the seniority list (§ 2585(4)).

Teachers are only entitled to reappointment within the tenure area in which they served, even if they hold certification for positions in other tenure areas (*Board of Educ. v. Barker Teachers Union*, 209 A.D.2d 945 (1994), *appeal denied*, 85 N.Y.2d 807 (1995); *Appeal of Allen*, 36 Educ. Dep't Rep. 299 (1997); *Appeal of Moravus*, 32 Educ. Dep't Rep. 419 (1992)). A collective bargaining agreement may not require that a teacher whose position has been abolished be appointed to any job opening in his or her tenure area or any position for which that teacher is certified (*Barker*). A teacher who is reappointed to a similar position within the district is entitled to appointment without reduction in salary or increment (§§ 2510(3)(a), 2585(4), 3013(3)(a)).

Regarding the period of preferred eligibility, one state appellate court ruled that a teacher whose preferred eligibility rights expired on June 30 of a particular year was not entitled to appointment to positions from which the incumbent teachers resigned effective that same June 30, because the court found that the vacancies created by the resignations did not occur until July "at the earliest" (*Matter of Raben v. Board of Educ. of Hauppauge UFSD*, 175 A.D.2d 286 (2d Dep't 1991), *appeal denied*, 79 N.Y.2d 754 (1992); see also *Matter of Lombardo v. Baldwin UFSD*, 150 A.D.2d 452 (2d Dep't 1989)); *Appeal of Principio*, 39 Educ. Dep't Rep. 11 (1998)).

8:149. What constitutes a "similar" position for purposes of reappointment from a preferred eligible list (PEL)?

Two positions are similar if *more than* 50 percent of the duties are same (*Appeal of Klein*, 43 Educ. Dep't Rep. ___, dec. no. 15,003 (2003); *Appeal of Allen*, 36 Educ. Dep't Rep. 299 (1997); see also *Greenspan v. Dutchess Co. BOCES*, 96 A.D.2d 1028 (2d Dep't 1983)). However, a teacher on a PEL is not entitled to reemployment if he or she is not certified to teach in the position sought. "Absent such certification, reemployment rights cannot attach" (*Davis v. Mills*, 98 N.Y.2d 120 (2002); see **8:157**).

A teacher has the burden of proving that a majority of the duties of the new position are similar to those of the former position (*Appeal of Jordan*, 37 Educ. Dep't Rep. 487 (1998); see also *Matter of Coates v. Ambach*, 52 A.D.2d 261 (3d Dep't 1976), *aff'd*, 42 N.Y.2d 846 (1977)).

According to the commissioner of education and one state appellate court, two positions will not be deemed "similar" if they are in different tenure areas (*Davis v. Mills*, 285 A.D.2d 703 (3d Dep't 2001), *aff'd on other grounds*, 98 N.Y.2d 120 (2002); *Brown v. Board of Educ.*, 211 A.D.2d 887 (3d Dep't 1995); *Appeal of Donato*, 41 Educ. Dep't Rep. 246 (2001)). However, another appellate court has ruled that there is no provision in the Education Law which requires that to be "similar," the vacant position exist within the excessed teacher's tenure area (*Levy v. Board of Educ. of Freeport U.F.S.D.*, 255 A.D.2d 459 (2d Dept 2000); *Leggio v. Oglesby*, 69 A.D.2d 446 (2d Dep't 1979), *appeal dismissed*, 53 N.Y.2d 704 (1981); see also *Board of Educ. v. Barker Teachers Union*, 209 A.D.2d 945 (4th Dep't 1994), *appeal denied*, 85 N.Y.2d 807 (1995)).

8:150. What rights of reappointment do excessed instructional employees in non tenure-bearing positions have?

Excessed instructional employees (and administrators) only qualify for preferred eligibility (PEL) rights if both the position from which they are excessed and the position to which they seek appointment are tenure-bearing. The employee need not have acquired tenure; rather, both positions must be tenure-track positions. For example, an instructional employee who is excessed from a tenure-bearing position may have PEL rights only to another tenure-bearing position (*Appeal of Strong* 41 Educ. Dep't Rep. 425 (2002); see also *Matter of Merz*, 21 Educ. Dep't Rep. 449 (1982)). However, assistant superintendents in small city school districts do not receive appointments to tenure-bearing positions and therefore do not have PEL rights (§ 2509(1)(b); *Appeal of Strong*).

8:151. Must teachers on a preferred eligible list (PEL) be offered substitute and/or part-time positions?

Yes. Teachers on the PEL also must be offered regular substitute positions of at least a five-month duration. Declining an offer of reinstatement to such a position does not adversely affect the teacher's preferred eligibility rights (§§ 2510(3)(b), 3013(3)(b)).

In addition, teachers on the PEL must be offered a part-time teaching position of shorter duration if one becomes available (*Abrams v. Ambach,* 43 A.D.2d 883 (3d Dep't 1974)). In fact, a teacher recalled from the PEL and placed in a part-time position after being excessed from a full-time position is entitled to a new seven-year period on the PEL from the date the school district abolishes his or her part-time position (*Avila v. Board of Educ. of the North Babylon UFSD,* 240 A.D.2d 661 (2d Dep't 1997), *appeal denied,* 91 N.Y.2d 801 (1997)).

8:152. How does retirement affect an excessed teacher's right to reappointment from a preferred eligible list (PEL)?

A teacher's retirement terminates the teacher's PEL rights (*Morehouse v. Mills,* 37 Educ. Dep't Rep. 428 (1998), *aff'd,* 268 A.D.2d 767 (3d Dep't 2000), *appeal denied,* 95 N.Y.2d 751 (2000); *Matter of Girard v. Board of Educ. of City Sch. Dist. of Buffalo,* 168 A.D.2d 183 (4th Dep't 1991) *Appeal of Donato,* 41 Educ. Dep't Rep. 246 (2001), unless the decision to retire was involuntarily made because of fraud, coercion, or duress (*Gould v. Bd. of Educ. of Sewanhaka Cent. High School Dist.,* 81 N.Y.2d 446 (1993); see also *Donato v. Mills,* ___ A.D.2d ___, 2004 N.Y. App. Div. LEXIS 4739 (3d Dep't 2004)). Similarly, acceptance of termination benefits terminates a teacher's PEL rights (*Morehouse; Matter of Gerson v. Board of Educ. of Comsewogue UFSD,* 214 A.D.2d 732 (2d Dep't 1995)). However, if a teacher retires under the disability retirement provisions of the Education Law then later recovers from the disability, the teacher is entitled to be placed on the PEL as of the date of the teacher's disability retirement (§ 2510(3)(a)).

8:153. Do teachers lose their right to remain on the preferred eligible list (PEL) if they accept a position in a different tenure area or refuse a particular offer of reemployment?

No. A teacher does not waive any right to reappointment within his or her tenure area by accepting a position in another tenure area in the district (*Matter of Mead,* 23 Educ. Dep't Rep. 101 (1983); or acceptance of other employment (*Donato v. Mills,* ___A.D.2d ___, 2004 N.Y. App. Div. LEXIS 4739 (3d Dep't 2004)). A teacher does not waive any right to reappointment from the PEL for refusing an offer of reemployment. A teacher who refuses an offer of reemployment because of a short-term commitment to another employer does not waive his or her seniority rights (*Lewis v. Cleveland Hill UFSD,* 119 A.D.2d 263 (4th Dep't 1986)).

8:154. Is there any particular order for recalling excessed teachers?

Yes. When several different teachers have been excessed, they must be offered reappointment in order of seniority (§§ 2510(3)(a), 2585(4), 3013(3)(a)). For purposes of determining seniority of teachers on preferred eligible lists, the length of service in the system, not length of service within a particular tenure area, is used (*Mahony v. Board of Educ.*, 140 A.D.2d 33 (2d Dep't 1988), *appeal denied*, 73 N.Y.2d 703 (1988)).

8:155. What are the rights of an improperly excessed teacher?

Such a teacher is entitled to reinstatement and back pay less any earnings from jobs worked at during normal school hours (*Matter of Lezette v. Board of Educ.*, 35 N.Y.2d 272 (1974); *Appeal of Lessing*, 34 Educ. Dep't Rep. 451 (1995)). In addition, the district may not offset the back pay it owes a reinstated teacher by the amount of unemployment benefits the teacher received. All or part of the unemployment benefits received by the teacher might be recovered by the Labor Department (*Appeal of Lessing*, 35 Educ. Dep't Rep. 116 (1995)).

8:156. Does an improperly excessed teacher have a duty to mitigate (lessen) any damages during the pendency of proceedings brought to review the abolition of his or her position?

Yes. The New York State Court of Appeals held that an improperly excessed teacher may not collect damages from his or her former employing school district to cover periods during which he or she refuses to accept comparable work (*Gross v. Board of Educ. of Elmsford UFSD*, 78 N.Y.2d 13 (1991)).

8:157. May a district recall from the preferred eligible list (PEL) a teacher who is not certified for the available position?

According to the New York Court of Appeals, teachers do not have a right to be reemployed from the PEL in a position for which they are not certified (*Davis v. Mills*, 98 N.Y.2d 120 (2002)).

However, if a district mistakenly recalls a tenured teacher from the PEL to teach a subject within that teacher's tenure area but outside his or her certification, it must continue to pay the teacher's full salary during the pendency of section 3020-a charges brought to remove that teacher for lack of certification (*Winter v. Board of Educ. for Rhinebeck CSD*, 79 N.Y.2d 1 (1992), *reconsideration denied*, 79 N.Y. 2d 978 (1992), see **8:194**). This is because teachers certified on the day they are initially hired by the district are deemed qualified under the Education Law for purposes of receiving a salary even if they are not specifically certified to teach in the position for which they are later mistakenly recalled to from the PEL (*Winter;* see **8:140**).

Professional Development

8:158. Does a school district or BOCES have any legal obligation to promote professional development among the teaching staff it employs?

Yes. Commissioner's regulations require that by September 1 each year, every school district and board of cooperative educational services (BOCES) must adopt a professional development plan designed to improve the quality of teaching by helping teachers stay current and meet the learning needs of students. This plan must include professional development opportunities for teaching assistants who hold level III certificates and long-term substitute teachers, as defined by commissioner's regulations (see 8 NYCRR §§ 80-5.4, 100.2(dd)(1)(i)).

A district may adopt its own professional development plan, or it may participate in a comprehensive plan adopted by the BOCES to which it belongs (8 NYCRR § 110.2(dd)(1)(ii)). Moreover, a school district or BOCES may include the local special education comprehensive system of professional development plan implemented pursuant to federal regulations as part of its professional development plan, provided that the plan meets all applicable legal requirements (8 NYCRR § 100.2(dd)(1)(iii)).

Similarly, the federal No Child Left Behind Act of 2001 (NCLB) requires that school districts have a plan to ensure that all public school teachers of core academic subjects receive high quality professional development to enable them to become highly qualified (see **8:2**) and effective classroom teachers (20 USC §§ 6319 (h); 7801(34); 34 CFR § 200.60 (a)(1)). According to the State Education Department, districts must plan and schedule compliance with this federal requirement through the PDP required by commissioner's regulations ("Updated Guidance on Implementing the NCLB's Requirements for Teachers," NY State Education Department, November 2003).

School districts may use Title I funds available under the NCLB to support ongoing training and professional development to assist both teachers and teaching assistants in meeting NCLB requirements (20 USC § 6319(h); 34 CFR § 200.60(a)(1)). Unless a lesser amount is sufficient, during fiscal years 2004 and 2005 districts must spend 5 percent of this Title I allocation on such efforts (20 USC § 6319(1); 34 CFR § 200.59(a)(1), (2)). Additional funds for professional development are available to school districts that apply for grants under Title II of the Act.

8:159. Can a school district or board of cooperative educational services (BOCES) obtain a variance from the requirement of adopting a professional development plan?

Yes, but only under one limited circumstance. The commissioner of education will grant a variance from the requirement of adopting a professional development plan to a school district or BOCES that, prior to October 7, 1999, executed an agreement negotiated pursuant to the Taylor Law, whose terms continue in effect and are inconsistent with this requirement (8 NYCRR § 100.2(dd)(7)).

8:160. Are there specific items that each school district and BOCES must include in its professional development plan?

Yes. Pursuant to the commissioner's regulations, each professional development plan must include a needs analysis, and a statement of the goals, objectives, strategies, activities and evaluation standards that the school district or BOCES will adopt and utilize as part of its professional development plan (8 NYCRR § 100.2(dd)(2)(i)). It must also include a description of:

- How the school district or BOCES will provide its teachers with professional development opportunities directly related to student learning needs, as identified by the school district or BOCES report card, or other sources, as determined by the school district or BOCES. For professional development plans covering the period of February 2, 2004 and thereafter, the plan must describe how the school district or BOCES will provide professional development opportunities that help teachers holding professional certificates maintain certification through the completion of 175 hours of professional development every five years in accordance with part 80 of the commissioner's regulations (8 NYCRR §§ 80-3.6, 100.2(dd)(2)(ii)(a)).
- Teachers' expected participation in professional development, including, at a minimum, the estimated average number of hours that each teacher will participate in professional development during the school year covered by the plan (8 NYCRR § 100.2(dd)(2)(ii)(b)).
- How the district or BOCES has aligned its professional development plan with New York standards and assessments, student needs (including but not limited to linguistic, cultural diversity, and special needs), and teacher capacities (8 NYCRR § 100.2(dd)(2)(ii)(c)).
- The articulation of professional development across grade levels (8 NYCRR § 100.2(dd)(2)(ii)(d)).
- The efforts that the school district or BOCES has made to ensure that professional development is continuous and sustained and that the methods and approaches for delivering professional development have been proven effective (8 NYCRR § 100.2(dd)(2)(ii)(e)).

- The manner in which the school district or BOCES will measure the impact of professional development on student achievement and teachers' practices (8 NYCRR § 100.2(dd)(2)(ii)(f)).
- Provision for training of employees holding a teaching certificate or license in classroom teaching service, school service, or administrative and supervisory service in school violence prevention and intervention (8 NYCRR § 100.2(dd)(2)(iii)); see **8:169**).

Beginning February 2, 2004, every professional development plan also must include provisions for a teacher mentoring program and describe how the district or BOCES will provide mentoring to teachers who fulfill the teaching experience requirement for a professional certificate by teaching in New York public schools. These teachers must participate in a mentored program in their first year of employment, unless they have completed two years of teaching prior to such service (8 NYCRR § 100.2(dd)(2)(iv); see **8:161–162**).

The professional development plan mentoring program is separate and district from the New York State Mentor Teacher-Internship Program (MIIP) authorized by section 3033 of the Education Law and part 85 of commissioner's regulations.

8:161. What is the purpose of the mentoring component of a professional development plan?

The purpose of the mentoring component is to provide support for new teachers in classroom teaching service to help ease the transition from teacher preparation to practice and thereby not only increase retention of teachers in public schools, but also improve student achievement in accordance with the new learning standards (8 NYCRR § 100.2(dd)(2)((iv)(a)).

8:162. What must be included in the mentoring program of a district's or BOCES' professional development plan?

The professional development plan must describe the following elements of its mentoring program:

- The procedure for selecting mentors, which must be made available to staff of the school district or BOCES, and upon request to members of the public.
- The role of mentors, including but not limited to, providing guidance and support to new teachers.
- The preparation of mentors, including but not limited to, the study of adult learning theory, the theory of teacher development, the elements of a mentoring relationship, peer coaching techniques, and time management methodology.

- Types of mentoring activities, including but not limited to, modeling instruction for the new teacher, observing instruction, instructional planning with the new teacher, peer coaching, team teaching, and orienting the new teacher to the school culture.
- Time allotted for mentoring, including but not limited to, scheduling common planning sessions, releasing the mentor and the teacher from a portion of their instructional and/or noninstructional duties, and providing for mentoring during superintendent conference days, before and after the school day, and during summer orientation.

8:163. Can school districts use information obtained about new teachers from their mentors to discipline them, or as part of their evaluation?

No. Unless authorized by a teacher's collective bargaining agreement, the information obtained by a mentor through interaction with a new teacher while engaged in mentoring activities cannot be used for evaluating or disciplining the teacher. The only exceptions to this rule are if withholding the information would endanger the life, health, or safety of any person, or if the mentor acquires information indicating that the teacher has been convicted of a crime or has committed an act that raises a reasonable question as to the teacher's moral character (8 NYCRR § 100.2(dd)(2)(iv)(d)).

8:164. What process must a school district or BOCES follow when formulating its professional development plan?

The plan must be developed in collaboration with a professional development team whose members are appointed by the board of education or board of cooperative educational services (BOCES) (8 NYCRR § 100.2(dd)(3)(i)(a); see **8:166**).

The school board or BOCES must convene the professional development team on or before October 1 each year, and thereafter must give the team at least 180 days in which to develop its recommended professional development plan (8 NYCRR § 100.2(dd)(3)(i)(c)). The professional development team then submits its recommended professional development plan to the school board or BOCES by a deadline specified by the school board or BOCES (8 NYCRR § 100.2(dd)(3)(i)(d)).

The school board or BOCES is free to accept or reject any part or all of the recommendations of the team. Any component of the recommended plan not approved by the school board or BOCES must be returned to the professional development team for further consideration. The team must submit any subsequent modifications to its recommended professional development plan to the school board or BOCES on or before June 1, and the school board or BOCES must act on the plan by June 30. The final determination on the content of the plan rests with the school board or BOCES (8 NYCRR § 100.2(dd)(3)(i)(d)).

The final professional development plan must be adopted by the school board or BOCES at a public meeting (8 NYCRR § 100.2 (dd)(3)(i)(e)). The school board or BOCES must review its effectiveness annually (8 NYCRR § 100.2 (dd)(3)(i)(e)).

8:165. What process must districts and BOCES follow in developing the mentoring component of their professional development plans?

The mentoring program must be developed and implemented consistent with the employer's collective bargaining obligations to the affected employees (8 NYCRR § 100.2(dd)(2)(iv)(c)).

Districts and BOCES may follow the same process used to develop and adopt their professional development plan (see **8:164**), or they may choose to collectively bargain the mentoring program into the professional development plan. Regardless of which process is followed, districts and BOCES must collectively negotiate mandatorily negotiable aspects of their mentoring programs (8 NYCRR § 100.2(dd)(2)(iv)(c)), such as pay for mentor training, time allocated for mentoring activities, and pay for activities occurring beyond the hours of a regular teacher work day.

8:166. Who are the members of the professional development team, and how are they chosen?

The school board or BOCES appoints the members of the professional development team. A majority of the team members must be teachers. The team must include the superintendent of schools, or the superintendent's designee, or in the case of a BOCES, the district superintendent or district superintendent's designee. The team also must include school administrators designated by the administrators' collective bargaining organization; teachers designated by the teachers' collective bargaining organization; at least one parent designated by the teachers' collective bargaining organization, and at least one parent designated by the established parents groups in the district, or in their absence, by the superintendent of schools, or the case of a BOCES, by the district superintendent; and one or more curriculum specialists (meaning a teacher or administrator whose primary job responsibility involves the development or evaluation of curricula) designated by the district or the teachers' collective bargaining organization, or both. In school districts or BOCES in which the teachers or administrators are not represented by a collective bargaining organization, teachers or administrators who serve on the professional development team must be designated by their peers in the manner prescribed by the school board or BOCES.

In addition, the professional team also must include at least one representative of an institution of higher education, provided that the school board or BOCES determines, after conducting a reasonable search, that a qualified candidate is available.

The team may include other nonmandated members, including representatives of professional development organizations or the community at large (8 NYCRR § 100.2(dd)(3)(i)(a)).

In schools under registration review (SURR), the members of the professional development team shall be the same as those indicated above. However, the members are not appointed as described above, but instead, are appointed by the school board upon the recommendation of the superintendent of schools (8 NYCRR § 100.2(dd)(3)(i)(b)).

The members of the professional development team in the New York City school system are appointed pursuant to separate, specific provisions of the regulations of the commissioner of education (see 8 NYCRR § 100.2(dd)(3)(i), (ii)).

8:167. May a school district or BOCES adopt a multi-year professional development plan?

Yes. The school board or BOCES may adopt an annual plan or a multi-year plan. However, in either case, the school board or BOCES must annually evaluate the effectiveness of the plan. Moreover, in the case of a multi-year plan, the professional development team must review the plan annually and submit recommended revisions to the school board or BOCES for its approval or rejection (8 NYCRR § 100.2(dd)(3)(i)(e)).

Each year, the superintendent of schools, or in the case of a BOCES, the district superintendent, must certify to the commissioner of education, in the form and within the timetable prescribed by the commissioner, that the district or BOCES has complied with the regulations requiring it to have a professional development plan in place for the succeeding school year, and that it has complied with the professional development plan applicable to the current school year (8 NYCRR § 100.2(dd)(4)(i)(a)).

The commissioner may require the school district or BOCES to submit a copy of its professional development plan for review. The commissioner may recommend changes to the plan to meet the learning needs of students (8 NYCRR § 100.2(dd)(4)(i)(b)).

8:168. Can teachers be required to participate in professional development outside of regular working hours?

In general, no. The commissioner's regulations provide that teachers' participation in professional development outside the regular school day or regularly scheduled working days of the school year shall be voluntary, unless the teachers' collective bargaining agreement makes such participation an agreed upon term or condition of employment (8 NYCRR § 100.2(dd)(6)).

8:169. Are school districts and BOCES required to provide staff with training on school violence prevention and intervention?

Yes. Employees holding a teaching certificate or license in classroom teaching service, school service, or administrative and supervisory service must complete at least a two-hour training course in school violence prevention and intervention. Upon request, the school district or BOCES must provide an employee who has successfully completed such a course with a certificate of completion. Such a course must include, but is not limited to, study in:

- the warning signs in a developmental and social context relating to violence and other troubling behaviors in children;
- the statutes, regulations, and policies relating to safe nonviolent school climate;
- effective classroom management techniques and other academic supports;
- integration of social and problem-solving skill development for students within the regular curriculum;
- intervention techniques designed to address a school violence situation; and
- effective school/community referral processes for students exhibiting violent behavior (8 NYCRR § 100.2(dd)(2)(iii)).

8:170. Are the professional development requirements suspended while a teacher is on active military duty?

Yes. In fact, no person in military service, who was licensed, registered, or certified to engage in a profession or occupation prior to entering into military service is required to complete the continuing education requirements for such profession or occupation during such period of military service (Mil. Law § 308-a; see also **8:32**).

8:171. Does a school district or BOCES have any obligation to keep records on the professional development of its teachers?

Yes. Each school district and BOCES must maintain a record of professional development successfully completed by certificate holders who are subject to the professional development requirements set forth in section 80-3.6 of the commissioner's regulations, and who take professional development courses offered by the school district or BOCES or by other entities on behalf of the school district or BOCES. This record must include the name of the professional certificate holder, his or her teacher certification identifying number, the title of the program, the number of hours completed, and the date and location of the program. The applicable school district or BOCES must maintain these records for a period of seven years from the date of completion of the professional development by the professional certificate holder, and must make them available for review by the State Education Department (SED) (8 NYCRR § 100.2(dd)(5)).

In addition, each school district and BOCES must maintain documentation concerning the mentoring program that it develops as part of its professional development plan (see **8:160–162**), including, but not limited to: the name of each teacher receiving mentoring and the teacher's certificate I.D. number, the type of mentoring activity, the number of clock hours successfully completed in that activity, and the mentor's name and teacher's certificate I.D. number. This documentation must be maintained and readily available for review by SED for a period of at least seven years from the date the mentoring activity was completed (8 NYCRR § 100.2(dd)(5)(ii)).

8:172. Are school districts required to make progress reports on the professional development activities completed by the certificate holders in their employment?

Yes. Each school district and BOCES must report to SED, in a form and within the timetable prescribed by SED, information concerning the completion of professional development by "regularly employed" certificate holders who are subject to the professional development requirements set forth in section 80-3.6 of the commissioner regulations. Prior to reporting this information, the school district or BOCES must consult with the certificate holder to verify the accuracy of the information.

A "regularly employed" certificate holder is one who is employed by a school district or BOCES in a position requiring teaching certification for at least 90 days during the July 1 through June 30 professional development year prescribed in section 80-3.6 of the commissioner's regulations. In computing the number of days employed, a day of employment includes a day worked in whole or in part or a day not actually worked but a day paid (8 NYCRR § 100.2(dd)(4)(b)(ii)).

Performance Evaluation

8:173. Are school districts and BOCES required to evaluate the performance of the teachers they employ?

Yes. The commissioner's regulations require that each school board and board of cooperative educational services (BOCES) provide for annual performance reviews of teachers who provide instructional services or "pupil personnel services." These same regulations specifically exempt from the requirement of annual performance reviews evening school teachers of adults enrolled in nonacademic, vocational subjects, as well as "supplementary school personnel" (8 NYCRR § 100.2(o)(2)(ii); see also 8 NYCRR §§ 80.1(w); 80.33 for definitions of teachers of "pupil personnel services" and "supplementary services," respectively). While school superintendents generally perform annual evaluations, neither the Education Law nor commissioner's regulations reserve this authority exclusively to school superintendents (*Appeal of Fusco*, 39 Educ. Dep't Rep. 836 (2000)). A purported performance evaluation may not include a reprimand (*Fusco*).

8:174. Are school districts and BOCES required to formally develop and adopt plans for reviewing teacher performance?

Yes. By September 1 of each year, each school board and BOCES must adopt an annual or multi-year plan for evaluating the performance of its teachers who provide instructional services or pupil personnel services (8 NYCRR § 100.2(o)(2)(iii)(a)(1)).

This professional performance review plan must be developed by the superintendent of schools, or in the case of a BOCES, by the district superintendent, in collaboration with teachers, pupil personnel professionals, administrators, and parents selected by such superintendent. Prior to its adoption, each school board and BOCES must give organizations representing parents and recognized representatives of the teachers' bargaining unit an opportunity to comment on the plan. Upon its completion, the plan must be formally adopted by the school board or BOCES and filed in the district office or BOCES office. The plan must then be made available for review by any individual by September 10 each year (8 NYCRR § 100.2(o)(2)(iii)(a)(2)).

The plan must describe how the school district or BOCES will deal with teachers whose performance is evaluated as unsatisfactory. It must provide for the development of teacher improvement plans for the benefit of, and in consultation with, each teacher who receives an unsatisfactory evaluation (8 NYCRR § 100.2(o)(2)(iii)(b)(4)). Moreover, each school district and BOCES must make an annual report to the State Education Department (SED) describing its efforts to address unsatisfactory teaching performance through teacher improvement plans and other means (8 NYCRR § 100.2(o)(2)(iv)).

The professional performance review plan also must describe how the district or BOCES trains staff who perform professional performance evaluations in the use of good evaluation practices. In the alternative, the plan must state that the school district or BOCES permits the appropriate staff to participate in evaluator training offered by SED (8 NYCRR § 100.2(o)(2)(iii)(b)(5)).

Each school district and BOCES must determine the formal procedures that it uses to review teacher performance in accordance with the Taylor Law (8 NYCRR § 100.2(o)(2)(vi)).

8:175. What specific criteria for evaluating teachers must school districts and BOCES include in their professional performance review plans?

The commissioner's regulations require that the professional performance review plans adopted by school districts and boards of cooperative educational services (BOCES) must include at least the following criteria for evaluating the performance of teachers who provide instructional services:

- *Content Knowledge* — the teacher must demonstrate a thorough knowledge of the subject matter and curriculum.
- *Preparation* — the teacher must demonstrate appropriate preparation employing the necessary pedagogical practices to support instruction.
- *Instructional Delivery* — the teacher must demonstrate that the delivery of instruction results in active student involvement, appropriate teacher/student interaction and meaningful lesson plans resulting in student learning.
- *Classroom Management*— the teacher must demonstrate classroom management skills supportive of diverse student learning needs that create an environment conducive to learning.
- *Student Development* — the teacher must demonstrate knowledge of student development, an understanding and appreciation of diversity, and the regular application of developmentally appropriate instructional strategies for the benefit of all students.
- *Student Assessment* — the teacher must demonstrate that he or she implements assessment techniques based on appropriate learning standards designed to measure students' progress in learning.
- *Collaboration* — the teacher must demonstrate that he or she develops effective collaborative relationships with students, parents, or caregivers, as needed, and appropriate support personnel to meet the learning needs of students.
- *Reflective and Responsive Practice* — the teacher must demonstrate that practice is reviewed, effectively assessed, and that appropriate adjustments are made on a continuing basis (8 NYCRR § 100.2(o)(2)(iii)(b)(1)).

The commissioner will grant a variance from using these specific criteria if he finds that the school district or BOCES has a local model for the evaluation of teachers that has produced successful results (8 NYCRR § 100.22(o)(2)(vii)(b)).

With respect to teachers who provide pupil personnel services, school districts and BOCES are free to determine what criteria to include in their professional performance review plans for evaluating these teachers (8 NYCRR § 100.2(o)(2)(iii)(b)(2)).

8:176. Must the professional performance review plan include information about the particular methods of assessment that the school district or BOCES will utilize to evaluate teachers' performance?

Yes. The professional performance review plan must describe the methods that the school district or board of cooperative educational services (BOCES) will utilize to assess teachers' performance. Such methods include, for example, classroom observation, peer review, self review, videotape assessment, and portfolio review.

School districts may not prohibit either a current or prospective candidate for permanent certification from videotaping a classroom presentation for the purpose of meeting the performance assessment of teaching skills requirement for permanent certification (8 NYCRR § 80-1.5(2)).

For teachers who possess a transitional or initial certificate, the plan must require evaluation of the teacher based on the portfolio review method, which may include, but is not limited to, a sample lesson plan, a sample of student work, a video of teaching performance, and/or the teacher's own assessment of his or her classroom performance (8 NYCRR § 100.2(o) (2)(iii)(b)(3)).

8:177. May a school district or BOCES obtain a variance from the commissioner's regulations on evaluating teachers?

Yes, under limited circumstances. The commissioner will grant a variance from compliance to a school district or BOCES, which, prior to September 3, 1999, entered into a collective bargaining agreement pursuant to the Taylor Law whose terms continue in effect and are inconsistent with the commissioner's regulations (8 NYCRR § 100.22 (o)(2)(vii)(a)).

Disciplining Tenured Teachers

Editor's Note: For more information on this subject including discussion of decisions rendered by 3020-a hearing officers and three-member panels since 1994 see Disciplining Tenured Teachers and Administrators, *published by the New York State School Boards Association (2004) and distributed by LexisNexis.*

8:178. May a school district fire a teacher?

A probationary teacher may be fired at any time, on the recommendation of the superintendent of schools, by a majority vote of the school board (§§ 2509(1)(a), 2573(1)(a), 3012(1)(a)), and subject to certain restrictions (see **8:125–131**).

A tenured teacher may not be fired unless the school district follows certain rules under section 3020-a of the Education Law, or at the written election of the teacher, rules specified in the collective bargaining agreement between the teachers union and the district (§§ 3020, 3020-a; see also 8 NYCRR Part 82; **8:179–201**).

8:179. Under what circumstances may a tenured teacher be fired or disciplined?

Tenured teachers have the right to retain their teaching positions as long as they exhibit good behavior and competent and efficient service (§§ 2509(2), 2573(5), 3012(2)). A tenured teacher may only be disciplined or discharged for "just cause" (§ 3020(1)).

Before a teacher is disciplined, that teacher is entitled to a hearing, often called a section 3020-a hearing, on the charges brought by the district. All school districts, including New York City, follow the disciplinary procedures established in section 3020-a, or alternative procedures contained within a negotiated collective bargaining agreement (§ 3020(1); see **8:182, 8:198**).

The New York State Court of Appeals has ruled that section 3020-a is constitutional (*Board of Educ. v. Gootnick*, 49 N.Y.2d 683 (1980)).

8:180. What is the procedure for removing or otherwise disciplining tenured teachers?

The procedure for removing or otherwise disciplining tenured teachers is mandated by section 3020-a of the Education Law. Any person, but usually the superintendent, files written charges, and the school board (except in New York City (see **8:183**)) votes to prefer charges against the teacher (*Matter of Van Dame*, 15 Educ. Dep't Rep. 63 (1975); *Matter of Arcuri*, 20 Educ. Dep't Rep. 178 (1980)). The teacher is notified of the charges and is entitled to request a hearing on the charges (§ 3020-a(2)(a), (c); 8 NYCRR § 82-1.3(b)). A pre-hearing conference must be held (§ 3020-a(3)(c)(ii); 8 NYCRR § 82-1.6(e)).

The 3020-a hearing is usually conducted before a single hearing officer who determines the guilt or innocence of the teacher and orders any penalty to be imposed. However, when the charges against the teacher concern pedagogical incompetence or issues involving pedagogical judgment, the teacher may choose either a single hearing officer or a three-member panel, often called a 3020-a panel (§ 3020-a(2)(c); 8 NYCRR §§ 82-1.3(d), 82-1.4).

A teacher's resignation after the conclusion of a hearing but prior to the hearing officer's decision does not preclude a school district from continuing the disciplinary proceedings and placing a record of the final determination in the teacher's personnel file (*Folta v. Sobol*, 210 A.D.2d 857 (3d Dep't 1994)).

8:181. Is the 3020-a hearing held in public or private?

Unless the employee notifies the hearing officer at least 24 hours before the first day of the hearing that he or she demands a public hearing, the hearing will be in private. However, the pre-hearing conference must be in private (8 NYCRR § 82-1.9).

8:182. May a tenured teacher waive his or her rights, including the right to a hearing, under section 3020-a?

Yes. A teacher may waive his or her right to a hearing under the law as part of a stipulation of settlement in a 3020-a case, provided the waiver is made knowingly and freely (*Abramovich v. Board of Educ.*, 46 N.Y.2d 450 (1979), *reconsideration denied*, 46 N.Y.2d 1076 (1979), *cert. denied*, 444 U.S. 845 (1979)).

A teacher may also choose, under the law, to proceed under alternative disciplinary procedures contained within a negotiated collective bargaining agreement. Such a negotiated alternative must also result in a disposition of the charges within the same time frames established under section 3020-a (§ 3020(1); except under certain collective bargaining agreements covering teachers in the City of New York, which are not bound by these time frames (§ 3020(4)).

A teacher who fails to request a hearing within 10 days of receiving the charges is deemed to have waived his or her right to a hearing, and the board must proceed, within 15 days by a majority vote of the board to determine the case and fix the penalty, if any, to be imposed (§ 3020-a(2)(d), *Matter of Gagnon v. Wappingers CSD*, 268 A.D.2d 472 (2d Dep't 2000); 8 NYCRR § 82-1.5(e)). A district's decision to proceed without a hearing is not appealable to the commissioner of education. A teacher challenging any such decision must initiate proceedings in State Supreme Court (*Appeal of Frajer*, 41 Educ. Dep't Rep. 403 (2002)).

In addition, a tenured teacher who initially requests a 3020-a hearing but subsequently fails to appear at the scheduled hearing waives the right to a hearing on the merits of his or her case. The school board then is free to vote on the charges and determine the penalty or punishment as if the teacher had never requested a hearing (*Matter of Syracuse City Sch. Dist.*, 21 Educ. Dep't Rep. 461 (1982)).

In general, districts must continue to pay the salary of teachers suspended while section 3020-a charges are pending (see **8:194–195**).

8:183. How are section 3020-a charges filed?

Detailed charges specifying the grounds for discipline must be filed in writing with the school district clerk or the secretary of the district or employing board (§ 3020-a(1)). The superintendent of schools usually files the charges, although any individual may file them (see **8:180**). Charges must be brought during the school year during which the employee is normally required to serve (§ 3020-a(1)).

Upon receiving the charges, the school board must vote to determine whether there is probable cause to bring the charges. The vote must be conducted in executive session within five days of submission of the charges and must be carried by a majority of the membership of the board (§ 3020-a(2)(a)).

However, in New York City, community school superintendents exercise all the duties of the employing board with respect to 3020-a charges, including making the determination of whether probable cause exists to bring charges against a tenured teacher in the first place (*Matter of Garzilli v. Mills and Bd. of Educ. of the City of New York*, 250 A.D.2d 131 (3d Dep't 1998)).

The teacher must be notified by certified or registered mail, return receipt requested, or personal service, and a copy of the charges must be forwarded to the commissioner of education by first-class mail. Such notice must specify in detail the charges filed against him or her, the maximum penalty that would be imposed by the school board if a hearing is not requested or that will be sought by the board if the teacher is found guilty of the charges after a hearing, and the teacher's rights under the law (§ 3020-a(2)(a)). The teacher has 10 days to request a hearing and, if the charge concerns pedagogical incompetence or issues of pedagogical judgment, to indicate whether a hearing before a single hearing officer or three-member panel is preferred (§ 3020-a(2)(c); 8 NYCRR §§ 82-1.3(b), 82-1.4).

If the teacher requests a hearing, the district must forward the charges to the commissioner within three working days of receipt of the request (§ 3020-a(2)(d); see also 8 NYCRR § 82-1.5).

8:184. Is there a time limitation for the filing of 3020-a charges?

Yes. Charges may not be brought more than three years after the occurrence of the alleged misconduct, unless it constitutes a crime when committed (3020-a(1), 2590-j(7)(c)). The United States Court of Appeals, Second Circuit, with jurisdiction over New York upheld the termination of a teacher found guilty of engaging in illegal sexual misconduct with two of his former students over 20 years earlier (*DeMichele v. Greenburgh CSD 7 and Arnold B. Green*, 167 F.3d 784 (2d Cir. N.Y. 1999), see also *Tasch v. Board of Educ. of City of New York*, 3 A.D.3d 502 (2d Dep't 2004); *Board of Educ., Saquoit Valley CSD v. Johnson*, Ben Falcigno, Hearing Officer (2000)).

However, in large city school districts, charges may not be brought more than three years after the occurrence of the alleged misconduct, unless the charge is of misconduct that resulted in conviction of a crime (§ 2573(8)). (*Matter of [Redacted]*), Richard Adelman, Hearing Officer, (1999); *Matter of D.*, James Walsh, Hearing Officer (1995)).

8:185. Is a school district required to disclose to the teacher in a 3020-a proceeding the nature of its case and the evidence against the teacher?

Yes. The teacher must be given the opportunity to defend himself or herself and the district must fully and fairly disclose the nature of its case and the evidence it will use against the teacher (§ 3020-a(3)(c)(i)).

Some hearing officers have ruled that the hearing officer may grant limited disclosure rights to school districts in 3020-a proceedings, sometimes referred to as "reciprocal" or "reverse" discovery (*Board of Educ., Starpoint CSD v. Townsend*, Eric W. Lawson, Hearing Officer, (2000); *Board of Educ., Abbott UFSD v. Walthall*, Howard C. Edelman, Hearing Officer (1997); *Board of Educ. of the City of New York v. Midy*, Arthur A. Riegel, Hearing Officer (1996); see § 3020-a(3)(c)(iii)).

However, other hearing officers have held that only the teacher has the right to disclosure (e.g., *Marcus Whitman CSD v. Kevin L.F.*, Douglas J. Bantle, Hearing Officer (1996)).

8:186. How is a section 3020-a hearing conducted?

The hearing officer or panel presides over the hearing. The rules of procedure and evidence used in a 3020-a hearing are not as strict as those followed in a court. The district and the teacher have the right to call witnesses to testify, to cross-examine witnesses, and to have an attorney present at the hearing. The teacher must be given an opportunity to testify but may not be required to do so (§ 3020-a(3)(c)(i); 8 NYCRR § 82-1.10). In addition, a teacher may not be prevented from discussing the case with his or her attorney during adjournments of a 3020-a hearing even during cross-examination of the teacher (*Matter of Elmore v. Plainview-Old Bethpage CSD*, 273 A.D.2d 307 (2d Dep't 2000); see connected cases at 296 A.D.2d 704 (3d Dep't 2002); and 299 A.D.2d 545 (2d Dep't 2002), *appeal denied*, 99 N.Y.2d 509 (2003).

Furthermore, a teacher cannot be required to speak to persons investigating allegations of misconduct for which he or she could be subjected to discipline under 3020-a, because any statements he or she made during the course of such an investigation would be admissible against the teacher at the 3020-a hearing. Therefore, requiring the teacher to cooperate with investigators would violate that teacher's right against self-incrimination under 3020-a (*Board of Educ. of the City of New York v. Mills*, 250 A.D.2d 122 (3d Dep't 1998), *appeal denied*, 93 N.Y.2d 803 (1999)).

In presenting its evidence, a school district may not access court records of a teacher who has been acquitted of misdemeanor charges even if the disciplinary hearing charges the teacher with the same conduct (*In re Joseph M.*, 82 N.Y.2d 128 (1993)). Taped telephone conversations between a student and a teacher charged with maintaining an inappropriately close relationship with the student have been ruled admissible by the commissioner if the tape is authentic and unaltered (*Appeal of Malone CSD*, 33 Educ. Dep't Rep. 108 (1993)).

A transcript of the hearing must be made and a copy provided free of charge to the teacher and the board, upon request (§ 3020-a(3)(c)(i)).

Within 30 days of the last day of the hearing, or within 10 days of an expedited hearing of a teacher charged with a revoked certification, the hearing officer must issue a written decision. The decision must include whether the teacher is guilty or innocent of each charge, the hearing officer's finding of fact on each charge, and what penalty or other action, if any, should be taken by the board (§ 3020-a (4)(a); 8 NYCRR § 82-1.10(g)). (See also **8:190**.)

8:187. How is the hearing officer selected?

Once the hearing is requested and the charges have been forwarded to the commissioner of education, the commissioner contacts the American Arbitration Association (AAA) to obtain a list of eligible labor arbitrators to conduct the hearing. The school board and the employee jointly must agree on a hearing officer from the list provided by AAA within 10 days. In the event they cannot agree, the commissioner will request AAA to select the hearing officer (§ 3020-a(3)(b)(iii)).

The hearing officer may not be a resident of the school district, except in New York City, and may not currently be serving as a mediator or fact finder in the school district. Additionally, the hearing officer may not be an agent or employee of the school board or of the teachers' union, or have served as an agent or employee in the last two years (§ 3020-a(3)(b); see also 8 NYCRR § 82-1.6).

Hearing officers are paid the customary AAA fee (§ 3020-a(3)(b)(i)). However, where a hearing is conducted under a contractual alternative procedure that alters the way the hearing officer is selected but otherwise provides the hearing be conducted in accordance with the provisions of section 3020-a, the fees paid the hearing officer may not exceed $200 per day (Laws of 1996, Ch. 474 § 134).

8:188. May 3020-a charges be heard by a three-member panel instead of a single hearing officer?

Teachers charged with pedagogical incompetence or issues involving pedagogical judgment can choose to have 3020-a hearings before a three-member panel rather than a single hearing officer (§ 3020-a(2)(c)).

The panel chairperson is selected in the same manner as a single hearing officer, and the school board and teacher each chooses one panel member from a list of hearing panelists maintained by the commissioner of education (§ 3020-a(3)(b)(iv); see also 8 NYCRR §§ 82-1.7, 1.8). The commissioner establishes the hearing panel list from names submitted by statewide organizations, including the New York State School Boards Association.

A panel hearing may not proceed without all three members present (8 NYCRR § 82-1.10(d)).

In a hearing before a three-member panel, the panelists selected by the board and the teacher each receives $100 per day plus expenses for service on the panel. Parties may not supplement a panelist's $100 per diem compensation with extra money because these additional payments would give the appearance of bias (*Syquia v. Board of Educ. of Harpursville CSD*, 80 N.Y.2d 531 (1992)). Where a panel is appointed under a contractual alternative procedure that alters the way panel members are selected, the fee paid a panel chairperson may not exceed $200 per day. The other panelists are to be paid the same as additional panel members in all other school districts (Laws of 1996, Ch. 474 § 134).

For additional information on reimbursable hearing expenses, see the commissioner's regulations at 8 NYCRR section 82-1.11.

8:189. Must the 3020-a hearing officer or panel conduct a pre-hearing conference?

Yes. The pre-hearing conference must take place within 10 to 15 days of the hearing officer's agreement to serve (§ 3020-a(3)(c)(ii); 8 NYCRR § 82-1.6(e)). The hearing officer at the pre-hearing conference issues subpoenas; rules on all motions by the district and the teacher, including motions to dismiss the charges; and rules on requests for bills of particulars or other requests for materials and documents by the parties (§ 3020-a(3)(c)(iii)).

Pre-hearing motions must be made on written notice to the hearing officer and adverse party at least five days before the pre-hearing conference, except for good cause, as determined by the hearing officer (§ 3020-a(c)(iv)).

The hearing officer at that time also determines the number of days required for the final hearing and schedules the final hearing dates. The dates of the final hearing must be scheduled on consecutive days. The law requires the final hearing to be completed no later than 60 days after the pre-hearing conference has concluded, unless the hearing officer determines that extraordinary circumstances warrant a limited extension (§ 3020-a(3)(c)(vi); 8 NYCRR § 82-1.10(f)).

If the school district presents evidence at the pre-hearing conference that the teacher's certification has been revoked, the hearing officer must conduct an expedited hearing within seven days (§ 3020-a(3)(c)(v)).

8:190. What happens if a teacher is acquitted of the 3020-a charges?

If acquitted, the teacher must be restored to his or her teaching position, with full pay for any period of suspension without pay, and the charges must be removed from the teacher's personnel record (§ 3020-a(4)(b)). If the hearing officer finds that any or all charges filed against the teacher were frivolous, he or she must order the school board to reimburse the State Education Department for all or a portion of the costs of the hearing, and to reimburse the teacher for all or a portion of the reasonable costs incurred in defending the charges (§ 3020-a(4)(c) see, e.g., *Board of Educ. of Florida UFSD v. De Pace*, 301 A.D.2d 521 (2d Dep't 2003), *appeal denied*, 99 N.Y.2d 511 (2003)).

8:191. How is the penalty determined when a teacher is found guilty of misconduct?

The hearing officer, or a three-member panel in cases of pedagogical incompetence, decides the appropriate penalty to be imposed if a teacher is found guilty of charges following a 3020-a hearing. At the request of the teacher, the hearing officer must consider the extent to which the school board has made efforts to correct the teacher's behavior, including remediation, peer intervention, or an employee assistance program (§ 3020-a(4)(a); see also *In re Carroll (Pirkle)*, 296 A.D.2d 755 (3d Dep't 2002), *appeal denied*, 98 N.Y.2d 764 (2002)).

The penalties authorized by the Education Law include a written reprimand, a fine, a suspension without pay for a specified period, or dismissal. In addition, the hearing officer can order remedial action, such as continuing education, counseling or medical treatment, or leaves of absence with or without pay (§ 3020-a(4)(a)). The hearing officer or panel may not impose more than one penalty at the same time (*Matter of Arbitration between Bernstein and Norwich City Sch. Dist.* (Sup. Ct., Chenango County,

J. Dowd, n.o.r.) (error to impose fine and written reprimand), *aff'd on other grounds,* 282 A.D.2d 70 (3d Dep't 2001), *appeal denied,* 96 N.Y.2d 937 (2001)), or an unauthorized penalty (*Adrian v. Board of Educ.,* 60 A.D.2d 840 (2d Dep't 1978) (error to impose suspension without pay and fine)), although the law permits combinations of remedial actions to be imposed (§ 3020-a(4)(a)). If a teacher who is suspended from employment is incarcerated, the period of suspension does not begin to run until the date of the teacher's release from incarceration (*Appeal of Manning,* 38 Educ. Dep't Rep. 458 (1999)).

The school board must implement the penalty imposed by the 3020-a hearing officer within 15 days of receipt of the decision (§ 3020-a(4)(b)). If the board disagrees with the penalty imposed by the hearing officer, its sole recourse is to appeal the decision (§ 3020-a(5); see also **8:193**).

Permitting a silent resignation or secret suspension generally is ill advised, and under some circumstances, may even subject school officials to criminal liability. Effective July 1, 2001, school districts may not enter into any agreement to withhold from law enforcement authorities the fact that an allegation of child abuse in an educational setting (see **12:82**) has been made against a school volunteer or employee (including teachers) in exchange for that individual's resignation or voluntary suspension (§ 1133(1)). Any such agreement is a class E felony and is punishable by a civil penalty of up to $20,000 (§ 1133(2)).

8:192. May a teacher be disciplined for off-campus, off-duty conduct?

It depends. Generally, a teacher may be disciplined for off-campus, off-duty conduct only if it can be established that there is a connection, or nexus, between the off-campus conduct and the teacher's performance of his or her duties. According to the New York Court of Appeals, there is such a nexus "if the off-campus conduct in question directly affects the performance of the professional responsibilities of the teacher, or if, without contribution on the part of school officials, the conduct has become the subject of such public notoriety that it significantly and reasonably impairs his or her ability to discharge the responsibilities of the position" (*Matter of Jerry,* 35 N.Y.2d 534 (1974)).

Noting the important role that a teacher serves as a role model, one state appellate court upheld the two-year suspension without pay of a teacher convicted of criminally negligent homicide for a "hit and run" accident that caused the death of a teenager. According to the court, the nature of the crime coupled with the widespread publicity of the case were sufficient grounds for discipline under 3020-a (*Ellis v. Ambach,* 124 A.D.2d 854 (1986)).

In *Melzer v. Board of Educ. of the City Sch. Dist. of the City of New York,* (336 F.3d 185 (2d Cir. 2003), *cert. denied,* 124 S.Ct. 1424 (2004)), the U.S. Court of Appeals for the Second Circuit with jurisdiction over New York upheld the dismissal of a tenured teacher for his active participation in a group that advocates for the release of all convicted pedophiles as well as the abolition of child pornography laws and all laws preventing consensual sexual relations between men and boys (see **8:86**).

8:193. Can either party appeal the 3020-a hearing officer's or panel's decision?

Yes. Both the teacher and the school district have a right to appeal the 3020-a hearing officer's or panel's decision to the courts under Article 75 of the Civil Practice Law and Rules (§ 3020-a(5)). Under this type of court review, the decision of the hearing officer can only be reversed on very narrow grounds, namely, if it were proven that there was corruption, fraud or misconduct in obtaining the decision, that the hearing officer exceeded his or her statutory power, or that the hearing officer (or the neutral hearing officer on a three-member panel) had not been impartial. Since it is unusual for a court to reverse a decision under these standards, the decision of the hearing officer is likely to be final in most cases (CPLR § 7511(b), see, e.g., *Austin v. Board of Educ. of City S.D. of New York*, 280 A.D. 2d 365 (1st Dep't 2001); *Matter of Bd. of Educ. of the Great Neck UFSD v. Brandman*, Sup. Ct, Nassau County, Franco, J. (2000) (not reported), *aff'd*, 286 A.D.2d 735 (2d Dep't 2001)).

However, at least two state appellate courts have held that where the parties are forced to engage in compulsory arbitration, as in a 3020-a proceeding, judicial review under Article 75 "requires that the award be accorded with due process and supported by adequate evidence in the record" which are principles typically applied in an Article 78 review (*Bernstein v. Norwich City Sch. Dist. Bd. of Educ.*, 282 A.D.2d 70 (3d Dep't 2001), *leave to app. dismissed*, 96 N.Y. 2d 937 (2001); *Matter of Carrol (Pirkle)*, 296 A.D.2d 755 (3d Dep't 2002); *Hegarty v. Board of Educ. of the City of New York*, 5 A.D.3d 771 (2d Dep't 2004); *Matter of Board of Educ. of Great Neck UFSD (Brandman)*, 286 A.D.2d 735 (2d Dep't 2001); *Matter of Elmore v. Plainview-Old Bethpage CSD*, 273 A.D.2d 307 (2d Dep't 2000)); see connected cases at 296 A.D.2d 704 (3d Dep't 2002); and 299 A.D.2d 545 (2d Dep't 2002), *appeal denied*, 99 N.Y.2d 509 (2003); *Matter of Fischer (Smithtown CSD)*, 262 A.D.2d 560 (1999)).

In contrast, another state appellate court has ruled that the broader Article 78 standard of review cannot be applied in an appeal from a 3020-a decision, because the law explicitly provides for Article 75 review (*Austin v. Board of Educ. of the City Sch. Dist. of the City of New York*, 280 A.D.2d 365 (1st Dep't 2001)). A similar view was adopted by at least one federal district court, which found it "plainly reasonable to limit a teacher's right to appeal an adverse [3020-a] hearing decision to the same scope of review generally applicable in actions seeking to challenge arbitration awards" (*Roemer v. Board of Educ. of the City Sch. Dist. of the City of New York*, 290 F.Supp.2d 329 (E.D.N.Y. 2003)).

8:194. May a teacher be suspended while a 3020-a charge is pending?

Yes. A school superintendent may suspend a tenured teacher with pay prior to the actual filing of charges, until the board meets to consider the charges (*Appeal of Williams*, 39 Educ. Dep't Rep. 643 (1998)). After the board votes to charge the teacher with misconduct under 3020-a, it may suspend the teacher until the case is resolved (§ 3020-a(2)(b); *Matter of Almeter*, 30 Educ. Dep't Rep. 439 (1991)). Generally, the teacher must be given full pay and benefits during suspension (§ 3020-a(2)(b); *Jerry v. Board of Educ.*, 35 N.Y.2d 534 (1974)). According to one court, such payments are not an unconstitutional gift of public funds (*Brady v. A Certain Teacher*, 166 Misc.2d 566 (1995)).

A district can reduce a teacher's pay during the pre-hearing suspension period by the amount of income the employee has earned in another job (*Jerry*; see also *Matter of Caravello v. Board of Educ. of Norwich CSD*, 48 A.D.2d 967 (3d Dep't 1975); *Matter of Wolfson v. Board of Educ. of Wappinger CSD*, 47 A.D.2d 748 (2d Dep't 1975)). However, a tenured teacher is not required to mitigate or reduce damages by seeking other employment (*Hawley v. South Orangetown CSD*, 67 N.Y.2d 796 (1986)).

8:195. Can a teacher be suspended without pay while 3020-a charges are pending?

Yes, under certain circumstances. For example, a district need not pay a suspended teacher where a collective bargaining agreement provides for suspension without pay (*Elmore v. Plainview-Old Bethpage CSD*, 299 A.D.2d 545 (2d Dep't 2002), *appeal denied*, 99 N.Y.2d 509 (2003); *Romano v. Canuteson*, 11 F.3d 1140 (2d Cir. 1993); *Board of Educ. v. Nyquist*, 48 N.Y.2d 97 (1979)); or where the teacher faces charges for lack of certification for the course he or she has been hired to teach (*Meliti v. Nyquist*, 41 N.Y.2d 183 (1976); *Matter of Cutler v. Board of Educ. of Poughkeepsie City Sch. Dist.*, 104 A.D.2d 988 (2d Dep't 1984), *aff'd*, 65 N.Y.2d 797 (1985); see also *Smith v. Andrews*, 122 A.D.2d 310 (3d Dep't 1986); **8:157**). A district is not required to pay a suspended teacher who has pleaded guilty to or been found guilty of a felony drug crime or a felony crime involving the physical or sexual abuse of a minor or student (§ 3020-a(2)(b)).

However, a district cannot withhold a teacher's pay during the pendency of 3020-a charges when delays are caused by the teacher's good faith request for adjournments (*Derle v. North Bellmore UFSD*, 77 N.Y.2d 483 (1991); see also *McCreery v. Babylon UFSD*, 827 F.Supp. 136 (E.D.N.Y. 1993)). Delays based on documented medical excuses, scheduling conflicts rendering the teacher's attorney unavailable or unavailability of essential witnesses are examples of good faith grounds for an adjournment (*Macroni v. Board of Educ. of the Seaford UFSD*, 215 A.D.2d 659 (2d Dep't 1995), *motion denied*, 87 N.Y.2d 892 (1995), *appeal denied*, 90 N.Y.2d 811 (1997)).

Similarly, a district cannot withhold a teacher's pay during the pendency of a 3020-a proceeding to terminate a teacher for lack of certification when the district itself reassigns a teacher a course he or she is not certified to teach (*Winter v. Board of Educ. for Rhinebeck CSD*, 79 N.Y.2d 1 (1992), *reconsideration denied*, 79 N.Y.2d 978 (1992); **8:157**).

8:196. May a teacher who has been suspended be given other, nonteaching assignments pending the outcome of a 3020-a proceeding?

Yes. A teacher suspended pending the outcome of a section 3020-a case may be given a nonteaching assignment provided the duties assigned "bear reasonable relationship to the suspended teacher's competence and training, and are consistent with the dignity of the profession." (*Matter of Adlerstein v. Board of Educ.*, 64 N.Y.2d 90 (1984)); *Hawley v. South Orangetown CSD*, 67 N.Y.2d 796 (1986)).

A teacher who refuses to accept reassignment forfeits the right to payment of salary during the remainder of the suspension (*Adlerstein; Brady v. Board of Educ. of Patchogue-Medford UFSD*, 166 Misc.2d 566 (1995)). Moreover, the board of education may prefer an additional charge against the teacher for insubordination. The same is true if a teacher accepts reassignment, but fails to adequately perform the reassigned duties (*Brady*).

8:197. Is a teacher who was suspended with pay pending the outcome of a 3020-a disciplinary proceeding and is subsequently discharged entitled to unemployment insurance benefits?

To be eligible for unemployment insurance benefits, a discharged teacher must establish that he or she was paid an amount of remuneration during a set base period of time, pursuant to a formula set forth in the Labor Law (Lab. Law § 527(1)(d)).

8:198. What legal alternatives to section 3020-a may a district use to discipline teachers?

Districts and their bargaining units may implement alternatives to the 3020-a process. However, except for certain collective bargaining agreements covering teachers in the City of New York, any alternatives negotiated after

September 1, 1994 must allow an employee to choose either those alternatives or the 3020-a process, as long as the charges are disposed of within the time constraints of 3020-a. Negotiated alternatives to 3020-a may remain in effect until they are changed by collective bargaining (§§ 3020(1); 3020(4)).

In addition, according to the commissioner of education, there was nothing improper about a district offering a teacher a cash incentive to retire in lieu of prosecuting 3020-a charges against the teacher for alleged incompetence. Moreover, according to the commissioner, payment of the incentive did not constitute an improper gift of public funds in violation of Art. VIII., sec. 1 of the New York State Constitution, but rather, "a proper exercise of the board's authority to negotiate a settlement of a potential claim to avoid expensive, time-consuming and uncertain litigation" (*Appeal of Allard*, 43 Educ. Dep't Rep. ___, dec. no. 14,957 (2003)).

The fact that an employee is subject to 3020-a discipline does not affect whether restrictions imposed on the employee must be negotiated. In *Port Jefferson UFSD*, 33 PERB ¶ 3047 (2000), the Public Employment Relations Board (PERB) ruled that a school district could not unilaterally impose a sign in, sign out procedure on a suspended employee during the pendency of a 3020-a proceeding.

8:199. May a district counsel a teacher to refrain from particular misconduct conduct without actually disciplining the teacher?

Yes. A district may place a counseling letter (known as a *"Holt"* letter) critical of a tenured teacher's performance in the teacher's personnel file (*Holt v. Board of Educ.*, 52 N.Y.2d 625 (1981); see also *Matter of Richardson*, 24 Educ. Dep't Rep. 104 (1984)). A *Holt* letter, however, may not be used as a reprimand, which is one of the statutory penalties under 3020-a, and as such, requires a hearing (*Appeal of Irving*, 39 Educ. Dep't Rep. 761 (2000); see *Appeal of Fusco*, 39 Educ. Dep't Rep. 836 (2000)).

8:200. Does every type of employer action that is deemed disciplinary in nature trigger a tenured teacher's right to formal due process under section 3020-a?

Yes. For example, in one case, the commissioner ruled that a superintendent's involuntary transfer of a principal to the position of assistant principal at another school, based on the superintendent's conclusion that the principal had engaged in misconduct, was a disciplinary action in violation of section 3020-a (*Appeal of Irving*, 39 Educ. Dep't Rep. 761 (2000)).

In contrast, a school board's decision to reassign a tenured employee based on the district's educational needs does not constitute discipline for which procedural due process must be provided under section 3020-a, as long as the employee's rights are not infringed (*Appeal of Dillon*, 43 Educ. Dep't Rep. ___, dec. no. 15,010 (2004); *Appeal of Gaul*, 40 Educ. Dep't Rep. 105 (2000)).

8:201. Are 3020-a decisions or settlement agreements available to the public under the Freedom of Information Law (FOIL)?

Yes. Generally, agreements settling disciplinary charges are subject to disclosure under FOIL. However, certain portions of such agreements should be reviewed and edited before disclosure to the public in order to protect privacy, including charges that were denied and charges mentioning the names of other employees or students (*LaRocca v. Board of Educ. of Jericho UFSD*, 220 A.D.2d 424 (2d Dep't 1995); *Western Suffolk BOCES v. Bay Shore UFSD*, 250 A.D. 2d 772 (2d Dep't 1998); *Buffalo Evening News, Inc. v. Board of Educ. of the Hamburg CSD* (Sup. Ct. Erie County 1987); but see *Anonymous v. Board of Educ. for the Mexico CSD*, 162 Misc.2d 300 (Sup. Ct. Oswego County 1994)).

A 3020-a panel or hearing officer decision with a finding of guilt is not exempt from FOIL as part of an employee's "employment history" and as such, may be disclosed pursuant to a FOIL request (*DeMichele v. Greenburgh CSD No. 7*, 167 F.3d 784 (2d Cir. 1999); see **2:84–87, 2:89**). Again, certain portions of the decision should be reviewed and edited before redisclosure to the public in order to protect privacy, including charges that were dismissed and those parts of the decision mentioning the names of other employees or students.

Teachers' Compensation and Benefits

8:202. Are teachers guaranteed minimum salaries under state law?

No. There are no state-mandated minimum salaries for teachers. Often these are established locally by the school board after collective bargaining with the teachers' union. However, the Education Law does impose other requirements on the payment of teachers' salaries.

Except as otherwise provided by law, the school district must pay extra salary to teachers who work more than the regular 10-month school year (§ 3101(3)). For each summer month a teacher works, the school district must pay that teacher at least an additional 1/10th of his or her annual salary (§ 3101(3); *Matter of Walsh*, 21 Educ. Dep't Rep. 467 (1982)). If a teacher works additional days instead of a whole month, the extra salary is one 1/200th of the annual salary for each day (§ 3101(3)).

8:203. Are substitute teachers entitled to a minimum salary?

No. There is no state-mandated minimum salary for substitutes. Each school district establishes the salary for its own substitutes.

If a district has given substitutes reasonable assurance of continued employment, the substitutes may be represented by a recognized or certified employee organization that will negotiate on their behalf over terms and conditions of employment, including compensation (Civ. Serv. Law § 201(7)(d)). Generally, a long-term substitute who is assigned to cover for a teacher who is on an extended leave for a definite period of time may be placed in the regular teachers' bargaining unit, because according to the Public Employment Relations Board (PERB), they perform the same professional duties under similar conditions (*Unatego CSD*, 15 PERB ¶ 3097 (1982); *Connetquot CSD,* 34 PERB ¶ 4001 (2001)). However, itinerant substitutes who teach on an ad hoc basis generally are not a part of the teachers' collective bargaining unit. They generally are placed in their own bargaining unit (*Bethpage UFSD*, 15 ¶ 4040, *aff'd*, 15 PERB ¶ 3094 (1982)).

If substitutes are represented by a recognized or certified employee organization, their compensation is a mandatory subject of bargaining with the district (see **10:25**).

8:204. What types of salary issues must be negotiated with a teachers' union?

The Taylor Law requires school districts to negotiate with recognized or certified employee organizations over salaries, wages, hours, and other terms and conditions of employment (Civ. Serv. Law §§ 201(4), 204(2), (3); see **chapter 10**). School districts are required to negotiate over increases in salaries (*Huntington UFSD, No.3,* 16 PERB ¶ 3061 (1983)) and/or decreases in salaries (*County of Monroe*, 10 PERB ¶ 3104 (1977)).

Additional salary issues that must be negotiated include longevity pay (*Triborough Bridge and Tunnel Authority*, 27 PERB ¶ 3076 (1994); merit pay (*County of Ulster*, 14 PERB ¶ 3008 (1981)); overtime pay (*Town of Henrietta*, 19 PERB ¶ 4565, *aff'd*, 19 PERB ¶ 3067 (1986); pay for summer work (*Saugerties CSD*, 10 PERB ¶ 4529 (1977)); and premium pay for extra work, such as teaching large classes (*West Irondequoit Teachers Ass'n v. Helsby*, 35 N.Y.2d 46 (1974)).

Determining salaries for newly created positions that have not been filled is not a mandatory subject of bargaining and thus need not be bargained (*Churchville-Chili CSD*, 17 PERB ¶ 3055 (1984)). However, once the new positions are filled, the salaries must be negotiated upon the union's demand (*New York City Sch. Dist.*, 22 PERB ¶ 3011 (1989)).

8:205. Must a school board recognize teaching experience outside the school district when determining a new teacher's placement on a salary schedule or longevity increments under a collective bargaining agreement?

A school board may choose to recognize prior teaching experience outside the district, but it is not legally required to do so (§ 3101(4)). However, transfer credits granted to teachers before April 12, 1971, when a state law that required districts to recognize outside teaching experience was repealed, are irrevocable and must continue to be recognized (*UFSD v. Nyquist*, 38 N.Y.2d 137 (1975); § 3102(6), repealed by Laws of 1971, Ch. 123). Districts often recognize other experience, such as service in the armed forces or Peace Corps, depending on their teachers' collective bargaining agreement.

The placement of new teachers on the salary schedule based on prior experience is a mandatory subject of bargaining (*Somers CSD*, 9 PERB ¶ 3014 (1976); *Bellmore UFSD*, 34 PERB ¶ 3009 (2001)).

8:206. May a school district make salary adjustments when a teacher fails to provide services under a contract?

Yes. Salary adjustments are calculated based on section 3101(3) of the Education Law. For teachers who fail to render services during the school year, that law defines salary as being at least 1/10th of the annual salary for each full month of service and a daily rate of 1/200th of the salary (*Matter of Sarmiento*, 18 Educ. Dep't Rep. 108 (1978)).

The calculation of salary adjustments under this definition poses a problem of inequity when the number of workdays in one month does not equal 20 days. For this reason, the commissioner of education has adopted the Huntington formula (*Matter of Swaim*, 9 Educ. Dep't Rep. 23 (1969)). This formula directs that salary adjustments for a teacher who has failed to serve at some time during the school year be calculated differently, depending on whether a teacher misses less than or more than half of the working days of the month (*Board of Educ. v. Ambach*, 97 A.D.2d 188 (3d Dep't 1983), *aff'd*, 63 N.Y.2d 780 (1984)).

If a teacher works for more than half of the working days of the month, the district may deduct 1/200th of his or her annual salary for each day of unauthorized absence. If a teacher works for half of the working days of the month or less, the district need only pay the teacher 1/200th of the annual salary for each day of service rendered. These calculations apply regardless of the number of working days in the particular month.

8:207. Must a school district pay teachers' salary for days a school is closed because of an emergency?

The usual practice is to pay salaries when schools are closed because of an emergency or inclement weather. However, in these cases, schools may require that teachers work additional school days, such as during vacation periods.

A district's collective bargaining agreement may cover payment of teachers' salaries for periods when school is closed (see *Orchard Park Teachers' Ass'n v. Board of Educ. of Orchard Park CSD*, 71 A.D.2d 1 (4th Dep't 1979)).

8:208. When are teachers entitled to be paid?

The salary of a teacher employed for a full school year must be paid in at least 10 installments (§ 3015(2); see *Matter of Schwartz*, 7 Educ. Dep't Rep. 130 (1968)). In addition, if a school district employs a teacher after July 1 in any school year, the district must pay the teacher's salary at least once in each month during the school year in which the teacher is employed (§ 3015(2)).

Neither a school district nor a board of cooperative educational services (BOCES) can pay teachers in advance for service they have not yet rendered (§ 3015(3); see also Opn. St. Comp. 82-363; 1 Educ. Dep't Rep. 730 (1951), Opn. of Counsel #28; 1 Educ. Dep't Rep. 736 (1951), Opn. of Counsel #37; 1 Educ. Dep't Rep. 796 (1951), Opn. of Counsel #88 (1954)). For example, a school district cannot pay teachers returning to duty at the beginning of the school year two weeks' salary, before they work for two weeks (*Board of Educ. v. Ramapo Teachers Ass'n*, 200 A.D.2d 62 (3d Dep't 1994), *appeal denied*, 84 N.Y.2d 806 (1994)).

8:209. May teachers be required to sign a waiver or release as a condition of a salary payment?

No. Teachers and other employees of a school district may not be required or even requested to make a general release or waiver as a condition of any salary payment (§ 3108).

8:210. May a district reduce a teacher's salary to contribute to a tax-sheltered annuity plan, if the teacher so requests?

Yes. Any school district or BOCES may include a provision in its teachers' collective bargaining agreement to reduce the annual salary of a teacher in order to invest in an annuity for that employee (§§ 3109, 3109-A). The annuity fund must meet specific requirements of the Internal Revenue Code (see 26 USC § 403(b)).

8:211. May a teacher be reimbursed by a school board for work-related traveling expenses?

Yes. A school board is authorized to reimburse a teacher for work-related expenses and to make rules and regulations concerning expenses, including the establishment of a mileage rate (§ 1604(27)). The establishment of a mileage rate for reimbursement is a mandatory subject of collective bargaining (*County of Tompkins*, 17 PERB ¶ 4575 (1984); see **10:52–53**).

School districts also are authorized to pay for convention, conference, and school expenses for teachers, including travel expenses (Gen. Mun. Law § 77-b; see also **19:16–17**).

8:212. Must school boards adopt rules and regulations governing leaves of absence for teachers and other school district employees?

Yes. School boards have both the authority and the obligation to adopt rules and regulations concerning excused absences and leaves of absences for teachers and other staff members (§§ 1709(16), 3005, 3005-a). For example, school districts are required by the federal Family and Medical Leave Act (FMLA) to provide all employees, including teachers, with unpaid leave for medical or family care purposes, and to adopt policies concerning such leaves (see 29 USC § 2601 *et seq.*; **10:84–92**). Such family and medical leaves are limited to 12 weeks in duration (29 USC § 2612), and the district must provide health insurance coverage at the usual cost to the employee during the leave (29 USC § 2614(c)).

A district may adopt a policy of allowing certain employees to take two days paid leave each school year to engage in consulting arrangements with other school districts (*Appeal of Morris,* 38 Educ. Dep't Rep. 427 (1998)).

Generally, leaves of absences and other types of leaves are mandatory subjects of bargaining under the Taylor Law (*City of Albany,* 7 PERB ¶ 3078 (1974), *aff'd,* 48 A.D.2d 998 (3d Dep't 1975), *aff'd,* 38 N.Y.2d 778 (1975); see **10:52–53**).

8:213. Are teachers entitled to paid leave for time spent as disaster relief volunteers for the American Red Cross?

Yes, up to 20 days of paid leave in each calendar year, subject to the approval of the superintendent of schools. In fact, all school district officers and employees, not just teachers, are entitled to such leave under qualifying circumstances.

The American Red Cross must certify that the employee is a disaster relief volunteer and must submit a written request for the employee's services to the superintendent of the employing district.

If leave is approved by the superintendent, it must be provided at the employee's regular rate of pay for those regular work hours during which the employee is absent from work while participating in authorized disaster relief operations. Moreover, such leave must be provided without loss of seniority, compensation, sick leave, vacation leave, or overtime compensation to which the employee is otherwise entitled. (Gen. Mun. Law § 92-c).

8:214. Are there any legal requirements applicable to sick leaves for teachers?

Yes. School districts, with the exception of New York City, must provide at least 10 sick days per year with pay for each teacher; any unused sick leave shall accumulate to at least 150 sick days (§ 3005-b).

Sick leave is a mandatory subject of bargaining (*City of Albany v. Helsby*, 48 A.D.2d 998 (3d Dep't 1975), *aff'd*, 38 N.Y.2d 777 (1975); *Village of Spring Valley*, 14 PERB ¶ 3010 (1981)), and the provisions of collective bargaining agreements are often more generous than those of section 3005-b or the federal Family and Medical Leave Act (FMLA); see **10:84–92**).

A teacher who is entitled to medical leave under the FMLA because he or she has a serious health condition that prevents the teacher from performing his or her job, or to care for a spouse, child, or parent who has a serious health condition, may elect to use (or the district may require the use of) available, accrued paid vacation, personal, or medical or sick leave for all or part of the maximum 12-week period of medical leave. However, accrued paid family or sick leave may not be used under the FMLA in any situation in which the district would not normally provide any such paid leave (see 29 USC § 2612(d)(2)(B); *Santos v. Knitgoods Workers' Union*, 252 F.3d 175 (2d Cir. 2001); see **10:84–92**).

8:215. Must school districts provide teachers leave to care for family members?

Yes. The Family and Medical Leave Act (FMLA) requires school districts to permit employees, including teachers, to take up to 12 work weeks of unpaid leave to care for a spouse, parent, or child who has a "serious health condition" (29 USC § 2612(a)(1)(C)). However, under FMLA, an eligible teacher may elect, or the district may require the teacher to substitute his or her accrued vacation leave, personal leave or medical leave for any part of the 12 weeks (29 USC § 2612(d)(2)(A)).

The district must provide health insurance to the teacher at the teacher's usual cost (29 USC § 2614(c); **10:84**).

8:216. May a school district require a pregnant teacher to take sick leave?

No. The United States Supreme Court has rejected as unconstitutional school district rules that set cutoff dates, such as four or five months before the due date of birth, for the purpose of imposing mandatory sick leave for pregnant teachers (*Cleveland Bd. of Educ. v. La Fleur*, 414 U.S. 632 (1974)). In addition, the Executive Law prevents an employer from compelling a pregnant employee to take a leave of absence unless she cannot reasonably perform duties related to her job as a result of the pregnancy (Exec. Law § 296(1)(g)).

8:217. How can school districts handle maternity leaves?

School districts can treat maternity leaves in a number of ways, including as unpaid leaves under the federal Family and Medical Leave Act (FMLA) (29 CFR § 825.114(c); see **10:84–92**), unpaid leaves of absence for a fixed duration of more than 12 weeks, or paid leaves that last only for the actual period of disability. Under FMLA, an eligible teacher may elect, or the district may require the teacher to substitute his or her accrued vacation leave, personal leave or family leave for any part of the 12 weeks (29 USC § 2612(d)(2)(A)).

The state Human Rights Law requires that a pregnant teacher who takes a maternity leave must be permitted to use her sick leave to the same extent as if she were suffering from some other physical disability (*Board of Educ. v. State Div. of Human Rights*, 35 N.Y.2d 675 (1974)). In addition, a school district must treat sick or disability leave taken for pregnancy in the same manner as other leave in determining credit for time served by probationary teachers (*Schwabenbauer v. Board of Educ.*, 667 F.2d 305 (2d Cir. 1981)). However, if no such credit is given to probationary teachers for any type of leave, those on maternity leave may not demand special treatment. FMLA provides that pregnancy is an authorized basis for medical leave.

Any personnel policy that singles out pregnancy, among all other physical conditions, as a category for special treatment in determining when a leave may commence violates the Human Rights Law (*Board of Educ. v. New York State Div. of Human Rights*, 35 N.Y.2d 673 (1974); *Union Free Sch. Dist. v. New York State Human Rights Appeal Bd.*, 35 N.Y.2d 371 (1974), *reargument denied*, 36 N.Y.2d 807 (1975)).

A district may not refuse to permit a teacher on FMLA leave from returning to the classroom except under limited circumstances that occur near the end of a semester (see 29 USC § 2618(d); **10:91**). It may not establish a minimum time after birth, such as three months, before allowing a teacher to return. However, a district may require that a teacher provide a physician's statement that she is physically able to work and require a physical examination to ensure her fitness, but only if the district requires this for other types of temporary disabilities (*Cleveland Board of Educ. v. La Fleur*, 414 U.S. 632 (1974)).

In addition, a school district properly denied two teachers' proposed use of a sick leave bank for extended post-pregnancy leave because they did not qualify as seriously ill or injured under the terms of the agreement establishing the bank, according to the Appellate Division, Second Department (*Matter of Pocantico Hills CSD v. Pocantico Hills Teachers Ass'n*, 264 A.D.2d 397 (2d Dep't 1999), *leave to app. denied*, 94 N.Y.2d 759 (2000)).

8:218. What leave rights are afforded to teachers who are adoptive or foster parents?

A teacher who adopts a child or who takes in a foster child is entitled to take up to 12 work weeks of unpaid leave under the Family and Medical Leave Act, within one year of the adoption of a child (under 18 years of age) or the placement of a foster child in the teacher's home (see 29 USC § 2612(a); **10:88**). However, under FMLA, an eligible teacher may elect, or the district may require the teacher to substitute his or her accrued vacation leave, personal leave, or family leave for any part of the 12 weeks (29 USC § 2612(d)(2)(A)).

Additionally, under the state Labor Law, any employer who permits an employee to take a leave of absence when a child is born must afford that same leave to an adoptive parent of a preschool child at the time the child is placed in the home by an authorized agency, or upon filing court papers for adoption if the adoption is not sponsored by an authorized agency (Lab. Law § 201-c).

8:219. Must a school district make reasonable accommodations for teachers who request time off to commemorate religious holidays or observances?

Yes. In general, New York State law prohibits employers, including school districts, from requiring any person to violate or forego a sincerely held practice of his or her religion as a condition of obtaining or retaining employment (including opportunities for promotion, advancement, or transfer). Therefore, a school district is required by law to make reasonable accommodations for teachers and other district employees who desire time off for religious observance (*Ansonia Bd. of Educ. v. Philbrook*, 479 U.S. 60 (1986); *Sherbert v. Verner*, 374 U.S. 398 (1963)), including observance of a particular day or days or any portion thereof as a Sabbath or other holy day, in accordance with the requirements of a person's religion.

However, an employer does not have to provide the required accommodation if it can demonstrate, after engaging in a bona fide effort, that providing the accommodation would cause it "undue hardship," as that term is defined in law (Exec. Law § 296(10)(a-d).

In one case, an administrative law judge ruled a school district violated the state human rights law when it refused to grant a teacher the district's perfect attendance award because she was absent from work to observe certain religious holidays (*Resnick v. Saranac CSD, State Div. of Human Rights*, Case No. 40E0C-89-137953E, Roberts, H. (1995)).

8:220. Can an employer require employees to make up absences taken for religious observations?

Yes. As practicable in its reasonable judgment, an employer may require employees to make up an absence resulting from a religious accommodation with an equivalent amount of time and work at some other mutually convenient time. Alternatively, the employer may require the employee to charge the absence against any available leave with pay, other than sick leave, or may treat the absence as an excused absence without pay. In addition, although the law does not require an employer to provide paid leave, a district may obligate itself by contract to provide paid leave for religious observances (see **8:221**).

An employee who makes up work in return for a religious accommodation during hours when "premium wages" (e.g., overtime pay) or "premium benefits" (e.g., additional seniority credit) ordinarily would be available is not entitled to such premium wages or benefits (Exec. Law § 296(10)(a-d)).

8:221. May a school district agree to a contractual provision that grants paid leave to teachers for observance of religious holidays and occasions?

It depends. Two separate state appellate courts have rendered conflicting rulings that have not been reconciled by the New York State Court of Appeals.

As a general rule, allowing employees use of paid "personal time" for religious purposes is a mandatory subject of bargaining under the Taylor Law (*Wappingers CSD*, 18 PERB ¶ 3039 (1985)). However, one state appellate court upheld a school district's refusal to recognize a provision in a collective bargaining agreement that authorized teachers to take as paid leave any religious holiday designated by the commissioner of education, without charging the leave time to any of their leave accruals. According to the court, this contract provision violated the Establishment Clause of the First Amendment of the federal constitution, because it made more paid days off available to teachers who "claimed to be religiously observant" than to teachers who were "agnostics, atheists, or simply less religiously observant" (*Port Washington UFSD v. Port Wash. Teachers Ass'n*, 268 A.D.2d 523 (2d Dep't 2000), *appeal denied*, 95 N.Y.2d 761 (2000)).

Similarly, the Public Employment Relations Board (PERB) has ruled in two cases that a school district did not violate its duty to bargain in good faith by unilaterally rescinding a "past practice" of allowing employees to take extra-contractual paid leave for religious observances separate and distinct from other types of leave, finding that it was an unconstitutional practice and therefore not mandatorily negotiable (*Auburn Enlarged City Sch. Dist.*, 30 PERB ¶ 3033 (1997); *Eastchester UFSD,* 29 PERB ¶ 3041 (1996)).

By comparison, another state appellate court upheld a provision in a collective bargaining agreement, which permitted teachers to receive up to three days of paid leave for religious observances, upon written request. According to the court, this type of contractual provision "does not offend the Establishment Clause in that it does not impermissibly advance religion by coercing members of the union to profess a religious belief." The court found the contractual provision at issue distinguishable from the one invalidated by the Second Department in the *Port Washington* case, because the religious leave clause before it did not impose any limitation on which religious holidays qualify for paid leave. Therefore, the contract provision did not impermissibly favor any one religion, but rather, provided "a reasonable accommodation of the teachers' religious beliefs. . . ." However, the court did not address the concern raised by the Second Department that such a provision provides more leave to employees who are religiously observant than to those who are not (*Maine-Endwell Teachers' Ass'n v. Board of Educ. of Maine-Endwell CSD,* 3 A.D.3d 685 (3d Dep't 2004)).

8:222. Is a school district required to give a teacher time off to vote?

Yes. A school district must allow up to two hours of paid time off from work for any employee who does not have sufficient time outside of work to vote (Elec. Law § 3-110(1)). This time must be taken at the beginning or the end of a shift. However, any employee who has four consecutive hours before or after work when the polls are open has sufficient time to vote and is not entitled to paid leave (Elec. Law § 3-110(2)).

A teacher who wants time off with pay to vote must notify the district between two and 10 days before Election Day (Elec. Law § 3-110(3)). Districts must post notices advising employees of their right to time off to vote (Elec. Law § 3-110(4)).

8:223. May a teacher be given a leave of absence to become an exchange teacher?

Yes. A teacher who has taught in the district for more than five years may be given up to two years' paid leave to serve as an exchange teacher in another state or foreign country, provided the state or country sends an exchange teacher with corresponding qualifications. Exchange teachers are paid by their employer; however, districts may supplement the income of foreign teachers. A teacher who is granted a leave of absence to serve as an exchange teacher must be granted the same compensation, retirement protection, and seniority rights as if he or she had served within the district (§ 3005).

Although a teacher with less than five years of service with a district may serve as an exchange teacher, the provisions of section 3005 of the Education Law do not apply to that teacher (*Dreyfuss v. Board of Educ.*, 76 Misc.2d 479 (1973), *aff'd*, 45 A.D.2d 988 (2d Dep't 1974)).

8:224. Must a district pay cash for unused leave time to teachers who resign?

A district is not required to provide employees with a cash payment for accumulated unused vacation, sick, and other leave time. However, districts may adopt a resolution to grant cash payments for unused time (Gen. Mun. Law § 92; see also *Karp v. North Country Community College*, 258 A.D.2d 775 (3d Dep't 1999); *Gratto v. Board of Educ. of the Ausable CSD*, 271 A.D.2d 175 (2000)). Absent passage of a board resolution in advance, such payments would constitute a gift of public funds in violation of Article VIII, section 1 of the state Constitution (*Karp, Gratto*).

Payment for accumulated sick, vacation, and leave time is a mandatory subject of collective bargaining (*Village of Lynbrook*, 10 PERB ¶¶ 3065, 3067 (1977), *aff'd*, 64 A.D.2d 902 (2d Dep't 1978), *aff'd*, 48 N.Y.2d 398 (1979)); see **10:53**). Many collective bargaining agreements oblige the employer to pay for unused leave time.

8:225. Is a teacher entitled to continued coverage in the district's group health plan if employment with the district is terminated?

Yes. Under most circumstances, an employee can continue coverage in a group health plan under the federal Comprehensive Omnibus Budget Reconciliation Act of 1985 (COBRA) (42 USC § 300bb-1 *et seq.*). This law requires school boards with 20 or more employees to offer participants in group health plans and their covered dependents an opportunity to buy back into continued coverage should they cease to be covered because of termination, reduced hours, retirement, resignation, or when their dependents would otherwise cease to be covered because of the participants' death, divorce, legal separation, Medicare entitlement, or ineligibility for dependent coverage under the group plan. This continued coverage must be offered for at least 18 months, in the case of termination or reduced hours, and up to 36 months in other instances.

In addition, the State Health Insurance Plan provides for continued health insurance coverage under certain circumstances, such as when an employee is on authorized leave without pay, is suspended and placed upon a preferred list, up to a period of one year, or when an employee who was hired prior to April 1, 1975 retires after completion of at least five years of service with the employer and the employer elected to participate in the plan prior to March 1, 1972 (4 NYCRR § 73.2(a)(3); Civ. Serv. Law §§ 163, 165). However, an employer may elect not to provide continued coverage to retiring employees hired on or after April 1, 1977, if such a decision is applied to all employees who meet certain specified conditions upon retirement (4 NYCRR § 73.2(a)(3)(iv); Civ. Serv. Law § 163).

In some instances, continued coverage may also be available to dependents upon the death of an employee or retiree (Civ. Serv. Law § 165-a; 4 NYCRR § 73.2(b)(1), (3)).

An employee on leave pursuant to the Family Medical Leave Act (FMLA) is entitled to coverage under COBRA when (1) the employee (spouse or dependent) is covered under an employer's group health plan on the day before the first day of FMLA leave or becomes covered during the FMLA leave; (2) the employee does not return to employment with the employer at the end of the FMLA leave; and (3) the employee (spouse or dependent) would in the absence of COBRA continuation coverage lose coverage under the employer's group health plan before the end of what would be the maximum coverage period.

Given the complexity and highly technical nature of this law, districts are encouraged to consult with their school attorneys or other COBRA advisers to better understand their obligations in applying these laws to specific situations.

9. Noninstructional Employees

The Civil Service

9:1. What is the civil service?

The civil service includes all offices and positions in the service of the state or any of its civil divisions, including school districts (*Palmer v. Board of Educ.,* 276 N.Y. 222 (1937), *motion to amend denied,* 276 N.Y. 682 (1938); *In re Holt,* 26 Misc.2d 247 (Sup. Ct. Kings County 1953), *aff'd, Holt v. Jansen,* 283 A.D. 796, *appeal denied,* 283 A.D. 815 (2d Dep't), *motion for leave to appeal denied,* 307 N.Y. 939 (1954); see §§ 17(1)–(2), 35(g)), except offices or positions in the military departments (§ 2(4)–(8)). The civil service is divided into two broad categories: the unclassified service (§ 35) and the classified service (§§ 40–44; see figure below).

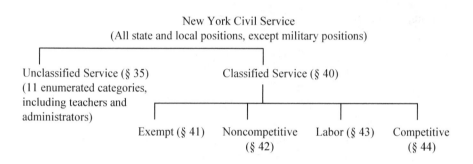

New York Civil Service
(All state and local positions, except military positions)

Unclassified Service (§ 35)
(11 enumerated categories, including teachers and administrators)

Classified Service (§ 40)

Exempt (§ 41)   Noncompetitive (§ 42)   Labor (§ 43)   Competitive (§ 44)

9:2. Are teachers and school administrators governed by the Civil Service Law?

No. Public employees whose principal functions are teaching or the supervision of teaching in a school district or board of cooperative educational services (BOCES) are in the unclassified service (§ 35(g), (j); see **9:1**). This includes employees such as superintendents, principals, teachers, teaching assistants, and other positions that have been certified by the commissioner of education to the State Civil Service Commission. The Education Law, not the Civil Service Law, governs the employment of persons in these unclassified positions (see, e.g., Educ. Law §§ 2509, 2510, 2573, 3001, 3002, 3003, 3004, 3012, 3013, 3019-a, 3020, 3020-a, 3031).

All statutory references in this chapter are to the New York State Civil Service Law unless noted otherwise.

9:3. What is the unclassified service?

The *unclassified* service comprises all positions in 11 categories listed in the Civil Service Law, including teachers and supervisory personnel in school districts and boards of cooperative educational services, the State University and certain community colleges, elective offices, legislative officers and employees, and members and employees of boards of election (§ 35). If a position is not included in one of the enumerated categories of positions in the unclassified service, the position is, by definition, in the classified service (§ 40; see *Ficken v. Vocational Educ. and Extension Bd. of the County of Suffolk*, 201 A.D.2d 481 (2d Dep't 1994), *dismissed*, 238 A.D.2d 589 (2d Dep't 1997), *appeal denied*, 90 N.Y.2d 908 (1997)).

9:4. What is the classified service?

The *classified* service comprises all offices and positions not included in the unclassified service. The classified service is further divided into four subcategories or "jurisdictional" classes: the competitive class, the noncompetitive class, the labor class and the exempt class (§ 40; see **9:6**). Unless otherwise specifically designated by law or administrative action of the local civil service agency, all positions are automatically in the competitive class (§ 44).

Article 5, section 6, of the New York State Constitution provides that appointments and promotions in the classified civil service must be made according to merit and fitness to be determined by examination, which, as far as practicable, must be competitive. The New York State Civil Service Law was enacted to carry out this purpose.

The Classified Service

9:5. What kinds of positions in school districts are in the classified civil service?

In school districts, virtually all noninstructional support staff positions are in the classified service. Thus, nonteaching administrative positions such as school tax collector, district treasurer, internal auditor, business manager, and labor relations director are generally in the classified service. So, too, are all clerical and noninstructional student-related positions, such as teacher aide and school monitor, as well as positions related to building maintenance, school security, school bus operation and the school lunch program. All local civil service agencies maintain an appendix to their local rules setting forth all positions under their jurisdiction that have been classified in other than the competitive class (see **9:9**).

9:6. How do the four classes (exempt, labor, noncompetitive, and competitive) within the classified service differ?

The *exempt* class includes all positions for which competitive or noncompetitive examination to determine the merit and fitness of applicants is found to be not practicable (§ 41(1)(e); N.Y. Const. Art. 5, § 6). Exempt class positions are so named because they are exempt from virtually all civil service limitations and restrictions. School boards have complete discretion in filling such positions.

An important factor to consider in determining whether a civil service position should be classified as exempt is whether the position involves highly confidential duties. However, the need for confidentiality, by itself, does not compel the classification of a particular position as exempt (*Dillon v. Nassau County Civil Serv. Comm'n*, 43 N.Y.2d 574 (1978)). School district positions typically placed in the exempt class include the secretary to the superintendent of schools, school tax collector, school district treasurer, internal auditor, and school district attorney (i.e., where the attorney is an "employee" and not an independent contractor).

There is no examination for exempt class positions. Nor are there are any set minimum qualifications for such positions. Instead, the person or body having the power to make the appointment, including a school board, determines the qualifications for the position and which person possesses such qualifications.

The *labor* class includes unskilled positions, with no minimum qualifications, although applicants may be required to demonstrate their ability to do the job (§ 43). Typically, appointments to positions in the labor class simply require notification to the local civil service agency of the employment, unless the local civil service agency decides to impose additional requirements such as the filing of an application (§ 43(2), see **9:9**). School district positions typically placed in the labor class include school monitor, cleaner, and food service helper.

The *noncompetitive* class includes all positions that are not in the exempt class or the labor class for which it is not practicable to ascertain the merit and fitness of applicants by competitive examination (§ 42(1); *Condell v. Jorling*, 151 A.D.2d **88** (3d Dep't 1989)). In the noncompetitive class, candidates' abilities are simply assessed against established qualifications for the position rather than being placed in competition with other candidates for the highest test score.

The noncompetitive class consists primarily of skilled trade positions. It also includes certain positions of a high-level administrative, scientific, or technical character involving a confidential relationship between the incumbent and the employer or which may require the performance of functions influencing policy.

Candidates for appointment to positions in the noncompetitive class need only meet the minimum qualifications for the position set by the local civil service agency. Generally, no written or oral examination is required. Instead, the local civil service agency compares the candidate's qualifications to the qualifications that it has issued for the position. If the agency determines that the candidate meets those qualifications, the employer is free to make the appointment. School district positions typically placed in the noncompetitive class include school nurse, school bus driver, teacher aide, custodial worker, building maintenance mechanic, groundskeeper, automotive mechanic, cook and baker.

The *competitive* class includes all positions not in the exempt, labor, or noncompetitive classes (§ 44). Candidates for competitive class positions must meet minimum qualifications established by the local civil service agency and are subject to competitive (ranked) examination to show their merit and fitness for the position (§ 50(1), (4)(a); *Professional, Clerical, Technical Employees Ass'n (Buffalo Bd. of Educ).*, 90 N.Y.2d 364 (1997)). Unless otherwise specifically designated by law or administrative action of the local civil service agency, all positions are automatically in the competitive class (§ 44). School district positions typically found in the competitive class include business manager, safety officer, secretary, keyboard specialist, clerk, custodian, supervisor of building maintenance, director of transportation, head bus driver, bus dispatcher, and school lunch manager.

No position shall be deemed to be in the exempt or noncompetitive class unless it appears under that class in the rules of the local civil service agency (§§ 41(2), 42(1); see **9:9**). The rules must also specify which positions in the noncompetitive class are confidential or involve functions influencing policy (§ 42(2-a)).

9:7. Who administers and enforces the Civil Service Law with respect to school district staff employed in the classified civil service?

The administration and enforcement of the civil service system for local governments in New York State is decentralized and is primarily the responsibility of local civil service agencies (§§ 15, 17). Every county, some cities, and a few towns in the state have either a local or regional civil service commission or a personnel officer (§ 15). The county civil service commission or personnel officer is responsible for civil service administration with respect to all positions in the classified service of the county and all the local governments within the county, including school districts, except for cities that have elected to operate their own local civil service agency (§ 17(1)). A regional civil service commission or personnel officer administers the civil service for classified service positions in counties and cities under its jurisdiction (§ 17(3)). Currently, there is only one regional civil service commission in the state: it administers the civil service for classified service positions in Chemung County and the city of Elmira.

For purposes of this chapter, the term *local civil service agency* encompasses the appropriate local or regional civil service commission or personnel officer.

9:8. Who administers and enforces civil service law with respect to staff employed on the classified civil service by a BOCES or multi-county district?

With respect to a board of cooperative educational services (BOCES) or any school district that operates in more than one county, the provisions of Civil Service Law section 19 govern. As a general rule, the BOCES board or multi-county school board is responsible for deciding which county civil service agency will have jurisdiction over its employees. The board must make the decision within 90 days after the BOCES or multi-county district is established. If it fails to make a decision within that period, the BOCES or district will be subject to the jurisdiction of the local civil service agency in which the greatest territorial area of the BOCES or district is located. Once the designation is made, it is final (§ 19).

9:9. What rules govern the administration of the classified civil service?

Each local civil service agency is responsible for adopting rules that govern the administration of civil service (§ 20). The local rules cover matters such as how positions will be classified, examinations, appointments, promotions, transfers, resignations, and reinstatements (§ 20(1)). These rules frequently reflect issues and concerns unique to that area. Since they are not uniform, they should always be reviewed in connection with any civil service question involving a position under the jurisdiction of the local civil service agency.

The local rules also contain appendices that list all positions under the local civil service agency's jurisdiction that have been classified in other than the competitive class.

The adoption or modification of any local rules, except a modification required because of a change in statute, may occur only after a public hearing. Local rules, including those dealing with placing positions in other than the competitive class, are not effective until approved by the State Civil Service Commission and filed with the secretary of state (§ 20(2); see also *Matter of Trager v. Kampe*, 99 N.Y.2d 361 (2003)).

The rules and regulations duly adopted by a local civil service agency have the force and effect of law (§ 20(2); *Albano v. Kirby*, 36 N.Y.2d 526 (1975)).

9:10. What is the school board's role in making appointments to positions in the classified service?

The school board is legally responsible for making appointments to all school district positions, including positions in the classified service, except in New York City where the chancellor has the power to appoint and set salaries for staff in nonrepresented managerial titles (Educ. Law §§ 1604(8), 1709(15), (16), 1711(1), 1804(1), 1903, 1950(4)(e), 2503(5), 2554(2), 2573(3), 2590-g(2), 2590-h(17), (41), 3011, 3012(1)(b); *Appeal of Brown*, 32 Educ. Dep't Rep. 212 (1992)). As the appointing authority, the board is required to notify the local civil service agency of all classified service appointments on a form prescribed by the local agency (§ 97(1); see **9:9**).

In addition, the school board is required to comply with all provisions of the Civil Service Law when making appointments to classified service positions. If the board fails to select or appoint classified service employees in accordance with the law, the board members may be personally responsible for paying that employee's salary (§ 95).

The school board must also ensure that prospective classified service employees, like all other prospective district employees, submit two sets of fingerprints for processing of their criminal history by the state Division of Criminal Justice Services and the Federal Bureau of Investigation, and for clearance for employment by the commissioner of education (Educ. Law §§ 305(30), 1604(39), (40), 1709(39), (40), 1804(9), (10), 1950(4)(ll), (mm), 2503(18), (19), 2554(25), (26), 3035; see **7:2, 8:66–79**).

9:11. May a school district assign an employee hired to perform services in one title of the classified service to the duties of another position?

Generally, no. Except in cases of temporary emergency, it is improper for an employer to assign out-of-title work to an employee hired to perform services in one position to the duties appropriate to another position (§ 61(2); *Kuppinger v. Governor's Office of Employee Relations*, 203 A.D.2d 664 (3d Dep't 1994)).

For example, requiring a school nurse to be responsible for monitoring security monitors and/or allowing persons into the school on an on-going basis has been found not to fall within the general statement of duties of a registered professional school nurse and therefore a violation of the Civil Service Law prohibition against out-of-title work (*CSEA v. New Hyde Park/Garden City Park UFSD*, 230 A.D.2d 702 (2d Dep't 1996)). Further, assigning an employee duties beyond the inherent nature of the position is a mandatory subject of negotiations (*Village of Scarsdale*, 8 PERB ¶ 3075 (1975); see **10:52–53**).

9:12. Can a school board create a new civil service position or reclassify an existing position for its school district?

Yes. A school board may create new positions in existing titles. However, the district must submit a proposal for reclassification, including a statement of the duties of the position, to the local civil service agency. The local civil service agency must furnish a certificate stating the appropriate civil service title for the position. Any new position in a reclassified title may be created only if the reclassified title was approved and certified by the local civil service agency (§ 22). The requirement that a school board get the approval of the local civil service agency before any new position is created is mandatory and non-negotiable. Failure to comply is fatal to the creation of the position (*CSEA v. Town of Harrison*, 48 N.Y.2d 66, *reargument denied*, 48 N.Y. 882 (1979)).

9:13. Are noninstructional employees in the classified service required to file a constitutional oath of office?

Yes. Every person employed by a school district, except employees in the labor class, must take an oath of affirmation in support of the United States and New York State constitutions before he or she starts work.

This oath need only be taken once, at the time of the original appointment, provided that the employee remains continuously employed by the same employer; if there is an interruption in employment, followed by a new appointment, then the employee must take the oath again (Opn. Att'y Gen. I 84-2).

However, a Native American Indian enrolled in or affiliated with an Indian nation recognized by the United States or State of New York may choose to affirm that he or she will perform his or her duties in a manner consistent with the United States and New York constitutions, rather than declaring his or her support of these constitutions (§ 62).

The Competitive Class

9:14. How are appointments or promotions to positions in the competitive class made?

An appointment or promotion to a position in the competitive class of the classified civil service can be made only by selection of one of the three persons certified by the local civil service agency as standing highest on the appropriate eligible list who is willing to accept such an appointment or promotion (§ 61(1); *Cassidy v. Mun. Civil Serv. Comm'n of the City of New Rochelle*, 37 N.Y.2d 526 (1975)). An eligible list is a list prepared by the local civil service agency (or in some cases by the State Civil Service

Department), which lists in rank order the names of all persons who have passed the required civil service examination for the position to which an appointment is to be made (see *Deas v. Levitt*, 73 N.Y.2d 525, *cert. denied*, 493 U.S. 933 (1989)). "Appointments and promotions [are] made from the eligible list most nearly appropriate for the position to be filled" (§ 61(1)) based on the qualifications of the position (*Samboy v. N.Y.S. Liquor Auth.*, 52 A.D.2d 1016 (3d Dep't 1976)).

If there are fewer than three candidates on an eligible list, a school board cannot be compelled by the Civil Service Law to make an appointment from that list. Instead, the board may make a provisional appointment from outside the list (see § 65(1); *Valentin v. New York State Dep't of Taxation and Finance*, 992 F.Supp. 536 (E.D.N.Y. 1997), *aff'd*, 175 F.3d 1009 (2d Cir. 1999); *Heslin v. City of Cohoes*, 74 A.D.2d 393 (3d Dep't 1980), *rev'd on other grounds*, 53 N.Y.2d 903 (1981); see **9:16**).

However, a collective bargaining agreement may contain a provision that requires a board of education to make an appointment from a list of fewer than three candidates (*Heslin*).

9:15. May a collective bargaining agreement provide alternative procedures for the appointment or promotion of competitive class staff?

Yes. Even though the Civil Service Law gives public employers the flexibility to appoint any one of the three highest scoring individuals on an eligible list (*Cassidy v. Mun. Civil Serv. Comm'n of the City of New Rochelle*, 37 N.Y.2d 526 (1975)), some public employers have, through collective bargaining, agreed to appoint the highest scoring individual, even though they are not required to enter into such negotiations (*Town of West Seneca*, 29 PERB ¶ 3024 (1996)). The courts have upheld such agreements.

For example, in *Professional, Clerical, Technical Employees Ass'n (Buffalo Bd. of Educ.)*, 90 N.Y.2d 364 (1997), the state Court of Appeals held that "there is nothing in our State's Constitution, the Civil Service Law or decisional law that prohibits an appointing authority from agreeing through collective bargaining negotiations on the manner in which it will select one of the top three qualified candidates from an eligible list for promotion." The court noted that the appointment of the highest scoring candidate, where compelled by a collective bargaining agreement, does not violate public policy, since appointees are required to serve a probationary term before their appointments become permanent, during which time the appointing authority has the ability to assess other traits not measurable by competitive examination.

9:16. May a school district appoint someone to a competitive class position if there is no appropriate eligible list of candidates?

Yes. A school district may make a provisional appointment to a competitive class position when there is no eligible list available (§ 65(1)), either because an examination has not been given or the eligible list expired (*Davey v. Dep't of Civil Serv.*, 60 A.D.2d 998 (4th Dep't 1978)) or the existing eligible list contains fewer than three names (*Valentin v. New York State Dep't of Taxation & Fin.*, 992 F. Supp. 536 (E.D.N.Y. 1997), *aff'd*, 175 F.3d 1009 (2d Cir. 1999)).

As a general rule, provisional appointments do not ripen into permanent appointments, no matter how long they exist (*Snyder v. Civil Serv. Comm'n of State of New York*, 72 N.Y.2d 981 (1988); *Becker v. New York State Civil Serv. Comm'n*, 61 N.Y.2d 252 (1984); *Haynes v. County of Chautauqua*, 55 N.Y.2d 814 (1981)), and the appointee can be terminated at any time for any lawful reason (*Preddice v. Callanan*, 69 N.Y.2d 812 (1987)). In addition, provisional appointees must be terminated within two months after the establishment of an appropriate eligible list, unless there is a large number of persons in a particular title serving on a provisional basis. In this case, the appointment can continue, with the approval of the local civil service agency, for a maximum of four months after the establishment of the eligible list to avoid programmatic disruption (§ 65(3)).

9:17. What rules govern provisional appointments within the competitive class?

To be appointed provisionally to a competitive class position, the candidate must demonstrate to the local civil service agency, by way of a noncompetitive examination, that he or she is qualified for the position. The noncompetitive examination may consist of a review and evaluation of the candidate's training, experience, and other qualifications, without written, oral, or other performance tests (§ 65(1)). A provisional appointment, which is typically made to an unencumbered position (i.e., one to which no one is returning or has a superior claim), allows the provisional appointee to serve in that position while he or she is awaiting the opportunity to take a competitive exam, or is awaiting the results of an exam.

The duration of a provisional appointment is limited to nine months (§ 65(2)). However, under extenuating circumstances it may be extended, provided there is no valid eligible list available (§ 65(4)). Once a provisional appointment is made, the local civil service agency must order a competitive examination within one month or as soon as practicable to ensure that the provisional appointment does not exceed nine months (§ 65(2)). Notwithstanding the specific statutory mandate, provisional appointments regularly exceed nine months.

A school district cannot make successive provisional appointments to circumvent the Civil Service Law (§ 65(4); *Riggi v. Blessing*, 9 A.D.2d 423 (3d Dep't 1959), *aff'd*, 10 N.Y.2d 917 (1961)). If, however, an examination for a position or group of positions fails to produce a list adequate to fill all positions being held on a provisional basis, or if the eligible list is immediately exhausted following its establishment, a new provisional appointment may be made to any such position that has not been filled by permanent appointment. In such a case, a school district may appoint a current or former provisional appointee to the position. If the current or former provisional appointee eventually becomes eligible for permanent appointment (i.e., he or she becomes one of the three highest scoring individuals on the then current eligible list willing to accept appointment), and the district wants to continue that employee in the position, the district must give the employee a permanent appointment (§ 65(4); *Becker*; *Haynes*).

9:18. May a school district appoint someone to a competitive class position on a temporary basis?

Yes. A temporary employee is essentially a substitute in a position that is encumbered (i.e., one to which someone else is returning or may have a superior claim). A school district may make a temporary appointment to a competitive class position (1) on an emergency basis for a period not exceeding three months; (2) to replace a permanent appointee who is on leave of absence for the duration of the leave; or (3) for up to six months when a position is not expected to exist for a longer period. If a position that is not expected to last more than six months does indeed remain in existence beyond the six-month period, the local civil service agency may authorize an extension for a period not to exceed an additional six months (§ 64(1)).

If the appointment is to be for three months or less, use of an eligible list is not required. However, if the appointment is to last between three and six months, the appointment must be made from the appropriate eligible list, but the appointee does not have to be among the top three on the list (see **9:14**). On the other hand, a temporary appointment for a duration of six months or longer does require that the appointee be among the three highest scoring candidates on the list willing to accept the appointment (§ 64(2)).

In addition, a local civil service agency can authorize a temporary appointment, without examination, when the person appointed will render professional, scientific, technical, or other expert services on either an occasional basis or on a full-time or regular part-time basis in a temporary position established to conduct a special study or project for not longer than 18 months (§ 64(3)).

Irrespective of the duration of the position to which a temporary appointment is made, the candidate must meet the stated minimum qualifications for the position and file an application with the local civil service agency.

9:19. May a school board establish a preference for residents of the school district when hiring competitive class employees?

Yes. Although a school board may not absolutely require that the candidates for a competitive class position be residents of the local school district, it may require that district residents be certified for hiring from an eligible list before nonresidents (§ 23(4-a); see also *Matter of Altamore v. Barrios-Paoli*, 90 N.Y.2d 378 (1997)). Establishing such a residency preference is a nonmandatory subject of bargaining under the Taylor Law (*Rensselaer City Sch. Dist.*, 13 PERB ¶ 3051, *aff'd*, 87 A.D.2d 718 (3d Dep't 1982); see **10:52–53**).

Once the district makes an appointment from among certified residents, it must continue to do so until the list of residents is exhausted. After exhausting the list of district residents, selection must be made from the entire eligible list without regard to residency.

On the other hand, a local civil service agency may establish a residency requirement for competitive and noncompetitive class employees, even over the objection of a local school board (§ 23(4-a); see *Buffet v. Municipal Civil Serv. Comm'n of City of Plattsburgh*, 58 A.D.2d 362 (3d Dep't 1977), *aff'd*, 45 N.Y.2d 1003 (1978)). However, a local civil service commission cannot establish a residency rule simply by listing such a requirement in the examination announcement. The local commission first must publish notice of the proposed residency rule and then conduct a public hearing. Thereafter, the rule becomes valid only upon approval by the state Civil Service Commission (§ 20; see also *Matter of Trager v. Kampe*, 99 N.Y.2d 361 (2003); see **9:9**).

9:20. Are veterans entitled to preference regarding appointment, promotion, or retention in a competitive class position?

Yes. The New York State Constitution authorizes a preference for veterans as an exception to the rule that appointments and promotions be made on the basis of merit and fitness (N.Y. Const. Art. 5, § 6; § 85). Disabled veterans, as defined by the Civil Service Law (§ 85(1)(b)), are entitled to 10 additional points on competitive examinations for original appointment and five additional points for promotion. Veterans who are not disabled are entitled to five additional points on a competitive examination for original appointment and two-and-one-half additional points for promotion (§ 85(2)(a)). Veterans are entitled, as well, to preference in retention upon the abolition of positions (§ 85(7)).

To be eligible for the preference, the veteran must have been a member of the armed forces of the United States who served in time of war and was honorably discharged or released under honorable circumstances from such service. He or she also must be a citizen of the United States or an alien lawfully admitted for permanent residence in the United States and a resident of New York State when applying for preference (§ 85(1)(a)).

Before additional credits can be added to a veteran's grade, the veteran must have obtained a passing grade on the examination. In other words, additional credits may not be used to change a veteran's rating from failing to passing (§ 85(2)(b)).

Veteran's credit may be used only once to obtain an appointment or promotion (*Matter of Marlow v. Tully*, 63 N.Y.2d 918, *rehearing denied*, 64 N.Y.2d 775 (1984), *cert. denied*, 472 U.S. 1010, *rehearing denied* 473 U.S. 924 (1985)). Thus, if a veteran has been permanently appointed or promoted to a position by means of additional credits that affected his or her position on the appropriate eligible list, he or she is not entitled to receive any additional credit in future examinations (§ 85(4)(a)).

9:21. Can a competitive class employee in one school district transfer to a similar position in another school district without further examination?

Yes. Local civil service agencies have rules that permit transfers to similar positions in other school districts or other units of government (§ 70(1)). Requests for transfer should be referred to the local civil service agency for approval.

As a general rule, an employee cannot be transferred without his or her consent (§ 70(1)). Exceptions to this general rule apply when there has been a "transfer of functions" (§ 70(2)) and in any city with a population of one million or more where the city and the authorized union have negotiated an agreement under the Taylor Law providing for involuntary transfers (§ 70(6)).

9:22. Is a board of cooperative educational services (BOCES) takeover situation considered a transfer under the Civil Service Law?

Yes. A BOCES' takeover of a program or service formerly provided by a school district or by a county vocational education and extension board is considered a transfer under Civil Service Law § 70. Classified service employees employed by a school district or county vocational educational extension board at the time of the takeover are considered BOCES employees entitled to protection under the Civil Service Law (Educ. Law § 3014-a(5); *Vestal Employees Ass'n v. PERB*, 94 N.Y. 2d 409 (2000)).

9:23. Does a person appointed to a competitive class position from an eligible list automatically attain permanent status?

No. Permanent appointments to positions in the competitive class require satisfactory completion of a probationary term. The probationary term is established by the local civil service agency and is included in the local civil service rules (§ 63(2); see, e.g., *Matter of Block v. Franklin Square UFSD*, 72 A.D.2d 602 (2d Dep't 1979). Because the length of the term may vary from one jurisdiction to another, the local civil service agency should be contacted for specific information.

Once a probationary competitive class employee attains permanent status, he or she can be terminated only for cause, after a hearing held in accordance with section 75 (see **9:34**) or with collectively bargained disciplinary procedures that supplement, modify or replace section 75 (see **9:40**).

In general, a probationary employee whose conduct or performance is not satisfactory may be terminated at any time after completion of the minimum period and before completion of the maximum period without a hearing so long as the decision is not made in bad faith, or for unconstitutional or illegal reasons (see *Albano v. Kirby*, 36 N.Y.2d 526 (1975); *Williams v. Commissioner of Office of Mental Health of State of N.Y.*, 259 A.D.2d 623 (2d Dep't 1999); *Tomlinson v. Ward*, 110 A.D.2d 537 (1st Dep't), *aff'd*, 66 N.Y.2d 771 (1985); *Macklin v. Powell*, 107 A.D.2d 964 (3d Dep't 1985)). However, local civil service rules may impose certain requirements, such as minimum notice and the opportunity to be heard (see *Albano*; *Saulpaugh v. Diehl*, 148 A.D.2d 928 (4th Dep't 1989)).

9:24. May "applicants" for a competitive class position be required to submit to fingerprinting and a criminal history record check?

Yes. State law gives municipal civil service commissions the authority to promulgate rules that require applicants for examination and competitive class positions to submit fingerprints for state and national criminal history records check to be conducted by the State Division of Criminal Justice Services (DCJS) and the Federal Bureau of Investigation (FBI). Adequate notice must be provided to applicants informing them that such criminal history records checks may be required, and the procedures involved.

Such fingerprinting requirements may not be applied to current employees, to any person who is considered an "applicant" because he or she is transferring pursuant to section 70 (i.e., to a position involving essential test on qualifications different from or higher than those required in the position held by the employee), to any person who is on a section 81 preferred list (i.e., a list of persons suspended or demoted from either competitive class or noncompetitive class positions because their position was abolished or reduced, who have a right to reinstatement to the same or a similar position in the same jurisdictional class if one becomes available), or to any person on a section 56 eligible list (which provides preferred eligibility rights for a period of one to four years) who has successfully completed a promotion exam pursuant to section 52 of the Civil Service Law (which sets forth examination requirements for competitive class promotion) (§ 50(4)).

Compensation and Leave Entitlements

9:25. Are school district noninstructional employees entitled to minimum wage and overtime?

School district employees are covered by the federal minimum wage and overtime standards in the federal Fair Labor Standards Act (FLSA), even though exemptions from the overtime standards may apply to certain executive, administrative, and professional employees (29 USC §§ 206(a)(1), 207(a)(1), 213(a)(1); *Garcia v. San Antonio Metro. Transit Auth.*, 469 U.S. 528 (1985)). They are also covered by the New York State Minimum Wage Act (Lab. Law, Art. 19). The minimum wage under both New York State and federal law is $5.15 per hour (Lab. Law § 652(1) and 29 USC § 206(a)(1)).

FLSA requires employers to pay their nonexempt employees overtime wages of one-and-one-half times the employees' regular rates of compensation for each hour they work in excess of 40 hours per week (29 USC § 207(a)(1)).

However, public employers may provide for paid leave or "compensatory time" in lieu of overtime compensation, so long as the benefit is equal to one-and-one-half hours off for each hour over 40 worked in a week (29 USC § 207(o)(1), (7)(B)). They can pay compensatory time in lieu of cash only where there is an agreement or understanding to do so prior to the performance of work; and, where the employees have a collective bargaining representative, the agreement must be between the employer and the collective bargain representative (29 USC § 207(o)(2)(A); 29 CFR § 553.23(a)(1)). No more than 240 hours of compensatory time off may be accrued (29 USC § 207(o)(3)(A)). If an employee has accrued 240 hours of compensatory time, any additional overtime must be paid at one-and-one-half times the employee's regular rate of compensation (29 USC § 207(o)(3)(A)).

Employees must be allowed to use compensatory time off on request within a reasonable period, as long as the employer's operations will not be unduly disrupted (29 USC § 207(o)(5)). An employee may be required to take compensatory time off unless the school district has agreed to the contrary (*Christensen v. Harris County*, 529 U.S. 576 (2000)).

Districts that fail to comply with FLSA may come under investigation by the U.S. Department of Labor (29 USC § 211). Both the Department of Labor and individual employees can sue school districts for back pay, overtime back payments, interest, liquidated damages (i.e., double the amount of unpaid wages), and equitable relief (29 USC §§ 216-17). Civil penalties of up to $1,100 per employee may be assessed against the employing school district for repeated or willful violations of FLSA (29 CFR §§ 578, 580). Moreover, repeated or willful violations may also result in criminal penalties of up to six months in prison and/or fines up to $10,000 (29 USC § 216). A school district may also be required to pay the attorneys' fees for a litigant who prevails in a lawsuit against it (29 USC § 216).

9:26. Must school districts submit employee payrolls to the local civil service agency?

Yes, for employees in the classified civil service. The local civil service agency with jurisdiction (see **9:7–9**) must certify at least annually that each person on the payroll list has been employed in accordance with law (§ 100(1)(a), (2)(a)). Such certification remains in effect until the next certification. However, with certain limited exceptions, the names of new or reinstated employees whose payroll status changed after the last certification must be submitted for certification on their first payroll (§ 100(2)(a)).

It is a misdemeanor for any school officer to willfully pay or authorize the payment of salary to any person in the classified service, if he or she knows that the local civil service agency has refused to certify the payroll because the individual in question has been appointed, employed, transferred, assigned to perform duties, or reinstated in violation of the Civil Service Law (§ 101; see also *Matter of Gillen v. Smithtown Lib. Bd. of Trustees*, 94 N.Y.2d 776 (1999); see **9:10**).

9:27. Are noninstructional school employees entitled to a set time period for lunch?

Yes. A noninstructional employee working more than six hours in a shift that extends over the time from 11 a.m. to 2 p.m. must receive at least 30 minutes for a lunch period (Lab. Law § 162(2)). Those working a shift shortly before 11:00 a.m. and continuing later than 7:00 p.m. are entitled to an additional meal period of at least 20 minutes between 5:00 and 7:00 p.m. (Lab. Law § 162(3)). Noninstructional employees who work more than six hours in a shift between 1 p.m. and 6 a.m. must be given a 45-minute meal period midway in the shift (Lab. Law § 162(3)). However, the state commissioner of labor may permit a shorter meal period to be fixed (Lab. Law § 162(5)). Moreover, while school districts and their employees cannot completely bargain away the lunch or meal period, it may be modified in a collective bargaining agreement (see *American Broadcasting Co. v. Roberts*, 61 N.Y.2d 244 (1984)). However, school districts may not unilaterally change the duration of meal breaks (*County of Nassau*, 24 PERB ¶ 3029 (1991)).

9:28. Are noninstructional employees who serve as volunteers in disaster relief operations entitled to paid leave?

Yes. In fact, all public officers and employees (not just noninstructional employees) who work for a school district and who are certified by the American Red Cross as disaster volunteers may be granted a leave of absence from work of up to 20 days per year, with pay, to participate in specialized disaster relief operations, upon written request from the American Red Cross, and upon approval of the school superintendent. Upon such approval, the officer or employee is entitled to compensation at his or her regular rate of pay during those work hours that the volunteer participates in authorized disaster relief operations. Moreover, no such volunteer shall lose seniority, sick leave, vacation, or overtime compensation to which he or she is otherwise entitled during the period of approved leave (Gen. Mun. Law § 92-c; see **7:30**).

9:29. Are noninstructional school employees entitled to leave under the federal Family and Medical Leave Act?

Yes. Under the federal Family and Medical Leave Act (FMLA) (29 USC §§ 2601–2654; 29 CFR Part 825), employers with more than 50 employees within 75 miles of their worksite must provide up to 12 weeks of unpaid leave to any eligible employee who works more than 1,250 hours a year, as needed for certain personal or family illness, or for the birth, adoption, or foster care placement of a child (29 USC §§ 2611(2), (4); 2612, 2618(a)(1)). The law also requires the employer to continue any health insurance it provides to employees during the period of leave, except as otherwise provided by law and regulations, and prohibits any collective bargaining agreement from reducing this benefit (29 USC §§ 2614(c)(1), 2562(b); 29 CFR § 825.209). Generally, upon return from FMLA leave, the employee must be restored to the same position he or she held prior to the absence, or one equivalent to it (see 29 USC § 2614(a)(1); 29 CFR § 825.214(a)).

The law allows employers to designate periods of paid leave as FMLA leave if employees are properly informed (see 29 USC § 2612(d)(2); 29 CFR § 825.208(b), (c)).

Because employers are prohibited from reducing the rights granted by this law (see 29 USC § 2652(b)), a school district should consult with its school attorney to ensure that its leave policies meet the law's requirements.

School districts should also afford the appropriate employee organization the opportunity to negotiate over specific issues relating to FMLA leave, such as substitution of paid leave for FMLA leave and procedures for applying for FMLA leave. Although FMLA prohibits the implementation of leave benefits that would be less than those mandated by FMLA, any proposal regarding FMLA leave, such as procedures that are not mandated by the statute or its regulations, must be negotiated (see *Rome Hospital*, 27 PERB ¶ 4575 (1994)), even if it duplicates the benefits promised by statute (*City of Cohoes*, 31 PERB ¶ 3020 (1998), *aff'd*, *Uniform Firefighters of Cohoes, Local 2562 v. Cuevas*, 276 A.D.2d 184 (3d Dep't 2000), *appeal denied*, 96 N.Y.2d 711 (2001)).

For more information on FMLA, see **10:84–92**.

9:30. Are noninstructional employees of school districts entitled to military leaves of absence?

Yes. In fact, under federal and state law, *all* public employees (not just noninstructional employees) who are required to perform "ordered" military duty are entitled to take a leave of absence from work for the duration of their military duty (38 USC § 4311(a); Mil. Law §§ 242(2), 243(1)(a),(2)(a), (19); see also Opn. Att'y Gen. F90-13). Military leave is a mandatory subject of bargaining (*City of Albany*, 7 PERB ¶ 3078 (1974), *aff'd*, 48 A.D.2d 998 (3d Dep't), *aff'd*, 38 N.Y.2d 778 (1975)), even if the proposal duplicates the benefits provided by statute (*City of Cohoes*, 31 PERB ¶ 3020 (1998), *aff'd*, *Uniform Firefighters of Cohoes, Local 2562 v. Cuevas*, 276 A.D.2d 184 (3d Dep't 2000), *appeal denied*, 96 N.Y.2d 711 (2001)).

Under state law, an employee absent from regular duties at a school district because of ordered military duty is entitled to be paid his or her usual pay for 30 calendar days, or 22 working days, whichever is greater, per calendar year and in any one continuous period of such absence (Mil. Law § 242(5); see also Opn. State Comp. 91-40). All such service, even if beyond the period of mandated paid leave, is to be treated as regular service with the school district and, as such, is counted as time served towards completion of a probationary period (Mil. Law § 243(5), (9)). In addition, employees on military leave may not suffer any loss of vacation, holiday, or any other right or privilege or be prejudiced regarding their employment status, including retention, reappointment, reemployment, reinstatement, transfer, or promotion (Mil. Law § 242(4), (6)).

A school board may, upon passage of board resolution, provide additional paid leave for school employees engaged in the performance of ordered military duty in excess of the paid leave mandated by state law. Such leave must be offered equally to all employees who are "similarly situated." However, to avoid a "gift of public funds" violation under Art. VIII, section 1 of the New York State Constitution, the board resolution providing for such additional paid leave must be approved prior to the time such leave is taken. When authorized in advance, such additional paid leave does not constitute a gift, but rather compensation for employment, the purpose of which is to "induce continued, faithful and competent service" (Opn. Att'y Gen I 90-57; see also Gen. Mun. Law § 92(1)).

Federal law (38 USC § 4301 *et seq.*) also grants specific employment rights to public employees required to perform military service, including the right to reemployment provided the employee's ordered military service does not exceed five years (38 USC § 4312(a), (c)).

Termination and Discipline
of Noninstructional Employees

9:31. Are classified service employees entitled to due process protection prior to being terminated or disciplined?

Only certain employees in the classified service are entitled to such protection and may be terminated or disciplined only pursuant to the provisions of section 75 of the Civil Service Law. All others may be disciplined or discharged without a hearing for any legal, nondiscriminatory reason, not made in bad faith (see *Tyson v. Hess*, 109 A.D.2d 1068 (4th Dep't), *aff'd*, 66 N.Y.2d 943 (1985); see also **9:23**). However, a collective bargaining agreement may afford employees alternative disciplinary protections and procedures (*Auburn Police Local v. Helsby*, 62 A.D.2d 12 (1978), *aff'd*, 46 N.Y.2d 1034 (1979); see **9:40–41**).

The following types of classified service employees are entitled to protection under section 75 of the Civil Service Law:

Persons holding a position by permanent appointment (as opposed to provisional or temporary appointment) in the competitive class (§ 75(1)(a)).

- Honorably discharged or honorably released veterans and exempt volunteer firefighters (as defined in the General Municipal Law) employed permanently in the classified service, regardless of the employee's jurisdictional classification, except for persons holding the positions of private secretary, cashier, or deputy of any official or department (§ 75(1)(b); see *Matter of Wamsley v. E. Ramapo CSD Bd. of Educ.*, 281 A.D.2d 633 (2d Dep't 2001)).

- Employees holding positions in the noncompetitive class who have completed at least five years of continuous service in that class, provided the employee's position has not been designated as confidential or policy-making by the local civil service agency (§ 75(1)(c); *Matter of Wamsley*).

9:32. Is there any time limit for bringing disciplinary charges against an employee under section 75?

Yes. No removal or disciplinary proceeding may be commenced more than 18 months after the occurrence of the misconduct or incompetency alleged in the charge. However, this limitation does not apply where the charges would, if proved in the appropriate court, constitute a crime (§ 75(4); see *Matter of Wojewodzic v. O'Neill*, 295 A.D.2d 670 (3d Dep't 2002)).

9:33. Are there any special procedures a district must observe when investigating whether disciplinary charges should be brought up against a noninstructional employee covered by section 75?

Yes. A noninstructional employee with section 75 protection is entitled to union representation when questioned, if it appears that the employee may be the subject of disciplinary action. The affected employee must be notified in advance, in writing, of that right. The employee is entitled to a reasonable period of time to obtain a representative. If the employee is unable to obtain a representative within a reasonable period of time, the district has the right to then question the employee without representation (§ 75(2)).

9:34. How is a noninstructional employee covered by section 75 terminated or disciplined?

Persons entitled to protection under section 75 of the Civil Service Law (i.e., persons holding the types of positions identified in **9:31**) have the right to notice of any charges against them and a hearing prior to discipline (§ 75(1)). They also are entitled to at least eight days to respond to the charges in writing (§ 75(2)).

At the hearing, the employee may be represented by counsel or by a representative of a recognized or certified employee organization and may present witnesses on his or her behalf. The burden of proving incompetency or misconduct by the employee is on the district (§ 75(2)). A finding of guilt must be supported by "substantial evidence" (*Cassilano v. Steisel*, 64 N.Y.2d 674 (1984)) which consists of proof that is "[m]ore than seeming or imaginary [but] less than a preponderance of the evidence, overwhelming evidence or evidence beyond a reasonable doubt" (*People ex rel. Vega v. Smith*, 66 N.Y. 2d 130 (1985), and a reasonable mind may accept as adequate to support a conclusion or ultimate fact" (*Matter of WEOK Broadcasting v. Planning Bd. of the Town of Lloyd*, 79 N.Y.2d 373 (1992)).

The required hearing is conducted by the school board or a designated hearing officer who makes a recommendation to the school board as to the guilt or innocence of the person against whom the charges are lodged and as to the penalty, if any (§ 75(2)). If the school board decides to designate a hearing officer, the board must make that designation in writing (§ 75(2)). The board's failure to make such a designation may leave it without jurisdiction to discipline the employee if someone other than the board itself conducts a hearing or another person who has the power to remove the employee against whom the charges are preferred. In one case where a board failed to officially designate the hearing officer who conducted the hearing, an appellate court annulled the hearing officer's determination and directed the district to reinstate the employee with back pay (*Matter of Payton v. Buffalo City Sch. Dist.*, 299 A.D.2d 825 (4th Dep't 2002); see also *Matter of Wiggins v. Bd. of Educ. of City of N.Y.*, 60 N.Y.2d 385, 387 (1983), *remanded*, 112 A.D.2d 1043 (2d Dep't 1985)).

The hearing officer or the school board making the final determination of guilt or innocence and setting the penalty must be unbiased. They should have no personal knowledge of the events surrounding the charge and should not have brought or prosecuted the charges (see *Memmelaar v. Straub*, 181 A.D.2d 980 (3d Dep't 1992)). A departure from this standard violates the employee's right to due process.

A school administrator may not make an agreement to withhold from the commissioner of education or law enforcement authorities the fact that an allegation of child abuse in an educational setting has been made against a district employee in exchange for a resignation or voluntary suspension. Any such agreement is subject to both criminal and civil penalties (Educ. Law § 1133(1); see **7:16, 8:191**).

9:35. Does a change in an employee's work assignment constitute discipline that requires a section 75 hearing?

It may, depending on the facts and circumstances. In one case, where a bus driver worked a second job that made her unavailable for her regularly assigned bus route, the district unilaterally demoted her from a permanent position of "assigned driver" (which entitled her to enhanced benefits) to that of an "unassigned driver." According to an appellate court, the reassignment resulted in a diminution of benefits and, therefore, was a form of demotion or discipline that required compliance with section 75, even though the district provided the driver the new assignment as an accommodation designed to enable her to work both jobs (*Matter of Bailey v. Susquehanna Valley CSD. Bd. of Educ.*, 276 A.D.2d 963 (3d Dep't 2000)).

In a different case, due to concerns about alleged misconduct by a bus driver, a district decided not to reassign him to an additional bus run that was not part of his regular duties, but would have enabled him to earn additional income. The same appellate court that decided the *Matter of Bailey* case determined that this did not constitute discipline. Even though the district's decision to deprive the driver of the additional assignment was based on the driver's alleged misconduct, the district's action was not disciplinary in nature because the driver did not have a protected property interest in the additional bus run, and the driver "did not suffer a reduction in title, grade, regular annual salary or benefits" (*Matter of Nydam v. Franklin CSD*, 303 A.D.2d 828 (3d Dep't 2003)).

9:36. Does the placement of a critical letter in the file of a noninstructional employee who is entitled to section 75 protection constitute discipline that would require a hearing as described in 9:34?

No. Civil Service Law section 75 does not insulate noninstructional school district personnel from all written critical comments from their supervisors. Documents such as critical administrative evaluations or admonitions that are intended to warn or instruct a given employee may be placed in an employee's file without resort to a formal hearing (*Tomaka v. Evans-Brant CSD*, 107 A.D.2d 1078 (4th Dep't), *aff'd*, 65 N.Y.2d 1048 (1985); see *CSEA v. Southhold UFSD*, 204 A.D.2d 445 (2d Dep't 1994)).

However, a letter that addresses more serious allegations may be treated as a disciplinary reprimand, requiring a hearing conducted under section 75. In deciding whether a particular written communication constitutes a reprimand that will require a hearing, no single factor will be determinative. A court will likely consider a number of factors, including the identity of the author, the subject matter of the document, the tenor of the document, the employer's characterization of the document, and whether the document's focus is on punishment or warning and instruction (*CSEA*).

9:37. May an employee facing discipline under section 75 be suspended without pay pending the outcome of the hearing?

Yes. The Civil Service Law allows for the suspension without pay of an employee for up to 30 days pending the hearing and determination of charges (§ 75(3)). If the employee is acquitted at the hearing or later reinstated after appeal to the local civil service agency or to the courts (see **9:39**), that employee is entitled to back pay for the period during which he or she was off the payroll, less the amount of any unemployment benefits he or she may have received during such period (§§ 75(3), 76(3), 77; see *Matter of CSEA, Local 1000, AFSCME, AFL-CIO v. Brookhaven-Comsewogue UFSD*, 87 N.Y.2d 868 (1995)).

9:38. What penalty or punishment may be imposed after a section 75 hearing?

The penalty or punishment imposed after a section 75 hearing may consist of: (1) a reprimand; (2) a fine not to exceed $100 to be deducted from the employee's wages; (3) suspension without pay for a period not exceeding two months; (4) demotion in grade and title; or (5) dismissal. Any time period during which an employee was suspended without pay prior to the outcome of the hearing (see **9:37**) may become part of the penalty (§ 75(3)).

9:39. May an employee who has been disciplined under section 75 file an appeal?

Yes. An employee may appeal any penalty to the local civil service agency or to the courts except an official reprimand that is accompanied by a remittance of compensation lost during suspension. The commissioner of education has no jurisdiction over this type of case (*Appeal of McGregor*, 35 Educ. Dep't Rep. 363 (1996)).

If the employee chooses to appeal to the local civil service agency, the agency's decision is final and conclusive and not subject to further review in any court (§ 76(3)). However, even though the Civil Service Law proscribes judicial review of a local agency's decision, the courts still have the power and the duty to review the decision to determine if it was unconstitutional, illegal or outside the agency's jurisdiction (*New York City Dep't of Envtl. Protection v. New York City Civil Serv. Comm'n*, 78 N.Y.2d 318 (1991)).

An employee wishing to appeal his or her discipline or discharge to the courts in an Article 78 proceeding must serve a notice of claim upon the school district within three months of the imposition of the discipline (*Harder v. Board of Educ., Binghamton City Sch. Dist.*, 188 A.D.2d 783 (3d Dep't 1992), citing Educ. Law § 3813(1)). According to some appellate courts, the four-month statute of limitations generally applicable to Article 78 proceedings is extended 30 days when a notice of claim is filed under Education Law § 3813(1) (see *Perlin v. South Orangetown CSD*, 216 A.D.2d 397 (2d Dep't), *appeal dismissed*, 86 N.Y.2d 886 (1995)).

The courts will review the findings of fact from a hearing by determining whether there is "substantial evidence" to support the charges (*Cassilano v.*

Steisel, 64 N.Y.2d 674 (1984); see **9:34** for a definition of substantial evidence).

The courts may also review the disciplinary penalty imposed, but the penalty may not be set aside unless it is "so disproportionate to the offense, in the light of all the circumstances, as to be shocking to one's sense of fairness" (*Pell v. Board of Educ.*, 34 N.Y.2d 222 (1974); see also *Scahill v. Greece* CSD, 2 N.Y.3d 754 (2004); *Winters v. Bd. of Educ.*, 99 N.Y.2d 549 (2002); *Will v. Frontier CSD Bd. of Educ.*, 97 N.Y.2d 690 (2002)).

9:40. Is Civil Service Law section 75 the only source of due process protection available to employees in the classified service?

No. While school districts must comply with the procedures specified in this section to discipline or discharge employees covered by the law, they may also collectively negotiate alternative disciplinary procedures with the union representing employees in recognized bargaining units (see *Barrera v. Frontier CSD*, 249 A.D.2d 927 (4th Dep't 1998)). If separate contractual procedures exist, they should be consulted prior to the discipline of any employee in the bargaining unit.

9:41. What due process protection is available to noninstructional employees not covered by section 75?

Such employees may have job protections under a collective bargaining agreement. Employees who do not have section 75 or collective bargaining agreement protections are "at will" employees, meaning that they can be discharged without cause and without a hearing. Simply stated, such employees can be disciplined or discharged for any reason, except an illegal reason (e.g., because of race, religion, sex, disability) (see *Tyson v. Hess*, 109 A.D.2d 1068 (4th Dep't), *aff'd*, 66 N.Y.2d 943 (1985); see also **9:23**).

9:42. Are noninstructional employees entitled to a name-clearing hearing?

Any public employee, regardless of whether the employee is entitled to the protection of Civil Service Law section 75, is entitled to a hearing to challenge his or her dismissal if the alleged reason for the dismissal puts the employee's good name, reputation, honor, or integrity in question (*Board of Regents v. Roth*, 408 U.S. 564 (1972); see *Wisconsin v. Constantineau*, 400 U.S. 433 (1971); see, e.g., *Brandt v. BOCES III, Suffolk County*, 820 F.2d 41 (2d Cir. 1987), *appeal after remand, Brandt v. Board of Co-op. Educ. Servs.*, 845 F.3d 416 (2d Cir. 1988)) (teacher charged with engaging in sexual conduct with autistic children); see also *Patterson v. City of Utica*, 307 F.3d 322 (2d Cir. 2004)). Such a hearing is referred to as a "name-clearing" hearing (see *Lentlie v. Egan*, 61 N.Y.2d 874 (1984)).

The right to a name-clearing hearing is available to both tenured and nontenured employees (*Goetz v. Windsor CSD*, 698 F.2d 606 (2d Cir. 1983), *remanded*, 593 F.Supp. 526 (N.D.N.Y. 1984); *Lutwin v. Alleyne*, 86 A.D.2d 670 (2d Dep't 1982), *modified on other grounds*, 58 N.Y.2d 889 (1983); *Salvatore v. Nasser*, 81 A.D.2d 1012 (4th Dep't 1981)).

In order to be entitled to a name-clearing hearing, the employee must establish that the stigmatizing statements made by the public employer have been publicly disclosed (*Bishop v. Wood*, 426 U.S. 341 (1976); *Patterson; Lentlie*). The disclosure requirement can be satisfied where the stigmatizing charges are placed in the discharged employee's personnel file and are likely to be disclosed to prospective employers (*Brandt; Donato v. Plainview-Old Bethpage CSD*, 96 F.3d 623 (2d Cir. 1996), *cert. denied*, 519 U.S. 1150, *remanded*, 985 F.Supp. 316 (E.D.N.Y. 1997); see also *Matter of Swinton v. Safir*, 93 N.Y.2d 758 (1999))).

Allegations of professional incompetence will support a right to a name-clearing hearing only when they "stigmatize" and denigrate the employee's competence as a professional and impugn his or her reputation to the point of significantly hampering the employee's continued ability to practice his or her profession (*Board of Regents; Donato*). If a name-clearing hearing is unlikely to remedy any ill effects caused by the employer's stigmatizing actions, a terminated employee may be able to recover monetary damages (*Patterson*).

9:43. What is the procedure in a name-clearing hearing?

The right to a meaningful opportunity to refute charges in a name-clearing hearing does not require a full, formal proceeding. However, a school district must offer the employee notice of the charges and a fair hearing to refute the charge before school district officials, which includes the right to counsel, to call witnesses on the employee's behalf, and to confront and cross examine witnesses supporting the allegations (*Board of Regents v. Roth*, 408 U.S. 564 (1972); *Donato v. Plainview-Old Bethpage CSD*, 96 F.3d 623 (2d Cir. 1996), *cert. denied*, 519 U.S. 1150, *remanded*, 985 F.Supp. 316 (E.D.N.Y. 1997), see also *Goldberg v. Kelly*, 397 U.S. 254, 266–71 (1970)).

At the hearing, the employee has the burden of proving that the charges are false (*Marzullo v. Suffolk County*, 97 A.D.2d 789 (2d Dep't 1983)).

Following the hearing, the employer need not rehire the employee even if the employee can prove the inaccuracy of the stigmatizing allegations. If the charges are proven false, however, the employer may be liable to the employee for damages (*Donato*).

9:44. What is the so-called "whistle-blower law"?

Section 75-b of the Civil Service Law, the so-called "whistle-blower law," prohibits public employers, including a school district, from taking retaliatory personnel action against an employee who discloses to a governmental body information concerning either a violation of law, rule, or regulation, which creates a substantial and specific danger to the public health or safety, or which the employee reasonably believes to be true and reasonably believes constitutes an improper governmental action (§ 75-b(2)(a)).

If disciplinary action is brought under an applicable statute (such as section 75 of the Civil Service Law) or under a collective bargaining agreement against an employee who reveals such information, the employee may assert a defense based on this statute in the disciplinary proceedings, which must be addressed by the hearing officer or arbitrator (§ 75-b(3)). Employees who do not have the right to such procedures may instead bring an action in court within one year after the alleged retaliatory action using the procedures set forth in section 740 of the Labor Law (§ 75-b(3)(c); see *Hanley v. New York State Executive Dep't, Div. for Youth*, 182 A.D.2d 317 (3d Dep't 1992); see also *Dobson v. Loos*, 277 A.D.2d 1013 (4th Dep't 2000)).

The protection afforded by the "whistleblower" law is not available where the employer has "a separate and independent basis" for alleged adverse actions taken against the employee (See *Matter of Brey v. Bd. of Educ.*, 245 A.D.2d 613 (3d Dep't 1997)).

Abolition of Noninstructional Positions

9:45. May a school board abolish a noninstructional position?

Yes. School boards may abolish noninstructional positions for reasons of economy, consolidation, abolition of functions, or curtailment of activities (§ 80(1); see *Aldazabal v. Carey*, 44 N.Y.2d 787 (1978); *Della Vecchia v. Town of North Hempstead*, 207 A.D.2d 484 (2d Dep't 1994), *appeal denied*, 84 N.Y.2d 812, 1018 (1995)).

School boards must act in good faith when such positions are abolished. These positions may not be abolished to circumvent the Civil Service Law (*Aldazabal*; *James v. Broadnax*, 182 A.D.2d 887 (3d Dep't 1992)). The burden of proving that a position was abolished in bad faith rests with the employee, who must show that the employer had no bona fide reason for eliminating the position, achieved no costs savings, hired someone else as a replacement, or that the abolition was otherwise motivated by bad faith (*Matter of Mucci v. Binghamton*, 245 A.D.2d 678 (3d Dep't 1997), *appeal dismissed*, 91 N.Y.2d 921, *appeal denied*, 92 N.Y.2d 802 (1998)).

Generally, noninstructional employees' positions are abolished in inverse order of original permanent appointment in the classified civil service (§ 80(1)). Employees who are blind, veterans, or spouses of disabled veterans are given preference in layoff situations (§ 85(7)).

In a layoff situation, competitive class employees may have an opportunity to "bump" other less senior employees in the same direct line of promotion or "retreat" back to a position the employee last served on a permanent basis (§ 80(6)).

After a layoff has occurred, it is the superintendent's responsibility to provide the name, title or position, date of appointment, and the date of and reason for the layoff to the local civil service agency. Laid-off or "excessed" noninstructional employees are placed on a preferred list and given preference over others in reinstatement to positions within their jurisdictional class (i.e., competitive, noncompetitive, labor, and exempt classes; see 9:6). Such excessed employees remain on the preferred list for four years (§ 81(1)).

9:46. Is an employee covered by section 75 entitled to notice and a hearing before his or her position is abolished?

As a general rule, no. A school district can lay off an employee entitled to the protection of section 75 without giving that employee notice and a hearing. However, if a school district seeks to abolish a single employee's position and there is no indication that the employer acted for reasons of economy or efficiency but rather it is alleged that the district targeted the employee for termination to avoid the requirements of section 75, the district has an obligation under the due process clause of the United States Constitution to provide the employee a hearing prior to removing the employee from his or her position, provided the employee requests such a hearing (*Dwyer v. Regan*, 777 F.2d 825 (2d Cir. 1985), *modified*, 793 F.2d 457 (2d Cir. 1986); see also *Cifarelli v. Village of Babylon*, 93 F.3d 47 (2d Cir. 1996)). Such a hearing must be held before a neutral fact finder, not the employer (*Dwyer*). The burden is on the employee to prove that the abolition was done in bad faith (*Bianco v. Pitts*, 200 A.D.2d 741 (2d Dep't 1994); see *Cifarelli*).

9:47. Where may additional information about civil service matters affecting schools be obtained?

Contact the city or county civil service commission or personnel officer in the city or county in which your school district is located. A complete listing of all local civil service agencies, as well as other technical assistance about the Civil Service Law, is available through the New York

State Department of Civil Service Web site at http://www.cs.state.ny.us. Click on "Programs and Services" and then "Municipal Service."

Security Guards

9:48. Is a school district required to comply with the requirements of the Security Guard Act of 1992?

Yes. If a school district employs at least one security guard, then the district is subject to the Security Guard Act of 1992 (Gen. Bus. Law § 89-f(5), (7)). Under section 89-o of the General Business Law, the secretary of state is empowered to adopt rules and regulations implementing the provisions of the act.

Any security guard employed by a school district must be registered by the Department of State (Gen. Bus. Law § 89-g(1)(b); see § 89-h). Registration for a security guard is effective for two years (Gen. Bus. Law § 89-m(1)).

A district employing a security guard must provide proof of self-insurance or liability insurance coverage to the Department of State. The insurance must cover death, personal injury, false arrest, false imprisonment, malicious prosecution, libel, slander, and violation of the right of privacy in the amount of $100,000 per occurrence and $300,000 in the aggregate (Gen. Bus. Law § 89-g(6)).

9:49. Whom should a school district contact for additional information or with questions regarding the Security Guard Act of 1992?

Questions about the Security Guard Act of 1992 should be directed to the Department of State at 518-474-4429. Information can also be found through the Department of State's Web site at http://www.dos.state.ny.us.

10. Employee Relations

Contracts of Employment

10:1. What is an individual contract of employment?

An *individual contract of employment* is an agreement, usually in writing, that contains a set of promises between an employer and an employee. Contracts of employment typically set forth terms of employment, duties of the position, salary, and employment benefits such as health insurance, retirement benefits, paid vacation and sick leave.

10:2. How are individual contracts of employment formed?

Following a period of negotiation during which an agreement is reached, a contract usually is executed or formed when both parties sign the written document. Although the school board is the entity that appoints all district personnel, except in New York City where the chancellor enjoys certain appointment authority (see, for example, Educ. Law §§ 1604(8), 1709(16), 1950(4)(e), 2503(5), 2509(3), 2554(2), 2573(3), 2590-g(2), 2590-h(17), (41); see also **9:10**), a common practice in many districts is for the board to approve the contract by resolution and to specify in that resolution the individual authorized to sign the contract on the board's behalf, such as the board president or the superintendent.

10:3. What is the difference between an individual contract of employment and a collective bargaining agreement?

An *individual contract of employment* is an agreement between the school district and an individual employee. A *collective bargaining agreement* is a contract between the school district, executed by the superintendent acting as the chief executive officer of the school district, and an employee organization (or union) that represents a group of employees included within a bargaining unit (see § 201(12); **10:22**).

Employees who are covered by the terms of a collective bargaining agreement are appointed to their positions by resolution of the board, and the agreement serves to describe the terms and conditions of that employment. However, employees covered by an individual contract of

---

All statutory references in this chapter are to the New York State Civil Service Law unless noted otherwise. The acronym PERB used throughout this chapter refers to the New York State Public Employment Relations Board. The Taylor Law (§§ 200–214) regulates the employee relations of public employers and employees in New York State, including school districts.

employment derive the right to the appointment to their positions from the contract itself.

Board policies, as well as employee manuals or handbooks, may give employees who are not covered by an individual contract of employment or a collective bargaining agreement protections and assurances regarding their terms and conditions of employment, including rights regarding discipline and discharge. These policies, manuals, and handbooks may also supplement the benefits or rights of employees covered by individual contracts of employment or collective bargaining agreements. Such rights may be enforceable as contracts or create other grounds for challenging an employment decision in court (see *Weiner v. McGraw-Hill, Inc.*, 57 N.Y.2d 458 (1982)). However, these rights may be limited or extinguished through the use of a disclaimer (*Lobosco v. NYNEX*, 96 N.Y.2d 312 (2001)). Districts should exercise care and consult with their school attorneys to avoid unintentionally creating such rights.

10:4. What school employees typically have individual contracts of employment?

Most school district employees do not have individual contracts of employment with the district but are covered by a collective bargaining agreement. However, some employees, such as the superintendent of schools, have an individual employment contract specifying their terms and conditions of employment (see **7:22–24**). Employees designated as either "managerial" or "confidential" under the Taylor Law are precluded from being members of a bargaining unit and therefore are not covered by a collective bargaining agreement (see §§ 201(7)(a), 202, 203, 214; see **10:39–41**).

10:5. What powers do school boards have in connection with collective bargaining agreements?

Under the Taylor Law, a school board's role regarding collective bargaining agreements is limited. It is the superintendent, as chief executive officer of the school district (§ 201(10)), and not the board, as the district's legislative body, who is technically responsible for negotiating and executing collective bargaining agreements (§ 201(12)). However, as a practical matter, given the employment relationship between the board and the superintendent (a relationship that does not exist between most chief executives and legislative bodies), school boards frequently play an active role in the negotiations process.

In addition, the school board also plays two distinct roles at the conclusion of the negotiations process. First, the board may ratify a tentative agreement reached by the district and the union before execution of the agreement (provided the right has been reserved to the board by the district's negotiator) (*Town of Dresden*, 17 PERB ¶ 3096 (1984)). Second, a board has the right to legislatively approve certain provisions of the executed agreement (§§ 201(12), 204-a(1); *Buffalo City Sch. Dist.*, 24 PERB ¶ 3033 (1991), *aff'd*, 191 A.D.2d 985 (4th Dep't 1993), *appeal dismissed*, 82 N.Y.2d 656 (1993)).

In a case where a board adopted a resolution directing its superintendent to execute an agreement, as ordered by PERB, the resolution constituted legislative approval, notwithstanding a statement to the contrary (*Board of Educ. for the City School Dist. of the City of Buffalo v. Buffalo Teachers Federation, Inc.*, 89 N.Y.2d 370 (1996); see **10:11**).

10:6. What is the difference between a school board's contract ratification and legislative approval powers?

Legislative approval and contract ratification are two related concepts that are often confused (*City of Saratoga Springs*, 20 PERB ¶ 3031 (1987)).

Contract ratification is a voluntary process under which a tentative agreement is submitted to a school board and/or union membership for a vote to accept or reject the tentative agreement. School boards do not have an inherent or automatic right of ratification (see *Town of Dresden*, 17 PERB ¶ 3091 (1984)). The right of ratification is created by agreement or through understanding between the parties' negotiators. It is not a right that a school board or any other party may unilaterally reserve to itself (see, for example, *Town of Dresden*; *Falconer CSD*, 6 PERB ¶ 3029 (1973); *Jamestown City Sch. Dist.*, 6 PERB ¶ 3075 (1973)). It may be waived by a board's failure to make a ratification decision (*Utica City Sch. Dist.*, 27 PERB ¶ 3023 (1994); *Jamesville-DeWitt CSD*, 22 PERB ¶ 3048 (1989); see **10:9**).

Legislative approval is a right and duty of the board created by statute (§§ 201(12), 204-a(1)). Unlike the negotiated right of ratification, which allows the board to approve or reject the entire tentative agreement, the statutory right of legislative approval only allows the board to act on those contract provisions that require an amendment of board policy or additional funding (§ 204-a(1)). As a general rule, those provisions of an executed agreement do not become binding on the school district until the board has given its approval (§ 201(12)). However, a school board's prior actions may result in a waiver of the right of legislative approval (see **10:11**).

Legislative approval of a multi-year agreement may not be conditioned upon or subject to annual appropriations. Once legislative approval has been given, the school district is bound by the agreement for its full, specified term (*Association of Surrogates & Supreme Court Reporters v. State of New York*, 78 N.Y.2d 143 (1991)).

10:7. What is involved in the ratification process?

The ratification process involves at least the following elements: First, the ratifying body (that is, the school board or the union membership) must be aware that negotiations have been completed and that its negotiators have reached an agreement subject only to ratification. Second, while the members of the ratifying body may differ on reasons for ratifying or rejecting the agreement, the agreement must be ratified or rejected as a whole and not on a piecemeal basis. Third, the negotiators must affirmatively support ratification, unless they have made the other party aware of their opposition to the tentative agreement. Finally, a decision to ratify must be clearly and unequivocally made and communicated (*Jamesville-DeWitt CSD*, 22 PERB ¶ 3048 (1989); see *Copiague UFSD*, 23 PERB ¶ 3046 (1990)).

10:8. What happens if district negotiators fail to reserve at the bargaining table the school board's right to ratify a negotiated agreement?

A school board has no automatic or inherent right to ratify a negotiated agreement, although it is common for district and employee organization negotiators to agree to require ratification by the school board and/or union membership in the ground rules established for negotiation of a collective bargaining agreement or within the collective bargaining agreement itself (see **10:5, 10:50**).

According to PERB, it is an improper practice for either a school board or an employee organization to attempt to reject an agreement after their respective negotiator has given assent, unless the parties have agreed that the board and/or union membership have reserved the right to ratify or reject the terms of a tentative agreement (see *Town of Greece*, 32 PERB ¶ 3059 (1999), *aff'd*, 280 A.D.2d 967 (4th Dep't 2001); *Town of Dresden*, 17 PERB ¶ 3096 (1984); *Falconer CSD*, 6 PERB ¶ 3029 (1973)).

10:9. Can a school board lose its properly reserved right to ratify an agreement?

Yes. The right of a school board to ratify an agreement, even though properly reserved (see **10:6**), can nonetheless be lost by the conduct of the district's negotiators. For example, all members of the district's negotiating team have a duty to support and affirmatively seek ratification of a tentative agreement, unless a team member has explicitly given advance notice to the union that he or she does not intend to support it (*Copiague UFSD*, 23 PERB ¶ 3046 (1990)). This is considered an indication of good faith at the bargaining table. Failure to perform this duty, which may be breached simply by silence on the part of a negotiator in the face of board opposition to the tentative agreement or by neutrality during the ratification process (see *Copiague UFSD*), will result in the loss of an employer's right to ratify the agreement (*City of Saratoga Springs*, 20 PERB ¶ 3031 (1987)).

The right to ratify an agreement also may be lost if the negotiators fail to provide the school board with the agreement (see *Town of Greece*, 32 PERB ¶ 3059 (1999), *aff'd*, 280 A.D.2d 967 (4th Dep't 2001)). In addition, a school board can lose its right to ratify an agreement if it fails to conduct a ratification vote "with reasonable expedition," which is also a violation of the district's duty to negotiate in good faith (*Utica City Sch. Dist.*, 27 PERB ¶ 3023 (1994)).

10:10. What happens if a school board loses or otherwise waives its right to ratify an agreement?

If PERB finds a waiver of the right to ratify, then it can direct a district to execute the agreement (*Utica City Sch. Dist.*, 27 PERB ¶ 3023 (1994); see **10:18–21** in regard to the powers and duties of PERB). For example, when a board loses its right of ratification because a negotiator improperly fails to affirmatively support ratification of an agreement (see **10:9**), the school superintendent can be required to execute that agreement. This occurred in a case where one of the district's negotiators distributed material to certain members of the school board in opposition to a tentatively reached agreement on the settlement of a new contract. PERB considered this evidence of failure to negotiate in good faith, which is an improper practice (see **10:70**), and directed the superintendent to execute the agreement without the board's ratification (*Buffalo City Sch. Dist.*, 24 PERB ¶ 3033 (1991), *aff'd*, 191 A.D.2d 985 (4th Dep't 1993), *appeal denied*, 82 N.Y.2d 656 (1993)).

10:11. Can a school board lose its statutory right to legislatively approve a contract?

Yes. For example, in one case, PERB determined that a school board had exercised its right of legislative approval when all the members of the board served on the negotiating team that came to an agreement with the union (*Sylvan-Verona Beach Common Sch. Dist.*, 15 PERB ¶ 3067 (1982), *appeal dismissed*, 16 PERB ¶ 7004 (Sup. Ct. Oneida County), *aff'd*, 16 PERB ¶ 7029 (4th Dep't 1983)). In another case, the state Court of Appeals ruled that a school board that had lost its right to ratify a contract because one of its negotiators failed to support ratification, did not have a separate right to legislatively approve the funding provisions of the contract (*Board of Educ. for the City Sch. Dist. of the City of Buffalo v. Buffalo Teachers Fed'n*, 89 N.Y.2d 370 (1996), *rehearing denied*, 89 N.Y.2d 983 (1997); see **10:6** for a discussion on the difference between ratification and legislative approval of a contract).

10:12. Can changes be made in the terms of a contract of employment or a collective bargaining agreement during the period of the contract or agreement?

Generally, the parties to a contract of employment or a collective bargaining agreement must adhere to all the specifications contained therein for the duration of the contract or agreement, unless the parties agree mutually to changes in such terms (see **10:49**). A board may change the terms of a contract of employment or a collective bargaining agreement only with the consent of the employee or the employee organization, respectively, that is, by renegotiating the terms of the contract or agreement (see generally, *Town of Greece*, 32 PERB ¶ 3059 (1999), *aff'd*, 280 A.D.2d 967 (4th Dep't 2001)).

Additionally, all the terms of an expired collective bargaining agreement, except those that sunset automatically, must be continued until a new agreement is negotiated pursuant to the *Triborough* Amendment to the Taylor Law (§ 209-a(1)(e); see **10:65**).

The Taylor Law

10:13. What is the Taylor Law?

The Taylor Law, officially entitled the Public Employees' Fair Employment Act, is codified as article 14 of the Civil Service Law. Enacted in 1967, the Taylor Law governs labor relations between public employers and public employees in New York State. The law is named after Prof. George W. Taylor of the University of Pennsylvania, chairman of Gov. Nelson Rockefeller's Committee on Public Employee Relations (also known as the Taylor Committee), whose report and recommendations formed the basis for the law. A copy of this report is appended to Chapter 1 of *Public Sector Labor and Employment Law*, 2nd ed., published by the New York State Bar Association (1998).

The Taylor Law's purpose is to promote harmonious and cooperative labor relations in the public sector and to avoid strikes (§ 200; *City of Newburgh v. Newman*, 69 N.Y.2d 166 (1987)).

10:14. What are the rights of a school district as a public employer under the Taylor Law?

As a public employer, a school district has the right to recognize (or withhold recognition of) employee organizations for the purpose of negotiating collectively and the right to enter into collective bargaining agreements (§§ 204(1), 207(3); *Town of Clay v. Helsby*, 45 A.D.2d 292 (4th Dep't 1974); *appeal after remand*, 51 A.D.2d 200 (4th Dep't 1976); see **10:27**).

In addition, while a school district is required to negotiate collectively with a certified or recognized employee organization (see **10:44, 10:46**), the district has the right to insist that the employee organization participate in good faith bargaining with the district (§§ 204(2), (3); 209-a(2)(b)). Although a school district must engage in negotiations over mandatory subjects of bargaining, negotiations cannot be conditioned on negotiating nonmandatory permissive subjects (*Board of Educ. of the City Sch. Dist. of the City of New York v. PERB*, 75 N.Y.2d 660 (1990)).

A district also has the right to negotiate free from strike activities, such as concerted stoppage of work or slowdown, or threats of strikes, and the right and the obligation to invoke the Taylor Law's procedures concerning strikes if a strike or strike activity occurs (§§ 201(9), 210; see **10:72, 10:74–76**).

10:15. What rights are given to public employees under the Taylor Law?

Public employees are guaranteed the rights of self-organization and representation for collective negotiations (§§ 202, 203). *Self-organization rights* enable public employees to join or refrain from joining unions (referred to in the Taylor Law as "employee organizations") of their choice (§ 202). *Representation rights* enable employees to designate an employee organization as their representative in collective negotiations with their public employer over terms and conditions of employment, and in the administration of grievances arising from their negotiated agreements (§ 203).

The rights given to employees under the Taylor Law do not extend to all persons employed by a public employer. Classes of employees to whom the law does not extend include managerial or confidential employees (§ 201(7)(a)) or to "casual" employees (*BOCES III, Suffolk County*, 15 PERB ¶ 3015, *aff'd, BOCES III Faculty Assoc. v. PERB*, 92 A.D.2d 937 (2d Dep't 1983)) and per diem substitute teachers who have not been given a reasonable assurance of continued employment by the district (§ 201(7)(d) and (f)) (see **10:25, 10:39**).

10:16. What penalties may be imposed on public employers that use state funds either to encourage or discourage employees from union organization?

Any employer, including a school district, that uses state funds for any of the prohibited purposes listed below is subject to a civil penalty ranging from $1,000 to $3,000, or three times the amount unlawfully expended, whichever is greater. These civil penalties may be imposed if state funds are used to:

- Train managers, supervisors, or other administrative personnel how to encourage or discourage union organization.
- Encourage or discourage any employee from participating in a union organizing drive.
- Pay attorneys, consultants, or others to encourage or discourage union organizational drives or employee participation in such drives.
- Hire or pay employees whose principal job is to engage in any of these activities.

In addition, employers found violating these provisions must maintain appropriately audited financial records, for a period of at least three years from the date of any such unlawful expenditures, sufficient to show that state funds were not thereafter used for any of the purposes prohibited by law. If requested, such financial records must be made available to the state entity that provided the funding and/or to the Attorney General within 10 business days.

The state Attorney General has the power to enjoin or restrain an employer from engaging in such activities (Lab. Law § 211-a).

10:17. Does the Taylor Law employee right to representation include the right to union representation during questioning by an employer?

Yes, if the employee reasonably believes that the investigatory interview may lead to discipline. According to PERB, "there is no clearer expression of participation in an employee organization than the request for union representation at an investigatory interview which may result in discipline, such as an employee's suspension, loss of pay or termination." To deny such representation constitutes an "improper practice" in violation of section 209-a(1)(a). (*New York City Transit Auth.*, 35 PERB ¶ 3029 (2002), *confirmed*, 196 Misc. 2d 526, 36 PERB ¶ 7009 (Sup. Ct. Kings County 2003). An employee's belief that an investigatory interview may lead to discipline will be deemed reasonable "if the interview is 'calculated to form the basis for taking discipline or other job-affecting actions against such employee because of past misconduct,' or incompetence" (*New York City Transit Auth.*, 36 PERB ¶ 3049 (2003)).

This right to representation, named a *Weingarten* right, after a 1975 U.S. Supreme Court decision in *National Labor Relations Board v. Weingarten* (420 U.S. 251), is codified in section 75 of the Civil Service Law and has long been invoked by school employees who enjoy section 75 job protections (see **9:31**). However, until PERB's ruling in *New York City*

Transit Auth., this right was not uniformly extended to unionized employees who did not have section 75 protections.

PERB has refused to extend *Weingarten* rights to staff asked to submit to a medical exam by their employer finding such an exam does not constitute an investigatory interview (*New York City Transit Auth.*).

10:18. Who administers the Taylor Law?

The Taylor Law is administered by the Public Employment Relations Board (PERB) (see § 205). The PERB Board consists of three members appointed by the governor and confirmed by the New York State Senate, one of whom serves as the chairperson of the board (§ 205(1)). In addition, PERB has a staff consisting of administrators, attorneys, administrative law judges (ALJs), mediators and fact finders (see § 205(4)(a), (5)(i)).

To help administer the Taylor Law, PERB employs ALJs to consider charges of improper practices by employee organizations or employers, to certify bargaining units, and to enforce other provisions of the Taylor Law (see § 205(4)(a); 4 NYCRR Part 212). PERB hears appeals (called "exceptions") from the decisions of ALJs (4 NYCRR Part 213).

10:19. What are PERB's powers and duties under the Taylor Law?

PERB's powers and duties include establishing bargaining units, certifying employee organizations as the exclusive representatives of such units, remedying improper practices by employers and employee organizations (including obtaining injunctions, when appropriate), administering some strike penalty provisions, presiding over hearings, assigning mediators and fact finders to help resolve negotiation impasses, conducting research, and establishing a staff to assist in all of these powers and duties (§§ 205(4), (5), 207, 209(3), 209-a, 210(3)).

PERB, however, generally has no authority to enforce a school district's collective bargaining agreement or to exercise jurisdiction over an alleged violation of such an agreement, unless an alleged contract violation would also constitute an improper practice (§ 205(5)(d); see also *Matter of Roma v. Ruffo*, 92 N.Y.2d 489 (1998)).

10:20. Does PERB have the authority to issue "declaratory" rulings?

Yes. PERB, however, has conferred this authority on its Director of Employment Practices and Representation who may issue such rulings when doing so "would be in the public interest," in furtherance of the policies fostered by the Taylor Law (4 NYCRR § 210.2(a)).

According to PERB, "[t]he purpose of a declaratory ruling proceeding is to provide a less adversarial means than an improper practice proceeding for resolving an existing justiciable issue between parties in two areas:

whether an employee, an employer or an employee organization is covered by the [law], or whether . . . a matter is a subject of mandatory negotiations. . . ." (*Town of Henrietta*, 25 PERB ¶ 6501 (1992)).

There must be a genuine and not merely hypothetical dispute between the parties concerning a subject for which declaratory relief may be granted (*City of Hornell and New York State Conference of Mayors and Municipal Officials*, 36 PERB ¶ 3033 (2003)).

10:21. Are PERB decisions subject to court review?

Yes. PERB's decisions are reviewable pursuant to article 78 of the Civil Practice Law and Rules (CPLR), which authorizes judicial review of determinations by administrative boards. Final orders of PERB are enforceable by the state supreme court upon petition by PERB in a special proceeding. An order by PERB that determines whether an employer or employee is subject to the Taylor Law may be deemed final when made (§ 213(a); CPLR § 7803). An Article 78 proceeding to challenge a PERB order must be filed within 30 days after service of the order (§ 213(a); *PERB v. Bd. of Educ. of City of Buffalo*, 39 N.Y.2d 86 (1976)).

Employee Representation under the Taylor Law

10:22. What is a bargaining unit?

As it pertains to school districts, a *bargaining unit*, or *negotiating unit*, is a group of employees organized for the purpose of collective negotiations and typically represented by an employee organization (union) (see **10:26**). Three typical bargaining units in schools would be administrators and supervisors, teachers and other instructional staff, and noninstructional staff. Employees need not be members of the union representing members of their bargaining unit (§ 202), but the union has the same duty of fair representation towards them as it has towards its members (§§ 204(2), 209-a(2)(c); see **10:34**).

10:23. How is the composition of a bargaining unit determined?

When defining a bargaining unit, the positions to be included in the unit must have a sufficient "community of interest" based on a variety of factors such as similar professional interests and/or terms and conditions of employment as well as locality of work, general supervision and interaction in the performance of work (§ 207(1)(a); *New York City Sch. Dist.*, 27 PERB ¶¶ 3026, 3067 (1994); but see *Dutchess County BOCES*, 25 PERB ¶ 3048 (1992)). The law also requires that the appropriate unit be defined or drawn along lines that permit public officials at the level of the unit to agree or to make effective recommendations with regard to the terms and conditions of employment to be negotiated (§ 207(1)(b)). Moreover, the unit must be compatible with the joint responsibilities of the public employer and the public employees to serve the public (§ 207(1)(c); see **10:27**).

10:24. May the same bargaining unit include supervisory and non-supervisory staff?

PERB has declined to automatically place supervisors and rank-and-file employees into separate bargaining units (*Dutchess County BOCES*, 25 PERB ¶ 3048 (1992)).

Instead, PERB will consider whether members of the same unit have significant supervisory responsibilities over others in the unit and whether there are other existing or potential conflicts of interest among members of the unit (*Dutchess County BOCES*; *Uniondale UFSD*, 21 PERB ¶ 3060 (1988)). For example, in one PERB case, a BOCES teachers' bargaining unit included teaching assistants. The teachers in that bargaining unit evaluated the teaching assistants. PERB found that a bargaining unit composed of teachers and teaching assistants in this case did not pose a conflict of interest because the teachers did not make any employment decisions concerning the teaching assistants (*Dutchess County BOCES*).

10:25. May substitute teachers be included in a bargaining unit under the Taylor Law?

Yes, if they are the type of substitutes considered to be public employees within the meaning of the Taylor Law. Specifically, the Taylor Law covers substitute teachers who have received a "reasonable assurance of continued employment" so as to be disqualified from receiving unemployment insurance benefits during summer vacation periods. Substitutes who have not been given a reasonable assurance of continued employment from a district are not eligible for inclusion in a collective bargaining unit in that district (§ 201(7)(d)).

Long-term substitutes are also covered, and are generally placed in the same bargaining unit as teachers (*Unatego CSD*, 15 PERB ¶ 3097 (1982); *Broome-Tioga BOCES*, 31 PERB ¶ 4016 (1998)). Per diem substitutes are generally placed in their own bargaining unit (*Bethpage UFSD*, 15 PERB ¶ 4040, *aff'd*, 15 PERB ¶ 3094 (1982); *Wellsville CSD*, 30 PERB ¶ 4011 (1997)).

10:26. What is an employee organization and how does an employee organization become the authorized representative of public employees?

An "employee organization" is a union. The Taylor Law, however, does not use the term "union" to refer to the entity authorized to represent a group of public employees in collective negotiations; instead, it uses the term "employee organization" (§ 201(5)).

There are basically two procedures by which an employee organization can become the authorized representative of a group of public employees: *recognition* by the employer upon agreement with the union over a unit definition, or *certification* by PERB after determining the most appropriate unit (see **10:27–29**; §§ 204(1), 207).

Following either recognition or certification , an employer must negotiate with the employee organization with respect to terms and conditions of employment (§ 204(2)).

10:27. How does the process of employer recognition work?

Recognition is the voluntary designation by the legislative body of a public employer of an employee organization as the negotiating representative of employees in an appropriate unit (4 NYCRR § 200.8). An employer, however, is not required to recognize any employee organization (*Town of Clay v. Helsby*, 45 A.D.2d 292 (4th Dep't 1974), *appeal after remand*, 51 A.D.2d 200 (4th Dep't 1976)). But if an employee organization requests recognition and that request is denied, the employee organization may seek certification from PERB (4 NYCRR § 201.3(b); see **10:29**). Both terms are used interchangeably in this chapter.

The recognition process begins with a request for recognition by an employee organization to the public employer (see **10:26**). Once an employer receives a request for recognition, it must determine the appropriateness of the bargaining unit proposed by the employee organization (§ 207(1), see **10:23**). There is no steadfast rule for the definition of an appropriate bargaining unit, although public policy is in favor of large rather than fragmented bargaining units (see *New York City Sch. Dist.*, 27 PERB ¶ 3067 (1994)). It is important to examine the professional status of the employees to be included in the bargaining unit, the employer's organizational hierarchy, conflicting interests among the positions to be included, and the employer's administrative convenience (see *New York City Sch. Dist.*, 27 PERB ¶¶ 3026, 3067 (1994)). PERB has ruled, for instance, that registered nurses may split off from a bargaining unit of noninstructional employees because the professional status of nurses is incompatible with the status of non-professional employees in the same bargaining unit (*Ichabod Crane CSD*, 33 PERB ¶ 3042 (2000), *transferred* *to the Appellate Division*, 34 PERB ¶ 7030 (Sup. Ct. Albany County 2001), *aff'd*, 300 A.D.2d 929 (3d Dep't 2002)).

After the unit has been defined, the employer must be satisfied that a majority of the employees in that bargaining unit have selected the employee organization (a union) which seeks recognition as their representative. Selection may be evidenced a number of different ways, including by employees' individual authorizations for the deduction of dues from their paychecks (called dues check off) (§ 207(2)).

Once the employer is convinced that the union represents a majority of the employees in the unit and the union affirms that it does not assert the right to strike against any government, to assist or participate in any strike, or to impose an obligation on employees to conduct, assist or participate in a strike, the union is then designated by the employer as the exclusive negotiating representative of the employees in the unit (§§ 204(2), 207(3)).

10:28. Are there any specific procedures that districts must follow when recognizing a union?

PERB has issued regulations that set forth the procedures that an employer must comply with to voluntarily recognize a union (4 NYCRR § 201.6). An employer must:

1. Post a written notice of recognition in a conspicuous place at suitable offices of the public employer for at least five working days.
2. Include the notice in a public advertisement of a newspaper of general circulation in the employer's area for at least one day.
3. Send notification to any employee organizations that have, in a written communication within a year preceding the recognition, claimed to represent any of the employees in the unit (4 NYCRR § 201.6(a)).

The information published must include the name of the union that has been recognized, the job titles included in the recognized unit, and the date of recognition (4 NYCRR § 201.6(b)).

10:29. How does the process of certification work?

If an employer refuses a request for recognition or does not respond to such a request, an employee organization (union) may file a *petition for certification* with PERB within the time frame prescribed by PERB (4 NYCRR § 201.3(a), (b)). A petition for certification must be supported by a showing of interest of at least 30 percent of the employees within the unit alleged to be appropriate (4 NYCRR § 201.3(a)–(e)). An employee organization can establish a showing of interest with evidence of dues deduction authorizations from employees that have not been revoked, or evidence of current membership, original designation cards or petitions that were signed and dated within six months of submission, or a combination of the three (4 NYCRR § 201.4(b); see § 207(2)). If necessary, the director of employment practices and representation may order an investigation and/or a hearing on the petition for certification (4 NYCRR §§ 201(4)(e); 201.9(a)(1),(2)).

An election will be held whenever more than one employee organization is seeking certification of the same bargaining unit or where an employee organization seeking certification is unable to show majority support of the employees in the unit (4 NYCRR § 201.9(g)(2)).

An employee organization may be certified without an election if the organization is the only organization seeking certification and it establishes that a majority of the employees within the unit choose to be represented by the organization (4 NYCRR § 201.9(g)(1)). Although PERB's regulations describe only two types of evidence that may be used in support of certification without an election, the director may also consider other types of evidence, such as a current employee organization membership list (*Beaver River CSD*, 35 PERB ¶ 3003 (2002); see 4 NYCRR § 201.9(g)(1)).

Certification will not be issued to a union that already has been "recognized" (see **10:27–28**), because the same rights are acquired by either process (see *Village of Sloatsburg*, 20 PERB ¶ 3014 (1987)).

10:30. Are employees who are hired after the recognition or certification of an employee organization included within the bargaining unit?

Generally, all employees whose positions fall within the unit's definition are considered members of the unit, regardless of when they are hired (see *State of New York (Dep't of Audit & Control)*, 24 PERB ¶ 3019 (1991)). The school district must negotiate the terms and conditions of employment of all such employees with the appropriate employee organization (§ 204(2)).

However, a new position may be created that does not fall within the definition of the bargaining unit. In this case, the district is not required to negotiate the terms and conditions of employment with respect to that position (see *North Shore UFSD*, 11 PERB ¶ 3011 (1978)). In such cases, the employee organization may request the district to add the new position to the unit by recognition or file a unit placement petition with PERB seeking an order to add the new position to its existing bargaining unit (4 NYCRR §§ 201.2(a), (b); 201.3).

10:31. What happens if there is a dispute between employee organizations about which of them represents a particular job title?

Either one or both of the competing employee organizations may file a unit clarification petition and/or a unit placement petition with PERB, asking PERB to determine which bargaining unit a particular title belongs to (see, for example, *Harrison CSD*, 36 PERB ¶ 3046 (2003)). The school district then has an opportunity to respond to the petition by indicating which unit it believes properly represents the job title at issue.

PERB's analysis begins with a review of the collective bargaining agreement between the district and the employee organization that claims to represent the job title(s) at issue (*Clinton Community College*, 31 PERB ¶ 3070 (1998)). If the "unit recognition clause" (the language in the collective bargaining agreement that defines the bargaining unit) specifically includes the job title at issue, PERB will grant that employee organization's unit clarification petition without further inquiry (*Monroe-Woodbury CSD*, 33 PERB ¶ 3007 (2000)). However, if the unit recognition clause does not expressly include the job title(s) at issue, or if the unit recognition clause is ambiguous, PERB will examine the evidence regarding the parties' practices regarding representation of the title(s) at issue (*County of Niagara*, 21 PERB ¶ 3030 (1988)).

If PERB finds that a particular title has not been included in any bargaining unit, then upon a proper petition, PERB may order placement of that title in the appropriate bargaining unit (see **10:30**).

10:32. What are the rights of a recognized or certified employee organization?

A recognized or certified employee organization is guaranteed the exclusive right to represent in collective bargaining the employees in the bargaining unit that it is designated to represent (§§ 204(2), 208(1)(a)). The organization also has the right to represent those employees in grievance proceedings (§§ 204(2), 208(1)(a)); to dues checkoff for those employees who authorize the dues checkoff (§ 208(1)(b)); to agency shop fees from those employees who are included within the bargaining unit but who are not members of the union (§ 208(3)(b); see **10:36**); and the right not to be challenged by a rival union until seven months before the expiration of a negotiated collective bargaining agreement (§ 208(2)).

10:33. May employees be forced to join an employee organization?

No. Section 202 of the Taylor Law guarantees public employees the right to join or refrain from joining employee organizations. However, amendments to the Taylor Law and the General Municipal Law give all public employee organizations the right to demand that bargaining unit members who are not also dues-paying members of that organization pay agency shop fees (§§ 201(2)(b), 208(3)(b); Gen. Mun. Law § 93-b(3); see **10:36**).

10:34. May employees who are not members of the employee organization be excluded from the bargaining unit?

No. Nonmembership in the employee organization is not a basis for exclusion from the bargaining unit, or for nonrepresentation by the employee organization. Employees covered by the unit's definition who are not members of the union are still bound by and enjoy the benefits of the collective bargaining agreement (see §§ 203, 204(2), 209-a(2)(c)) and are required to pay an agency shop fee to the employee organization (see § 208(3)(b); **10:36**).

10:35. Is a recognized or certified employee organization entitled to dues deductions?

Yes. A public employer must deduct employee organization dues from employees' salaries upon the presentation of cards authorizing deduction of dues signed by the individual employees (§§ 201(2)(a), 208(1)(b)).

Once the employer has received these cards, authorization to deduct dues may remain effective until withdrawn or changed by the member employee in a written document presented to the employer (see Gen. Mun. Law § 93-b; *Erie County*, 5 PERB ¶ 3021 (1972)). This member employee right of revocation cannot be restricted (see *Rochester City Sch. Dist.*, 10 PERB ¶ 3097 (1977)).

Failure to deduct membership dues and transmit them to the union is a per se violation of the Taylor Law (*City of Troy*, 28 PERB ¶ 3027 (1995)). Moreover, it is improper for a school district faced with competing claims from different employee organizations for dues money to hold such dues in escrow pending a resolution of the dispute. An employer may not refuse to remit dues to a certified employee organization unless that employee organization has been decertified (*Bd. of Educ. of City Sch. Dist. of City of Long Beach*, 35 PERB ¶ 3020 (2002)).

However, an employee organization may lose the right to dues checkoff if it is determined to have violated the Taylor Law's prohibition against strikes (§ 210(3)(a), (f); see **10:75**).

10:36. May employees whose positions are included within a bargaining unit, but who choose not to join an employee organization, be required to pay fees to the organization?

Yes. Employees who choose not to join the employee organization whose positions are included in its bargaining unit are required to pay agency shop fees to the organization (§§ 201(2)(b), 208(3)(b); Gen. Mun. Law § 93-b(3)).

Agency shop fees are representation fees deducted from the pay of nonunion members in an amount equivalent to the membership dues paid by members of the employee organization. The employer must collect the agency shop fees and pay them to the employee organization (§§ 201(2)(b), 208(3)(b)).

However, agency shop fee payers who object to any portion of their fees being spent "in aid of activities or causes of a political or ideological nature only incidentally related to terms and conditions of employment" are entitled to be refunded that portion of such fees (§ 208(3)(b)). The employee organization must maintain a refund procedure, and at the request of such employees, it must provide them with financial information sufficient to determine whether a refund may be sought, and in what amount; if the employee organization fails to establish and maintain such a refund procedure, it has no authority to collect agency shop fees (§ 208(3)(b); *Civil Serv. Employees Ass'n (Hartog)*, 32 PERB ¶ 3080 (1999); see *Hampton Bays Teachers Ass'n (Sullivan)*, 14 PERB ¶ 3018 (1981)). If the employee organization fails or refuses to provide this disclosure, the fee payer may be entitled to a full refund of all agency shop fees he or she has paid (see *St. Lawrence-Lewis County BOCES Teachers Ass'n (Baker)*, 15 PERB ¶ 3113 (1982)).

10:37. Are there any limitations on the use of agency shop fees?

Yes. Agency shop fees cannot be used over the objection of the fee payer for purposes other than the collective bargaining rights afforded to unions by the Taylor Law such as grievance adjustment and contract administration, including lobbying or other political activity or for public relations efforts to promote the teaching profession and public unionism in general (see *Lehnert v. Ferris Faculty Ass'n*, 500 U.S. 507 (1991), *rehearing denied*, 501 U.S. 1244 (1991), *remanded*, 937 F.2d 608 (6th Cir. 1991); *Abood v. Detroit Bd. of Educ.*, 431 U.S. 209 (1977), *rehearing denied*, 433 U.S. 915 (1977)). However, such fees may be applied to the cost of social activities, conventions, publications, and a local union's affiliation with state and national union organizations, other than the pro rata share of the political or ideological expenditures of such affiliate, even over the objections of nonunion members of the bargaining unit (*Ellis v. Brotherhood of Railway, Airline & Steamship Clerks*, 466 U.S. 435 (1984); *remanded*, 736 F.2d 1340 (9th Cir. 1984); *Lehnert*).

10:38. Do former employees or retirees enjoy representation rights under the Taylor Law.

Not generally. The law affords representational rights to public employees (§ 209-a(2)(c)). However, in rare cases, PERB has ruled that an employee organization may have a continuing duty to represent former employees under circumstances where their "severance from employment is contested or there is some other basis upon which to conclude that there is a continuing nexus to employment. . . ." (*Westchester County Correction Officers' Benevolent Ass'n, Inc.*, 30 PERB 3075 (1997)).

PERB has never extended this duty to retirees (*Greece CSD*, 28 PERB ¶ 3048 (1995), *aff'd, Lanzillo v. PERB*, 29 PERB ¶7003 (Sup. Ct. Albany County 1996)). However, one appellate court has found that a "continuing nexus" to employment warranted an extension of the "duty of fair representation" to retirees (see *Baker v. Bd. of Educ., Hoosick Falls CSD*, 194 Misc.2d 116 (2002), *aff'd*, 3 A.D.3d 678 (3d Dep't 2004)).

10:39. Are there any employees excluded from coverage under the Taylor Law?

An employee may be excluded from a bargaining unit and excluded from coverage under the Taylor Law if he or she is properly designated as a "managerial" or "confidential" employee under the Taylor Law. Such a designation must be requested by the employer and have been granted by PERB (§ 201(7)(a); 4 NYCRR § 201.10; see **10:40**).

In addition, some district employees, such as continuing education teachers, may not be entitled to representation under the Taylor Law because they are considered "casual employees" who lack the regular and continuing employment relationship required for covered public employee status under the Taylor Law (see *BOCES III, Suffolk County*, 15 PERB ¶ 3015 (1982), *aff'd, BOCES III Faculty Assoc. v. PERB*, 92 A.D.2d 937 (2d Dep't 1983)). However, "casual" employment cannot be claimed simply because a school employee provides services only during the school year (§ 201(7)(f)).

Managerial and Confidential Employees

10:40. How are employees designated as managerial or confidential under the Taylor Law?

Employers, including school boards, must file an application with PERB, pursuant to PERB's rules of practice, for designation of an employee as managerial or confidential (§ 201(7)(a); 4 NYCRR § 201.10). A school board may not unilaterally make this designation (*Wappingers CSD*, 16 PERB ¶ 3029 (1983)).

Applications may be filed at any time except for employees represented by a recognized or certified employee organization (4 NYCRR § 201.10(b)). For these employees, only one application may be made during an employee organization's period of unchallenged representation, which lasts until seven months prior to the expiration of the contract between the district and the union (§ 208(2); 4 NYCRR § 201.10(b)).

Even after the designation is made, it does not take effect with respect to employees covered by a negotiated agreement until the termination of the period of unchallenged representation enjoyed by the employee organization (§ 201(7)(a)).

10:41. What are the criteria for designating someone as a managerial employee?

An employee may be designated as *managerial* only if (1) he or she formulates policy (see *State of New York*, 36 PERB ¶ 3029 (2003)); or (2) the school district might reasonably require that employee to directly assist in preparing for and conducting collective negotiations or have a major role in the administration of collective bargaining agreements or in personnel administration, provided that the employee's role is not routine or clerical, and requires the exercise of independent judgment (§ 201(7)(a)).

"Managerial" has been defined to be more than giving mere input. A PERB administrative law judge has stated that "managerial status depends upon the exercise by the personnel involved of broad authority directly resultant from their intimate relationship 'to the top' (e.g., to a board of education or a superintendent of schools), while supervisory status is manifested by an individual's relationship to (and direct control over) 'rank and file' employees. The distinction is substantive, not semantic; those individuals who perform managerial functions will in all likelihood possess either direct or indirect supervisory authority, but the reverse is not true. And it is the Legislature's will that only those individuals whose authority in labor relations matters goes beyond traditional supervisory concerns are to be excluded from rights under the [Taylor Law]" (*Beacon Enlarged City Sch. Dist.*, 4 PERB ¶ 4024 (1971)).

Accordingly, building principals generally have not been designated as "managerial" (*New York City Sch. Dist.*, 6 PERB ¶ 3040 (1973), but see *Ellenville CSD*, 16 PERB ¶ 3066 (1983)). In small school districts, however, principals may be designated "managerial" because they are more likely to have a significant role in formulating policy and personnel administration (*McGraw CSD*, 21 PERB ¶ 3001 (1988)).

10:42. What are the criteria for designating someone as a confidential employee?

An employee may be designated *confidential* only if he or she serves in a confidential relationship to a managerial employee who directly assists in collective bargaining or has a major role in contract or personnel administration (§ 201(7)(a)).

According to PERB case law, "an employee is confidential . . . only when in the course of assisting a managerial employee who exercises labor relations responsibilities, that employee has access or is privy to information related to collective bargaining, contract administration, or other aspects of labor-management relations on a regular basis which is not appropriate for the eyes and ears of rank and file personnel or their negotiating representative" (*Penfield CSD*, 14 PERB ¶ 4044, *aff'd*, 14 PERB ¶ 3082 (1981)), and has a confidential relationship with a managerial employee (*Town of DeWitt*, 32 PERB ¶ 3001 (1999); *North Rose-Wolcott CSD*, 33 PERB ¶ 3002 (2000)). Clerical staff may be designated as "confidential" if they are privy to confidential information related to collective bargaining (see *Rockland County BOCES*, 34 PERB ¶ 3032 (2001)).

The Collective Bargaining Process

10:43. What is collective bargaining?

According to the Taylor Law, *collective bargaining*, also known as *collective negotiations*, is the process for fulfilling the mutual obligation of an employer and an employee organization to meet at reasonable times and confer in good faith over the wages, hours and other terms and conditions of employment of public employees, or the negotiation of an agreement, or any question arising thereunder, and the execution of a reached agreement (§ 204(3)).

10:44. Are public employers required to engage in collective bargaining?

Yes. The Taylor Law requires public employers to negotiate in "good faith" (see **10:46**) with an employee organization that has been recognized or certified as the exclusive representative of a bargaining unit of its public employees (§ 204(2), (3); see **10:26–29**).

An employer's refusal to negotiate in good faith is an "improper practice" (§ 209-a(1)(d); see **10:70**).

10:45. Do public employers have to continue bargaining once an agreement is reached?

Not generally. Once a collective bargaining agreement (CBA) is reached, unless the CBA contains a re-opener clause that unambiguously provides for a full re-opening of negotiations on a particular subject or subjects, the parties no longer have an obligation to negotiate during the duration of the CBA concerning any subject that is expressly covered by the CBA (*Matter of Roma v. Ruffo*, 92 N.Y.2d 489 (1998); see also *County of Nassau*, 31 PERB ¶ 3064 (1998)).

However, a newly certified or recognized employee organization has the "immediate right to negotiate for employees in the unit even though there may still be in existence an unexpired agreement entered into with the former representative . . . (*County of Rockland*, 20 PERB ¶ 3017 (1987); see also § 208(1)(a)).

In addition, public employers must negotiate over the impact of managerial decisions that affect terms and conditions of employment (see **10:59–60**).

10:46. What does it mean to negotiate in "good faith"?

PERB has stated that good faith requires a party to "approach the negotiating table with a sincere desire to reach agreement" (*Town of Southampton*, 2 PERB ¶ 3011 (1969)) and to actively participate in negotiations indicating a "present intent to find a basis for agreement" (*Deposit CSD*, 27 PERB ¶ 3020 (1994), *aff'd*, 214 A.D.2d 288 (3d Dep't 1995), *reconsideration denied*, 29 PERB ¶ 7001 (3d Dep't), *appeal denied*, 88 N.Y.2d 866 (1996)).

However, the obligation to bargain in good faith under the Taylor Law does not compel either party to agree to a proposal or require the making of a concession (§ 204(3)). What is required is "a continuing willingness to submit one's demands to the consideration of the bargaining table where argument, persuasion and the free interchange of views can take place" (*East Meadow UFSD*, 16 PERB ¶ 3086 (1983)).

PERB has held the good faith requirement, for example, to prohibit misrepresentations at the bargaining table (*County of Rockland*, 29 PERB ¶ 3009 (1996)); to require each party to listen to and respond to the other party's proposals (*City of Mount Vernon*, 11 PERB ¶ 3095 (1978); *City of Yonkers*, 7 PERB ¶ 3006 (1974)); to require each party, upon request, to supply the other party with information that the other party needs to evaluate its bargaining demands (*Bd. of Educ. of the City Sch. Dist. of the City of Buffalo*, 36 PERB ¶ 3034 (2003); and to require each party to give its negotiator sufficient authority to reach agreement on open issues (*County of Niagara*, 23 PERB ¶ 3003 (1990); see also *Sachem CSD No. 5*, 6 PERB ¶ 3014 (1973)).

The duty to negotiate in good faith also encompasses the obligation of negotiators to support a tentative agreement reached at the bargaining table unless they explicitly give notice to their opposition that they do not agree with certain proposals and do not intend to support those proposals at a ratification vote (*Copiague UFSD*, 23 PERB ¶ 3046 (1990); see also **10:7, 10:9**).

10:47. Does the "good faith" requirement impose an obligation to negotiate issues in a particular order?

No. Good faith negotiations do not require the parties to discuss issues in any particular order of priority or to negotiate any particular issue, such as wages, to the point of agreement before resolving other issues, but it does require them to be willing to discuss all issues (*Town of Haverstraw*, 9 PERB ¶ 3063 (1976)).

10:48. Who participates in collective bargaining?

Generally, a negotiating team for the school district and a team for the employee organization engage in collective bargaining. The school district's negotiating team typically consists of a chief spokesperson, a recorder to take notes, an individual who is familiar with the district's educational program, and an individual who is familiar with the financial needs and resources of the district. The chief spokesperson, for example, could be an attorney, a board of cooperative educational services (BOCES) negotiator, or an administrator.

Generally, the school board designates the individuals who will serve on the negotiating team, with the advice of the superintendent.

10:49. May a school board choose anyone it wishes to serve on its negotiating team?

Yes. Although the superintendent, as chief executive officer of the school district, is responsible for the collective bargaining agreement with the employee organization (§ 201(10), (12); *Utica City Sch. Dist.*, 27 PERB ¶ 3023 (1994)), a school board may generally choose whomever it pleases to serve on its negotiating team, so long as the selection is not intended to frustrate bargaining, either because of ill will or conflicting interest (*Erie County Water Auth.*, 25 PERB ¶ 3030 (1992); *City of Newburgh*, 16 PERB ¶ 4590, *aff'd*, 16 PERB ¶ 3081 (1983)).

10:50. What are ground rules and negotiation procedures?

Although not specifically mentioned in the Taylor Law, ground rules and negotiation procedures are agreements between a school district and a union on how negotiations will be conducted. PERB has held that negotiation procedures and ground rules are nonmandatory subjects, that they are preliminary and subordinate to substantive negotiations, and that they should not interfere with the commencement or progress of negotiations (*Marcellus CSD*, 21 PERB ¶ 3035 (1988)).

Examples of the issues that may be agreed to by the parties are the time and place for negotiating sessions, the length of sessions, the procedures for ratification of the agreement by one or both parties, and the authority of the parties to reach an agreement. Reserving the right of ratification may be important if a school board considers such final approval important before the contract becomes binding (see **10:5–10** for a detailed discussion of ratification).

Although ground rules and negotiation procedures can be very helpful in guiding the parties through the negotiations process, PERB will consider it an improper practice if a party insists on any ground rule at the expense of commencement or progress of substantive negotiations (see *Madison CSD*, 22 PERB ¶ 3057 (1989)). Violation of a ground rule is not an improper practice as long as the two parties are able to continue negotiating in good faith (*Board of Educ., CSD No. 1*, 6 PERB ¶ 3049 (1973), *aff'g* 6 PERB ¶ 4526 at 4591 (1973)).

10:51. Can a school district set a deadline for an employee organization's submission of items to be negotiated?

No public employer has the power to unilaterally set a deadline for submission of the items to be negotiated. However, the employee organization and the district may agree in the collective bargaining agreement or in their ground rules for negotiations to establish a submission date for demands for future agreements. Such agreements are enforceable, and parties may waive their rights to make new demands if submitted after the date agreed upon (*Heuvelton CSD*, 12 PERB ¶ 3007 (1979)).

On the other hand, even absent such an agreement, it may be an improper practice for either party to submit new or previously withdrawn demands after impasse (see, e.g., *Schenectady County Community College*, 6 PERB ¶ 3027 (1973); see also **10:62**).

10:52. What subjects usually are negotiated in collective bargaining?

Subjects of collective bargaining negotiations may include salary and other wage issues, hours of employment, health insurance and other benefits, leaves of absence, grievance procedures, and other terms and conditions of employment (see §§ 201(4), 204(3)).

Issues that may arise during collective bargaining can be categorized into three groups:

- *mandatory subjects*, over which both the employer and the union have an obligation to bargain in good faith until agreement is reached or until the party that demanded negotiations withdraws the issue from the table;
- *permissive, or nonmandatory subjects*, over which either party may, but is not obligated to negotiate; and
- *prohibited subjects*, about which neither party may lawfully negotiate (*Board of Educ. of the City Sch. Dist. of the City of New York v. PERB*, 75 N.Y.2d 660 (1990)).

Each party must negotiate with respect to mandatory subjects upon demand by the other party (*Board of Educ. of the City Sch. Dist. of the City of New York v. PERB*, 75 N.Y.2d 660 (1990)). Any change relating to mandatory subjects of bargaining must be negotiated prior to the adoption of any such change. A willingness to negotiate after the change is immaterial (*Great Neck Water Pollution Control Dist.*, 28 PERB ¶ 3030 (1995)). It is permissible, however, for an employee organization to waive the right to demand negotiations over changes to a mandatory subject of bargaining by agreeing to a "management rights" clause. The intent to waive must be sufficiently plain and clear (*Town of Greece*, 28 PERB ¶ 3078 (1995); *County of Livingston*, 26 PERB ¶ 3074 (1993)).

The Taylor Law itself does not clearly delineate most mandatory, nonmandatory, or prohibited subjects of collective bargaining. PERB and the courts resolve disputes about the "scope of bargaining" or whether a particular subject is a mandatory, nonmandatory, or prohibited subject of bargaining (§§ 205(5)(d), 213(a); see **10:53**).

10:53. How are mandatory, prohibited, and nonmandatory (permissive) subjects of bargaining distinguished from one another?

A *mandatory* subject of bargaining is one which falls within section 201(4) of the Taylor Law that defines terms and conditions of employment as "salaries, wages, hours and other terms and conditions of employment." Examples of mandatory subjects of bargaining, other than those listed in section 201(4), include benefits, leave provisions, workload, disciplinary procedures, and other related issues, such as the implementation of drug testing procedures and the consequences thereof (see, respectively, *City of Cohoes*, 31 PERB ¶ 3020 (1998), *aff'd, Uniform Firefighters of Cohoes, Local 2562 v. Cuevas*, 276 A.D.2d 184 (3d Dep't 2000), *appeal denied*, 96 N.Y.2d 711 (2001); *City of Albany*, 7 PERB ¶ 3078 (1974), *aff'd, Albany v. Helsby*, 48 A.D.2d 998 (3d Dep't), *aff'd*, 38 N.Y.2d 778 (1975); *County of Rockland & Rockland County Sheriff*, 31 PERB ¶ 3062 (1998); *Patchogue-Medford UFSD*, 30 PERB ¶ 3041 (1997); *County of Nassau*, 27 PERB ¶ 3054 (1994)). In addition, previously nonmandatory terms incorporated into a collective bargaining agreement become mandatory subjects for purposes of negotiating the next agreement (*Greenburgh No. 11 UFSD*, 32 PERB ¶ 3024 (1999)) or any time negotiations on a current contract are reopened (*City of Troy*, 33 PERB ¶ 4589 (2000)).

Prohibited subjects of bargaining include subjects that are expressly prohibited by law or reserved to management by public policy. For instance, the Taylor Law specifically prohibits bargaining over retirement benefits to be provided by a public retirement system (§ 201(4); but see *Baker v. Bd. of Educ., Hoosick Falls CSD*, 194 Misc.2d 116 (2002), *aff'd*, 770 N.Y.S.2d 782 (3d Dep't 2004); see also **10:38**). Also, New York State courts have held that law and/or public policy prohibit school districts from agreeing to delegate the board's power to grant or deny tenure (*Cohoes City*

Sch. Dist. v. Cohoes Teachers Ass'n, 40 N.Y.2d 774 (1976)); to preclude a board from inspecting teacher personnel files (*Board of Educ., Great Neck UFSD v. Areman*, 41 N.Y.2d 527 (1977)); or to prepay the salaries of teachers on return to work in the fall because the Education Law prohibits the payment of teacher salaries in advance of the performance of services (*Board of Educ. v. Ramapo Teachers' Ass'n*, 200 A.D.2d 62 (3d Dep't 1994), *appeal denied*, 84 N.Y.2d 806 (1994). On the otherhand, according to the commissioner of education in *Appeal of Totolis & Richard*, 36 Educ. Dep't Rep 476 (1997), the payment of health insurance benefits for July and August to teachers retiring at the beginning of September does not constitute prepayment for services during the upcoming school year but, rather, payment for services rendered during the preceding school year.

Permissive or *nonmandatory* subjects of negotiation include matters that are not terms and conditions of employment but do not violate a statute or strong public policy (*Board of Educ. of the City Sch. Dist. of the City of New York v. PERB*, 75 N.Y.2d 660 (1990)). Examples include transfer of work to BOCES (*Vestal Employees Ass'n v. PERB*, 94 N.Y.2d 409 (2000); *Webster CSD v. PERB*, 75 N.Y.2d 619 (1990)) and demands regarding employees outside the bargaining unit, student scheduling, class size, hiring of substitutes, and staff reductions (see *Somers CSD*, 9 PERB ¶ 3014 (1976)).

10:54. Can certain issues involve more than one subject of collective bargaining?

Yes. Some general subjects may fall into more than one category. For example, determination of the criteria by which teachers are evaluated is a nonmandatory (permissive) subject of bargaining, but procedures and forms for the evaluation of teachers are mandatory subjects of negotiations (see *Newburgh City Sch. Dist.*, 21 PERB ¶ 3036 (1988), *aff'd*, 22 PERB ¶ 7009 (Sup. Ct. Albany County), *appeal dismissed*, 25 PERB ¶ 7008 (3d Dep't 1992); *Elwood UFSD*, 10 PERB ¶ 3107 (1977); *Somers CSD*).

However, any single proposal that has both mandatory and nonmandatory aspects is considered a nonmandatory subject of bargaining in its entirety (see *City of White Plains*, 33 PERB ¶ 3051 (2000)). For example, a proposal that would allow grievances over mandatory and nonmandatory subjects of bargaining is a nonmandatory subject of bargaining (*City of Schenectady*, 21 PERB ¶ 3022 (1988)). This is different from otherwise nonmandatory subjects of bargaining previously incorporated into a collective bargaining agreement which become mandatory subjects of bargaining during negotiations of a subsequent agreement (*Greenburgh No. 11 UFSD*, 32 PERB ¶ 3024 (1999), or reopened negotiations on a current agreement (*City of Troy*, 33 PERB ¶ 4589 (2000)).

10:55. Are fingerprinting costs for job applicants a mandatory subject of bargaining?

No. The fingerprinting costs that school districts generally require job applicants to assume before employment are not a mandatory subject of bargaining because they are applicable to the public at large and not just school district employees represented by employee organizations under the Taylor Law (*Newark Valley Cardinal Bus Drivers*, 35 PERB ¶ 3006 (2002); *aff'd* 36 PERB 7005, *aff'd, Newark Valley Cardinal Bus Driver, Local 4360, NYSUT, AFT, AFL-CIO*, 303 A.D.2d 888 (3d Dep't 2003), *appeal denied*, 100 N.Y.2d 504 (2003)).

10:56. Must a school board negotiate its decision to subcontract bargaining unit work to a private firm or individual or to assign unit work to nonunit personnel?

The decision to transfer work from a bargaining unit to individuals outside the bargaining unit or to subcontract work to outside employers generally is considered a mandatory subject of bargaining (see *Niagara Frontier Transp. Auth.*, 18 PERB ¶ 3083 (1985)). Here, PERB can order reinstatement of employees who were terminated as a result of a unilateral decision (as opposed to a negotiated agreement) (§ 205(5)(d); see *Saratoga Springs City Sch. Dist.*, 11 PERB ¶ 3037 (1978), *aff'd, Saratoga Springs City School Dist. v. New York State PERB*, 68 A.D.2d 202 (3d Dep't 1979), *appeal denied*, 47 N.Y.2d 711 (1979)); and restoration of work to the bargaining unit (see *County of Onondaga*, 27 PERB ¶ 3048 (1994)).

10:57. Are there any exceptions to the duty to negotiate subcontracting decisions?

Yes. A school district may not be required to negotiate a decision to transfer work under certain circumstances, such as where the decision to transfer unit work is directly related to a decision to alter the level of services provided by the employer to its constituency (see *New Rochelle City Sch. Dist.*, 4 PERB ¶ 3060 (1971)); where there is a substantial change in the nature of the duties to be performed by the nonunit workers (see *Hewlett-Woodmere UFSD*, 28 PERB ¶ 3039 (1995), *aff'd, Hewlett-Woodmere UFSD v. PERB*, 232 A.D.2d 560 (2d Dep't 1996); *Hyde Park CSD*, 21 PERB ¶ 3011 (1988)); where there are significant changes in the qualifications of the workers necessary to perform the work (see *County of Erie*, 29 PERB ¶ 3045 (1996); *West Hempstead UFSD*, 14 PERB ¶ 3096 (1981)).

Also, a school district does not have to negotiate a decision to transfer work where the work at issue has been performed by nonunit employees in the past (see *Hammondsport CSD*, 28 PERB ¶ 3059 (1995)); where the work was previously performed for such a limited time, and with such infrequency, that it cannot be established as "exclusive" unit work (see *Dreyden Central School Dist.*, 36 PERB ¶ 3005 (2003); or where the employee organization has agreed to language authorizing the district to subcontract unit work (see *Garden City UFSD*, 27 PERB ¶ 3029 (1994)).

Subcontracting may also be permitted without negotiation where the action is authorized by law. For example, a school district's decision to have a board of cooperative educational services (BOCES) take over academic programs pursuant to section 1950(4)(bb) of the Education Law is not a mandatory subject of bargaining (*Webster CSD v. PERB*, 75 N.Y.2d 619 (1990)). Similarly, a district's transfer of printing services pursuant to a contract with the local BOCES has been found to be a nonmandatory subject of negotiation (*Vestal Employees Ass'n v. PERB*, 94 N.Y.2d 409 (2000)). Because the legislative intent of the statute was not to require bargaining over the decision to subcontract work to the BOCES, districts need only negotiate over the impact of the decision and not the decision itself (see **10:59–60**).

10:58. Can a school district contract out its cafeteria and restaurant services without engaging in collective bargaining?

Probably not. In the past, school cafeteria and restaurant services were not an "ordinary contingent expense," which meant that these services had to be self-sustaining through state and federal aid and meal fees unless the voters approved the expenditure as part of the district's budget. Therefore, if a district's budget was defeated by the voters, the district could continue to operate cafeteria and restaurant services only if the district could finance these operations without using local taxpayer dollars.

Accordingly, in one case, a school district that was forced to end its cafeteria program after a budget defeat by the voters caused the board to adopt a contingency budget, hired a contractor to provide lunches on a self-sustaining financial basis, without district funding. An appellate court ruled that subcontracting was permissible without negotiations because the budget defeat had caused the loss of union members' jobs, not the decision to hire a contractor. In so ruling, the court reversed a prior PERB decision to the contrary (see *Germantown CSD v. PERB*, 205 A.D.2d 961 (3d Dep't 1994)).

However, subsequent amendments to the Education Law that make school cafeteria and restaurant services an "ordinary contingent expense" (see Educ. Law §§ 1604(28), 1709(22), 2023(1)) cast doubt on the continued viability of that case.

10:59. What are impact negotiations?

Although school districts need not bargain over managerial decisions involving permissive or nonmandatory subjects of bargaining (see **10:52–53**), they are required to negotiate over the impact of such decisions on the terms and conditions of employment (*County of Nassau*, 27 PERB ¶ 3054 (1994); see *West Irondequoit Teachers Ass'n v. Helsby*, 35 N.Y.2d 46 (1974)). This requirement most often is triggered when an employer takes unilateral action that indirectly affects terms or conditions of employment, such as elimination of positions (see *New Rochelle City Sch. Dist.*, 4 PERB ¶ 3060 (1970)).

PERB has stated: "A demand for impact bargaining permits negotiation about those mandatorily negotiable effects which are inevitably or necessarily caused by an employer's exercise of a managerial prerogative" (*County of Nassau*). For example, where a BOCES unilaterally assigned its teachers additional teaching duties during previously unassigned portions of their workday, PERB ruled that the BOCES had properly exercised a "management prerogative" but reminded the BOCES that it had an obligation to engage in impact bargaining upon demand, which would involve "other mandatory subjects of negotiations" (*Capital Region BOCES*, 36 PERB ¶ 3004 (2003)).

10:60. When are public employers and unions required to engage in impact negotiations?

A school district is obligated to engage in impact bargaining only if the union makes a demand that it do so. A union's demand to negotiate impact must be "clearly made, and cannot be inferred from a demand to negotiate a decision" (*Lackawanna City Sch. Dist.*, 28 PERB ¶ 3023 (1995)).

The requirement that a school district negotiate impact does not mean that the district is prevented from initiating its decision unless and until an agreement is reached on the terms and conditions of employment actually or potentially affected by those decisions. In fact, a district may implement the decision before it negotiates with the union over the impact (*Niagara Frontier Transit Metro Sys., Inc.*, 36 PERB ¶ 4538(2003); see also *State of New York (SUNY Binghamton)*, 27 PERB ¶ 3018 (1994)).

10:61. What is a past practice and how does it impact collective bargaining?

A *past practice* involves a mandatory subject of bargaining which has not been included in a written agreement, but which is unequivocal and has been in existence for a substantial period of time, and which affected employees could reasonably expect to continue without change (*Canastota CSD*, 32 PERB ¶ 3003 (1999)). A proposed change in an established past practice relating to a mandatory subject of bargaining must be negotiated with the employee organization representing the affected employees before that change is decided upon by the district (see *County of Genesee*, 18

PERB ¶ 3016 (1985), *aff'd, Bork v. Newman*, 122 A.D.2d 329 (3d Dep't 1986); see **10:70**).

For a practice to be "unequivocal" it must be "clear and unambiguous; expressed in full and definite terms; carrying no implications for future change" (*Sherburne-Earlville CSD*, 36 PERB ¶ 3011 (2003)). Therefore, even if a practice has continued for a significant period of time, if it is not unequivocal, the parties can have no reasonable expectation that it will continue. Thus, in *Sherburne-Earlville CSD*, PERB ruled that a supervisor's unauthorized practice of allowing a select few senior custodians to borrow school district equipment and tools did not establish an unequivocal practice evincing mutual agreement between the district and the employee organization.

10:62. What is an impasse?

Impasse is a stalemate or deadlock in collective bargaining. It is the point at which either or both parties to the negotiation determine that there is no reasonable expectation that further negotiations would be fruitful without third-party assistance (see *City of Newburgh*, 15 PERB ¶ 3116 (1982), *aff'd, Newburgh v. PERB*, 97 A.D.2d 258 (3d Dep't 1983), *aff'd*, 63 N.Y.2d 793 (1984)). Under the Taylor Law, an impasse may be deemed to exist if, despite efforts to bargain in good faith, the parties fail to reach an agreement at least 120 days prior to the end of the school district's fiscal year (§ 209(1)), which is commonly the final effective date of a collective bargaining agreement. However, the courts and PERB have recognized that impasse may be declared by either party at any time before, during, or after the 120-day period, so long as a true impasse exists (§ 209(3); *City of Mount Vernon*, 11 PERB ¶ 3095 (1978); see *New York City Sch. Dist.*, 34 PERB ¶ 3016 (2001); *City of Schenectady v. Helsby*, 57 Misc.2d 91 (Sup. Ct. Schenectady County 1968)). Impasse cannot be declared before the parties' proposals have been considered (*Village of Johnson City*, 12 PERB ¶ 3020 (1979)).

10:63. What happens when a school district and an employee organization reach an impasse?

Districts and employee organizations may agree to procedures on resolution of impasses, such as submission of open issues to impartial arbitration (§ 209(2); see *City of Newburgh v. Newman*, 69 N.Y.2d 166 (1987)). Such procedures may include a provision on how the costs of a mediator or arbitrator will be shared and, once agreed upon, must be followed.

In the absence of such agreed-upon impasse procedures or in the event that these procedures are unsuccessful, either party may request assistance from PERB, or PERB may render such assistance on its own (§ 209(2), (3); see **10:19, 10:64**).

The obligation to negotiate in good faith extends to participation in the mediation and fact-finding process. As such, refusal to participate in the mediation or fact-finding process constitutes an improper practice (*Poughkeepsie City Sch. Dist.*, 27 PERB ¶ 3079 (1994); *City of Mount Vernon*, 11 PERB ¶ 3095 (1978); see **10:67**).

10:64. What role does PERB have in settling an impasse?

If there is no agreement on procedures to resolve an impasse in collective bargaining, or these procedures fail, either party may formally request PERB, or PERB on its own may determine to assist in resolving the impasse (§ 209(2), (3)). Such assistance may include the services of a mediator, and if mediation fails, the services of a fact finder (§ 209(3)(a), (b)). The fact finder's report of recommendations must be released to the public five days after the report is given to the school superintendent and employee organization (§ 209(3)(c)). Either party may accept or reject any or all of the fact finder's recommendations. If the impasse continues, additional mediation, called "conciliation," may be provided (§ 209(3)(d)).

There are no charges to either the employer or the employee organization for these PERB services.

10:65. What happens if the current collective bargaining agreement expires before a successor agreement is negotiated?

In such situations, all the provisions of the expired agreement continue in full force and effect until the parties agree to a new agreement. This is because section 209-a(1)(e) of the Civil Service Law, commonly referred to as the *Triborough* Amendment, makes it an improper practice for an employer to refuse to continue all the terms of an expired agreement until a new agreement is negotiated.

This obligation ends, however, if the employee organization has violated section 210(1) of the Civil Service Law by striking or by causing, instigating, encouraging, or condoning a strike. In case of such a violation, the district may be able to unilaterally change certain policies and practices (see **10:75**).

The New York State Court of Appeals has found that the *Triborough* Amendment has the effect of extending the obligations of the agreement until a new agreement is reached (*Association of Surrogates & Supreme Court Reporters v. State of New York*, 79 N.Y.2d 39 (1992)). However, PERB has ruled that this is a statutory obligation, and collective bargaining agreements actually do expire for purposes of the Taylor Law, since to conclude otherwise would make it impossible for any union to ever establish the element of an "expired contract," which is necessary to state a claim for relief under the

Triborough Amendment, and thus, would effectively repeal the *Triborough* Amendment (*State of New York (Office of Parks and Recreation)*, 27 PERB ¶ 3001 (1994)).

10:66. Do all provisions in an expired agreement have to continue in effect during negotiations for a successor contract?

No. Certain obligations contained in a collective bargaining agreement may be made to end with the contract's expiration even under the *Triborough* Amendment by use of what is known as a "sunset clause" (see *Waterford-Halfmoon UFSD*, 27 PERB ¶ 3070 (1994)). Such a clause simply attaches a final effective date to a specific provision in the contract, such as one which determines the conditions upon which salary increments or step advances are to take place (see *Schuylerville CSD*, 29 PERB ¶ 3029 (1996)). The effectiveness of these clauses is based on the idea that the *Triborough* Amendment requires only that the contract, as written, continue in effect until a new contract is negotiated (§ 209-a (1)(e); *Waterford-Halfmoon*).

Improper Practices

10:67. What is an improper practice?

An *improper practice* is an action by either an employee organization or a public employer that is prohibited by section 209-a of the Civil Service Law. Most improper practices infringe on another party's ability to exercise rights granted by law (see **10:70–72**).

A party who files an improper practice charge also may petition PERB for injunctive relief pending a decision on the merits. That party must show reasonable cause to believe that an improper practice has occurred, and that immediate and irreparable injury, loss, or damage will result that would render a subsequent judgment on the merits ineffectual. Upon such a showing, PERB either will issue an order permitting the charging party to seek injunctive relief from state Supreme Court, or will itself petition the court for such injunctive relief on behalf of the charging party (§ 209-a).

10:68. Is there a deadline for filing improper practice charges?

Yes. For an improper practice charge to be timely, it must be filed within four months of either the date when the decision to take the action complained of is announced or the date when the action is implemented (4 NYCRR § 204.1(a)(1); *City of Oswego*, 23 PERB ¶ 3007 (1990)). However, if the relief sought is fundamentally private and the issue does not have significant public policy implications, the school district must be served a notice of claim within three months after the basis for the claim arose (Educ. Law § 3813(1); *Board of Educ. of the Union-Endicott CSD v. PERB*,

197 A.D.2d 276 (3d Dep't), *appeal denied*, 84 N.Y.2d 803 (1994); *Deposit CSD v. PERB*, 214 A.D.2d 288 (3d Dep't 1995), *appeal denied*, 88 N.Y.2d 866 (1996); see *Sidney CSD*, 28 PERB ¶ 3066 (1995); compare *Mahopac CSD*, 28 PERB ¶ 3045 (1995), where an improper practice charge that the district intentionally interfered with its employees' right to representation was ruled not subject to the notice of claim requirements).

The improper practice charge itself provides sufficient notice to meet this requirement if it is actually served within the three-month period. A school district does not waive a notice of claim defense if it fails to raise it in its original answer to the improper practice charge, as long as it raises the issue before PERB (*Deposit CSD*).

10:69. What happens if PERB agrees that an improper practice was committed?

PERB is authorized to order the offending party to cease and desist from that improper practice and to "take such affirmative action as will effectuate the policies" of the Taylor Law, including ordering payment of lost wages with interest and reinstatement of employees with or without back pay. Punitive damages are not authorized, although under "exceptional circumstances," attorneys' fees may be awarded (§ 205(5)(d); see *City of Troy*, 28 PERB ¶ 3027 (1995); *Town of Henrietta*, 28 PERB ¶ 3079 (1995)).

10:70. What types of improper practices might a public employer commit?

An employer commits an improper practice when it:
- Fails to negotiate collectively in good faith (§ 209-a(1)(d); see § 204(2), (3); **10:46**). Under certain circumstances, an employer's practice on a mandatory subject of bargaining that is not incorporated in a contract may become a term and condition of employment that cannot be altered unilaterally (*Canastota CSD*, 32 PERB ¶ 3003 (1999); see *County of Genesee*, 18 PERB ¶ 3016 (1985), *aff'd, Bork v. Newman*, 122 A.D.2d 329 (3d Dep't 1986); see **10:61**).
- Fails to continue all the terms of an expired agreement until a new one is negotiated, unless the employee organization has engaged in, caused, instigated, encouraged, or condoned a strike (§ 209-a(1)(e), see § 210(1)).
- Deliberately interferes with the rights of public employees to participate in or refrain from participating in employee organizations of their own choosing (§ 209-a(1)(a); see § 202, *Greenburgh 11 UFSD*, 33 PERB ¶ 3018 (2000); see also *City of Syracuse*, 36 PERB ¶ 3047 (2003); **10:15, 10:22**).

- Dominates or interferes with the formation or administration of employee organizations (§ 209-a(1)(b)).
- Discriminates against any employee for the purpose of encouraging or discouraging membership or participation in an employee organization (§ 209-a(1)(c)).
- Uses state funds appropriated for any purpose to train supervisors or other administrators in methods to discourage union organization or to discourage an employee from participating in a union-organizing drive (§ 209-a(1)(f); see also **10:16**).

10:71. Does an employer's refusal to provide an employee with information for use in preparation for grievance arbitration constitute an improper practice?

It may. Both employers and employee organizations have a reciprocal obligation, as part of the duty to bargain in good faith, to provide each other with information that is necessary and relevant to collective bargaining. The failure to do so may constitute an improper practice. According to PERB, this employer obligation to provide information extends through grievance processing and continues after a demand for arbitration has been filed, even though the same information also may be available by way of subpoena from an arbitrator (*Greenburgh No. 11 UFSD*, 33 PERB ¶ 3059 (2000); see also **10:77–83** for a discussion on grievances).

10:72. What are some examples of possible improper practices by an employee organization?

An employee organization (union) commits an improper practice when it interferes with the right of public employees to participate in or refrain from participating in employee organizations of their own choosing (§§ 209-a(2)(a), 202; see also Lab. Law § 211-a), when it refuses to negotiate collectively in good faith with a public employer as it is required to do (§§ 209-a(2)(b), § 204(2), (3)), or when it breaches its duty of fair representation to public employees under the Taylor Law (§ 209-a(2)(c)).

It also is an improper practice for an employee organization to make a credible threat of a strike in order to create pressure in negotiations (see *East Meadow UFSD*, 16 PERB ¶ 3086 (1983)), or to threaten to "work to rule," which is a concerted refusal to participate in "voluntary" activities, such as escorting students on field trips, writing recommendation letters for students or attending faculty meetings, where the school district has a reasonable expectation of participation (see *Haverling CSD*, 22 PERB ¶ 4554 (1989); see **10:74**).

It is also an improper practice for an employee organization to fail or refuse to provide to an agency shop fee payer an independently audited statement of its expenses and those of its affiliates, upon refund of a portion of such fees, along with an explanation of how the refund amount was determined, to allow an individual to object to the amount refunded (*Public Employees Fed'n (Raterman)*, 15 PERB ¶ 3024 (1982), *aff'd, Public Employees Fed'n v.* PERB, 93 A.D.2d 910 (3d Dep't 1983); *United Univ. Professions v. Newman*, 146 A.D.2d 273 (3d Dep't), *appeal denied*, 74 N.Y.2d 614 (1989); *Civil Serv. Employees Ass'n (Hartog)*, 32 PERB ¶ 3080 (1999); see **10:36**).

10:73. Does a union commit an improper practice in violation of its duty of fair representation if it does not obtain the exact same benefits for every member of the bargaining unit?

No. The duty of fair representation does not require an employee organization to obtain the same treatment for everyone it represents. "Where a union undertakes a good faith balancing of the divergent interests of its membership and chooses to forego benefits which may be gained for one class of employees in exchange for benefits to other employees, such accommodation does not, of necessity, violate the Union's duty of fair representation" (*Matter of Civil Serv. Bar Ass'n, Local 237 v. City of New York*, 64 N.Y.2d 188 (1984); but see, *Baker v. Bd. of Educ., Hoosick Falls CSD*, 194 Misc.2d 116 (2002), *aff'd*, 770 N.Y.S.2d 782 (3d Dep't 2004)).

10:74. What types of activities constitute a prohibited strike?

Any strike activity is prohibited activity. Specifically, the Taylor Law defines prohibited strike activity as "any strike or other concerted stoppage of work or slowdown by public employees" (§ 201(9)). It also states that "an employee who is absent from work without permission, or who abstains wholly or in part from the full performance of his duties in his normal manner without permission, on the date or dates when a strike occurs, shall be presumed to have engaged in such strike on such date or dates" (§ 210(2)(b)). For instance, an abnormally high absentee rate among employees may be deemed a strike (*Orleans-Niagara BOCES Teachers Ass'n*, 28 PERB ¶ 3050 (1995); *CSEA of Yonkers*, 13 PERB ¶ 3026 (1980), *aff'd*, 78 A.D.2d 1016 (2d Dep't 1980)).

A violation of this prohibition can be found in many forms of conduct, including a boycott of voluntary assignments or other work, such as field trips (*Pearl River UFSD*, 11 PERB ¶ 4530, *aff'd*, 11 PERB ¶ 3085 (1978)) and parent orientation sessions (see *Horseheads Teachers Ass'n and New York State United Teachers*, 15 PERB ¶ 3110 (1982)); a boycott of faculty meetings (see *Webutuck Teachers Ass'n*, 13 PERB ¶ 3041 (1980)); refusal to help students or volunteer for extracurricular assignments (see *Baylis v. Seaford UFSD*, 22 PERB ¶ 7533 (Sup. Ct. Nassau County 1989)); or even to threaten to "work to rule," which is a boycott of "voluntary" activities (see **10:72**).

A union's responsibility for an unlawful strike can be established through circumstantial evidence (*Orleans-Niagara BOCES Teachers Ass'n*).

10:75. What types of sanctions and penalties may be imposed against employees and employee organizations in the event of a strike?

There are court-imposed, PERB-administered, and school district-imposed sanctions and penalties against striking employees and their employee organizations.

- A court may issue an injunction against a strike, and if the injunction is violated, impose penalties for contempt (§ 211; Jud. Law §§ 750–751).

- PERB may determine that the employee organization will lose its automatic dues checkoff and any agency shop fee checkoff privileges (§ 210(3)(a), (f); see §§ 208(1)(b), 208(3)(b); see, for example, *Yonkers Fed'n of Teachers*, 32 PERB ¶ 3075 (1999)). But a settlement between a union and a school district that involves a suspension of any checkoff privileges in exchange for the union's agreement to refrain from further strike activities before the next agreement is negotiated is permissible (*Buffalo City Sch. Dist.*, 34 PERB ¶ 3012 (2001)).

- School districts are required to make certain deductions from the pay of each employee found in violation (§ 210(2)(f); also see **10:76**). Specifically, employees who strike are to be penalized twice their daily rate of pay for each day they are engaged in the strike (§ 210(2)(f)), as well as being subject to disciplinary action and penalties for misconduct (§ 210(2)(a)).

Furthermore, when an employee organization engages in prohibited strike activities, the district is no longer obligated to comply with the *Triborough* Amendment, which otherwise requires the continuation of the terms of an expired agreement until a new agreement is reached (§ 209-a(1)(e); see also **10:65**). The employee organization also may lose its right to charge an employer with an improper practice for making unilateral changes in mandatory subjects of bargaining (see *Somers CSD*, 9 PERB ¶ 3061 (1976)).

10:76. What are a school district's responsibilities in the event of a strike by school district employees?

Section 211 of the Civil Service Law provides that when it appears that public employees are threatening to strike, are about to strike, or have gone out on strike, the public employer, through its chief legal officer, must immediately apply to the New York State Supreme Court for an injunction against the strike. A temporary restraining order forbidding the strike may be issued by the court immediately (CPLR §§ 6301, 6313). Those who continue to strike despite the restraining order are in contempt of court and subject to penalties of up to $1,000 and/or 30 days' imprisonment, at the discretion of the court (Jud. Law § 751(1)).

Furthermore, school officials must impose the "two-for-one" payroll penalty on strikers. This penalty is a loss of twice the daily rate of pay for every day the employee strikes (§ 210(2)(f)). If the strike involved only limited activities, such as extracurricular and coaching activities, the district may be limited to withholding compensation for those activities only (see *Baylis v. Seaford UFSD*, 22 PERB ¶ 7533 (Sup. Ct. Nassau County 1989); **10:74**). These deductions must be made between 30 and 90 days after a determination that employees have violated the law prohibiting strikes, and cannot be made outside this statutory time period (§ 210(2)(f); see *King v. Carey*, 57 N.Y.2d 505 (1982)). Measurement of the 30- to 90-day time period does not start until the affected employees have been notified individually of the determination that they have committed a violation (*Plainview-Old Bethpage Congress of Teachers v. Bd. of Educ. of the Plainview-Old Bethpage CSD*, 100 A.D.2d 849 (2d Dep't), *aff'd*, 63 N.Y.2d 921, *rehearing denied*, 64 N.Y.2d 755 (1984)).

Separate from the imposition of the payroll penalty, the Taylor Law prohibits the payment by the employer of any compensation to a public employee for any day or any part of a day in which he or she engages in such prohibited activities (§ 210(3)(h)).

Finally, the school district is responsible for notifying and providing information to PERB concerning the strike violations (§ 210(3)(b)). School officials also should give PERB's Office of Counsel sufficient information so that it may begin proceedings to revoke the offending employee organization's dues and agency shop fee deduction privileges (see § 210(3)(a), (f)).

Grievances

10:77. What is a grievance?

Generally, a *grievance* is a claim that a specific provision (or provisions) of a collective bargaining agreement has been violated. However, contractual grievance procedures may be extended by mutual agreement to apply to a broad range of actions and decisions outside the contract, such as the application of district policies (see, e.g., *City of Schenectady*, 21 PERB ¶ 3022 (1988); *Pearl River UFSD*, 11 PERB ¶ 3085 (1978)).

The grievant, the party bringing the grievance, seeks a determination that the other party has violated the contract and that specific remedial action should be taken.

A school district's use of intimidating and coercive measures, such as installing metal detectors at grievance hearings or changing the location of grievance hearings or other grievance procedures, without union agreement, may violate an employee's rights under the Taylor Law to have grievances heard (*Greenburgh 11 UFSD*, 33 PERB ¶ 3018 (2000)).

10:78. How are grievances resolved?

In most cases, procedures for resolutions of grievances, or grievance procedures, are provided in school district collective bargaining agreements. The Taylor Law provides that a certified or recognized employee organization has the right to represent employees in the settlement of grievances (§§ 203–204, 208(1)(a)).

Most grievance procedures involve several different levels or steps that are progressively invoked to satisfy both parties. If a grievance cannot be resolved internally between the parties, such agreements usually provide for a final settlement by either advisory or binding arbitration (see **10:79–83**).

In addition, article 15-C of the General Municipal Law (which predates the Taylor Law) specifies rules regarding grievance procedures. Specifically, any political subdivision of the state, including school districts, that has 100 or more full-time employees, except the city of New York, must establish certain minimal grievance procedures (Gen. Mun. Law §§ 682(1), 684(1)).

These mandated grievance procedures must consist of at least two stages and cover any grievance relating to employees' health or safety, physical facilities, materials or equipment furnished to employees or supervision of employees. The law does not require that grievance procedures address issues of an employee's rate of compensation, retirement benefits, disciplinary proceedings or other matters that can be appealed to the commissioner of education or through a contractual grievance procedure (see Gen. Mun. Law § 682(4)).

If a school district does not adopt a grievance procedure, the procedure established by section 684, which consists of two stages and an appellate stage, goes into effect automatically under the law's requirement (Gen. Mun. Law § 684(1)).

The law calls for final resolution of grievances by advisory arbitration by a grievance board appointed by the superintendent (Gen. Mun. Law § 684(4), (7)). Because the arbitration is advisory, the school board either may accept or reject the grievance board's recommendations.

10:79. May a school board agree to arbitration for the resolution of grievances?

Yes. As there are no prohibitions from the constitution, statute, or common law principles, arbitration under the terms of a collective bargaining agreement is a permissible form of resolving disputes between a board of education and its employees (*Board of Educ. of Watertown City Sch. Dist. v. Watertown Educ. Ass'n*, 93 N.Y.2d 132 (1999)). However, where there is an agreement to arbitrate grievances arising under a collective bargaining agreement, a particular grievance may not be arbitrated if it falls outside of the agreement to arbitrate (*Pocantico Hills CSD v. Pocantico Hills Teachers Ass'n*, 264 A.D.2d 397 (2d Dep't 1999), *appeal denied*, 94 N.Y.2d 759 (2000)). Moreover some duties or responsibilities are so important that a school district will not be permitted to delegate them or to bargain them away. For example, a school board cannot surrender its statutory authority and allow an arbitrator to determine whether a teacher is to be granted tenure (see *Cohoes City Sch. Dist. v. Cohoes Teachers Ass'n*, 40 N.Y.2d 774 (1976)); or be divested of its right to inspect teacher personnel files (*Board of Educ., Great Neck UFSD v. Areman*, 41 N.Y.2d 527 (1977)); or be bound by contractual provisions that interfere with a school board's responsibility to maintain adequate classroom standards (see *Honeoye Falls-Lima CSD v. Honeoye Falls-Lima Educ. Ass'n*, 49 N.Y.2d 732 (1980)).

On the other hand, although ill advised, it does not offend public policy for a district to bargain away its right to choose between qualified applicants for a particular teaching assignment (*Matter of United Fed'n. of Teachers v. Bd. of Educ. of the City School Dist. of the City of N.Y.*, 1 N.Y.3d 72 (2003)).

10:80. Is arbitration of a grievance dispute binding or advisory?

The parties involved in a grievance may agree that arbitration either will be advisory, where the arbitrator's decision has limited legal effect, or binding, where the arbitrator's decision will be final and binding and can be appealed only under certain limited circumstances (see **10:81**).

10:81. May grievance decisions rendered after binding arbitration be appealed in court?

Yes. An arbitrator's award may be challenged in court. However, the standard by which a court will overturn or reject a decision rendered after arbitration is difficult to meet.

In a review of a binding arbitration decision, errors of law or fact are generally not grounds to vacate the arbitrator's award, and courts will grant a petition to vacate the award only in cases where:

- There was corruption, fraud, or misconduct in procuring the award.
- The arbitrator was biased.
- The arbitrator exceeded his or her power or so imperfectly executed that power that a final and definite award was not made.
- The arbitrator failed to follow procedure (CPLR § 7511(b)(1)).

An arbitrator exceeds his or her power if an award violates a strong public policy, is "totally" or "completely" irrational, or exceeds a specifically enumerated limitation on his or her power (*Silverman v. Benmor Coats, Inc.*, 61 N.Y.2d 299 (1984); *Rochester City Sch. Dist. v. Rochester Teachers Ass'n*, 41 N.Y.2d 578 (1977)).

10:82. May grievance decisions rendered after advisory arbitration be appealed in court?

Advisory arbitration awards themselves usually may not be appealed. As a general rule, a court will not confirm an award issued following advisory arbitration (*Benjamin Rush Employees United v. McCarthy*, 76 N.Y.2d 781 (1990)). However, in certain circumstances, the parties may, by their conduct, convert an arbitration award issued pursuant to an agreement providing for advisory arbitration into a binding determination (*Board of Educ. of the Yonkers City Sch. Dist. v. Yonkers Fed'n of Teachers*, 46 N.Y.2d 727 (1978); *Hempstead Classroom Teachers Ass'n v. Board of Educ. of the Hempstead UFSD*, 79 A.D.2d 709 (2d Dep't 1980)).

On the other hand, once a school board has made a final decision on an advisory arbitration award, that determination may be overturned by a court if the board acted in an "arbitrary" or "capricious" manner when accepting or rejecting the award (CPLR § 7803; *Pell v. Bd. of Educ. of UFSD No. 1 of the Towns of Scarsdale & Mamaroneck*, 34 N.Y.2d 222 (1974)).

10:83. How are arbitrators selected?

Arbitration clauses usually designate one of a number of organizations, usually the American Arbitration Association (AAA) or PERB, as the administrator of an arbitration agreement. Thereafter, the organization may do most of the selection and scheduling work, including sending the parties one or more lists of names of arbitrators for each party to rank or veto, and appointing the highest-ranking arbitrator who was not vetoed by either party (see, for example, 4 NYCRR § 207.7; AAA Labor Arbitration Rule 12).

Family and Medical Leave Act

10:84. What is the Family and Medical Leave Act?

The Family and Medical Leave Act (FMLA) is a federal law that requires school districts with more than 50 employees within 75 miles of their work site (see 29 USC §§ 203(v),(w),(x), 2611(2)(B)(ii), (4)(A)(iii); 2618(a)(1); 29 CFR §§ 825.104(a), 825.110(a)(3), 825.600(b)) to provide up to 12 weeks of unpaid leave to eligible employees for medical or child-care purposes during a designated 12-month period (see 29 USC § 2612(a)(1), (c), (d)(1)). The 12-month period during which 12 weeks of leave may be taken is measured either against the calendar year, any fixed 12-month "leave year" (such as a fiscal year), or a rolling 12-month period measured either forward from the date of an employee's first FMLA leave or backwards from the date an employee uses FMLA leave (29 CFR § 825.200(b)). Failure by the employer to select any one of these methods allows employees to use the most beneficial method for them until the employer designates the appropriate measure (see 29 CFR § 825.200(e)).

Absences of one or more weeks when school is closed and employees are not expected to report to work do not count against FMLA leave entitlements. However, when a particular holiday falls during a week taken as FMLA leave, the entire week is counted as FMLA leave (see 29 CFR § 825.200(f)).

Although the family and medical leave is generally unpaid (see 29 USC § 2612(c), (d); 29 CFR § 825.207(a); see **10:90**), school districts must continue normal health insurance benefits during the leave except as otherwise provided by law and regulations (see 29 USC § 2614(c)(1); 29 CFR § 825.209).

10:85. What makes an employee eligible for FMLA Leave?

An employee is eligible under the law to take family and medical leave if he or she has been employed for at least 12 months and has worked at least 1,250 hours in the 12 months immediately preceding commencement of leave (see 29 USC § 2611(2)(A); 29 CFR § 825.110(a)). When the need for family or medical leave is foreseeable, the employee must give 30 days' notice of his or her intention to take the leave (29 USC § 2612(e); 29 CFR § 825.302(a)).

10:86. May an employee sue an employer for alleged violations of FMLA?

Yes. An employee may sue a school district in state or federal court, or file a complaint in an administrative proceeding for violations of the law (29 USC § 2617(a)(2), (b)(1); 29 CFR § 825.400(a)). If the court rules in favor of the employee, that employee may recover wages, salary and benefits, compensation for actual monetary loss (as for example the cost of providing care), job reinstatement or promotion, as well as attorneys' fees and costs (29 USC § 2617(a)(1), (3); 29 CFR § 825.400(c)).

10:87. Are school districts required to give employees notice of their rights under FMLA?

Yes. All school districts, regardless of the number of people they employ, are required to post notices on FMLA (29 USC § 2619; 29 CFR § 825.300(a)). School districts that have employees who are eligible for FMLA leave must include information on FMLA in any handbook that provides information on employee benefits (29 CFR § 825.301(a)(1)). In addition, districts must provide information on FMLA whenever an employee requests a FMLA-qualified leave, whether or not the employee actually requests FMLA leave, including notice of their decision to designate leave as FMLA leave (29 CFR §§ 825.301(b), (c), 825.302(c)).

10:88. What is the difference between family leave and medical leave under FMLA?

Family leave is available for the birth and care of an infant, adoption and care of a child, and the placement with the employee of a child in foster care (29 USC § 2612(a)(1)(A), (B); 29 CFR § 825.112(a)(1), (2); see also **8:183–188**). An employee may only take family leave during the 12-month period beginning with the birth or placement of a child (29 USC § 2612(a)(2); 29 CFR § 825.201).

Medical leave is available to an employee who has a serious health condition that prevents the employee from performing his or her job, or to care for a spouse, dependent child, or parent who has a serious health condition (29 USC §§ 2611(7), (11), (12), (13), 2612(a)(1)(C),(D); 29 CFR §§ 825.112(a)(3), (4), 825.113(c)). A serious health condition is defined generally by FMLA as "an illness, injury, impairment, or physical or mental condition" that involves hospitalization or other inpatient care or continuing treatment by a health care provider (29 USC § 2611(11)), and in more detail in FMLA's implementing regulations (see 29 CFR §§ 825.114, 825.800). A district can require an employee requesting a medical leave to produce a certificate from his or her health care provider that gives the basis for and anticipated duration of the medical leave (29 USC § 2613(a), (b); 29 CFR §§ 825.305, 825.306). If the district doubts the validity of the doctor's certification, the law provides a method for obtaining a second and, if necessary, a third medical opinion (29 USC § 2613(c), (d); 29 CFR § 825.307).

10:89. May employees take FMLA leave on an intermittent basis?

It depends. Employees may take intermittent leave for family leaves only if the employer agrees to permit intermittent leave; employees are not entitled to intermittent family leave (29 USC § 2612(b)(1); 29 CFR § 825.203(b)).

Unlike family leave, medical leave may be taken on an intermittent basis (29 USC § 2612(b)(1); 29 CFR § 825.203(c)). The district may temporarily transfer the employee to a position with equal pay and benefits if the intermittent leave is foreseeable and the position better accommodates recurring periods of leave (29 USC § 2612(b)(2); 29 CFR § 825.204). Additionally, for instructional employees whose absences due to foreseeable medical treatment will exceed 20 percent of the working days of the period over which that leave will occur, the district can require the employee either to take a block leave (take the time all at once) or accept a temporary transfer to another position with equal pay and benefits which better accommodates recurring periods of leave and for which the employee is qualified (29 USC § 2618(c); 29 CFR § 825.601).

10:90. Can a school district require an employee to use accrued paid leave time under a collective bargaining agreement rather than take an unpaid FMLA leave?

Yes. Unless otherwise agreed to in a collective bargaining agreement, an employee may choose or a school district may require an employee to use accrued paid vacation, personal or family leave for purposes of a family leave or a medical leave to care for a spouse, dependent child, or parent with a serious health condition (29 USC § 2612(d)(2)(A); 29 CFR § 825.207). However, although leave under a disability plan may count as FMLA leave, paid leave may not be substituted if the employee is receiving workers' compensation (see 29 CFR § 825.207(d)).

In addition, an employee may choose or a district can require an employee to use accrued paid vacation, personal, or medical/sick leave for purposes of a medical leave (29 USC § 2612(d)(2)(B); 29 CFR § 825.207).

Furthermore, under FMLA, an employee cannot use accrued family or sick leave when he or she would not otherwise be able to use such leave under the terms of a collective bargaining agreement or board policy (see 29 USC § 2612(d)(2)(B); 29 CFR § 825.207(b), (c)).

10:91. Does an employee who takes a FMLA leave have the right to return to his or her job after the leave is over?

Yes. At the end of the leave the employee is entitled to return to the position he or she held when the leave commenced or to an equivalent position (see 29 USC § 2614(a)(1); 29 CFR § 825.214(a)). For school district employees, the determination of how an employee will be restored to an equivalent position must be made on the basis of established school board policies and practices and the collective bargaining agreement (29 USC § 2618(e); 29 CFR § 825.604). For example, school districts are free under the law to assign a returning elementary teacher to a different grade from the class he or she taught prior to the leave consistent with any applicable district policy or the collective bargaining agreement.

Generally, employers may not require employees to take more FMLA leave than necessary, and employees may return to work earlier than anticipated (29 CFR § 825.309(c)). However, special limitations apply with respect to instructional employees returning from leave near the conclusion of an academic term (see 29 USC § 2618(d); 29 CFR § 825.602). Depending on the duration of the leave and the length of time remaining until the end of the school term, the district can require the employee to wait until the next term to return. The additional time is not counted as FMLA leave (see 29 CFR § 825.603(b)).

An employee does not lose any previously accrued employment benefits as a result of the leave, but he or she is not entitled to accrue seniority or additional benefits for the period of the leave (29 USC § 2614(a)(2), (3); 29 CFR § 825.215(d)(2)).

10:92. What are the collective bargaining implications of FMLA?

The leave entitlements established by FMLA do not diminish any employee benefits established in a collective bargaining agreement (29 USC § 2652(a)). Thus, if a contract provides greater leave benefits, the provisions of the contract apply.

Conversely, no collective bargaining agreement may diminish the benefits provided by FMLA (29 USC § 2652(b)). Thus, FMLA provides a minimum floor of benefits for all eligible employees, even if a collective bargaining agreement provides lesser benefits.

Any proposal for negotiations on FMLA leave is a mandatory subject of bargaining under the Taylor Law (see *Rome Hosp.*, 27 PERB ¶ 4575 (1994)), even if it duplicates the benefits promised by statute (see generally *City of Cohoes*, 31 PERB ¶ 3020 (1998)).

11. Retirement

11:1. Is there a mandatory retirement age for school district employees?

No. There is no mandatory retirement age for most public employees in New York State (§ 530; Exec. Law § 296(3-a)(a); see Age Discrimination in Employment Act (ADEA), 29 USC §§ 621(b), 623(a)(1); *Johnson v. State of New York*, 49 F.3d 75 (2d Cir. 1995)).

11:2. Does an early retirement incentive violate the federal Age Discrimination in Employment Act?

It depends. The federal Age Discrimination in Employment Act (ADEA) broadly prohibits age-based discrimination in the workplace (see 29 USC § 623(a)). However, it also specifically allows voluntary early retirement incentives that do not arbitrarily discriminate on the basis of age (29 USC § 623(f)(2)(B)(ii), see 29 USC § 621(b)).

Applying these principles, a federal appeals court with jurisdiction over New York upheld an early retirement incentive contained in a teachers' collective bargaining agreement. Participation in the program, which offered teachers additional benefits if they retired when they first became eligible to retire, was triggered by years of service, not age, and therefore did not arbitrarily discriminate on the basis of age. In addition, it was truly voluntary, and was made available for a reasonable amount of time. The court also ruled that the ADEA does not require that employers offer identical early retirement incentives for employees of different ages (*Auerbach v. Board of Educ. of the Harborfields CSD of Greenlawn*, 136 F.3d 104 (2d Cir. 1998)).

On the other hand, one federal district court with jurisdiction over part of New York found that an early retirement incentive which required that teachers retire at the end of the school year in which they first became eligible to retire or suffer a reduction in payments for already accumulated sick leave benefits violated the ADEA because it diminished their accrued benefits as they got older (*O'Brien v. Board of Educ. of Deer Park UFSD*, 127 F. Supp. 2d 342 (E.D.N.Y. 2001)).

All statutory references in this chapter are to the Retirement and Social Security Law unless otherwise noted.

11:3. Under what circumstances are school district employees entitled to health benefits when they retire?

Generally, the entitlement of school district employees to health benefits when they retire derives from either contractual provisions in an applicable collective bargaining agreement or school district policy. The contributions made by a school district to its retired teachers' health insurance premiums are not constitutionally protected pension benefits (*Lippman v. Board of Education*, 104 A.D.2d 123 (1984), *aff'd* 66 N.Y.2d 313 (1985)). However, if a school district provides health insurance benefits to employees after they retire based on a contractual obligation, those retirees will be entitled to those benefits at the same contribution rate until the district negotiates a decrease in benefits or an increase in contribution rate from its active employees. At that point, the district may require a corresponding diminution in benefits or an increase in contribution rate from its retirees, unless prohibited from doing so by the terms of a collective bargaining agreement (Laws of 2004, ch. 25).

One state Supreme Court judge ruled that this law even prevents school districts from eliminating reimbursement to Social Security-eligible retirees for their Medicare B premiums. The court rejected the school district's argument that it could not make a corresponding reduction for active employees who do not receive Medicare Part B coverage. According to the court, the law does not require that the "exact same benefit be taken from both groups (retirees and active employees), but only that there be a 'corresponding diminution of benefits. . . .'" (*Bryant v. Bd. of Educ. of Chenango Forks CSD*, 777 N.Y.S.2d 883 (Sup. Ct. Broome Co. 2004)).

Once employees have retired, they may not be able to make changes to their health insurance coverage, if that right is only extended to active employees in a district benefit plan (*Odorizzi v. Otsego Northern Catskill BOCES*, 307 A.D.2d 490 (2003)).

11:4. Can a school district deduct from an employee's salary the cost of participating in a tax-sheltered annuity plan to increase his or her retirement income?

Yes. The local school board must approve a tax-sheltered annuity plan, pursuant to a written agreement (usually the collective bargaining agreement between the employee's union and the district) by which the district reduces the employee's annual salary for the purpose of purchasing the annuity (Educ. Law §§ 3109, 3109-A; 26 USC § 403(b); see **8:181**).

Overview of Public Retirement Systems

Editor's Note: As a result of the federal No Child Left Behind Act of 2001 (NCLB) some teachers aides have been reclassified as teaching assistants. By law, teacher aides join the New York State and Local Employees' Retirement System (ERS), and teaching assistants join the New York State Teachers' Retirement System (TRS). For information on the impact of the NCLB reclassification on membership in the retirement system, please refer to a Fact Sheet issued by the State Retirement System that is available at http://www.nystrs.org/main/library/TeacherAides.pdf. For additional information on the NCLB, see Leaving No Child Behind in New York, 2nd Edition, *a handbook published by the New York State School Boards Association and distributed by LexisNexis.*

11:5. What state retirement plans are available for school district employees?

Outside New York City, noninstructional employees participate in the New York State and Local Employees' Retirement System (ERS) (§§ 40(b), (c), 500(b)(4), 600(b)(3)); while teachers participate in the New York State Teachers' Retirement System (TRS) (§§ 40(e), 500(b)(2), 600(b)(2); Educ. Law §§ 501(4), 503(1)). Public school employees in New York City are covered by the New York City Teachers' Retirement System or the Board of Education Retirement System of the City of New York (BERS) (Educ. Law § 2575(1)(a); NYC Admin. Code §§ 13-501(7)(a), 13-503).

11:6. Can the benefits of a member of a state retirement plan be changed to the member's disadvantage?

No. The state constitution makes membership in any pension or retirement system of the state or a municipality a contractual relationship and, thus, the system's benefits may not be diminished or impaired (N.Y. Const. Art. V, § 7). This constitutional provision guarantees statutory benefits in place on the date of an individual's employment (*Kleinfeldt v. New York City Employees' Ret. Sys.*, 36 N.Y.2d 95 (1975); *Birnbaum v. New York State Teachers' Ret. Sys.*, 5 N.Y.2d 1 (1958)).

For example, the New York State Court of Appeals invalidated any reductions in Tier III benefits that purportedly were made by Chapter 414 of the Laws of 1983. The 1983 law attempted to alter previous benefits by reducing the system's death benefit and by preventing members from withdrawing their contributions to the system until age 62, even if they left service earlier (*Public Employees Fed'n v. Cuomo*, 62 N.Y.2d 450 (1984)).

This constitutional provision also has been held to require that the mortality table in effect on the date a member joins the Teachers' Retirement System is guaranteed to the member in the calculation of her or his benefits and may not be changed (*Birnbaum*).

11:7. Do all members of state retirement plans have the same obligations and benefits?

No. The obligations and benefits of members of the Teachers' Retirement System and the Employees' Retirement System vary, depending on the tier in which an employee belongs. For convenience, the systems use a tier concept to distinguish these groups. The same tier structure is used for members in all state retirement plans. Tiers are established to ensure that members' benefits are not reduced or impaired, since the New York State Constitution prohibits diminishment of benefits (see **11:6**). Participation in a particular tier is based on the date the employee joined the system.

Members in *Tier I* include employees with a date of system membership before July 1, 1973 (see § 440(a); 2 NYCRR § 325.2(a)).

Tier II members include those employees with a date of system membership between July 1, 1973 and July 26, 1976 (2 NYCRR § 325.2(b)). Although Tier II expired on June 30, 1976 (see § 440(a)), anyone with a date of system membership between July 1 and July 27, 1976 became a member in Tier II, because Chapter 890 of the Laws of 1976, which created Tier III, was not signed into law until July 27, 1976 (*Oliver v. County of Broome*, 113 A.D.2d 239 (3d Dep't. 1985), *motion for leave to appeal denied*, 67 N.Y.2d 607, *appeal on constitutional grounds denied*, 67 N.Y.2d 1027 (1986); 2 NYCRR § 325.1).

Members in *Tier III* include those employees with a date of system membership between July 27, 1976, and September 1, 1983 (§§ 500(a), 520; 2 NYCRR § 325.2(c)).

Members in *Tier IV* generally include those employees with a date of system membership on or after September 1, 1983 (2 NYCRR § 325.2(d)).

Information on tier membership related to the reclassification of teacher's aides as teaching assistants as a result of the federal No Child Left Behind Act of 2001 (NCLB) is available at: http://www.nystrs.org/main/library/TeacherAides.pdf.

11:8. What are the requirements for service retirement and benefits for members in Tier I?

Tier I TRS members may retire at any age with 35 years of total credited service (Educ. Law § 535(1)(a)). Tier I TRS and ERS members may retire after age 55 with the equivalent of five or more years of credited service (§§ 75-c(a)(1)(b), 75-g(c), 75-i(a), 76(a); Educ. Law § 535(1)(b) and (c)).

11:9. What are the requirements for service retirement and benefits for members in Tier II?

The normal retirement age for members in Tier II is 62 years (§ 442(a)).

Retirement is permitted between the ages of 55 and 62, but with a reduction in benefits according to the following formula:

- One half of 1 percent per month for each of the first 24 full months by which retirement predates age 62 (§ 442(a)(1).
- One quarter of 1 percent per month for each full month by which retirement predates age 60. In no event is retirement allowed before age 55 (§ 442(a)(2)).

A Tier II member, however, may retire without reduction in benefits if he or she is at least 55 years old and has completed 30 or more years of service (§ 442(b)(1)).

11:10. What are the requirements for service retirement and benefits available to members in Tier III?

Members in Tier III are covered by the provisions of the Coordinated-Escalator Retirement Plan (CO-ESC), as set forth in Article 14 of the Retirement and Social Security Law, or the Coordinated Retirement Plan, as set forth in Article 15 (§§ 500(a), 600(a)). The Article 14 plan integrates Social Security benefits with service retirement. Members must contribute 3 percent of their wages until they have 10 years of membership or 10 years of service credited with the retirement system (§§ 517(a), 613(a), 902(b)(1)). Members must render at least five years of credited service and attain age 62 to be eligible for normal retirement (§§ 503(a), 516(a), 603(a), 612(a)).

Members who retire between the ages of 55 and 62 with less than 30 years of credited service have their benefits reduced based on their age at retirement (§§ 504(a)-(c), 603(i), 604(a), (b)). In addition to these reductions, if a member elects to retire under Article 14, his or her retirement benefits commencing at age 62 will be reduced by 50 percent of the primary Social Security benefit (§§ 504(a)-(c), 511(a)). However, a member may retire under Article 15 at age 55 and 30 years of service with no reduction in benefits (§ 603(a)).

11:11. What are the requirements for service retirement and benefits available to members in Tier IV?

Members in Tier IV are covered by the provisions of the Coordinated Retirement Plan, as set forth in Article 15 of the Retirement and Social Security Law. Members in Tier IV must contribute 3 percent of their wages until they have 10 years of membership or 10 years of service credited with the retirement system (§§ 613(a), 902(b)(1)). Members will be eligible for a normal retirement benefit at age 62, if they have a minimum of five years of credited New York State service, or at age 55, if credited with 30 years of service (§§ 603(a), 612(a)).

Members may retire between the ages of 55 and 62 with less than 30 years of service, with a reduced retirement allowance (§§ 603(i), 604(a), (b)).

11:12. What is meant by vesting?

Vesting occurs when an employee is legally entitled to receive retirement benefits without the need to render additional service. Generally, employees become vested after five years of service in one of the retirement systems (§§ 76(a)(1), 502(a), 516(a), 602(a), 612(a); Educ. Law §§ 503(3), 535(1)(b)). Once vested, an employee may receive benefits under one of the retirement systems upon retiring at the statutorily specified age, depending on the tier to which he or she belongs. However, retirement after five years, but less than the statutorily required number of service years, will result in a reduced retirement benefit (see **11:9–11**).

11:13. What is meant by final average salary and how does it affect a member's retirement benefit?

Final average salary is the highest average annual compensation earned during any three years of credited service (§§ 2(9), 443(a), 512(a), 608(a); Educ. Law § 501(11)(b)). The retirement systems use the concept of final average salary as one factor in computing pensions for retiring members (see **11:26–29**).

The calculation of final average salary may be limited in some cases. Depending on a member's tier and date of membership, earnings for any 12-month period that exceed certain amounts may be excluded from a member's calculation of final average salary. The limitations are set forth below:

- For Tier I members who joined on or after June 17, 1971, any amount of salary in a particular 12-month period that exceeds the salary base of the previous 12 months by more than 20 percent (§ 431(4); see *Kleinfeldt v. New York City Employees' Ret. Sys.*, 36 N.Y.2d 95 (1975)).
- For Tier II members, salary earned in any one year that exceeds the average of the previous two years by more than 20 percent (§ 443(a)).
- For Tier III and IV members, salary earned in any one year that exceeds the average of the previous two years by more than 10 percent (§§ 512(a), 608(a)).

For Tier I members, lump sum payments for unused sick leave or vacation, and any other form of termination payments or retirement bonuses or incentives, are included in the computation of final average salary only if the member joined a retirement system before June 17, 1971. For Tier I members who joined after June 17, 1971 and for the members of all the other tiers, final average salary does not include these payments (§§ 431, 443(a); *Kleinfeldt*). Such payments may not be included in any three-year final average salary calculation for any TRS member.

Retirement benefits for Tier I TRS members who joined before June 17, 1971 may be based, in the alternative, on a five-year final average salary, including termination pay, if it constitutes compensation earned as a teacher (21 NYCRR §§ 5003.1, 5003.2; see also *Van Haneghan v. New York State Teachers' Ret. Sys.*, 6 A.D.3d 1019 (3d Dep't 2004)).

11:14. How do early retirement incentives offered by the state affect the age requirements for retirements in the various tiers?

Periodically, the state offers early retirement incentive plans that allow public employees to retire at an earlier age than that at which they would normally be allowed to retire. For example, in 2002, under a state early retirement incentive, employees other than superintendents who were at least 50 years of age with at least 10 years of service could take advantage of an incentive pursuant to which an employee would receives one month of additional service credit for each year of service, up to 36 months (Laws of 2002, ch. 69, Part A §§ 1(f),5, 6(a)). However, employees could not receive both the state incentive and a locally negotiated incentive contained in a collective bargaining agreement, unless the employer exempted its eligible employees from the waiver (Laws of 2002, ch. 69, § 4(b)). In addition, the early retirement incentive contained reductions, which varied by tier, for individuals who retired before the age at which they were eligible for a full and unreduced pension (Laws of 2002, ch. 69, § 6(a)). School boards could only provide the benefits of the state early retirement incentive to their employees by resolution (Laws of 2002, ch. 69, § 4(a)).

Employees who submit their resignations prior to a school board's decision to participate in a state early retirement incentive program are not entitled to participate in the program (*Dodge v. Board of Educ. for the Schodack CSD*, 237 A.D.2d 806 (3d Dep't 1997)).

11:15. Are Tier III and Tier IV member contributions subject to taxation?

Under 26 USC section 414(h) of the Internal Revenue Code, as implemented by sections 517(f) and 613(d) of the state Retirement and Social Security Law, the 3 percent contribution made by Tier III and Tier IV members is not subject to federal income tax. Those contributions are still subject to New York State taxation (Tax Law § 612(b)(26)). The 3 percent contributions are included in gross income for federal income tax purposes when they are distributed at retirement or upon withdrawal from a retirement system (26 USC §§ 61(a)(11), 72, 402(a)).

11:16. May a member borrow from his or her accumulated deposits in the Teachers' Retirement System (TRS) or Employees' Retirement System (ERS)?

Any member who has credit for at least one year of service may borrow from their contributions (§§ 50(a)(1), 517-b(a), 517-c(b), 613-a(a), 613-b(b); Educ. Law § 512-b(1)). The loan for members in Tiers I and II may not be less than $25 for ERS members or $300 for TRS members or exceed three-fourths of the member's accumulated contributions. TRS members must not have received a loan within the previous six months (§ 50(a)(1); Educ. Law § 512-b(1); 2 NYCRR § 351.2; 21 NYCRR § 5004.2). Members who are in Tiers III and IV may borrow an amount no less than $1,000 and up to 75 percent of their accumulated contributions (§§ 517-b(a), 517-c(b), 613-a(a), 613-b(b); see also New York State and Local Retirement Systems Employer Guide at http://www.osc.state.ny.us/retire/emplguid/loans.pdf).

In addition, the Legislature has authorized TRS to adopt rules and regulations permitting a loan at any time prior to retirement to a teacher who is not in active service or on a leave of absence (Educ. Law § 512-b(8)).

A loan must be repaid in equal installments that are at least 2 percent of the member's contract salary, and sufficient to repay the total amount due together with interest paid on the unpaid balance within five years (§§ 517-b(b), 517-c(c), 613-a(b), 613-b(c); Educ. Law § 512-b(2); 2 NYCRR § 351.6(a); 21 NYCRR § 5004.4(c)). However, provisions in effect through July 1, 2005 at the time this book went to press, authorized a public retirement system to suspend the loan repayment obligation of a member who is absent on military duty, for as long as the member is absent for such duty. Any such suspension extends the time for repayment of the unpaid balance of the loan for the same length of time that the loan is suspended (Laws of 2004, ch. 127).

11:17. May a member remove his or her contributions from the Teachers' Retirement System (TRS) or the Employees' Retirement System (ERS)?

Yes, in some cases. Tier I and II members may withdraw their voluntary contributions at any time with interest (§ 51(c), see Educ. Law § 512(a)).

Tier III and IV members may only withdraw their contributions after they have left public employment, if they have less than 10 years of service credit, and are ineligible to receive other benefits (§§ 517(b), (c), 613(c)). Upon withdrawal of Tier III and IV contributions, membership in the retirement system ceases (§§ 517(c), 517-a(4), 613(c); Educ. Law § 503(3)). Tier III and IV members with 10 or more years of service credit may not withdraw their contributions (§§ 517(c), 613(c)).

Except in limited circumstances, any member who has less than five years of credited service, has left public employment for at least seven years, and has not withdrawn his or her contributions will have his or her membership in TRS or ERS cancelled (§§ 40(f)(1), 517-a(1); Educ. Law § 503(3); see Educ. Law § 512-a(1); 21 NYCRR § 5006.2(a)). After the required notice has been given, any contributions left unclaimed may be declared abandoned (§ 109(a), (b); Educ. Law § 531(1)).

Unclaimed contributions may be reclaimed upon presentation of a valid claim by the former member or his or her estate (§ 109(c); Educ. Law § 531(4); see **11:16** in reference to a member borrowing against his or her contributions).

11:18. Can retired school district employees authorize automatic deductions from their retirement allowance?

Yes. Retired school district employees may have the cost of participating in union employee benefit plans and the cost of membership dues automatically deducted from their retirement allowance (§ 110-c; Educ. Law § 536). Retirees participating in the New York State Health Insurance Plan (NYSHIP) may also have the cost of contributions deducted from their retirement allowance (Civ. Serv. Law § 167(3)). Retired employees may also authorize voluntary contributions from their retirement allowance to the political action committee of their union (Educ. Law § 536(2); Administrative Code of the City of New York § 13-561).

11:19. Can a member of a retirement system buy credit for prior public service?

Yes. An active member of a retirement system who previously was a member of a public retirement system, and whose earlier membership ceased because of insufficient service credit (see **11:12**), withdrawal of accumulated contributions (see **11:17**), or withdrawal of membership, may be deemed to be a member of his or her current retirement system beginning with the original date of membership in the previous retirement system. If the date of earlier membership would place the member in a different tier, the member would then be deemed to be a member of that tier (§ 645(2)).

To be eligible for such prior service credit, the member must apply for such credit and repay with interest at the rate of 5 percent compounded annually any amount refunded to the member when he or she left the previous retirement system (§ 645(2)). Otherwise, the prior service is provided to the member without payment. Any active member or retiree who became a member of Tiers I or II by paying for such credit is entitled to a refund of those payments with interest at the rate of five percent compounded annually (§ 645(3)). Any amount paid by a member or retiree for service within Tiers III and IV are not entitled to a refund for such payment (§ 645(2)).

Members in Tier I can buy prior in-state public service for time that they were not previously members, under certain circumstances (§ 41(c), see § 2(17); Educ. Law § 509(2)(a)(5)).

Members in Tiers II, III and IV can buy credit for service that pre-dated their entry into a retirement system (§§ 446(b), 513(b), 609(b)).

11:20. Can a member of a retirement system buy credit for prior public service performed out of state?

In many cases members of TRS Tier I can buy up to 10 years of out-of-state service in a public school on a matching basis with their credited New York State service (Educ. Law § 509(5)). Teachers in Tier II may receive credit for out-of-state service if it had been credited under a previous Tier I TRS membership. Teachers in Tiers III and IV may not receive credit for out-of-state service (Educ. Law § 509(8)(a)).

11:21. Can a member of a retirement system buy credit for military service?

Yes. Members of New York State's public retirement systems may be eligible for up to three years of additional credit for military service rendered during periods of military conflict (§ 1000). Members should contact the appropriate retirement system for detailed eligibility requirements (see **11:47, 11:55**). The amount paid by the member for the purchase of military service credit will be refunded with interest if the military service purchased does not result in a larger death benefit or retirement allowance than would have been payable had the member not purchased the additional credit (§ 1000(9)).

11:22. Can a member of a public retirement system transfer membership between retirement systems?

Yes. An individual who joins a new state retirement system may transfer his or her active membership in another state retirement system within a designated period of time after joining the new system, usually one year (§ 43(a), (b), (k); Educ. Law § 522(2)).

Information on the transfer of membership for teacher's aides reclassified as teaching assistants as a result of the federal No Child Left

Behind Act of 2001 is available at: http://www.nystrs.org/main/library/ TeacherAides.pdf.

11:23. Can a member be reinstated to an earlier date of membership after leaving one of the public retirement systems and subsequently rejoining?

Yes. The Retirement and Social Security Law allows a member to obtain prior credit, even though that person may have had the right to transfer and failed to do so. The granting of previous service credit will alter the individual's date of membership and possibly his or her tier status. To be eligible, a member must apply for such prior service credit with the administrative head of his or her current retirement system. The member must also repay, with interest at the rate of 5 percent compounded annually, the amount refunded, if any, when he or she left the previous retirement system (§ 645(2); see **11:19**).

11:24. Can members of the Teachers' Retirement System (TRS) or Employees' Retirement System (ERS) retire on disability?

Yes. To be considered for an ordinary disability allowance, members must be credited with 10 years of service within New York State, except for members in Tier III, who need only five years of service if they are eligible for a primary Social Security disability benefit (§§ 62(aa)(1), 506(a), 605(b)(1); Educ. Law § 511(3)). Members who become disabled through job-related accidents may be eligible, under certain conditions, for accidental disability benefits (§§ 63, 507, 605(b)(3)).

Members of the New York City Teachers' Retirement System who are not eligible for workers' compensation will receive a disability benefit equal to two-thirds of their final average salary (§ 605(f)). Such disability benefits are considered payment in lieu of a workers' compensation benefit (§ 605(g)).

The TRS Board may approve the disability retirement application of an eligible member who would have been entitled to retire for disability, but died before the application could become effective. The eligible member's death must be as a result of the disability (Educ. Law § 511(8)(b)).

11:25. Is an in-service death benefit available to retirement system members?

Yes. The retirement systems provide ordinary and accidental death benefits. The benefit depends on a number of factors including the member's date of membership, salary and length of service (see §§ 60, 60-b, 61, 448, 508, 509, 606, 607; Educ. Law § 512(b)(5)).

In addition, a pre-retirement death benefit is available to members of the state retirement systems who are out of public service and who die on or after January 1, 1997 but prior to retirement, having at least 10 years of credited service at the time of death (§§ 60-c(a), 448-a(a), 508-a(a), 606-a(a); Educ. Law § 512(e); Laws of 1998, ch. 388, § 8). The death benefit is equal to one-half of the benefit payable if the member had died in active service on the last date of employment (§§ 60-c(c), 448-a(c), 508-a(c), 606-a(c); Educ. Law § 512(e)).

11:26. What retirement plans are available to Tier I and II members?

The retirement plans available to Tier I and II members depends on the type of plan the member's employer elected.

There are four noncontributory retirement plans available to members in Tiers I and II of the Employees' Retirement System (ERS). Employees enrolled in any one of these plans are not required to contribute to it (§ 75-b(a)). If an employer does not elect a noncontributory plan, Tier I and II members have a choice of two plans, both of which require employee contributions.

11:27. What are the noncontributory retirement plans available to Tier I and Tier II members?

Tier I and II members of the Employees' Retirement System (ERS) have a choice of four noncontributory plans.

The Noncontributory Plan (1/60th Plan). At retirement, a member will receive a pension equal to 1/60th of his or her final average salary for each year of service rendered as a member on and after April 1, 1960 (§ 75-c(a)(1)(a)), plus 1/120th of final average salary for each year of service rendered as a member before April 1, 1960 (§ 75-c(a)(1)(b)), plus an annuity from any accumulated contributions left on deposit with the system (§ 75-c(a)(5)). Each year of prior service (up to a maximum of 35 years) will increase the pension by 1/60th of the member's final average salary (§§ 2(24), 75-c(a)(1)(b)).

The Noncontributory Plan with Guaranteed Benefits (Improved 1/60th Plan). At retirement, a member will receive a pension equal to 1/60th of his or her final average salary for each year of service since April 1, 1960 (see §§ 75-c(a)(1)(a), 75-e(b)(1)), plus a pension that will produce, when added to the annuity purchasable by required member contributions, a retirement allowance of 1/60th of his or her final average salary for each year of service between April 1, 1938 and April 1, 1960 (§ 75-e(b)(1)). All members' contributions in excess of the contributions required under this plan will, if left in the system, increase the member's retirement allowance (§ 75-e(b)(3)). Each year of prior service (to a maximum of 35 years) will increase the pension portion of the retirement allowance by 1/60th of final average salary (§§ 75-c(a)(1)(b), 75-e(b)(1), see § 2(24)).

The Career Plan (25 years). A member retiring with at least 25 years of total service will receive a retirement allowance of 1/50th of final average salary for each of the first 25 years of service, plus 1/60th of final average salary for each year in excess of 25 (§ 75-g(a)(1), see § 75-c(a)(1)).

The Improved Career Plan. The employer may elect to reduce the number of years of total service required for career retirement benefits to 20, and the employee will receive a retirement allowance of 1/50th of the member's final average salary for each year of service, provided that the maximum pension payable does not exceed three-quarters of final average salary (§ 75-i(a)).

11:28. What contributory retirement plans are available to Tier I and II members?

If a member's employer has not elected a noncontributory plan (see § 75-b(a)), the employee has a choice between the Age 55 Plan and the Age 60 Plan.

The Age 60 Plan. A member in Tier I may retire at or after age 60, regardless of length of service, with a pension of 1/140th of final average salary for each year of his or her service as a member, plus 1/70th of final average salary for each year of prior service (to a maximum of 35 years), plus an annuity purchased by his or her contributions (§ 75(a), see § 2(24)). The same benefit formula applies to members in Tier II, but those members must meet the criteria described in **11:9**.

The Age 55 Plan. A member in Tier I may retire at or after age 55, regardless of length of service, with a pension of 1/120th of final average salary for each year of service as a member, plus 1/60th of final average salary for each year of prior service (to a maximum of 35 years), plus an annuity purchased by member contributions (§ 75(d), see § 2(24)). The same benefit formula applies to members in Tier II, but those members must meet the criteria described in **11:9**.

In contrast, there is only one noncontributory plan available to Tiers I and II of the Teachers' Retirement System (TRS), the *TRS Career Plan.* At retirement, a member will receive a pension equal to 1.8 percent of final average salary for each year of New York state service rendered prior to July 1, 1959, and 2 percent of final average salary for each year of New York state service rendered after June 30, 1959, and 1 percent of final average salary for each year of out-of-state service (Educ. Law § 535(5)(a)). The out-of-state service is limited to the number of years necessary to equal 35 total years of service credit (Educ. Law § 535(5)(a)(3)). A member who retires with less than 20 years of full-time New York state service will have their pension reduced by 5 percent for every year less than the 20-year requirement, but this amount cannot be less than half of what the full pension would be (Educ. Law § 535(5)(b)). In addition to the pension benefit, a member will also receive an annuity based on his or her accumulated contributions at retirement (Educ. Law § 535(8)).

See question **11:9** for a discussion of the reduction of pension benefits applicable to members in Tier II.

11:29. What are the retirement plans available to Tiers III and IV members?

The availability of retirement plans depends on a member's tier. Tier III members may opt for benefits under the Coordinated-Escalator Retirement Plan or CO-ESC (article 14) or under the Coordinated Retirement Plan (article 15, see §§ 500(a), 600(a)). Tier IV members are only entitled to the benefits under the Coordinated Retirement Plan (article 15, see § 600(a)).

The Coordinated-Escalator Retirement Plan — CO-ESC (Article 14). Normal retirement age is 62 years (§ 501(17)). A member at normal retirement age will receive a pension equal to 1/50th of final average salary times years of credited service if the member is credited with 20 or more years of service. No more than 30 years may be applied to a pension (§ 504(a)). A member at normal retirement age with less than 20 years of credited service will receive a pension equal to 1/60th of final average salary times years of credited service (§ 504(b)). Members who retire between the ages of 55 and 62 with less than 30 years of credited service will have their pensions reduced based on their age at retirement (§ 504(c)). Regardless of the number of years of service rendered, a member's pension will be reduced by 50 percent of the member's Social Security benefit at age 62 (§§ 504(a)-(c), 511). Once retired, a member's benefits are increased annually at a rate equal to 3 percent or the amount computed on a cost-of-living index, whichever is less. In the event of a decrease in the cost-of-living index, the annual benefit will also decrease, but not below the initial benefit level (§ 510(c)).

The Coordinated Retirement Plan (Article 15). Normal retirement age is 62 years (§ 601(h)). A member at normal retirement age will receive a pension equal to 1/50th of final average salary times years of credited service if the member is credited with 20 to 30 years of service. Any years in excess of 30 years shall provide an additional retirement allowance equal to 3/200th of final average salary times years of credited service (§ 604(b)). A member at normal retirement age with less than 20 years of credited service will receive a pension equal to 1/60th of final average salary times years of credited service (§ 604(a)). Members who retire between the ages of 55 and 62 with less than 30 years of credited service will have their pensions reduced based on their age at retirement (§ 603(i)).

11:30. Are some retired employees entitled to supplemental pensions or cost of living adjustments (COLAs)?

Yes. Noninstructional employees who retired before 1961 are entitled to the more generous of two supplemental pensions provided by law (articles 4 and 6). Teachers who retired before July 1, 1970 receive the supplemental pension available to noninstructional employees or a supplemental pension provided under the Education Law, whichever is greater (Educ. Law § 532(e), (g)).

However, in lieu of these supplemental pensions, a retired employee who is (1) age 62 and retired for five years or (2) age 55 and retired for 10 years or (3) on disability retirement for five years (regardless of age) may receive an annual cost-of-living adjustment (COLA) (§ 78-a(a)(i), (ii), (iii), (h); Educ. Law § 532-a(a)(i), (ii), (iii), (h)). The COLA is 50 percent of the consumer price index and applies to the first $18,000 of a retiree's pension (§ 78-a(b)-(d); Educ. Law § 532-a(b)-(d)). The minimum annual increase is one percent and the maximum increase is three percent (§ 78-a(d); Educ. Law § 532-a(d)).

11:31. Is the retirement allowance of a retired school district employee subject to federal and New York State income tax?

There is no New York State income tax on any part of the retirement allowance (§ 110(1)). There is federal income tax on the retirement allowance (26 USC §§ 61(a)(11)). When the employee retires, a statement is furnished giving the necessary data for income tax purposes. In January of each year, a 1099-R statement is sent to each retiree (see 26 USC § 6041(a), (d)). The 1099-R gives the taxable portion of the allowance received during the previous year (see Instructions to 1099-R form and IRS Publication 575, Pension and Annuity Income). Check with the United States Internal Revenue Service for information about other changes. The Web site address is http://www.irs.ustreas.gov.

11:32. Can a school district employee who is retired from service return to public employment without the loss of his or her retirement allowance?

Generally, a retiree's allowance is suspended when he or she returns to work for the state or a local government (§ 101(a); Civ. Serv. Law § 150; Educ. Law § 503(5)).

However, under specified conditions, a retiree may return to public employment without loss of retirement allowance. Commencing with the calendar year in which he or she reaches age 65, a member retired from service is not subject to restrictions on his or her earnings (§ 212(1)). Starting in 2004, any retiree under 65 can earn up to $27,500 without prior approval from the appropriate state official and without loss, suspension, or diminution of his or her retirement allowance (§ 212(2).

Except as provided above, if the retiree is a retired teacher employed in a regular position in public service, the retiree's allowance will be suspended unless the employer obtains the approval of the appropriate state official listed below (§ 211(2); Educ. Law § 503(5); 21 NYCRR § 5023.1(a); see **11:33**). If a retired teacher's compensation for a temporary or occasional position exceeds the salary limitation above, then his or her retirement allowance will be suspended for the period an excess amount is earned (21 NYCRR § 5023.1(b), (c)).

11:33. Is a waiver available for retirees wanting to return to public service at a salary that exceeds the limitation applicable to avoid loss of a retirement allowance?

Yes. If a retiree will earn more than the applicable amount (see **11:32**), the employer must obtain approval from the commissioner of education for a retiree to work as a teacher or administrator, or from the state civil service commission for a retiree to work as a noninstructional employee (§ 211(2)(a), (b)).

Approval will only be granted if: (1) the retiree is qualified, competent, and physically fit for performance of the duties in question; (2) there is need for their services in such a position; (3) there are not readily available for recruitment persons qualified to perform the duties of the position; and (4) their employment is in the best interests of the employer. Approvals are granted for periods up to two years each (§ 211(2)(b)).

New York's waiver process is designed to prevent a retiree from collecting a pension from one job while accruing additional pension benefits from a second job, known as "double dipping." Thus, the waiver system has a rational basis, and does not violate equal protection principles. Moreover, since a claimant is not legally entitled under state law to a second set of benefits, the waiver system does not violate the right to substantive due process (*Connolly v. McCall*, 254 F.3d 36 (2d Cir. 2001)).

11:34. Can a retired school district employee who returns to public employment rejoin a state retirement system?

Yes. If a formerly retired employee has not received the approval of the appropriate state official and/or earns a salary above the applicable earnings limitation (see §§ 211, 212; **11:32**), the retirement allowance is suspended

(§ 101(a); Civ. Serv. Law § 150; Educ. Law § 503(5)) and membership in the state retirement system resumes (§ 101(a); Educ. Law § 503(11)(a)).

11:35. What happens if a retiree returns to work for a private employer?

Work for a private employer, an out-of-state employer (public or private) or the federal government does not affect a service retiree's retirement allowance (see §§ 101, 210(e), 211, 212).

Teachers' Retirement System

11:36. Who is covered by the Teachers' Retirement System?

The Teachers' Retirement System (TRS) includes teachers in the public and charter schools of New York State, except New York City teachers, and some members of the State University of New York teaching staff (Educ. Law art. 8-B, §§ 501(4), 503(4), 2854(3)(c)). New York City teachers are covered by the New York City Teachers' Retirement System (NYC Admin. Code §§ 13-501(7)(a); 13-503).

The term *teacher* is defined broadly in the law to include regular teachers, special teachers, superintendents, principals, school librarians and other members of the teaching and professional staff of public schools (Educ. Law § 501(4)).

Although the New York Charter Schools Act of 1998 states that charter school teachers are deemed to be employees of the local school district for the purpose of membership in TRS (Educ. Law § 2854(3)(c)), TRS regulations provide for admission of individual charter schools as participating employers in the retirement system. Following admission to the retirement system, a charter school may not withdraw as a participating employer (21 NYCRR §§ 5026.1, 5026.2).

11:37. May substitute or other part-time teachers join the Teachers' Retirement System (TRS)?

Yes. Membership for substitute or other part-time teachers is at the individual employee's option (Educ. Law § 503(2); 21 NYCRR § 5000.1(d)). Employers must notify part-time teachers in writing of their right to membership in the system, and teachers must acknowledge receipt of such notice in writing (Educ. Law § 520(2)(b)).

11:38. Who is responsible for operating the Teachers' Retirement System (TRS)?

Primary responsibility for the proper operation of the TRS rests with its board and staff (Educ. Law §§ 504(1), 507(1)). Additional supervision is provided by the New York State Department of Insurance (Educ. Law § 523). TRS funds may be invested only in accordance with statutory specifications (see § 177; Educ. Law § 508). An actuarial valuation is made each year to determine whether the system has the resources to meet its obligations (see Educ. Law §§ 508(5), 517(2)(a)). Any deficiency must be made up by increasing the contributions made by school districts (Educ. Law §§ 517(2), 521(2)).

11:39. How many members are on the Teachers' Retirement System's (TRS) board, and how are they chosen?

The TRS board has 10 members (Educ. Law § 504(2)). Three of them are elected by the New York State Board of Regents. One of those members must be or have been an executive officer of a bank authorized to do business in the state and may not be an employee of the state (Educ. Law § 504(2)(a)). The other two members must be current or former school board members who have experience in finance and investment. Neither may be an employee of the state. One of those members must also be or have been an executive officer of an insurance company. These two members are chosen from a list of five presented to the Board of Regents by the New York State School Boards Association (Educ. Law § 504(2)(b)).

Two school administrators are chosen by the commissioner of education (Educ. Law § 504(2)(c)). The state comptroller or his or her appointee also sits on the board (Educ. Law § 504(2)(d)). Three active teachers are elected from among TRS's members (Educ. Law §§ 504(2)(e), 505), and one retired teacher is elected from among the retired members of the retirement system (Educ. Law §§ 504(2)(f), 505-a). The affirmative vote of a majority of the board and the concurrence of one of the active teacher members of the board is required to adopt, amend, or repeal any rule or regulation relating to member benefits (Educ. Law § 506(5)).

All members, with the exception of the comptroller or his appointee, serve for a term of three years (Educ. Law § 504(2)).

11:40. How is the Teachers' Retirement System (TRS) funded?

The TRS is funded through members' contributions (§§ 517(a), 613(a)), school district employers' contributions (Educ. Law §§ 517(2), 519(2), 521(2)) and investment income (Educ. Law § 508(2)).

11:41. How much do school districts contribute to the Teachers' Retirement System (TRS)?

The amount a school district contributes to the TRS varies from year-to-year, depending on actuarial analysis (Educ. Law §§ 517(2), 521(2)). The employer's contribution rate payable by school districts jumped considerably from .36 percent of a member district's payroll for the 2002–03 school year to 2.52 percent during the 2003–04 school year. At the time this book went to press, the employer contribution rate for the 2004-05 school year was an estimated 5.63 percent. TRS's board sets the rate annually, based on the recommendations of the system's actuary (for rates, see TRS Web site (http://www.nystrs.org/); see also **11:38**).

11:42. When are school districts' contribution payments to the Teachers' Retirement System (TRS) due?

Pursuant to changes made in the payment schedule for employer contributions during the 1990 state budget, school districts' payments to the TRS are made in the fall for salaries paid during the previous school year (Educ. Law § 521(h)).

11:43. How are payments made to the Teachers' Retirement System (TRS)?

Payments are credited directly to TRS by the state comptroller from each district's state aid apportionment in three equal installments due on September 15, October 15, and November 15 of each fiscal year (Educ. Law §§ 521(2)(b)-(d), (h), 3609-a(1)(a)(1)). Employers who receive no state aid or whose state aid payments are insufficient to pay the amount due the system are billed directly by the system (Educ. Law § 521(2)(h); see also **21:3**).

11:44. What happens if an employer underpays its obligation to the Teachers' Retirement System (TRS)?

The amount of the underpayment is deducted from the employer's state aid apportionment for the following year, on April 15. Employers whose payments from such appropriation are insufficient to pay the amount due, or who do not receive such payments, will be billed by the system for the underpayment (Educ. Law § 521(h)). Payments that are not made within 30 days will accrue interest (Educ. Law § 521(f)).

11:45. May a member of the Teachers' Retirement System (TRS) receive a lump sum retirement payment?

Yes. A member of TRS who is entitled to receive a retirement allowance, other than for disability, may elect at retirement to receive, in lieu of a retirement allowance, a lump sum payment which is of actuarial equivalent value to the retirement allowance if the allowance is less than $2,400 per year. Payment of the lump sum would complete the retirement system's obligation to the member (Educ. Law § 537).

11:46. May members of the Teachers' Retirement System (TRS) change their retirement option selections after their retirement date?

Yes. TRS members as well as members of the New York City Teachers' Retirement System and the Board of Education Retirement System of the City of New York may change retirement options up to 30 days after the date of their retirement (Educ. Law §§ 539(6), 2575 (17)(q); Administrative Code of the City of New York, § 13-558(e)).

11:47. Where can further information about the Teachers' Retirement System (TRS) be obtained?

For more information about the TRS, contact the system's offices at 10 Corporate Woods Drive, Albany, N.Y. 12211-2395; telephone 518-447-2900 or 1-800-348-7298; Web site at http://www.nystrs.org/.

Employees' Retirement System

11:48. What school district employees are covered by the Employees' Retirement System?

The New York State and Local Employees' Retirement System (ERS) includes noninstructional employees in districts where a school board elects to provide retirement coverage to such employees by participating in ERS. There is no law that requires a district to do so; however, participation by an employer, once made, may not be revoked (§ 30(a)). The law likewise precludes the establishment of any retirement system for a civil service employee other than the ERS (§ 113(a)).

Any noninstructional employee in the service of the district on the date the system is adopted may or may not elect to become a member (§ 40(c)(1)). All persons appointed to full-time noninstructional positions on and after the date of adoption must become members of the ERS as of their dates of appointment (§ 600(b)(3)).

11:49. May part-time noninstructional employees join the Employees' Retirement System (ERS)?

Yes. However, membership for part-time employees is optional (§ 600(b)(3)(a)). Employers must notify part-time employees in writing of their right to membership in the system, and employees must acknowledge receipt of such notice in writing (§ 45).

11:50. Who is responsible for operating the Employees' Retirement System (ERS)?

The state comptroller serves as the sole trustee and administrative head of the ERS (§§ 11(a), 13(b)).

11:51. How is the Employees' Retirement System (ERS) funded?

The ERS is funded through member and employer contributions, as determined by the Retirement and Social Security Law (see §§ 17, 21-24, 517(a), 613(a)), and investment income (§ 13(b), (c)).

11:52. How much do school districts contribute to the Employees' Retirement System?

Each September, employers are provided with information for estimating the employer contribution for the next fiscal year. Recent legislation provides for the establishment of final employer contribution rates based on the value of the retirement system fund as of the previous April 1. This legislation requires a minimum employer contribution of 4.5 percent of salaries (§§ 23-a, 323-a). More information on contribution rates may be found on the system's Web site(see **11:55**).

11:53. How are payments made to the Employees' Retirement System (ERS)?

Employees' contributions are paid into ERS by payroll deductions each payroll period (§§ 517(f), 613(d)).

Employers' contributions to ERS are paid once each year following receipt of a bill from the state comptroller (§ 17(a)). Payment cannot be required before February 1 of the calendar year following the calendar year in which the statement is received (§ 17(c)).

Under legislation designed to ease the burden of significant increases to employer contribution rates, school districts may amortize a portion of their payments to the retirement system for up to 10 years (§§ 23-a(b), 323-a(b), 17-b, 317-b; see **19:79**).

11:54. What happens if an employer underpays its obligation to the Employees' Retirement System (ERS)?

If payment is not made by February, interest is added to the amount beginning the first day after the date that the payment is required to be paid (§ 17(c), (d)). The state comptroller has the authority to bring suit in a state supreme court against any participating employer to recover any sum due the system (§ 17(e)).

11:55. Where can more information about the Employees' Retirement System (ERS) be obtained?

More information about the ERS can be obtained by contacting the New York State and Local Employees' Retirement System, 110 State Street, Albany, N.Y. 12244-0001, telephone 518-474-7736 or 866-805-0990. Retirement-related information may also be found at the Office of the State Comptroller's homepage at: http://www.osc.state.ny.us/retire.

Social Security

11:56. Are teachers in New York State covered by Social Security?

Yes. Almost all teachers in New York State now have Social Security coverage. The few exceptions are:

- Teachers who were members of the New York State Teachers' Retirement System before the Social Security referendum on December 12, 1957, and who rejected coverage or who did not sign a declaration accepting coverage before the referendum, and who did not accept Social Security during the 1959 or 1961–1962 reopenings.
- Teachers whose employment began after December 31, 1957, who are eligible to become retirement system members and who have not done so.

All newly employed teachers must participate (§ 138-a).

11:57. Are noninstructional employees of school districts covered by Social Security?

Yes. Almost all noninstructional employees of school districts are covered by Social Security. Exceptions are:

- Employees who were members of the Employees' Retirement System before the Social Security referendum on December 2, 1957, and either rejected coverage or failed to accept it before the referendum and did not accept Social Security during the 1959 or 1961-62 reopenings.

- Employees whose employment began after December 31, 1957, other than those in positions that exclude them from membership in a retirement system and who are provided with Social Security as the result of action completed before December 1957, who are eligible to become members of ERS, but whose positions do not require membership and who have not filed a membership application.

11:58. Can a school district withdraw entirely from the Social Security system?

No. The federal Social Security Act prohibits the state or any of its political subdivisions from discontinuing coverage of its employees by the Social Security system (42 USC § 418(f)).

11:59. At what age can an employee retire and receive a Social Security benefit?

An employee can retire as early as age 62 and receive a Social Security benefit (42 USC § 402(a)(2)). However, that benefit will be reduced by as much as 30 percent unless the employee delays retirement until full retirement age (42 USC § 402(q)(1), (9)). Conversely, an employee may receive a credit worth up to 8 percent of the normal benefit if he or she defers collecting a benefit past full retirement age (42 USC § 402(w)).

Full retirement age is increasing from 65 in 2000 to 67 in 2022. From 2000 to 2005, the full retirement age is being increased by two months per year until it is 66 years of age. The full retirement age will remain 66 from 2005 until 2016. In 2017, it will again be increased for two months per year until 2022 when the full retirement age will be 67 (42 USC § 416(1)(l)(1)).

11:60. Are there limits on earnings, after retirement, for Social Security benefits?

Yes, for Social Security beneficiaries who are less than full retirement age (see **11:59**). If an individual is less than full retirement age, his or her benefits are reduced by one dollar for every two dollars earned above an annual earnings limitation set by the Social Security Administration (42 USC § 403(f)(3), (8)(A), (B)). The earnings limitation applicable to those under full retirement age in 2004 is $11,640 (http://www.socialsecurity. gov/pressoffice/factsheets/colafacts2004-alt.htm).

In the year an individual reaches full retirement age, one dollar in benefits will be deducted for every three dollars earned over an annual earnings limitation set by Congress. In 2004, the limitation was $31,080 (42 USC § 403(f)(3), (8)(D); see also http://www.socialsecurity.gov/ pressoffice/factsheets/colafacts2004-alt.htm.

There is no reduction of benefits for earnings beginning with the month that a person reaches full retirement age (42 USC § 403(f)(3),(8)(E), (9)).

11:61. Should employees who intend to work beyond age 65 contact the Social Security Administration?

Yes. To enroll in Medicare, these individuals should contact the Social Security Administration, even though no retirement benefits will be paid until actual retirement (see 42 USC §§ 426, 1395c; 42 CFR §§ 406.6(c)(4)), 406.10(a)(3).

11:62. Where can further information about Social Security be obtained?

More information about Social Security can be obtained by calling the Social Security Administration at 1-800-772-1213, or at 1-800-325-0778 (for TTY users), or at http://www.ssa.gov.

12. Students

Editor's Note: This chapter includes brief discussions on applicable provisions of the No Child Left Behind Act, and both federal and New York State regulations implementing that statute. For more information on this subject, see Leaving No Child Behind in New York, 2nd Edition, *a handbook published by the New York State School Board's Association and distributed by LexisNexis.*

School Attendance

12:1. Must children in New York State receive academic instruction?

Yes. Minors who turn six years old on or before December 1 in any school year must receive full-time instruction from the first day school is in session in September of such school year. Minors who turn six years old after December 1 of a school year must receive full-time instruction from the first day of school in the following September. All children must remain in attendance until the last day of the school year in which they reach the age of 16 (§ 3205(1)(c)).

A school board has the authority to require minors from ages 16 through 17 who are not employed to attend school until the last day of the school year in which they become 17 years of age (§ 3205(3)).

Instruction may take place in a public, private or parochial school, or at home (§§ 3202, 3204(1), (2), 3210(2)). A minor who has completed a four-year high school course of study is not required to attend school (§ 3205(2)(a)).

12:2. Are there any exemptions from the compulsory education requirements?

The landmark case regarding exemption from compulsory school requirements is *Wisconsin v. Yoder*, 406 U.S. 205 (1972), where the United States Supreme Court permitted Amish children to be exempted from compulsory school attendance after the eighth-grade level. However, the exemption was based exclusively on the recognition that the preservation of Amish society depended on its children learning how to maintain an agrarian way of life free from modern technology.

According to the court, the accommodation afforded the Amish did not contravene the principles of public education; rather, it allowed Amish children to be educated in the ways necessary to preserve the Amish way of life.

The U.S. Court of Appeals, Second Circuit, which has jurisdiction over New York State, expressly declined to expand the holding of *Yoder* beyond the facts of that case when a parent argued a school district was required to accommodate his religion beliefs and exempt his son from the seventh grade health-education curriculum. The district allowed students to opt out from the portion of curriculum related to family-life instruction and AIDS education. However, the parent wanted his child excused entirely from the health education program (*Leebaert v. Harrington*, 332 F.3d 134 (2d Cir. 2003)). According to the Second Circuit, the claim made by the Amish is one that few other religious groups or sects can make. Parents do not have a right "to tell a public school what his or her child will and will not be taught."

12:3. Is a student under 16 or 17 years of age who marries subject to the compulsory education law?

Yes. Attendance is compulsory for minors (see **12:1**). There is no exception for students under the ages of 16 or 17 who are married. However, 16- or 17-year-old students who have a certificate of full-time employment may attend school not less than 20 hours per week instead of full time (§ 3205(2)(b); for more detail on employment of students, see **12:149–156**).

12:4. Is a child five years of age entitled to go to public school?

Yes. The law provides that a person over five and under 21 years of age who does not possess a high school diploma is entitled to attend the public schools maintained in the district where he or she resides (§ 3202(1); see **12:1** for compulsory education age requirements). A child over five years of age is entitled to attend the public schools in the district regardless of whether or not the district maintains a kindergarten program. That child would be entitled to be admitted to the first grade (*Appeal of Carney*, 15 Educ. Dep't Rep. 325 (1976); *Formal Opinion of Counsel No. 75*, 1 Educ. Dep't Rep. 775 (1952)).

The law does not require a school district to admit a child who becomes five years old after the school year has commenced unless his or her birthday occurs on or before December 1. School boards may, at their discretion, admit children at an earlier age (§ 3202(1)).

If a school district maintains a policy that would delay the admission to kindergarten of any child who becomes five after December 1, it need not alter such policy on an individual basis for particular students (*Frost v. Yerazunis*, 53 A.D.2d 15 (3d Dep't 1976); *Appeal of Sollitto*, 31 Educ.

Dep't Rep. 138 (1991); *Appeal of Tommasetti*, 39 Educ. Dep't Rep. 513 (2000); *Appeal of S.H.*, 40 Educ. Dep't Rep. 527 (2001)).

In *Matter of Benjamin*, 26 Educ. Dep't Rep. 533 (1987), the commissioner of education held that a school district may not enact a policy requiring that a child be at least five years of age by September 1 of the school year he or she begins school.

12:5. Are all children who attend public schools required to go to kindergarten?

No. Transfer students to upper grades may avoid kindergarten. However, within certain legal limitations, the age of entrance and the grade placement of children are matters for local education authorities to decide. A local school board may:

- Require any child entering school under the age of six to attend and complete a year of kindergarten, provided that the child has not already done so in another kindergarten, such as a private one, substantially equivalent to that of the local public school. Even in such a case, a school board can require the child to be tested and evaluated before making any determination with respect to placement. If the testing indicates that the child will be unable to perform at a first-grade level, the board may require the child to remain in kindergarten (*Matter of Pleener*, 30 Educ. Dep't Rep. 55 (1990); *Matter of Kitchen*, 12 Educ. Dep't Rep. 20 (1972)).
- Delay until the following September the admission of any child who becomes five after December 1 (§ 3202(1)).
- Base the initial entrance of children into kindergarten on chronological age within the statutory limitations.
- Decide the date and place of enrollment of children in school.

A nonpublic school kindergarten may not admit a child who is younger than the age of entrance into the public schools established by the district in which the child resides (8 NYCRR § 125.9).

12:6. May a child who attended kindergarten elsewhere be denied admission to a public school first-grade class, based solely on that child's age?

No. The commissioner of education has held that a school board policy that uses age as the sole criterion for admission of kindergarten students into the first grade contravenes the legal right of a child to be graded in the school system in accordance with ability. However, a school board may require the child be tested and evaluated before determining the child's placement (*Matter of Kitchen*, 12 Educ. Dep't Rep. 20 (1972); *Matter of*

Lazar, 6 Educ. Dep't Rep. 7 (1966), see also *Appeal of Bruce A. M.*, 32 Educ. Dep't Rep. 335 (1992)).

12:7. At what age may children attend a prekindergarten program?

Under the universal prekindergarten legislation, school boards may, but are not required to, adopt a plan to provide prekindergarten services to resident children (§ 3602-e(4)). If such a plan is adopted by the school board and approved by the commissioner of education, resident children who are four years of age on or before December 1 of the year in which they are enrolled or who will otherwise be first eligible to enter public school kindergarten commencing with the following year will be eligible to receive pre-kindergarten services (§ 3602-e(1)(c), see also *Appeal of Ahn*, 41 Educ. Dep't Rep. 413 (2002)). For a summer only universal prekindergarten program, resident children who are five years of age on or after December 1 of the year in which they are enrolled or who will otherwise be first eligible to enter kindergarten with the current school year are eligible to participate. (8 NYCRR § 151-1.2(d)). Once a child is enrolled in a prekindergarten program, an attendance policy must be applied to the child (8 NYCRR § 151-1.2(d)).

12:8. May a student of compulsory education age attend a school other than a public school?

Yes. However, the compulsory attendance law requires that instruction given to a minor elsewhere than a public school must be "at least substantially equivalent to the instruction given to minors of like age and attainments at the public schools of the city or district where the minor resides" (§ 3204(2)).

For more information on what constitutes substantially equivalent instruction for nonpublic and home-schooled students, see **chapter 24**.

12:9. May parents home-instruct students?

Yes. However, a student who is instructed at home must be provided with a substantially equivalent education to that of the public schools where he or she resides, with instruction by a competent instructor (§§ 3204(2), 3210(2(d)). Instructors need not be certified teachers (see 8 NYCRR § 100.10).

For more information on home-instruction of students, see **24:19–36**.

12:10. Can students attend public school part time and receive home instruction for the balance of the school day?

No. According to the commissioner of education, the Legislature has not authorized partial attendance at a public school except under certain specified circumstances (*Appeal of Pope,* 40 Educ. Dep't Rep. 473 (2001); *Appeal of Sutton,* 39 Educ. Dep't Rep. 625 (2000); *Matter of Mayshark,* 17 Educ. Dep't Rep. 82 (1977)). One of those circumstances is detailed in section 3602-c of the Education Law, commonly referred to as the dual-enrollment law, which permits instruction in the areas of career education, gifted and talented education, education for students with disabilities, and counseling, psychological and social work services related to instruction. The dual-enrollment law does not apply to home-instructed students (*Appeal of Pope*; "Questions and Answers on Home Instruction," NY State Education Department: Revised March 2004, question 20).

12:11. May individuals who have obtained a high school diploma attend public school?

Yes. A school board must admit an individual who has received a high school diploma and is under 21 years of age to classes in the district. Any such person who is not a veteran must pay tuition except that the school board may waive the payment of such tuition. However, if this is done, the student may not be counted for state aid purposes (§ 3202(1); 8 NYCRR § 174.3; *Matter of Brown,* 15 Educ. Dep't Rep. 79 (1975)).

12:12. May individuals who have obtained a high school equivalency diploma, but not a high school diploma, attend public school?

Yes. According to the State Education Department, an otherwise qualified individual who has received a high school equivalency diploma, but not a high school diploma, may still attend the public schools in his or her district of residence, without paying tuition, until the age of 21, or until that person has obtained a high school diploma (see "School Executive's Bulletin," Office of Elementary, Middle and Secondary Education, State Education Department, June 1989).

12:13. May a student who is over the compulsory school attendance age and who does not possess a high school diploma be dropped from school enrollment?

Yes. Students over the age of compulsory school attendance in the school district may be dropped from enrollment if they have been absent 20 consecutive school days and the district has complied with the following procedure:

The principal or superintendent must schedule an informal conference and notify both the student and parent or guardian of this situation in writing at their last known address. At that conference, the principal or superintendent must determine the reasons for the student's absence and whether reasonable changes in the student's educational program would encourage and facilitate his or her continuance of study. The student and parent or guardian must be informed orally and in writing of the student's right to re-enroll at any time in the school maintained in the district of residence, as long as the student remains qualified to attend.

If, after reasonable notice, the student and parent or guardian fail to attend the informal conference, the student may be dropped from enrollment, provided there is notification in writing of the right to re-enter at any time, as long as the student is qualified for attendance (§ 3202(1-a)).

12:14. How may an adult over 21 years of age secure a high school diploma?

Section 100.7 of the commissioner's regulations provides that an adult may secure a high school equivalency diploma by achieving an acceptable score on the comprehensive examinations under the New York State Equivalency Diploma program. The individual must have lived in New York State at least one month before the examination (8 NYCRR § 100.7(a)(1)). Inmates of a state correctional institution also may take these examinations (8 NYCRR § 100.7(a)(1)(ii)(c)).

Additionally, as an alternative to the comprehensive examinations, candidates may qualify by completion of 24 college credits (semester hours) at an approved institution of higher education (8 NYCRR § 100.7(a)(2)(iii)). Beginning with applications made on or after September 1, 2000, the 24 credits shall be distributed as follows: six credits in English language arts including writing, speaking and reading (literature); six credits in mathematics; three credits in natural science; three credits in social science; three credits in humanities; and three credits in career and technical education and/or foreign languages (8 NYCRR § 100.7(a)(2)(iii)).

World War II and Korean War veterans who did not obtain a high school education may be awarded a high school diploma based on knowledge and experience gained while in service, under a program developed by the commissioner (§ 305(29), (29-a)).

12:15. Are public schools required to provide educational services to youths who are incarcerated in county correctional facilities?

Yes. The Education Law and the commissioner's regulations require school districts to provide educational services to youths under age 21 who do not have high school diplomas and who are incarcerated in county correctional facilities located within their districts (see § 3202(7)(a); 8 NYCRR Part 118; *Handberry v. Thompson*, 92 F.Supp.2d 244 (S.D.N.Y. 2000)). These districts receive state aid for such programs (§ 3602(35)).

12:16. Must school districts provide pregnant students with educational opportunities equal to those provided to students who are not pregnant?

Yes. Schools may not discriminate against students based on their parental and/or marital status (Title IX of the Educ. Amendments of 1972, 20 USC § 1681; 45 CFR § 86.40). Pregnant students should be encouraged to remain in school and to participate in programs designed especially for them. All programs for pregnant students should be developed in cooperation with the school physician and student personnel staff to best provide for each individual. Homebound instruction should be made available to pregnant students when necessary.

12:17. May school districts preclude students from attending district schools on the basis of race, creed, color, or national origin?

No. The Education Law provides that no person may be refused admission to or be excluded from any public school in New York State because of race, creed, color, or national origin (§ 3201(1)). In addition, segregation of students by race is prohibited by the federal constitution (*Brown v. Board of Educ.*, 347 U.S. 483 (1954); *Lee v. Nyquist*, 318 F.Supp. 710, *aff'd*, 402 U.S. 935 (1971)).

In *Brown*, the United States Supreme Court held that statutorily imposed separate school facilities for blacks and whites were unconstitutional. However, the mere existence of racially segregated schools does not constitute a federal constitutional or statutory violation (*United States v. Yonkers Bd. of Educ.*, 624 F.Supp. 1276, *aff'd*, 837 F.2d 1181 (2d Cir. 1987), *cert. denied*, 486 U.S. 1055 (1988)).

De facto segregation is segregation that is inadvertent and without assistance of school authorities and not caused by any state action but rather by social, economic and other factors (*Hart v. Community Sch. Bd. of Educ.*, 512 F.2d 37 (2d Cir. 1975)). Since the *Brown* decision, New York state and federal courts and the commissioner of education have held that, although alleged de facto racial segregation does not constitute a sufficient basis for a court to order a racial integration plan, school officials can adopt voluntary plans to remedy the effects of de facto segregation (see *Balaban v. Rubin*, 14 N.Y.2d 193 (1964), *cert. denied*, 379 U.S. 881 (1964); *Van Blerkom v. Donovan*, 15 N.Y.2d 399 (1965); *Matter of Barnhart*, 21 Educ. Dep't Rep. 126 (1981); see also *United States v. Yonkers Bd. of Educ.*, 624

F.Supp. 1276, *aff'd*, 837 F.2d 1181 (2d Cir. 1987), *cert. denied*, 486 U.S. 1055 (1988); *Brewer v. West Irondequoit CSD*, 212 F.3d 738 (2d Cir. 2000)). In some circumstances, the commissioner has required districts to take action to counteract de facto racial imbalance (*Matter of Fishburne*, 12 Educ. Dep't Rep. 5 (1972); *Appeal of Gray*, 6 Educ. Dep't Rep. 92 (1967); but see *Appeal of Bennardo*, 33 Educ. Dep't Rep. 178 (1993)).

Nonetheless, the fact that a substantial number of students in a school district live below the federal poverty line does not deprive those students of their State Constitutional rights to a sound basic education (*Paynter v. State of New York* 290 A.D.2d 95(4th Dep't 2002), *aff'd*, 100 N.Y.2d 434 (2003)).

A school district attempting to counteract racial imbalance must be careful in how it attempts to do so if it adopts an admissions policy. Under recent cases from the United State Supreme Court a school may not make race a decisive factor of the admissions process by administering bonus points based on race or ethnicity but can consider race among several factors such as geographic residence and socioeconomic standing when seeking to enroll a critical mass of minorities (*Grutter v. Bollinger*, 539 U.S. 306, (2003) and *Gratz v. Bollinger*, 539 U.S. 244 (2003)).

12:18. Are school districts required to facilitate the enrollment of students released from residential facilities?

Yes. Districts of residence are required to promptly enroll any student released or conditionally released from a residential facility operated by the Office of Children and Family Services, the Office of Mental Health, the Office of Mental Retardation and Developmental Disabilities or a local department of social services. Moreover, school districts must designate at least one employee to facilitate the prompt enrollment of these students, receive student records, and serve as the district contact person with residential facilities and state and local agencies. Districts must also implement the education plan for any such student's release as submitted to Family Court (8 NYCRR § 100.2(ff)).

12:19. What is truancy?

Truancy is the willful violation by a student of the compulsory attendance provisions in Article 65 of the Education Law, which require minors from six to 16 or 17 years of age to attend school full time (§ 3205).

12:20. Is truancy a violation of law?

Yes. An attendance officer may arrest a truant without a warrant (§ 3213(2)(a)). Habitual truancy is grounds for filing a person in need of supervision (PINS) petition in family court. Children under age eighteen may be the subject of a PINS petition (Family Court Act §§ 712(a), 732). The filing of a PINS petition involving a child classified as a student with disabilities may constitute a change in educational placement subject to the procedural safeguards of the federal Individuals with Disabilities Education Act if the PINS petition contemplates a change in the child's educational placement (*Matter of Beau II*, 95 N.Y.2d 234 (2000)).

However, the commissioner has ruled that school authorities may not suspend students from school for truancy (*Appeal of Ackert*, 30 Educ. Dep't Rep. 31 (1990); see **12:116**). An in-school suspension for truancy is acceptable if the alternative education provided is adequate (*Appeal of Miller*, 35 Educ. Dep't Rep. 451 (1996), see **12:143**).

Section 3213(2)(c) of the Education Law requires an attendance officer or other person authorized by the school district to notify the parent of an elementary-grade student of his or her child's absence from school, if the parent so requests. The obligation to notify a parent arises only after a parent has submitted a request to be notified.

12:21. What level of school attendance is prescribed for minors who are required to attend school?

Minors who are required to attend school must do so regularly, as prescribed by the school board where the student resides or is employed, for the entire time the appropriate public schools or classes are in session (§ 3210(1)). In addition, school boards must adopt a comprehensive attendance policy that establishes record keeping procedures and intervention strategies to ensure sufficient attendance by all students to permit them to succeed at meeting the state learning standards (8 NYCRR § 104.1; see **12:22**).

12:22. Must a school district have a policy regarding attendance?

Yes. Every school district is required to have in place a comprehensive attendance policy. The policy must serve to provide for the maintenance of an adequate record verifying the attendance of all children upon instruction, establish a mechanism for examining patterns of pupil absence and developing effective intervention strategies to improve school attendance (8 NYCRR § 104.1(i)). It must:

- state the overall objectives to be accomplished and describe the specific strategies that will be used to achieve those objectives;
- specify the type of absences, tardiness, and early departures that will be deemed excused or unexcused, and the coding system that will be used to identify the reason for such absences, tardiness, and early departures;

- establish a minimum standard of attendance if the district opts to have a policy regarding attendance and eligibility for course credit (see **12:22**). In such an instance, the policy must also describe the notice to be given to parents and specific intervention strategies to be used prior to the denial of course credit;
- describe incentives to encourage attendance and discourage absences, tardiness and early departures;
- describe the notice to be given to parents of students who are absent, tardy or leave school early without excuses;
- describe the process to develop specific intervention strategies to address identified patterns of unexcused absences, tardiness and early departures; and
- identify the individual(s) at each school building responsible for reviewing attendance records and initiating intervention strategies (8 NYCRR § 104.1 (i)(2)).

A school board must review student attendance records annually and revise the policy as necessary to improve attendance if the attendance records show a decline in student attendance (8 NYCRR § 104.1(i)(3)).

To promote community awareness of the policy, districts must:

- provide a plain language summary of the policy to parents before each school year and take other steps necessary to help them understand the policy;
- provide each teacher with a copy of the policy and any amendments thereto; and
- make copies of the policy available to other members of the community upon request (8 NYCRR § 104.1(i)(4)).

12:23. Must districts maintain student attendance records?

Yes. School attendance records must be kept for use in the enforcement of the Education Law (§§ 3024, 3211(1)), and as the source for the average daily attendance used to help determine a district's state aid allocation (§ 3025(1)).

A school must maintain a register of attendance for each pupil which includes the child's name; date of birth; home address; names of parents/guardians; phone numbers to contact parents/guardians; date of enrollment; record of pupil's attendance on days of instruction; and the date of withdrawal or date dropped from enrollment (8 NYCRR § 104.1(d)).

The commissioner of education can prescribe the form and manner of keeping such records (§§ 3024, 3025(1), 3211(1)).

12:24. Who is responsible for maintaining student attendance records?

A teacher, supervisory staff or other suitable employee designated by the board shall make entries into a register of attendance and verify the entries by oath or affirmation (§ 3211(i); 8 NYCRR §§ 104.1(b)(4), (5), (f), (g)). Entries will include all excused and unexcused absences, tardiness and early departures (8 NYCRR § 104.1(d)(7)).

Starting with the 2003-04 school year, each building principal and the staff member designated to initiate intervention strategies to improve attendance must review the attendance records for the purpose of taking any indicated action (8 NYCRR § 104.1(h)).

In nondepartmentalized schools (K–8) attendance shall be taken once per day and if students are dismissed from lunch, again upon their return (8 NYCRR § 104.1 (d)(7)(i)). In grades 9–12 and departmentalized schools attendance shall be taken each period of instruction (8 NYCRR § 104.1(d)(7)(ii)).

12:25. May a school board adopt a minimum attendance policy for students to receive academic credit?

Yes. The commissioner of education has upheld the adoption and implementation of minimum attendance policies for students to receive academic credit (*Appeal of Hansen*, 34 Educ. Dep't Rep. 235 (1994); *Appeal of Peter C.*, 34 Educ. Dep't Rep. 171 (1994)). A minimum attendance policy may distinguish between excused and unexcused absences (*Appeal of a Student with a Disability*, 41 Educ. Dep't Rep. 380 (2002)).

A policy may not deny credit to a student who has taken all tests and secured a passing grade, but has exceeded the allowable number of absences for that course (*Appeal of Johnston*, 35 Educ. Dep't Rep. 154 (1995), *Appeal of Shepard*, 31 Educ. Dep't Rep. 315 (1992); *Matter of Burns*, 29 Educ. Dep't Rep. 103 (1989)). A school district with a minimum attendance policy may determine that a properly excused absence for which the student has performed any assigned make up work shall not be counted as an absence for the purpose of determining course credit (8 NYCRR § 104.1(i)(2)(v)).

A minimum attendance policy adopted by a school district must include a description of the notice to parents about the policy and specific intervention strategies to be used prior to the denial of course credit (8 NYCRR § 104.1(i)(2)(v)). If a school district does not follow the procedures set out in its policy, it may not deny course credit to a student (*Appeal of Adriatico*, 39 Educ. Dep't Rep. 248 (2000)).

Although not required, a minimum attendance policy should contain an appeal process which is available to challenge the number of absences on record, ensure that no violation of the federal Individuals with Disabilities Education Act or section 504 of the Rehabilitation Act has occurred, and to provide an opportunity to waive the maximum allowable absence limit for "extenuating circumstances" — without regard to whether the absences were excused or unexcused. Such an appeal process must be administered in a neutral manner and comply with applicable law (*Appeal of Ehnot*, 37 Educ. Dep't Rep. 648 (1998)).

12:26. May a school district count the days when a student is suspended from school as absences?

No. A school may not count days when a student is suspended from school as absences, unless the student is offered alternative instruction and fails to attend such instruction (*Appeal of Shepard*, 31 Educ. Dep't Rep. 315 (1992)).

12:27. May a student be absent from school, in violation of the school district's attendance policy, if that student's parent consents to such an absence?

No. The commissioner of education has ruled that parental consent to a student's absence does not preclude the school district from enforcing its attendance policy against the student for violating the district's attendance policy (*Matter of Auch*, 33 Educ. Dep't Rep. 84 (1993)). A school board can establish rules concerning the order and discipline of the schools, as it may deem necessary (§ 1709(2)). These rules are not subject to parental consent (*Matter of Auch*).

12:28. May a student be absent from school for observance of religious occasions?

Yes. The Education Law recognizes school days missed for religious observance or any other reason as "absences" (§ 3210(1)(b)). A student's absence from school during school hours for religious observance outside the school building and grounds will be excused upon a written request signed by his or her parent or guardian (8 NYCRR § 109.2(a)).

The commissioner of education has upheld a school board's policy requiring completion of compensatory work when a student exceeded seven absences in any quarter, when applied to a student whose eighth absence was due to the student's observance of a religious holiday (*Matter of Hegarty*, 31 Educ. Dep't Rep. 232 (1992)).

12:29. May a student be released for religious instruction?

Yes. A student may be released during school hours for religious instruction upon a written request by his or her parent or guardian (8 NYCRR § 109.2(a)). The courses in religious education must be maintained and operated by or under the control of duly constituted religious bodies (8 NYCRR § 109.2(b)). Students must be registered for the courses and a copy of the registration must be filed with the local public school authorities (8 NYCRR § 109.2(c)). The attendance of students enrolled in such religious classes must be reported to the public school principal at the end of each semester (8 NYCRR § 109.2(d)).

Absence for release-time programs for kindergarten through 12th grade cannot be for more than one hour each week at the close of either the morning or afternoon session, or both, at a time to be fixed by the local school authorities. The time designated for each separate unit — the primary grades (kindergarten–grade 3), intermediate grades (grades 4–6), junior high school grades (grades 7–9), and senior high school grades (grades 10–12) — must be the same for all students in that unit in each separate school (8 NYCRR § 109.2(e)).

If there is more than one school offering religious education within the district, the hours for absence from each particular public elementary or secondary school in that district must be the same for all such religious schools (8 NYCRR § 109.2(e)).

A school board may establish an optional program for high school students in grades 9 through 12, permitting them to enroll in a course in religion in a registered nonpublic high school, with the written approval of the student's parent or guardian. This is subject to prior approval of the public high school principal with respect to course schedule, student attendance and reporting of student achievement. Absence to attend such a course may be excused for the number of periods per week that the course is scheduled in the nonpublic school, provided that the excused absences must be at the beginning or close of the public school session and are mutually agreed upon by the school officials (8 NYCRR § 109.2(f)).

School districts have no authority to transport students released for religious instruction from the public school to a church or parochial school. (*Appeal of Fitch*, 2 Educ. Dep't Rep. 394 (1963); see also *Appeal of Santicola*, 37 Educ. Dep't Rep. 79 (1997)).

12:30. What can be done for children who are absent from school because of lack of suitable clothing, food and other necessities?

Public welfare officials, except as otherwise provided by law, must furnish indigent children with suitable clothing, shoes, books, food, transportation and other necessities to enable them to attend upon instruction required by law (§ 3209(6)).

12:31. Do students have a right to transfer to another school?

Generally, a school board has the power to assign students to a particular school, to prescribe their courses of study and to regulate their transfer from one class or department to another (§ 1709(3)). However, consistent with the federal No Child Left Behind Act of 2001 (NCLB), students attending a school identified as in need of improvement, corrective action or restructuring have the right to transfer to another school at the same grade level within the district that has not been identified as such, or designated as persistently dangerous. This right is subject to health and safety code requirements regarding facility capacity (20 USC § 6316 (b)(1)(E); 34 CFR §§ 200.39(a)((1), 200.44(a); 8 NYCRR §§ 100.2 (p)(6)(vi), 120.3). It does not automatically entitle students to transfer to a magnet school or special focus schools (i.e., math or science schools or other similar school that has entrance requirements based on academic or other skills (8 NYCRR § 120.3(a)). For more information on schools in need of improvement, corrective action or restructuring see **14:89–103**; see also *Leaving No Child Left Behind in New York, 2nd Edition*, published by the New York State School Boards Association and distributed by LexisNexis.

In addition, students attending a school designated as persistently dangerous or who become victims of a violent criminal offense that occurs at the public school they attend have the right to transfer to a safe public school at the same grade level within the district (20 USC § 7912(a); § 2802(7); 8 NYCRR § 120.5).

A *persistently dangerous school* is one so identified by the commissioner of education based on objective information, including data submitted over a two-year period through the state's uniform violent incident reporting system established under the Safe Schools Against Violence in Education Act (SAVE) (8 NYCRR § 120.5(a)).

A *violent criminal offense* includes the infliction of serious physical injury, a sex offense involving forcible compulsion or any other offense involving the use or threatened use of a deadly weapon as defined in the penal law. (§ 2802(7)(b), 8 NYCRR § 120.5 (b). Possible violent criminal offenses are listed in the State Education Department's Web site at: http://emsc.nysed.gov/ deputy/Documents/unsafeschool/criminaloffenseslist.html.

For additional information on unsafe schools and public school choice under the NCLB, see *Leaving No Child Behind in New York, 2nd Edition*, published by the New York State School Boards Association and distributed by LexisNexis.

12:32. Can students be transferred involuntarily from one school to another in the same district?

Yes. The school board, the superintendent of schools or the district superintendent may transfer a student from regular classroom instruction to an appropriate educational setting in another school on the written recommendation of the school principal and following an independent review (§ 3214(5)(a); *Appeal of a Student Suspected of Having a Disability*, 40 Educ. Dep't Rep. 212 (2000)).

Before the school principal may initiate an involuntary transfer, he or she must provide the student and his or her parents with written notification of the consideration of transfer recommendation. The notice must set forth the time and place for an informal conference with the principal, and specify their right to be accompanied by an attorney or an individual of their choice (§ 3214(5)(b)).

After the conference is held, and if the principal believes the student would benefit from the transfer or receive an adequate and appropriate education in another school program or facility, the principal may recommend that course of action to the superintendent. These transfers are usually recommended because of behavior or academic problems. The recommendation must include reasons indicating the need for transfer and other supporting information. A copy must be sent to the parent and the student (§ 3214(5)(c)).

Once the superintendent receives the recommendation, he or she must notify the parents and the student of the proposed transfer, their right to a fair hearing on the issue, and other procedural rights. The written notice must include a statement that the student or parents have 10 days to request a hearing (§ 3214(5)(d)).

A hearing to determine whether a student should be transferred is not the same as a hearing for disciplinary reasons. While the purpose of a disciplinary hearing is to punish a student for wrongdoing, the purpose of a transfer hearing is to determine whether the proposed transfer would be beneficial for the student (*Appeal of K.B.*, 41 Educ. Dep't Rep. 431 (2002); *Appeal of a Student Suspected of Having a Disability; Appeal of Reeves*, 37 Educ. Dep't Rep. 271 (1998), § 3214(5); see **12:150**). Unless the parents consent to the transfer, the proposed transfer may not take place until the 10-day period to request a hearing has elapsed, or a formal decision is rendered following a hearing, whichever is later (§ 3214(5)(d)). Ultimate responsibility for the assignment of students rests with the school board (§ 1709(3)). Students with disabilities may not be involuntarily transferred without the participation of the committee on special education (CSE) (*Appeal of Wanda D.*, 34 Educ. Dep't Rep. 556 (1995)).

Involuntary transfers, for the purposes of this question, do not include transfers made to reduce racial imbalance or to change attendance zones (§ 3214(5)(a)).

12:33. May students be charged fees such as textbook fees, yearbook fees, or locker fees as a condition of attendance?

No. As a general rule, no fee or charge may be required as a condition of school attendance, credit in a required course, or for materials or activities that are part of a course requirement. However, school districts may rent, sell, or loan supplies to students attending the public schools on such terms and under such rules and regulations as may be prescribed by the school board (§ 701(5)). Thus, a school board may require students who are financially able to pay a fee for supplies provided by the school (*Matter of Posman*, 12 Educ. Dep't Rep. 51 (1972)).

A school district operating under a contingency budget is not required to furnish instructional supplies to the district's school children free of charge (*Sodus CSD v. Rhine*, 63 A.D.2d 820 (4th Dep't 1978); *Reiss v. Abramowitz*, 39 A.D.2d 916 (2d Dep't 1972)).

12:34. Is a school district required to pay the tuition for a high school student who elects to go to a vocational high school if the district of residence does not have vocational courses?

Yes. If a student resides in a district where high school courses are offered but no vocational high school is available, or if vocational high school courses are not available in the academic school or schools designated by the district, the student may select and attend any other academic school within the state in which vocational courses are available. The tuition charge, if any, in excess of the difference between the cost of educating the student and the apportionment of public monies on account of the attendance of such student, is charged to the district in which the student resides. The district of the student's residence does not need to pay for the the student's transportation costs (§ 2045(2)).

Student Residency

12:35. May a school district refuse to admit nonresident students?

Yes. School districts are required to admit only district residents who are over five and under 21 years of age who have not received a high school diploma (§ 3202(1)). However, if a student is forced to temporarily relocate outside the district due to a parent or guardian being called to active military duty, the student may continue to attend school in their original district without the payment of tuition. In such circumstances, the district is not required to provide transportation to the relocated student. (§ 3202(1)).

But where a district has contracted with another district to receive that district's students under the nonresidence attendance provision of section 2045(1) of the Education Law, it may not refuse to receive nonresident students without demonstrating valid and sufficient reasons (*Appeal of the Bd. of Educ. of the Eastport/South Manor CHSD*, 40 Educ. Dep't Rep. 695 (2001); *Matter of Bd. of Educ. of South Manor UFSD*, 14 Educ. Dep't Rep. 412 (1975); *Matter of Brunswick CSD*, 14 Educ. Dep't Rep. 33 (1974)).

12:36. May a school district admit nonresident students?

Yes. A school district may accept nonresidents on terms prescribed by the school board, including the payment of tuition within limits set forth in commissioner regulations (§ 3202(2); 8 NYCRR Part 174; *Appeal of Fuller*, 41 Educ. Dep't Rep. 86 (2001) see **12:37, 12:40**).

School districts that admit nonresident students may not exclude students with disabilities or charge nonresident students with disabilities a different tuition rate. Such an action would be a violation of section 504 of the Rehabilitation Act (29 USC § 794) and the Americans with Disabilities Act (42 USC § 12132), which prohibit discrimination on the basis of disability (Letter from the Assistant Secretary for Civil Rights, United States Department of Education, Office for Civil Rights, Aug. 10, 1994; see also *Appeal of Taylor*, 43 Educ. Dep't Rep. 1, dec. no. 14,897 (2003)).

12:37. What constitutes residency for purposes of attending a particular school district?

Residency means domicile, which requires one's physical presence and the intention to remain (*Longwood CSD v. Springs UFSD*, 1 N.Y.3d 385(2004); *Appeal of Smith*, 40 Educ. Dep't Rep. 126 (2000)).

Physical presence alone is insufficient to establish residence for purposes of attending the school in that district on a tuition-free basis (*Longwood; Appeal of Ritter*, 31 Educ. Dep't Rep. 24 (1991), including presence in a homeless shelter at the time social services takes over a child's maintenance and support (*Longwood*).

A person does not lose his or her legal residence or domicile until another residence is established through both intent and action expressing such intent (*Appeal of Reifler*, 31 Educ. Dep't Rep. 235 (1992); *Matter of Aufiero*, 26 Educ. Dep't Rep. 406 (1987)). A temporary absence does not constitute the abandonment of a permanent residence where actions reflect an intent to return to the district (*Appeal of Berliner*, 38 Educ. Dep't Rep. 181(1998); *Appeal of Lokkeberg*, 38 Educ. Dep't Rep. 134 (1998); *Matter of Aufiero*). To determine intent, it becomes necessary to look at factors such as continuing ties to the community and the nature of the efforts to return (*Appeal of Berliner; Appeal of Mountain*, 35 Educ. Dep't Rep. 382 (1996)).

12:38. How is a student's legal school district of residence determined?

Generally, a student's legal school district residence is presumed to be that of his or her parents or legal guardian (*Appeal of Smith*, 40 Educ. Dep't Rep. 126 (2000); *Appeal of Reynolds*, 37 Educ. Dep't Rep. 58 (1997)). If a student does not live with a parent or legal guardian but there has been no surrender of parental control, that student's legal residence still may be that of the parent or guardian, depending on the particular set of circumstances. A natural parent does not need a formal custody determination before his or her children are admitted to public school (*Appeal of Rivers*, 42 Educ. Dep't Rep. 86 (2002)).

In making residency determinations, the commissioner and the courts have considered financial support, the child's day-to-day care, delegation of parental authority and whether it may be revoked at will (*Catlin v. Sobol*, 77 N.Y.2d 552 (1991); see also *Catlin v. Sobol*, 93 F.3d 1112 (2d Cir. 1996) (presumption of residence with parents not unconstitutional)). A temporary transfer of custody and control during a parent's illness does not suffice to overcome the presumption that a child resides with his parents. *Appeal of Mario D.*, 41 Educ. Dep't Rep. 24 (2001)). However, a continued relationship between a child and a parent who has otherwise relinquished custody and control or continued coverage under a parent's health insurance policy are not necessarily dispositive in resolving the question of a child's residency (*Appeal of Donohue*, 41 Educ. Dep't Rep. 26 (2001)).

Students also may rebut the presumption that their residence is with their parents by establishing their emancipated minor status. A student is considered emancipated if he or she is beyond the compulsory school age, is living separate and apart from his or her parents in a manner inconsistent with parental custody and control, is not receiving financial support from his or her parents, and has no intent to return home (*Appeal of Kehoe*, 37 Educ. Dep't Rep. 14 (1997)).

A student's living in a district solely for the purpose of attending a particular school has been rejected as a basis for establishing residency in such district (*Appeal of DeGorge*, 39 Educ. Dep't Rep. 590 (2000); *Appeal of Brown*, 38 Educ. Dep't Rep 159 (1998); *Appeal of Ritter*).

12:39. How does one determine whether a child is a resident entitled to attend the schools of a particular district?

The school board or its designee will determine whether a child is entitled to attend the schools of the district. Any decision by a school official, other than the board or its designee, that a child is not entitled to attend the schools of the district must include notification of the procedures to obtain review of the decision within the district.

Prior to reaching such a decision, the board or its designee must allow the parent or guardian the opportunity to submit information concerning the child's right to attend school in the district. If the board determines that the child is not entitled to attend its schools, it must, within two business days, provide written notice of its decision to the child's parent, person in parental relation, or to the child as appropriate (8 NYCRR § 100.2(y); *Appeal of Cortes*, 37 Educ. Dep't Rep. 114 (1997)). The written notice must state the following:

- The child is not entitled to attend the public schools of the district.
- The basis for the determination that the child is neither a resident of the district nor entitled to attend its schools as a homeless child.
- The date as of which the child will be excluded from school.
- The board's determination may be appealed to the commissioner of education, in accordance with section 310 of the Education Law, within 30 days of the date of the determination, and that the procedure for taking such an appeal may be obtained from the Office of Counsel, State Education Department, State Education Building, Albany, N.Y., 12234, or by calling 518-474-8927 (8 NYCRR § 100.2(y)).

12:40. Can foreign students qualify as district residents for purposes of receiving a public education on a tuition-free basis?

Yes. The commissioner of education has ruled federal immigration status alone does not preclude a nonimmigrant from establishing residency for the purpose of attending public school on a tuition-free basis. A child living in a district under a business/pleasure visa may be able to establish residency within the district even though one of the conditions for the granting of such a visa is that the visa holder express an intent to return to his or her home country upon expiration of the visa. According to the commissioner, if an individual has a subjective intent to remain despite the assurance given to obtain the visa, that is a matter for federal immigration law, not New York school residency law. Federal immigration status is only one factor to be considered in the making of a residency determination (*Appeal of Plata*, 40 Educ. Dep't Rep. 552 (2001); see **12:37–38**).

However, a foreign student who attends a public secondary school under an F-1 visa must reimburse the school district for the full unsubsidized per capita cost of providing education at the school during the student's attendance (8 USC § 1184(m)(1)(B)(ii)).

School districts should also be aware the USA Patriot Act (see Pub. Law 107-56), primarily applicable to institutions of higher education, requires the monitoring of nonimmigrant foreign students, including students attending public schools under an exchange program authorized to issue type J visas (Pub. Law 107-56; 8 USC § 1372(a)(1), (h)(2)). The act also establishes that the Family Educational Rights Privacy Act (FERPA) (20 USC § 1232g) does not apply to aliens to the extent the U.S. Attorney General determines necessary to carry out the monitoring program.

12:41. What is the legal school district of residence for students of divorced parents?

Where a child's parents are divorced and a court awards custody to one parent, the child's residence is presumed to be that of the custodial parent (*Appeal of Juracka*, 31 Educ. Dep't Rep 282 (1992); *Appeal of Forde*, 29 Educ. Dep't Rep. 359 (1990)). This presumption is rebuttable. In determining whether that presumption is rebutted, a school board must consider several factors, including the extent of the time the child actually lives in the district and the intent of family members to have the child reside in the district (*Appeal of Marilyn J.*, 41 Educ. Dep't Rep. 78, (2001); *Appeal of Weaver*, 39 Educ. Dep't Rep. 588 (2000)); *Appeal of Petrie*, 37 Educ. Dep't Rep. 200 (1997); *Appeal of O'Brien*, 35 Educ. Dep't Rep. 46 (1995)).

Where a child's parents are divorced and the child's time is essentially divided between the households of the parents, with both parties assuming day-to-day responsibility for the child, the determination of the child's residence ultimately rests with the family. In such cases, the parents may designate the child's residence (*Appeal of Marilyn J.*; *Appeal of Weik*, 41 Educ Dep't Rep. 80 (2001); *Appeal of Cortes*, 37 Educ. Dep't Rep. 114 (1997); *Appeal of Juracka*; *Appeal of Barron*, 31 Educ. Dep't Rep. 1 (1991); *Appeal of Forde*). If parents are unable to decide which district their child should attend and ask a family court to make the decision, a school district must honor the court's order designating the district of school attendance (*Appeal of T.K.*, 43 Educ. Dep't Rep. ___, dec. no. 14,935 (2003)).

12:42. What is the legal school district of residence for students placed by social services?

In the case of a nonresident student placed in a family home by a social services district or a state department or agency, the cost of instruction must be paid by the district in which the student resided at the time the agency assumed responsibility for the student's support. Short-term physical presence in a homeless shelter at the time of placement by social services does not suffice to establish residency which requires physical presence plus an intent to remain (§ 3202(4)(a); see also *Longwood CSD v. Springs UFSD*, 1 N.Y.3d 385, (2004); **12:37**). However, when the home is the actual and only residence of the student and the student is not supported and maintained by the agency, the student is considered a resident of the district in which the family home is located and no tuition may be charged (§ 3202(4)(b)).

12:43. May a parent who has more than one residence choose either as his or her legal residence for purposes of securing a child's attendance in a particular school district?

No. Residence in this context means permanent domicile, as distinguished from a temporary abode (see **12:37**).

When a person claims legal residency in a place where he or she does not remain all year, it becomes necessary to look for some overt act that indicates the individual has made a choice to consider this his or her domicile, such as whether or not the parent registers and votes from that place or whether that parent uses it as his or her residence on income tax returns.

The payment of school taxes does not necessarily make a person a legal resident of that district. Any such amount, however, must be deducted from the tuition charged to a nonresident student (§ 3202(3)).

12:44. How is tuition determined for the instruction of nonresident students?

Tuition is computed according to a formula established by the commissioner of education (8 NYCRR Part 174; see also *Appeal of the Board of Educ. of the Harrison UFSD*, 43 Educ. Dep't Rep. ___, dec. no. 15,017 (2004); *Appeal of the Board of Educ. of the East Quogue UFSD*, 43 Educ. Dep't Rep. ___, dec. no. 15,026 (2004)). The Education Law also provides that the school tax payments of nonresidents who own assessable property in the school district must be deducted from any tuition charges levied against any such nonresident (§ 3202(3)).

Districts that contract with other districts to provide education for some of their students must designate the receiving district by April 1 (8 NYCRR § 174.4). Tuition becomes due at the completion of each school year (*Appeal of the Bd. of Educ. of the Marcellus CSD*, 26 Educ. Dep't Rep. 510 (1987)).

Homeless Children

Editor's Note: For additional information on the education of homeless children under the McKinney-Vento Homeless Education Assistance Improvement Act of the federal No Child Left Behind Act of 2001, see Leaving No Child Behind in New York, 2nd Edition, *a handbook published by the New York State School Boards Association an distributed by LexisNexis. See also the U.S. Department of Education Draft non-regulatory Guidance on Education for Homeless Children and Youth Program, March 28, 2003, available at http://www.ed.gov/nclb/landing.jhtml.*

12:45. What is the definition of a homeless child within the Education Law?

Except as otherwise provided by law, a *homeless child* is a child who does not have a fixed, regular, and adequate nighttime residence or whose primary nighttime location is in a public or private shelter designated to provide temporary living accommodations, or a place not designed for, or ordinarily used as, regular sleeping accommodation for human beings. Consistent with the provisions of the McKinney-Vento Homeless Education Assistance Improvement Act of the federal No Child Left Behind Act of 2001, this definition encompasses a child who is

- sharing the housing of other persons due to a loss of housing, economic hardship or a similar reason
- living in motels, hotels, trailer parks, or camping grounds due to the lack of alternative adequate accommodations
- living in a car park, public space, abandoned building, substandard housing, bus or train station or similar setting
- abandoned in a hospital or awaiting foster care placement
- a migratory child who qualifies as homeless

(42 USC § 11434a(2); § 3209(1)(a); 8 NYCRR § 100.2(x)(1); see also *Appeal of P.L.*, 40 Educ. Dep't Rep. 84 (2000); *Appeal of Gannon*, 37 Educ. Dep't Rep. 135 (1997)). An inadequate nighttime residence includes a motel room with no kitchen accommodation (*Appeal of R.G.*, 41 Educ. Dep't Rep. 428 (2002)).

Although children awaiting foster care placement fall under the definition of homeless, children already placed in foster care do not (§ 3209(1)(a-1); 8 NYCRR § 100.2(x)(1)(i)(c)).

Children who live with a parent in an apartment subsidized by a federal program that provides rental assistance grants and does not require that grant recipients leave their home when the grant expires are not homeless.

They have an adequate fixed regular nighttime residence that is not temporary or transitional (*Appeal of D.R.*, 43 Educ. Dep't Rep. ___, dec. no 14,944 (2003)).

Children for whom no parent or person in parental relation is available are considered *unaccompanied youth* (8 NYCRR § 100.2(x)(1)(vi)).

12:46. Where may a homeless child attend school?

A homeless child may attend school within the school district of his or her current location, the school district of origin, or a school district participating in a regional placement plan.

The school "*district of origin*" is the district within New York State where the homeless child was attending a public school on a tuition-free basis or was entitled to attend when circumstances arose that caused the child to become homeless (§ 3209(1)(c); 8 NYCRR § 100.2(x)(1)(iii)).

The school *district of current location* is the district within New York State where the temporary housing arrangement or the residential program for a homeless or runaway child is located, which may be different from the school district of origin (§ 3209(1)(d); 8 NYCRR § 100.2(x)(1)(iv)).

A *regional placement plan* is a comprehensive regional approach to the provision of educational placements for homeless children, which must be approved by the commissioner of education (§ 3209(1)(e); 8 NYCRR § 100.2(x)(1)(v)).

A homeless child may attend school in the district he or she was entitled to attend before becoming homeless for the duration of homelessness if that district is the same district in which the child is temporarily housed (42 USC § 11432(g)(3)(A); 8 NYCRR § 100.2 (x)(2)(ii)).

The designation as to where a homeless child will attend school is made by the child's parent or guardian, the homeless child together with the homeless liaison designated by the school district if no parent or guardian is available, or the director of a residential program for runaway and homeless youth, where applicable, in consultation with the homeless child (§ 3209(1)(b); 8 NYCRR § 100.2(x)(1)(ii)).

A parent who disagrees with a school district's recommended placement must be notified of the right to appeal the placement decision through the district's dispute resolution procedures. (42 USC § 11432(g)(3)(B); 8 NYCRR § 100.2(x)(7)(b). However, the district must enroll the child in the school requested by the parent while resolving any dispute regarding school selection or enrollment (42 USC § 11432(g)(3)(E)).

12:47. Once a district is designated as the district of attendance for a homeless child, may it subsequently be changed?

Yes. The homeless child's district of attendance may be changed if the person so deciding (see **12:46**) finds that the original designation to be educationally unsound. The change must be made before the end of the first semester of attendance or within 60 days after commencing attendance at a school, whichever occurs later (8 NYCRR § 100.2(x)(2)(vi)).

12:48. Is a homeless child who previously resided in a school district outside New York State entitled to enroll in a public school in New York State on a tuition-free basis?

Yes. The homeless child is a resident of the district where the temporary housing arrangement is located and is entitled to attend school on a tuition-free basis (§ 3209(2)(b)(2); 8 NYCRR § 100.2(x)(2)(iv)).

12:49. What procedures must be followed to admit homeless children into the designated school district?

A designation form provided by the commissioner of education must be completed by the person responsible for designating a homeless child's district of attendance (§ 3209(2)(d); 8 NYCRR § 100.2(x)(3)). All school districts must provide a form to any homeless child or parent or guardian who seeks to enroll a child in school (8 NYCRR § 100.2(x)(3)).

The school district must immediately review the designation form to assure that it has been completed, admit the homeless child and provide the child with access to all of its programs, activities, and services to the same extent as they are provided to resident students. The district must admit the child even if he or she is unable to produce records normally required for enrollment, such as academic records, medical records, proof of residency, or other documentation (8 NYCRR § 100.2(x)(4)(ii)).

The designated district must also make a written request to the school district where the child's records are located for a copy of such records. The district must then forward the designation form to the commissioner of education and the school district of origin where applicable (§ 3209(2)(e); 8 NYCRR § 100.2(x)(4)).

The district where the child's records are located must forward a complete copy of the homeless child's records, including, but not limited to, proof of age, academic records, evaluations, immunization or medical records, and guardianship papers, if applicable, within five days of receiving a written request (§ 3209(2)(f); 8 NYCRR § 100.2(x)(5)).

12:50. What other responsibilities does a district have with regard to homeless students?

School districts cannot segregate homeless students in a separate school or a separate program within a school based on their status as homeless, unless such placement is necessary for a short period of time because of health and safety emergencies or the need to provide temporary, special, and supplementary services that meet the unique needs of the child (8 NYCRR § 100.2(x)(7)(a)(i)).

The school district must also appoint a liaison to, in part, work with local social service agencies and other programs providing services to homeless and with school districts about transportation concerns. The liaison must also inform parents of homeless children about the educational and related opportunities available to them and their rights, and assist in the placement of unaccompanied youth (those with no parent or guardian) and notify the student of the right to appeal placement decisions (42 USC § 11432(g)(6); § 3209(2-a); 8 NYCRR § 100.2(x)(7)(c), (d)).

12:51. Who is responsible for the payment of a homeless child's tuition?

If the parent or guardian of the homeless child, or the homeless child, if no parent or guardian is available, designates a school district other than that of the child's last residence, the district providing instruction will be eligible for reimbursement by the State Education Department (SED) (§ 3209(3)(a)). The district where the child last attended school then must reimburse SED for its expenditure for educational services on behalf of that child. Reimbursement will be equal to the school district's basic contribution, pro-rated for the period of time for which the services are provided by a school district other than the one in which the child last attended school (§ 3209(3)(b)).

12:52. May a homeless child attend any school within the school district he or she chooses to go to?

If the homeless child attends school in the district of origin, consistent with a parent or guardian's wishes, and to the extent feasible, the district is required to keep the child in the school of origin (8 NYCRR § 100.2(7)(a)(ii). The child may choose to attend the school building in the attendance zone where the child is temporarily located, or the child may choose to remain in the public school building he or she previously attended until the end of the school year. The homeless child may attend the same school building for an additional year if that year constitutes the child's last year in such a building (§§ 3209(1)(c), 3209(2)(b)(1); 8 NYCRR § 100.2(x)(2)(ii), (v)).

If the child goes to school in the district of current location, that child may attend the school in the zone of his or her temporary location or any other school that nonhomeless students who live in the same attendance zone may attend (§ 3209(1)(d); 8 NYCRR § 100.2(x)(2)(v)).

12:53. What happens when a homeless child who attends school in the district of current location is subsequently relocated to a different temporary housing arrangement outside that district or to a different attendance zone within that district?

The homeless child may continue to attend the same school building until the end of the school year and for one additional year if that year constitutes the child's last year in such building (§ 3209(2)(c); 8 NYCRR § 100.2(x)(2)(iii)).

12:54. Are homeless children entitled to receive school transportation services?

Yes. When a homeless child designates the school district of current location to attend school, that district must provide transportation to the child on the same basis as it is provided to resident students (§ 3209(4)(d); 8 NYCRR § 100.2(x)(6)(iii)).

If the child attends the school district of origin or a school district participating in a regional placement plan, then that district must provide transportation to and from the child's temporary housing and school (§ 3209(4)(c)).

If a homeless child attends the public school building where he or she previously attended, then that district must provide transportation to and from the temporary housing location and the school the child legally attends if the temporary housing location is located in a different attendance zone or community school district within such district (§ 3209(4)(e); 8 NYCRR § 100.2(x)(6)(iv)).

However, a social services district is responsible for providing transportation to homeless children who are eligible for benefits under section 350-j of the Social Services Law and who are placed in temporary housing arrangements outside their designated districts. To the extent funds are available, the state Division for Youth must provide transportation for each homeless child who lives in a residential program for runaway and homeless youth located outside the designated district.

The social services district or division of youth may contract with a school district or board of cooperative educational services (BOCES) to provide such transportation services (§ 3209(4)(a), (b)). Any homeless child not entitled to receive transportation from the Department of Social

Services or the Division for Youth must be transported by the designated school district (§ 3209(4)(c); 8 NYCRR § 100.2(x)(6)).

Homeless children are entitled to transportation even if a district does not provide transportation to nonhomeless students and during on going disputes regarding school selection and enrollment (U.S. Department of Education Draft Non-Regulatory Guidance on Education for Homeless Children and Youth, March 28, 2003).

12:55. Are there any mileage limitations that apply to the provision of transportation to homeless children?

Yes. A designated school district that must provide transportation to a homeless child may not provide transportation in excess of 50 miles one way, unless the commissioner determines that it is in the best interest of the child (§ 3209(4)(c); 8 NYCRR § 100.2(x)(6)(ii)).

12:56. Is state aid available for districts that provide transportation to homeless children?

Yes. A school district may receive state aid to offset expenditures incurred by the district for the transportation of homeless children under certain circumstances (§ 3209(4)(c)).

Student Health and Welfare

12:57. Are school districts required to employ a school physician or school nurse?

Each district must employ either a competent physician or a duly licensed nurse practitioner as a medical inspector to make inspections of students attending the public schools in the city or district (§ 902(1)(a); 8 NYCRR § 136.2(c)).

However, there is no requirement that schools employ other types of nurses. The only requirement is that a nurse (other than a nurse practitioner) hired by a district be a registered nurse, have graduated from a school of nursing registered by the Board of Regents, and be authorized to practice as such (§ 902(1)).

Additionally, the state has no requirement mandating schools to employ the services of school nurse-teachers. A school nurse-teacher is a registered nurse who is a certified teacher or teaching assistant, qualified, and trained to perform, in addition to nursing services, other educational services in the classroom (*Bork v. North Tonawanda City Sch. Dist.*, 60 A.D.2d 13 (4th Dep't 1977), *appeal denied*, 44 N.Y.2d 647 (1978); *Matter of Festa*, 21 Educ. Dep't Rep. 374 (1982)).

12:58. Are school districts required to provide a health service program?

Yes. Each school district must provide a health service program. (8 NYCRR Part 136, article 19, § 901 *et seq.*). These programs are not intended to supplant the provision of medical services from the student's primary physician (see Opn. Counsel No. 98, 1 Educ. Dep't Rep. 824 (1961); Opn. Counsel No. 67, 1 Educ. Dep't Rep. 766 (1952)). As part of any such program, school districts must conduct medical inspection of all students attending the public schools (except in the cities of New York, Buffalo, and Rochester). The purpose of a medical inspection is to examine for the existence of disease or physical defects and to test the eyes and ears of students (§ 901; 8 NYCRR § 136.2(b)).

The term *health service* refers to the several procedures including medical examinations, dental inspection and/or screening, vision screening and audiometer tests, used to ascertain the health status of students and prevent and correct defects and diseases; handle accident or illness; and address the health and safety aspects of the school plant and the hygiene of instruction (8 NYCRR § 136.1(d)).

Each child enrolled in a school (except in Buffalo, New York City, and Rochester) must have a satisfactory health examination as required under law and regulations (§§ 903–905) and any special health examinations as may be essential (8 NYCRR § 136.3(a)(2)). Districts are authorized to conduct physical examinations of students (§ 903; 8 NYCRR § 136.3(a)(2)) except in Buffalo, New York City, and Rochester, which have their health services provided by county health departments.

Every district is required to provide approved and adequate personnel and facilities, maintain for each child's cumulative records covering the essential features of the health service program, and make reports to the State Education Department on forms prescribed by the commissioner of education (8 NYCRR § 136.2(d)).

12:59. Are school districts required to provide health and welfare services to students attending private schools?

At the request of a private school, a school board is required to provide any or all of the health and welfare services and facilities available to students attending the public schools. Services may include those performed by a physician, dentist, dental hygienist, nurse, school psychologist, school social worker, school speech therapist, or nurse practitioner. They may also include dental prophylaxis, vision and hearing tests, the taking of medical histories, and the administration of health-screening tests, the maintenance of cumulative health records, and the administration of emergency-care programs for ill or injured students (§ 912; see **12:57**).

These services are mandatory only for residents of the district (§ 912). The district where the nonpublic school is located, however, must contract with the district(s) where the nonresident students of such school reside for payment of the agreed-upon amount for health services (§ 912). Provision for this expenditure must be included in the annual budget.

While the law requires school districts to provide health services to nonpublic school students equivalent to those provided to the public school students, it does not require a school district to provide full-time nursing services for a nonpublic school (*Appeal of Burke*, 34 Educ. Dep't Rep. 3 (1994)).

12:60. What requirements must school districts comply with when providing a health service program?

The Education Law and the commissioner's regulations require, among other things, that each district do the following:

- Record the results of the health examinations (the dental inspection and/or screening, hearing, vision and scoliosis screening) on approved forms that will be kept on file in the school.
- Require the physician or nurse practitioner making the examination to sign the health record card and make approved recommendations.
- Advise, in writing, the parent or guardian of each child in whom any aspect of the total school health service program indicates a defect, disability, or other condition that may require professional attention with regard to health.
- Keep confidential health records of children except when the records must be used by approved school personnel and, with the consent of the parents or guardians, for use by appropriate health personnel of cooperating agencies.
- Require adequate health inspections of students by teachers, school nurse-teachers and other approved school personnel.
- Maintain a suitable program of education to inform school personnel, parents, nonschool health agencies, welfare agencies, and the general public regarding school health conditions, services, and factors relating to children's health.
- Provide adequate guidance to parents, children, and teachers in procedures for preventing and correcting defects and diseases and in the general improvement of children's health.
- Furnish appropriate instruction to school personnel in procedures to follow in case of accident or illness.
- Provide suitable inspections and supervision of the health and safety aspects of the school building.

- Provide adequate health examinations before student participation in strenuous physical activity and periodically throughout the season.
- Provide health examinations necessary for issuing employment certificates, vacation work permits, newspaper carrier certificates, and street trades badges.
- Provide scoliosis screening for each child between the ages of eight and 16 years of age, regardless of the child's grade, at least once each school year (8 NYCRR § 136.3; see article 19)).

Students and their parents cannot sue school districts for money damages when districts fail to screen students for scoliosis. However, the commissioner of education may withhold public funding from districts that fail to comply with the medical and health care requirements of article 19 (§ 911; *Uhr v. East Greenbush CSD*, 94 N.Y.2d 32 (1999)).

12:61. Are students required to furnish certificates of health in New York State public schools?

Yes. Every student who initially enters school, and thereafter begins first, third, seventh, and 10th grades (except in Buffalo, New York City, and Rochester) is required to present a health certificate signed by a duly licensed physician authorized to practice medicine in New York State (§ 903; 8 NYCRR § 136.3(a)(2)).

For students who attend a city school district, the examination for a certificate must include a one-time test for sickle-cell anemia. In all other school districts, the test for sickle-cell anemia is performed at the discretion of the physician. This testing requirement does not apply to students who refuse to take the test because of religious beliefs (§ 903).

The certificate, which must state whether or not the student's condition of bodily health is fit enough to permit his or her attendance in the public schools, must be submitted to the principal or teacher in charge of the school within 15 days of entrance to the school or the grades cited above. This certificate then is filed with the clerk of the district (§ 903).

If a student does not present a health certificate, a notice must be sent to the student's parents or guardian stating that, if the required health certificate is not furnished within 15 days from the date of that notice, the student will be given a medical examination (§ 903).

Parents do not have the right to withhold a student from all school medical examinations (including those testing sight, hearing, etc.) and to refuse to transmit certificates from their family physician in these cases (Opn. Counsel No. 54, 1 Educ. Dep't Rep. 750 (1952)). The student must either submit to the exam or provide a health certificate from his or her family physician.

12:62. Must school districts conduct medical examinations of students who have not furnished certificates of health?

Yes. Except in the Buffalo, New York City, and Rochester schools, the school district's physician or nurse practitioner must examine all students who have not furnished certificates, or who are disabled, to determine whether they have defective sight or hearing or any other disability that might prevent them from doing well in school. This is also done to determine whether a possible condition might require modification of the student's education program to prevent possible injury or to ensure that student does well in school (§ 904; 8 NYCRR §§ 136.2(b), 136.3(a)(2)).

For students who attend a city school district, the examination must include a one-time test of all students between the ages of four and nine to determine the presence of sickle-cell anemia. In all other school districts, the test for sickle-cell anemia is performed at the discretion of the school district's physician. This testing requirement does not apply to students who refuse to take the test because of religious beliefs (§ 904).

Parents or guardians must be notified of the existence of defective sight or hearing or other physical disability. If a student's parent or guardian is unable or unwilling to provide the necessary relief and treatment for a student's condition, the principal, or teacher must report this to the school district's physician, whose duty it will be to provide the relief (§ 904).

12:63. What other medical tests must be performed by school districts?

Student hearing tests must be performed once a year in grades 7 and below, in grade 10, and at other times deemed necessary by the school physician, principal or teachers (§ 905(1)).

Student eye tests must be performed once a year for all students (§ 905(1)). In addition, all students, regardless of grade level, must be tested for color perception, distance acuity, and near vision, within six months of admission to school. Students whose parents or guardians object to these eye tests on the grounds that they conflict with their sincerely held religious beliefs are exempt from these requirements (§ 905(4)). These test results must be made available to the students' parents and teachers within that school and kept in a permanent file for at least as long as the student is enrolled in the school (§ 905(4)).

Student scoliosis examinations must be performed once a year for students between the ages of eight and 16, except those students whose parents or guardians are bona fide members of a recognized religious organization whose teachings are contrary to this requirement (§ 905(1)). These results must be provided in writing to a parent or person in parental relation within 90 days if a finding of the presence of scoliosis is made (§ 905(2)). Students and their parents cannot sue school districts for money damages when districts fail to screen students for scoliosis. Responsibility for enforcing the scoliosis screening requirement is specifically vested in the commissioner of education who may withhold funds from a district that willfully or negligently fails to comply with the statute (*Uhr v. East Greenbush CSD*, 246 A.D.2d 37 (3d Dep't 1998), *aff'd*, 94 N.Y.2d 32 (1999)).

Local school authorities may require an examination of a child at any time, at their discretion, to promote that child's educational interest (§ 903).

12:64. May school district staff administer medication to students?

Only health care practitioners licensed or certified in New York State, including, for example, physicians, nurse practitioners, physicians assistants, registered professional nurses and licensed practical nurses may administer medication under Title VIII of the Education Law. Districts should establish policy and procedures for the administration of medication to students during the regular school day or while participating in school-sponsored activities such as field trips and athletics in accordance with guidelines issued by the New York State Education Department on the Administration of Medication in the School Setting, last revised April 2002.

A written order from a duly licensed prescriber and written parental permission to administer medication (including nonprescription drugs) are required.

School districts must permit students who have been diagnosed by a physician or a duly authorized health care provider with a severe asthmatic condition to carry and use a prescribed inhaler during the school day, with the written permission of a physician or a duly authorized health care provider and parental consent. The diagnosis of a severe asthmatic condition must be based on the physician's determination that the student is subject to sudden asthmatic attacks severe enough to debilitate the student. A record of this permission must be maintained in the school office (§ 916).

12:65. Must children be immunized in order to attend the public schools?

Yes. Children must be immunized against poliomyelitis, mumps, measles, diphtheria, rubella, varicella, Haemophilus influenzae type b (Hib), pertussis, tetanus, and hepatitis B (Pub. Health Law § 2164(2), (2-a) (7)(a), 10 NYCRR § 66-1.1, 66-1.3).

If there is no proof or record of a child's immunization, the principal or teacher must direct the child's parent or person in parental authority to have the child immunized by any health practitioner. The child may also be immunized without charge by the county health officer, if the parent or guardian consents (Pub. Health Law § 2164(6); see **12:66** for exceptions).

The immunizing physician must provide an immunization certificate to the person in parental relation to the child (Pub. Health Law § 2164(5)).

No child may be admitted to school or allowed to attend school for more than 14 days without an appropriate immunization certificate or acceptable evidence of immunization. This period may be extended to 30 days on a case-by-case basis by the principal if a student has transferred from another state or country and can show a good faith effort to get the necessary certification or other evidence of immunization (Pub. Health Law § 2164(7)(a)).

The principal must forward a report to the local health authority and to the parent, and notify the parent to have the child immunized in a case where a student is refused admission to or continued attendance at a school for failure to provide appropriate proof of immunization (Pub. Health Law § 2164(8-a)(a)). In addition, the principal must send an immunization consent form to the parent and cooperate with the local health authority in scheduling a time and place for immunizing a child for whom consent has been obtained.

A student may appeal a denial of admission to or continued attendance at school to the commissioner of education (Pub. Health Law § 2164(7)(b)).

12:66. Are there any exceptions to the immunization requirements?

Yes. Students may be admitted to school or continue attendance without a certificate or proof of immunization if:

- A physician will testify or certify that administering a vaccine to a specific student will be detrimental to that student's health (Pub. Health Law § 2164(8)); or
- In the case of varicella, either a health care provider documents the child has already had varicella, or there is serologic evidence the child has immunity to varicella (Pub. Health Law § 2164(2-a); 10 NYCRR § 66-1.3(a)(9)); or
- The student, or the student's parents or guardian, hold genuine and sincere religious beliefs that prohibit immunization (Pub. Health Law § 2164(9)).

Parents may oppose immunizations on religious grounds without belonging to an organized religion. However, the opposition to immunization must be based on religious beliefs instead of merely framed in terms of religious belief (*Lewis v. Sobol*, 710 F.Supp. 506 (S.D.N.Y. 1989); *Sherr v. Northport-East Northport UFSD*, 672 F.Supp. 81 (E.D.N.Y. 1987); *Farina v. Board of Educ. of New York City*, 116 F.Supp.2d 503 (S.D.N.Y. 2000); *Appeal of Quigley*, 41 Educ. Dep't Rep. 399 (2002); *Appeal of Swett*, 34 Educ. Dep't Rep. 492 (1995)).

A school district cannot reject a request for an exemption from only one vaccine without an investigation (*Appeal of M.E.F.*, 43 Educ. Dep't Rep. ___, dec. no. 14,987 (2003)).

12:67. Must school districts participate in surveys on student immunizations directed by the state commissioner of health?

Yes. Each school district must participate in surveys directed by the state commissioner of health and provide any records or reports so requested (§ 914(3)). Furthermore, the commissioner of health must conduct an annual audit of the immunization level of children attending schools (Pub. Health Law § 613(2)).

12:68. May public school students be tested for the use of illegal drugs?

Yes, but only upon the written request or consent of the child's parent or legal guardian (§ 912-a(2); *Appeal of Studley*, 38 Educ. Dep't Rep. 258 (1998); see also **12:111**). If parental authorization is obtained, the Education Law permits urine testing of students in grades 7–12 for detection of use of "dangerous drugs" as defined in the Penal Law (§ 912-a(1)). These tests must be conducted without notice to the student (§ 912-a(2)). If the test result indicates that the student is using dangerous drugs, the district must report such information to the local social services department and to the parent or legal guardian, including a statement as to available programs and facilities to combat dangerous drug usage (§ 912-a(2)).

The test results may not be used for law enforcement purposes and must be kept confidential (§ 912-a(3)). The law also contains an exemption from testing based on religious considerations (§ 912-a(4)).

12:69. Must students who have contracted contagious diseases be prohibited from attending school?

Yes. Whenever a student in a public school shows symptoms of any contagious, or infectious disease, as defined in section 2(1)(l) of the Public Health Law, he or she must be sent home immediately. Before that student is allowed to return to school, he or she must either present a certificate from the city or town health officer or family physician, or be examined by the district medical officer (§ 906).

A district may be obligated to provide temporary home instruction for a student suffering from a short-term physical disability (§ 1709(24); *Appeal of Douglas and Barbara K.*, 34 Educ. Dep't Rep. 214 (1994); *Appeal of Anthony M. and D. M.*, 30 Educ. Dep't Rep. 269 (1991)). However, the commissioner of education has ruled that a district was not obligated to provide home instruction to students who missed approximately one and one half months of school because of head lice, a condition that could normally be alleviated in one or two days, because the students' parent contributed to the excessive absence by failing to follow the recommended course of treatment to rid her children of the lice (*Appeal of Douglas and Barbara K.*).

12:70. Does New York State regard acquired immune deficiency syndrome (AIDS) as a contagious, communicable or infectious disease?

No. AIDS has not been defined in the regulations of the New York State Department of Health as a contagious, communicable or infectious disease, and its exclusion from this category has been upheld by the New York State Court of Appeals (*New York State Soc. of Surgeons v. Axelrod*, 77 N.Y.2d 677 (1991)).

12:71. May a student with AIDS or any other human immunodeficiency virus (HIV)-related illness be prohibited from attending public school solely because he or she has an HIV-related illness?

No. A student with AIDS or another HIV-related illness cannot be denied the opportunity to attend school, continue his or her education, or take part in school-related activities, solely on the basis of having been diagnosed with AIDS or becoming infected with HIV. Automatic exclusion from school of children infected with HIV or who have contracted AIDS would violate those students' rights under section 504 of the Federal Rehabilitation Act of 1973 (*District 27 Community Sch. Bd. v. Board of Educ.*, 130 Misc.2d 398 (Sup. Ct. Queens County 1986); see 29 USC § 794).

Several federal courts with jurisdiction outside of New York have held that children infected with HIV are disabled for purposes of the Rehabilitation Act and otherwise are qualified to attend classes in the absence of evidence that they pose a significant risk of harm to classmates or teachers (see *Martinez v. Sch. Bd. of Hillsborough County*, 861 F.2d 1502 (11th Cir. 1988); *Thomas v. Atascadero Unified Sch. Dist.*, 662 F.Supp. 376 (C.D. Cal. 1987)).

The Americans with Disabilities Act (ADA) also prohibits school districts from denying students with disabilities the benefits of or participation in the services, programs, and activities of the district on the basis of disability (42 USC § 12132). The United States Supreme Court has ruled that asymptomatic HIV infection is a disability under the ADA (*Bragdon v. Abbott*, 524 U.S. 624 (1998)).

The regulations implementing the ADA also state that HIV, whether symptomatic or asymptomatic, is included in the definition of "disability" (28 CFR § 35.104). The regulations prohibit discrimination in the provision of educational and other services against individuals infected with HIV (see 28 CFR § 35.130(a)).

12:72. Must information concerning HIV and/or AIDS be kept confidential?

Yes. Current law and regulations strictly limit the disclosure of confidential information about HIV or AIDS (Pub. Health Law article 27-F; 10 NYCRR Part 63). In most circumstances, disclosure of such information concerning a student is contingent on obtaining an authorization for release form signed by the student, or if the student lacks the "capacity to consent," by a person legally authorized to consent on behalf of the student (Pub. Health Law § 2782; 10 NYCRR § 63.5(a)).

Disclosure of such information also is permitted if a court order has been issued requiring its release because of the presence of a clear and imminent danger to another person who unknowingly may be at significant risk as a result of contact with the student (Pub. Health Law § 2785(2)(b); 10 NYCRR § 63.6(a)(12), (b)(4)). This information can be given only to persons identified in the court order, only for the reasons provided in the court order (Pub. Health Law § 2785(6)).

12:73. Are there any precautions school districts are required to observe to prevent the spread of HIV and other diseases communicable through contact with blood and other bodily fluids?

Yes. School districts must have a written "exposure control plan." The plan must provide for employee training on how to deal with body fluids and other materials, and the keeping of accurate medical and training records. The plan must also identify positions, such as nurses, coaches, and custodians, and tasks likely to come into contact with blood and other bodily fluids. In addition, it must set forth the procedures to be followed, including "universal precautions," which require, for instance, that all bodily fluids and material be treated as infectious, and the wearing of protective equipment (29 CFR § 1910.1030(c)(1)).

12:74. Are safety glasses required in school shops or lab courses?

Yes. School boards must provide that students and teachers participating in certain vocational, shop, and laboratory courses wear eye safety devices (§ 409-a(1); 8 NYCRR § 141.10(a)). This requirement also extends to visitors to such courses (§ 409-a(3); 8 NYCRR § 141.10(a)).

12:75. Are school districts required to have automated external defibrillator (AED) equipment in their schools?

Yes. There must be AED equipment on site at each instructional school facility to ensure ready and appropriate access for use during emergencies. Each AED device must be approved by the Food and Drug Administration and be used according to the manufacturer's instructions (8 NYCRR § 136.4(b)).

When determining the number of devices a school needs and where they should be placed, consideration shall be given to the number and ages of individuals in the building, the size and physical layout of the facility, types and locations of athletic, curricular, and extracurricular events and any unique design features of the building. (§ 917(1); 8 NYCRR § 136.4(b); State Education Department Q & A Regarding Automated External Defibrillators in Schools Round 1)). The State Education Department has stated that each school facility should have as its goal "a specific response plan that targets a victim's collapse to defibrillation time less than or equal to four to five minutes" (SED Q & A Regarding Automated External Defibrillators Round 1)).

At least one staff member trained in the operation and use of an AED must be present whenever school facilities are used for school-sponsored or school-approved curricular or extracurricular events or activities and whenever a school-sponsored athletic contest is held at any location. Activities such a board meetings, PTA meetings, and activities sponsored by outside groups such as 4-H or Girl/Boy Scouts are excluded from the AED mandate and the school does not need to provide AED coverage at these events (SED Q & A Regarding Automated External Defibrillators in Schools, Round 2). School officials must ensure that AED equipment and a trained staff person are provided on-site whenever a school-sponsored competitive athletic event is held at a site other than a public school facility (§ 917(2); 8 NYCRR § 136.4(c), (d)).

12:76. Are public schools required to maintain home telephone numbers of each student?

Yes. The Education Law requires each school to maintain the telephone numbers of each student enrolled, and of their parent or guardian, including both residential and business telephone numbers, for emergency notification purposes (§ 3212-a(1)). The law allows parents and students to refuse to supply their telephone numbers, and exempts those districts whose school boards adopt resolutions providing these records need not be maintained (§ 3212-a(1), (2)).

Missing and Abused Children

12:77. What is a school district's responsibility in relation to the identification and finding of missing children?

The commissioner of the Division of Criminal Justice Services (CJS) is required to regularly give the State Education Department (SED) a bulletin with information about the children listed in the statewide register. SED then must forward this bulletin to every public and private school where parents, guardians, or others legally responsible for such children have given consent (Exec. Law § 837-f(10)).

The CJS commissioner also must cooperate with public and private schools to develop education and prevention programs concerning child safety; to operate a toll-free, 24-hour hotline for the public to use to relay information concerning missing children; and to provide other assistance to local agencies in the investigation of these cases (Exec. Law § 837-f(5), (8), (11)).

A school district which is notified by CJS that a child has been listed as missing must flag the schooling record of the child in such a manner that whenever a copy of or information concerning that record is requested, the person authorized to issue such record is alerted to the fact that the child has been reported as a missing child. The school then must immediately report any such requests to the local law enforcement authority and CJS (§ 3222(4)).

Once CJS has notified the school that a reported missing child has been recovered, the school must remove the flag from the child's schooling record (§ 3222(4)).

A school must immediately notify CJS if it discovers that a child who is reported missing by the division is currently enrolled in that school (§ 3222(5)).

12:78. Is a school district required to provide instruction to prevent the abduction of children?

Yes. All students in kindergarten through eighth grade must receive instruction designed to prevent the abduction of children. Such instruction must be provided either by a regular classroom teacher or be under the teacher's direct supervision, if it is provided by a public or private agency (§ 803-a(1)).

In providing for a course of study, the school board may establish a local advisory council or use the school-based shared-decision-making committee to recommend the content and implementation of such courses. Alternately, school districts may use courses of instruction developed by others, such as other school districts, boards of cooperative educational services (BOCES), or any other public or private agency. Advisory councils shall consist of, but not be limited to, parents, school board members and trustees, appropriate school personnel, business and community representatives, and law enforcement personnel having experience in the prevention of child abduction (§ 803-a(3)).

School districts must provide appropriate training and curriculum materials for those teachers who provide the instruction (§ 803-a(4)).

12:79. To whom may a student be released from school?

Section 3210(1)(c) of the Education Law provides that a person who requests the release of a student from school must be identified against a list of names provided by the student's parent or guardian at the time of the child's enrollment in the school.

A school district may adopt procedures for submitting a list of names at a later date or updating the list of names provided by the person or persons in parental relation to the student. If someone whose name is not on the list attempts to obtain the release of a student, that student may not be released. There is an exception for an emergency release, provided that the student's parent or guardian agrees.

12:80. What is the school's responsibility concerning a child's release from school in cases where the child's parents are separated or divorced?

A school district may presume that either parent of a child has authority to obtain the child's release, unless the district has been provided with a certified copy of a legally binding instrument, such as a court order or decree of divorce, separation, or custody, that indicates the noncustodial parent does not have the right to obtain such release (§ 3210(1)(c)).

12:81. What is a school district's responsibility to report abused or maltreated school children?

School officials must make a report to child protective services when they have reasonable cause to suspect a student is abused or maltreated. If the person who suspects abuse or maltreatment is a school staff member, he or she must notify the head of the school immediately, who must then make the report (Soc. Serv. Law § 413(1)).

The law also states that, in addition to those persons legally required to report suspected child abuse or maltreatment, any person who has reasonable cause to suspect child abuse or maltreatment may make such a report (Soc. Serv. Law § 414).

Reports of child abuse or maltreatment must be made immediately by telephone or fax on a form supplied by the commissioner of social services. An oral report must be followed by a written report within 48 hours. Oral reports must be made to the statewide central register of child abuse and maltreatment, unless an appropriate local plan provides these reports should be made to the local child protective service. Except in specified instances, written reports also must be made to the local child protective service (Soc. Serv. Law § 415).

The Social Services Law provides legal penalties for failure to report cases of suspected child abuse, including liability for damages proximately caused by such failure (Soc. Serv. Law § 420, see *Matter of Catherine G.*, 307 A.D.2d 446, (3d Dep't 2003), *appeal granted*, 1 N.Y.3d 503 (2003)). The law also provides immunity from liability for the school official making such a report in good faith (Soc. Serv. Law § 419).

The hotline telephone number to report a case of suspected abuse or maltreatment is 800-342-3720. An additional hotline telephone number for school administrators and teachers to report suspected abuse or maltreatment is 800-635-1522.

The Education Law requires that school districts develop, maintain, and disseminate written policies and procedures on reporting child abuse, pursuant to the Social Services Law and the Family Court Act. These must include procedures for mandatory reporting of child abuse or neglect; obligations of persons required to report; taking a child into protective custody; mandatory reporting of deaths; a statement of immunity from liability; penalties for failure to report; and providing services and procedures necessary to safeguard the life or health of a child. In addition, every board must establish and maintain a training program for all current and new school employees regarding these policies and procedures (§ 3209-a).

12:82. What is a school district's responsibility to report suspected child abuse in an educational setting?

The Education Law requires that school districts report to law enforcement authorities allegations of child abuse in an educational setting by a district employee or volunteer. The term *child abuse* refers to the intentional or reckless infliction of physical injury, serious physical injury, or death, as well as conduct that creates a substantial risk of such injuries or death. It also includes any child sexual abuse as defined under sections 130 or 263 of the Penal Law, and the dissemination of or attempts to disseminate indecent materials to minors under article 235 of the Penal Law (§ 1125(1), (9)). The term *educational setting* means building and grounds of a public school district, vehicles used to transport students to and from school, and field trips, co-curricular and extracurricular activities, as well as sites where those activities take place. It also includes any other location where direct contact occurs between students and employees or volunteers (§ 1125(5)).

Teachers, school nurses, guidance counselors, school psychologists and social workers, administrators, school board members, or other school personnel required to hold a teaching or administrative license must file a written report with the school principal upon receipt of any oral or written allegation of child abuse in a educational setting.

Where there is reasonable suspicion to believe that an act of child abuse has occurred, the school principal must take action as required by law, including promptly notifying parents of the allegation and their rights, responsibilities and procedures to be followed; forwarding a copy of the report to the superintendent of schools; and notifying appropriate law enforcement officials without delay (§§ 1126, 1128). A copy of the report itself is not given to the parents (see *Appeal of S.S.*, 42 Educ. Dep't Rep. 273 (2003)). Where there is a determination that no reasonable suspicion exists, the parents are not entitled to notification of their rights (*Appeal of S.S.*). Where the alleged child abuse occurred outside the district, the report must be submitted to the superintendent of both the district of attendance and the district where the abuse allegedly occurred. In this case, both superintendents are responsible for contacting law enforcement authorities without delay and for taking other actions required by law (§§ 1126(2), 1128, 1128-a)).

Willful failure to comply with the child abuse in an educational setting reporting requirements constitutes a class A misdemeanor. The failure to contact law enforcement authorities is also punishable by a civil penalty of up to $5,000 (§ 1129).

12:83. What must be included in a district's notice of parental rights in a situation involving suspected child abuse in an educational setting?

The notice of parental rights to be provided to the parents of a child allegedly subjected to child abuse in an educational setting must include a description of the following: the duties of school district personnel upon receipt of an allegation; notification by the district attorney and the action that will be taken upon criminal conviction of a licensed or certified school employee; duties of the commissioner; the confidentiality of records; penalties for failure to comply with reporting requirements; and the prohibition and penalty against unreported resignations of school employees or volunteers involved in a child abuse allegation (referred to as "silent resignations") (8 NYCRR § 100.2(hh)(1)).

12:84. Must school districts train employees on their duties regarding child abuse in an educational setting?

Yes. School districts must provide an annual written explanation to each teacher and all other school officials and ongoing training regarding the law on child abuse in an educational setting to all current and new teachers, school nurses, school counselors, school psychologists, school social workers, school administrators, other personnel required to hold a teaching or administrative certificate or license and school board members. The training program shall include duties of all school personnel, confidentiality of records, notification to the district attorney and action taken upon conviction and the prohibition of silent resignations (8 NYCRR § 100.2(hh)(2), (3)).

Sex Offender Registration Act
("Megan's Law")

12:85. What is the Sex Offender Registration Act?

The Sex Offender Registration Act (commonly referred to as "Megan's Law") is a law that requires convicted sex offenders to register with the Division of Criminal Justice Services (CJS) upon discharge, parole, or release (Correct. Law § 168 *et seq.*). Based on the recommendations of a Board of Examiners of Sex Offenders, convicted sex offenders will be designated either as "sex predators," "sexually violent offenders" or "predicate sex offenders" and assigned to one of three risk classifications, which will determine the extent of public notification of their return to the community (Correct. Law §§ 168-a(7), 168-l(6)).

Public notification ranges from notification to law enforcement agencies only, to authorizing the law enforcement agencies to disseminate such information as a photograph and description of the offender, which may include the offender's name, address, employment address, modus of operation, and the crime for which the offender was convicted (Correct. Law § 168-l(6)).

The United States Court of Appeals for the Second Circuit has upheld the community notification provisions of the Sex Offender Registration Act (*Doe v. Pataki*, 120 F.3d 1263 (2d Cir. 1997), *cert. denied*, 522 U.S. 1122 (1998)). Furthermore, Megan's laws in general have withstood constitutional challenge and been upheld by the U.S. Supreme Court (see *Smith v. Doe*, 538 U.S. 84 (2003); *Connecticut Dep't of Pub. Safety v. Doe*, 538 U.S. 1 (2003).

12:86. Are school districts automatically notified of the release of a sex offender into their school community?

No. However, local law enforcement agencies are given authority, at their discretion, to release information on a sex offender related to the nature of the offense committed to any community with vulnerable populations (Correct. Law § 168-l(6)).

12:87. May a school district disclose information it receives under the Sex Offender Registration Act to members of the public?

Under the law, any entity, including a school district, receiving information on a sex offender may disclose or further disseminate such information at their discretion (Correct. Law § 168-l(6)(b), (c)).

An agency, its officials, and employees will be immune from civil or criminal liability for any decision on their part to release what they believe to be relevant and necessary information, unless it is proven they acted with gross negligence or in bad faith. The law further provides that no civil or criminal liability will be imposed against any agency, official, or employee for failing to release the information unless it is shown that they acted with gross negligence or in bad faith (Correct. Law § 168-r). However, the knowing simulation or dissemination of a purportedly official notice that falsely suggests an individual is a registered sex offender shall constitute a class A misdemeanor (Penal Law § 240.48).

Students' Constitutional Rights

12:88. What constitutional rights do students enjoy while they attend public school?

Certain constitutional rights, as set forth in the Bill of Rights of the United States Constitution, and listed below, are of special importance to students who attend public schools.

- The *First Amendment* provides, in part, that Congress will make no law prohibiting the free exercise of religion, freedom of speech, the right of people to assemble peaceably and to petition the government for a redress of grievances.
- The *Fourth Amendment* guarantees in part the right of people to be secure in their persons, houses, papers and effects against unreasonable searches and seizures.
- The *Fifth Amendment* maintains that no person shall be compelled in any criminal case to be a witness against himself or herself, nor be deprived of life, liberty or property without due process of law.

The questions that follow illustrate the impact of these constitutional rights in the day-to-day activities of a public school system. See **chapter 23** for more information on the role of religion in the schools.

12:89. Can a school district censor or curtail student publications?

Yes, if they are school-sponsored. In *Hazelwood Sch. Dist. v. Kuhlmeier*, 484 U.S. 260 (1988), the United States Supreme Court held that a school need not tolerate student speech that is inconsistent with its "basic educational mission." Such a determination rests with its school board and is supported by the distinction between "a student's personal expression that happens to occur on school premises" and a school's "authority over school-sponsored publications, theatrical productions, and other expressive activities" that are viewed by students, parents, and the community, and could reasonably be considered part of the school curriculum. According to the court, educators may constitutionally exercise "editorial control over the style and content of student speech in school-sponsored expressive activities so long as their actions are reasonably related to legitimate pedagogical concerns" (484 U.S. at 273, 274).

Based on the rationale in *Hazelwood*, a school district could reject an advertisement from a family-planning group in school district newspapers, yearbooks, and programs for athletic events (*Planned Parenthood of Southern Nevada, Inc. v. Clark County Sch. Dist.*, 941 F.2d 817 (9th Cir. 1991)).

On the other hand, a school district may establish a policy granting students broader protection for free speech than required, which then becomes the standard to be applied. A board policy, for instance, may limit the school district's authority to censor a school-sponsored student publication to those situations where there is an imminent threat to disrupt the education process or where the literary work is libelous or obscene even though such a policy is more restrictive of a school's authority than the standard set in the *Hazelwood* case (*Matter of Brenner*, 28 Educ. Dep't Rep. 402 (1989); see also *Appeal of Doro*, 40 Educ. Dep't Rep. 281 (2000); *Appeal of Miller*, 39 Educ. Dep't Rep. 348 (1999)).

12:90. Do students have the right to distribute on school grounds literature written and produced off school premises?

Yes. School authorities, however, may regulate the time, manner, place, and duration for distributing literature on school grounds (see, e.g., *Appeal of Doro*, 40 Educ. Dep't Rep. 281 (2000)). In addition, school authorities may regulate the content of literature to be distributed on school grounds to the extent necessary to avoid material and substantial interference with the requirements of appropriate discipline in the operation of the school (*Eisner v. Stamford Bd. of Educ.*, 440 F.2d 803 (2d Cir. 1971); see also **12:89** on a school district's right to control school-sponsored expressive activities).

Guidelines for the distribution of literature on school grounds should specify the time, place, and duration of distribution, and provide a method of distribution that will not interfere with normal school operations. For example, it should be made clear that those individuals who distribute literature may not block pedestrian traffic or the entrance to a building, and must remove any litter they create. The guidelines also may provide for sanctions against those who violate the prescribed procedures.

The guidelines may establish procedures for the submission of literature to the district for prior approval. Any predistribution review procedures must identify to whom the material is to be submitted, the criteria by which the material is to be evaluated, and a limitation on the time within which a decision must be made (see *Eisner*).

Although there are no New York cases with respect to whether students have a right to distribute written religious materials in school, federal courts in other jurisdictions have concluded that the same constitutional standards apply to student distribution of religious and nonreligious literature (*Hedges v. Wauconda Community Unit Sch. Dist. No. 118*, 9 F.3d 1295 (7th Cir. 1993); *Hemry v. School Bd. of Colorado Springs Sch. Dist. No. 11*, 760 F.Supp. 856 (D. Colo. 1991)).

12:91. Can school officials discipline students for the off-campus production and distribution of student publications?

No. School officials have no authority to punish students for the publication and distribution of student magazines or papers produced and distributed off school property (*Thomas v. Board of Educ.*, 607 F.2d 1043 (2d Cir. 1979), *cert. denied*, 444 U.S. 1081 (1980); but see *Appeal of Roemer*, 38 Educ. Dep't Rep. 294 (1998)).

12:92. Can a school district discipline students for the distribution on-campus of student publications produced off school premises?

Yes, if such distribution may cause a material or substantial disruption to the school environment. In *Board of Educ. of Monticello CSD v. Commissioner of Educ.*, 91 N.Y.2d 133 (1997), the New York Court of Appeals upheld the 10-day suspension of a student who distributed on school grounds a publication he produced on a home computer that encouraged other students to destroy school property and to engage in acts of insubordination, because there was sufficient evidence that the student's conduct endangered the safety, health, and welfare of others. However, a student who distributed unflattering essays produced on a home computer about a teacher could not be suspended on the grounds that the distribution of the essays threatened the health, safety, and welfare of persons in the school (*Appeal of Roemer*, 38 Educ. Dep't Rep. 294 (1998)).

The commissioner of education upheld the long-term suspension of a student who e-mailed a bomb threat message to the district's Web site because the school was "seriously disrupted" when it was forced to cancel classes due to the bomb threat (*Appeal of B.B.*, 38 Educ. Dep't Rep. 666 (1999)). Similarly, although not binding in New York, in another state a high school student suspended from school for one year after publishing an article in an underground newspaper on how to "hack" into the school's computer was denied preliminary injunctive relief to reinstate his attendance at school because the appeals court agreed that the school authorities had reason to believe the student's article would be disruptive (*Boucher v. School Bd. of Greenfield*, 134 F.3d 821 (7th Cir. 1998)).

12:93. Can public school students peacefully protest or demonstrate their views during school hours?

Yes. The United States Supreme Court has ruled that students have a constitutional right to demonstrate peacefully during school hours, as long as there is no disruption of the educational process of the school.

In the landmark case in this area, the court upheld the right of three students who were suspended from school in 1965 to wear black armbands as a protest against the Vietnam War. The court stressed that the student's actions were a form of protected free speech that did not disrupt regular schoolwork or intrude on the rights of others. It suggested that the decision could not be applied to aggressive, disruptive action. The court decided the armbands were "the type of symbolic act" protected by the constitutional guarantees of free speech and that an "apprehension of disturbance is not enough to overcome the right to freedom of expression" (*Tinker v. Des Moines Indep. Community Sch. Dist.*, 393 U.S. 503 (1969)).

Most litigation regarding students' free expression rights centers on children of high school age. However, according to a federal appellate court outside of New York elementary students have more limited rights because instilling values in young students, a primary goal of public schools, requires a greater level of guidance. Therefore, in one case, it was permissible for a school to stop a third grader from circulating a petition protesting a class trip to the circus after a student fell on an icy playground during the gathering of signatures. According to the court, there is no constitutional right to circulate a petition in class or an icy playground. The court was careful to note it was not saying there never is a right to gather signatures. However, such a right may be restricted when it interferes with the educational process or the right of other students (*Walker-Serrano v. Leonard*, 168 F.Supp.2d 332, (M.D. Pa. 2001), *aff'd*, 325 F.3d 412 (3d Cir. 2003)).

Similarly, the right of students to demonstrate their views does not include the right to distribute pencils with a religious message during an in-class party (*Walz v. Egg Harbor Township Bd. of Educ.*, 342 F.3d 271 (3d Cir. 2003), *cert. denied*, ___ U.S. ___, 124 S. Ct. 1658 (2004)). Neither does it include the right to say "I'm going to shoot you" while on a playground (*S.G. v. Sayreville Bd. of Educ.*, 333 F.3d 417(3d Cir. 2003)).

12:94. Can students wear or display armbands, buttons, or other badges of symbolic personal expression in school buildings?

Yes. Students may wear or display buttons, armbands, flags, decals, or other badges symbolic of personal expression, where the manner of expression does not materially intrude on the orderly process of the school or the rights of others. The buttons, armbands, and other badges of personal expression must not contain lewd, offensive, or libelous material or advocate racial or religious prejudice (*Tinker v. Des Moines Indep. Community Sch. Dist.*, 393 U.S. 503 (1969); *Frasca v. Andrews*, 463 F.Supp. 1043 (E.D.N.Y. 1979); *Appeal of Parsons*, 32 Educ. Dep't Rep. 672 (1993)).

12:95. Can a school district ban student speech that is not religious or political in nature?

Yes. The United States Supreme Court upheld the right of a school district to discipline a student who gave a nominating speech containing sexual innuendos in support of a fellow student's candidacy for a school office even though there was no evidence of material or substantial disruption caused by the speech. In upholding the suspension, the court noted that the penalties imposed in this case, in contrast to *Tinker*, were unrelated to any political point of view. The court also held that the First Amendment does not prevent school officials from determining that the use of vulgar and lewd speech would undermine the school's basic educational mission in teaching civility and mature conduct. According to the court, the sexual innuendo was plainly offensive to teachers and students, insulting, and potentially seriously damaging to its less mature audience (*Bethel Sch. Dist. v. Fraser*, 478 U.S. 675 (1986)).

In *Poling v. Murphy*, 872 F.2d 757 (6th Cir. 1989), *cert. denied*, 493 U.S. 1021 (1990), a federal appellate court held that school officials did not violate the constitutional rights of a student when they disqualified him from a student council election for making discourteous and rude remarks about an assistant principal at a school assembly. However, another federal appellate court found that there is a First Amendment right to "disparaging speech" and ruled one school district's anti-harassment policy exceeded its authority to govern student speech. The district's policy exceeded the scope of existing federal laws prohibiting harassment based on sex, race, color, national origin, age, and disability because it also prohibited negative comments about other personal characteristics and values such as clothing, social skills and intellect. The policy was not a permissible regulation of student speech under *Fraser* because it did not confine itself to lewd and vulgar speech, and could not be justified under *Tinker* because there was no particularized reason for anticipating a "substantial disruption" (*Saxe v. State College Area Sch. Dist.*, 240 F.3d 200 (3d Cir. 2001).

12:96. Can a school district regulate a student's use of the district's computer system?

Yes. The commissioner of education has upheld the suspension of a student who admitted to preparing an e-mail bomb threat message addressed to the district's Web site. Although the student claimed the message was sent inadvertently, she knew about it for two days before the actual threat and never notified the school. As a result, the school day was "seriously disrupted" when the school was forced to cancel classes due to the bomb threat (*Appeal of B.B.*, 38 Educ. Dep't Rep. 666 (1999), see **12:92**; see also *Appeal of T.N.*, 42 Educ. Dep't Rep. 235 (2003); *Appeal of David and Cynthia L.*, 40 Educ. Dep't Rep. 297 (2000)).

The commissioner has also upheld a district's actions in suspending a student and barring his use of any school computer after the student used a school-issued laptop computer to attempt to gain unauthorized access to a number of servers around the country, including the district's server. The student had also used the school-issued laptop to load on some servers programs that can be used to sabotage a server by flooding it with data (*Appeal of J.C.*, 41 Educ. Dep't Rep.395 (2002)).

12:97. Can a school district regulate a student's use of the Internet off-campus?

Yes. The commissioner of education upheld the suspension of a student who e-mailed a message with anti-Semitic contents and a threat of violence from a home computer to other students' home computers. According to the commissioner, the district reasonably interpreted the e-mail as a threat to student safety, and it substantially disrupted school operations. There was a nexus between the e-mail and a disruption of normal school operation because school administrators, board members, parents, community members, and the police were all involved in responding to the e-mail. Thus the district was authorized to pursue the disciplinary action subsequently taken (*Appeal of Ravick*, 40 Educ. Dep't Rep. 262 (2000)).

12:98. May a school district prescribe the way students must dress while they attend school?

Generally, school officials may not prescribe students' dress while they attend school in cases where fashion or taste is the sole criterion. However, a dress code may be adopted when there are legitimate educational concerns (*Appeal of Pintka*, 33 Educ. Dep't Rep. 228 (1993), *see Appeal of Conley*, 34 Educ. Dep't Rep. 376 (1995)).

Accordingly, the commissioner has ruled that the wearing of hats cannot be prohibited in school hallways unless the display is vulgar and indecent, imposes a health risk, is disruptive, or implicates other compelling educational concerns. Hats may be banned in the classroom for the same reasons, and also if they are considered disrespectful and improper under community standards (*Appeal of Pintka*). An unwritten policy prohibiting the wearing of vests and outerwear by students was found not to violate student First Amendment rights where there was no evidence that a student's vest was protected as symbolic speech of either political or religious expression (*Appeal of Mangaroo*, 33 Educ. Dep't Rep. 286 (1993)).

A dress code may not be vague, subjective, or overly broad (*Appeal of Parsons*, 32 Educ. Dep't Rep. 672 (1993)). In addition, it should be developed in consultation with teachers, administrators, other school service professionals, students, and parents (8 NYCRR § 100.2(l)(2)(i), (ii)(a)) to ensure that it reflects "current community standards" on "proper decorum and deportment" (*Appeal of Pintka*; see also *Appeal of Phillips*, 38 Educ. Dep't Rep. 297 (1998)). Districts may regulate students' dress when such rules relate to a specific educational purpose, such as teaching students socially appropriate behavior, or health, safety, or full participation in school activities, such as in science laboratories and physical education classes (*Matter of Scally*, 16 Educ. Dep't Rep. 243 (1977); see also *Appeal of Bartlett*, 33 Educ. Dep't Rep. 234 (1993)). However, clothing worn to make a religious or political statement cannot be banned, unless it is disruptive of the educational process, lewd, or offensive (*Tinker v. Des Moines Indep. Sch. Dist.*, 393 U.S. 503 (1969)).

School districts must be particularly wary of creating dress codes that are overbroad even when relating to socially appropriate behavior, health, and safety. A federal appellate court outside of New York overturned a district's ban on clothing that contained messages related to weapons when there was no evidence that clothing with such messages disrupted school operations or interfered with the rights of others. Furthermore, the provision had the effect of banning lawful nonviolent, non threatening symbols such as the fighting insignia of military units in overseas operations in which parents or siblings of students may serve (*Newsom v. Albemarle County Sch. Bd.*, 354

F.3d 249 (4th Cir. 2003); see also *Sypniewski v. Warren Hills Regional Bd. of Educ.*, 307 F.3d 243 (3d Cir. 2003)).

12:99. May a school district require that students wear a school uniform?

No. The commissioner of education has ruled that under New York law, a school district lacks authority to compel students to wear a uniform or particular kind of clothing or force exclusion from school (*Appeal of Dalrymple*, 5 Educ. Dep't Rep. 113 (1966)).

However a federal district court upheld a New York City Board of Education mandatory uniform policy for students in prekindergarten through grade 8, which allowed parents to secure an exception from the policy. The policy also provided that discipline for noncompliance could not include suspension from class or school, or affect an academic grade or participation in an extracurricular activity. Instead, the policy limited corrective measures to parent or student-teacher conferences and reprimands (*Lipsman v. New York City Bd. of Educ.*, 1999 U.S. Dist. LEXIS 3574 (S.D.N.Y. Mar. 23, 1999)).

Similarly, an Arizona state court ruled that a particular school's mandatory uniform policy did not violate student First Amendment rights because it allowed students who did not wish to wear a uniform to transfer to another district school without a mandatory uniform policy or to a school outside the district (*Phoenix Elementary Sch. Dist. No. 1 v. Green*, 943 P.2d 836 (Ariz. App. Div. 2, 1997)).

According to one federal appellate court, a mandatory school uniform policy implemented to reduce student behavior problems and improve the educational process did not violate student First Amendment rights (*Canady v. Bossier Parish Sch. Bd.*, 240 F.3d 437 (5th Cir. 2001)).

12:100. Can a district ban "gang-related" clothing and accessories?

Although there are no New York cases with respect to bans on gang-related apparel, federal courts in other jurisdictions have addressed the question.

A school board policy that prohibited earrings on male students as part of an effort to curb the presence and influence of gangs in the school was upheld because the district provided evidence to the court of gang presence, activity, and violence in the schools. Under those circumstances, the board's concern for the safety and well-being of its students and the curtailment of gang activities was rational and did not violate the First Amendment (*Olesen v. Board of Educ. of Sch. Dist. No. 228*, 676 F.Supp. 820 (N.D. Ill. 1987)). But a racial harassment policy that prohibited written material that creates ill will was used impermissibly to bar a student from wearing a t-shirt with comedian Jeff Foxworthy's "Top Ten Reasons You Might Be a Redneck Fan" on it. There was no particular or concrete basis for banning the t-shirt, which had been worn several times without incident, and was not related to the gangs at the school (*Sypniewski v. Warren Hills Regional Board of Educ.*, 307 F.3d 243 (3d Cir. 2002)).

Absent proof of associated gang activity or facts that might reasonably lead school authorities to forecast substantial disruption of school activities, a broad ban on "gang-related apparel," such as rosaries or clothing with professional or college team logos, violates the First Amendment (*Chalifoux v. New Caney Indep. Sch. Dist.*, 976 F.Supp. 659 (S.D. Tex. 1997); *Jeglin v. San Jacinto Unified Sch. Dist.*, 827 F.Supp. 1459 (C.D. Cal. 1993)).

In addition, a regulation stating, without further clarification, that "[g]ang related activities such as display of colors, symbols, signals, signs, etc., will not be tolerated on school grounds" was unconstitutionally vague because it failed to provide adequate notice regarding unacceptable conduct and failed to offer clear guidance of its application (*Stephenson v. Davenport Community Sch. Dist.*, 110 F.3d 1303 (8th Cir. 1997)). However, a school rule that prohibited specified activities, such as recruiting students for membership, threatening, or intimidating students to commit acts in furtherance of the purpose of the gang, survived a constitutional challenge, because unlike *Stephenson,* it was sufficiently clear what activities were banned (*Fuller v. Decatur Pub. Sch. Bd., Board of Educ. of Sch. Dist. No. 61,* 251 F.3d 662 (7th Cir. 2001)).

12:101. Can school districts ban fraternities or sororities from public schools?

Yes. Under the Education Law, school boards may adopt rules and regulations to abolish and/or prohibit any fraternity, sorority, or secret society in any secondary school under their jurisdiction (§§ 1709-a(1), 2503-a(1), 2554-a(1)).

Before taking such action, a board must find that the group has, by virtue of its activities, caused or created a disruption of or interference with the academic processes of any secondary school, or caused or created such interference with the progress of any student or students in any secondary school within the district's jurisdiction (§§ 1709-a(1(a)), 2503-a(2), 2554-a(2)).

Such groups are defined as those where the decision to accept new members is made by the group's membership rather than by the free choice of the student who wishes to enter. Certain organizations, such as the Boy

Scouts and the Girl Scouts, are exempt from this definition (§§ 1709-a(2), 2503-a(3), 2554-a(3)).

After such a regulation has been adopted and disseminated, the board may discipline any student who promises to join, becomes a member of, remains a member of, or solicits any person to join the group in question (§§ 1709-a(3), 2503-a(4), 2554-a(4); for information on fraternity initiations, see sections 120.16 and 120.17 of the Penal Law, which concern hazing).

12:102. May public school officials search a student's belongings while in attendance at school?

Yes. In *New Jersey v. TLO*, 469 U.S. 325 (1985), the United States Supreme Court held that a student may be searched by a school official if the official has "reasonable suspicion" to believe that a search of that student will result in evidence that the student violated the law or a school rule. In that case, the court upheld a search of a student's purse after she denied smoking at school in violation of school policy. The court ruled that the principal had reasonable cause to search the student's purse based on a teacher's report that the student was smoking in the bathroom. The court also upheld an extended search of the pocketbook for drugs, after the principal found rolling papers in the student's purse.

Under New York cases, the reasonableness of a search is predicated upon the reliability of a proven informant tipping off the school authorities (see *People v. Scott D.*, 34 N.Y.2d 483 (1974); *People v. Singletary*, 37 N.Y.2d 310 (1975)).

To be reasonable, a search under *TLO* must not only be justified at its inception, but the scope must also be reasonably related to the circumstances that justified the search in the first place. The reasonableness of the scope of a search may depend, for example, on the area searched in relation to the area where one could reasonably expect to find evidence of a violation of law or school rule; the time and place of the search and its proximity to when and where the alleged violation occurred; the duration of the search; and the intrusiveness of the search.

The New York State Court of Appeals held that a less intrusive search conducted by school officials, such as the touching of the outside of a book bag, requires a less strict justification than that of reasonable suspicion (*In re Gregory M.*, 82 N.Y.2d 588 (1993)).

12:103. May public school officials search a student's person while in attendance at school?

Yes. In *People v. Singletary*, 37 N.Y.2d 310 (1975), the New York State Court of Appeals upheld the search of a high school student by the dean in charge of security. The court found that the search had been based upon "concrete, articulable facts" supplied by a student informant who had provided accurate and reliable information in five prior occasions and informed the dean the student was selling drugs at school. When the dean searched the student, he found 13 glassine envelopes of heroine in his sock.

Similarly, a state appellate court upheld the "pat down" of a student, which led to the discovery of a gun. In *Matter of Haseen N.*, 251 A.D.2d 505 (2d Dep't 1998), school officials patted down students on Halloween to search for eggs because of prior egg-throwing incidents. The pat down was upheld because it was the least intrusive, most practical means of locating eggs and represented a reasonable balance between the students' privacy rights and the school's interest in maintaining order.

It must be noted, however, that, as the level of the intrusiveness of the search increases, a higher standard of suspicion is required. In a case that predated *New Jersey v. TLO*, 469 U.S. 325 (1985) (see **12:102**), the New York Court of Appeals ruled that school officials can search a student's person only when "sufficient cause" for such a search exists. The search in *People v. Scott D.*, 34 N.Y.2d 483 (1974), was unlawful because even though a teacher reported seeing a student go into the bathroom with another student twice within one hour and leaving within five to 10 seconds, the alleged unusual behavior could be explained by innocent activities. In addition, the district failed to establish the basis of the information that the student was a drug dealer or the reliability of the informants. The fact that the student had lunch with another student associated with drugs did not contribute to reasonable suspicion. Therefore, a strip search of the student that led to the discovery of cocaine envelopes was unlawful.

Since *People v. Scott D.*, the United States Court of Appeals for the Second Circuit held that a teacher who conducts a strip search of a student must have probable cause (*M. M. v. Anker*, 607 F.2d 588 (2d Cir. 1979)).

12:104. May school officials search student lockers?

Yes. The New York State Court of Appeals held that although a student may have exclusive use of a locker as far as other students are concerned, he or she "does not have such exclusivity over the locker as against the school authorities" (*People v. Overton*, 20 N.Y.2d 360, *aff'd on reh'g*, 24 N.Y.2d 522 (1969)).

School authorities should include in their student handbooks a provision that states that lockers, desks, and other such storage spaces remain the exclusive property of the school, and that students have no expectation of privacy with respect to these areas. It was significant to the court's decision in *People v. Overton,* that students were told they had exclusive possession of their lockers only in relation to other students. They were also required to give their lock combinations to their teachers, and school officials retained a master key for access to all lockers.

12:105. May public school officials search a student's hotel room and belongings while on a school-sponsored trip?

Yes. The reasonableness standard set by *New Jersey v. TLO*, 469 U.S. 325 (1985) (see **12:102**), applies to student property searches conducted by school officials when "off campus" on a school-sponsored excursion, such as a class or field trip. In *Rhodes v. Guarricino*, 54 F.Supp.2d 186 (S.D.N.Y. 1999), a federal district court in New York upheld the search of student hotel rooms by a chaperone during a school-sponsored trip to Disney World after the chaperone smelled a strong odor of marijuana outside one of the student's room. The court rejected the student's argument that *TLO*'s reasonableness standard did not apply "off campus."

12:106. Can school authorities confiscate dangerous and illegal weapons, such as knives and guns, brought to school by students?

Yes. If possible, these articles should be taken from students, and the police and parents should be notified. School authorities have the same responsibility as every other citizen to report violations of law. A school official has the right to search a student based on a reasonable suspicion that he or she has a gun (*In re Ronald B.*, 61 A.D.2d 204 (2d Dep't 1978); see also *New Jersey v. TLO*, 469 U.S. 325 (1985), *In re Gregory M.*, 82 N.Y.2d 588 (1993); see **12:150–156** regarding the Gun-Free Schools Act).

In addition, school officials should be aware that 13- and 14-year-olds who possess a loaded firearm, as defined in the Penal Law, on school grounds may be criminally prosecuted as adults (Crim. Proc. Law §§ 1.20(42) 190.71(a) and Penal Law §§ 10(18), 30(2), 70.05(2), all as amended by Laws of 1998, Ch. 435; Penal Law § 220(14)).

12:107. May child welfare agency workers remove a student from school in connection with a report to the Central Register of Child Abuse and Maltreatment?

The U.S. Court of Appeals for the Second Circuit, with jurisdiction over New York, has ruled that state officials may not remove a child from school without first obtaining a court order, if there is sufficient time to obtain such an order (*Tenenbaum v. Williams*, 193 F.3d 581 (2d Cir. 1999), *cert. denied,* 529 U.S. 1089 (2000)). In *Tenenbaum*, a government official removed a child from her school to conduct an examination for signs of sexual abuse. The child was taken to a hospital where she remained for several hours before being examined and returned to her parents. The school district had filed a report with the Central Register of Child Abuse and Maltreatment after the child had indicated to a teacher her father had hurt her in the groin area.

According to the court, the child's removal from school constituted a "seizure" under the Fourth Amendment. The court further found that in an emergency situation, where a state officer would reasonably believe that a child is subject to the danger of abuse if not removed from school before court authorization can reasonably be obtained, the state officer would be permitted to remove the child without a warrant (or its equivalent, a court order) and without parental consent.

12:108. Do police have the right to enter schools?

Yes. Police can enter schools if a crime has been committed, if they have a warrant for arrest or search, or if they have been invited by school officials.

However, counsel for the State Education Department has indicated that police authorities have no power to interview children in schools or to use school facilities in connection with police department work, and that a school board has no right to make children available for such purposes. Law enforcement officers do not have a legal right to interrogate a student in the school without the permission of the parents, nor would any officer or employee of the school have the right to authorize this, since custody of the child by the school is limited to education purposes (Opinion of Counsel, 1 Educ. Dep't Rep. 800 (1959)).

12:109. May a police officer assigned to a school as a liaison search students and their belongings?

Yes. However, it is unclear whether police officers who are assigned to schools may conduct such searches using the same reasonable suspicion standard that applies to school officials. According to one state appellate court, a school safety officer assigned exclusively to school security did not require probable cause in order to search a student (*Matter of Stephen A.*, 308 A.D.2d 359 (1st Dep't 2003); see also *Shade v. City of Farmington*, 309 F.3d 1054 (8th Cir. 2002)). However, courts in other state have required police officers to have probable cause when involved in searches on school grounds (*State v. Tywayne H.*, 93 P.2d 251 (N.M. 1997); F.P. v. State, 528 So.2d 1253 (Fl. 1988); *Picha v. Wielgos*, 410 F.Supp 1214 (N.D. Ill. 1976)).

12:110. May a school district use trained narcotics dogs to search for drugs in school buildings?

The use of scent dogs to detect the scent of drugs, alcohol or other contraband in public schools is still an open question in New York State. But federal-level cases outside New York have upheld a school district's use of trained dogs to sniff students' lockers and cars for drugs or alcohol by ruling this type of action did not constitute a search under the Fourth Amendment (*B.C. v. Pumas Unified Sch. Dist.*, 192 F.3d 1260 (9th Cir. 1999); *Horton v. Goose Creek Indep. Sch. Dist.*, 690 F.2d 470 (5th Cir. 1982), *cert. denied*, 463 U.S. 1207 (1983); *Zamora v. Pomeroy*, 639 F.2d 662 (10th Cir. 1981)).

However, courts differ on the use of scent dogs to sniff students. In *Horton* and *B.C.*, the courts ruled that the districts' use of scent dogs to sniff students was a search under the Fourth Amendment and therefore, dog sniffing of a student without a reasonable suspicion that the student possessed drugs violated the Fourth Amendment.

In contrast, the Seventh Circuit Court of Appeals ruled that sniffing of students by scent dogs is not a "search" under the Fourth Amendment and upheld the sniffing of students without individualized suspicion that a particular student possessed drugs (*Doe v. Renfrow*, 475 F.Supp. 1012, *aff'd*, 631 F.2d 91 (7th Cir. 1980), *cert. denied*, 451 U.S. 1022 (1981)).

12:111. May a school district require students to submit to mandatory drug testing without reasonable suspicion that a particular student is using illegal drugs?

Not in New York State, unless the student's parent or legal guardian freely consent to such drug testing of his or her child (§ 912-a(2); *Appeal of Studley*, 38 Educ. Dep't Rep. 258 (1998); see also **12:68**). This is true, even though the U.S. Supreme Court has ruled that such drug testing does not violate a student's constitutional rights, (*Vernonia Sch. Dist. 475 v. Acton*, 515 U.S.646 (1995) because New York law provides greater protection to students in this instance than the federal constitution.

In 1995, the United States Supreme Court upheld an Oregon school district's policy that authorized mandatory random urinalysis drug testing of student athletes, with no requirement of reasonable suspicion that the particular student tested is involved in illegal drug use. The policy required students and their parents to sign a form consenting to the testing in order to participate in the district's sports program. The court recognized the nature and immediacy of the district's concern for eradicating illegal drug use in athletic competition where the risk of physical harm to the user and other players is high. The district demonstrated that it had a severe problem with illegal drug use by student athletes and that district officials had attempted lesser intrusive means prior to implementing the drug-testing policy (*Vernonia*).

Thereafter in *Board of Educ. of Indep. Sch. Dist. No. 92 of Pottawatomie County v. Earls*, 536 U.S. 822 (2002), the Supreme Court also upheld a district policy that required all middle school and high school students participating in extracurricular activities to consent and submit to suspicionless drug testing. The court explained that a student's privacy interest is limited in a public school environment where there are concerns for maintaining discipline, health, and safety. It examined the "negligible" intrusion of the process followed to collect urine samples and confidentiality safeguards used, and the nature and immediacy of the school's concerns in addressing drug abuse problems. In the Court's view, it would make little sense to wait until a substantial portion of students begin using drugs before a school is allowed to establish a drug testing program to deter their use.

However, in *Appeal of Studley*, the commissioner of education ruled that New York school districts lack statutory authority to mandate that student athletes submit to suspicionless drug testing, absent parental consent. Moreover, according to the commissioner, since the law only permits schools to drug test students upon the consent or request of a parent, the refusal of parents to give such consent cannot result in a student being prohibited from participating in sports.

12:112. Are school administrators required to give *Miranda* warnings before questioning a student?

No. There is no requirement for any sort of *Miranda*-type warning during informal, noncustodial discussions with administrators (*Pollnow v. Glennon*, 594 F.Supp. 220, *aff'd*, 757 F.2d 496 (2d Cir. 1985); see also *People v. Butler*, 188 Misc.2d 48 (Kings County, 2001)). In addition, neither the Education Law nor the federal constitution requires school officials to contact the parents of a student before questioning that student concerning an alleged infraction of a school rule (*Appeal of M.F. and P.F.*, 43 Educ. Dep't Rep. ___, dec. no. 14,960 (2003); *Appeal of Lago*, 38 Educ. Dep't Rep. 723 (1999); *Appeal of Pronti*, 31 Educ. Dep't Rep. 259 (1992)). A statement obtained from a student during the course of an investigation may be used as evidence for disciplinary purposes (*Appeal of M.F. and P.F.*).

12:113. May a school district require students to perform community service as a requirement for graduation?

Yes. In *Immediato v. Rye Neck Sch. Dist.*, 73 F.3d 454 (2d Cir. 1996), *cert. denied*, 117 S.Ct. 60 (1996), a board of education established a graduation requirement that high school students complete 40 hours of community service for an organization of their choice and participate in a classroom discussion of their projects. The United States Court of Appeals for the Second Circuit, in reviewing a student's challenge of the graduation requirement, held that the service mandated by the district did not violate the Thirteenth Amendment to the federal constitution (which bans slavery and involuntary servitude). The court also ruled that the graduation requirement did not violate any constitutional liberty, parental, or privacy rights protected by the Fourteenth Amendment to the federal constitution.

Student Discipline

12:114. Must a school district adopt a code of conduct?

Yes. The Education Law and commissioner's regulations require school districts, boards of cooperative educational services (BOCES), and county vocational extension boards to adopt and implement a code of conduct for the maintenance of order on school property and at school functions. This code must be developed, in cooperation with student, teacher, administrator, and parent organizations; and school safety and other school personnel (§ 2801(3); 8 NYCRR § 100.2(l)(i)). It must govern the conduct of students, teachers and other school personnel, as well as visitors. In New York City community district education councils may adopt and implement additional policies consistent with the citywide code of conduct, provided that the chancellor approves such additional provisions (§ 2801(3)).

The Education Law requires that the code of conduct include, at a minimum, provisions regarding conduct, dress, and language deemed appropriate and acceptable, as well as what will be considered inappropriate and unacceptable on school property and at school functions. It must stipulate acceptable civil and respectful treatment of teachers, school administrators, other school personnel, students, and visitors on school property and at school functions.

The code must also include the following:

- An appropriate range of disciplinary measures that may be imposed for violations of the code.
- The roles of teachers, administrators, other school personnel, the school board, and parents.
- Standards and procedures to assure the security and safety of students and school personnel, including the removal of students and other persons who violate the code from the classroom and school property.
- The period for which a disruptive student may be removed from a classroom for each incident.
- Disciplinary measures for incidents involving the possession or use of illegal substances or weapons, the use of physical force, vandalism, violation of another student's civil rights and threats of violence.
- Provisions for the detention, suspension, and removal of students from the classroom, including the establishment of policies and procedures to ensure their continued educational programming and activities.

- Procedures for reporting and determining violations of the code and for imposing and carrying out disciplinary measures.
- Procedures for compliance of the code and its enforcement with state and federal laws relating to students with disabilities.
- Procedures for notifying local law enforcement agencies of code violations that constitute a crime, and for notifying parents of code violations.
- The circumstances and procedures for filing a complaint in criminal court, and a juvenile delinquency or person in need of supervision petition in family court.
- The circumstances and procedures for making referrals to appropriate human service agencies.
- A bill of rights and responsibilities of students to be publicized and explained to all students annually.
- Guidelines and programs for in-service education programs for all district staff to ensure effective implementation of the code.
- The minimum suspension period for violent students and students who repeatedly are substantially disruptive of the educational process or substantially interfere with the teacher's authority over the classroom. This minimum suspension period may be reduced on a case-by-case basis to be consistent with any other state and federal law (§ 2801(2), 8 NYCRR 100.2(l)(2)(ii)).

A *violent pupil* is an elementary or secondary school student under age 21 who commits an act of violence upon a teacher, administrator, or other school employee; or while on school district property does so upon another student or any other person lawfully there; or while on school property possesses a gun, knife, explosive or incendiary bomb, or other dangerous instrument capable of causing physical injury or death, or displays or threatens to use any such instrument; or knowingly and intentionally damages or destroys district property or the personal property of a teacher, administrator, other school district employee or any person lawfully on school property (§ 3214(2-a(a))).

A student who is repeatedly disruptive of the educational process or substantially interferes with the teacher's authority over the classroom is one who engages in conduct that results in the removal of the student from the classroom by a teacher on four or more occasions during a semester, or three or more occasions during a trimester, as applicable (8 NYCRR § 100.2(l)(2)(ii)(m)).

12:115. Is there a process districts must follow to adopt or revise a code of conduct?

School boards and BOCES may adopt the required code of conduct only after at least one public hearing that provides for the participation of school personnel, parents, students, and other interested parties. The code must be reviewed and updated annually if necessary and filed with the commissioner of education no later than 30 days after adoption. Districts may establish a committee to facilitate review of the code consisting of the same types of individuals involved in the development of the code (§ 2801(2), ((3), (5); 8 NYCRR § 100.2(l)(2)(iii)(a)).

In addition, districts must ensure community awareness of their code by providing copies of their respective code of conduct to all students at a general assembly at the beginning of each school year, mailing a plain language summary of the code to all parents and guardians before the beginning of each school year, providing all current and new teachers with updated copies of the code and making copies available for review by any who request it (§ 2801(4); 8 NYCRR 100.2(l)(2), (i)(iii)(b)).

12:116. What types of discipline may be imposed upon students for violations of student disciplinary codes?

The following are among the types of discipline that may be imposed:
- Verbal warning.
- Written warning.
- Written notification to parents or guardians.
- Probation.
- Reprimand.
- Detention.
- Suspension from transportation.
- Suspension from participation in athletic events.
- Suspension from social or extracurricular activities.
- Suspension from other privileges.
- Exclusion from a particular class.
- In-school suspension.
- Suspension not in excess of five days.
- Suspension in excess of five days.

The commissioner of education has ruled that a student behavior code that imposed an automatic suspension on a student for certain behavior without regard to the circumstances giving rise to the offense was invalid (*Appeal of Nuttall*, 30 Educ. Dep't Rep. 351 (1991); 8 NYCRR § 100.2(l)(1)(f)). However, a school district's code of conduct must provide minimum suspension periods for students who repeatedly and substantially disrupt the educational process or who substantially interfere with a teacher's authority over the classroom, and for violent pupils as defined by law and commissioner's regulations. These minimum periods of suspension may be reduced on a case-by-case basis (§§ 2801(2)(l), (m), 3214(2-a(a)); 8 NYCRR § 100.2(l)(2)(ii)(m), (n)).

A district may not impose a harsher penalty on a student merely because the student does not cooperate with the district's investigation of an incident and does not admit guilt (*Appeal of Kier*, 39 Educ. Dep't Rep. 210 (1999)).

In addition, although a properly implemented school board policy that provides for a loss of credit for nonattendance is appropriate (see **12:25**), a school district may not suspend a student for truancy. According to the commissioner, suspending a student for truancy is inconsistent with the educational goal of encouraging children to regularly attend and participate fully in school (*Appeal of Ackert*, 30 Educ. Dep't Rep. 31 (1990)). However, an in-school suspension for truancy is acceptable if the alternative education provided is adequate (*Appeal of Miller*, 35 Educ. Dep't Rep. 451 (1996), see **12:116, 12:143**).

12:117. Is corporal punishment forbidden in schools?

Yes. Corporal punishment is any act of physical force upon a student for the purpose of punishing that student (8 NYCRR §§ 19.5(b), 100.2(l)(3)(i)). The Rules of the Board of Regents specify that no teacher, administrator, officer, employee, or agent of a school district may use corporal punishment against a student (8 NYCRR § 19.5(a)).

However, in situations where alternative procedures and methods not involving the use of force cannot reasonably be employed, the use of reasonable physical force is permissible to:

- Protect oneself, another student, teacher, or any person(s) from physical injury.
- Protect the property of the school or others.
- Restrain or remove a student whose behavior interferes with the orderly exercise and performance of school district functions, powers, and duties, if that student has refused to refrain from further disruptive acts (8 NYCRR §§ 19.5(c), 100.2(l)(3)(i)).

12:118. Must a school district submit a report if a complaint about corporal punishment has been filed?

Yes. The commissioner's regulations require every school board to submit a written report to the commissioner on complaints about corporal punishment by January 15 and July 15 each year. The report must include the substance of each complaint about the use of corporal punishment received by local school authorities during the reporting period, the results of each investigation, and the action, if any, taken by the school authorities in each case (8 NYCRR § 100.2(l)(3)(ii)).

12:119. Under what conditions may a student be suspended from school or removed from a classroom?

A student may be suspended from required attendance for insubordination or disorderly student conduct that otherwise endangers the safety, morals, health or welfare of others (§ 3214(3)(a)). (See **13:49–59** concerning the suspension of students with disabilities.)

In addition, the Education Law authorizes a teacher to remove a disruptive pupil from the classroom (§ 3214(3-a)). A *disruptive pupil* is an elementary or secondary school student under age 21 who substantially disrupts the educational process or interferes with the teacher's authority in the classroom (§ 3214(2-a)(b)).

School officials lack authority to suspend a student who permanently withdraws from school before imposition of the suspension because there is no longer any relationship between the former student and the school district (*Appeal of Rosenkranz*, 37 Educ. Dep't Rep. 330 (1998)).

12:120. Are students entitled to due process when suspended from school?

Yes. In *Goss v. Lopez*, 419 U.S. 565 (1975), the United States Supreme Court held that once a state provides public schools and requires its children to attend, this right may not be taken away without at least some minimal due process.

Due process requires that a student be given oral or written notice of the charges against him or her, and, if the charges are denied, an explanation of the evidence the authorities have and an opportunity to present the student's side of the story. In the majority of cases, the school administrator may be able to discuss the alleged misconduct with the student informally minutes after it has occurred. In being given an opportunity to explain his or her version of the facts at this discussion, the student must first be told what he or she is accused of and the basis of the accusation.

12:121. May students be suspended or removed from a particular class?

Yes. But district administrators who suspend students from a particular class must provide the same due process rights as would be provided if the student was being suspended from school for the same duration (*Appeal of Trombly*, 26 Educ. Dep't Rep. 214 (1986); but see *Mazevski v. Horseheads CSD*, 950 F.Supp. 69 (W.D.N.Y. 1997)).

In addition, the Education Law authorizes teachers to remove disruptive students from the classroom (§ 3214 (3-a); see **12:119, 12:123**).

12:122. Who may suspend a student?

The school board, the superintendent of schools, the board of cooperative educational services (BOCES) district superintendent of schools, or a building principal may suspend a student (§ 3214(3)(a) see also *Appeal of V.R. and C.R.*, 43 Educ. Dep't Rep ___, dec. no. 14,934 (2003)). However, in no case may a principal suspend a student for a period exceeding five school days (§ 3214(3)(b)(1)).

12:123. May a teacher suspend a student?

No, but a teacher may remove a disruptive student from class (§ 3214(3-a).

A teacher removing a disruptive student (see **12:119**) from the classroom must inform the student and the principal of the reasons for the removal. Prior to removal, the teacher must give the student an explanation of the basis for the removal and an opportunity to informally present the student's version of relevant events within 24 hours of the removal, unless the teacher finds that the student's presence in the classroom poses a continuing danger to persons or property or an ongoing threat of disruption to the academic process (§ 3214(3-A)(a); see also *Appeal of R.F.*, 43 Educ. Dep't Rep. ___, dec. no. 14,972 (2003)).

The principal must inform the student's parents of the removal and the reasons therefore within 24 hours of the removal and, on request, give the student and the student's parents an opportunity to meet with the principal and discuss the reason for the removal. If the student denies the charges, the principal must provide an explanation of the basis for the removal and an opportunity for the student and/or the student's parents to present the student's version at an informal hearing to be held within 48 hours of the student's removal (§ 3214(3-a)(b)).

The principal may set aside the teacher's disciplinary action only upon finding that the charges against the student are unsupported by substantial evidence; or that the removal constitutes a violation of law; or that the conduct warrants suspension from school and a suspension will be imposed. The principal must make this determination by the close of business on the day after the 48-hour period for an informal hearing (§ 3214(3-a)(c)).

12:124. What procedures must be followed to suspend a student for five days or less?

The Education Law requires that the suspending authority (see **12:112**) must notify the student of the charged misconduct, and if the student denies the charges, provide the student with an explanation of the suspension. On request, the student and the student's parents must be given an opportunity for an informal conference with the building principal.

At the informal conference, the student and/or the student's parent has a right to present the student's version of the incident and to question the complaining witnesses against the student (§ 3214(3)(b); *Appeal of a Student with a Disability,* 40 Educ. Dep't Rep. 47 (2000); *Appeal of Alan G.,* 38 Educ. Dep't Rep. 46 (1998)). It is insufficient to only provide an opportunity for the parent to speak with the principal without the complaining witness present or to speak with the complaining witness without the principal present (*Appeal of Alan G.*).

The required notice and opportunity for an informal conference must take place prior to suspension. Only if the student's presence in school is a continuing danger to persons or property or an ongoing threat of disruption to the academic process, can the requisite notice and opportunity for an informal conference take place as soon after the suspension as is reasonably practicable (§ 3214(3)(b); 8 NYCRR § 100.2(l),(4); *Appeal of R.F.,* 43 Educ. Dep't Rep. ___, dec. no. 14,972 (2003); *Appeal of V.R. and C.R.,* 43 Educ. Dep't Rep. ___, dec. no. 14,934 (2003)).

12:125. What procedures must be followed when giving parents notice of their right to an informal conference prior to a student suspension of five days or less?

When suspension of a student for five days or less is proposed, parents must be provided with written notice delivered by personal messenger, express mail, or an "equivalent means reasonably calculated to assure receipt" within 24 hours of the decision to propose suspension (§ 3214(3)(b); 8 NYCRR § 100.2(l), (4)). Although notification of the proposed suspension must be provided where possible by telephone if the district has the parent's phone number, oral notification is not sufficient notice even when followed by same day regular mail notification (*Appeal of R.F.,* 43 Educ. Dep't Rep. ___, dec. no. 14,972 (2003)). Neither is notice sent registered mail return receipt requested (*Appeal of V.R. and C.R.,* 43 Educ. Dep't Rep. ___, dec. no. 14,934 (2003).

The notice must include a description of the incident(s) for which suspension is proposed and must inform the parent or guardian of his or her right to request an immediate informal conference with the principal. The notification must be in the parent's dominant language or mode of communication (§ 3214(3)(b); 8 NYCRR § 100.2(l),(4); *Appeal of R.F.*; *Appeal of V.R. and C.R.*).

12:126. What procedures must be followed in order to suspend a student in excess of five days?

No student may be suspended in excess of five school days unless the student and his or her parent or guardian has had an opportunity for a hearing on reasonable notice (§ 3214(3)(c)). A school district may not unilaterally postpone a student disciplinary hearing and keep a student out of school beyond the initial five-day suspension pending the hearing (*Appeal of N.S.*, 42 Educ. Dep't Rep. 190 (2002)).

Although the law does not define "reasonable notice," the commissioner of education has held that a single day's notice of a suspension hearing is unreasonable (*Appeal of Eisenhauer*, 33 Educ. Dep't Rep. 604 (1994)). In another case, three days' verbal notice prior to the hearing was found to be sufficient (*Appeal of DeRosa*, 36 Educ. Dep't Rep. 336 (1997); see also *Appeal of J.D.*, 39 Educ. Dep't Rep. 593 (2000)).

In addition, students are entitled to fair notice of the charges against them so that they can prepare and present an adequate defense. Notice that repeats the general statutory language of section 3214 of the Education Law — which contains the bases upon which a student may be suspended — or merely sets forth a statement that a student violated school rules or disrupted school activities, is not "reasonable" because it fails to provide the student with enough information to prepare an effective defense. However, the charges in a student disciplinary hearing need only be sufficiently specific to advise the student and his or her counsel of the activities or incidents that have given rise to the proceeding and that will form the basis for the hearing (*Board of Educ. v. Commissioner of Educ.*, 91 N.Y.2d 133 (1997), see also *Appeal of K.B.*, 41 Educ. Dep't Rep. 431 (2002)).

The student may bring his or her parents or guardians to the hearing and has the right to be represented by an attorney or other counsel, to testify on his or her own behalf, to present witnesses and other evidence on his or her own behalf, and to cross-examine witnesses against him or her (§ 3214(3)(c); *Appeal of K.D.*, 37 Educ. Dep't Rep. 702 (1998); *Appeal of Johnson*, 34 Educ. Dep't Rep. 62 (1994)). Without deciding whether telephone testimony is permissible in a section 3214 hearing, the commissioner of education has stated that such a practice raises "serious questions" given a student's statutory right to a fair hearing and to question witnesses presented by the district (*Appeal of K.D.*).

12:127. What type of evidence must be introduced at a student disciplinary hearing to support a decision to suspend a student in excess of five days?

The decision to suspend a student from school following a student disciplinary hearing must be based on competent and substantial evidence that the student participated in the objectionable conduct (*In the Matter of the Bd. of Educ. of the City Sch. Dist. of the City of New York*, 293 A.D.2d 37 (3d Dep't 2002); *Appeal of G.M.*, 41 Educ. Dep't Rep. 479 (2002); *Appeal of Timothy R. and Janice A. Blake*, 37 Educ. Dep't Rep. 250 (1997)). This standard requires that a district prove a student's guilt by presenting persuasive evidence of such "quality and quantity" as to allow a "fair and detached fact finder" to conclude the student engaged in the alleged misconduct "reasonably, probatively and logically" (*In the Matter of the Bd. of Educ. of the City Sch. Dist. of the City of New York*).

At the hearing, persons having personal knowledge of the facts should be called to testify. There must be some direct evidence of guilt of the charges. Hearsay evidence alone is not sufficient, notwithstanding the administrative nature of the proceeding (see *Appeal of Parker*, 34 Educ. Dep't Rep. 379 (1995); *Appeal of Swingle*, 32 Educ. Dep't Rep. 245 (1992); *Appeal of Normand*, 26 Educ. Dep't Rep. 389 (1987); *Matter of Dennis*, 19 Educ. Dep't Rep. 235 (1979); but see *Appeal of D.J.*, 42 Educ. Dep't Rep. 382 (2003); *Appeal of D.C.*, 41 Educ. Dep't Rep. 277 (2002); *Appeal of a Student Suspected of Having a Disability*, 39 Educ. Dep't Rep. 476 (1999); *Appeal of Hamet*, 36 Educ. Dep't Rep. 174 (1996)). As in a court of law, the burden of proof rests on the person making the charge against the student, and the student is entitled to a presumption of innocence of wrongdoing unless otherwise proven (*Matter of Montero*, 10 Educ. Dep't Rep. 49 (1970)).

It should be noted that a witness' written statement submitted to a disciplinary hearing is not eligible for consideration by the hearing officer unless that student is made available for cross-examination (*Appeal of D.C.; Appeal of R.C.*).

12:128. May a student's anecdotal record be submitted into evidence at a student disciplinary hearing involving a decision to suspend a student in excess of five days?

Yes. However, a student's anecdotal record may be considered only when fixing a penalty, and only after a finding of guilt already has been made. A student and his parents must be given notice whenever the student's anecdotal record will be considered in setting the penalty (*Appeal of a Student Suspected of Having a Disability (Somers, CSD)*, 41 Educ.

Dep't Rep. 253 (2002)). In addition, a penalty may not be based on conclusions unrelated to the actual charges preferred against a student (*Appeal of A.Q.*, 41 Educ. Dep't Rep. 331(2002); *Appeal of G.M; Appeal of R.C.*, 41 Educ. Dep't Rep. 446 (2002)).

12:129. Who conducts a student disciplinary hearing?

Generally, it is the superintendent of schools who conducts a student disciplinary hearing. However, both the superintendent and the school board are authorized to appoint a hearing officer to conduct student disciplinary hearings. The hearing officer's report is advisory only, and the superintendent or board may accept or reject all or any part of it (§ 3214(3)(c)).

12:130. May a superintendent or hearing officer admit into evidence at a student discipline hearing evidence that was suppressed by a court in another action or proceeding?

Yes. In one case, the New York State Court of Appeals ruled a judge's determination that certain evidence could not be used against a student in a family court proceeding because it was obtained as a result of an illegal search was not binding in a student disciplinary proceeding (*Matter of Juan C. v. Cortines*, 89 N.Y.2d 659 (1997)). Subsequent to this decision, amendments to the Education Law now provide that if a student is being suspended, in whole or in part, for the possession on school grounds or property of any firearm, rifle, shotgun, dagger, dangerous knife, dirk, razor, stiletto, or any weapon, instrument, or appliance set forth in section 265.01 of the Penal Law, the superintendent or hearing officer may consider the admissibility of such evidence even if a court in a criminal or juvenile delinquency proceeding previously has determined that the evidence was obtained as a result of an unlawful search or seizure (§ 3214(3)(c)(1)).

12:131. May a student facing a suspension in excess of five days waive the right to a disciplinary hearing?

Yes. A school district may utilize a disciplinary system whereby students who face a suspension in excess of five days, may, together with their parents, elect either to accept the districts' proposed disposition without a section 3214 hearing, or to request such a hearing. Any waiver must be made knowingly and voluntarily and intelligently (*Appeal of McMahon*, 38 Educ. Dep't Rep. 22 (1998); see also *Appeal of a Student Suspected of Having a Disability*, 41 Educ. Dep't Rep. 390 (2002)).

The law only requires school districts to afford students an opportunity for a hearing, which opportunity may be waived by a student and his or her parent(s) as long as certain safeguards are provided. For a waiver to be voluntary, knowing, and intelligent, the student and his or her parents must be fully informed, in writing, of the right to a hearing, as well as the consequences of waiving that right (*Appeal of a Student Suspected of Having a Disability*, 41 Educ. Dep't Rep. 390 (2002)).

In addition, districts may not interpret a parent's failure to request a hearing as a waiver of the right to a hearing. Absent a binding and written waiver, districts must schedule a hearing and notify both parents and student of the hearing. The only penalties available under such a waiver system are those penalties that would be available if a hearing were actually held. The range of possible penalties must be identified in any waiver letter provided to parents and students (*Appeal of McMahon;* see also *Appeal of L.M.*, 43 Educ. Dep't Rep.___, dec. no. 15,005 (2003)).

12:132. What happens if a student is suspended for more than five days without a hearing?

If a superintendent is forced to postpone a hearing and the five-day suspension already has expired, the student must be allowed to return to school in the interim, unless the student's parents have consented to the delay (*Appeal of N.S.*, 42 Educ. Dep't Rep. 190 (2002)). A student who is suspended more than five days without a hearing may request an order of the commissioner of education directing reinstatement, pending a hearing and a determination of the charges (*Appeal of Knispel*, 35 Educ. Dep't Rep. 145 (1995)).

In addition, the United States Supreme Court determined that public school students who are suspended without a hearing can collect damages from school officials for the violation of their constitutional rights (*Carey v. Piphus*, 435 U.S. 247 (1978)). Even if school officials can demonstrate that their suspensions were justified, students deprived of their due process rights are entitled to recover nominal damages not to exceed one dollar without proof of actual injury. The court also held that school districts may be liable for other damages if students suspended without a hearing can prove actual injury derived from the denial of due process.

12:133. Are there any limitations on the duration of a student's suspension?

No. However, the commissioner of education has ruled that permanent suspensions (expulsions) should be reserved for extraordinary circumstances, such as where the student's behavior poses a danger to the safety and well-being of other students (*Appeal of Dale C.*, 40 Educ. Dep't Rep. 70 (2000); *Appeal of Osoris*, 35 Educ. Dep't Rep. 250 (1996); *Appeal of Sole*, 34 Educ. Dep't Rep. 270 (1994); *Matter of McDonald*, 8 Educ.

Dep't Rep. 32 (1968)). For example, in one case, the commissioner stated the general rule that a single fight, without more, is an insufficient basis to permanently suspend a student from school (*Appeal of Khan*, 35 Educ. Dep't Rep. 322 (1996)). The commissioner has also found that permanent suspension was not warranted in a case where a student was accused of smoking marijuana on school grounds and had over 80 previous disciplinary incidents because none of the prior suspensions, including one where the student brought a razor blade to school, exceeded five days. If the prior incidents did not warrant more severe penalties, they could not create a basis for a permanent suspension (*Appeal of Y.M.*, 43 Educ. Dep't Rep. ___, dec. no. 14,968 (2003)).

Although a student may be permanently suspended under certain circumstances, there is no authority under the Education Law to permanently banish a student from school grounds (*Appeal of MacNamara*, 37 Educ. Dep't Rep. 326 (1998)).

12:134. May a student's period of suspension be continued into the next school year(s)?

Yes. A school district may carry over a suspension to the following school year when misconduct occurs at the end of the school year (Appeal of R.D., 42 Educ. Dep't Rep. 237 (2003)).

12:135. What are a school district's responsibilities after a student has been suspended?

In the case of a student of compulsory attendance age who has been suspended after a hearing for insubordination or disorderly conduct, immediate steps must be taken for his or her supervision or detention as provided by the Family Court Act, or for his or her attendance for instruction elsewhere (§ 3214(3)(e)).

Under the Education Law, school boards must furnish alternative education to all students of compulsory school age (see **12:126**) (*Turner v. Kowalski*, 49 A.D.2d 943 (1975); *Appeal of McMahon*, 38 Educ. Dep't Rep. 22 (1998); *Appeal of Bridges*, 34 Educ. Dep't Rep. 232 (1994); *Appeal of Klug*, 20 Educ. Dep't Rep. 134 (1980)). Alternative instruction need not match in every respect the instructional program previously offered to the student. However, it must be sufficient so that the student can complete the required coursework in all of the student's academic subjects (*Matter of Lee D.*, 38 Educ. Dep't Rep. 262 (1998); *Appeal of Camille S.*, 39 Educ. Dep't Rep. 574 (2000); *Matter of Malpica*, 20 Educ. Dep't Rep. 365 (1981); *Matter of Gesner*, 20 Educ. Dep't Rep. 326 (1980)). School districts must also ensure the continued educational programming of students removed from the classroom by their teacher for disruptive behavior (§ 2801 (2)(e); see **12:119, 12:121, 12:123**).

A district is not required to provide instruction for a suspended student over the compulsory school age (§ 3205(3); *Matter of Reid v. Nyquist*, 65 Misc.2d 718 (1971); *Matter of Chipman*, 10 Educ. Dep't Rep. 224 (1971)).

Effective until June 30, 2005, if a student is expelled or seeks to enroll in another school district rather than serve out a suspension, the district must facilitate the transfer of disciplinary records relating to the suspension or expulsion of the student to any public or nonpublic school in which the student enrolls, seeks, intends, or is instructed to enroll on a full-time or part-time basis (§ 3214(7)).

12:136. How soon after a student is suspended must a district provide alternative instruction?

A school district is required to take immediate steps to provide the required alternative instruction (§ 3214(3)(e)). The term "immediate" does not mean instantaneously, but it does mean that the district should act promptly, with due regard for the nature and circumstances of the particular case (*Turner v. Kowalski*, 49 A.D.2d 943 (2d Dep't 1975); *Appeal of A.G.*, 41 Educ. Dep't Rep. 262 (2002); *Appeal of a Student with a Disability*, 40 Educ. Dep't Rep. 47 (2000); *Appeal of McMahon*, 38 Educ. Dep't Rep. 22 (1998); *Appeal of Benkelman*, 34 Educ. Dep't Rep. 250 (1994)).

For example, a school district policy which stated that the district would not provide alternative instruction for students suspended for five days or less was ruled invalid (*Turner v. Kowalski*). In *Appeal of Bridges*, 34 Educ. Dep't Rep. 232 (1994), the commissioner of education also admonished a district for having a policy which stated that the district would not provide alternative instruction if the period of suspension was for less than three days.

12:137. May a school board revoke a student's suspension?

Yes. Where a student has been suspended for cause, the suspension may be revoked by the school board whenever it appears to be in the best interests of the school and the student to do so (§ 3214(3)(e)).

12:138. May a student avoid suspension by signing a probation agreement?

Yes. The commissioner of education has ruled that a school district has the authority to offer a student facing long-term suspension the option of signing a "contract of conduct" under which the district would agree to stay the suspension in return for the student's promise to strictly abide by all school disciplinary rules. If the student violates the contract of conduct, the district would reinstate the original suspension after a conference with the superintendent (*Appeal of Spensieri*, 40 Educ. Dep't Rep. 51 (2000)).

Prior to executing a contract of conduct, a district must still conduct a student disciplinary hearing, which after a finding of guilt, authorizes a district to suspend a student long-term in the first place. Before revoking a contractual probation a district must provide a minimal amount of due process including written notice, the right to request a conference, and an opportunity to contest a determination that the student violated the conditions of probation (*Spensieri*).

The contract in *Spensieri* provided that the district would readmit the student to class upon the condition that the student (1) diligently complete his courses, (2) abide by all school rules and regulations including the rules of conduct in the student handbook, and (3) not engage in the particular types of conduct that caused the suspension. If the student violated any of these conditions, the district would mail written notice of the violation to the student and his guardians, and the superintendent could reimpose the original period of suspension. The contract also gave the student an opportunity to request a conference with the superintendent to contest any alleged violation, after which the superintendent would issue a written determination on whether the suspension should continue to be stayed or reimposed.

To be valid, a conduct contract must serve to stay an original suspension and allow a student to return immediately. It may not extend an initial suspension period effectively resulting in a suspension of indefinite duration (*Appeal of R.M. and L.M.*, 43 Educ. Dep't Rep. ___, dec. no. 14,951 (2003). Neither may such a contract extend an original suspension for new misbehavior without the benefit of superintendent's hearing or require parents to waive their child's right to due process as a condition of attending public school (*Appeal of a Student with a Disability*, 42 Educ. Dep't Rep. 192 (2002)). In addition, a contract of conduct may not include provisions for anger management counseling (*Appeal of M.F. and P.F.*, 43 Educ. Dep't Rep. ___, dec. no. 14,960 (2003)).

12:139. May a student appeal his or her suspension?

Yes. The Education Law allows students to appeal long-term suspensions — in excess of five days — to the local board of education and then to the commissioner of education (§ 3214(3)(c)); *Appeal of Amara S.*, 39 Educ. Dep't Rep. 90 (1999)). The time for filing an appeal with the commissioner begins to run when the final decision of the school board is made, rather than when the parents' attorney receives a copy of the decision (*Appeal of R.A. and D.A.*, 43 Educ. Dep't Rep. ___, dec. no. 14,995 (2003)).

However, students who are suspended from school for five days or less may appeal their suspension directly to the commissioner, unless a school district has adopted a policy that would require students to appeal short-term suspensions to the board of education before appealing to the commissioner (*Appeal of Amara S.*).

12:140. May a district suspend a student from school transportation?

Yes. Moreover, a suspension from transportation services does not require a full, formal hearing as is required under section 3214 of the Education Law, because such a suspension does not, per se, affect a student's right to attend school. All that is required is an opportunity to discuss the facts underlying the threatened discipline (*Appeal of Hale*, 30 Educ. Dep't Rep. 26 (1990)).

However, the commissioner of education has held that where suspending a student from school transportation amounts to a suspension from attending school because of the distance between home and school, and there is no alternative public or private means of transportation, the school district must make "appropriate arrangements" to provide for the student's education (*Matter of Stewart*, 21 Educ. Dep't Rep. 654 (1982)).

Similarly, if a district provides transportation to a school-sponsored event such as a field trip, extracurricular activity, or other event, it must provide students with transportation back to the point of departure or the appropriate school in the district. Parents may furnish alternative transportation for their child if, in accordance with district policy, they provide written notice of the alternative transportation arrangements. If intervening circumstances occur while at the school-sponsored event that require a student to remain behind (e.g., a student is caught shoplifting on a field trip) then a school district representative must remain with the student until his or her parent or legal guardian has been notified of the event and the student is delivered to them (§§ 1604(41), 1709(41), 1804(11),1903(2), 1950(19), 2503(20), 2554(27), 2590-e(10)).

12:141. May a district suspend or exclude a student from extracurricular activities for disciplinary reasons?

Yes. Under the Education Law, a school board has the authority to establish reasonable academic standards as prerequisites for eligibility for extracurricular activities (§ 1709(3); *Matter of Clark*, 21 Educ. Dep't Rep. 542 (1982)). School boards also have the authority to establish reasonable standards of conduct for participation in extracurricular activities (*Appeal of Wright*, 38 Educ. Dep't Rep. 756 (1999); *Appeal of Douglas and Judy H.*, 36 Educ. Dep't Rep. 224 (1996)).

In addition, a school district does not discriminate against a student athlete, if the discipline imposed on the athlete is more severe than the penalty imposed on nonathletes involved in the same disciplinary incident. For example, in *Appeal of Wright*, a basketball player was suspended from the team for the remainder of the season in addition to the one-day suspension from school imposed on him and two other nonathletes for smoking marijuana. The commissioner of education upheld the penalty even though athletes had more to lose because school policy expressly provided for team suspension of athletes involved in smoking, drinking, or illegal drugs.

A full due process hearing does not apply to the exclusion or suspension of a student from extracurricular activities. However, the student and his or her parents must be given an opportunity to discuss the factual situation informally with the district official in charge (*Appeal of C.V.,* 42 Educ. Dep't Rep. 3 (2002); *Appeal of N.C.,* 42 Educ. Dep't Rep. 119 (2002), *Matter of Clark*).

In lieu of a suspension from extracurricular activities, the commissioner of education has upheld a board policy that required attendance at 10 "insight" classes for students who consumed alcohol during an extracurricular activity (*Appeal of Douglas and Judy H.*).

12:142. May a school district discipline a student for off-campus misconduct?

Yes. In one case, the commissioner of education upheld the long-term suspension and exclusion from graduation exercises of a high school senior who fired a BB gun at another student's car and three other students off-campus. He also brought a BB gun to a dinner held for school football players and their families (*Appeal of Orman,* 39 Educ. Dep't Rep. 811 (2000)). In another case, the commissioner also upheld the long-term suspension of a student who e-mailed an offensive, threatening message from his home computer to other student's home computers (*Appeal of Ravick,* 40 Educ. Dep't Rep. 262 (2000)), and students who agreed to meet to fight a few blocks from school (*Appeal of K.S.,* 43 Educ. Dep't Rep. ___, dec. no. 15,063 (2004)).

The commissioner also upheld the suspension of students who purchased handguns off-campus (*Appeal of R.C.,* 41 Educ. Dep't Rep. 446 (2002)) and of students who agreed to fight a few blocks from school (*Appeal of K.S.,* 43 Educ. Dep't Rep. ___, dec. no. 15,063 (2004)).

12:143. What is in-school suspension, and what procedures are required for its implementation?

In-school suspension is the temporary removal of a student from the classroom and his or her placement in another area in the school building designated for such a suspension where that student will receive substantially equivalent, alternative education. A study hall does not satisfy the obligation to provide alternative instruction (*Appeal of Forster*, 31 Educ. Dep't Rep. 443 (1992); *Appeal of Ackert*, 30 Educ. Dep't Rep. 31 (1990)).

This kind of suspension does not require the more formal procedures required for out-of-school suspensions. However, with an in-school suspension, the student and his or her parents must be provided with a reasonable opportunity for an informal conference with the individual who imposed the suspension in order to discuss the conduct and the penalty involved (*Appeal of M.C.*, 43 Educ. Dep't Rep.___, dec. no. 14,993 (2003); *Appeal of Denis*, 40 Educ. Dep't Rep. 306 (2000); *Appeal of Lynn I.*, 39 Educ. Dep't Rep. 76 (1999); *Appeal of Kainz*, 38 Educ. Dep't Rep. 339 (1998); *Appeal of Gaslow*, 34 Educ. Dep't Rep. 293 (1994); *Matter of Danison*, 31 Educ. Dep't Rep. 169 (1991); *Matter of Watts*, 23 Educ. Dep't Rep. 459 (1984)).

Unlike suspensions from school, in-school suspensions may be imposed by someone other than the building principal (*Appeal of M.C.*, 43 Educ. Dep't Rep. ___, dec. no. 14,993 (2003) see **12:143**).

12:144. May a district use detention as a penalty?

Yes. A district may use detention as a penalty for certain student conduct when suspension would be inappropriate. Teachers and administrators may keep a student after school, provided there is no parental objection and the student has appropriate transportation home (State Education Department Memorandum on Detention to District Superintendents, April 28, 1995). They may also have the authority to prohibit students from participating in such activities as recess, interscholastic athletics, and field trips (*Matter of Kubinski*, 26 Educ. Dep't Rep. 348 (1987)).

12:145. May a district use community service as a penalty in a student disciplinary proceeding?

No. A school district has no authority to impose a community service requirement as a penalty under section 3214 of the Education Law (*Appeal of X. H.*, 43 Educ. Dep't Rep. ___, dec. no. 15,005 (2003); *Appeal of R.M and L.M*, 43 Educ. Dep't Rep.___, dec. no. 14,951 (2003); *Appeal of Cynthia and Robert W.*, 37 Educ. Dep't Rep. 437 (1998); see **12:116**).

12:146. May a school district impose counseling as a penalty in a student disciplinary proceeding?

No. A school district has no authority to condition a student's return to school from a suspension on participation in counseling services. Districts, however, are not precluded from recommending counseling in circumstances where a student may benefit from such services (*Appeal of X. H.*, 43 Educ. Dep't Rep. ___, dec. no. 15,005 (2003); *Appeal of R..M. and L.M.*, 43 Educ. Dep't Rep. ___, dec. no. 14,951 (2003); *Appeal of Jayme K.*, 40 Educ. Dep't Rep. 114 (2000); *Appeal of McMahon*, 38 Educ. Dep't Rep. 22 (1998); see **12:116**).

12:147. May a school district require a psychological or psychiatric examination as a penalty in a student disciplinary proceeding?

No, a school district is not permitted to order a psychological or psychiatric examination as part of a penalty for a suspension. If the district determines that such an examination is warranted, the proper avenue is to refer the student to the district's committee on special education (*Appeal of Pinckney*, 37 Educ. Dep't Rep. 284 (1998)).

12:148. Can a school board lower a student's grade as a disciplinary measure?

No. A student may not be disciplined by having his or her grades lowered, unless the student's misconduct is related to his or her academic performance, such as cheating on an examination or being illegally absent to avoid taking a test (*Appeal of Pappas,* 39 Educ. Dep't Rep. 310 (1999), *Matter of Augustine,* 30 Educ. Dep't Rep. 13 (1990); *Matter of Caskey,* 21 Educ. Dep't Rep. 138 (1981); *Matter of MacWhinnie,* 20 Educ. Dep't Rep. 145 (1980)).

12:149. May a district involuntarily transfer a student from one school to another as a penalty in a student disciplinary proceeding?

No. Involuntary transfers may not be imposed as a penalty in a student disciplinary proceeding, because the purpose of the procedure for involuntarily transferring a student is to determine whether the proposed transfer would be beneficial to the student (*Matter of Reeves,* 37 Educ. Dep't Rep. 271 (1998); see also *Appeal of a Student Suspected of Having a Disability,* 40 Educ. Dep't Rep. 212 (2000); *Appeal of Mangaroo,* 37 Educ. Dep't Rep. 578 (1998); see § 3214(5); see **12:32**).

12:150. What is the Gun-Free Schools Act?

The Gun-Free Schools Act is a federal law which requires that all states receiving funds under the No Child Left Behind Act of 2001 (NCLB) have a law that requires school districts to suspend students who bring a weapon or firearm to school or possesses a firearm at school for a minimum of one calendar year (20 USC § 7151(b)(1)). The term *school* means any setting under the control and supervision of a school district for student activities approved and authorized by the district (20 USC § 7151(f)). The term *firearm* means the same as such term is defined by federal law (18 USC § 921(a)(3) 18 USC § 930(g)(2); 20 USC § 7151(b)(3); § 3214(3)(d)(3); see **12:151**).

12:151. What is a firearm under the Gun-Free Schools Act?

For the purposes of the Gun-Free Schools Act, a firearm means the same as that term is defined in section 921 of Title 18 of the United States Code (20 USC § 7151(b)(3)). The following are included within the definition:

- Any weapon (including a starter gun) which will or is designed to or may readily be converted to expel a projectile by the action of an explosive.
- The frame or receiver of any weapon described above.
- Any firearm muffler or firearm silencer.
- Any destructive device, which is defined as any explosive, incendiary, or poison gas, such as a bomb, grenade, rocket having a propellant charge of more than four ounces, a missile having an explosive or incendiary charge of more than one-quarter ounce, a mine, or other similar device.
- Any weapon which will, or which may be readily converted to, expel a projectile by the action of an explosive or other propellant, and that has any barrel with a bore of more than one-half inch in diameter.
- Any combination of parts either designed or intended for use in converting any device into any destructive device described in the two immediately preceding examples, and from which a destructive device may be readily assembled.

The Gun-Free Schools Act expressly does not apply to a firearm lawfully stored inside a locked vehicle on school property, or if it is for activities that are school approved and authorized and the district has appropriate safeguards to ensure student safety (20 USC § 7151(g); § 3214(3)(d)(2)).

A dangerous weapon is defined under federal law as any device, instrument, material, or substance that is used for or is readily capable of causing death or serious bodily injury. Pocketknives with a blade of less than two-and-one-half inches in length are excluded from the definition of dangerous weapon (18 USC § 930(g)(2)).

The commissioner of education has ruled that a BB gun is not a weapon within the meaning of the Gun-Free Schools Act because the gun uses a spring mechanism to propel the projectile instead of an explosive charge (*Appeal of Eddy*, 36 Educ. Dep't Rep. 359 (1997)). However, in another case where a school district included BB guns within the definition of "weapons" set forth in school policy, the commissioner upheld the one-year suspension of a student who brought a BB gun to school and fired it at a school bus as students were boarding (*Appeal of C.D.*, 43 Educ. Dep't Rep. ___, dec. no. 15,041 (2004)).

12:152. What are a school district's responsibilities under the Gun-Free Schools Act?

All school districts must suspend a student who brings or possesses a firearm at school for a period of not less than one calendar year. The superintendent of schools, district superintendent of schools or community superintendent may modify, in writing, the suspension requirement on a case-by-case basis (see *Appeal of R. S.*, 38 Educ. Dep't Rep. 419 (1998)). A superintendent's determination may be appealed to the school board and the commissioner of education (20 USC § 7151(b)(1); § 3214(3)(d)(1)).

All school districts must have a policy which requires superintendents to refer students under the age of 16 who have been determined to have brought a firearm to school to the county attorney for a juvenile delinquency preceding, and students 16 years of age or older to the appropriate law enforcement officials (§ 3214(3)(d)(1); 20 USC § 7151(h)(i)).

In addition, each school district that receives state funding must provide an assurance within its application for state aid that it is in compliance with section 3214(3)(d) of the Education Law (20 USC § 7151(d)(1)). The application must include a description of the circumstances surrounding any suspension imposed under the state law implementing the Gun-Free Schools Act, including the name of the school concerned, the number of students suspended from school, and the types of firearms concerned (20 USC § 7151(d)(2)).

12:153. Does the suspension requirement of the Gun-Free Schools Act apply only to violations occurring within school buildings?

No. The one-year suspension requirement applies to students who bring or possess a firearm in any setting that is under the control and supervision of the school district for student activities approved and authorized by the district (20 USC § 7151(f); *Appeal of J.D.*, 39 Educ. Dep't Rep. 593 (2000)).

12:154. Is a student entitled to due process before a school district may impose the one-year suspension required under the Gun-Free Schools Act?

Yes. A student charged with bringing or possessing a firearm at school is entitled to the same due process protection afforded to other students who have been suspended in excess of five days (*Appeal of J.D.*, 39 Educ. Dep't Rep. 593 (2000); see **12:126–128, 12:130–132, 12:135–136, 12:139**).

12:155. Are school districts required to provide alternative educational services to students who have been suspended for bringing a weapon to school?

Yes. While the Gun-Free Schools Act neither requires nor prohibits the provision of alternative educational services to students that have been suspended, under state law, school boards are required to furnish alternative education to students who have been suspended until the last day of the school year in which they turn age 16, (or 17 in some districts, see **12:1**), (§ 3214(3)(e); 20 USC § 7151(b)(2); see **12:135–136**).

12:156. Does the Gun-Free Schools Act apply to students with disabilities?

Yes. However, the Gun-Free Schools Act must be construed to be consistent with the Individuals with Disabilities Education Act (IDEA) and section 504 of the Rehabilitation Act (20 USC § 7151(c); § 3214(3)(d); for further information on the discipline of students with disabilities, see **13:49–59**).

12:157. May a school board offer a reward for information related to vandalism of school property?

Yes. School boards may offer monetary rewards in sums not to exceed $1,000 for information leading to the arrest and conviction of persons who have committed felonious or misdemeanor acts of vandalism of school district property (§ 1709(38)).

Student Employment

12:158. May students work while they attend school?

Yes. Students may work while they attend school, provided they obtain a valid employment certificate and do not work in excess of the number of hours prescribed by law (see §§ 3215–3228).

12:159. Under what circumstances may students be issued employment certificates?

Minors who are 14 or 15 years old may secure employment permits and may work while school is in session or when school is not in session. They are prohibited from working in factories (§ 3216(1); Lab. Law § 131(1), (2)).

Minors who are 14 to 16 years of age must have a farm work permit for employment on a farm operated by an individual other than their parents or guardians (§ 3226(1); Lab. Law § 131(3)(f)), (3)(a)(4)). To obtain a farm work permit, a child must present evidence of age, written consent of a parent or guardian, and a certificate of fitness (§ 3226(3)(a)-(c)). A farm work permit is only valid when signed by an employer (§ 3226(4)). A child over the age of 12 may obtain a farm work permit to assist in the harvest of berries and fruits by hand under certain circumstances (§ 3226(2); Lab. Law § 130(2)(e)).

An employment certificate is not required for babysitting, caddying, shoveling snow, or other so-called casual employment (§ 3215(4); Lab. Law § 131(3)(a); 8 NYCRR § 191.1).

The minimum age for a newspaper carrier is 11 (§ 3228(1); Lab. Law § 130(2)(c)). A newspaper carrier must possess a newspaper carrier permit issued by the commissioner of education or school physician (§ 3228(2), (3)).

Under certain conditions, a minor who is 15 years old may secure a special employment certificate and leave school to work (§§ 3216(5), 3225(1); 8 NYCRR § 190.2). See **12:172** for information about student employment in school lunch programs.

12:160. What special rules apply to the issuance of an employment certificate for child performers?

Employment permits for child performers are valid for six months from the date of issuance by the Department of Labor (Lab. Law § 151, Arts. and Cult. Affairs Law § 35.01(4)). In order to renew a permit, the child performer must show proof that he or she is receiving the required educational instruction and maintaining satisfactory academic performance (Lab. Law §§ 151, 152). A child performer must either attend full day instruction at school or be tutored by a certified teacher if his or her work schedule prevents regular school attendance (Lab. Law § 152(2)(a)). No child performer shall be declared absent from school while working with a permit in accordance with legal requirements. A child performer who is required by law to attend school shall not be without educational instruction and unemployed for a period of more than 10 consecutive days while the school where the child is enrolled is in session (Lab. Law § 152(2), (3).

Employers are required to keep on file all permits and certificates to work and to employ issued under the labor or education laws and these must be open for inspection at all times by school attendance and probation officers, the state board of education, and the labor department (Lab. Law § 151(3)).

12:161. What is the maximum number of hours 14- and 15-year-old students are legally allowed to work?

When school is in session, 14- and 15-year-old minors may not work:

- more than three hours on any school day;
- more than eight hours on any day when school is not in session;
- more than 18 hours per week, or no more than six days per week;
- after 7:00 p.m. or before 7:00 a.m (Lab. Law § 142(1), (2)).

12:162. Do 16- and 17-year-old students need employment certificates?

Yes. Minors 16 to 17 years old may not be employed unless they have standard employment certificates. These certificates are valid for work in factories or any other trade, business, or service (§ 3216(2); Lab. Law § 132(2)) when attendance upon instruction is not required.

12:163. What hours are 16- and 17-year-old students legally allowed to work?

The general rule is that when school is in session, 16- and 17-year-old minors may not be employed more than four hours on any day preceding a school day other than on a Sunday or a holiday; no more than eight hours on a Friday, Saturday, Sunday or holiday; no more than 28 hours per week; no more than six days a week and before 6:00 a.m. (Lab. Law § 143(1)).

Employers who schedule minors who are 16 or 17 years old to work between 10:00 p.m. and midnight on any day preceding a school day must obtain written permission from the student's parent or guardian and a certificate from the school at the end of each marking period that indicates the student's academic performance is satisfactory, as measured by district standards (Lab. Law § 143(1)(e)). Employers who employ 16- and 17-year-olds between 10:00 p.m. and midnight on any day preceding a nonschool day need only secure written permission from the student's parent or guardian (Lab. Law § 143(1)(f)).

A 17-year-old employed as a counselor, junior counselor or counselor-in-training at a camp for children during the months of June, July and August is not limited in the number or hours they may work (Lab. Law § 143(4)).

Before processing requests for students' certificates of academic standing, districts should make certain that students are afforded all of the rights and consent they would receive for any other requests for disclosures of information from their student records, under the federal Family Educational Rights and Privacy Act (FERPA) (see **2:88, 26:1**).

12:164. Who issues employment certificates in New York State?

Employment certificates and vacation work permits are issued by the superintendent of schools, or his or her designee. In New York City, the city school district chancellor or his or her designee issues the employment certificates or permits. The district superintendent may issue such certificates and permits for students attending classes operated by a BOCES. In registered nonpublic secondary schools, the principal may issue these certificates (§ 3215-a(1)).

12:165. Must a student be issued an employment certificate for each new job?

No. An employment certificate is valid not only for initial employment but also for subsequent employment in work permitted by the particular type of certificate (§ 3216(6)).

12:166. Are illegally employed students and their beneficiaries entitled to workers' compensation and death benefits?

Yes. Section 14-a of the Workers' Compensation Law provides double compensation and death benefits for illegally employed minors and their beneficiaries. The employer alone, not the insurance carrier, is liable for the increased compensation or increased death benefits provided for by this section.

School Lunch and Breakfast Programs

12:167. May school districts operate and maintain a school lunch program?

Yes. School districts may operate and maintain a school lunch program pursuant to the National School Lunch Act of 1946, as amended (42 USC § 1751 *et seq.*). In addition, school districts can provide, maintain, and operate a cafeteria or restaurant for the use of students and teachers while they are at school (§ 1709(22)). Expenses for cafeteria or restaurant services are now considered ordinary contingent expenses (§ 2023(1)).

The Child Nutrition Act of 1966, as amended (see 42 USC § 1772), and section 1709(23) of the Education Law also authorize school districts to provide milk for students within the limitations of the congressional budget appropriation made for such purpose.

12:168. May school districts operate and maintain a school breakfast program?

Yes. School districts may operate and maintain breakfast programs pursuant to the Child Nutrition Act of 1966 (42 USC § 1771 *et seq.*), and part 114 of the commissioner's regulations. Districts must submit an application to the commissioner of education before establishing this type of program (8 NYCRR § 114.1(c), (e)). Approval may be granted for selected schools rather than an entire district (8 NYCRR § 114.1(c)).

State law and regulations require school districts that provide a school lunch program on or after January 1, 1993 to establish and maintain school breakfast programs in public elementary schools (Laws of 1976, Ch. 537, as amended by Laws of 1993, Ch. 614 and Ch. 615; 8 NYCRR § 114.1(a)(5), (i)(2)). Annual exemptions to this requirement may be granted by the commissioner because a school district lacks a need for such a program due to low school enrollment or participation in the program, because of economic hardship, or for other good cause that makes the establishment of a breakfast program impractical (Laws of 1980, Ch. 798; Laws of 1993, Ch. 57 § 389, Ch. 614 § 3, and Ch. 615 § 3; 8 NYCRR § 114.1(i)(4)).

To the extent that state and federal funds are available, school districts eligible to participate in breakfast programs are reimbursed monthly for breakfasts served that meet meal pattern requirements and for their first year of operation for approved expenses exceeding revenues, subject to the commissioner's approval. Claims for reimbursement will be made on the basis of claims submitted to the commissioner in the form he requires (Laws of 1980, Ch. 798, § 4; 8 NYCRR § 114.1(g), (j)).

12:169. May a school district be exempted from or terminate a school breakfast program?

Yes. A school district that is required to establish a school breakfast program may seek an exemption from participation or may terminate the program under certain circumstances by applying to the commissioner of education for an annual exemption (Laws of 1980, Ch. 798 § 4 as amended by Laws of 1993, Ch. 615 § 4; see 8 NYCRR § 114.1(i)(3)-(7)). Parents and taxpayers must be made aware of the district's intent to request an exemption by May 1 of each year and be offered an opportunity to share their concerns with school officials (8 NYCRR § 114.1(i)(8); see also Laws of 1980, Ch. 798 § 4, as amended by Laws of 1993, Ch. 615 § 4).

A school district that is not required to establish a school breakfast program may terminate its participation in the program by majority vote of the school board. A resolution to terminate the program is not effective prior to June 30 of the school year within which the vote was taken (Laws of 1980, Ch. 798 § 4, amended by Laws of 1993, Ch. 615 § 4).

In addition, no school district is required to operate a school breakfast program if the state elects to terminate participation in the National School Breakfast Program, the corresponding federal program ceases to exist, or if federal funding for the program is withdrawn for any reason whatsoever (Laws of 1976, Ch. 537 § 1(g)).

12:170. Are school meals subject to sales tax?

Sale of food and drink to students on school premises are exempt from taxation. However, sale of food and drink to adults is subject to sales tax (Tax Law § 1105(d)(ii)(B)).

12:171. How is a student's eligibility to participate in a school district's breakfast program on a free or reduced-price basis determined?

A student's eligibility to participate in a school district's breakfast program on a free or reduced-price basis is determined according to income eligibility guidelines issued annually by the State Education Department and sent to school superintendents (Laws of 1976, Ch. 537 § 1(e); 8 NYCRR § 114.1(d)).

12:172. May a school district employ students to work in its food-service program?

Yes. Children at least 14 years old may be employed in a school's food-service program if the student presents a valid employment certificate (Lab. Law §§ 131(3)(g), 132(3)(c); see **12:159–166**).

12:173. May school districts employ a food-service management company to operate their breakfast and lunch programs?

Yes. School districts may contract with a private food-service management company for the purpose of managing and operating, in whole or in part, its food-service program (7 CFR § 210.16(a); 8 NYCRR § 114.2). However, the food-service program remains the legal responsibility of the school district, in accordance with the written agreement required by federal regulations (8 NYCRR § 114.2(a); 7 CFR § 210.9). This agreement is available from the State Education Department (8 NYCRR § 114.2(a)(1)).

Any contract with a food-service management company may not exceed one year and must conform to the commissioner's regulations (8 NYCRR § 114.2(c), (d)). In addition, the contract must be awarded to the lowest responsible bidder. Under certain circumstances, the competitive bidding requirement does not apply to annual, biennial, or triennial extensions of a contract (§ 305(14)(a); 8 NYCRR § 114.2(c), (g)). Furthermore, all food-service management company contracts must be reviewed and approved by the commissioner of education, including annual extensions of contracts (§ 305(14)(a); 8 NYCRR § 114.2(d)(1), (g)).

If contracting is being considered and the school district is subject to the terms of a collective bargaining agreement, the proposal may have to be negotiated with the bargaining unit (see **10:56**).

12:174. Do school districts contracting with a food-service management company remain eligible for reimbursement of funds expended in their breakfast and lunch programs?

Yes. Where a school district contracts with a private food-service management company, it nonetheless remains eligible to receive both federal and state reimbursement and food, in the same way it does for school-operated programs, provided the requirements in the commissioner's regulations are observed (8 NYCRR § 114.2).

12:175. Are school districts eligible to receive federally donated surplus foods and price-support commodities for their breakfast and lunch programs?

Yes. Schools participating in the National School Lunch and Breakfast programs are eligible to receive such food available for distribution (42 USC § 1777; 7 USC § 1431). However, schools must pay the transportation costs for trucking the goods from the district warehouse to the school. In addition, the cost of warehousing is prorated on the basis of the number of case lots allocated to the school. This charge is made once a year and deducted from the claim for reimbursement. The New York State Office of General Services, Bureau of Government Donated Foods, handles the operation of the Commodity Distribution Program.

12:176. Can school districts be reimbursed for meals served to preschool students?

Yes. School districts are eligible to be reimbursed for meals that meet the standards of the lunch meal pattern served to preschool children in school-sponsored classes, just as they are for meals provided to other school children, provided funds are not available from other sources to meet this need (see Laws of 1976, Ch. 537 § 1(a), (d)).

12:177. May a school district make its cafeteria facilities available for meals to community groups such as parent-teacher associations?

Yes, if permission is granted by the school board. Section 1709(22) of the Education Law permits use of the cafeteria by the community for school related functions and activities and to furnish meals to the elderly residents of the district who are 60 years of age and older.

It is recommended that a school cafeteria employee be available to ensure that facilities and equipment are used properly. The agency or group using the facilities should compensate this employee.

School districts should establish rules and regulations concerning, for example, the personnel to be involved, the number of activities during the year it is permissible for personnel to be involved in, and other pertinent matters (§ 414).

12:178. Are a school district's cafeteria and food-service programs subject to sanitation rules and regulations?

Yes. Federal regulations require all schools to abide by all state and local laws and regulations for proper sanitation and health (7 CFR § 210.13(a); see 10 NYCRR Subpart 14-1).

13. Students with Disabilities

Editor's Note: At press time, the Individuals with Disabilities Education Act was before Congress for reauthorization. Therefore, the answers to the questions below are subject to change in accordance with any revisions Congress might make.

Basic Definitions and Applicable Laws

13:1. What laws govern the education of children with disabilities?

The following statutes and their accompanying regulations govern the education of children with disabilities:

- The Individuals with Disabilities Education Act (IDEA), formerly known as the Education of Handicapped Children Act (EHA), which imposes on school districts an obligation to provide all children with disabilities, including children with disabilities who have been suspended or expelled from school, with a free, appropriate public education in the least restrictive environment. The IDEA was amended and reauthorized on June 4, 1997 (20 USC §§ 1400–1487). New IDEA regulations became effective May 11, 1999 (34 CFR Part 300).
- Section 504 of the Rehabilitation Act of 1973 and the Americans with Disabilities Act of 1990, which prohibit discrimination on the basis of disability (29 USC §§ 706, 794–794(a); 42 USC §§ 12101–12213; 34 CFR Part 104).
- Article 89 of the New York State Education Law and part 200 of the commissioner's regulations, which are also the vehicles that implement federal law governing the rights of children with disabilities in New York State. New part 200 regulations became effective January 6, 2000 (8 NYCRR Part 200).

On occasion, there is a lag between changes in the federal statutes and the incorporation of those changes into state law. During such lags, school districts nonetheless are bound by the new federal requirements. In addition, New York State law may at times confer greater rights on students with disabilities than the federal statutes. In such cases, New York State law must be followed. Therefore, it is important for school districts to be familiar with all of the applicable laws.

This chapter addresses, primarily, a district's responsibilities under the IDEA and New York law and regulations.

13:2. What is the definition of children with disabilities applicable to the provision of education to such children?

Generally, *children with disabilities* are those who fall within one of the classifications set forth in the Individuals with Disabilities Education Act (IDEA) and section 200.1(zz) of the commissioner's regulations, and who, because of this, need special education and related services (20 USC § 1401(3)(A); 34 CFR § 300.7; 8 NYCRR § 200.1(zz); see also Educ. Law § 4401(1)).

These classifications include children who suffer from mental retardation; hearing impairment, including deafness, speech or language impairment; visual impairment, including blindness; emotional disturbance; orthopedic impairment; autism; traumatic brain injury; other health impairments; or learning disabilities (20 USC § 1401(3)(A)(i); 8 NYCRR § 200.1(zz); see also § 4401(1)).

The New York State Education Law still contains references to children with handicapping conditions, but pursuant to federal law, references in this chapter will be to children with disabilities.

Notwithstanding the IDEA's definition of children with disabilities, under section 504 of the Rehabilitation Act of 1973, an individual with a disability is defined as "any person who has a physical or mental impairment which substantially limits one or more of such person's major life activities, has a record of such an impairment, or is regarded as having such an impairment" (29 USC § 706(8)(B); see also Educ. Law § 4401(1)).

Similarly, the Americans with Disabilities Act (ADA) extends its benefits to disabled individuals "who, with or without reasonable modifications to rules, policies or practices, the removal of architectural, communication or transportation barriers, or the provision of auxiliary aids and services, meets the essential eligibility requirements for the receipt of services or the participation in programs or activities provided by a public entity" (42 USC § 12131(2)).

It is important for school districts to be aware of this broader definition of individuals with disabilities because section 504 and the ADA prohibit discrimination solely on the basis of disability.

In addition, under section 504 and the ADA, school districts may be responsible for providing education and related services to children with disabilities who do not fall under any of the classifications set forth in the IDEA or the commissioner's regulations (*Appeal of a Child with a Handicapping Condition*, 32 Educ. Dep't Rep. 56 (1992); *Application of a Child Suspected of Having a Handicapping Condition*, SRO dec. no. 92-12 (1992)). For example, according to the United States Department of Education's Office of Civil Rights, all students infected with HIV or who have HIV-related conditions, including those who are currently asymptomatic, are handicapped within the definition of section 504. School districts must provide for proper procedures in the evaluation and placement of these students, as well as for proper procedural safeguards (*Fairfax County (Va.) Public Schs.*, 19 IDELR 649 (1992)).

13:3. What is meant by a "free appropriate public education," which school districts must provide to children with disabilities?

A free appropriate public education (FAPE) consists of special education and related services provided to a student with a disability at public expense under public supervision or direction in conformity with an individualized education program (IEP), which is tailored to meet the unique needs of that student (20 USC § 1401(8); 34 CFR § 300.13(a)(d)). However, school districts are not required to maximize the potential of each disabled child. Districts must provide each child with a disability with a "basic floor of opportunity" consisting of "personalized instruction with sufficient support services to permit the child to benefit educationally from that instruction" (*Board of Educ. v. Rowley*, 458 U.S. 176 (1982); *Walczak v. Florida UFSD*, 142 F.3d 119 (2d Cir. 1998)).

The educational benefit afforded a disabled student must be more than minimal (*Polk v. Central Susquehanna Intermediate Unit 16*, 853 F.2d 171 (3d Cir. 1988), *cert. denied*, 488 U.S. 1030 (1989)).

In addition, a school district is not obligated to provide an optional program or to match or surpass a program offered by a private school (*Matter of a Handicapped Child*, 26 Educ. Dep't Rep. 70 (1986)).

13:4. What is an individualized education program (IEP)?

An *individualized education program* (IEP) is a written statement outlining the plan for providing an educational program for a disabled student based on the unique needs of that student. It must include, for example:

- The classification of the student's disability.
- The present levels of the student's educational performance and the individual needs of the student, according to the child's level of academic or educational achievement and learning characteristics, levels of social and physical development, and management needs.
- The recommended special education program; the class size, if appropriate; and the extent to which the student will participate in regular education programs and an explanation of the extent to which the child will not participate with nondisabled children in the regular class and in extracurricular and nonacademic activities.
- The measurable annual goals, including benchmarks or short-term objectives, related to involving the child in the general curriculum.

- A statement of how the child's progress toward the annual goals will be measured and how the child's parents will be regularly informed of the child's progress.
- The special education, related services and supplementary aids and services to be provided to the child, or on behalf of the child.
- The program modifications or supports for school personnel that will be provided for the child to advance appropriately toward attaining the annual goals, to be involved and progress in the general curriculum and to participate in extracurricular and other non-academic activities; and to be educated and to participate with other students with disabilities and nondisabled students.
- The individual modifications needed in the administration of state or districtwide assessments of student achievement for that child to participate in such assessments.
- The projected date the student will begin receiving special education and related services, the frequency, location and amount of time per day he or she will receive services, whether the student is eligible for a 12-month educational program (and the name of the service provider for July and August), and a projected date to review his or her need for these services.
- Beginning at age 14 and updated annually, a statement of the transition services needs of the child under the applicable components of the child's IEP that focuses on the child's course of study during the student's secondary school experience such as participation in advanced placement or vocational education courses.
- Any necessary transition services beginning at age 15 (or younger, if appropriate), which focus on activities designed to promote the child's movement from school to post-school experiences and any needed linkages.
- Beginning at least one year before the child reaches age 18, a statement that the child has been informed of his or her rights under IDEA, if any, that will transfer to the child on reaching 18.
- The student's recommended placement (20 USC § 1414(d)(1)(A); 34 CFR § 300.347; 8 NYCRR §§ 200.1(y), 200.1(fff), 200.4(d)).

School districts must ensure that personnel responsible for implementing or assisting in the implementation of an IEP understand their responsibilities and receive a copy of the IEP or are provided an opportunity to review it prior to implementation (§ 4402(n); 8 NYCRR §§ 200.2, 200.4(e), 200.16)).

13:5. What is meant by the term "least restrictive environment" in which federal and state laws require students with disabilities be educated?

The requirement that students with disabilities be educated in the *least restrictive environment* (LRE) appropriate to their individual needs means that to the maximum extent appropriate, children with disabilities must be educated with nondisabled children, as close as possible to their home. Children with disabilities may not be removed from regular classroom instruction unless it is determined that they cannot be educated satisfactorily in that environment, even with the use of supplementary aids and services (20 USC §§ 1412(a)(5)(A); 34 CFR §§ 300.55(c), 300.130, 300.550–556; 8 NYCRR § 200.1(cc); *Mavis v. Sobol*, 839 F.Supp. 968 (N.D.N.Y. 1993)). These are aids, services and other supports that are provided in regular education classes or other education-related settings to enable children with disabilities to be educated with non-disabled children to the maximum extent appropriate, in accordance with the LRE requirement (20 USC § 1401(29); 8 NYCRR § 200.1(bbb); 34 CFR § 300.28). They may include, but are not limited to, specially designed instructions (see **13:6**) and consultant teacher services and other group or individual supplemental or direct special education instruction (8 NYCRR § 200.6(a)(1)).

School districts may not remove a student with disabilities from education in an age-appropriate classroom solely because of needed modification in the general curriculum (34 CFR § 300.552 (e)). However, students who must be removed from regular classroom instruction must be provided services within a "continuum of alternative placements" including, for example, resource rooms, related services or itinerant instruction in conjunction with regular class placement, and instruction in regular classes and special classes (8 NYCRR § 200.6). They also must be educated in public school buildings so they may interact with children who are not disabled in areas such as music, art, gym, recess and lunch (see *Application of a Child with a Handicapping Condition*, 30 Educ. Dep't Rep. 108 (1990); *Application of a Child with a Handicapping Condition*, 29 Educ. Dep't Rep. 1 (1989)).

LRE requirements apply as well to nonacademic and extracurricular activities including, for example, meals and recess periods, athletics, transportation, recreational activities and school sponsored clubs (34 CFR §§ 300.553, 300.306)

13:6. What is specially designed instruction?

Specially designed instruction means adapting the content, methodology or delivery of instruction, as appropriate to meet the unique needs that result from a student's disability, and to ensure the student has access to the general curriculum to meet the educational standards applicable to all students (34 CFR § 300.26(b)(3); 8 NYCRR § 200.1(vv)).

13:7. What are related services?

Related services consist of transportation and such developmental, corrective and other supportive services as may be required to assist a child with a disability to benefit from special education, and includes the early identification and assessment of disabling conditions in children. Related services also include speech-language pathology and audiology services; psychological services; physical and occupational therapy; recreation, including therapeutic recreation; school social work services; counseling services, including rehabilitation counseling; orientation and mobility services, medical services for diagnostic and evaluation purposes only; parent counseling and training; school health services; assertive technology services, other appropriate developmental or corrective support services; appropriate access to recreation and other appropriate support services (20 USC § 1401(22); 34 CFR § 300.24(a); 8 NYCRR § 200.1(qq)).

13:8. What are assistive technology services?

Assistive technology services means "any service that directly assists a child with a disability in the selection, acquisition, or use of an assistive technology device" (20 USC § 1401(2); 34 CFR § 300.6; 8 NYCRR § 200.1(f)). *Assistive technology device* means "any item, piece of equipment, or product system, whether acquired commercially off the shelf, modified, or customized, that is used to increase, maintain, or improve functional capabilities of a child with a disability" (20 USC § 1401(1); 34 CFR § 300.5; 8 NYCRR § 200.1(e)). School districts must permit students with disabilities to use school-purchased assistive technology devices at home or in another setting if the committee on special education (CSE) determines the student needs to access the device in nonschool settings to receive a free appropriate public education (see **13:3**) to complete homework, for example (34 CFR Part 300, Appendix A).

The School District's Responsibilities

13:9. What are the school district's basic responsibilities in providing services to children with disabilities?

School districts must provide all eligible children with disabilities a free appropriate public education in the least restrictive environment appropriate to meet their individual needs in conformity with their individualized education program and regardless of the severity of their disabilities (20

USC §§ 1412(a)(1)(A), 1412(a)(5)(A); *Board of Educ. v. Rowley*, 458 U.S. 176 (1982); *Timothy W. v. Rochester Sch. Dist.*, 875 F.2d 954 (1st Cir. 1989), *cert. denied*, 493 U.S. 983 (1989); *Application of a Child with a Handicapping Condition*, 30 Educ. Dep't Rep. 64 (1990), or their ability to benefit from special education (*Timothy W. v. Rochester Sch. Dist.*).

Districts must also provide procedural safeguards for children with disabilities and their parents (20 USC § 1415(b), (d); 34 CFR § 300.504; 8 NYCRR § 200.5) and notice of the procedural safeguards available (20 USC § 1415(d)(2); 8 NYCRR § 200.5(f); see **13:20–21**).

In addition, school boards must:

- Provide for the identification, location, evaluation and maintenance of information about all children with disabilities residing within their districts, including children with disabilities attending private schools (20 USC § 1412(a)(3)(A); 34 CFR §§ 300.125, 300.451; 8 NYCRR § 200.2(a)).

- Appoint a committee on special education (CSE), CSE subcommittees, as appropriate, and a committee on preschool special education (CPSE) to assure the timely identification, evaluation and placement of eligible school age students with disabilities and preschool children with disabilities (20 USC § 1414(b)(4)(A), (d)(1)(B); Educ. Law §§ 4402(1)(b), 4410(3); 8 NYCRR § 200.3(a), (c)).

- Ensure testing and evaluation materials and procedures for identifying and placing children with disabilities are neither racially nor culturally discriminatory and meet the requirement of federal and state law and regulations (20 USC §§ 1412(a)(6)(B), 1414; 34 CFR §§ 300.530–300.543; 8 NYCRR § 200.4(b)(4)).

- Arrange for special education programs and services based upon completion of a student's IEP and the recommendation of the CSE or CPSE (8 NYCRR §§ 200.2(d), 200.4(e)(1), (2)).

- Prepare plans by September 1 of every other year which outline the district's special education programs and services, as required by commissioner's regulations in order to receive state aid (8 NYCRR § 200.2(c)).

- Appoint impartial hearing officers to hear appeals over the school district's actions concerning the identification, evaluation and placement of students with disabilities (§ 4404(1); 8 NYCRR §§ 200.2(b)(9), 200.2(e), 200.5(i)).

13:10. Are school boards required to adopt any specific policies for providing services to children with disabilities?

Yes. School boards must adopt written policies that establish:

- Administrative practices and procedures to ensure that, to the maximum extent appropriate to their needs, all children with disabilities have the opportunity to participate in school district programs available to all other public school students and preschool children to participate in preschool programs (20 USC § 1413(a)(1); 8 NYCRR § 200.2(b)(1), (2)) and have an appropriate amount of space to meet their special education program and service needs (8 NYCRR § 200.2(c)(2)(iv), (v); see also 8 NYCRR §§ 155.1(a), 155.2(b), 155.12(b), (d), 155.15 (c), 200.2(g)).

- Practices and procedures for appointing and training appropriately qualified personnel, including members and chairpersons of the committee on special education (CSE) and committee on preschool special education (CPSE) (20 USC § 1413(a)(3); 8 NYCRR § 200.2(b)(3)). On an annual basis and by a date set by the commissioner of education, school boards must submit to the State Education Department a local comprehensive system of personnel development (CSPS) plan which shows all personnel providing services to students with disabilities are adequate as prescribed by the commissioner (8 NYCRR § 200.2(h)).

- Administrative practices and procedures that provide special education services and programs to the extent appropriate to students' needs within a continuum of services to enable those students to be involved in and progress in the general education curriculum (8 NYCRR § 200.2(b)(4)).

- A plan for implementing school-wide approaches and pre-referral interventions in order to remediate a student's performance prior to referral for special education (8 NYCRR § 200.2(b)(7)).

- Plans and procedures for the appropriate declassification of students with disabilities as required by applicable law and regulations (8 NYCRR § 200.2(b)(8)).

- Administrative practices and procedures that ensure personnel responsible for implementing or assisting in the implementation of a student's individualized education plan (IEP) both receive a copy of the IEP or are provided an opportunity to review it, and are informed of their responsibility prior to implementation as required by commissioner's regulations (§ 4402(7); 8 NYCRR §§ 200.2, 200.4(e), 200.16).

- Mechanisms to ensure the observance of procedural safeguards afforded students with disabilities and their parents (20 USC § 1415; see 8 NYCRR § 200.5).
- Practices and procedures that ensure the confidentiality of a student's IEP and other personally identifiable data, information or records pertaining to students with disabilities (8 NYCRR § 200.2(b)(6)).
- Parents are provided a copy of their child's IEP at no cost (8 NYCRR §§ 200.4(e), 200.16).

13:11. When do a school district's responsibilities towards students with disabilities end?

The general rule is that school districts must provide special education services to students with disabilities until they obtain a local high school or Regents diploma, or until the end of the school year in which the child turns 21, whichever occurs first (20 USC § 1412(a)(1)(A); Educ. Law § 4402(5); 8 NYCRR §§ 200.1(h), 200.1(zz); *Application of Herman and Fanny M.*, 18 Educ. Dep't Rep 127 (1978)).

However, districts have been ordered to provide compensatory education to disabled students beyond the statutory age. According to the Office of Special Education Programs (OSEP) at the U.S. Department of Education, whether a student graduates or ages out does not negate the relevancy of, and the need for, compensatory services that might assist a student in participating in further education, obtaining employment, and/or living independently (*Letter to Riffel*, 34 IDELR 292 (OSEP 2000)).

Generally, the denial of a free appropriate public education does not necessarily entitle a student to compensatory education. There has to have been a gross violation of the Individuals with Disabilities Education Act that denied or excluded the student from educational services for a substantial period of time (*Application of the Bd. of Educ. of the Smithtown CSD*, SRO dec. no. 02-097 (2003); see also *Application of the Bd. of Educ. of the Gowanda CSD*, SRO dec. no. 04-016 (2004)). At least one court outside New York State has determined that the provision of services by unlicensed, unqualified personnel warrants an award of compensatory education (*Evanston Comm. CSD No. 65 v. Michael M*, 40 IDELR 175 (7th Cir. 2004).

13:12. What specific "child find" responsibilities does a school board have for identifying and maintaining data on children with disabilities?

Each school board must locate and identify all children with disabilities who reside in the district, whether they are of preschool or school age, including children with disabilities enrolled in private schools; highly mobile children with disabilities (such as migrant and homeless children);

and children suspected of being a child with a disability and in need of special education even though they are advancing from grade to grade (20 USC §§ 1412(a)(3)(A), (10)(A)(ii); 34 CFR §§ 300.125(a)(2), 300.451; 8 NYCRR § 200.2(a)(1)). A register of such children must be maintained and revised annually by the district's committee on special education (CSE) for school-age children or the committee on preschool special education (CPSE) for younger children (Educ. Law § 4402(1)(a); 8 NYCRR § 200.2(a)(1)).

Procedures must be implemented to ensure the availability of statistical data to determine the status of each child with a disability in the identification, location, and evaluation, placement and program review process. Data must be reported by October 1 to the CSE or CPSE (8 NYCRR § 200.2(a)(1)).

Procedures must be designed to record data on each child with a disability and shall include at least the following types of data:

- The child's name, address and birth date.
- The child's parents' names and address or addresses and the native language spoken in the child's home.
- The child's suspected disability.
- The dates of referral and evaluation, recommendations of the CSE or CPSE, actual placement, and annual program reviews.
- The site where the child currently is receiving an educational program.
- In certain instances, any reasons why the child is not receiving an appropriate public education.

This data must be organized so that it can be determined readily whether the child is receiving an appropriate public education, a partial education or no education at all (8 NYCRR § 200.2(a)(2)).

Anyone who collects this data must receive training and written information on the procedures for collecting the data (8 NYCRR § 200.2(a)(3)).

13:13. What must school districts do to locate children with disabilities attending private schools?

School districts must undertake "child find" activities with respect to private school children with disabilities, which are comparable to those undertaken for children with disabilities in public schools (34 CFR § 300.451(a); 8 NYCRR § 200.2(a)(7)) including, for example, the wide distribution of informational brochures, regular public service announcements, staffing exhibits at community activities (OSEP Questions and Answers, May 4, 2000, 34 IDELR 263). According to one federal appellate court, however, school districts do not have to do an individualized mailing to all private school students and their parents as part of their child-find efforts (*Doe v. Metropolitan Nashville Pub. Schs.*, 157 Ed. Law Rep. 583 (6th Cir. 2001)).

In addition, districts must consult with appropriate representatives of private school children with disabilities on how to carry out the required child-find activities (34 CFR § 350.451(b); 8 NYCRR § 200.2(a)(7)). These representatives may include representatives of organizations of nonpublic schools, selected parents of students with disabilities enrolled in nonpublic schools, and selected representatives of nonpublic schools in the district (8 NYCRR § 200.2(a)(7)).

13:14. Must school districts report the data collected on children with disabilities?

Yes. Data on children with disabilities must be reported according to the following rules:

- School districts must prepare and keep on file summary reports of data on students and preschool children, including the number of children who were served, the number of those who were not served and the reasons why they were not served.
- School districts must submit a summary report of the children they served to the State Education Department (SED) on prescribed forms.

Each year, the school board or trustees of each school district, with the exception of cities with 125,000 or more inhabitants, must report the register of children with disabilities who are under the age of 21 to the district superintendent of the board of cooperative educational services (BOCES) of which the district may be a part. In addition, the data must be reported to the district's committee on special education (CSE) or committee on preschool special education (CPSE), as appropriate, by October 1 of each year (see **13:12**). The regular census must be filed on or before October 15 of each year (see **2:26**). The register also must be available to SED representatives (Educ. Law §§ 3241, 3242; 8 NYCRR § 200.2(a)(4)).

13:15. Are school districts required to provide year-round services to disabled students?

Yes, to students whose disabilities require a structured learning environment of up to 12 months' duration to prevent "substantial regression." This means the inability to maintain developmental levels due to a loss of skill or knowledge, during the months of July and August, severe enough to require an inordinate period of review at the beginning of the school year to reestablish and maintain the individualized education program's (IEP) goals and objectives mastered at the end of the previous school year (34 CFR § 300.309; 8 NYCRR §§ 200.1(aaa), 200.1 (eee); *Appeal of a Child with a*

Handicapping Condition, 31 Educ. Dep't Rep. 17 (1991)). This standard does not require that children with disabilities actually regress in their skills before they are eligible for summer programs and services; what is required is a "reasonable basis" for concluding that regression would occur without these services *(Application of a Child with a Disability*, SRO dec. no. 93-28 (1993)).

School districts may not unilaterally limit the type, amount, or duration of year-round services for students with disabilities, or limit such services to particular categories of disabilities (34 CFR § 300.309(a)(3)). Programs providing services during the months of July and August must operate at least 30 school days. However, programs providing only related services must be provided with the frequency and duration specified in the student's IEP (8 NYCRR § 200.1(eee)).

13:16. Are school districts responsible for providing medical services to students with disabilities?

School districts are not required to provide medical services except for diagnostic and evaluative purposes (20 USC § 1401(22); 8 NYCRR § 200.1(ee)). However, districts must provide necessary school health-related services to students with disabilities (20 USC § 1401(22); 34 CFR § 300.306; 8 NYCRR § 200.1(qq), (ss)).

Medical services for evaluative and diagnostic purposes refers to services provided by a licensed physician or registered health professional in consultation with or under the supervision of a licensed physician to determine whether a student has a medically-related disability which may result in the student's need for special education and related services (8 NYCRR § 200.1(ee)).

School health services refer to services provided by a qualified nurse or other qualified person (8 NYCRR § 200.1(ss)).

The United States Supreme Court has ruled that school districts must provide health services to students with disabilities as long as the services do not have to be performed by a licensed physician and are necessary for the student to attend school and benefit from special education *(Cedar Rapids Community Sch. Dist. v. Garrett F.*, 526 U.S. 66 (1999*); Irving Indep. Sch. Dist. v. Tatro*, 468 U.S. 883 (1984)).

13:17. Must school districts ensure that students with disabilities have an opportunity to participate in extracurricular activities?

Yes. School districts must adopt and implement procedures for ensuring that students with disabilities can participate in extracurricular activities (8 NYCRR § 200.2(b)(1)) and are provided an equal opportunity for participation (*Rose Tree Media (PA) Sch. Dist.*, OCR Decision, 40 IDELR 188 (2003)).

Actual knowledge by the disabled students' parents of district extracurricular programs and activities does not relieve the district of its obligation to notify students with disabilities and their parents of these activities (*Application of a Child with a Handicapping Condition*, 30 Educ. Dep't Rep. 293 (1991)).

School districts, however, are not obligated to ensure that disabled children participate in all extracurricular activities which the parents or the child choose (*Application of the Board of Educ. of the East Syracuse-Minoa CSD*, SRO dec. no. 92-11 (1992)).

Districts may make an individual determination concerning the physical capacity of a student with a disability to participate in an extracurricular athletic activity. If refused participation, the student then may commence a special court proceeding to appeal the district's decision preventing the student from participating (§ 3208-a(1)). If the court mandates participation, the law absolves the district from liability for injuries sustained during participation in the activity if the injury is attributable to the physical impairment involved in the court order (§ 3208-a(4)).

13:18. Must school districts provide special education and related services to students with disabilities who are placed by their parents in private schools?

Yes. Under both the Individuals with Disabilities Education Act and the dual-enrollment provisions of the state Education Law, districts must provide special education and related services to private school students with disabilities (20 USC § 1412(a)(10)(a)(i); 34 CFR § 300.452; § 3602-c; see *Benjamin P. v. City of Lackawanna*, 23 IDELR 430 (W.D.N.Y. 1995); see also *Board of Educ. of the Hyde Park CSD*, SRO dec. no. 02-024 (2003)).

A school district, however, is not responsible for the student's tuition at the private school unless the parents have placed the student at the private school because they disagree with the program or placement recommended by the district, and they meet certain other conditions (see **13:45**).

If a student with disabilities attends a private school located outside his or her district of residence, the district of residence must contract with the district of location for the provision of special education services to the student. The district of residence may not insist on providing those services only at one of its own schools (*Board of Educ. of the East Islip UFSD*, SRO dec. no. 02-035 (2003).

13:19. May school districts provide on-site special education and related services to students with disabilities who attend private schools, including parochial schools?

Yes. Under the federal Individuals with Disabilities Education Act (IDEA), special education services may be provided to students with disabilities on the premises of private schools, including parochial schools, to the extent consistent with law (20 USC § 1412(a)(10)(A)(i)). The United States Supreme Court has ruled that the federal constitution does not prevent a school district from providing services to students on-site at the premises of their parochial school (*Agostini v. Felton*, 521 U.S. 203 (1997)).

A school district is not required under federal law to provide on-site special education services to children with disabilities voluntarily enrolled in private schools. However, it is still an open question as to whether New York state law requires public school districts to provide such on-site services. A case addressing the issue was dismissed as moot by a federal appellate court with jurisdiction over New York without a discussion of the issue (*Russman v. Board of Educ. of Enlarged City Sch. Dist. of City of Watervliet*, 260 F.3d 114 (2d Cir. 2001)).

In an earlier case, the New York State Court of Appeals ruled that a public school district was not required to provide special education services to students voluntarily enrolled in a private school on the private school premises (*Board of Educ. of Monroe-Woodbury CSD v. Wieder*, 72 N.Y.2d 174 (1988)).

According to New York's State Review Officer, services that must be provided in a classroom setting, such as consultant teacher and full-time aide services, must be provided on-site in the student's private school classroom. Services such as counseling and occupational therapy, which do not require a classroom setting, do not have to be provided on-site (*Board of Educ. of the Hyde Park CSD*, SRO dec. no. 02-024 (2003)).

13:20. What procedural safeguards must a school district provide to students with disabilities and their parents?

The federal Individuals with Disabilities Education Act (IDEA) and state law and regulations require that school districts afford students with disabilities and their parents procedural safeguards that include the right to:

- Receive prior written notice whenever the district proposes or refuses to initiate or change the identification, evaluation, educational placement or provision of a free appropriate public education to the child.
- Examine all records pertaining to the child conducted by a qualified examiner not employed by the school district.

- Consent to evaluations and reevaluations, the initial provision of special education, the initial provision of services in a 12-month program, the release of personally identifiable information in accordance with the Family Educational Rights and Privacy Act (20 USC § 1232(g); 34 CFR Part 99), and district access to a parent's private insurance proceeds.
- Participate at each committee on special education (CSE) and committee on preschool special education (CPSE) meeting with respect to the identification, evaluation and educational placement of the child.
- Receive at least five days notice prior to a CSE or CPSE meeting related to the development or review of a student's individualized education program (IEP), or the provision of a free appropriate public education to the student, including the purpose, date, time, and location of the meeting, and title of persons expected to attend, along with other required information.
- Receive notice of procedural safeguards.
- Obtain an independent evaluation of the child conducted by a qualified examiner who is not employed by the public agency responsible for the education of the student.
- Present complaints to the school district and initiate due process hearings over the identification, evaluation or educational placement of a disabled child, or the provision of a free appropriate public education.
- Appeal adverse findings and decisions in an impartial hearing, including the right to disclosure of evaluation results and recommendations.
- Have the student remain in his or her then-current educational placement during the pendency of due process proceedings, subject to certain exceptions.
- An explanation of the procedures for students who are subject to placement in an interim alternative educational setting.
- An explanation of the requirements for unilateral placement by parents in private schools at public expense.
- Mediation.
- Attorneys' fees.
- Request a school physician to participate in committee meetings. Request an interpreter, translator or reader for the meeting and be accompanied at such meetings by such individuals as the parent may desire.
- Request information on obtaining free or low-cost legal assistance and other relevant services at no expense to the district (20 USC

§ 1415(d); 34 CFR §§ 300, 345(b), 300.500–300.517; 8 NYCRR § 200.5; see also 8 NYCRR § 200.1(z)).

Federal regulations implementing Section 504 of the Rehabilitation Act of 1973 also require that districts receiving federal education funds establish a system of procedural safeguards concerning the identification, evaluation, and/or educational placement of children believed to need special instruction or related services, and give parents notice of their rights under Section 504 (34 CFR § 104.36; *Plainfield (CT) Pub. Sch.*, OCR Decision, 40 IDELR 118 (2003)).

13:21. Must a school district provide written notice of the procedural safeguards?

Yes. A school district must give parents written notice of the procedural safeguards upon:

- A child's referral for evaluation.
- Reevaluation.
- Each notification of an individualized education program (IEP) meeting.
- Each registration of a parental complaint or request for an impartial hearing relating to the identification, evaluation, or educational placement of the child, or the provision of a free appropriate public education.
- Each notification of a decision to place a child with a disability in an interim alternative placement as permitted by law, or take disciplinary action that involves a change in placement (20 USC §§ 1415(d)(2), 1415(k)(4)(A)(i); 8 NYCRR § 200-1.7(a)).

A school district must use the procedural safeguards notice prescribed by the commissioner of education (8 NYCRR § 200.5(f)(1)) and provide it in the native language of the parent or other mode of communication used by the parent, unless it is clearly not feasible to do so (8 NYCRR § 200.5(f)(2)). If the parent has no written language, notice must be given orally or by other means or mode of communication, and the district must ensure the parent understands the content of the notice and maintain written evidence that the parent has received notice of procedural safeguards (8 NYCRR § 200.5 (f)(2)).

The procedural safeguards notice prescribed by the commissioner of education applies only to children with disabilities eligible to receive special education and related services under the federal Individuals with Disabilities Education Act. School districts must give parents separate notice of their rights under Section 504 of the Rehabilitation Act of 1973 (34 CFR § 104.36; *Plainfield (CT) Pub. Sch.*, OCR Decision, 40 IDELR 18(2000)).

The Committee on Special Education

13:22. What is the function of a school district's committee on special education?

The primary function of the committee on special education (CSE) is to identify, evaluate, review the status of, and make recommendations concerning the appropriate educational placement of each school-age child with a disability, or thought to have a disability, who resides within the school district (8 NYCRR §§ 200.3, 200.4).

The CSE must also make an annual report to the school board on the status of services and facilities made available by the district for children with disabilities (Educ. Law § 4402(1)(b)(3)((f)). The CSE is also responsible for maintaining and annually revising the register of children with disabilities who are entitled to attend public school during the next school year or those referred to the committee (8 NYCRR § 200.2(a)).

13:23. Who comprises a school district's committee on special education?

A committee on special education (CSE) must include the following members:

- The parent of the child with a disability.
- At least one regular education teacher of the student (if the child is, or may be, participating in the regular education environment). The regular education teacher must be someone who is certified to teach the student under consideration and who teaches in one of the regular education programs, which might be appropriate for the student. A kindergarten teacher would not be an appropriate CSE member for a student being considered for a regular middle school class (*Board of Educ. of the Arlington CSD*, SRO dec. no. 02-080 (2003)).
- A special education teacher of the student or, where appropriate, a special education provider of such child.
- A school psychologist.
- A representative of the school district who is:
    (1) qualified to provide or supervise special education;
    (2) knowledgeable about the general curriculum, and
    (3) knowledgeable about the availability of resources of the district.
  (This individual may also be the special education teacher/provider or school psychologist if they meet the above qualifications.)
- An individual who can interpret the instructional implications of evaluation results (may also be one of the above district team members or a person having knowledge or special expertise regarding the student so determined by the district).

- At the discretion of the parent or the district, other individuals who have knowledge or special expertise regarding the child, including related services personnel. A parent's right to invite such individuals does not include the right to reimbursement and compensation related to their attendance (*Board of Educ. of the Greene* CSD, SRO dec. no. 02-009 (2003)). However, a CSE that chooses to resolve an impasse in reaching consensus by taking a vote is required to count the vote of every participant at the CSE meeting, including those invited by parents as having knowledge of special expertise about their child (*Sackets Harbor CSE v. Munoz*, 283 AD2d 756 (3d Dep't 2001)).
- A school physician, if requested in writing by the parents or the school district 72 hours before a meeting.
- A parent of another child with a disability residing in the district or a neighboring district. The parent of a declassified student no longer eligible for special education or of a disabled child who has graduated my serve as the additional parent member for up to five years beyond their child's declassification or graduation. This additional parent may not be employed or under contract with the current school district. The original student's parent may wave the participation of this CSE member.
- Where appropriate, the child with a disability (20 USC § 1414(d)(1)(B); Educ. Law § 4402(1)(b)(1); 8 NYCRR § 200.3(a)).

Whenever the CSE is considering a student's transition services needs, needed transition services, or both, it must invite the student and a representative of any agency likely to provide or pay for transition services (34 CFR § 300.344(b)). Additional prescribed members are required for any CSE determining whether a student suspected of having a specific learning disability is a child with a disability (34 CFR § 300.540).

13:24. May a school district have more than one committee on special education (CSE)?

Yes. Buffalo, New York City, Rochester, Syracuse and Yonkers must establish CSE subcommittees to the extent necessary to ensure the timely evaluation and placement of students with disabilities. Other school districts also may establish CSE subcommittees but are not required to do so (Educ. Law § 4402(1); 8 NYCRR § 200.3(c)). The CSE, however, is responsible for overseeing and monitoring the activities of each subcommittee to assure compliance with the requirements of applicable law and regulations (§ 4402(1)(b)(1)(b)).

13:25. Is there any difference in function between a committee on special education (CSE) and a CSE subcommittee?

A CSE subcommittee performs the same functions as a CSE, except that the CSE remains responsible for deciding cases concerning the initial placement of a student in a special class, in a special class outside of the student's school of attendance or in a school primarily serving children with disabilities or a school outside the student's district (Educ. Law § 4402; 8 NYCRR § 200.3(c)(4)).

In addition, a CSE subcommittee must report to the CSE annually on the status of each student with a disability under its jurisdiction (8 NYCRR § 200.3(c)(6)). Upon written parental request, the CSE subcommittee also must refer to the CSE for review any of its recommendations not acceptable to the parent (8 NYCRR § 200.3(c)(5)).

13:26. Who are the members of a CSE subcommittee?

A CSE subcommittee must include the following members:
- The parent of the child with a disability.
- One regular education teacher (if the child is, or may be, participating in the regular education environment).
- A special education teacher of the student, or where appropriate, a special education provider of such child.
- A school psychologist, whenever a new psychological evaluation is reviewed or a change to a program option with a more intensive staff/student ratio, as set forth in part 200.6(g)(4) of the commissioner's regulations, is considered.
- A representative of the school district who is:
    (1) qualified to provide, administer or supervise special education,
    (2) knowledgeable about the general curriculum, and
    (3) knowledgeable about the availability of resources of the district.
  (This individual may also be the special education teacher/provider or school psychologist if they meet the above qualifications)
- At the discretion of the parent or the district, other individuals who have knowledge or special expertise regarding the child, including related services personnel.
- An individual who can interpret the instructional implications of evaluation results (may also be one of the above district team members).
- Where appropriate, the child with a disability (20 USC § 1414(d)(1)(B); Educ. Law § 4402(1)(b)(1); 8 NYCRR § 200.3(c)).

13:27. What happens if the school board disagrees with the recommendation of the committee on special education or the CSE subcommittee?

If a school board disagrees with either committee's recommendation, it may follow one of the following procedures:

- Return the recommendation to the committee with a statement of the board's objections or concerns. The committee must then consider the board's objections or concerns, revise the individualized education program (IEP) where appropriate, and resubmit a recommendation to the board. If the board continues to disagree with the recommendation, it may either continue to return the recommendation to the original committee for additional review or establish a second committee to develop a new recommendation.

- Establish a second committee to develop a new recommendation. If the board disagrees with the recommendation of the second committee, it may return the recommendation to the second committee with a statement of its objections or concerns. The second committee then must consider the board's objections or concerns, revise the IEP where appropriate and resubmit a recommendation to the board. If the board continues to disagree with the revised recommendation, it may continue to return the recommendation to the second committee for additional review.

Once a school board establishes a second CSE, the board may not select the recommendation of the initial CSE.

Under either procedure, the school board must arrange for the programs and services in accordance with an IEP within 60 school days of receiving the consent to evaluate a student not previously identified as a student with a disability, or within 60 school days of the referral for review of the child with a disability (8 NYCRR § 200.4(e)).

Only a CSE may determine the content of a student's IEP and a student's placement (*Application of the Board of Educ. of the Gowanda CSD*, SRO dec. no. 04-016 (2004)).

13:28. Must the school board notify the parents of a student with disabilities of its disagreement with the recommendations of the committee on special education or CSE subcommittee?

Yes. In addition, the notice must be in writing and set forth the school board's reasons and indicate that the recommendations will be sent back to the committee on special education or CSE subcommittee with notice of the need to schedule a timely meeting to review the board's concerns and revise the student's individualized education program as appropriate (8 NYCRR § 200.5(a)(5)(ii)).

13:29. Is a school district required to notify parents of its proposal or refusal to initiate or change the identification, evaluation or placement of a child with a disability?

Yes. A school district is required to give parents written notice of its proposal or refusal to initiate or change the identification, evaluation or placement of a child with a disability, or the provision of a free appropriate public education along with a description of:

- An explanation of its decision.
- Other options considered and why they were rejected.
- Each evaluation procedure, test, record, or report used as a basis for its action, as well as other factors relevant to the district's decision.

The notice must also include a statement that parents of a student with a disability have procedural protections under the Individuals with Disabilities Education Act (IDEA). Additionally, if the notice is not about an initial referral for evaluation, it must also inform the parent how to obtain a copy of the procedural safeguards, and where to obtain assistance in understanding parental rights under IDEA (20 USC § 1415(c); 34 CFR § 300.503(b); 8 NYCRR § 200.5(a)(1), (2), (3)).

Notice involving referral for initial evaluation or revaluation must include a description of the proposed evaluation or reevaluation and the uses to be made of the information, and indicate that the parent may submit evaluation information for CSE consideration.

In cases involving a reevaluation, the notice must also inform parents of their rights to request a test or assessment as part of the reevaluation to determine the student's continued eligibility (8 NYCRR § 200.5(a)(5)(i)).

Furthermore, if the proposed action involves placement in an approved private school, the notice must also include a copy of the private school's policy on the use of psychotropic medication if the school uses it (8 NYCRR § 200.5(a)(5)(vii)).

13:30. Is parental consent required before the committee on special education (CSE) conducts an initial evaluation of a child suspected of having a disability or for any reevaluation of a child with a disability?

Yes. The parent must provide written consent for both an initial evaluation of a child suspected of having a disability and for any reevaluation of a child with a disability before the initial evaluation or reevaluation is conducted (20 USC §§ 1414(a)(1)(C), 1414(c)(3); 34 CFR §§ 300.500(b)(1), 300.505(a)(1); 8 NYCRR §§ 200.1(1), 200.5(b)(1)).

If a parent fails to give consent for an initial evaluation, a school district may have to go to mediation and/or due process. The district must give the parent an opportunity to attend an informal conference with the CSE or other prescribed individuals and ask questions about the proposed evaluation. If the parent does not request to attend such a conference or continues to withhold consent for 30 days after receipt of a referral, the board of education must commence an impartial hearing to determine whether the initial evaluation should be conducted without parental consent (20 USC § 1414(a)(1)(C)(ii); 34 CFR § 300.505(b); 8 NYCRR § 200.5 (b)(1)(i)(c)).

13:31. Are there any exceptions to the evaluation/reevaluation consent rule?

Yes. Parental consent for a reevaluation is not necessary if a school district has taken reasonable measures to obtain such consent and the child's parent has failed to respond (20 USC § 1414(c)(3); 8 NYCRR § 200.5(b)(1)(i)(b)). The district must have a record of its attempts to obtain parental consent (8 NYCRR § 200.5(b)(1)(i)(b)(1)).

In addition, consent is not required before reviewing existing data as part of an evaluation or reevaluation, or before administering a test or other evaluation administered to all children without a need for parental consent (34 CFR § 300.505(a)(3); 8 NYCRR § 200.5(b)(1)(i)(a)).

13:32. Is parental consent necessary before a district can provide special education programs and services to a child with a disability?

Yes. Consent for initial evaluation does not constitute consent for initial provision of special education services (20 USC § 1414(a)(1)(c); 34 CFR § 300.505(a)(2); 8 NYCRR § 200.5(b)(1)(ii)(a)). Therefore, a school district must obtain parental consent prior to initially providing special education services to a child who has not previously been identified as having a disability. Likewise, consent is also required for the initial provision of special education service in a 12-month special service and /or program (8 NYCRR § 200.5(b)(ii), (iii)).

According to the Office of Special Education Programs (OSEP) at the U.S. Department of Education, a school district may not initiate due process to override a parent's refusal to consent to the initial provision of special education and related services (*Letter to Cox*, 36 IDELR 66 (OSEP 2001)). But a district does not have to apply the disciplinary protections available to students eligible for services under the Individuals with Disabilities Education Act when a student is not receiving special education because the student's parents refuse to consent to the initial provision of services. There is no difference between a refusal to consent and a failure to respond to a request for consent (*Letter to Gantwerk*, 39 IDELR 215 (2003)).

13:33. Can parents revoke their consent to an initial evaluation, reevaluation or initial provision of special education programs and services?

Yes. Parental consent is voluntary and may be revoked at anytime. However, revocation of the consent does not negate district actions undertaken after consent was given but before it was revoked (34 CFR § 300.500(b)(1); 8 NYCRR § 200.1(1)(3).

13:34. How often must a school district's committee on special education (CSE) review a student's individualized education program (IEP)?

Each student's IEP must be reviewed at least annually. It may be reviewed and revised more often if appropriate. The review must be based on an assessment of the IEP and other current information pertaining to the student's performance. The review must consider the educational progress and achievement of the student and the student's ability to participate in instructional programs in regular education and in the least restrictive environment (20 USC § 1414(d)(4); 8 NYCRR § 200.4(f)).

In addition, the CSE must arrange for an appropriate reevaluation of each student with a disability if conditions warrant a reevaluation or if the child's parent or teacher requests a reevaluation, and at least every three years (20 USC § 1414(a)(2); 34 CFR § 300.536(b); 8 NYCRR § 200.4(b)(4)).

A school district may continue to develop and review a student's IEP and placement during the pendency of litigation concerning a prior IEP or placement. According to one federal court, to prohibit such efforts would require school districts to violate their statutory duties under the Individuals with Disabilities Education Act (*Norma P. v. Pelham Sch. Dist.*, 19 IDELR 938 (1993)).

13:35. Must a school district evaluate a child with a disability prior to declassification?

Yes, unless the committee on special education (CSE) determines that it does not require additional data to decide whether the child continues to be a child with a disability. In such an instance, the district must notify the child's parent of its determination and the reasons thereof, as well as the parent's right to request an assessment. The school district is not required to conduct the assessment unless requested by the child's parent (20 USC § 1414 (c)(4); 34 CFR § 300.533(d); 8 NYCRR § 200.4(b)(5)(iv)).

A declassification evaluation is not required when a student's eligibility for special education programs and services ends as a result of the student's graduation with a local high school or Regents' diploma, or because the student ages out (34 CFR § 534(c)).

13:36. Must a parent of a disabled student be present at the committee on special education (CSE) or CSE subcommittee meeting where his or her child is being discussed?

A parent of a child with a disability is a mandated member of the CSE or the CSE subcommittee and should be present at all meetings of the committee in which his or her child is being discussed (20 USC § 1414(d)(1)(B); 34 CFR §§ 300.344(a)(1), 300.345; 8 NYCRR §§ 200.3(a)(1)(i), 200.3(d)). In addition, the school district must ensure the parent understands the proceedings at the meetings, including arranging for an interpreter for deaf parents and parents whose native language is other than English (34 CFR §§ 300.345(e), 300.501(c)(5); 8 NYCRR § 200.5(d)(5)).

However, a CSE or CSE subcommittee may meet without the parent if it cannot convince the parent to attend, and has a record of its attempt to do so at a mutually agreed upon time and place (8 NYCRR § 200.5(d)(3)).

If neither parent can participate in a meeting regarding the student's educational placement, the district must use other methods to ensure their participation, including individual conference calls or video conferencing (34 CFR § 300.501(c)(3)). However, the CSE or CSE subcommittee may make a placement decision without parental involvement if the school is unable to obtain the parents' participation and has records of its attempts do so, including records of telephone calls made or attempted, copies of correspondence sent to the parents and any responses received, and records and results of visits made to the parent's home or place of employment (34 CFR §§ 300.345(c), 300.501(c)(3); 8 NYCRR § 200.5(d)(4)).

A CSE meeting does not include informal or unscheduled conversations among school personnel and conversations about teaching methodology, lesson plans, or coordination of services provision if those issues are not addressed in the student's individualized education program. A CSE meeting does not include either preparatory activities by school personnel to develop a proposal or response to a parental proposal that will be discussed at a later meeting (34 CFR § 300.501(b)(2)).

13:37. May a parent tape-record his or her child's committee on special education (CSE) or CSE subcommittee meeting?

Yes. A parent may tape-record his or her own child's CSE or CSE subcommittee meeting without approval by the CSE, CSE subcommittee or school board. However, the parent may forfeit the right to tape-record future proceedings if there are circumstances that indicate this right is being abused. A school district also must be permitted to tape-record CSE or CSE subcommittee meetings (*Application of a Child with a Handicapping Condition*, 30 Educ. Dep't Rep. 178 (1990)).

13:38. May the school attorney attend the district's committee on special education (CSE) or CSE subcommittee meetings?

The U.S. Department of Education discourages the attendance at CSE or CSE subcommittee meetings of either a school attorney or an attorney accompanying a student's parent, even if the attorney has knowledge or special expertise about the student (Appendix A to IDEA Regulations, Question 29, 34 CFR Part 300).

School attorneys should attend such meetings only on those rare occasions when the committee's ability to perform its functions depends on the immediate resolution of critical legal issues. The school attorney should not become a listening post for the school board, nor may he or she attend CSE or CSE subcommittee meetings to intimidate parents or undermine the decision-making process (*Application of a Child with a Handicapping Condition*, 30 Educ. Dep't Rep. 286 (1991)).

Parental Challenges

13:39. May the parents of a disabled student challenge the actions taken by the committee on special education (CSE), CSE subcommittee or the school board regarding the classification, evaluation or placement of the student?

Yes. Parents who disagree with the actions taken by either the committee on special education (CSE), CSE subcommittee, and/or the school board concerning the classification, evaluation or placement of their child may request, in writing, an impartial due process hearing. The school board then must appoint an impartial hearing officer (IHO) to hear the appeal and make appropriate recommendations to resolve the issue (20 USC §§ 1415(b)(6); 1415(f); 34 CFR §§ 300.507, 300.508, 300.509; Educ. Law § 4404(1); 8 NYCRR § 200.5(i)). The IHO may schedule a pre-hearing conference with the parties to simplify or clarify the issue, establish dates of the completion of the hearing, identify evidence and witnesses, and address any other administrative matters necessary to complete a timely hearing (8 NYCRR § 200.5(i)(3)(xi)). Each party will have up to one day to present its case unless the IHO determines that additional time is necessary for a full, fair disclosure of the facts to arrive at a decision (8 NYCRR § 200.5(i)(3)(xiii)).

School districts must inform parents requesting an impartial due process hearing of the availability of mediation and of any free or low cost legal and other relevant services in the area (20 USC § 1415(e); 34 CFR § 300.507(a)(z); 8 NYCRR § 200.5(i)(2)).

13:40. How are impartial hearing officers selected?

School districts appoint impartial hearing officers (IHO) on a rotation basis, from a list provided by the State Education Department and maintained in alphabetical order, beginning with the first name after the IHO who last served, or the first name on the list if no IHO on the list has served (Educ. Law § 4404(1); 8 NYCRR § 200.2(e)(1)(ii)). The appointment process must be commenced immediately but no later than two business days after the district receives a written request for a hearing (8 NYCRR § 200.5(i)(3)(i)(a)). An IHO may not accept appointment if he or she is unable to start the hearing within the first 14 days after being appointed by the district (8 NYCRR § 200.5(i)(3)(i)(b)).

A district must offer appointment to each successive IHO on the list whenever an IHO declines appointment or fails to respond or is unreachable within 24 hours after documented, independently verifiable, reasonable efforts by the district (8 NYCRR § 200.2(a)(1)(ii)).

A school board must appoint an IHO immediately. It may designate one or more of its members to appoint an IHO (8 NYCRR § 200.5(i)(3)(ii)).

A board must rescind an IHO appointment and appoint a new IHO if after a hearing commences the parents and the district agree that the IHO has become incapacitated or otherwise unavailable or unwilling to continue the hearing or issue a decision (8 NYCRR § 200.5(i)(3)(iii)).

Individuals employed by a school district, school, or program serving disabled students placed by a committee on special education (CSE) may not serve as impartial hearing officers while employed as such and for a period of two years after they cease working for these employers (8 NYCRR § 200.1(x), *Application of a Child with a Disability (Canastota CSD)*, SRO dec. no. 96-84 (1996)).

13:41. May an impartial hearing officer's determination be appealed?

Yes. The hearing officer's decision may be appealed to the state review officer (SRO) at the State Education Department (§ 4404(2); 8 NYCRR § 200.5(j)). However, the SRO will dismiss any appeal by a school district that is not supported by official school board action authorizing the appeal (*Board of Educ. of the Carmel CSD*, SRO dec. no. 00-004 (2001)).

Staff at the Office of State Review may schedule a telephone conference with the parties' attorneys to consider the possibility of settlement, simplify the issues, resolve procedural problems, or discuss any matters that may help expedite the appeals process. Failure to attend and participate in such a conference may result in dismissal of the petition for appeal (8 NYCRR § 279.14).

The state review officer's decision may, in turn, be appealed to the New York State Supreme Court or federal district court (20 USC § 1415(i)(2); § 4404(3); 8 NYCRR § 200.5(j)(3)).

13:42. What is the status of a student with a disability while proceedings regarding his or her classification, evaluation or academic placement take place?

With the exception of certain disciplinary proceedings, during the pendency of any proceedings challenging the classification, evaluation and placement of a student with a disability, that student must remain in his or her current educational placement unless the school district and the parent agree otherwise. This is what is referred to as the "stay-put" requirement. A student applying for initial admission to a public school must be placed in the public school program until all such proceedings have been completed (20 USC § 1415(j); 34 CFR § 300.514; Educ. Law § 4404(4); 8 NYCRR § 200.5(l); see **13:57–58**).

In a case where parents challenging their child's placement enroll the child in a private school, the private school becomes the child's stay-put placement if, on appeal, New York's State Review Officer (see **13:40**) agrees with the parents that the child's placement should be changed. In such an instance, the school district becomes financially responsible for maintaining the child at the private school during the pendency of any further appeals (*Board of Educ. of the Pawling CSD v. Schutz*, 290 F.3d 476 (2d Cir. 2002)). However, that would not be the case if the child's parents subsequently enroll the child in a new private school and there is no evidence that the educational programs of both private schools are substantially similar (*Board of Educ. of the Arlington CSD*, SRO dec. no. 02-031(2002)).

According to one federal district court in New York, the stay-put provisions do not apply during the pendency of an appeal from an order of compensatory education for a student who has aged out (see **13:10**) and is no longer otherwise eligible to receive services under the Individuals with Disabilities Education Act (*Cosgrove v. Board of Educ. of the Niskayuna CSD*, 35 IDELR 8 (N.D.N.Y. 2001)). In another ruling, a federal appellate court held that the stay-put provisions do not apply where a student relocates from one state to another, even if the student is forced to cope in regular education without supports while the parents resolve their differences with the district in the new state (*Michael C. v. Radnor Township Sch. Dist.* 202 F.3d 642 (3d Cir. 2000)).

In addition, the stay-put provisions have been found not to apply when a child's current educational placement is no longer functionally available. That was the case where a Lovass service provider who had the only state approval program that would satisfy the requirements of the student's IEP became unavailable to provide the services. In such an instance, parents and their school district remain free to agree on a new placement. Absent an agreement, a court may award relief seeking a change in placement where such a change is shown to be warranted (*Wagner v. Board of Educ. of Montgomery County*, 39 IDELR 122 (4th Cir. 2003)).

13:43. Are school districts liable for money damages when parents challenge their determination regarding their child's classification, evaluation or placement?

Not in a lawsuit brought directly under the Individuals with Disabilities Education Act (IDEA). However, parents may recover money damages if they prevail in lawsuit under Section 1983 of the Civil Rights Act of 1964 alleging a violation of IDEA (*Polera v. Board of Educ. of the Newburgh City Sch. Dist.*, 288 F.3d 478 (2d Cir. 2002)).

13:44. Are school districts liable for the cost of attorneys' fees and expert witnesses incurred by the parents of a child with a disability during an appeal of the district's determination regarding the classification, evaluation or placement of the student?

Yes, if the parents are the prevailing party on an action or proceeding (20 USC § 1415(i)(3); 34 CFR § 300.513)). However, attorneys' fees are not available to parents who file an informal state complaint review procedure (CRP) with the State Education Department instead of commencing an impartial due process hearing, which always remains an option (*Vultaggio v. Board of Educ., Smithtown CSD*, 39 IDELR 261 (2d Cir. 2003)). In addition, parents are not deemed prevailing parties entitled to attorneys' fees when they enter into a voluntary settlement of their differences with their school district, unless the agreement provides for court enforcement of the settlement. A settlement agreement that is enforceable by a court through a consent decree order also would entitle parents to attorneys' fees (*Roberson v. Giuliani*, 40 IDELR 3 (2d Cir. 2003); *J.C. v. Regional Sch. Dist. 10 Bd. of Educ.*, 278 F.3d 119 (2d Cir. 2002)).

Fees awarded must be based on rates prevailing in the community where the action or proceeding arose for the kind and quality of services furnished (20 USC § 1415(i)(3)(c); 34 CFR § 300.513(c)(1); *I.B. v New York City Dep't of Educ.*, 39 IDELR 155 (2d Cir. 2003)). Prevailing rates refer to the amount actually charged by the attorneys and not the rate a school board pays when it agrees to pay attorneys' fees (*R.E. v. NYC Board of Educ.*, 38 IDELR 66 (S.D.N.Y. 2003)).

In addition, attorneys' fees may be awarded even if their amount exceeds the cost of the settlement of a parent's claim (*Elliott v. Board of Educ. of the*

Rochester City Sch. Dist., 40 IDELR 151 (W.D.N.Y. 2003)). They may include the costs of services provided by a litigation consultant that helped the parents' attorney prepare for trial and with jury selection. Westlaw computer research charges are not recoverable (*BD v. DeBuono*, 130 F.Supp.2d 401 (S.D.N.Y. 2002)).

Attorneys' fees may not be awarded for an attorney's attendance at a CSE meeting unless it is convened as a result of an administrative proceeding or judicial action, or at the discretion of the state, for mediation that is conducted prior to the filing of a complaint (20 USC § 1415(i)(3)(D)(ii); 34 CFR § 300.513(c)(2)(ii)) According to one federal district court in New York, attorneys' fees are available if the CSE meeting is convened as a result of a parent's request for an impartial due process hearing (*F.R. and K.R. v. Board of Educ., Plainedge Public Schs.*, 31 IDELR 77 (E.D.N.Y. 1999). Attorneys' fees may not be awarded either under certain circumstances for services performed after a written offer of settlement is made to a parent (20 USC § 1415(i)(3)(D)(i), (E); 34 CFR § 300.513(c)(2)(i)). In addition, attorneys' fees may be reduced under certain circumstances (20 USC § 1415(i)(3)(F), (G); 34 CFR § 300.513(c)(4)).

Courts have refused to award attorneys' fees to pro se litigants (litigants who represent themselves) even when the litigant is an attorney (*Rappaport v. Vance*, 19 IDELR 770 (1993)). However, attorneys' fees may be awarded despite the fact that the parents were represented by a publicly-funded attorney (*Yankton Sch. Dist. v. Schramm*, 93 F.3d 1369 (1996)). In addition, attorneys' fees are not available to a lay advocate, except that a lay advocate may receive fees incurred at due process hearings as an educational consultant or as a witness (*Connors v. Mills*, 29 IDELR 946 (N.D.N.Y. 1998)).

13:45. May parents unilaterally place their child with a disability in a private school and be reimbursed by the district for the cost if they disagree with the school district's determination concerning their child?

Yes, subject to certain conditions. A parent who disagrees with a school district's placement and proceeds to enroll his or her child in a private school may be entitled to tuition reimbursement if a court or hearing officer determines that the school district did not make a free appropriate public education available to the child in a timely manner and that the private placement is appropriate (20 USC § 1412(a)(10)(C)(ii); 34 CFR § 300.403(c)).

The appropriateness of a private placement must be based on objective evidence regarding the students' performance. Least restrictive environment requirements (see **13:5**) may be considered in determining the appropriateness of the parents' private placement (*M.S. v. Board of Educ. of the City of Yonkers*, 231 F.3d 96 (2d Cir. 2000); cf. *Board of Educ. of the*

Irvington UFSD, SRO Dec. No. 01-035 (2002); *Board of Educ. of the North Salem Sch. Dist.*, SRO Dec. No. 00-056 (2001)). The parent bears the burden of proving that the private placement is appropriate (*M.S.*).

However, a court or hearing officer may deny or reduce the reimbursement if the parents failed to give the school district notice at the most recent individualized education program (IEP) meeting that they rejected the proposed placement, and stated their concerns and their intent to enroll the child in a private school at public expense, or failed to provide 10 business days (including any holidays that occur on a business day) written notice to the district prior to removing the child (20 USC § 1412(a)(10)(C)(iii)(I); 34 CFR § 300.403(d)(1); see *Berger v. Medina City Sch. Dist.*, 40 IDELR 31 (6th Cir. 2003); *Rafferty v. Cranston Pub. Sch. Comm.*, 38 IDELR 31 (1st Cir. 2002); *Pollowitz v. Weast*, 2001 U.S. App. LEXIS 6729 (4th Cir. Md. Apr. 17, 2001).

Parental notice will be excused if the parent is illiterate and cannot write English, if compliance would likely result in physical or serious emotional harm to the child, if the school prevented the parent from providing such notice or if the parents were not notified of the notice requirement (20 USC § 1412(a)(10(C)(iv); 34 CFR § 300.403(e); see *Mrs. M. v. Portland Sch. Comm.*, 40 IDELR 228 (1st Cir. 2004)).

In addition, tuition reimbursement may be reduced or denied if the school district gave the parents written notice of its intent to evaluate the child and the reasons for the evaluation prior to the parents' removal of the child, but the parents failed to make the child available for the evaluation (20 USC § 1412(a)(10)(C)(iii)(II); 34 CFR § 300.403(d)(2)). Tuition reimbursement may also be denied to parents who fail to cooperate with a school district by not allowing the district a reasonable opportunity to evaluate their child (*Patricia P. v. Board of Educ. of Oak Park and River Forest High Sch. Dist. No. 200*, 203 F.3d 462 (7th Cir. 2000)).

13:46. May parents who disagree with a school district's determination concerning their child with a disability unilaterally place their child at a private school that is not approved by the state and be reimbursed for the cost of the school?

Yes. According to the United States Supreme Court, the parents of a student with a disability may be awarded reimbursement for private school placement (see **13:45**), even if the private school does not meet state educational agency standards. Courts, however, may consider whether the private school costs are reasonable (*Florence County Sch. Dist. Four v. Carter*, 510 U.S. 7 (1993)). Further ruling that parents are not required to place their children at state-approved schools, the United States Supreme Court in *Carter* explained that parents cannot be held to the same standards as public school districts when arranging for the placement of their children.

13:47. May parents unilaterally place their child with a disability in another public school district and be reimbursed for that placement, if they disagree with the school district's determination concerning their child?

Yes. Parents may be entitled to reimbursement for tuition paid to another public school district and for reasonable transportation costs after the parents remove their child from the school district of residence because they are dissatisfied with the special education services provided to their child. However, they must establish that the district of residence failed to make a free appropriate public education available to their child in a timely manner and that their choice of placement is appropriate (*Northeast CSD v. Solo*, 79 N.Y.2d 598 (1992)).

13:48. Do parents of a child with a disability have a right to an independent educational evaluation (IEE) of their child at public expense?

Yes, if they disagree with the evaluation obtained by the school district. However, the district may initiate a hearing to show that its evaluation is appropriate or that the evaluation obtained by the parent does not meet school district criteria. If the hearing officer agrees with the school district, the parents still have a right to an IEE but not at public expense (20 USC § 1415(d)(2)(A); 34 CFR § 300.502; 8 NYCRR § 200.5(g)).

Independent educational evaluations obtained by the parent at public expense must be subject to the same criteria that the school district uses when it initiates an evaluation, including the location of the evaluation and the qualifications of the examiner (34 CFR § 300.502(e); 8 NYCRR §§ 200.1(z), 200.5(g)(1)(ii)). Such evaluations must be conducted by a qualified examiner who is not employed by the public agency responsible for the education of the student (8 NYCRR § 200.1(z)). Upper limits on the costs of particular tests may not simply be an average of fees customarily charged by professionals in the area, but must permit parents to choose from among qualified individuals in the area (*Application of a Child with a Handicapping Condition*, SRO dec. no. 92-35 (1992), 93-26 (1993)).

A school district may ask, but not require, that parents tell why they disagree with the district's evaluation (34 CFR § 300.502(b)(4); 8 NYCRR § 200.5 (g)(1)(iii)).

Disciplining Students with Disabilities

13:49. May a student with a disability be suspended or removed from school?

School districts may suspend or remove a disabled student from school in accordance with the procedures and safeguards set forth in both federal and state law and regulations (20 USC § 1415(k)(l)(A)(i); 34 CFR §§ 300.519–00.529; Educ. Law § 3214(g), 4404 (1); 8 NYCRR subpart 201).

Generally, a suspension or removal of a student with a disability constitutes a disciplinary change in placement that requires parental consent if it is for

- more than 10 consecutive school days, or
- 10 consecutive school days or less if the student is subjected to a series of suspension or removal that constitutes a pattern because they add to more than 10 school days in a school year, and because of factors such as the length of each suspension, the total amount of time the child is removed, and the proximity of the suspension to one another (34 CFR § 300.519; 8 NYCRR § 201.2(e)).

Nonetheless, a student with disabilities may be removed without parental consent to an interim alternative educational (IAES) setting for periods of up to 45 days at a time for behavior involving weapons, illegal drugs, controlled substance, or conduct which poses a risk of harm to the student or others (see **13:51**).

A school district may also impose a suspension which would otherwise result in a disciplinary change in placement if the committee on special education determines that the student's misconduct was not a manifestation of the student's disability (20 USC §§ 1415(k)(1)(A), 1415(k)(2), (5); 34 CFR §§ 300.121(d), 300.519(a), 300.520(a)(1), 300.521, 300:524, 300.506(c)(3), (4); Educ. Law §§ 3214(3)(g)(iv), (vii); 8 NYCRR §§ 201.7(e), 201.8(a), (b), (d), (f), 201.9(c)(3); see **13:55**).

Under New York law, the school district must conduct a disciplinary hearing to determine if the student is guilty of the misconduct before a suspension penalty beyond five school days can be imposed (§ 3214(3)(g)). The same applies to students presumed to have a disability for discipline purposes and to declassified students (20 USC § 1415(k)(8)(A); 34 CFR § 300.527; Educ. Law § 3214(g)(2); 8 NYCRR § 201.5); *Appeal of a Student Suspected of Having a Disability*, 35 Educ. Dep't Rep. 492 (1996); see **13:58**).

Students with disabilities attending summer school are entitled to the same discipline safeguards applicable during the regular school year (*LIH v. New York City Bd. of Educ.*, 33 IDELR 1 (E.D.N.Y. 2000).

13:50. What is an interim alternative education setting (IAES)?

An interim alternative education setting is a temporary educational placement for a period of up to 45 days, other than the student's current placement at the time the behavior precipitating the IAES occurred (8 NYCRR § 201.2(k); see **13:53** for a description of the level of services that must be provided in an IAES).

13:51. Under what circumstances may a student with disabilities be placed in an interim alternative education setting?

A superintendent of schools may place a student in an interim alternative educational setting (IAES) for the same amount of time that a child without a disability would be subject to discipline but not more than 45 days for each separate instance where:

- The child possesses a weapon in school, or at a school function.
- The child knowingly possesses or uses illegal drugs or sells or solicits the sale of a controlled substance while at school or a school function.

In addition, an impartial hearing officer may order the placement of a child in an IAES for up to 45 days at a time if the school district shows by substantial evidence that maintaining the child in his or her current placement is substantially likely to result in injury to the child or others, and that it has taken steps to minimize the risk of harm in the child's current placement (20 USC §§ 1415(k)(1)(A), 1415(k)(2); 34 CFR §§ 300.519(a), 300.521; 300.526(c)(3), (4); Educ. Law § 3214(3)(g)(iv), (vii); 8 NYCRR §§ 201.7(e), 201.8(a), (b), (d)).

A student may be placed in an IAES on grounds of dangerousness and for misconduct relating to weapons, illegal drugs or controlled substance even if the behavior triggering the placement was a manifestation of the student's disability (8 NYCRR §§ 201.9(c)(3), 201.8(f); see **13:53**).

13:52. Who determines the interim alternative educational setting for a student with disabilities being removed for misconduct involving weapons, illegal drugs or controlled substances, or on grounds of dangerousness?

The committee on special education (CSE) determines the IAES for a student removed for weapons, illegal drugs or controlled substances.

The impartial hearing officer determines the IAES for a student being removed on grounds of dangerousness based on consideration of a setting proposed by school personnel in consultation with the child's special education teacher (20 USC § 1415(k)(2)(3); 34 CFR §§ 300.521, 300.522; 8 NYCRR §§ 201.8(c), 201.10(e)).

13:53. What level of services must an appropriate interim alternative educational setting offer a student with a disability?

A student placed in an interim alternative educational (IAES) setting must receive services that enable that student to continue to participate in the general curriculum, although in another setting, and to receive services and modifications, including those in his or her current individualized education program (IEP), that will allow the child to meet the goals of the IEP. The IAES must include services and modifications designed to address the behavior so that it does not reoccur (20 USC § 1415(k)(2), (3); 34 CFR §§ 300.521, 300.522; 8 NYCRR §§ 201.8(c), 201.10(e)).

13:54. What level of services must be offered to students with disabilities during suspensions other than those involving placement in an interim alternative educational setting?

During suspensions for periods of up to 10 school days in a school year that do not constitute a disciplinary change in placement (see **13:49**), a school district must provide students with disabilities of compulsory education age with alternative instruction on the same basis as nondisabled students. With respect to students who are not of compulsory education age, a district must provide services only to the extent they are provided to nondisabled students of the same age who have been similarly suspended (8 NYCRR § 201.10(b)).

During subsequent suspensions for periods of 10 consecutive school days or less that in the aggregate total more than 10 school days in a school year but do not constitute a disciplinary change in placement (see **13:49**), students must receive services necessary to enable them to appropriately progress in the general curriculum and appropriately advance toward achieving the goals in their individualized education program (IEP). The building principal, superintendent of schools or other school official imposing the suspension, in consultation with the student's special education teacher, makes the determination regarding the extent to which services are necessary to enable the student to appropriately progress in the general curriculum and advance toward achieving the IEP goals.

The same level of services applies for students suspended in excess of 10 school days in a school year where the suspension constitutes a disciplinary change of placement for behavior determined by the committee on special education (CSE) not to be a manifestation of student's disability. However, in this last situation, it is the CSE that determines the extent to which services are necessary (34 CFR §§ 300.520(a)(1)(ii), 300.121(d); 8 NYCRR § 201.10(c), (d)).

13:55. When must a committee on special education conduct a manifestation determination of the student's behavior?

The CSE must conduct a review regarding the relationship between the child's disability and his or her behavior whenever a school district decides to place the child in an interim alternative educational setting (IAES) for one of the following reasons:

- The child's misconduct involves weapons, illegal drugs or controlled substances.
- The child's current placement in his or her current educational setting poses a risk of harm to the student or others.
- The district decides to impose a suspension that constitutes a disciplinary change in placement.

The purpose of this review is to determine whether the student's behavior is related to, or a manifestation of, his or her disability in accordance with the criteria set forth in law and regulations. If the behavior is a manifestation of the student's disability, no further disciplinary action may be taken, except placement in an IAES in cases involving weapons, illegal drugs or controlled substances, or dangerous behavior.

The CSE must conduct the manifestation determination immediately if possible, but no later than 10 days after the date on which the decision to take action is made (20 USC § 1415(k)(4)(B); 34 CFR § 300.523(a)(2), (b); Educ. Law § 4402(1)(b)(3)(j); 8 NYCRR § 201.4(a)(1), (2), (3)).

13:56. Must a committee on special education conduct a functional behavioral assessment of a student with disabilities subjected to disciplinary action?

The CSE must develop an assessment plan and conduct a functional behavioral assessment to address the student's behavior if it had not conducted such an assessment and implemented a behavioral intervention plan for the student before the behavior in question occurred. Or, if the child already has a behavioral intervention plan, the CSE must review and modify the plan, as necessary, to address the behavior.

A functional behavioral assessment involves the process of determining why a student engages in behaviors that impede learning and how the student's behavior relates to the environment (8 NYCRR § 200.1(r)).

In either case, this meeting must take place no later than 10 business days after the district first suspends the student for more than 10 school days in a school year or imposes a suspension that constitutes a disciplinary change in placement, including placement in an interim alternative educational setting for behavior involving weapons, illegal drugs, or controlled substances (20 USC § 1415(k)(1)(B); 34 CFR § 300.520(b); Educ. Law § 4402(1)(b)(3)(1); 8 NYCRR §§ 201.3, 201.2(r)).

13:57. May parents challenge the placement of their child in an interim alternative educational setting (IAES) and/or the determination of a committee on special education that the child's behavior is not a manifestation of his or her disability?

Yes, In such an instance, the school district must conduct an expedited due process hearing which must be completed within 15 business days of the district's receipt of a parental request for a hearing (8 NYCRR § 201.11(c)).

During the pendency of the hearing or appeal, the child remains in the IAES pending the outcome of the decision or until expiration of the IAES, whichever occurs first, unless the parents and the district agree otherwise (20 USC § 1415(k)(7)(A); 34 CFR § 300.526(a); 8 NYCRR § 201.11(d)).

13:58. Are the procedures that apply to the discipline of disabled students also applicable to students who have not been classified as students with disabilities?

Yes, if the student is a student presumed to have a disability for discipline purposes, i.e., the school district is deemed to have had knowledge, as defined by statute, that the child was a child with a disability before the misconduct occurred (20 USC § 1415(k)(8)(A); 34 CFR § 300.526(7); Educ. Law § 3214(g)(2); 8 NYCRR §§ 201.2(m), 201.5)).

In addition, certain due process safeguards apply to students who have been declassified but later exhibit behavioral problems (*Appeal of a Student Suspected of Having a Disability (South Country CSD)*, 35 Educ. Dep't Rep. 492 (1996)).

If a request for an individual evaluation is made on behalf of a student subject to disciplinary removal who is not presumed to have a disability for disciplinary purposes, the CSE must conduct and complete an expedited evaluation within 15 school days after receipt of the request and make an eligibility determination within five school days after completion of the expedited evaluation (20 USC § 1415(k)(8)(C); 34 CFR § 300.527 (d)(1), (2); 8 NYCRR § 200-1.6). Until that evaluation is completed, the student remains in the educational placement determined by the district, which can include suspension (20 USC § 1415(k)(8)(C)(ii); 34 CFR § 300.527(d)(1), (2)(ii); 8 NYCRR § 201.6(c)).

13:59. Are students with disabilities subject to a school district's attendance policy?

Yes. However, a school district may not apply its attendance policy to a student with disabilities in order to deny the student course credit where the absences are related to the student's disability or to a medical condition which would constitute a handicap under section 504 of the Rehabilitation

Act (*Appeal of a Child with a Handicapping Condition*, 32 Educ. Dep't Rep. 56 (1992)).

Preschool Children with Disabilities

13:60. What are school districts' responsibilities in regard to preschool special education?

School boards must adopt a written policy that establishes administrative practices and procedures to ensure that each preschool child with a disability can participate in preschool programs approved by the commissioner of education (8 NYCRR § 200.2(b)(2)). School districts, for instance, must identify, evaluate, refer, place and review the placement of preschool children (ages three and four) with disabilities, including children enrolled in Head Start programs (20 USC § 1400 *et seq.*; Educ. Law § 4410; 8 NYCRR §§ 200.2(a)(1), 200.16).

Every school board also must appoint and train qualified personnel to a committee on preschool special education (CPSE), which makes recommendations on the identification, evaluation, and appropriate services for these children (20 USC § 1413(a)(3); Educ. Law § 4410(3); 8 NYCRR §§ 200.2(b)(3), 200.3(a)(2), 200.16(b)), and ensure the allocation of appropriate space within the district for special education programs that meet the needs of preschool students with disabilities (Educ. Law § 4410; 8 NYCRR § 200.2(c)(2)(v)).

13:61. What types of services and programs must school districts provide to preschool children with disabilities?

Preschool children with disabilities are entitled, for example, to special education itinerant services, special classes in a half- or full-day program, and related services available to school-age children with disabilities (Educ. Law § 4410(1)(j), (k) 8 NYCRR §§ 200.1(nn), 200.16(h)). Special education itinerant services may be provided as part of an approved program given by a certified special education teacher in accordance with the regulations of the commissioner of education, at sites determined in the same way as for the provision of related services (§ 4410(1)(k); 8 NYCRR § 200.16(h)(3)(ii)).

Related services need not be provided in conjunction with a program at a facility approved or licensed by a government agency. They can be provided at a site determined by the school board, including, but not limited to, an approved or licensed prekindergarten or Head Start program, the work site of the provider, a hospital, a state facility, or a child-care location, including the child's home or a place where care for less than 24 hours a day is provided on a regular basis, such as day care centers, family day care homes and in-home care by persons other than parents. A preschool child with disabilities is entitled to receive services at home if the documented medical or special needs indicate the child should not be transported to another site (§ 4410(1)(j); 8 NYCRR § 200.16(h)(3)(i)).

Prior to recommending any program, the CPSE should consider the appropriateness of providing related services or special education itinerant services only, related services in coordination with special education itinerant services, and a half-day or full-day program. Special education services must be provided consistent with least restrictive environment requirements (§ 4410(5)(b)(i); 8 NYCRR § 200.16(d)). Whenever possible, school districts should select related service providers employed by a single agency (8 NYCRR § 200.16(e)(2)).

13:62. Who is responsible for coordinating the provision of related and itinerant special education services to preschool children with disabilities?

When the committee on preschool special education (CPSE) recommends two or more related services, the school board designates one of the providers as coordinator. When special education itinerant services are provided in conjunction with one or more related services, the special education itinerant service provider must serve as the coordinator (8 NYCRR § 200.16(e)(2)).

13:63. What is the difference between a committee on special education (CSE) and a committee on preschool special education (CPSE)?

Generally, the CSE addresses the needs of school-age children with disabilities, while the CPSE focuses on the needs of preschool children with disabilities. However, generally speaking, parental rights and district responsibilities governing the CSE also apply to the CPSE.

A CSE and a CPSE also are made up of different members. The CPSE must include the following members:

- The parent of the preschool child with a disability.
- A regular education teacher (if the child is, or may be, participating in the regular education environment).
- A special education teacher, or where appropriate, a special education provider of such child.
- A representative of the school district who
    (1) is qualified to provide or supervise special education;
    (2) is knowledgeable about the general curriculum; and
    (3) is knowledgeable about the availability of preschool special education programs and services and other resources of the district

and the municipality. This individual serves as the chairperson of the committee.

- A parent of a child with disabilities who resides in the district or a neighboring district and whose child is enrolled in a preschool or elementary-level education program, as long as that parent is not employed by or under contract with the school district or municipality responsible for the child. The child's parent may waive the participation of this CPSE member.
- At the discretion of the parent or the district, other individuals who have knowledge or special expertise regarding the child, including related services personnel.
- An individual who can interpret the instructional implications of evaluation results. (This individual may also be one of the above district team members or the school psychologist.)
- For a child in transition from early intervention programs and services (infant and toddler programs), the appropriate professional designated by the agency that has been charged with the responsibility for the preschool child. This professional must attend all meetings of the CPSE conducted prior to the child's initial receipt of services.

An appropriately certified or licensed professional from the municipality where the child resides should also attend; however, attendance of the appointee of the municipality is not required for a quorum of the CPSE.

Parents and the district have the right, to invite the child's evaluator to attend and participate at any CPSE meeting held to review or reevaluate the status of a preschool child (Educ. Law § 4410(3)(a), (f); 8 NYCRR § 200.3(a)(2); see **13:23**, **13:25** for the membership of the CSE). Specific responsibilities for each CSE and CPSE are set forth in the Education Law sections 4402 and 4410; and part 200 of the commissioner's regulations.

14. Instruction and Curricula

14:1. Is there an official school year for instruction?

The Education Law defines the school year as the period commencing on the first day of July in each year and ending on June 30 of the next year (§ 2(15)). However, court decisions have recognized that the normal instructional year extends from September through June (see *Schneps v. Nyquist*, 58 A.D.2d 151 (3d Dep't), *appeal denied*, 42 N.Y.2d 808 (1977); see also *Appeal of Lease*, 39 Educ. Dep't Rep. 215 (1999)).

14:2. Who determines the exact length of a school district's school year?

Local school districts determine the number of days that their schools will be in session and when personnel must report for duty. The State Education Department does not determine the local school year.

Additionally, individual school boards may divide the school year into semesters and marking periods and, following negotiation with the appropriate bargaining units, expand the number of instructional days for their districts (*City Sch. Dist. v. Helsby*, 42 A.D.2d 262 (3d Dep't 1973)).

14:3. Is there a minimum number of school days in a school year?

Yes. Section 3204(4) of the Education Law provides that school must be in session 190 days each year for instructional purposes, inclusive of legal holidays that occur during the school term and exclusive of Saturdays.

The law also requires 180 days of instruction for state aid purposes (§ 3604(7)). The financial apportionment from the state will be reduced by 1/180th for each day less than 180 days the school actually is in session. However, the commissioner of education may disregard this reduction for up to five days for certain reasons, such as adverse weather or a breakdown of school facilities, where it is demonstrated that the district cannot make up such lost days of instruction during the school year (§ 3604(7)).

Upon approval by the commissioner of education, the chancellor of the New York City Board of Education may establish an alternative school calendar pilot program with some of the 180 days of instruction taking place in July and August. Student enrollment in the program must be voluntary. Employment issues to ensure appropriate staffing are subject to collective bargaining (Laws of 2002, Ch. 75).

14:4. May school be in session during a legal holiday?

In general, no school may be in session on a Saturday or a legal holiday, except Election Day and Washington's and Lincoln's birthdays. However, driver education classes may be held on Saturdays (§ 3604(8)). Also, school authorities in a district having fewer than 600 students may provide classes for the disadvantaged on any day of the week, including Saturday and Sunday (§ 3604(8-b)).

14:5. What are the legal holidays in New York State?

Section 24 of the General Construction Law lists the following public holidays in New York:

- New Year's Day (January 1)
- Dr. Martin Luther King, Jr. Day (third Monday in January)
- Lincoln's Birthday (February 12)
- Washington's Birthday (third Monday in February)
- Memorial Day (last Monday in May)
- Flag Day (second Sunday in June)
- Independence Day (July 4)
- Labor Day (first Monday in September)
- Columbus Day (second Monday in October)
- Veterans Day (November 11)
- Thanksgiving Day (fourth Thursday in November)
- Christmas Day (December 25)

In addition, each general election day and any day appointed by the president of the United States or by the governor of New York State "as a day of general thanksgiving, general fasting and prayer, or for other general religious observances" may be declared public holidays (Gen. Constr. Law § 24). This generally has been interpreted to include Sundays.

14:6. Is there a minimum number of hours in a school day for public schools in New York State?

Yes. Section 175.5 of the commissioner's regulations lists the minimum daily session lengths for students. To qualify for apportionment of state aid, schools must be in session as follows:

- The daily sessions for students in half-day kindergarten must be a minimum of two-and-one-half hours.
- The daily sessions for students in full-day kindergarten and grades 1–6 must be a minimum of five hours, exclusive of the time allowed for lunch.
- The daily sessions for students in grades 7–12 must be a minimum of five-and-one-half hours, exclusive of the time allowed for lunch (8 NYCRR § 175.5(a)).

There is no maximum number of hours in a school day and there is no requirement in law concerning the time of day classes must be held.

14:7. Are there minimum school-day hours for schools that operate on double or overlapping (split) sessions?

To qualify for apportionment of state aid, schools that operate on double or overlapping (split) sessions, with prior written approval by the commissioner of education, must meet the following minimum-hours requirements:

- The daily sessions for students in half-day kindergarten must be a minimum of two hours.
- The daily sessions for students in full-day kindergarten and grades 1–6 must be a minimum of four hours, exclusive of the time allowed for lunch.
- The daily sessions for students in grades 7–12 must be a minimum of four-and-one-half hours, exclusive of the time allowed for lunch (8 NYCRR § 175.5(c)).

14:8. Are school districts required to offer a kindergarten program?

No. It is within the discretion of the school board to offer a kindergarten program to students between the ages of four and six. The school board may fix a higher minimum age for admission to kindergarten (§ 1712).

However, children over the age of five are entitled to attend the public schools in the district, regardless of whether or not the district maintains a kindergarten program. These children are entitled to attend first grade. A board is not required to admit a child who becomes five after the school year has commenced unless the child's birthday occurs on or before December 1 (§ 3202(1); *Appeal of Carney*, 15 Educ. Dep't Rep. 325 (1976); *Formal Opinion of Counsel 75*, 1 Educ. Dep't Rep. 775 (1952); see **12:4**)).

14:9. Are school districts required to offer a prekindergarten program?

No. It is up to each local school board to decide whether or not to offer a prekindergarten program. Some school districts qualify for the New York State Targeted Prekindergarten Program, created to provide early intervention services related to school preparation to disadvantaged or at-risk children. This program still operates in approximately 97 school districts and BOCES throughout the state.

In addition, Chapter 436 of the Laws of 1997 established a universal prekindergarten program, which serves eventually those four-year-olds who are not served by the targeted prekindergarten program or a full-day special education prekindergarten program. The program is optional at the discretion of the school board. All school districts in the state are eligible to participate (§ 3602-e).

Further information on this program may be obtained from the State Education Department's Child, Family and Community Services Team at 518-474-5807 or at http://www.nysed.gov. See also **12:7** for more specific student age eligibility requirements.

14:10. Who determines whether or not a school district will offer a prekindergarten program?

The school board is ultimately responsible for determining whether or not to offer a prekindergarten program. However, under the law, all eligible districts must form a prekindergarten policy advisory board appointed by the superintendent which must include members of the school board, teachers employed by the district as selected by their respective collective bargaining unit, parents of children who attend the district's schools, community leaders and childcare and early education providers (§ 3602-e(3), (4)).

14:11. When must an eligible school district form a prekindergarten policy advisory board?

School districts are not required to form the advisory board until the school year immediately preceding the school year in which funds will first become available to the district (Memorandum from James Kadamus, Deputy Commissioner for Elementary, Middle, Secondary and Continuing Education, State Education Department, March 1998). The commissioner of education will notify eligible districts by November 15 of each year (§ 3602-e(3), (9)).

14:12. What is the role of the prekindergarten policy advisory board?

The advisory board must recommend to the school board as to whether or not the district should offer a prekindergarten program. Prior to reaching its determination, the advisory board must hold at least one public hearing to provide an opportunity for input from parents, school personnel, childcare providers and other interested members of the community. In reaching its recommendation, the advisory board must consider a number of factors set forth in the statute (§ 3602-e(3)(b); 8 NYCRR § 151-1.8(b)).

If the advisory board determines that it will recommend the implementation of a prekindergarten program, it must develop and submit a prekindergarten program to the school board by a date determined by the commissioner of education (§ 3602-e(3)(c); 8 NYCRR § 151-1.8(a)).

14:13. Is a school board required to accept the recommendation of the prekindergarten policy advisory board?

No. The school board has 30 days from receiving such recommendation to adopt, reject or modify the recommendation and/or plan. However, if the board is considering modifying or rejecting the advisory board's recommendation and/or plan, it must hold a public meeting with the advisory board to discuss it (§ 3602-e(4)).

If the board adopts a plan to implement a prekindergarten program, it must submit an application pursuant to the rules and regulations of the Board of Regents and the commissioner of education (§ 3602-e(5); 8 NYCRR Subpart 151-1).

14:14. Can a school district offer a "summer only" universal prekindergarten program?

Yes. A school district may operate a summer-only prekindergarten program during July and August, but only when the commissioner finds the district is unable to operate the program during the regular school session because of a lack of available space in both district buildings and eligible agencies. The district must demonstrate that it made diligent efforts to identify, recruit, and collaborate with eligible agencies during the regular school session and was unable to operate the program during the regular school session (8 NYCRR §§ 151-1.4 (d), 151-1.8 (19) see **12:7** for information on student age eligibility requirements).

14:15. Must school districts provide programs for the education of gifted and talented students?

No, there is no state mandate requiring that such education be provided. However, article 90 of the Education Law and part 142 of the commissioner's regulations contain guidelines for the education of gifted and talented students in districts that provide this kind of education. Additionally, the commissioner's regulations provide for screening of students entering the public schools for gifted abilities, as well as for disabilities and limited English proficiency, and require a student identified as possibly gifted to be reported to the superintendent no later than 15 calendar days after completion of the screening (8 NYCRR § 117.3(c)(3), (f)). Beyond these requisites, school districts have considerable discretion as to the scope and content of programs for gifted and talented students.

To identify gifted students and determine their eligibility to participate in a gifted program, a school district may provide for diagnostic tests or other evaluation mechanisms related to the program objectives of the district. Students may be referred for participation in a gifted program by, for example, a parent or a teacher (§ 4452; *Appeal of Pfeffer*, 38 Educ. Dep't Rep. 514 (1999)).

In the event a school district offers a gifted program, it must obtain the consent of a student's parents before conducting any tests or evaluations to determine the student's eligibility for the program. If the parents do not grant their consent, the child may not be tested or evaluated and may not participate in the program. In addition, the district may not impose a fee for the administration of such tests or evaluations (§ 4452(1)(e)).

14:16. What is the definition of a gifted student?

The Education Law establishes criteria for identifying gifted students, which include, for example, "high performance capability" and "exceptional potential in [specified] areas." The criteria encompass students "who require educational programs . . . beyond those normally provided by the regular school program in order to realize their full potential" (§§ 3602-c(1)(b), 4452(1)(a); 8 NYCRR § 142.2; *Appeal of Pfeffer*, 38 Educ. Dep't Rep. 514 (1999)).

14:17. Must a school district accept nonpublic school students into its gifted program?

Yes. A school district that offers a gifted program must accept nonresident students attending a private school located within its boundaries, upon the request of the student's parent, as long as the student is a New York State resident. The parent's request must be filed with the school board of the school district of residence by June 1 of the preceding year (*Appeal of Pfeffer*, 38 Educ. Dep't Rep. 514 (1999); see *Appeal of Goodman*, 38 Educ. Dep't Rep. 824 (1999)).

14:18. Can a high school principal or guidance director prevent a student from taking a high school course because, in that person's judgment, the student could not pass the course?

Ordinarily, no. School authorities do not have the legal authority to prevent students from taking a specific subject when the students maintained passing grades in any earlier courses that may be viewed as prerequisites. The commissioner of education has held, however, that a school board may require completion of a certain curriculum in order for a student to be eligible for admission to a BOCES vocational program (*Matter of Tripi*, 21 Educ. Dep't Rep. 349 (1981); *Appeal of a Student Suspected of Having a Disability (Rockville Center CSD)*, 41 Educ. Dep't Rep. 329 (2002)).

Also, no legal basis exists for denying a student admission to a particular subject course on the basis of test results, other than tests for preceding courses. However, a district may apply reasonable criteria for selection to honors classes including, for example, teacher recommendations, standardized test scores, IQ scores and course grades (*Appeal of Dawn H.*, 39 Educ. Dep't Rep. 635 (2000); *Appeal of Julio I*, 39 Educ. Dep't Rep. 509 (2000)).

14:19. May students be excused from courses or lessons that conflict with the religion of their parents or guardian?

Students may be excused from courses or lessons only in accordance with the rules and regulations of the Board of Regents and the commissioner's regulations.

A student may be excused, consistent with the requirements of public education and public health, from any study of health and hygiene that conflicts with the religion of his or her parents or guardian. While the Education Law and the Regents Rules specifically require parents to submit a petition certified by a proper representative as defined by section 2 of the Religious Corporation Law, this requirement has been determined in another context to be unconstitutional (§ 3204(5); 8 NYCRR § 16.2; see generally *Sherr v. Northport-East Northport UFSD*, 672 F.Supp. 81 (E.D.N.Y. 1987); *Lewis v. Sobol*, 710 F.Supp. 506 (S.D.N.Y. 1989)).

Students also may be excused from instruction on AIDS prevention if the parent or guardian has file a written request with the school principal, in which the parent agrees that the student will receive AIDS instruction at home (8 NYCRR § 135.3(b)(2); see *also Ware v. Valley Stream High Sch. Dist.*, 75 N.Y.2d 114 (1989)).

However, mere exposure to courses and lessons with which someone disagrees does not burden a person's right to the free exercise of religion, and is not a violation of the Free Exercise Clause of the First Amendment of the United States Constitution (*Mozert v. Hawkins County Bd. of Educ.*, 827 F.2d 1058 (6th Cir. 1987), *cert. denied*, 484 U.S. 1066 (1988)). Parents do not have a right to tell a school what their children "will and will not be taught" (*Leebaert v. Harrington*, 332 F.3d 134 (2d Cir. 2003); see **12:2, 23:3**).

14:20. Can districts limit student participation in academic programs and other school activities on the basis of sex?

No. Title IX of the Federal Educational Amendment of 1972 (20 USC § 1681 *et seq.*) and its related regulations forbid sexual discrimination in any activity or program receiving federal funds, including all of the operations of a local educational agency, vocational school system or any other type of school system that receives federal aid (see 20 USC § 1687).

Likewise, the Education Law and commissioner's regulations prohibit school districts from denying membership or participation in any school program or activity not only on the basis of sex, but also on the basis of race, marital status, color, religion, national origin or disability (§§ 313, 3201, 3201-a). However, in the case of students with disabilities, the activity must be appropriate to a student's special educational needs (8 NYCRR § 200.2(b)(1)).

14:21. Can school districts limit student participation in interscholastic sports on the basis of sex?

No. With respect to school athletes, courts generally apply a three-part test to assess whether an institution is violating Title IX of the Federal Education Amendments of 1972 (20 USC § 1681 *et seq.*; see **14:20**) in the area of interscholastic sports by failing to effectively "accommodate" the interests and abilities of members of both sexes. A school district need only pass one part to be in compliance. The three parts are:

1. Whether interscholastic level participation opportunities for male and female students are provided in numbers substantially proportionate to their respective enrollments.
2. Where the members of one sex have been and are underrepresented among interscholastic athletes, whether the institution can show a history and continuing practice of program expansion that is demonstrably responsive to the developing interests and abilities of the members of that sex.
3. Where the members of one sex are underrepresented among interscholastic athletes, and the institution cannot show a history and continuing practice of program expansion as described above, whether the district can demonstrate that the interest and abilities of the members of that sex have been fully and effectively accommodated by the present program (44 Fed. Reg. § 71,413 *et seq.*; "Clarification of Intercollegiate Athletics Policy Guidance: The Three-Part Test," U.S. Department of Education (1996); see also "Further Clarification of Intercollegiate Athletics Policy Guidance Regarding Title IX Compliance", U.S. Department of Education (2003)).

However, in a case that departed from traditional "accommodations" claims, the U.S. Court of Appeals for the Second Circuit ruled that two New York State school districts violated the "equal treatment" provisions of Title IX by scheduling girls' high school soccer in the spring, thereby depriving its participants of the opportunity to compete in the state and regional interscholastic championship games, held in the fall. Meanwhile, the district scheduled boys' soccer in the fall, thereby affording its participants the opportunity to engage in championship competition. According to the court, "[s]cheduling the girls' soccer season out of the championship game season sends a message to the girls on the team that they are not expected to succeed and that the school does not value their athletic abilities as much as it values the abilities of the boys." However, the court stopped short of ruling that scheduling girls' soccer in the spring always will violate Title IX, holding that another district may be able to justify such a scheduling decision if it can provide adequate non-discriminatory reasons for its decision (*McCormick ex rel. McCormick v. Sch Dist. of Mamaroneck*, 307 F.3d 275 (2d Cir. 2004)).

In addition, New York's Education Law provides students may not be disqualified from athletic teams by reason of their sex, except pursuant to the commissioner's regulations (§ 3201-a). The commissioner's regulations require boys and girls be given equal opportunity to participate in interscholastic competition, either on separate teams or in mixed competition. When a school provides separate teams, the superintendent of schools may permit girls to participate on boys' teams. However, when a school provides a team for girls, the superintendent can determine whether to allow one or more boys to participate on the girls' team, based on whether such participation would have a significantly adverse effect on the opportunity for girls to participate successfully in interscholastic competition (8 NYCRR § 135.4(c)(7)(ii)(c)(4); *Lantz v. Ambach*, 620 F.Supp. 663 (S.D.N.Y. 1985); *Appeal of Martin*, 38 Educ. Dep't Rep. 130 (1998)).

14:22. Can districts limit student participation in academic programs and other school activities on the basis of sexual orientation?

No. Both the Education and Executive Laws provide protection against discrimination based on sexual orientation (Educ. Law § 313; Exec. Law § 291 *et seq.*), The term sexual orientation means "heterosexuality, homosexuality, bisexuality, or asexuality both actual and perceived" (Exec. Law § 292(27)). A student is protected from such discrimination in admission policies and access to educational programs.

Curriculum

14:23. Are there state-mandated learning standards?

Yes. The term *learning standards* refers to the level of "knowledge, skills, and understandings that individuals can and do habitually demonstrate over time as a consequence of instruction and experience" adopted by the Board of Regents and set forth in commissioner's regulations (8 NYCRR § 100.1(t)).

The learning standards are organized into seven general curriculum areas, including English/language arts (8 NYCRR § 100.1(t)(1)(i)), mathematics, science and technology (8 NYCRR § 100.1(t)(1)(ii), social studies (8 NYCRR § 100.1(t)(1)(iii)), languages other than English (8 NYCRR § 100.1(t)(1)(iv)), the arts (8 NYCRR § 100.1(t)(1)(v)), health and physical education, and family and consumer sciences (8 NYCRR § 100.1(t)(1)(vi)), and career development and occupational studies (8 NYCRR § 100.1(t)(1)(vii)).

In the area of mathematics and science, the learning standards require, for example, that students be able to use "mathematical analysis, scientific inquiry and engineering design, as appropriate, to pose questions, seek answers and develop solutions" (8 NYCRR § 100.1(t)(1)(ii)(a)). Students must also understand the relationships and common themes that connect mathematics, science and technology and apply these themes to other areas of learning (8 NYCRR § 100.1(t)(1)(ii)(f)). Regarding English/language arts, students will, for example, "listen, speak, read and write for information and understanding, . . . for critical analysis and evaluation, and for social interaction" (8 NYCRR § 100.1(t)(1)(i)(a), (c), (d)).

The learning standards in each of the seven general curriculum areas are further organized into four levels. These include the elementary or elementary-level state learning standards which encompass the knowledge, skills, and understandings all students are expected to know and be able to do by the end of grade four; the intermediate or intermediate-level learning standards applicable through the end of grade eight; the commencement or commencement-level standards for a high school diploma; and the alternate performance level for students with disabilities who have limited cognitive abilities combined with behavioral and/or physical limitations, and who require highly specialized education and services (8 NYCRR § 100.1(t)(2)).

School boards, however, are empowered to authorize the general courses of study offered in the schools, provided the course requirements are not arbitrary, capricious nor unreasonable, and do not supplant the state-mandated minimum requirements (*Appeal of O'Neill*, 29 Educ. Dep't Rep. 297 (1990); see **14:25–32**). The authority of school boards to determine what instructional programs will be offered is not subject to a public vote (*Appeal of Brush*, 34 Educ. Dep't Rep 273 (1994)).

Consistent with the federal No Child Left Behind Act of 2001 (NCLB), the learning standards apply to all public elementary and secondary school students (20 USC §§ 6301(1), (6), 6311(b)(1)). The standards may be subject to change in the future as New York continues to take steps to ensure compliance with the NCLB.

14:24. Do the learning standards apply to students with disabilities?

Yes. Students with disabilities entering the ninth grade after the 2001–02 school year will be held to the same learning standards as nondisabled students. Students with disabilities and nondisabled students alike must pass the required courses based on the state's commencement level of standards and take the required Regents examinations.

However, students with disabilities who entered ninth grade prior to September 2010, and do not pass a required Regents examination may take the Regents Competency Test in that subject (8 NYCRR § 100.5(a)(3), (5)(i), (b)(3), (c)(3), (d)(3), (e)(3); see "Extension of the RCT Safety Net for Students with Disabilities," NY State Education Department (October 2003)). Certain students with disabilities may be eligible to take the state's alternate assessment instead (see **14:73**).

In addition, a student with a disability that adversely affects the ability to learn a language may be excused from the foreign language requirements if the student's individualized education program indicates that such instruction would not be appropriate to the student's special educational needs. The student must still meet the requirements for the total number of credits required for a high school diploma (8 NYCRR § 100.5(b)(2)(ii)(b)), 100.5(b)(7)(iv)(g), (vi)).

School districts may continue to award high school individualized education program diplomas to a student with a disability, pursuant to section 200.1(mm) of the commissioner's regulations. However, students with disabilities must first be provided with appropriate opportunities to earn a high school diploma in accordance with section 100.5 of the commissioner's regulations (8 NYCRR § 100.9)).

14:25. What are the program requirements for prekindergarten and kindergarten students?

Each school operating a prekindergarten and kindergarten program must provide an education program based on and adapted to the ages, interests and needs of the children. Required learning activities in such programs include development of communication skills and exposure to literature; dramatic play, creative art, and music activities; participation in group projects, discussion and games; science and mathematical experiences; large-muscle activities in prekindergarten and instruction in physical education in kindergarten; and instruction in health education for students in kindergarten (8 NYCRR § 100.3(a)(1)).

In addition, each school operating a prekindergarten and/or kindergarten program must establish and provide an early literacy program based on and adapted to the needs, ages, and interests of the students. The elements of the program must include, but are not limited to, the use of reading to obtain meaning from print; frequent, intensive opportunities to read for learning and pleasure; activities that teach regular spelling-sound relationships; learning about the nature of the alphabetic writing system; and understanding the structure of spoken words (8 NYCRR § 100.3(a)(2)).

School districts must also develop procedures that invite the active participation of each child's parents or guardians in these programs (8 NYCRR § 100.3(a)(3)).

14:26. What are the program requirements for students in grades 1–6?

All students in grades one through six must receive instruction in:
- Mathematics, including arithmetic, science, and technology.
- English/language arts.
- Social studies, including geography and United States history.
- Languages other than English.
- The arts, including visual arts, music, dance, and theatre.
- Career development and occupational studies.
- Health education, physical education, and family and consumer sciences.

If student need is established, bilingual education and/or English as a second language instruction must also be provided (8 NYCRR § 100.3(b)).

14:27. What are the program requirements for students in grades 7 and 8?

By the end of the eighth grade, students must complete the following:
- Two units of study each in English language arts, social studies, science, and mathematics.
- One unit of study in technology education.
- Three-quarters of a unit in home and career skills.
- One-half unit of study in health education.
- Physical education (not less than three times per week in one semester and two times per week in the other semester).
- One-half unit study in the visual arts and one-half unit in music.
- The equivalent of one period a week in library and information skills.
- Instruction in career development and occupational studies (8 NYCRR § 100.4; see **14:36** for foreign language requirements).

A unit of study consists of at least 180 minutes of instruction per week throughout the school year or its equivalent (8 NYCRR § 100.1(a)).

Students who have been determined to need academic intervention services may have the unit of study requirements for one or more subjects reduced by the principal, if certain criteria specified in the commissioner's regulations have been met (8 NYCRR § 100.4(b)(4); see **14:76–83** for a more detailed discussion of academic intervention services).

14:28. May students in grade 8 take high school-level courses?

Yes, provided that the superintendent has determined that the eighth-grade student demonstrates readiness in each subject to be taken at the high school level. The district must provide eighth-grade students the opportunity to take high school courses in mathematics and at least one of the following: English, social studies, languages other than English, art, music, career and technical education, or science. Eighth-grade students may be awarded credit for such a course only if they meet one of the following conditions:

- Attend the class in a high school with high school students and pass the course on the same basis as the high school students, and credit is awarded by the high school.
- Pass the course and the applicable state proficiency examination or Regents examination, credit for which must be accepted as transfer credit by all registered New York State high schools.
- If no state proficiency examination or other appropriate assessment is available, pass a course that has been approved for high school credit by the district superintendent, or his designee, of the district where the middle, junior, or intermediate school, and high school are located.

To receive high school credit for the course, the student must pass the applicable Regents or state proficiency examination, or if no such examination is available for the course, the student must pass a locally developed examination, which establishes student performance at a high school level, as determined by the principal (8 NYCRR § 100.4(c)).

14:29. What program requirements must students in grades 9–12 complete to receive a high diploma?

Program requirements for a diploma depend upon the year in which a student first enters grade 9. However, a student who completes the diploma requirements in less than four years is subject to the diploma requirements applicable to students who entered grade nine four years prior to the school year in which the accelerated diploma will be awarded. Moreover, an accelerated diploma student graduating at the end of the fall semester is subject to the diploma requirements in effect for the preceding school year (8 NYCRR § 100.5(a), (e)).

Students entering ninth grade before the 2001–02 school year — All students who entered ninth grade prior to the 2001–02 school year are required to earn 18.5 units of credit for either a local or Regents diploma (8 NYCRR § 100.5(a)(2)). Core requirements for both diplomas include four units of credit in English, four units of social studies (including one unit in American history and one half unit each in government participation and economics or their equivalent), two units of science, two units of mathematics, one-half unit of health education and one unit of art and/or music (8 NYCRR § 100.5(a)(2), (6), (7), (8)). For a local diploma, the balance of units will be met through electives taken to fulfill sequence requirements (8 NYCRR § 100.5(c)(2)). For a Regents diploma, students must complete three units of a second language in addition to sequence requirements (8 NYCRR § 100.5(b)(2)(i), (ii)). All students must earn the equivalent of two units of physical education, which do not count toward the required units of credit (8 NYCRR § 100.5(a)(4); see **14:36** for foreign language requirements). Therefore, a student will need to earn 20.5 credits in order to graduate (18.5 academic credits and 2 physical education credits).

Students entering ninth grade in and after the 2001–02 school year — Core requirements for a Regents or local high school diploma applicable to students first entering grade nine in the 2001–02 but prior to the 2005–06 school year school year include 22 credits broken down as follows:

- Four units of credit in English.
- Four units of social studies (including one unit of American history, one half unit of participation in government, and one-half unit of economics or an equivalent course).
- Three units of science (at least one unit must be life sciences, at least one in physical sciences, and the third may be in either life or physical sciences).
- Three units of mathematics.
- One unit of visual arts and/or music, dance, or theatre.
- One-half unit of health education (8 NYCRR §§ 100.5(a)(3)).

All students must earn the equivalent of two units of physical education, which count toward the required total of credits (8 NYCRR § 100.5 (a)(4)). All students must attain state learning standards in parenting skills through either the health or family and consumer sciences programs or a separate course (8 NYCRR § 100.5(a)(3)(vi); see **14:58**). In addition to the core requirements, a student must complete one unit of commencement-level credit in a language other than English, which can be earned by passing the "second language proficiency" (SLP) examination and additional units to total 22 units of credit (8 NYCRR §§ 100.2(d), 100.5(b)(7)(iv)(g), (iv)(i)).

Students entering ninth grade in and after the 2005–06 school year — Local diplomas will not be available for students entering ninth grade in or after the 2005–06 school year (8 NYCRR §§ 100.5(a)(3), § 100.5(b)(7)). The only diplomas available to them will be a Regents diploma, a Regents diploma with advanced designation, a state high school equivalency diploma, or a high school individualized education program diploma available to students with disabilities in accordance with the commissioner's regulations (8 NYCRR §§ 100.5(b)(7), 100.7, 100.9).

14:30. What are the program requirements for a Regents diploma with advanced designation?

A student may obtain a Regents diploma with an advanced designation by completing the requirements for the Regents diploma, completing two additional foreign language units and the Regents comprehensive assessment in that language and passing additional Regents math and science examinations. The student must pass the Regents Mathematics A and Mathematics B exams or the three Regents exams for Course I, Course II, and Course III, or the Regents exam for Mathematics A and Course III. One of the two Regents science exams required for a Regents diploma with advanced designation must be in life science, and the other in physical science (8 NYCRR § 100.5(b)(7)(v)).

14:31. May a school district award a unit of credit to a high school student who has not taken a course but passes the Regents examination in that subject?

It depends. Generally, a unit of credit is earned by mastery of the learning outcomes for a given subject after completing a unit of study that consists of at least 180 minutes of instruction per week throughout a school year (8 NYCRR § 100.1(b)(1)). Passing a Regents exam in any given subject will not be construed as having earned a unit of credit in that subject unless the student also passes the course as offered in a registered high school (8 NYCRR § 100.5(a)(5)(v)).

However, a student may earn up to six and one half units of credit toward a Regents or local diploma without taking a course if the student scores at least 85 or its equivalent on a Regents exam or state-approved examination, and successfully completes either an oral exam or a special project that shows proficiency in such knowledge, skills, and abilities normally developed in the course but not measured by the relevant Regents exam or state-approved test, as determined by the principal (8 NYCRR §§ 100.1(b)(2), 100.5(a)(5)(v), (d)(1)(ii), (iii)). A student is eligible to earn credit for examination only if the superintendent of schools or the chief administrative officer of a registered nonpublic school determines that, based on the student's past academic performance, the student will benefit academically from this alternative. In addition, the student must attend school, or receive substantially equivalent instruction elsewhere until age 16 as required by the compulsory education law (8 NYCRR §§ 100.1(b)(2), 100.5(d)(1)(i), (iv)).

For more information on Regents examinations and other state assessments, see **14:65–75.**

14:32. May school districts establish curriculum requirements for a diploma above and beyond the minimum units of credit required by the state for graduation?

Yes. School districts may impose, as part of a credit-bearing course of study, requirements that exceed the state's minimum requirements, provided the additional requirements are not arbitrary, capricious, or unreasonable (*Appeal of O'Neill*, 29 Educ. Dep't Rep. 297 (1990)).

For example, in *Immediato v. Rye Neck CSD*, 73 F.3d 454 (2d Cir. 1996), *cert. denied*, 519 U.S. 813 (1996)), the United States Court of Appeals for the Second Circuit upheld a district's community service program which required students to complete 40 hours of community service sometime during their four high-school years and to participate in corresponding classroom discussion about their service in order to earn a high school diploma. The program had no exceptions or opt-out provisions for students who objected to performing community service. The court recognized the district's interest in teaching students the values and habits of good citizenship, and introducing them to their social responsibilities as citizens.

The commissioner of education had reached a similar conclusion previously in *O'Neill*. However, the *Immediato* court cautioned that if students were required to wash their teachers' cars, paint their houses or weed their gardens, the extent, nature, and conditions of "service" and the more exploitive purpose of the program might warrant a finding of involuntary servitude in violation of the 13th Amendment of the United States Constitution.

14:33. What authority does the State Education Department hold over the local school district in the matter of curriculum?

Before a district is entitled to receive state aid, the commissioner of education must be satisfied that proper instruction is given by qualified teachers for the required time (§ 3604(7)).

The Rules of the Board of Regents also state that no school district will receive any apportionment unless it submits all required reports, maintains an approved course of study, provides a school building and site that are in conformity with the Education Law, the commissioner's regulations and the Regents' rules, and meets all other requirements of law (8 NYCRR § 3.35). Lack of compliance also may result in loss of a school's charter or registration.

Under the federal No Child Left Behind Act (NCLB) of 2001, each state receiving Title I assistance must assist school districts in developing or identifying "high-quality effective curricula aligned with state academic achievement standards," and must disseminate such curricula to each school district and school (20 USC § 6311(b)(8)(D)). Each school district receiving

Title I grants must adopt "high quality" curriculum content and student academic achievement standards and assessments which meet all Title I criteria and are applicable to all students served by each school district (20 USC §§ 6311(b)(5)(B), 6312(c)(1)(O)), 6315(c)(1)(C)(ii); 34 CFR § 200.1).

In addition, if a school is identified as in need of corrective action (see **14:99**), a school district must take at least one specified corrective action, which may include instituting and fully implementing a new curriculum (20 USC § 6316 (b)(7)(C)). Similarly, if the State Education Department (SED) takes corrective action with regard to a school district (see **14:105**), it may institute and fully implement a new curriculum based on state and local academic content and achievement standards (20 USC § 6316(c)(10)(C)(ii)).

14:34. Are public schools required to follow specific state syllabi?

Generally no, although the commissioner's regulations recommend the use of a state syllabus where available (8 NYCRR § 100.2(b)). However, schools must make use of state syllabi in certain circumstances in mathematics, science, and occupational education in grades 9–12 (8 NYCRR §§ 100.5(a)(7), (8), 100.5(b)(6), 100.5(d)(3)(ii)).

In addition, the use of state syllabi may be required for individual schools identified as requiring academic progress or in need of improvement based on student performance in state assessments and other factors set forth in the commissioner's regulations (8 NYCRR §§ 100.2(b), (m)(3), 100.2(p)(9); (see also **14:89–107**).

For further information on state syllabi, contact the Office of Curriculum and Instruction, Education Building Annex Room 681, State Education Department, Albany, N.Y. 12234.

14:35. Are there any legal requirements concerning homework in the instructional programs of schools?

No. Although homework generally is considered an important part of a student's education because of the knowledge of subject matter gained, the reinforcement of school learning and the development of independent thinking and good work habits, there are no state requirements concerning the assignment or completion of homework by students. A school board may establish a policy providing that homework be assigned to students for the purpose of reinforcing, preparing, supplementing, and reviewing concepts that have been or will be taught (see, e.g., *Appeal of Human*, 36 Educ. Dep't Rep. 351 (1997)).

A school board also may adopt a policy that subjects students to a required summer reading program from a designated list as long as the books to be used as part of the mandatory assignment are reasonably available to all students. Although a district may require that students demonstrate understanding of the books they read over the summer during the first weeks of school, it may not ask students to submit written assignments upon their return to school (*Appeal of Lahm*, 41 Educ. Dep't Rep. 193 (2002)).

14:36. Are school districts required to provide instruction in a language other than English?

Yes. Public school students are required to complete two units of study in a language other than English (LOTE) by the end of ninth grade. At least one unit of study must be in the same language. Public school districts may start LOTE instruction at any grade level but must do so no later than the beginning of eighth grade so that students are provided the required two units of study by the end of ninth grade. Students who pass an approved proficiency examination by the end of the ninth grade will be awarded the first unit of academic credit in LOTE instruction (8 NYCRR § 100.2(d)).

For students entering ninth grade in and after 2001–02, a Regents diploma requires one unit of commencement-level credit in a language other than English, which can be earned by passing the state "second language proficiency" (SLP) examination (8 NYCRR §§ 100.2(d), 100.5(b)(7)(iv)(g)).

A student with a disability that adversely affects the ability to learn a language may be exempted from these requirements by his or her individualized education program (IEP) (8 NYCRR §§ 100.2 (d)(1)(iii), 100.5(b)(7)(iv)(g); for more information about LOTE requirements, see "Languages Other Than English (LOTE) Part 100 Q & A," NY State Education Department (March 2001), available at http://www.emsc.nysed.gov/part100/pages/policyq&alote.htm).

14:37. Must school districts provide bilingual education or English as a second language (ESL) programs?

No. However, every district must screen all new students for proficiency in the English language as part of their overall diagnostic evaluation (8 NYCRR §§ 117.2(b), 117.3).

Furthermore, school districts must have a policy setting forth how limited English proficient (LEP) students will be educated (§ 3204(2-a); 8 NYCRR § 154.3). This policy must include:

- The district's philosophy for the education of LEP students.
- Administrative practices and procedures to screen students diagnostically for LEP, to identify LEP students and to evaluate each such student annually, including his or her performance in content areas to measure academic progress.

- An assurance of access to appropriate instructional and support services for such students, including guidance programs.
- An assurance that each LEP student has equal opportunities to participate in all school programs and extracurricular activities as non-LEP students.
- A description of the nature and scope of the instructional programs and services currently available to LEP students to help them acquire English proficiency (8 NYCRR § 154.3(a)).

School districts must provide a written copy of the policy to the commissioner of education, along with reports by building principals on those students initially identified as being limited English proficient and the number of LEP students served in the preceding school year, the number of students annually evaluated as being limited English proficient in the preceding school year; the number and qualifications of teachers and support personnel providing services to LEP students, and a description of the curricular and extracurricular services provided to LEP students (8 NYCRR § 154.3(b)). For information pertaining to state aid for LEP programs, see **21:12.**

In addition, under the federal No Child Left Behind Act of 2001 (NCLB), school districts receiving Title I funds must provide all LEP students with an annual assessment of English proficiency which measures such students' oral language, reading, and writing skills in English (20 USC § 6311 (b)(7)). New York's annual assessment of English proficiency is the New York State English as a Second Language Achievement Test (NYSESLAT).

Academic intervention services provided pursuant to part 100 of the commissioner's regulations to LEP students must supplement and may not replace those services provided pursuant to part 154 of the commissioner's regulations (8 NYCRR § 100.1(g); see **14:76–83** for more information on academic intervention services).

14:38. Are school districts required to notify parents if their child is given language instruction to attain English proficiency?

Commissioner's regulations and the federal No Child Left Behind Act of 2001 require that each school district using Title I or Title III funds to provide a language instruction educational program to limited English proficient (LEP) students, must, no later than 30 days after the beginning of the school year, inform the parents of such student that he or she has been identified for participation in such a program (20 USC § 6312(g)(1); 8 NYCRR § 154.4(g)). The notice must state:

- the reasons for the identification of their child as LEP and in need of placement in the program;

- the student's level of English proficiency, how such level was assessed, and the status of the student's academic achievement;
- the method of instruction used in the program, and the methods of instruction used in other available programs, including how such programs differ in content, instruction goals, and use of English and a native language in instruction;
- how the program in which their child is participating will meet his or her educational strengths and needs;
- how the program will specifically help their child learn English, and meet age-appropriate academic achievement standards for grade promotion and graduation;
- for high schools: the specific exit requirements for the program, the expected rate of transition from the program into classrooms that are not tailored for limited English proficient children; and
- in the case of a student with a disability, how the program meets the objectives of the student's individualized education program (20 USC § 6312(g)(1)(A)).

The parents must also be notified of their rights to decline to enroll their child in an instructional bilingual education program, to have the child immediately removed from such program upon their request, or to choose another program or method of instruction such as a free-standing English as a second language program, if available. If a district offers more than one program or method of LEP instruction, it must assist parents in choosing one. LEP students in a school building that does not offer bilingual education may transfer to another district school that does (20 USC § 7012(a); 20 USC § 6312(g)(1)(A)(viii); 8 NYCRR § 154.4(g)(2)).

In addition, if the school district has failed to make progress on the annual measurable achievement objectives for LEP students (see **14:94**), the district must separately inform the parents of LEP students identified for participation, or participating in such program, of such failure no later than 30 days after such failure occurs (20 USC § 7012(b), 20 USC § 6312(g)(1)(B)).

All notices to parents of LEP students must be provided in an understandable and uniform format and in English and a language that the parent can understand (20 USC § 7012(c), 20 USC § 6312(g)(2); 8 NYCRR § 154.4(g)(1)).

For students who are identified for participation in a LEP program after the beginning of the school year, school districts must provide this notice to the students' parents within two weeks of the student child being placed in such program (20 USC § 7012(d), 20 USC § 6312(g)(3)). Parents of new entrants must be provided with an orientation session (8 NYCRR § 154(g)(4)).

For further information on this subject and other NCLB requirements see *Leaving No Child Behind in New York, 2nd Edition*, a handbook published by the New York State School Boards Association and distributed by LexisNexis.

14:39. Must students take physical education?

Yes. Education Law and the commissioner's regulations require that all students receive physical training as part of the required course of study each year they attend school, from kindergarten through grade 12 (§§ 803, 3204(3)(a)(1); 8 NYCRR § 135.4; however, see **14:41** for alternatives to regularly scheduled physical education classes). The commissioner's regulations specify that the frequency of such required physical education classes varies based on grade level (8 NYCRR § 135.4(c)(2)).

Students who are temporarily or permanently unable to participate in the regular physical education program must be provided with adapted activities that meet the needs of the particular student. A certified physical education teacher must teach adaptive physical education programs (8 NYCRR § 135.4 (c)(1)(iv)). Teaching assistants may teach adaptive physical education provided that they are under the general supervision of a certified teacher (*Appeal of Branschback*, 38 Educ. Dep't Rep. 493 (1999)). Temporary or short-term adaptations should be made by the physical education teacher in consultation with appropriate medical personnel. Permanent or long-term program adaptations should be based on the recommendation of the student's family physician.

Students classified by the committee on special education may not be able to participate safely or successfully in the activities of the regular physical education program and must be provided with adaptive physical education. A written individualized education program (IEP) must include a prescriptive physical education program for a student in need of special education. The physical education teacher should be involved in the development of the IEP (8 NYCRR § 200.4(d)(2)(vii)(c); see also **chapter 13**).

14:40. Is physical education required for a high school diploma?

Yes. Two units of physical education will be required as part of the 22 core credits required for a high school diploma, for students entering ninth grade in the 2001–02 school year and thereafter (8 NYCRR § 100.5(a)(3)).

For students who entered ninth grade prior to 2001–02, the two units of physical education required are in addition to the 18.5 credits required for a diploma (8 NYCRR § 100.5(a)(4)).

A student who graduates in fewer than eight semesters is not required to continue enrollment in high school for the sole purpose of completing the physical education requirement. However, he or she must have fulfilled the physical education requirement successfully each semester up to that time (8 NYCRR § 100.5 (a)(4)).

If a student does not meet the physical education requirement, he or she should be given an incomplete until the requirement is fulfilled. A school district should offer reasonable makeup opportunities to complete the requirement. Students may not be dropped from their regular physical education program (8 NYCRR § 135.4(c)(3)).

14:41. May districts offer their students alternatives to regularly scheduled physical education classes?

Yes. Districts may offer such alternatives only to students in grades 7–12. Students in grades 10–12, for example, may be permitted to use an "extra-class" athletic program for physical education credit. However, before using this option, students must demonstrate they have achieved acceptable levels of physical fitness and have acquired the skills and knowledge of physical education instructional activities (8 NYCRR § 135.4(c)(2)(ii)(c)). Once the extra-class athletic program has ceased, the students must return to class. Program options other than those set forth in the commissioner's regulations must be approved by the commissioner of education (8 NYCRR § 135.4(c)(2)(i)(b), (ii) (e)).

14:42. Are school districts required to provide instruction on acquired immune deficiency syndrome (AIDS)?

Yes. Section 135.3 of the commissioner's regulations includes provisions for mandated instruction about AIDS in kindergarten through 12th grade. This instruction must be designed in an age-appropriate manner and provide accurate information to students on the nature of the disease, methods of transmission, and methods of prevention.

In public schools, the school board is required to establish an advisory council to be responsible for making recommendations concerning content, implementation, and evaluation of an AIDS instructional program. The council must consist of parents, school board members, appropriate school personnel, and community representatives, including representatives from religious organizations (8 NYCRR § 135.3(b) (2), (c)(2)). The New York State Court of Appeals upheld the requirement for participation of representatives of religious organizations on the council (*New York State Sch. Bds. Ass'n v. Sobol*, 79 N.Y.2d 333 (1992), *cert. denied*, 506 U.S. 909 (1992)). However, the commissioner has upheld a district's decision to deny a member of its AIDS advisory council access to observe health education classes because the presence of a noninstructional adult could stifle open classroom discussion. The advisory council member's role does not entitle him or her to "unfettered access" to district classrooms (*Appeal of Canazon*, 33 Educ. Dep't Rep. 124 (1993)).

Recommended guidelines for HIV/AIDS instruction are available from the State Education Department. According to the commissioner, "peer" teaching may be used to present AIDS education, but if it is to be incorporated into the district's curriculum, it should first be reviewed by the district's advisory council and be implemented consistently with the commissioner's regulations (*Appeal of Akshar*, 35 Educ. Dep't Rep. 424 (1996)).

A school district may also incorporate into its AIDS instructional program workshops on AIDS-related issues provided by a board of cooperative educational services (BOCES). However, the district retains the ultimate responsibility for complying with the applicable commissioner's regulations (*Appeal of Szymkowiak*, 36 Educ. Dep't Rep. 204 (1996)).

In addition, a student may be excused from instruction concerning the methods of preventing contraction of AIDS if the parent or guardian has filed with the school principal a written request that includes an assurance that the student will receive AIDS instruction at home (8 NYCRR § 135.3(b)(2), (c)(2); see also *Ware v. Valley Stream High Sch. Dist.*, 75 N.Y.2d 114 (1989); **14:44**).

The No Child Left Behind Act of 2001 prohibits school districts from using any Title I funds or any other funds available under the act to provide sex education or HIV-prevention education in schools "unless that instruction is age appropriate and includes the health benefits of abstinence" (20 USC § 7906).

14:43. May school districts distribute condoms to students as part of the AIDS instruction curriculum?

No. A state appellate court ruled that a school district policy or regulation that directs schools to make condoms available upon a student's request violates Public Health Law section 2504, which requires parental consent for children's health services. Such a policy or regulation would also deny parents their constitutional rights "to influence and guide the sexual activity of their children without state interference." But in making this ruling, the court also rejected the parents' claim that condom distribution should be prohibited because it violated their religious beliefs (*Alfonso v. Fernandez*, 195 A.D.2d 46 (2d Dep't 1993), *appeal dismissed without opinion*, 83 N.Y.2d 906 (1994)).

Furthermore, the federal No Child Left Behind Act of 2001 prohibits school districts from using any Title I funds or any other funds available under the act to operate a program of contraceptive distribution in schools (20 USC § 7906(a)(4)).

14:44. May school districts conduct demonstrations on the use of condoms as part of the AIDS instruction curriculum?

Yes. The commissioner of education has explained that school boards may exercise considerable discretion in prescribing an AIDS curriculum, in consultation with its AIDS advisory council, in a case where extensive public comment was solicited as well. However, the opt-out provision, which requires the parent or guardian to assure that their child will receive AIDS instruction at home (see **14:42**) does not dictate that the parent must provide a condom demonstration at home (*Appeal of O'Shaughnessy*, 35 Educ. Dep't Rep. 57 (1995)).

14:45. Are schools required to provide instruction on the methods of preventing and detecting certain cancers?

Yes. As part of a required health education course at the senior high school level, school districts must provide instruction regarding methods of preventing and detecting certain types of cancers, such as breast, skin and testicular cancers and others cancers, "where certain preventative measures have become generally accepted and adopted and recommended generally to the public." Such instruction must be taught by a teacher certified to teach health (§ 804(3-a)).

14:46. Are schools required to provide instruction on drug, alcohol, and tobacco abuse?

Yes. The Education Law and the commissioner's regulations mandate a program of instruction regarding the misuse and abuse of alcohol, tobacco and other drugs for all students in kindergarten through 12th grade (§§ 804, 806-a, 3028-a; 8 NYCRR §§ 100.2(c)(3), 135.3(a)).

The State Education Department has developed an integrated K–12 health-education curriculum that includes instruction on the physical and psychological impact of substance abuse, with an emphasis on nonuse as a means of avoiding health problems. Districts may choose to develop local syllabi that incorporate state and local criteria.

14:47. Is instruction about the environment required in the public schools?

Yes. Section 810 of the Education Law requires that all public school students receive instruction relating to the conservation of the natural resources of the state on Conservation Day, which is the last Friday of April of each year. The commissioner of education may prescribe a course of exercises and instruction that must be adopted and observed by school authorities on Conservation Day (8 NYCRR § 100.2(c)(9)).

14:48. Are schools required to provide instruction about human rights issues?

Yes. Section 801 of the Education Law requires courses of instruction in human rights issues, with particular attention to the study of the inhumanity of genocide, slavery, including the freedom trail and the Underground Railroad, the Holocaust, and the mass starvation in Ireland from 1845 to 1850.

14:49. Are schools required to provide instruction in civility, citizenship, and character education?

Yes. Section 801-a of the Education Law requires instruction in kindergarten through 12th grade in civility, citizenship, and character education. Such instruction is to be incorporated into existing curricula. Students are to be taught the principles of honesty, tolerance, personal responsibility, respect for others, observance of laws and rules, courtesy, dignity, and other traits.

Grants are available under the federal No Child Left Behind Act of 2001 for certain partnership programs in character education (see 20 USC § 7247).

14:50. Are schools required to provide instruction about the prevention of child abduction?

Yes. Section 803-a of the Education Law requires that all students in grades K–8 in all public schools receive instruction designed to prevent the abduction of children. The instruction must be provided under the direct supervision of regular classroom teachers; however, it may be given by any other public or private agency. In developing and implementing these courses of study, a school board may establish local advisory councils or employ the school-based shared-decision-making teams to make recommendations to the board.

14:51. Are schools required to provide instruction in the humane treatment of animals?

Yes. Students in elementary school must receive instruction in the humane treatment and protection of animals and the importance of the part they play in the "economy of nature" as well as the necessity of controlling the proliferation of animals that are subsequently abandoned and caused to suffer extreme cruelty. This instruction may be joined with work in literature, reading, language, nature study, or ethnology (§ 809(1); 8 NYCRR § 100.2(c)(8)).

14:52. Must students participate in dissections of animals that are part of the curriculum?

No. Any student expressing a moral or religious objection, substantiated in writing by his or her parent or guardian, to the performance or witnessing of the dissection of an animal must be allowed to complete an alternative project approved by the student's teacher. Students who perform alternative projects shall not be penalized (§ 809(4)).

14:53. Must school districts provide instruction and training in fire drills?

Instruction and training in fire drills must be provided in all public and private schools. These fire drills must be held at least 12 times in each school year. Eight of the drills must be held between September 1 and December 1 of each year. Two additional drills during summer school must be held in buildings where summer school is conducted. One of these must be held during the first week of summer school. Students also must be instructed at one of the drills about procedures to be followed if a fire occurs during a lunch period (§ 807).

Every school year, three fire drills must also be held on each school bus, and include, for example, practice and instruction in the location, use and operation of the emergency door, fire extinguishers, first-aid equipment, and windows as a means of escape in case of fire or accident (§ 3623(1); 8 NYCRR § 156.3(f); see **22:50**).

In addition, instruction in fire and arson prevention must be given to all students for at least 45 minutes in each month school is in session. The course of instruction must relate to the protection of life and property against loss or damage as a result of criminally initiated or other preventable fires. The course must also include materials to educate children on the dangers of falsely reporting a criminal incident or impending explosion or fire emergency involving danger to life or property or impending catastrophe (§ 808).

14:54. Are school districts required to provide instruction relating to the flag?

Yes. School districts must provide instruction regarding respect for the flag of the United States of America, including its display and use (§ 802; 8 NYCRR §§ 100.2(c)(7), 108.4, 108.6, 108.7; see **16:45–47**).

14:55. Is military instruction permitted in the public schools?

Yes. School boards may offer, during school hours, a junior reserve officer training program in conjunction with the United States Department of Defense to students in grades 9–12 who are at least 14 years of age.

Enrollment and participation in such a program must be voluntary on the part of the student, and each student must obtain written consent of a parent or guardian. However, instruction in or the presence within any school of any type of current or future weaponry as part of such a program is prohibited (§ 802(3)).

14:56. Is instruction on the use of firearms permitted in the public schools?

Yes. School boards may authorize instruction within their schools on the safe and proper use of firearms that are allowed by law to be used in hunting wild game, and on the study of game laws and proper hunting and conservation practices. However, both the State Education Department and the Department of Environmental Conservation must approve this course(§ 809-a).

Although the federal Gun-Free Schools Act (20 USC § 7151) and state law (§ 3214(3)) prohibit firearms on school grounds, neither applies to activities that are school approved and authorized where a district has adopted appropriate safeguards to ensure student safety (see **12:141**).

14:57. May schools teach about religion?

Yes. Although the federal and state constitutions forbid the teaching of religion in the public schools, they do not prevent teaching about religion. The schools have a responsibility to teach about religion and its place in civilization, which may be a positive force in the inculcation of moral values in youths and in the development of a respect for religion and for religious beliefs (*Matter of Rubinstein*, 2 Educ. Dep't Rep. 299 (1962); see **chapter 23**).

School districts may not require that creation science be taught as a counterbalance to the teaching of evolution (*Edwards v. Aguillard*, 482 U.S. 578 (1987)). Evolution science may not be taught as a religion either, to counterbalance the religious doctrine of creationism (*Peloza v. Capistrano Unified Sch. Dist.*, 37 F.3d 517 (9th Cir. 1994), *cert. denied*, 515 U.S. 1173 (1995)).

14:58. Must schools offer instruction in parenting skills?

Yes. Students entering ninth grade in 2001 and thereafter must achieve state parenting education standards prior to graduation. Schools must offer instruction regarding child development and parental skills and responsibility in either the health or family and consumer sciences programs or a separate course ((§ 804-b, 8 NYCRR § 100.5(a)(3)(vi)).

The State Education Department (SED) does not plan to establish a curriculum for parenting skills. School authorities are authorized to vary the course contents to meet the needs of their particular districts, using the

"Scope of Instruction" recommended by SED. More information about suggested curricula is available from the SED Parenting Project Office at the Coordinated School Health Network, Erie 1 BOCES, 1050 Maryvale Drive, Cheektowaga, N.Y. 14225, 716-630-4233.

14:59. May high schools offer automobile driver education and training courses for credit towards a diploma?

Yes. Authority for this is granted under section 507(1) of the Vehicle and Traffic Law (see also "Driver and Traffic Safety Education Guidelines; Program Description and Requirement," NY State Education Department, February 2003, available at www.emsc.nysed.gov/ciai/drive.html). Any vehicle used for driver training must bear identification indicating that the car is being driven by a student driver (see also Veh. & Traf. Law § 375(44)).

The Education Law requires all schools that offer driver education courses to include a driver safety component, based on curriculum established by the commissioner of education. The safety component should emphasize the effects of drug and alcohol use. It must also include motorcycle safety awareness (§ 806-a). The class time spent actually driving under the supervision of the instructor may be counted towards the 20 supervised hours the holder of a learner's permit needs before taking a driving test. The instructor is required to issue a certificate detailing the time the student spent driving under instructor supervision upon request (Educ. Law § 806-a(2); Veh. & Traf. Law § 502(2)(d), and 8 NYCRR § 107.2).

14:60. May high schools offer automobile driver education and training outside the regular school day and curriculum?

Yes. A school district may also offer driver education courses outside of the regular school day, which are supplemental and not part of the regular school curriculum, and do not count as credit towards a diploma (§ 3604(8)). In addition, if such a course is not offered as part of an adult or continuing education program, the district may charge a fee, provided no student is denied access if he or she cannot pay the fee. Certified teachers must be used as instructors for such a course (State Education Department Memorandum from Terry Schwartz, dated June 1992).

14:61. May a school offer students training in health care services?

The Education Law authorizes the commissioner of education, in cooperation with the Board of Regents, to establish a program of credit for health care service training for those secondary school students interested in such a career. The program may be instituted by any school district seeking to provide its secondary school students with an opportunity to participate in a health care facility or agency training program. Students receive academic credit for work-related training received at the health care facilities or agencies (§ 812).

14:62. Are there any programs available to school districts to provide instruction on the prevention of childhood obesity?

Yes. The Department of Health is charged with establishing a school-based childhood obesity prevention program. The program emphasizes instruction on nutrition and physical activity and is linked to current health and physical education courses (Public Health Law § 2599-b(2)). The Department of Health must periodically collect and analyze information from schools to determine the success of the program (Public Health Law § 2599-b(3)).

14:63. May districts create a student credit union to teach students about saving money?

Yes. School districts can authorize a credit union to open and maintain a student branch within elementary and secondary schools. The credit unions may only be open to students. Students interested in learning the skills needed for a job with a bank can apply to be tellers (Banking Law § 450-b).

14:64. Are school districts required to provide school-to-work programs?

No. School districts are not required to offer students opportunities for work-based learning experiences. However, the federal School-to-Work Opportunities Act (20 USC §§ 6101–6251) provides money for state, local school district, and business partnerships to develop and implement a combination of vocational education and on-the-job training, to give students the skills needed to find work after high school. Most states, including New York, have received implementation grants for statewide coordination of school-to-work programs and for subgrants to local school/business partnerships to implement grants at the local level. In New York, these programs are monitored by the state School-to-Work Opportunities Advisory Committee.

School districts may also receive funds under the federal Job-Training Partnership Act (JTPA) (29 USC § 1517(c)).

Any questions regarding participation in the school-to-work initiative should be directed to the State Education Department, Office of Workforce Preparation and Continuing Education, EBA Room 319, Albany, N.Y. 12234.

Academic Achievement

Editor's Note: Additional information on the impact of the federal No Child Left Behind Act of 2001 on this subject is available in Leaving No Child Behind in New York, 2nd Edition, *a handbook published by the New York State School Boards Association and distributed by LexisNexis.*

14:65. Are public school students required to participate in any state assessments?

Yes. All public school students at the elementary, intermediate, and high school level must participate in state assessments that reflect the knowledge, skills, and understandings that all students are expected to know and be able to do at certain specified grade levels, and for receiving a high school diploma. This requirement applies, as well, to students with disabilities and the knowledge, skills, and understandings they are expected to know and be able to do as indicated in their individualized education program (8 NYCRR § 100.1(t)(2)).

However, the commissioner of education may approve the use of alternative assessments, which measure an equivalent level of knowledge and skill (8 NYCRR § 100.2(f)). The commissioner may also approve alternative testing procedures subject to conditions set forth in the commissioner's regulations (8 NYCRR § 100.2(g)).

The federal No Child Left Behind Act of 2001 requires that states assess all public school students in mathematics, reading or language arts and, starting with the 2007–08 school year, science (20 USC § 6311(b)(3); 34 CFR § 200.5(a)).

14:66. What examinations are students required to take at the elementary level?

Currently, students must take the following elementary assessment examinations in the fourth grade: English/language arts, mathematics, and science. Students who score below the state designated performance level on the fourth grade English language arts and/or the mathematics assessment must receive at least one semester of academic intervention services (see **14:76–83**), and must be retested no later than the completion of fifth grade (8 NYCRR 100.3(b)(2)(i), (iii)).

In the fifth grade, students must take the social studies elementary assessment (8 NYCRR § 100.3(b)(2)).

However, the federal No Child Left Behind Act (NCLB) of 2001, will require yearly assessments in reading or language arts and mathematics in grades 3–8 beginning no later than the 2005–06 school year. It will also require that assessment examinations in science be administered at three levels — third to fifth grade, sixth to ninth grade, and 10th to 12th grade — no later than the 2007–08 school year (20 USC § 6311(b)(3)(C); 34 CFR §§ 200.2(a)(1), 200.5). A state may use additional academic assessment measures, but cannot use them in lieu of the required academic assessments. Such additional assessment measures cannot be used to reduce the number of or change schools otherwise subject to school improvement, corrective action, or restructuring; but can be used to identify additional schools for school improvement, corrective action, or restructuring (20 USC § 6311(b)(2)(D), (4); 34 CFR § 200.2(c); see **14:89–107**).

Students home-schooled by their parents may, but are not required to, participate in these assessments (20 USC § 7886(b); 8 NYCRR § 100.3(b)(2)(ii)).

14:67. What examinations are students required to take at the intermediate level?

Currently, eighth-grade students must take the English language arts, mathematics, social studies, and science intermediate assessments (8 NYCRR § 100.4(d)). However, the federal No Child Left Behind Act of 2001 imposes additional testing requirements, some of which will go into effect no later that the 2005–06 school year and others by the 2007–08 school year (see **14:66**). Students may also be required to take such other assessments as the commissioner of education may determine appropriate (8 NYCRR § 100.4(d)(5)).

Students home-schooled by their parents may, but are not required to, participate in these assessments (20 USC § 7886(b); 8 NYCRR § 100.4(e)).

14:68. What examinations are students required to obtain a high school diploma?

State assessment requirements for a high school diploma depend on the year students first enter the ninth grade and whether a student is a student with disabilities. Students who take more than four years to earn a diploma must satisfy the requirements applicable to the year they first entered grade 9 (8 NYCRR § 100.5(a)).

For example, students who enter grade 9 before September 2005 must take the Regents Comprehensive English exam and pass with a score of at least 65 for a Regents diploma, or 55–64 for a local diploma as determined by the school board. On the other hand, students with disabilities entering the ninth grade before September 2010 who fail the Regents Comprehensive English exam may earn a local diploma by passing, instead, the Regents Competency Tests (RCT) in Reading and Writing or their equivalents. This is often referred to as the "Safety Net"). There is no

Regents science exam requirement for students entering grade nine prior to September 1999 (8 NYCRR § 100.5 (a)(5)(i)(a)).

REQUIRED REGENTS EXAM SCHEDULE

Students Entering 9th Grade in 1997	Students Entering 9th Grade in 1998	Students Entering 9th Grade in 1999 and after
English/ Lang. Arts	English/ Lang. Arts	English/ Lang. Arts
Math	Math	Math
	Global History	Global History
	U.S. History And Gov't	U.S. History And Gov't
		Science

Through the 2004-05 school year, the Regents exams listed above must be successfully completed with a score of 65 for a Regents endorsed diploma. A modified score determined by the school board ranging from 55 to 64 may be considered passing for a local diploma.

Students with disabilities who enter ninth grade prior to September 2010 and who do not achieve a passing score on a required Regents examination may fulfill the requirement for a local diploma by passing the RCT in that subject (8 NYCRR § 100.5(a)(5)). For more information, contact the State Education Department's Office of Curriculum, at 518-473-4698.

14:69. Are New York State public high schools required to use Regents examinations?

Yes. Rules of the Board of Regents pertaining to apportionment provide, in part, that secondary schools receiving state aid must use Regents examinations or approved equivalent examinations in the senior high school grades (8 NYCRR § 3.35). As the state moves toward an all-Regents curriculum and the new graduation requirements are fully phased in, all students will be required to take the Regents exams in English/language arts, mathematics, global history and geography, U.S. history and government, and science (8 NYCRR § 100.5(a)(5)(i)).

Alternative assessments that measure an equivalent level of knowledge and skill may be substituted for state assessments, with the approval of the commissioner. Alternative assessments for the required Regents examinations must measure the state learning standards for the respective content area and must be at least as rigorous as the corresponding state assessment; must be consistent with technical criteria for validity, reliability, and freedom from bias; must be developed by an entity other than a local school board or district; must be available for use by any school, or district in New York; and must be administered under secure conditions approved by the commissioner (8 NYCRR §§ 100.2 (f), 100.5(a)(5)(ii)).

14:70. Who may be admitted to Regents examinations?

All students who have studied a subject at an approved school for at least a period of time not less than what has been prescribed by the commissioner of education have the right to take a Regents examination at the school they attend. However, students taking the Regents science examination must have satisfactorily met the laboratory requirements as stated in the state syllabus for that science (8 NYCRR § 8.2(a)(c)).

Students who wish to demonstrate academic proficiency acquired through independent, out-of-school or other study may also be admitted to a Regents examination, but only at the discretion of the principal of the school administering the examination (8 NYCRR § 8.2(b)).

14:71. May a student be prohibited from taking a Regents examination because of a failure to pass a local qualifying examination?

No. While school boards may set requirements for admissions and for high school graduation that are more stringent than those prescribed by the state, they may not prohibit a student who has not met those requirements from taking a Regents examination, provided that student meets the requirements set by the Board of Regents (8 NYCRR § 8.2).

14:72. What can a school district do if a student commits fraud in a Regents exam?

The commissioner's regulations allow full discretion and latitude to local school administrators when fraud is found in regard to a Regents examination. If a local administrator responsible for giving the examination concludes there is sufficient evidence of a student committing, or attempting to commit, fraud, he or she may cancel that student's examination. The administrator may exclude that student from further exams until that student has demonstrated to the administrator's satisfaction that he or she is entitled to the restoration of this privilege.

In each instance where fraud has been established, the administrator must promptly file a brief report with the commissioner of education, giving the name of the student and describing the circumstances and the action taken.

A student accused of fraud must have a full opportunity for a hearing before the local school board or person(s) designated by the board, if requested, and in the presence of his or her parents and legal counsel, if desired (8 NYCRR § 102.4; see *Matter of Pellinger,* 20 Educ. Dep't Rep. 53 (1980), in regard to "substantial evidence" needed in such cases).

14:73. Are there any alternatives to the state assessments that can be used for students with disabilities?

The federal Individuals with Disabilities Education Act of 1997 (IDEA) requires that each state develop and implement an alternate assessment for students with disabilities who cannot participate in the regular assessment system, even with accommodations. School districts may use the New York State Alternate Assessment (NYSAA) for certain students who the committee on special education (CSE) determines have a severe cognitive disability with significant deficits in communication/language and adaptive behavior; require a highly specialized educational program that facilitates the acquisition, application, and transfer of skills across natural environments; and require educational support systems, such as assistive technology, personal care services, or behavioral intervention.

The federal No Child Left Behind Act of 2001 also requires states to provide alternate assessments and accommodations for students with disabilities (20 USC § 6311(b)(3); 34 CFR § 200.6).

The NYSAA consists of a collection of the student's work and parent/teacher observations, called a "datafolio," used to demonstrate what the student can or cannot do based on the learning standards for all students. It measures student progress toward meeting the alternate performance indicators for each standard, which are educational outcomes on a basic functional level. It includes information collected over several months, in a variety of ways, such as photographs and videotapes, evidence of social interactions, interviews, data collection forms, and surveys. The NYSAA also includes surveys of the student's parents for their perception of the student's performance. For additional information, see "The Learning Standards and Alternate Performance Indicators for Students with Severe Disabilities," available at http://www.vesid.nysed.gov/specialed/.

14:74. Are there any exceptions from state assessments for students with limited English proficiency?

No. The federal No Child Left Behind Act of 2001 (NCLB) requires that limited English proficient (LEP) students be included in all required assessments. However, LEP students must be provided reasonable accommodations on the assessments, including, to the extent practicable, assessments "in the language and form most likely to yield accurate data on what such students know and can do in academic content areas, until such students have achieved English language proficiency" (20 USC § 6311(b)(3)(C); 34 CFR § 200.6(b)).

Students who have attended school in the U.S. (excluding Puerto Rico) for three or more consecutive school years must be tested in English in the reading and language arts state assessments. If the school district determines, on a case-by-case basis, that academic assessments in another language or form would likely yield more accurate and reliable information on what such students know and can do, the district may make a determination to assess such students in the appropriate language other than English for no more than two additional consecutive years (20 USC § 6311(b)(3)(C); 34 CFR § 200.6(b)(2)).

The NCLB further requires that states assess the English proficiency of all LEP students on a yearly basis to measure their oral language, reading, and writing skills in English (20 USC § 6311(b)(7)). In New York, that assessment consists of the New York State English as a Second Language Achievement Test (NYSESLAT).

14:75. Are there any exceptions from state assessments for newly enrolled students?

No. The federal No Child Left Behind Act of 2001 requires that school districts include students who have attended schools in the district for a full academic year even if they have not attended a single school for a full academic year. However, the performance of students who have attended more than one school in the district in any academic year will be used only in determining the progress of the school district (20 USC § 6311(b)(3)(C)(xi); see **14:91** regarding adequate yearly progress).

14:76. Are school districts required to provide services designed to help students meet the learning standards reflected in state-mandated assessments?

Yes. School districts must provide *academic intervention services* (AIS) that supplement the general curriculum instruction to assist students in meeting the learning standards, as well as student support services, which may include guidance, counseling, attendance, and study skills needed to support improved academic performance. AIS programs are intended to assist students who are at risk of not achieving the learning standards in English language arts, mathematics, social studies, and/or science, or who are at risk of not gaining the knowledge and skills needed to meet or exceed designated performance levels on state assessments.

Academic intervention services must supplement and not replace those services provided to students with limited English proficiency pursuant to part 154 of the commissioner's regulations, or special education services and programs as defined in Education Law sections 4401 (1) and (2). However, they may include diagnostic screening for vision, hearing, and physical disabilities pursuant to article 19 of the Education Law, and screening for possible limited English proficiency or possible disabilities pursuant to part 117 of the commissioner's regulations (8 NYCRR §§ 100.1(g), 100.2(ee)(1), (2), (3)).

In addition, the federal No Child Left Behind Act of 2001 requires that school districts provide supplemental educational services to eligible students after a school and/or school district has failed to make adequate yearly progress for three consecutive school years (20 USC § 6316(e)(12); see **14:98**).

14:77. Must school districts provide academic intervention services to students with disabilities?

Yes. Academic intervention services must be made available to students with disabilities on the same basis as nondisabled students, provided that the services are consistent with the student's individualized education program pursuant to Education Law section 4402 (8 NYCRR § 100.1(g)).

14:78. Are students required to participate in academic intervention services?

Yes. A school district has the authority and responsibility to place students in appropriate academic programs during the regular school day, and this includes placement in an academic intervention services program. A district has the authority, by board resolution, to set the hours of compulsory attendance and to extend the school day (§ 1709 (2), (3), (5) (33); § 2503 (1), (2), (3), (4)(a); § 2554(1), (9), (11), (13)(a)).

In contrast, attendance in summer school programs and academic intervention services offered outside of the regular school year is voluntary. However, the State Education Department recommends that districts provide opportunities for academic intervention services in the summer.

14:79. What role do parents play in academic intervention services?

Once a student has been determined to need academic intervention services (AIS), the principal must notify the parent or person in parental relation to the student in writing, in the native language of the parent. The notice must include a summary of the AIS to be provided to the student, the reason the student needs such services, and the consequences of not achieving expected performance levels.

The student's parent must be provided with an opportunity at least once per semester during the regular school year to consult with the student's regular classroom teacher(s) and other professional staff providing AIS. At least once each quarter during the regular school year, reports on the student's progress must be sent to the student's parent(s) by mail, telephone, or other means in a language or other mode of communication understood by the parents. In addition, parents must be provided with information on ways to work with their child and educators to improve the child's achievement, and ways to monitor their child's progress (8 NYCRR § 100.2(ee)(6)).

14:80. Must school districts develop a description of the academic intervention services they will offer eligible students?

Yes. Each school district must develop and each school board must approve a description of academic intervention services (AIS) to be provided, including any variations in services in schools in the district. The plan must describe the districtwide procedures used to determine the need for AIS, whether AIS are offered during the regular day or during an extended school day or year, and the criteria for ending the services, including the performance levels, if any, that students must obtain on district-selected assessments. Beginning July 1, 2002, and every two years thereafter, each district must review and revise its AIS description based on student performance results (8 NYCRR § 100.2(ee)(4)).

Based on performance criteria developed by the commissioner, certain school districts may be required to submit their description of their AIS services to the State Education Department for review and approval (8 NYCRR § 100.2(ee)(4)(iv)).

14:81. How does a district determine if a student is eligible for academic intervention services?

The requirements for providing academic intervention services (AIS) differ according to a student's grade level. For example, at the kindergarten through grade 3 level, districts must provide academic intervention services to students who lack reading readiness or are at risk of not achieving the state-designated performance level in English/language arts and/or mathematics (8 NYCRR § 100.2(ee)(1)).

In grades 4–8, students are eligible to receive AIS if, for example, they score below the designated performance level on either of the state elementary assessments in English/language arts, mathematics, social studies or science, or are at risk of not meeting state standards in those areas. Students who score below the state designated performance level on the fourth-grade English language arts and/or the mathematics assessment must receive at least one semester of academic intervention services and must be re-tested no later than the completion of fifth grade (8 NYCRR

§ 100.3(b)(2)(iii)). In addition, students of limited English proficiency are also eligible if they are at risk of not meeting state standards in those areas through English or their native language (8 NYCRR § 100.2(ee)(2)).

Students in grades 9–12 are eligible for AIS if, for example, they score below the designated performance level on either of the state intermediate level assessments in English/language arts, mathematics, social studies or science, or are at risk of not meeting state standards in those areas. Students in grades 9–12 are also eligible if they score below the designated performance level on any one of the state examinations required for graduation. Students of limited English proficiency are also eligible if they are at risk of not meeting state standards in English language arts, mathematics, social studies and/or science through English or their native language (8 NYCRR § 100.2(ee)(3)).

14:82. Is there a schedule districts must follow when providing an eligible student with academic intervention services?

Academic intervention instructional and/or support services must start no later than the beginning of the semester following a determination that a student needs such services. The services must continue until the student's performance meets or exceeds the state-designated performance level on the next state assessment, or the student's achievement on district-selected assessment demonstrates the student is likely to meet or exceed state-designated performance levels on the next state assessment (8 NYCRR § 100.2(ee)(5)(iv)).

Academic intervention services may be offered during the regular school day, an extended school day, or an extended school year (8 NYCRR § 100.2(ee)(5)). They must be provided by qualified staff certified pursuant to part 80 of the commissioner's regulations (8 NYCRR § 100.2(ee)(5)(iii)).

14:83. Can a school district eliminate instruction in a learning standards area in order to provide academic intervention services in another area?

No. However, students in grades 7 and 8 who have been determined to need academic intervention services may have the unit of study requirements for one or more subjects reduced, but not eliminated, by the principal, if certain criteria specified in the commissioner's regulations have been met (8 NYCRR § 100.4(b)(4)(ii)).

14:84. Are school districts required to issue student progress reports, in the form of report cards, to parents or guardians?

No. However, most school districts provide parents or guardians with progress reports, generally prepared by the students' teachers, which provide information on grades, attendance, conduct, and other relevant data. Report cards are issued each quarter in most districts. Districts also may send out additional information on student progress or lack of progress in the form of interim reports when a student is failing a course or has attained a noteworthy achievement.

Nonetheless, for students who are receiving academic intervention services, school districts are required to provide progress reports at least once each quarter during the regular school year. The reports must be sent to the student's parent(s) by mail, telephone, or other means in a language or other mode of communication understood by the parents. In addition, parents must be provided with information on ways to work with their child and educators to improve the child's achievement, and ways to monitor their child's progress (8 NYCRR § 100.2(ee)(6)).

Furthermore, districts must ensure that the providers of "supplemental services" required under the federal No Child Left Behind Act of 2001 (see **14:98**), regularly inform parents of their child's progress (20 USC § 6316(e)(3); 8 NYCRR § 120.4(f)(8)(vii)).

14:85. Must school districts report the results of state tests?

Yes. As part of the district's school report card, each public school district must annually provide to the State Education Department the results of state assessments as part of the records required to be submitted to the commissioner of education (8 NYCRR § 100.2(bb)(2)(i)).

In addition, section 3211-a of the Education Law requires that schools must report the standardized reading test result of any student scoring at or below the 23rd percentile to his or her parents or guardian. School districts also must provide either a certified teacher of reading or other appropriate school district personnel to interpret the score of a child whose parents have requested an interpretation of such test results.

14:86. Is the state required to issue a school report card?

Yes. Under commissioner's regulations, the State Education Department (SED) issues an annual report card for each public school and school district to measure students' progress based on information it receives annually on educational programs and services, student performance and fiscal data from each public school district and each nonpublic school (8 NYCRR § 100.2(m)). In New York City, the chancellor produces a New York City School Report Card, as approved by the commissioner of education.

The New York State School Report Card consists of four reports: an overview of School Performance and Analysis of Student Subgroup Performance, the Comprehensive Information Report, the School

Accountability Report, and for public school districts, the Fiscal Supplement (8 NYCRR § 100.2(m)(1)). It includes, in part:

- aggregate data on student achievement at each proficiency level on the state academic assessments;
- results disaggregated by race, ethnicity, gender, disability status, migrant status, English proficiency, and status as economically disadvantaged (unless the number of students in a subgroup is insufficient to yield statistically reliable information or the results would reveal personally identifiable information about an individual student);
- the percentage of students not tested disaggregated by the same categories and subject to the same exception above; and
- a comparison between the actual achievement levels of each group of students above and the state's annual measurable objectives for each such group of students on each of the required academic assessments (see 20 USC § 6311(h); 34 CFR §§ 200.2(b)(10), 200.7, 200.8; see 8 NYCRR § 100.2(m)).

14:87. Is a school district required to distribute its school report card?

Yes. Under state law, each school board must transmit the four reports in the state school report card for its district and the schools within the district to local newspapers of general circulation, and append it to the proposed school budget that must be available for distribution to the public at least 14 days before the budget vote. Copies must also be available for distribution at the annual meeting (§§ 1716(6), 2554(24), 2590-e(8), 2601-a(7); 8 NYCRR § 100.2(bb); 8 NYCRR § 100.2 (m)(3)).

In addition, the parent of each student attending a school receiving federal education funds under Title 1 of the No Child Left Behind Act (20 USC §§ 6301–7941) is entitled to a copy of the school report card in an understandable and uniform format and, to the extent practicable, in a language that the parents can understand. A district may include with the school report card additional information, which must be made widely available through such means as posting on the Internet, distribution to the media, and distribution through public agencies. If a school district issues a report card for all students, it may include this information as part of the students' report cards (20 USC § 6311(h)(2)(B), (E); 8 NYCRR § 100.2(m)(4)).

14:88. Are BOCES required to prepare a report card?

Yes. The board of cooperative educational services (BOCES) report card must include measures of academic performance by students on a school-by-school or program-by-program basis in the following:

- Measures of program participation, completion and placement in areas including, but not limited to, special education, occupational education, alternative education and adult and continuing education.
- The aggregate performance of students of component school districts on statewide evaluation tests in reading, mathematics, science and vocational courses, and Regents exams in English, mathematics, science and social studies.
- The percentage of students in the BOCES region who graduate with Regents and other diplomas.
- A comparison of such measures of academic performance to statewide averages for all BOCES.
- Other measures that support the achievement of higher standards, such as curriculum and staff development activities, and a comparison of the same to statewide averages for all BOCES (8 NYCRR § 100.2(cc)).

BOCES report cards must also include a summary of the district's annual violent or disruptive incident reports, in a form prescribed by the commissioner (8 NYCRR § 100.2(cc)(4))).

The report card must also include measures of fiscal performance of the supervisory district, including expenditures per pupil and a summary of BOCES administration, program, and capital expenditures. These fiscal measures shall also be compared to statewide averages for BOCES.

The BOCES report card must be transmitted to newspapers of general circulation and be appended to copies of the administrative budget made publicly available. Copies must also be available for distribution at the annual meeting (§ 1950(4)(kk); 8 NYCRR § 100.2(cc)).

Consequences for Low Student Academic Achievement

Editor's Note: For further information on the consequences of low student academic achievement under the federal No Child Left Behind Act of 2001 see Leaving No Child Behind in New York, 2nd Edition, *a handbook published by the New York State School Boards Association and distributed by LexisNexis.*

14:89. Are public schools and school districts held accountable for the academic performance of their students?

Yes. Each year, the commissioner of education reviews the performance of all public schools, school districts and charter schools within the state to determine whether they have made adequate yearly progress (AYP) on specified accountability performance criteria and additional accountability indicators set forth in commissioner's regulations (8 NYCRR § 100.2(p)(4);

see **14:92-96**). Failure to make adequate yearly progress for two consecutive years or more causes a school and/or district to be designated as "requiring academic progress" (8 NYCRR §§ 100.2(p)(5)(vi),(6), (7)), as well as "in need of improvement, corrective action or restructuring" if they receive federal educational funds under Title I of the No Child Left Behind Act of 2001 (20 USC §§ 6316(b), (c)(3); 34 CFR §§ 200.33(a), 200.39(b), 200.50(d); 8 NYCRR §§ 100.2(p)(6)(vi),(vii),(viii),(ix), (7)(iii),(iv); see **14:91, 14:97-102**; see also *Ass'n of Community Organizations for Reform Now v. NYC Dep't of Educ.*, 269 F.Supp.2d 338 (S.D.N.Y. 2003).

In addition, schools that the commissioner determines are farthest from meeting his benchmarks for measuring the performance of "all students" in the aggregate may be identified as a *school under registration review* (SURR) (8 NYCRR § 100.2(p)(9)). Schools placed under registration review risk having their registration revoked and declared an unsound educational environment (8 NYCRR § 100.2(p)(10)(i),(vi)). Schools that, in addition to failing to meet or exceed the commissioner's SURR benchmarks, also have conditions that threaten the health, safety, and/or educational welfare of students or have been the subject of persistent parental complaints may be designated as a *poor learning environment* (8 NYCRR § 100.2(p)(9)).

The commissioner also may identify and place under registration review any school for which a district fails to provide in a timely manner student performance data required by the commissioner to conduct the annual assessment of the school's performance. The commissioner may include, as well, any school with an excessive percentage of students failing to participate in state assessments (8 NYCRR § 100.2(p)(9)).

14:90. Are public schools and school districts held accountable for the performance of every student?

No. Only the performance of continuously enrolled students is included in adequate yearly progress (AYP) determinations (8 NYCRR § 100.2(p)(5)(iii); see **14:92–96**). In grades 3–8 this means students whose latest date of enrollment occurred after the date prescribed by the commissioner of education for completion of basic educational data systems (BEDS) forms. For grades 9-12 it means students in the annual high school cohort (8 NYCRR § 100.2(p)(1)(ix)).

AYP determinations on accountability performance criteria — When making AYP determinations regarding accountability performance criteria (see **14:92–94**) at an individual high school, the annual high school cohort consists of students who first enrolled in ninth grade three years previously anywhere and who were enrolled in the school on the first Wednesday in October of the previous school year. It does not include students who transferred to another high school or approved alternative high school equivalency or high school equivalency preparation program, or a criminal justice facility. It does not include either students who left the United States or its territories, or who have died.

When making similar AYP determinations at the district level, the annual district high school cohort consists of students who first enrolled in ninth grade three years previously anywhere and who were enrolled in the district or placed in educational programs out of district by the district's committee on special education or a school official on the first Wednesday in October of the previous year (8 NYCRR § 100.2(p)(16)(i)).

AYP determinations measuring the annual high school cohort's graduation rate — When making AYP determinations related to use of the cohort's graduation rate as an additional accountability indicator (see **14:96**), the annual high school cohort at both an individual high school and district level consists, until 2005–06, of all members of the cohort for the previous school year plus any students excluded from the cohort solely because they transferred to an alternative high school equivalency or high school equivalency preparation program (8 NYCRR § 100.2(p)(16)(ii)).

14:91. What happens if a public school or school district fails to make adequate yearly progress (AYP)?

A school that fails to make AYP for two consecutive years in the same accountability performance criterion or additional accountability indicator must be designated as a *school requiring academic progress: year 1* (SRAP 1) (8 NYCRR § 100.2(p)(5)(vi),(6)). A school that received federal educational funds under Title I of the No Child Left Behind Act of 2001 (NCLB) during those two years will also be designated as a *school in need of improvement* (SINI) (20 USC § 6316(b)(1); 34 CFR § 200.32(a);8 NYCRR § 100.2(p)(6)(vi); see also *Ass'n of Community Organizations for Reform Now v. NYC Dep't of Educ.*, 269 F.Supp.2d 338 (S.D.N.Y. 2003).

The continuous failure of a school to make AYP on the same performance criterion or additional indicator that caused its initial designation as requiring academic progress and in need of improvement will cause the school to move along a continuum described in the chart below (8 NYCRR § 100.2(p)(6); 20 USC §§ 6316(b), (c)(3); 34 CFR §§ 200.33(a), 200.39(b), 200.50(d); 8 NYCRR §§ 100.2(p)(6); see also *Ass'n of Community Organizations for Reform Now v. NYC Dep't of Educ.*, 269 F.Supp.2d 338 (S.D.N.Y. 2003).

AYP Failure Designations

Years of Consecutive AYP Failure	School Requiring Academic Progress Status	NCLB Status
2	SRAP: Year 1	SINI: Year 1
3	SRAP: Year 2	SINI: Year 2
4	SRAP: Year 3	Corrective Action
5	SRAP: Year 4	In Need of Restructuring
6	SRAP: Year 5	Restructuring

A school district that fails to make AYP for two consecutive years will be designated as a *district requiring academic progress*. A district that received federal educational funds under Title I of the NCLB during those two years will also be designated as a *district in need of improvement* (20 USC § 6316(c)(3); 34 CFR § 200.50(d); 8 NYCRR 100.2(p)(7)(i),(iii)). The continued failure of a school district to make AYP on the same performance criterion or additional indicator that caused its initial designation will also cause the district to move along a designation continuum similar to that applicable to schools (see **14:104–05**).

14:92. On what basis are public schools and districts deemed to have made adequate yearly progress (AYP) regarding the performance of their students?

In each year, public schools, school districts, and charter schools will be deemed to have made AYP if each of certain specified accountability groups separately makes AYP on pre-set accountability performance criteria and additional accountability indicators (8 NYCRR § 100.2(p)(5)(i),(v); see also **14:94–96**).

The *accountability groups* include those groups of students for each grade level or annual high school cohort comprised of:
- all students,
- students from major racial and ethnic groups,
- students with disabilities,
- students with limited English proficiency, and
- economically disadvantaged students.

At the school district level, the accountability groups include all students enrolled in a public school within the district and students placed out of district for educational services by the district's committee on special education or a school official (8 NYCRR § 100.2(p)(1)(i)).

14:93. On what basis are accountability groups deemed to have made adequate yearly progress (AYP)?

An accountability group makes AYP if the following three conditions are met. First, the district submits required data files to the commissioner of education within the time frames and in the format prescribed by the commissioner. Second, 95 percent of students in accountability groups with 40 or more students who are enrolled at the elementary and middle school level on the first day of test administration, or in at least their fourth year of high school at the high school level, receive valid scores on the required English/language arts and math state assessments. Third, the students in accountability groups with 30 or more students both meet or exceed, or do not differ significantly from the annual measurable objective set for the accountability performance criteria, and meet or exceed the additional accountability indicator applicable at the group's grade level (8 NYCRR § 100.2(p)(5); see **14:94–96**).

14:94. What performance criteria is used to make adequate yearly progress (AYP) determinations?

Accountability performance criteria used to make AYP determinations depends on the grade level and type of state assessment involved. In general, student performance on required state assessments in English/language arts and mathematics must meet or exceed, or not differ significantly from *annual measurable objectives* (AMOs) designed to achieve a score of 200 in the 2013–14 school year on the performance index (PI) used by New York State to measure adequate yearly progress.

The chart below illustrates AMOs through the 2013–14 school year that ensure a PI score of 200 in 2013–14 (see also 8 NYCRR § 100.2(p)(14)).

Annual Measurable Objectives for 2002–03 to 2013-14

School Year	Elementary-Level		Middle-Level		Secondary-Level	
	ELA	Math	ELA	Math	English	Math
2002-03	123	136	107	81	142	132
2003-04	123	136	107	81	142	132
2004-05	131	142	116	93	148	139
2005-06	138	149	126	105	154	146
2006-07	146	155	135	117	159	152
2007-08	154	162	144	129	165	159
2008-09	162	168	154	141	171	166
2009-10	169	174	163	152	177	173
2010-11	177	181	172	164	183	180
2011-12	185	187	181	176	188	186
2012-13	192	194	191	188	194	193
2013-14	200	200	200	200	200	200

Limited English proficient students in grades 4 and 8 may be deemed to meet the English/language arts (ELA) performance criteria if they show a specified increment of progress on the New York State English as a Second Language Achievement Test (NYSESLAT) for their grade level if they meet certain criteria. First, they must have attended school in the United States (not including Puerto Rico) for fewer than three consecutive years. Second, the district determines to administer the NYSESLAT to such students in lieu of the ELA required state assessment. A district may determine on a case-by-case and annual basis to allow students attending U.S. schools for more than three but less than six years to take the NYSESLAT in lieu of the ELA. However, no ELA exemptions are available beyond a student's fifth year in U.S. schools (8 NYCRR § 100.2(p)(14)(vi)).

14:95. How are the performance index (PI) scores calculated for the accountability performance criteria used to make adequate yearly progress (AYP) determinations?

Performance index scores are calculated based on four student performance levels. Students scoring at Level 1 are credited with 0 points, those scoring at Level 2 with 100 points and students scoring at Levels 3 or 4 with 200 points. The performance index for each accountability group (see **14:92**) is calculated by summing the points and dividing by the number of students in the group (8 NYCRR § 100.2(p)(1)(iv)).

The four student performance levels used to calculate performance index scores differ for each type of assessment and grade level. Consistent with the requirements of the federal No Child Left Behind Act of 2001, Level 1 aligns with performance at the basic level, Level 2 basic proficiency, Level 3 proficient, and Level 4 advanced (8 NYCRR § 100.2(p)(1)(v); see 20 USC § 6311(b)(1)(D)(ii)).

Generally, at the high school level, a score below 55 on a Regents exam would constitute Level 1 or basic performance, a score of 55-64 Level 2 or basic proficiency performance, a score of 65-84 Level 3 performance, and a score of 85-100 Level 4 performance (8 NYCRR § 100.2(p)(1)(v)).

14:96. What are the additional accountability indicators used to make adequate yearly progress (AYP) determinations?

The additional accountability indicators used to make AYP determinations depend on the grade level involved. At the elementary level and middle school level, the additional accountability indicator consists of either a science index of 100 that the commissioner of education may increment annually, or progress in relation to performance in the previous school year. At the high school level, the additional accountability indicator consists of either the high school graduation rate established annually by the commissioner, or progress in relation to the previous school year's graduation rate. The graduation rate consists of the percentage of the annual graduation rate cohort that earns a local diploma by August 31 of the fourth calendar year after first entering grade 9, unless the majority of students participate in a state-approved five-year program (8 NYCRR § 100.2(p)(15); see **14:90**).

14:97. What steps must a school and district take when the school fails to make adequate yearly progress (AYP) for two consecutive years?

A school designated as requiring academic progress (SRAP): year 1 and as in need of improvement (SINI) under the federal No Child Left Behind Act of 2001 (NCLB) (see **14:91**) must develop a two-year school improvement plan in consultation with parents, school staff, the school district, and outside experts. The plan must be approved by the school board within three months of the designation. It must be implemented by the first day of regular student attendance of the next school year after the school year in which the school was so designated. If the school board has not approved the plan by that date, it must be implemented immediately upon approval (20 USC § 6316(b)(3),(4); 34 CFR §§ 200.40, 200.41; 8 NYCRR § 100.2(p)(6)(i),(vi)).

A school district with one or more schools designated as in need of improvement under the NCLB must offer all students in those schools the opportunity to transfer to another school within the district that has not been identified as in need of improvement, corrective action, or restructuring, or designated as persistently dangerous, by the first day of the school year following identification (20 USC § 6316(b)(1)(E); 34 CFR §§ 200.39(a)(1)(i), 200.44(a); 8 NYCRR §§ 100.2(p)(6)(vi)); 120.3); see **14:91, 14:98-102**).

Students transferring to another school enjoy the same rights and benefits as other students already enrolled in that school. They also have the right to remain at the school they transfer to until they complete that school's highest grade level (20 USC § 6316(b)(1)(E),(F), (13); 34 CFR § 200.44(f),(g)(1); 8 NYCRR §§ 120.3(e)).

14:98. What steps must a school and district take when the school fails to make adequate yearly progress (AYP) for three years in a row?

Schools designated as requiring academic progress (SRAP): year 2 and as in need of improvement, year 2 under the federal No Child Left Behind Act of 2001 (NCLB) (see **14:91**), must update their school improvement plan (see **14:97**). The updated plan must be approved by the school board and implemented no later than the first day of regular student attendance for the next upcoming school year (8 NYCRR § 100.2(p)(6)(i)).

A school district with a school designated as in need of improvement (SINI), year 2 under the NCLB must continue to offer all the students at that school the opportunity to transfer to another school (see **14:97**). It also must offer supplemental educational services to eligible students from low-income families attending that school (20 USC § 6316(b)(5); 34 CFR § 200.39(b); 8 NYCRR §§ 100.2(p)(6)(vii), 120.3(a), 120.4(b)).

Supplemental educational services (SES) include tutoring and other supplemental academic enrichment services that are additional to instruction provided during the school day. They must be high-quality, research-based, and specifically designed to improve student academic achievement on state assessments in English/language arts (including reading) and/or mathematics, and attain proficiency in meeting state academic standards (20 USC § 6316(e)(12) (C); 34 CFR § 200.45; 8 NYCRR §§ 120.4(a)(5), (d)(2)(iv)). School districts must give parents of SES-eligible students notice of the availability of services, information about approved providers in the area and, upon request, assistance in selecting a provider (20 USC § 6316(e)(2); 8 NYCRR §§ 100.3(c), 120.4(f)). Parents choose their child's SES provider from a list of state-approved providers for their area. Districts then arrange for services with the provider selected by a child's parents (20 USC § 6312(e)(3)(1), (2); 34 CFR §§ 200.45(c), 200.46(b)(1); 8 NYCRR § 120.4(b)).

14:99. What steps must a school and district take when the school fails to make adequate yearly progress (AYP) for four consecutive years?

When a school is designated as requiring academic progress (SRAP): year 3 and as in need of corrective action under the federal No Child Left Behind Act of 2001 (NCLB) (see **14:91**), the school superintendent must develop a corrective action plan, which must be approved by the school board within three months following the identification. The plan must be implemented by the first day of regular student attendance the next school year after the school year in which the school was so identified. If the board has not approved the corrective action plan by that time, then the plan must be implemented immediately upon approval.

The corrective action plan must include at least one of the following actions:

- Replacement of school staff relevant to the school's failure to make AYP, subject to any existing applicable collective bargaining provisions, and tenure termination rights under section 3020-a of the Education Law.
- Institution and full implementation of a new curriculum, including providing appropriate professional development for all relevant staff that relies on scientifically based research, and offers substantial promise of improving educational achievement for low-achieving students and enabling the school to make AYP.
- Significant decrease in management authority at the school level, subject to any existing applicable collective bargaining provisions.
- Appointment of an outside expert to advise the school on its progress toward making AYP, based on the school plan.
- Extension of the school year or school day for the school, subject to collective bargaining under the Taylor Law.
- Restructuring of the internal organization structure of the school (20 USC §§ 6316(b)(3)(b)(i), (7)(C); 34 CFR 200.42(b)(4); 8 NYCRR § 100.2(p)(6)(iii),(viii)).

In addition, a school district with one or more schools identified as in need of corrective action under the NCLB must continue to provide students the opportunity to transfer to another school (see **14:97–98**), and to make supplemental educational services (see **14:98**) available to eligible students in that school (20 USC § 6316(b)(7)(C); 34 CFR §§ 200.42(b)(1),(3), 200.44(a), 200.45(c); 8 NYCRR 100.2(p)(6)(viii), 120.3(a), 120.4(b)).

14:100. What steps must a school and district take when the school fails to make adequate yearly progress (AYP) for five consecutive years?

When a school is designated as requiring academic progress (SRAP): year 4 and as in need of restructuring under the federal No Child Left Behind Act of 2001 (NCLB) (see **14:91**), the school superintendent must develop a restructuring plan in a format prescribed by the commissioner of education, which must be approved by the school board no later than June 30 of the school in which the school is so designated. The plan, which need not be implemented unless the school fails to make AYP for one additional year, must make fundamental reforms such as significant changes in the school's staff, governance, or organization. It also may include a plan to close or phase out the school and replace it with a new one (20 USC § 6316(b)(8)(B); 34 CFR § 200.43(b)(3); 8 NYCRR § 100.2(p)(6)(iv),(ix)).

A school district with one or more schools identified as in need of restructuring under the NCLB must continue to provide students the opportunity to transfer to another school (see **14:97–99**) and to make supplemental educational services (see **14:98**) available to eligible students in that school (20 USC § 6316(b)(8)(A); 34 CFR §§ 200.43(b), 200.44(a), 200.45(c); 8 NYCRR 100.2(p)(6)(viii), 120.3(a), 120.4(b)). It also must provide teachers and parents with prompt notice and adequate opportunity to comment before it takes any action, and allow them to participate in the development of the restructuring plan (20 USC § 6316(b)(8)(C); 34 CFR § 200.43(b)(4); 8 NYCRR § 100.2(p)(6)(ix)).

14:101. What steps must a school and district take when the school fails to make adequate yearly progress (AYP) for six consecutive years?

A school that is designated as requiring academic progress (SRAP): year 5 and that has been previously identified as in need of restructuring under the federal No Child Left Behind Act of 2001 (NCLB) (see **14:91**) must implement its restructuring plan (see **14:100**) no later than the first day of regular school attendance of the school year following the administration of the assessments that caused the school to be so designated (8 NYCRR § 100.2(p)(6)(v)).

14:102. What happens if a school continues to fail to make adequate yearly progress (AYP) after implementing a restructuring plan?

When a school continues to fail to make AYP for two consecutive years during the three school years following implementation of a restructuring plan, the school superintendent must develop a revised restructuring plan. The revised restructuring plan must be approved by the school board by June 30 of the school year in which such plan is required (8 NYCRR § 100.2(p)(6)(v)).

14:103. Are there any circumstances under which a school that fails to make adequate yearly progress and is subject to the requirements of the federal No Child Left Behind Act of 2001 (NCLB) does not have to develop an improvement, corrective action, or restructuring plan?

Yes, if the school has been placed under registration review (SURR) and the corrective action plan and comprehensive action plan developed as a result of such placement complies with NCLB requirements (8 NYCRR § 100.2(p)(10)(iv); see **14:107**)

14:104. What happens when a school district fails to make adequate yearly progress (AYP)?

In addition to being designated as a *district requiring academic progress* and possibly as *in need of improvement* under the federal No Child Left Behind Act of 2001 (NCLB) (see **14:91**), the district must develop a district improvement plan in a format prescribed by the commissioner of education, and in consultation with parents, school staff, and others. The plan must be approved by the school board no later than three months following identification, and submitted to the commissioner for approval. It must be implemented by the beginning of the next school year after the school year in which the district was identified as requiring academic progress (20 USC § 6316(c)(7); 34 CFR § 200.52(a); 8 NYCRR § 100.2(p)(7)(i),(iii)).

14:105. Are school districts that fail to make adequate yearly progress (AYP) subject to corrective action?

Yes. The commissioner may identify a school district for corrective action at any time after it has been identified as in need of improvement under the NCLB (see **14:91**). However, the commissioner must identify a district for corrective action if the district fails to make AYP by the end of the second full school year after it was identified for improvement (20 USC § 6316(c)(10)(B); 34 CFR §§ 200.50(e)(1), 200.53(c); 8 NYCRR § 100.2(p)(7)(iv)).

When a school district is identified for corrective action under the NCLB, the state must take at least one of the following steps:

- Defer programmatic funds or reduce administrative funds.
- Institute and fully implement a new curriculum that is based on state and local academic content and achievement standards, including providing appropriate professional development based on scientifically based research for all relevant staff, that offers substantial promise of improving educational achievement for low-achieving students.

- Replace district personnel relevant to the failure to make AYP, subject to existing applicable collective bargaining provisions and tenure termination rights under section 3020-a of the Education Law.
- Remove particular schools from the jurisdiction of the district and establish alternative arrangements for public governance and supervision of such schools.
- Appoint a receiver or trustee to administer the affairs of the district in place of the superintendent and school board.
- Abolish or restructure the district.
- Authorize students to transfer from district schools to higher-performing public schools in another district, and provide to such students transportation or the cost of transportation, in conjunction with at least one other of the corrective actions specified above (20 USC § 6316(10)(C); 34 CFR § 200.53(c)(2)).

14:106. Can a school or district lose its designation as either requiring academic progress or in need of improvement, corrective action, or restructuring under the No Child Left Behind Act of 2001 (NCLB)?

A school or district requiring academic progress will be removed from such status if it makes adequate yearly progress for two consecutive years on the same performance criteria or additional indicator that caused it to be so identified. The same applies to a school or district identified for improvement, corrective action or restructuring under the NCLB (20 USC §§ 6316(c)(11); 34 CFR §§ 200.32(d), 200.33(c), 200.35(b), 200.50(h); 8 NYCRR §§ 100.2(p)(6)(xv)(xvi), (7)(ii),(v)).

14:107. What happens if a school is identified and placed under registration review?

The commissioner of education will place a school under registration review (SURR) if its students are found to be the farthest from benchmarks established to measure the performance of the "all students" accountability group (see **14:92**). Following identification of such a school, the commissioner will appoint a team to undertake a resource, planning, and program audit of the school and the district where the school is located.

Based on the results of the audit, the commissioner may require that the school superintendent develop a correction action plan in consultation with school staff, parents, and community members to address the findings of the audit. The plan must be approved by the school board and submitted to the commissioner for review and approval (8 NYCRR § 100.2(p)(9),(10)(i)).

In addition, the school must develop a comprehensive education plan or modify any such existing plan in accordance with the district's school-based management and shared decision making plan. The corrective action plan and the comprehensive education plan must be submitted to the commissioner by July 31 of the school year next following the school year in which the commissioner placed the school under registration review (8 NYCRR § 100.2(p)(10)(ii),(iii)).

Unless the period is shortened or extended by the commissioner, a SURR school has three full academic years to show progress. If it doesn't, the commissioner will recommend to the Board of Regents that its registration be revoked, and the school be declared an unsound educational environment (8 NYCRR § 100.2(p)(10)(vi)).

For SURR schools that receive Title I funds under the federal No Child Left Behind Act of 2001, the corrective action plan and comprehensive education plan serves in lieu of a school improvement plan, corrective action plan or restructuring, provided they comply with NCLB requirements (8 NYCRR § 100.2(p)(10)(iv)).

Instructional Resources

14:108. What is a textbook?

A *textbook* is defined as "any book, or a book substitute, which shall include hard covered or paperback books, workbooks, or manuals" and for expenses incurred after July 1, 1999, "any courseware or other content-based instructional materials in an electronic format, as such terms are defined in the regulations of the commissioner, which a pupil is required to use as a text, or a text-substitute, in a particular class or program in the school he or she legally attends" (§ 701(2)).

14:109. Does a district have a duty to provide free textbooks to students?

Yes. School boards have the power and duty to purchase and to loan, upon individual requests, textbooks to all children residing in the district enrolled in kindergarten through 12th grade. These textbooks are to be loaned free to such students, subject to rules and regulations that are or may be prescribed by the Board of Regents and the school board (§ 701(3); *Appeal of Lease*, 39 Educ. Dep't Rep. 215 (1999)).

For information on the purchase and loan of textbooks for nonpublic school students, see **24:14.**

14:110. Does a district have a duty to provide alternative instructional materials to students with disabilities?

Yes, each school board and board of cooperative educational services (BOCES) must establish a plan to ensure that every student with a disability who needs instructional materials in an alternative format not only will receive those materials but also at the same time instructional materials are available to nondisabled students. *Alternative format* is defined to mean any medium or format other than a traditional print textbook that is needed as an accommodation for a disabled student, including but not limited to, Braille, large print, open and closed caption, audio, or electronic files.

The plan must specify:

- a procurement policy giving a preference to vendors who agree to provide such alternative formats;
- how students will access electronic files, if needed, and how electronic files will be converted if necessary;
- the process to be used when ordering materials to identify the needs of students with disabilities residing in the district who will need alternative instructional materials;
- ordering timelines to ensure such materials are available at the same time as regular format materials;
- procedures to avoid delay in ordering such materials when students with disabilities move into the district or enroll in a BOCES program (§§ 1604(29-a), 1709(4-a), 1950(4-a), 2503(7-a), 2554(7-a), 3602(10)(b); as amended by Chapter 377 of the Laws of 2001; 8 NYCRR § 200.2(b)(10), (i); State Education Department Memorandum from Lawrence C. Gloeckler, "Amendment to Section 200.2 of the Commissioner's Regulations Implementing Chapter 377 of the Laws of 2001: Plans to Provide Instructional Materials in Alternative Formats to Students with Disabilities").

School districts must also have a plan to supply textbooks in alternative formats to preschool children with disabilities (8 NYCRR § 200.2(c)(2)(vi)).

14:111. Can the state dictate the use of certain textbooks in the public schools?

No. The school board, or whatever body or officer that performs the function of the board, designates the textbooks to be used (§ 701; Opn. Att'y Gen. 1919; 18 St. Dep't Rep. 456 (1919)).

14:112. Is there any limitation on how frequently textbooks may be changed in a school system?

Yes. After a textbook has been designated for use, the district is prohibited from replacing it with any other book within a five-year period from the time of its designation, unless three-fourths of the school board or whatever body or officer that performs the function votes to do otherwise (§ 702).

14:113. Do parents have a right to inspect classroom materials?

Under the Hatch Amendment (20 USC § 1232h), parents have the right "to inspect, upon request, any instructional material used as part of the educational curriculum for the student" (20 USC § 1232h(c)(1)(C)(i)). However, the Hatch Amendment does not give parents the right to inspect course materials because they find such materials offensive or just because the school receives federal aid.

In addition, parents have the right to inspect, upon request, any instrument used in the collection, disclosure, or use of personal information before the instrument is administered or distributed to a student (20 USC § 1232h (c)(1)(E), (F)), except for personal information collected from students for the exclusive purpose of developing, evaluating, or providing educational products or services for students or educational institutions, such as college or military recruitment, book clubs or magazines providing low-cost literary products or curriculum, tests and or other instructional materials used by schools (20 USC § 1232h (c)(4)(A)).

Parents also have the right to inspect survey[s] created by a third party before the survey is administered or distributed by a school to a student, except a survey administered to a student in accordance with the Individuals with Disabilities Education Act (20 USC § 1232h (c)(1)(A)(i), (5)(A)).

Students may not be required to submit to a survey, analysis, or evaluation that reveals information regarding the following: political affiliation; mental or psychological problems potentially embarrassing to the student or his or her family; sex behavior and attitudes; illegal, anti-social, self-incriminating and demeaning behavior; critical appraisals of other individuals with close family relationship, legally recognized or analogous privileged relationship; religious practices, affiliations, or beliefs of the student or student's parent; or income. Participation in survey instruments soliciting such information requires the consent of the student, or his or her parent, if the student is a minor (20 USC § 1232h(b)). School districts must give parents and students annual notice of this right (20 USC § 1232h(c)).

14:114. Do parents have the right to require that certain alleged controversial books or other curricular materials not be used or given to their child?

No. The school board has broad authority to determine what books will be used in its courses, and parents of a student cannot compel a board to use a particular textbook or to discontinue the use of one (*Appeal of Dimasio*, 39 Educ. Dep't Rep. 827 (2000); *Appeal of Carney*, 39 Educ. Dep't Rep. 255 (1999); *Appeal of Smith*, 34 Educ. Dep't Rep. 346 (1994)). The only exceptions are for students who may be excused from that part of the study of health that conflicts with their religious beliefs, and from instruction about

AIDS (§ 3204(5); 8 NYCRR §§ 16.2, 135.3(b)(2); see also **14:19, 14:40**). In addition, parents may not compel a school district to assign an alternate curriculum to their child either based on their disapproval of classroom assignments (*Appeal of Carney*).

The courts have also upheld the broad discretion of school boards in selecting instructional materials against parental challenges that the use of particular materials violates the First Amendment rights of both them and their children. For example, despite the claim by parents in two separate cases that the use of the "Impressions" reading series fostered a pagan belief in the occult, in direct opposition to their Christian beliefs, two federal appellate courts have ruled that the school districts' use of the book did not violate either the Establishment or Free Exercise Clause of the First Amendment (*Brown v. Woodland Joint Unified Sch. Dist.*, 27 F.3d 1373 (9th Cir. 1994); *Fleischfresser v. Directors of Sch. Dist. 200*, 15 F.3d 680 (7th Cir. 1994)).

14:115. May a school board remove a previously approved textbook because of objections to the material contained in it, without violating the First Amendment?

Yes. However, according to a decision from the United States Court of Appeals for the Eleventh Circuit, the removal and the methods used must be "reasonably related to legitimate pedagogical concerns." In *Virgil v. School Bd.*, 862 F.2d 1517 (11th Cir. 1989), the court reviewed the removal of a textbook used in an elective humanities course designed for 11th- and 12th-grade students because of the explicit sexuality and excessively vulgar language and subject matter contained in selections within the textbook of Aristophane's "Lysistrata" and Chaucer's "The Miller's Tale." Neither of these selections was required or assigned during the course. The book remained available in the school library for students' use, along with other adaptations and translations of "Lysistrata" and "The Miller's Tale."

In upholding the removal, the court applied the standard set by the United States Supreme Court in *Hazelwood Sch. Dist. v. Kuhlmeier*, 484 U.S. 260 (1988). The case focused on a permissible school board regulation of expression that "may fairly be characterized as part of the school curriculum," provided such regulation is "reasonably related to legitimate pedagogical concerns." (The *Hazelwood* case had involved school censorship of a school-sponsored student newspaper.) In *Virgil*, the court found that the selections were part of the school curriculum because it was reasonable to think that the public may perceive them to bear the school's imprimatur, and that the motivation for the removal presented a legitimate concern regarding the appropriateness of the selections for the student audience in question.

The United States Court of Appeals for the Ninth Circuit held that a parent could not proceed on a civil rights liability action claiming a First

Amendment violation based on a school district's refusal to remove from a required reading list Mark Twain's *The Adventures of Huckleberry Finn* and William Faulkner's *A Rose for Emily.* The student and her parent found the books offensive because of their repeated use of racially derogatory terms (*Montiero v. Tempe Union High Sch. Dist.*, 158 F.3d 1022 (9th Cir. 1998)).

Although New York is under the jurisdiction of the Second Circuit, these cases may have some persuasive value in this state.

14:116. Are schools required to have a library?

Yes. The commissioner's regulations require each school to maintain a library that meets the needs of students and serves as an adequate complement to the instructional program in the various areas of the curriculum.

The commissioner's regulations also provide the following direction as to the number of holdings that junior and senior high schools of different sizes must maintain:

- The library of a junior high school with fewer than 200 students must contain at least 1,000 titles.
- The library of a high school with fewer than 200 students must contain at least 1,000 titles.
- The library of a junior-senior high school with fewer than 200 students must contain at least 2,000 titles.
- The library of a secondary school in which the average daily attendance is between 200 and 500 students must contain at least 3,000 titles.
- The library of a secondary school in which the average daily attendance is between 500 and 1,000 students must contain at least 5,000 titles.
- The library of a secondary school in which the average daily attendance is more than 1,000 students must contain at least 8,000 titles (8 NYCRR § 91.1).

14:117. Are schools required to have a school librarian?

Yes. Each district with a secondary school must employ a certified school library-media specialist, unless equivalent service is provided by an alternative arrangement approved by the commissioner of education, in accordance with specified standards contained in the commissioner's regulations (8 NYCRR § 91.2; *Appeal of Walker,* 43 Educ. Dep't Rep. ___; dec. no. 15,074 (2004)).

14:118. May a school board remove books from the school library without violating the First Amendment?

The constitutional issues in the removal of books from a school library are focused on the school board's motivations in taking such action. In *Board of*

Educ. v. Pico, 457 U.S. 853 (1982), the United States Supreme Court held that although a school board has the authority to remove certain books it deems inappropriate from the school library, the board may not remove such books to restrict access to certain social, political, and moral ideas which the board simply disapproves. In its decision, the court said that the school board would have been within its rights to remove the books if they contained vulgar language or if the school board had established a policy setting forth criteria, such as "educational suitability," for keeping books in the district's libraries.

Prior to *Pico*, a federal appeals court had ruled that a district's removal of a film version of "The Lottery" by Shirley Jackson from the school library violated the First Amendment rights of students because the decision to remove the film was based on the fact that a majority of the board and some parents found the film's ideological and religious themes offensive (*Pratt v. Independent Sch. Dist. No. 831*, 670 F.2d 771 (8th Cir. 1982)).

Following *Pico*, the United States Court of Appeals for the Second Circuit (which includes New York State) dismissed a student's complaint that the school board had violated the First Amendment by removing certain library books because of their vulgar and obscene language (*Bicknell v. Vergennes Union High Sch. Bd. of Directors*, 638 F.2d 438 (2d Cir. 1980)). Here there was no dispute that the board had not removed the books in question simply because of the ideas they contained or that there was any political motivation on the part of the board. Rather, the court stated the school board had the right to remove those books because of their vulgar and sexually explicit content.

14:119. May teachers duplicate copyrighted material in books or musical compositions for their classes or student groups without prior permission?

With certain restrictions, yes. Federal law prohibits any "infringing use" of copyrighted works, that is, the use of copyrighted works without the consent of the author or owner of the copyright (see 17 USC §§ 101, 106, 107, 117).

The law specifically states, however, that the "fair use" of such works for teaching purposes, including making "multiple copies for classroom use," as well as for criticism, comment, scholarship or research, is not an infringing use. Fair use is not a rigidly defined term, but rather is based on a number of factors, including the purpose and character of the use, whether such use is of a commercial nature or is for nonprofit educational purposes, the nature of the original work, the size of the portion used, and the effect on the value or market of the original work (see *Basic Books, Inc., v. Kinko's Graphics Corp.,* 758 F.Supp. 1522 (S.D.N.Y. 1991); Notes of Committee on the Judiciary, House Report No. 94-1476, in note following 17 USC § 107).

Based on guidelines for classroom copying by the House Judiciary Subcommittee, teachers may reproduce materials if four tests are passed:

brevity (a single short poem, story, essay or illustration, or a short excerpt of a larger work); spontaneity (a decision made by the teacher making the copy close to the time the material is to be used); cumulative use (generally no more than nine occasions per teacher per term); and notice (each copy must include the name of the copyright owner, year of publication and a (c) or © symbol).

Copyrighted, or "proprietary," computer software and documentation may not be reproduced other than to make archival back-ups or because the copy is an essential step to use the computer program in conjunction with a machine (see 17 USC § 117). "Shareware," which is software in the public domain, is not subject to this restriction (37 CFR § 201.26).

It is important to note that classroom and instructional fair use for plays and musical numbers does not include public performances, especially if an admission fee is charged (17 USC § 110).

Violation of copyright may result in fines and injunctive actions against a school district. Particularly in the case of computer software, violation of a license agreement may void any applicable warranty or continued service arrangement, even if the copyright laws have not been violated (17 USC §§ 501–505).

14:120. What is the law regarding use and possession of hypodermic syringes for instructional purposes?

In accordance with section 811 of the Education Law and part 137 of the commissioner's regulations, school personnel may procure, use, and possess hypodermic syringes and needles for educational purposes, provided school authorities file a certificate of need for such equipment with the commissioner of education and the New York State Department of Health.

Authorized use of hypodermic syringes and needles by school districts is limited to actual educational demonstrations or other educational purposes designated in the certificate of need. Any other use is unauthorized and prohibited.

A certificate of need must designate specified information including the individuals responsible for the custody of hypodermic syringes and needles used in the institution, the names of individuals designated as responsible for supervising the use of such hypodermic syringes and needles, and the safeguards to be taken to prevent such instruments from falling into the hands of unauthorized persons (§ 811; 8 NYCRR § 137.1).

A record of all hypodermic syringes and needles purchased, lost, stolen, or destroyed must be maintained and kept for a period of two years (8 NYCRR § 137.3).

School Assistance to College-bound Students

14:121. May school districts restrict the number of college applications students may submit for processing by their high schools?

No. School districts may, however, establish rules of procedures for submission of such requests (§ 209-a).

14:122. What funds are available for college scholarships for New York State high school graduates?

The Pell Grant is a federal aid program for undergraduates. It is the "floor" of the aid package, designed to be combined with other aid sources. Like the Tuition Assistance Program (TAP), it is based on a family's resources, is noncompetitive and does not need to be repaid.

The Tuition Assistance Program (TAP) is a state grant. It is based on a family's taxable income balance, adjusted to take into account other family members attending college, tuition costs and the receipt of other financial aid. Neither a qualifying examination nor repayment is required. Awards are made to all eligible applicants. Students who are in an approved postsecondary program are eligible to receive annual TAP grants for up to eight years of combined undergraduate and graduate study.

Children, spouses, and financial dependents of individuals who are either killed or severely disabled while on active military duty and the military members themselves are also eligible for Military Enhanced Recognition, incentive and tribute scholarships (MERIT) (NY Educ Law § 608-a).

Similarly, children of Vietnam veterans born with spina bifida are entitled to an annual award of $450 for four or five years depending upon the length of study required for their academic program (8 NYCRR § 2201.4).

In addition, children, spouses, and financial dependents of firefighters, volunteer fire fighters, police officers, peace officers and emergency medical service workers who have died as a result of an injury sustained in the line of duty in service of New York state are eligible to receive scholarships as well (Educ. Law § 604, 668-b).

World Trade Center Memorial Scholarships are available to individuals, children, and financial dependents whose parent or spouse were either killed or permanently disabled in the attack on the World Trade Center (Educ. Law § 604, 608).

The New York State Higher Education Services Corporation's Guaranteed Student Loan Program enables students to borrow money from New York State lending institutions at a low interest rate.

For information about TAP, state-supported scholarship assistance programs and/or medical, dental and veterinary school loan programs, please consult the Higher Education Services Corporation, 99 Washington Avenue, Albany, N.Y. 12210; telephone: 518-474-5642; Web site: http://www.hesc.com.

15. School District Reorganization

15:1. What is school district reorganization?

School district reorganization is the term used to define the statutory processes by which two or more school districts are merged into a single district or a school district is dissolved. The various methods of school district reorganization include centralization, annexation, consolidation, and dissolution, each of which has a different purpose and implication. Each reorganization procedure is limited in its application to one or more of the organizational types of school districts: for example, union free, central, common, and city school districts.

15:2. What is centralization?

Centralization is the most common form of reorganization. A new central school district is created by the merger of two or more contiguous districts, with a new school board and boundaries that encompass the area of the districts being reorganized (see **15:11**). Under the Education Law, city school districts are not eligible for centralization (§§ 1801(2), 1804(1)).

15:3. What is annexation?

Annexation is a reorganization procedure whereby any school district, other than a city school district, is dissolved and its territory annexed to a contiguous central school district (§ 1802(2); see **15:12**) or to a union free school district (§ 1705; see **15:13**). The dissolution of the annexed district is a part of the annexation process and is different from the dissolution of a school district ordered by the district superintendent (§ 1505; see **15:16**).

Unlike in centralization, annexation does not result in the creation of a new district, nor is a new school board elected. The operation of the annexing school district remains basically the same before and after the annexation. Residents of the annexed district become eligible to vote and may be elected to the school board of the annexing district in subsequent elections (see § 1705).

15:4. What is consolidation?

Consolidation is a reorganization procedure that may involve the merger of any combination of common or union free school districts to form a new

---

Editor's Note: In addition to the Education Law, A Guide to the Reorganization of School Districts in New York State *(Albany, N.Y.: State Education Department, 1998) has been used as a primary reference throughout this chapter.*

common or union free school district (§ 1510; see **15:14**). Central and city school districts may not participate in the consolidation of union free and/or common school districts.

However, consolidation may also involve the incorporation of districts contiguous to city school districts of cities with populations of less than 125,000 residents into the city school district. The resulting school district becomes known as an enlarged city school district (§§ 1524, 1526; see **15:15**). Similar to annexation, the district to be consolidated will cease to exist.

15:5. What is dissolution?

Dissolution is a seldom-used form of reorganization in which a district superintendent by order dissolves one or more districts within his or her supervisory district and forms a new district from such territory. Alternatively, the district superintendent may dissolve a district and unite the territory with an adjoining district or districts, other than a city school district (§ 1505(1)).

A district superintendent may also partition existing union free, central, central high school and enlarged city school districts, dissolve and reform the district if necessary, and form a new union free or city school district out of such territory upon certain specified conditions set forth in the Education Law section 2218 (see **6:23**).

15:6. What is the Master Plan and its impact on school district reorganization?

The Master Plan, codified in 1972 in section 314 of the Education Law under the name State Plan, is an administrative and statutory effort intended to advance school district reorganization so as to provide education facilities in the most efficient and economical manner, while also serving the best interests of children. The plan was originally adopted by the State Education Department in 1947 and was designed to encourage consolidation, annexation, and centralization, in order to improve the functioning of public schools. The result was massive reorganization of districts, a reduction in the number of school districts in the state, and the creation of larger districts.

15:7. Is there a legal procedure whereby a school district can be broken up and divided into two or more smaller districts?

Yes. An example of this was the creation of community school districts in New York City, which was accomplished by a change in the Education Law that required enactment of a specific law by the state Legislature (see Art. 52-A).

The Education Law also allows district superintendents to partition off, dissolve, and reform and form a new union free or city school district from certain existing districts and under certain specified conditions (§ 2218; see 6:23).

15:8. What is the role of the commissioner of education in school district reorganizations?

While the commissioner of education is not authorized to compel a reorganization of school districts without voter approval (§§ 1705(1)(a), 1801(4) the commissioner does play a pivotal role in school district reorganization. This role includes, but is not limited to, preliminary activities conducted prior to voter consideration of district reorganization (§§ 314(2), (3), 1705(1)(b), 1801(1), (2), (3)).

In most circumstances, the process of district reorganization begins with an order issued by the commissioner. For example, the commissioner issues an order laying out the new district boundaries for a centralized school district (§ 1801). The order laying out the new school district does not constitute the establishment of a new district, but is a proposal made by the commissioner upon which the residents of the new proposed district will vote.

In an annexation, the commissioner issues an order dissolving one or more common, union free, or central school districts and annexing the territory of such district(s), or portion thereof, to one or more adjoining central or union free school districts, subject to the approval of the voters of each affected district (§§ 1705(1)(a), 1801(2)).

Although the commissioner has the statutory authority to independently issue orders concerning reorganization, the practice has been that the commissioner will not issue these orders until an adequate feasibility study has been conducted and indicates that the proposal is desirable, that the people in the district have been informed of the potential reorganization, and that there is evidence that the majority of the voters in the affected district or districts support the proposal.

Reorganization Procedures

15:9. Are there any preliminary steps school districts must take before they can reorganize?

Generally, the first step toward reorganization includes joint meetings between the affected school boards to gain information and to determine whether reorganization offers sufficient benefits to warrant formal study.

If the boards agree that reorganization might be beneficial, they then typically undertake a joint feasibility study, also known as an efficiency study, which is a written report commissioned by a school district considering reorganization. Its purpose is to describe how a specific combination of districts may operate if reorganization were to be implemented. The commissioner of education has ruled that the authority to order a feasibility study rests solely with the school board; district voters may not compel the board to conduct such a study (*Appeal of Leman*, 32 Educ. Dep't Rep. 579 (1993); § 3602(14)(h)).

A feasibility study should include:

- Current and projected student enrollments.
- Current and projected professional staffing plans.
- Current and projected housing plans.
- A plan for educational programs and curricula in the proposed district.
- A plan for transportation in the proposed district.
- Fiscal implications of the reorganization, including changes in state aid, expenditures, and local tax effort.

Once the study has been conducted, the affected boards inform their residents of the potential reorganization and assess the public's support for the proposed reorganization. The established practice is that the commissioner will not take formal action to authorize a reorganization unless there is evidence of support in each of the districts included in the proposed reorganization. Public support may be assessed through the use of petitions or advisory referendums (straw votes).

15:10. Is state aid available to school districts that conduct a feasibility study?

No. The costs of feasibility studies are not eligible for state aid reimbursement (§ 3602(14)(h)(4)).

15:11. What are the procedures involved in centralization?

After an adequate study is performed indicating that the proposed centralization is desirable and that a majority of the voters in the affected districts support it, the commissioner of education may then issue an order laying out the territory of the new central school district (§ 1801(1), (2)). The order constitutes only a proposal (§ 1801(4)).

Within 10 days of making and entering the order of consolidation, the commissioner shall transmit a certified copy to the clerk of each affected district. Within five days of receipt, the clerk of each affected district must post a certified copy of the commissioner's order in five conspicuous places within each district (§ 1801(3)).

At this point, a petition requesting the commissioner to call a special meeting may then be filed. The petition must be signed by at least 100 voters or by the number of voters equal to at least 10 percent of the student population of the combined districts, whichever is less (§ 1802(1)). The commissioner may then call a special meeting to allow the qualified voters in the affected districts to determine whether or not the new district will be created (§§ 1801(4), 1802(1)(b)).

The Education Law authorizes two types of special meetings: one in which either the votes of all districts are combined, or an alternative procedure in which the votes of each district are separately tabulated, to determine if voter approval exists (§§ 1803, 1803-a).

15:12. What are the procedures involved in annexation to a central school district?

After an adequate study is performed indicating that the proposed annexation is desirable and that a majority of the voters in the affected districts support it, the commissioner of education may issue an order annexing an existing school district to a contiguous central school district. Within five days of receiving a certified copy of the commissioner's order, the clerk of each affected district must post a certified copy of the commissioner's order in five conspicuous places within each district (§ 1801(3)). The order becomes effective in 60 days (§ 1802(2)).

However, the voters of any school district affected by the proposed annexation to a central school district may, within 60 days after the filing of the commissioner's annexation order, submit a petition requesting a referendum, signed by at least 100 qualified voters or by a number of voters equal to at least 10 percent of the student population in the district per the last census, whichever is less (§ 1802(2)(b)). Within 30 days of receipt of such petition, the commissioner must schedule a referendum and provide notice of the referendum in each district that has requested one to determine whether or not the annexation will occur (§ 1802(2)(b)). The notice of the referendum must be posted in 10 conspicuous places at least 10 days before the meeting. It must also be published in a newspaper at least three days before the meeting (§ 1802(2)(b)).

A majority of the voters in each district must vote in favor of the annexation in order for it to be valid (§ 1803(1)). If the voters reject annexation, the question may not be presented again for one year except as otherwise provided by law. If the question of annexation is not again presented within two years, the original commissioner's order becomes null and void (§ 1803(8)).

15:13. What are the procedures involved in an annexation to a union free school district?

After an adequate study is performed indicating that the proposed annexation is desirable and that a majority of the voters in the affected districts support it, the commissioner of education may issue and file with each affected district an order annexing an existing school district to a contiguous union free school district.

In this type of annexation, the law requires voter approval of the commissioner's order proposing the annexation in order for the reorganization to become effective (§ 1705(1)(a)). Therefore, no petition by the voters is necessary. The commissioner must fix a time and place for a special meeting for residents to vote on an annexation resolution (§ 1705(1)(b)). If the voters reject the resolution, the question may not be presented to the voters again for one year. If no meeting is called within two years after the resolution's defeat, the commissioner's order becomes null and void (§ 1705(2)(b)).

15:14. What are the procedures involved in the consolidation of union free and/or common school districts?

Upon receipt of a petition signed by at least 10 qualified voters of each affected school district requesting a meeting to consider the consolidation of one or more school districts, the respective school boards of the affected districts must submit a consolidation proposal to the commissioner of education. Upon the commissioner's approval, a special meeting is called in each district to gain the approval for the consolidation by the qualified voters of each district (§§ 1511, 1512). Each board must give public notice that a meeting of such districts will be held at a centrally located place in order to vote upon the consolidation. The meeting must be held not less than 20 nor more than 30 days after publication of the notice (§ 1511(1)). If the consolidation is approved, a new district is created and a new school board is elected. If consolidation is rejected, the question may not be raised again for one year (§§ 1512, 1513, 1702).

15:15. What are the procedures for consolidations involving city school districts?

In this form of reorganization, after an adequate study is performed indicating that the proposed consolidation is desirable and that a majority of the voters in the affected districts support the proposed consolidation, it must then be approved by the school board of the city district and the qualified voters of the adjoining district (§§ 1524(1), 1526). If so approved, the adjoining district is dissolved and the territory is added to the city school district. A new district is not created, nor is a new school board elected (§ 1524(1)).

15:16. What are the procedures for dissolving a district?

After an adequate study is performed indicating that the proposed dissolution is desirable and that a majority of the voters in the affected districts support the proposed dissolution, the district superintendent issues an order dissolving one or more districts within his or her supervisory district and annexing the territory to an adjoining district (§ 1505(1)). If the territory of more than one district superintendent is affected by the dissolution, approval by a majority of the district superintendents is required (§ 1505(1)).

Dissolution is the only reorganization process that does not specifically provide an opportunity for the qualified voters of the affected district or districts to make the final determination as to whether or not a reorganization will be implemented. However, the Education Law establishes a process by which voters may contest the dissolution by filing their objections with the local county court judge, who then appoints a committee to determine whether the dissolution should occur (§ 1505(2)).

15:17. Is there a limit to the number of times a proposal to reorganize may be submitted to the voters within a given time period?

Yes. If a reorganization proposition is defeated by the voters, a revote on the same proposal cannot be called within one year after the original vote (§§ 1512(1), 1705(2)(b), 1803(8), 1803-a(6)). Additionally, the commissioner's order for reorganization is deemed null and void if a second special meeting is not called within two years of the original meeting at which the voters rejected the reorganization, or if a second meeting is held and the proposal is again defeated (§§ 1705(2)(b), 1803(8), 1803-a(6)).

Impact of Reorganization

15:18. How is the name of a newly created central school district selected?

The commissioner of education designates the name of a newly centralized district in the centralization order (§ 1801(2)). Subject to the commissioner's approval, school boards of new or reorganized central school districts may select a different name by filing a written request for a name change with the commissioner no later than 14 days before the centralization order is to become effective (§ 315). However, reorganized districts must comply with the commissioner's regulations concerning the use of simplified names (see 8 NYCRR Part 240).

15:19. What happens to the property and debts of former school districts after a reorganization?

Under all forms of reorganization, the newly reorganized district assumes the debts of the former school district, such as bonds or notes or those relating to school building construction (§§ 1517, 1705(3), 1804(5)(b)). Any other debts of the defunct district must be paid off out of that district's assets (§§ 1518, 1705(3), 1804(5)(a)).

In a centralization or annexation, the new central school district or annexing district "shall succeed to all the property rights" of the defunct district (§§ 1705(3), 1804(5)).

In a dissolution under section 1505 of the Education Law, the dissolved school district's property must be sold and the net proceeds of the sale are apportioned to the taxpayers of the dissolved district based on the latest assessment roll (§ 1520).

Special rules apply, however, to reorganizations conducted pursuant to section 2218 of the Education Law.

15:20. How does a school district reorganization affect employment contracts?

If a teacher has an employment contract with a school district, that contract is a property right subject to the normal rules of property distribution in a reorganization (*Barringer v. Powell*, 230 N.Y. 37 (1920)). For example, in a centralization, the employment contract would be an obligation assumed by the new district.

However, one court has ruled that a collective bargaining agreement is not a contract assumed by an annexing district. In this situation, the teachers from the annexed district become covered by the collective bargaining agreement between the teachers and the annexing district, and the contract between the annexed district and its union is not enforceable against the annexing district (*Cuba-Rushford CSD v. Rushford Faculty Ass'n*, 182 A.D.2d 127 (4th Dep't 1992)).

15:21. What employment rights are provided to employees of districts that have been dissolved or reorganized pursuant to annexation to a union free school district?

The Education Law only specifies the employment rights of employees in cases of dissolution of a school district and annexation to a union free school district and reorganization conducted pursuant to section 2218. However, a separate section applicable to annexations to a union free school district provides that the employees of the annexed district become employees of the annexing district and retain their tenure status and seniority (§ 1705(4)). If fewer teaching positions are necessary following the annexation, the teachers from both districts with the greatest seniority within each tenure area are retained in positions in the annexing district, and excessed teachers from both districts are placed on preferred eligible lists based on seniority (§ 1705(4)). To determine "salary, sick leave and any other purpose" in the annexing district, service in the annexed district will be credited as service in the annexing district (§ 1705(4)).

Other sections applicable generally to school district dissolution and reorganization further provide that where a district is dissolved and added to more than one school district, the teachers of the dissolved district are entitled to select the district in which they wish to be employed. Based on their preferences and seniority, they will be appointed to positions in the newly created district (§ 1505-a(1)). A district that employs teachers from dissolved districts is required to accept the seniority credit acquired in the dissolved district and credit such seniority as if the teacher had served in the annexing district to determine "salary, sick leave and any other purpose" (§ 1505-a(3)). If there are more teachers than positions available, the teachers of a dissolved district are entitled to be placed on the preferred eligible list of the annexing district, in order of seniority acquired in the dissolved district. The teachers would then fill any future vacancies in the annexing district at the payment schedule set by that district (§ 1505-a(2), (3)).

15:22. What employment rights exist for employees of districts that have been reorganized pursuant to centralization, consolidation, or annexation to a central school district?

Although the Education Law does not specify the employment rights of employees in school district reorganizations involving centralization, consolidation, or annexation to a central school district, the State Education Department (SED) has clarified those rights. According to SED, in a centralization or consolidation, teachers in the former school district become employees of the newly created district. Thus, the teachers from both districts with the greatest seniority within each tenure area are retained in positions in the new district and excessed teachers from both districts are placed on preferred eligible lists based on seniority.

In an annexation to a central school district, the more senior teachers from the annexed district do not displace teachers in the annexing district. However, teachers from the annexed district are entitled to fill any new positions created by the annexation in the annexing district based on the seniority credit earned at the annexed district. Former teachers of the annexed district not employed by the annexing district are entitled to be placed on the preferred eligible list of the annexing district.

According to SED, similar rights are applicable in a consolidation with a city school district.

15:23. How are superintendents affected by reorganization?

A superintendent under contract, other than one in an annexing district, does not have employment rights in the reorganized district. However, that superintendent's employment contract is considered a property right and becomes an obligation of the reorganized school district (see *Matter of Foster*, 28 Educ. Dep't Rep. 29 (1988)). Thus, the reorganized district must pay that superintendent's salary and benefits under his or her contract.

15:24. Is state aid available to school districts that reorganize?

Yes. Additional operating aid and building aid is available to certain school districts that reorganize and comply with particular requirements of the Education Law (§ 3602(14)).

15:25. Where can more information be obtained about reorganization?

Information about reorganization can be obtained by contacting the State Education Department, Office of Management Services: School District Organization and BOCES Services, Room 876, Education Building Annex, Albany, N.Y. 12234; or by calling the office at 518-474-3936. See also *A Guide to the Reorganization of School Districts in New York State* (Albany, N.Y.: State Education Department, 1998).

16. School Buildings, Grounds and Equipment

16:1. Are school districts required to prepare long-range plans on educational facilities?

Yes. Section 155.1 of the commissioner's regulations requires each school district to prepare and keep on file a comprehensive long-range plan pertaining to educational facilities.

The plan must be reevaluated and updated at least annually. It must include an appraisal of the following: the educational philosophy of the district with resulting administrative organization and program requirements; current and projected student enrollments; use of space and state-rated student capacity of existing facilities; the allocation of instructional space to meet the current and future special education program and service needs, and to serve students with disabilities in settings with nondisabled peers; priority of need of maintenance, repair or modernization of existing facilities, including consideration of the obsolescence and retirement of certain facilities; and the provision of additional facilities.

The numbers, types, space requirements and pupil capacities of facilities must relate to the present and projected needs of the school district programs, including mandated educational requirements and the current and future special education program and service space needed to serve all students with disabilities.

In addition, each school district must prepare a five-year capital facilities plan, as prescribed by the commissioner of education. The plan, which must be updated annually, must identify critical maintenance needs based upon consideration of the safety rating of each occupied building (§§ 409-d (2)(d); 8 NYCRR § 151.1(a), 155.3(c); see **17:18**).

16:2. Must the voters approve the designation of a site for a new school building?

Sometimes. Voter approval is required in a common school district and in any other school district that has a population of less than 5,000 (§§ 401(2), 2512(1), 2556(2)). However, although certain districts are not required to get voter approval for site selection, the board may still submit the issue of site selection to the voters (*Matter of Albanese*, 11 Educ. Dep't Rep. 166 (1972)).

16:3. Must the commissioner of education approve the site for construction and enlargement of school district facilities?

Yes. Pursuant to section 408 of the Education Law, section 155.1(c) of the commissioner's regulations requires that sites for the construction or enlargement of facilities be approved by the commissioner of education. This regulation also requires the district to consider the following when selecting a site:

- The size and location of a site must be consistent with the long-term building plans of the district (8 NYCRR § 155.1(c)(1)).
- The educational adaptability of the site must take into account the placement of the building and development of the grounds for outdoor educational programs and related activities, without excessive initial or development costs. Sites must also include the following minimum usable acres, unless otherwise approved by the commissioner: elementary school (K–6) — a three-acre base plus one acre for each 100 students, or fraction thereof; and secondary schools (7–12) — a 10-acre base plus one acre for each 100 students, or fraction thereof (8 NYCRR § 155.1(c)(2)).
- Sites must be developed to conserve natural resources and avoid environmental problems within the limits of the educational program. Care must be taken to ensure that the site and facilities are consistent with and contribute to the school and community environment and provide for the health and safety of occupants (8 NYCRR § 155.1(c)(3)).

The New York State School Boards Association recommends that a district considering a site contact the State Education Department's Office of Facilities Planning prior to purchase.

Acquisition and Disposal of School Property

16:4. How may a school district acquire real property for school purposes?

A school district may acquire real property for school purposes by gift, grant, devise (a clause in a will disposing of real property) or purchase; and by involuntary acquisition under some circumstances if an agreement cannot be made with the owner for the purchase (§ 404).

The school board as a corporate body holds title to real property (§§ 406, 1603, 1709(9)). In city school districts with fewer than 125,000 inhabitants, the school board holds title to real property purchased by it in the name of the school district (§ 2511(1)). In a Big 5 city school district, the school board takes title to real property in the name of the city, which holds the property in trust for use by the school district (§ 2557).

Special provisions regarding purchase and sale of real and personal property apply to large city school districts, as indicated in section 2556 of the Education Law.

16:5. Once a site has been properly selected, must the voters approve the purchase of real property?

Yes, except in city school districts with a population over 125,000 inhabitants, the purchase of real property is subject to the approval of the voters (§§ 416(1), 2511(1), 2556(1)).

16:6. Can a school board enter into an option agreement for the purchase of a school site without the voters' authorization or consent?

Yes, provided that the amount paid for the option is reasonable (Opn. of Counsel No. 65, 1 Educ. Dep't Rep. 764 (1952)). In such instances, the district is purchasing the option to buy the site at a later date, and not the site itself.

16:7. If a school district is given a site as a gift, must the district still get the voters' approval to accept it?

No. Voter approval is not necessary to accept the property as a gift (§ 404). However, except in large city school districts, voter approval is necessary before a school building can be erected on the property (§§ 416(1), 2512(1), 2556(1)).

16:8. Can a school district enter into a lease for a school building?

Yes. The school board in any union free, central or city school district, and the chancellor of the New York City school district, may authorize the lease of a school building from either another school district or from any person, partnership or corporation (§§ 403-b(1), 1726, 2503(8), 2554(6), 2590-h(17)).

If the lease is between two school districts, the leased building must be within a reasonable distance of the leasing district, as determined by the commissioner of education (§ 403-b(1)). If the lease is between a school district and a non-school entity, the leased building or facility must be located within the school district (§ 403-b(1)).

All leases and leased facilities must meet the following requirements:

- No lease shall become effective until approved by the commissioner of education (§ 403-b(1)(c)).
- The lease may not exceed five years unless the district voters have approved a longer term. The initial term of lease, however, cannot exceed the period of probable usefulness as prescribed by law (§ 403-b(1)(a); Local Fin. Law § 11.00(a)(2)).

- The voters in the lessee district must approve any renewal of the lease, except for those leases made by a large city school district (§§ 403-b(1)(d), 2503(8), 2554(6)).
- The voters in the lessee district must approve any capital project to be undertaken in a leased building or facility during the term of the lease subject to prior approval by the commissioner after the need for such project has been established, except for those leases made by a large city school district (§§ 403-b(1)(b), 2503(8), 2554(6)).
- The leased facility must meet all applicable standards for the health, safety and comfort of its occupants.
- The leased facility must be educationally adequate.
- The school district must have a current five-year facilities plan or other applicable long-range facilities plan that includes such lease (§§ 403-b(1)(c), 2503(8), 2554(6)).
- To be eligible for state aid, any leased facility must meet the requirements for access by individuals with disabilities and, when the purpose of the leased space includes special education programs and services, the leased space must be consistent with the district's comprehensive long-range plan for the allocation of instructional space to meet the current and future special education program and service needs and to serve students with disabilities in settings with nondisabled peers. (§§ 403-b(1)(e), 2503(8), 2554(6)); 8 NYCRR §§ 155.12(b)(6), (d)(5)(i)).

16:9. May a school district enter into a lease-purchase agreement for the purchase of school buildings?

Yes. A school board may enter into agreements for the lease-purchase of buildings for school purposes, either to be placed or erected on a district-owned site. Such an agreement is subject to the requirements in section 1726 of the Education Law. Approval by the district voters and the commissioner of education is also required. However, no lease-purchase agreement may be made for a period exceeding the applicable period of probable usefulness for the property (§§ 1726, 2503(8); Local Fin. Law § 11.00(a)(2); Gen. Mun. Law § 101; *Appeal of Brousseau*, 37 Educ. Dep't Rep. 295 (1998)).

16:10. May a school district sell its property?

Yes. A school board may, as prescribed by law, sell the real and personal property owned by the school district (§§ 1604(36), 1709(11), 1804(6)(a), (c), 2511, 2557).

In union free and small city school districts, voter approval is required to sell real property (§§ 1709(11), 2511). In central school districts that have been centralized for at least seven years, voter approval is not necessary unless a petition requesting a vote is submitted to the board, signed by at least 10 percent of the voters (§ 1804(6)(c)). Large city school districts do not need voter approval to sell real property (§ 2557).

Private sale of surplus equipment to a school board member or other school official or employee who is involved in the purchasing function is generally prohibited (Gen. Mun. Law Art. 18; Opn. St. Comp. 58-120).

In addition, school boards have a fiduciary responsibility to obtain the best price possible when selling or disposing of school district property (*Matter of Ross v. Wilson*, 308 N.Y. 605 (1955); *Matter of New City Jewish Center v. Flagg*, 111 A.D.2d 814 (2d Dep't 1985); *Matter of Baker*, 14 Educ. Dep't Rep. 5 (1974)). However, the board may exercise its judgment and discretion in good faith concerning the method of sale that will bring the best price.

A school board may, in its discretion, use the proceeds from the sale of real property to set up a reserve fund to reduce real property taxes in the district for a period of up to ten school years (§ 1709 (37); see also **19:29**).

With respect to the sale of unneeded personal property, such as a used station wagon, the sale must be bona fide and for adequate consideration. Bids at a public auction are not required (Opn. St. Comp. 58-120).

16:11. May a school district donate its property as a gift?

The Education Law authorizes a school district to donate unused school buildings and sites, but only to a *public corporation* for its use. The gift may be made on terms and conditions determined by the school board, and may or may not involve a money transaction. Except in large city school districts, voter approval is required (§ 405).

The term *public corporation* includes counties, cities, towns, villages, district corporations (territorial divisions of the state with the power to issue obligations and levy taxes or require the levy of taxes) and public-benefit corporations. This last category includes such units as the various bridge and housing authorities (Gen. Constr. Law § 66).

16:12. Can a school board rent out a school building or other school property?

Yes. A school board may adopt a resolution which states that the real property to be leased is not currently needed for school district purposes and that the leasing of such real property is in the best interest of the school district (§ 403-a(1); see also *Camillus v. West Side Gymnastics Sch., Inc.*, 109 Misc.2d 609 (Sup. Ct. Onondaga County 1981); *Appeal of Brousseau*, 37 Educ. Dep't Rep. 295 (1998)).

The terms of the lease must reflect a fair market rental value as determined by the school board; must not exceed a 10-year term; and require the lessee to restore the real property to its original condition, less ordinary depreciation, upon termination of the lease. The lease may be renewed for a period up to 10 years, upon approval of the commissioner of education (§ 403-a, *Yeshiva of Spring Valley, Inc. v. Board of Educ. of East Ramapo CSD*, 132 A.D.2d 27 (2d Dep't 1987); *Matter of Hollister*, 39 Educ. Dep't Rep. 109 (1999)).

There is no requirement for voter approval of lease terms once the district has properly complied with the requirements of section 403-a of the Education Law (*Matter of Hollister*, 33 Educ. Dep't Rep. 294 (1993)). However, voter approval must be sought for any proposed lease agreement that will exceed 10 years in length (§ 403-a(5)).

In addition, school boards and BOCES, without voter approval, may convey a right-of-way over school property for public utilities services to any municipality, municipal district, authority or public utility. This is known as granting an easement (§ 405).

Construction and Renovation of Facilities

16:13. Must the district voters approve the construction of new facilities?

Yes. Except in large city school districts, a majority of the voters at a school district must authorize and approve taxes for the addition, alteration, repair or improvement to the sites or buildings belonging to the district (§ 416(1), (7)).

In addition, the Education Law prohibits resubmission of propositions for construction of new school buildings (or additions at the same site) more than twice in a one-year period and prohibits the resubmission of the same or similar proposition within 90 days. However, if the proposition is to approve an additional amount necessary to carry out an already approved building project, this restriction does not apply (§ 416(6)).

16:14. Can a school board print and distribute to the voters an informational brochure relating to a bond issue for a new school building to be approved at a district election?

Yes. However, the New York State Court of Appeals held that although a school board may use public funds to pay for an advertisement or newsletter to explain a proposed district budget or bond issue, it may not include subjective statements in such publications that, for example, urge district residents to vote "yes" because the board believes that particular budget or bond issue to be in the best interest of the school district (*Phillips v. Maurer*, 67 N.Y.2d 672 (1986); see also **4:44–50**).

In order to avoid any appearance of impropriety, any informational materials sent to district voters should be kept strictly factual and impartial (*Appeal of Hubbard,* 39 Educ. Dep't Rep. 363 (1999); *Appeal of Meyer*, 38 Educ. Dep't Rep. 285 (1998); *Appeal of Friedman*, 37 Educ. Dep't Rep. 363 (1998); *Appeal of Moessinger*, 33 Educ. Dep't Rep. 487 (1994)).

16:15. May a school district contract with an architect for the preparation of preliminary plans and specifications for a school building construction project before submitting the building project to the voters?

Yes. The school board may so contract with an architect, whose fee may legitimately be paid by the district. However, before an architect prepares final plans, voter approval must be obtained at a school district meeting, except in large city school districts (Formal Opn. of Counsel No. 1, 1 Educ. Dep't Rep. 701 (1951)).

16:16. Can the cost of construction of a new public school building exceed the amount authorized by the school district's voters?

No. Where the voters of a school district have approved a maximum expenditure for the construction of a school, the district may not exceed the maximum amount authorized (Local Fin. Law § 37.00; 12 Opn. St. Comp. 4 (1956)).

Additional funds may be authorized only with the voters' approval either in a regular budget vote or by special referendum (see § 416). If the school board deems it an emergency situation, then, within certain restrictions, a budget note can be issued to cover the excess cost (Local Fin. Law § 29.00). For information on the issuance of bonds in a construction project, see **19:94**.

16:17. Are there required specifications on the construction of school buildings in New York State?

Yes. Details on construction of public school buildings may be found in Part 155 of the commissioner's regulations and in the "Manual of Planning Standards" and "Instruction Guide for Public School Districts and BOCES Obtaining Building Permits for Capital Construction Projects." Both of these publications are available from the State Education Department's Office of Facilities Planning in Albany. Construction information is also available from the Office of Facilities Planning website at http://www.emsc.nysed.gov/facplan/.

16:18. Must plans and specifications for school buildings be approved by the commissioner of education?

Yes. Plans and specifications for the construction, enlargement, repair or remodeling of school facilities of a school district (other than in a city school district having at least one million residents), and a board of cooperative educational services district, must be submitted for the commissioner's approval when the cost of the work is anticipated to be at least $10,000, and for all projects that affect the health and safety of students (§ 408, 8 NYCRR § 155.2(b)).

Plans and specifications must show detailed requirements of design and construction, space layout, circulation and exits, smoke and fire control, accident protection, visual and thermal environment and related electrical and mechanical work, sanitation features and related plumbing work (8 NYCRR § 155.2(b)(1)(i)). All plans and specifications for new instructional space must be consistent with the region's special education space requirements plan (8 NYCRR § 155.2(b)(2); see 8 NYCRR § 200.2(g)). They must conform to the State Uniform Fire Prevention and Building Code (9 NYCRR Parts 600-1250) and Part 155 of the commissioner's regulations including, but not limited to, the uniform safety standards for school construction and maintenance projects (see 8 NYCRR §§ 155.2, 155.5). In addition, any construction or remodeling project costing at least $5,000 also must comply with the state Uniform Fire Prevention and Building Code (8 NYCRR § 155.2(b), (c), (d)).

The commissioner's approval of school building plans signifies only that the plans and specifications meet the minimum requirements of sections 408 and 409 of the Education Law, the commissioner's regulations, and policies of the Office of Facilities Planning relating to educational requirements, heating, ventilation, lighting, sanitation and health, and fire and accident protection. It does not signify approval of architectural or structural design, choice of building materials, any contracts that may be awarded or executed, or any features that will go beyond the minimum requirements. Additionally, this approval gives no assurance that this project qualifies for state aid for education in accordance with the provisions of section 3602 of the Education Law.

Upon approval of plans and specifications, the commissioner will issue a building permit, provided that a licensed architect or engineer properly supervise the project during construction (8 NYCRR § 155.2(b)(5)).

16:19. What is the process for a school district to obtain approval and a building permit for a school construction project?

Approval of building projects is the responsibility of the State Education Department (SED). Receipt of a building permit from SED is evidence of official approval of a building project and is obtained according to the following procedure:

- A district sends one of four letter of intent (LOI) forms depending upon the project:
  o New buildings, additions to existing buildings, or reconstruction work to be done in or on an existing building;
  o Leasing building space off district property or buildings that have been constructed or placed on district property without first obtaining a Building Permit for SED;
  o Placing manufactured buildings on district property; or
  o Setting up districtwide projects.
- The Office of Facilities Planning sends a letter to the district acknowledging receipt of the letter of intent and informing the district of their assigned 15-digit control number and the name of the project manager assigned to their project. The project manager coordinates all aspects of the project and serves as the district's contact with SED.
- The district must then complete the State Environment Quality Review (SEQR) process. Under the SEQR process the district must determine if the building project will have an effect on the environment such that an environmental impact statement (EIS) should be completed. Once the SEQR is completed, the district will submit copies of all SEQRA documents used by the district to make the final determination as to the type of action for each capital project proposed by the district.
- The district must then consult with the State Historic Preservation Office (SHPO) as to whether historic or archaeological resources will be impacted and, if so, how any substantial adverse impacts can be avoided or mitigated. If adverse environmental impact cannot be avoided or adequately mitigated, an agreement must be reached between SHPO and the district, if possible.
- Final plans are submitted to a district's project manager. Only if a project involves the construction of a new instructional facility or the addition to an existing instructional facility, will the district need to make a preliminary submission prior to the final submission. The project manager has the authority to waive a preliminary submission. Final plans are reviewed by bureau staff, architects, and engineers.
- Upon approval, the district will be sent a set of final approval documents, including the building permit for each approved project, a bond certificate when required, a certificate of approval plans and specifications, a certification of substantial completion form and any other documents necessary for final inspection and certification. (See 8 NYCRR § 155.9; see also "Guidelines for School District Implementation of State Environmental Quality Review" and

"Instruction Guide for Public School Districts and BOCES Obtaining Building Permits for Capital Construction Projects " available from the Office of Facilities Planning Web site at http://www.emsc.nysed.gov/facplan/.)

16:20. Can the commissioner revoke a building permit for a school construction project?

Yes, in the event of violations of the State Uniform Fire Prevention and Building Code, Part 155 of the commissioner's regulations or other safety standards imposed by law or regulation (8 NYCRR § 155.2(b)(5)(ii)).

16:21. Must school districts advertise for bids for construction projects?

Yes. In addition, section 101 of the General Municipal Law, more commonly referred to as the Wicks Law, requires that school districts bid out separate specifications for plumbing and gas fitting, steam heating, hot water, ventilating and air conditioning apparatus; and electrical wiring and standard illuminating fixtures on any construction program exceeding $50,000. Separate contracts must be awarded in these areas in accordance with the competitive bidding requirements of the General Municipal Law (see **19:56–62**).

However, districts may not advertise bids for school building construction projects that exceed $10,000 until the plans and specifications have been submitted to and approved by the commissioner of education. There is an exception for city districts with populations of one million or more (§ 408(1); 8 NYCRR § 155.2(b)). Furthermore, the uniform standards for school construction and maintenance projects require that bid specifications and contract documents must address the issue of safety during construction before contract documents are advertised for bid (8 NYCRR § 155.5(c)).

16:22. Are there legal restrictions in determining wages for workers on school construction contracts?

Yes. The state Labor Law requires that the "prevailing rate of wages" be paid to all workers on public school building projects in the state. This includes construction, alterations and repairs (Lab. Law § 220(3)), even when the work is performed by staff from a board of cooperative educational services (BOCES) (*Cayuga-Onondaga Counties Bd. of Coop. Educ. Servs. v. Sweeney*, 89 N.Y.2d 395 (1996)). However, BOCES students who participated in the construction of an office building as part of their educational experience were not employees of a contractor and therefore were not entitled to payment of prevailing wages for public work

(*Onondaga-Cortland-Madison BOCES v. McGowan* 285 A.D.2d 36 (3d Dep't 2001)).

The determination of prevailing wages must be made in accordance with the rates of wages paid pursuant to collective bargaining agreements in the locality in which the work is done (Lab. Law § 220(5)(a)).

16:23. May new school buildings be occupied before they are completely finished?

Yes, but be aware that conditions may exist that could compromise the health and safety of students when new schools are occupied before they are completed (see **17:20–21**).

At the time of substantial completion of the project (when the work is sufficiently complete for occupancy of the building for its intended use), the architect or engineer must submit a certification of substantial completion form to the commissioner of education and certify that the project was completed in conformance with the State Uniform Fire and Prevention and Building Code, part 155 of the commissioner's regulations, and the project plans and specifications previously approved by the commissioner (8 NYCRR § 155.2(b)(6)). Following receipt and posting of the certificate of occupancy, the building can be fully used. In addition, the district's health and safety committee must have the opportunity for a walk through to confirm the area is ready to be opened for use (see 8 NYCRR § 155.5(n)).

16:24. Must school buildings be accessible to persons with disabilities?

Yes. Under the federal Americans with Disabilities Act (ADA), school districts must ensure that all new construction or alterations to existing facilities are accessible to persons with disabilities. However, districts are not required to make structural changes to existing facilities if other methods would make their programs accessible to individuals with disabilities (42 USC § 12101 et seq.).

16:25. Is a school district subject to zoning regulations with regard to its buildings or proposed buildings?

No. School districts are not subject to town, city or village zoning provisions regulating setback, selection of a school building site, school building construction and the size of the open areas surrounding school buildings. A district is not required to obtain a municipal building permit (Opn. St. Comp. 68-426). Similarly, a school district is not subject to a municipal noise ordinance that requires application for a building permit to engage in construction activities after 5:30 p.m. and on weekends (Opn. Atty. Gen. No. 99-20). It also does not have to comply with the provisions of a town building code (*Board of Educ. v. Buffalo*, 32 A.D.2d 98 (4th

Dep't 1969); *Camillus v. West Side Gymnastics Sch., Inc.*, 109 Misc.2d 609 (Sup. Ct. Onondaga County 1981); see also **16:18**).

16:26. May a public school rent highway equipment from a county highway department to construct or repair school roads or for snow removal?

Yes, as provided in section 133-a of the Highway Law. The state comptroller has indicated that loaning an operator for the equipment is also an implied authorization (Opn. St. Comp. 58-328).

16:27. Can a school district receive building aid for a leased building?

Yes. A district can receive building aid if the leased school or facility meets requirements for access by individuals with disabilities to both facilities and programs, and is consistent with the special education space requirement, as defined in the commissioner's regulations (§ 403-b(1)(e); 8 NYCRR §§ 155.12(b)(6)(i)). The leased space must be used to house programs for students in grades prekindergarten through 12, with minimal associated administrative and support services space, as approved by the commissioner of education (§§ 3602(6), 2503(8), 2554(6)).

In addition, space leased for special education programs and services is eligible for building aid if the space is consistent with the district's comprehensive long-range plan for the allocation of instructional space to meet the current and future special education program and services needs and to serve students with disabilities in settings with nondisabled peers (8 NYCRR § 155.12(d)(5)(i)).

Closing of School Buildings

16:28. Can the commissioner of education declare certain areas of a school building unsafe and unusable?

Yes. If the commissioner judges the general condition of a school building, or any part or area, would be detrimental to the health and safety of its occupants, he may designate an area or areas of the building as unusable or may limit the number of occupants allowed in that area (8 NYCRR § 155.7(j)).

16:29. Does a school board have the right to close school buildings and create new attendance zones without voter approval?

Yes. Decisions about the assignment of students and the establishment of reasonable methods of zoning for the purpose of school attendance rest with the school board under section 1709 of the Education Law (see *Matter of*

Lanfear, 31 Educ. Dep't Rep. 340 (1992); *Matter of Furman*, 15 Educ. Dep't Rep. 70 (1975)).

16:30. Are there any specific procedures a school board must follow before closing down a school building?

Yes. According to section 402-a of the Education Law, a notice of the proposed closing must be published in a newspaper in the community, posted conspicuously in the affected school district, and circulated to elected state and local public officials who represent the affected communities. The school board must also hold a public hearing to evaluate the impact of the proposed closing on the affected district before rendering a decision (§ 402-a).

However section 402-a only applies when a district intends to discontinue use of a school building for any purpose. If a district simply wants to convert a building to a different use, such as administrative offices, then section 402-a does not apply at all (*Appeal of Patashnich and Waters*, 39 Educ Dep't Rep. 236 (1999); *Appeal of Malone and Trombley*, 39 Educ. Dep't Rep. 135 (1999)).

In addition, the Education Law authorizes and recommends, but does not require, that a district establish an advisory committee on school building utilization to investigate the educational impact of the closing six months prior to the scheduled closing. The decision to establish such an advisory committee rests with the board (§ 402-a(1); *Appeal of Patashnick and Waters; Appeal of Seligman*, 31 Educ. Dep't Rep. 131 (1991)). The final responsibility for adopting a reorganization plan rests with the board, even if an advisory committee is established (*Appeal of Seligman*).

If a committee is established, it must review, at least, the following factors:

- The current and projected pupil enrollment, the prospective need for such a building, the ramifications of such closing upon the community, initial costs and savings resulting from such closing, and the potential disposability of the closed school.
- The possible use of the school building for other educational programs or administrative services.
- The effect of the closing on personnel needs, and on the costs of instruction, administration, transportation and other support services.
- The type, age and physical condition of the building, outstanding indebtedness, maintenance and energy costs, recent or planned improvements for the building, and the building's special features.
- The ability of the other schools in the affected district to accommodate students if the building closes.

- The possible shared utilization of space in the building during or after regular school hours, pursuant to the Education Law (§ 402-a(2)).

The committee's educational impact statement findings must be filed with the school board (§ 402-a(1)).

Use of Public School Buildings, Grounds, and Equipment

16:31. Who has the final authority in granting use of a public school building?

Section 414 of the Education Law gives a school board the authority to adopt reasonable regulations with regard to granting the use of school buildings to outside organizations.

No association or organization has the right to use a school building without the express permission of the board. For example, local teachers' associations or organizations are not entitled as a matter of right to use a school building for meetings (*Matter of Charlotte Valley*, 18 PERB ¶ 3010 (1985)).

The board has the authority to prescribe the terms of use of a school building, including a rental fee sufficient to cover expenses resulting from the prescribed use (with limited exceptions) (see **16:41**), and may also refuse to grant an organization's request for use. For example, if it can be proven that a "clear and present danger" of possible damage to the building exists, the board can deny access to the organization (*Matter of Ellis*, 77 St. Dep't Rep. 32 (1956)).

16:32. What uses of school buildings may be permitted by a school board under the Education Law?

Section 414(1) of the Education Law sets forth the permissible uses of school buildings. As long as the school board determines that the particular use will not disrupt normal school operations, school buildings and grounds and other property of the district may be used for the following:

- Instruction in any branch of education, learning or the arts.
- Public libraries or stations of public libraries.
- Social, civic and recreational meetings and entertainments, and other uses pertaining to the welfare of the community that are nonexclusive and open to the general public (*Appeal of Emilio*, 33 Educ. Dep't Rep. 75 (1993)).
- Meetings, entertainments and occasions where admission fees are charged, when the proceeds are to be expended for an educational or charitable purpose. However, these uses are not permitted if they

are under exclusive control and the proceeds are to be applied for the benefit of a society, association or organization of a religious sect or denomination, or of a fraternal, secret or exclusive society or organization other than organizations of veterans of the military, naval and marine service of the United States and organizations of volunteer fire fighters or volunteer ambulance workers.

- Polling places for holding primaries and elections, for the registration of voters and for holding political meetings. However, no meetings sponsored by political organizations are permitted unless authorized by the voters' approval, or, in cities, approved by the school board. Except in cities, it is the school board's duty to call a special meeting for these purposes upon the petition of at least 10 percent of the qualified electors of the district (see § 414 (1)(e); Elec. Law § 4-104).
- Civic forums and community centers (see § 414(1)(f)).
- Classes of instruction for mentally retarded minors operated by a private organization that is approved by the commissioner of education.
- Recreation, physical training and athletics, including competitive athletic contests of children attending a private, nonprofit school.
- Child-care programs when school is not in session, or when school is in session for the children of students attending schools of the district and, if there is additional space available, for children of employees of the district, to be determined by the school board.
- Graduation exercises held by not-for-profit elementary and secondary schools, provided that no religious service is performed.

School districts and building principals need to be mindful of ensuring compliance with the State's Uniform Fire Prevention and Building Code during assembly events, which include any activities conducted in a school's large public places such as cafeterias, pools, gymnasiums, and auditoriums. At such events there should be no blocked exits and obstructions in corridors, and fire access lanes should be clear to ensure the ability of emergency responders to reach the scene ("Evening Assembly Event" Alert, NY State Education Department, February 9, 2004 available at http://www.emsc.nysed.gov/facplan/FireSafety).

A district permitting community use of school property for after-school programs must ensure such programs are open to all children in the school district, regardless of whether they attend public or private school (see § 414(2)).

16:33. Can a school building be used as a polling place in a general election?

Yes. A school building can be designated as a registration and polling place if this use of the building will not interfere with its customary use, and if it is conveniently situated for the voters residing in the election district. Any expense incurred as a result of this use must be paid like the expenses of other registration and polling places (§ 414).

If an election board selects a public school as a polling place, school officials are required to make available a room suitable for registration and voting as close as possible to the main entrance (Elec. Law § 4-104(3)).

16:34. May school property be used to provide child-care services?

Yes. Section 410-c(5) of the Social Services Law and section 414 of the Education Law authorizes child-care programs for school-age children during hours school is not in session and permits school buildings to be used for this purpose. In addition, section 414(1)(i) of the Education Law authorizes the use of school facilities for child-care services during school hours for children of students attending school. These services may also be made available to school employees, depending on space availability and as determined by the school board.

16:35. Can a school district allow games of chance such as bingo and raffles in its school buildings?

Only in limited circumstances. Generally the organization conducting the game of chance must be domiciled in a municipality (including a city, town, or village) that has passed a local law allowing games of chance. In addition, the organization must apply for and obtain a games of chance identification number from the New York State Racing and Wagering Board. Lastly, the proceeds must be disbursed for one of the lawful purposes allowed in the General Municipal Law (Exec. Law Art. 19-B; Gen. Mun. Law Art. 9-a, 14-H).

Only bona fide religious, charitable, or nonprofit organizations are permitted to conduct these games, as long as the entire net proceeds are devoted to the lawful purposes of the organization. However, section 414 of the Education Law prohibits the use of a school building by exclusionary groups. Therefore, the only types of outside groups that could use a school building for this purpose would be charitable or nonprofit organizations, such as parent-teacher associations, veterans, volunteer fire fighters or volunteer ambulance workers. Proceeds from the games would go to benefit these groups, and only after the city, town or village approved the games.

More information on charitable gaming is available from the New York State Racing and Wagering Board Web site at http://www.racing.state.ny.us/charitable/char.home.htm.

16:36. May the military use school facilities to recruit students?

Yes. Section 2-a of the Education Law provides such authority. In addition, the federal No Child Left Behind Act of 2001 (NCLB) requires that any district receiving financial assistance under the act provide military recruiters the same access to secondary school students it provides to post secondary educational institutions and prospective employers (20 USC § 908(a)(3)).

The New York State Court of Appeals upheld the rights of districts to adopt and implement a policy that bars access to groups that engage in discriminatory practices (see *Lloyd v. Grella*, 83 N.Y.2d 537 (1994)). The court held that no special status set forth in section 2-a of the Education Law was granted to the military, and, therefore, the school district's policy was not illegal so long as all groups with discriminatory policies were equally barred from access on that basis. However, the continued validity of the *Lloyd* decision is questioned in light of the NCLB provisions.

16:37. May a school district deny the Boy Scouts of America use of its facilities because of its discrimination practices?

No. Under the federal No Child Left Behind Act of 2001 (NCLB), a school district may not deny use of its facilities to any group affiliated with the Boy Scouts of America or any other youth group listed as a patriotic society in federal law, including, for example, the Girl Scouts and the Boys and Girls Club, based solely on the group's membership or leadership criteria or oath of allegiance to God and country (20 USC § 905(b)(1)).

16:38. May a school building be used for religious instruction during school hours?

No. The use of a school building for religious instruction is prohibited by article 11 of the New York State Constitution (*see Illinois ex rel. McCollum v. Board of Educ.*, 333 U.S. 203 (1948); see also **23:1; 23:4**). However, schools may offer comparative religion courses so long as such courses teach about religion as opposed to proselytizing religious messages.

16:39. May a school building be used by an outside religious organization?

Yes. A school building may be used by an outside religious organization just like any other community group. However, it may not be used by such an organization if a meeting, entertainment or occasion sponsored by such an organization is under its exclusive control and any proceeds from its activity are to be applied for the benefit of the religious organization (§ 414(1)(d)).

The United States Supreme Court has ruled that school districts cannot deny access to religious organizations solely on the basis that they would present a religious perspective, where the school would permit other groups to present their views on the same topic (*Lamb's Chapel v. Center Moriches UFSD*, 508 U.S. 384 (1993)).

The U.S. Supreme Court followed *Lamb's Chapel* when it ruled a school district acted unconstitutionally when it refused to allow a Christian youth group to hold meetings on school grounds, even though it allowed the Boy Scouts, the Girl Scouts and the 4-H Club to meet. Similar to the aforementioned groups, the youth group taught character development and morals. However, it utilized Bible stories and prayer. The court found the exclusion of the group was viewpoint discrimination and rejected the district's claim that allowing the group access to the school would present an Establishment Clause violation. The court held there was no credible evidence the public would perceive the club meetings as an endorsement of religion (*The Good News Club v. Milford CSD*, 533 U.S. 98 (2001)).

A district may enact a policy that prohibits any organization from using school facilities for lectures, presentations, demonstrations, political events or seminars. The key requirement is that such a restriction be applied uniformly to all applicants, regardless of their viewpoints (*Saratoga Bible Institute, Inc. v. Schuylerville CSD*, 18 F. Supp. 2d 178 (N.D.N.Y. 1998)).

16:40. May school districts permit outside religious groups to use school facilities for purposes of conducting religious worship services or to conduct religious instruction?

The use of school property for religious worship or instruction is not among the uses expressly authorized in the Education Law (§ 414). Prior to the U.S. Supreme Court decision in *The Good News Club v. Milford CSD*, 533 U.S. 98 (2001) (see **16:39**), the United States Court of Appeals for the Second Circuit, with jurisdiction over New York State, upheld a school district's policy and regulation, based on section 414 of the Education Law, which prohibited an outside organization or group from conducting religious services or religious instruction on school premises (*Bronx Household of Faith v. Community Sch. Dist. No. 10*, 127 F.3d 207 (2d Cir. 1997), *cert. denied*, 523 U.S. 1074 (1998)). However, following *Good News*, the Second Circuit revisited the issue and ruled against a school district that barred a church from using its school premises to conduct Sunday worship services because they also involved activities related to teaching moral values (*The Bronx Household of Faith v. The Board of Educ. of the City of New York & Community Sch. Dist. No. 10*, 331 F.3d

342, 2003 U.S. App. LEXIS 11379 (2d Cir. N.Y. 2003)). In *Bronx Household*, the district had permitted access to outside groups such as the Boy Scouts, who provided a moral message to members of the community. Therefore, the church had to be given the same opportunity.

16:41. May students use a school building for Bible study meetings and prayer?

Yes, under the federal Equal Access Act (20 USC § 4071). Generally, the act requires that public secondary schools which receive federal financial assistance provide students equal access and may not deny them use of school facilities during noninstructional time on the basis of the religious, political, philosophical or other content of the speech that can be expected to take place at the meeting if it permits student groups to use school premises for any noncurriculum-related purpose (see **23:7**). The United States Supreme Court held the act is constitutional in *Board of Educ. of Westside Community Schs. v. Mergens*, 496 U.S. 226 (1990).

The act also requires that:

- Meetings be voluntary and initiated by the students.
- There be no sponsorship of the meeting by the school, the government, or its agents or employees.
- Employees or agents of the school or government attend only in a nonparticipatory capacity.
- Meetings do not interfere materially and substantially with the orderly conduct of educational activities within the school.
- Nonschool people do not direct, conduct, control or regularly attend activities of student groups.

The United States Court of Appeals for the Second Circuit ruled that a school district may not preclude a student Bible club from meeting on school premises by claiming that the club violated the district's non-discrimination policy because the club's constitution required that only Christians could serve as officers of the club (*Hsu by & through Hsu v. Roslyn UFSD No. 3*, 85 F.3d 839 (2d Cir. 1996), *cert. denied*, 519 U. S. 1040 (1996)).

Under the federal No Child Left Behind Act of 2001, school districts receiving funds under the act may not prevent or otherwise deny student participation in constitutionally protected prayer (20 USC § 904(b)). The U.S. Secretary of Education is responsible for issuing guidance on what constitutes constitutionally protected prayer in the public schools (20 USC § 7904(a)).

16:42. May a school district charge for the use of its facilities by outside organizations?

Yes. The Education Law provides that a school board may adopt reasonable regulations for the use of its buildings and grounds, including a schedule of fees as prescribed by such regulations (§ 414; see also **16:46**). For instance, a school district is authorized to charge for the cost of maintaining its facility or property (i.e., heat, electricity, custodian/maintenance costs). Although this issue has not yet come before the courts, failure to charge for such costs might be deemed to violate the state constitutional prohibition against gifts of public funds (Art. 8. Sec. 1; see **19:14**).

A school board may also charge a nonresident for the use of district property (e.g., jogging track), since the commissioner of education has interpreted the Education Law to require that any meeting, entertainment or other use for the benefit of the community be non-exclusive and open only to the general public of the school district, that is, to the residents of the school district (*Matter of Emilio*, 33 Educ. Dep't Rep. 75 (1993)). According to the commissioner, it would be highly unusual to interpret the language of section 414(1)(c) as compelling school districts to open up the uses of its property intended to promote the welfare of the community served by the school district to those who did not reside in the community.

16:43. May a school district charge churches higher fees than other nonprofit organizations for the use of school facilities?

No. To charge churches higher fees than other nonprofit organizations would discriminate against religious speech and interfere with or burden the church's right to speak and practice religion as protected by the free exercise clause (*Fairfax Covenant Church v. Fairfax County Sch. Bd.*, 17 F.3d 703 (4th Cir. 1994), *cert. denied*, 511 U.S. 1143 (1994)).

16:44. May a school district allow admission fees to be charged to school-sponsored athletic events held on school grounds and permit the broadcasting of such events?

Yes. A school board may allow admission fees to be charged to school-sponsored athletic events held on school grounds as long as the proceeds are expended for school purposes (§ 414(1)(d); Opn. St. Comp. 81-18). A board also may allow radio and television stations to broadcast reports on high school games and other events, even though the broadcasts may be commercially sponsored (Arts & Cult. Aff. Law § 61.09).

Display of Flag on School Grounds

16:45. Must school districts display the American flag?

Yes. The Education and Executive Laws require that a district purchase and display the American flag on or near the public school building during school hours every school day (§ 418; Exec. Law § 403(5)). However, the flag may not be displayed in inclement weather, in which case it is to be displayed in the "principal room of the schoolhouse" (§ 420; Exec. Law § 403(3)). Outside display, except on special occasions for patriotic effects, is limited to the hours from sunrise to sunset (Exec. Law § 403(1)).

16:46. When must school districts display the American flag?

The Executive Law requires that the flag be displayed, weather permitting, on holidays, including:
- New Year's Day (January 1)
- Dr. Martin Luther King, Jr., Day (third Monday in January)
- Lincoln's Birthday (February 12)
- Washington's Birthday (third Monday in February)
- Memorial Day (last Monday in May)
- Flag Day (second Sunday in June)
- Independence Day (July 4)
- Labor Day (first Monday in September)
- POW/MIA Recognition Day (third Friday in September, or if this is in conflict with a religious observance, the second Friday in September)
- Columbus Day (second Monday in October)
- Veterans Day (November 11)
- Thanksgiving Day (fourth Thursday in November)
- Pearl Harbor Day (December 7)
- Christmas Day (December 25)

If any of these holidays fall on a Sunday (except for Flag Day), the flag should be displayed the next day. In addition, the flag must be displayed on any general election day and on any day designated by the president of the United States or the governor of New York State as a day of general thanksgiving or for displaying the flag (Exec. Law § 403(2)).

The flag is to be displayed at full staff except that it must be flown at half-mast on December 7 (Pearl Harbor Day); on days commemorating the death of a personage of national or state standing, of a local serviceman, or of an official or public servant who, in the opinion of the school district, contributed to the community; and it may be flown at half-mast on days designated by the president of the United States or the governor of New York State as special periods of mourning (Exec. Law § 403(21)). One court has held, however, that it is improper for a district to fly its flag at half-mast as an expression of political dissent (*Lapolla v. Dullaghan*, 63 Misc.2d 157 (1970)).

In addition, the flag must be displayed in all assembly rooms of the school (i.e. the auditorium), pursuant to the commissioner's regulations (§ 419; 8 NYCRR §§ 108.1–108.3). The willful failure to comply with section 419 of the Education Law is a misdemeanor.

16:47. Must school districts establish rules for the proper care of the American flag?

Yes. The Education Law requires that school authorities establish rules and regulations governing the proper care, custody and display of the flag (§ 420). Both the United States Code and the Executive Law provide guidance regarding the proper display and care of the flag (4 USC §§ 5–10; Exec. Law § 403). In addition, the commissioner's regulations provide the requirements for the material and size of the flag, care of the flag, and for its display in assembly rooms (8 NYCRR Part 108).

16:48. Must the salute to the flag and the pledge of allegiance to the flag be recited daily in school?

Yes. Section 802 of the Education Law requires that the commissioner of education prepare a program for public schools that provides for the salute to the flag and a daily pledge of allegiance to the flag, and for instruction in its correct use and display (§ 802; 8 NYCRR § 108).

The official text of the pledge and the manner in which it must be recited is contained in the commissioner's regulations. The text is: "I pledge allegiance to the Flag of the United States of America and to the Republic for which it stands, one Nation, under God, indivisible, with liberty and justice for all" (8 NYCRR § 108.5).

16:49. Can students and teachers abstain from reciting the pledge of allegiance?

Yes. Students have the right to abstain from reciting the pledge and teachers have the right to stand silently during the daily recitation of the pledge. In *West Virginia State Bd. of Educ. v. Barnette*, 319 U.S. 624 (1943), the United States Supreme Court ruled that requiring teachers and students to stand in salute of the flag and recite the pledge of allegiance against their religious beliefs constituted a violation of their rights under the Free Exercise Clause of the First Amendment to the U.S. Constitution (see also *Russo v. CSD No. 1*, 469 F.2d 623 (2d Cir. 1972), *cert. denied, CSD No. 1 v. Russo*, 411 U.S. 932 (1973)).

In addition, those refusing to salute the flag may not be required to either stand or leave the room, according to the United States Court of Appeals for the Second Circuit, which has jurisdiction over New York State. According to the court, the act of standing itself is a "gesture of acceptance"; the option of leaving the room, "punishment [for] nonparticipation" (*Goetz v. Ansell*, 477 F.2d 636 (2d Cir. 1973)).

The U.S. Supreme Court dismissed, on procedural grounds, a lawsuit claiming that it violates the Establishment Clause of the federal constitution to require students to listen daily to the recitation of the Pledge of Allegiance, because the Pledge contains the words "One Nation, **Under God**" within its text (*Elk Grove Unified Sch. Dist.*, 124 S.Ct. 2301 (2004)). By declining to rule on the merits of the claim, the court left the substantive constitutional question for another day.

Conduct on School Property

16:50. May school boards regulate conduct on school district property?

Yes. School boards must adopt rules and regulations for the maintenance of public order on school property and ensure they are enforced (§ 2801). These rules and regulations must govern the conduct of students, teachers and other staff, as well as visitors and other licensees and invitees. They must be filed with the Board of Regents and the commissioner of education. This requirement also applies to any amendments, which must be filed no later than 10 days after their adoption. If a board fails to follow these filing requirements, the district may not be eligible to receive any state aid or assistance until the regulations are filed.

The penalties for violations must be clearly set forth and must include provisions for ejecting a person from school property, and, in the case of a student or teacher, his or her suspension, or other appropriate disciplinary action. The law states that this section of the Education Law is not intended to limit or restrict anyone's freedom of speech or right to peaceful assembly (§ 2801).

However, the Federal District Court for the Northern District of New York found that a school district which barred a reporter from school grounds did not violate the reporter's First Amendment rights to freedom of the press, speech or association, where the reporter had attempted to initiate personal contacts of a sexual nature with two female coaches and then failed to stop at the district's directive. The court found the district's order to bar the reporter from attending athletic events and restricting his contact with coaches to written and telephone contact through the main office or athletic office was a reasonably tailored time, place and manner regulation that did not restrict all forms of news gathering access (*Hone v. Cortland City Sch. Dist.*, 985 F. Supp. 262 (N.D.N.Y. 1998)).

Similarly, a New York appellate court upheld a school district's decision to temporarily bar a parent from entering her child's school building following an incident where the parent twice entered the school building carrying a handgun (that she was licensed to carry in connection with her employment as a probation officer) in violation of district policy requiring prior written permission to bring a gun into the schoolhouse, and in violation of the building principal's directive communicated to her personally to remove her gun prior to entering the school building to attend a parent-teacher conference (*Cina v. Waters*, ___ A.D.3d ___, 779 N.Y.2d 289 (3d Dep't 2004)).

16:51. May school districts bar from school events parents who engage in aggressive behavior?

Yes. The commissioner of education upheld a school district's decision to bar a parent from attending future athletic events practices, because the parent persisted in engaging in threatening and aggressive behavior, even after the district's athletic director and superintendent met with him to discuss complaints about him and gave him written warning that his continued misbehavior would result in the district barring him from future events. The commissioner also held that the parent was not entitled to a full hearing and that he did not have a "right" of access to school property (*Appeal of Mayer*, 39 Educ. Dep't Rep. 198 (1999)).

16:52. Is it unlawful to loiter or trespass on school grounds?

Yes. To loiter has been interpreted to mean to be slow in moving, to delay, to be dilatory, to saunter or to lag behind. Section 240.35(5) of the Penal Law states that any person who is not a parent or legal guardian of a student in regular attendance, who loiters on or about any school building or grounds, public or private or a school bus, without written permission or a specific, legitimate purpose for being there, is guilty of violating the law.

In addition, a person may be charged with criminal trespass if he or she enters or remains in a school building in violation of conspicuously posted rules regarding entry and use of the building (Penal Law § 140.10).

"School grounds" are defined by the Penal Law (Penal Law § 240.00(3)).

16:53. Is it unlawful to draw graffiti upon school property?

Yes. Sections 145.60 and 145.65 of the state Penal Law establish the making of graffiti as a class A misdemeanor and the possession of graffiti instruments a class B misdemeanor. The Education Law states that school districts may offer monetary rewards of no more than $1,000 to individuals for information leading to the arrest and conviction of any person or persons for felonies or misdemeanors directly connected to vandalism of district property (§ 1604(38)).

16:54. May a school district establish its own traffic and parking regulations on school property?

Yes. School districts may regulate, restrict or prohibit parking or standing, the direction and speed of traffic, and movement of motor traffic on any parking fields, driveways or public ways accessory to any school, playground or facility under their jurisdiction (Veh. & Traf. Law § 1670). Any violation of district traffic regulations will be considered a traffic infraction (Opn. St. Comp. 79-26).

Section 1174 of the Vehicle and Traffic Law prohibits motorists from passing stopped school buses while they are boarding or discharging school children on school property. In addition, motorists may not exceed maximum school speed limits established on a highway adjacent to a school during school days at the times indicated on the school zone speed limit sign, or when beacons attached to the school zone speed limit sign are flashing and indicate the speed limit is in effect. Beacons may only flash during student activities at the school and up to 30 minutes immediately before and up to 30 minutes immediately after such student activity (Veh. & Traf. Law § 1180 (c)).

16:55. Can a school district prohibit the sale of sweetened foods to students in school?

Yes. Section 915 of the Education Law prohibits the sale of certain sweetened foods, including, but not limited to, soda, chewing gum and candy, from the beginning of the school day until the end of the last scheduled meal period.

16:56. What are drug-free school zones?

A *drug-free school zone* is an area within 1,000 feet of a private or public school, including nursery, prekindergarten, kindergarten, elementary, intermediate, junior high, vocational, or high school, and child-care center facilities, as defined by law (Penal Law § 220.44).

Under the Penal Law it is a felony to sell drugs in any school building, structure, athletic playing field, playground or land contained within a drug-free zone school, or in any area accessible to the public or any parked vehicle located within such zone (Penal Law §§ 220.00, 220.34, 220.44).

Signs designating the drug-free school zone may be erected upon the request of a school district and in cooperation with those entities having jurisdiction over the highways (High. Law § 317).

16:57. Are there funds available to help school districts prevent violence and drug abuse within the community?

Yes. Under the Safe and Drug-Free Schools and Communities Act (20 USC § 7101 et seq.), local school districts are eligible to receive funds to develop comprehensive drug and violence prevention programs that are designed to:

- foster a safe and drug free learning environment that supports academic achievement
- prevent or reduce violence, the use possession and distribution of illegal drugs, and delinquency
- promote the involvement of parents and community groups (20 USC § 115(b)(1)

To further these goals, the act provides funds for a number of initiatives, including "safe zones of passage" for students between home and school through such measures as drug-free school zones, enhanced law enforcement and neighborhood patrols (20 USC § 7116(b)(2)).

Commercialism in the Public Schools

16:58. Can a school district allow the sale of student photographs by a private business firm on school grounds?

Ordinarily, no, because this action would violate the New York State Constitution (Art. 8, § 1). However, where photographs are taken "for a valid school purpose," such as for the school yearbook, they may be taken on school premises during school hours. But school personnel may not solicit or collect money for this purpose (*Matter of Fusare*, 20 Educ. Dep't Rep. 14 (1980); *Matter of Hoyt*, 17 Educ. Dep't Rep. 173 (1977); *Matter of Albert*, 7 Educ. Dep't Rep. 7 (1967); see also memo of August 27, 1974, from Counsel for State Educ. Dep't: "Sale of School Photographs").

School rings may be sold on the school premises if certain specific conditions are met (*Matter of Gary Credit Corp.*, 26 Educ. Dep't Rep. 414 (1987)).

16:59. Can a school district allow commercial television or radio programming in its schools?

No. Part 23 of the Rules of the Board of Regents prohibits a school district from entering into a contract that, in whole or in part, promises the district will permit commercial promotional activity on school premises through electronic media, such as the promotion or sale of products and services on television or radio (8 NYCRR § 23.2). However, the rules state that this should not be construed as prohibiting commercial sponsorship of school activities.

16:60. Can a school district enter into a contract that gives a specific beverage manufacturer the exclusive right to sell its beverages on campus in exchange for a fee?

Yes, with certain limitations. Commercialism on school property is generally prohibited. However, an agreement with a commercial vendor for the exclusive right to sell its beverage on campus, known as a "pouring rights" contract, may be permissible if the contract complies with all applicable New York laws, including but not limited to, the state constitution, the competitive bidding requirements of the General Municipal Law, the Freedom of Information Law, and provisions restricting the hours of operation of beverage vending machines (see *Appeal of American Quality Beverages LLC I and II*, 42 Educ. Dep't Rep. 144,153 (2002); *Appeal of Citizens for Responsible Fiscal and Educational Policy*, 40 Educ. Dep't Rep. 315 (2000); NYS Const., Art. VIII, § 1; Gen. Mun. Law Article 5-A; Pub. Off. Law Article 6; § 915).

Pouring rights contracts are not subject to approval by the commissioner of education because they do not involve private food service management companies. According to the commissioner, although the sale of pre-sweetened beverages does not violate a school district's obligation to provide physical and health education in an environment conducive to healthful living, districts should consider whether the installation of vending machines in school is in the best interest of student's health, particularly at the elementary level (*Id.*).

16:61. What must be included in a pouring rights contract?

The State Education Department's model "pouring rights" contract offers guidance on framing these type of contracts ("Contracts for Exclusive 'Pouring Rights'", Memorandum to District Superintendents and Superintendents of Schools, Kathy Ahearn, Deputy Commissioner for Legal Affairs, SED Office of Counsel, July 10, 1998). A copy of the model contract is available from SED's Office of Counsel. However, it should be noted the commissioner invalidated a provision in *Appeal of Citizens for Responsible Fiscal and Educational Policy*, 40 Educ. Dep't Rep. 315 (2000), that contained similar language to that of the model contract. The provision allowed the vendor to sell its products to fundraising groups "based on a presale of cases of products to students' family and friends." Individual buyers would redeem their orders at school by exchanging a receipt for the beverages. The commissioner found "no statutory authority for the use of school premises or school district staff to facilitate the sale of a vendor's products or fundraising groups."

In addition, the commissioner has cautioned that districts should not accept any advance payment on pouring rights that they would be required to pay back in the event of early termination (*Appeal of American Quality Beverages LLC I and II*, 42 Educ. Dep't Rep. 144 (2002)).

16:62. Do lighted panels on vending machines constitute unlawful advertising?

No. According to the commissioner of education, the advertising effect of lighted panels that simply illuminate static pictures is incidental. However, districts need to consider whether promotional statements on the panels are appropriate for school environments and whether plain panels should be used instead (*Appeal of American Quality Beverages LLC I and II*, 42 Educ. Dep't Rep. 144,153 (2002)).

16:63. Can a school district allow the collection of money from students for charitable donations in the schools?

No. Section 19.6 of the Rules of the Board of Regents prohibits the direct solicitation of charitable donations from children in the public schools during the school day. However, there are three types of activities that this section does not proscribe:

- Fund-raising activities that take place off school premises or outside of the regular school day. Thus, recruiting children during the school day for participation in fundraising activities is permissible as long as the activities themselves occur off school premises or outside of the school day.
- Arms-length transactions where the contributor receives something for his or her donation. Thus, this rule does not prohibit the sale of goods or tickets for concerts or admission to social events where the proceeds go to charity, because the purchaser receives a consideration; the concert or admission to a social event for the funds expended.
- Indirect forms of charitable solicitation on school premises that do not involve coercion, such as having a bin or collection box in a hallway or other common area for the donation of food, clothing or money. In these instances, the collection activity is passive, and no pressure is exerted upon students to participate.

What the rule does prohibit is approaching students in their classrooms or homerooms and asking them directly to donate money or goods to charity (see *Appeal of Ponte*, 38 Educ. Dep't Rep. 280 (1998); "Guidelines Relating to Solicitation of Charitable Donations from School Children," NY State Education Department, January 1994).

16:64. Can school districts allow fund-raising activities involving the participation of students during school hours?

No. The solicitation of charitable donations cannot become intertwined with a school's educational responsibilities. That happened in a case where students shot baskets to raise money for the American Heart Association in a "Hoop for Hearts" program during physical education class. Although the students solicited and collected pledges from the community off school grounds, and parent volunteers collected the funds in the school's hallway, the commissioner of education determined that the funds raised accrued during class time on school grounds. In addition, students were awarded prizes during the school day for achieving the pledge goals. According to the commissioner, this level of activity belied the intent and purpose of section 19.6 of the Rules of the Board of Regents (see **16:63**). It was irrelevant that the activity was sponsored by the Parent-Teacher Association (*Appeal of Ponte*, 38 Educ. Dep't Rep. 280 (1998)).

17. School Building Safety

Emergency Management

17:1. Must school districts have school safety plans?

Yes. The Education Law requires that public school districts and boards of cooperative educational services (BOCES) adopt a comprehensive districtwide school safety plan and building-level school safety plans on crisis intervention, and emergency response and management (§ 2801-a(1); 8 NYCRR § 155.17(b)). Districts having only one school building are required to develop only a single building-level school safety plan that also satisfies the requirements for a districtwide plan (8 NYCRR § 155.17(b).

These plans must be designed to prevent or minimize the effects of serious violent incidents and emergencies and to facilitate the coordination of schools and school districts with local and county resources in the event of such incidents or emergencies (8 NYCRR § 155.17(e)).

An *emergency* comprises a situation, including but not limited to a disaster, that requires immediate action, occurs unpredictably, and poses a threat of injury or loss of life to students or school personnel or of severe damage to school property (8 NYCRR § 155.17(c)(4)).

A *disaster* refers to an occurrence or imminent threat of widespread or severe damage, injury, or loss of life or property resulting from any natural or manmade causes such as fire, flood, drought, windstorms, hurricane, tornado, wave action, earthquake, high water, chemical accident, explosion, epidemic, air and water contamination, landslide, mudslide, war or civil disturbance (8 NYCRR § 155.17(c)(3)).

A *serious violent incident* refers to an incident of violent criminal conduct that is, or appears to be, life threatening and warrants the evacuation of student and/or staff because of an imminent threat to their safety or health. Examples include a riot, hostage-taking, kidnapping and/or the use or threatened use of a firearm, explosive, bomb, incendiary device, chemical or biological weapon, knife, or other dangerous instrument capable of causing death or serious injury (8 NYCRR § 155.17(c)(17)).

17:2. Who is responsible for developing and updating school safety plans?

The districtwide and building-level school safety plans must be developed respectively by a districtwide and building-level school safety team in accordance with a form prescribed by the commissioner of education (§ 2801-a(1); 8 NYCRR § 155.17(b)).

Each building-level school safety team must be appointed by the building principal, or the chancellor of education in New York City, in accordance with board-established guidelines or regulations and must include at least representatives of teacher, administrator and parent organizations; school safety personnel and other school personnel; community members; local law enforcement officials; local ambulance or other emergency response agencies; and any other representatives the school board or chancellor deem appropriate (§ 2801-a(4); 8 NYCRR § 155.17(c)(11)).

The districtwide school safety team must be appointed by the school board, or the chancellor of education in New York City, and include board representatives, representatives of student, teacher, administrator and parent organizations; school safety personnel; and other school personnel (§ 2801-a(4); 8 NYCRR § 155.17(c)(13)).

Each team also is responsible for reviewing their respective plan at least annually and updating it as needed (8 NYCRR § 155.17(b)).

17:3. What is the process for adopting school safety plans?

A board of education or the chancellor of education in New York City must adopt the plans after a public comment period of at least 30 days and at least one public hearing. Current copies of the districtwide plan and any amendments thereto are to be filed with the commissioner within 30 days of adoption. Building-level plans and any amendments thereto must be filed with the state police and local law enforcement within 30 days of adoption.

Building-level plans are confidential and are not subject to release under the Freedom of Information Law or any other provision of law. Therefore, only a summary of a building-level plan can be made available for public comment. A sample summary can be found in the "Project SAVE Guidance Document for School Safety Plans," issued by the State Education Department, April 2001. It is available through the department Web site at http://www.emsc.nysed.gov/facplan/HealthSafety.htm (8 NYCRR § 155.17(e) (3)).

Each safety plan must be reviewed at least annually and updated as needed (§ 2801-a(5); 8 NYCRR § 155.17(b)). In addition, the school safety plan must be updated to reflect any changes necessary to accommodate school construction projects, including an updated emergency exit plan indicating temporary exits required due to construction, and provisions for the emergency evacuation and relocation or release of students and staff in the event of a construction incident. The district must familiarize students and staff with any temporary exits and emergency procedures established as a result of the construction project (8 NYCCR § 155.5(c)(3), (4); see also **17:20**).

Superintendents and building principals are required to provide written information to all students and staff regarding emergency procedures by October 1 of each year (8 NYCCR § 155.17(i)).

Except in the case of routine snow emergency days, districts must notify the commissioner of education whenever the emergency plan or building-level school safety plan is activated and results in the closing of a school building as prescribed by commissioner's regulations (8 NYCRR § 155.17(h)).

17:4. What must be included in a districtwide school safety plan?

A districtwide school safety plan, which consists of a comprehensive, multi-hazard school safety plan that covers all school buildings and addresses crisis intervention, emergency response and management at the district level (8 NYCRR § 155.17(c)(12), must:

- Identify sites of potential emergency.
- Include appropriate prevention and intervention strategies as specified in commissioner's regulations.
- Identify appropriate responses to emergencies, including protocols for responding to bomb threats, hostage-takings, intrusions, and kidnappings.
- Include strategies for improving communications among students and between students and staff and reporting of potentially violent incidents.
- Describe the duties of hall monitors and any other safety personnel, the training required of all personnel acting in a school security capacity, and the hiring and screening process for all personnel acting in a school security capacity (8 NYCRR § 155.17 (e)(1)(i), (v), (xvi), (xvii), (xviii)).

In addition, a districtwide school safety plan must include policies and procedures for:

- Responding to implied or direct threats of violence, as well as actual acts of violence, by students, teachers, other school personnel, and visitors to the school.
- Contacting parents, guardians or persons in parental relation to district students in the event of a violent incident or an early dismissal.
- School building security including, where appropriate, the use of school safety officers and/or security devices or procedures.
- Disseminating informative materials regarding the early detection of potentially violent behaviors as specified in commissioner's regulations.
- Annual multi-hazard school safety training for staff and students.

- Review and the conduct of drills and other exercises to test components of the emergency response plan (8 NYCRR § 155.17(e)(1)(iii), (iv), (xi), (xii), (xiii), (xiv), (xv), (xvi), (xvii), (xviii)).

Furthermore, except in the case of New York City, districtwide school safety plans must also:

- Describe plans for ordering school cancellations, early dismissal, evacuation, and sheltering.
- Describe arrangements for obtaining assistance during emergencies from emergency services organizations and local governmental agencies.
- Include procedures for obtaining advice and assistance from local government officials.
- Identify district resources that may be available for use during an emergency.
- Describe procedures for coordinating the use of school district resources and manpower during emergencies (8 NYCRR § 155.17(e)(1)(ii); (vii), (viii), (ix), (x)).

School districts, other than New York City, must also include in their districtwide school safety plan a system for informing all educational agencies within the district of a disaster, and information about them, including their school population, number of staff, transportation needs, and the business and home telephone numbers of key officials at each such agency (8 NYCRR § 155.17(e)(1)(xix), (xx)). *Educational agencies* include public and nonpublic elementary and secondary schools, public and private nursery schools, approved private schools for the education of students with disabilities, and public and private schools for the education of preschool children with disabilities (8 NYCRR § 155.17 (c)(1)).

The plan also must be updated to reflect any changes necessary to accommodate school construction projects, including an updated emergency exit plan indicating temporary exits required due to construction; and provisions for the emergency evacuation and relocation or release of students and staff in the event of a construction incident. The district must familiarize students and staff with any temporary exits and emergency procedures established as a result of the construction project (8 NYCCR § 155.5(c)(3), (4); see also **17:21**).

17:5. What must be included in a building-level school safety plan?

A building-level school safety plan, which consists of a building-specific school emergency response plan that addresses crisis intervention, emergency response, and management at the building level (8 NYCRR § 155.17(c)(10)), must:

- Designate an emergency response team, other appropriate incident response teams, and a post-incident response team.
- Establish internal and external communication systems in emergencies.
- Define the chain of command consistent with the national interagency incident management system (NIMS)/incident command system (ICS).
- Coordinate the school safety plan with the statewide plan for disaster mental health services to assure access to federal, state, and local mental health resources in the event of a violent incident (8 NYCRR § 155.17(e)(2)(ii), (iv), (v), (vi)).

A building emergency response plan must also include policies and procedures for the safe evacuation of students, teachers, other school personnel, and visitors to the school in the event of a serious violent incident or other emergency as specified in commissioner's regulations, and for securing and restricting access to a crime scene. It also must contain procedures for assuring that crisis response, fire and law enforcement officials have access to floor plans, blueprints, schematics and other maps of the school interior, school grounds, and road maps of the immediate surrounding area, and for an annual review and conduct of drills and other exercises to test components of the plan (8 NYCRR § 155.17(e)(2)(i), (iii), (vii), (viii)).

17:6. Who makes the decision to close schools because of an emergency?

Schools may be closed in response to an emergency in accordance with the districtwide school safety plan (8 NYCRR § 155.17(e)(1)(ii); see **21:20** for the impact closing schools may have on state aid payments). While schools are not allowed to operate without electricity, water, or sanitation systems, in emergencies it is up to local school officials to determine whether an emergency will result in school closings pursuant to the districtwide school safety plan (8 NYCRR § 155.7(e), (g); SED Office of Facilities Planning Newsletter #46, December 2003).

17:7. Who is responsible for notifying educational agencies of local or state emergencies?

During the occurrence of a local or state emergency, the district (BOCES) superintendent serves as the chief communications liaison to notify all educational agencies within his or her geographic jurisdiction. The superintendent of schools in the cities of Buffalo, Rochester, Syracuse, and Yonkers perform this function for all educational agencies within their respective city district (8 NYCRR § 155.17(g)).

Both public and nonpublic schools must inform students and staff about emergency procedures in writing by October 1 of each school year (8 NYCRR § 155.17(i)). Except in New York City, all educational agencies must provide the school superintendent of the public school district within which they are located with information about their school population, number of staff, transportation needs, and the business and home telephone number of their key officials (8 NYCRR § 155.17(k); see **17:3**)).

17:8. What is an emergency response team?

An *emergency response team* is a building-specific team designated by the building-level safety team to assist the school community in responding to a serious violent incident or emergency and providing the initial response to all emergency situations. It must include appropriate school personnel, local law enforcement officials, and representatives from local, regional and/or state emergency response agencies.

Outside New York City there should be an emergency response team for each school building. In New York City, a unique team for each school building is not required, emergency response teams can be developed at the district level with participation from building-level personnel (8 NYCRR 155.17(c)(14); see also "Project SAVE Guidance Document for School Safety Plans," State Education Department, April 2001).

17:9. What is a post-incident response team?

A *post-incident response team* is a building-specific team designated by the building-level school safety team to assist the school community in coping with the aftermath of an emergency or serious violent incident. This team is comprised of appropriate school personnel, medical personnel, mental health counselors, and others who can assist the school community in coping during the aftermath. Each school building is required to have its own team. In New York City, however, there may be a districtwide post-incident response team with building-level participation instead of a unique team for each school (8 NYCRR § 155.17(c)(15)).

The post-incident response team has both short- and long-term responsibilities. Its short-term responsibilities include developing procedures for mental health counseling of students and staff, building security, facility restoration, and it must perform a post-incident response critique. Long-term, the team must monitor for post-traumatic stress, ensure building security and perform mitigation (reduce the likelihood of occurrence and impact if situation does occur again) ("Project SAVE Guidance Document for School Safety Plans," State Education Department, April 2001).

17:10. Are school districts required to conduct emergency drills?

Yes. School districts must conduct fire drills at least 12 times each school year (eight between September 1 and December 1) to ensure that, in the event of an emergency, students will be able to leave the school building in the shortest possible time and without confusion or panic (§ 807(1)).

At least one-third of the drills shall make use of the fire escapes on buildings (§ 807(1)). Moreover, fire drills must be conducted during construction projects to familiarize students and staff with temporary exits and revised emergency procedures whenever temporary exits and revised emergency procedures exist (8 NYCRR § 155.5(c)(4); see **14:53**).

In addition, at least once every school year, each school district and BOCES must conduct a test of its emergency plan or its emergency response procedures under each of its building-level school safety plans a (at a time no earlier than 15 minutes before normal dismissal), in cooperation with local county emergency-preparedness-plan officials if possible. The drill also must test the usefulness of the communications and transportation systems during emergencies. Parents or guardians must be notified of the drill at least one week in advance (8 NYCRR § 155.17(j)).

17:11. Are school districts required to hold emergency drills for after-school programs?

No. However, a principal or other person in charge of the school building during an after-school program, event, or performance must notify the participants who are not regular occupants of the building of the procedures to be followed, should an emergency occur (§ 807(1-a)).

17:12. What should a school district do if it receives a bomb threat?

A school district should respond to a bomb threat in accordance with the response protocols set forth in its school safety plan.

According to the "Revised Bomb Threat Response Guidelines," issued jointly in February 1999 by the New York State Education Department and the New York State Police, the district should keep in mind the following:

- All bomb threats must be taken seriously and no bomb threat may be treated as a hoax.
- Schools must have a consistent, unified plan of action to deal with bomb threats. Bomb threat plans must be included in the district's school safety plan.
- Anyone receiving information about a bomb threat must immediately notify the school building administrator or his or her designee who, in turn, will notify law enforcement officials and initiate the planned actions to move all occupants out of harm's way.

- A school's specific response to a bomb threat depends upon information regarding the location of the bomb and the time left to reach a place of safety. Evacuating a building may not be the safest response. Potential shelter locations must be pre-established in cooperation with local law enforcement. Sheltering areas and routes of egress and evacuation must be thoroughly searched for suspicious objects before or during an evacuation in accordance with the process set forth in the district's emergency management plan. The search for something unusual does not involve touching or handling the suspect object.
- A bomb threat is a criminal act and must be treated as one. Appropriate state, county, and/or local law enforcement authorities must be notified immediately upon receiving a bomb threat. Law enforcement officers will contact fire and/or county emergency coordinators as the situation requires, and, upon finding suspicious objects, will call for appropriate bomb technicians. Any person caught reporting a bomb threat will be prosecuted to the fullest extent of the law (see **17:13**).
- Staff should be trained on how to handle telephone and written bomb threats and how to handle mail bombs and suspicious packages.

School officials must inform parents and guardians as soon as possible of any incident that activates the school emergency management plan, along with actions taken to protect students, staff and property.

As soon as possible after the conclusion of a bomb threat incident, schools must complete a "New York State School Bomb Threat Report Data Sheet" and send it to the State Education Department, Office of Facilities Planning, Room 1060, EBA, Albany, N.Y. 12234. This is in addition to reporting requirements regarding activation of school safety plans (see **17:14**).

Questions regarding school emergency planning and the "Revised Bomb Threat Response Guidelines" may be directed to Laura Sahr at 518-474-3906 or via e-mail at lsahr@mail.nysed.gov.

17:13. What penalties can be imposed on persons who falsely report a bomb threat or place a false bomb on school grounds?

Any person who knowingly reports false information or initiates or circulates a false warning of an impending occurrence of a fire or explosion as well as the release of a hazardous substance to an official organization that deals with emergencies is guilty of a Class E felony for a first offense and a class D felony for two or more offenses (Penal Law §§ 240.50, 240.55, 240.60).

Any person who places upon school grounds a device or object that he believes will appear to be or to contain a bomb, destructive device, or explosive but is actually inoperative is guilty of a class D felony (Penal Law § 240.62). A person convicted of making a false report in the first degree or placing a false bomb on school grounds will have his driving license suspended for one year (Veh. & Traf. Law § 510(2)(b)(xii)).

In addition, a school district can seek restitution from the parent or legal guardian of a minor child between the ages of 10 and 18 who falsely reports a bomb threat or places a bomb for the expense of responding to such false report or incident. The total expense recoverable may not exceed $5,000 (Gen. Oblig. Law § 3-112).

17:14. Must school districts report any activation of their school safety plans?

Yes. Except in the case of routine snow emergency days, each superintendent must notify the commissioner of education as soon as possible whenever its districtwide or a building level school safety plan is activated and results in a school building closing. Districts within a supervisory district must notify the BOCES superintendent who is responsible for passing on the information to the commissioner (8 NYCRR § 155.17(h)).

17:15. May the commissioner of education order school districts to take emergency response actions?

Yes. The commissioner may order individual school districts to take emergency response actions if local officials are unable or unwilling to take action deemed appropriate under county or state emergency preparedness plans or directions (8 NYCRR § 155.17(m)).

Building Structure Safety

17:16. Who promulgates health and safety regulations for public school buildings in New York State?

The commissioner of education is authorized to promulgate health and safety regulations for all educational facilities (§ 409; see 8 NYCRR Part 155). The commissioner also is authorized to establish, develop, and monitor a comprehensive public school building safety program (§ 409-d; see 8 NYCRR § 155.3; see also **17:18**) and a uniform code of public school building inspections, safety rating, and monitoring (§ 409-e; see 8 NYCRR § 155.4; see also **17:19**).

Furthermore, for districts other than the Big 5, the commissioner has the power to designate a school building or a particular area within a school building as unusable for pupil occupancy when, based on these regulations, the general conditions of the building indicate it would be detrimental to the health and safety of its occupants (8 NYCRR § 155.7(j)).

When approving new lease agreements by union free or central school districts, the commissioner must determine whether the leased facility meets all applicable standards for the health, safety, and comfort of occupants, is educationally adequate and has a five-year capital facilities plan (§ 403-b(1)(c); see also **16:17**; **17:18**).

17:17. What school building health and safety subjects are covered by the commissioner's regulations?

The commissioner's regulations detail safety requirements for a broad range of subjects such as building exits (8 NYCRR § 155.7(a)); fire and smoke control (8 NYCRR § 155.7(b)); accident protection (8 NYCRR § 155.7(c)); mechanical equipment, including heating, ventilation and air conditioning (HVAC) systems (8 NYCRR § 155.7(d)); water and sanitation systems (8 NYCRR § 155.7(e)); natural gas (8 NYCRR § 155.7(f)); and electrical systems (8 NYCRR § 155.7(g)). For example, the regulations forbid the obstruction of emergency exits and mandate that safety glass be used in certain areas of school buildings.

The regulations also cover fire and building safety inspections (8 NYCRR § 155.8) and school safety plans (8 NYCRR § 155.17; see **17:1**). Additionally, they establish a comprehensive public school safety program (8 NYCRR § 155.3); a uniform code of public school building inspections, safety rating and monitoring (8 NYCRR § 155.4); and uniform safety standards for school construction and maintenance projects (8 NYCRR § 155.5).

17:18. What is the comprehensive public school safety program?

The comprehensive public school safety program serves to ensure that all occupied school facilities, whether owned, operated or leased by a district, are properly maintained and preserved and provide suitable educational settings (§ 409-d; 8 NYCRR § 155.3). It has four basic components:

1. Building condition surveys initially completed by all schools in the manner prescribed by the commissioner of education by November 15, 2000. A report of the survey results was submitted to the commissioner of education by January 15, 2001. Surveys must be completed every five years thereafter under the same November and January deadlines. Nonetheless, an initial building condition survey is not required until November 15, 2005 for new buildings that received a certificate of substantial completion between August 31, 1995 and September 30, 1999. New buildings that receive a certificate of

substantial completion dated October 1, 1999 or thereafter must have a building condition survey completed every five years, starting with the second survey following the certificate's issue.

The surveys must cover at least the items identified in the commissioner's regulations. A team that includes at least a licensed architect or engineer must conduct physical inspections in order to complete a survey (8 NYCRR §§ 155.3(a), 155.4(b)(1)).

2. Annual visual inspections to be conducted by a team including a Department of State-certified code enforcement official, the district director of facilities or his or her designee, and a member of the district's health and safety committee. A separate visual inspection is not necessary in the years when a building condition survey is performed. Visual inspections must be completed by November 15 and a report filed with the commissioner by January 15 of the following year. If a problem is detected during a visual inspection, which renders the building unsatisfactory or unsafe or unhealthful, the district must hire a licensed architect or engineer to perform a detailed inspection and develop a corrective plan (8 NYCRR §§ 155.3(b), 155.4(b)(2)).

3. Five-year capital facilities plan developed by July 1, 2001 and updated annually, using the safety rating of each occupied building. The plan, to be prepared in a manner and format prescribed by the commissioner, must identify critical maintenance needs and information designed to evaluate the safety and health conditions in school facilities. It must be submitted to the commissioner upon request (8 NYCRR §§ 155.1(a)(4), 155.3(c)).

4. Procedures to monitor the safety and condition of all occupied public school buildings. As part of these procedures, districts must establish a health and safety committee comprised of representatives from district officials, staff, bargaining units, and parents, and, during a construction project, the architect, construction manager, and project contractors, as well. Districts also must establish a comprehensive maintenance plan for all major building systems to ensure the building is maintained in a state of good repair, provide for a least toxic approach to integrated pest management, and maintenance procedures and guidelines concerning acceptable indoor air quality. School boards must annually review and approve annual building inspection reports and the five-year building condition surveys.

In addition, monitoring systems procedures must ensure that annual safety inspections are conducted for each school building, and that a current and valid certificate of occupancy is maintained and posted conspicuously. The procedures must ensure a process that allows for a health and safety committee to participate in the investigation and disposition of complaints related to health and safety, and that the district takes and reports to the commissioner immediate action to remedy serious conditions affecting health and safety. They must ensure that all construction and maintenance activities comply with the uniform safety standards for school and maintenance projects set forth in the commissioner's regulations (8 NYCRR §§ 155.3(d), 155.4(d), 155.5(c)(2)).

17:19. What is the uniform code of public school buildings, inspections, safety rating, and monitoring?

The uniform code of public school buildings, inspections, safety rating, and monitoring provides standardized procedures for periodic inspections and the monitoring system required by the comprehensive public school safety program (§ 409-e; 8 NYCRR § 155.4; see **17:18**). It also requires that school districts provide an annual safety rating of occupied school buildings keyed to the structural integrity and overall safety of the building. Each district must establish a safety rating in consultation with the district's health and safety committee and in accordance with the commissioner's regulations.

Each building's safety rating must identify and assess the condition of every major building component in one of the following categories: excellent, satisfactory, unsatisfactory, unsafe/unhealthful, or indeterminate. Building system deficiencies must be categorized as health and safety, structural, comfort, or aesthetic.

The overall rating of a building is determined by a weighted system developed by the commissioner of education and includes the following categories: excellent, good, satisfactory, and unsafe/unhealthful. A rating of unsafe/unhealthful will cause the revocation of the building certificate of occupancy (8 NYCRR § 155.4(c)).

Further information is available through the State Education Department's Office of Facilities Planning at 518-474-3906 or at http://www.emsc.nysed.gov/facplan.

17:20. What are the uniform safety standards for school construction and maintenance projects?

The uniform safety standards for school construction and maintenance projects establish standardized procedures for ensuring the safety of school buildings and their occupants during construction and maintenance projects (see **16:17**). They address the following issues:

- The monitoring of construction and maintenance activities.
- The investigation and disposition of complaints.
- Pre-construction testing, planning, and notification of construction projects.
- General safety and security standards.
- Separation of construction from occupied spaces.

- Maintenance of exits and ventilation.
- Fire and hazard prevention.
- Noise abatement during construction and maintenance.
- Control of chemical fumes, gases, and other contaminants.
- Asbestos abatement and lead paint protocols (see **17:51, 17:61–75**).
- School radon responsibilities.
- Post-construction inspections (§ 409-e(4)(b); 8 NYCRR § 155.5; see **17:18**).

17:21. What are some examples of the specific procedures school districts must follow under uniform safety standards for school construction and maintenance projects?

The uniform safety standards for school construction and maintenance projects provide that school boards must ensure, for example:

- Occupied portions of any school buildings undergoing construction comply with the minimum requirements to maintain a certificate of occupancy, and that school district personnel monitor the occupied areas during construction and maintenance activities for any safety violations (8 NYCRR § 155.5(a)).
- Effective September 30, 1999, all bid specifications and contract documents address safety issues before contract documents are advertised for bid. All areas disturbed during renovation or demolition must be tested for lead and asbestos. District school safety plans must be updated as necessary, including emergency exit plans during construction, and provisions for emergency evacuations of students and staff during a construction incident (8 NYCRR § 155.5(c)).
- Establish procedures to notify parents, staff, and the community of a construction project costing $10,000 or more in an occupied building at least two months in advance of initial date of construction or in the case of emergency construction, as far in advance of the start of construction as practicable (8 NYCRR § 155.5(d)).
- Construction materials are stored safely and securely; gates to construction areas must be locked; workers must wear photo-identification badges at all times while working at occupied sites (8 NYCRR § 155.5(e)).
- Construction areas are separated from occupied spaces including designation of separate stairways and elevators for construction workers during work hours. In addition, provisions must be made to prevent the passage of dust and contaminants into occupied parts of a building and for the removal of debris through enclosed chutes or a similar sealed system (8 NYCRR § 155.5(f)).

- Proper exiting and adequate ventilation are maintained (8 NYCRR § 155.5(g)).
- School district personnel conduct daily inspections of district occupied areas to ensure that fire exits and emergency egress windows are not blocked by construction materials, equipment or debris. Also, no smoking rules must be strictly enforced on school property, including construction areas (8 NYCRR § 155.5 (h)).
- Noise in excess of 60 dba in occupied spaces occurs only when the building or affected building spaces are unoccupied or when acoustical abatement measures are taken (8 NYCRR § 155.5(i)).

Further information on the uniform safety standards for construction and maintenance projects can be found at the State Education Department's Office of Facilities Planning, at 518-474-3906 or http://www.emsc.nysed.gov/facplan.

For information on the additional requirements imposed by the state's uniform fire prevention and building code, contact the New York State Department of State at 518-474-4750 or http://www.dos.state.ny.us.

17:22. Are school districts required to maintain a minimum temperature in schools?

Yes. The "Property Maintenance Code of New York State," part of the "New York State Uniform Fire Prevention and Building Code," requires that "indoor occupiable work spaces be supplied with heat during the period from September 15 to May 31 to maintain a minimum temperature of 65°F (18°C) during the period the spaces are occupied." However, there are exceptions for areas of vigorous physical activity (gymnasiums) and processing spaces (coolers or freezers) (19 NYCRR § 1220-1226; see also Office of Facilities Planning Newsletter #37, March 2003).

17:23. Are school districts required to issue school facility report cards?

Yes. Each district is required to prepare a school facility report card for each occupied building. The school board must review the school facility report card for each building and report the results in a public meeting. The report card must provide information as prescribed by the commissioner of education on items such as a building's age, size, enrollment, useful life, safety rating, and visual inspection and building condition survey results (8 NYCRR § 155.6).

17:24. Are electrically-operated partitions or doors covered by safety rules?

Yes. School districts that have electrically-operated doors or partitions must post conspicuous notices in the immediate vicinity of the operating mechanism concerning their safe and proper operation and supervision, must have established procedures concerning notification on their operation to employees and others who regularly use the area, and must inform those employees of the penalties for disabling safety devices on the doors or partitions. Any person who disables or directs another to disable such a safety device is subject to a fine and up to 15 days in jail or both. In addition, every electrically-operated partition or door must have safety devices to stop the motion of the partition or door if a body or other object is in its path (§ 409-f; 8 NYCRR § 155.25(c)(3)).

The commissioner's regulations further require every partition to be equipped with two key-operated control stations so that two people must simultaneously activate the controls and apply constant pressure to open or close the partition. The control stations must be located at opposite ends of and opposite sides of, and in view of, the partition. The partition must be capable of being reversed at any point while opening or closing, and must be installed such that the failure of any safety device renders the partition inoperable until such device is fixed (8 NYCRR § 155.25(c)(1), (2)).

Students are not permitted to operate such partitions, and all students present during partition operation must be directly supervised by trained staff, must keep away from the partition, and are not allowed to cross the path of the moving partition. Staff members who regularly use the partitions must be trained in the safe operation of the partition and its safety features. Training must include discussion of past accidents and the potential and possibility of serious injury or death. Records of such training must be maintained (8 NYCRR § 155.25(d)).

Any district with an electrically operated partition not in compliance with the commissioner's regulations may not use the partition until the proper safety devices are installed (SED Office of Facilities Planning Newsletter #42, August 2003).

17:25. Are fire safety inspections required for school buildings?

Yes. Annual inspections are required for fire and safety hazards that may endanger the lives of students and district employees. Boards of cooperative educational services (BOCES) and school districts, except for the Big 5, must have all their school buildings inspected by a qualified inspector under procedures established by the State Fire Administrator. This inspection report must be filed in the district offices and with the commissioner of education. The annual inspection must be conducted in accordance with a schedule established by the commissioner of education. That schedule breaks the state into zones, each with a fire inspection period during which the inspection must take place and a deadline for filing inspection reports. Each building, including any owned, leased or used in any manner by the district, must have a separate fire safety inspection (§ 807-a; see also 8 NYCRR § 155.8; 19 NYCRR Part 1225; Manual for Fire and Building Safety Inspections in Public and Nonpublic Schools, SED, Revised January 2004).

In addition, the commissioner may order a fire safety inspection at any reasonable time. School authorities may not refuse the inspector access to the school building. Further, any public school building may be inspected at any reasonable time by the local fire chief or a fire fighter assigned to do so by the fire chief. A school administrator has the right to be present during this inspection (§ 807-a(6), (7)).

For further information on fire inspection, see the State Education Department's Manual for Fire and Building Safety Inspections in Public and Nonpublic Schools, Revised January 2004, available on-line at http://www.emsc.nysed.gov/facplan.

17:26. Who is responsible for enforcing fire safety requirements in the public schools?

The commissioner of education has the responsibility to administer and enforce the New York State Uniform Fire Prevention and Building Code (see 19 NYCRR Parts 1220-1226) with respect to buildings, premises, and equipment in the custody of school districts and boards of cooperative educational services (BOCES) (8 NYCRR § 155.8(a)–(c)).

The commissioner has the authority to issue a certificate of occupancy to public school districts that indicates that a school building is in compliance with part 155 of the commissioner's regulations and with the state Uniform Fire Prevention and Building Code (8 NYCRR § 155.8(e)(1)). The commissioner also has the power to issue temporary certificates of occupancy, and to deny or revoke certificates of occupancy to school districts that fail to comply with these standards (8 NYCRR § 155.8(e)(2), (3)).

17:27. What happens if a public school building does not pass a fire inspection?

If a school building fails to pass a fire inspection, the school board must adopt a plan, approved by the commissioner of education, to correct all violations. The commissioner may issue a temporary certificate of occupancy pending these corrections and, particularly when the building is not suitable for occupancy or intended use, he may refuse to issue or he may revoke an existing certificate of occupancy (8 NYCRR § 155.8(c), (e)).

17:28. Must the school district inform the public of the results of fire-safety inspections?

Yes. Fire inspection reports must be filed in the school district and with the commissioner of education (see **17:18**). All such reports shall be retained as public record for at least three years. Within 20 days, school districts also must publish a notice in a local newspaper stating the report has been filed (§ 807-a(5)(a-c)).

17:29. Must a school's fire alarm system be connected with the community's fire departments?

Yes, wherever practical. The school's fire alarm system must be connected if the school building is located in a fire district that has an electrically-operated, general municipal fire alarm box system so that sounding the school-building fire alarm system automatically relays the alarm to the fire department (§ 807-c; 8 NYCRR § 155.7(g)(4)). Additionally, wherever practical, a fire alarm box compatible with the municipal system must be located and accessible on the site or in the school building.

In a case where a fire district may not have an electrically-operated, general municipal fire alarm system, it is up to the board and the governing body of the local fire department to decide whether to connect the school building to the fire department (§ 807-c; see also 8 NYCRR § 155.7(g)(4)).

17:30. What authority does the local fire department have if a school building fire alarm is activated?

If a school building's fire alarm goes off, the fire department has the authority to enter the school building to determine whether the fire is out and whether the building is safe for occupancy, even in the event of a false alarm (Gen. Mun. Law § 204-d). School officials may not deny fire fighters access to the school building or order them to leave (Inf. Opn. Att'y Gen. 81-13).

If a school building's fire alarm sounds, students may not reenter the building until the fire department determines the building is safe for occupancy. Only the fire department, not the police department or school district, has the authority to order students back into the building (Inf. Opn. Att'y Gen. 81-13, 83-67).

Workplace Safety

17:31. Are school districts required to provide a safe workplace for school employees?

Yes. However, while the employer is required to furnish a workplace that is free from recognized hazards to employees, employees also must comply with safety and health standards and other regulations that are applicable to their own actions and conduct (Lab. Law § 27-a(3)(b); see also Lab. Law § 884 for information on workplace safety training and education programs).

17:32. Must school districts comply with workers' safety rules established by the federal Occupational Safety and Health Administration (OSHA)?

Yes. The Public Employees' Safety and Health (PESH) Bureau adopts all OSHA regulations through state rule-making procedures (Lab. Law § 27-a(4); 12 NYCRR § 800.3), even though OSHA itself has jurisdiction only over private employers. School districts must comply with PESH regulations; therefore, indirectly they are complying with OSHA regulations. Thus, PESH is responsible for enforcement and interpretation of these rules.

17:33. Who is responsible for enforcing workplace safety requirements?

Schools are governed by the Public Employees' Safety and Health (PESH) Bureau of the New York State Department of Labor, which was established by the State Occupational Safety and Health Act (SOSHA) (Lab. Law § 27-a), to protect public employees from hazards in their workplaces. PESH's jurisdiction covers public employers and employees, including both instructional and noninstructional employees of school districts.

17:34. What does the Public Employees' Safety and Health (PESH) Bureau require of school districts with regard to worker safety rules?

School districts must comply with worker safety rules adopted by PESH that run the gamut from very general to explicitly precise. In general, districts are required to maintain a safe workplace under what is known as the general duty clause (Lab. Law § 27-a(3)(a)(1)). Other PESH rules are more detailed and precise, such as the Hazard Communication Standard (see **17:39–41**) and the chemical laboratory safety rules (see **17:45**).

17:35. What happens if a school district violates a workers' safety rule established by the Public Employees' Safety and Health (PESH) Bureau?

PESH is authorized to issue stringent monetary penalties for safety violations committed by public employers. However, the procedures adopted by PESH permit school districts to correct their mistakes before fines are imposed (Lab. Law § 27-a(6)).

Initially, an employer is cited by a PESH safety inspector for a safety violation that is labeled at the time of the citation as either "serious" or "nonserious." Then the employer is given a certain period of time to correct the violation. If the employer fails to correct this problem by a set deadline, then PESH can assess a fine (Lab. Law § 27-a(6)).

The fine for a nonserious violation can be up to $50 per day beyond the deadline; for a serious violation, it could be as high as $200 per day. A state formula for calculating penalties also takes into account other mitigating factors, such as the district's good faith efforts to remediate (Lab. Law § 27-a(6); New York State Department of Labor's *Field Operations Manual* for penalty guidelines; see also *Matter of New York City Transit Auth. v. NYS Dep't of Labor*, 88 N.Y.2d 225 (1996)).

The seriousness of a violation is decided in part by a determination of the extent of injury that could occur to workers exposed to the hazard in question (Lab. Law § 27-a(6)). Because a majority of hazards could result in injury, many violations may be considered serious by PESH.

17:36. Is financial assistance available to comply with a citation from the Public Employees' Safety and Health (PESH) Bureau?

Yes. Section 27-a of the state Labor Law provides grants under certain circumstances in conjunction with the State Occupational Safety and Health Act (SOSHA). Under this section, the state Department of Labor is authorized to provide school districts with 75 percent of the cost of capital abatement projects incurred in order to comply with a SOSHA citation (Lab. Law § 27-a(16)(A)).

17:37. Do worker safety rules apply to shop classes and other instructional locations?

Yes. Under the federal Occupational Safety and Health Administration (OSHA) rules adopted by PESH, school districts must ensure that teachers and other instructional employees in shop classes and other instructional locations are protected by fundamental safety measures. In machine technology or shop classes, these safety measures include, for example, adequate guards for radial-arm saws and grinders; disconnecting switches for power driven woodworking machines and safety guards for abrasive wheel machines (see 29 CFR §§ 1910.213, 1910.215).

School districts also must implement a chemical hygiene plan capable of protecting employees from health hazards in all chemical laboratories (29 CFR § 1910.1450(b), (e); see **17:46**).

In addition, school districts must determine if hazards that necessitate the use of personal protective equipment are present or likely to be present in the workplace, including asbestos (see **17:62**). The district must provide this information to its employees and must have a written certification of making this assessment (29 CFR §§ 1910.132(d), 1910.1001(h)).

17:38. What is a school district's responsibility for protecting employees from exposure to the human immunodeficiency virus (HIV) and hepatitis infections?

The Public Employees' Safety and Health (PESH) Bureau has adopted federal Occupational Safety and Health Administration (OSHA) standards for workers' protection from blood-borne pathogens such as HIV and hepatitis B. These require public employers, including school districts, to develop, implement, and evaluate exposure-control plans to eliminate or minimize employees' exposure to blood-borne diseases, and to use various methods of compliance to protect workers. Methods of compliance include requiring employees to wash their hands, handle needles properly, use plastic gloves made available by the employer in the workplace, and ensure work areas contaminated by blood or body fluids are properly decontaminated. For further information, see "An Implementation Package for HIV/AIDS Policy in New York State School Districts," New York State HIV/AIDS Prevention Education Program, June 17, 1996.

Employers must provide additional protection to certain employees who encounter "occupational exposure" to blood-borne pathogens. These include participation in special training programs and free hepatitis B vaccinations for employees who choose to be vaccinated. In addition, employers having "occupationally exposed" employees must establish a written exposure control plan accessible to all employees and must review it annually.

Employers must also identify tasks associated with any job classification that occupationally exposes or may expose employees. Employees are "occupationally exposed" to blood-borne pathogens if "reasonably anticipated" skin, eye, mucous membrane, or parenteral contact with blood or body fluid "may result" from an employee's performance of his or her duties. Under these regulations, school nurses are probably occupationally exposed, and other school employees, such as special education teachers and coaches, may be exposed (see 29 CFR § 1910.1030).

Hazardous Materials and Toxic Substances

17:39. What are a school district's responsibilities regarding the presence of hazardous materials and toxic substances on school premises?

Districts must comply with the federal Occupational and Safety Health Administration (OSHA) Hazard Communication Standard (29 CFR § 1910.1200), adopted by the Public Employees' Safety and Health (PESH) Bureau, concerning hazardous substances, and New York State's Right-to-Know Law concerning toxic substances (Lab. Law §§ 875–883; Pub. Health Law §§ 4800–4808; see 9 NYCRR Part 1174). Both laws require school districts to develop and maintain a written hazard-communication program that includes information and training about materials that pose potential health and/or safety hazards. Both also apply to materials commonly used by employees as part of a daily occupational routine, such as cleaning fluids, photocopier toner, glues, and photographic developing fluids.

The hazard-communication program must ensure containers that hold hazardous materials are properly labeled to identify their contents and warn of any hazards that may be related to their use. It also must provide for the maintenance of material safety data sheets at the work site, as well as employee training at the work site. In addition, school districts must make available for inspection a list of all hazardous chemicals to which employees might be exposed and document employee training in hazardous-materials management and protection, as well as any incident that involves an employee's exposure to hazardous materials (29 CFR § 1910.1200(e)(1)).

Under OSHA regulations, school districts also must report the exposure of any employee to any of 13 listed carcinogens (see 29 CFR § 1910.1003(a) for the list of carcinogens). Incidents that result in the release of any of these carcinogens into areas where employees may be potentially exposed must be reported to the nearest OSHA area director within 24 hours. This report must state what happened and include information on any medical treatment of affected employees. A more detailed written report must be filed within 15 days (29 CFR § 1910.1003(f)(2)). In addition, OSHA regulations require school districts to adopt and implement a written respiratory protection program (29 CFR § 1910.134 (a)(2), (c)), which includes effective engineering control methods to prevent employee breathing of contaminated air, and provisions for employee use of respirators, if necessary, to protect health and safety.

Districts may not use paradichlorobenzene as a school bathroom deodorizer (§ 409-g).

17:40. Must school districts maintain material safety data sheets on hazardous materials?

Yes. The federal Hazard Communication Standard requires a material safety data sheet (MSDS) for each known hazardous material on school district property, which includes information such as the name of the chemical or compound, any possible ill effects a worker may experience from exposure to it, and instructions on how to handle a related hazard, should one occur.

The supplier or manufacturer of a chemical or compound usually provides an MSDS. They also are available through the New York State Department of Health, the Environmental Protection Agency or the National Institute of Occupational Safety and Health. However, it is the district's responsibility to obtain an MSDS for each chemical or compound, if one has not been automatically supplied (Lab. Law § 876; 29 CFR § 1910.1200(g)).

The state Right-to-Know Law requires that information about known hazardous materials in the workplace, such as an MSDS, be provided to an employee requesting such information within 72 hours, excluding weekends and public holidays, of the district's receipt of the request (Lab. Law § 876(7)).

17:41. What happens if a district fails to comply with the Hazard Communication Standard or provide employees access to material safety data sheets under the Right-to-Know Law?

Employers who violate the Hazard Communication Standard are subject to fines imposed by the Public Employees' Safety and Health (PESH) Bureau for violation of state regulations (Lab. Law § 27-a(6); *New York City Transit Auth. v. NYS Dep't of Labor*, 88 N.Y.2d 225 (1996); see also **17:35**; see also New York State Department of Labor's *Field Operations Manual* for the state penalty guidelines).

In addition, if a school district fails to provide timely information on known hazardous materials (see **17:39–40**), the employee is permitted under the state's Right-to-Know Law to refuse to work with the material until the information is furnished (Lab. Law § 876(7)). This provision is known as the right-to-strike provision.

17:42. What are a school district's responsibilities regarding the use of pesticides on school premises?

The comprehensive public school safety program and the uniform code of public school building inspection, safety, ratings, and monitoring require that school districts establish a comprehensive maintenance plan that includes provisions for a least toxic approach to integrated pest management (8 NYCRR §§ 155.3(d), 155.4 (d)(2)).

Integrated pest management (IPM) is a systematic approach to managing pests that focuses on long-term prevention or suppression with minimal impact on human health, the environment, and nontargeted organisms (6 NYCRR § 325.1 (al)).

IPM is offered as a state contract under the state Office of General Services. Information is available from the Office of General Services at 518-474-3899 and http://www.ogs.state.ny.us.

The Department of Environmental Conservation (DEC) provides guidelines for integrated pest management for school districts in its book, "IPM Workbook for New York State Schools" (Cornell Cooperative Extension Community IPM Program with support from New York State Department of Environmental Conservation, August 1998). Copies are available from DEC's Bureau of Pesticides Management at 518-402-8781.

The DEC also has issued regulations regarding the use of pesticides that are applicable to school districts (6 NYCRR Part 325). These regulations require the following:

- A copy of the label of each indoor or outdoor pesticide must be provided to the facility where it is being used. This information must be made available to anyone who requests it.
- Contracts with contractors taking care of the grounds must state which chemicals are going to be used.
- Contractors must post on the grounds visible signs prior to and at least 24 hours after pesticide application, warning of the pesticide use. By January 1, 2005 the signs must be made of rigid material with black letters at least 4 inches by 5 inches in size on a yellow background.
- An apprentice may not apply pesticides on any school premises without the direct supervision of a certified applicator.
- Districts using pesticides must register and file an annual report with the DEC, which includes the quantity of pesticide product used (6 NYCRR §§ 325.23, 325.25, 325.40).

In addition, Environmental Conservation Law section 33-0725 requires that a pesticide be used only in accordance with its labeling (exceptions provided are for agricultural purposes only).

For more information concerning pesticides, refer to 6 NYCRR Part 325 and Environmental Conservation Law Article 33, contact the nearest regional office of the Department of Environmental Conservation, or visit its Web site at http://www.dec.state.ny.us. The Environmental Protection Agency's Office of Pesticide Programs offers the publication "Pest Control in the School Environment: Adopting Integrated Pest Management" (August 1993) available at 703-305-7035 or http://www.epa.gov/pesticides/ipm/brochure/.

17:43. Must school districts give notice of pesticide applications?

Yes. School districts must give prior written notice of pesticide applications to anyone who has asked to receive such notice, in accordance with notification provisions set forth in the Education Law and commissioner's regulations (§ 409-h; 8 NYCRR § 155.24). For example, at the beginning of each school year or summer school session the school district must provide written notification to all staff and parents that pesticides may be used periodically throughout the school year or summer school session, that the district is required to maintain a list of those people who wish to receive 48-hour notice prior to the application of pesticides and how to register for the list and the name and phone number of the school pesticide representative (§ 409-h (2); 8 NYCRR § 155.24(b)).

Further information and training is available through the Health and Safety Office of local boards of cooperative educational programs (BOCES), as well as Cornell Cooperative Extension (800-635-8356) and the Office of Facilities Planning at the New York State Education Department at 518-474-3906 or http://www.emsc.nysed.gov/facplan/.

17:44. Are there any restrictions on the use of pressure treated lumber in public school facilities?

Yes. School districts and BOCES are prohibited from using lumber that has been pressure treated with chromated copper arsenate (CCA) in the construction of playground structures owned or operated by the district or BOCES. (Envtl. Conserv. Law § 37-0109(1)) This is due to the possible risk of contamination and poisoning by arsenic and chrome, which are two known human carcinogens.

Moreover, school districts and BOCES must maintain and operate all existing playground structures previously constructed using CCA pressure treated lumber and any surrounding ground cover including gravel, wood chips or rubber in a manner that minimizes the leaching of the CCA from such structures (Envtl. Conserv. Law § 37-0109(2)). This can be done by staining or painting the structures with certain penetrating coatings as advised by the state Department of Environmental Conservation (DEC). (SED memorandum from Carl Thurnau to District Superintendents, Superintendents of Schools, et al., November 2002).

The DEC commissioner must compile and publish information on the dangers and hazards to public health and to the environment in connection with the use of CCA-treated lumber. The commissioner also is required to publish a list of less toxic materials that may be used as an alternative. Finally, the DEC is required to publish and widely disseminate to the public information about non-toxic methods and materials that are available to adequately maintain playground structures to as the minimize leaching of CCA from such structures (Envtl. Conserv. Law § 37-0109(3)).

The DEC has published some of this information on its Web site http://www.dec.state.ny.us (search for "chromated"). Information may also be obtained at the DEC's Division of Solid and Hazardous Materials, Bureau of Solid Waste, Reduction and Recycling at 518-402-8660 or 625 Broadway, Albany, NY 12233.

There are several products that may be used in place of CCA-treated lumber. The EPA has registered a number of alternate wood preservatives. In addition, untreated wood (e.g., cedar and redwood) and non-wood alternatives, such as plastics, metal, and composite materials, are available (SED memorandum from Carl Thurnau to District Superintendents, Superintendents of Schools, et al., November, 2002).

17:45. Are there any safety concerns with respect to using construction and demolition debris as fill for athletic fields?

Yes. Construction and demolition debris (C&D debris) generally includes uncontaminated solid waste resulting from construction, remodeling, repair, and demolition of structures or roads. However, if the debris has been mechanically processed it may be contaminated with lead or other harmful materials. If a school is contemplating using C&D debris as fill for an athletic field the debris should only contain concrete and concrete products, asphalt, pavement, brick, glass, soil, and rock. (Marc Moran, Regional Director, Region 3, NYS Department of Environmental Conservation (DEC); Letter to Superintendents September 26, 2003; see also NYS DEC Region 3 Solid Waste Program; Construction and Demolition Debris FAQ September 2003) see also 6 NYCRR Part 360).

Recent problems with use of contaminated C&D debris at schools has resulted in the State Education Department mandating that in the case of a major field reconstruction where the elevation of the playing field surface is to be raised significantly the project will require a full review by the Office of Facilities Planning. Previously site work did not require review and issuance of a building permit (Carl Thurnau, Coordinator Office of Facilities Planning, Letter to Superintendents August 11, 2003).

17:46. What rules apply to the use of chemicals in school laboratories by district employees?

Districts must comply with federal Occupational Health and Safety Administration (OSHA) regulations governing the use of certain hazardous chemicals in school laboratories (29 CFR § 1910.1450). The state Public Employees' Safety and Health (PESH) Bureau has interpreted these regulations to be applicable only to chemicals used in science laboratories and not to the use of compounds in industrial arts and other school subjects (see 29 CFR § 1910.1450(a)(3)).

Under the regulations, school districts must adopt a chemical hygiene plan that includes practices, policies, and procedures to ensure that employees are protected from all potentially hazardous chemicals in their work areas, including keeping exposures below regulatory limits (29 CFR § 1910.1450(b), (e)). In addition, districts must:

- Monitor employees' exposure to chemicals (29 CFR § 1910.1450(d)).
- Provide permanent and temporary employees with training and information (29 CFR § 1910.1450(f)).
- Provide updated training when a new toxic substance is introduced into the workplace (29 CFR § 1910.1450(f)).
- Provide employees with medical consultations and examinations under certain circumstances (29 CFR § 1910.1450 (e);(g)).
- Identify hazards of chemicals used in the workplace, including the maintenance of labels and material safety data sheets (MSDSs) of chemicals (29 CFR § 1910.1450(h)).
- Provide employees with respirators when required (29 CFR § 1910.1450(i)).
- Maintain certain records proving compliance with the regulations (29 CFR § 1910.1450(j)).

In addition, section 305(19) of the Education Law requires school districts to follow certain procedures to ensure safety in school science laboratories and directs the commissioner of education to adopt regulations on chemical laboratory safety. It requires that all schools store chemicals in locked, secured rooms and cabinets, and provides for the arrangement, ventilation, and fire protection of chemicals in accordance with guidelines issued by the commissioner.

School districts also must take an annual inventory of all chemicals used in their science laboratories, including specific information on each substance, and must retain the inventory and make it available to the commissioner for inspection (§ 305(19); 29 CFR § 1910.1200(e)(1)(i)).

17:47. What are a school district's responsibilities regarding the disposal of hazardous waste?

A school district is obligated to properly dispose of hazardous waste (42 USC § 9601 *et seq.*; Envtl. Conserv. Law § 27-0900 *et seq.*). A district's liability for the disposal of hazardous waste is far-reaching. Under federal "cradle-to-grave" liability policies, one who arranges for the disposal of hazardous wastes may be liable for the cost of cleaning up those substances forever, even though the person or entity lawfully disposed of the waste with a licensed waste hauler. Continuing liability stems from the interwoven obligations created by numerous federal hazardous waste laws and regulations, including the Resource Conservation and Recovery Act (RCRA) (42 USC § 6901 *et seq.*), and the Comprehensive Environmental Response, Compensation, and Liability Act (CERCLA) (42 USC § 9601 *et seq.*).

17:48. What are a school district's responsibilities for underground storage tanks for petroleum?

The state Department of Environmental Conservation (DEC) has adopted regulations applicable to owners of both underground and above-ground storage tanks for petroleum to prevent and/or minimize damage from leaks and spills from tanks. The federal Resource Conservation and Recovery Act (RCRA) and the Environmental Protection Agency (EPA), the federal agency that enforces RCRA, impose additional requirements on owners of underground storage tanks. Local and county health departments may impose additional restrictions.

The regulations adopted by DEC require school districts that own underground and above-ground storage tanks containing petroleum to register and pay a registration fee for storage tanks (6 NYCRR §§ 612.2, 612.3). In addition, owners of tanks must:

- Employ practices for preventing transfer spills and accidental discharges (6 NYCRR § 613.3(a)).
- Install secondary containment systems and gauges for above-ground tanks (6 NYCRR § 613.3(c)).
- Test underground storage tanks for leaking and damage when the tank is 10 to 15 years old, depending on the type of tank (6 NYCRR § 613.5).
- Retest underground storage tanks for tightness every five years from the date of the last test (6 NYCRR § 613.5).
- Inspect above-ground storage tanks for leakage and damage each month (6 NYCRR § 613.6).
- Prepare daily inventory records for underground storage tanks (6 NYCRR § 613.4).

- Conduct an extensive inspection of above-ground storage tanks when the tank is 10 years old (6 NYCRR § 613.6).
- Conduct an extensive reinspection of above-ground storage tanks every 10 years from the date of the last test (6 NYCRR § 613.6).

The regulations also contain provisions about record-keeping and reporting requirements in the event of a spill or leak from a tank (6 NYCRR §§ 613.4; 613.5(a)(4); 613.6(c); 613.8). Finally, the regulations impose strict requirements for new underground storage tanks, new above-ground tanks and for closing out-of-service tanks (6 NYCRR § 613.9 and Part 614).

The federal law and regulations require owners of underground storage tanks to meet strict standards designed to prevent leaks and to ensure financial responsibility for clean-up costs and third-party damage claims (40 CFR Part 280). The financial responsibility requirement of the EPA regulation requires school districts and other owners of underground storage tanks to demonstrate their ability to pay for site clean-up and any liability to others for leak damage (40 CFR § 280.93). The regulations relieve a district of the obligation to carry special insurance policies for such coverage if it can meet one of two alternative requirements: a bond-rating test or a worksheet test. The bond-rating test requires the district to have at least $1 million of general obligation bonds of investment grade or better outstanding. The worksheet test involves the calculation of financial ratios (40 CFR §§ 280.104, 280.105)

In addition, federal regulations required that bare steel tanks of 110 gallons or larger (except on-site heating tanks) were to be upgraded by December 22, 1998. To upgrade the tank means essentially that the old system either must be retrofitted or closed, or a new system installed (40 CFR § 280.21).

Radon

17:49. What are a school district's responsibilities over the presence of radon in schools?

The uniform safety standards for school construction and maintenance projects require that school districts take responsibility to be aware of the geological potential for high levels of radon and to test and mitigate as appropriate (8 NYCRR § 155.5(m)).

Radon is a naturally occurring colorless, odorless, tasteless gas in the ground and atmosphere created by the natural breakdown (radioactive decay) of uranium deposits in the earth. When it is present in the air, it causes ionization (or splitting) of the molecules that make up the air. This ionization process results in the release of uranium, lead, and other substances in the environment, often called radon progeny or radon's daughters.

Based upon current scientific studies, radon and its progeny can affect cell development adversely in humans and exposure can lead to cancer. Some scientists believe radon is the leading cause of lung cancer among nonsmokers. Children would be particularly susceptible to damage from radon because their cells are developing and reproducing at a much more rapid rate than adults' cells.

The state Department of Health has identified areas around the state as having high concentrations of radon. This information is available from the Department of Health's Radon Measurement Database, on-line at http://www.health.state.ny.us/nysdoh/radon/radonhome.htm (8 NYCRR § 155.5(m)).

17:50. Is there assistance available to school districts regarding radon detection and control?

Yes. The State Education Department (SED) has issued a program guideline for radon detection and control that includes recommendations for school districts. These recommendations address testing for radon in school buildings, devices used during testing, training for school district personnel conducting testing, and response actions to testing results. Testing methods that can measure the presence of radon include charcoal canisters, alpha-track detectors and electrets. SED recommends, for example, against the use of charcoal canisters to test for radon; instead it supports the use of an electret, a small air chamber encompassed by an electromagnetic field, or alpha-tract detectors, to conduct radon testing. SED's Office of Facilities Planning advises school districts to call them at 518-474-3906, before conducting any testing to prevent districts from incurring any unnecessary expenses.

For more information, see "Environmental Quality of Schools" (Albany, N.Y.: State Education Department, 1994), "Reducing Radon in Schools: A Team Approach" (Environmental Protection Agency, April 1994, http://www.epa.gov/iaq/schools/redrnsch.html), and "Radon Prevention in the Design and Construction of Schools and Other Large Buildings (EPA, June 1994, http://www.epa.gov/iaq/schools/rnprevnt.html). Or contact SED's Office of Facilities Planning, Room 1060, Education Building Annex, Albany, N.Y. 12234 (http://www.emsc.nysed.gov/facplan/) or the New York State Department of Health's Bureau of Environmental Radiation Protection, 547 River Street, Room 530, Troy, N.Y. 12180, 518-402-7550 (http://www.health.state.ny.us). The New York State Department of Health also has a radon hotline for consumers at 800-458-1158 and a Web site at http://radon@health.state.ny.us.

Lead

17:51. What are a school district's responsibilities over the presence of lead in the schools?

Lead is a naturally occurring toxic metal that is harmful to health and can cause damage to the brain and nervous system resulting in reduced attention span, behavioral problems, impaired hearing and a lowered IQ. Lead is especially dangerous to young children, pregnant women, and fetuses. Lead enters the human body through inhalation (by breathing particles of lead-contaminated dust) and by ingestion (by drinking lead-contaminated water). Common sources of exposure to lead include paint chips and dust from paint that contains lead, and lead leached in water from lead solder or pipes.

The uniform safety standards for school construction and maintenance projects require that school districts test all areas to be disturbed during renovation or demolition and areas of flaking and peeling paint for the presence of lead (8 NYCRR § 155.5(c), (1)). Any construction or maintenance operations that will disturb lead-based paint must be abated in accordance with federal "Guidelines for the Evaluation and Control of Lead-Based Paint Hazards in Housing" (U.S. Department of Housing and Urban Development, Washington D.C., Revised June 1997). Areas of flaking and peeling paint must be abated or encapsulated in accordance with the same guidelines (8 NYCRR § 155.5(l)). According to commissioner's regulations, abatement involves mitigation of the lead hazard in accordance with guidelines from the federal Housing and Urban Development (HUD) Department (8 NYCRR § 155.5 (l)) which differ from the Environmental Protection Agency (EPA) at 40 CFR Part 745.

Copies of the guidelines and additional information are also available through the State Education Department, Office of Facilities Planning, EBA, Room 1060, Albany, N.Y. 12234 (http://www.emsc.nysed.gov/facplan or at http://www.hud.gov/offices/lead/guidelines/hudguidelines/).

17:52. What are a school district's responsibilities over the presence of lead in its water supply?

A school district that supplies its own water from wells it owns must test for lead under the federal Safe Drinking Water Act of 1974, which limits lead content to five parts per billion or less (42 USC § 300f *et seq.*).

Districts connected to a public water system need not test for lead in the drinking water. The New York State Department of Health oversees the public water supply program in the state. However, the federal Environmental Protection Agency (EPA) has issued a guidance document that recommends school districts do a plumbing profile to test for lead, and describes appropriate response actions (see "Testing Schools and Day Care Centers for Lead in the

Drinking Water" http://www.epa.gov/safewater/lead/testing.htm (Washington, D.C: EPA, 2004) and "Lead in drinking water in schools and non-residential buildings"   http://www.epa.gov/safewater/consumer/leadinschools.html (Washington, D.C.: EPA, 1994).

For information on a district's water responsibilities, contact the Department of Health at the state or local level (800-458-1158 or http://www.health.state.ny.us).

17:53. What is the law concerning water coolers with lead-lined tanks in school buildings?

Under the U. S. Lead Contamination Control Act of 1988, the Consumer Product Safety Commission is directed to recall water coolers with lead-lined tanks. Manufacturers must repair, replace, or refund the cost of the tanks (42 USC § 300j-22). The Environmental Protection Agency (EPA) is directed to publish a list of manufacturers of lead-containing water coolers (42 USC § 300j-23(a)). The sale of lead-containing water coolers is banned (42 USC § 300j-23(b)). School districts must disseminate to staff, students, and parents the results of any tests conducted (42 USC § 300j-24(d)(2)).

17:54. What steps can a school district take to reduce the presence of lead in indoor rifle ranges?

The erosion of the lead bullet base by propellant gases, lead bullet fragments, improper range cleaning, and home ventilation can generate lead dust in indoor rifle ranges. Based on the discovery of lead contamination in and around indoor firing ranges, the State Education Department recommends that school districts ensure that:

- Indoor rifle ranges are properly cleaned at least annually using wet methods and high-efficiency particulate air (HEPA) vacuums.
- Indoor rifle ranges are negatively pressurized and that adequate airflow through the range should move in a uniform (non-turbulent) manner from the firing line to the bullet trap and main exhaust plenum.
- Obstructions are kept out of the airflow path between the air inlet and the firing line. Obstructions include solid doors, windows, as well as stationary crowds of people.
- The air exhaust for the range is not located near any air intakes.
- The area of exhaust discharge outside the building is carefully monitored.
- In booths with half-height doors, shooters are prevented from contacting the shelf with their bodies by installing a bar between the shooter and the shelf.
- Persons working in or using an indoor rifle range are cautioned about carrying lead home on clothing, skin, and hair. Shoes worn on the

range should not be worn home and clothing should be laundered separately. No food or beverages should be permitted in the range. Wash hands and face before leaving the range (State Education Department Memorandum from Carl Thurnau to District Superintendents, Superintendents of School *et al.*, Nov. 16, 1999).

For other recommendations and information, contact the State Education Department, Office of Facilities Planning, EBA, Room 1060, Albany, N.Y. 12234 (http://www.emsc.nysed.gov/facplan/), or the NYS Department of Health Environmental Infoline at 800-458-1158.

Indoor Air Quality

17:55. What is indoor air quality?

Indoor air quality refers to the numerous environmental and psychological elements that affect the purity of air or the perceived purity of air within enclosed structures. Factors that influence indoor air quality include temperature, humidity, air movement or lack thereof, and contaminants such as dust, tobacco smoke, fumes from paints, cleaning materials, fumes from copy or print machines, mold, and formaldehyde. Building exhausts, car exhausts, mowing equipment and dust, paving, roofing and other activities may cause pollution to come into school buildings and affect the quality of air within.

Regarding mold, the State Education Department (SED) recommends that school districts take prompt action at first signs of excess moisture to prevent mold growth. Waiting for mold problems to develop can cost much more to correct, in terms of money, time, absenteeism, building closures, and poor morale (SED Office of Facilities Planning Newsletter #37, March 2003). The Environmental Protection Agency (EPA) offers guidance, information and resources at http://www.epa.gov/mold. See also "Mold Remediation in Schools and Commercial Buildings", EPA, Office of Air and Radiation, Indoor Environments Division, March 2001.

The heat, ventilation, and air-conditioning (HVAC) system in a school building may affect its indoor air quality under certain circumstances. SED encourages school districts to periodically clean their ducts and filters. Districts should pay special attention to changes in and around school buildings due to plant growth (trees and shrubs) and during construction and maintenance activities.

17:56. What laws apply to indoor air quality?

The comprehensive public school safety program and the uniform code of public school building inspection, safety and monitoring require that school districts establish a comprehensive maintenance plan that includes maintenance procedures and guidelines that will contribute to acceptable indoor air quality (8 NYCRR §§ 155.3, 155.4(d)(2)).

The uniform safety standards for school construction and maintenance projects require that all plans and specifications for construction projects in occupied facilities include a plan detailing, in part, how adequate ventilation will be maintained during construction (8 NYCRR § 155.5(g)). It also requires that districts make provisions to prevent the passage of dust and contaminants into occupied areas (8 NYCRR § 155.5(f), and the control of chemical fumes, gases, and other contaminants during construction and maintenance projects (8 NYCRR § 155.5(f), (j)).

In the past, the commissioner of education has ordered a school district to monitor students' physical symptoms when the air quality of a school building allegedly caused health problems (*Appeal of Anibaldi*, 33 Educ. Dep't Rep. 166 (1993)).

An appellate court has held that, while a teacher's allergic reaction to dust and mold in the work environment does not constitute an "occupational disease" when the condition does not result from some distinctive feature of employment, it may constitute an "occupational injury" compensable under Workers' Compensation Law (*Matter of Martin v. Fulton City Sch. Dist., et al.*, 300 A.D.2d 901 (2002)).

The New York State Energy Research and Development Authority (NYSERDA) offers technical assistance to help school districts address their indoor air-quality problems. For more information, contact NYSERDA at 518-862-1090 or 866-697-3732 (http://www.nyserda.org) or the State Education Department, Office of Facilities Planning, EBA, Room 1060, Albany, N.Y. 12234 (http://www.emsc.nysed.gov/facplan/).

17:57. Is smoking permitted in school buildings?

No. The federal Pro-Children Act of 1994 prohibits tobacco use in an indoor facility used for the routine provision of education or library services for students in schools receiving federal education aid. This prohibition extends to the entire school building, not just the classrooms used for instruction (20 USC § 6083(a)). For example, teachers' lounges located in elementary school buildings must be smoke-free.

The Education Law further restricts smoking in schools by prohibiting smoking in school buildings and on school grounds during school hours, meaning whenever there is a student activity that is supervised by faculty or staff, or any officially school-sanctioned event taking place (§ 409(2)). The Education Law defines school grounds as "any structure, and surrounding outdoor grounds contained within a public school's legally-defined property boundaries as registered in a county clerk's office" (§ 409(2)). The Public Health Law adds to that definition "and any vehicles used to transport children or school personnel" (Pub. Health Law § 1399-n(6)). The commissioner's regulations require strict enforcement of the no-smoking policy on public school property in construction areas (8 NYCCR § 155.5(h)(1)).

The provisions of the state law do not supersede any collective bargaining agreement, during its term, in existence on the effective date of the act, August 25, 1994 (Laws of 1994, Ch. 565, § 8).

In addition to federal and state laws specifically addressing smoking in school settings, New York's Clean Indoor Air Act prohibits smoking in certain workplaces (Pub. Health Law §§ 1399-n, 1399-o).

17:58. How does collective bargaining affect the rules concerning smoking in the workplace?

State law does not allow smoking on any school grounds or in certain places of employment, including school districts (§ 409(2); Pub Health Law §§ 1399-n, 1399-o). There is no longer an exception for designating smoking areas in noninstructional buildings during nonschool hours.

Asbestos

17:59. What is asbestos?

Asbestos is a group of naturally occurring minerals that can be processed into fibers, which may cause several medical problems, including cancer and lung damage. Its presence can be detected only through the use of laboratory analysis.

Asbestos-containing materials (ACM) were used widely in school building construction from the 1940s to the 1970s. They commonly included acoustical material, wall board, sprayed-on fireproofing, air cell pipe wrap, and floor and ceiling tiles. ACM may be potentially harmful if it is sanded, sawed, or subjected to any action that would release asbestos fibers and render them airborne.

Information on asbestos is available from the following New York State Education Department publications: "New York State Elementary & Secondary Schools Asbestos Guidebook for the Schools and the Community" (Central Services Team 1, undated), and "Designated Person's Guide to the Asbestos Hazard Emergency Response Act (AHERA)" (Central Services Team 1, 1994). Information and financial assistance is also available through the Environmental Protection Agency (EPA) under the federal Asbestos School Hazard Abatement Act (ASHA) (20 USC §§ 4011-4022).

17:60. What is friable asbestos?

Under New York State law, *friable asbestos* is a "condition of crumbled, pulverized, powdered, crushed or exposed asbestos which is capable of being released into the air by hand pressure" (Lab. Law § 901(11)).

In its rule entitled "Damaged Friable Surfacing ACM" (asbestos-containing material), the federal Environmental Protection Agency (EPA) defines damaged friable surfacing ACM to include the following: deteriorated or physically injured material such that the internal structure of the material is inadequate; or the bond of the lamination to its substrate is inadequate; or a lack of fiber cohesion or adhesion qualities; flaking, blistering, or crumbling; water damage, significant water stain, scraped, gouged, marred or other signs of physical injury (see 40 CFR § 763.83).

17:61. What laws govern a school district's obligations regarding asbestos-containing material?

The federal Asbestos Hazard Emergency Response Act (AHERA) and Article 30 of the New York State Labor Law (see 15 USC §§ 2641-2656) govern requirements regarding asbestos management for school districts.

AHERA is administered by the federal Environmental Protection Agency (EPA). The EPA has adopted regulations concerning asbestos-containing material (ACM) in schools (see 40 CFR Part 763, Subpart E; see **17:63-64** for more information about AHERA). The State Education Department is the AHERA designee for New York State's schools and, thus, serves a role in providing information to schools and in collecting information, such as asbestos-management plans.

In addition, the state Department of Labor has adopted work rules concerning asbestos known as Industrial Code Rule 56 (see 12 NYCRR Part 56; see also **17:62** and **17:71** for more information about Industrial Code Rule 56).

AHERA and the EPA regulations describe requirements concerning inspection and management of asbestos-containing material in school buildings, while the state Labor Law and Industrial Code Rule 56 control work practices for interaction with asbestos-containing material. The asbestos laws and regulations seek to reduce or eliminate potential risks associated with asbestos fibers.

Furthermore, uniform safety standards for school construction and maintenance projects which require that all school areas to be disturbed during renovation or demolition be treated for the presence of asbestos and which prohibit certain asbestos abatement projects are found in the commissioner's regulations (see 8 NYCRR § 155.5(c), (k); see also **17:20**).

More information on AHERA is available from the State Education Department's publication, "Designated Person's Study Guide to the

Asbestos Hazard Emergency Response Act (AHERA)" (Central Services Team 1, 1994).

17:62. What are some of the specific requirements school districts must comply with regarding asbestos-containing materials (ACM)?

The federal Asbestos Hazard Emergency Response Act (AHERA) requires that school districts:

- Identify all friable and nonfriable asbestos-containing material (ACM) in school buildings (40 CFR §§ 763.85–763.88).
- Appoint an individual as asbestos designee to ensure that AHERA requirements are implemented (40 CFR § 763.84 (g)(1)).
- Conduct an initial inspection and subsequent reinspection once every three years (40 CFR § 763.85(a), (b)).
- Conduct a periodic asbestos surveillance in each building at least once every six months (40 CFR § 763.92 (b).
- Prepare, administer and maintain an asbestos-management plan (40 CFR 763.93(a)).
- Adopt and execute appropriate response actions (40 CFR § 763.90).
- Notify workers and building occupants or their legal guardians about inspections, response actions and post-response actions at least once each school year (40 CFR §§ 763.84(c), 763.93(e)(10)).
- Notify short-term workers such as telephone repair workers, electricians and plumbers of the specific location of asbestos-containing materials in a building (40 CFR § 763.84(d)).

State aid is not available for costs incurred after July 1, 1989 for the completion of asbestos inspections and management plans (see 8 NYCRR § 155.18(a)).

In addition, AHERA requires that school districts clearly post warning labels on all materials containing asbestos fibers, at and approaching each regulated area and in maintenance and custodial locations (29 CFR § 1910.1001(j)(3), (4); 40 CFR § 763.95), and properly train all custodial and maintenance employees annually (29 CFR § 1910.1001(j)(7); 40 CFR §§ 763.92(a)(1), 763.84(b)). Two hours of asbestos awareness training must be provided for new employees (29 CFR § 1910.1001(j)(7), 40 CFR § 763.92(a)(1)).

In addition, school districts must provide personal protective equipment, including the use of respirators where necessary, for housekeeping and other employees who are exposed to dangerous levels of ACM (29 CFR § 1910.1001(g), (h), (j)).

School districts must also ensure that the various records required under AHERA regulations are properly maintained and distributed as required by law. For example, school officials must keep a copy of the asbestos management plan in the district's administrative office. Each building also must have a copy of that building's asbestos management plan in its administrative office (40 CFR § 763.93(g)(2), (3)).

The management plan must be made available without cost for inspection by the Environmental Protection Agency (EPA) and state representatives, as well as to workers before work begins in any area of a school building. It also must be made available to the public, school personnel and their representatives, and parents or legal guardians; in this case, the district may charge a reasonable fee for copying the plan. Except for requests for inspection from workers, the district must provide a copy of the management plan within five working days after receipt of the request for inspection of the plan. (40 CFR § 763.93(g)(2), (3)). In addition, school districts are required to keep AHERA asbestos records for at least three years after the last required inspection (40 CFR § 763.94(a)).

New York State Industrial Code Rule 56, which conforms with AHERA, requires that persons employed in any aspect of an asbestos project, as well as those who supervise them, be trained appropriately and certified. In addition, Industrial Code Rule 56 sets standards and procedures for the removal, enclosure, application, encapsulation, or disturbance of friable asbestos and the handling of asbestos or asbestos-containing material (ACM) in a manner that prevents the release of asbestos fibers (see **17:64**). For example, school districts must conduct an asbestos survey and removal project of all asbestos identified when a school building is scheduled for demolition (12 NYCRR § 56-1.9). This rule also establishes an inspection and enforcement program administered by the New York State Department of Labor and sets forth record-keeping, reporting, and retention requirements for asbestos contractors (12 NYCRR Part 56).

17:63. Are school districts responsible for conducting ongoing asbestos reinspections?

Yes. The asbestos management plans required by the Asbestos Hazard Emergency Response Act (AHERA) (see **17:62**) must contain a time schedule for the triennial reinspection and periodic visual surveillance of school buildings. A certified inspector or management planner must physically and visually reinspect the buildings in all areas that contain either known or assumed asbestos-containing material (ACM). With each reinspection, a state-certified inspector must visually and physically inspect material that was previously considered nonfriable and determine whether it has become friable since the last inspection (40 CFR § 763.85(b)(3)(ii)). The asbestos designee must be satisfied that the reported information is accurate and complete and must sign a statement to that effect (40 CFR § 763.93(i)).

The management plan's time schedule should outline surveillance of all friable and nonfriable known or assumed ACM every six months (40 CFR § 763.92(b)). This surveillance need not be performed by a certified inspector, but the person who performs the surveillance must have undergone at least two hours of asbestos-awareness training. Since this is a visual inspection, no additional training is necessary (only required for handling ACM) (40 CFR § 763.92 (a)(1)).

17:64. What response actions may school districts take regarding the presence of asbestos in the schools?

There are five federally approved response actions or methods of responding to the presence of asbestos from which school officials may choose: removal, encapsulation, enclosure, repair, and operations and maintenance (40 CFR §§ 763.90, 763.91).

- *Removal* involves taking out or stripping of any asbestos-containing materials (ACM) from an area in a school building (40 CFR § 763.83; see 12 NYCRR § 56-1.4(bm)).
- *Encapsulation* is the application of either a penetrating material that penetrates the ACM and binds the components together or a bridging agent that surrounds the asbestos fibers or embeds them in an adhesive matrix, creating a membrane over the surface of the ACM (40 CFR § 763.83; see 12 NYCRR §§ 56-1.4(ag), 56-13.1).
- *Enclosure* involves the construction of airtight walls, ceilings, and floors between the ACM and the facility's environment, or around surfaces coated with asbestos material or any other appropriate procedure that prevents the release of asbestos fiber (40 CFR § 763.83; 12 NYCRR § 56-1.4(ah); 56-14.1). The goal of enclosure is to create an airtight, impermeable, permanent barrier around the ACM to prevent release of asbestos fibers into the air (see 40 CFR § 763.83).
- *Repair* consists of returning damaged ACM to an undamaged condition or an intact state to prevent the release of asbestos fibers (40 CFR § 763.83). The state Department of Labor defines repair as corrective action using required work practices to control the release of asbestos fiber from damaged ACM (12 NYCRR § 56-1.4(bn)).
- *Operation and maintenance* is a program of work practices to maintain ACM in good condition, ensure cleanup of asbestos fibers previously released, and prevent further release by minimizing and controlling ACM disturbance or damage (40 CFR § 763.83).

The Environmental Protection Agency (EPA) requires school districts to select from these options a response action that protects human health and the environment and is the "least burdensome method" (40 CFR

§ 763.90(a)). Currently, the EPA suggests that the safest and most cost-effective response action is to manage the asbestos in place.

The state Labor Law and Industrial Code Rule 56 authorizes asbestos projects to be undertaken by a licensed contractor, which involves any aspect of the removal, encapsulation, enclosure, or disturbance of friable asbestos or any handling of asbestos material that may result in the release of asbestos fiber (Lab. Law § 901(7); 12 NYCRR § 56-1.4(o)). The contractor's obligations may depend on the amount of square and/or linear feet of asbestos or ACM, and whether the asbestos project is defined as a large, small or minor asbestos project (12 NYCRR § 56-1.4(au), (bs), (aw); see **17:65**). In addition, certain asbestos projects may qualify as "emergency asbestos projects" or a "repair," resulting in slight variance from some of the general rules concerning asbestos projects (12 NYCRR §§ 56-1.4(ae), (bn), 56-3.2).

17:65. Are school officials required by law to remove all asbestos-containing material to make a school safe?

No. In fact, an asbestos-removal project may, on occasion, increase the amount of airborne asbestos fibers in a building if it is not conducted and monitored properly. Therefore, removal should be considered only as a last resort.

In addition, the uniform safety standards for school construction and maintenance projects that require that all asbestos abatement work comply with all applicable federal and state laws, forbid large and small asbestos projects (see **17:71**) while a school building is being occupied. However, minor projects involving the removal, disturbance, repair, encapsulation, enclosure, or handling of 10 square feet or less, or 25 linear feet or less, of asbestos or asbestos material are permissible in unoccupied areas of an occupied building in accordance with applicable law and regulations (8 NYCRR § 155.5(k)).

17:66. Once asbestos has been removed from a school district, does all liability cease?

No. A school district still must concern itself with how the material is handled, where it is to be stored, how it is to be transported, and whether it is transported to an approved dumping site. If the abatement contractor violates any of the rules regarding these matters, the school district may share liability for an Environmental Protection Agency (EPA) fine.

Additionally, diseases attributed to exposure to asbestos have long periods of latency, perhaps as much as 40 years. Under the current statute of limitations on certain personal injury lawsuits, injured persons now have up to three years after they discover they have an asbestos-related disease to bring a lawsuit against a school district or other party that they allege has wrongfully exposed them to asbestos (Civ. Prac. L. & R. § 214-c).

However, the discovery of the mere presence of asbestos is not the same as the discovery of an asbestos-related disease for statute of limitation purposes (*Germantown CSD v. Clark* 294 A.D.2d 93 (2002)).

17:67. Who is responsible for ensuring a school district's compliance with the asbestos laws?

An asbestos designee appointed by the school district is responsible for coordinating the asbestos program in the district and for keeping the district in compliance with all asbestos mandates (see 40 CFR § 763.84(g)). The asbestos designee must be knowledgeable about the federal, state, and local laws and regulations concerning asbestos.

The asbestos designee need not be a separate position within the district, but may be added to the responsibilities of an existing position. The overall size of the district and the size of its asbestos project or projects should determine whether the school board should create a separate position to perform these duties.

17:68. Who may conduct asbestos inspections, develop asbestos management plans and effectuate response actions on behalf of a school district?

School district employees or a person or person or company from outside the school district may conduct inspections, management plans, and response actions. If a district uses a member of its own staff to perform these duties, it must obtain a New York State contractor's license, and the person who reinspects a school building or performs a response action must obtain the appropriate certification from the state Department of Labor. This certification requires special training that may be available through a board of cooperative educational services (BOCES) health and safety office or through a private organization whose courses have been approved by the state Department of Health.

If a district employs outside personnel to perform these duties, school officials must take special care to be sure that the outside company's certification is valid in New York State; that the laboratories used for testing purposes are certified and approved by the state Department of Health's Environmental Laboratory Approval Program; and that the company has adequate facilities and properly trained, certified personnel to fulfill the requirements of all laws and regulations pertaining to the potential disturbance of asbestos (Pub. Health Law § 502; see 12 NYCRR §§ 56-2.1, 56-2.2, 10 NYCRR Part 55).

17:69. Can a school district proceed on an asbestos-abatement project if it has underestimated the cost and does not have voter approval for the project?

Yes. If the project is necessary to render a building safe, asbestos abatement is an ordinary contingent expense and voter approval is not required for such expenditure. However, voter approval would be required before a district could issue bonds or capital notes to fund such a project (see Opn. of Counsel, 1 Educ. Dep't Rep. 792 (1954)).

17:70. How can a school district finance an unanticipated asbestos-abatement project?

There are several ways to finance an asbestos-abatement project. The school board first must declare, by resolution, the project's costs to be a contingent expense. By a second resolution, the board may assign the balance of any unappropriated funds for this purpose (see 8 NYCRR § 170.2(l)). Any remaining debt that ensues could be financed in the subsequent year by increasing taxes (see § 2023).

Another way the board may finance a large-scale asbestos project is to request voter approval of a bond issue for asbestos abatement. Voters would actually decide on the bond, not the project itself. If the voters approve the bond issue, then the district could finance the project over a period of years (see § 416). If the voters determine not to approve the bond issue, however, the entire sum would be taxable on the next tax roll.

17:71. Are there any notice requirements that must be met before an asbestos project begins?

Yes. In a large asbestos project, defined as one involving more than 260 linear feet or 160 square feet of material, the contractor must notify both the Environmental Protection Agency's (EPA) Hazardous Materials Division and the commissioner of the New York State Department of Labor's Asbestos Control Bureau at least 10 days before beginning the project (Lab. Law § 904(2); 12 NYCRR § 56-1.6(b)(1)). If an asbestos hazard is present that requires immediate attention, or if emergency conditions make it impossible to give 10 days notice, the owner, owners' agent, consultant, or contractor must notify the Program Manager's office at the Asbestos Control Bureau in Albany by telephone at 518-457-1255, or in person (Bldg. 12, State Campus, Albany, NY 12240), prior to beginning the project (12 NYCRR § 56-1.7(a)).

In addition, Labor Law and Industrial Code Rule 56 requires all contractors engaged in the abatement portion of an asbestos project to provide "business occupants" written notice 10 days prior to beginning any work on any asbestos project in a building. With regard to projects being conducted in school buildings, the faculty, staff and students attending such school are considered "business occupants" (Lab. Law § 904(4); 12 NYCRR § 56-1.8(a)). If the contract is signed less than 10 days prior to scheduled work, contractors are required to give three-days notice (Lab. Law § 904(4); 12 NYCRR § 56-1.8(b)). In an emergency, written notice to business occupants must be given as soon as practicable (Lab. Law §904(4); 12 NYCRR § 56-1.8(c)).

17:72. Must air sampling be performed during an asbestos-abatement project?

Yes. Air sampling is the process of measuring the asbestos fiber content of a known volume of air collected during a specific period of time (12 NYCRR § 56-1.4(f)). Air sampling is performed in conjunction with an abatement project in order to determine the asbestos fiber content in the air in the vicinity of the project. The size of the abatement project, as defined under Industrial Code Rule 56, determines when air sampling must be performed (12 NYCRR § 56-17.1).

Under Industrial Code Rule 56, monitoring the same methodology for air sampling and analysis of asbestos must be used for all pre-abatement, abatement and post-abatement (12 NYCRR § 56-17.1).

17:73. How is a containment area formed around an asbestos-abatement project?

There are extensive rules and regulations about the type and quantity of plastic to be used in an asbestos-abatement project and the number of layers of plastic to be placed on floors, walls, ceilings and other surfaces to prevent any possible release of asbestos fibers from the containment area. Negative air pressure helps to ensure that air from inside the containment area flows through high-efficiency particulate air (HEPA) filters before being discharged back into the air as clean air. In addition, workers leaving the work area must comply with detailed procedures to prevent contamination outside the project area (see 12 NYCRR subparts 56-4 through 56-11).

17:74. Must an asbestos contractor and its employees be licensed and certified?

Yes. The state Department of Labor issues licenses to contractors who wish to conduct asbestos-abatement projects in this state. In addition, the department issues a variety of certificates for workers who wish to work for asbestos-abatement contractors (see 12 NYCRR § 56-2), which are valid for one year and cost from $30 to $150 (see Lab. Law § 903).

All contractors who engage in an asbestos project, as well as any business that provides management planning, project design, monitoring, inspection and/or air-monitoring services, must have an asbestos-handling license. This license costs $300 and must be renewed annually (Lab. Law §§ 902(1), 903(2), (3), (4); 12 NYCRR § 56-2.1(a)).

Although the Department of Labor actually issues the license or certification, the state Department of Health has the responsibility for approving training programs (12 NYCRR § 56-2.2 (a)).

17:75. Must an asbestos contractor keep records on asbestos projects?

Yes. Every contractor must maintain, for at least 30 years, records on each asbestos project in which the contractor was engaged. These records must include the name, address, and Social Security number of the supervisor of the project; the location and description of the asbestos project; the amount of asbestos material that was abated or disturbed; the starting and ending dates of the project; the name and address of each waste-disposal site where asbestos waste material was deposited; the name and address of any site used for interim storage of asbestos waste materials; the name and address of any transporter of asbestos waste material; and the names, addresses, and Social Security numbers and asbestos license and certificate numbers of all the people who worked on the project (Lab. Law § 904(1); 12 NYCRR § 56-1.6(a)(1)).

18. School District Liability and School Insurance

18:1. Are school districts exempt from lawsuits?

No. The concept of sovereign immunity, which prevented lawsuits against the state and other governmental entities, has been abolished in New York State by virtue of the Court of Claims Act (Court of Claims Act § 8).

A school district may be liable as a corporate entity for its own negligence and other improper actions such as breach of contract, as well as the wrongful actions of school board members. It may also be liable for the negligence of its employees under the doctrine of *respondeat superior*, which makes the master responsible for the negligence of its employees when the negligence occurs during the performance of their employment responsibilities and results in injury to others (*Helbig v. City of New York Bd. of Educ.*, 212 A.D.2d 506 (2d Dep't 1995)).

Liability entails the financial responsibility to pay a person or entity, or to otherwise remedy a wrong, when there is injury or damage to such person or entity due to the wrongful action or inaction of the school district, school board members or their employees.

School districts carrying liability insurance generally are protected to the limits of such insurance. Above these limits, and under any applicable deductible in the insurance policy, the responsibility to pay the claim rests with the school district.

18:2. Are school board members exempt from lawsuits brought against them personally?

No. However, there is immunity for school board members when they carry out official functions within the context of a school board meeting. For immunity to apply, these functions cannot be exclusively ministerial. They must involve the exercise of discretion or expert judgment in policy matters (see *Haddock v. City of New York*, 75 N.Y.2d 478, 484–85 (1990); see **18:24–25**).

18:3. Is there a procedure for bringing a lawsuit against a school district?

Yes. The Education Law provides that no action or special proceeding relating to district property or claim against the district or involving the rights or interests of the district may be brought unless the claimant files a written verified claim, or notice of claim, that describes the basis of the lawsuit, within three months after the incident occurred on which the claim is based

(§ 3813(1)). The three-month period also applies to certain improper practice proceedings under the Taylor Law (see also **10:45**). This is true even where the claimant has complied with the four-month statute of limitations under PERB rules (see 4 NYCRR § 204.1(a)(1); *Matter of Palka v. Union Endicott CSD*, 2 A.D.3d 1174 (3d Dep't 2003); *Board of Educ. of Union Endicott CSD v. New York State Pub. Employment Relations Bd.*, 250 A.D.2d 82 (3d Dep't 1998), *appeal denied*, 93 N.Y.2d 805 (1999); *Board of Educ. v. New York State PERB*, 197 A.D.2d 276 (3d Dep't 1994), *leave to app. den.*, 84 N.Y.2d 803 (1994)).

Where the lawsuit involves a claim for the payment of money owed, the party bringing the lawsuit must serve a summons and complaint on the school district, indicating that a notice of claim was served and that the officer or body having the power to approve the payment of the claim refused to do so within 30 days of its receipt (§ 3813(1)). This 30-day waiting period has been found to extend the four-month statute of limitations for bringing an Article 78 proceeding (*Perlin v. South Orangetown CSD*, 216 A.D.2d 397 (2d Dep't 1995), *motion for leave to app. dismissed*, 86 N.Y.2d 886 (1995)).

In order to bring tort claims for personal injury against school officials, teachers, or other employees, the claimant must comply with the provisions of the General Municipal Law. These require, for instance, that a notice of claim be made and served upon the school district within 90 days after the claim arose (Educ. Law § 3813(2); Gen. Mun. Law §§ 50-e, 50-i).

Where the person entitled to commence an action is an infant at the time the cause of action accrues, the statute of limitations for filing a claim against a municipality, including a school district, is tolled (frozen in time) until the child turns 18 (C.P.L.R. § 208). This is so even when a parent files a notice of claim pursuant to the General Municipal Law during the period of infancy (*Henry v. City of New York*, 94 N.Y.2d 275 (1999)).

18:4. Can a lawsuit against a school district proceed if the required notice of claim is not filed in a timely manner?

Yes. Upon application, a court, at its discretion, may extend the time to serve the notice of claim on the school district, but not beyond the statute of limitations for the bringing of the lawsuit, and never beyond one year (§ 3813(2-a), (2-b); Gen. Mun. Law § 50-e(5); *Sainato v. Western Suffolk BOCES*, 242 A.D.2d 301 (2d Dep't 1997); *Chanecka v. Board of Educ. Broome-Tioga BOCES*, 243 A.D.2d 1011 (3d Dep't 1997)).

In granting an extension, a court will consider, for example, whether the district acquired knowledge of the facts of the claim within the three-month period, whether the claimant was an infant or physically or mentally incapacitated, whether the claimant died before the time limited for service of the notice of claim, and whether the delay prejudiced the district in maintaining its defense (§ 3813(2-a); Gen. Mun. Law § 50-e(5); *Sica v. Board of Educ. of the City of New York*, 226 A.D.2d 542 (2d Dep't 1996)).

18:5. Can a lawsuit against a school district proceed without the filing of a notice of claim at all?

Sometimes. Under certain limited exceptions, the notice of claim requirement does not apply, as for example, where the action or proceeding against the district "seeks to vindicate a public interest" rather than a private right (*Board of Educ. v. New York State PERB*, 197 A.D.2d 276 (3d Dep't 1994), *motion for leave to appeal denied*, 84 N.Y.2d 803 (1994)); *Union Free Sch. Dist. v. New York State Human Rights Appeal Bd.*, 35 N.Y.2d 371 (1974), *rehearing denied*, 36 N.Y.2d 806 (1975)).

Moreover, the notice of claim requirements are inapplicable to claims of employment discrimination filed with the New York State Division of Human Rights (DHR) (*Freudenthal v. County of Nassau*, 99 N.Y.2d 285 (2003)).

Similarly, the notice of claim provisions of the Education Law do not apply to appeals to the commissioner of education (*Appeal of Hollister*, 39 Educ. Dep't Rep. 109 (1999); *Appeal of Sole Trustee of Hickory South Mountain*, 38 Educ. Dep't Rep. 577 (1999); *Appeal of Shusterman*, 18 Educ. Dep't Rep. 516 (1979)) or to declaratory judgments (*Levert v. Central Sch. Dist.*, 24 Misc.2d 832 (1960)).

18:6. Can the commencement of other types of proceedings substitute for service of a notice of claim upon a school district?

Sometimes. In a case where a district was served with an improper practice charge and answered the charge within the requisite three-month period, an appellate court ruled the union's failure to file a notice of claim was not fatal because the district had received constructive notice of the claim (*Deposit CSD v. PERB*, 214 A.D.2d 288 (3d Dep't 1995), *appeal denied*, 88 N.Y.2d 866 (1996)).

Similarly, a notice of issuance of a right-to-sue letter sent by the Equal Employment Opportunity Commission will constitute effective service of a notice of claim (*Kushner v. Valenti*, 285 F.Supp.2d 314 (E.D.N.Y. 2003)).

In addition, two separate state appellate courts have determined that a petition to the commissioner of education also can serve as the "functional equivalent" of a notice of claim (*Menella v. Uniondale UFSD*, 287 A.D.2d 636 (2d Dep't 2001); see also *Matter of Bd. of Educ. of Westbury UFSD*, 81 A.D.2d 691 (3d Dep't 1981)). "[A]" paper that is not denominated a notice of claim may satisfy the requirement if it "gives notice of the nature of the claim, and the essential facts underlying the claim" (*Menella*).

Negligence

18:7. What is negligence?

Negligence is a legal principle that imposes liability on entities and individuals who breach a duty they owe to others, thereby causing them injury (see *Prosser & Keaton on the Law of Torts* § 30 (5th ed. 1984)).

In general, school districts have a duty to supervise students in their care and to maintain the school premises and any equipment in a safe working condition. A school district has the duty to exercise the same degree of care toward its students as would a reasonable, prudent parent under comparable circumstances (*Mirand v. City of New York*, 84 N.Y.2d 44 (1994); *Shante D. by Ada D. v. City of New York*, 190 A.D.2d 356 (1st Dep't 1993), *aff'd*, 83 N.Y.2d 948 (1994); *Lawes v. Board of Educ.*, 16 N.Y.2d 302 (1965)). Should a breach of this duty by either the school system, board members or their employees result in an injury to a student, the school district may be held liable (see, for example, *Ernest v. Red Creek CSD*, 93 N.Y. 2d 664 (1999), where a district was exposed to liability for releasing a student into reasonably foreseeable hazard of crossing a street while school buses were pulling out; see also, *Maracallo v. Board of Educ. of the City of New York*, 2 Misc.3d 703 (St. Sup. Ct. Bronx Co. 2003), where a district was held liable after a student drowned in a wave pool at a water park during a school field trip).

18:8. Can a school district be held liable for negligently failing to protect students from criminal acts committed by third parties?

Yes. A school district may be held liable for harm to a student caused by a criminal act of a third party when the crime is a "reasonably foreseeable" consequence of circumstances created by the school district. For example, a school district was found negligent for its failure to protect two students, where school personnel had knowledge of threats against them and the potential for harm (*Mirand v. City of New York*, 84 N.Y.2d 44 (1994)).

In another case, a school district was liable for the sexual assault of a kindergartner by an older student in the school bathroom when the kindergartner was allowed by his teacher to go to the bathroom unaccompanied despite two memoranda instructing staff to the contrary (*Garcia v. City of New York*, 222 A.D.2d 192 (1st Dep't 1996), *leave to appeal denied*, 89 N.Y.2d 808 (1997); see also *Shante D. by Ada D. v. City of New York*, 190 A.D.2d 356 (1st Dep't 1993), *aff'd*, 83 N.Y.2d 948 (1994)).

In still another case, the New York State Court of Appeals upheld a jury verdict based on negligent supervision against a school district for injuries sustained by a student who was raped off school premises while on a school field trip *(Bell v. Board of Educ. of City of New York*, 90 N.Y.2d 944 (1997)).

However, in a case decided after *Bell*, a state appellate court ruled that a school district could not be held liable for a sexual assault by two male students upon a female student that occurred on school grounds during the school day because the male students' actions were so "extraordinary and intervening" that they were not "foreseeable" by the district (*Schrader v. Board of Educ. of Taconic Hills CSD*, 249 A.D.2d 741 (3d Dep't 1998), *appeal denied*, 92 N.Y.2d 806 (1998); *see also Marshall v. Cortland Enlarged City Sch. Dist.*, 265 A.D.2d 782 (3d Dep't 1999)). Moreover, the same court has ruled that a school district may not be held vicariously liable for a sexual assault committed by its employee, since liability arises from the failure to adequately supervise (see *Dia CC. v. Ithaca City Sch. Dist.*, 304 A.D.2d 955 (3d Dep't 2003)).

It is unlikely a district could escape liability for its own negligence by requiring from parents or guardians a waiver of liability or a permission slip frequently used by schools when children participate in certain school-sponsored events. Although a signature on a permission slip indicates a parent or guardian is aware the student will participate in a particular activity, it may not release the school from liability. Liability will depend on whether there was negligent supervision by school personnel.

18:9. Can a school district be held liable in negligence for educational malpractice?

No. The New York State Court of Appeals has held that actions for educational malpractice are barred by public policy considerations because the courts will not second-guess the professional judgments of school officials and educators in selecting and implementing educational programs and evaluating students (*Torres v. Little Flower Children's Servs.*, 64 N.Y.2d 119, 126–27 (1984), *cert. denied*, 474 U.S. 864 (1985); *Hoffman v. Board of Educ.*, 49 N.Y.2d 121 (1979); *Donohue v. Copiague UFSD*, 47 N.Y.2d 440 (1979)).

For example, where a high school graduate who could not read or write sufficiently to complete a job application sued the district for its failure to provide him with adequate teachers, administrators, and psychologists in order to evaluate his progress, the Court of Appeals explained it is not for the courts to make a judgment on the validity of school board policies or to review day-to-day implementation of these policies (*Donohue v. Copiague UFSD*).

On the other hand, where a principal willfully and intentionally falsified test scores as a result of which a student was denied remedial and special education, a state appellate court dismissed the educational malpractice claim against the school district, but gave permission to the student's parent to proceed against the principal on the basis of intentional wrongdoing as well as against the school district, under the doctrine of respondent superior, in the event the principal's actions were reasonably foreseeable (*Helbig v. City of New York*, 212 A.D.2d 506 (2d Dep't 1995)).

18:10. Can a school district be held liable for negligence in its hiring or retention of staff?

A school district may be held liable for negligence in its hiring or retention of an employee if it fails to follow its own established procedures for making employment decisions, such as those which might require investigating the criminal history of new employees (*Haddock v. New York*, 75 N.Y.2d 478 (1990)). However, where there is no violation of internal procedures and policies, a school district enjoys immunity with respect to the exercise of discretion in deciding whether to hire a particular employee (*Mon v. New York*, 78 N.Y.2d 309 (1991)).

In *Haddock*, the City of New York failed to comply with its own policy of investigating employees with a known criminal record. Therefore, city officials lost their immunity in connection with their decision to hire and retain the employee.

18:11. Can a school district be held liable if one of its teachers sexually molests students off school grounds, at a nonschool event?

Each case will depend upon its own facts. But in one notable case, a New York State appellate court dismissed a lawsuit against a school district that claimed district officials negligently hired and supervised a teacher who allegedly sexually molested two students at their home after being invited to a holiday party at the students' home by their parents. According to the court, any connection between the teacher's employment with the district and his alleged sexual molestation of the students at their home "was severed by time, distance, and the intervening independent acts of their parents" (*Anonymous v. Dobbs Ferry UFSD*, 736 N.Y.S.2d 117 (2d Dep't 2002); see also *K.I. v. New York City Bd. of Educ.*, 256 A.D.2d 189 (1st Dep't 1998)).

18:12. Can a school district that provides a false or misleading recommendation about a former employee be held liable if the employee injures students in another district?

Not according to two New York State appellate courts. The Appellate Division, Second Department, dismissed a negligence claim against a public school district in New York State, under circumstances where the district recommended a former employee to another public school district for a position as a grammar school teacher, without disclosing that the teacher had been charged with sexual misconduct. Many years later, when the same teacher injured a student at the new school district, the student sued the district that recommended the teacher, claiming the district was negligent in its failure to warn the hiring district of the teacher's past history (*Cohen v. Wales*, 133 A.D.2d 94 (2d Dep't 1987), *appeal denied*, 70 N.Y.2d 612 (1987); *see also K.I. v. New York City Bd. of Educ.*, 256 A.D.2d 189 (1st Dep't 1998)).

The court rejected the claim, writing:

> The common law imposes no duty to control the conduct of another or to warn those endangered by such conduct, in the absence of a special relationship between either the person who threatens harmful conduct or the foreseeable victim (*citation omitted*). The mere recommendation of a person for potential employment is not a proper basis for asserting a claim of negligence where another party is responsible for the actual hiring (*citation omitted*). Nor are there sound policy reasons warranting the expansion of the common-law duty of the schools since the plaintiffs have an adequate remedy at law as against the school district which had custody of the infant at the time of the injury and also against the wrongdoer (*citation omitted*) (*Cohen*, 133 A.D.2d at 95).

18:13. Can school districts be held liable for negligently failing to protect teachers from students or other third parties?

Not generally. The courts have not held school districts liable for injury to teachers who are assaulted by students at school, ruling that districts do not owe a duty to teachers to protect them from harm by third parties (*Verra v. City of New York*, 217 A.D.2d 577 (2d Dep't 1995), *appeal denied*, 86 N.Y.2d 710 (1995); *Krakower v. City of New York*, 217 A.D.2d 441 (1st Dep't 1995), *appeal denied*, 87 N.Y.2d 804 (1995)). Furthermore, a district does not assume such a duty merely because it implements security measures (*Bonner v. City of New York*, 73 N.Y.2d 930 (1989); *Bain v. New York City Bd. of Educ.*, 268 A.D.2d 451 (2d Dep't 2000); *Johnson v. New York City Bd. of Educ.*, 270 A.D.2d 310 (2d Dep't 2000)).

However, a district may be held liable for injuries to a teacher by a student, if the district has entered into a "special relationship" with the teacher by undertaking an affirmative duty to the teacher upon which the teacher reasonably relies (*Pascuccui v. Board of Educ. of the City of New York*, 305 A.D.2d 103 (1st Dep't 2003)).

In addition, in one civil rights lawsuit (see **18:21–26**) a federal district court in New York allowed a case commenced by a teacher alleging students harassed him because of his nationality (including throwing paper balls at him) to go to trial based on a claim of hostile work environment. According to the teacher, the situation continued "virtually unabated" despite his repeated complaints to school administrators. In the court's view, administrators and school board officials have greater disciplinary authority over students than a classroom teacher. It was up to the jury to decide the existence of a hostile work environment and whether the district took appropriate remedial action based on all the circumstances. (*Peries v. New York City Bd. of Educ.*, 2001 U.S. Dist. LEXIS 23393 (E.D.N.Y. Aug. 6, 2001)).

18:14. Can a school district be held liable for the negligence of an independent contractor it hires?

The general rule is that an employer is not liable for the negligence of an independent contractor, because the employer has no control over how the independent contractor performs the work. Thus, the independent contractor is held accountable for its own improper actions. There are exceptions, however, such as when the employer owes a nondelegable duty to the individual harmed by the independent contractor, or when such individual would be left without a remedy if the general rule was applied strictly (*Feliberty v. Damon*, 72 N.Y.2d 112 (1988); *Prosser & Keaton on the Law of Torts* § 71 (5th ed. 1984)).

The New York State Court of Appeals applied the general rule in favor of school districts in a case where it ruled that a district was not liable for the negligent actions of a bus company with which it had contracted for the transportation of school children to and from school. In *Chainani by Chainani v. Board of Educ.*, 87 N.Y.2d 370 (1995), a student was injured by a school bus driven by the employee of an independent contractor when the bus drove over the student after dropping her off at her stop. The parents sued the district for damages based on the negligence of the driver. The court ruled the parents could not recover damages from the district.

However, in *David "XX" v. St. Catherine's Center for Children* (267 A.D.2d 813 (3d Dep't 1999)), the Appellate Division, Third Department, held that the general rule will not apply where a student is released to an independent contractor into circumstances that pose a foreseeable risk of harm. Therefore, if the district is aware of an unreasonable risk posed by the conduct of the contractor and fails to take steps to minimize the risk, even though it is in the best position to minimize that risk, the district may be held liable. In *David "XX"*, it was alleged that a student was repeatedly sexually abusing another student while on a school bus over the course of six weeks. The contract between the district and the independent contractor required the presence of an aide on the bus while students were transported. The student's parent sued both the independent contractor bus company and the district. The Third Department refused to dismiss the case against the district because the parent alleged he had repeatedly advised the district that his son was being abused, that there were allegedly no aides on the bus during the incidents, and that the alleged abuser appeared to have a documented history of aggressive sexual behavior.

18:15. On what basis can a school district be found negligent when there is an accident involving children on their way to and from school?

In general, school districts have no legal responsibility for children before they arrive on school grounds at the start of the school day and after they leave school grounds at the end of the school day (*Chainani by Chainani v. Board of Educ.*, 87 N.Y.2d 370 (1995)), and therefore cannot be found negligent for any injuries sustained by students on their way to and from school.

However, where a district transports students to and from school, it may be liable for its own negligence in failing to provide a "reasonably safe mode of conveyance" (*Williams v. Board of Trustees*, 210 A.D. 161 (1924); see also *Blair v. Board of Educ.*, 86 A.D.2d 933 (3d Dep't 1982)), even though generally it will not be liable for the negligent acts of an independent contractor hired to transport students to and from school (*Chainani by Chainani v. Board of Educ.*; but see *David "XX" v. St. Catherine's Center for Children*, 699 N.Y.S.2d 827 (3d Dept 1999)).

The district's responsibility begins when a child is picked up and ends when he or she has been properly discharged from the bus (see *Pratt v. Robinson*, 39 N.Y.2d 554 (1976); *Hanley v. East Moriches UFSD II*, 275 A.D.2d 389 (2d Dep't 2000); *Fornaro v. Kerry*, 139 A.D.2d 561 (2d Dep't 1988); Veh. & Traf. Law § 1174(b); 8 NYCRR § 156.3(d)). However, the district's duty of care continues when the student is released without further supervision into a foreseeably hazardous situation the district played a role in creating (*Ernest v. Red Creek CSD*, 93 N.Y. 2d 664 (1999)). In *Ernest*, a student was hit by a pickup truck when walking home after school and crossing the road in front of the school while school buses were still departing. The driver's view was obstructed by a moving school bus. Normally, the district waited to release students who walked home until all the school buses were gone, but did not do so on the day of the accident.

A school district is not liable for injuries sustained by a student who leaves the custody of the district by exiting from a school bus prior to reaching school, or getting off before his or her regular bus stop at the end of the school day even if that student's conduct violates school policy (*Bushnell v. Berne-Knox-Westerlo Sch. Dist.*, 125 A.D.2d 859 (3d Dep't 1986), *appeal denied*, 69 N.Y.2d 609 (1987); *Hurlburt v. Noxon*, 149 Misc.2d 374 (Chenango County Sup. Ct. 1990)).

Similarly, a school district ordinarily will not be found negligent where a student who fails to get on the school bus gets injured, because there is no duty to assure that students get on the school bus. However, if school officials were to promise a parent they would ensure that his or her child takes the school bus, then a court could find that by making the promise, the district assumed a special duty to protect the child, and the district could be found negligent for any injuries sustained by the student as a result of its failure to do so (see *Wenger v. Goodell*, 288 A.D.2d 815 (3d Dep't 2001), where the court applied this legal test, but found no such promise, and therefore no duty; see also *Briggs v. Rhinebeck CSD*, 2 A.D.3d 383 (2d Dep't 2003), holding that "[i]t was not reasonably foreseeable that . . . allowing [a] 17-year-old . . . to leave [school district] premises in the automobile of a fellow student who possessed a driver's license, would have resulted in his being injured in an automobile collision").

18:16. On what basis can school districts be found negligent when there is an accident involving students who leave school grounds during the school day?

Generally, the school district has no duty to supervise a student who leaves school grounds without permission, although the courts will examine all the circumstances, such as the student's age and whether school authorities provided or should have provided supervision.

For example, a court refused to find a school district negligent where a 14-year-old student was involved in a car accident at 5:00 p.m. the same day he had left school without permission. The court rejected the parents' argument that the district had breached its duty of supervision, finding that "once a student is beyond its lawful control, the school district owes no legal duty to supervise the activities of a student." In addition, the court refused to rule that a school district must impose security measures to prevent students from leaving the premises (*Palella v. Ulmer*, 136 Misc.2d 34 (Rensselaer County Sup. Ct. 1987), *rev'd on other grounds by Palella v. State*, 141 A.D.2d 999 (3d Dep't 1988)).

In another case, a state appellate court found a school district was not negligent for injuries to third parties caused by a 10th-grade student who drove his own car from his home district to a BOCES in violation of school policy, which required that he take the school bus (*Thompson v. Ange*, 83 A.D.2d 193 (4th Dep't 1981)). The court refused to find that the school district assumed a legal duty to prevent injury to the public by the mere adoption of its no-driving policy.

18:17. On what basis can school districts be found negligent when student participants in school-sponsored athletic events are injured?

School districts must exercise "reasonable care" to protect student athletes from injuries that may result from unassumed, concealed or unreasonably increased risks (see *Benitez v. Board of Educ.*, 73 N.Y.2d 650 (1989); *Reed v. Pawling*, 245 A.D.2d 281 (2d Dep't 1997), *leave to app. denied*, 91 N.Y.2d 809 (1997)). In *Benitez*, for example, a high school athlete who was paralyzed during a football game claimed that the district owed him the same duty of care as a prudent parent in warning him not to play because he was fatigued. The court found that "injury and fatigue are inherent in team competitive sports" and the student had assumed the risk of competition as he was properly equipped, well trained, and had played voluntarily.

Similarly, a district was not found negligent for injuries to a varsity wrestler who was struck in the jaw by an opponent in a weight classification one category higher, because the student reasonably could be found to have assumed the risk (*Edelson v. Uniondale UFSD*, 219 A.D.2d 614 (2d Dep't 1995)). In another case, a court dismissed a lawsuit by an experienced football player who was injured during a tackling drill, finding that the player voluntarily assumed the risk of injury (*Hagan v. Northport-East Northport UFSD No. 4*, 273 A.D.2d 441 (2d Dep't 2000)). In still another case, a court dismissed a claim by an experienced high school cheerleader who was injured while performing a straddling jump during practice, finding that she had voluntarily assumed the risk of injury *(Weber v. William Floyd Sch. Dist.*, 272 A.D.2d 396 (2d Dep't 2000); see also *Fisher v. Syosset CSD*, 264 A.D.2d 438, *appeal denied*, 94 N.Y.2d 759 (2000)).

By contrast, one appellate court refused to dismiss a lawsuit against a school district by an inexperienced student pole-vaulter who injured his knee under circumstances where he landed on a seam in the mat, and where the pole was placed six inches higher than he ever had cleared. According to the court, the student had not necessarily assumed the risk because the seam was concealed and the student was not accustomed to attempting the sport at that level of difficulty (*Laboy v. Wallkill CSD*, 201 A.D.2d 780 (3d Dep't 1994)). Similarly, another appellate court refused to dismiss a lawsuit where a student was injured by a hidden spike that was positioned in the base path of a softball field, finding no evidence that the student was aware of the existence of the spike, and therefore that she did not assume the risk of being injured by the spike (*Simmons v. Smithtown CSD*, 272 A.D.2d 391 (2d Dep't 2000)).

Several appellate courts have refused to dismiss lawsuits against school districts by students who were injured during an athletic activity where the district may have failed to provide adequate supervision of the activity or take reasonable steps to ensure that the equipment used by the student did not unreasonably increase the risk of injury (*Hubbard v. East Meadow UFSD*, 277 A.D.2d 353 (2d Dep't 2000); *Neu v. Helm Middle Sch.*, 262 A.D.2d 1040 (4th Dep't 1999); *Kane v. North Colonie CSD*, 273 A.D.2d

526 (3d Dep't 2000); *Merson v. Syosset CSD*, 286 A.D.2d 668 (2d Dep't 2001)).

18:18. On what basis can school districts be found negligent when nonstudent participants at school-sponsored events are injured?

Assumption of risk principles applicable to student athletes (see **18:17**) apply also to nonstudent participants in school-sponsored athletic events. For example, in *Arbegast v. Board of Educ.*, 65 N.Y.2d 161 (1985), a student teacher was injured when the donkey she was riding in a donkey basketball game put its head down and she fell off. The participants had been told they might fall off and that they were participating at their own risk. The court held that the teacher had assumed the risk and found the school district not liable.

18:19. Are school districts liable for spectator injuries at school-sponsored events?

It depends. Generally, spectators are deemed to have assumed the normal risks associated with attendance at a game. For instance, in *Akins v. Glens Falls City Sch. Dist.*, 53 N.Y.2d 325 (1981), *rehearing denied*, 54 N.Y.2d 831 (1981), a spectator sitting and watching a school's baseball game was injured. The court held the district was not liable, explaining that the owner of a baseball field is only required to exercise reasonable care and need only provide screening for the area of the field behind home plate, where the danger of getting hit by a ball is the greatest.

18:20. Can a school district be held liable for injuries occurring during the use of school facilities by an outside organization?

Yes, if it has been found that the school district was negligent in some manner. The requirement of some school boards that outside organizations carry liability insurance when they use school property may relieve the school district from liability in the event of an accident to either a participant or a spectator (see *Ambrosio v. Newburgh Enlarged City Sch. Dist.*, 5 A.D.3d 410 (2d Dep't 2004). In the alternative, the district's own liability insurance policy may cover this type of situation.

Civil Rights Liability

18:21. What does civil rights liability consist of and how do school districts become exposed to it?

Civil rights liability arises under section 1983 of the Civil Rights Act of 1876. Accordingly, a civil rights lawsuit is also referred to as a section 1983 action. Liability attaches to any person who, "acting under color of state law" (be it statutory law, custom, policy or practice), deprives a person of his or her federal constitutional and/or statutory rights. However, section 1983 is not available to enforce federal regulations if the underlying federal statute does not itself create a private right of action. That was the case in *Alexander v. Sandoval*, 532 U.S. 275 (2001). Here an employee alleged a violation of federal regulations promulgated under Title VI of the Civil Rights Act of 1964 prohibiting "disparate impact" discrimination, and the U.S. Supreme Court found Congress did not intend to authorize private enforcement of those regulations. Similarly, the U.S. Supreme Court has ruled that the Family Education Rights and Privacy Act (FERPA) does not authorize private lawsuits for violations of its provisions (*Gonzaga v. Doe*, 122 S. Ct. 2268 (2002)). Following the U.S Supreme Court's reasoning in *Gonzaga*, a federal district court in New York has ruled that the No Child Left Behind Act (NCLB) also does not authorize private lawsuits to enforce its provisions either (*Ass'n of Community Organizations for Reform Now v. NYC Dep't of Educ.*, 269 F.Supp.2d 338, 341 (S.D.N.Y. 2003)).

An individual bringing a section 1983 lawsuit against a school district must establish not that the district or its officials or employees were negligent, but rather that the individual enjoyed a protected federal right, that a school district official or employee deprived him or her of that right, and that the cause of that deprivation was a statute, official practice, policy or custom (42 USC § 1983; *Monell v. Department of Social Servs.*, 436 U.S. 658 (1978)). "Policy" includes policies and decisions officially adopted and promulgated by the school board; regulations and decisions adopted and promulgated by school officials to whom the board has delegated final policy-making authority in the particular area in question; and widespread practices of officials and employees which, although not authorized by adopted policy, are so common and well settled as to constitute a custom that fairly represents district policy (*St. Louis v. Praprotnik*, 485 U.S. 112 (1988)).

The U.S. Supreme Court has indicated that as a general rule, a single hiring decision by an employee of a municipality, which does not itself violate federal law, does not rise to the level of a municipal "policy" under which a municipality can be held liable under section 1983 (*Board of the County Comm'rs of Bryan County, Oklahoma v. Brown*, 520 U.S. 397 (1997)).

18:22. Are there any additional theories of liability upon which a district may be held liable for an alleged civil rights violation?

Yes. The courts have established numerous theories, including the following, for imposing civil rights liability:

Deliberate Indifference. This theory requires a finding of governmental conduct that reflects a "deliberate" or "conscious" choice that can be deemed to amount to a deliberate indifference toward the constitutional or federal statutory rights of the individual injured. Deliberate indifference cases have involved, for example, the failure to properly train staff (*Canton v. Harris*, 489 U.S. 378 (1989); see *Hot v. Carmel CSD*, 994 F.Supp. 225 (S.D.N.Y. 1998)). Deliberate indifference may be established through the existence of a continuing, widespread, persistent pattern of unconstitutional misconduct by government officials and employees; a deliberate indifference to or tacit authorization of such conduct by policy-making officials after notice to the officials of the misconduct; and evidence that the complaining party was injured by conduct undertaken pursuant to official policy or custom; in other words, the policy or custom was the moving force behind the constitutional violation (*Johnson v. Newburgh Enlarged Sch. Dist.*, 239 F.3d 246 (2d Cir. 2001); *Jane Doe "A". v. Special Dist.*, 901 F.2d 642 (8th Cir. 1990); *Baynard v. Malone*, 268 F.3d 228 (4th Cir. 2001), *cert. denied, Baynard v. Alexandria City Sch. Board*, 122 S.Ct. 1357 (2002); *Doe v. Taylor Indep. Sch. Dist.*, 15 F.3d 443 (5th Cir. 1994), *cert. denied sub nom. Lankford v. Doe*, 513 U.S. 815 (1994)).

Special Relationship. Another theory of civil rights liability requires the existence of a special relationship that imposes on governmental authorities an affirmative duty of care and protection with respect to the individual injured (*DeShaney v. Winnebago County Dep't of Social Servs.*, 489 U.S. 189 (1989)). The courts have limited special relationship cases to situations where the government has deprived individuals of their liberty and ability to defend themselves as in the case of prisoners and involuntarily institutionalized patients (see, e.g., *DeShaney; Stoneking v. Bradford Area Sch. Dist.*, 856 F.2d 594 (3d Cir. 1988), *vacated sub nom. Smith v. Stoneking*, 489 U.S. 1062 (1989), *on remand*, 882 F.2d 720 (3d Cir. 1989), *cert. denied*, 493 U.S. 1044 (1990)).

Courts have refused to consider state compulsory education laws as placing students in the "functional custody" of school authorities with a concurrent affirmative duty to protect students from injury (*Armijo; Wright v. Lovin*, 32 F.3d 538 (11th Cir. 1994); *Johnson; Walton v. Alexander*, 44 F.3d 1297 (5th Cir. 1995); *Stoneking v. Bradford*). In New York, however, there have been several federal district court decisions where school districts have been found to have a special relationship with students subject to civil rights liability, based on the state's compulsory education law (see, e.g., *Lichtler v. County of Orange*, 813 F.Supp. 1054 (S.D.N.Y. 1993); *Robert G. v. Newburgh City Sch. Dist.*, 1990 U.S. Dist. LEXIS 91 (S.D.N.Y. Jan. 8, 1990 (unreported)); see also *Pagano v. Massapequa Pub. Schs.*, 714 F.Supp. 641 (E.D.N.Y. 1989); but see *Robertson v. Arlington CSD*, 31 IDELR 236 (S.D.N.Y. 2000), where the court held that compulsory school attendance laws do not establish a special relationship giving rise to a constitutional duty to protect students against violence from other students).

Violations of Substantive Due Process. Some types of misconduct by governmental actors, including school officials and employees, are so extreme and so outrageous that they "shock the conscience." Citizens are deemed to have an inherent and fundamental right under the due process clause of the Fourteenth Amendment not to be victimized by such misconduct. However, the legal standard for establishing a violation of the right to substantive due process is very high. It has been stated that "not all wrongs perpetrated by a government actor violate due process. The protections of due process are available only against egregious conduct which goes beyond merely 'offend[ing] some fastidious squeamishness or private sentimentalism' and can fairly be viewed as so 'brutal' and 'offensive to human dignity' as to shock the conscience" (*Smith v. Half Hollow Hills CSD*, 298 F.3d 168 (2d Cir. 2002); see also *County of Sacramento v. Lewis*, 523 U.S. 847, n.8 (1998), wherein the U.S. Supreme Court asserted that the Constitution should not "be demoted to . . . a font of tort law").

State-Created Danger. In addition, some federal appellate courts have found liability on a related theory of "state-created danger" where injury was caused by the state's reckless or intentional action so egregious so as to "shock the conscience." The courts have ruled that in order to prevail on a "danger creation" theory, the plaintiff must show a substantially dangerous environment was created by state actors, the danger was known to the state actors, and state authority was used to create an opportunity that would not have otherwise existed for the injury to occur (*Armijo v. Wagon Mound Pub. Sch.*, 159 F.3d 1253 (10th Cir. 1998); *Johnson v. Dallas*, 38 F.3d 198 (5th Cir. 1994), *cert. denied*, 514 U.S. 1017 (1995); *Reed v. Gardner*, 986 F.2d 1122 (7th Cir. 1993); but see *Dwares v. New York*, 985 F.2d 94 (2d Cir. 1993); and *Shrum v. Kluk*, 249 F.3d 773 (8th Cir. 2001)). In *Armijo*, for example, the Tenth Circuit Court of Appeals refused to dismiss a lawsuit against school officials who suspended and sent home alone, without notifying his parents, a special education student who had, to the officials' knowledge, voiced suicidal thoughts that same day and displayed depression in prior months.

Even where there is no civil rights violation, however, a student may have a claim against a school district if the district's negligence is the proximate cause of the student's injuries (see **18:7–20).**

18:23. Can a school district be required to pay a "prevailing party's" attorneys' fees in a civil rights lawsuit?

Yes. A "prevailing party" in a civil rights lawsuit is entitled to have his or her attorneys' fees paid by the district (42 USC § 1988). According to the U.S Supreme Court, when a court enters a judgment on the merits in favor of a plaintiff or orders a consent decree (i.e., a court ordered settlement) that favors the plaintiff, the plaintiff is deemed a prevailing party (*Buckhannon Bd. & Care Home, Inc. v. W. Va. Dep't of Health & Human Res.*, 532 U.S. 598 (2001)). In contrast, a private settlement between parties, even if on terms favorable to the plaintiff, generally will not confer prevailing party status on the plaintiff, because such settlements are not judicially sanctioned (*Buckhannon*).

However, according to the U.S. Court of Appeals for the Second Circuit, a judgment on the merits or court-ordered consent decree are only examples of judicial action that convey prevailing party status. The court held that other types of judicial action can support an award of attorneys' fees, "so long as the action carries with it sufficient judicial imprimatur."

Thus, where a trial court retained jurisdiction over a private settlement by including the terms of the settlement agreement in its dismissal order, the Second Circuit found the trial court's retention of jurisdiction sufficient judicial imprimatur to support an award of attorneys' fees, because the trial court's retention of jurisdiction meant that a breach of the settlement agreement also would constitute a breach of the dismissal order (*Roberson v. Guiliani*, 346 F.3d 75 (2d Cir. 2003)).

18:24. May a school board member be held personally liable for the violation of an individual's civil rights when performing legislative activities?

No. The United States Supreme Court ruled that local legislators, such as school board members, have absolute immunity from civil liability in connection with lawsuits arising out of their performance of legislative activities (*Bogan v. Scott-Harris*, 523 U.S. 44 (1998)). This case does not shield board members from lawsuits for actions which are not legislative in nature. For example, the Court distinguished the abolition of a position, which it determined to be legislative, from the hiring or firing of a particular employee. (See also *Harhay v. Town of Ellington Bd. of Educ.*, 323 F.3d 206 (2d Cir. 2003).)

18:25. May school board members and district employees be held personally liable for the violation of an individual's civil rights?

Yes. School board members and other district employees may be held individually liable in a civil rights action if they knew or should have known that their actions would violate the federal constitutional or federal statutory rights of a person (see **18:24** for exception pertaining to school board members and legislative activities). Government officials enjoy "qualified immunity" which protects them from liability only when their actions or their performance of "'discretionary functions' . . . do not violate a clearly established constitutional or statutory right of which a reasonable person would have known" (*Davis v. Scherer*, 468 U.S. 183, 191 (1984), *rehearing denied*, 468 U.S. 1226 (1984); *Harlow v. Fitzgerald*, 457 U.S. 800, 818 (1982)).

According to the U.S. Court of Appeals, Second Circuit, whether or not a person is entitled to qualified immunity in a particular case depends on the answers to the following three-step inquiry:

1. Has the plaintiff alleged a violation of a constitutional right?
2. If yes, was that right "clearly established" at the time of the alleged violation of that right?
3. If a clearly established, constitutionally protected right was violated, were the defendant's actions "objectively reasonable?"

According to the Second Circuit, this inquiry should be followed in sequential order, since a plaintiff's failure to establish any one part typically will result in a grant of qualified immunity to the defendant (*Harhay v. Town of Ellington Board of Educ.*, 323 F.3d 206 (2d Cir. 2003)).

18:26. Can school district officials search employees' offices and/or office computers without violating their constitutional right to be free from unreasonable search and seizure?

Yes, under certain circumstances. While public employees are protected by the Fourth Amendment from unreasonable search and seizure, "[t]he 'special needs' of public employers may . . . allow them to dispense with probable cause and warrant requirements when conducting workplace searches related to investigations of work-related misconduct" (*Levanthal v. Knapek*, 266 F.3d 64 (2d Cir. 2001)).

The nature and extent of the search that a district may conduct without violating an employee's Fourth Amendment rights depends upon the employee's "expectation of privacy" in his or her work space, including items within the work space, such as a computer. A school district employee's expectation of privacy depends not only upon the law, but also upon a district's policies and practices.

According to the United States Court of Appeals for the Second Circuit, public employees can have a "substantial" expectation of privacy in private possessions kept in their workplace, but this expectation can be diminished by workplace realities such as work-related visits by fellow employees and others (*Shaul v. Cherry Valley-Springfield CSD*, 363 F.3d 177 (2d Cir. 2004)).

However, an employer still may search an area or materials in which an employee has a justifiable "expectation of privacy" if the search is "reasonable." A search will be deemed reasonable if it is "justified at its inception and appropriate in scope" (*Levanthal*). A search will be deemed appropriate in scope if the search methods employed are "reasonably related to the objective of the search and not excessively intrusive" in view of the purpose of the search (*Levanthal*).

Therefore, according to the Second Circuit, even where a teacher has an expectation of privacy in his or her classroom, school authorities have a right to search the teacher's classroom for evidence pertaining to an investigation into work-related misconduct by that teacher. They also may search a teacher's classroom for appropriate, noninvestigatory, work-related purposes, such as cleaning and preparing a teacher's classroom for use by a substitute (*Shaul*).

A teacher who fails to avail himself or herself of a reasonable opportunity to remove personal items from his or her classroom may lose all expectation of privacy in the contents of the classroom (*Shaul*).

Employment Discrimination

18:27. What constitutes employment discrimination?

Generally, employment discrimination consists of practices that impair employment opportunities for individuals who meet certain protected characteristics such as race, sex or disability, in violation of federal and/or state law. For example, on the federal level, Title VII of the Civil Rights Act of 1964 (42 USC § 2000e-2) prohibits all employers with 15 or more employees from discriminating in the hiring, firing, demotion or promotion of employees on the basis of race, sex, religion and national origin.

The United States Supreme Court has interpreted Title VII as protecting former employees who have filed employment discrimination complaints from retaliation by their former employer. In one case, a former employee was permitted to sue his former employer for providing unfavorable job recommendations to prospective employers (*Robinson v. Shell Oil Co.*, 519 U.S. 337 (1997)). Generally, an employee who prevails in a Title VII lawsuit is granted reinstatement and back pay. However, 1991 amendments to the act grant the right to a jury trial and also permit a court to award compensatory and punitive damages (*Landgraf v. USI Film Prod.*, 511 U.S. 244 (1994)).

The Pregnancy Discrimination Act of 1978 (PDA) (42 USC § 2000e (k)) amended Title VII to also prohibit discrimination in employment against pregnant women and to require that they be treated no differently than any other temporarily disabled employee. For conditions to be afforded protection by the PDA they must be unique to women (see *Saks v. Franklin Covey, Co.*, 316 F.3d 337 (2d Cir. 2003) (employer exclusion of surgical procedures to treat infertility did not violate PDA)). School districts and their attorneys must be sure to apply leave provisions and other terms and conditions of employment equally to all employees, with no greater burden on women who take leave in order to give birth.

In addition, the Age Discrimination in Employment Act (ADEA) (29 USC § 621 *et seq.*) prohibits age discrimination in employment (see **18:29–31**). The American with Disabilities Act (ADA) (42 USC § 12101 *et seq.*; see **18:32–40**) and section 504 of the Rehabilitation Act (29 USC § 794) prohibit discrimination on the basis of disability.

18:28. Is there a timeframe within which employment discrimination claims alleging violations of Title VII must be filed?

Yes. In general, employees who wish to sue their employers for employment discrimination alleging violations of Title VII must file a complaint with the Equal Employment Opportunity Commissioner (EEOC) within 300 days after the alleged unlawful employment practice, or lose their right to sue.

However, the U.S. Supreme Court has created a judicial exception to this rule where the complainant asserts a claim alleging "hostile environment" employment discrimination. A hostile work environment claim, by its very nature, alleges a series of separate acts that collectively constitute a single unlawful employment practice. Therefore, for the purpose of complying with the 300-day timeline for filing a complaint with the EEOC, it does not matter if some of the acts alleged to have created a hostile work environment occurred more than 300 days prior to filing, provided that at least one of the alleged acts that is part of the employee's hostile environment discrimination claim occurred within the 300 day window for filing. (*National Railroad Passenger Corp. v. Morgan*, 536 U.S. 101 (2002); see also **18:41**).

In contrast, a claim based upon an alleged "discrete" act of discrimination or retaliation (i.e., one that creates a basis for a lawsuit by itself, without regard to other incidents, such as a refusal to hire, failure to promote, denial of a transfer, or termination) must be filed within the 300-day window. "Each discrete act starts a new clock for filing charges alleging that act" (*National Railroad Passenger Corp.*).

18:29. What is the Age Discrimination in Employment Act?

The Age Discrimination in Employment Act (ADEA) (29 USC § 621 *et seq.*) is a federal law applicable to employers with 20 employees or more, which protects employees over the age of 40 from discrimination based on age. The ADEA only provides protection to those over age 40 from discrimination favoring younger workers. For example, the U.S. Supreme Court ruled that an employer did not commit an unlawful act of discrimination when it eliminated retiree health insurance benefits for workers under 50 but retained them for workers over 50. According to the court, the grant of greater benefits to an older subgroup within the protected class of older workers does not constitute age discrimination (*General Dynamics Land Systems Inc. v. Cline*, 124 S.Ct. 1236 (2004)).

An employee alleging a violation of the ADEA must prove that the employee's age played a motivating role in, or contributed to, an employer's employment decision (*Rentz v. Grey Advertising*, 135 F.3d 217 (2d Cir. 1997); *Gordon v. New York City Bd. of Educ.*, 232 F.3d 111 (2d Cir. 2000)). The ADEA may be violated even if the worker hired to replace an older employee is himself or herself over 40 (*O'Connor v. Consolidated Coin Caterers Corp.*, 517 U.S. 308 (1996); *see also Byrnie v. Town of Cromwell Bd. of Educ.*, 243 F.3d 93 (2d Cir. 2001)).

If an employee makes out a prima facie case of age discrimination, then the burden shifts to the employer to offer a legitimate nondiscriminatory reason for the adverse employment action. However, if the court believes that a jury could properly find that the reason offered by the employer is a pretext, then the court will submit the case to a jury to determine whether age discrimination occurred under the facts presented (*Byrnie v. Town of Cromwell Bd. of Educ.*).

One New York appellate court ruled the ADEA applied to a town assessor as well, even though that position is considered a public office (*Matter of Scopelliti v. Town of New Castle*, 210 A.D.2d 308 (2d Dep't 1994)).

The United States Supreme Court ruled in *Kimel v. Florida Bd. of Regents* (528 U.S. 62 (2000)) that the ADEA did not annul a state's sovereign immunity under the Eleventh Amendment. Therefore, states cannot be sued under the ADEA. However, a federal district court in New York has ruled that a school district is not immune from an ADEA suit despite the Supreme Court's ruling in *Kimel* (*Gavigan v. Clarkstown CSD*, 84 F.Supp.2d 540 (S.D.N.Y. 2000)).

18:30. Are former employees precluded from commencing a lawsuit under the Age Discrimination in Employment Act (ADEA)?

No. According to the United States Supreme Court, workers may sue former employers under the ADEA, even when they have signed a release of all claims against the employer if the release does not meet the specific requirements of the Older Workers Benefit Protection Act (OWBPA) (29 USC § 626(f)); 29 CFR § 1625.23; *Oubre v. Entergy Operations, Inc.*, 522 U.S. 422 (1998)).

Furthermore, employees cannot be required to tender back severance pay received in exchange for signing a legally defective release as a condition to commencing a lawsuit against their former employers. Such a requirement "might tempt employers to risk noncompliance with the OWBPA's waiver provisions, knowing it will be difficult [for employees to repay the moneys]" (*Oubre*; see **18:43**). Furthermore, even if an employee accepts a cash severance payment or other consideration from the employer as a condition of agreeing to such a release, the employer cannot require the employee to "tender back" (i.e. return, or offer to return) the severance payment prior to challenging the waiver and suing the employer (29 CFR § 1625.23; *Oubre;* see also *Hodge v. New York College of Podiatric Med.*, 157 F.3d 164, 165 (2d Cir. 1998); and *Tung v. Texaco, Inc.*, 150 F.3d 206, 209 (2d Cir. 1998)).

18:31. Does a retirement incentive program for teachers violate the Age Discrimination in Employment Act (ADEA)?

It depends. For example, the United States Court of Appeals for the Second Circuit ruled that a school district did not violate the ADEA when it negotiated a retirement incentive program with the teachers' union because eligibility to participate in the program was triggered by years of service, not age. The plan was offered to all teachers with at least 10 consecutive years of service with the district if they retired at the end of the school year in which they turned 55 and had completed 20 years of service in the state Teachers' Retirement System (TRS) (*Auerbach v. Board of Educ. of the Harborfields CSD*, 136 F.3d104 (2d Cir. 1998); but see *Abrahamson v. Board of Educ. of the Wappingers Falls CSD*, 374 F.3d 66 (2d Cir. 2004); *O'Brien v. Board of Educ. of Deer Park UFSD*, 127 F.Supp.2d 342 (2d Cir. 2001); see **11:2**).

For a retirement incentive plan to be lawful under the ADEA it must meet the following criteria: the incentive must be voluntary; it must available for a reasonable period of time, and it may not arbitrarily discriminate on the basis of age. However, the ADEA does not require an employer to provide identical early retirement incentives for employees of different ages (*Auerbach*).

18:32. What is the Americans with Disabilities Act?

The Americans with Disabilities Act (ADA) (42 USC § 12101 *et seq.*) is a federal law that prohibits discrimination on the basis of disability. The ADA, which applies to both private and public employers with more than 15 employees, prohibits discrimination in employment against a "qualified" disabled person, one who can perform the essential functions of the position with or without a "reasonable accommodation" unless offering the reasonable accommodation would impose an undue hardship on the employer (42 USC § 12111(9), (10)). Employees suing under the ADA must prove the disability was a motivating factor in the adverse employment action. They do not need to show that the disability was the sole cause of the action (*Parker v. Columbia Pictures Entertainment, Inc.*, 204 F.3d 326 (2d Cir. 2000); see also *Parker v. SONY Pictures Entertainment, Inc.*, 260 F.3d 100 (2d Cir. 2001); and *McNely v. Ocala Star-Banner Corp.*, 99 F.3d 1068 (11th Cir. 1996), *cert. denied*, 520 U.S. 1228 (1997)). Punitive damages are not available as a remedy in private lawsuits under section 202 of the act (*Barnes v. Gorman*, 122 S.Ct. 2097 (2002)).

18:33. What is a disability under the Americans with Disabilities Act?

The term "disability" is defined by the Americans with Disabilities Act (ADA) as "a physical or mental impairment that substantially limits one or more major life activities . . . a record of such an impairment; or being regarded as having such an impairment" (42 USC § 12102). It does not include an impairment that is not substantially limiting when corrective measures are taken. For example, near sightedness corrected by the use of eyeglasses is not a disability under the ADA (*Sutton v. United Airlines*, 527 U.S. 471 (1999)).

The United States Supreme Court has ruled that the ADA applies to people infected with the human immunodeficiency virus (HIV) (*Bragdon v. Abbott*, 524 U.S. 624 (1998)). While other federal district courts have held otherwise, a federal district court in New York ruled that pregnancy and its complications are not protected under the ADA because they are temporary, nonchronic and of short duration with little or no long term (*Johnson v. A.P. Products, Ltd.*, 934 F.Supp. 625 (S.D.N.Y. 1996)).

Identifying physical criteria for a job, without more, does not violate the ADA. Employers may determine that certain physical attributes are appropriate for certain positions, for example, such as perfect vision for airline pilots (*Sutton*).

Similarly, restricting a colorblind person from driving a bus does not constitute disability discrimination that violates the ADA, because the ability to readily distinguish traffic signals is an essential function of driving a bus (*Shannon v. New York City Transit Auth.*, 332 F.3d 95 (2d Cir. 2003)).

In addition, employers do not have to hire or promote individuals who pose a direct threat to the health and safety of others in the workplace, or to their own health and safety (*Chevron U.S.A., Inc. v. Echazabal*, 536 U.S. 73 (2002)).

18:34. How is it determined whether a disability substantiality limits a major life activity under the ADA?

In *Toyota Motor Mfg., Ky., Inc. v. Williams*, 534 U.S. 184 (2002), the United States Supreme Court ruled that "when addressing the major life activity of performing manual tasks, the central inquiry must be whether the claimant is unable to perform the variety of tasks central to most people's daily lives, not whether the claimant is unable to perform the tasks associated with her particular job." Furthermore, the Court held that "the impairment's impact must also be permanent or long term." The Court found that repetitive work with arms extended at shoulder height (as the claimant was required to do in her job) was not an important part of most people's daily lives. Conversely, the Court listed tasks, such as brushing one's own teeth and bathing, as manual tasks that are central to daily living. Since the claimant could perform these tasks, she did not qualify as disabled under the act.

Similarly, at least one circuit court has found that cancer and the effects of chemotherapy did not substantially limit an employee's ability to work as required under the ADA, where his doctor specifically stated that he was not disabled by the cancer and admitted that he was fully capable of working (*Gordon v. E.L. Hamm & Assocs., Inc.*, 100 F.3d 907 (11th Cir. 1996), *cert. denied*, 522 U.S. 1030 (1997)).

18:35. Is it possible for a person who does not have a "disability" that is recognized under the ADA to have a disability that is recognized and protected under state law?

Yes. According to the United States Court of Appeals for the Second Circuit, which has jurisdiction over New York, a person who does not have a "disability" under the federal ADA still may have a disability under New York's Human Rights Law (Exec. Law § 290 *et seq.*). Under the ADA, the impairment must be one that "substantially limits a major life activity" (see **18:33–34**). However, under New York law, a person will be deemed to have a disability if the person can demonstrate a "physical or mental impairment through medically accepted clinical or laboratory diagnostic techniques" (Exec. Law § 292(21); *Reeves v. Johnson Controls World Servs., Inc.*, 140 F.3d 144 (2d Cir. 1998); see also **18:41**).

18:36. What is a "reasonable accommodation" under the ADA?

The term "reasonable accommodation," as defined in the ADA, includes making existing facilities used by employees readily accessible to and usable by individuals with disabilities, job restructuring, modifying work schedules, reassigning to a vacant position and modifying equipment, examinations, or devices (42 USC § 12111(9)). According to the United States Equal Employment Opportunity Commission (EEOC), the federal agency charged with enforcing the ADA, a reasonable accommodation is any reasonable change in the workplace to remove barriers to equal employment opportunities for disabled individuals. It allows an applicant to be considered for a position and an employee to perform the essential functions of a job and enjoy equal benefits and privileges.

According to the United States Supreme Court, an employer may deny a request for accommodation that conflicts with the rules of a seniority system observed by the employer. An employee "remains free to present evidence of special circumstances that make 'reasonable' a seniority rule exception in [a] particular case." According to the Court, an employee "might show, for example, that the employer, having retained the right to change the seniority system unilaterally, exercises that right fairly frequently, reducing employee expectations that the system will be followed" (*U.S. Airways, Inc. v. Barnett*, 535 U.S. 391 (2000)).

An employee who claimed "total disability" for purposes of receiving Social Security Disability benefits was precluded from claiming that his disability was one that could be reasonably accommodated under the ADA (*Mitchell v. Washingtonville CSD*, 992 F.Supp. 395 (1998), *aff'd*, 190 F.3d 1 (2d Cir. 1999)).

An employer's offer of reassignment to a lesser position is not a reasonable accommodation under the ADA, when another position becomes available which is comparable to an employee's prior job for which the employee is qualified (*Norville v. Staten Island Univ. Hosp.*, 196 F.3d 89 (2d Cir. 1999)). However, an employer was not required to assign a new supervisor as a reasonable accommodation for an employee who claimed she suffered from depression as a result of her supervisor's alleged mistreatment of her (*Kennedy v. Dresser*, 193 F.3d 120 (2d Cir. 1999), *cert. denied*, 528 U.S. 1190 (2000)). Nonetheless, the Court has refused to adopt a blanket rule that the replacement of a supervisor can never be a reasonable accommodation under the ADA, stating that the reasonableness of such an accommodation must be evaluated on a case-by-case basis (*Kennedy*; see also *Wernick v. Federal Reserve Bank of New York*, 91 F.3d 379 (2d Cir. 1996)).

18:37. Are part-time and probationary employees entitled to reasonable accommodations under the ADA?

Yes. Employers must provide reasonable accommodations to part-time, full-time and probationary employees alike ("U.S. Equal Employment Opportunity Commission Enforcement Guidance: Reasonable Accommodation and Undue Hardship Under the Americans with Disabilities Act," October 2002. A copy of this publication is available from the EEOC's Publications Center at 800-669-3362 or at http://www.eeoc.gov/policy/docs/accommodation.html).

18:38. May an employer offer different benefits for physical and mental and emotional disabilities?

The ADA does not prohibit an employer from offering more generous disability benefits for physical disabilities than for mental and emotional disabilities, according to the U.S. Court of Appeals, Second Circuit. Citing to other similarly held federal circuit courts of appeals decisions, the Second Circuit ruled that "so long as every employee is offered the same plan regardless of that employee's contemporary or future disability status, then no discrimination has occurred even if the plan offers different coverage for different disabilities" (*Equal Employment Opportunity Commission v. Staten Island Savings Bank*, 207 F.3d 144 (2d Cir. 2000); see also *Zervos v. Verizon N.Y., Inc.*, 2001 U.S. Dist. LEXIS 17061 (2001)).

Moreover, according to the New York State Court of Appeals, group insurance policies that provide more generous coverage for physical disabilities than for mental disabilities do not violate the anti-discrimination provisions of the New York State Insurance Law (*Polan v. State of New York Ins. Dep't,___ N.Y.3d ___, slip opn. 05765 (2004)).

18:39. May an employee bring a hostile environment lawsuit under the Americans with Disabilities Act?

According to at least one federal district court in New York, a claim of "hostile environment" employment discrimination is actionable under the ADA. The case involved an employee who informed his employer that he suffered from severe asthma and required a smoke-free work environment. Despite repeated requests for relief, his exposure to secondhand tobacco smoke from co-workers continued unabated. The employer ultimately terminated the employee, purportedly for poor performance. The employee sued under the ADA, contending that the employer's refusal to accommodate his need created a hostile environment, and the court allowed this cause of action under the ADA (*Hendler v. Intelecom USA, Inc.*, 963 F.Supp. 200 (E.D.N.Y. 1997)). Although the decision is binding only within the jurisdiction of the Eastern District of New York, it offers guidance to other courts.

All school grounds in New York State must be smoke free (see **17:57–58**) and therefore it is unlikely that a hostile environment claim would arise based on exposure to second-hand smoke in a school environment. However, the federal court's recognition of "hostile environment" discrimination claims commenced under the ADA potentially could be applied under different factual scenarios.

18:40. Can individuals be personally liable for discrimination claims brought under the Americans with Disabilities Act?

One federal district court in New York has ruled that individuals cannot be personally liable for discrimination claims brought by employees under the ADA. The ruling is consistent with several other federal court decisions outside of New York. However, the Court of Appeals for the Second Circuit, which has jurisdiction over New York, has not yet addressed the issue (*Doyle v. Columbia-Presbyterian Med. Ctr.*, 1998 U.S. Dist. LEXIS 11646, 5 Accom. Disabilities Dec. (CCH) P5-210 (S.D.N.Y. July 28, 1998)).

18:41. Are there any state laws that prohibit employment discrimination?

Yes. New York's Human Rights Law prohibits discrimination on the basis of age, race, creed, color, national origin, sexual orientation, military status, sex, marital status, disability, and prior arrest or conviction record (Exec. Law § 290 *et seq.*). It applies to all employers with four or more employees, and their unions. The law is enforced either by filing an administrative complaint with the State Division of Human Rights or bringing a lawsuit directly in state court. New York courts adjudicating claims of unlawful discriminatory practices prohibited by the state's Human Rights Law apply the same legal principles used to resolve federal discrimination claims under Title VII of the Civil Rights Act of 1964 (see *Mittl v. Rivera-Maldonado*, 100 N.Y.2d 326 (2003)). Under these principles, if an employer offers a business related reason for its alleged discriminatory action, an employee only needs to show that the explanation was a pretext. There is no requirement that the employee show the real motive was discrimination (*Classic Coach v. Mercado*, 280 A.D.2d 164, 166 (2d Dep't 2001), *appeal denied*, 97 N.Y.2d 601 (2001)).

Although the Human Rights Law makes it unlawful to discriminate on the basis of marital status, a domestic partnership does not constitute a protected marital status under the law. As such, a state appellate court ruled that a school district did not violate the state Human Rights Law when it refused to provide health insurance benefits to the same-sex domestic partner of a school district retiree (*Funderburke v. Uniondale UFSD No. 15*, 251 A.D.2d 622 (2d Dep't 1998), *leave to appeal denied*, 92 N.Y.2d 813 (1998)). Since the district did not make health insurance coverage available to the domestic partners of any of its unmarried retirees, it did not engage in unlawful discrimination when it refused to make coverage available to the same-sex domestic partner of its retiree in this case (compare with *Irizarry v. Bd. of Educ.*, 251 F.3d 604 (7th Cir. 2001), where the court held that a board of education's practice of extending health insurance benefits to homosexual partners but denying them to unmarried heterosexual partners had a rational basis, and therefore withstood legal challenge).

In addition, the state Correction Law makes it illegal to refuse to license or hire a person because that person has a criminal record, unless there is a direct relationship between the criminal offense and the license or employment sought, or there would be an unreasonable risk to property or the safety or welfare of specific individuals or the public (Correct. Law § 752). The law sets forth a number of factors to be considered in determining whether such an unreasonable risk is posed, such as the time elapsed since the crime was committed, the seriousness of the offense and the duties and responsibilities of the position sought. The law creates a presumption of rehabilitation if the applicant has obtained a certificate of relief from civil disabilities, but that presumption may be overcome by the weight accorded the other factors, on a case-by-case basis (Correct. Law § 753*); Matter of Arrocha v. Board of Educ. of the City of New York* (93 N.Y.2d 361 (1999)); *Matter of Camuliare v. New York City Bd. of Educ.* (unreported, N.Y.L.J. Sept. 9, 1998), see **8:53**).

Furthermore, the state "whistle-blower law" prohibits public employers from retaliating against employees for disclosing to a governmental body information regarding a violation of a law, rule or regulation when the violation "creates and presents a substantial and specific danger to the public health or safety" or for disclosing to a governmental body information "which the employee reasonably believes to be true and reasonably believes constitutes an improper governmental action." However, unless there is imminent and serious danger to public health or safety, prior to disclosing such information, an employee must make a good faith effort to provide his or her employer with the information to be disclosed and must give the employer a reasonable time to take appropriate action. It provides for reinstatement and back pay if the employee can show that the employer retaliated illegally for the protected activity (Civ. Serv. Law § 75-b). By comparison, in the private sector, an employee may be fired for reporting "possible" violations of law, because the protections of the anti-retaliation statute that apply to private sector employees (Lab. Law § 740) only apply to reports of actual violations of law (*Bordell v. General Electric Co.*, 88 N.Y.2d 869 (1996); see also **9:44**).

Finally, the state Legal Activities Law protects employees who engage in certain legal activities after work hours, such as consuming legal substances, recreational activities that do not involve compensation, and political activities (Lab. Law § 201-d). For example, membership in a union is protected,

(*Muhitch v. St. Gregory the Great Roman Catholic Church & Sch.*, 239 A.D.2d 901 (4th Dep't 1997)), as is off-duty political activity (*Baker v. City of Elmira*, 271 A.D.2d 906 (3d Dep't 2000); *Richardson v. City of Saratoga Springs*, 246 A.D.2d 900 (3d Dep't 1998); *Cavanaugh v. Doherty*, 243 A.D.2d 92 (3d Dep't 1998)).

However, according to New York's appellate courts, dating and romantic relationships, including extramarital affairs between co-workers, do not fall within the scope of the definition of "recreational activity" under the law (see *State v. Wal-Mart Stores*, 207 A.D.2d 150 (3d Dep't 1995); see also *Hudson v. Goldman*, 283 A.D.2d 246 (1st Dep't 2001); *Bilquin v. Roman Catholic Church*, 286 A.D.2d 409 (2d Dep't 2001)). The *Wal-Mart* case involved the discharge of two employees for violating a "fraternization policy" when they dated each other even though they each were married to others. Similarly, the *Hudson* case involved co-workers who were both terminated for allegedly having an extramarital affair. Notably, in a separate case, the United States Court of Appeals for the Second Circuit followed the *Wal-Mart* decision, holding that "romantic dating" is not a "recreational activity" within the meaning of New York Labor Law section 201-d (*McCavitt v. Swiss Reinsurance Am. Corp.*, 237 F.3d 166 (2d Cir. 2001)).

18:42. Can individual employees be held personally liable for employment discrimination?

Sometimes. The United States Court of Appeals for the Second Circuit ruled, for example, that two employees could be held personally liable for their use of gender stereotypes in discriminating against a female employee who had young children (*Back v. Hastings on Hudson UFSD*, 2004 WL 739846 (2d Cir. 2004)). However, in a sexual harassment case, the Second Circuit ruled that employees may not be held individually liable for acts of discrimination under Title VII of the Civil Rights Act of 1964 (*Tomka v. Seiler Corp.*, 66 F.3d 1295 (2d Cir. 1995)). This is the prevailing view among the federal circuit courts (see *Lissau v. Southern Food Serv.*, 159 F.3d 177, 181 (4th Cir. 1998)). (See also **18:40**.)

18:43. Can an employee waive the right to sue for employment discrimination in exchange for a severance package?

Yes. An employee can agree to waive the legal right to file a discrimination lawsuit in exchange for a severance package, but the waiver must be made knowingly and voluntarily.

Moreover, any time a current or former employee signs a release agreeing to waive the right to sue an employer for discrimination, the release must comply with applicable laws. For example, a release of claims against an employer for age discrimination must comply with the specific requirements of a federal law known as the "Older Workers Benefit Protection Act" (OWBPA) (29 USC § 626(f); 29 CFR § 1625.23; *Oubre v. Entergy Operations, Inc.*, 522 U.S. 422 (1998); see **18:30**). If a release under the OWBPA does not comply with specific requirements set forth in that law, then it may be invalid, and the employee may be able to sue the employer anyway.

One federal district court in New York ruled, in a case commenced under Title VII of the Civil Rights Act of 1964, that an employer may require an employee to execute a "binding undertaking" which requires the employee to pay back the employer (including possible interest) if the release is later ruled invalid (*Kristoferson v. Spunkmeyer, Inc.*, 965 F.Supp. 545 (S.D.N.Y. 1997)).

Sexual Harassment

18:44. What is sexual harassment?

Sexual harassment is a form of sex discrimination or gender-based employment discrimination that violates Title VII of the federal Civil Rights Act of 1964 (42 USC § 2000e-2; *Meritor Savings Bank, FSB v. Vinson*, 477 U.S. 57 (1986)). It is also a form of sex discrimination under Title IX of the 1972 Educational Amendments (20 USC § 1681), which prohibits discrimination in educational programs and activities that receive federal funds (*Davis v. Monroe County Bd. of Educ.*, 526 U.S. 629 (1999); *Franklin v. Gwinnett County Pub. Sch.*, 503 U.S. 60 (1992); *Bruneau v. South Kortright CSD*, 163 F.3d 749 (2d Cir. 1998), *cert. denied*, 526 U.S. 1145 (1999)).

If the sexual harassment is so pervasive that it is "calculated to drive someone out of the workplace," it also may be a constitutional violation (*Annis v. County of Westchester*, 36 F.3d 251 (2d Cir. 1994), *aff'd in part, vacated on other grounds*, 136 F.3d 239 (2d Cir. 1998); see **18:45–46** for discussion on peer sexual harassment and teacher-student sexual harassment).

In addition, sexual harassment is recognized as a form of sex discrimination under the New York State Human Rights Law, which prohibits discrimination in employment on the basis of certain immutable characteristics such as gender (Exec. Law § 290 *et seq.*; see also **18:41**). Damages may be awarded under both state and federal law if the complainant produces testimony as to hurt and humiliation derived from the acts of sex discrimination (*New York State Dep't of Correctional Servs. v. State Div. of Human Rights*, 215 A.D.2d 908 (3d Dep't 1995); *Cornwell v. Robinson*, 23 F.3d 694 (2d Cir. 1994)).

Men can be victims of sexual harassment by female supervisors (*Forte v. East Harlem Block Schs.*, 1994 U.S. Dist. LEXIS 7944, 65 Fair Empl. Prac. Case (BNA) 383 (S.D.N.Y. 1994); *Goering v. NYNEX Info. Resources Co.*,

209 A.D.2d 834 (3d Dep't 1994)). Sexual harassment directed at members of the same sex has also been found to be actionable (*Oncale v. Sundowner Offshore Services, Inc.*, 523 U.S. 75 (1998); compare with *Simonton v. Runyon*, 225 F.3d 122 (2d Cir. 2000), holding that harassment based on "sexual orientation" is not actionable under Title VII).

18:45. What are the characteristics of sexual harassment?

Sexual harassment consists of "unwelcome sexual advances, requests for sexual favors, and verbal or physical conduct of a sexual nature" (29 CFR § 1604.11; 34 CFR § 106.8; 29 CFR § 1609.1(b)).

In the employment context, the United States Supreme Court has recognized two types of sexual harassment: "quid pro quo" and "hostile environment" sexual harassment (*Meritor Savings Bank, FSB v. Vinson*, 477 U.S. 57 (1986)).

Quid pro quo sexual harassment involves situations where an employee's submission to or rejection of unwelcome sexual conduct is used by an employer to determine that person's terms or conditions of employment. Examples of this kind of sexual harassment would include being given or denied a raise, transfer, or being disciplined for refusing to accede to the sexual advances of a supervisor.

Hostile environment sexual harassment, on the other hand, can take many forms. Usually, it is a pattern of unwelcome sexual conduct sufficiently severe to interfere with an individual's performance or to create an intimidating, hostile, or offensive working environment. Examples of this would include repeated sexual remarks aimed at an individual who finds the remarks offensive.

18:46. Is it necessary for an employee to show serious psychological harm or economic loss in order to prevail in a sexual harassment lawsuit?

No. In *Harris v. Forklift Sys.*, 510 U.S. 17 (1993), the United States Supreme Court ruled that an employee need not prove serious psychological harm in order to succeed in a sexual harassment lawsuit.

18:47. What should a school district do to protect itself against claims of sexual harassment?

School districts should adopt comprehensive sexual harassment prevention programs that include the following elements: policies that condemn sexual harassment and which contain procedures for clearly and regularly communicating the district's strong disapproval of sexual misconduct; procedures for resolving complaints which encourage victims to come forward, and ensure their confidentiality and protect them against retaliation; and provisions for immediate and effective remedies. Districts also should take appropriate disciplinary action against offenders, and provide ongoing and comprehensive training for district employees and students.

In addition, school districts should be aware that Title IX of the 1972 Educational Amendments (20 USC § 1681) requires federal fund recipients not only to adopt a policy that condemns actions prohibited by the act, but also to appoint an employee responsible for ensuring compliance with Title IX. This policy must be posted and disseminated to all students and employees, as well as to the parents of students.

Prior to adopting or revising a sexual harassment policy and procedures, school districts may have an obligation to negotiate certain aspects of the policy and procedures relating to employee discipline with employee organizations (unions) (*Patchogue Medford UFSD*, 30 PERB ¶ 3041 (1997)).

18:48. May an employer be held liable for failing to protect an employee from sexual harassment by a supervisor?

Yes. The U.S. Supreme Court has ruled that in both *quid pro quo* and *hostile environment* sexual harassment, an employer may be liable for the harassment of an employee by a supervisor even if the employer did not know that the harassment was taking place (*Burlington Industries v. Ellerth*, 524 U.S. 742 (1998); *Faragher v. City of Boca Raton*, 524 U.S. 775 (1998)). Moreover, according to the United States Court of Appeals for the Second Circuit, an individual need not have the power to hire, fire, demote or promote to be considered a supervisor for purposes of establishing employer liability in a Title VII discrimination lawsuit, if that individual has dominion, in other respects, over the employee alleging the harassment (*Mack v. Otis Elevator Co.*, 326 F.3d 116 (2d Cir. 2003), *cert. denied*, 124 S.Ct. 562 (2003).

However, the Supreme Court also has ruled that if an employer has not taken any "tangible employment action" against the person complaining of the harassment, then the employer can successfully defend itself by proving that it exercised reasonable care to prevent and promptly correct sexually harassing behavior and that the employee "unreasonably failed to take advantage of preventive or corrective opportunities provided by the employer or to otherwise avoid harm" (*Faragher v. City of Boca Raton*, 524 U.S. 775, 807 (1998)).

Moreover, according to the Supreme Court, if workplace sexual harassment creates a hostile environment so intolerable that it is reasonable for an employee to resign (known as a "constructive discharge"), the employer still retains the affirmative defense established by *Ellerth* and

Faragher, unless a supervisor also took formal, employer-sanctioned, adverse employment action against the employee (such as demoting the employee or drastically reducing her pay) that precipitated her resignation (*Pennsylvania State Police v. Suders*, 124 S.Ct. 2342 (2004)).

Notably, in *Mack v. Otis Elevator*, the Second Circuit remanded the case to permit the employer to assert this affirmative defense.

18:49. May an school district be held liable for failing to protect an employee from sexual harassment if the employee insists that his or her complaint be kept confidential?

It depends. Where an employee insisted that her supervisor keep her complaint "confidential," the United States Court of Appeals for the Second Circuit ruled that the employer was not liable for failing to protect the employee from sexual and racial harassment. According to the court, the employer's decision to honor the employee's request for confidentiality was reasonable under the circumstances, but warned that its holding was limited to the particular facts of the case. It cautioned that there is a point at which harassing conduct could become so severe that a reasonable employer would be required to take action, despite an employee's request to the contrary (*Torres v. Pisano*, 116 F.3d 625 (2d Cir. 1997), *cert. denied*, 522 U.S. 997 (1997)).

18:50. May a school district be held liable when a teacher sexually harasses a student?

Yes. The United States Supreme Court has ruled that a school district may be held liable under Title IX for sexual harassment of a student by a teacher (*Franklin v. Gwinnett County Pub. Sch.*, 503 U.S. 60 (1992)). However, damages may not be recovered unless an official of the district who has authority to institute corrective measures on the district's behalf has actual notice of, and is deliberately indifferent to, the teacher's misconduct (*Gebser v. Lago Vista Indep. Sch. Dist.*, 524 U.S. 274 (1998); see also *Baynard v. Malone*, 268 F.3d 228 (4th Cir. 2001), *cert. denied by Baynard v. Alexandria City Sch. Bd.*, 122 S.Ct. 1357 (2002)).

18:51. Can a school district be held liable when a student sexually harasses another student?

Yes. The United States Supreme Court has ruled that school districts can be held liable for sexual harassment of students by fellow students that is "so severe, pervasive and objectively offensive" that it denies the victims equal access to education, when the district has the authority to take remedial action against the harasser but acts in a deliberately indifferent manner (*Davis v. Monroe County Bd. of Educ.*, 526 U.S. 629, 652 (1999)).

In *Davis*, a fifth-grade female student claimed she was repeatedly sexually harassed by a 10-year-old male student in her class over a five-month period, despite the fact that she and her parents made repeated reports of the harassment to her teacher and school administrators. The parents alleged the girl's grades dropped as a result of the harassment. The Supreme Court was particularly concerned that the alleged acts of harassment were prolonged in nature, that the harassment had a concrete negative effect on the female student's ability to receive an education, and that the school district never once disciplined the male student harasser even though he pled guilty to sexual battery for his misconduct.

In a case decided after *Davis*, a parent of a disabled high school student sued a school district under Title IX for failing to protect the student from sustained sexual harassment, assault, and battery by one of her fellow students. It was alleged that when teachers learned of the sexual assaults, they instructed the student not to tell her mother, and they informed the mother only that the girl had been battered. When confronted by the girl's mother, the teachers denied the assaults occurred. The principal refused to investigate the matter and suspended the female but not the male. The school did not inform the police of the alleged assaults. Relying on the factors established in *Davis*, the United States Court of Appeals for the 10th Circuit ruled that the parent sufficiently stated a claim of school district liability under Title IX and that the individual defendants actually knew of and acquiesced in the male student's behavior. Therefore, the principal and the teachers were not entitled to qualified immunity (see **18:25**) because the law was clearly established at that time under *Davis* that a person who exercises the state's supervisory authority may be held liable for consciously acquiescing in sexually harassing conduct by an actor over whom they had authority (*Murrell v. School Dist. No. 1*, 186 F.3d 1238 (10th Cir. 1999)).

In a pre-*Davis* case, the Second Circuit, which has jurisdiction over New York, upheld a finding that a school district did not violate the Title IX rights of a sixth-grade female student who alleged that the district failed to properly safeguard her from sexual harassment by her male classmates, based on a jury finding that the boys' treatment of the girl was misconduct but not sexual harassment. In addition, the district had responded adequately when it became aware of the situation (*Bruneau v. South Kortright CSD*, 163 F.3d 749 (1998), *cert. denied*, 526 U.S. 1149 (1999)). In *Bruneau*, the Second Circuit also affirmed the dismissal of the girl's claim under section 1983 alleging a violation of her civil rights (see **18:21**) after concluding that it was Congress' scheme that a claimed violation of Title IX be pursued under Title IX and not section 1983. The decision is significant because some claims available under section 1983 are not available under Title IX. Under section 1983, for example, a claim could be made against a school district, not only on the basis of deliberate indifference as in the *Davis* case, but also for failure to adequately train its employees (see **18:22**). However, the courts have not interpreted Title IX to allow for such claims.

Defense and Indemnification

18:52. Must a school district retain an attorney?

No. Although most school districts retain counsel to provide legal advice to the school board and represent it in matters pending before the courts or administrative tribunals (*Yorktown CSD v. Yorktown Congress of Teachers*, 42 A.D.2d 422 (2d Dep't 1973)), there is no requirement that every district retain counsel. Such a decision is within the discretion of the school board.

Some districts retain outside counsel for specific purposes, such as labor negotiations or disciplinary proceedings against tenured teachers; others appoint attorneys to handle any legal matters that arise. Some districts have attorneys on staff serving in this capacity.

Outside attorneys may be employed by a retainer agreement, which is terminable at any time, or pursuant to a contract at a fixed salary, provided, however, that a board of education cannot bind successor boards to an employment contract with an attorney (see *Harrison CSD v. Nyquist*, 59 A.D.2d 434 (3d Dep't 1977), *appeal denied*, 44 N.Y.2d 465 (1978)).

Furthermore, the appointment of a school attorney falls within the "professional services exception" to the competitive bidding requirements of the General Municipal Law (see **19:60**). Therefore districts need not subject the selection of their attorney(s) to a bidding process (*People ex rel. Smith v. Flagg*, 17 N.Y. 584 (1858)). However, districts are required to adopt and follow internal policies and procedures governing procurement of professional services, such as those provided by a school attorney, "so as to assure the prudent and economical use of public moneys in the best interests of the taxpayers" (Gen. Mun. Law § 104-b; see also **19:61-62**).

18:53. Are school districts responsible for defending and indemnifying school board members and employees who are sued for negligence and other improper actions?

Yes. Section 3811 of the Education Law requires school districts (other than New York City) and boards of cooperative educational services (BOCES) to defend and indemnify any superintendent, principal, teacher, other member of the teaching and supervisory staff, noninstructional employee, any school board member, any member of the committee on special education (CSE) or subcommittee thereof, or any person appointed to serve as a surrogate parent on local CSEs, for all reasonable costs and expenses, including awards resulting from any action or proceeding against him or her arising out of the exercise of his or her powers or the performance of his or her duties (other than one brought by a school district or a criminal action brought against the individual). Any such costs and expenses must be approved pursuant to board resolution, which also authorizes the levying of a tax for such purpose. Section 3812 provides for inclusion of these costs in the next annual budget so that they may be assessed against the school district.

With respect to New York City, section 2560 of the Education Law requires the New York City school district to provide legal representation and indemnification against claims to school board members, employees, members of CSEs, and authorized participants in school volunteer programs in the city, pursuant to section 50-k of the General Municipal Law.

In addition, section 3023 of the Education Law requires school boards and BOCES boards to indemnify and provide legal representation to teachers, practice or cadet teachers, members of the supervisory and administrative staff, other employees and authorized participants in volunteer programs against lawsuits for negligence, accidental bodily injury or property damage, provided those persons were performing their duties within the scope of employment or their authorized volunteer duties and under the direction of the board. Section 3023 also permits school boards to arrange for and maintain appropriate insurance with any appropriate insurance company or to self-insure to protect the district against the risk of claims under this sections of law.

An additional indemnification provision applies specifically to teachers and volunteers who are sued as a result of taking disciplinary action against students. Section 3028 of the Education Law requires all school boards and BOCES boards to provide an attorney and to pay the attorneys' fees and expenses incurred in the defense of teachers or authorized volunteers who are sued either in a civil or criminal action arising out of disciplinary action taken against any student of the district. As with most indemnification provisions, the protection applies only if the teacher or volunteer was discharging his or her duties within the scope of employment or authorized volunteer duties when the disciplinary action took place (see, for example, *Inglis v. Dundee CSD Bd. of Educ.*, 180 Misc. 2d 156 (Yates County Sup. Ct. 1999); see also *Cromer v. City School Dist. of Albany Bd. of Educ.*, NYLJ, April 15, 2002 (Albany County Sup. Ct. 2002)). One state supreme court ruled a physical education teacher was acting within the scope of employment when he grabbed a student by his sweatshirt and led him to a doorway after he refused to follow the teacher's directions, and used his feet and legs to move the student after the student fell through the gym doorway. According to the court, the teacher was "disciplining a student while engaged in his employment as a physical education teacher and his actions were generally foreseeable" (*Cromer*).

Because the Board of Regents has strictly limited the circumstances under which teachers may legally use physical force against students (see **8:92**), the New York State Insurance Department has indicated that insurance carriers may limit their coverage to damages arising out of the use of physical force as permitted by the Regents while not providing coverage for unauthorized corporal punishment. However, a school district's duty to provide a legal defense and/or pay attorneys' fees is not affected by the availability of liability insurance.

18:54. Are there any procedures that school board members and employees must comply with before a school district can defend and indemnify them?

Pursuant to section 3811 of the Education Law, the board member or employee must notify the board in writing of the commencement of the proceeding against him or her within five days after service of process. Thereafter, the school board has 10 days within which to designate and appoint legal counsel to represent the individual. In the absence of such a designation and appointment, the individual may select his or her own counsel.

In addition, for these protections to apply, the individual must obtain a "certificate of good faith" either from an appropriate court or from the commissioner of education, which certifies that the individual appeared to have acted in good faith with respect to the exercise of his or her powers or the performance of duties (§ 3811(1)).

If a district meeting or school board disputes the amount of costs claimed by an individual, it may be adjusted by the county judge in the county in which the district or any part of it is located (§ 3811(2)).

Under sections 3023 and 3028 (see **18:53**), the teacher or other employee or volunteer must deliver a copy of the summons and complaint or demand or notice to the board within 10 days of the time the complaint is served upon that person.

18:55. Are there any alternative provisions affecting a school district's responsibilities regarding indemnification and defense of school board members and district employees?

Yes. If a school board or BOCES board adopts a resolution as prescribed by section 18 of the Public Officers Law, board members, officers and employees acting within the scope of their employment or duties may be covered by this statute. This coverage may supplant or supplement the protection provided under the Education Law, depending on the language of the resolution passed by the board (see *Matter of Percy*, 31 Educ. Dep't Rep. 199 (1991)). In order to supplement the Education Law protection, the resolution must do so explicitly.

Section 18 also requires the district to pay for employees' legal defense costs and damages if the case is of the type covered by the statute, provided that the employee was acting within the scope of his or her duties when the allegedly wrongful act occurred. The employee must forward a copy of any summons or other court papers to the superintendent of schools or school attorney within 10 days after he or she is served in order to obtain protection under the statute, and must fully cooperate in his or her defense. It is not necessary for the employee to obtain a good faith certificate to be protected under the statute.

18:56. May an insurance carrier refuse to defend or indemnify a school district sued for "intentional" acts committed by its employees?

It depends on the nature of the claim, the type of insurance policy in effect, and the court that hears the claim. In one case, a state appellate court refused to grant an insurance company's motion to dismiss a school district's claim for defense and indemnification where the district was sued based on allegations that a district teacher engaged in sexual misconduct with students. The insurance company disclaimed coverage under the errors and omissions policy issued to the district on the grounds that both "assault and battery" and "bodily injury and emotional distress" were excluded from coverage under the policy, and that the alleged acts of sexual misconduct by the teacher would fall within these areas of exclusion. The court acknowledged that errors and omissions policies typically cover negligence claims and do not provide coverage for intentional acts such as sexual assault. However, the court found that the insurance company was obligated to defend and indemnify the school district in this case. The court noted the lawsuit against the school district claimed that the district should be held liable for its own negligence: 1) for hiring the teacher, allegedly without conducting an adequate background check (which may have alerted the district to the teacher's conviction of sex crimes in another state); and 2) for allegedly failing to aggressively investigate complaints of sexual misconduct by the teacher. While the teacher "may have intentionally perpetrated the alleged sexual assaults against students," the claim against the district was "predicated upon its conceptually independent negligent supervision." Under the circumstances, allowing the insurer to disclaim coverage in this case "would effectively eviscerate the errors and omissions policy altogether" (*Watkins Glen CSD v. Nat'l Union Fire Ins. Co.*, 286 A.D.2d 48 (2d Dep't 2001)).

In contrast, according to another state appellate court, "it is the nature of the underlying acts, not the theory of liability" that determines whether the insurance policy at issue requires the insurer to defend and indemnify the insured. Therefore, the court ruled that an insurance company was not obligated to defend or indemnify a school district that was sued for negligent hiring, retention and supervision of a teacher accused of assaulting and sexually abusing students. While the complaint alleged district negligence, the allegations stemmed from the underlying intentional acts of assault and sexual abuse. The insurance policy did not define covered "occurrences" to include intentional acts (*Sweet Home CSD v. Aetna Commercial Insur. Co.*, 263 A.D.2d 949 (4th Dep't 1999), *appeal withdrawn*, 94 N.Y.2d 915 (2000)).

Insurance

18:57. Must a school board have insurance or other protection against damage to school property?

Yes. Section 1709(8) of the Education Law states that a school board must "insure the schoolhouses and their furniture, apparatus and appurtenances, and the school library." School districts may establish a liability and casualty reserve fund for self-insurance purposes (Gen. Mun. Law § 6-n; see **19:29**).

18:58. What other types of insurance are commonly purchased by school boards to protect their districts?

Many school districts purchase what is known as special multi-peril insurance policies. These are package policies designed to provide a combination of property and general liability coverage. Other coverage often purchased by districts are floater policies to protect district property that is taken off school grounds; automobile coverage, which protects against vehicular accidents; and school board members' errors and omissions coverage, also known as school board legal liability coverage.

School districts also may purchase catastrophe-umbrella or excess policies to protect the district against large losses. The school district's administrative staff and insurance professionals can help the school board determine an adequate amount of coverage for the types of insurance they choose to purchase.

18:59. Are school districts required to carry workers' compensation insurance?

Yes. School districts must provide workers' compensation coverage for all teachers and other employees for injuries incurred in the performance of their duties and must post notifications of said insurance or be subject to a fine (§§ 1604(31), 1709(34), 2503(10); Work. Comp. Law § 51). The Workers' Compensation Law requires employers to provide benefits to employees for disability or death "arising out of and in the course of employment" (Work. Comp. Law § 10). However, it bars employees from suing their employers for accidental injuries that arise out of and occur in the course of employment, including claims for damages caused by negligent supervision or hiring, negligent failure to initiate or follow anti-discrimination policies, or negligently carrying out disciplinary action (see *Maas v. Cornell Univ.*, 253 A.D.2d 1 (3d Dep't 1999), *aff'd,* 94 N.Y.2d 87 (1999)).

One court found that an injury sustained by an elementary school teacher while volunteering as a stage hand in a high school play was sufficiently related to her employment to entitle her to benefits under the Worker' Compensation Law (*Walker v. Greene CSD*, 774 N.Y.S.2d 848 (3d Dep't 2004)).

In another case, where an employee was killed in an altercation with a co-worker in the stairwell of the employer's building, the Court of Appeals found that the employer tacitly condoned the conduct that lead to the fatality; therefore, the employee's death arose from the course of employment *(Rosen v. First Manhattan Bank*, 84 N.Y.2d 856 (1994)).

The courts also have recognized a "special errand" exception for injuries that occur while the employee is on an errand to or from work and home. If the employer encouraged the errand and obtained a benefit as a result of its performance, the injury will be deemed to have occurred in the course of employment (*Neacosia v. New York Power Auth.*, 85 N.Y.2d 471 (1995); *Dziedzic v. Orchard Park CSD*, 283 A.D.2d 878 (3d Dep't 2001)).

The law establishes a complex plan to determine the amount of such benefits based upon the employee's average weekly wage and the extent and permanency of the injury (Work. Comp. Law §§ 14–15). The school district's workers' compensation protection can be obtained through the State Insurance Fund, an insurance company authorized to provide worker's compensation insurance, or by self-insurance, either individually or as part of a group self-insurance plan (see Work. Comp. Law Arts. 4 and 5; practice commentary to Work. Comp. Law § 50).

In addition, section 212(2) of the Workers' Compensation Law provides that school districts may elect to cover their employees under the Disability Benefits Law. These benefits are provided to employees unable to work because of an injury unrelated to their employment.

18:60. Are school districts required to provide unemployment insurance coverage?

Yes. All school districts must provide unemployment insurance coverage. The federal government requires that unemployment insurance be provided to all employees of state and local governments, including public school employees, in order for states to be in conformity with federal law (see 26 USC § 3304; *County of Los Angeles v. Marshall*, 442 F.Supp. 1186 (D.D.C. 1977), *aff'd*, 203 U.S. App. D.C. 185 (1980), *cert. denied*, 449 U.S. 837 (1980); Lab. Law §§ 512, 565).

Section 565(7) of the Labor Law states that any two or more school districts may form a joint account to pay unemployment insurance benefits, pursuant to the rules and regulations of the commissioner of labor. In addition, school districts and boards of cooperative educational services (BOCES), along with other municipal corporations, are specifically authorized to establish reserve funds for unemployment insurance payments (Gen. Mun. Law § 6-m; see **19:29**).

Additionally, there are other special rules related to state and local governments regarding their responsibilities under the Federal Unemployment Tax Act. For example, state and local governments are specifically granted the option to pay on the reimbursement method instead of being subject to federal unemployment payroll tax (26 USC § 3309(a)(2); see Lab. Law § 565(5)). Thus, districts only pay for the actual benefits sent to former employees, rather than the administrative costs of the program.

18:61. Are all school district employees eligible for unemployment benefits?

No; not all school district employees are eligible for unemployment benefits. The general rule is that employees of educational institutions are not allowed unemployment insurance benefits for periods between academic years or terms, or vacation periods, or holiday recess periods, provided an employee has a contract or a reasonable assurance that he or she will perform services in such capacity for both such academic years or terms or for the period immediately following such vacation period or holiday recess (Lab. Law § 590(10), (11); *In re Claim of Bicjan*, 219 A.D.2d 751 (3d Dep't 1995); see also *In re Claim of Hammond*, 252 A.D.2d 638 (3d Dep't 1998)).

However, at least one court has ruled that when a school district enters into a contract with an independent agency which is responsible for compiling a list of available substitute teachers and for selecting the teacher to be hired for each job, using the agency's own criteria to make the selection, the employee was eligible for unemployment insurance because the district could not give "reasonable assurance" of employment (*Makis v. Owego-Apalachin CSD*, 233 A.D.2d 743 (3d Dep't 1996)).

The courts have held that individual notices taken together with their collective bargaining agreement constitute a contract within the meaning of section 590(11) of the Labor Law, resulting in the claimant's ineligibility for unemployment benefits over the summer vacation (*In re Claim of La Mountain*, 51 N.Y.2d 318 (1980)). However, federal law permits states to adopt legislation to permit noninstructional employees to receive unemployment benefits during the summer months (26 USC § 3304). New York has not adopted such legislation.

In the event that an employee successfully sues a district for reinstatement and back pay, a district may not deduct unemployment payments from the award of back pay, even where the district paid the unemployment tax directly to the state Labor Department's Unemployment Insurance Division on behalf of the employee (*Appeal of Lessing*, 35 Educ. Dep't Rep. 116 (1995)).

18:62. How much insurance should a school board maintain for its district?

Since the risks of liability differ in all districts, depending on such issues as the number of students and employees, programs operated and other factors, there is no simple answer to this question that is appropriate for all school boards. It is possible that a board could go many years without being sued, or it could face several lawsuits in a short span of time. In addition, the possible cost to a district of a lawsuit varies greatly, in part, depending upon the type of lawsuit and the damages the plaintiff is seeking. Predicting the outcome of multiple lawsuits is even more difficult. Therefore, the New York State School Boards Association recommends that the board examine the risks faced by the district and consult with its school attorney and professionals in the insurance field to determine appropriate coverage for itself.

In most situations where a school board and/or its employees are sued, the school district has an obligation to defend and indemnify the school board members as long as the lawsuit arose out of the exercise of its powers or the performance of its duties (see **18:52–56**).

Thus, if the district has an insurance policy for school board members, commonly referred to as an errors and omissions or school board legal liability policy, and the limit of the insurance policy is too low to cover the costs involved in the settlement or verdict, the district still will retain these obligations. The district will have to find the funds to pay, even if it means raising taxes. In such a situation, a school board member is not obligated to pay amounts, out of his or her own pocket, above the district's policy limits.

18:63. Do the legal requirements on competitive bidding apply to the purchase of school insurance?

No. Section 103 of the General Municipal Law does not cover service contracts, and a school district is not obligated to submit its insurance coverage to competitive public bidding (*Lynd v. Heffernan*, 286 A.D. 597 (1955); *Surdell v. Oswego*, 91 Misc.2d 1041 (1977); Opn. St. Comp. 61-233).

However, the General Municipal Law requires that school districts adopt internal policies and procedures governing the procurement of professional services, such as insurance, so they are procured "in a manner so as to assure the prudent and economical use of public moneys in the best interests of the taxpayers" (Gen. Mun. Law § 104-b).

18:64. How may a school board secure information on the reliability or financial status of an insurance company with whom it wishes to do business?

A school board can receive information that would be helpful in evaluating an insurance company by consulting an insurance reference such as Best's Key Rating Guide, or the New York State Insurance Department, 25 Beaver Street, New York, N.Y. 10004-2319, 212-480-6400; or 200 Old Country Road, Mineola, N.Y. 11501, 516-248-5886; or the Web site, http://www.ins.state.ny.us.

18:65. May a school district act as a self-insurer for protection against claims?

Yes. A self-insurance fund may be established by any school district or board of cooperative educational services (BOCES) except one in a city with a population of 125,000 or more. This fund may be used to pay for almost any loss, claim, action or judgment for which the district is authorized or required to purchase or maintain insurance (Gen. Mun. Law § 6-n (1),(2)). The amount paid into such fund may not exceed the greater of $33,000, or 5 percent of the total district budget for the fiscal year (Gen. Mun. Law § 6-n(4); see **19:29**).

The law provides for oversight and regulation of municipal cooperative health insurance plans and self-funded health insurance consortia by the State Insurance Department and provides legal and regulatory requirements, safeguards, and other conditions for the plans (Ins. Law Art. 47).

18:66. Are school districts permitted to arrange group insurance programs for district employees?

Yes. Sections 1604(31-a), 1709(34-a) and 2503(10-a) of the Education Law permit the establishment of group insurance programs applying to teachers and other employees on life insurance, accident and health insurance, medical and surgical benefits, and hospital benefits (See also Gen. Mun. Law § 92-a). These sections of the law make it permissible, at the discretion of the board, to pay all or part of the cost of group insurance for school employees.

For unionized employees, most changes in benefits first must be negotiated with their bargaining agent (*Genesee-Livingston-Steuben-Wyoming BOCES*, 29 PERB ¶ 3065 (1996), *confirmed*, 30 PERB ¶ 7009 (Sup. Ct. Livingston County (1997)).

18:67. Can school boards legally withhold funds for the payment of various group insurance programs from employees' salaries?

Yes. School boards have the legal right to withhold, at the written request of individual employees, a portion of their salaries to pay group insurance premiums (§§ 1604(31-a), 1709(34-a), 2503 (10-a)).

18:68. Are school board members permitted to participate in school employee hospitalization and medical service plans?

Yes. Section 92-a(4) of the General Municipal Law permits school board members to participate in hospitalization and medical service plans, but they must pay the total cost for both themselves and their family members.

Retired school board members with at least 20 years of service in such a position are also eligible for these plans, as long as they pay the total cost (Gen. Mun. Law § 92-a(1-a)).

18:69. May a school board insure its students against personal accidents regardless of whether or not the district is responsible for the accident?

Yes. School boards may, at their discretion, purchase insurance against accidents to students occurring in school; on school grounds; during physical education classes; during intramural and interscholastic sports activities, while students are being transported between home and school in a school bus; and during school-sponsored trips. The premiums may be paid from district funds (§§ 1604(7-a), (7-b), 1709(8-a), (8-b)).

18:70. May a school require students to purchase insurance as a prerequisite for participation in a school program?

No. Although school boards are authorized to insure students against injuries sustained while participating in school programs, they may not lawfully pass on to their students the cost of such insurance or require the students to purchase it themselves. In addition, a school board may not use its staff to solicit the purchase of insurance, because this is considered an unconstitutional use of public moneys, property and services in aid of a private corporation (*Matter of Shapnek*, 3 Educ. Dep't Rep. 99 (1963); *Matter of Countryman*, 1 Educ. Dep't Rep. 538 (1960)).

18:71. Can a bidder on a school construction job be required to secure surety bonds from a particular insurance company or broker?

No. This would be a violation of section 2504 of the New York State Insurance Law.

19. Fiscal Management

Editor's Note: The New York State Education Department, through its office of General Educational Management Services, makes a number of guidance documents and worksheets available on its Web site that school board members, superintendents, business officials and others may find helpful in meeting the legal requirements described in this chapter. For a menu of these items, go to: http://www.emsc.nysed.gov/mgtserv/gensho.htm.

19:1. What is the fiscal year of a school district?

The fiscal year of a school district runs from July 1 to June 30 (see, for example, Educ. Law § 2515).

19:2. Who is legally responsible for the fiscal management of a school district?

The board of education constitutes the corporate body of the school district (Educ. Law §§ 1601, 1701, 2502), and as such, is legally responsible for fiscal management of the district (§§ 1604, 1709, 1804, 2503).

However, the Local Finance Law identifies the president of the school board as the chief fiscal officer and chief executive officer of the school district (Local Fin. Law § 2.00(5)(e), (5-a)(e)). Moreover, the Education Law identifies the superintendent of schools as the chief executive officer of the district (§ 1711(2)(a)).

The board may delegate certain fiscal responsibilities to the board president as chief fiscal officer, such as, for example, the issuance and/or renewal of certain notes (Local Fin. Law § 30), and to the superintendent as chief executive officer (see, for example, **19:44**). In addition, other school officers whom the board is required by law to appoint including, for instance, the treasurer and auditor, play a role in the fiscal management of the district (see **19:3**).

19:3. What other district officers play a role in the fiscal management of the district?

Except in union free school districts whose limits correspond with those of an incorporated village or city, or in districts wholly located in a first-class town or towns, the board must appoint a tax collector. Moreover, except in union free school districts whose limits correspond with those of an incorporated village or city, the board must appoint a treasurer

(§ 2130(4); 8 NYCRR § 170.2 (a)). The same person cannot hold these two offices (8 NYCRR § 170.2(a); see also **3:9, 3:14**.)

Each school board also must designate individuals to be responsible for purchasing and the certification of payrolls (8 NYCRR § 170.2 (b)).

A board may choose to appoint a deputy treasurer (§ 1720(2), see also **3:15**) and an internal auditor (§§ 1709(20-a), 2509(4); 8 NYCRR § 170.2(a); see also **3:20**).

19:4. What is a school board's primary fiscal responsibility?

The board must ensure that district expenditures do not exceed the budget approved by the voters or otherwise authorized by law (§ 1718; 8 NYCRR § 170.2 (k); see also **19:21**). The board must require the treasurer to provide it with a monthly bank reconciliation statement for all funds showing the cash balance on hand at the beginning of the month, receipts by source during the month, total disbursements during the month, and the cash balance on hand at the end of the month (8 NYCRR § 170.2(o)).

In addition, the treasurer is required to provide the board with a budget status statement, at least quarterly (monthly if budget transfers have been made since the last report), showing the status of the district's revenue accounts and appropriations accounts. At a minimum, the status report on the district's revenue accounts must show estimated revenues, amounts received as of the date of the report, and estimated revenues for the balance of the fiscal year. The status report on the district's appropriations accounts must show, at a minimum, original appropriations, transfers and adjustments, revised appropriations, expenditures to date, outstanding encumbrances, and unencumbered balances (8 NYCRR § 170.2(p)).

For additional detailed information about a school board's fiscal responsibilities, see *Fiscal Fitness: A Guide to Monitoring Your School District's Budget*, available online for download at http://www/nyssba.org /ScriptContent/VA_Custom/PDFs/fscal_fitness_online_book.pdf.

19:5. Are school boards required to publish an annual financial statement?

Yes. In union free, central and central high school districts, the board of education is required to publish an annual financial statement, including the items of expenditure in full, during either July or August. The law requires that the financial statement be published in one public newspaper that is "published" in the district. If no public newspaper is "published" in the district, then the district must use a newspaper "having general circulation" in the district. If no public newspaper is published in the district, and there is no newspaper having general circulation in the district, then the school district must post copies of the statement in five public places in the district

(§ 1721; see also 8 NYCRR § 170.2(s); *Appeal of Maxam*, 34 Educ. Dep't Rep. 289 (1994)).

In small city school districts, the board of education is required to annually publish its financial statement within three months of the close of the fiscal year. The statement must include "a full and complete statement of any bonds issued the preceding year for school purposes and the disposition made or to be made of the proceeds of such bonds." The law requires that this statement be published in at least one newspaper, or two if available, "having general circulation in the city school district," or in pamphlet form for general distribution, as prescribed by the commissioner. However, if the report is published in pamphlet form, then the board is required to publish notice in a newspaper or newspapers having general circulation in the district, indicating when and where the pamphlets will be made available (§ 2528).

In common school districts, the trustees present the financial statement at the annual meeting (see **4:13**).

In addition, the Governmental Accounting Standard Board (GASB) requires school districts to prepare annual financial statements that contain more detailed information about the financial condition of the school than that which is required in the annual financial statement published pursuant to state law. For more information about GASB, school board members should consult their school business official and/or visit the GASB Web site at http://www.gasb.org.

19:6. Are school districts required to file financial reports with the state comptroller?

Yes. Each school district must file an annual report of its financial condition on forms prescribed by the comptroller. The comptroller, in turn, will examine the report and issue a review to the school district (Gen. Mun. Law § 30). The district must then give public notice of the examination report, as set forth in law (Gen. Mun. Law §§ 34–5).

In preparing this annual report, districts must use the Uniform System of Accounts for School Districts prescribed by the state comptroller, including specific forms for recording the district's financial transactions (8 NYCRR § 170.2(f)). Refusing or neglecting to comply with the comptroller's directive to keep accounts as prescribed, within a reasonable time, constitutes a misdemeanor (Gen. Mun. Law § 36).

19:7. Are school districts subject to financial audits?

Yes. There are three types of audits that are conducted in school districts:
- *Internal Audits*. The Education Law provides for the establishment of an Office of Internal Auditor and the appointment of such auditor. The

auditor has the powers and duties of the school board with respect to allowing or rejecting all accounts, charges, claims or demands against the school district (see **19:3** and **19:8**). The purpose is to detect and correct any errors at the time the transactions occur (§§ 1709(20-a), 2526; 8 NYCRR § 170.2(a)).

- *State or Federal Audits.* Governmental agencies may review the records of a school district. The purpose is usually to determine that legal provisions prescribed by the government agency are being followed. For example, the General Municipal Law authorizes the state comptroller to examine the financial affairs of school districts (Art. 3, § 30 *et seq.*; see also *McCall v. Barrios-Paoli*, 93 N.Y.2d 99 (1999); see also **19:6**).

- *Independent Audits.* The Education Law and commissioner's regulations require that all school districts obtain an independent audit by an outside certified public accountant or public accountant. The purpose of this audit is to verify the accuracy of invoices, purchase orders, payroll, claims and contracts transacted by the school district during the school year. The independent auditor will review the documentary evidence and thus determine the district's compliance with all laws, policy, rules and regulations regarding the expenditure of money. A copy of the certified audit in a form prescribed by the commissioner of education must be furnished to the State Education Department (SED). School districts with fewer than eight teachers are not included in this requirement. The auditor must carry out the audit in conformity with SED's guidelines. The auditor's final report must be adopted by a board resolution, and a copy must be filed with the commissioner of education by October 1 of each year; for large city school districts, it must be filed by January 1 (§ 2116-a(3); 8 NYCRR § 170.2(r)).

In addition, in the City of Buffalo, the city comptroller has the power to examine the financial affairs of the city's public schools and to audit any and all school district accounts (Gen. Mun. Law § 34-a).

19:8. How does the appointment of an internal auditor affect a school board's fiscal responsibilities?

When a board of education appoints an internal auditor, the board gives up its auditing power. Thereafter, the internal auditor has the exclusive authority to audit accounts and charges and to allow or reject claims against the district. The internal auditor continues to have this power until and unless the board abolishes this position (§§ 1709(20-a), 2526; 8 NYCRR § 170.2(a)).

19:9. Must a school district's treasurer, deputy treasurer, tax collector and internal auditor be bonded?

Yes. The Education Law and commissioner's regulations require that the school district treasurer, deputy treasurer, tax collector and internal auditor execute and deliver to the board an "official undertaking." Bonds must be received by the board within 10 days after each officer is notified of appointment and before each assumes his or her duties. In districts under the jurisdiction of a district superintendent, the district superintendent also must approve the bonds (§§ 1720, 2130(5), 2527, 8 NYCRR § 170.2(d)).

The bond required must be in an amount fixed and approved by the school board. There is no law that specifies the amount of each bond. Treasurers, collectors and certain other public officers may be covered by a blanket bond (Pub. Off. Law § 11(2); see also **3:21**).

19:10. Can a school board accept gifts of money and/or real and personal property from private parties?

Yes. Section 1709(12) of the Education Law authorizes a board "[t]o take and hold for the use of the . . . schools or of any department of the same, any real estate transferred to it by gift, grant, bequest or devise, or any gift, legacy or annuity, of whatever kind, given or bequeathed to the . . . board, and apply the same, or the interest and proceeds thereof, according to the instructions of the donor or testator" (see also § 404(1)).

However, any gift accepted by a school district must be free of restrictions or requirements that are contrary to law or district policy. A district may refuse gifts outright or accept gifts on the condition that the school board will honor the donor's wishes if the board determines, in its discretion, that any restrictions or requirements attached to the gift are lawful, appropriate, and consistent with district policy.

Districts must invest gifts of money not required for immediate expenditure pursuant to General Municipal Law § 11 (Opn. St. Comp. I 94-15; see also **19:36–38**).

19:11. Can a school board accept a gift of money to be used for a specific program?

Yes, a school board may accept a gift of money to be used for a specific program, provided that the board does not delegate to a third party the decision of whether or not to offer the program in the first place and does not delegate any control over the manner in which the program is offered (*Appeal of DeMasi*, 18 Educ. Dep't Rep. 320 (1978)).

19:12. Can a school board accept and administer a gift to be held in trust for a school purpose?

Yes. Real and personal property "may be granted, conveyed, devised, bequeathed and given in trust and in perpetuity or otherwise to . . . any school district or its trustees or board of education, for the support and benefit of public schools . . . or for the support and benefit of any particular school therein" (§ 3701; see also Est. Powers & Trusts Law § 8-1.1 *et seq.*, which sets forth rules governing charitable trusts).

Districts must report to the commissioner of education the existence of any trusts held for school purposes by the board of education, by school district officers or employees, or by any other persons (that the district is aware of). Moreover, districts must transmit to the commissioner an "authenticated copy of every will, conveyance, instrument or paper embodying or creating the trust. . . ." (§ 3703).

A district may refuse gifts made in trust, or may accept such gifts subject to the condition that the school board will honor the donor's wishes if the board determines, in its discretion, that any restrictions or requirements attached to the trust are lawful, appropriate, and consistent with district policy.

Districts must invest trust funds pursuant to Estates, Powers and Trusts Law section 11-2.2 (Opn. St. Comp. I 94-15).

19:13. Can a school board accept and administer a gift to be held in trust for awarding scholarships?

Yes. Section 1709(12-a) of the Education Law authorizes a board of education "[t]o take and hold in trust for the purpose of awarding scholarships in [the] schools any real estate transferred to it by gift, grant, bequest or devise, or any gift, legacy or annuity, of whatever kind, given or bequeathed to said board and apply the same, or the interest and proceeds thereof, according to the instructions of the donor or testator."

As with other gifts, trusts accepted and/or administered by a school district must be free of restrictions or requirements that are contrary to law or district policy. For instance, Title IX of the Federal Educational Amendment of 1972 prohibits school districts from engaging in practices or activities that discriminate on the basis of sex (20 USC § 1681 *et seq.*; see also **14:20**). Therefore, districts should not accept or administer a trust that by its terms provides scholarships only to male or female students.

However, a trust established to provide scholarships for students of a particular gender does not necessarily violate the law. New York's highest court has ruled that "gender restrictions in private trusts do not necessarily violate public policy" [emphasis added]. Moreover, such discrimination by private parties does not violate the Equal Protection Clause of the U.S.

Constitution in the absence of action by public officials in furtherance of the discrimination (*Matter of Wilson*, 59 N.Y.2d 461 (1983)).

In fact, the New York State Court of Appeals specifically ruled that a testamentary trust that creates a scholarship fund solely for the benefit of male students may be reformed by naming a private trustee in place of the school board, if the school board is "unwilling or unable to fulfill the discriminatory terms of the trust." In the same decision, the court also ruled that where a testamentary trust established a scholarship open only to male students certified by the superintendent of schools as having the highest grades in certain subjects, and the superintendent refused to play a role in furtherance of the discriminatory purpose of the trust by certifying the required information, the trust could be reformed by allowing students to apply directly to the bank named as the trustee and to themselves submit the required grade information (*Wilson*).

19:14. May a school district make contributions from district funds to a charitable organization or a scholarship fund?

No. This would be considered an improper gift of public funds under Article VIII, section 1 of the New York State Constitution, which prohibits the disbursement, gift or loan of public moneys and resources for the benefit of private groups or individuals (see, for example, 29 Opn. St. Comp. 154 (1973); see also *Appeal of LaLonde*, 31 Educ. Dep't Rep. 408 (1992)).

19:15. May school boards in New York State legally pay dues to the New York State School Boards Association?

Yes. This is authorized by section 1618 of the Education Law.

19:16. May a school district pay for the expenses incurred by members of its school board and district employees in attending a convention of the New York State School Boards Association or other conferences?

Yes. The General Municipal Law authorizes municipalities, including school districts, to permit and pay for the attendance of board members, officers and staff at conferences. The term conference includes conventions, conferences or seminars for the benefit of the municipality (Gen. Mun. Law § 77-b(1)(c), (3); see also *Matter of Cappa*, 18 Educ. Dep't Rep. 373 (1978)). The authorization must be by a board resolution adopted prior to attendance and entered in the board minutes, or the board may delegate the power to authorize attendance at conferences to any executive officer (Gen. Mun. Law § 77-b(2); see also Opn. St. Comp. No. 93-12 (1993)).

In addition, the Education Law provides that school district officers, including school board members, may be reimbursed for "expenses actually and necessarily incurred in the performance of their official duties" (§ 2118; see also § 1604(27)).

19:17. Are there any restrictions on the reimbursement of expenses associated with attendance at conferences or meetings?

Yes. School board members are not entitled to reimbursement "for expenses incurred in traveling to meetings at which the full attendance of the board is required or where the meeting convenes at the official place of duty of the board" (Opn. St. Comp. 80-138 (1980)).

Moreover, it is considered improper to reimburse district officers and employees for the cost of alcoholic beverages consumed at an otherwise authorized meeting or conference (Opn. St. Comp. 82-213 (1982)).

19:18. Is a school board responsible for providing for the protection and supervision of the financial affairs of student clubs and extracurricular activities?

Yes. An "extraclassroom" activity encompasses any organization within the district that is conducted by students and that receives no financial support from district voters or the board of education (8 NYCRR § 172.1). Part 172 of the commissioner's regulations provides that the school board of each school district outside New York City that has an educational program beyond grade six not only must make rules and regulations for the conduct, operation and maintenance of extraclassroom activities, but also for the safeguarding, accounting and audit of all moneys received and derived from such activities (8 NYCRR § 172.2; see also *Appeal of Keely*, 14 Educ. Dep't Rep. 396 (1975); and *Appeal of Vagnarelli*, 20 Educ. Dep't Rep. 566 (1981)). At a minimum, such rules and regulations must include:
- The method to be followed in establishing an organization.
- The records of receipts and expenditures to be maintained and the reports to be made at least quarterly to the board of education (see also *Appeal of Hall and Cooper*, 32 Educ. Dep't Rep. 377 (1992)).
- A provision that the authority to expend moneys shall be distinct and separate from the custody of those moneys.
- A provision that an independent and impartial audit of the accounts shall be made at least annually in conjunction with the audit of the district records.
- The method of disposing of funds of defunct organizations (8 NYCRR § 172.3).

The school board must direct that the moneys received from the conduct, operation or maintenance of any extracurricular activity be deposited with an official designated by the board as the treasurer of the extraclassroom activity fund (8 NYCRR § 172.4). Extraclassroom activity funds held in the custody of a school district treasurer must be invested pursuant to General Municipal Law § 11 (Opn. St. Comp. 94-15).

For additional detailed information, see "The Safeguarding, Accounting and Auditing of Extraclassroom Activity Funds: Finance Pamphlet 2, Revised 1999," available online via the State Education Department's Office of Educational Management Services Web site, http://www.emsc.nysed.gov/mgtserv/extrclas_old.pdf.

Cash Management

19:19. Must a school board designate a bank or trust company for the deposit of school funds?

Yes. The school board must designate at least one bank or trust company for the deposit of all funds received by the treasurer and collector, by a resolution adopted by board majority (see § 2129; Gen. Mun. Law § 10(2)(a); 8 NYCRR §§ 170.1(a), 170.2(c); see **3:17**).

The resolution must specify the maximum amount that may be kept on deposit in each particular bank or trust company, subject to change at any time by further board resolution (Gen. Mun. Law § 10(2)(a)).

Deposits in excess of the amount insured under the Federal Deposit Insurance Act (FDIC) must be secured in accordance with the provisions of General Municipal Law section 10(3).

19:20. What are the major accounting funds maintained by school districts?

As defined by the Uniform System of Accounts for School Districts, the general fund is the principle fund of the school district and includes all operations not required to be recorded in other funds.

Special aid funds include the following:

- School store fund — accounts for revenues and expenditures of stores maintained and operated by school boards for the sale of textbooks and other school supplies (Note: Stores operated by student organizations are accounted for in the extraclassroom activity fund; see **19:18**).
- School lunch fund — accounts for revenues and expenditures of the school district's food service program.
- Insurance reserve fund — accounts for appropriation and expenditures in connection with a district's self-insurance program, if one has been established.
- Special aid fund — provides accounts for special projects or programs supported in whole or in part by federal funds and/or state-funded grants, except capital projects.

- Public library fund — records transactions of a library established and sponsored by the school district. The Education Law requires that money received for library purposes must be kept in a separate fund (§ 259(1)).
- Capital project fund — accounts for capital improvements and acquisitions.
- Debt-service fund — accounts for the payment of interest and principal on long-term debt.
- Trust and agency funds — account for assets held in a trustee capacity and/or as agent for individuals, private organizations, other governmental units and/or other funds. These include agency funds, expendable trust funds and nonexpendable trust funds (principle must be preserved).

19:21. Is a school board authorized to spend district funds in excess of the budget appropriations approved by the voters?

Yes, but only under certain limited circumstances. Section 1718 (1) of the Education Law expressly provides that "no school board shall incur a district liability in excess of the amount appropriated by a district meeting unless the board is specially authorized by law to incur such liability." Section 2023 provides such authorization in the case of ordinary contingent expenses, including but not limited to, teachers' salaries and the purchase of library books (see also § 2022(5); *Appeal of Clark*, 37 Educ. Dep't Rep. 386 (1998); Opn. St. Comp. 81-401 (1981); **19:45–55**).

In addition, grants in aid received from the state and federal governments for specific purposes, other state grants in aid identified by the commissioner of education for general use as specified by the school board, gifts which are required to be expended for particular objects or purposes, and insurance proceeds that are used to repair or replace lost, stolen, damaged or destroyed real or personal property, may be appropriated by board resolution at any time for such objects and purposes (§§ 1718(2) 3713; see also *Appeal of Leman*, 39 Educ. Dep't Rep. 35 (1999); *Appeal of Cook*, 32 Educ. Dep't Rep. 71 (1992); *Matter of Cappa and Motoyama*, 11 Educ. Dep't Rep. 128 (1971)).

19:22. Must vouchers be submitted with bills and invoices to a school board or internal a editor for approval before payment?

Yes. With few exceptions, a claim against a school district may not be paid unless an itemized voucher has been presented to the school board and audited and approved (§§ 1604(13), 1724, 2524). Payment before board approval is permissible, however, under certain circumstances (see **19:23–24**).

In school districts with an internal auditor, the responsibility for auditing, rejecting or allowing any and all claims rests with the auditor, not with the school board (§§ 1709(20-a), 2523(2), 2525, 2526(2); see **19:8**).

19:23. May a school board authorize the payment of certain claims against the school district in advance of audit and approval by the board of education or internal auditor?

Yes. A school board may authorize, by resolution, the payment in advance of audit of claims for public utility services (including electric, gas, water, sewer and telephone services), postage and freight, and express charges. All such claims must be presented at the next regular meeting for audit, and the claimant and the officer incurring or approving the claim are jointly and severally liable for any amount not allowed by the school board (§§ 1724(3), 2524(2)).

19:24. May a school district's treasurer ever issue payment of an invoice before the board's approval?

Yes. The Education Law and commissioner's regulations authorize boards of education to establish petty cash funds and to designate school district officers and employees to pay out of a petty cash fund, in advance of the board's authorization, properly itemized bills for materials, supplies or services furnished to the school district under conditions calling for immediate payment to the vendor upon delivery of such materials, supplies or services (§§ 1604(26), 1709(29); 8 NYCRR § 170.4(d)).

19:25. Must a school board adopt rules for using petty cash funds?

Yes, upon its establishment (§§ 1604(26), 1709(29)). Such rules and regulations must designate the school district's officers and employees who will administer and be responsible for petty cash funds and also must prescribe the method of record keeping (8 NYCRR § 170.4(a)(1), (3)). In addition, no such fund may exceed $100 at any one time in school districts with eight or more teachers, or $5 in districts employing fewer than eight teachers. Deposits to petty cash funds may not exceed the amount paid out from the fund (8 NYCRR § 170.4(b), (c)).

Petty cash funds provided for buildings, cafeterias, school stores or other activities that do not operate during July and/or August must be closed out by June 30 (8 NYCRR § 170.4(e)).

19:26. May a school district's checks be signed with a facsimile signature, reproduced by a check signer or other machine?

Yes. When authorized by board resolution, district checks may be signed by facsimile signature of the treasurer and other district officers whose signatures may be required (§§ 1720(2), 2523(2); see also Gen. Constr. Law § 46; Formal Opinion of Counsel No. 83, 1 Educ. Dep't Rep. 786 (1952); 8 Opn. St. Comp. 110, No. 5256 (1952); Opn. St. Comp. 79-665 (1979)).

Where a facsimile signature is used, however, it should be affixed under the supervision and control of the person whose signature it represents (25 Opn. St. Comp. 79 (1969); 10 Opn. St. Comp. 326 (1954)).

19:27. May a school district accept payment by credit card?

Yes. Section 5 of the General Municipal Law authorizes school districts, upon passage of a board resolution, to contract with financing agencies or card issuers for the acceptance of credit cards as a means of payment of fines, taxes, fees, charges, and other financial obligations and amounts owed to the district (Gen. Mun. Law § 5).

Reserve Funds

19:28. What is a reserve fund?

A *reserve fund* is a separate account established by a school district to finance the cost of various objects or purposes of the district. Reserve funds can be thought of as self-imposed savings accounts for particular purposes into which funds will be deposited over a period of time until the desired amount is accrued.

19:29. What kinds of reserve funds are school districts authorized to establish?

In addition to a retirement contribution reserve funds (Gen. Mun. Law § 6-r; see **Introduction**), districts may establish the following:

Reserve Funds for Objects and Purposes for Which a District May Issue Bonds (§ 3651)

Section 3651 of the Education Law authorizes school districts to establish reserve funds to finance any object or purpose for which the district may issue bonds pursuant to the Local Finance Law (Educ. Law § 3651(1)). Any interest earned or capital gains realized on the reserve fund deposits or investments must accrue to the fund. The separate identity of each reserve fund established pursuant to this section of law must be maintained regardless of whether the assets consist of cash or investments, or both (§ 3651(2)). However, the moneys in such funds need not be deposited in separate bank accounts (Laws of 1996, Ch. 140, § 3).

No school district located wholly or partly within the Adirondack Park, which has within its boundaries state lands subject to taxation assessed at more than 30 percent of the aggregate taxable assessed valuation of the real property located in the district, may establish this type of reserve fund, unless upon the recommendation of the commissioner of education, the state comptroller consents to the establishment of the reserve (§ 3651(8)(b)). Other characteristics:

- Pays the cost of any object or purpose for which bonds may be issued.
- Established through voter approval (§ 3651(1)); voter approval is not required in city school districts with a population of at least 125,000 inhabitants (§ 3651(9)).
- Funds spent through voter approval (§ 3651(3)); voter approval is not required in city school districts with a population of at least 125,000 inhabitants (§ 3651(9)).
- All or part of funds may be transferred to any other reserve funds established under this section, with voter approval (§ 3651(4)); voter approval is not required in city school districts with a population at least 125,000 inhabitants (§ 3651(9)).
- If the voters determine that the reserve fund is no longer needed, the board of education may liquidate the fund by applying the proceeds to any outstanding bonded indebtedness of the district and applying the remaining balance, if any, to reduce the annual tax levy, subject to certain limitations set forth in law (§ 3651(5)).
- Accounted for in the capital project fund (see also **19:31–34**).

Tax Certiorari Reserve (§ 3651(1-a))

- Pays judgments and claims resulting from tax certiorari proceedings under Article 7 of the Real Property Tax Law.
- Amount of money held in this reserve may not exceed amount "reasonably necessary" to pay anticipated judgments and claims arising out of tax certiorari proceedings.
- Established without voter approval (Opn. St. Comp. 89-17).
- Funds may be spent without voter approval (Opn. St. Comp. 89-17).
- Accounted for in the general fund. Any moneys in this reserve fund which are not used to pay tax certiorari claims and judgments for the tax roll in the year the moneys are deposited to the fund, and which will not reasonably be required to pay such judgments and claims, must be returned to the general fund no later than July 1 four years after the deposit of such moneys into the reserve fund (see also *Appeal of Goldin*, 43 Educ. Dep't Rep. ___, dec. no. 14,904 (2003)).

Reserve Fund for Uncollected Taxes (applies only to small city school districts) (§ 3651(1-b))

- Offsets amount of uncollected real property taxes due and owing to a small city school district, where the city or county is not required, pursuant to Real Property Tax Law section 1332, to pay the amount of unpaid taxes to the treasurer of the school district.

- The amount of the reserve cannot be less than the estimated amount of unpaid taxes for the fiscal year for which the budget is being prepared. Such estimate must be based on the ratio of unpaid taxes during the last completed fiscal year compared to the principal amount of the school district's tax levy for the last completed fiscal year. For example, if 5 percent of the total amount of property taxes remained unpaid during the last completed fiscal year, then the district may establish a reserve fund for uncollected taxes based on an estimate of 5 percent of the total tax levy for the fiscal year for which the budget is being prepared.
- Established without voter approval.
- Funds may be spent without voter approval.
- Accounted for in the general fund.

Property Loss Reserve and Liability Reserve (§ 1709(8-c))

- Separate reserve funds must be established for property loss and for liability claims. The separate identity of each fund must be maintained, whether its assets consist of cash or investments, or both.
- These two types of reserve funds pay for property loss and liability claims incurred.
- Once established, such a reserve fund may not be reduced (other than by payments for losses for which the reserve was established) below the estimated amount necessary to cover unsettled claims or suits.
- The portion of reserve funds not allocated for unsettled claims or suits may be used, upon dissolution of a district's self-insurance plan, to pay insurance premiums for policies purchased to insure subsequent losses in areas previously self-insured.
- Established without voter approval.
- Funds may be spent without voter approval for the purpose for which the reserve fund was established, but may not be spent without voter approval for any other purpose.
- Accounted for separate and apart from all other funds of the school district in the same manner as provided in General Municipal Law section 6-c(10).
- Funds may be invested pursuant to General Municipal Law section 11 (§ 1723-a).

Note: Total funds in of the property loss reserve and liability reserve may not exceed 3 percent of the annual budget or $15,000, whichever is greater.

Reserve for Tax Reduction (§§ 1604(36), 1709(37))

- Returns to taxpayers, over a period of not more than 10 years, the proceeds from the sale of school district real property, where the proceeds are not needed to pay any debts.
- Established without voter approval.
- Funds spent without voter approval.
- Funds may be invested pursuant to General Municipal Law section 11 (§§ 1604-a, 1723-a).
- Accounted for in the general fund.

Note: Revenue from the sale of real property purchased with obligations that are still outstanding at the time of the sale must be deposited in a mandatory reserve for debt service pursuant to General Municipal Law section 6-l (see the discussion on page 724 on Mandatory Reserve for Debt Service herein). However, revenue in excess of the amount needed to retire the debt may be used for any lawful school purpose (Opn. St. Comp. 86-26 (1986); see also 29 Opn. St. Comp. 126, Opn. 73-792 (1973)).

Repair Reserve Fund (Gen. Mun. Law § 6-d)

- Covers repairs to capital improvements or equipment of a type not recurring annually or at shorter intervals (Gen. Mun. Law § 6-d(3)(a); see also Opn. St. Comp. 84-8; 26 Opn. St. Comp. 225 (1970)). Funds in the repair reserve fund also may be appropriated to a reserve fund established pursuant to Education Law section 3651 (Gen. Mun. Law § 6-d(3)(d)).
- Established without voter approval, but may not be funded without voter approval (Opn. St. Comp. 81-401 (1981)).
- Funded by budgetary appropriation or other revenues not required by law to be paid into any other fund or account (Gen. Mun. Law § 6-d(1)).
- Funds spent without voter approval. Expenditures in non-emergency situations require a public hearing, following publication of a notice in the official newspaper(s) or other newspaper designated by the district, at least five days in advance of the public hearing, describing the purpose of the proposed expenditure and the time and place of the public hearing (Opn. St. Comp. 85-20). In emergency situations expenditures from the fund may be authorized without a public hearing by a two-thirds vote of the school board. One-half the amount expended in an emergency situation must be repaid to the fund during the next fiscal year, and the remainder must be repaid to the fund by the end of the second fiscal year following the fiscal year in which the moneys were expended (Gen. Mun. Law § 6-d(2)).

- Accounted for separate and apart from all other funds of the school district in the same manner as provided in General Municipal Law section 6-c(10) (Gen. Mun. Law § 6-d(4)).
- Funds may be invested pursuant to General Municipal Law section 11 (Gen. Mun. Law § 6-d(4)).
- Any interest or capital gains on moneys deposited or invested accrue to the fund (Gen. Mun. Law § 6-d(4)).
- The members of the board of education commit a misdemeanor if they authorize a withdrawal from or expend money withdrawn from a repair reserve fund for any purpose not authorized by law (Gen. Mun. Law § 6-d(6)).

Workers' Compensation Reserve (Gen. Mun. Law § 6-j)

- Pays for compensation benefits and other expenses authorized by article 2 of the Workers' Compensation Law and for payment of expenses of administrating this self-insurance program (Gen. Mun. Law § 6-j(4)).
- Established without voter approval (Gen. Mun. Law § 6-j(1)).
- Funded by budgetary appropriation and such other sums as may legally be appropriated (Gen. Mun. Law 6-j(3)).
- Funds spent without voter approval.
- Accounted for separate and apart from all other funds of the school district in the same manner as provided in General Municipal Law section 6-c(10) (Gen. Mun. Law § 6-j(3)).
- If a school district ceases to be a self-insurer for its workers' compensation claims, the board of education may transfer any amounts in the reserve fund in excess of that which is needed to satisfy accrued and contingent claims to any other reserve fund authorized under Article 2 of the General Municipal Law, or to any reserve fund authorized under Education Law section 3651 (Gen. Mun. Law § 6-j(6)). Similarly, at the end of any fiscal year, the board may transfer funds in excess of amounts needed to satisfy existing obligations and pending workers compensation claims to any other fund authorized under Article 2 of the General Municipal Law, or to any reserve fund authorized under Education Law section 3651, and/or may apply all or part of the excess funds to the budgetary appropriation for the next fiscal year (Gen. Mun. Law § 6-j(5)).

Mandatory Reserve for Debt Service (Gen. Mun. Law § 6-l)

- Used for retiring outstanding obligations remaining at the time of the sale of district property that was financed by obligations (Gen. Mun. Law § 6-l(3)).
- Established without voter approval.

- Funded with the proceeds from the sale of district property. However, the proceeds of the sale in excess of the amount needed to retire the outstanding obligations on the property sold may be used by the school district for any lawful purpose (Gen. Mun. Law § 6-l(2)).
- Funds spent without voter approval.
- Accounted for in the debt service fund in the manner specified in Gen. Mun. Law § 6-l(4)).
- The separate identity of the fund must be maintained regardless of whether its assets consist of cash or investments, or both (Gen. Mun. Law § 6-l(6)).
- Funds may be invested pursuant to General Municipal Law section 11 (Gen. Mun. Law § 6-l(6)).
- Any interest or capital gains on moneys deposited or invested accrue to the fund (Gen. Mun. Law § 6-l(6)).
- School board members commit a misdemeanor if they authorize a withdrawal from or expend money withdrawn from a mandatory reserve fund for any purpose not authorized by law (Gen. Mun. Law § 6-l(7)).

Unemployment Insurance Payment Reserve Fund (Gen. Mun. Law § 6-m)

- Pays for the cost of reimbursement to the State Unemployment Insurance Fund for payments made to claimants (Gen. Mun. Law § 6-m(4)).
- Established without voter approval.
- Funded by budgetary appropriation, with funds from other reserve funds authorized under Article 2 of the General Municipal Law by resolution subject to "permissive referendum," and with such other funds as may be legally appropriated by the board of education (Gen. Mun. Law § 6-m(2)).
- Funds spent without voter approval.
- Accounted for in the general fund. However, the separate identity of the fund must be maintained regardless of whether its assets consist of cash or investments, or both (Gen. Mun. Law § 6-m(3)).
- Funds may be invested pursuant to General Municipal Law section 11 (Gen. Mun. Law § 6-m(3)).
- Any interest or capital gains on moneys deposited or invested accrue to the fund (Gen. Mun. Law § 6-j(3)).
- If a school district that has established an unemployment reserve fund later decides to cease being liable for payments in lieu of contributions, the board of education may transfer any moneys in the reserve fund in excess of the amount needed to satisfy all pending claims to any other reserve fund authorized under Article 2 of the General Municipal Law, or to any reserve fund authorized under

Education Law section 3651 (Gen. Mun. Law § 6-m(6)). Similarly, at the end of any fiscal year, the board may transfer funds in excess of amounts needed to satisfy existing obligations and pending unemployment claims to any other fund authorized under Article 2 of the General Municipal Law, or to any reserve fund authorized under Education Law section 3651, and/or may apply all or part of the excess funds to the budgetary appropriation for the next fiscal year (Gen. Mun. Law § 6-m(5)).

Insurance Reserve (Gen. Mun. Law § 6-n)

- Pays liability, casualty and other types of losses, except those incurred for which certain types of insurance may be purchased, such as life insurance, accident and health insurance. Moreover, a school district may not expend moneys from the insurance reserve fund for any type of claim for which the district has established a reserve under any other provision of law (Gen. Mun. Law § 6-n(2)(a)).

- The board of education may pass a resolution to discontinue another reserve fund that previously was established to cover the same types of claims for which moneys may be expended from an insurance reserve fund and may transfer any unexpended balance from such other reserve fund to the insurance reserve fund, subject to any liabilities incurred or accrued against the other reserve fund (Gen. Mun. Law § 6-n(2)(b)).

- Established by board approval.

- Funded by budgetary appropriation, with funds from other reserve funds authorized under Article 2 of the General Municipal Law by resolution subject to permissive referendum, and with such other funds as may be legally appropriated by the board of education (Gen. Mun. Law § 6-n(3)).

- Funds spent through board approval.

- Accounted for separate and apart from all other funds of the school district, in the manner set forth in General Municipal Law section 6-n(6).

- Funds may be invested pursuant to General Municipal Law section 11 (Gen. Mun. Law § 6-n(5)).

- Any interest or capital gains on moneys deposited or invested accrue to the fund (Gen. Mun. Law § 6-n(5)).

- If the board of education decides that it no longer needs an insurance reserve fund established under this section of law, the board may transfer the moneys remaining in the fund to any other reserve fund (that is comprised of moneys raised on the same tax base as the moneys in the reserve fund) authorized under Article 2 of the General Municipal Law or by Education Law section 3651, subject to any liabilities incurred or accrued against the fund (Gen. Mun. Law § 6-n(13)).

- School board members commit a misdemeanor if they authorize a withdrawal from or expend money withdrawn from the insurance reserve fund for any purpose not authorized by law (Gen. Mun. Law § 6-n(12)).

Note: The annual contribution to the insurance reserve may not exceed $33,000 or 5 percent of the budget, whichever is greater (Gen. Mun. Law § 6-n(4)). Settled or compromised claims up to $25,000 may be paid without judicial approval (Gen. Mun. Law § 6-n(11)).

Employee Benefit Accrued Liability Reserve Fund (Gen. Mun. Law § 6-p)

- Pays the cash payment of the monetary value of accrued and accumulated but unused sick leave, personal leave, holiday leave, vacation time, time allowances granted in lieu of overtime compensation and any other forms of payment of accrued but unliquidated time earned by employees (Gen. Mun. Law § 6-p(7)). However, a school district may not make an expenditure from this reserve fund for any employee benefit for which the district has established a reserve fund under any other provision of law (Gen. Mun. Law § 6-p(2)(a)).
- The board of education may pass a resolution to discontinue another reserve fund that previously was established to cover the same types of claims for which moneys may be expended from an employee benefit accrued liability reserve fund and may transfer any unexpended balance from such other reserve fund to the employee benefit accrued liability reserve fund, subject to any liabilities incurred or accrued against the other reserve fund (Gen. Mun. Law § 6-p(2)(b)).
- Established without voter approval.
- Funded by budgetary appropriation, with funds from other reserve funds authorized under article 2 of the General Municipal Law by resolution subject to permissive referendum, and with such other funds as may be legally appropriated by the board of education (Gen. Mun. Law § 6-p(3)).
- Funds may be spent without voter approval.
- Accounted for separate and apart from all other funds of the school district in the manner set forth in Gen. Mun. Law § 6-p(5).
- Funds may be invested pursuant to General Municipal Law section 11 (Gen. Mun. Law § 6-p(4)).
- Any interest or capital gains on moneys deposited or invested accrue to the fund (Gen. Mun. Law § 6-p(4)).

- If the board of education decides that it no longer needs this reserve fund, the board may transfer the moneys remaining in the fund to any other reserve fund (that is comprised of moneys raised on the same tax base as the moneys in the reserve fund) authorized under article 2 of the General Municipal Law or by Education Law section 3651, subject to any liabilities incurred or accrued against the fund (Gen. Mun. Law § 6-p(9)).
- School board members commit a misdemeanor if they authorize a withdrawal from or expend money withdrawn from the employee benefit accrued liability reserve fund for any purpose not authorized by law (Gen. Mun. Law § 6-p(8)).

Nuclear Facility Tax Stabilization Reserve (unconsolidated law)

- May be established by the board of education in any school district in which a nuclear-powered electric generating facility is located.
- Funded by budgetary appropriation, except that such appropriation is limited to the amount of annual tax payments or payments in lieu of taxes (PILOTs) made by the nuclear-powered generating facility to the school district in excess of the tax payments or PILOTs paid to the school district by that same facility during the fiscal year prior to the fiscal year in which the reserve fund was established (excluding tax payments or PILOTs made by nuclear-powered generating facilities that were exempt from taxation pursuant to Public Authorities Law § 1012).
- Moneys in the fund must be deposited and secured in the manner provided by section 10 of the general municipal law.
- Funds may be invested pursuant to General Municipal Law section 11; any interest earned or capital gain realized on the moneys so invested must accrue to and become a part of the fund.
- Funds may be expended to lessen or prevent any projected increase in the amount of the real property tax levy needed to finance the eligible portion of the school district budget for the next fiscal year, as disclosed in the annual budget that is presented to the voters for approval.
- The board president must account for this fund separate and apart from all other funds of the school district, and must, within 60 days after the end of the fiscal year, provide the board of education and the state comptroller a detailed report of the operation and condition of the fund during the preceding fiscal year.
- If the board of education decides that it no longer needs this reserve fund, the board may transfer the moneys remaining in the fund to any other reserve fund authorized by Education Law section 3651, or to the general fund of the school district that is comprised of moneys

raised on the same tax base as the moneys in the reserve fund. However, prior to discontinuance of the fund, the school board president must certify to the entire board of education that such reserve funds are no longer needed.

- School board members are deemed trustees of the fund and commit a misdemeanor if they willfully and knowingly authorize a withdrawal from or expend money withdrawn from, the nuclear facility tax stabilization reserve fund for any purpose not authorized by law (Laws of 2001, Ch. 202).

19:30. Is voter approval required to establish reserve funds?

Some reserve funds require voter approval to be established (see **19:29**).

The proposition to establish a reserve fund pursuant to Education Law section 3651 must specify the purpose, the ultimate amount, the probable term and the source from which the funds will be obtained (§ 3651(1)(b); see also *Appeal of Kackmeister*, 40 Educ. Dep't Rep. 577 (2001); *Appeal of Goldin*, 43 Educ. Dep't Rep. __, dec. no. 14, 904 (2003)).

The following is a suggested resolution that may be used to establish a particular capital reserve fund:

> RESOLVED, that the Board of Education of the Blanktown Central School District hereby is authorized and directed to establish a reserve fund to be known as the Garage Construction Reserve Fund, which shall be for a part of the construction of a school bus garage. The ultimate amount of such fund shall be $25,000, of which amount there shall be raised annually by installments by taxes levied on the taxable property of the district the sum of $5,000 for five successive years.

The details of each resolution should be different in order to cover the particular items to be included in the establishment of each fund. A school district attorney should be consulted on the exact wording.

19:31. Is voter approval required to spend money from a reserve fund established under Education Law section 3651?

Yes, except where specifically exempted by law. For example, moneys may be spent from a tax certiorari reserve without voter approval (§ 3651(1-a), see **19:29**).

According to the commissioner of education, Education Law section 3651 mandates that "each and every expenditure must be authorized separately by the voters, so that the voters can evaluate the expenditure in light of circumstances at the time each expenditure is to be made."

Moreover, "expenditures from reserve funds should be for the specific purpose(s) for which the fund was established, and the proposition to approve the expenditure should explicitly state the purpose of the proposed expenditure (§ 3651(3)). Although the stated purpose(s) of a reserve fund may be somewhat broad, the spending authorization should be specific and give the voters adequate notice of the particular intended use of the funds." (*Appeal of Kackmeister*, 40 Educ. Dep't Rep. 577 (2001)).

19:32. May a school district make deposits into a reserve, that in the aggregate, exceed the maximum amount of the reserve authorized by the voters, as long as the amount in reserve at any one time does not exceed the maximum?

No. The total of the funds paid into the reserve over the lifetime of the fund cannot exceed the maximum amount authorized by the voters.

Suppose, for example, that the voters authorize a board of education to establish a $1 million reverse fund by levying a tax of $200,000 each year for five years and depositing this amount into the reserve. Further suppose that once the reserve fund reaches the desired $1 million mark, the district appropriates $600,000 from the fund, leaving $400,000 in the reserve.

Could the district replenish the $600,000 that it appropriated, as long as it stays within the $1 million maximum authorized by the voters? No. The commissioner found that this practice violates Education Law section 3651 inasmuch as it amounts to an unauthorized "rolling reserve" (*Appeal of Kackmeister*, 40 Educ. Dep't Rep. 577 (2001); *Appeal of Goldin*, 43 Educ. Dep't Rep. __, dec. no. 14,904 (2003)).

19:33. May a school district add moneys to a section 3651 reserve fund after the expiration of its "probable term"?

No. When a district submits a proposition to the voters asking for permission to establish a reserve fund, the proposition must state the "probable term" of the reserve (see **19:30**) in order to apprise the electorate of the length of time the reserve will continue in existence.

If, after establishing a reserve fund, a district decides that the probable term should be extended, the district can submit a new proposition to the voters asking for permission to extend the probable term, provided that any such proposition is submitted to the voters prior to the expiration of the original probable term approved by the voters.

"[O]nce the established probable term has expired, the reserve fund is essentially defunct except as a vehicle to hold the accumulated funds. No more funds may be added, no amendment can be made to the terms of the fund, and it simply must be spent down by appropriate propositions to expend the accumulated balance" (*Appeal of Kackmeister*, 40 Educ. Dep't Rep. 577 (2001); see also *Appeal of Goldin*, 43 Educ. Dep't Rep. ___, dec. no. 14,904 (2003)).

19:34. May a school district appropriate moneys from a section 3651 reserve fund during the same fiscal year in which the reserve was created?

No. "[A] reserve fund is intended as a mechanism to reserve and accumulate funds over time for a future project, not as a vehicle to finance a current project or current needs. There is no sense whatsoever in depositing money received from current tax levies into a reserve fund, and then conveying the money via an interfund transfer to the district's capital fund to expend the money during the same fiscal year. If there is money from current tax levies available for such current needs, the money should simply be deposited directly into the capital fund for expenditure" (*Appeal of Kackmeister*, 40 Educ. Dep't Rep. 577 (2001)).

19:35. Are school districts authorized to transfer excess funds from certain reserve funds?

Yes. Money remaining in the workers' compensation, unemployment insurance reserve, and insurance reserve funds, after required payments are made, may be transferred to certain reserve funds or applied to the budget appropriation for the next fiscal year (Gen. Mun. Law §§ 6-j(5), 6-m(5), 6-n(13)).

Investment of School District Funds

19:36. May the school board temporarily invest school district funds that are not required for immediate expenditure?

Yes. A school district may temporarily invest district funds that are not required for immediate expenditure in a number of ways, including:

- In special time-deposit accounts or in certificates of deposit issued by banks or trust companies and guaranteed under the provisions of the Federal Deposit Insurance Act, or otherwise secured pursuant to section 10(3) of the General Municipal Law (Gen. Mun. Law 11(2)).
- In obligations guaranteed by the United States or obligations of the State of New York. Moreover, certain reserve funds may be invested in obligations of the school district that established the fund (Gen. Mun. Law § 11(3); see **19:37**). Unless they are registered or inscribed in the name of the school district, these obligations can only be purchased, delivered and redeemed if accompanied by written instructions from the board of education or the chief fiscal officer (school board president) if the school board has delegated the duty of making investments to this officer (Gen. Mun. Law § 11(3)(b)).

These investments may be made or purchased only if they are payable or redeemable at the option of the school district within such time as the proceeds will be needed to meet expenditures for which the reserve was established (Gen. Mun. Law § 11(2), (3)).

Except as otherwise provided by contract with bond or note holders, moneys invested by a school district pursuant to this section of law may be commingled for investment purposes, provided, however, that the district must at all times maintain records showing the separate identity of the sources of such funds. Income received on commingled moneys must be credited, on a pro rata basis, to the fund or account from which the moneys were invested (Gen. Mun. Law § 11(6)).

19:37. May a school district invest the money it holds in its reserve funds?

Yes. A school district may invest its reserve funds in the same types of accounts and obligations in which it is authorized to invest other district funds that are not required for immediate expenditure (see **19:36**). In addition, moneys in any reserve fund established pursuant to section 6-d, 6-f, 6-j, 6-l, 6-m, or 6-n of the General Municipal Law may even be invested in obligations of the school district that established the fund (Gen. Mun. Law § 11(3)).

19:38. Must a school board adopt a policy for the investment of school district funds?

Yes. Section 39 of the General Municipal Law requires a school board to adopt a comprehensive investment policy that sets forth both the district's general operative policy as well as instruction to its administrators and staff regarding the investing, monitoring and reporting of the district's investments. The district school board must review the investment policy annually.

The District Budget

19:39. Are school districts required to have a budget?

Yes. The Education Law requires that school districts other than large city school districts present an annual budget to the district voters for their approval. If the voters refuse to approve a budget, the school board must adopt a contingency budget (Educ. Law §§ 2022(4), (5), 2023(1), 2601-a(4), (5); see **4:1**; see also **19:45–55**). For more information on school district budget votes and the components of a school district budget, see **4:13–49**).

19:40. May school district residents delete budgetary items from the board's proposed budget and call for a separate vote on the deleted items at a special meeting?

No. The Education Law provides that district residents may file a petition with the school board requesting a vote on one or more propositions regarding items that are within the powers of the voters to approve, such as capital construction and/or changes in the mileage limitations for the transportation of students. This section does not, however, include the right to delete corresponding items from the board's own proposed budget (*Matter of Amsel,* 28 Educ. Dep't Rep. 406 (1989); see also *Appeal of Krause,* 27 Educ. Dep't Rep. 57 (1987)).

19:41. May a school board include a fund in its budget to cover unanticipated expenses?

No. There is no authority for a school board to include in its budget what would amount to an "unofficial reserve fund" to pay for previously unbudgeted expenses (*Appeal of Clark,* 37 Educ. Dep't Rep. 386 (1998); see **19:29** for information on authorized reserve funds).

19:42. May a school board retain a fund balance from unexpended funds that remain in the general fund at the end of the fiscal year?

Yes, within certain limitations. At the end of each fiscal year, a school board may retain unexpended, unreserved funds remaining in the district's general fund in an amount equal to 2 percent of the district budget for the upcoming school year. This is known as the district's fund balance. The board may use these funds to pay for items that constitute ordinary contingent expenses (Real Prop. Tax Law § 1318; see also *Appeal of Silletti,* 40 Educ. Dep't Rep. 426 (2000)).

The school board must use any unexpended, unreserved funds in excess of the 2 percent limit to reduce the district's tax levy for the upcoming school year (Real Prop. Tax Law § 1318; see also *Appeal of Liberties,* 42 Educ. Dep't Rep. 321 (2003)). Funds properly retained under other sections of law as, for example, a reserve fund established pursuant to the Education Law or the General Municipal Law, are excluded from the 2 percent limitation (Real Prop. Tax Law § 1318(1); see also **19:29**).

The tax collector's warrant must "state the amount of unexpended surplus funds in the custody of the board" and also must state "that except as authorized or required by law, such unexpended surplus funds have been applied in determining the amount of the school tax levy" (Real Prop. Tax Law § 1318; see also *Appeal of Silletti*).

19:43. May a school district levy a tax to create a planned balance?

Yes. With voter approval, school districts may levy a tax in one fiscal year to be appropriated during the next fiscal year (*Appeal of Rabideau*, 38 Educ. Dep't Rep. 359 (1998); see also *Matter of Gardner*, 22 Educ. Dep't Rep. 94 (1982)). This levy of such a tax establishes a planned balance. The primary purpose of a planned balance is to avoid the cost of borrowing to meet expenses during the first part of the fiscal year before state aid is received (*Matter of Wozniak*, 11 Educ. Dep't Rep. 63 (1971)).

Section 2021(21) of the Education Law provides that the planned balance of a district budget is limited to the amount necessary to meet expenses during the first 120 days of the fiscal year following the fiscal year in which such tax is collected.

School districts in Suffolk County should consult the Suffolk County Tax Act regarding different provisions in that area.

19:44. May a school district legally transfer funds between budget categories without voter approval?

Yes. Section 170.2(l) of the commissioner's regulations provides that "the board of education of every union free school district shall have the power and it shall be its duty: . . . (l) to make transfers between and within functional unit appropriations for teachers' salaries and ordinary contingent expenses" (see also *Appeal of Lauterback*, 30 Educ. Dep't Rep. 223 (1990)). "Boards of education may, by resolution, authorize the chief school officer to make transfers within limits as established by the board" (8 NYCRR § 170.2(l); see also *Appeal of Gargan*, 40 Educ. Dep't Rep. 465 (2000)).

From an accounting standpoint, this regulation allows districts to transfer funds between contingent expenditure codes and/or to transfer funds from non-contingent expenditure codes to contingent expenditure codes. However, the regulation does not allow districts to transfer funds from contingent expenditure codes to non-contingent expenditure codes, or to transfer funds between non-contingent expenditure codes.

See section 170.1 of the commissioner's regulations for rules pertaining to financial accounting in common school districts.

Contingency Budgets

19:45. What is a contingency budget?

A *contingency budget* is prepared and adopted by the school board when the voters reject the board's proposed budget. The contingent budget funds only teachers' salaries and those items the board determines to be "ordinary contingent expenses" (§§ 2022(5), 2023(1), 2601-a(4), (5); see **19:50–55** for more information on ordinary contingent expenses).

A contingency budget must have the same degree of specificity by both function and object that is required for budgets that are presented to the voters (*Appeal of Hubbard*, 43 Educ. Dep't Rep. ___, dec. no. 14,898 (2003)).

The board is authorized to levy a tax to fund these expenses if the proposed budget is defeated (§§ 2022(5), 2023(1), 2601-a(4), (5)). When adopting a contingency budget, the board may still submit to the voters separate propositions on specific items that require their approval, such as expanding the district's transportation mileage limitations (§§ 2022(2), 2601-a(3)). However, a board may not submit a proposition involving the expenditure of money more than twice (§§ 2022(4), 2601-a(4); see **4:32**).

19:46. When must a district adopt a contingency budget?

A school board must adopt a contingency budget after the proposed budget has been defeated twice by the voters. A board may adopt a contingency budget after the voters defeat the proposed budget once (§§ 2022(4), (5), 2023(1), 2601-a(4), (5)).

In any event, as a practical matter, the school board either must adopt a contingency budget for the ensuing fiscal year by July 1 or must pass resolutions to approve contingency budget appropriations for specific purposes, as needed, until the board adopts the overall contingency budget. This is because all district appropriations expire at the end of the fiscal year on June 30.

Moreover, as an additional practical matter, the board must adopt a contingency budget prior to the issuance of the tax levy, in order to ensure the collection of taxes sufficient to fund the ordinary contingent expenditures for which the board will make appropriations during the fiscal year.

19:47. Is there a cap on the total amount of district spending during a contingency budget?

Yes. A contingency budget may not result in a percentage increase in total spending over the district's total spending under the district budget for the prior year that exceeds the lesser of (1) the result obtained when computing 120 percent of the Consumer Price Index, or (2) 4 percent over the prior year's budget.

However, the following types of expenditures may be excluded in determining total spending:

- Expenditures resulting from a tax certiorari proceeding.

- Expenditures resulting from a court order or judgment against the school district.
- Expenditures for emergency repairs that are certified by the commissioner of education as necessary as a result of damage to, or destruction of, a school building or school equipment.
- Capital expenditures, including debt service and leases resulting from projects approved by the voters.
- Expenditures attributable to projected increases in public school enrollment, including new prekindergarten enrollment.
- Non-recurring expenditures in the prior year's budget (§ 2023 (4)(a), (b)).

The school board's contingency budget resolution must refer to a statement indicating the projected percentage increase or decrease in total spending for the school year, together with an explanation of the reasons that the board disregarded any portion of an increase in spending in formulating its contingency budget (§ 2023(4)(c)).

19:48. Are there other separate caps on district spending during a contingency budget?

Yes. In addition to the cap on total district spending during a contingency budget (see **19:47**), the administrative component of a contingency budget is capped at the lesser of (1) the percentage that the administrative component had comprised in the prior year's budget exclusive of the capital component, or (2) the percentage that the administrative component had comprised in the last defeated budget, excluding the capital component.

For example, if the program component for the 2004-05 budget was $10 million and the administrative component was $1.5 million, the administrative component of a contingency budget for the following year is capped at 15 percent, or less if the administrative component of the last purposed defeated budget comprised a smaller percentage (§§ 2023(3), 2601-a(5)).

19:49. May a school board amend and/or revise the final contingency budget after its adoption by majority vote of the board?

Yes. In fact, even an incoming board, as newly constituted at the annual organizational meeting, may make adjustments to the contingency budget adopted by the predecessor board, provided that the district continues "to maintain the educational program as required by statute and regulation" (*Appeal of Citizens for Education*, 36 Educ. Dep't Rep. 12 (1996)).

However, the Education Law precludes amendments or revisions to a final contingency budget that would exceed the spending limitations of the contingency budget caps (§ 2023(4)(d); see **19:47–48**). There are limited exceptions to this. For example, the law authorizes school boards to add to the final contingency budget appropriations in excess of the budgetary caps for expenditures caused by actual enrollment over the projected enrollment used to develop the contingency budget (§ 2023(4)(d)(ii). It also permits added appropriations exceeding the contingency budget caps for the expenditure of gifts, grants in aid for specific purposes or for general use or insurance proceeds authorized pursuant to Education Law section 1718(2) (§ 2023(4)(d)(iii)).

19:50. What constitutes an "ordinary contingent expense" for purposes of a school budget?

Ordinary contingent expenses have been defined under law to include: 1) legal obligations; 2) expenditures specifically authorized by statute; and 3) other items necessary to maintain the educational program, preserve property and ensure the health and safety of the students and staff (§ 2601-a (5); Formal Opn. of Counsel 213, 7 Educ. Dep't Rep. 153 (1967)).

The school board is responsible for initially determining what items constitute ordinary contingent expenses (*Matter of Gouverneur CSD*, 15 Educ. Dep't Rep. 468 (1976)). A school board's determination of which items to include in its contingency budget is subject to review by the commissioner of education if the board's decision is challenged (§ 2024; see also *Appeals of Gorman*, 39 Educ. Dep't Rep. 377 (1999) and *Board of Educ. of Freeport UFSD v. Nyquist*, 71 A.D.2d 757 (3d Dep't 1979), *aff'd*, 50 N.Y. 2d 889 (1980)).

However, the commissioner will not overturn a school board's contingency budget decisions on appeal "unless there is a clear showing that the board's decision was illegal or arbitrary and unreasonable" (*Appeal of Baisch*, 40 Educ. Dep't Rep. 405 (2000)).

19:51. What are some examples of ordinary contingent expenses?

Examples of ordinary contingent expenses include the following. Legal obligations (based on Educ. Law § 2601-a(5)(c); Formal Opinion of Counsel 213, 7 Educ. Dep't Rep. 153 (1967)):

- Debt service (both principal and interest payments).
- Judgments from courts and orders of the commissioner of education and other administrative bodies or officers.
- Social Security and retirement obligations, as well as other payroll taxes and assessments.
- Pre-existing contractual obligations, including collective bargaining agreements under the Taylor Law (see, for example, *Matter of Powell*, 22 Educ. Dep't 353 (1983); see also *Appeals of Gorman*, 39 Educ. Dep't Rep. 377 (1999), where the commissioner of education upheld a

district's entry into a lease of photocopying machines during a contingency budget, among other reasons, because the collective bargaining agreement between the district and the teachers union required the district to maintain a certain number of photocopying machines for teachers' use; see also *Appeal of Johnson*, 38 Educ. Dep't Rep. 327 (1998), in which the commissioner upheld as an ordinary contingent expense a district's undisputed past practice of allowing certain secretaries to take time off for emergency snow days without requiring them to charge their leave accruals).

- Payments made to a former superintendent in settlement of claims arising from a contract (*Appeal of Gallagher*, 39 Educ. Dep't Rep. 697 (2000); see also *Matter of Rowley*, 22 Educ. Dep't Rep. 385 (1983)).

Expenditures specifically authorized by statute:

- Teachers' salaries (§§ 2022(5), 2023(1), 2601-a(5)(a)).
- Interschool athletics, field trips and other extracurricular activities (§§ 2023(1), 2601-a(5)(f)); see also *Appeal of Baisch*, 40 Educ. Dep't Rep. 405 (2000)).
- Transportation within the state-mandated mileage limitations (K-8 students: 2-15 miles; 9-12 students: 3-15 miles (§ 3635(1)); children with disabilities: up to 50 miles (§§ 4401(4), 4402(4)(d)).
- Transportation to and from school under the mileage limitations last approved by the voters if more generous than the minimum mileage limitations required under state law (§§ 2023(2), 2503(12), 2601-a(5)(b); see also *Appeal of Wenger*, 37 Educ. Dep't Rep. 5 (1997)).
- Transportation related to interschool athletics, field trips and extracurricular activities (§§ 2023(1)(2), 2601-a(5)(f)).
- Expenses for cafeteria or restaurant services (§§ 1604(28), 1709(22), 2023(1)).
- Textbooks (§§ 701(3), 2601-a(5)(b)).
- Expenses in connection with membership in the New York State School Boards Association, Inc. (§ 1618).
- Convention and conference expenses (Gen. Mun. Law § 77-b; see also *Matter of Cappa*, 18 Educ. Dep't Rep. 373 (1978)).
- Under limited circumstances: youth bureaus, recreation and youth service projects, and other youth programs (Exec. Law §§ 422–423).
- The district's share of BOCES services (§§ 1950, 2601-a(5)(b); see also *Matter of New Paltz CSD*, 30 Educ. Dep't Rep. 300 (1991)).
- Health and welfare services (§§ 912, 2601-a(5)(b)).
- Grants in aid received from either the state or federal government, other gifts, and insurance proceeds not involving the expenditure of local money (§§ 1718(2), 2023(4)(d)(iii); see also, *Appeal of Baisch*, 40 Educ. Dep't Rep. 405 (2000)).

- Kindergarten, nursery and night schools (§§ 1712, 2601-a(5)(b)).
- Prekindergarten, if the board chooses to offer a prekindergarten program (§ 3602-e(11)).
- Accident insurance for students (§ 1709(8-a), (8-b)).
- In-service training for teachers (§ 1709(32)).
- Eye safety devices (§ 409-a).
- Library books and other instructional materials associated with a library (§§ 2023(1), 2601-a(5)(d)).
- Energy performance contracts entered into by either a school district or a BOCES (Energy Law § 9-103(3); see also *Appeals of Gorman*, 39 Educ. Dep't Rep. 377 (1999)).

Other items necessary to maintain the educational program, preserve property and assure the health and safety of students and staff. The following, based on Formal Opinion of Counsel 213, 7 Educ. Dep't Rep. 153 (1967), as well as the specific statutes and cases noted, is a partial list:

- Necessary travel expenses of board members and employees on official business (§§ 1604(27), 2118).
- Amounts needed to pay for necessary legal services (§ 2601-a(5)(e)).
- "Teacher supplies" but not "student supplies."
- Salaries for necessary non-teaching employees (§ 2601-a(5)(e); *Appeal of Berry*, 34 Educ. Dep't Rep. 325 (1995); *Appeal of Blizzard*, 34 Educ. Dep't Rep. 268 (1994); *Matter of Gouverneur CSD*, 15 Educ. Dep't Rep. 471 (1976)).
- Utilities, including fuel, water, light, power, and telephone (§ 2601-a(5)(e)).
- Use of school buildings for teachers' meetings and PTA meetings with school-connected purposes. However, this does not include programs of entertainment or of a social nature (see *Appeal of Forlani*, 23 Educ. Dep't Rep. 325 (1984)).
- Emergency repairs of school plant (see, for example, *Appeals of Gorman*, 39 Educ. Dep't Rep. 377 (1999); and *Appeal of Ryman*, 29 Educ. Dep't Rep. 74 (1989), upholding necessary roof repairs; see also *Matter of Mitzner*, 31 Educ. Dep't Rep. 142 (1991), upholding replacement of lighting fixtures required for safety reasons).
- Maintenance of necessary, sanitary facilities.
- Necessary expenditures for complying with the commissioner's regulation pertaining to such items as fire alarm systems and fire escapes (see *Gorman*; see also *Appeal of Gargan*, 40 Educ. Dep't Rep. 465 (2000)).
- Rental of temporary classroom facilities with approval of the commissioner, in the case of an unforeseeable emergency (§§ 1726(5), 2601-a(5)(e)). But in the absence of an unforeseeable emergency,

voter approval is required (*Appeal of Wiesen*, 35 Educ. Dep't Rep. 157 (1995)).

- Required civil defense equipment.
- Certain expenses, such as for emergency repairs, or to equip a classroom or classrooms where it is essential to house additional students. This does not include equipment (but see *Gorman* and *Appeal of Mitzner*, 31 Educ. Dep't Rep. 142 (1991)).
- Materials used in classes by students where uniformity is essential to the program or to preserve health and safety.
- Newspapers and periodical subscriptions for libraries and classroom use where essential for instruction or to preserve continuity of sets.
- Expenditures necessary to advise district voters concerning school matters (§ 2601-a(5)(e)). However, hiring a public relations firm to assist the district in promoting its image to district residents is not an ordinary contingent expense (*Appeal of Nolan*, 35 Educ. Dep't Rep. 139 (1995); see also *Appeal of Mitzner*, where the commissioner provided guidance on what is meant by "necessary" information).
- Preliminary plans and specifications needed to submit propositions to voters.
- Options on land where the price of land is nominal.

Although equipment purchases generally do not constitute an ordinary contingent expense, in one case the commissioner ruled that it was permissible for a board of education to replace obsolete computer equipment with new computers while on contingency budget, because technology was a "significant element" of the district's curriculum, and the superintendent asserted that the purchase was "necessary to the district's educational mission and ability to meet the new learning standards required by the Board of Regents" (*Appeal of Schadtle, Jr.*, 40 Educ. Dep't Rep. 60 (2000); see also *Matter of Mitzner*, 31 Educ. Dep't Rep. 142 (1991)).

19:52. Are there any items of expenditure that do not constitute ordinary contingent expenses?

Yes. Examples of items that do not constitute ordinary contingent expenses include the following:

- New equipment, such as school buses.
- Public use of school buildings and grounds, except where there is no cost to the district (see *Appeal of Forlani*, 23 Educ. Dep't Rep. 325 (1984), but a district may charge a fee that meets or exceeds its actual costs (§ 414(2); see also *Appeal of Emilio*, 33 Educ. Dep't Rep. 75 (1993)).
- Nonessential maintenance.

- Capital expenditures, except in an emergency (*Appeals of Gorman*, 39 Educ. Dep't Rep. 377 (1999)).
- Consultant services to review district operations and make recommendations necessary for the creation of the budget (*Appeal of Shravah*, 36 Educ Dep't Rep. 396 (1997), *aff'd*, *Matter of Education Alternatives v. Mills*, 175 Misc.2d 105 (1997); see also *Appeal of Gallagher*, 39 Educ. Dep't Rep. 697 (2000)).

This list is based on Formal Opinion of Counsel 213, 7 Educ. Dep't Rep. 153 (1967), as well as the specific cases cited.

19:53. Can a school board increase teachers' salaries while the district is operating on a contingency budget?

Yes. Increases in teachers' salaries are authorized by the Education Law (§ 1709(16); *Matter of New Paltz CSD*, 30 Educ. Dep't Rep. 300 (1991); Formal Opn. of Counsel 213, 7 Educ. Dep't Rep. 153, 154 (1967)). Moreover, Education Law section 2023 authorizes expenditures for teachers' salaries during a contingency budget. The commissioner of education has applied the definition of teacher found in Education Law section 3101(1) to include school superintendents, principals, and teaching assistants within the class of persons to whom a school board may grant salary increases during a contingency budget (see *Appeal of Berry*, 34 Educ. Dep't Rep. 325 (1995); see also *Appeal of Reinhardt, Jr.*, 16 Educ. Dep't Rep. 448 (1977)).

19:54. Can a school board increase noninstructional employees' salaries while the district is operating on a contingency budget?

Yes, in most cases. Increases in salaries for noninstructional employees who are subject to a collective bargaining agreement are authorized as a contractual obligation of the district (*Matter of Powell*, 22 Educ. Dep't Rep. 353 (1983)). However, noninstructional employees who are not members of a collective bargaining unit and employees designated by the Public Employment Relations Board (PERB) as management or confidential may not receive a salary increase during a contingency budget "unless it is impossible to assure qualified personnel for the minimum service, in which case these employees may also be paid necessary amounts" (*Appeal of Lauterback*, 30 Educ. Dep't Rep. 223 (1990); *Appeal of Reinhardt, Jr.*, 16 Educ. Dep't Rep. 448 (1977); *Matter of Gouverneur CSD*, 15 Educ. Dep't Rep. 468 (1976)).

Additional pay to employees not covered by a collective bargaining agreement may be provided if they are assigned new duties (*Appeal of Berry*, 34 Educ. Dep't Rep. 325; see also *Appeal of Parsons*, 32 Educ. Dep't Rep. 444 (1993)).

The commissioner of education has recognized other exceptions as well. In one case, the commissioner ruled that a board of education had the authority to grant a salary increase to the district treasurer while operating on a contingency budget, because Education Law section 2130(4) gives school boards specific authority to "fix the compensation of the treasurer." In another case, the commissioner dismissed a challenge to a district's hiring of additional noninstructional staff for its special education programs during a contingency budget, where the district demonstrated that the staff increase was necessitated by a substantial increase in the number of special education students served by the district (*Appeal of Blizzard*, 34 Educ. Dep't Rep. 268 (1994)).

19:55. How does the adoption of a contingency budget affect a school district's transportation requirements?

The Education Law requires that school districts that adopt a contingency budget continue the mileage limitations for the transportation of students last approved by the district voters. The mileage limits can be changed only by a special proposition passed by a majority of the district voters. In addition, transportation to and from interscholastic athletic events, field trips and other extracurricular activities is permissible under a contingency budget (§§ 2023(1), (2), 2503(12), 2601-a (5)(b), (f); see also, *Appeal of Wenger*, 37 Educ. Dep't Rep. 5 (1997)).

Purchasing

19:56. Are school district purchases subject to competitive bidding?

Yes. All contracts for public works (for example, services, labor and construction) in excess of $20,000 and purchase contracts (for example, commodities, materials, supplies and equipment) in excess of $10,000 must be awarded, after advertising for sealed bids, to the lowest responsible bidder who furnishes the required security ((Gen. Mun. Law § 103(1); Educ. Law §§ 1619, 2513, 2556(10); see, for example, *Appeal of World Network Servs., Inc.*, 38 Educ. Dep't Rep. 800 (1999)).

The board may not restrict its bids to residents of the school district (Opn. St. Comp. 92-50)).

School districts cannot avoid competitive bidding by signing a series of separate contracts for the same item, each for less than the $10,000 or $20,000 limit (Opn. St. Comp. 91-64).

Special rules apply to competitive bidding on construction projects (see **16:21**).

19:57. Is the lease of personal property by a school district subject to competitive bidding?

Yes. Section 1725 of the Education Law requires that any agreement by a school board for the lease of personal property is subject to the bidding requirements of the General Municipal Law for purchase contracts.

19:58. What is involved in the bidding process?

Generally, school boards must advertise in a newspaper designated for such purpose. At least five days must elapse between the first publication of the advertisement and the date specified for the opening of bids. The board may designate any officer or employee to open the bids at the time and place specified in the notice (Gen. Mun. Law § 103(2)).

In cases where two or more responsible bidders furnishing the required security submit identical bids as to price, the contract may be awarded to any of the bidders. The designated officer may, at his or her discretion, reject all bids and re-advertise for new bids (Gen. Mun. Law § 103(1)).

19:59. Can a school board reject a low bid for apparel manufactured by a "sweatshop"?

Yes. A board of education may reject a bid for apparel on the grounds that the bidder is not a "responsible bidder," based upon either or both of the following considerations: (1) the labor standards applicable to the manufacture of the apparel, including, but not limited to: a)employee compensation, b)working conditions, c)employee rights to form unions, and d)the use of child labor; and/or (2) the bidder's failure to provide sufficient information to enable the district to determine the labor standards applicable to the manufacture of the apparel (Gen. Mun. Law § 103(12); see also **19:64**).

19:60. Are there any exceptions to the competitive bidding requirements?

Yes. The competitive bidding law need not be followed if there is an emergency, accident or unforeseen occurrence whereby the life, health, safety or property of persons living within the school district require immediate action (Gen. Mun. Law § 103(4); Opn. St. Comp. 81-267; Opn. St. Comp. 81-224; Opn. St. Comp. 71-543).

Competitive bidding is not required, either, when there is only one possible supplier or source from which to procure goods or services, such as in the case of a public utility or patented item (*Harlem Gas v. Mayor*, 33 N.Y. 309 (1865); see also *Williams v. Bryant*, 53 A.D.2d 229 (4th Dep't 1976)). However, the mere likelihood that only one company will bid on a contract does not justify procuring the goods or services without competitive bidding.

When a school district invokes this exception, school officials should be prepared to offer proof that the goods and/or services in question only were available from one source (Opn. St. Comp. 83-124)).

In addition, surplus and secondhand supplies, material or equipment may be purchased without competitive bidding from the federal government, New York State, or from any other political subdivision, district or public benefit corporation (Gen. Mun. Law § 103(6); see **19:66-69**). School districts may make direct purchases of fresh farm products such as eggs, livestock, fish, dairy products, juice, grains, fresh fruit and vegetables directly from producers and growers without competitive bidding (Gen. Mun. Law § 103(9), (10); 8 NYCRR § 114.3), and milk in some instances (Gen. Mun. Law § 103(9), (10); 8 NYCRR § 114.4).

Competitive bidding is not required either with respect to contracts for "professional services" requiring, for example, special skill or training, legal services, medical services, property appraisals or insurance (*Trane Co. v. Broome County*, 76 A.D.2d 1015 (3d Dep't 1980); *Appeal of Lombardo*, 38 Educ. Dep't Rep. 730 (1999); Opn. St. Comp. 92-33).

At the school board's discretion, contracts for mobile instructional units and contracts for the transportation of students that involve an annual expenditure in excess of $10,000 may be awarded through the competitive bidding process or through an evaluation of proposals process, subject to the approval of the commissioner of education (§ 305(14)(a), (e); 8 NYCRR §§ 155.21, 156.12; see **22:96-102**).

Districts also may extend contracts for cafeteria and restaurant service, transportation of students, maintenance of school buses and for mobile instructional units, for periods of up to five years, without observing competitive bidding requirements, subject to certain limitations on annual cost increases and subject to the approval of the commissioner of education (§ 305(14); see also *A.C. Transp., Inc. v. Board of Educ. of the City of New York*, 253 A.D.2d 330 (1st Dep't 1999), *leave to appeal denied*, 93 N.Y.2d 808 (1999)).

19:61. Are there alternative procedures a school district must follow when competitive bidding is not required?

Yes. Section 104-b of the General Municipal Law requires districts purchasing goods or services that are not subject to the requirements of the competitive bidding law to take measures to ensure the "prudent and economical use of public moneys" (Gen. Mun. Law § 104-b(1)).

Alternative proposals or quotations must be secured by a procurement process involving requests for proposals (RFPs), written or verbal quotations, or other appropriate methods of procurement, except for procurement under a county contract, under a state contract of items manufactured in state correctional institutions, or from agencies for the blind and severely disabled (see **19:66–70**). Districts must evaluate proposals received, prior to awarding a contract, to ensure that any proposal accepted would be "in the best interest of the taxpayers" (*Appeal of Leman & Sluys*, 39 Educ. Dep't Rep. 407 (1999)).

Districts must develop standards for the methods of competition to be used and the sources of documentation to be maintained in the most cost-effective manner possible when soliciting non-bid procurement. District purchasing policies and regulations must require adequate documentation of actions taken, particularly if contracts are awarded to an offerer other than the lowest responsible dollar offerer (Gen. Mun. Law § 104-b(2)).

The unintentional failure of a school district to fully comply with the procurement processes prescribed by law shall not be grounds to void action taken by the district, and neither the district nor its officers and employees may be successfully sued based on such unintentional failure (Gen. Mun. Law § 104-b(5)).

19:62. Are there procedures that must be followed for determining whether a particular purchase is subject to competitive bidding or an alternative procurement process?

District policies must set forth the procedures for determining whether a particular purchase is subject to competitive bidding. If it is not subject to competitive bidding (see **19:60–61**), then the district must document the basis for such determination (Gen. Mun. Law § 104-b(2)).

Comments must be solicited periodically from those administrators involved in the procurement process including before enactment of a district's policies and regulations regarding purchasing (Gen. Mun. Law § 104-b(3)). These policies and regulations must then be adopted by a board resolution and reviewed by the school board at least annually (Gen. Mun. Law § 104-b(1), (4)).

19:63. Must school districts give a preference in their procurement polices to vendors who agree to provide instructional materials in "alternative formats" for students with disabilities?

Yes. Each school district and BOCES must develop a plan to ensure that its instructional materials are available (at the same time that such instructional materials are available to non-disabled students) in a usable alternative format for students with disabilities. As part of this plan, each school district and BOCES also must amend its procurement policy to include a provision giving preference to vendors who agree to provide instructional materials in alternative formats.

An *alternative format* means any "medium or format for the presentation of instructional materials, other than a traditional print textbook, that is needed as an accommodation for a disabled student enrolled in the school district, including, but not limited to Braille, large print, open and closed captioned, audio, or an electronic file in an approved format, as defined in the regulations of the commissioner."

If an electronic file is provided, the BOCES' or district's plan must explain how students with disabilities will access the format and/or how the BOCES or district will convert to an accessible format.

Each district's overall plan must identify the needs of students residing in the district for alternative format materials. Moreover, the plan must specify ordering timelines to ensure that alternative format materials are available at the same time as regular format materials (Educ. Law §§ 1604(29-a), 1709(4-a), 1950(4-a), 2503(7-a), 2554(7-a), 3602(10)(b), 8 NYCRR § 200.2(b)(10)).

19:64. Can school boards refuse to purchase apparel manufactured by "sweatshops"?

Yes. In addition to being able to reject a low bid for apparel manufactured by a "sweatshop" (see **19:59**), boards of education may include in their procurement policies and procedures (see **19:61**) a prohibition against purchasing apparel from any vendor based upon either or both of the following considerations: (1) the labor standards applicable to the manufacture of the apparel, including, but not limited to: a) employee compensation, b) working conditions, c) employee rights to form unions, and d) the use of child labor; and/or (2) the vendor's failure to provide sufficient information to enable the district to determine the labor standards applicable to the manufacture of the apparel.

The inclusion of such a prohibition in a district's procurement policy will apply only when a district makes purchases of apparel that are not subject to the state's competitive bidding laws. However, through another corollary provision of law, districts also may be able to refuse to purchase apparel manufactured by "sweatshops" even when competitive bidding does apply (see **19:59**) (Gen. Mun. Law § 104-b(6).

19:65. May a school district enter into a cooperative purchasing agreement?

Yes. School districts may join together to purchase materials and supplies in bulk to get the benefit of lower prices. An agreement entered into by school districts for joint purchasing should contain provisions relative to the manner of making and awarding these contracts. This arrangement must conform to the competitive bidding law (Gen. Mun. Law § 119-o(1), (2)(d); 18 Opn. St. Comp. 381, dec. no. 62-803).

19:66. May a school district make purchases through the state Office of General Services?

Yes. Section 104 of the General Municipal Law authorizes schools to purchase materials, equipment or supplies, except for printed materials, through the state Office of General Services (OGS), provided the purchase exceeds $500 and the school districts accept sole responsibility for any payment due the vendor. Where bids are received by a district, a purchase may still be made through OGS if it can be made on the same terms, conditions and specifications, but at a lower price.

19:67. May a school district make purchases through county government?

Yes. A school district may purchase materials, equipment or supplies, or contract for services (other than services subject to article 8 or 9 of the Labor Law) through the county in which the district is located, or through any adjoining county, subject to local rules established under County Law section 408-a(2)).

The school district accepts sole responsibility for any payment due the vendor. No school district shall make any purchase or contract for such services where the district already has received bids for purchase or contract, unless it can be made on the same terms, conditions and specifications at a lower price through the county (Gen. Mun. Law § 103(3)).

19:68. Must school districts make purchases from correctional institutions of needed goods that are manufactured at these institutions?

Generally, yes. Under section 184 of the Correction Law, school districts are required to purchase goods manufactured in prisons from the Department of Correctional Services, unless the commissioner of corrections certifies that such goods are not available upon requisition.

The competitive bidding requirements under the General Municipal Law do not apply to purchases made pursuant to the Correction Law (Opn. St. Comp. 86-55).

A school district can appeal the purchase price of an item on the grounds that it "unreasonably exceeds the fair market price." (Correction Law § 186(3); Opn. St. Comp. 86-55). In addition, a district may apply to the department for a waiver which would permit it to purchase an item or items from other sources pursuant to normal bidding requirements (see the State Comptroller's Financial Management Guide 8.3020, updated annually).

19:69. Are school districts encouraged to procure products and services from the state and/or from organizations that serve the disabled?

School districts are encouraged, and sometimes required (see **19:68**) to procure available products and services from the state Department of Corrections, from qualified nonprofit organizations that serve the blind and individuals with severe disabilities, from qualified special employment programs for the mentally ill and from qualified veterans' workshops (State Fin. Law § 162(1)(2)). The commissioner of general services, in consultation with the commissioners of correctional services, social services, education and mental health, compiles a list of products and services provided by preferred sources and makes this list available to political subdivisions, including school districts (State Fin. Law § 162(3)). The law sets forth an order of priority for procuring such products and services.

Products. School districts first must purchase available products from the Department of Correctional Services' correctional industries program (State Fin. Law § 162(4)(a)(i)). Next in order of priority, districts must purchase available products from qualified nonprofit agencies for the blind (State Fin. Law § 162(4)(a)(ii)). Finally, if the products in question are not available from either of these two sources, then the district may procure them from qualified nonprofit agencies for the severely disabled, qualified special employment programs for the mentally ill, or qualified veterans' workshops (State Fin. Law § 162(4)(a)(iii)).

Services. Equal priority is given to the procurement of services provided by qualified nonprofit agencies for the blind, qualified non-profit agencies for the severely disabled, qualified special employment programs for the mentally ill, and qualified veterans' workshops (State Fin. Law § 162(4)(b)).

The commissioner of correctional services sets the prices for products produced by the Department of Correctional Services' correctional industries program (State Fin. Law § 162(5)). The commissioner of general services sets the prices for all other products and services under this section of law (State Fin. Law § 162(6)).

19:70. May a school district award a paper products contract to a company that uses recycled paper, even if this company is not the lowest responsible bidder?

Yes, as long as the recycled product is reasonably competitive and costs no more than 10 percent more than the nonrecycled product, or 15 percent more than the nonrecycled product if at least 50 percent of the secondary material used to make the product was generated from the waste stream in New York State.

Each document printed on recycled paper must include the official state recycling emblem if such product has been approved by the state Department of Environmental Conservation (DEC). If the product has not been approved by the DEC, then it must contain a printed statement indicating the percentage of pre-consumer and post-consumer recycled material content of the product (Gen. Mun. Law § 104-a).

19:71. May a school district purchase farm products directly from New York farmers?

Yes. The commissioners of education, and agriculture and markets have created a farm-to-school program to facilitate and promote the purchase of New York farm products. As part of the program, districts that are interested in purchasing farm products will be given information about the availability of farm products and in turn will have their contact information distributed to interested farmers. (§ 305(31); Agriculture & Markets Law § 16 (5-b)).

19:72. May a school board enter into a lease-purchase agreement for instructional equipment?

Yes, for limited purposes. Section 1725-a of the Education Law permits school boards to enter into lease-purchase agreements for instructional equipment, with the payment to be applied against the purchase price of the equipment. These agreements must have the prior written approval of the commissioner of education and are subject to the bidding requirements of the General Municipal Law.

Under the commissioner's regulations, applications for approval of these agreements must be submitted between 30 and 90 days before the execution of the agreement. A variance can be granted upon a showing of good cause.

The regulations define *instructional equipment* to mean instruments, machines, apparatus or other types of equipment that are used directly in the instruction of students and are not consumed in use and retain their original shape and appearance with use; are not expendable items, such as textbooks or supplies; are not capital improvements, as such term is defined in section 2(9) of the Local Finance Law; and do not lose their identity through incorporation into a different or more complex unit (8 NYCRR § 170.7).

19:73. May a school district enter into installment contracts to purchase equipment?

Yes. Under the conditions set forth in section 109-b of the General Municipal Law, districts can enter into installment contracts to purchase "equipment, machinery or apparatus." No payments may be financed by the proceeds of municipal bonds or bond anticipation notes (BANs). The contract term may not exceed the useful life of the item or items purchased (subject to a maximum term of 30 years).

Installment purchase contracts are subject to competitive bidding (Gen. Mun. Law § 109-b(3)(a)). In addition, if voter approval is required to issue obligations to finance the equipment machinery or apparatus, it is required in order for the school board to enter into an installment purchase contract (Gen. Mun. Law § 109-b(5)).

19:74. Does the state sales tax law apply to school districts?

School districts, in their role as purchasers, users or consumers, are exempt from sales tax, as they are when they sell services or property of a kind not ordinarily sold by private persons (Tax Law § 1116).

All school lunch fund sales to students are tax-exempt. All lunch sales to adults are subject to the sales tax (Tax Law § 1105(d)(ii)(B)).

Hotel or motel rooms and meal charges for school district officials and employees who are traveling on official business for their school districts and whose travel expenses are paid from or fully reimbursed from school district funds are exempt from state and local sales taxes (Tax Law § 1116).

19:75. Are school districts exempt from federal excise taxes?

Yes. School districts generally are exempt from federal excise taxes. School districts should so advise vendors of this and furnish a tax exemption certificate, which may be duplicated.

For more information, see individual sections of the Internal Revenue Code for exemptions regarding specific excise taxes.

Borrowing

19:76. Can a school district borrow money?

Yes. School districts may issue long-term obligations, including serial bonds (§ 21.00) and statutory installment bonds (§ 62.10).

They may also issue short-term obligations, including bond anticipation notes (BANs) (§ 23.00), tax anticipation notes (TANs) (§ 24.00), revenue anticipation notes (RANs) (§ 25.00), capital notes (§ 28.00) and budget notes (§ 29.00).

School districts are authorized to issue zero coupons and capital appreciation bonds (§ 57.00(e)). They may also issue variable rate

---

All of the statutory references in the section "Borrowing" are to the New York State Local Finance Law unless noted otherwise.

obligations up to July 15, 2006 (§ 54.90) and discounted bonds at negotiated sales through July 15, 2006, subject to rules and regulations promulgated by the state comptroller and the comptroller's prior approval except as provided in the rules and regulations.

In addition, school districts are authorized by the state and federal government to issue qualified zone academy bonds (QZABs) which are available to qualified schools for use in repair, and rehabilitation of buildings, purchasing equipment for such facilities, developing course materials for at such schools and training teacher at qualified schools. School districts that issue QZABs receive interest free financing and purchasers of the bonds receive a federal tax credit instead of interest payments (26 USC § 1397E; 8 NYCRR § 155.22).

19:77. Is there any limit to the amount of money that school districts may borrow?

Yes. In school districts that have an aggregate assessed valuation of taxable real property of $100,000 or over, no bonds or bond anticipation notes (BANs) can be issued if the indebtedness of the school district will exceed 10 percent (5 percent in city school districts) of the full valuation of the taxable real property in the district. Details of and exceptions to this rule, including computing the debt limit for city school districts, are found in section 104.00 of the Local Finance Law. Additional limitations applying to the issuance of budget notes are found in section 29.00(3) (see **19:84**).

19:78. What is the 50 percent rule and how does it affect a school district's ability to borrow money?

According to the 50 percent rule, no installment of a bond issue may be more than 50 percent in excess of the smallest previous installment. The purpose of this rule is to prevent the ballooning of bond issue installments close to the date of maturation, while earlier installments are minimized.

School districts may also use level or declining debt financing as an alternative to the 50 percent rule for the purpose of retiring debt (NYS Const. Art. 8, § 2; Local Fin. Law § 21.00(d)).

19:79. When are long-term borrowing instruments used?

Section 11.00 of the Local Finance Law describes more than 90 purposes for which municipalities may issue long-term obligations, many of which are applicable to school districts. For each purpose listed, there is a period of probable usefulness, and districts may not borrow for longer than the period of probable usefulness of the object or purpose. For example, the period of probable usefulness for school buses is five years (§ 11.00(29)). Recent amendments have added retirement incentive programs and retirement contributions to the items that may be bonded, under certain circumstances (§ 11.00(85-b); (99); see also **11:53**). School districts may use a "weighted average period of probable usefulness" for two or more objects or purposes under the same bond issue (§ 11.00(a)).

Serial bonds are used primarily to finance capital projects and are issued in accordance with the provisions of section 11.00 of the Local Finance Law. A serial bond must mature in annual installments (§ 21.00(b)). The last installment of a serial bond must mature by the expiration of the period of probable usefulness of the object or purpose for which it was issued, as computed from the date such bonds were issued, or if bond anticipation notes were issued in anticipation of the serial bonds, as computed from the date the BANs were issued, which-ever date is earlier (§ 21.00(c)). Districts are authorized to issue bonds or notes with a maximum maturity equal to the weighted average period of probable usefulness of all projects being financed in a multi-purpose issue (§ 11.00(a)).

A single bond, known as a statutory installment bond, may be issued for the full principal amount when the principal amount of the objects or purposes to be financed does not exceed $1 million in the aggregate, and the issue is to be sold at private sale (§ 62.10).

19:80. When are short-term borrowing instruments used?

Short-term borrowing instruments, which include bond anticipation notes (BANs), capital notes, tax anticipation notes (TANs), revenue anticipation notes (RANs) and budget notes, are used as follows:

Bond anticipation notes (BANs) most commonly are used for temporary financing before the issuance of serial bonds. This gives the district flexibility in timing the actual bond sale. The adoption of a serial bond resolution is a prerequisite to issuing a BAN. The total amount of the note may not exceed the amount of the bond in anticipation of which it is issued.

A BAN may be renewed, but this note or renewal may not extend more than five years beyond the original date of issue. Section 23.00 of the Local Finance Law sets forth the method for redeeming BANS that are issued in anticipation of bonds having substantially level or declining debt service payments and are outstanding for more than two years.

Capital notes may be issued to finance all or part of the cost of the purposes listed in section 11.00 of the Local Finance Law. They must mature not later than the last day of the second fiscal year succeeding the fiscal year in which such notes are issued. However, an installment of 50 percent of the amount of such notes must mature in the first fiscal year succeeding the fiscal year in which such notes are issued, unless such notes are authorized and issued during a fiscal year at a time subsequent to the date of the adoption of the annual budget for the next succeeding fiscal year (§ 28.00).

Tax anticipation notes (TANs) and revenue anticipation notes (RANs) are used, respectively, to borrow in anticipation of the collection of taxes and the receipt of revenues, other than real property taxes, by the school district. TANs and RANs must mature within one year from the date of their issuance. Although provision is made in the law for their renewal, in most school districts TANs and RANs would be retired within one year after their issuance because the district would have received the anticipated taxes and revenues. The law requires such taxes and revenues to be used to pay off a note (§§ 24.00, 25.00; see also *Appeal of Aarseth*, 33 Educ. Dep't Rep. 522 (1994)).

Budget notes may be issued during the last nine months of the fiscal year to finance required expenditures for which either no or insufficient provision was made in the annual budget or to provide temporary school buildings or facilities in a year when an unforeseeable public emergency, such as an epidemic, riot or storm, prevents the use of all or part of the district's buildings and facilities.

Budget notes may be renewed, but these notes, including renewals, may not mature later than the close of the fiscal year succeeding the fiscal year in which they are issued. However, if the notes are authorized and issued during the fiscal year at a time subsequent to the date of adoption of the annual budget for the next succeeding year, they may mature not later than the close of the second fiscal year succeeding the fiscal year in which they were issued (§ 29.00).

19:81. Are there any special rules regarding the finance of capital projects through bonds or bond anticipation notes (BANs)?

With limited exceptions, the Local Finance Law requires a "down payment" from current funds of at least 5 percent of the estimated cost of a capital improvement or equipment purchase (§ 107.00(b)(2), (d)).

The "down payment" requirement does not apply, for example, to capital improvements estimated to exceed $20 million (§ 107.00(d)(3)(g)), and does not apply to the financing of any object or purpose for which the period of probable usefulness as prescribed in section 11 is five years or less (§ 107.00(d)(5)).

However, through July 15, 2003, districts may issue bonds or BANs for capital improvements or the acquisition of equipment or make expenditures from the proceeds of these instruments for capital improvements without complying with this "down payment" requirement (§ 107.00(d)(9)).

19:82. Are there any limits on the rates of interest for school borrowing?

In general, sections 57.00(b), 60.00(b) and 63.00(b) of the Local Finance Law authorize the sale of bonds and notes without limitation on the rate of interest.

19:83. Must a school board adopt a resolution to authorize the issuance of bonds and notes?

Yes, according to section 31.00 of the Local Finance Law.

19:84. Must the school district's voters approve the issuance of bonds and capital notes?

Yes. With limited exceptions, before a school board can adopt a resolution authorizing the issuance of bonds or capital notes, voters must approve a tax to be collected in installments for the bonds that are to be issued (§ 37.00; see also Educ. Law § 416). Different restrictions can be found in sections 37.00 and 104.00 of the Local Finance Law.

19:85. Does a school district need the consent of the Board of Regents or the state comptroller to issue bonds?

The consent of the Board of Regents to issue bonds is necessary when a district, other than a city school district, having an aggregate assessed valuation of real property of $100,000 or more (excluding the payment of judgments or settled or compromised claims), proposes to issue bonds or bond anticipation notes, which would cause the school district's indebtedness, as determined pursuant to Local Finance Law section 137.00, to exceed 10 percent of the valuation of the real property subject to taxation by the school district. Moreover, under such circumstances, the tax voted to be collected in installments to satisfy the indebtedness, or the proposition for the approval of the bond resolution, must be approved by at least 60 percent of the qualified voters who vote at the election called for such purposes (§ 104.00(d)).

In school districts located wholly within the Adirondack Park that have within their boundaries state lands subject to taxation, the full valuation of which is more than 30 percent of the full valuation of real property subject to taxation by the school district, the consent of the state comptroller also is required (§ 104.00(d)(3)).

In city school districts, the consent of both the Board of Regents and the state comptroller is necessary before the district can contract indebtedness (including existing indebtedness) that exceeds 5 percent of the average valuation of real property in the school district. Under such circumstances, the tax voted to be collected in installments to satisfy the indebtedness, or the proposition for the approval of the bond resolution, must be approved by at least 60 percent of the qualified voters who vote at the election called for such purposes. The proposition presented to the voters must contain a statement indicating that the obligations to be issued may exceed the constitutional debt limit of the school district (§ 104.00(b)(8), (c); see also **19:76**).

19:86. How are bonds and notes sold?

Generally, bonds must be sold at public sale (§ 57.00). Sections 57.00 (2 NYCRR Part 25), 58.00 and 59.00 of the Local Finance Law describe, respectively, the procedure for the public sale of bonds, requirements for notice of sale of bonds and bidding regulations related to the sale of bonds.

Bonds may be sold at private sale in the following instances:

- The bonds are sold to the United States government or to the New York State Municipal Bond Bank Agency or to certain sinking funds or pension funds (§ 57.00(a)).
- The bonds are issued in an amount not to exceed $1 million (§ 63.00). The total amount of bonds that may be sold at private sale in any one fiscal year of the school district is $1 million.
- The sale is of a statutory installment bond or bonds that does not exceed $1 million in the aggregate (unless sold to the United States government) and that may be issued for the full principal amount (§ 62.10).

All notes may be sold at either public or private sale without limitation on interest rates (§§ 60.00, 60.10).

19:87. Is a school district required to file a debt statement with the state comptroller before it issues bonds?

A school district must file a debt statement with the state comptroller before it sells any bonds that are required to be sold at public sale. A school district may file a debt statement in connection with the issuance of bond anticipation notes (BANs) (Local Fin. Law § 109.00, Art. II, Title 10, § 130 *et seq.*).

19:88. May a school district combine a number of projects into a single bond issue?

Yes. Section 57.00(c) of the Local Finance Law permits a school district to combine a number of projects such as the purchase of a school bus, reconstruction of a school building or construction of another building into a single bond issue. By selling such a single issue, it is frequently possible to obtain a lower interest rate as well as save on legal expenses, printing and advertising.

19:89. May a school district sell bonds and notes to a bank where an officer or employee of the school district is also an officer, director or stockholder of that bank?

Yes. School district bonds and notes may be sold to a bank under these circumstances at private sale without limitation as to rate of interest, provided that at least two other banks are unwilling or unable to purchase the notes at a rate of interest equal to or less than that at which the bank in which the officer or employee has an interest proposes to purchase such notes. However, the school district officer or employee who has an interest in the sale must disclose that interest in accordance with section 803 of the General Municipal Law.

Under these circumstances, the aggregate principal amount of notes purchased or held by the bank and bonds held by the bank must not exceed $100,000. Any school district officer who willfully participates in violating these provisions may be found guilty of a misdemeanor (§ 60.10).

19:90. Must the money received from the sale of bonds and notes be deposited in a special bank account?

Yes. With the exception of the proceeds of capital notes issued in amounts of $100,000 or less and budget notes, all proceeds from the sale of bonds, bond anticipation notes (BANs), budget notes and capital notes must be deposited in a special account in the bank or trust company and may not be combined with the other funds of the district (§ 165.00(a)(1)).

The law does permit the deposit of proceeds from the sale of any two or more such obligations in a single special account; however, a separate accounting record must be maintained for each issue (§ 165.00(a)(2)).

19:91. May a school district temporarily invest the proceeds from the sale of bonds pending actual use of the money?

Yes. Section 165.00(b) of the Local Finance Law provides that the proceeds from the sale of bonds, bond anticipation notes (BANs) and capital notes may be invested pursuant to section 11 of the General Municipal Law. For example, such funds may be invested in obligations of the United States and agencies of the United States where the principal and interest are guaranteed by the federal government, in obligations of New York State and special time-deposit accounts, or in certificates of deposit issued by a bank or trust company located and authorized to do business in this state. This is known as arbitrage. Its purpose is to earn interest by temporarily investing the proceeds at a better rate than the rate at which the funds were borrowed.

19:92. Is the interest earned from temporary investments subject to the provisions of the Internal Revenue Code?

Yes. The Internal Revenue Code imposes rebate (return of investment profits to the federal government) requirements on income from arbitrage that relate to the time period during which all gross proceeds must be spent on the purpose for which the funds were borrowed (§ 165.00(b); see also **19:90**). For more information, contact a bond counsel, and/or consult the Internal Revenue Code.

19:93. May a school district use proceeds from a bond sale for a different purpose than that for which the bonds were issued?

No. "Local Finance Law section 165.00(a) provides, in pertinent part: 'In the event that any portion of the proceeds, inclusive of premiums, from the sale of bonds . . . is not expended for the object or purpose for which such obligations were issued, such portion shall be applied only to the payment of the principal of and interest on such obligations respectively . . .'" (*Appeal of Goldin*, 40 Educ. Dep't Rep. 628 (2001); see also *Appeal of Kirschenbaum*, 43 Educ. Dep't Rep. ___, dec. no. 15,020 (2004)).

19:94. What happens if the school district voters refuse or fail to appropriate the amount of money needed to pay the district's bonds and interest?

The state constitution requires school districts to appropriate the amount of their debt service requirements annually. If a district fails to appropriate the money, the constitution provides that upon the suit of a bondholder, the first revenues received by the district shall be "applied to such purposes" (NYS Const. Art. 8, § 2).

19:95. What is the role of bond counsel when a school district plans to issue a bond?

A school district hires an attorney, referred to as bond counsel, on a fee basis to obtain a professional opinion with respect to the legality of a bond issue. Such an opinion is required by dealers and investors. Bond counsel prepares papers and reviews procedures affecting the sale of the bonds, expedites borrowing, advises on meeting technicalities and furnishes appropriate forms. A careful distinction should be made between the functions of bond counsel and those of the school attorney.

19:96. Where may school boards obtain additional information about school district borrowing?

Additional information about school district borrowing may be obtained from the school district attorney, who should be consulted on all major borrowing proposals of the district; bond counsel; and the Office of the State Comptroller. Also, consult the New York State Local Finance Law.

20. Assessment and Collection of Taxes

20:1. Do all school districts levy taxes?

Most do, but not all. Fiscally independent school districts levy taxes for school purposes. The state's common, union free, central, central high school, and small city school districts are all fiscally independent. They all submit their budgets to the voters for approval and levy school taxes for authorized purposes, with the exception that in central high school districts, such taxes are levied by the component school districts on behalf of the central high school district (Educ. Law §§ 1608, 1716, 1908, 2022).

Fiscally dependent school districts do not levy taxes. Only the Big 5 city school districts are fiscally dependent. They are Buffalo, New York, Rochester, Syracuse and Yonkers. They are dependent on municipal tax revenue to fund education (Educ. Law § 2576). Municipal governments levy a single real property tax for school and nonschool purposes and allocate a portion of their tax revenues for education. Fiscally dependent districts also may receive income from other local taxes, such as income taxes and sales taxes (see, for example, **20:4**).

20:2. Which district levies taxes on a residential property that is split between two different school districts?

Under Education Law section 3203, when a residential property is intersected by the boundary line between two school districts, the owner may designate either school district as the district for attendance by his or her children. Once this designation is made, both school districts continue to levy school taxes based upon the assessments in their respective taxing jurisdictions (see 9 Opn. Counsel SBRPS No. 22 (1987); see also **20:37**), but the district that does not provide instruction to the children must pay over the school taxes that it has collected on the property to the school district where the children receive instruction.

This is true regardless of how much of the property is located in the affected districts. In one case, the commissioner of education ordered a school district where the bulk of a particular split residential property was located to pay over more than $6,000 in school taxes to the district designated by the owners for attendance by their children, even though only

---

All statutory references in this chapter are to the New York State Real Property Tax Law unless otherwise noted. The material in the chapter refers chiefly to school districts other than the Big 5 city school districts. For selected legal opinions by statute (or by subject), visit the New York State Office of Real Property Services (ORPS) Web site at: http://www.orps.state.ny.us/legal/opinions/index.ctm.

one square foot of the entire property was located in the designated district (see *Board of Educ. of the Harborfields CSD*, 41 Educ. Dep't Rep. 15 (2001); see also same case at 41 Educ. Dep't Rep. 113 (2001)).

20:3. Are there state constitutional limits on taxes levied by school districts in New York State?

No. A prior constitutional limit on taxes levied by small city school districts was repealed in 1985 (NYS Const. Art. 8, § 10). Corresponding sections of the Education Law (see Educ. Law § 2701 *et seq.*) that regulated the constitutional tax limits in small city schools districts were repealed by Chapter 171 of the Laws of 1996.

20:4. Are there any sources of tax revenue for school districts other than real property?

Yes. The Tax Law authorizes certain municipalities, including some school districts under certain limited circumstances (see, for example, Tax Law § 1212) to levy non-realty taxes for both education and general purposes. These can be, for example, taxes on utilities, real estate sales, food and drinks in restaurants and bars, vending machines, and admissions to places of amusement, and general sales taxes (Tax Law §§ 1200–1263).

20:5. May school districts receive a portion of the county sales tax?

Yes. The Tax Law authorizes counties to allocate a portion of their sales tax revenues to school districts and other localities (Tax Law § 1262).

20:6. What are some key definitions related to the assessment and collection of school taxes?

Assessment is the determination, by assessors, of the valuation of real property, including exempt real property, as well as the determination of whether such real property is subject to taxation or special *ad valorem* levies (§ 102(2)).

The *assessment roll* is the list of each parcel of property in the municipality and its assessed value as it exists before a warrant for the collection of taxes is attached to it (§ 550(1)).

Real property is land, above and under water; buildings and other structures affixed to the land, including bridges and wharves; underground and elevated railroads and railroad structures; telephone and telegraph lines; mains, pipes and tanks; mobile homes and trailers; and other property (see § 102(12) for a complete definition).

The *state equalization rate* is the percentage of full value at which taxable real property in a county, city, town or village is assessed as determined by the New York State Board of Real Property Services (§ 102(19)).

The *tax roll* is a final assessment roll to which tax amounts have been added and to which a warrant has been attached (§ 904(1)).

A *tax warrant* empowers the tax collector to collect the taxes (§ 904(4)).

Assessment

20:7. Who has oversight responsibility over the assessment of taxes?

The New York State Board of Real Property Services, formerly known as the State Board of Equalization and Assessment, is the five-member state oversight board for the real property tax system (§ 200). The Office of Real Property Services (ORPS) effectuates the policies of the board (§ 201). It assesses special franchises; establishes state equalization rates; approves assessments of taxable state lands; generally supervises the function of assessing throughout the state; and furnishes assessors with information, instructions, and training (§ 202).

For additional information about ORPS, visit their Web site at: http://www.orps.state.ny.us/.

20:8. Who conducts property assessments for tax purposes?

Property assessments for tax purposes are made by local municipal, town, or county assessors, or boards of assessors charged with the duty of assessing real property within an assessing unit for purposes of taxation or special levies (§§ 102(3), 1302(1)).

Assessors may be appointed or elected (§§ 102(3), 310, 329). Appointed assessors serve for six years. However, they may serve an indefinite term if the office of assessor is a full-time position or has been classified in the competitive class of the civil service (§ 310(2), (7)).

Elected town assessors serve for six-year terms unless the town retains a board of assessors. In that case the term of office is four years. No more than two assessors are elected at the biennial election, except when the unexpired balance of a term is being filled, then three assessors may be elected (Town Law § 24).

All assessors must obtain state board certification of successful completion of the basic course of training prescribed by the New York State Board of Real Property Services (§ 310(5)(a)). In addition, all appointed assessors and elected assessors who serve a six-year term must complete a continuing training and education program (§ 310(5)(b)).

20:9. What is the timetable for the administration of the assessment system?

January 1 is the *valuation date*, which is the date by which the value of the real property must be determined in most cases. However, the valuation date for a city or town may differ under separate sections of law applicable to such cities and towns (§ 301; see *SKM Enters. v. Town of Monroe*, 2 Misc. 3d 1004A, 2004 N.Y. Misc. LEXIS 187, 2004 NY Slip Op 50138U (2004)).

March 1 is the *taxable status date* for real property in most cities and towns, which is the date by which assessors must complete an inventory of all real property in the community. The taxable status date may differ for some cities and towns under separate sections of law applicable to such cities and towns (§ 302(1)). The taxable status date of cities, towns, and counties is controlling for school district purposes (§§ 302(2), 1302(3), (4)). The taxable status date in villages is usually January 1 (§ 1400)).

May 1 is the date by which the assessor(s) must publish the tentative assessment roll and make it available for public inspection until the fourth Tuesday in May (§§ 506, 526).

The fourth Tuesday in May (or other date established by city or county charter, county tax act, or other special law), also known as *grievance day*, is the date on which the Board of Assessment Review must begin hearing assessment complaints (§ 512(1)). In addition, the governing body of an assessing unit that employs an assessor who is at the same time employed by another assessing unit may set another date or dates for the meeting of the board of assessment review. Such date, or the first date in cases where the board meets on more than one date, must be between the fourth Tuesday in May and the second Tuesday in June (§ 512(1-a)).

July 1 is the deadline for filing the final assessment roll (§ 516).

20:10. Who prepares a copy of the appropriate portion of the town or county assessment roll for school district tax-collection purposes?

Because municipalities usually are not contiguous with school districts, different portions of each municipality's tax roll contain properties that are attributed to different school districts. Therefore, once the assessment roll for town or county purposes has been completed, a duplicate assessment roll is prepared and the assessor delivers a copy of the appropriate portion to the clerk, trustee or other proper official of each school district within five days after the completion and certification of the assessment roll. The expense of preparing this document is charged to the city, town or county except when prepared for a city school district, which must reimburse the municipality preparing the duplicate assessment role (§ 1302(2)).

20:11. Who is responsible for the accuracy of the assessment roll?

Each school district is responsible for determining whether certain parcels of real property are within its boundaries (§ 1302(2); see also *Matter of Hudson Falls CSD v. Town of Moreau Assessor*, 202 A.D.2d 716 (3d Dep't 1994), *appeal denied*, 83 N.Y.2d 760 (1994)). The district superintendent of a board of cooperative educational services (BOCES) district has the authority to determine the legal boundaries between adjoining school districts within his or her jurisdiction (Educ. Law § 2215(1); *Appeal of Bd. of Educ. of Fort Edward UFSD*, 33 Educ. Dep't Rep. 457 (1994); see also **6:20, 6:23**).

20:12. What is the law regarding the correction of assessment rolls and tax rolls?

Title 3 (Corrections of Assessment Rolls and Tax Rolls) of the Real Property Tax Law defines and describes the procedures for correcting clerical errors, unlawful entries, errors in essential fact, the assessment of omitted property and other errors (§§ 550–559).

A school board may authorize a designated official to approve the correction of the tax roll and tax bill where the correction does not exceed $2,500 (§ 554(9)).

20:13. Who is responsible for resolving assessment complaints?

The board of assessment review is the body of officers empowered to hear and determine complaints about assessments (§ 102(4)). Members are appointed by the legislative body of the local government (523(1)(b)).

20:14. What are the procedures for reviewing and changing assessments?

Complaints regarding assessments are filed with the assessor prior to a hearing of the board of assessment review, or with the board at a hearing, but cannot be filed in the first instance at an adjourned hearing conducted by the board (§ 524(1)).

Where a complaint is filed within three business days preceding the hearing, the board of assessment review must grant the assessor's request for an adjournment to permit the assessor to prepare a response to the complaint (§ 524(1)). Once the response has been considered, the board makes a determination of the final assessed valuation and prepares a verified statement showing any changes (§ 525(3), (4)).

As soon as possible after receiving the statement from the board, the assessor makes the changes in the assessment on the assessment roll (§ 526(5)).

Tax Certiorari Proceedings

20:15. What are the procedures for challenging a local assessment review board's refusal to reduce a property tax assessment?

A taxpayer (a person – corporate or otherwise) initiates a property tax *certiorari*. This is a legal proceeding whereby the taxpayer who has been denied a reduction in assessment by a local assessment review board challenges his or her property tax assessment on the grounds of excessiveness, inequality, illegality, or misclassification (§§ 700, 701, 706(1)).

Procedural laws regarding *certiorari* actions are contained in Article 7 of the Real Property Tax Law.

If, alternatively, a taxpayer opts to pursue a remedy through the small claims assessment review procedure (§§ 729–739, Title 1-A), they waive their right to commence a tax certiorari under Article 7 title I, but may still seek judicial review pursuant to Article 78 of the Civil Practice Law and Rules (§ 736).

20:16. How does a school district learn of the filing of a real property tax *certiorari* proceeding?

Under the Real Property Tax Law, when a taxpayer files a tax *certiorari* petition with the appropriate court challenging a tax assessment, the taxpayer must mail a copy of the petition and notice to the superintendent of schools of any school district in which any part of the real property at issue is located within 10 days from the date of service of the petition and notice on the clerk of the assessing unit. The taxpayer also must file proof of this mailing with the court within 10 days (§ 708(3)).

20:17. May a school district become a party to a real property tax *certiorari* proceeding?

Yes, at the school board's discretion. Most requests by residential property owners for reductions in assessment are settled by local assessment review boards or in small claims courts. Generally, the minor reductions that result from these procedures are not problematic for school districts. However, the large reductions in assessment granted to businesses, industries, multiple dwellings, and other commercial property owners as a result of certiorari actions may present a problem for individual school districts.

20:18. How does a school district become a party to a real property tax *certiorari* proceeding?

Following the superintendent's receipt of the tax *certiorari* petition and notice by mail (§ 708(3)), a school board must take a vote to become a party to the action, and then serve a verified answer to the petition *or* a notice of appearance in the action within the time frame set by statute. If a district serves a "notice of appearance" instead of a verified answer, then all allegations set forth in the taxpayer's petition are deemed denied by the school district (§ 712(2-a)).

20:19. What are the rights of a school district that chooses to become a party to a tax certiorari proceeding?

According to at least one appellate court, a school district that invokes its option to become a party to a tax *certiorari* proceeding enjoys the same rights as other parties, "including the right to reject an unacceptable settlement offer" among the other parties to the proceeding (*Liberty Mgmt. of N.Y., Inc. v. Assessor of Glenville*, 284 A.D.2d 61 (3d Dep't 2001)).

20:20. What happens if a taxpayer fails to notify the affected school district(s) of the commencement of the proceeding as set forth in law?

Failure to mail a copy of the notice and petition to the superintendent of schools of each school district in which any part of the real property at issue is located, as required by law (see **20:16**), may result in dismissal of the petition, "unless excused for good cause shown" (§ 708(3)).

In one case, an appellate court found that "good cause" had been shown under circumstances where a taxpayer's failure to mail the petition and notice to the correct school district resulted from misinformation the taxpayer received from the assessor's office (*Village Square of Penna, Inc. v. Semon*, 290 A.D.2d 184 (3d Dep't 2002), *appeal denied*, 98 N.Y.2d 647 (2002)). Another appellate court found no good cause existed in the absence of prejudice to the school district in a case where no answers had been served, no appraisals exchanged, and no negotiations had taken place (*Bloomingdale's, Inc. v. City Assessor*, 294 A.D.2d 570 (2d Dep't 2002), *appeal denied*, 99 N.Y.2d 553(2002)).

20:21. What happens if a school district receives a tax *certiorari* notice and petition late?

According to one appellate court, if a school district simply receives the petition and notice late, then the district must intervene in the proceeding and make a motion to dismiss the petition for lateness. If the district fails to do this, then it waives its objection to late service and must comply with any court order or settlement reached in the matter (*Brookview Apts. v. Stuhlman*, 278 A.D.2d 825, 826 (4th Dep't 2000)). But another appellate court has ruled that a *certiorari* petition should not be dismissed for lateness absent prejudice to the school district as a result of a late delivery of the notice and petition (*Bloomingdale's, Inc. v. City Assessor*, 294 A.D.2d 570 (2d Dep't 2002), *appeal denied*, 99 N.Y.2d 502 (2002)).

20:22. Is a school district that never receives the tax *certiorari* notice and petition in the manner set forth by law obligated to refund back taxes under a settlement or court order from the proceeding?

No. The two New York appellate courts that have squarely addressed the issue have ruled that if a school district *never* is served with the tax *certiorari* petition and notice before trial or settlement, then the district is not required to refund any back taxes pursuant a court order or settlement (*Brookview Apts. v. Stuhlman*, 278 A.D.2d 825, 826 (4th Dep't 2000); see also *Macy's Primary Real Estate, Inc. v. Assessor of City of White Plains*, 291 A.D.2d 73 (2d Dep't 2002), *appeal denied*, 99 N.Y.2d 502 (2002)).

Tax Exemptions

20:23. What kinds of property are wholly exempt from real property taxation?

Examples of property wholly exempt from real property taxation include:
- Real property of the United States, except by permission of Congress (§ 400).
- Real property of New York State, other than property expressly subjected to taxation (§ 404, § 530 *et seq.*).
- Real property of a municipal corporation, within its corporate limits, held for public use (§ 406(1); but see **20:30**).
- Real property of a school district or a board of cooperative educational services (BOCES) (§ 408).
- Real property on Native American reservations (§ 454).
- Real property owned by corporations or associations organized exclusively for religious, charitable, hospital, or educational purposes, for example, as specified by law (§ 420-a(1)). This property is exempt only to the extent of the value of the portion of the property so used (§ 420-a(2)).
- Real property of an agricultural society that permanently uses it for a meeting hall or exhibition grounds (§ 450).
- Real property of a municipal corporation, not located within its corporate limits, used for fire protection services (provided that some fire protection services are available within the municipality), or used

as a public park, public aviation field, highway, or for flood control and soil conservation purposes, provided the school board agrees to the exemption in writing (§ 406(2)).

- Real property of a corporation, association, or post composed of veterans of the Grand Army of the Republic, Veterans of Foreign Wars, Disabled American Veterans, the American Legion, and other veterans' organizations (§ 452).
- The homes of clergy owned by religious corporations (§ 462).
- Under certain conditions, improvements related to the accessibility of the property by an owner or member of the owner's household who is disabled (§§ 459, 459-b).
- Certain real property located on farms, including silos and farm feed storage bins, commodity sheds, bulk milk tanks and coolers, and manure storage and handling facilities (§ 483-a).
- Farm or food processing labor camps or commissaries, as defined in article seven of the Labor Law (§ 483-d).
- School districts wholly or partly within a city with a population of at least 50,000 but fewer than 1 million that has adopted a local law to exempt real property converted from nonresidential use to residential use, or to mixed-use, may by resolution likewise exempt such property (§ 485-a).

For a complete overview of exemptions, see sections 400–494 of the Real Property Tax Law.

20:24. What kinds of property are partially exempt from real property taxation?

Examples of property that is partially exempt from real property taxation includes:

- Real property of a minister, priest, or rabbi under certain circumstances, and the property of his or her unremarried surviving spouse, up to $1,500 (§ 460).
- Real property owned by an industrial development agency (IDA), including certain railroad property (§§ 412-a, 412-b).
- Under certain conditions, real property owned by a person who is 65 years old or older, if authorized by the school board (§ 467; see **20:27–28**).
- Under certain conditions, real property constructed, altered, installed, or improved for the purpose of commercial, business, or industrial activity (§ 485-b).
- Under certain conditions, and subsequent to passage of a resolution by the local school board, some home improvements may be partially exempt from real property taxes for a limited period (§ 421-f).

- Under certain conditions, and if authorized by a resolution adopted by the local board of education, newly constructed primary residences for first-time home buyers and improvements made to such properties in excess of 1,000, subject to limitations on household income as set forth in law (§ 457).
- Under certain conditions, and if authorized by the school board, real property altered, installed, or improved subsequent to the Americans with Disabilities Act (ADA) to remove architectural barriers for persons with disabilities (§ 459-a).
- Under certain conditions, and if authorized by the school board, real property owned by one or more persons with disabilities, or real property owned by a husband, wife, or both, or by siblings, at least one of whom has a disability, with limited income, and persons 65 years of age or older, as set forth in statute (§ 459-c).
- Under certain conditions, any increase in the value attributable to the construction or reconstruction of structures and buildings essential to the operation of lands actively devoted to "agricultural or horticultural" use, which includes the raising, breeding, and boarding of livestock, including commercial horse boarding operations (§ 483).
- Certain property owners are entitled to a partial tax exemption under the New York State School Tax Relief Program (STAR) (see **20:32–44**).

For a complete overview of exemptions, see sections 400–494 of the Real Property Tax Law.

In instances where the assessor wholly discontinues a partial exemption, as opposed to reducing it, granted to a parcel on the preceding year's assessment role, notice must be given to the taxpayer by the assessor (§ 510-a).

20:25. Are there any special rules pertaining to a real property tax exemption for nuclear powered electric generating facilities, for solar or wind energy systems, and for railroad property?

Yes. A nuclear powered electric generating facility may be exempt from school taxation for up to 15 years if authorized by resolution adopted by the board of education in the district(s) in which the facility is located, except that such facility may be obligated to make payments in lieu of taxes (PILOTs) to the school district, as set forth in law (§§ 485, 490, 1227).

Exemptions for certain solar and wind energy systems in school districts shall be granted upon proper application for a period of 15 years unless by resolution a school district opts to prohibit such exemptions. Districts opting out may instead require the property owner to enter into a contract for PILOTs that provides for annual payments in an amount not to exceed the amounts which would otherwise be payable but for the exemption. The

Big 5 city school districts are excluded from the provisions of this section of law (§ 487(9)).

Approved capital project investments of interstate railroads for certain rail service improvements would become exempt from real property taxation over a 10-year phase out period ending in 2012–13. State payments to local governments to offset lost tax revenue would be provided according to a transitional adjustment schedule, which would hold harmless school districts through 2004–05. For the remaining eight years of the phase out, half of lost school district revenue would be offset (Chapter 698 of 2003).

20:26. Are there any special rules pertaining to a real property tax exemption for persons age 65 or over?

Currently, section 467 of the Real Property Tax Law enables school districts to grant persons age 65 or over, by board resolution, the following exemptions:

- a 50 percent exemption for these who have up to $24,000 in personal income, as defined by law (§ 467(3)).
- an exemption of between 5 and 45 percent along a sliding scale for those whose income is above the income ceiling adopted by the school district, as set forth by statute.

For example, if a district adopts the maximum income ceiling of $24,000 for the purpose of granting the 50 percent exemption, persons over age 65 whose personal income exceeds this amount, up to a maximum of $32,400, still will qualify for a 5 percent exemption if the district also adopts the sliding scale exemption.

In addition, any county, city, town, village or school district may adopt a local law, ordinance, or resolution to grant up to a 50 percent tax exemption on the assessed value of real property owned by one or more persons age 65 or over, or real property owned by a husband and wife or siblings, one of whom is age 65 or over. A school board must hold a public hearing prior to adopting such a resolution (§ 467(1)(a)). The board then must give a copy of the resolution to the assessor, who prepares the tax roll that will be affected by the tax exemption. The exemption cannot be granted under certain circumstances, such as in the case of real property where a child resides, if that child attends a public elementary or secondary school, unless the board of education of the school district in which the property is located, after a public hearing, adopts a resolution providing for such exemption. The requirement for such a hearing and resolution is separate from, and in addition to, the requirement that a board of education hold a public hearing before approving a resolution to offer the exemption to persons age 65 and over in the first place (§ 467(2)).

Furthermore, certain persons 65 years of age or older may also qualify for the enhanced STAR program tax exemption (see **20:34**).

20:27. Must a board of education give notice of the availability of a tax exemption for persons age 65 or over?

Yes. The school board must notify property owners of the availability of this exemption, if the board has adopted a resolution providing for the exemption. The statute provides a sample notice that districts may use (§ 467(4)). Those who wish to take advantage of the exemption must file an application with the assessor on or before the appropriate taxable status date (§ 467(5)).

A school board may, after holding a public hearing on the matter, adopt a resolution eliminating the requirement of filing an application annually for any person who has previously been granted the exemption on five consecutive assessment rolls, provided that the person includes a sworn statement with his or her tax payment indicating that he or she continues to be eligible for the exemption (§ 467(6)(b)); see also 9 Opn. Counsel SBRPS No. 36 (1990)).

20:28. Are there any special rules pertaining to real property tax exemptions for person age 65 or over who purchase real property after the taxable status date?

Yes. A person who purchases real property after the taxable status date and qualifies for an exemption may file a late application for an exemption with the assessor within 30 days of the transfer of title (§ 467(9)(a)(i)). Upon approval of the application, the new property owner may receive a pro rata exemption credit to reduce the amount of taxes due on the property for the following year (§ 467(9)(a)(ii)). School districts that receive notice of pro rata exemption credits from the assessor must include such sums in the budget appropriations for the subsequent fiscal year (§ 467(9)(a)(iii)).

20:29. Are there any special rules pertaining to exemptions from school taxes that apply to property owned by veterans?

Yes. See sections 458 and 458-a of the Real Property Tax Law (see also **20:58**).

20:30. Is a municipality exempt from paying school taxes on real property it acquires on a tax foreclosure sale?

No. A municipality is liable for school taxes on real property it acquires by deed, a referee's deed in a tax foreclosure, or pursuant to a deed made in lieu of a tax foreclosure (§ 406(5); *Union Free Sch. Dist. v. Steuben County*, 178 Misc. 415 (1942), *aff'd*, 264 A.D. 945 (4th Dep't 1942)).

20:31. Is school district property located outside a city and village subject to special assessments or *ad valorem* taxes from that city or village?

No. Section 490 of the Real Property Tax Law exempts school district real property from certain special assessments and *ad valorem* levies (§§ 408, 490).

20:32. What is the New York State School Tax Relief Program (STAR)?

STAR is a state-funded exemption from school property taxes for owner-occupied, primary residences. To be eligible for the exemption, the property must be a one-, two-, or three-family residence, a farm home, or a residential condominium or cooperative apartment (§ 425(3)). The program has two components: the enhanced program for income-eligible senior citizens and the basic program for all other property owners (§ 425 (2)(a), (3), (4)). The STAR exemption must be applied after any other applicable exemptions have been applied to the property's assessed value (§§ 425(7)(b), 467(1)(c)).

20:33. What rights does a taxpayer have if his or her STAR application is denied?

If a STAR application is denied, the applicant may seek administrative and judicial review of the denial, subject to the same time constraints that apply to the review of assessments appearing on the current year's assessment roll (§ 425(6)(d)(ii)). Similarly, if a previously recognized exemption is discontinued or revoked, the taxpayer may seek administrative and judicial review of the action (§ 425 (11)(b), (12)(c)).

20:34. What is the enhanced STAR program?

The enhanced STAR program is available to eligible senior citizens. The enhanced exemption is $50,000 (§ 425(2)(b), (4)).

To be eligible for the enhanced exemption, property owners must all be at least 65 years of age, unless they are husband and wife, or siblings, in which case only one owner need be at least 65 years of age as of December 31, but the property must serve as the primary residence of that owner (§ 425 (4)(a)(i)). In addition, the combined annual "income" of all of the owners and their spouses residing in the premises must not exceed the applicable income limits set forth in law (§ 425(4)(b)(i)). "Income" means

"adjusted gross income" as reported for federal income tax purposes
(§ 425(4)(b)(ii)).

20:35. What is the basic STAR program?

The basic STAR program applies to all primary-residence homeowners,
regardless of age or income, and provides a $30,000 base exemption
(§ 425(2)(b),(iv), (3)). Senior citizens whose income exceeds the applicable
income limits set forth in law for the enhanced STAR exemption (**20:34**)
still may be eligible for the basic STAR exemption (§ 425 (2)(b)(iv),
(4)(a),(b)(i)).

20:36. May a husband and wife who own more than one home claim a STAR exemption on each home?

Generally no. To be eligible for the exemption, the property must serve
as the "primary residence" of one or more of the owners (§ 425(3)(b)).
However, if husband and wife are "living apart due to legal separation,"
each spouse may be eligible to claim the STAR exemption on the property
that serves as his or her primary residence (§ 425 (4-a)(a)).

20:37. Does the STAR exemption apply to a residence split by municipal boundaries?

Yes. When an applicant's primary residence (i.e., the actual residential
structure itself) is located in two or more municipalities, each portion of the
residence is eligible for the STAR exemption, provided that the eligibility
requirements are otherwise satisfied. The exemption is pro-rated — just as
the full value of the property is apportioned between each municipality by
its assessor(s) — such that the total STAR savings does not exceed the
STAR savings available if the property were located entirely within one
municipality (§ 425(4-a)(c); see also **20:2**).

20:38. Does the STAR exemption apply to library taxes levied by school districts on behalf of such libraries?

No. According to an opinion of counsel issued by New York's State
Board of Real Property Services, which oversees the STAR exemption
process, the STAR exemption does not apply to taxes or charges levied for
library purposes (10 Opn. Counsel SBRPS No. 59 (1998)).

20:39. How do district residents obtain either the enhanced STAR program exemption or the basic STAR program exemption?

In general, all owners of the property who primarily reside thereon must
jointly file an application for the exemption with the assessor on or before

the appropriate taxable status date (§ 425(6)(a)). However, such application may be filed after the appropriate taxable status date, but in no event later than the last date on which a petition with respect to complaints of assessment may be filed, under circumstances where the failure to file a timely application resulted from:

- death of the applicant's spouse, child, parent, brother, or sister; or
- an illness of the applicant or of the applicant's spouse, child, parent, brother, or sister, which actually prevented the applicant from filing on a timely basis, as certified by a licensed physician.

If either of these conditions is satisfied, then the assessor approves or denies the application as if it had been filed on or before the taxable status date (§ 425(6)(e)).

Where school district taxes are levied upon prior year assessment rolls, the assessing unit may adopt a local law allowing the submission of STAR applications for each school year on or before the taxable status date of the current year's assessment roll (§ 425(6)(d)(i)). When such a local law is in effect, the eligibility of property for a STAR exemption for a particular school year is based on the condition of the property as of the taxable status date of the prior year's assessment roll, and ownership of the property is determined as of the taxable status date of the current year's assessment roll (§ 425(6)(d)(ii)).

If the assessor is satisfied that the applicant(s) are entitled to an exemption, he or she will approve the application and such real property shall thereafter be partially exempt from school district taxation, without further application (§ 425(6)(b), (9-a)). However, the enhanced program exemption for eligible senior citizens only applies for one year, and a renewal application must be submitted each year, unless: 1) the taxpayer has elected to participate in the STAR income verification program (see **20:40**); or 2) the property continues to be eligible for the senior citizen exemption pursuant to Real Property Tax Law section 467, in which case the enhanced exemption continues to apply automatically (see **20:27**) (§ 425(9-b)).

20:40. Can taxpayers have their income eligibility for the enhanced STAR exemption verified without having to reapply each year?

Yes. The application form for the enhanced STAR exemption must give applicants the opportunity to have their income eligibility verified annually by the state Department of Taxation and Finance, pursuant to an agreement between their assessor and the department (§ 425(4)(b)(iv); Tax Law § 171-k).

Thereafter, the taxpayer's income eligibility will be verified annually by Department of Taxation and Finance, and the taxpayer will not need to provide income documentation to the assessor unless the Tax Department informs the assessor that it is unable to verify the taxpayer's income eligibility, or that the taxpayer does not qualify for the enhanced exemption under the income eligibility guidelines (§ 425(4)(b)(iv)).

The Department of Taxation and Finance is prohibited from providing any other information about the income of the taxpayer other than that which is necessary to verify income eligibility for the enhanced STAR exemption. Moreover, the assessor and other municipal officials must keep such information confidential, subject to removal from office and/or other penalties authorized by law. Consistent with this requirement of confidentiality, the Freedom of Information Law is inapplicable to this information (Tax Law § 171-k).

Income documentation still must be submitted to the assessor with

- the initial application for the enhanced exemption;
- renewal applications by taxpayers who previously have not participated in the income verification program;
- any application to resume the enhanced exemption after it has been discontinued;
- an application submitted in a new assessing jurisdiction (even if same the applicant previously qualified in another jurisdiction) (§ 425(4)(b)(vi)).

Taxpayers who do not participate in the income verification program must file a renewal application with the assessor each year in order to continue receiving the enhanced exemption (§ 425(9-b); see also **20:39**).

20:41. What are a school district's responsibilities under the STAR program?

School districts are required to provide information about the STAR exemption to each person who owns a residence in the school district. The statute provides a sample notice that districts may use (§ 425(5)).

20:42. How do school districts set their tax rates under the STAR program?

The amount of taxes to be levied and the tax rate must be determined without regard to the STAR exemption (§ 1306-a(1)).

20:43. How will the state reimburse school districts for the tax shortfall attributable to the STAR exemption?

Under the law, the total tax savings from the STAR program must be incurred by the state. Each school district must submit an application to the State Board of Real Property Services, which must approve the application and certify to the commissioner of education the amount of state aid payable to the district (§ 1306-a(3); Educ. Law § 3609-e).

20:44. Where can further information about the STAR program be obtained?

Contact your local tax assessor's office or contact the New York State Office of Real Property Services at 16 Sheridan Avenue, Albany, N.Y. 12210-2714; telephone 888-697-8275 or 518-474-2819, or at http://www. orps.state.ny.us/.

Determining the Tax Rate

20:45. How is the amount of tax to be imposed on each parcel of property in the school district determined?

There are three methods of determining the tax amount.

1) In a district that is completely within or coterminous with a single taxing jurisdiction, the amount of the tax is determined by multiplying the assessed value of the parcel by the tax rate per thousand dollars of assessed value. The school tax rate per thousand is determined by dividing the total amount of the tax levy by the total assessed value of the property in the town and multiplying that result by 1,000. For example, if the total amount of the levy is $8 million, and the total assessed value of all taxable property is $135 million, the tax rate per 1,000 is $59.25. The school tax on a parcel assessed at $50,000 is $2,962.96.

2) In a district that embraces two or more towns or other local taxing jurisdictions, the full value of assessed real property in each jurisdiction is calculated by dividing the assessed valuation determined by each local assessor by the equalization rate established by the State Board of Real Property Services for that locality (full value) (§ 1314).

3) In the case of a school district located in more than one city or town where all affected municipalities opt to use the special large parcel equalization process for a "designated large property" (as that term is defined in law), the state board must notify the appropriate school district and assessing unit and provide instructions for the apportionment of the tax levy (§ 1316).

20:46. What is tax equalization, and what is its role in the process of setting tax rates?

Tax equalization, simply stated, is the ratio between the actual current market value of property and the assessed value of that property. *Full value*, or *market value*, is the price a piece of property would command if it were sold. *Assessed value* is the value of a piece of property established by taxing authorities on the basis of which the tax rate is applied. The assessed value is often a fraction of the actual market value.

Tax equalization is a method of computation used with the aim of equitably apportioning the tax burden where a district encompasses parts of two or more tax districts that assess property at different fractions of full value. The end result of the use of the state equalization rate is supposed to be the determination of the full market value of property and tax rate on full value. (The process for establishing the equalization rate is set forth in section 1314 of the Real Property Tax Law.)

20:47. Are residential and commercial properties taxed at the same rate?

Under the homestead/nonhomestead property-classification system, residential and commercial properties can be taxed at different rates in approved assessing units (those that have undergone reassessment of all parcels at full market value and have been approved by the State Board of Real Property Services). This ensures against a disproportionate tax burden for residential taxpayers by reducing tax rates on residential properties.

Article 19 of the Real Property Tax Law regulates the adoption and implementation procedures of the homestead tax system.

20:48. How are school districts affected by the homestead/non-homestead property-classification system?

If a locality elects this option, it must provide a copy of the local law establishing the homestead classification system to the authorities of each school district located wholly or partially within that locality. When adopted by an approved assessing unit (a town, village, or city), the homestead system applies to taxes levied on all real property by each school district wholly contained within the approved assessing unit (§ 1903(1)(a)(b)). However, an affected district may adopt a resolution rejecting this kind of property-classification system in its district (§ 1903(1)(a)).

20:49. Can the homestead/nonhomestead property-classification system apply to school districts located in more than one city or town?

Yes, if one or more cities or towns within the school district has adopted a homestead/nonhomestead property-classification system. A school board may, by resolution, adopt such a classification system, upon filing a notice of intent, as set forth in law (§ 1903-a(1)(a), (b)), and following a public hearing to be held at any time prior to the levy of school taxes (§ 1903-a(3)).

School districts may cancel notice of intent to adopt such a system by filing a notice of cancellation, as set forth in law (§ 1903-a(1)(c)). They may also, by board resolution and without a public hearing, rescind any prior action adopting such a system at any time prior to the levy of taxes for the fiscal year to which the resolution is applicable. Any such rescission must also be filed in accordance with law (§ 1903-a(5)).

Tax Collection

20:50. Are there specific procedures and deadlines for authorizing the collection of taxes?

Yes. After the tax roll has been prepared by applying the property tax rates against the properties assessed, the list must be confirmed by school board resolution. At the date and time at which this resolution is adopted, the school taxes become a lien on the properties (§ 1312).

The next step is to execute the warrant, which serves as a directive to the tax collector to collect taxes in accordance with the confirmed tax list and provides authorization for making collection (§ 1318(1)). In most school districts, the tax warrant must be affixed to the tax list on or before September 1 (§ 1306(1)). In small city school districts, the tax warrant must be affixed to the tax roll no later than 90 days after the start of the fiscal year, which begins July 1 (§ 1306(2), see also Educ. Law § 2515). At least a majority of the school board is required to sign the warrant for the collection of taxes (§ 1318(1)).

The state does not fix a limit on the number of times a tax warrant may be renewed. However, warrants of school tax collectors must be returnable in time for the school authorities to transmit necessary information regarding unpaid taxes to the county treasurer by November 15 (§§ 1318(3), 1330(2)).

20:51. How are taxpayers notified of their school taxes?

Upon receipt of a warrant for the collection of taxes, the collecting officer must publish a notice in a newspaper, or two newspapers, if there are two, having general circulation in the school district, which states that the warrant has been received and all taxes due must be received within one month from the time of the first published notice (§§ 1322(1), 1324).

The notice must be published at least twice and as many additional times as the school authorities may direct (§§ 1322(1), 1324). If there is no newspaper having general circulation in the district, the notice must be posted immediately in at least 20 public places in the district (§ 1322(1)).

In addition, the collecting officer also must mail a statement of taxes to each real property owner on the tax list (§§ 1322(1), (2), 1324, 922(1)). Where the school district has levied a tax for the purpose of a public library or on behalf of a library district, the amount of the taxes attributable to library purposes must be separately stated on each statement of taxes (§§ 1322(1), 1324; see also **20:38**).

The tax collector also must give a like notice by mail or personally to all nonresident taxpayers whose post offices may be known or ascertained, and to all railroads and utility corporations. The notice should bear the date of the posting of the notice. The tax collector is required to give such notice at least 20 days prior to the expiration of the one-month period of tax collection (§ 1322(2)).

In a school district where the board of education has adopted a resolution authorizing the payment of taxes in installments, the notice that the collecting officer is required to give also must state that taxes may be paid by installments in the manner specified in the board resolution (§§ 1326(2), 1336(3); see also **20:54**).

20:52. May residential taxpayers who are age 65 or over or disabled designate a third party to receive a duplicate tax statement from the tax collector?

Yes. The tax collector must enclose with each statement of taxes a notice that taxpayers who are age 65 or over, or disabled, and who are owner-occupants of residential real property consisting of no more than three family dwelling units, are eligible for the third-party notification procedure. This notice must explain the application procedure and other aspects of the provision (§ 1325(1)).

20:53. What kind of informational materials may a tax collector(s) include along with tax bills mailed or delivered to real property owners?

Section 1826 of the Tax Law makes it a misdemeanor for "[a]ny person, firm, corporation, or association, or employee thereof, who mails or delivers or causes to be mailed or delivered, any notice, circular, pamphlet, card, hand-bill, printed or written notice of any kind other than that which is *authorized or required by law* with a . . . tax bill or notification of a tax to be levied by the state of New York or any political subdivision thereof. . . ." [emphasis added].

Various authorities have interpreted the phrase "authorized or required by law" to include not only general state statutes, but also local laws (see 9 Opn. Counsel SBRPS No. 14 (1985); and 9 Opn. Counsel SBRPS No. 98 (1993)). However, since school districts do not have the power to adopt "local laws," school districts may only include information with tax bills that is authorized or required by state law (9 Opn. Counsel SBRPS No. 14 (1995), footnote 2).

A school board may, by resolution, require the collecting officer to enclose a summary of the adopted budget and an explanation of the computation of the tax rate (§§ 1322(1), 1324; see also **20:51**).

Also, subdivision 4 of section 467 of the Real Property Tax Law *requires* school districts that offer senior citizens a real property tax exemption pursuant to that section of law to notify real property owners of the availability of the exemption by means of a "notice or legend sent on or with each tax bill. . ." (see also 9 Opn. Counsel SBRPS No. 14 (1985)).

20:54. May school taxes be paid in installments?

Yes, but the law is different for city and non-city school districts.

City school districts may adopt a resolution stating that school taxes may be paid in a specified number of installments, but no more than six. The installments must be as equal as possible, and the resolution must state the number of installments and the dates on which installments are due to be paid. Each installment subsequent to the first includes interest on the balance due calculated from the date the first installment was due, at the rate of interest determined pursuant to section 924-a (§ 1326(1)). Or the board may adopt a resolution to assess interest on the balance due at the same rate of interest that is applicable to unpaid city taxes in the city in which the district is located (§ 1326(3); the amount of any unpaid interest becomes part of the amount of unpaid tax (§ 1326(1)).

City districts also may limit installment payments to qualified senior citizens and persons with physical disabilities (§ 1327).

Non-city school districts may adopt a resolution by a two-thirds vote allowing school taxes to be collected in three installments. The minimum amount per installment is set by statute and the due date for each installment must be specified in the school board's resolution (§ 1326-a(1)). In addition, the school district may choose to limit the installment program to certain types of property as provided in the law (§ 1326-a(4)).

Moreover, in a non-city school district, upon enactment of a local law by a county pursuant to section 972, the school board may pass a resolution prior to the date of the annual district meeting, which authorizes the payment of tax in installments as to any taxes in excess of $50 levied by the district on any parcel of real property located within the county that also is located within the school district (see also §§ 1338, 1340). This resolution must be certified by the district clerk to the clerk of the board of supervisors by August 1 following the annual meeting. The warrant for the collection of taxes levied while this resolution is in effect must explain that the property owner may elect to pay the taxes due, in installments, and must contain instructions regarding the payment of taxes in the manner specified by the local law enacted by the county (§§ 972, 1336, 1338(2)).

20:55. Can a school board restrict the property tax installment payment option to certain taxpayers?

Yes. A school board may limit installment payments of school property taxes to senior citizens who qualify for the senior citizen exemption and/or to those taxpayers who are disabled as defined by law (§§ 1327, 1326-a(4)(b), (c)).

In addition, non-city school districts can limit installment payments of school property taxes to one-, two- and three-family residential properties (§ 1326-a(4)(a)).

20:56. May the tax collector accept payment of taxes on only part of a parcel of real property?

Yes, provided the taxpayer furnishes certain specifications, including apportionment, regarding the assessment of the parcel (§ 932). Once a written request is submitted by a party interested in an affected property, an assessor must apportion an assessment under the law (9 Opn. Counsel SBEA No. 13 (1990)).

20:57. What happens if school taxes are inadvertently paid to the wrong collector?

School taxes inadvertently paid to the collector of a district that does not include the assessed property within its boundaries, should be refunded by that district (§ 556).

20:58. What happens if a real property owner who is in military service fails to pay a property tax bill on time?

The law provides special protections to real property owners in active military service. Under both state and federal law, interest on delinquent taxes for properties owned by persons in military service is imposed at a reduced rate of 6 percent annually (i.e., one-half percent per month), or less pursuant to a resolution adopted by the local board of education (Mil. Law § 314(4); see also 50 USC § 560(4); and 9 Opn. Counsel SBRPS No. 64

(1991)). Furthermore, the deadline for payment of any such interest penalties owed to a municipal corporation (including a school district) by a person who has been deployed to active military duty, or by the spouse or domestic partner of that individual, shall be extended for 90 days after the end of such deployment, provided the school board passes a resolution authorizing such an extension (§ 925-d).

Both state and federal law provide additional protections to real property owners in military service, including protections against foreclosure (see Mil. Law § 314; and 50 USC § 560).

20:59. What happens if any taxes remain unpaid at the time the collecting officer is required to return a warrant to the school authorities?

The collecting officer must return the tax roll and warrant with a statement of the unpaid taxes and a description of the property upon which taxes remain unpaid (§ 1330(1), 1332(2)). When the school authorities receive this statement, they must compare it with the original tax roll. If it is correct, they must certify the statement as such (§ 1330(2), 1332(3)).

The school authorities then immediately transmit the statement and certificate in time for the county treasurer to receive it no later than November 15 (§ 1330(2)). Different rules apply to the transmittal of this statement and certificate in city school districts (§ 1332(3)).

On or before April 1 of the next year, the county treasurer must pay the school district the amount of unpaid school taxes (§ 1330(4); see § 1332(5) for city school districts, § 1342 relating to taxes paid in installments).

20:60. Does the return of unpaid school taxes by the county to the school district include any interest paid to the county by delinquent taxpayers?

Yes. School districts that have school tax collectors employed on a salary basis are entitled to receive, in addition to the unpaid taxes, interest at a rate set by the commissioner of taxation as set forth in law. If the school district's tax collector is compensated on a fee basis, the district receives no fees (§§ 1328(2), 1330(5); Opn. St. Comp. 81-420; 8 Opn. Counsel SBEA No. 58 (1982); see also **20:62**).

20:61. What happens to the tax roll and warrant after they have been returned to the school authorities by the collecting officer?

The school authorities must deliver the tax roll and warrant to the school district clerk within 15 days (20 days in city school districts) of their return by the collecting officer. School districts under a district superintendent, however, deliver the tax list and warrant to the district superintendent who, in turn, delivers it to the school district clerk by July 1 (§§ 1330(3), 1332(4)).

20:62. How are tax collectors paid?

Some school districts employ tax collectors on a salary basis, with the salary determined by the school board (§ 1328(2); Educ. Law § 2130(4)). In other districts, the tax collector receives 1 percent of the amount of taxes collected during the first month after the publication of notice and not more than 5 percent of the amount collected after the first month (§ 1328(1)).

Industrial Development Agencies

20:63. What is an industrial development agency?

An *industrial development agency* (IDA) is an independent public benefit corporation created through state legislation at the request of one or more sponsoring municipalities. Article 18-A of the General Municipal Law sets forth powers, jurisdiction and requirements for IDAs. Legislation creating a specific IDA may contain provisions different from or in addition to the general legislation contained in the General Municipal Law.

20:64. May school board members serve on an IDA board?

Yes. The General Municipal Law states that school board members, municipal officials, and representatives of organized labor and business may serve on IDA governing boards (Gen. Mun. Law § 856(2)).

20:65. What is the taxable status of real property owned by industrial development agencies, bonds and notes issued for IDA projects, and purchases made for IDA projects?

All property titled to an IDA, as well as any bonds or notes issued by an IDA, are exempt from taxation, except for transfer and estate taxes (§ 412-a; Gen. Mun. Law § 874(1), (2)).

However, an IDA is authorized to negotiate payments in lieu of taxes (PILOTs) with the private developers participating in IDA projects (Gen. Mun. Law § 858(15)). PILOT moneys received from an IDA are to be included in the school budget as if they were tax dollars (Opn. St. Comp. 82-174). Furthermore, PILOTs must be included as estimated in the annual preparation of the school district's budget (Educ. Law §§ 1608(3), 1716(3), 2601-a(3)). PILOTs received by the IDA must be given to the school district within 30 days of receipt (Gen. Mun. Law § 874(3)).

In addition, all IDAs must adopt a uniform tax exemption policy with input from affected tax jurisdictions, including school districts, which states what tax exemptions are available to those interested in seeking IDA assistance for commercial enterprises. This policy must include guidelines for the claiming of real property, mortgage recording, and sales tax exemptions. The policy must also indicate the extent to which a proposed project will require additional services, including educational services, and the extent to which the proposed project will provide additional sources of revenue for school districts (Gen. Mun. Law § 874(4)(a)).

20:66. Can IDAs distribute PILOT revenues as they see fit?

No. Unless otherwise agreed to by the school board and municipal governments affected by an IDA project, payments in lieu of taxes (PILOTS) must be distributed in proportion to the amount of real property and other taxes which would have been received had the project not been tax-exempt (Gen. Mun. Law § 858(15)).

20:67. What responsibilities do IDAs have with respect to notifying school districts about their IDA-assisted projects?

IDAs must provide written notice to the chief executive officer of each affected school district within which any pending project is located that requires more than $100,000 in IDA financial assistance of a public hearing on the proposed project, at least 10 days prior to the hearing. In addition to stating the time and place of the hearing, the notice of the hearing must include a general description of the project (including its location), the identify the initial owner, operator or manager of the project, and a description of the financial assistance contemplated by the IDA with respect to the project (Gen. Mun. Law § 859-a)).

IDAs also must notify school boards and municipalities within 15 days of an agreement reached for payments in lieu of taxes (PILOTS) on an IDA-assisted project (Gen. Mun. Law § 858(15)).

21. State Aid

Editor's Note: At the time this publication went to press the governor and the Legislature were finalizing the details of their 2004 school budget agreement. They had not reached agreement on reforms necessary to comply with the New York State Court of Appeals decision in Campaign for Fiscal Equity Inc. v. State, *100 N.Y.2d 893 (2003). The finalized budget and any reforms eventually adopted will affect the contents of this chapter. Look for developments in* On Board, *other New York State School Boards Association publications, and posted on the NYSSBA Web site at http://www.nyssba.org.*

21:1. How is public elementary and secondary education financed in New York State?

Public education in New York State is funded through a combination of local tax revenues, aid from the state government, and a small amount of assistance from the federal government. The most current information available indicates that local revenues provide approximately 46.9 percent of all school district revenues. The state share is approximately 47.3 percent and the federal share is approximately 5.8 percent.

21:2. What is the source of money used to pay state aid?

The bulk of the money used to pay state aid is derived from state tax revenues. These include the personal income tax, the sales and use tax, the corporate franchise tax, the motor fuel tax and corporation utility taxes.

Proceeds from the New York State Lottery support elementary, middle and secondary education. A share of the lottery proceeds is computed according to an equalized formula based on each school district's taxable property wealth per pupil to support the general state aids otherwise payable to a school district. Under the State Finance Law, all revenues from the state lottery, after prizes and the cost of administration have been accounted for, must be used for the support of education (State Fin. Law § 92-c). School districts receive a portion of their fall state aid payment in the form of a check directly from the lottery fund by September 1 (§ 3609-a(1)(a)(2)). A portion of the lottery funds ($15 per resident pupil) is added to regular textbook aid, which is included in the check districts receive from the lottery fund. Lottery aid also includes a $10 payment for each blind and deaf student attending state-supported schools for the blind and deaf (State Fin. Law § 92-c(4)(b)). In actuality, however, lottery funds are used to supplant, not to supplement, general fund spending for education as originally intended.

21:3. When is state aid actually paid to local school districts?

The state aid payment schedule, as amended by Chapter 53 of the Laws of 1992, provides school districts with funds beginning in the fall of each year (§ 3609-a; see also **21:2**). The school district fiscal year begins July 1 and ends on June 30.

The payment schedule includes the following features:

- The state sends payments to the New York State Teachers' Retirement System (TRS) on behalf of districts in September, October and November (§ 3609-a(1)(a)(1)). The relative amount of a district's TRS obligation does not affect monthly aid payment calculations.
- Lottery aid is paid in full by September 1 (§ 3609-a(1)(a)(2)).
- Fixed payments are paid in the months of October, November and December. These payments guarantee a fixed percentage of a district's total aid, after TRS payments, by a given date: 12.5 percent by October 15, 18.75 percent by November 15, and 25 percent by December 15 (§ 3609-a(1)(a)(4)).
- Individualized payments are paid during the months of January through June. These are calculated to guarantee that each district receives 50 percent of its state and local revenues by the first business day of January, 60 percent by February, 70 percent by March, 80 percent by April, 90 percent by May and 100 percent in the June payment (§ 3609-a(1)(b)(2)). Any amount in excess of 100 percent of aid projections will be paid in September (§ 3609-a(1)(b)(3)(vii)).
- Boards of cooperative educational services (BOCES) aid is provided to school districts for services purchased from BOCES. After deducting payments due to TRS on behalf of BOCES, 25 percent of BOCES aid is paid on or before February 1, 55 percent is paid in June, and the remainder in September (§ 3609-d(1)).
- Growth aid is paid in full in June (§ 3609-a(1)(b)(3)(v)).
- Public and private excess cost aid payments for students with disabilities are separated from the general aid payment schedule. There are four guaranteed dates for reimbursement. The calculated sum of aids is apportioned according to the following schedule: 25 percent by December; 70 percent by March; 85 percent by June; 100 percent by August; and any amount in excess of 100 percent of aid projections by September (§ 3609-b(2)(a)).
- The School Tax Relief (STAR) program, created in 1997, provides homeowners with a real property tax exemption. In turn, the state reimburses school districts for the lost revenue through payments directly to school districts. STAR payments are paid in the months of October, November, December and January.
- For districts that participate in the federal Medicaid reimbursement program, reimbursement for excess cost aids will be paid in

conjunction with the scheduled payment of federal share moneys for Medicaid reimbursement (§ 3609-b(1)(a)).

21:4. What is the process for school districts to submit claims for state aid?

The superintendent of schools or district superintendent generally submits claims for aid to the Office of Management Services of the State Education Department. That office and the New York State Department of Audit and Control process claims for payment.

Prior year aid claims are subject to an amount appropriated by the Legislature. Eligible claims are payable in the order the payments have been approved by the commissioner of education. No claim may receive more than 40 percent of the amount appropriated. In the event the number of prior year claims outweigh available funding, partial payments are to be made with the balance of the late aid payment to be made in the next state fiscal year (§ 3604(5)(c)).

Chapter 83 of the Laws of 2002 allows the Big 5 city school districts (New York City, Buffalo, Rochester, Syracuse, and Yonkers) and 14 other school districts with prior year aid claims over $1 million to access financing through the Municipal Bond Bank to provide additional revenue during the current fiscal crisis without imposing additional debt on the districts or the State (Laws of 2002, Ch. 83, pp. 76–84).

21:5. Is state aid available to nonpublic schools in New York State?

Yes. In 1979, the United States Supreme Court upheld the constitutionality of chapters 507 and 508 of New York State's Laws of 1974, the so-called mandated services law. This law requires payment of state financial aid to nonpublic schools for costs incurred by them in complying with certain state mandates, such as testing, pupil evaluation, achievement tests and attendance records (*Committee for Pub. Educ. & Religious Liberty v. Regan*, 444 U.S. 646 (1980)).

In 1973, the court had struck down such statutes as being violations of the Establishment Clause of the First Amendment because they contained no requirement that nonpublic schools account for funds received and how they were spent (see *Levitt v. Committee for Pub. Educ. & Religious Liberty*, 413 U.S. 472 (1973)). The present laws provide a means for auditing payments of state funds, thus ensuring that state funds are used only for secular services.

Nonpublic schools also secure state aid in the form of services and equipment including school transportation, health services, career education, services for gifted students and children with disabilities, textbooks, computer software, and library materials (§§ 3635, 912, 3602-c, 701(3), 752, 712).

Since April 1975, an office of nonpublic school services in the State Education Department has dealt specifically with state services to nonpublic schools.

Types of State Aid

21:6. What types of state aid are available to school districts?

There are two basic types of state aid available to school districts.

Unrestricted (or general) aid may be used by districts for any purpose as determined by local priorities and needs. Comprehensive operating aid is the major unrestricted aid (§ 3602(12); see **21:7, 21:10**). Other types of unrestricted aid are the extraordinary needs component of comprehensive operating aid, growth aid, tax effort aid and tax equalization aid (§ 3602 (12)(e), (13), (16)(b),(c); see **21:11**). The 2002–03 state budget consolidated operating aid, tax effort aid, tax equalization aid, and the transition adjustment. For the 2003–04 school year, school districts received $6.8 billion in comprehensive operating aid. Comprehensive operating aid is a compilation of aid formerly grouped into comprehensive operating aid, gifted and talented aid, operating standards aid, and academic support aid (Big 5 cities). The amount received by each district was a reduction of the amount received in the 2003–04 school year of between 2.25 and 6.30 percent, depending on the district's relative wealth. Beyond this, the formulas used to generate these aids were not changed nor were the variables used to generate the funding.

Categorical aid is provided to districts for particular purposes and must be spent for the purpose specified. For example, in 1999–2000, an estimated 40 categorical grants and aids were available to school districts; however, not all districts are eligible for all categorical aids. Some categorical aids are distributed according to formulas; others are awarded on a grant basis (see **21:12** for major aids, categorical aids, and grant programs).

21:7. What is comprehensive operating aid and how is it calculated?

Comprehensive operating aid is unrestricted aid. It is spent according to a district's priorities as determined by the school board, not for specifically legislated purposes. Historically, operating aid has been the largest single category of allocation. In more recent years, two programs were appropriated at greater levels than operating aid — building aid and LADDER (Learning, Achieving, Developing by Directing Educational Resources).

For operating purposes, the state shares in allocating aid to the public schools through an aid-ratio formula. Comprehensive operating aid is generated up to a certain ceiling level per pupil in inverse proportion to a district's wealth, as represented by the value of its real property and adjusted gross income of the community. Districts with low wealth receive a relatively high amount of aid, while districts with high wealth receive a relatively low amount of aid.

Comprehensive operating aid is calculated and distributed in accordance with an equalized formula based on a district's selected operating aid ratio. The formula calls for a district's aid per pupil to be multiplied by the number of total aidable pupil units (TAPU) (§ 3602(8)), as defined in **21:9**. For those districts in which the formula generates less than $400 per pupil, the statute guarantees $400 per-pupil minimum comprehensive operating aid, often referred to as the flat grant (§ 3602(12)(c)). For 2003–04, the operating aid limit was $3,900.00 per pupil.

21:8. How is operating aid actually calculated?

The formula for operating aid can be expressed mathematically (see "2003–2004 Guidebook to State Aid Formulas for Elementary and Secondary Education," State Education Department, November 2003):

The sum of .5 (full-value wealth ratio) and .5 (income-wealth ratio) = Combined Wealth Ratio (CWR)

A district's selected operating aid ratio is the greatest of:
1.37 – (1.23 × CWR), 1.00 – (0.64 × CWR), 0.80 – (0.39 × CWR), 0.51 – (0.22 × CWR)

The maximum aid ratio is .90. Based on this model, for a district of average wealth (1.0 CWR), the aid ratio is 41 percent. Thus, the state share of the first $3,900 a district spends per pupil will be 41 percent.

Operating aid ratio × ceiling ($3,900) = formula aid per pupil (§ 3602(12)(d))

Approved operating expenses (up to $8,000) per pupil $3,900 × 7.5 percent. This product × district aid ratio = formula operating aid

The greater of formula aid per pupil plus aid ratio per pupil or per pupil flat grant ($400) = total operating aid per pupil

Total operating aid per pupil × selected TAPU (see **21:9**) = total operating aid

21:9. What is the pupil count used in computing comprehensive operating aid?

Comprehensive operating aid is determined by multiplying aid per pupil unit, as computed in the formula, by the total aidable pupil units (TAPU) (§ 3602(8); see **21:8**).

The base pupil count for TAPU is based on average daily attendance (ADA) (§ 3602(1)(d)). ADA is the average number of pupils served during the calendar year, determined by dividing the total number of attendance days of all pupils by the number of days school was in session for the previous year.

For any given school year, districts are permitted to use the higher of the previous year's (base year) TAPU or a two-year average of the base year and the year prior to the base year (§ 3602(8)(iii)). The count chosen is called selected TAPU for payment. School districts are required to treat charter schools like nonpublic schools in areas such as textbook, computer software and school library materials aid (§ 2853(4)(a)). For these aids, charter school students are included in the calculation of TAPU.

The table below shows how different students are weighted in the calculation of TAPU for payment. For the calculation of aid in the 2003–04 school year, average daily attendance (ADA) will be calculated using the year prior to the base year, plus an enrollment adjustment.

Basic Pupil Weightings

Half-day Kindergarten	.50
ADA (K-6)	1.00
ADA (7-12)	1.25
Dual Enrollment*	1.00
Additional Weightings	
Secondary (including PSEN** but excluding certain students with disabilities)	.25
PSEN (K-12 including pupils with disabilities)	.25
Summer School	.12

*See **21:23** for information about dual enrollment.
**Pupils with special educational needs, § 3602(1)(e).

21:10. What is the transition adjustment for purposes of calculating comprehensive operating aid?

A *positive transition adjustment* prevents districts from receiving less total operating aid in the current year than its total operating aid paid in the base year. A *negative transition adjustment* limits, or caps, allowable increases in total operating aid.

The group of aids that are subject to the transition adjustment include operating aid, tax effort aid and tax equalization aid. The transition adjustment varies from year to year. For example, under the Laws of 1999, no district could receive less aid than the previous year. In the 2000–01 state budget, districts subject to the negative transition adjustment were allowed a maximum increase of 4.27 percent (from 2.8 percent) over 1999–2000 or to provide an increase of 18.1 percent (from 7.8 percent) of the difference over the previous year (§ 3602(18)). The 2001–02 state budget suspended the use of formulas altogether and resulted in districts receiving a lump-sum payment that was the same as what they had received the year prior. The 2002–03 state budget perpetuated certain inequities by consolidating operating aid, tax effort aid, tax equalization aid, and the transition adjustment. Transition adjustments result in an inequitable distribution of school aid, because the wealth-equalized formula is not permitted to work. The 2003–04 state budget reduced operating aid between 2.25 and 6.30 percent, based on relative district wealth.

21:11. What other unrestricted state aid may districts receive in addition to comprehensive operating aid and extraordinary needs aid?

Districts may receive tax equalization and tax effort aids, both of which replace high tax aid (§ 3602(16)). Tax equalization aid is based on a district's per pupil expense (up to $8,000), minus its comprehensive operating aid per pupil. If the difference between these two measures would require a full value tax rate greater than $19.50, equalization aid is provided, according to Chapter 53 of the Laws of 1994. Tax effort aid is based on residential property taxes and income, and measures the residential tax levy against the district's ability to raise revenue. These aids were consolidated into comprehensive operating aid in 2002–03.

The Legislature introduced a new aid, tax limitation aid, in the 1999–2000 budget, that is currently available to school districts. The purpose of this aid is to ensure that school districts with high residential property tax burdens can continue to provide local support for education without increasing property taxes. For 2003–04, $30 million was appropriated for districts experiencing a high tax effort. Districts with a "tax effort ratio" (greater than 3.9 percent of 2000 adjusted gross income) and "pupil wealth ratio" less than one and one half the estate average are eligible for tax limitation aid. This aid is paid on a current year basis, with 70 percent paid before March 15 and the rest paid after April 1.

21:12. What are the major categorical aids available to school districts?

The major categorical aids are:

- *Boards of cooperative educational services (BOCES) aid*, provided to help school districts pay for the services they purchase from BOCES (§ 1950(5)). Component school districts are eligible to receive BOCES aid for services like occupational education, teacher training, curriculum development and administrative and management services. For the 2003–04 the state allocated approximately $522 million for BOCES aid.

- *Transportation aid*, provided to pay between 6.5 percent and 90 percent of a district's approved transportation expenditures, depending upon one of three aid ratios. For instance, one is derived from the operating aid ratio; another from the resident weighted average daily attendance ratio), adjusted by a sparsity factor (§ 3602(7)). Chapter 145 of the Laws of 1999 provides for the cost of transporting nonpublic school students for particularly hard-hit districts. In addition, the state budget provides up to $5 million for transportation reimbursement to district-run summer school programs. For 2003–04 the state expended approximately $1.88 million for transportation aid. Transportation aid is separated into capital expenses, which include bus purchases and non-capital expenses, which include salaries, operating and maintenance expenses, contractual expenses, equipment, uniforms, health and life insurance, retirement benefits and other costs of operation. Transportation expenditures for athletic and field trips are not eligible for aid.

- *Building aid*, provided to districts for building purposes (§ 3602(6)). Certain conditions are placed on those districts scheduled for reorganization (§ 3602(14)). The building aid ratio falls between 0 and .90, except that under additional incentive aid approved in 1998 districts may qualify for a ratio of between .10 and .98. Building aid is also available for stationary metal detectors, security cameras, safety devices for electronically operated partitions and room dividers, and other security devices approved by the commissioner of education (§ 3602(6-c)). Projects costing less than $10,000 are not generally eligible for building aid. Beginning in the 2000–01 state fiscal year, state aid payments to school districts are delayed until the first payment on a bond is due for projects approved by the voters after July 1, 2000. School districts will still be able to use a selected building aid ratio (the best aid ratio between 1982–83 and 1999–2000). However, the building aid ratio will be determined without consideration of the .10 incentive aid authorized in the 1997–98 state budget for all projects. The incentive aid will be added onto the higher of the selected building aid ratio or the current building aid ratio. Also, swimming pool projects will no longer be eligible for the .10 incentive aid. Projects without instructional space are not generally eligible for building aid. Leases for a district-owned bus garage are eligible for building aid. The state is expected to spend approximately $1.178 billion on building aid in 2003–04. Projects approved by the State Education Department on or after December 1, 2001 and projects for which no bonds were issued prior to that date are subject to an assumed amortization schedule of 30 years for new buildings, 20 years for additions to existing buildings and 15 years for renovations, rehabilitation and reconstruction of existing buildings. School districts are required to notify the SED any time that obligations have been issued to fund the cost of capital construction.

- *Minor maintenance and repair aid*, provided to repair schools, based on their age, square footage, and a growth index (§ 3602(6-d)). $49.7 million was allocated for 2003–04, with New York City receiving approximately two-thirds of the amount.
- *Gifted and talented aid*, provided to defray the cost of special programs to meet the learning needs of gifted and talented students (§ 3602(23)) has been combined into comprehensive operating aid.
- *Limited English Proficiency (LEP) aid*, provided for students who cannot benefit from the regular instructional program because of their limited ability to speak, read and write English (§ 3602(22)). These students must receive a program of either bilingual education or English as a second language (ESL) so that they master English as well as learn their academic subjects. In order to qualify for LEP aid, the commissioner's regulations say that a district must develop a comprehensive plan detailing how it will implement and budget for these programs. The plan must be filed with SED no later than August 31 of the service year. A district must provide other information, including the number of LEP students it serves, the criteria it uses to place ESL students in either a bilingual or a free-standing ESL program, the nature and scope of the programs currently offered to LEP students, an evaluation plan, and a description of its procedures for managing the programs (8 NYCRR § 154.4). Districts may operate their own programs or contract with BOCES.
- *Aid for children with disabilities*, provided to partially defray the excess cost involved in educating children with disabilities, both in public school districts and for BOCES programs (public excess cost aid) and in private schools (private excess cost aid) (§ 3602(19)). Public excess cost aid is paid for students with disabilities placed in a public special education program by the committee on special education. In 2003–04, the state expended approximately $2.075 billion on public excess cost aid. For 2003–04, "save harmless" was reduced to 95 percent of aid paid in 2002–03. Private excess cost aid

is paid for students with disabilities placed by the committee on special education at SED-approved private schools.

- *Educationally-related support service (ERSS)*, provided to support services to non-disabled students in order to maintain their placement in a regular education program. Speech therapy aid, which provides speech and language improvement services for students with speech impairments, was combined with this aid in 1993–94 (§ 3602(32)).

- *Summer school aid*, provided to support the cost of summer programs aimed at improving pupil performance. Summer school aid is available for district-operated academic programs only. Eligible programs must be constructed to prepare students to take or retake Regents examinations or portions or Regents examinations, or improve student performance in required academic subjects.

- *Employment preparation education (EPE) aid*, used to fund adult education programs such as literacy, basic skills and high school equivalency programs (§ 3602(24)). Both BOCES and component district programs serving persons 21 years of age and older who have not yet received a high school or high school equivalency diploma are eligible for EPE aid. All EPE programs need prior SED approval to receive aid.

- *Reorganization incentive aid*, provided for both operating and building expenses incurred by those school districts scheduled for reorganization (§ 3602(14)). For qualifying districts that reorganized prior to July 1, 1983 the aid is equal to 25 percent of regular building aid. For districts qualifying after July 1, 1983, the maximum allowable aid is 30 percent. Total building and reorganization incentive aid may not exceed 95 percent of assumed annual expenses or project costs.

- *Textbook aid*, provided to reimburse districts for the current-year costs of the purchase of textbooks and other approved instructional materials. All textbooks owned or acquired by a district must also be loaned to all resident pupils enrolled in kindergarten through 12th grade in public and nonpublic schools on an equitable basis. Software for educational purposes is also eligible for reimbursement under textbook aid (§ 701; see **14:108**). Home instruction students may not be included for purposes of textbook aid. The 2003–04 state budget limited textbook aid (including the lottery portion) to $57.30 per pupil for the 2003–04 school year. This aid is paid to districts in September. The cost of biweekly newspapers and news magazines are allowable expenditures under textbook aid.

- *Computer software aid*, provided for the purchase and loan of computer software. Software programs designed for use in public schools must also be loaned on an equitable basis to nonpublic school students (§§ 751–752)). The 2003–04 state budget limited software aid to $14.98 per pupil.

- *Computer hardware and technology equipment aid*, apportioned to districts for the lease, repair or purchase of mini- and microcomputers, computer terminals or certain other technology equipment, such as lasers, robotics equipment and solar energy equipment, for instructional purposes (§ 3602(26)). Training and staff development expenses are allowed at the rate of 20 percent. In order to qualify, districts must file a technology plan. Districts on a contingency budget may use up to the total allocated in the previous year's budget for such purchases, repair and, lease or training.
- *Instructional computer technology expenses aid*, apportioned to districts to provide additional funding for acquisition and maintenance of education technology (§ 3602(26-a)).
- *Library materials aid*, allocated to districts to purchase library materials, which must also be loaned on an equitable basis to nonpublic school students (§§ 711(4), 712). Library books and instructional materials are ordinary contingent expenses.
- *Special services aid*, provided to the Big 5 city school districts and other non-component districts of BOCES, are eligible for occupational education and computer services (§ 3602(17)).
- *Universal pre-kindergarten aid*, allocated to enhance existing programs and establish new pre-kindergarten programs (§ 3602-e, 8 NYCRR § 151.13(a)). The grant for 2003–04 was fixed at the 2002–03 level, making districts eligible to receive a grant equal to the grant received in that prior year. The allocation for 2003–04 is $201 million.
- *Full-day kindergarten incentive aid*, provided to school districts that do not currently offer a full-day kindergarten program as an incentive to do so (§ 3602(12-a)). In order to qualify, districts must offer full-day kindergarten to all students.
- *Early grade class size reduction aid*, provided to reduce the class size of grades K-3 to an average of 20 students (§ 3602(37)). The amount of aid payable in 2003–04 was equal to the amount the district received in 2002–03.
- *Teachers of Tomorrow Recruitment and Retention Program,* awarded as grants to districts to aid in their recruitment and retention of teachers, with consideration given to such factors as the degree of the district's teacher shortage, the number of temporarily and provisionally licensed teachers in the district, the district's fiscal capacity and geographic sparsity, and the number of new teachers the district intends to hire (§ 3612).
- *Small cities aid* is available for small cities with populations under 250,000. In 2003–04 approximately 50 received roughly $82 million in small cities aid. Districts qualified for eligibility in 1987–88 and all districts are currently projected to be on "save harmless." In 2003–04 districts received the same aid as they received in 2002–03.

- *High cost aid* is included in public excess cost aid and is available for students with disabilities served in the public school or BOCES program at an annualized costs exceeding three times the district's approved operating expense.
- *Integrated settings excess cost aid* may be claimed for students with disabilities who receive special education services for 60 percent or more of the school day in a general education classroom. This aid may be claimed in addition to public excess cost aid.
- *Extraordinary needs aid (ENA)* is available to districts with income wealth less than 2.5 times the state average. ENA is based on the income wealth ration, the adjusted operating aid ceiling and a pupil count reflecting student need. $704.9 million in ENA was projected in 2003–04.
- *Full-day kindergarten conversion aid* is available to districts that offer full-day kindergarten to all students and have previously offered either half-day kindergarten or no kindergarten in order to qualify for full-day kindergarten conversion aid.
- *Legislative initiatives* or "member items" are submitted by districts to individual members of the state Legislature and are made available at the discretion of the leaders of each house of the state Legislature. The amount allocated for legislative initiatives in the state budget is subject to negotiation between the Legislature and governor each year.

21:13. How are approved expenditures for debt service eligible for building aid determined?

There are two forms of debt service expenditures eligible for capital notes: bond anticipation notes and bonds and capital notes. Approved expenditures for bond anticipation notes (BANS) will be limited to actual expenditures for principal and interest related to financing of a school construction project through BANS. Such expenditures may not include expenditures for principal for the first 23 months after issuance and expenditures on principal or interest on BANS issued or reissued after a certificate of substantial completion is issued (§ 3602(6)(i)(1)). The 2000–01 state budget changed the timing on payments for BANs. Payments on BANs that districts had received in June will be received in July of the following year.

For projects approved by the commissioner of education on or after December 1, 2002, or for projects approved sooner but for which no debt has yet been issued, approved expenditures for bonds and capital notes are computed based on an amortization period equal to its period of probable usefulness or 30 years for new construction, 20 years for additions, and 15 years for reconstruction projects. If the district does not use a bond issue of this length, the commissioner will compute the state aid payments as if the district had done so (§ 3602(6)(i)(2), as amended by Laws of 2001, Ch. 383).

The first assumed principal and interest payment is made the later of 18 months after approval by the State Education Department's Office of Facilities Planning or on the date the general construction contract is certified to the Education Department (SED guidance document "Overview of State Building Aid Changes with Questions and Answers," March 2002, p. 1).

While the state share will be paid according to the assumed amortization schedule, local districts may finance their projects in any way they choose. The former penalty for early borrowing is eliminated for projects subject to prospective assumed amortization (SED guidance document, p. 2).

Beginning with building aid due districts in the 2002–03 school year, projects approved by the commissioner before December 1, 2001 and for which debt has already been issued are also subject to assumed amortization for the state share of their related debt.

Districts may avail themselves of several options to manage the change in building aid for existing projects. They can refinance only the state portion of existing debt. In this case, state aid will cover the entire cost of refinancing the state share. The local share is paid off by the district under the same terms and schedule as existing debt.

Alternatively, districts may refinance both the state and local share of debt. State building aid will only cover the cost of refinancing state debt. The district would pay off the local share under the same terms and schedule as the state share.

Finally, a district may choose to absorb the difference in state building aid payments or to seek a waiver consistent with the guidelines developed by the commissioner in consultation with the Director of the Budget. Information regarding waivers is available at http://www.stateaid.nysed.gov (SED guidance document, pp. 2–3).

21:14. How can districts receive allocations for "qualified zone academies" from the state?

In 2002, the commissioner's regulations were amended to include a detailed description of the procedures necessary for school districts to receive an allocation for qualified zone academies from the state. Qualified zone academy bonds are available to eligible schools for use in repair and rehabilitation of buildings, purchasing equipment for such facilities, developing course materials for use at schools and training teachers and other personnel at these schools. School districts can qualify for the program if at least 35 percent of their students are eligible for free or reduced-price lunches under the National School Lunch Act.

As a part of the application process, school districts must certify that the schools and bonds to be issued meet certain requirements, and provide copies of commitments from private entities to make qualified contributions and the written approval of the board and superintendent for such bond issue (8 NYCRR § 155.22).

The regulations also say that 50 percent of the state limitation amount allocation, which will be determined annually by the commissioner, shall be allocated to qualified zone academies in New York City, and the remaining 50 percent shall be allocated to those in the rest of the state. If the state does not exhaust its allocation limitation amount in any given year because school districts that have received an allocation have failed to spend it, the State can then distribute the remaining funds to districts in proportion to the percentage of students who are eligible for free and reduced-cost lunches under the national school lunch program (8 NYCRR § 155.22).

Calculation and Distribution of State Aid

21:15. How relevant to the calculation of state aid is the school district code number that appears on the state income tax form?

The school district code identifies the school district to which the income of the taxpayer is attributed.

As explained in **21:17**, income is a major factor in the calculation of a district's wealth and, therefore, in the calculation of state aid to be received by a district. It is crucial that the school district code number be accurate so that the correct amount of total income can be assigned to each district. If more than the actual amount of income per pupil is attributed to a district, it appears wealthier on paper than it actually is and may get less state aid than it deserves. Conversely, if less than the actual amount of income per pupil is attributed to a district, the district may get more state aid than it deserves.

For the purposes of annual aid distribution, a computerized income verification process is used to verify the match between addresses and school district codes reported on income tax returns used to determine district wealth (§ 3602(1)(k)(2)).

21:16. On what basis is state aid distributed?

There are a number of different bases on which state aid is distributed, depending on the type of aid. Some aid is distributed according to wealth-equalizing formulas. This means that the wealthier a district is, in terms of the property value and adjusted gross income behind each pupil, the less aid per pupil it receives. The poorer a district, the more aid per pupil it should receive.

Other aid is allocated based on a certain amount per pupil. Grants are allocated in a variety of ways. For example, the aid may cover a specific portion of the district's budgeted program costs, or lump sum amounts may be awarded to a limited number of districts. The latter method of allocation is often used when a grant is available only to certain districts, such as the

Big 5 city school districts (see **21:16**). Certain categories of aid, like transportation, BOCES, and building aid, reimburse districts for a portion of these costs.

The pupil count used to distribute aid is based on each district's average daily attendance (ADA) (§ 3602(1)(d)). ADA represents the average number of pupils present on each regular school day in a given period. The average is determined by dividing the total number of attendance days of all pupils by the number of days school was in session for the previous year (§ 3602(1)(d); see **21:9**).

21:17. On what basis is state aid distributed to the Big 5 city school districts?

Buffalo, New York City, Rochester, Syracuse, and Yonkers, each with populations over 125,000, are the Big 5 city school districts (§ 2550). These city school districts do not levy taxes to raise revenues as do the rest of the state's school districts. Rather, they are dependent on the portion of the city budget devoted to education each year for the local share of their budgets (§ 2576). Each of these cities also receives state and federal aid. The categorical state aids are accounted for separately by the cities, and each aid must be used entirely for its designated categorical purpose. The same is true for nearly all federal aid, since it is also categorical.

General-purpose state education aid becomes city revenue and is used to fund the schools; however, the cities do not necessarily allocate to the schools the exact amount of this aid received from the state. The cities differ in the extent to which general-purpose state education aid is used to supplement the municipal contribution to the schools.

21:18. How is a school district's wealth measured for purposes of school aid?

A school district's wealth, or ability to pay, is measured by comparing its property value per pupil with the state average property value per pupil, and the district's adjusted gross income per pupil with the state average adjusted gross income per pupil. The ratios derived from these comparisons are multiplied by .5 and added together to form the combined-wealth ratio (CWR) (§ 3602(1)(l)). Wealth is measured based on a prior year's data.

21:19. Can attendance for state aid purposes be excluded for days when school district employees are on strike?

No. Occasionally, legislation has been enacted on a year-by-year basis that allows a district to exclude the attendance for days on which there was a strike or for days on which attendance was affected adversely because of a strike. By being able to exclude the generally lower attendance on these days, a district was not penalized on the computation of weighted average daily attendance (WADA) (§ 3602(2)), upon which state aid is based (see **21:15**). This legislation has not been enacted in recent years.

21:20. Is a school penalized by the state aid formula for days on which it must be closed because of an emergency that results in the district providing less than 180 days of instruction?

Not necessarily. The commissioner of education is authorized to excuse a reduction of up to five days of instruction below 180 days for certain reasons, such as adverse weather or impairment of heating facilities, if the days cannot be made up by using scheduled vacation days. The 2002–03 state budget also exempted days on which schools had to be closed due to the events of September 11, 2001. Ordinarily, the apportionment of operating aid must be reduced by 1/180th for each day less than the required 180 days of instruction (§ 3604(7)).

21:21. Do districts receive aid for increased student enrollments?

Yes. Growth aid is available to districts with growth exceeding 0.4 percent. For example, a district experiencing 5 percent growth would receive an additional 4.6 percent of formula operating aid as growth aid. Growth aid is paid in the spring, separately from the general aid payment schedule (§ 3602(13)(b)).

21:22. Does state aid distribution reflect the needs of disadvantaged students?

Yes, to a degree. Chapter 57 of the Laws of 1993 enacted the extraordinary needs component of comprehensive operating aid. Extraordinary needs aid is distributed on the basis of student need using measures of poverty, such as the number of K–6 students eligible for free and reduced-priced lunch, the number of students who have limited English proficiency, and the number of students in geographically sparse areas (§ 3602(1)(s), (12)(e); see "Description of 2001–02 New York State School Aid Programs," State Education Department, November 2001, p. 23).

21:23. Is there special financial aid for those public schools that incur increased costs because of nonpublic school closings in their district?

Yes. There are two types of relief for public school districts experiencing enrollment increases resulting from the closing of nonpublic schools. The first type of relief is an impact aid, which is paid for each of the first two years the new students are in a district's public schools (§ 3602(5)).

The second type of relief, which is more indirect, comes from an immediate inclusion of students who formerly attended nonpublic schools in the definitions of total wealth pupil units (TWPU) (§ 3602(2-b)(c)) and resident weighted average daily attendance (RWADA) (§ 3602(2)(f)). The addition of these new students normally would not be reflected in a district's computations of TWPU and RWADA until two years after they had begun attending public schools. However, this two-year lag has been eliminated (§ 3602(2-b)(c)). Since the addition of these students is more quickly recognized in pupil wealth measures used in calculating those aids that use these measures, these aids are more accurately distributed.

21:24. Can districts receive aid for providing services required by the dual enrollment provision in the Education Law?

Yes. The dual enrollment provision requires school boards to provide instruction in the areas of gifted students, career education, education for students with disabilities, and counseling, psychological, and social work services related to such instruction to students who attend nonpublic schools, provided that such instruction is also given to students enrolled in the public school district (§ 3602-c).

Students receiving gifted or career education must be transported between the nonpublic school they legally attend and the public school where these services are offered, if the distance exceeds a quarter of a mile. Students with disabilities must receive transportation in accordance with the needs of such students (§ 3602-c(4)).

State aid for operating expenses is based on a formula that reflects the portion of the school day a nonpublic school student spends in a public school program (§ 3602-c(1)(e)). Districts that contract for these services with a board of cooperative education services (BOCES) receive aid based on the BOCES aid formula (§ 3602-c(3)). In addition, districts are reimbursed between 6.5 and 90 percent of approved transportation expenditures, depending upon the selected aid ratios plus a sparsity adjustment (§§ 3602(7)), 3602-c(4)).

Districts providing services to nonresident students under this provision are entitled to recover tuition from the students' home districts, according to the commissioner of education.

21:25. What are some common aid names and their abbreviations?

Here are some of the more common names and abbreviations for state aid and formulas:

Combined Wealth Ratio	(CWR)
Average Daily Attendance	(ADA)
Ratio of Weighted Daily Attendance	(RWADA)
Teachers Retirement System	(TRS)
Total Aidable Pupil Unit	(TAPU)
Total Wealth Pupil Unit	(TWPU)

21:26. Is New York's state aid system for funding public education constitutional?

In *Campaign for Fiscal Equity, Inc. v. State*, 719 N.Y.S.2d 475 (2001), a state Supreme Court ruled that New York State has consistently violated the state constitution by failing to provide the opportunity for a "sound basic education" to New York City public school students.

Subsequently, the New York State Court of Appeals, the state's highest court, ordered the state to ascertain the actual cost of providing a sound basic education in New York City and to ensure that schools receive the necessary funding by July 30, 2004. The court refrained from issuing specific orders saying it had "neither the authority nor the ability nor the will to micromanage education funding" (*Campaign for Fiscal Equity, Inc. v. State*, 100 N.Y.2d 893 (2003)). At the time this publication went to press the governor and both houses of the state legislature had issued plans to respond to the court imposed compliance deadline of July 30, 2004. No agreement among the parties was imminent.

21:27. Where can additional information about the distribution of state aid and details of aid formulas be found?

More detailed descriptions of aid, formulae and dollar allocations can be obtained from the Education Unit of the New York State Division of the Budget.

For questions about individual districts, contact the State Education Department's Office of Management Services State Aid Workgroup at 518-473-8364 or at http://www.nysed.gov.

22. Transportation

22:1. Must a school district furnish school bus transportation for students residing within the district?

Yes. School districts, except city school districts, are required to transport all students in grades kindergarten through 12, including those attending nonpublic schools and charter schools (§§ 2853(4)(b), 3635; see **22:109–10**). They do not have to, nor are they authorized to, provide transportation for children attending prekindergarten (*Appeal of Neubauer*, 32 Educ. Dep't Rep. 320 (1992)).

City school districts may, but are not required to, provide transportation (§ 3635(1)(c)). If it is provided, the transportation must be based on a reasonable and consistent policy that treats all children "in like circumstances" in a similar manner. However, students in different grade levels are not considered to be in "like circumstances." Therefore, a city school district may, for instance, provide transportation to students in certain grades and not others, based on its policy (*Appeal of Cassin*, 32 Educ. Dep't Rep. 373 (1992)).

Similarly, students receiving transportation services under section 3635 may be treated differently than to children transported to and from school under other statutes (*Appeal of Neubauer*). For example, a school district which provides transportation to students with disabilities under the provisions of article 89 of the Education Law is not required to transport students attending regular education beyond the distance limitations of section 3635 (see **22:12**), even if students with disabilities are transported a longer distance (*Appeal of Guiney*, 34 Educ. Dep't Rep. 410 (1995)).

In enlarged city school districts, transportation is required only for students residing outside the city limits, but it also may be provided to children living within the city limits (§ 2503(12)). An enlarged city school district may distinguish, in its transportation policy, between students residing within the city limits and those residing in areas of the enlarged city school district outside of the corporate boundaries of the school district (*Matter of Collar*, 14 Educ. Dep't Rep. 327 (1975)).

A district may use private carriers and/or public transportation to transport students to and from school (see *Appeal of Clancy*, 37 Educ. Dep't Rep. 280 (1998); *Appeal of Bruner*, 32 Educ. Dep't Rep. 276 (1992); *Appeal of Lavin*, 32 Educ. Dep't Rep. 249 (1992) (see **22:8**)).

22:2. Must a school district provide transportation to students who move to the district after the district budget has been passed and bus routes approved?

Yes, if the parents or guardians submit a written request within 30 days after establishing residency in the district. No late request may be denied if a reasonable explanation is provided for the delay. A statement by the parents that they were not aware of their obligation to submit a timely transportation request normally would not constitute a reasonable explanation for delay (§ 3635(2); *Appeal of Mogilski*, 37 Educ. Dep't Rep. 446 (1998)).

22:3. Must a school district furnish school bus transportation for resident students attending school outside their attendance zone?

Yes. Except as otherwise provided (see **22:1**), the Education Law requires that school districts transport students to and from the school "they legally attend" (§ 3635(1)). According to the commissioner of education, if a district allows a child to attend a district school other than the one the child would normally be assigned to, the school outside the child's attendance zone becomes the school the child legally attends. As such, the district has a legal obligation to transport that child to and from school (*Appeal of Nicotri*, 38 Educ. Dep't Rep. 80 (1998)).

However, when a child is permitted to attend a nonattendance zone school, the child's parent may agree to waive the provision of transportation that would otherwise be required (§ 3635(7)). The waiver must be voluntary (*Appeal of Jongebloed*, 16 Educ. Dep't Rep. 385 (1977)). The agreement to waive transportation must be renewed annually in writing (§ 3635(7)).

22:4. Must a district provide transportation for a student attending summer school?

No. In *Appeal of Stamler*, 38 Educ. Dep't Rep. 292 (1998), the commissioner of education ruled that a school district did not have to transport a district resident attending summer school in a neighboring district, even when the district had voluntarily agreed to pay the summer school tuition. The commissioner also noted that a school board is not obligated to provide transportation to and from any summer school program, except for students with disabilities in accordance with state law.

However, transportation to and from approved summer school programs operated by a school district is eligible for state aid, subject to a prorated share of a statewide cap of $5 million (§ 3622-a(6)).

22:5. Must a school district transport children of divorced parents to different locations on different days of the week?

No. According to the commissioner of education, a student can only have a single residence for school purposes even when that student's parents are divorced (see **12:41**). There is no statutory or regulatory requirement that a district transport a student whose parents share joint custody to one parent's home on some days of the week and to the other parent's home on different days of the week (*Appeal of Dickinson*, 39 Educ. Dep't Rep. 41 (1999); *Appeal of VanDerJagt*, 33 Educ. Dep't Rep. 517 (1994)).

22:6. Must a school district transport back to school all students attending a field trip or extracurricular activity?

When a school district or board of cooperative education services (BOCES) provides students with transportation to a school-sponsored field trip, extracurricular activity or any other similar event, it must transport those students back to either the point of departure, or an appropriate school, unless the student's parent or guardian has provided the school district with written notice, consistent with district policy, authorizing an alternative form of return transportation for the student. If the parent has not authorized alternative return transportation and intervening circumstances make such return transportation by the school district impractical, a district representative must contact the student(s)' parents and inform them of such intervening circumstances, and remain with the student(s) until each has been delivered to his or her parent (§§ 1604(41), 1709(41), 1804(11), 1903(2), 1950(19), 2503(20), 2554(27), 2590-e(10)).

22:7. May a school district provide transportation between school and child care centers?

Yes. A school board may provide, at its discretion, transportation to any child attending kindergarten through eighth grade between a child's school and before and/or after-school child care locations in accordance with the district's general transportation mileage limitations. The Education Law defines a child care location as a place within the district, other than the child's home, where care for less than 24 hours a day is provided on a regular basis (§ 3635(1)(e)). "A regular basis" does not necessarily mean on a daily basis and a district may not deny transportation to a child care location just because a student is not to be transported there every day. Upon request, a district providing transportation to a child care location would have to transport a student to his or her child care location on some days and his or her home on other days where both locations are within the district's mileage limitations (*Appeal of Seibt*, 40 Educ. Dep't Rep. 186 (2002)).

The child's parents must request child care transportation in writing no later than April 1 preceding the next school year, except where the family moves into the district later than April 1. In that case, the request must be made within 30 days of establishing residency in the district (§ 3635(1)(e)).

Once a board determines the district will provide transportation to child care locations, the transportation must be provided in accordance with the requirements of section 3635(1)(e) of the Education Law (*Appeal of Berkins,* 39 Educ. Dep't Rep. 620 (2000)).

When a child receives transportation from a before-school child care location to the school he or she attends, the child is entitled to be transported from the school to his or her home or to an after-school child care location only if the distance from the school to such location is within the district's mileage limitations. Similarly, when a child receives transportation from school to an after-school child care location, he or she is entitled to be transported from home to school only if the distance between home and school is within the district's mileage limitations. This is so even if the child is otherwise ineligible for transportation between home and school under a district's transportation policy (*Appeal of Berkins).* Furthermore, a child receiving both before- and after-school child care is eligible for transportation to a designated bus stop near the child care location if the child care location is within the district's mileage limits, even if the child's home is not (*Appeal of Bernes,* 39 Educ. Dep't Rep. 620 (2000)).

However, a board may limit transportation to child care locations located within the attendance zone of the school the child attends and anywhere within the district for child care locations licensed pursuant to section 390 of the Social Services Law (§ 3635(1)(e); *Appeal of Grove,* 33 Educ. Dep't Rep. 176 (1993)). There is no statutory authority for a school district to provide transportation to a child care location outside of the district (*Appeal of a Student Suspected of Having a Disability,* 38 Educ. Dep't Rep. 507 (1999)).

The cost of providing transportation between school and child care centers is state-aidable.

22:8. May a school district use a public carrier for student transportation?

Yes. The commissioner of education has ruled that a district's use of an existing public transportation system to transport students from school is neither illegal nor unreasonable (*Appeal of Clancy,* 37 Educ. Dep't Rep. 280 (1998)). Occasionally some districts do this by providing the students with bus tickets, a bus pass or railroad tickets (*Appeal of Del Vecchio,* 39 Educ. Dep't Rep. 258 (1999); *Matter of Tomasso,* 23 Educ. Dep't Rep. 120

(1983); *Matter of Farrell*, 18 Educ. Dep't Rep. 506 (1979)). However, they may not advance cash for this purpose.

In addition, the mere fact that some students are transported on private buses does not mean that all must be (*Appeal of Clancy; Appeal of Tomasso*).

22:9. Can a regional transportation system be organized and operated to cover a number of different school districts?

Yes. A regional transportation system may include transportation between home and school, as well as cooperative bus maintenance. These regional services may be conducted jointly with other school districts or boards of cooperative educational services (BOCES) (§§ 1709(25)(g), 1950(4)(q), 3621(8), (9)). BOCES are authorized to provide transportation to and from BOCES classes at a district's request (§ 1950(4)(q)).

22:10. Can a school district compensate parents for transporting their own children?

Yes, under certain circumstances. Although a district legally can contract with a parent for a student's transportation, this contract may not exceed the actual cost of the services provided (*Matter of Antonette*, 18 Educ. Dep't Rep. 413 (1979)). It should be done only if the district, through competitive bidding or the request for proposal process, has been unable to secure a regular contractor. The child also must be within the required transportation mileage limits. Unless an exemption is granted, the parent must satisfy the requirements of Article 19-A of the Vehicle and Traffic Law and part 156 of the commissioner's regulations.

According to the New York State Department of Transportation, parents' vehicles used in the transportation of their own children to and from school, and where the parents are being reimbursed accordingly, are not subject to a Department of Transportation inspection. However, if a parent's vehicle is used to transport his or her own children and other children to and from school, and the parent is being reimbursed for transporting other children, that vehicle is subject to a Department of Transportation inspection. Under either scenario, the vehicles will be subject to the Department of Motor Vehicles' inspection program.

22:11. Can a school district charge a fee to transport students?

There is no statute that specifically authorizes the board to charge a fee for this purpose. However, a commissioner's decision that a school district may not charge a fee or require a donation as a condition for participation in interscholastic athletic activities implies that such a charge is not permissible (*Matter of Ambrosio*, 30 Educ. Dep't Rep. 387 (1991)).

22:12. Are there any distance limitations for the transportation of students?

Yes. Although, door-to-door transportation is not required (*Matter of Boyar*, 21 Educ. Dep't Rep. 286 (1981); see **22:20**), eligibility for transportation is determined by the distance between a child's home and the school a child attends (§ 3635(1); *Studley v. Allen*, 24 A.D.2d 678 (3d Dep't 1965); *Appeal of Wenger*, 39 Educ. Dep't Rep. 5 (1997); *Appeal of Neubauer*, 32 Educ. Dep't Rep. 320 (1992); see **22:13**). A district may require children in grades kindergarten through eight to walk a distance of up to two miles, and children in grades nine through 12 to walk a distance of up to three miles, from their homes to their schools. The district must provide bus transportation up to a distance of 15 miles (§ 3635(1)(a), (c)).

However, transportation for distances less than two miles in the case of children in kindergarten through the eighth grade, or less than three miles in the case of students in grades nine through 12, and for distances greater than 15 miles may be provided, if the voters approve (*Appeal of Wenger*, 37 Educ. Dep't Rep. 5 (1997); *Matter of Zakrzewski*, 22 Educ. Dep't Rep. 381 (1983); *Matter of Silver*, 1 Educ. Dep't Rep. 381 (1959)). If transportation is provided, it must be offered equally to all children in like circumstances residing in the district (§ 3635(1)(a); see **22:1**).

The law does not require a district to provide transportation to or from a point other than a student's residence, child care location if such transportation is provided by the district (see **22:7**), or pickup point established by school authorities along the route from a student's home to the school legally attended (§ 3635(1)(e); see *Matter of Wasserman*, 15 Educ. Dep't Rep. 278 (1978)).

For information on distance limitations applicable to nonpublic school students, see **22:109**.

22:13. How are transportation distance limitations measured?

Distances to determine eligibility for transportation must be measured from home to school by the nearest available publicly maintained route from home to school (§ 3635(1)(a); *Matter of Kluge*, 31 Educ. Dep't Rep. 107 (1991); *Matter of Now*, 22 Educ. Dep't Rep. 91 (1982)). For example, a district's use of a footpath through a publicly owned and maintained park for purposes of determining the distance from home to school has been upheld by the commissioner of education and at least one court (*Arlyn Oaks Civic Ass'n v. Brucia*, 171 Misc.2d 634 (Sup. Ct. Nassau County 1997); *Appeal of Rosen*, 37 Educ. Dep't Rep. 107 (1997)).

In addition, school boards have broad discretion in selecting measuring points on school property for the purposes of determining eligibility for transportation. For example, the commissioner has upheld a district policy of measuring distance limitations from "the nearest school exit to the beginning of a residential property line." According to the commissioner, a district may measure transportation distance from any part of the school, including a corner of school property, the side rather than front entrance, the midpoint of the school or other point, as long as it does so fairly and consistently (*Appeal of Mogel*, 41 Educ. Dep't Rep. 127 (2001); see also *Appeal of Porzio*, 42 Educ. Dep't Rep. 166 (2002)).

Similarly a school district has broad discretion when selecting the measuring point on a student's property as long as it consistently uses the same measuring point (*Appeal of Flemming*, 43 Educ. Dep't Rep. ___; dec. no. 15,028 (2004).

A district's distance determination will be upheld so long as the means of measurement are reasonable. The use of a calibrated automobile odometer to measure distance is legally reasonable and sufficient (*Appeal of Adamitis*, 38 Educ. Dep't Rep. 765 (1999); *Appeal of Jagoda*, 34 Educ. Dep't Rep. 154 (1994)). Proof of calibration is a reasonable response to a bona fide challenge to the accuracy of the odometer as a measuring device (*Appeal of Jagoda*). In addition, a district's use of an aerial survey has also been viewed as reasonable by the commissioner (*Appeal of Canossa*, 37 Educ. Dep't Rep. 456 (1998)).

22:14. Can a school district provide transportation to students who reside at a lesser distance from school than the minimum limitations solely on the basis of a hazard?

Yes. The Child Safety Act of 1992, which is scheduled to sunset June 30, 2005 unless extended by the Legislature, allows all districts except city school districts with more than 125,000 inhabitants (the Big 5), with voter approval, to establish a child safety zone and provide transportation to students who live less than two or three miles from school but must walk along hazardous zones (§ 3635-b).

A child safety zone is determined based on regulations established by the commissioner of transportation and in consultation with local law enforcement officials (See 17 NYCRR Part 191). Children living within this zone may be transported without regard for distance or the "like circumstances" requirement contained in section 3635(1)(a) of the Education Law (§ 3635-b(2); see **22:1**).

The cost of providing transportation within a child safety zone is not state-aidable. It is also not considered an ordinary contingent expense (§ 3635-b(10)).

22:15. Are there any restrictions on the length of time a student should ride to or from school?

No. Neither the Education Law nor the commissioner's regulations specify a maximum time limit for the transportation of students. The commissioner of education has ruled that, depending on the circumstances, one-way trips of up to one-and-one-half hours are not necessarily excessive (*Appeal of McCarthy and Bacher*, 42 Educ. Dep't Rep 329 (2003); *Appeal of Devore*, 36 Educ. Dep't Rep. 326 (1997); *Matter of Capozza*, 25 Educ. Dep't Rep. 15 (1985); *Matter of Rouis*, 20 Educ. Dep't Rep. 493 (1981); *Appeal of Polifka*, 31 Educ. Dep't Rep. 61 (1991)).

According to the commissioner, the school board is legally responsible for determining transportation routes and modes of transportation. A school board's transportation determination will be upheld unless the board's actions can be proven to be arbitrary or unreasonable (*Devore; Polifka; Rouis*; *Matter of Lauth*, 2 Educ. Dep't Rep. 484 (1963)).

On the same basis, the commissioner ruled against a parent who argued the school district should adopt a "first on, first off" policy to prevent students who are picked up early in the morning from being the last to be dropped off in the afternoon (*Appeal of Fullam*, 38 Educ. Dep't Rep. 227 (1998); *Appeal of Reich*, 38 Educ. Dep't Rep. 565 (1999); *Appeal of Byrne*, 34 Educ. Dep't Rep. 389 (1995)).

22:16. May a student's transportation privileges be suspended?

Yes. The school board and/or the superintendent of schools, not the bus driver, have the authority to suspend the transportation privileges of children who are disorderly and insubordinate. Students' rights to minimal due process applicable in classroom situations are not necessarily applicable to such student transportation cases (*Appeal of R.D.*, 42 Educ. Dep't Rep. 237 (2003); *Appeal of McGaw*, 28 Educ. Dep't Rep. 84 (1988)). However, a student and his or her parents or guardian must be granted an opportunity to appear informally before the person or body authorized to impose discipline to discuss the factual situation underlying the threatened suspension from transportation (*Appeal of McGaw*; *Matter of Roach*, 19 Educ. Dep't Rep. 377 (1980)).

When a district suspends a student's transportation privileges, the parents or guardian of the child involved become responsible for seeing that the child gets to and from school.

However, a district must consider the effect of a suspension of transportation on the student's attendance and must make appropriate arrangements for the student's education where the suspension of transportation is tantamount to a suspension from attendance because of the distance between the home and the school and there is no alternate public or private means of transportation. According to the commissioner of education, a suspension of transportation privileges may not have the effect of depriving the student of education (*Matter of Stewart*, 21 Educ. Dep't Rep. 654 (1982); *Matter of Roach*, 19 Educ. Dep't Rep. 377 (1980)).

According to the U.S. Department of Education's Office of Civil Rights (OCR), where transportation is a related service, revocation of school bus transportation for an unruly student with disabilities is subject to the same due process protection that applies to the discipline of disabled students unless a school district provides transportation by other means (OCR Response to Inquiry, 20 IDELR 864, 867 (1993)).

Bus Routes and Pick-up Points

22:17. May a school bus be routed on private roads?

The commissioner of education has held that a school district is not required to provide transportation to students over privately maintained roads (see *Matter of Cohen*, 21 Educ. Dep't Rep. 280 (1981)). However, a district may provide transportation to students over privately maintained roads with the landowner's consent (*Appeal of Taylor*, 26 Educ. Dep't Rep. 255 (1986)).

22:18. Must a school bus travel roads that may be impassable or unsafe?

The commissioner of education has held that a school board may refuse to use a public road to provide transportation to students if the board can establish its use would involve an "unreasonably hazardous condition" (*Matter of Clark*, 15 Educ. Dep't Rep. 260 (1976)).

In *Matter of McGibbon*, 14 Educ. Dep't Rep. 271 (1975), for example, the district verified that a road where a parent wanted her child to be picked up by district transportation was so narrow that a school bus and another vehicle could not pass each other, the road did not have safe shoulders, and it included steep grades that buses had been unable to negotiate without skidding into trees. Based on this information, the commissioner held that it was not unreasonable or illegal for the student to walk a mile to a pick-up point, rather than authorize the school bus to travel on an unsafe road.

In *Appeal of Warner*, 37 Educ. Dep't Rep. 469 (1998), the commissioner upheld the district's decision to deny transportation along a particular roadway after district officials visited the site and hired an accident investigation expert to evaluate the roadway. The expert told the district the sight distance and roadway width were inadequate and unsafe. An alternate pick-up point on another road was more consistent with student safety than traveling along the requested roadway (see also *Appeal of Gulla*, 39 Educ. Dep't Rep. 716 (2000)).

22:19. Does a school district have a duty to act with reasonable care to other motorists when routing its buses and designating pick-up points for school buses?

Yes, according to one state supreme court that refused to dismiss a case alleging that an accident where a child riding in a car was killed and others injured occurred because a school district was negligent toward other motorists when it placed a bus stop in an area with hilly terrain and obscure visibility for eastbound drivers (*Black v. Homer CSD*, 190 Misc.2d 17, (N.Y. Sup. Ct. 2002)). According to the court, "It would be unreasonable to hold that a school district owes absolutely no duty whatsoever to other motorists, when determining where to place a bus stop." However, a finding of liability would depend on whether "the risk to the public safety is both consequential and unreasonable," the availability of alternative bus stop locations, "the relative efficiency and cost" of the alternatives, and whether a safer alternative was available.

22:20. May a school board designate pick-up points for school buses?

Yes. School districts are not required to provide transportation to students directly to and from home (§ 3635(1)(d)). A school board is authorized to exercise its discretion in designating pick-up points after considering and balancing issues of student safety, convenience, routing efficiency and cost (*Appeal of Icenogle*, 34 Educ. Dep't Rep. 406 (1995)).

To afford the greatest possible protection to school children, the school board or superintendent may designate drive-off places on public highways for school buses to drive off the highway to receive or discharge students. The state or municipality having jurisdiction over a highway so designated is authorized to provide construction and maintenance of drive-offs (§ 3635(5)). However, the fact that a pick-up point is located on a heavily traveled road or may require students to wait or travel on unlit narrow roadways with no sidewalks or walkways is insufficient to prove that the pick-up point is unsafe (*Appeal of DiNapoli*, 38 Educ. Dep't Rep. 269 (1998); *Appeal of Behan,* 34 Educ. Dep't Rep. 368 (1995); *Appeal of Krauciunas*, 35 Educ. Dep't Rep. 107 (1995); *Appeal of Jett,* 33 Educ. Dep't Rep. 446 (1994)).

It is the responsibility of the parent, not the school district, to see that his or her child reaches the pick-up point safely (*Pratt v. Robinson*, 39 N.Y.2d 554 (1976); *Appeal of Rheame-Wellenc*, 37 Educ. Dep't Rep. 83 (1997); *Appeal of Pauldine*, 35 Educ. Dep't Rep. 54 (1995), *application to reopen denied,* 38 Educ. Dep't Rep. 101 (1998)). However, a district may not require a parent to transport their child to a pick-up point, which is farther away than the distance limitations for pick-up points set by the district policy (*Appeal of Zwickel*, 42 Educ. Dep't Rep. 346, (2003)).

22:21. What is the distance a student can be made to walk to a pick-up point?

The policy on walking distance established for a school district may be applied to side roads as well as to the distance from the student's home to the school itself. For example, if a school policy provides that student who lives more than 4/10ths of a mile will be transported to school, then students can be required to walk up to 4/10ths of a mile to reach the pick-up point (*Appeal of Marsh*, 36 Educ. Dep't Rep. 134 (1996), see **22:12**).

22:22. May a school district establish and maintain shelters for students who take school buses at various places along its bus routes?

There is nothing in the law that prevents school districts from doing this. A district may be ordered to provide additional transportation for children who live off a main route in cases where it is unwilling to provide these children with suitable shelter to wait for the bus, and where the district provides transportation for all other children at a point near their homes (*Matter of Spicer*, 73 St. Dep't Rep. 167 (1952)).

School Buses

22:23. What is the statutory definition of a school bus?

A *school bus* may be any "motor vehicle owned by a public or governmental agency or private school and operated for the transportation of pupils, children of pupils, teachers, and other persons acting in a supervisory capacity, to or from school or school activities, or privately owned and operated for compensation for the transportation of pupils, children of pupils, teachers and other persons acting in a supervisory capacity to or from school or school activities" (Veh. & Traf. Law § 142).

Under the commissioner's regulations for school bus driver, monitors, attendants and pupils, a school bus includes every vehicle owned or contracted for by a public school or board of cooperative educational services (BOCES) and operated for the transportation of pupils, children of pupils, teachers and other persons acting in a supervisory capacity to or from school or school activities (8 NYCRR § 156.3(2)).

22:24. May a school district standardize its fleet with certain makes of school buses?

Yes. A school board may adopt a resolution, by a vote of at least three-fifths of all board members, which states that for reasons of efficiency or economy, it will standardize the bus fleet. This resolution must include the reasons for its adoption (Gen. Mun. Law § 103(5)).

A need for standardization does not permit a school district to dispense with competitive bidding. It merely authorizes it to specify a particular type or brand. For further information, see "Competitive Bidding under General Municipal Law Section 103" (Opn. St. Comp., 1982, Research Paper, pp. 3017, 3034).

22:25. Must all school buses be painted the same color?

Yes. All school buses, regardless of ownership, having a seating capacity of more than seven passengers, must be painted the yellow color known as "national school bus chrome" (Veh. & Traf. Law § 375(21)).

22:26. Must school buses be equipped with exterior reflective material?

Yes, every school bus manufactured for use in New York on or after April 1, 2000, and used to transport 10 or more passengers on or after September 1, 2002, must be equipped with exterior reflective markings that comply with rules and regulations promulgated by the Department of Motor Vehicles. State aid is available for the purchase of buses with exterior reflective markings and for the purchase and installation of exterior reflective markings on older school buses (Veh. & Traf. Law § 375(21-h); § 3623-a(2)(c); 15 NYCRR § 46.12(a)).

To further enhance highway safety, strobe lights may be affixed on school buses for use when students are being picked up, discharged, or transported to and from school or school functions and conditions impair the visibility of the school bus. Installation and operation of school bus strobe lights must comply with regulations issued by the Department of Motor Vehicle (15 NYCRR § 56.12).

22:27. Must a school bus be identified by a sign?

Yes. Buses having a seating capacity greater than seven passengers must have the designation "School Bus" displayed conspicuously on two signs located on the exterior of the bus. The black letters must be at least eight inches high, and each stroke of each letter must be at least one inch wide. The background of the signs must be a yellow color known as "national school bus chrome" (Veh & Traf. Law § 375(20)(b)(1); see **22:25**).

These signs must be mounted securely on top of the bus. One must face forward and one must face backward, and each sign must be visible and readable from a distance of at least 200 feet. While the bus is being operated at night, the signs must be illuminated to be visible from a distance of at least 500 feet (Veh. & Traf. Law § 375(20)(c)).

In addition, the flashing red signal lamps with which school buses must be equipped must be attached securely in the proper position (15 NYCRR § 46.2(g)). This law applies to vehicles with a seating capacity of seven or more passengers used exclusively to transport pupils, teachers, and other persons acting in a supervisory capacity to and from school or school activities (15 NYCRR § 46.2(a)).

22:28. Must a school bus identify the owner and/or operator of the vehicle?

All school buses purchased, leased, or acquired on or after September 1, 1997 must have the area code and telephone number of the owner and/or operator printed in three-inch bold type on the left rear of the bus (Veh. & Traf. Law § 1223-a).

22:29. Must school buses have safety equipment, such as special mirrors in front of the bus body?

Yes. Under section 375(20-e) of the Vehicle and Traffic Law, each school bus with a seating capacity of more than 12 and with the engine located ahead of the driver must be equipped with a convex mirror mounted in front of the bus. In this way the seated driver can observe the road directly in front of the bus. This is for the protection of students passing in front of the bus after they leave the bus.

School buses must also be equipped with safety glass and those manufactured after April 1, 1990, must have backup beepers to alert others when the bus is put in reverse, in addition to other safety equipment (Veh. & Traf. Law §§ 375(11), 375(21-g), 15 NYCRR § 46.8).

With certain exceptions, school buses used by contractors that provide transportation to a school district must meet the same safety specifications and requirements as district-owned buses (§ 3623(1)(b)).

22:30. Must other vehicles owned by a school district and used to transport students meet the same requirements that apply to regular school buses?

Only vehicles used "exclusively" or "primarily" to transport pupils to and from school must meet the school vehicle requirements of the Vehicle and Traffic Law (Veh. & Traf. Law § 375 (20), (21); see *Sigmond v. Liberty Lines Transit, Inc.*, 261 A.D.2d 385 (2d Dep't 1999)).

There are certain requirements for vehicles having seating capacities in excess of seven passengers and other requirements for those with seating capacities in excess of 12 and/or 15 passengers. In addition, special requirements exist for mirrors for vehicles with engines located in front of the driver (see **22:29**). However, the commissioner of transportation is authorized to grant exemptions from the requirements (see Veh. & Traf. Law § 375(20), (21)).

22:31. Who has ultimate authority for regulating safety and certification of school buses?

The commissioner of transportation in consultation with the commissioner of education is responsible for the adoption, promulgation, and the enforcement of rules, standards, and specifications regulating and controlling the efficiency and equipment of school buses used to transport students. Particular attention is made toward the safety and convenience of students and adaptability of such school buses to the requirements of the school district. No school bus shall be purchased by a school district or used to transport students unless and until it has been approved by the commissioner of transportation as complying with the rules, standards and specifications (§ 3623).

22:32. Must school buses in New York State be inspected regularly?

Yes. School buses in New York State must be inspected every six months. State Department of Transportation regulations provide that school buses cannot be operated unless they carry a certificate of inspection for the preceding six months, prominently displayed in the lower right-hand corner on the interior surface of the windshield (17 NYCRR § 721(3)).

22:33. Besides transporting students, what else may district-owned school buses be used for?

In addition to the transportation of students to and from school and/or school activities, district-owned buses and conveyances may be used legitimately for the following:

- Transportation for students and teachers to school-related events such as field trips and athletic events (*Cook v. Griffin*, 47 A.D.2d 23 (4th Dep't 1975); *Matter of O'Donnell*, 18 Educ. Dep't Rep. 259 (1978); see also § 2023(1)).
- Lease to another school district or Native American tribe for certain recreation projects or youth service projects (§ 1709(25)(c)).
- Lease to another school district, to a board of cooperative educational services (BOCES), to a county vocational education and extension board or to a Native American tribe for educational purposes (§ 1709(25)(b)).

- Rent or lease to any senior citizens' center that is recognized and funded by the office for the aging (§ 1501-b(1)(a)).
- Rent or lease to any nonprofit incorporated organization serving senior citizens (§ 1501-b(1)(b)).
- Rent or lease to any nonprofit incorporated organization serving the physically or mentally disabled (§ 1501-b(1)(c)).
- Rent or lease to any nonprofit organization that provides recreation youth services or runs neighborhood playgrounds or recreation centers (§§ 1501-b(1)(d), 1604(21)).
- Rent or lease to any municipal corporation, as defined in the General Construction Law (§ 1501-b(1)(e)).
- Rent or lease to a fire company as defined in the Volunteer Firefighters' Benefit Law, or an ambulance company as defined in the Volunteer Ambulance Workers' Benefit Law (§ 1501-b(1)(i)).
- Transportation for certain infants and toddlers of students enrolled in school district or BOCES programs. This is eligible for state aid (§ 3635(1)(f)).
- For districts wholly or partially located in rural areas, transportation to district residents enrolled in educational, job-training or other programs; children under age five traveling between home and day-care or preschool programs; and employees of school districts or other educational institutions (§ 1502(1)).

22:34. What rules apply when a school district leases its school buses to others?

Whenever a bus is leased or rented, the consideration paid by the lessee may not be less than the full amount of the costs and expenses incurred as a result thereof. In addition, the lessee must maintain insurance on each bus so leased, protecting the lessor district from all claims by reason of personal injury to persons and property damage. The lessee also is required to carry fire insurance as well as compensation insurance on the driver of the leased bus. To protect the lessor district against further loss, the lessee also is required to carry collision insurance in the amount of the value of the bus. The cost of this insurance must be paid by the entity that leases the bus (§§ 1501-b(4), 1604(21), 1709(25)(f)).

22:35. What are some examples of impermissible uses of school buses?

There is no authority for a district to use school buses to transport residents to parent-teacher meetings or on shopping trips.

A district may not use its school buses to transport senior citizens from a senior citizens housing facility to a polling place for a school election (*Appeal of Jordan*, 39 Educ. Dep't Rep. 551 (2000)).

22:36. Can advertisements or public service messages be displayed on school buses?

No. It is unlawful for any motor vehicle having a seating capacity of more than seven passengers, that is used primarily to transport students and teachers to and from school, to have any sign, placard or other display mounted, placed or installed on the vehicle, other than signs required by law, such as indicating that the vehicle is a school bus, and the ownership of the school bus. This provision does not apply to cities with a population of 1 million or more (Veh. & Traf. Law § 375 (21-h); see **22:27–28**).

School Bus Safety

22:37. Is there an established speed limit for school buses?

Yes. Although the Vehicle and Traffic Law specifies a maximum speed limit of 55 miles per hour, and 65 miles per hour on certain stretches of specified state highways located in rural areas, the Education Law specifies that the maximum speed at which school vehicles engaged in student transportation may be operated shall be 55 miles per hour (§ 3624).

Other restrictions on speed in populated areas and elsewhere, as conditions warrant, are imposed by cities, villages, and the state Department of Transportation. School bus drivers should observe these regulations conscientiously at all times, and also should operate at speeds that are reasonable in terms of prevailing road, traffic and weather conditions. Speed should be reduced at curves, blind crossings, crests of hills, in fog, or wherever the view is curtailed so the bus will be able to stop within the distance of clear vision.

22:38. Must a school bus keep its headlights illuminated at all times?

Yes. School buses must keep their lights on at all times they are operated, even when they are not transporting students (Veh. & Traf. Law § 375(20)(i)).

22:39. How many stop arms must a school bus have?

Every school bus manufactured for use in New York on or after January 1, 2002, with a capacity of 45 persons or more, must be equipped with a second stop arm that has to be located on the driver's side as close as practical to the rear corner of the bus (Veh. & Traf. Law § 375(21-c); 15 NYCRR § 46.7).

22:40. Are two-way radios and strobe lights required equipment on school buses?

No. However, these devices are authorized as allowable transportation expenses (§ 3623-a(2)(c); 15 NYCRR §§ 46.6, 46.7, 56.12; see **22:26**).

22:41. Is a school bus permitted to turn right at a red traffic signal?

If the school bus is transporting students, the driver cannot turn right for any purpose if the bus is facing a steady red signal (Veh. & Traf. Law § 1111(d)(5)).

22:42. Must school buses stop at all railroad crossings?

Yes. Publicly and privately owned school buses must stop at all railroad crossings, whether or not they carry students, and proceed only when the driver can do so safely. While crossing the tracks, the driver must not shift gears (Veh. & Traf. Law § 1171(a)).

Section 3636 of the Education Law provides a school district may not use an unguarded railroad crossing when transporting students to and from school or other places unless a public hearing has been held and a resolution adopted by the school board has determined using another route would be impractical. This resolution must be filed with the State Education Department and the state Department of Transportation. Additionally, the district must prepare and maintain a map indicating the bus route used and must make it available for inspection by any resident of the district at a place designated by the school board.

22:43. Are seat belts for students required equipment on all school buses?

All school buses manufactured after July 1, 1987 must be designed to include seat belts and increased seat padding on the passenger seats. In addition, all motor vehicles weighing 10,000 pounds or less and used to transport students must have seat belts, regardless of the date of first use. The seat belts must be approved by the commissioner of transportation (15 NYCRR § 49.6; Veh. & Traf. Law § 383(5)(a)). Drivers' seat belts are required on all school bus vehicles owned or leased by the district (Veh. & Traf. Law § 383(4-a)).

22:44. Are school districts required to compel students to wear seat belts while on the school bus?

No. Furthermore, according to section 3813(4) of the Education Law, when a lawsuit is brought against a school district, a school bus operator under contract with a district, or an operator of a school bus (including a driver, matron or teacher serving as a chaperon), no such person shall be held liable solely because the injured party was not wearing a seat belt (see *O'Connor v. Mahopac CSD*, 259 A.D.2d 530 (2d Dep't 1999)). However, after a public hearing, a school board may choose to adopt a resolution that provides for the use of seat belts on school buses (§ 3635-a).

22:45. Are school districts required to provide students with instruction on the use of seat belts?

Districts that transport students on school buses equipped with seat belts must insure that all students who are transported on any school bus owned, leased, or contracted for by the district or board of cooperative educational services (BOCES) receive instruction on the use of seat belts. Instruction must be provided to both public and nonpublic school students at least three times a year (8 NYCRR § 156.3(g)).

22:46. Are "child safety seats" required on school buses?

All children under the age of four who are passengers on a school bus must be restrained in a federally-approved child safety seat or another restraining device approved by the commissioner of motor vehicles, (Veh. & Traf. Law § 1229-c (11)). This statutory requirement applies to all school buses that are owned and operated by public or private schools or privately owned and operated for compensation.

22:47. What is the law regarding standees on a school bus?

Generally, there may be no standing passengers on school buses owned or contracted to a school district when used exclusively to transport students, teachers and other persons acting in a supervisory capacity to and from school or school activities. However, this prohibition does not apply during the first 10 days of session in each school year, nor in the event of a bus breakdown, accident or other unforeseen occurrence that necessitates the transportation of standing passengers. City school districts with a population of one million or more may adopt and enforce local laws that comply with these provisions (§ 3635-c, Veh. & Traf. Law § 1229-b(2)). In addition, section 1229-b of the Vehicle and Traffic Law makes unlawful the operation of a camp or charter omnibus for 10 miles or more with any passenger standing.

22:48. Must students cross in front of the school bus when they are being picked up or discharged from it?

Yes. The driver of the school bus must instruct those students who must cross the highway or street to cross 10 feet in front of the bus. The driver must keep the school bus halted with red signal lights flashing until they have reached the opposite side of the highway or street (Veh. & Traf. Law § 1174(b); 8 NYCRR § 156.3(d)(4)).

22:49. May the school district employ a school crossing guard to direct traffic for school buses on a public highway?

No. However, section 208-a of the General Municipal Law gives any city, town or village the authority to appoint school crossing guards for these purposes (see *Ernest v. Red Creek CSD,* 93 N.Y.2d 664 (1999); Inf. Opn. Att'y Gen. 84-30; see also § 806(3); *Matter of Glasner,* 7 Educ. Dep't Rep. 15 (1967)).

22:50. Are emergency drills required on school buses?

Yes. The commissioner's regulations (8 NYCRR § 156.3(f)) require emergency drills on school buses. These drills must include practice and instruction in the location, use and operation of the emergency door, fire extinguisher, first-aid equipment and windows as a means of escape in case of fire or accident (§ 3623)(1)(c)).

Drills also must include instruction in safe boarding and exiting procedures with specific emphasis on when and how to approach, board, disembark and move away from the bus after disembarking. They must include specific instructions for students to advance at least 10 feet in front of the bus before crossing the highway after disembarking. They must address specific hazards encountered by students during snow, ice, rain and other inclement weather, including, but not necessarily limited to, poor driver visibility, reduced vehicular control and reduced hearing. They must include instruction in the importance of orderly conduct by all school bus passengers, with emphasis on student discipline. This instruction and the conduct of the drills must be given by a member or members of the teaching or student transportation staff.

Students attending public and nonpublic schools who do not participate in these drills must also be provided with drills on school buses, or, as an alternative, must be provided with classroom instruction covering their content. A minimum of three drills must be held during the school year, the first to be conducted during the first seven days of school, the second between November 1 and December 31, and the third between March 1 and April 30. No drills may be conducted when buses are en route.

School authorities must certify in their annual report to the State Education Department that their district has complied with this requirement.

22:51. What is the state law in relation to vehicles overtaking or meeting buses transporting children to or from school?

Section 1174 of the Vehicle and Traffic Law prohibits motorists from passing stopped school buses while they are boarding or discharging school children. A vehicle overtaking or meeting a bus transporting children to and from school that is stopped to receive or discharge passengers on a public highway must come to a complete stop and remain stationary until the bus resumes motion or until signaled by the driver or a police officer to proceed, provided the bus carries flashing red signal lights and signs designating it as a school bus that are displayed as required by law (Veh. & Traf. Law § 1174). Failure to obey this traffic rule can result in either a fine of between $250 and $400 or 30 days imprisonment, or both for a first offense. Penalties increase with repeat offenses (Veh. & Traf. Law § 1174(c)).

22:52. Is it unlawful to loiter on a school bus?

Yes. To loiter has been interpreted to mean to be slow in moving, to delay, to be dilatory, to saunter or to lag behind. The Penal Law states that any person not having any reason or relationship involving custody of or responsibility for a student, who loiters, remains in or enters a school bus, not having written permission or a specific, legitimate purpose for being there, is guilty of loitering, a violation of law (Penal Law §§ 240.00, 240.35(5), (7)).

22:53. What is the law regarding eating and drinking by school staff on school buses?

Bus drivers, monitors and attendants are not allowed to eat or drink on a school bus while the vehicle is transporting students. Moreover, they may not perform any act or conduct themselves in a manner, which may impair the safe operation of the bus (8 NYCRR § 156.3(e)(5)).

22:54. May a school district restrict the type of objects students may bring onto a school bus?

Yes. State Department of Transportation regulations provide that the main aisle and the aisle to the door of a school bus may not be obstructed (17 NYCRR § 721.4(a)(11))). The commissioner of education upheld a district policy which prohibited students from carrying items on the bus which could not fit on their laps, including all musical instruments other than flutes or clarinets, hockey sticks, lacrosse sticks, baseball bats, ski equipment, large equipment bags, large art displays, and any other item of similar size and shape (*Appeal of Moyer*, 37 Educ. Dep't Rep. 335 (1998)).

22:55. Who is responsible for the supervision and safety of students taking the school bus?

School districts are liable for the supervision and safety of students who are within their physical custody or authority. Generally, they are not liable for the supervision and safety of students prior to boarding or after disembarking from a school bus. Custodial control and responsibility at those times rest with the parents (*Pratt v. Robinson*, 39 N.Y.2d 554 (1976); see **22:20**).

In one case, however, an appellate court initially refused to dismiss a lawsuit against a district where a parent alleged that a district representative had promised to ensure that the student rode the school bus home rather than travel in another student's car. The court held that while a school district does not have a duty to compel students to ride the school bus home, if the district representative had made the promise, the district may have undertaken a special duty to the student (*Wenger v. Goodell*, 220 A.D.2d 937 (3d Dep't 1995)). However, after the facts were presented in the *Wenger* case, the district again moved to dismiss the case because the parent had not established that the district had in fact undertaken a special duty to the student. The appellate court agreed, and dismissed the action against the district (*Wenger v. Goodell*, 288 A.D.2d 815 (3d Dep't 2001), see also *Cerni v. Zambrana*, 271 A.D.2d 566 (2d Dep't 2000)).

In another case, a district was found liable when a student was hit by a pickup truck when walking home after school and crossing the road in front of the school while school buses were still departing. The driver's view was obstructed by a moving school bus. Normally, the district waited to release students who walked home until all the school buses were gone, but did not on the day of the accident. According to the state Court of Appeals, while a district's duty of care toward a student generally ends when it relinquishes custody of the student, the duty of care continues when the student is released without further supervision into a foreseeably hazardous situation the district played a role in creating (*Ernest v. Red Creek CSD*, 93 N.Y. 2d 664 (1999)).

22:56. Who is responsible for the supervision and safety of students when a district hires an independent contractor for the transportation of students?

A school district ordinarily is not liable where it hires an independent contractor to provide transportation services and a student is injured in connection therewith (*Chainani v. Board of Educ. of the City of New York*, 87 N.Y.2d 370 (1995); *Thomas v. Board. of Educ. of the Kingston City Sch. Dist.*, 291 A.D.2d 710 (3d Dep't 2002)). In *Chainani*, a district was sued by the parent of a student who suffered severe injuries when struck by her school bus after she had disembarked. The school bus was driven by the employee of a bus company serving as an independent contractor. The New York Court of Appeals ruled that the district was not directly liable for the student's injuries because the student was not within the custody of the school district at the time of the accident but rather was in the custody of the independent contractor. The court also refused to hold the school district vicariously liable for the student's injuries because the activity of transporting students is not inherently dangerous and the district was not aware that the independent contractor had created a peculiar unreasonable risk (but see *David XX v. St. Catherine's Ctr. for Children,* 267 A.D.2d 813 (3d Dep't 1999)).

22:57. Does a district's code of conduct apply to students transported to and from school by an independent contractor?

Yes. A school district remains responsible for enforcing its code of conduct while students are traveling on school buses whether or not the transportation is independently contracted for (*Appeal of M.H.,* 43 Educ. Dep't Rep. __, dec. no. 14,973 (2003); see **12:114** for further discussion on the code of conduct).

22:58. Who is responsible for ensuring no children are left behind on a school bus at the completion of a bus run?

School bus drivers, monitors, and attendants all share in this responsibility. They must check the vehicle at the conclusion of the bus route to ensure that no child is left on board unattended (8 NYCRR § 156.3(e)(4)).

22:59. May a school district use video cameras on school buses to ensure the safety of the driver and passengers?

Yes, video cameras may be used on school buses that transport students (8 NYCRR § 156.9(d)(1)). These cameras may be used to record the students' conduct to ensure their safety and to serve as evidence of their conduct for disciplinary purposes, if necessary (see *Appeal of Burrows,* 39 Educ. Dep't Rep. 212 (1999)).

School Bus Drivers

22:60. What is the definition of a school bus driver?

A *school bus driver* is any person who drives a school bus owned, leased, or contracted for by a public school district or board of cooperative educational services (BOCES) for the purpose of transporting students.

However, a driver of a passenger or suburban type of vehicle is not considered a school bus driver if he or she is a school district employee who does not ordinarily transport students and is operating that vehicle to transport one or more students to a hospital or other medical facility, a physician's office, or home for medical treatment or because of illness. Likewise, a driver of a suburban inter-city coach or transit bus who transports students on trips other than between home and school, such as field trips and athletic trips, is not considered to be a school bus driver. A parent who transports only his or her own children is also excluded from this definition (8 NYCRR § 156.3(a)).

22:61. What are the qualifications for a school bus driver?

Although the superintendent of schools must approve in writing, on a form prescribed by the commissioner of education, the employment of each bus driver for each bus owned or operated within the district, the qualifications of school bus drivers are determined by regulations of the commissioner of education and the commissioner of motor vehicles (Educ. Law § 3624; 8 NYCRR § 156.3(b); 15 NYCRR Part 6).

For an individual to be qualified as a school bus driver, he or she must:

- Be at least 21 years of age (8 NYCRR § 156.3(b)(2)).
- Have a currently valid driver's license or permit that is valid for the operation of a bus in New York State (8 NYCRR § 156.3(b)(4)).
- Pass a physical examination established by the commissioners of education and motor vehicles (8 NYCRR § 156.3(b)(3)).
- Pass a physical performance test established by the commissioner of education (8 NYCRR § 156.3(b)(3)(iii)(a)).
- Furnish to the superintendent at least three statements from three different persons not related to the applicant assessing his or her moral character and reliability (8 NYCRR § 156.3(b)(6)).
- Have no conviction, violation or infraction listed in section 509-c or section 509-cc of the Vehicle and Traffic Law, or under any other provision of article 19-A of that law. In order to determine an applicant has no such convictions the applicant must submit fingerprints for a state criminal history check. The fingerprints also may be submitted to the FBI for a national check (Veh. & Traf. Law §509-cc(5); see **22:74**).
- Meet all other licensing and training requirements for driving a school bus (Veh. & Traf. Law §§ 501, 509-b, 509-c; 8 NYCRR § 156.3).

22:62. What are the licensure requirements for school bus drivers?

Licensure requirements for all school bus drivers currently are covered by article 19-A of the Vehicle and Traffic Law (§ 509-a to 509-o), part 6 of the rules and regulations of the commissioner of motor vehicles and part 156 of the regulations of the commissioner of education.

Federal and state laws require all school bus drivers to be issued a commercial driver's license (CDL) (Veh. & Traf. Law §§ 501-a(1), 509-b; 49 USC § 31308). This CDL is required of all commercial drivers, including school bus drivers. The Education Law allows schools to receive transportation aid for certain approved costs associated with the licensing regulations such as the training of drivers for the CDL and the expenses incurred in fingerprinting drivers for background checks (Educ. Law §§ 3602(7)(b), 3623-a(1)(e)(6); see also **22:74**).

The commissioner's regulations require each driver of a motor vehicle conveying school children to have the appropriate operator's or commercial driver's license (8 NYCRR § 156.3(b)(4)).

22:63. Are school bus drivers required to meet any physical requirements?

Yes. Each school bus driver must meet the requirements of section 6.11 of the regulations of the commissioner of motor vehicles, and the basic minimum physical requirements specified in the regulations of the commissioner of education, concerning, for example, vision and hearing. The superintendent must consider a physician's or nurse practitioner's written report in determining the driver's fitness to operate or continue to operate any transportation vehicle used by students (Educ. Law § 3624; 15 NYCRR § 6).

Restricting a colorblind person from driving a school bus does not constitute disability discrimination under the American with Disabilities Act. Moreover, such a person would not be entitled to an accommodation under that act that would not otherwise enable him to perform the essential function of distinguishing traffic signals (see *Shannon v. New York City Transit Auth.*, 332 F.3d 95 (2d Cir. 2003)).

22:64. Are school bus drivers required to pass a physical performance test?

Yes. After September 1, 1997, all bus drivers must pass a physical performance test approved by the commissioner of education, at least once every two years. In no case shall the interval between physical performance tests exceed 24 months. Drivers employed as of that date had until July 1, 2000 to take and pass the test.

The test shall be readministered to each driver after an absence of 60 days or more (8 NYCRR § 156.3(b)(3)(iii)).

The test must be conducted by a certified school bus driver instructor. To pass the test, a bus driver must be able to perform the following functions:

- Repeatedly open and close a manually operated bus entrance door.
- Climb and descend bus steps.
- Operate hand controls simultaneously and quickly.
- Have quick reaction time from throttle to brake.
- Carry or drag individuals in a bus emergency evacuation.
- Repeatedly depress clutch and/or brake pedals.
- Exit quickly oneself and students from an emergency door.

A bus driver who fails any part of the test may not operate a school bus until he or she passes a re-examination test. The re-examination must be taken no sooner than three days from the prior test. The employer will be responsible for paying for the re-examination if the bus driver passes; the bus driver is responsible for the cost if he or she fails the re-examination (8 NYCRR § 156.3(b)(3)(iii)(a); see also "School Bus Driver Physical Performance Test Guidelines," State Education Department (SED), August 1997, available from SED's office of Pupil Transportation Services 518-474-6541 or on their Web site at http://www.emsc.nysed.gov/mgtserv/ptransho.htm).

22:65. Are school bus drivers required to undergo physical examinations?

Yes. Each regular or substitute driver of a school bus owned, leased, or contracted for by a school district or BOCES must be examined every year by a physician or nurse practitioner. When a driver is initially hired, he or she must be examined within four weeks prior to the beginning of service. The results of these physical examinations must be reported immediately to the superintendent on forms prescribed by the commissioner of education (8 NYCRR § 156.3(b)(3)(ii); see **22:61**).

22:66. Are school bus drivers required to have school bus safety training?

Each school bus driver initially employed by a school board or transportation contractor after July 1, 1973 must complete at least two hours of instruction on school bus safety practices. Each driver initially employed after January 1, 1976 who transports only students with disabilities must receive an additional hour of instruction concerning the special needs of such students (8 NYCRR § 156.3(b)(5)(i)).

During his or her first year of employment, each driver must complete a basic course of instruction in school bus safety practices approved by the commissioner of education that includes two hours of instruction concerning the special needs of students with disabilities. All school bus drivers must complete a minimum of two hours of refresher instruction in school bus safety at least two times a year, at sessions conducted between July 1 and the first day of school and between December 1 and March 1 of each school year. Refresher courses for drivers who transport students with disabilities exclusively also must include instruction relating to the special needs of such students (8 NYCRR § 156.3(b)(5)(ii), (iii).

All training must be provided by or under the direct supervision of a school bus driver instructor certified by the commissioner of education, with the exception of pre-service training (8 NYCRR § 156.3(b)(5)(v)). An approved school bus driver instructor's physical presence is not required during training conducted on the initial employment of a school bus driver by the board or transportation contractor, provided such training is conducted under the general supervision of such an instructor (8 NYCRR § 156.3(b)(5)(v)(a)).

Each driver's compliance with the training requirements described above should be verified through the district's record-keeping system.

Drivers who operate transportation vehicles owned, leased, or contracted for by nonpublic schools also must receive safety training (§ 305(34)).

22:67. Must occasional drivers receive the training specified in 22:66?

No. Under the commissioner's regulations, an occasional driver is defined as a certified teacher employed by a school district or board of cooperative educational services (BOCES) who is not primarily employed as a school bus driver or substitute school bus driver on either a full-time or part-time basis. Occasional drivers used for other than regular routes are not required to fulfill the training described in **22:66** (8 NYCRR § 156.3(b)(5)(iv)).

22:68. Are school bus drivers subject to alcohol and drug testing?

Yes. School bus drivers who operate a commercial motor vehicle and are required to have commercial driver's licenses (CDLs) are subject to alcohol and drug testing, according to federal regulations adopted to implement the Omnibus Transportation Employee Testing Act of 1991 (49 CFR Parts 382, 391) and part 40 of the Code of Federal Regulations, Procedures for Transportation Workplace Drug and Alcohol Testing Programs (49 CFR Part 40). A school bus driver is subject to this requirement only when driving a vehicle that is designed to transport 16 or more passengers, including the driver (49 CFR §§ 382.103, 382.107).

A school district may terminate a bus driver who fails an alcohol test even if it is an isolated incident because a district has "a special obligation to safeguard the well-being of the students" and a bus driver's alcohol-related conduct "jeopardizes public safety and the safety of school children" in the driver's charge (*Will v. Frontier CSD Bd. of Educ.*, 97 N.Y.2d 690 (2002). In addition, operating a school bus while under the influence of alcohol or drugs is a crime under state law, punishable by fines, imprisonment or both, as well as license suspension and/or license revocation. If a school bus driver is convicted of operating any vehicle while under the influence of alcohol or drugs, his or her license will be suspended or revoked and he or she will also be disqualified as a school bus driver for the period of that revocation or suspension. Such disqualification will be no less than six months (Veh. & Traf. Law §§ 509-cc(1)(g), 1193(1)(d)(1-a), (4-a), (2)(b)(4-a); see also **22:61** & **22:74**).

22:69. When must bus drivers submit to alcohol and drug testing?

The regulations require school districts to have programs in place that will test school bus drivers for alcohol and drugs under the following circumstances:

- Before they are employed as bus drivers (49 CFR § 382.301; see *The Federal Register*, vol. 60, no. 90, 24765 (May 10, 1995)).
- After a bus accident has occurred, if there was a fatality, or if the driver was cited for a moving violation in connection with the accident and there is an injury treated away from the scene of the accident or a disabled vehicle is towed away from the scene (49 CFR § 382.303(a)(1), (2); see **22:78**).
- If there is reasonable suspicion that the driver has used drugs or alcohol (49 CFR § 382.307).
- Randomly, a minimum percentage of a district's average number of bus drivers per year— 10 percent for alcohol and 50 percent for drugs. These percentages may vary, according to the Federal Highway Authority. Random tests must be unannounced and spread reasonably throughout the year (49 CFR § 382.305(b)(1)).
- Drivers who have previously tested positive for alcohol and/or substance abuse must submit to a "return to duty" test for before returning to work (49 CFR §§ 40.305, 382.309).
- Unannounced follow-up tests on drivers referred by substance abuse professionals for alcohol or drug counseling and who have returned to work (49 CFR §§ 40.307, 40.309, 382.311).

Prior to implementing the testing programs, school districts must provide school bus drivers with information regarding the policy and regulation requirements, as well as information on alcohol and drug treatment programs and resources (49 CFR §§ 382.113, 382.601).

22:70. Are bus driver alcohol and drug testing results confidential?

The general rule is that alcohol and drug testing records are confidential and may not be revealed to anyone other than the employer without the driver's consent. However, under federal regulations, employers must make these records available to an authorized representative of the U.S.

Department of Transportation, when requested, or any local or state official with regulatory authority over the employer or drivers. In addition, an employer may disclose the test results in proceedings related to benefits sought by the employee, such as worker's compensation or unemployment insurance compensation. Post-accident records may also be disclosed to the National Transportation Safety Board in the course of an accident investigation, or as required by state law (49 CFR § 382.405; News Alert, U.S. Department of Transportation, Federal Highway Administration, Region One, Mar. 27, 1998).

22:71. May a school bus driver be precluded from driving a school bus based upon alcohol and/or drug consumption?

Yes. In accordance with federal and state law, a school bus driver must not drive a school bus if he or she:

- Possesses, consumes or is reasonably believed to possess or have consumed alcohol or a controlled substance, while on duty.
- Uses or is under the influence of alcohol or a controlled substance within six hours or less before duty.
- Has an alcohol concentration of 0.02 or higher, or tests positive for a controlled substance; or refuses to take a required alcohol or controlled substance test.

Any employee who is tested and found to have an alcohol concentration of at least 0.02, but less than 0.04, will be removed from the position until his or her next regularly scheduled duty period, but not less than 24 hours following the test.

If the driver has an alcohol concentration of 0.04 or greater, or has engaged in prohibited alcohol or controlled substance use, he or she will be removed from driving duties and referred to a substance abuse professional. No driver who has abused controlled substances or alcohol may return to duty unless he or she has successfully passed a required return-to-duty test (49 CFR § 40, Subpart O, 49 CFR §§ 382.307(e), 382.309, Veh. & Traf. Law § 509-l).

22:72. May a bus company be held liable if a bus driver operates a school bus while intoxicated?

Yes. No motor carrier shall permit a driver to be on duty or operate a bus, if by the driver's general appearance or conduct he or she appears to have consumed an intoxicating liquor within the past six hours (Veh. & Traf. Law § 509-l (2)(b), 15 NYCRR § 6.25). In *In re Northland Transportation, Inc. v. Jackson* (271 A.D.2d 846 (3d Dep't 2000)), a school bus driver was en route to pick up children when her bus broke down. A state trooper who came to the aid of the disabled bus observed the driver was glassy-eyed and smelled strongly of alcohol. The driver failed four field sobriety tests, was placed under arrest for driving while intoxicated, and a later breathalyzer test revealed a blood alcohol content of 0.07 percent. The driver was later convicted of the charge.

The driver's employer was convicted of permitting the driver to drive that day, in violation of section 509-l of the Vehicle and Traffic Law, and was fined $2,500. On appeal, a state appellate court held that a motor carrier may be found guilty of violating the statute if it knew, or through reasonable diligence or simple observation, should have known that one of its drivers appeared to have consumed alcohol in the preceding six-hour period. In this case, the court concluded the company had no procedure in place to address the clear mandates of the statute. If it had, the driver's "obvious intoxicated appearance and conduct would have been observed and she would not have been permitted to drive the bus that morning."

22:73. Are school districts required to pay for the rehabilitation of bus drivers who fail an alcohol or drug test?

No. Any treatment or rehabilitation program must be provided in accordance with the employer's policy or labor/management contracts. The regulations do not require the employer to provide rehabilitation, pay for treatment or reinstate the employee (49 CFR § 40, Subpart O; 382.605).

22:74. Must school bus drivers be fingerprinted?

Yes. The Vehicle and Traffic Law and Department of Motor Vehicles regulations require all school bus drivers to be fingerprinted so a school district may obtain any criminal record from state and federal authorities (Veh. & Traf. Law §§ 509-d(2); 509-cc(5); 15 NYCRR § 6.4(b)). In addition, driving and employment records must be obtained (see 22:75–77).

Districts can obtain reimbursement for most costs associated with fingerprinting school bus drivers (Educ. Law §§ 3602(7) 3623-a(1)(e)(6); see 22:62).

22:75. Is a school district required to check a person's employment record before employing that person as a school bus driver?

Yes. The school district must conduct an investigation of the driver's employment record during the preceding three years, in a manner prescribed by the commissioner of motor vehicles (Veh. & Traf. Law § 509-d(1)(iii)).

22:76. Is a school district required to check a person's driving record before employing that person as a school bus driver?

Yes. A school district must obtain the driving record of each bus driver it employs from the appropriate agency in every state in which that driver resided or worked and/or held a driver's license or learner's permit during the preceding three years, in a manner prescribed by the commissioner of motor vehicles (Veh. & Traf. Law § 509-d(1)(ii)). A copy of the response by each state, showing the driving record or certifying that no driving record exists for that driver, must be kept on file by the school district for three years (§ 509-d(3)). The driving record must be updated annually by the bus driver, and such information must be kept in the employer's record (§ 509-f).

22:77. Is a school bus driver required to report his or her convictions for violations of the Vehicle and Traffic Law to his or her employer?

Yes. A school bus driver who is convicted of a misdemeanor or felony under the Vehicle and Traffic Law, or who has his or her driver's license revoked, suspended or withdrawn, must notify his or her employer by the end of the business day following the date when the driver received notice of such action. Failure to provide this notice will subject the driver to a suspension of five working days or a suspension equivalent to the number of working days that the driver was not in compliance with this requirement, whichever is longer (Veh. & Traf. Law § 509-i(1)).

A school bus driver convicted of a traffic infraction in any jurisdiction must notify his or her employer within five working days of such a conviction. Failure to provide such notice within the required time period will subject the driver to a suspension of five working days (Veh. & Traf. Law § 509-i(1-a); see *In re Smith v. Board of Educ. of Taconic Hills CSD*, 235 A.D.2d 912 (3d Dep't 1997)).

22:78. Is a school bus driver required to report his or her involvement in an accident to his or her employer?

Yes. A driver who is involved in an accident as defined in section 509-a of the Vehicle and Traffic Law, in any jurisdiction, must notify his or her employer within five working days from the date of the accident. Failure to so notify within the required time period will subject the driver to a suspension of five working days (Veh. & Traf. Law §§ 509-d(1-b), 509-i(1-b); see also **22:69**).

22:79. Does the school bus driver have responsibility to maintain order on the bus?

Yes. School bus drivers, monitors and attendants are all responsible for reasonable behavior of students in transit (8 NYCRR § 156.3(d)). However, drivers have no authority to suspend students for disorderly conduct. They should report those students who violate established rules to the school principal who should take appropriate action (see **22:16**).

School Bus Monitors and Attendants

22:80. What is the definition of a school bus monitor?

A *school bus monitor* is any person employed to assist children to safely enter and exit from a school bus owned, leased, or contracted for by a school district or board of cooperative educational services (BOCES), and to assist the school bus driver in maintaining proper order on the school bus (8 NYCRR § 156.3(a)(3)).

22:81. What is the definition of a school bus attendant?

A *school bus attendant* is any person employed to assist students with a disabling condition on a school bus owned, leased, or contracted for by a school district or BOCES (8 NYCRR § 156.3(a)(4)).

22:82. What are the qualifications for a school bus monitor or attendant?

All school bus monitors and attendants must:

- Be at least 19 years of age.
- Have the physical and mental ability to satisfactorily carry out their duties.

Each monitor or attendant may be examined by a physician upon the order of the school superintendent within two weeks prior to the beginning of each school year. The school superintendent will consider the physician's report to determine the fitness of the monitor or attendant to carry out his or her functions (8 NYCRR § 156.3(c)(1), (2), (3)).

22:83. Are school bus monitors and attendants required to pass a physical performance test?

Yes. School bus monitors and attendants hired prior to July 1, 2003 had until July 1, 2004 to take and pass a physical performance test. Those hired after July 1, 2003 must take and pass the test before they may assume their duties (8 NYCRR § 156.3(c)(3)(iii)).

The physical performance test must be administered by a certified school bus driver instructor who shall assess the ability of the school bus monitor or attendant to, for example, climb and descend bus steps, carry or drag students in a bus emergency evacuation, and exit quickly from an emergency door (8 NYCRR § 156.3(c)(3)(iii)(a)).

School districts, BOCES or transportation contractors that do not have enough school bus driver instructors on staff to administer the physical performance tests, may apply for a waiver to have Department of Motor Vehicles certified examiners administer the tests, provided they are conducted under the general supervision of a certified school bus driver instructor (8 NYCRR § 156.3(c)(3)(iii)(b)).

22:84. Are school bus monitors and attendants required to have safety training?

Yes. Specifically, all school bus monitors and attendants must receive three hours of pre-service instruction that includes at least school bus safety practices, child management techniques and the proper techniques for assisting children to safely enter and exit a school bus (8 NYCRR 156.3(c)(5)(i)). Those monitors and attendants working in a district on July 1, 2003 had until July 1, 2004 to take the required safety training. Those hired after July 1, 2003 must complete the required training prior to beginning service.

In addition, school bus monitors and attendants serving students with a disabling condition must receive instruction relating to special needs transportation including proper techniques for assisting disabled students in entering and exiting the school bus. Those hired as of January 1, 2004 had until July 1, 2004 to complete this additional training. School bus monitors and attendants hired after January 1, 2004 must complete the special needs training prior to assuming their duties (Veh. & Traf Law § 1229-d; 8 NYCRR § 156.3(c)(5)(i)).

Furthermore, school bus monitors and attendants hired after July 1, 2003 must complete within their first year of employment a "Basic Course of Instruction for Monitors and Attendants" that provides at least 10 hours of instruction on topics prescribed by the commissioner (8 NYCRR § 156.3(c)(5)(iii).

All monitors and attendants must receive a two hour refresher training annually at sessions conducted between July 1 and the first day of school, and between December 1 and March 1 of each school year (8 NYCRR § 156.3(c)(5)(iv)).

22:85. Must school bus monitors and attendants be certified in cardiopulmonary resuscitation?

Only school bus attendants who serve students with a disabling condition are required to have and maintain certification in cardiopulmonary resuscitation (CPR), when such skills are required as part of a student's individualized education program (IEP). Those attendants employed as of January 1, 2004 had until July 1, 2004 to obtain a CPR certification. Those hired after January 1, 2004 must be CPR certified prior to assuming their duties (Veh. & Traf. Law § 1229-d(3); 8 NYCRR § 156.3(c)(4)).

Schools districts, BOCES, or contractors may also require both school bus monitors and attendants to maintain certification in first aid (8 NYCRR § 156.3(c)(4)).

22:86. Are school bus monitors and attendants permitted to leave a school bus when children are inside?

Yes, but only to help children enter or exit the school bus and to safely cross the street. Otherwise, when children are inside the bus, monitors and attendants must remain on the bus with them, except in an emergency (8 NYCRR § 156.3(e)(4)).

22:87. Can school districts require that school bus attendants be fingerprinted?

Yes. Section 1229-d of the Vehicle and Traffic Law authorizes school districts to require that applicants for a position as school bus attendant submit fingerprints for a criminal history check.

Purchase and Lease of School Buses and Transportation Services

22:88. Must a school district competitively bid the purchase of a school bus?

Yes, if the purchase involves an expenditure of more than $10,000 (Gen. Mun. Law § 103; see 19:56–62 for more information on the bidding process). Financing must be approved by the school board and may be by a bond, note or authorized as a specific item in the budget.

22:89. Must a school bus purchase be approved by the commissioner of education?

Yes. Any school bus purchase by a district must be approved by the commissioner of education. Transportation aid will not be apportioned for the purchase cost of the bus unless the district has obtained the required purchase approval (see 8 NYCRR § 156.4).

22:90. May school districts participate in cooperative purchasing of school buses?

Yes. School districts may purchase school buses and other items cooperatively (Gen. Mun. Law Article 5-G, §§ 119-m–119-oo). This method requires the adoption of specifications that will be agreeable to all in the group. The voters of each district must grant the necessary appropriation or authorization to borrow money. The major benefit is the possibility of securing lower prices through quantity buying. Each district must award its own contract for purchase.

22:91. May a school district purchase a school bus through an installment purchase contract?

Yes. However, these contracts are subject to competitive bidding requirements, and installment payments may not be financed by the issuance of bonds or notes (Gen. Mun. Law § 109-b). For further information, see "Competitive Bidding Under General Municipal Law Section 103" Opn. St. Comp., 1998, Research Paper, pp. 3014–17; see also **19:73**).

A school board may replace a school bus because of damage or loss without voter approval, using any unencumbered funds or by using budget notes (§ 1709(25)(a)); Loc. Fin. Law § 29.00).

22:92. May school districts lease school buses?

Yes. A school board may lease a motor vehicle to transport students for a one school year term. However, when authorized by the voters, the lease may be for up to a five-year term. Once the initial lease expires, any additional lease for the same or equivalent replacement vehicle(s) requires voter approval (§§ 1604(21-a), 1709(25)(i), 2503(12-a); see *Appeal of Shafer*, 43 Educ. Dep't Rep. ___, dec. no. 14,900 (2003)). No voter approval is required in the Big 5 school districts (§ 2554(19-a)).

In addition, subject to approval by the commissioner of education, school buses may be leased under emergency conditions for up to 90 days (unless the emergency continues). Emergency conditions include, but are not limited to, strikes, delay in delivery date, theft, vandalism, fire and accident (§ 1709(25)(e); (8 NYCRR § 156.6).

22:93. What transportation-related items may districts purchase through state contracts?

The state Division of Standards and Purchases gives school districts the opportunity to purchase, through state contracts, items such as school buses, gasoline, tires, spark plugs and motor oil, all at considerable savings. The purchase or series of purchases of a specific item must exceed $500; however, the amount need not be spent at any one time but may be spread over a period of time. Nonpublic schools may purchase such state contract items through local school districts (Gen. Mun. Law § 109-a).

Inquiries about state contracts can be directed to the Office of General Services, Division of Purchasing, Empire State Plaza, Albany, N.Y. 12242.

22:94. What insurance must be carried on a school bus?

Minimum and maximum levels for public liability and property damage insurance for school buses are contained in section 370 of the Vehicle and Traffic Law. The law establishes a minimum amount of indemnity for damages and injuries to persons and for property damage.

Each school board must determine whether the statutory minimum sufficiently protects the district. If a board desires insurance in excess of the minimum, the amount of coverage must be specified in the district's advertisement for transportation contract bids. No-fault automobile insurance applies to school vehicles, although this law does not apply to losses incurred through property damage.

22:95. May a school district contract for the maintenance of school buses?

Yes. The process for entering into and extending any such contract is the same process applicable to contracts for the transportation of students (Educ. Law § 305(14)(a); see 8 NYCRR § 156.12; see also **22:96–98, 101**).

22:96. May a school district contract for the transportation of students?

Yes. In addition, through June 30, 2007, contracts for the transportation of students that annually run more than $10,000 may be either competitively bid or secured through a request for proposals process (Educ. Law § 305(14)(a), (e); 8 NYCRR § 156.12; see **19:56-62** for more information on the bidding process).

For more information on pupil transportation contracts, visit the State Education Department's Office of Pupil Transportation Services Web site at http://www.emsc.nysed.gov/mgtserv/ptransho.htm).

22:97. Must transportation contracts be approved by the commissioner of education?

Yes. A transportation contract does not become valid and binding upon either party until it has been approved by the commissioner of education (§§ 3625(4); 305(14)(a), (e); 8 NYCRR § 156.12(d)).

Transportation contracts may be made for a period not exceeding five years if the terms are approved by the district voters (§§ 1604(23), 1709(27)). These must be in writing, approved by the school superintendent, and signed by the superintendent and the school board president (§ 3625(1), (2)).

A contract extension may exceed the maximum amount specified, referenced by the consumer price index, to compensate for the criminal history and driver licensing testing fees attributable to special requirements for school bus drivers pursuant to articles 19 and 19-a of the Vehicle and Traffic Law. These costs must be approved by the commissioner (§ 305(14)(c)).

The state comptroller also is authorized to audit the financial records relating to contracts of school bus contractors that provide school transportation to districts (§ 3625(2)).

The contract must state the contractor agrees to come to a full stop before crossing any railroad track or state highway (§ 3625(1), (2); see **22:42**).

22:98. What procedures must a school district follow to award a transportation contract by the competitive bidding process?

When a school board awards a transportation contract through competitive bidding, the transportation contract must be advertised in the same manner as purchase contracts under section 103 of the General Municipal Law (Educ. Law § 305(14)(a)). All advertisements for bids must be published in a newspaper or newspapers, designated by the school board or trustees, with general circulation within the district. The advertisement must state when and where bids will be publicly opened and read, either by school authorities or their designee. At least five days must elapse between the first publication of the advertisement and the opening of bids (§ 305(14)(a)).

A school board may solicit bids in alternative categories, such as soliciting bids for contracts for individual school bus routes and alternative bids for contracts for all of the district's school bus routes in the aggregate. The district may then select the lowest responsible bidder in either category. *Acme Bus Corp. v. Board of Educ. of the Roosevelt UFSD*, 91 N.Y.2d 51 (1999); *Appeal of Mitchell*, 40 Educ. Dep't Rep. 88 (2000)).

If a district is faced with an emergency affecting student transportation services and must take immediate action, the school board may negotiate interim transportation contracts for a period not to exceed one month. During this time, the board or a district trustee must advertise for bids and award a contract as required by the law. The approved costs of the interim contracts will be eligible for transportation aid (§ 305(14)(b)).

22:99. What procedures must a school district follow to award a transportation contract through a request for proposals process?

When a board of education awards a transportation contract through a request for proposals process, it must specify in its public notice soliciting proposals all the criteria it will use in evaluating the proposals and the weightings assigned to each criterion (8 NYCRR § 156.12(c)).The board must evaluate each proposal based upon the following criteria:

- previous experience of the contractor in transporting pupils;
- name of each transportation company of which the contractor has been an owner or manager;
- a description of any safety programs implemented by the contractor;
- record of accidents in motor vehicles under control of the contractor;
- the driving history of the contractor's employees;
- inspection records and model year of each of the motor vehicles under the control of the contractor;
- maintenance schedules of the motor vehicles under the control the contractor;
- a financial analysis of the contractor;
- documentation of compliance with motor vehicle insurance requirements; and
- total cost of the proposal (8 NYCRR § 156.12(b)).

Proposals for contracts to meet anticipated needs during the following school year must be requested by June 1, except for contract proposals for the transportation of students with disabilities, which must be requested by July 1. If an emergency or other unforeseen situation prevents compliance with these deadline, the proposals must be requested at least 30 days prior to the beginning date of service (8 NYCRR § 156.12(e),(g)).

22:100. Are there any exceptions to the competitive bidding or request for proposal process for awarding transportation service contracts?

Yes, within certain specified restrictions. When an emergency arises, or there is an unforeseen occurrence or condition affecting student transportation services that requires immediate action and cannot await competitive bidding or responses to request for proposals, a district may enter into an "interim contract." However, an interim contract may not exceed one month in duration, pending the award of a contract in compliance with the competitive bidding or request for proposal process (§ 305(14)(b); 8 NYCRR § 156.12(f).

22:101. May a school board extend an existing transportation contract?

Yes. Moreover, a school board choosing to extend an existing transportation contract is not required to undergo competitive bidding or a request for proposals process if it chooses to extend such a contract for up to five years.

A board electing to extend a transportation contract may, in its discretion, increase the amount to be paid in each year of the contract extension by an amount not to exceed the regional consumer price index increase for the New York, N.Y.-Northeastern New Jersey area, based upon the index for all urban consumers (CPI-U) during the preceding 12-month period, provided it has been satisfactorily established by the contractor that there has been at least an equivalent increase in its costs of operation during the period of the contract (§ 305(14)(a); *A.C. Transportation, Inc. v. Board of Educ. of the City of New York*, 253 A.D.2d 330 (1st Dep't 1999)).

The commissioner of education has the authority to reject any contract extension if he finds the amount in the proposed extension fails to reflect any decrease in the regional consumer price index for the New York, N.Y.-Northeastern New Jersey area, based upon the CPI-U during the preceding 12-month period, or, if in his opinion, the extension is not in the district's best interests. If the commissioner does reject a proposed extension, he may order the board to seek, obtain and consider other bids (§ 305(14)(a)).

22:102. May a school board amend an existing transportation contract?

Yes, in certain cases. Through January 1, 2005 school boards have authority to amend existing student transportation contracts when necessary to comply with federal, state or local laws, rules or regulations imposed after execution of the contract, or to enhance the safety of pupil transportation. Any such amendments are subject to approval by the commissioner of education and require demonstrable enhancements in pupil safety and/or increased savings consistent with maintaining student safety. In addition, any such amendment may not cause additional cost to the state, locality or school district, circumvent competitive bidding requirements or other provisions of law, or fail to increase or maintain student transportation safety (§ 305(14)(d)).

22:103. May a school district provide regional student transportation services?

Yes. Such services may be provided jointly with other school districts or BOCES boards (§ 1709(25)(g)). School districts may also contract with another school district, a county, municipality, or the state division for youth to provide transportation for students if the contract cost is appropriate (§ 1709(25)(h)).

State Aid for Transportation

22:104. How is student transportation aid calculated?

Transportation aid is paid on general operations and on bus purchases. All school districts are entitled to transportation aid, between 6.5 percent and 90 percent of their approved transportation expense (§§ 3602(7), 3622-a, 3623-a).

If the voters approve transportation beyond the state-mandated mileage limitations, the transportation for the distance beyond one and one-half and two or three miles and over 15 miles is eligible for transportation aid (§§ 3621(2)(a), 3635(1)(a); 8 NYCRR § 156.2(a)).

The amount of state aid payable on the purchase of a school bus is limited to the actual cost of the bus or the state contract price for a similar bus, whichever is less, or, if no similar bus is available under a state contract, to the statewide median cost of similar buses. Aid on bus purchases may be reduced based on calculations made by the State Education Department (§ 3602(7)(c)).

Sections 3602(7)(b) and 3623-a(e) of the Education Law makes the following additional expenses eligible for transportation aid: health, life and other insurance premiums for transportation personnel for whom salaries are approved; premiums for collision and other insurance coverage; uniforms; equipment; and other expenses approved by the commissioner's regulations.

22:105. Can a school district count students enrolled in nonpublic schools in the formula to determine state transportation aid for the district?

Yes. Except for cities with populations of more than 1 million, the resident nonpublic school district enrollment must be included in the district's computation of the wealth per pupil formula used to determine state aid for transportation (§ 3602(7)(a)).

22:106. Is state aid available for the transportation of students above grade 6 to another school district when the district does not furnish instruction for these grades?

Yes. Districts that do not maintain a secondary school must provide transportation, when necessary, for their students who have completed the work in the sixth grade and are receiving instruction in another district.

These districts are eligible for transportation aid under the same rules that apply to other transportation (§ 3622-a(2)).

22:107. Is state aid available for the transportation of students with disabilities?

Yes. The Education Law provides that school districts transporting students with disabilities to and from school are eligible for state aid reimbursement of between 6.5 percent and 90 percent of the approved cost of such transportation provided.

However, it also provides that this transportation may not be in excess of 50 miles from the home of such a student to the appropriate special service or program, unless the commissioner of education certifies that no appropriate nonresidential special service or program is available within 50 miles. In this case, the commissioner may establish, by regulation, a maximum number of trips between a student's home and the private residential school that provides special services or programs (§§ 4401(4), 4402(4)(d); see also 8 NYCRR § 200.12).

22:108. Do school districts receive state aid for out-of-district transportation of students to nonpublic schools?

Yes. State aid for transportation of students to nonpublic schools is based on the same criteria as that of aid to public schools (§ 3622-a(4)).

Transportation for Nonpublic School Students

22:109. Are school districts required to provide transportation to nonpublic school students?

Yes. The Education Law requires that school districts must provide transportation to nonpublic school students within the same mileage limits established for resident students attending public schools (§ 3635). If a district transports public school students beyond what is legally required, it must do the same for nonpublic school students (§ 3635(1); *Appeal of Defeis*, 34 Educ. Dep't Rep. 408 (1995); *Appeal of Whitaker*, 33 Educ. Dep't Rep. 59 (1993); *Matter of Eberhardt*, 25 Educ. Dep't Rep. 263 (1986); *Matter of McIntyre*, 25 Educ. Dep't Rep. 156 (1985)). A school district is not required to transport students to a nonpublic school by private carrier rather than public transportation (*Appeal of Clancy*, 37 Educ. Dep't Rep. 280 (1998); *Appeal of Lavin*, 32 Educ. Dep't Rep. 249 (1992)).

To determine eligibility, the distance to be measured is from the student's home to the nonpublic school (see **22:13**). If a student lives within the mileage limitations, then the school district must provide direct transportation for the child to the nonpublic school (*Appeal of Hurd*, 41

Educ. Dep't Rep. 473 (2002)). If a student lives outside the mileage limitations but the district provides transportation to others who attend that student's nonpublic school and live within the mileage limits, the district must designate one or more public schools as a centralized pick-up point to transport nonpublic school students who live outside the mileage limits (§ 3635(1)(b)(i); *Appeal of Del Prete*, 40 Educ. Dep't Rep. 141 (2000); *Appeal of Defeis*). Those students then must be transported from the centralized pick-up point to their respective nonpublic schools (see **22:111**).

In addition, a school district may elect to provide transportation from a centralized pick-up point to a nonpublic school student whose school is located more than 15 miles from the student's residence if the district has provided transportation to that school in at least one of the three prior years, and the distance between the pick-up point and the nonpublic school is not more than 15 miles (§ 3635(1)(b)(ii); *Appeal of Porzio*, 42 Educ. Dep't Rep. 166 (2002); *Appeal of Lucente,* 40 Educ. Dep't Rep. 455 (2000); *Defeis*). A district does not have to provide transportation from centralized pick-up points to any nonpublic school to which regular home-to-school transportation is not already being provided (*Appeal of Porzio*; *Appeal of Lucente*).

Once children are transported to the nonpublic school, responsibility for their supervision belongs to the nonpublic school even if the children arrive before the start of the school day (*Appeal of Hamilton*, 21 Educ. Dep't Rep. 30 (1981)).

The cost of providing transportation between centralized pick-up points and nonpublic schools is an ordinary contingent expense (§ 3635(1)(b)(ii)).

22:110. Are school districts required to provide transportation to charter school students?

Yes. A charter school is deemed a nonpublic school for transportation purposes. Therefore, a school district must provide transportation to charter school students who reside in the district to the same extent transportation is provided to resident students who attend nonpublic schools (§§ 2853(4)(b), 3635; *Appeal of New Covenant Charter Sch.* (39 Educ. Dep't Rep. 610 (2000)). Requests for transportation must be submitted by April 1 of the preceding school year, even if parents have not yet enrolled their child in the charter school (*Appeal of New Covenant Charter School*, 41 Educ. Dep't Rep. 358 (2002)).

22:111. Are school districts responsible for providing transportation to nonpublic school students between their home and a centralized pick-up point?

No. A district is not obligated to provide transportation to nonpublic school students to and from the centralized pick-up point. A district may provide a nonpublic school student residing outside the district's mileage limits with transportation to the centralized pick-up point if the student lives on an established school bus route to the centralized pick-up point, and from there on to the nonpublic school, provided such transportation does not result in additional costs to the district (§ 3635(1)(b)(i)).

22:112. May a school district deny transportation to otherwise eligible nonpublic school students?

Yes. A parent must submit a request in writing for transportation to a nonpublic school no later than April 1, unless the family moves into the district after April 1, in which case the request must be made within 30 days of establishing residency (§ 3635(2)).

The filing of a late request may result in a denial of transportation, even where the district has previously accepted late requests (*Appeal of Beer*, 33 Educ. Dep't Rep. 620 (1994)).

No late request may be denied, however, if a reasonable explanation is provided for the delay. The school board has discretion to determine the reasonableness of the excuse, and its decision will not be set aside unless it constitutes an abuse of discretion (*Appeal of Aguanno*, 41 Educ. Dep't Rep. 326 (2002); *Appeal of Gabay*, 39 Educ. Dep't Rep. 492 (2000); *Appeal of Tarricone*, 38 Educ. Dep't Rep. 623 (1999)).

Even in the absence of a reasonable explanation for the delay, a late request must be granted if it can be provided under existing transportation arrangements at no additional cost to the district (*Appeal of Mendoza*, 34 Educ. Dep't Rep. 402 (1995); *Appeal of Frasier*, 34 Educ. Dep't Rep. 404 (1995)). For example a school district did not abuse its discretion when it denied a late request for private school transportation to a student who had three siblings already receiving transportation to that school. The district contracted for transportation on a per-seat basis and it would have cost the district an additional $513.95 per month to grant the late transportation request (*Appeal of Aguanno*).

22:113. What are some examples of reasonable excuses for a late transportation request?

A change in designation of a nonpublic school different than the nonpublic school originally specified after the April 1 deadline constitutes a separate request (*Appeal of Galvani*, 34 Educ. Dep't Rep. 370 (1995);

Appeal of McNair, 33 Educ. Dep't Rep. 418 (1994)). However, there would be a reasonable excuse for failing to meet the April 1 deadline where a student is admitted to a private boarding school but is subsequently denied enrollment by the private school after April 1 (*Appeal of Lamba*, 32 Educ. Dep't Rep. 473 (1993); *Application to Reopen the Appeal of Lamba*, 32 Educ. Dep't Rep. 611 (1993)).

Similarly, the commissioner found a reasonable excuse for a transportation request to a charter school submitted after the April 1 deadline where the charter school did not receive formal approval to operate until after the deadline. However, parents of the charter school students would not be exempted from making timely requests in future years (*Appeal of New Covenant Charter School* (39 Educ. Dep't Rep. 610 (2000)). The fact that a charter school might be subject to an enrollment cap at the time of the April 1 deadline is not a reasonable excuse for late requests for transportation either (*Appeal of New Covenant Charter School*, 41 Educ. Dep't Rep. 358 (2002)).

A transportation request that is mailed prior to the April 1 deadline but is not received until later may still be a valid timely request even if the postmark is dated after April 1 (*Reopening Appeal of Calabrese*, 43 Educ. Dep't Rep. ___, dec. no. 14,982 (2003)).

22:114. What are some examples of unreasonable excuses for late transportation requests?

A board need not accept ignorance or forgetfulness of the April 1 deadline as a reasonable excuse (*Appeal of Mogilski*, 37 Educ. Dep't 446 (1998); *Appeal of Haque*, 34 Educ. Dep't Rep. 496 (1995)). Similarly, a belated parental decision to enroll a child in a nonpublic school is not a reasonable excuse (*Appeal of Aguanno*, 41 Educ. Dep't Rep. 326 (2002); *Appeal of R.O.*, 40 Educ. Dep't Rep. 137 (2000); *Appeal of Attubato*, 38 Educ. Dep't Rep. 511 (1999); *Appeal of Hause*, 34 Educ. Dep't Rep. 374 (1995)).

Reliance on a nonpublic school to submit a list of students requiring transportation is not a reasonable excuse for filing a late request either (*Matter of Hendricks*, 21 Educ. Dep't Rep. 302 (1981); see **22:115**).

22:115. May a nonpublic school submit a list of students who require transportation?

Yes. However, while the nonpublic school may submit a list of nonpublic students requiring transportation, it is the responsibility of the parent or guardian of a nonpublic school student to ensure a written request is filed on time or transportation may be denied (see **22:114**).

This list should contain the name, address, age and grade of each child, and a signed affidavit that states that the school has been authorized by the parents or guardian of each child to act as his or her representative. This affidavit also should indicate that a copy of this authorization duly signed by the parents is on file in the school office (see *Appeal of Lucente*, 39 Educ. Dep't Rep. 244 (1999); *Matter of Hendricks*, 21 Educ. Dep't Rep. 302 (1981)).

22:116. Must public school districts provide transportation to nonpublic schools on days when public schools are not in session?

No. However, New York City must provide transportation to nonpublic schools for a maximum of five days, or a maximum of 10 days in any year in which the last day of Passover and Easter Sunday are separated by more than seven days, when public schools are not in session. Such five or 10 additional days are limited to the Wednesday, Thursday and Friday after Labor Day; Rosh Hashanah; Yom Kippur; the week in which public schools are closed for spring recess; and the week between Christmas Day and New Year's Day (§ 3635(2-a)).

22:117. Are school districts required to alter their schedule to accommodate the transportation needs of nonpublic school students?

No. However, the commissioner of education has noted repeatedly that public and nonpublic schools have an obligation to cooperate in a reasonable manner in the scheduling of classes and transportation (*Appeal of Frasier*, 35 Educ. Dep't Rep. 499 (1996); *Appeal of Post*, 33 Educ. Dep't Rep. 151 (1993); *Matter of Jeffers*, 26 Educ. Dep't Rep. 408, 411 (1987); *Matter of Berger*, 22 Educ. Dep't Rep. 443 (1983)).

While public school authorities may not dictate the opening or closing hours for a nonpublic school (*Berger*), they are not required to alter their own schedules in order to provide transportation to nonpublic school students. Accordingly, the commissioner has ruled that a transportation scheme that delivers nonpublic school students to their school just five minutes (*Berger*) or even 20 minutes (*Matter of Stickley*, 27 Educ. Dep't Rep. 328 (1988)) before the start of the school day does not impose an unreasonable burden on the nonpublic school.

However, a transportation scheme that consistently delivers students late to nonpublic schools and on time to public schools is not reasonable (*Appeal of Pallos*, 39 Educ. Dep't Rep. 650 (2000); *Matter of Hacker*, 28 Educ. Dep't Rep. 141, 143 (1988); *Matter of Osgood*, 25 Educ. Dep't Rep. 274 (1986); *Matter of Tyo*, 20 Educ. Dep't Rep. 384 (1981)).

In addition, the adoption of an "unreasonable" schedule by a nonpublic school will not result in an obligation on the part of the public school district to provide special transportation services at additional expense in order to meet that schedule. This was the case, for example, where a nonpublic school dismissed its elementary and middle school students at 3:20 p.m., but classes for high school students didn't end until 5:00 p.m. (*Berger*).

22:118. May a school district transport students who attend release-time religious instruction from the public school to a church or parochial school?

No. School districts have no legal authority to provide this service (*Appeal of Fitch*, 2 Educ. Dep't Rep. 394 (1963); see also *Appeal of Santicola*, 37 Educ. Dep't Rep. 79 (1997)).

23. Religion and Public Education

23:1. What constitutional provisions govern the role of religion in the public schools?

The Establishment and Free Exercise Clauses of the First Amendment of the United States Constitution primarily govern the role of religion in the public schools. New York's Blaine Amendment also imposes certain limitations on the relationship between government authorities (including school districts) and religious schools.

23:2. What is the Establishment Clause?

The Establishment Clause states: "Congress shall make no law respecting an establishment of religion." It has been interpreted to require the separation of church and state and is applicable to the states and their subdivisions, including school districts. It requires that government pursue a course of "complete neutrality toward religion," and not promote religion or entangle itself in religious matters (see *Board of Educ. of the Kiryas Joel Village Sch. Dist. v. Grumet*, 512 U.S. 687 (1994); *Lee v. Weisman*, 505 U.S. 577 (1992); *Wallace v. Jaffree*, 472 U.S. 38, 60 (1985); *Larson v. Valente*, 456 U.S. 228 (1982), *reh'g denied*, 457 U.S. 1111 (1982)).

However, not all governmental conduct that confers a benefit on or gives special recognition to religion is automatically prohibited. It depends on all the circumstances surrounding the particular church-state relationship (*Lynch v. Donnelly*, 465 U.S. 668, 678–79 (1984); see **23:5**).

23:3. What is the Free Exercise Clause?

The Free Exercise Clause addresses the freedom of individual belief and religious expression. It states: "Congress shall make no law prohibiting the free exercise" of religion. This clause is also applicable to the states and their political subdivisions, and prohibits government from restricting the right of an individual to believe in whatever he or she may choose. This right, however, may not be read "to require the Government to conduct its own internal affairs in ways that comport with the religious beliefs of particular citizens" (*Bowen v. Roy*, 476 U.S. 693, 699–700 (1986); *Lyng v. Northwest Indian Cemetery Protective Ass'n*, 485 U.S. 439 (1988)). Although "government may accommodate the free exercise of religion," it may not "supersede the fundamental limitations imposed by the Establishment Clause" (*Lee* at 587; see also *Kiryas Joel v. Grumet*).

23:4. How does New York's Blaine Amendment affect religion and public education?

In addition, article 11, section 3 of the New York State Constitution, also known as the Blaine Amendment, provides that neither the state nor any state subdivision, which includes school districts, may authorize the use of its property, credit or public funds, directly or indirectly, to assist any school under the control of any religious denomination or which teaches any denominational tenet or doctrine. The purpose of this article is to prevent state aid to religion, but the article has been interpreted as not prohibiting every state action that may provide some benefit to religious schools (*Board of Educ. v. Allen*, 392 U.S. 236 (1968)). For example, this article specifically exempts the *transportation* of students to and from nonpublic schools, and the district's examination or inspection of such schools.

The U.S. Supreme Court has not ruled directly on the validity of state constitutional provisions that are stricter than the Establishment Clause (see, e.g., *Witters v. Washington Dep't of Servs.*, 474 U.S. 481 (1986)). It avoided doing so in 2004 in a case involving a Washington State law that prohibited the use of state scholarship funds to pursue a degree in theology, ruling that although states may fund theological studies, they are not required to do so (*Locke v. Davey*, ___ U.S. ___, 124 S.Ct. 1307 (2004)).

23:5. Are there standards to determine whether a certain government action violates the Establishment Clause?

The most commonly used standard to determine whether governmental action violates the separation of church and state principles of the Establishment Clause is the Lemon test, a three-pronged test established by the United States Supreme Court and named after the lawsuit that gave rise to it, *Lemon v. Kurtzman* (403 U.S. 602 (1971), *reh'g denied*, 404 U.S. 876 (1971), *on remand*, 348 F.Supp. 300 (E.D. Pa. 1972), *aff'd*, 411 U.S. 192 (1973)). To be constitutional, an action: (1) must not have a religious purpose; (2) must not have a principal or primary effect of advancing or inhibiting religion; and (3) must not foster excessive government entanglement with religion.

However, since the early 1990s, the Supreme Court has decided a number of cases without reference to the *Lemon* test. During this time, several justices have questioned the continued appropriateness of the test (see *Board of Educ. of the Kiryas Joel Village Sch. Dist. v. Grumet*, 512 U.S. 687 (1994); *Zobrest v. Catalina Foothills Sch. Dist.*, 509 U.S. 1 (1993); *Lambs Chapel v. Center Moriches UFSD*, 508 U.S. 384 (1993), *remanded without op.*, 17 F.3d 1425 (2d Cir. 1994); *Lee v. Weisman*, 505 U.S. 577 (1992)).

The high court has not overruled *Lemon* (see *Doe v. Santa Fe Indep. Sch. Dist.*, 530 U.S. 290 (2000); *Agostini v. Felton*, 521 U.S. 203 (1997)), but it also uses an Establishment Clause analysis that focuses on global principles of neutrality not linked to a specific test. Under these neutrality principles, the Establishment Clause is violated when government acts in a non-neutral manner toward religion by favoring (1) religion over nonreligion, (2) nonreligion over religion, or (3) a particular denomination over another (see, e.g., *Kiryas Joel v. Grumet*; *Wallace v. Jaffree*, 472 U.S. 38, 60 (1985); *Larson v. Valente*, 456 U.S. 228 (1982), *reh'g denied*, 457 U.S. 1111 (1982)).

In *Zelman v. Harris*, 536 U.S. 639 (2002), the Supreme Court applied the neutrality test in ruling that a voucher program did not violate the Establishment Clause because vouchers were provided directly to a broad range of income-eligible parents who, in turn, endorsed the check over to the participating school of their own private choice. Both public and private schools were allowed to participate in the program.

23:6. Are there standards to determine whether a certain government action violates the Free Exercise Clause?

Claims of violations of the Free Exercise Clause in an educational context traditionally have been measured by balancing the state's interest in providing public education against the right of the parent, student, or employee to freely exercise or practice his or her religion. However, the right to exercise one's religion freely is not burdened simply by mandating one to be exposed to ideas with which that person disagrees (*Mozert v. Hawkins County Bd. of Educ.*, 827 F.2d 1058 (6th Cir. 1987), *cert. denied*, 484 U.S. 1066 (1988)).

Prayer and Moments of Silence

Editor's Note: The federal No Child Left Behind Act of 2001 (NCLB) prohibits all school districts from maintaining and implementing any policy or practice that denies participation in constitutionally protected prayer in the public schools. The U.S. Secretary of Education has issued a guidance on constitutionally protected prayer that is available at http://www.ed.gov/policy/gen/guid/ religion and schools/index.html. Districts should consult with their school attorney to ensure their policies are compliant with the guidance and applicable court decisions. Additional information on the NCLB is available in NYSSBA's publication Leaving No Child Behind in New York, 2nd Edition, *distributed by LexisNexis.*

23:7. Is it constitutional for boards of education to open their public meetings with a prayer?

This issue has not yet been answered by any court with jurisdiction over the school districts in New York State. However, at least one federal appellate court has ruled such practice unconstitutional (*Coles v. Cleveland Bd. of Educ.*, 171 F.3d 369 (6th Cir. 1999)). The court rejected the argument that opening prayers at school board meetings are constitutionally permissible because prayers at sessions of the state legislature have been ruled constitutional (see *Marsh v. Chambers*, 463 U.S. 783 (1983)). According to the court, the school board is an integral part of the public school system. School board meetings can and are attended by students who may actively participate in the discussions.

Even though prayers at school board meetings differ from the graduation prayers ruled unconstitutional in *Lee v. Weisman*, 505 U.S. 577 (1992) (see **23:13**), because prayers at school board meetings are not said in front of the student body as a whole, "the school-board setting is arguably more coercive to participating students than the graduation ceremony at issue in *Lee*." In contrast, however, one federal appellate court ruled that a district did not violate the Establishment Clause when a school board member recited the Lord's Prayer at a graduation ceremony. According to the court, at the time, the board member was engaged in private speech. There was no involvement by the district in determining that the board member would speak, and the autonomy afforded to him in determining the contents of his remarks deemed his speech private (*Doe v. School Dist. of the City of Norfolk*, 340 F.3d 605 (8th Cir. 2003)).

23:8. May a public school district organize or require class participation in daily prayer?

No. Policies promoting school-sponsored prayer in public schools consistently have been struck down as unconstitutional acts of government. The United States Supreme Court has ruled repeatedly that the separation of church and state principles embodied in the Establishment Clause of the First Amendment prohibit school-sponsored prayers and religious exercises, even when the prayer is nondenominational and participation is voluntary.

For example, the high court ruled unconstitutional a prayer endorsed by the New York State Board of Regents for use in public schools (*Engle v. Vitale*, 370 U.S. 421 (1962)). It also struck down a state statute requiring readings from the Bible, even if students were not required to engage in such prayers (*School Dist. v. Schempp*, 374 U.S. 203 (1963)).

23:9. May a public school district organize or require students to participate in moments of silent meditation?

In 1985, the United States Supreme Court struck down a state statute requiring a one-minute period of silence for "meditation or voluntary prayer during the school day" (*Wallace v. Jaffree*, 472 U.S. 38 (1985)). In *Jaffree,* the legislative history of the statute reviewed by the court made it clear that the purpose was to permit prayer. Therefore, the statute was found to be unconstitutional.

Similarly, a federal appeals court struck down a New Jersey moment-of-silence statute that required public schools to permit students to observe one minute of silence "for quiet and private contemplation or introspection" because it violated the Establishment Clause. The Supreme Court declined to rule on the merits of the case (*Karcher v. May*, 780 F.2d 240 (3d Cir. 1985), *appeal dismissed for lack of jurisdiction*, 484 U.S. 72 (1987)).

In contrast, other federal appeals courts have upheld state laws requiring a one-minute period of quiet reflection in public classrooms (*Brown v. Gilmore*, 258 F.3d 265 (4th Cir. 2001); *Bown v. Gwinnet County Sch. Dist.*, 112 F.3d 1464 (11th Cir. 1997)).

New York's Education Law allows for a moment of silence in the public schools at the opening of school every school day (§3029-a). It specifically provides: "The silent meditation authorized . . . is not intended to be, and shall not be conducted as, a religious service or exercise, but may be considered an opportunity for silent meditation on a religious theme by those who are so disposed, or a moment of silent reflection on the anticipated activities of the day." Students may remain seated and may not be required to stand.

New York's statute has not been challenged in the courts. According to a 1964 Formal Opinion of Counsel from the State Education Department, the application of the statute would be impermissible if the statutory moment of silence were prefaced with the statement: "We will now have a moment of silence to acknowledge our Supreme Being" (Opn. Educ. Dep't, 3 Educ. Dep't Rep. 255 (1964)). Since the legislative history of that statute does not indicate that it was enacted to foster organized religious prayer, it may pass constitutional scrutiny.

23:10. May a public school district permit students to lead their peers in organized prayer during school hours?

No. Although the United States Supreme Court has not ruled on this question, other courts have found this to violate the separation of church and state requirements of the Establishment Clause. For example, where a student club was allowed to broadcast inspirational readings from the Bible and sectarian prayers over the school intercom system after the school's morning announcements, and where student-initiated prayers were allowed in individual classrooms during classroom hours, the courts perceived the school district as endorsing such religious messages (*Herdahl v. Pontotoc County Sch. Dist.*, 887 F.Supp. 902 (N.D. Miss. 1995); see also *Ingebretsen v. Jackson Pub. Sch. Dist.*, 88 F.3d 274 (5th Cir. 1996), *cert. denied*, 117 S.Ct. 388 (1996)).

23:11. May student groups meet on school premises and openly pray or conduct Bible study activities?

Yes. The federal Equal Access Act (20 USC §§ 4071–74) requires that public schools allow such use of its facilities, but only during noninstructional time, if the students are high school students, if the meeting or activity is not school-sponsored, and if the school district already allows other student-run, noncurriculum-related student groups to meet on school premises during "noninstructional time."

Noninstructional time generally means before or after school. However, one federal appellate court has ruled that a public high school's lunch break was "noninstructional time," rejecting the district's position that only time set aside before and after school constituted "noninstructional time" (*Ceniceros v. Board of Trustees of San Diego Unified Sch. Dist.*, 66 F.3d 1535 (9th Cir. 1995)). According to another federal appellate court, an activity period between homeroom and the first period of instruction is also noninstructional time (*Donovan v. Punxsutawney Area Sch. Bd.*, 336 F.3d 211 (3d Cir. 2003)).

A student group is noncurriculum-related unless the subject matter of that group is actually taught or concerns the body of courses as a whole, or participation in such a group is a course requirement or provides the participants with academic credit (*Board of Educ. of Westside Community Schools v. Mergens*, 496 U.S. 226 (1990)).

According to the United States Supreme Court, the Equal Access Act does not violate the Establishment Clause, because, under the act, schools are not endorsing religious speech; they are merely permitting such speech on a nondiscriminatory basis (*Board of Educ. of Westside Community Schools v. Mergens*).

A related issue involves the question of whether a student religious group using school property under the Equal Access Act may limit participation in the group to members who share the same religious beliefs. In *Hsu v. Roslyn UFSD No. 3*, 85 F.3d 839 (2d Cir. 1996), *cert. denied*, 117 S.Ct. 608 (1996), the United States Court of Appeals for the Second Circuit, with jurisdiction over New York, ruled that a school district could not enforce a pre-existing nondiscrimination policy to prohibit a student Bible club from meeting on school property under the act because the group allowed only Christians to serve as officers of the club.

23:12. May school personnel attend student group meetings where students openly pray or conduct Bible study activities?

Under the federal Equal Access Act (20 USC §§ 4071–74), school personnel may attend such meetings only as monitors, not as advisors or participants, and the meetings may not interfere materially or substantially with the orderly conduct of school activities. Furthermore, non-school persons or groups may not direct, control or regularly attend these student group meetings and activities. See **16:39** for information on the right of outside organizations to conduct, on public school premises, after-school religious activities involving public school students.

23:13. May a school district allow religious leaders to deliver benedictions and invocations at public school graduation ceremonies?

No. The United States Supreme Court ruled that it is unconstitutional for public schools to permit invocations and benedictions delivered by religious leaders at graduation ceremonies because of a potential coercive effect on the impressionable students who attend these ceremonies (*Lee v. Weisman*, 505 U.S. 577 (1992)). In so ruling, the high court rejected the argument that attendance at graduation ceremonies is voluntary. According to the court, "high school graduation is one of life's most significant occasions [and] a student is not free to absent herself from the graduation exercise in any real sense of the term voluntary."

23:14. May a school district allow students to deliver prayers at public school graduation ceremonies?

The United States Supreme Court has not addressed the issue of whether student-initiated prayer at graduation ceremonies is constitutional. However, some believe that the high court would invalidate a school district policy that allows student-initiated prayers at graduation ceremonies based on its decision in *Santa Fe Indep. Sch. Dist. v. Doe*, 530 U.S. 290 (2000), where the court ruled against a school district that allowed students to deliver prayer at a football game (see **23:15**).

Lower federal courts have been split on the issue. For example, in *Jones v. Clear Creek Indep. Sch. Dist.*, 977 F.2d 963 (5th Cir. 1992), *cert. denied*, 508 U.S. 967 (1993), the Fifth Circuit Federal Court of Appeals ruled that student-initiated and student-led nonsectarian graduation prayers are permissible because they solemnize the occasion.

Likewise, in *Adler v. Duval County Sch. Bd.*, 250 F.3d 1330 (11th Cir. 2001), *petition for cert. denied*, 122 S.Ct. 664 (2001) in a hearing *en banc*, the 11th Circuit ruled constitutional a school board policy that allowed a graduating senior elected by the class to deliver an unrestricted message at graduation. Students in the district were permitted to choose to elect a speaker to present a message at graduation with the school having no control over the content of the student's message. The 11th Circuit distinguished the *Santa Fe* case based upon "the total absence of state involvement in deciding whether there will be a graduation message, who will speak, or what the speaker may say." The court also considered "the student speaker's complete autonomy over the content of the message" and the fact that the message delivered, whether "secular, sectarian or both," was not state sponsored.

The Third Circuit took an opposing view in *American Civil Liberties Union of New Jersey v. Black Horse Pike Regional Bd. of Educ.*, 84 F.3d 1471 (3d Cir. *en banc* 1996).

23:15. May a public school district permit students to deliver prayers before, during, or after school-sponsored extracurricular activities?

The United States Supreme Court, in *Santa Fe Indep. Sch. Dist. v. Doe*, 530 U.S. 290 (2000), ruled that a school policy that allowed student-initiated, student-delivered, nonsectarian, nonproselytizing prayer at high school football games violates the separation of church and state.

The school district unsuccessfully argued that the policy was constitutional because it merely supported private religious speech, which was not controlled by the district; students were permitted to vote on whether a prayer would be recited; and the policy did not have an unconstitutional coercive effect upon students to adhere to religious practices they disagreed with simply because the invocations were delivered by fellow students.

According to the high court, the policy involved "both perceived and actual endorsement of religion. . . . The degree of school involvement makes it clear that the pregame prayer bears the imprint of the State and thus put school-aged children who objected in an untenable position." In addition, "members of the listening audience must perceive the pre-game message as a public expression of the issues of the majority of the student body with the approval of school administrators." As such, the pre-game prayer would be inevitably perceived as being stamped with the school's seal of approval.

The court further determined that "adolescents will often submit to pressure from their peers towards conformity, and that the influence is strongest in matters of social connection. . . . The constitutional command will not permit the district to exact religious conformity from a student as the price of joining classmates at a varsity football game."

Teaching of Religion

23:16. May a school district allow the teaching of creationism in its schools?

No. In addition, the United States Supreme Court has well established that a school district cannot prohibit the instruction of evolution or require that instruction of evolution be balanced with instruction of creation science (*Epperson v. Arkansas*, 393 U.S. 97 (1968); *Edwards v. Aguillard*, 482 U.S. 578 (1987)).

Furthermore, according to one federal appellate court outside of New York State, a school district may not require that a disclaimer be read before the teaching of evolution in its schools. In *Freiler v. Tangipahoa Parish Bd. of Educ.*, 185 F.3d 337 (1999), the U.S. Court of Appeals for the Fifth Circuit invalidated a disclaimer, which read:

> It is hereby recognized by the . . . board of education that the lesson to be presented regarding the origin of life and matter, is known as the Scientific Theory of Evolution and should be presented to inform students of the scientific concept and not intended to influence or dissuade the Biblical version of Creation. . . . It is the basic right of each student to form his/her own opinion and maintain beliefs taught by parents. Students are urged to exercise critical thinking and gather all information possible and closely examine each alternative toward forming an opinion.

The court rejected the district's argument that its purpose was to encourage critical thinking and that any benefit to religion was incidental to that purpose. Instead, the court found that the purpose and effect of the disclaimer was to protect and maintain belief in the Biblical version of creation.

23:17. May a school district impose limitations on teacher references to religion in the classroom?

Yes. In *Marchi v. Board of Cooperative Educational Services (BOCES) of Albany, Schoharie, Schenectady and Saratoga Counties*, 173 F.3d 469 (2d Cir. 1999), *cert. denied*, 528 U.S. 869 (1999), the United States Court of Appeals for the Second Circuit, with jurisdiction over New York State, upheld a BOCES directive instructing one of the employees to stop using "references to religion in the delivery of [his] instructional program unless it is a required element of a course of instruction and . . . has prior approval by [his] supervisor."

According to the Second Circuit, a public school risks violating the separation of church and state "if any of its teachers' activities gives the impression that the school endorses religion." In order to avoid such a violation, a school may prohibit teacher religious expressions and teacher-parent interactions that "risk giving the impression" that the district endorses religion.

The teacher, who had recently converted to Christianity, admitted modifying his instructional program to discuss such matters as "forgiveness, reconciliation, and God." He also played a religious music tape in class called "Wee 2 Sing the Bible," given to him by one of his student's parents to help calm the student. The teacher wrote back to the parent: "I thank you and the LORD for the tape; it brings the Spirit of Peace to the classroom . . . may God Bless you all richly!"

Similarly, in another case, found a school district lawfully terminated a substitute teacher for speaking with students about her religious views in class after hearing that a student had died. Even if her religious discussion had addressed an issue of "public concern," the school board's "'compelling interest in avoiding Establishment Clause violations' justified its actions" in terminating her (*Rosario v. Does 1–10*, 2002 U.S. App. LEXIS 11127 (2d Cir. 2002)).

23:18. May members of the clergy participate as volunteer staff in public school educational programs?

There is no specific case in New York that addresses this issue. However, one federal appellate court outside New York ruled that a school district violated the separation of church and state when it implemented a "Clergy in Schools" volunteer counseling program because it recruited volunteers exclusively from among the local clergy to provide counseling to students in school, during school hours (*Doe v. Beaumont Indep. Sch. Dist.*, 173 F.3d 274 (5th Cir. 1999)).

The district's failure to include lay professionals well qualified to mentor students concerning morals and virtue nullified the secular character of the program, even though the clergy were told to focus on civic values, refrain from discussing sex and abortion, and not to pray with students. The absence of lay volunteers indicated that the selection of volunteers was based on the fact that they were religious representatives rather than on their alleged listening and communications skills.

Similarly, a federal district court ruled a school district violated the Establishment Clause when it arranged a panel comprised exclusively of clergy members to discuss homosexuality and religion at a program held during its diversity week (*Hansen v. Ann Arbor Pub. Schs.*, 293 F.Supp.2d 780 (E.D. Mich. 2003)).

Religious Observances

23:19. May a school district close school for the observance of a religious holiday?

Although courts with jurisdiction over New York have not yet ruled on this matter, the United States Court of Appeals for the Seventh Circuit declared unconstitutional an Illinois statute that required all public schools to close on Good Friday because its legislative history reflected that the statute was intended to "accord special recognition to Christianity beyond anything . . . necessary to accommodate the needs of [Illinois'] Christian majority (*Metzl v. Leininger*, 57 F.2d 618 (7th Cir. 1995)). However, the court explained its decision might have been different if the state had shown that the majority of students were Christians and would not attend school on Good Friday. Under such circumstances, the court noted it would make sense to close school to prevent the wasteful expenditure of resources.

23:20. May a school district acknowledge the observance of religious holidays through plays, pageants, and other programs containing religious themes?

School districts may acknowledge religious holidays in programs that have religious significance as long as these programs also contain some educational or cultural purpose (*Florey v. Sioux Falls Sch. Dist. 49-5*, 619 F.2d 1311 (8th Cir. 1980), *cert. denied*, 449 U.S. 987 (1980)).

In *Matter of Rosenbaum*, 28 Educ. Dep't Rep. 138 (1988), the commissioner of education upheld a school district's policy permitting religious music and art where it was taught as part of a genuine secular program of education and where the policy excused students from participating in those parts of the curriculum which conflicted with their religious beliefs. The U.S. Court of Appeals for the Second Circuit, with jurisdiction over New York, ruled that Earth Day celebrations did not impermissibly endorse religion in a case where the record showed no one attending the ceremonies "worshipped" the earth or attached any significance of a religious nature to the celebration activities (*Altman v. Bedford CSD*, 245 F.3d 49 (2d Cir. 2001)).

However, the commissioner has also ruled that a school board's resolution to change the name of its "Winter" music concert to the "Christmas" concert violated the Establishment Clause. The resolution began: "We, being a Christian community . . .", which the commissioner found indicated an unconstitutional religious purpose (*Appeal of Sebouhian*, 31 Educ. Dep't Rep. 397 (1992)).

A school district may adopt guidelines for the treatment of religious and cultural holidays in the instructional program (Appeal of Pasquale, 30 Educ.

Dep't Rep. 361 (1991)). According to the commissioner, the adoption of such guidelines falls within the broad statutory authority of school boards to adopt bylaws and rules for the governance of the schools (§ 1709)). In this regard, a federal appellate court has ruled that a school district did not violate the Free Exercise of religion rights of an elementary school student when it denied the student permission to distribute gifts containing religious messages at an in-class holiday party. According to the court, an elementary school classroom . . . is not a place for student advocacy." Moreover, because young impressionable students could easily misinterpret a fellow student's message, schools must be able to restrict student expression that contradicts or distracts from a curricular activity." The court found significant that the student had not been asked to express his news about the personal significance of the holiday, in which case he would have been attempting to respond to a class assignment or activity.

The singing of "God Bless America" at a general school assembly memorializing the tragic events of September 11, 2001 does not violate the Establishment Clause (*Appeal of Cayot*, 42 Educ. Dep't Rep. 97 (2002)).

In another case, the U.S. Supreme Court dismissed, on procedural grounds, a lawsuit claiming that it violates the Establishment Clause of the federal constitution to require students to listen daily to the recitation of the Pledge of Allegiance, because the Pledge contains the words "One Nation, *Under God*" within its text (*Elk Grove Unified Sch. Dist.*, 124 S.Ct. 2301 (2004)). By declining to rule on the merits of the claim, the court left the substantive constitutional question for another day.

23:21. May a school district excuse or release a student from school attendance for religious observance or religious instruction?

Yes. School absences for the observance of religious holidays outside of the official state holidays and for attendance at religious instruction are permitted by state law and regulation upon written request from a parent or guardian (§ 3210(1)(b); 8 NYCRR § 109.2(a)). Students may be released to take such religious instruction in accordance with the commissioner's regulations (8 NYCRR § 109.2), as long as that instruction is not provided at the public school (*Zorach v. Clauson*, 343 U.S. 306 (1952)).

23:22. Must school districts accommodate an employee's request for time off for religious observances?

Title VII of the Civil Rights Act of 1964 prohibits discrimination by an employer on the basis of an employee's religion. It requires that reasonable accommodations be made for an employee's desire to observe religious holidays, unless to do so would create an undue hardship.

Generally, courts have permitted teachers to take approximately five to 10 days off for religious reasons, even where substitutes must be hired (see *Wangsness v. Watertown Sch. Dist.*, 541 F.Supp. 332 (D.S.D. 1982); *Niederhuber v. Camden County Vocational & Technical Sch. Dist. Bd. of Educ.*, 495 F.Supp. 273 (D.N.J. 1980), *aff'd without op.*, 671 F.2d 496 (D.N.J. 1980)). Presumably, more than five or 10 teacher absences for religious observances would be considered an undue hardship for a school district and outside the scope of an employee's Title VII protection.

As with Title VII, the New York State Human Rights Law (Exec. Law § 296(10)) also makes it unlawful for any employer to discriminate against an employee because the employee observes a particular Sabbath day or days in accordance with his or her religious beliefs. Moreover, except in emergencies, a district cannot require a teacher to work on a Sabbath or holy day and must allow the teacher time to travel to his or her home or to places of religious observance (Exec. Law § 296(1)(b)).

In *New York City Transit Auth. v. Div. of Human Rights*, 89 N.Y.2d 79 (1996), the New York State Court of Appeals held that an employer unlawfully discriminated against an employee by firing her when she refused to work at any time from sundown on Friday to sundown on Saturday because the tenets of her religion. The Court of Appeals ruled that the law requires employers to make a "good-faith" effort to accommodate Sabbath observing employees, even though an accommodation ultimately may not be available. The employer argued that it could not accommodate the employee, because the collective bargaining agreement required it to give senior employees preference in selecting days off. The court determined that the employer still had an obligation under the law to attempt to accommodate the employee's religious observance, despite this provision of the collective bargaining agreement, and that the employer had not made any effort to do so.

23:23. Must school districts pay employees for leave taken for religious observances?

There is a difference of opinion among New York courts. Although one court has ruled that paid leave for religious observance is a permissive subject of bargaining (*Binghamton City Sch. Dist. v. Andreatta*, 30 PERB ¶ 7504 (Broome County Sup. Ct. 1997)), another held that a school district's unilateral decision to no longer comply with a collective bargaining contract provision that allowed teachers upon request to take paid religious holidays was not arbitrable because the provision was unconstitutional (*Matter of Port Washington UFSD v. Port Washington Teachers Ass'n*, 268 A.D.2d 523 (2d Dep't 2000), *appeal dismissed,* 95 N.Y.2d 790, *leave to appeal denied,* 95 N.Y.2d 761 (2000)). Still another court upheld a clause in a collective bargaining agreement that provided three days of paid leave for religious observances because there was no requirement regarding which holidays could be taken. The clause merely provided a religious accommodation (*Maine Endwell Teachers Ass'n v. Bd. of Educ. of the Maine Endwell CSD*, 3 A.D.3d 685 (3d Dep't 2004)).

According to the United States Supreme Court, public employers must permit an employee to use unpaid leave for religious observances if the days required are in excess of personal days already provided (*Ansonia Bd. of Educ. v. Philbrook*, 479 U.S. 60 (1986)).

23:24. Must school districts negotiate over leave for religion observation?

The Public Employment Relations Board (PERB) has ruled in two cases that a school district did not violate its duty to bargain in good faith by unilaterally rescinding a past practice of allowing employees to take extra paid leave for religious observances, finding that it was an unconstitutional practice and therefore not mandatory negotiable (*Auburn Teachers Ass'n v. Auburn Enlarged City SD*, 29 PERB ¶ 4671 (1997); *CSEA v. Eastchester UFSD*, 29 PERB ¶ 3041 (1996)). Similarly, one court has ruled that paid leave for religious observance is a permissive subject of bargaining (*Binghamton City Sch. Dist. v. Andreatte*, 30 PERB ¶ 7504 (*Broome County Sup. Ct.* 1997)). Even though there is a difference of opinion as to whether paid leave for religious observances is constitutionally permissible (see **23:23**).

Religious Symbols

23:25. May school districts display religious symbols?

A school district's temporary display of religious symbols associated with religious holidays does not violate the Establishment Clause, according to one federal appeals court, if the display is not proselytizing in nature and merely acknowledges cultural and historical aspects of the holiday (*Florey v. Sioux Falls Sch. Dist. 49-5*, 619 F.2d 1311 (8th Cir. 1980), *cert. denied*, 449 U.S. 987 (1980)).

By contrast, another federal appeals court ruled that a school district violated the Establishment Clause when it displayed for 30 years a portrait of Jesus Christ in the hallway of a public school (*Washegesic v. Bloomingdale Public Sch.*, 33 F.3d 679 (6th Cir. 1994), *cert. denied*, 514 U.S. 1095 (1995)). However, the court indicated that its decision would have been different if the school had placed representative symbols of many of the world's religions on a common wall.

Similarly, a federal district court in New York ordered a school district to remove a mural depicting a crucifixion that was painted by a former student and displayed on a wall in the school auditorium (*Joki v. Board of Educ. of Schuylerville CSD*, 745 F.Supp. 823 (N.D.N.Y. 1990)). The court held that since the mural was patently religious, it violated the Establishment Clause because impressionable students might assume school sponsorship of religion.

These decisions are consistent with a number of cases regarding religious displays on municipal property, including the United States Supreme Court decision in *Stone v. Graham*, 449 U.S. 39 (1980), *reh'g denied*, 449 U.S. 1104 (1981), *on remand*, 612 S.W.2d 133 (Ky. 1981), which invalidated a statute requiring the posting of the Ten Commandments inside public classrooms under the Establishment Clause.

23:26. What factors do courts consider when determining if a particular type of display violates the Establishment Clause?

Courts have considered a variety of factors when determining what types of displays pass scrutiny under the Establishment Clause. Particularly in *County of Alleghaney v. American Civil Liberties Union, Greater Pittsburgh Chapter*, 492 U.S. 573 (1989), the United States Supreme Court noted several factors that included:

- The location of the display.
- Whether the display is part of a larger configuration that includes nonreligious items.
- The religious intensity of the display.
- Whether the display is shown in connection with a general secular holiday.
- The degree of public participation in the ownership and maintenance of the display.
- The existence of disclaimers of public sponsorship. Most notably, the court indicated that a greater level of sensitivity must be exercised with respect to the public schools.

In *Allegheny*, the high court found that a nativity scene inside a county courthouse by itself violated the separation of church and state. However, the display of a large Christmas tree and a Hanukkah menorah with the message "A Salute to Liberty" outside that same county courthouse did not.

Other court cases reflect application of the *Allegheny* factors including a case where a city's inclusion of a nativity scene in its Christmas display, along with a Santa Claus, a Christmas tree, a reindeer, a clown, a teddy bear, and other holiday items, did not to violate the Establishment Clause (*Lynch v. Donnelly*, 465 U.S. 668 (1984), *reh'g denied*, 466 U.S. 994 (1984)).

Similarly, in *Elewski v. City of Syracuse*, 123 F.3d 51 (2d Cir. 1997), *cert. denied*, 118 S.Ct. 1186 (1998), the United States Court of Appeals for the Second Circuit, which has jurisdiction over New York State, ruled that the display of a city-owned crèche in a downtown public park at public expense did not violate the Establishment Clause. According to the court, the relevant inquiry is whether a reasonable observer would perceive a message of endorsement from the display. In this case, the government-owned display, when viewed together with a privately sponsored menorah displayed nearby, and other traditional religious and secular decorations in the area, did not endorse religion, but instead celebrated the "diversity of the holiday season."

In yet another case, the United States Court of Appeals for the Seventh Circuit upheld a complete ban by a local government on all displays in the lobby of a government building, finding that the policy was a content-neutral law of general applicability, which did not violate the First Amendment (*Grossbaum v. Indianapolis-Marion County Building Auth.*, 100 F.3d 1287 (7th Cir. 1996), *cert. denied*, 117 S.Ct. 1822 (1997)).

23:27. May a school district display items associated with Halloween?

In a case that the United States Supreme Court declined to hear, a Florida state court ruled that the depiction of witches, cauldrons and brooms, and related costumes during a school Halloween celebration did not violate the Establishment Clause (*Guyer v. School Bd. of Alachua County*, 634 So.2d 806 (Fla. App. 1 Dist. 1994), *cert. denied*, 513 U.S. 1044 (1994)). The Florida court rejected the argument that use of the symbols and costumes endorsed and promoted "Wicca" (a religion based on witchcraft and religious principles), after finding that the symbols were not "singularly" or "distinctively" religious. Although the decision is not binding in New York, it might be persuasive to courts with jurisdiction over the state.

23:28. Can the use of certain symbols as school mascots be unconstitutional?

Litigation on the issue of school mascots and the religion clauses of the First Amendment of the United States Constitution has been scarce. However, the focus has been on whether the use of a particular symbol advances religion and violates the separation of church and state. For example, in *Kunselman v. Western Reserve Local Sch. Dist. Bd. of Educ.*, 70 F.3d 931 (6th Cir. 1995), parents unsuccessfully argued that use and display of a "blue devil" as the school's mascot violated the Establishment Clause by encouraging devil worship. In the court's opinion, "No reasonable person would think that the school authorities here are advocating Satanism . . . when they use the name and symbol" (*Kunselman* at 933).

Aside from the constitutionality issue, a determination as to the appropriateness of a school mascot rests with the local school board. Such a determination will be put aside only upon a showing that the board has abused its discretion (*Appeal of Tobin*, 25 Educ. Dep't Rep. 301 (1986), 30 Educ. Dep't Rep. 315 (1991)). However, the commissioner of education has advised school districts to examine whether district mascots that are based upon Native American themes are inappropriate or offensive (see *Appeal of D'Orazio*, 41 Educ. Dep't Rep.292 (2002); see also Memorandum from Education Commissioner Richard P. Mills on Public School Use of Native American Names, Symbols and Mascots dated Feb. 5, 2002; *Appeal of Eurich*, 37 Educ. Dep't Rep. 707 (1998)).

23:29. May school districts prevent a teacher from wearing religious garb while teaching?

In a decision from the turn of the last century, the New York State Court of Appeals upheld a prohibition against the wearing of religious clothing by teachers (*O'Connor v. Hendrick*, 184 N.Y. 421 (1906)). The court found that the teacher's religious attire might unduly influence impressionable students, and that this sectarian influence was unconstitutional.

However, at least one modern court has struck down a school's prohibition against teachers' religious garb as violating Title VII and the duty to make a reasonable accommodation for an employee's religious practices (*United States v. Board of Educ. for Sch. Dist.*, 911 F.2d 882 (3d Cir. 1990)). Consequently, in order to continue to ban religious garments, a school district may have to show that an accommodation of the teacher's wishes would cause undue hardship to the district.

In addition, one federal district court in New York upheld the right of a prison guard who was a Native American and practitioner of the traditional religion of the Mohawk Nation to wear long hair, because it was an important spiritual tenet of his religion (*Rourke v. New York State Dep't of Correctional Servs.*, 915 F.Supp. 525 (N.D.N.Y. 1995), *remanded*, 224 A.D.2d 815 (3d Dep't 1996)). Therefore, it is questionable whether the *O'Connor* decision is still a valid legal precedent.

24. Nonpublic Schools and Home Instruction

Nonpublic Schools

24:1. Must a school district allow students of compulsory education age to withdraw from its public schools and attend a nonpublic school?

Yes. A school district must permit a child of compulsory education age to attend a nonpublic school (see § 3204(1)). However, parents withdrawing a child of compulsory education age from the public school must furnish proof that their child is receiving required instruction elsewhere. Failure to furnish such proof raises a presumption that the child is not receiving the required instruction, which is a violation of the Education Law, and which may result in a finding of educational neglect (§ 3212(2)(d); *Appeal of Brown*, 34 Educ. Dep't Rep. 33 (1994); *Appeal of White*, 29 Educ. Dep't Rep. 511 (1990), *citing Matter of Christa H.*, 127 A.D.2d 997 (4th Dep't 1987) and *In re Andrew "T. T.,"* 122 A.D.2d 362 (3d Dep't 1986); see also Fam. Ct. Act § 1012(f)(i)(A)).

24:2. Do school districts owe any responsibility to resident children who attend nonpublic schools?

Yes. Public school boards must ensure that resident children attending schools other than a public school receive instruction from "competent teachers" that is "at least substantially equivalent," in terms of both "time and quality," to the instruction they would receive if they attended the public schools in the district where they reside (§§ 3204(2), 3210(2); *In re Adam D.*, 132 Misc.2d 797 (Fam. Ct. 1986); *Appeal of Brown*, 34 Educ. Dep't Rep. 33 (1994)).

The responsibility for determining substantial equivalency rests with the local school board (*Appeal of Brown*; *Appeal of Lynn*, 29 Educ. Dep't Rep. 128 (1989); *Formal Op. of Counsel No. 78*, 1 Educ. Dep't Rep. 778 (1952)). However, the board may delegate the responsibility for making any such initial determination to the superintendent of schools (see *In re Adam D.*; *In re Kilroy*, 121 Misc.2d 98 (Fam. Ct. 1983); *Appeal of Brown*, 34 Educ. Dep't Rep. 33 (1994); § 1711(3)).

24:3. How can a school district determine if a student attending a nonpublic school is receiving a substantially equivalent education?

The superintendent of schools may visit the nonpublic schools of resident children to evaluate the educational programs they are receiving outside the public schools. The substantial equivalency of unregistered nonpublic schools must be determined through local review. However, if the nonpublic school is registered with the State Education Department (SED), the school board of the district where that nonpublic school is located should accept the registration as evidence that the nonpublic school has an equivalent program of instruction, if SED has not placed it "under review." Such placement, however, does not necessarily mean a lack of equivalency or require such a determination ("Guidelines for Determining Equivalency of Instruction in Nonpublic Schools," NY State Education Department, January 2004, available at http://www.emsc.nysed.gov/nonpub; see also **24:6**). Nonpublic schools that are not registered with SED may be presumed to have an equivalent program.

24:4. What steps should be taken if the school district determines that a nonpublic school does not provide a substantially equivalent education to that provided in the public school?

The superintendent and the nonpublic school administrator should discuss any perceived deficiencies, determine whether these deficiencies can be corrected within a reasonable period of time, and create a schedule for the corrections to be made. If the nonpublic school is unable or unwilling to remedy its deficiencies, and the superintendent determines that the program does not provide a "substantially equivalent education," the superintendent should notify his or her board and the school boards of other districts in which students attending the nonpublic school live. The superintendent also may share the information with the board of cooperative educational services (BOCES) district superintendent ("Guidelines for Determining Equivalency of Instruction in Nonpublic Schools," NY State Education Department, January 2004).

24:5. Are nonpublic schools subject to the same legal requirements that apply to public schools?

Generally, nonpublic schools are not bound by all of the requirements that apply to public schools. For example, the law does not require that nonpublic teachers and administrators meet the state's requirements for certification. In addition, the rights of students in private schools generally are governed by the contractual arrangement between the school and the parents or by regulations or procedures set forth in a student handbook or school catalogue. Accordingly, nonpublic schools may impose tighter restrictions on students' speech and conduct than those possible within the public schools (see **12:88–113; 12:114–157**).

However, where nonpublic schools receive federal funds, they may become subject to various federal civil rights laws, such as:

- Title IX of the Federal Education Amendments of 1972, which bars sexual discrimination in education programs.

- Title VI of the Civil Rights Act of 1964, which bans discrimination by race, color, religion or national origin in federally funded programs.
- Section 504 of the Rehabilitation Act of 1973, which prohibits discrimination against students with disabilities in such programs.
- The Family Educational Rights and Privacy Act, 20 USC § 1232g, which requires parental review of and consent to the release of student educational records.

In addition, certain state laws are applicable to nonpublic schools, such as section 807-a of the Education Law, which requires that nonpublic elementary or secondary schools enrolling 25 or more students file a fire inspection report with the state. The Education Law and commissioner's regulations also require that any registered nonpublic nursery school or kindergarten attended by six or more pupils meet certain safety standards to prevent fire, health, or other safety hazards (§ 807-a (10)(a)(b); 8 NYCRR § 125.3).

While a public school board is not responsible for enforcing these provisions, if a fire inspection reveals "an apparently serious deficiency," the board may take appropriate steps to inform the parents of nonpublic school students ("Guidelines for Determining Equivalency of Instruction in Nonpublic Schools," NY State Education Department, January 2004).

In addition, commissioner of education regulations on school bus safety practices that apply to public school districts also apply to nonpublic schools. This includes instruction and retraining requirements for school bus drivers who operate student transportation owned, leased, or contracted for by public school districts (§ 305(34); see **22:66–67**).

24:6. Must nonpublic schools be registered with the State Education Department?

Nonpublic schools are not required to be registered with the State Education Department (see 8 NYCRR § 100.2(p)). However, the commissioner's regulations provide for the voluntary registration of nonpublic nursery schools and kindergartens (8 NYCRR Part 125). In addition, nonpublic high schools may be registered by the Board of Regents upon the recommendation of the commissioner of education. Only registered nonpublic high schools may issue diplomas and administer Regents examinations (8 NYCRR § 100.2(p)).

Inquiries concerning the requirements and procedures for the registration of nonpublic secondary schools or nursery schools and kindergartens should be addressed to the State Education Department's Office of Nonpublic School Services, The Education Building, Albany, N.Y. 12234.

24:7. Does the State Education Department review registered nonpublic high schools?

Yes. A registered nonpublic high school shall be placed under review by the commissioner of education under the following conditions:

- whenever the school scores below the registration review criteria on one or more of the measures adopted by the Board of Regents, and the student achievement on such measures or other appropriate indicators has not shown improvement over the preceding three school years; or
- when other sufficient reason exists to warrant registration review, as determined by the commissioner (8 NYCRR § 100.2(p)(6)(i)(a), (b)).

The school then develops an improvement plan with technical assistance from the commissioner if needed (8 NYCRR § 100.2(p)(6)(ii)). If the school does not show progress on the criteria in question, the commissioner notifies the school that it is at risk of having its registration revoked. If after a further period of time the school still does not show progress, the commissioner will recommend to the Board of Regents that it revoke the school's registration. If the Board of Regents revokes the school's registration, the commissioner and nonpublic school officials will develop a plan to protect the educational welfare of the students (8 NYCRR § 100.2(p)(6)(iii), (iv)).

24:8. Is there any State Education Department review of unregistered nonpublic schools?

Yes. The State Education Department (SED) may review any unregistered nonpublic school when the school scores below one or more of the review criteria on indicators of student achievement as provided in the commissioner's regulations, has not shown improvement on such indicators over the preceding three school years, and has not otherwise demonstrated satisfactory performance on other student achievement indicators determined by the commissioner in consultation with the appropriate nonpublic school officials (8 NYCRR § 100.2(z)).

Nonpublic schools under SED review are required to notify parents, develop a school improvement plan (with technical assistance from SED if requested), and submit the plan to SED. If, after a time period established by the commissioner in consultation with the appropriate nonpublic school officials, the school has not demonstrated progress, the commissioner will formally notify the nonpublic school officials that the school is at risk of being determined to be an "unsound educational environment." If the commissioner later determines there is still insufficient progress, he will determine that the school is an unsound educational environment. The commissioner and the nonpublic school officials must then develop a plan to ensure that the educational welfare of the students is protected (8 NYCRR § 100.2(z)).

24:9. Are there any steps a public school district should take when a new nonpublic school is established within its boundaries?

Yes. Public school officials must determine whether the new nonpublic school building is a safe place by reviewing, for example, building structure reports and fire inspection reports, whether the length of the school day and school calendar are substantially equivalent to that required for public schools, and whether the program of instruction covers essentially the same subject areas as are covered in the public schools (see §§ 807-a, 3204(2), 3210(2)).

The superintendent of schools should ask to visit the new school prior to its opening and ask the administrator of the nonpublic school for information such as the names and grade levels of students from the district, the school calendar and curriculum guides.

If public school officials determine these all are satisfactory and that the new nonpublic school will provide a substantially equivalent education, the superintendent should notify the public school board of this in writing, forward a copy of the notification to the nonpublic school and, where appropriate, notify the board of cooperative educational services (BOCES) district superintendent of the findings of the review. The superintendent should contact the State Education Department's (SED) Office of Nonpublic School Services to ensure that the new school will be placed on SED's mailing list and that its head will be invited to the annual fall conference for nonpublic school administrators ("Guidelines for Determining Equivalency of Instruction in Nonpublic Schools," NY State Education Department: January 2004, see also **24:2–4**).

24:10. Are nonpublic schools entitled to any state aid?

Yes. Nonpublic schools are eligible for state financial aid for costs incurred by them in complying with state mandates relating to the administration of state testing and evaluation programs and participation in state programs for the reporting of basic educational data (Laws of 1974, Chs. 507 and 508).

Although the New York State Constitution provides that neither the state nor any state subdivision may provide funding or use its property or credit to assist a nonpublic school (NYS Const. Art. 11, § 3), the authorized apportionment of state aid funds for nonpublic schools is limited to the services they are required to perform for the state in connection with the state's own responsibility to evaluate students through a system of uniform testing and reporting procedures to ensure students are being adequately educated (Laws of 1974, Chs. 507 and 508). The United States Supreme Court has upheld the constitutionality of these provisions under separation of church and state principles of the Establishment Clause of the First Amendment of the United States Constitution (§ 3601; *Committee for Public Education and Religious Liberty v. Regan*, 444 U.S. 646 (1980)).

Services for Nonpublic School Students

24:11. Are there any type of services that public school districts must provide to nonpublic school students?

Yes. As authorized by law, public school districts must provide nonpublic school students with, for instance, health and welfare services (§ 912, see **12:58**) and transportation (§ 3635, see **22:109–118**); and loan them textbooks (§ 701(3); **24:14–15**), computer software (§ 752, see **24:17**) and library materials (see **24:16**) (see also "Handbook on Services to Pupils Attending Nonpublic Schools," NY State Education Department, Revised March 2004. The handbook can be found at http://www.emsc.nysed.gov/nonpub).

In addition, under section 3602-c of the Education Law (also known as the dual-enrollment law), and upon parental request, school districts must provide students attending nonpublic schools located in the district with educational services in the areas of instruction for the gifted, career education, and special education and related services for students with disabilities (§ 3602-c (1)).

Parental requests for dual-enrollment services must be filed with the student's school district of residence by June 1 preceding the school year for which services are requested (§ 3602-c(2)). School districts may contract for such services with boards of cooperative educational services (BOCES) or the school district in which the nonpublic school is located (§ 3602-c(2), (3)). Transportation must be furnished between the nonpublic school and the site where the program is offered if the distance is more than one-fourth of a mile. The district may claim state aid for this transportation (§ 3602-c(4)).

Under federal law, school districts also may be required to provide educational services to students attending nonpublic schools, such as remedial instruction, counseling and other supplementary services where federal funds are appropriated and distributed in accordance with programs proposed by local school districts and approved by the State Education Department (20 USC § 6320, see § 3602(10); 8 NYCRR subpart 149-1, *et seq.*).

24:12. Are school districts required to provide dual-enrollment services on site at the nonpublic schools?

No. The dual-enrollment law indicates that the services be provided in the regular classes of the public schools, with public school students in attendance (§ 3602-c(9); see **24:13**).

24:13. Is a school district required to provide on-site special education and related services to students with disabilities who attend private schools, including parochial schools?

The United States Supreme Court has ruled that the federal constitution does not prevent a school district from providing services to students on site at the premises of their parochial school (*Agostini v. Felton*, 521 U.S. 203 (1997)). Under the Individuals with Disabilities Education Act (IDEA), special education services may be provided to students with disabilities on the premises of private schools, including parochial schools, to the extent consistent with law (20 USC § 1412(a)(10)(A)(i)).

However, a school district is not required under federal law to provide on-site special education services to children with disabilities voluntarily enrolled in private schools. No court has answered the question of whether state law requires public school districts to provide such services on the premises of the private school (see **13:19**).

24:14. Must public school districts purchase and loan textbooks to students attending nonpublic schools?

Yes. Section 701 of the Education Law requires all school boards to purchase and to loan "upon individual request" textbooks, workbooks, and manuals, for example, to all children residing in the district who attend kindergarten through 12th grade in any public school and in any nonpublic school that complies with the Education Law. Items such as encyclopedias, almanacs, atlases, certain audiovisual materials, and review books are not considered "textbooks" (see 8 NYCRR § 21.2(a)).

Textbooks may be purchased only for resident students (see 8 NYCRR § 21.2(a)). Children who reside outside of the district in which the nonpublic school they attend is located must have their textbooks provided by their district of residence (§ 701(3)).

Under the statute, both the power and the duty to purchase and loan textbooks depend upon individual requests to the school board for such textbooks. To comply with the law, the nonpublic school may either forward individual student requests as a group to the school board or keep the requests on file and forward a summary of the requests to the school board (see 8 NYCRR § 21.2(b)). Section 701(6) of the Education Law provides that school districts receive an additional apportionment of state aid to comply with the statute. No school district is required to spend more on purchasing textbooks than the amount of state aid it receives for this purpose (§ 701(4)).

The commissioner of education has held that a school board must establish a procedure to ensure equitable distribution of all available textbooks, "both those on hand from prior years and those newly purchased." This "procedure must assure that in each subject area students are treated equally regardless of the school attended" (*Matter of Gross*, 25 Educ. Dep't Rep. 382, 384 (1986); see also *Appeal of Kelly*, 35 Educ. Dep't Rep. 235 (1996); *Matter of Caunitz*, 30 Educ. Dep't Rep. 396 (1991); § 701(4); 8 NYCRR § 21.2(c)).

Although the Education Law requires public schools to loan textbooks upon individual request, it does not authorize school districts to reimburse individuals who have purchased textbooks on their own (*Appeal of Kelly*, 35 Educ. Dep't Rep. 235 (1996)).

For more information, see "New York State Textbook Loan Program: Recommended Procedures for Textbook Purchases, Loans and Inventory Control," NY State Education Department, State Aid, January 2003. This document can be found on the Web at http://stateaid.nysed.gov/txtbk03.pdf.

24:15. Is it constitutionally permissible for a public school district to purchase and loan textbooks to students attending parochial schools?

Yes. The United States Supreme Court has upheld the constitutionality of New York State's Education Law textbook provisions (*Board of Educ. v. Allen*, 392 U.S. 236 (1968); see also *Mitchell v. Helms*, 530 U.S. 793 (2000)). However, textbooks purchased and loaned to parochial school students must be nonsectarian and designated for use in any public elementary or secondary school of the state or approved by any school board (§ 701(3)).

24:16. May nonpublic school students borrow library materials?

Yes. School library materials owned or acquired by a public school district pursuant to section 711 of the Education Law must be made available on an equitable basis to all eligible students enrolled in grades kindergarten through 12 in both public and nonpublic schools located within the public school district (8 NYCRR § 21.4(d)).

Such library materials must be required for use as a learning aid in a particular class or program, and loaned for individual student use only (8 NYCRR § 21.4(b)). They must be loaned free of charge upon the individual request of eligible nonpublic school students. Requests may be presented directly to the lending district, or with the consent of the district, to an appropriate official at the nonpublic school attended by the student (8 NYCRR § 21.4(c)).

School authorities must establish lending procedures consistent with the commissioner's regulations and must inform authorities at the nonpublic schools within the boundaries of the public school district of these procedures (8 NYCRR § 21.4(d)).

24:17. May school districts purchase and loan computer software programs to nonpublic school students?

Yes. The law provides that school districts may purchase computer software programs and must loan these software programs upon individual request to nonpublic school students (§§ 751–752; 8 NYCRR § 21.3(c)). This software must be made available on an equitable basis to all eligible pupils, in both public and nonpublic schools (8 NYCRR § 21.3(d)).

Computer software does not include microcomputers, blank diskettes, cassettes or tapes, chips, computer correction devices, consoles, cords, disk drives, or other similar items of hardware (8 NYCRR § 21.3(a)). Moreover, a public school district may purchase only computer software programs that do not contain material of a religious nature (8 NYCRR § 21.3(b); see also *Mitchell v. Helms*, 530 U.S. 793 (2000); *Board of Educ. v. Allen*, 392 U.S. 236 (1968)).

No school district is required to purchase or otherwise acquire software programs that will cost more than the "software factor" multiplied by the sum of the public school district enrollment and the enrollment of nonpublic school students within the school district (§§ 751(3), (4), 3602(n)(2), (3)).

24:18. May nonpublic school children participate in extracurricular activities at the public schools in their district of residence?

According to the commissioner of education, school boards have authority to limit participation in extracurricular activities to students enrolled in the district. Although there is no legal requirement that nonpublic school children be granted permission to participate in extra-curricular activities, a school board may establish a policy that allows for participation of nonpublic school students. Nonpublic school students have no right to attend public school on a part-time basis, however. Accordingly, a district may not allow a nonpublic school student to participate in band when doing so would, in essence, be allowing the student to participate in its school program on a part-time basis (*Appeal of Ponte*, 41 Educ. Dep't Rep. 174 (2001)).

Unlike with other extracurricular activities, a public school board may not authorize the participation of nonpublic school students on public school athletic teams. The regulations governing interscholastic sports require a pupil to be a "bona fide" student enrolled in a public school in regular attendance 80 percent of the time (8 NYCRR § 135.4(c)(f)(ii)(b)(2)). Therefore participation in interscholastic sports by nonpublic school students is limited to those offered by the nonpublic school the student attends.

Home Instruction

24:19. Are parents permitted to educate their children at home?

Yes. The Education Law permits the education of children at home, provided that children of compulsory education age receive full-time instruction, and are taught by competent teachers and receive instruction that is substantially equivalent to that provided at the public schools of the student's district of residence (§§ 3204(2), 3210(2), 3212(2); 8 NYCRR § 100.10; see *In the Matter of Andrew T.T.*, 122 A.D.2d 362 (1986); *In re Franz*, 55 A.D.2d 424, 427 (2d Dep't 1977); *People v. Turner*, 277 A.D. 317, 319 (4th Dep't 1950)). However, state law does not require any specific credentials for the person providing home instruction ("Questions and Answers on Home Instruction," NY State Education Department, Revised March 2004, question 8. The Questions and Answers on Home Instruction may be accessed on the Internet at http://www.emsc.nysed.gov/nonpub).

24:20. Must parents educating their children at home adhere to laws and regulations regarding home instruction?

Yes. The Education Law imposes upon parents a duty to ensure that their children receive appropriate instruction (§ 3212(2); *Appeal of Brown*, 34 Educ. Dep't Rep. 33 (1994); *Matter of White*, 29 Educ. Dep't Rep. 511 (1990); *Matter of Thomas H.*, 78 Misc.2d 412, 413 (1974)). Further, the state has a legitimate and compelling interest in ensuring that its children receive an education that will prepare them to be productive members of society (*Blackwelder v. Safnauer*, 689 F.Supp. 106 (N.D.N.Y. 1988), *appeal dismissed*, 866 F.2d 548 (2d Cir. 1989)).

When a school district is unable to obtain information from parents regarding home instruction and has insufficient evidence that appropriate instruction is taking place, it is obligated to report the case to the central registry as a case of suspected educational neglect pursuant to Social Services Law section 413 (*Appeal of the Bd. of Educ. of the Lynbrook UFSD*, 41 Educ. Dep't Rep. 17 (2001)). The commissioner of education has no authority to review appeals by school districts against parents.

24:21. What specific provisions govern home instruction?

Sections 3204(2), 3210(2)(d), and 3212(2) of the Education Law, and section 100.10 of the commissioner's regulations, set forth the requirements that must be met by parents who wish to educate their children at home. Parents must, for instance, develop an individualized home instruction plan (IHIP) (8 NYCRR § 100.10(c), (d); *Appeal of Brown*, 34 Educ. Dep't Rep. 33 (1994); *Matter of White*, 29 Educ. Dep't Rep. 511 (1990)); submit quarterly reports (8 NYCRR § 100.10(g)); and file an annual assessment indicating the student's progress (8 NYCRR § 100.10(h)). The regulations also provide detailed requirements for courses to be taught, required attendance, and student evaluation (8 NYCRR § 100.10(e–h)).

24:22. What are the responsibilities of parents who educate their children at home?

The parents or other persons in parental relation to students of compulsory education age wishing to educate their children at home must do the following:

- Notify the superintendent of schools in writing each year by July 1 of their intention to educate their child at home. If they move into the district or decide to educate their child at home after the start of the school year, they must provide notice within 14 days of commencing home instruction (8 NYCRR § 100.10(b)).
- Submit an individualized home instruction plan (IHIP) for each child of compulsory attendance age to be instructed at home within four weeks of receipt of the form provided by the district or by August 15, whichever is later (8 NYCRR § 100.10(c)(2)). The plan must contain, among other items, a list of the syllabi, curriculum materials, textbooks or plan of instruction to be used in each of the required subjects noted in the regulations, and the names of the person(s) to provide instruction (8 NYCRR § 100.10(d); see 8 NYCRR § 100.10(e) for a list of required courses). The school district will provide assistance in developing the IHIP, if the parent so requests (8 NYCRR § 100.10(c)(2)).
- Submit quarterly reports for each child to the school district on the dates specified in the IHIP. Each report must contain the number of hours of instruction; a description of the material covered in each subject; either a grade for the child in each subject or a written narrative evaluating the child's progress; and a written explanation if less than 80 percent of the course material set out in the IHIP was covered in any subject (8 NYCRR § 100.10(g)).
- File an annual assessment of the student at the same time as the fourth quarterly report. The assessment must be based on the results of a

commercially published norm-referenced achievement test, such as the Iowa or California Test, or an alternative form of evaluation that meets the regulatory requirements. The test must be administered by the professional staff at a public or nonpublic school or at the child's home by a certified teacher or other qualified person, including the child's parent. The superintendent's consent is required when such a test is administered at a nonregistered nonpublic school or at the child's home (8 NYCRR § 100.10(h); "Questions and Answers on Home Instruction," NY State Education Department, Revised March 2004, question 64). The commissioner of education has ruled that a student must take a commercially prepared achievement test despite his parents' objection that the test "conflicted with their personal philosophy" (*Appeal of Abbokire*, 33 Educ. Dep't Rep. 473 (1994)).

24:23. What are the school district's responsibilities with respect to the individualized home instruction plan (IHIP) developed by parents educating their children at home?

Within 10 business days of receiving notice from a child's parents of their intention to educate their child at home, the school district must send to the parents a copy of the home instruction regulations, along with a form on which the parents must submit an IHIP for any child educated at home (8 NYCRR § 100.10(c)(1)).

Within 10 business days of receipt of the IHIP or by August 31, whichever is later, the school district must either notify the parents that the IHIP is satisfactory or give the parents written notice of any deficiencies (8 NYCRR § 100.10(c)(3)).

The superintendent of schools is responsible for ensuring the home-schooled student's IHIP complies with the commissioner's regulations, subject to review on an appeal to the board (8 NYCRR § 100.10(c)). If there are deficiencies, the parent must, within 15 days of receipt of such notice or by September 15, whichever is later, submit a revised IHIP that corrects the deficiencies (8 NYCRR § 100.10(c)(4)). The superintendent then reviews the revised IHIP. If he or she determines the indicated deficiencies have not been corrected, he or she will issue a notice of noncompliance within 15 days of receipt of the revised IHIP or by September 30, whichever is later (8 NYCRR § 100.10(c)(5)).

24:24. What happens if a school district determines that the individualized home instruction plan (IHIP) of a home-schooled student is deficient?

If the parents disagree with the school superintendent's determination of noncompliance (see **24:23**), they have a right to appeal to the school board

(8 NYCRR § 100.10(c)(5)). If the board upholds the superintendent's determination, the parents may appeal to the commissioner of education within 30 days of receipt of notice of the board's decision (8 NYCRR § 100.10(c)(6)).

If parents lose their appeal or fail to contest the determination that their child's IHIP is deficient, they must "immediately provide for the instruction of their children at a public school or elsewhere in compliance with the Education Law." Further, the parents must provide to the superintendent written notice of the arrangements they have made, unless they have enrolled their child in the public school (8 NYCRR § 100.10(c)(7), (8)).

24:25. May home-schooled students receive instruction at a location outside their parents' primary residence?

Yes. Instruction for students educated at home may be provided outside the parents' primary residence, provided the building where instruction takes place is in compliance with the local building code (8 NYCRR § 100.10(f)(5)).

24:26. May parents engage a tutor to provide home instruction?

Yes. Parents may engage the services of a tutor to provide instruction for all or part of the home instruction program. Moreover, parents providing home instruction to their children also can arrange to have their children receive group instruction in particular subjects. But where parents organize to have a "majority" of their children's education provided by a tutor in a group setting, they will be deemed to be operating a nonpublic school and no longer providing home instruction. As such, they will have to satisfy state law and regulations ensuring the substantial equivalency of instruction provided by nonpublic schools ("Questions and Answers on Home Instruction," NY State Education Department, Revised March 2004, questions 4–5).

24:27. Are there any attendance requirements for home-schooled students?

Yes. Children in grades 1–6 must receive 900 hours of instruction and those in grades 7–12 must receive 990 hours, with attendance substantially equivalent to 180 days per school year. Absences are allowed on the same basis as prescribed by the school district for students attending the public schools. Parents must maintain records of attendance to be provided to the district upon request (8 NYCRR § 100.10(f)).

Instruction at home is usually given within the general timeframe of the normal school day, but greater flexibility in scheduling is possible. For example, parents may choose to provide instruction on weekends or in the evening. However, the total amount of instructional time per week should be generally comparable to that of the public school ("Questions and Answers on Home Instruction," NY State Education Department, Revised March 2004, question 7).

24:28. Are there any courses home-schooled students are required to take?

Yes. The commissioner's regulations set forth the courses that children in grades K–12 educated at home must study (8 NYCRR § 100.10(e)). In addition to courses in specific academic areas such as English, math, science, history, arts, physical education, and others, home instruction must also cover patriotism and citizenship; health education regarding alcohol, drug and tobacco misuse; highway safety and traffic regulation, including bicycle safety; and fire and arson prevention and safety (8 NYCRR § 100.10(e)(2)(v)). Although every student must have a physical education program, activities may differ provided that the outcomes are similar to those established for students in the public school.

24:29. Are home-schooled students required to take state mandated standardized tests?

No. Home-instructed students are not required to take, for instance, pupil evaluation program (PEP) tests, although the tests may be used to meet annual assessment requirements (8 NYCRR § 100.10(h); "Questions and Answers on Home Instruction," NY State Education Department, Revised March 2004, question 57; see **14:65–68**).

In addition, if a request is made, school officials are encouraged to admit a student receiving home instruction to a Regents examination. If a Regents examination has a lab requirement, the student may be admitted to the examination if there is evidence that the student has met the lab requirement. The student's individualized home instruction plan (IHIP), quarterly reports and/or verification from the student's teacher can provide such evidence. However, Regents examinations may only be administered at the public school or registered nonpublic school because they are secure examinations. The test results can be helpful to the student and also to public school officials ("Questions and Answers on Home Instruction," NY State Education Department, Revised March 2004, question 62).

24:30. What happens if a home-schooled student does not perform adequately on the annual assessment?

If a student does not receive an adequate score on an annual assessment, the home instruction program will be placed on probation for a period of up to two years. The parent must submit a plan of remediation to be reviewed by the school district (8 NYCRR § 100.10(i)(1)). To be adequate, a student's annual assessment must reflect a composite score above the 33rd percentile on national norms, or indicate one academic year of growth as compared to a test administered during or subsequent to the prior school year (8 NYCRR § 100.10(h)(1)(v)).

If the objectives of the remediation plan are not met, the superintendent of schools will issue a notice of noncompliance, subject to school board review (8 NYCRR § 100.10(i)(2)), and ultimately require that the parent enroll the child in a public or other school that meets the requirements of the Education Law (8 NYCRR § 100.10(c)(7)).

During the probation period, the superintendent may require one or more home visits, if he or she has reasonable grounds to believe that the home instruction program does not comply with the regulations. The superintendent may include members of a home instruction peer review panel in the home visit team (8 NYCRR § 100.10(i)(3)). If the home instruction program is not on probation, school officials may request a home visit, but the parents are not required to consent to the request ("Questions and Answers on Home Instruction," NY State Education Department, Revised March 2004, question 29).

24:31. May a home-schooled student be awarded a local or Regents diploma?

No. A high school diploma may only be awarded to a student enrolled in a registered secondary school who has completed all program requirements set by the Regents, the school or the district (8 NYCRR § 100.2(p); see also "Questions and Answers on Home Instruction," NY State Education Department, Revised March 2004, question 24).

24:32. Are home-schooled students granted the same right to borrow public school textbooks, computer software, and library materials as students enrolled in nonpublic schools?

No. The state law that requires districts to loan these items to nonpublic school students does not apply to students who receive home instruction because such students are not enrolled in a nonpublic school. However, school districts may voluntarily loan such items to home-schooled students, subject to availability after the district has satisfied its legal obligations ("Questions and Answers on Home Instruction," NY State Education Department, Revised March 2004, questions 15–16; see also **24:14–17**).

24:33. Do home-school students have the same right to dual enrollment services as students enrolled in nonpublic schools?

No. The dual-enrollment provisions that authorize partial attendance at a public school by nonpublic school students for the purpose of obtaining instruction in the areas of occupational and vocational education, gifted education, and education of students with disabilities, do not apply to home-schooled students (*Appeal of Pope*, 40 Educ. Dep't Rep. 473 (2001); see also "Questions and Answers on Home Instruction," NY State Education Department, Revised March 2004, question 20).

24:34. Are home-schooled students entitled to participate in public school interscholastic sports?

No. The commissioner's regulations require that participants in interscholastic sports must be enrolled in a public school (8 NYCRR § 135.4(c)(7); see "Questions and Answers on Home Instruction," NY State Education Department, Revised March 2004, question 11). In addition, a home-schooled student does not have a right to participate in sports, only a mere expectation. The regulation restricting participation to public school students serves the legitimate purpose of "promoting school spirit, providing role models, and maintaining academic standards" (*Bradstreet v. Sobol*, 165 Misc. 2d 931 (Sup. Ct. 1995), *aff'd*, 225 A.D.2d 175 (3d Dep't 1996); see also *Appeal of Pelletier*, 27 Educ. Dep't Rep. 265 (1988); 8 NYCRR §§ 135.1(g), 135.4(c)(7)(ii)(b)(2)).

However, home-schooled children may participate in the public school district's intramural activities and other school-sponsored club activities, at the discretion of the board of education, which should adopt a written policy in this regard ("Questions and Answers on Home Instruction," NY State Education Department, Revised March 2004, questions 11–12).

24:35. Are home-schooled students subject to the same immunization requirements as students attending school?

No. The provisions of Public Health Law section 2164, which require parents to submit proof of immunization prior to admission of their children to a school (see **12:65–66**), do not apply to students being educated at home. However, if the commissioner of health notifies school officials of the outbreak of a disease for which immunization is required, parents of home-schooled children who seek to participate in testing or other activities on the premises of a public or nonpublic school must produce proof of immunization or be denied access ("Questions and Answers on Home Instruction," NY State Education Department, Revised March 2004, question 14).

24:36. Are school districts entitled to state aid for home-schooled students?

No. School districts cannot claim state aid for students instructed at home by their parents ("Questions and Answers on Home Instruction," NY State Education Department, Revised March 2004, question 21).

Homebound Instruction

24:37. Is homebound instruction the same thing as home instruction?

No. Homebound instruction is provided on a temporary basis by the public school district when a student is unable to attend school because of short-term disability or discipline (see *Appeal of a Student Suspected of Having a Disability (Fayetteville-Manlius CSD)*, 40 Educ. Dep't Rep. 75 (2001), *Appeal of Douglas and Barbara K.*, 34 Educ. Dep't Rep. 214 (1994); *Appeal of Anthony M.*, 30 Educ. Dep't Rep. 269 (1991)). Home instruction is typically provided by parents who exercise the right to instruct their child(ren) at home instead of at a public or nonpublic school (see 8 NYCRR § 100.10(a), (b); see also **24:1**; **24:19**).

24:38. Under what circumstances is a student entitled to homebound instruction?

If a prolonged absence due to a short-term physical, mental or emotional illness is anticipated, the administrator of the student's school should talk with the student's parents about arranging for homebound instruction. According to the State Education Department, an absence of at least two weeks is considered a prolonged absence. The student's physician should verify any such absence due to illness (see "Handbook on Services to Pupils Attending Nonpublic Schools," NY State Education Department, Revised March 2004).

However, in one case, the commissioner of education excused a school district's obligation to provide homebound instruction where parents failed to respond to the district's initial offer for homebound instruction, and contributed to their children's absence from school by failing to follow a recommended course of treatment for lice (*Appeal of Douglas and Barbara K.*, 34 Educ. Dep't Rep. 214 (1994)).

24:39. Who is responsible for providing homebound instruction?

The district in which the student resides is responsible for providing an appropriately certified teacher to tutor the homebound student. However, the district of residence may contract with another district to provide this service. (see "Handbook on Services to Pupils Attending Nonpublic Schools," NY State Education Department, Revised March 2004).

24:40. Is a school district required to provide homebound instruction to nonpublic school students?

Yes. A nonpublic school student requiring homebound instruction should enroll in the public school during the time he or she receives homebound instruction from the public school, so that the district may count the student in its attendance report for state aid purposes (see "Handbook on Services to Pupils Attending Nonpublic School," NY State Education Department, Revised 2004).

24:41. Is there a minimum amount of instruction districts must offer homebound students?

Elementary school students on homebound instruction must receive at least five hours of instruction per week and secondary school students 10 hours per week. To the extent possible, homebound instruction should be staggered proportionately throughout the week (8 NYCRR § 175.21; see also "Handbook on Services to Pupils Attending Nonpublic School," NY State Education Department, Revised March 2004).

The U.S. Department of Education Office of Civil Rights determined, however, that a school policy that provided only four hours of instruction per week to homebound students and which failed to provide for makeup sessions when teachers were unable to provide the services during a particular week violated the Americans with Disabilities Act and section 504 of the Rehabilitation Act of 1973 (*Boston Pub. Sch.*, 21 IDELR 172 (1994)).

25. Charter Schools

Editor's Note: For further information concerning New York State's Charter Schools Law, consult Charter Schools in New York: An Analysis of New York State's New Charter School Legislation, *published by the New York State School Boards Association (1999) and available online at http://www.nyssba.org. Contact also the Charter Schools Unit of the State Education Department's Office of Elementary, Middle and Secondary Continuing Education at 518-474-1762, or online at http://www.emsc.nysed.gov/rscs/charter/charterschools.html or the State University of New York's Charter Schools Institute online at http://www.newyorkcharters.org/.*

Formation of Charter Schools

25:1. What is a charter school?

A *charter school* is an "independent and autonomous public school" established under the provisions of Article 56 of the Education Law, also known as the New York Charter Schools Act of 1998 (§§ 2850, 2853(1)(c)). It operates pursuant to an approved "charter" issued by the Board of Regents (§ 2851(3)(c)), and is eligible for funding from both private and public local, state, and federal funds (§ 2856; see **25:28**).

A charter school may be a newly created school, or it may be the result of the conversion of a previously existing public school (see § 2851(3); see also **25:4**)). The law expressly prohibits an existing private school from converting to a charter school (§ 2852(3)).

25:2. Where may a charter school be located?

A charter school may be located in part of an existing public school building, in space provided on a private work site, in a public building, or in any other suitable location. A charter school may own, lease, or rent its space (§ 2853(3)(a)).

At the request of a charter school or a prospective applicant, a school district must provide a list of vacant, unused school buildings and vacant, unused portions of school buildings, including private school buildings, within the district that may be suitable for the operation of a charter school (§ 2853(3)(c)).

For purposes of local zoning, land use regulation and building code compliance, the charter schools law treats charter schools as nonpublic schools (§ 2853(3)(a)). However, projects for the construction, renovation or repair of buildings for charter schools are subject to Labor Law provisions regarding prevailing wages and supplements. One exception might apply, for example, when the project is controlled and financed entirely by a private developer, and the lease of space for use by the charter school is for a period substantially shorter than the useful life of the building (Opn. Att'y Gen. F. 2000-3).

25:3. Who can form a charter school?

Teachers, parents, school administrators, community residents, or any combination thereof, may apply to establish a charter school. They may submit their application independently, or in conjunction with a college, university, museum, educational institution, not-for-profit corporation exempt from taxation under section 501(c)(3) of the Internal Revenue Code, or for-profit business or corporate entity authorized to do business in New York State (§ 2851(1)).

The law does not allow, however, an existing private school to convert to a charter school (§ 2852(3)). In addition, a charter may not be issued to any school that would be wholly or in part under the control or direction of any religious denomination, or in which any denominational tenet or doctrine would be taught (§ 2854(2)(a)).

25:4. What is the process for forming a charter school?

Those wishing to form a charter school must submit an application to one of three *charter entities* established by the charter schools law: the Board of Regents, the Board of Trustees of the State University of New York, or the local school board of the district where the charter school will be located, except in New York City where the law designates the chancellor of the New York City Board of Education as a charter entity instead of a school board. However, applications for converting an existing public school into a charter school must be submitted to, and may only be approved by, the local school board (§ 2851(3)).

A charter entity then reviews those applications submitted for its approval. During the review process, it may require applicants to modify or supplement their application as a condition of approval (§ 2852(3)). In the case of a conversion application, the law further requires that parents or guardians of a majority of the students then enrolled in the existing public school must vote in favor of converting the school to a charter school (§ 2851(3)(c)).

Upon approval of an application, applicants and the charter entity enter into a proposed agreement, known as the charter. The charter must set forth the conditions under which the charter school was approved to operate and the expectations it will have to meet to continue in operation (§ 2852(5);

Matter of the Bd. of Educ. of the Roosevelt UFSD v. Board of Trustees of the State University of New York, 282 A.D.2d 166 (3d Dep't 2001)).

Next, within five days after entering into a proposed charter, the charter entity other than the Board of Regents must submit to the Regents, for final approval, a copy of the charter along with the application and supporting documentation (§ 2852(5); *Matter of Bd. of Educ. of the Roosevelt UFSD*)).

The Board of Regents may approve and issue the charter, or it can return the proposed charter to the charter entity for reconsideration with written comments and recommendations (§ 2852(5-a)). The charter entity then can resubmit the proposed charter with or without modifications, or abandon the proposed charter. Any modifications to the charter require an applicant's written approval. However, the charter entity can abandon the proposed charter with or without applicant approval (§ 2852(5-b)).

The Board of Regents must approve and issue a charter resubmitted by the Board of Trustees of the State University of New York within 60 days of the resubmission. If the Regents do not act within 60 days, the charter will be deemed approved and issued (§ 2852(5-b); *Matter of the Bd. of Educ. of the Roosevelt UFSD*)). This limitation on the Regents' discretion to act on a resubmitted charter applies only to charters entered into by the Board of Trustees of the State University of New York.

25:5. Can a charter entity reject a charter school application?

Yes. Furthermore, a charter entity may not approve an application unless it determines that:

1. the proposed charter school meets all applicable statutory and regulatory requirements,
2. the applicant has the ability to operate the school in an education-ally and fiscally sound manner; and
3. approval of the application is likely to both improve student learning and achievement, and materially further the purposes of the charter school law (§ 2852(2); *Matter of the Bd. of Educ. of the Roosevelt UFSD,* 287 A.D.2d 858 (3d Dep't 2001)).

In addition to improving student learning and achievement, the purposes of the charter schools law include: (1) increasing learning opportunities for all students, particularly those at risk of academic failure; (2) encouraging the use of different and innovative teaching methods; (3) creating new professional opportunities for educators; (4) providing parents and students with expanded educational opportunity choices within the public school system; and (5) providing schools with a method to change from rule-based to performance-based accountability systems (§ 2850(2)).

The denial of an application must be in writing and state the reasons therefor (§ 2852(6)).

25:6. Can an applicant appeal the denial of a charter school application?

No. If a charter entity denies a charter school application, the denial is final and may not be appealed to any authority, including a court of law (§ 2852(3), (6)). However, nothing in the law prevents an applicant from submitting an application that has been rejected by one charter entity to another charter entity.

25:7. Can a school board challenge the approval of a charter school application?

Yes. In *Matter of the Bd. of Educ. of the Roosevelt UFSD v. Board of Trustees of the State University of New York* (282 A.D.2d 166 (3d Dep't 2001)), the Appellate Division, Third Department upheld the right of a school board to challenge a SUNY Trustees' determination to grant a charter on the grounds it was arbitrary and capricious because it failed to properly consider the fiscal impact granting charter would have on affected school districts. While the Charter Schools Act expressly prohibits an applicant from seeking judicial or administrative review of the denial of an application, no similar prohibition exists in law to prevent a school district or school board from seeking review of a determination to grant an application and issue a charter. However, the court also held that a school district is precluded, for lack of standing, from challenging the Charter Schools Act itself on constitutional grounds (see also, related proceeding, *Matter of the Bd. of Educ. of the Roosevelt UFSD v. Board of Trustees of the State University of New York*, 287 A.D.2d 858 (3d Dep't 2001)).

25:8. Is there a limit on the number of charter schools that may be established in New York State?

Yes. The New York Charter Schools Act of 1998 authorizes the Board of Regents to issue only 100 charters: 50 of those based on the recommendation of the Board of Trustees of the State University of New York, the other 50 upon recommendations by the other charter entities; in other words, the Board of Regents, the New York City schools chancellor, or local school boards elsewhere throughout the state (§ 2852(9); see **25:4**).

However, there is no limit on the number of existing public schools that may be converted into charter schools (§ 2852(9)).

25:9. Is there a limit on the lifetime of a charter school?

Yes. A charter school may exist for a maximum period of five years, unless its charter is renewed (§§ 2851(2)(p), 2851(4), 2853(1)(a)). However, charters may be renewed only upon application, and for time periods not to exceed five years each (§ 2851(4)).

25:10. Can a charter be revoked or terminated?

Yes. The Board of Regents or the charter entity which approved the charter school application can revoke or terminate a charter (1) if student achievement falls below the level that would allow the commissioner of education to revoke the registration of another public school and student achievement has not shown improvement over the preceding three years; (2) for serious violation of law; (3) for material and substantial violation of the charter, including fiscal mismanagement; or (4) violations of the Civil Service Law involving interference with or discrimination against employee rights (§ 2855(1); 8 NYCRR § 3.17).

Procedures applicable to charter revocation proceedings conducted by the Board of Regents require that the charter school receive written notice of any intention to revoke its charter at least 30 days prior to the effective date of the proposed revocation, along with the reasons for the proposed revocation and an opportunity to correct the problems associated with the proposed revocation (§ 2855(2); 8 NYCRR § 3.17(a)(1)).

In addition, the charter school must have an opportunity to submit a written response to the notice of intent to revoke and, upon request, for oral argument before a three-member panel of the Board of Regents (8 NYCRR § 3.17(a)(2), (3)).

The Board of Regents' panel is responsible for submitting a recommendation to the full board based on the charter school's written response and oral argument as to whether the charter should be revoked, placed on probationary status, or subjected to a remedial action plan or such other action as the panel deems appropriate. The full board may accept or reject, in whole or in part, the panel's recommendation. The decision of the full board is final. An order revoking a charter also revokes a charter school's certificate of incorporation (§§ 219; 2853(1); 2855(3); 8 NYCRR § 3.17(a)(4), (5)).

The above procedures do not apply to Board of Regents proceedings involving revocation of a charter school's certificate of incorporation after another charter entity revokes the school's charter (8 NYCRR § 3.17(b), (c)).

Operation of Charter Schools

25:11. Are charter schools subject to the same laws and regulations that apply to other public schools?

No. Charter schools must comply with all applicable federal constitutional provisions, statutes, and regulations. They are also bound by the same state health and safety, civil rights, and student assessment requirements as other public schools, except that their student discipline codes are governed by separate provisions of the Education Law instead of the SAVE legislation applicable to other public schools (§§ 2, 2801(2), 2851(2)(h)). The only specific requirement regarding student discipline is that the expulsion or suspension of students from school be consistent with the requirements of due process and with federal laws and regulations governing the placement of students with disabilities.

Charter schools are subject to the requirements of the compulsory education law (§ 2854(1)(b)), and student performance standards adopted by the Board of Regents. They may administer and their students must take Regents exams to the same extent required of other public school students (§ 2854(1)(d); 8 NYCRR § 100.2(p)).

In addition, charter schools are subject to the Open Meetings Law and the Freedom of Information Law (§ 2854(1)(e)). They must comply with commissioner's regulations regarding electrically operated partitions located in classrooms or other facilities used by students (8 NYCRR § 155.25) and automated external defibrillators (§ 917; 8 NYCRR § 136.4), and are subject to fingerprinting requirements (see **25:32**).

Nonetheless, charter schools are exempt from all other state and local laws, rules, regulations, or policies governing public or private schools, other than the charter schools law (§§ 2854(1)(b), 2855(5)). According to the attorney general, this does not mean that charter schools are exempt for all state laws, only those specifically applicable to public or private schools (Opn. Att'y Gen. F 2000-3).

25:12. Are charter schools subject to the federal No Child Left Behind Act (NCLB)?

Yes, including but not limited to the NCLB's public reporting requirement. Their annual report card must include basic educational data, a report on academic performances, and a report on fiscal performances. Charter schools must submit to the commissioner of education and the Board of Regents information regarding matters such as the professional qualifications of each teacher and the classes they teach, student demographic data, services provided, performance on state assessments, student attendance, documentation of transfers and dropouts at the secondary level, and violent and disruptive incidents (8 NYCRR § 119.3).

25:13. Are charter schools subject to oversight and supervision?

Yes. A charter school is subject to the supervision and oversight of both the Board of Regents and the charter entity that approved the charter school (§ 2853(1)(c), (2)).

The school district where a charter school is located is not required to but may visit, examine into, and inspect a charter school approved by the Board of Regents or the Board of Trustees of the State University of New York, and forward to the Board of Regents and the charter entity any evidence of non-compliance with applicable laws, regulations, and charter provisions for possible termination or revocation of the charter (§ 2853(2-a)).

25:14. Where should complaints about charter schools be directed?

Complaints about charter schools that would otherwise be presented to the Board of Regents should be directed to the commissioner of education. The Regents have delegated to the commissioner the authority to receive, investigate, and respond to complaints, issue appropriate remedial orders, place a charter school on probationary status, and develop and impose on a charter school a remedial action plan (§§ 2855 (1), (3), (4); 8 NYCRR § 3.16).

Student Admissions and Enrollment

25:15. Who may attend a charter school?

In general, any child who is qualified for admission to a public school under New York State laws may be admitted to a charter school (§ 2854(2)(b)). A charter school may not limit admission on the basis of intellectual ability, measures of achievement or aptitude, athletic ability, disability, race, creed, gender, national origin, religion, or ancestry (§ 2854(2)(a)).

However, a charter school must restrict admission to students within the grade levels it serves (§ 2854(2)(c)). In addition, it may limit admissions to students of a single gender or who are at risk of failure in school if the charter school was formed as a single-sex school or as a school designed to serve at-risk students, provided that such action would not constitute impermissible discrimination under federal law (§ 2854(2)(a)).

A charter school may also deny admission to any student who has been expelled or suspended from a public school until the period of suspension or expulsion from the public school has expired (§ 2854(2)(d)).

25:16. May a charter school have student admission preferences?

Yes. If the number of students who submit a timely application for enrollment exceeds the capacity of the grade level or building, a random selection process shall be used to admit students. In that case, however, the charter school must provide admission preference to students returning to that school, siblings of children already enrolled in the charter school, and children residing in the local school district in which the charter school is located (§ 2854(2)(b)).

25:17. Is there a minimum number of students required for a charter school?

Yes. A charter school must serve at least 50 students at a single site, unless the applicant presents a compelling justification such as the location of the charter school in a geographically remote area. In addition, the charter schools law allows a charter school to serve less than 50 students during its first year of operation (§ 2851(2)(i)).

Academic Program and Services

25:18. Are charter schools subject to the Board of Regents learning standards?

Yes. Charter schools must design their educational program to meet or exceed student performance standards adopted by the Board of Regents and must meet the same student assessment requirements as other public schools (§ 2854(1)(b), (d); 8 NYCRR § 100.2(p)).

25:19. Must charter school students take Regents exams?

Yes. Charter school students must take Regents examinations to the same extent as other public school students (§ 2854(1)(d); see *International High School Charter School v. Mills*, 276 A.D.2d 165 (3d Dep't 2000)).

25:20. May a charter school issue a high school diploma?

Yes. A charter school offering high school instruction may grant Regents diplomas and such other certificates and honors specifically authorized by its charter (§ 2854(1)(d); 8 NYCRR § 100.2(p)).

25:21. Are there any restrictions on the grade levels that a charter school can offer?

No. A charter school may serve one or more of the grades between 1 and 12. It may also offer a kindergarten program (§ 2854(2)(c)). However, there is no authority in the law that allows a charter school to offer only preschool instruction.

25:22. What is the length of the school year and school day of charter schools?

Both are determined by the individual charter school. However, the charter schools law requires that a charter school provide at least as much instruction time during the school year as required of other public schools (§ 2851(2)(n)).

25:23. Who is responsible for developing an individualized education program (IEP) for charter school students with disabilities?

The committee or subcommittee on special education (CSE or CSE subcommittee) of the student's school district of residence is responsible for developing an IEP for a student with disabilities attending a charter school, and the charter school must provide special education programs and services in accordance with the IEP (§ 2853(4)).

The charter school may arrange to have such services provided by the student's school district of residence, by the charter school itself, or by contract with another provider (§ 2853(4); see the State Education Department, Office of Elementary, Middle, Secondary, and Continuing Education, "Charter Schools and Special Education," available at http://www.emsc.nysed.gov/rscs/charter/charterschools.html).

25:24. Who is responsible for transporting charter school students to and from school?

For purposes of transportation, the charter schools law treats charter schools the same as nonpublic schools. This means that the student's school district of residence is responsible for providing a charter school student with transportation to and from school on the same basis as nonpublic school students — in other words, subject to the applicable minimum mileage limits for transportation in the school district of residence, and the requirement of the timely filing of a request for transportation pursuant to section 3635(2) of the Education Law (§ 2853(4)(b)).

A district is responsible for transporting resident students attending charter schools even in cases when during a charter school's first year of operation, the school is not approved and the request for transportation is not submitted until after the April 1 deadline for transportation requests by private school students (*Appeal of New Covenant Charter School*, 39 Educ. Dep't Rep. 610 (2000); see **22:110**). However, subsequent requests for transportation from an established charter school are subject to the April 1 deadline even when there is an enrollment cap on the school. In such a case, nothing prohibits the school from submitting by April 1 a list of students interested, but not yet enrolled (*Appeal of New Covenant Charter School*, 41 Educ. Dep't Rep. 358 (2002)).

The charter school's charter must provide for any needed supplemental transportation, which must comply with all transportation safety laws and regulations applicable to other public schools. A charter school may contract with a school district for the provision of supplemental transportation services to a charter school, at cost (§ 2853(4)(e)).

25:25. May charter school students participate in the athletic and extracurricular activities of their school district of residence?

Yes. However, it is at the discretion of the school district of residence to allow such children to participate in athletic and extracurricular activities of the district's schools (§ 2853(4)(b)).

25:26. Are there any services that a school district must make available to charter schools?

Yes. School districts must make available to charter schools textbooks, computer software, school library materials, and health and welfare services to the same extent as nonpublic schools (§ 2853(4)(a)).

Charter School Funding

25:27. Can charter schools levy taxes or charge tuition?

No. The charter schools law expressly denies charter schools the authority to levy taxes or charge tuition (§§ 2853(1)(e), 2854(2)(a)). Additionally, charter schools may not require the payment of fees except on the same basis and to the same extent as other public schools (§ 2854(2)(a)).

25:28. How are charter schools funded?

Charter schools receive public funding depending on the number of students the charter school serves, the adjusted expense per pupil of the various districts of residence for those students, and federal aid attributable to a student with a disability attending a charter school (§ 2856(1); 8 NYCRR § 119.1(d)(3), (4)). The school district of residence of a student who enrolls in a charter school must pay directly to the charter school the appropriate payment amounts no later than the first business day of July, September, November, January, March and May in accordance with the payment schedule set forth in the charter schools law and the commissioner's regulations (§ 2856(1); 8 NYCRR § 119.1(d)(1), (2)).

A school district must also pay directly to a charter school any federal or state aid received for a student with a disability attending the charter school, in proportion to the level of services that the charter school provides directly or indirectly to the student (§ 2856(1)).

The state comptroller is authorized to deduct an amount equal to the unpaid obligation from any state aid available to a school district that fails to make indicated payments to a charter school. The commissioner of education must certify to the comptroller the amount of state aid to be deducted (§ 2856(2); 8 NYCRR § 119.1(a)).

Additionally, individuals and organizations can provide funding or other assistance to the establishment and operation of a charter school. A charter school may accept gifts, donations, or grants of any kind as long as they are not subject to conditions contrary to any provision of law or a term of the charter school's charter (§ 2856(3)).

A school district may not submit to the voters an advisory proposition regarding increases to the proposed district budget to fund a newly formed charter school. "Advisory propositions and referenda are discouraged because they may infer voter determination of the issue." They are particularly ill-advised when a district is legally obligated to provide payments to a charter school in accordance with the Education Law and fails to adequately inform the voters of this obligation (*Appeal of Marshall,* 41 Educ. Dep't Rep. 219 (2001)).

25:29. Are there any restrictions on the use of moneys a charter school receives from a school district?

Yes. A charter school may not expend moneys received from a local school district (see **25:28**) for the purchase or construction, acquisition, reconstruction, rehabilitation, or improvement of a school facility (§ 2853(3)(b)). However, it may apply for assistance to the "charter school stimulus fund," which is made up of public or private donations, gifts, and grants to provide discretionary support, including grants and loans to applicants and charter schools, for start-up costs and costs associated with facilities (State Fin. Law § 97-sss).

Charter School Personnel

25:30. What is the minimum number of teachers required for a charter school?

A charter school must employ at least three teachers at the school, unless the applicant presents a compelling justification such as the location of the charter school in a geographically remote area. In addition, the charter schools law allows a charter school to employ less than three teachers during its first year of operation (§ 2851(2)(i)).

25:31. Must charter school teachers be certified by New York State?

Yes. With certain limited exceptions, a charter school must employ teachers certified in accordance with the requirements applicable to other public schools. In addition, the number of uncertified teachers employed by a charter school may not exceed 30 percent of its teaching staff or five teachers, whichever is less (§ 2854(3)(a-1)).

25:32. Are charter school teachers subject to fingerprinting and child abuse in an educational setting reporting requirements?

Yes. The Education Law and commissioner's regulations require charter schools to fingerprint prospective employees hired after July 1, 2001, for the purposes of a criminal history background check (§ 2854(3)(a-2), (a-3); 8 NYCRR § 87.1 *et seq.*).

Charter schools are also subject to child abuse in an educational setting reporting requirements (§ 1125 *et seq.*, 8 NYCRR § 100.2(hh); see State Education Department, Charter Schools Unit, "Questions and Answers Concerning the Applicability of SAVE and the School Employee Fingerprinting and Child Abuse Reporting Legislation to Charter Schools," available at http://www.emsc.nysed.gov/rscs/charter/charterschools.html; see **8:13–24; 12:80**).

25:33. Who do charter school employees work for?

Charter school staff members are employees of the charter school. However, they may be deemed employees of the school district where the charter school is located for the purpose of providing retirement benefits, including membership in the teachers' retirement and other retirement systems open to employees of public schools (§ 2854(3)(a), (c); 8 NYCRR § 119.2)). It is up to the charter school to determine whether it will treat its employees as private or public employees for retirement purposes, and to apply for admission as a participating employer in a public retirement system. The charter school and its employees are responsible for the financial contributions for such benefits (§ 2854(3)(c); 8 NYCRR § 119.2(b), (c)).

25:34. Do charter school employees enjoy collective bargaining rights?

Yes. Moreover, for purposes of collective bargaining, employees of a "converted charter school" (see **25:1**), other than "managerial" or "confidential" employees, are deemed included in the same negotiating unit containing like titles or positions for district employees. They are covered by the same collective bargaining agreement covering that school district negotiating unit, unless a majority of the charter school employees in the negotiating unit want to modify the agreement as it applies to them and negotiate changes to the agreement with the approval of the charter school's board of trustees (§ 2854(3)(b)). On the other hand, employees of a "newly created charter school" (see **25:1**) are not deemed members of any existing collective bargaining unit representing employees of the school district in which the charter school is located and are not subject to any existing collective bargaining agreement between the district and its employees (§ 2854(3)(b-1)).

In addition, charter schools must afford employees not represented by a union reasonable access to any employee organization, and remain neutral in a representation vote by employees (§ 2854(3)(c-1), (c-2)).

25:35. May teachers from a public school district teach in a charter school?

Yes. A teacher employed by a public school district may request a leave of absence to teach in a charter school. The charter schools law provides that a request for a leave of up to two years may not be unreasonably withheld (§ 2854(3)(d)).

In addition, a public school teacher on leave to teach at a charter school may return to the school district during the period of the leave without the loss of any right of certification, retirement, seniority, salary status or any other benefit provided by law or the applicable collective bargaining agreement. If an appropriate position is not available for the teacher, the teacher's name is to be placed on a preferred eligible list for appointment to a future vacancy that may occur in a position similar to the one the teacher immediately held prior to the leave of absence (§ 2854(3)(d)).

26. Federal Laws and Public Schools

Editor's Note: This chapter provides a brief overview of the No Child Left Behind Act of 2001 (NCLB) and is not meant to be exhaustive. Applicable provisions and their implementation in New York State have been incorporated into other chapters in this book. For more information see Leaving No Child Behind In New York, 2nd Edition, *published by New York State School Boards Association and distributed by LexisNexis. See also the U.S. Department of Education's Web site at http://www.ed.gov/ nclb/landing.html and the New York State Education Department's Web site at http://www.emsc.nysed.gov/deputy/nclb/nclbhome.htm/.*

26:1. Is the federal government responsible for the provision of public education within the individual states?

No. Education is a state function under the 10th Amendment of the United States Constitution, which reserves to the states those powers not delegated to the federal government. Furthermore, a number of United States Supreme Court decisions support the reserved powers of states in the field of public education. In *Brown v. Board of Educ.*, 347 U.S. 483 (1954), for example, the Court stated that education is perhaps the most important function of state and local governments. In 1972, the Court recognized that "providing public schools ranks at the very apex of the function of a state" (*Wisconsin v. Yoder*, 406 U.S. 205 (1972)).

Additionally, in 1970, the General Education Provisions Act (20 USC §§ 1221–1234i) was amended to include a "prohibition against federal control of education" including any "direction, supervision, or control over the curriculum, program of instruction, administration, or personnel of any educational institution, school, or school system, or over the selection of library resources, textbooks, or other printed or published instructional materials by any educational institution or school system" (20 USC § 1232a).

However, the federal role in public education has grown steadily as the availability of federal funds to state education departments and local school districts depends on local compliance with federal laws and regulations. For instance, if school districts accept federal funds, they must comply with, among others, the Hatch Amendment (20 USC § 1232h), which gives parents the right to inspect classroom materials used in connection with federally funded programs (see **14:113**); the Family Educational and Privacy Rights Act (also known as the Buckley Amendment) (20 USC § 1232g), which requires school districts to adopt policies to ensure student privacy rights (see **2:85**); the Individuals with Disabilities Education Act

(IDEA) (20 USC §§ 1400–1487), which requires schools to meet certain guidelines for serving children with disabilities (see **chapter 13**); and the Equal Access Act (20 USC § 4071), which declares that schools permitting student groups to use school facilities for noncurriculum-related purposes may not deny access to student religious or political groups based on anticipated content of the meeting (see **16:41**).

Moreover, the U.S. Constitution affects public education through its amendments, largely the First, Fifth, and 14th Amendments, protecting the rights of individuals. U.S. Supreme Court decisions interpreting these amendments have affected schools in areas such as school desegregation, separation of church and state, freedom of speech, corporal punishment, and compulsory attendance.

Although the U.S. Constitution does not guarantee the right of public education, it precludes states, when determining for whom education must be provided, from categorically denying education to students on the basis of race, national origin, alienage, indigence, or illegitimacy (*San Antonio Indep. Sch. Dist. v. Rodriguez*, 411 U.S. 1 (1973)). For instance, children who are illegal aliens may, in some circumstances, be entitled to a free public education (*Plyler v. Doe*, 457 U.S. 202 (1982)).

26:2. By what authority does the federal government legislate in the area of public education?

The authority of the federal government to legislate in the area of public education is derived from article 1, section 8, of the United States Constitution, which pertains to the power of Congress to provide for the general welfare and the Equal Protection Clause of the 14th Amendment.

26:3. What federal agency has responsibility for coordinating federal support of education?

The United States Department of Education was created by the 96th Congress to assume responsibility for education (20 USC § 3411). The department's budget of discretionary funds is mostly distributed to the states' education departments and local schools.

26:4. Must school districts accept federal funds?

No. School districts and states are not obligated to accept federal funds, but if they do, they must accept the conditions under which federal funds are granted (*Grove City College v. Bell*, 465 U.S. 555 (1984)). Congress may set these conditions (*Oklahoma v. United States Civil Service Comm'n*, 330 U.S. 127 (1947)).

26:5. What are the major programs through which federal education aid is allocated to elementary and secondary schools in New York State?

The following are the major federal education aid programs:

- **No Child Left Behind Act of 2001** (20 USC §§ 6301–7941). This law amended the Elementary and Secondary Education Act (ESEA), which became law in 1965. It encompasses and regulates all federal educational programs except for the Individuals with Disabilities Education Act.
- **Individuals with Disabilities Education Act (IDEA)** (20 USC §§ 1400–1487). This legislation provides various programs to strengthen the educational services received by students with disabilities.

26:6. What federal programs are contained in the No Child Left Behind Act (NCLB)?

The key federal funding programs encompassed in the NCLB are as follows:

- **Title I—Part A: Improving the Academic Achievement of the Disadvantaged.** This, the largest federal education program, provides states and local schools with funding to help improve instruction for disadvantaged students in high-poverty schools (20 USC § 6311).
- **Title II—Preparing, Training, and Recruiting High Quality Teachers and Principals.** Provides grants for professional development for teachers with significant set-asides for mathematics and science teachers. Authorizes a new state, formula-based grant program that combines the Eisenhower Professional Development State Grants and Class-Size Reduction programs into one program that focuses on preparing, training, and recruiting high-quality teachers (20 USC § 6601).
- **Title III—Language Instruction for Limited English Proficient and Immigrant Students.** Consolidates the 13 former bilingual and immigrant education programs into one state, formula-based program. Provides grants for programs designed to help non-English-speaking students attain English proficiency (20 USC § 6801).
- **Title IV—21st Century Schools.** Provides grants for safe schools through anti-drug, anti-tobacco, and anti-violence programs as well as for community learning programs. Includes the Safe and Drug-Free Schools and Communities Act and the Gun-Free Schools Act (20 USC § 7101).
- **Title V—Promoting Informed Parental Choice and Innovative Programs.** Provides funding for local educational innovation based on

"scientifically based research" (20 USC § 7201). Also includes funding for charter and magnet schools and for public school choice programs as well as grants for gifted and talented students (20 USC § 7215).

- **Title VI—Flexibility and Accountability.** Establishes demonstration programs regarding flexible use of federal funds by states and school districts (20 USC § 7305a). Also establishes the Rural Education Achievement Program (20 USC § 7341a).
- **Title VII—Indian, Native Hawaiian, and Alaska Native Education.** Provides funding for schools that serve Native American populations (20 USC §§ 7401–7402).
- **Title VIII—Impact Aid Program.** Provides aid to districts that educate children residing on federal property and whose parents are employed by the federal government, particularly by the military (20 USC § 7701).
- **Title IX—General Provisions.** Continues many of the provisions found in Title XIV of the predecessor law, such as flexibility provisions relating to consolidated plans and use of administrative funds, waivers, uniform provisions, and limitations on the federal role in education. Defines such key terms as "beginning teacher," "highly qualified teacher," "parental involvement," "poverty line," "professional development," and "scientifically-based research." Some of the significant new general provisions of Title IX include requirements regarding school prayer (see **16:41**), the Equal Access Act (see **16:41**), military recruiting (see **16:36**), and the "Unsafe School Choice Option" (see **12:31**).
- **Title X, Part C—Education for Homeless Children and Youth.** Amendments to the McKinney-Vento Homeless Assistance Act. Retains, with some changes, the current program to provide grants to states to give homeless children and youth access to the same free and appropriate public education, including preschool education, as other children and youth.

26:7. What learning standards are required under the NCLB?

The NCLB requires that states receiving Title I assistance, including New York, adopt "challenging academic content and student academic achievement standards" for all public elementary school and secondary school children, not limited to children served under Title I, in subjects determined by the state, including at least mathematics, reading or language arts, and (beginning in the 2005–06 school year) science, which must include the same knowledge, skills, and levels of achievement expected of all children (20 USC § 6311 (b)(1); 34 CFR § 200.1). See **14:23** for more information on New York's learning standards.

26:8. What state assessments are required under the NCLB?

Through the 2004–05 school year, school districts must assess students in reading or language arts and mathematics at least once in grades 3–5, 6–9 and 10–12. However, beginning with the 2005–06 school year, students in grades 3–8 will be required to take annual assessments in reading or language arts and mathematics. Students in grades 10–12 must continue to be tested at least once in English language arts and mathematics (20 USC § 6311(b)(3)(C); 34 CFR §§ 200.2(a)(1), 200.5(a)).

Beginning with the 2007–08 school year, students must be assessed at least once in science during three separate grade spans. At least one assessment will be required in grades 3–5, in grades 6–9, and in grades 10–12 (20 USC § 6311(b)(3)(C); 34 CFR §§ 200.2, 200.5).

These requirements apply to all students, including those with disabilities and those with limited English proficiency (20 USC § 6311(b)(3)(C)(ix); 34 CFR § 200.6). In addition, school districts must annually assess the English proficiency of limited English proficiency students (20 USC § 6311(b)(7)).

Every other year, states must also administer to a sample of fourth- and eighth-grade students the reading and mathematics exams of the National Assessment of Educational Progress (NAEP). The test scores will be used as an independent check on the rigor of state standards and will be paid for by the federal government (20 USC § 6311(c)(2)).

Each state assumes responsibility for developing and implementing its own tests as well as for establishing student proficiency requirements. State assessments must be aligned with the state's academic standards and must produce results that are comparable from year to year. They must yield results that can be used to determine whether students are meeting the state standards and to help teachers diagnose student academic needs (20 USC § 6311(b)(3)(C)). State assessment scores must be provided to school districts before the beginning of the following school year (20 USC § 6311(b)(10); see **14:65–75**).

26:9. How does the NCLB define "adequate yearly progress"?

The NCLB does not define what is meant by "adequate yearly progress." Instead, the law requires each state to define, based on the academic assessments it will be using, what constitutes adequate yearly progress in a statistically valid and reliable manner that applies the same high standards to all public school students and results in continuous, substantial academic improvement for all students. The state's definition must separately measure annual improvement for low-income students, major racial and ethnic groups, students with disabilities, and limited English proficiency students. It must also include graduation rates for secondary schools and at least one other academic indicator, as determined by the state, for all public elementary school students (20 USC § 6311(b)(2)(B), (C), (D); 34 CFR §§ 200.13(b), 200.19)); for more information on adequate yearly progress, see **14:89–105**).

26:10. What accountability does a school district have for underperforming schools?

School districts that have underperforming schools must take specified measures to improve the schools' performance or lose their federal funding. Underperforming schools are subject to a range of actions and remedies under the NCLB. Depending on the number of years a school fails to make adequate yearly progress, an underperforming school may be subject to classification as a school in need of improvement measures, corrective actions or complete restructuring of the school.

Schools failing to make adequate yearly progress for two consecutive years will be identified as being in need of improvement (20 USC § 6316(b)(1)(A), (B); 34 CFR § 200.32(a); 8 NYCRR § 100.2(p)(6)(vi)). Students attending such schools must be given the opportunity to enroll in another public school within the district, including a charter school, that has not been identified as needing improvement or designated as persistently dangerous (20 USC § 6316(b)(1)(E); 34 CFR §§ 200.39(a)(1)(i), 200.44(a); 8 NYCRR §§ 100.2(p)(6)(vi), 120.3(a)). Priority will be given to the lowest achieving students from low-income families who wish to transfer (20 USC § 6316(b)(E)(ii); 34 CFR § 200.44(e); 8 NYCRR § 120.3(b)).

Schools identified as needing improvement will have three months to develop a plan to improve the school within two years and must also ensure that at least 10 percent of their federal funds are used for professional development (20 USC § 6316(b)(3); 34 CFR §§ 200.40, 200.41)). The district must also provide a school identified as needing improvement with technical assistance to implement the improvement plan and improve student performance (20 USC § 6316(b)(4)(B); 34 CFR § 200.40(c)).

26:11. What are the supplemental educational services requirements under the NCLB?

If a school continues to fail to make adequate yearly progress the year after it is identified as needing improvement, it must still provide the transfer option (20 USC § 6316(b)(5); 34 CFR § 200.39(b)) and it must provide eligible students with the opportunity to obtain supplemental educational services from an outside provider, selected by parents from a state-approved list, but paid for the school district (20 USC § 6316(e)(2); 34 CFR § 200.45(c); 8 NYCRR § 120.4; see **14:98**).

Supplemental educational services (SES) are tutoring and other academic enrichment services, apart from instruction provided during the school day. They must be high-quality, research-based, and designed to increase the academic achievement of eligible children and assist them attain proficiency in meeting the state's academic achievement standards (20 USC § 6316 (e)(12)(c); 8 NYCRR § 120.4(a)(5), (d)(2)(iv)). A *provider* is a financially sound, nonprofit or for-profit entity, or a school district that has demonstrated effectiveness in increasing student academic achievement. (20 USC § 6316 (e)(12)(B); 34 CFR § 200.47(b)(1); 8 NYCRR § 120.4(a), (d)). An *eligible child* is a child from a low-income family, as determined by the school district pursuant to the NCLB (20 USC §§ 6313(c)(1), 6316(e)(12)(A); 34 CFR § 200.45(b)(1); 8 NYCRR § 120.4(a)(3), (b)).

School districts are required to spend an amount equal to 20 percent of their allocation under Title I, Part A on choice-related transportation, supplemental educational services, or a combination of both. If the costs of satisfying all SES requests exceeds an amount equal to 5 percent of that allocation, districts may not spend less than that 5 percent, but are not required to spend more. Districts may spend up to an additional 10 percent, unless they choose to spend the additional 10 percent exclusively for the transportation of students who transfer to another school because their school has been identified as in need of improvement, corrective action or restructuring status (20 USC § 6316(b)(10)(A), (B)).

26:12. When is a district identified for corrective action under the NCLB?

Schools failing to make adequate yearly progress by the end of the second full year of improvement status will be identified as needing "corrective action" (20 USC § 6316(b)(7)(C); 34 CFR § 200.33(a); 8 NYCRR §§ 100.2(p)(6)(viii), 120.2(h)). Schools that are identified as needing corrective action must continue to implement all measures required of schools identified for improvement and must also take at least one of the following corrective actions:

- replace school staff members who are "relevant" to the failure to make adequate yearly progress;
- institute and implement a new curriculum, including professional development;
- significantly decrease management authority at the school level;
- appoint an outside expert to advise the school on its progress toward making adequate yearly progress;
- extend the school day or year; or

- restructure the school's internal organizational structure (20 USC § 6316(b)(3)(B)(i), (7)(C); 34 CFR § 200.42(b)(4); see **14:99**).

26:13. When must a school district make plans to restructure a school?

If a school continues to fail to make adequate yearly progress after one full year of corrective action, the district must continue to offer students the option to transfer and supplemental services to eligible students. The school district must also prepare a plan and make arrangements for school restructuring (20 USC § 6316(b)(8)(A), (C); 34 CFR §§ 200.43(b), 200.44(a), 200.45(c); 8 NYCRR §§ 100.2(p)(6)(ix), 120.3(a)).

The plan, which must be implemented in the following school year, must involve one of the following alternatives:
- reopening the school as a charter school;
- replacing staff who are relevant to the failure to make adequate yearly progress;
- contracting with an outside company with a "demonstrated record of effectiveness" to operate the school;
- turning the school's operation over to the state; or
- implementing "any other major restructuring" that will improve student achievement and enable the school to make adequate yearly progress (20 USC § 6316(b)(8)(B); 34 CFR § 200.43(b)(3); see **14:100–101**).

26:14. Can a school challenge a district's decision to identify it as needing improvement or corrective action?

Yes. Before a school is identified as needing improvement or corrective action, the school district must provide it with an opportunity to review any data or assessment results on which the proposed classification is based. After it provides the school with an opportunity for review, the school district has 30 days in which to make a final determination on the school's status (20 USC § 6316(b)(2)(A), (B); 34 CFR § 200.31)).

Before the district's final determination is made, the school can present evidence that the proposed decision is in error for statistical or substantive reasons (20 USC § 6316(b)(2)(B)).

26:15. What are the NCLB requirements for teacher qualifications?

Under the NCLB, all new teachers of core academic subjects hired after the first day of the 2002–03 school year with federal Title I Part A funds must be "highly qualified" (20 USC § 6319(a)(1)). In addition, states must develop plans with annual measurable objectives to ensure all public school teachers teaching in core academic subjects meet the federal definition of "highly qualified" by the end of the 2005–06 school year (20 USC § 6319(a)(2)).

A "highly qualified" teacher is one who has obtained full state certification as a teacher, or has passed the state teacher licensing examination, and holds a license to teach in the state and has at least a bachelor's degree (20 USC § 7801(23)). To be highly qualified, teachers also must show subject matter competency in the subjects they teach. Different requirements apply for establishing subject matter competency depending on a teacher's date of hire and grade level taught and his or her newness to the profession (20 USC § 7801(23)). For more information on teacher qualifications, see **chapter 8**.

26:16. Do parents have a right to request information from school districts on teacher qualifications?

Yes. School districts receiving Title I, Part A funds, must at the beginning of each school year notify the parents of each student attending any school receiving such funds that the parents may request information regarding the professional qualifications of the student's classroom teachers, including at least the following:

- whether the teacher has met state qualification and licensing criteria for the grade levels and subject areas in which the teacher provides instruction;
- whether the teacher is teaching under emergency or other provisional status through which state qualification or licensing criteria have been waived;
- the baccalaureate degree major of the teacher and any other graduate certification or degree held by the teacher, and the field of discipline of the certification or degree;
- whether the child is provided services by paraprofessionals and, if so, their qualifications (20 USC § 6311(h)(6)(A); 34 CFR § 200.61(a)).

In addition, each school that receives Title I, Part A funds must provide to parents timely notice that their child has been assigned to, or taught for four or more consecutive weeks by, a teacher who is not highly qualified (20 USC § 6311(h)(6)(B); 34 CFR § 200.61(b)).

The district must also include in the annual school district report card information regarding the professional qualifications of teachers in the district, the percentage of such teachers teaching with emergency or provisional credentials, and the percentage of classes in the state not taught by highly qualified teachers (20 USC § 6319 (b)(1)(A)).

26:17. What are the NCLB requirements for paraprofessionals?

All new paraprofessionals hired after January 8, 2002 with federal Title I, Part A funds to provide instructional support services must have a high school diploma or its equivalent. They also must have either completed at least two years of post-secondary education or meet a "rigorous standard of quality" and demonstrate necessary knowledge and skills for assisting in the instruction of reading/language arts, writing or mathematics, or readiness therein, through a "formal state or local academic assessment" (20 USC § 6319(c); 34 CFR § 200.58(b), (c)).

All paraprofessionals paid with Title I Part A funds must meet this standard by January 8, 2006 (20 USC § 6319(d), (f); 34 CFR § 200.58(b), (d)). Title I paraprofessionals engaged in parental involvement or language translation activities only need to have a high school diploma or its equivalent (20 USC § 6319(c)(1), (2), (e); 34 CFR § 200.58(c)). Individuals performing only noninstructional duties such as technical support for computers, personal care service and clerical duties are not deemed Title I paraprofessionals and are not subject to the NCLB requirements (34 CFR § 200.58(a)(2)(i)).

26:18. What new requirements regarding the education of homeless children are there in the NCLB?

The NCLB retains, with some changes, the current McKinney-Vento Homeless Education Assistance program to provide grants to states to help ensure that homeless children and youth have access to the same free and appropriate public education, including preschool education, as other children and youth.

The NCLB specifies that school districts must, at the request of the child's parent or guardian, provide or arrange for transportation to the homeless child's school of origin when that school is within the district. When the school of origin is in a different district from the one where the homeless child is living, both districts must agree on a method for sharing transportation responsibility and costs.

Pending resolution of a dispute about school placement, a district must immediately enroll a homeless student in the student's school of choice and provide a written explanation of the rights of appeal to the parent or guardian and student.

All districts, not just districts receiving NCLB subgrants, must designate local liaisons for homeless children and youth (42 USC § 11431 *et seq.*, as amended by Title X, Part C, §§ 1031–1033 of the No Child Left Behind Act of 2001).

26:19. Can school districts apply for waivers of NCLB requirements?

Yes. School districts may apply to the U.S. Department of Education (DOE) for a waiver of any NCLB program that provides funds to state agencies or school districts (20 USC § 7861). However, the DOE cannot waive certain programs or requirements, including those relating to the allocation or distribution of funds to the states, maintenance of effort, comparability of services, equitable participation of private school students and teachers, parental participation and involvement, and civil rights requirements (20 USC § 7861(c)).

26:20. What are the NCLB provisions regarding the education of students with limited English proficiency (LEP)?

School districts receiving Title I funds must provide all LEP students with an annual assessment of English proficiency, which measures such students' oral language, reading, and writing skills in English (20 USC § 6311 (b)(7); 34 CFR § 200.6(b)(3)).

Each school district using Title I or Title III funds to provide a language instruction educational program to LEP students, must, no later than 30 days after the beginning of the school year, inform the parents of such student that he or she has been identified for participation in such a program. The parents must also be notified of their rights to decline to enroll their child in such program, to have the child immediately removed from such program upon their request, or to choose another program or method of instruction, if available. If a district offers more than one program or method of LEP instruction, it must assist parents in choosing one (20 USC § 6312(g)(1)(A), (B), (3)). In addition, if the school district has failed to make progress on the annual measurable achievement objectives for LEP students (see **14:94**), the district must separately inform the parents of LEP students identified for participation, or participating in such program, of such failure no later than 30 days after such failure occurs (20 USC § 6312(g)(1)(B); see **14:37–38**).

All notices to parents of LEP students must be provided in an understandable and uniform format and, to the extent practicable, in a language that the parent can understand (20 USC § 6312(g)(2); 34 CFR § 200.6(b)).

School districts must also include LEP students in all required state assessments (20 USC § 6311(b)(3)(C)). Students who have attended school in the U.S. (excluding Puerto Rico) for three or more consecutive school years must be tested in English in the reading and language arts state assessments, subject to certain exceptions ((20 USC § 6311(b)(3)(C)(x); 34 CFR § 200.6(b)(2)); see **14:74**).

26:21. What are the NCLB's requirements regarding private school students?

The extent to which private school students are entitled to equitable federally-funded services remains the same (see, 20 USC §§ 6320(a)(1), (b)(2); 7881(a)(1); 34 CFR § 200.62(a)(1)). The NCLB provides that the district has the final authority to determine the number of low-income children from private schools who qualify for funding, but it specifies a complaint process for private schools that disagree with the district's determination (20 USC § 6320(c), 34 CFR § 200.63(b)(7)).

In addition, the NCLB requires that a school district consult with private schools to a greater degree than previously required. In particular, a school district must ensure "timely and meaningful consultation" with appropriate private school officials during the design and development of the district's federally funded programs. The consultation must occur before the district makes any decision that affects the opportunities of eligible private school children to participate in programs, and must continue throughout implementation and assessment of these services. It must include issues such as how children's needs will be identified; what services will be offered; how services will be provided, academically assessed and improved; and the scope of the equitable services for eligible private school children. Furthermore, the district must obtain a written affirmation signed by private school officials that this consultation has occurred. If such consultation does not take place, a private school has the right to file a complaint with SED (20 USC §§ 6320(b); 34 CFR § 200.63(b), (e), (f)).

Consultation has to be timely and meaningful; it does not have to be face-to-face. While personal meetings may be the most effective means of communication, teleconferencing, video conferencing, e-mail, fax and correspondence are acceptable (NY State Education Department Consultation/Collaboration Requirements in Consolidated Application/DCEP Addendum Development; see also 34 CFR § 200.63 (c)(1)).

School districts retain final authority over the use of a third-party provider to deliver Title I services to private school students. However, if the district decides against this option, it must inform private school officials of their decision, and explain why and how they made that decision (20 USC §§ 6320(b)(1)(H), 881(c)(2); 34 CFR § 200.63(d)(2)).

26:22. What rights do parents have to sue school districts for violations of NCLB requirements?

In the first of its kind ruling, a federal district court in New York ruled that parents do not have a right to sue a school district for its alleged failure to comply with NCLB parental notice, school transfer, and supplemental educational services provisions. According to the court, responsibility to enforce the law rests with the U.S. Department of Education and the U.S. Secretary of Education who have authority to withhold federal funding from school districts that violate NCLB requirements (*Ass'n of Community Organizations for Reform Now v. NYC Dep't of Education*, 269 F. Supp. 2d 338 (S.D.N.Y. 2003)).

Index

A

BORROWING MONEY —Cont'd

Capital projects.

Bonds or bond anticipation notes to finance, 19:81.

Combination of multiple projects into single bond issue, 19:88.

Conflicts of interest.

Sale of bonds, etc., to financial institution with connections to district officers, etc., 19:89.

Debt statement, filing.

Required to issue bonds, 19:87.

50 percent rule, 19:78.

Information resources for district, 19:96.

Interest rates, 19:82.

Limits on indebtedness, 19:77.

Long term instruments, 19:79.

Proceeds.

Deposit, 19:90.

Investment pending use of money, 19:91.

Taxation of interest, 19:92.

Purposes for which used.

Fidelity to authorized purposes, 19:93.

Regents, board of.

Consent to issue bonds, 19:85.

Resolution to authorize issuance of bonds or notes, 19:83.

Sale of bonds and notes.

Conflicts of interest.

Sale of instruments to financial institution with connections to district officers, etc., 19:89.

Method, 19:86.

Proceeds.

Deposit, 19:90.

Investment pending use of money, 19:91.

Taxation of interest, 19:92.

Purposes for which used.

Fidelity to authorized purposes, 19:93.

School construction projects.

Construction of new facilities.

Distribution of informational materials, 16:14.

Short term instruments, 19:80.

State aid.

Building aid.

Debt service, expenditures for, 21:13.

State comptroller.

Consent to issue bonds, 19:85.

Taxation to finance.

Voter approval, 19:84.

BOYCOTTS.

See TAYLOR LAW.

BOYS SCOUTS OF AMERICA.

School buildings and grounds.

Use of facilities and equipment, 16:37.

BREAKFAST PROGRAMS, STUDENT, 12:167 to 12:178.

BRIBERY.

School board members, 2:46.

BROADCASTING.

School-sponsored athletic events, 16:44.

BUDGET, 19:39 to 19:44.

Advocacy as to budget, 4:44 to 4:56.

Annulment of results, 4:51.

Anonymous literature, distribution, 4:56.

Avoiding the appearance of impropriety, 4:52.

Dissemination of nonpartisan information by PTA and other organizations and individuals, 4:55.

Employee unions, staff or students, 4:54.

Examples of improper advocacy, 4:48.

Examples of permissible statements, 4:50.

Factual information to voters, 4:46.

Property values diminishing, stating as fact, 4:49.

Improper budget advocacy.

Avoiding the appearance of impropriety, 4:52.

Consequences, 4:51.

Examples, 4:48.

Permissible statements.

Examples of permissible statements, 4:50.

Personal capacity advocacy by board members, 4:45.

Private individuals and organizations, 4:53.

Prohibition, 4:44.

Property values.

Diminished property values, stating as fact, 4:49.

PTA and other organizations.

Use of district facilities or channels to disseminate nonpartisan information, 4:55.

Rejection of budget.

Statement of consequences not constituting advocacy, 4:44.

Removal from office for willful violation, 4:52.

Staff advocacy on behalf of budget, 4:54.

Student advocacy on behalf of budget, 4:54.

Teacher advocacy on behalf of budget, 4:54.

Videotape communication of budget information to voters, 4:47.

Austerity budget.

Rejection of proposed budget, 4:31.

Balanced budget.

Tax levy to create planned balance, 19:43.

Commissioner of education.

Imposition of budget by commissioner of education, 4:33.

Notes

Notes

Notes

Notes

Notes

Notes

Notes

Notes

Notes

Notes